# מחזור קורן לראש השנה • נוסח ספרד

# The Koren Rosh HaShana Maḥzor • Nusaḥ Sepharad

קורן ירושלים

THE ROHR FAMILY EDITION

# מחזור קורן לראש השנה

# THE KOREN ROSH HASHANA MAḤZOR

כי
אתה
שומע
קול
שופר

WITH INTRODUCTION, TRANSLATION AND COMMENTARY BY

Rabbi Lord Jonathan Sacks שליט״א

•

KOREN PUBLISHERS JERUSALEM

The Koren Rosh HaShana Maḥzor, Nusaḥ Sepharad
The Rohr Family Edition
First North American Hebrew/English Edition, 2014

Koren Publishers Jerusalem Ltd.
POB 4044, Jerusalem 91040, ISRAEL
POB 8531, New Milford, CT 06776, USA

www.korenpub.com



The creation of this Maḥzor was made possible through the generous support of Torah Education in Israel.



Standard Size, Hardcover, ISBN 978 965 301 666 8
Compact Size, Hardcover, ISBN 978 965 301 672 9

RHUSA01S

דּוֹר לְדוֹר יְשַׁבַּח מַעֲשֶׂיךָ...

*The Rohr Family Edition*
*of*
*The Koren Rosh HaShana Maḥzor*
*pays tribute to the memory of*

**Mr. Sami Rohr** ז״ל
ר׳ שמואל ב״ר יהושע אליהו ז״ל

who served his Maker with joy
and whose far-reaching vision, warm open hand, love of Torah,
and love for every Jew were catalysts for the revival and growth of
vibrant Jewish life in the former Soviet Union
and in countless communities the world over

*and to the memory of his beloved wife*

**Mrs. Charlotte Rohr (née Kastner)** ע״ה
שרה בת ר׳ יקותיאל יהודה ע״ה

who survived the fires of the Shoah to become
the elegant and gracious matriarch,
first in Colombia and later in the United States,
of three generations of a family
nurtured by her love and unstinting devotion.
She found grace in the eyes of all those whose lives she touched.

Together they merited to see all their children
build lives enriched by faithful commitment
to the spreading of Torah and *Ahavat Yisrael*.

*Dedicated with love by*
**The Rohr Family**
NEW YORK, USA

# CONTENTS


| | | |
|---|---|---|
| מבוא | ix | Preface |
| הקדמה | xiii | Introduction |
| **ערב ראש השנה** | | **ROSH HASHANA EVE** |
| התרת נדרים | 3 | Annulment of Vows |
| פרוזבול | 7 | Prozbul |
| עירובין | 9 | Eiruvin |
| הדלקת נרות | 11 | Candle Lighting |
| מנחה לערב ראש השנה | 13 | Minḥa for Erev Rosh HaShana |
| אחות קטנה | 51 | Aḥot Ketana |
| קבלת שבת | 57 | Kabbalat Shabbat |
| **ליל ראש השנה** | | **ROSH HASHANA EVENING** |
| מעריב לראש השנה | 65 | Ma'ariv |
| עמידה | 79 | The Amida |
| קידוש לליל ראש השנה | 117 | Kiddush |
| סימנים | 121 | Simanim |
| ברכת המזון | 125 | Birkat HaMazon / Grace after Meals |
| מסכת ראש השנה | 139 | Massekhet Rosh HaShana |
| **שחרית** | | **SHAḤARIT** |
| השכמת הבוקר | 209 | On Waking |
| ברכות התורה | 213 | Blessings over the Torah |
| עטיפת טלית | 217 | Tallit |
| הכנה לתפילה | 219 | Preparation for Prayer |
| ברכות השחר | 225 | Morning Blessings |
| תפילות השחר | 257 | Morning Prayers |
| פסוקי דזמרה | 283 | Pesukei DeZimra |
| נשמת | 305 | Nishmat |
| המלך | 309 | HaMelekh |
| ברכו | 315 | Barekhu |
| קריאת שמע | 333 | The Shema |
| עמידה | 343 | The Amida |

| | | |
|---|---|---|
| סדר ליום א׳ | 359 | FIRST DAY |
| חזרת הש״ץ לשחרית | 361 | Leader's Repetition for Shaḥarit |
| קדושה | 399 | Kedusha |
| אבינו מלכנו | 413 | Avinu Malkenu |
| סדר קריאת התורה | 429 | Reading of the Torah |
| סדר תקיעת שופר | 467 | The Blowing of the Shofar |
| הנני העני ממעש | 485 | Leader's Prayer |
| מוסף ליום א׳ | 489 | Musaf for First Day |
| חזרת הש״ץ למוסף | 529 | Leader's Repetition for Musaf |
| ונתנה תוקף / קדושה | 543 | Untaneh Tokef / Kedusha |
| קידושא רבה וברכה מעין שלוש | 639 | Kiddush & Al HaMiḥya |
| סדר ליום ב׳ | 643 | SECOND DAY |
| חזרת הש״ץ לשחרית | 645 | Leader's Repetition for Shaḥarit |
| קדושה | 691 | Kedusha |
| אבינו מלכנו | 703 | Avinu Malkenu |
| סדר קריאת התורה | 717 | Reading of the Torah |
| סדר תקיעת שופר ליום ב׳ | 749 | The Blowing of the Shofar |
| הנני העני ממעש | 761 | Leader's Prayer |
| מוסף ליום ב׳ | 765 | Musaf for Second Day |
| חזרת הש״ץ למוסף | 803 | Leader's Repetition for Musaf |
| ונתנה תוקף / קדושה | 543 | Untaneh Tokef / Kedusha |
| קידושא רבה וברכה מעין שלוש | 893 | Kiddush & Al HaMiḥya |
| מנחה | 897 | MINḤA |
| תשליך | 945 | Tashlikh |
| מעריב למוצאי ראש השנה | 957 | MA'ARIV FOR MOTZA'EI ROSH HASHANA |
| סדר ברית מילה | 997 | Brit Mila |
| פיוטים נוספים ליום א׳ | 1005 | Additional Piyutim for First Day |
| פיוטים נוספים ליום ב׳ | 1039 | Additional Piyutim for Second Day |
| הלכות תפילה | 1077 | Halakha Guide |
| קדיש דרבנן באותיות לועזיות | 1094 | Rabbis' Kaddish Transliterated |
| קדיש יתום באותיות לועזיות | 1095 | Mourner's Kaddish Transliterated |

## PREFACE

*Let us voice the power of this day's sanctity – it is awesome, terrible.*

On Rosh HaShana, we stand before God in judgment. We fear His *Din*, and crave His *Raḥamim*. We are both humbled and strengthened by the belief that our very future depends on our *tefilla*.

It is with this sense of humility, hope and the awesomeness of the task, that we offer *The Koren Rosh HaShana Maḥzor*. We have created this Maḥzor to mitigate the trepidation with which one enters the High Holy Days, and to highlight the transformative potential they hold. We hope that the Maḥzor helps those seeking to understand their place in the world, and their place before God, and serves as a steady guide through the encounter with God's majesty on Rosh HaShana.

A project of this scope would have been virtually impossible without the partnership of the Rohr family, who have dedicated this Maḥzor in memory of their dear parents, Charlotte and Sami Rohr. The Rohr family's passion for *Avodat HaShem* and books come together in their support for the creation of this Maḥzor. On behalf of the scholars, editors and designers of this volume, we thank you; on behalf of the users and readers of this Maḥzor, we are forever in your debt.

We could not have embarked on this project without the moral leadership and intellectual spark of Rabbi Lord Jonathan Sacks. Rabbi Sacks provides an invaluable guide to the liturgy through his remarkable translation, introduction and commentary. His work not only clarifies the text and explains the teachings of our sages, but uniquely and seamlessly weaves profound concepts of Judaism into the reality of contemporary life. It was our distinct privilege to work with Rabbi Sacks to create a Maḥzor that we believe appropriately mirrors the complexity and richness of life itself.

We only hope that Rabbi Sacks's contribution is matched by the scholarship, design and typography that have been hallmarks of Koren Publishers Jerusalem for more than fifty years. Raphaël Freeman led Koren's small but highly professional team of scholars, editors and artists. Rabbi David Fuchs supervised the textual aspects of the work. Rachel Meghnagi edited the English texts. Efrat Gross edited the Hebrew texts, and these were ably proofread by Barukh Brener and Naor Kahalani.

Jessica Sacks translated *Keriat HaTorah, Mishnayot Rosh HaShana,* and some of the festival prayers. Rabbi David Fuchs elucidated the *Mishnayot* commentary. Rabbi Eli Clark contributed the informative and useful Halakha Guide, and we are grateful to Binyamin Shalom and Adina Luber for their translation of the *piyutim*.

This new edition of the Koren Maḥzor continues the Koren tradition of making the language of prayer more accessible, thus enhancing the prayer experience.

One of the unique features of the Maḥzor is the use of typesetting to break up a prayer phrase-by-phrase – rather than using a block paragraph format – so that the reader will naturally pause at the correct places. No commas appear in the Hebrew text at the end of lines, but in the English translation, where linguistic clarity requires, we have retained the use of commas at the end of lines. Unlike other Hebrew/English maḥzorim, the Hebrew text is on the left-hand page and the English on the right. This arrangement preserves the distinctive "fanning out" effect of the Koren text and the beauty of the Koren layout.

We hope and pray that this Maḥzor, like all our publications, extends the vision of Koren's founder, Eliyahu Koren, to a new generation to further *Avodat HaShem* for Jews everywhere.

Matthew Miller, Publisher
Jerusalem 5774 (2014)

# INTRODUCTION

*The Story of Rosh HaShana*

*by*

RABBI LORD
JONATHAN SACKS

## INTRODUCTION

The ten days that begin on Rosh HaShana and culminate in Yom Kippur are the holy of holies of Jewish time. The atmosphere in the synagogue is intense. You can almost touch the Divine Presence. Isaiah said: "Seek God where He is to be found, call on Him when He is close" (Is. 55:6). The rabbis wrestled with this verse. What could it mean? God is the God of everywhere and all time. He is always to be found, always close. The verse seemed to make no sense at all.

This was their reply: "These are the Ten Days of Repentance between Rosh HaShana and Yom Kippur" – meaning, God is always close to us, but we are not always close to Him. He is always to be found, but we do not always seek Him out. To sense the closeness of God needs some special effort on our part. To reach out to the Infinite in finite space, to meet the Eternal in the midst of time, to sense what ultimately lies beyond the senses, requires a focus far beyond the ordinary.

It needs a drama of holiness, enacted in our holiest place, the synagogue, at the holiest of times, *Yamim Nora'im*, the Days of Awe. To begin it needs a sound – the shofar – so piercing and strange that it wakes us out of our everyday consciousness into an awareness of being present at something vast and momentous. We need to come close to God for God to feel close to us. That is what happens on the Ten Days of Repentance, and it begins on Rosh HaShana.

It is as if the world has become a courtroom. God Himself is the Judge. The shofar announces that the court is in session, and we are on trial, giving an account of our lives. Properly entered into, this is a potentially life-changing experience. It forces us to ask the most fateful questions we will ever ask: Who am I? Why am I here? How shall I live? How have I lived until now? How have I used God's greatest gift: time? Who have I wronged, and how can I put it right? Where have I failed, and how shall I overcome my failures? What is broken in my life and needs mending? What chapter will I write in the book of life? The unexamined life, a philosopher said, is not worth living. No one who has genuinely experienced Rosh HaShana and Yom Kippur lives an unexamined life.

These are days of reflection and introspection when we stand in the conscious presence of Infinity, knowing how short and vulnerable life

◂ really

really is, and how little time we have here on earth. This can be, and should be, a life-changing experience. Unfortunately, it not always is. The prayers are long. Some of them, especially the *piyutim*, the liturgical poems with their elaborate acrostics and obscure wordplays, are hard to understand. Others use imagery that can seem remote. The central image of Rosh HaShana is of God as King enthroned in the seat of judgment. That image would once have been self-evident, but there are fewer kings today than there once were, and even in the monarchies that remain, the role of royalty is often more symbolic than judicial. The prayers we say on Rosh HaShana span more than thirty centuries, and some need decoding if they are to speak to us today.

Yet Rosh HaShana and Yom Kippur have retained an undiminished hold on the Jewish imagination. They remain days on which even Jews estranged from Judaism for much of the year come to synagogue, and the world's longest courtroom drama continues: the extended argument between God and His people about the fate of justice and the justice of fate that has been running since the day when Abraham first called God "Judge of all the earth," and that led Albert Einstein to speak about that "almost fanatical love of justice" that made him thank his stars that he was born a Jew.

No people has believed as lucidly and long as have Jews, that life has a purpose; that this world is an arena of justice and human dignity; that we are, each of us, free and responsible, capable of shaping our lives in accordance with our highest ideals. We are here for a reason. We were created in love and forgiveness by the God of love and forgiveness who asks us to love and forgive. However many times we may have failed to live up to our aspirations, God always gives us the chance and the power to begin again. On Rosh HaShana and Yom Kippur, the holiest days of a holy people, God summons us to greatness.

I want in this introduction, to tell the story of Rosh HaShana and what it might mean for us.

### *The Mystery*

No sooner do we open the Torah, seeking to understand the significance of the day, than we are plunged into mystery. Only twice does the Torah touch on the subject, and in neither case does it provide much information:

> The LORD spoke to Moses, saying: Speak to the Israelite people thus: In the seventh month, on the first day of the month, you shall observe complete rest, a sacred occasion commemorated with loud blasts [*zikhron terua*]. (Lev. 23:23–24)

> On the first day of the seventh month you shall hold a sacred assembly. You shall do no laborious work, and you shall mark a Day of the Blowing of the Shofar [*yom terua*]. (Num. 29:1)

Other than details of the sacrifices to be offered, that is all. There is no explanation of what the day represents, or what the sound – *terua* – signifies. Nor does the Torah specify what instrument is to be used. It might be a horn. But equally it might refer to the silver trumpets the Israelites were commanded to make to summon the people (Num. 10:1–10). The central motifs of the other festivals, the unleavened bread and bitter herbs of Pesaḥ, the booth of Sukkot, the affliction (fasting) of Yom Kippur, all have symbolic value. We know what they mean and how they connect with the mood of the day. But the Torah does not tell us what the sound of *terua* symbolizes. Is it the sound of celebration, of warning, of fear or tears? We do not know (Rabbeinu Baḥye, *Kad HaKemaḥ, Rosh HaShana* [2]).

Nor does the Torah use the phrase *Rosh HaShana,* the beginning or "head" of the year, in this context or any other. The only time it appears in Tanakh, the Hebrew Bible as a whole, it refers to Yom Kippur: "In the twenty-fifth year of our exile, at the beginning of the year [*berosh hashana*], *on the tenth of the month,* in the fourteenth year after the fall of the city" (Ezek. 40:1). In fact the Torah seems to make it clear that Rosh HaShana is *not* the beginning of the year. It is the first day, not of the first, but the seventh month. The first month is Nisan.

How then do we arrive at the festival as we know it today?

In the earliest stages of an embryo, when a fetus is still no more than a small bundle of cells, already it contains the genome, the long string of DNA, from which the child and eventually the adult will emerge. The genetic structure that will shape the person it becomes is there from the beginning. So it is with Judaism. "Bible, Mishna, Talmud and Aggada, even what a senior disciple is destined to teach in the presence of his master, was already stated to Moses at Sinai" (Talmud Yerushalmi, *Pe'ah* 2:4). The evolution of Rosh HaShana was already prefigured at the outset, but to see how it developed we have to decipher the clues.

### *Creation's Anniversary*

The first thing we notice is that it is "the first day of the seventh month." The number seven, especially when applied to time, always signifies *holiness*. The first thing declared holy in the Torah is the seventh day, Shabbat (Gen. 2:1–3). The seventh or "sabbatical" year is likewise holy. There is to be no work in the fields. The land is to enjoy rest. Debts are released. A similar provision applies to the fiftieth or Jubilee year (at the end of seven seven-year cycles) when, in addition, most ancestral land returned to its original owners. The seventh month fits this pattern. It is to the year what Shabbat is to the week, the sabbatical to a cycle of years, and the Jubilee to an era. It is holy time.

What is specific about the holiness of the seventh in a sequence of time is that it is marked by a cessation of work. It marks a period during which we cease creating and remember that we are creations. We stop making and remember that we are made. We, the universe and time itself are the work of a hand greater than merely human, greater in fact than anything we can conceive. On the seventh, be it day, month or year, we focus our attention on God the Creator of all. Rosh HaShana is a festival of Creation.

No sooner have we said this than we see that in Judaism there is a dual structure of time, just as there is a unique duality in Judaism as a whole. On the one hand God is the *Creator*, who made heaven and earth and all that lives. But God is also the *Redeemer* who rescued His people from slavery in Egypt and led them through the wilderness to the Promised Land. He is the *Revealer* who appeared to the people at Mount Sinai, made a covenant with them, gave them laws, and from time to time sent them, through the prophets, His word.

God's creation is universal. God's redemption and revelation are particular to the people of Israel who, by their history and way of life, testify to His existence and involvement with the world. The two cycles of time in Judaism represent this duality. One cycle – Pesaḥ, Shavuot and

Sukkot – is about redemption and revelation, about the way God acts in history through the shaping events of the Jewish people. The other – the seventh day, seventh month and seventh year – is about creation, God in relation to the cosmos as a whole.

This is the first insight into the meaning of the day. Rosh HaShana is a celebration of the universe as God's work. The sages called it the anniversary of creation. This is the theme of the middle section of the Musaf Amida, *Zikhronot*, "Remembrances." "You remember all of creation, and all things that were formed… for this day is the opening of all Your works, a remembrance of the very first day" (page 508). It is echoed in the prayer *Hayom Harat Olam*, "This day is the birth of the world" (page 514).

Because it is about creation and humanity, the prayers of Rosh HaShana have a universalism not shared by Pesaḥ, Shavuot and Sukkot. The central section of the Amida on those days begins with the words, "You have chosen us from among all peoples," a declaration of Jewish chosenness. By contrast, in the Amida on Rosh HaShana we say, "And so place the fear of You… over all that You have made," an expression of complete universality. Pesaḥ, Shavuot and Sukkot are about what it is to be a Jew. Rosh HaShana is about what it is to be human.

## *The Kingship of God*

The next hint is given in the biblical names for the festival, *Yom Terua* and *Zikhron Terua*, "the day of *terua*" and "a commemoration or remembrance of *terua*." What is *terua*? In all other biblical contexts, it refers to a sound, usually produced by a wind instrument, though sometimes it may mean a shout or cry on the part of a crowd.

What instrument is the Torah referring to? The silver trumpets used by the Israelites in the wilderness were used to sound both a *tekia* and a *terua*, a *tekia* to summon the people and a *terua* to signal that it was time to begin a further journey (Num. 10:1–7). So the *terua* of Rosh HaShana might refer to a trumpet. The sages ruled out this possibility for a simple reason.

Rosh HaShana turns out not to be the only time that a *terua* was sounded in the seventh month. It was also sounded on the tenth of the month, Yom Kippur, in the Jubilee year, when slaves went free and ancestral land returned to its original owners. The Jubilee was the occasion

◂ of the

of the famous words, taken directly from the biblical text, written on the Liberty Bell of America, "Proclaim liberty throughout all the land unto all the inhabitants thereof" (Lev. 25:10). The previous verse (25:9) states specifically that one should sound the *terua* with a shofar:

> Then you shall sound the horn loud [*shofar terua*]; in the seventh month on the tenth day of the month, on the Day of Atonement, you shall have the horn sounded throughout the land.

Indeed the Hebrew word for Jubilee, *yovel,* also means a ram's horn (Ex. 19:13). It became a simple inference to conclude that this applied to the *terua* of the first day of the seventh month as well.

What was special about the shofar? In several places in Tanakh it is the sound of battle (see for example, Joshua 6; I Samuel 4; Jeremiah 4:19, 49:2). It could also be the sound of celebration. When King David brought the Ark into Jerusalem, he danced and the people rejoiced with "*terua* and the sound of the shofar" (II Samuel 6:15). But in a number of places, especially the historical books, the shofar was sounded at the coronation of a king. So we find at the proclamation of Solomon as king:

> Tzaddok the priest took the horn of oil from the sacred tent and anointed Solomon. Then they sounded the shofar and all the people shouted, "Long live King Solomon!" (I Kings 1:39)

Likewise when Jehu was appointed king:

> They quickly took their cloaks and spread them under him on the bare steps. Then they blew the shofar and shouted, "Jehu is King!" (II Kings 9:13)

When Absalom sought to have himself proclaimed king in the lifetime of his father, David, we read:

> Then Absalom sent secret messengers throughout the tribes of Israel to say, "As soon as you hear the sound of the shofar, then say, 'Absalom is King in Hebron!'" (II Samuel 15:10)

The book of Psalms associates the shofar not with a human king but with the declaration of God as King. A key text is Psalm 47, said in many congregations before the shofar blowing on Rosh HaShana:

◂ God has

> God has been raised up in sound;
> raised, the LORD, in the voice of the shofar [...]
> For God is King over all the earth... (Ps. 47:6, 8)

Psalm 98 makes a clear connection between God's kingship and his judgment:

> With trumpets and the sound of the shofar,
> shout for joy before the LORD, the King. [...]
> For He is coming to judge the earth.
> He judges the world with righteousness
> and all nations with equity. (Psalm 98:6, 9)

We have now arrived at the second great dimension of Rosh HaShana. It is the day on which we celebrate the kingship of God. This has left its mark throughout the Rosh HaShana prayers. The key word is *Melekh*, "King." The Leader begins in the morning service with a dramatic rendition of *HaMelekh* (page 309). The third blessing of the Amida, that normally ends with the words "the holy God," on Rosh HaShana and throughout the Ten Days of Repentance, becomes "the holy King." In particular, Musaf on Rosh HaShana begins with an entire section dedicated to *malkhiyot*, verses relating to divine kingship. Rosh HaShana is the day we celebrate God not just as Creator of the world, but its Ruler also.

### *The Coronation*

The concept of divine kingship sounds simple, even routine, but it is not. It made ancient Israel unique. Eventually it had an impact on the development of freedom in the West. It was a Jewish scholar, Philo, who lived in Alexandria in the first century, who realized how radical it was. Philo was writing about Judaism for a Greek-speaking audience, and when it came to the political structure of Jewry he found that the Greek language had no word for it. The Greeks had words for most things. They were the world's first systematic thinkers, and in Plato's *Republic* and Aristotle's *Politics* they surveyed every known type of political structure – tyranny, monarchy, oligarchy, aristocracy and democracy. But there was no word for the Jewish system, and Philo was forced to invent one to explain it.

The word he chose was *theocracy* – rule by God alone. This was the

◂ thought

thought expressed by Gideon, the man who led the Israelites to success in their battle against the Midianites. When the people sought to make him king, he replied: "I will not rule over you, nor will my son rule over you. The Lord will rule over you" (Judges 8:23).

Eventually the Israelites did appoint a king, and in the course of time they developed other systems of governance: judges, elders, patriarchs, exilarchs, city councils and, in the modern state of Israel, democracy. But the ultimate Ruler of the Jewish people was God alone. This meant that no human ruler had absolute authority. Prophets could criticize kings. People could disobey an immoral order. The sovereignty of God meant that there are moral limits to the use of power. Right is sovereign over might. These were, and remain, revolutionary ideas.

They were also responsible for the single most astonishing phenomenon of Jewish history, the fact that Jews retained their identity as a nation for two thousand years in exile, scattered across the world. Wherever they were, God remained their King. They remained His people. Rarely was this better expressed than in the great prayer, *Aleinu* (page 40), originally written for Rosh HaShana as a preface to the verses about God's kingship:

He is our God; there is no other.
Truly He is our King; there is none else.

There is an integral connection between kingship and creation, and it can be stated simply. God made the universe. Therefore God owns the universe. Therefore God is its ultimate Sovereign since He can specify the terms and conditions under which we exist within the universe. This applies to all humanity.

Hence the second paragraph of *Aleinu,* with its vision and hope of a time "when all humanity will call on Your name," and "all the world's inhabitants will realize and know that to You every knee must bow." The God of revelation and redemption is the God of Israel. The God of creation is the God of all humankind. But they are the same God. Hence the vision of Zechariah with which *Aleinu* ends, when "the Lord shall be King over all the earth; on that day the Lord shall be One and His name One" (Zech. 14:9).

Underlying this is perhaps the most remarkable idea of all. "There is no King without a people" (*Kad HaKemaḥ, Rosh HaShana* [2]). The fact

◂ that

that the people of Israel accepted God as their King, and His covenant as their constitution, means that they bear witness to Him by their very existence and way of life. That is what the psalm means when it says "You are the Holy One, enthroned on the praises of Israel" (Ps. 22:4). The praises of Israel are the visible symbol of God's majesty. That confers extraordinary dignity on us.

Rabbi Joseph Soloveitchik, doyen of Jewish thinkers in the twentieth century, used to explain this by telling the story of his first Hebrew teacher, a Chabad Hasid who made an indelible impression on him as a child by telling him that Rosh HaShana was God's coronation. "And who puts the crown on His head? We do." He spoke about his memories of praying as a child among the Hasidim on the first night of Rosh HaShana:

> I can feel the unique atmosphere which enveloped these Hasidim as they recited the prayers by which they proclaimed Him their King. The older Hasidim termed this night the "Coronation Night" as they crowned Him as their King. These poor and downtrodden Jews, who suffered so much during their daily existence, were able to experience the enthroning of the Almighty and the true meaning of the Kingship prayers of the Rosh HaShana liturgy.*

The shofar on Rosh HaShana is our way of participating in God's coronation.

## *Exile and Return*

The anniversary of creation; a kingship renewal ceremony – there Rosh HaShana might have remained had it not been for one overwhelming historical fact: the Babylonian exile. It is one thing to celebrate the harmony of the created universe when you are at home with the universe, another when you are reminded daily that you are not at home, when you are strangers in a strange land. It is one thing to celebrate divine sovereignty when you enjoy national sovereignty, another when you have lost it and are subject to another power. The destruction of the Temple and the Babylonian exile were a trauma for the Jewish people, physically and spiritually, and we have an indelible record of how the people felt: "By

* Aaron Rakeffet-Rothkoff, *The Rav*, Vol. 2 (Hoboken, NJ: KTAV Publishing House), p. 171.

◂ the rivers

the rivers of Babylon we sat and wept as we remembered Zion… How can we sing the LORD's song on foreign soil?" (Ps. 137:1–4).

Judaism and the Jewish people might have disappeared there and then, as had happened to the ten tribes of the northern kingdom, Israel, a century and a half before. There was one difference. The religious identity of the southern kingdom, Judah, was strong. The prophets, from Moses to Jeremiah, had spoken of exile and return. Once before, in the period between Joseph and Moses, the people had experienced exile and return. So defeat and displacement were not final. There was hope. It was contained in one word: *teshuva.*

There is no precise English translation of *teshuva,* which means both "return": homecoming, a physical act – and "repentance": remorse, a change of heart and deed, a spiritual act. The reason the Hebrew word means both is because, for the Torah, sin leads to exile. Adam and Eve, after they had sinned, were exiled from the Garden of Eden. Cain, after he had murdered his brother, was punished by being sentenced to eternal exile. (Gen. 4:12). The idea of justice in the Torah is based on the principle of *mida keneged mida,* "measure for measure." A sin, *ḥet,* is an act in the wrong place. The result, *galut,* is that the agent finds himself in the wrong place. Sin disturbs the moral harmony of the universe.

But God forgives. That one fact rescues life from tragedy. The sages said that God created repentance before He created humanity. (Nedarim 39b). What they meant was that God, in creating humanity and endowing the human person with freewill, knew that we would make mistakes. We are not angels. We stumble, we sin. We are dust of the earth and to dust we will one day return. Without repentance and forgiveness, the human condition would be unbearable. Therefore God, creating humanity, created the possibility of repentance, meaning that when we acknowledge our failings, we are forgiven. Exile is not an immutable fate. Returning to God, we find Him returning to us. We can restore the moral harmony of the universe.

It follows that on a national scale, *teshuva* means two things that become one: a spiritual return to God and a physical return to the land. This is how Moses put it in the key text of *teshuva betzibbur,* collective national repentance:

> When all these blessings and curses I have set before you come on you and you take them to heart wherever the LORD your God disperses

◂ you among

> you among the nations, and when you and your children return to the Lord your God and obey Him with all your heart and with all your soul according to everything I command you today, then the Lord your God will restore your fortunes and have compassion on you and gather you again from all the nations where He scattered you. Even if you have been banished to the most distant land under the heavens, from there the Lord your God will gather you and bring you back. (Deut. 30:1–4)

That was the theory and the hope. The question was: would it actually happen that way? It did, in the return of the Babylonian exiles to the land of Israel, and it was solemnized in one of the shaping events of Jewish history. It took place in the days of Ezra and Nehemiah on Rosh HaShana itself.

### *The Great Renewal*

Jews, not all but many, had returned from the Babylonian exile. The ruined Temple had been rebuilt. But the nation was in disarray. Religious knowledge was slight. Many had intermarried with local populations. They could not even speak Hebrew. "Half of their children spoke the language of Ashdod or the language of one of the other peoples, and did not know how to speak the language of Judah" (Neh. 13:24).

On the first day of the seventh month, Ezra the scribe and Nehemiah the governor convened a national assembly at the Water Gate in Jerusalem. Ezra, standing on a wooden platform, publicly read from the Torah while Levites were stationed throughout the crowd to translate and explain what was being said. As they began to realize how far they had drifted from the divine mission, the people started weeping:

> And all the people listened attentively to the Book of the Law… Then Nehemiah the governor, Ezra the priest and teacher of the Law, and the Levites who were instructing the people said to them all, "This day is holy to the Lord your God. Do not mourn or weep." For all the people had been weeping as they listened to the words of the Law. And he [Nehemiah] said, "Go and enjoy choice food and sweet drinks, and send some to those who have nothing prepared. This day is holy to our Lord. Do not grieve, for the joy of the Lord is your strength." The Levites calmed all the people, saying, "Be still, for this

◂ is a holy

> is a holy day. Do not grieve." Then all the people went away to eat and drink, to send portions of food and to celebrate with great joy, because they now understood the words that had been made known to them. (Neh. 8:3; 8:9–12)

That Rosh HaShana (which incidentally extended for two days: the people returned the next day to continue the reading) became the start of a period of national rededication, a covenant renewal ceremony. It was a turning point in Jewish history, and it is not too much to say that we owe to it the survival of Jews and Judaism.

What Ezra and Nehemiah had understood was that religious identity was at the heart of Jewish survival. The Israelites had undergone almost a controlled experiment into what enables a nation to endure. Following the split of the nation into two after the death of Solomon, the northern kingdom had been conquered by the Assyrians. Transported, its people had, for the most part, acculturated into the general population and disappeared, to become known to history as the Lost Ten Tribes. The southern kingdom of Judah, conquered and forced into exile by the Babylonians, had sustained their identity. Inspired by people like Ezekiel, they studied Torah. They prayed. They listened to the prophets, who told them that their covenant with God was still intact. They stayed Jews. Indeed the very fact that we are today called Jews (*Yehudim*, i.e. members of the southern kingdom of Judah) is testimony to this phenomenon.

Ezra and Nehemiah, seeing the sad state of Jewish identity among the Jews of Israel, realized that a major program of religious revival was called for, beginning with the public reading of the Torah that Rosh HaShana, the first ever national adult education seminar. The strength of the Jewish nation, they saw more clearly than any of their contemporaries, lay not just in armies and physical defense but in identity and spiritual defense. Ezra was a new type in history: a "scribe," the teacher as hero.

Slowly over the course of the next five centuries, new institutions emerged, most significantly the synagogue and the house of study, which would allow Jewry to survive even military and political defeat. By the first and second century of the common era, when Jews suffered two catastrophes at the hands of the Romans, they had become a people whose heroes were teachers, whose citadels were schools, and whose passion was study and the life of the mind. That transformation was responsible for a phenomenon that has no parallel, a people capable of surviving two thousand years of exile, their identity intact. It began with that gathering on the first of Tishrei, when Ezra recalled a people to its ancient mission, and the people wept as they became aware of how far they had drifted from the Torah, their constitution as a nation.

Thus was born the association of the day with *teshuva,* national return. It was Nahmanides in the thirteenth century who most clearly understood that the return of Jews from Babylon and their renewal of the covenant was the historical realization of Moses' prophecy about return, which was itself, for Nahmanides, the source of the command of *teshuva.* (commentary on Deut. 30:2).

### *Individual Responsibility*

The Babylonian exile had another effect as well. As a nation in their own land, the Jewish people experienced their fate collectively. War and peace, poverty and prosperity, famine or fruitfulness, these are things a nation experiences as a nation. The Torah is intimately concerned with the fate and dignity of individuals, but it was first and foremost a covenant with the nation as a whole.

Things are different in exile. The nation is no longer in charge of its destiny. It experiences fate primarily as a group of individuals. It remains a nation, but an injured nation, a nation not at home in the world. It was then that an idea present in Judaism from the beginning, took on a new significance. The key figure who brought this message to the exiles was a priest and prophet who was with them in Babylon: Ezekiel.

Ezekiel reminded the people of the power and possibility of individual responsibility. In so doing, he gave expression to the idea of *teshuva* in a way that has remained salient from his day to now. The first principle he taught the people had already been emphasized by his elder contemporary, Jeremiah. We are each responsible for our own sins, and no one else's:

> The one who sins is the one who will die. The child will not share the guilt of the parent, nor will the parent share the guilt of the child.

◂ The righteousness

> The righteousness of the righteous will be credited to them, and the wickedness of the wicked will be charged against them. (Ezek. 18:20)

Then he gives precise articulation to the idea of *teshuva*:

> But if a wicked person turns away from all the sins he has committed and keeps all My decrees and does what is just and right, that person will surely live; they will not die. None of the offenses they have committed will be remembered against them. Because of the righteous things they have done, they will live. Do I take any pleasure in the death of the wicked? declares the Sovereign LORD. Rather, am I not pleased when they turn from their ways and live? (Ezek. 18:21–23)

That is it. No Temple, no sacrifice, no sin offering, no ritual of atonement, but simply the act of turning – *teshuva* – understood as an abandonment of sin and a change of behavior to embrace the holy and the good. These and other verses from Ezekiel became key texts in the rabbinic understanding of *teshuva*.

Ezekiel relates this to the shofar:

> The word of the LORD came to me: "Son of man, speak to your people and say to them: 'When I bring the sword against a land, and the people of the land choose one of their men and make him their watchman, and he sees the sword coming against the land and blows the shofar to warn the people, then if anyone hears the shofar but does not heed the warning and the sword comes and takes their life, their blood will be on their own head… (Ezek. 33:1–4)

The task of the prophet is to sound the shofar as a warning to the people that their sins are about to be punished and that they must now do *teshuva* if they are to avert the coming catastrophe. Ezekiel is not the only one to speak of the shofar in these terms. As we read in Isaiah: "Raise your voice like a shofar. Declare to My people their rebellion and to the descendants of Jacob their sins" (Is. 58:1). Hosea (8:1), Joel (2:1, 15) and Amos (3:6) all understood the shofar as the sound of warning of imminent war, itself a sign that the nation had sinned. But Ezekiel, more lucidly than anyone else, set out the doctrine of *teshuva* in the way we understand

◂ it today

it today, as something done by individuals as well as a nation, as a change of mind and deed, initiated by the sound of the shofar.

*

So the basic shape of Rosh HaShana emerged from potentiality to actuality. What was originally a festival of divine creation and sovereignty, accompanied by the shofar as a clarion proclaiming the King, became also – through the prophets, the Babylonian exile, and the return – a day of national and individual rededication, a remembrance of sins and a turning with new commitment to the future.

The rabbis fleshed out this sketch with detail and color. First was the name Rosh HaShana itself. The sages knew of four New Years: the first of Nisan as the New Year for kings and festivals, the first of Elul for the tithe of cattle, the first or fifteenth of Shevat for trees, and the first of Tishrei for "years, and Sabbatical years and Jubilees" (Mishna, *Rosh HaShana* 1:1; see page 142). However it was the first of Tishrei that became known as the New Year per se.

The Mishna states that on Rosh HaShana all creatures pass before God (ibid. 1:2). How they do so depends on the precise text of the Mishna, which exists in two variants: *kivnei Maron* or *kivenumeron*. *Numeron* is thought to be derived from a Greek word meaning "a troop of soldiers." Accordingly the Talmud reads this as meaning "like the troops of the house of David." The alternative reading, "like the children of Maron," is given two interpretations in the Talmud. One is "like a flock of sheep" passing one by one through a wicket so that they can be counted by the shepherd, or "like the ascent of Beit Maron," a narrow pass through which only one person can go at a time.

The first reading, "like the troops of the house of David," sees the primary meaning of Rosh HaShana as a festival of divine kingship. God is King, the shofar proclaims His presence, and we, His retinue, gather to pay Him homage. The second and third see it as a day on which God judges us, one at a time. The biblical phrase about the land of Israel, "the eyes of the LORD your God are continually on it from the beginning of the year to its end" (Deut. 11:12) was understood to imply that "from the beginning of the year, sentence is passed as to what the end shall be" (*Rosh HaShana* 8a).

◂ The rabbis

The rabbis also articulated the concept of a book of life. Moses, pleading for the people after the making of the golden calf, says, "But now, please forgive their sin, but if not, then blot me out of the book You have written" (Ex. 32:32). In Psalms 69:29 David says about the wicked, "May they be blotted out of the book of life and not be listed with the righteous."

The book of Esther contains a famous episode in which, "That night the king could not sleep; so he ordered the book of records [*sefer hazikhronot*] … to be brought in and read to him" (Esther 6:1). There were times when the king read a record of events that had happened and passed verdict, whether for punishment or reward.

Rabbi Yoḥanan taught that on Rosh HaShana three books lie open in heaven: one for the completely wicked, one for the completely righteous, and one for the intermediate. The completely righteous are immediately inscribed in the book of life; the thoroughly wicked are immediately inscribed in the book of death; the verdict on the intermediate is suspended from New Year till the Day of Atonement. If they deserve well, they are inscribed in the book of life; if they do not deserve well, they are inscribed in the book of death (*Rosh HaShana* 16b). It became a particularly beautiful custom to wish people, on the first night of the year, that they be written and sealed immediately for life, implying that those around us are completely righteous. Those who judge others favorably are, we believe, themselves judged favorably.

Both the Babylonian Talmud and the Jerusalem Talmud specify that, whatever the decree, there are certain acts that have the power to avert or annul it, or at least mitigate its harshness. The Babylonian Talmud lists four: charity, prayer, change of name and change of deed – some add a fifth: change of place (*Rosh HaShana* 16b). The Jerusalem Talmud lists three: prayer, charity and *teshuva* (Talmud Yerushalmi, *Ta'anit* 2:1), deriving all three from God's answer to Solomon's prayer at the inauguration of the Temple:

> If My people, who are called by My name, will humble themselves and pray [= prayer] and seek My face [= charity] and turn from their wicked ways [= *teshuva*], then I will hear from heaven, and I will forgive their sin and heal their land. (II Chronicles 7:14)

◂ All of

All of these motifs – God's kingship, His sitting in the throne of judgment, opening the book in which our deeds and signatures are written, the sound of the shofar that makes even the angels tremble, the shepherd counting his flock, the verdict written on Rosh HaShana and sealed on Yom Kippur, and the power of repentance, prayer and charity to avert the evil decree – are brought together in the liturgical poem *Untaneh Tokef*, one of the great prayers and the most vivid image of Rosh HaShana as we might imagine it in the heavenly court.

We have traveled a long way from the starting point of Rosh HaShana as the anniversary of creation, yet there is a fine rabbinic midrash that brings us back to our starting point. According to Rabbi Eliezer, creation began on 25 Elul, making the first of Tishrei the day on which humanity was created. That day, Adam and Eve were made, and that day they sinned. Yet God forgave them, or at least mitigated their punishment. Initially He had said, "You must not eat from the tree of the knowledge of good and evil, for when you eat from it you will certainly die" (Gen. 2:17). Yet Adam and Eve ate but did not die. Evidently they were forgiven. The midrash continues:

> God said to Adam: This will be a sign to your children. As you stood in judgment before Me this day and were pardoned, so will your children in the future stand in judgment before Me and will emerge from My presence pardoned. When will that be? *In the seventh month, on the first day of the month.* (*Vayikra Raba* 29:1)

On Rosh HaShana we are like Adam and Eve, the quintessential representatives of the human condition. We may have sinned. We may have lost the paradise of innocence. We all do. But we are alive. We live in the radiance of God and the generosity of his compassion. In the simplest yet most moving of prayers, Rabbi Akiva turned to God and said, *Avinu Malkenu*, "Our Father, our King." (*Ta'anit* 25a) God is our King, Sovereign of the universe, Author of our laws, the Judge who administers justice. But He is also our Father and we are His children, and can a father withhold compassion from his children? Time and again He forgives us and never loses patience. Human parents may lose faith in a child but God never does: "Were my father and my mother to forsake me, the Lord would take me in" (Ps. 27:10).

◂ *Past, Present*

### *Past, Present and Future*

All of these ideas have left their mark on the Maḥzor and appear in our prayers, especially in the central section of the Musaf Amida. On all other festivals, there is one central blessing, *Kedushat HaYom*, "the special sanctity of the day." Uniquely Rosh HaShana has three central blessings, *Malkhiyot*, Kingship; *Zikhronot*, Remembrances; and *Shofarot*, verses about the Shofar. These correspond to the sentence (not found in Tanakh, but pieced together from biblical phrases), "The LORD is King, the LORD was King, the LORD will be King, forever and all time."

*Malkhiyot* refers to the present. *Zikhronot* is about memories of the past. *Shofarot* is about the future. The shofar is always a signal of something about to come: the imminent arrival of the king, a warning of impending danger, or the sound of a trial about to begin.

*Teshuva* sensitizes us to the full significance of time. There are those who live purely in the present, but their lives have no overarching meaning. They react rather than act. They travel with no ultimate destination. They are "like chaff blown by the wind" (Ps. 1:4). To be a Jew is to live poised between past and future: the past and future of our individual lives, of our ancient but still young people, and of humanity as a whole.

*Teshuva* tells us that our past does not determine our future. We can change. We can act differently next time than last. If anything, our future determines our past. Our determination to grow as human beings – our commitment to a more faithful, sensitive, decent life in the year to come – gives us the courage and honesty to face our past and admit its shortcomings. Our *teshuva* and God's forgiveness together mean that we are not prisoners of the past, held captive by it. In Judaism sin is what we do, not what we are. Therefore we remain intact, able to acknowledge our failures and then move on.

My predecessor Lord Jakobovits made a profound comment about Rosh HaShana. Given that it is the start of the Ten Days of Repentance, surprisingly it contains no explicit confessions, no penitential prayers. These form the text and texture of Yom Kippur but not Rosh HaShana. Why so? Because, he suggested, *teshuva* is driven by two different mindsets: commitment to the future and remorse about the past. Rosh HaShana is about the first, Yom Kippur about the second. *Rosh* means "head" and the default position of the head is looking forward not back.

◂ The placing

The placing of Rosh HaShana before Yom Kippur means that our determination to act better in the future is prior to our feelings of remorse about the past. To which we might add that this is why we blow shofar on Rosh HaShana. The shofar, too, turns our attention to what lies ahead, not behind.

### *What Rosh HaShana Says To Us*

What then does Rosh HaShana say to us? Of what is it a reminder? How can it transform our lives?

The genius of Judaism was to take eternal truths and translate them into time, into lived experiences. Other cultures have constructed philosophies and theologies, elaborate systems of abstract thought. Judaism prefers truth lived to truth merely thought. Ancient Greece produced the logical imagination. Judaism produced the chronological imagination, truth transposed into the calendar. Rosh HaShana, the anniversary of the creation of humanity, invites us to live and feel the human condition in graphic ways.

The first thing it tells us is that life is short. However much life expectancy has risen, we will not, in one lifetime, be able to achieve everything we might wish to achieve. *Untaneh Tokef* tells the poetry of mortality with haunting pathos:

> Man is founded in dust and ends in dust.
> He lays down his soul to bring home bread.
> He is like a broken shard,
> like grass dried up,
> like a faded flower,
> like a fleeting shadow,
> like a passing cloud,
> like a breath of wind,
> like whirling dust,
> like a dream that slips away.

This life is all we have. How shall we use it well? We know that we will not finish the task, but neither are we free to stand aside from it. That is the first truth.

The second is: life itself, each day, every breath we take, is the gift of God:

◂ Remember

Remember us for life,
O King who delights in life,
and write us in the book of life –
for Your sake, O God of life.

Life is not something we may take for granted. If we do, we will fail to celebrate it. God gives us one gift above all others, said Maimonides: life itself, beside which everything else is secondary. Other religions have sought God in heaven, or the afterlife, the distant past or the distant future. Here there is suffering, there reward; here chaos, there order; here pain, there balm; here poverty, there plenty. Judaism has relentlessly sought God in the here-and-now of life on earth. Yes, we believe in life after death, but it is in life before death that we truly find human greatness.

Third, we are free. Judaism is the religion of the free human being freely responding to the God of freedom. We are not in the grip of sin. We are not determined by economic forces or psychological drives or genetically encoded impulses that we are powerless to resist. The very fact that we can do *teshuva*, that we can act differently tomorrow than we did yesterday, tells us we are free. Philosophers have found this idea difficult. So have scientists. But Judaism insists on it, and our ancestors proved it by defying every law of history, surviving against the odds, refusing to accept defeat.

Fourth, life is meaningful. We are not mere accidents of matter, generated by a universe that came into being for no reason and will one day, for no reason, cease to be. We are here because a loving God brought the universe, and life, and us, into existence – a God who knows our fears, hears our prayers, believes in us more than we believe in ourselves, who forgives us when we fail, lifts us when we fall, and gives us the strength to overcome despair. The historian Paul Johnson once wrote: "No people has ever insisted more firmly than the Jews that history has a purpose and humanity a destiny." He concluded: "The Jews, therefore, stand right at the center of the perennial attempt to give human life the dignity of a purpose."* That too is one of the truths of Rosh HaShana.

Fifth, life is not easy. Judaism does not see the world through rose-tinted lenses. The sufferings of our ancestors haunt our prayers. The world

* Paul Johnson, *A History of the Jews* (London: Phoenix, 2004), Prologue, p. 2.

we live in is not the world as it ought to be. That is why, despite every temptation, Judaism has never been able to say the messianic age has come, even though we await it daily. But we are not bereft of hope because we are not alone. When Jews went into exile the *Shekhina,* the Divine Presence, went with them. God is always there, "close to all who call on Him in truth." (Ps. 145:18) He may hide His face, but He is there. He may be silent, but He is listening to us, hearing us and healing us in ways we may not understand at the time but which become clear in retrospect.

Sixth, life may be hard, but it can still be sweet, the way the *ḥalla* and the apple are on Rosh HaShana when we dip them in honey. Jews have never needed wealth to be rich, or power to be strong. To be a Jew is to live for simple things: the love between husband and wife, the sacred bond between parents and children, the gift of community where we help others and others help us and where we learn that joy is doubled and grief halved by being shared. To be a Jew is to give, whether in the form of *tzedaka* or *gemilut ḥasadim,* acts of loving kindness. It is to learn and never stop seeking, to pray and never stop thanking, to do *teshuva* and never stop growing. In this lies the secret of joy. Throughout history there have been hedonistic cultures that worship pleasure, and ascetic cultures that deny it, but Judaism has a different approach altogether: to sanctify pleasure by making it part of the worship of God. Life is sweet when touched by the divine.

Seventh, our life is the single greatest work of art we will ever make. Rabbi Joseph Soloveitchik, in one of his earliest works, spoke about *Ish HaHalakha,* the halakhic personality and its longing to create, to make something new, original. God too longs for us to create and thereby become His partner in the work of renewal. "The most fundamental principle of all is that man must create himself." That is what *teshuva* is, an act of making ourselves anew. On Rosh HaShana we step back from our life like an artist stepping back from his canvas, seeing what needs changing for the painting to be complete.

Eighth, we are what we are because of those who came before us. Our lives are not disconnected particles. We are each a letter in God's book of life. But single letters, though they are the vehicles of meaning, have no meaning when they stand alone. To have meaning they must be joined to other letters to make words, sentences, paragraphs, a story, and to be a Jew is to be part of the strangest, oldest, most unexpected and counter-intuitive story there has ever been: the story of a tiny people, never large and often homeless, who nonetheless outlived the greatest empires the world has ever known: the Egyptians, Assyrians, Babylonians, the Greeks and Romans, the medieval empires of Christianity and Islam, all the way to the Third Reich and the Soviet Union. Each in turn thought itself immortal. Each has gone. The Jewish people still lives.

So on Rosh HaShana we remember and ask God to remember those who came before us: Abraham and Isaac, Sarah, Hannah and Rachel, the Israelites of Moses' day, and the Jews of every generation, each of whom left some living legacy in the prayers we say or the melodies in which we sing them. And in one of the most moving verses of the middle section of Musaf we recall the great words said by God through the prophet Jeremiah: "I remember of you the kindness of your youth, your love when you were a bride; how you walked after Me in the desert, through a land not sown" (Jer. 2:2). Our ancestors may have sinned, but they never stopped following God though the way was hard and the destination distant. We do not start with nothing. We have inherited wealth, not material but spiritual. We are heirs to our ancestors' greatness.

Ninth, we are heirs to another kind of greatness too, that of the Torah itself and its high demands, its strenuous ideals, its panoply of mitzvot, its intellectual and existential challenges. Judaism asks great things of us and by doing so makes us great. We walk as tall as the ideals for which we live, and those of the Torah are very high indeed. We are, said Moses, God's children. (Deut. 14:1) We are called on, said Isaiah, to be His witnesses, His ambassadors on earth. (Is. 43:10) Time and again Jews did things thought impossible. They battled against might in the name of right. They fought against slavery. They showed that it was possible to be a nation without a land, to have influence without power, to be branded the world's pariahs yet not lose self respect. They believed with unshakable conviction that they would one day return to their land, and though the hope seemed absurd, it happened. Their kingdom may have been bounded by a nutshell yet Jews counted themselves kings of infinite space. Judaism sets the bar high, and though we may fall short time and again, Rosh HaShana and Yom Kippur allow us to begin anew, forgiven, cleansed, undaunted, ready for the next challenge, the next year.

◂ And finally

And finally comes the sound of the shofar, piercing our defenses, a wordless cry in a religion of words, a sound produced by breath as if to tell us that that is all life is – a mere breath – yet breath is nothing less than the spirit of God within us: "Then the Lord God formed man from the dust of the ground and breathed into his nostrils the breath of life, and man became a living being" (Gen. 2:7). We are dust of the earth but within us is the breath of God.

And whether the shofar is our cry to God or God's cry to us, somehow in that *tekia, shevarim, terua* – the call, the sob, the wail – is all the pathos of the Divine–human encounter as God asks us to take His gift, life itself, and make of it something holy, by so acting as to honor God and His image on earth, humankind. For we defeat death, not by living forever but by living by values that live forever; by doing deeds and creating blessings that will live on after us, and by attaching ourselves in the midst of time to God who lives beyond time, "the King – the living, everlasting God."

The Hebrew verb *lehitpalel*, to pray, more precisely means "to judge oneself." On Rosh HaShana we stand in judgment. We know what it is to be known. And though we know the worst about ourselves, God sees the best; and when we open ourselves to Him, He gives us the strength to become what we truly are.

Those who fully enter the spirit of Rosh HaShana emerge into the new year charged, energized, focused, renewed, knowing that to be a Jew is to live life in the presence of God, to sanctify life for the sake of God, and to enhance the lives of others – for where we bring blessings into other lives, there God lives.

Rabbi Jonathan Sacks
London, 5771 (2011)

# מחזור קורן לראש השנה

## THE KOREN ROSH HASHANA MAḤZOR

## ANNULMENT OF VOWS

*On the morning before Rosh HaShana, one should annul vows before three men, who sit as judges, saying:*

שִׁמְעוּ נָא Listen, please, my masters (expert judges): every vow or oath or prohibition or restriction or ban that I have vowed or sworn, whether awake or in a dream, or that I swore with one of the holy names that may not be erased, or by the holy four-letter name of God, blessed be He, or any naziriteship that I accepted on myself, even a naziriteship like that of Samson, or any prohibition, even against enjoyment, whether I forbade it to myself or others, by any expression of prohibition, whether using the language of prohibition or restriction or ban, or any positive commitment, even to perform a [non-obligatory] commandment, that I undertook by way of a vow or voluntary undertaking or oath or naziriteship or any other such expression, whether it was done by handshake or vow or voluntary undertaking or commandment-mandated custom I have customarily practiced, or any utterance that I have verbalized, or any non-obligatory commandment or good practice or conduct I have vowed and resolved in my heart to do, and have done three times without specifying that it does not have the force of a vow, whether it relates to myself or others, both those known to me and those I have already forgotten – regarding all of them, I hereby express my retroactive regret, and ask and seek their annulment from you, my eminences. For I fear that I may stumble and be trapped, Heaven forbid, in the sin of vows, oaths, naziriteships, bans, prohibitions, restrictions and agreements. I do not regret, Heaven forbid, the performance of the good deeds I have done. I regret, rather, having accepted them on myself in the language of vow, oath, naziriteship, prohibition, ban, restriction, agreement or acceptance of the heart.

Therefore I request annulment for them all.

---

Judaism is a religion that stresses the sanctity of language, especially when used to accept or impose obligations on oneself. Deep significance attaches to vows and the other verbal undertakings: "If a man makes a vow to God, or makes an oath to obligate himself, he must not break his word. He must do everything he said" (Num. 30:3). In general, it is preferable not to invest voluntary commitments with the sacred status of a vow. "If you refrain from making a vow, you will not be guilty" (Deut. 23:23). "It is better not to vow than to make a vow and not fulfill it" (Eccl. 5:4).

# התרת נדרים

*On the morning before* ראש השנה*, one should annul vows before three men, who sit as judges, saying:*

שִׁמְעוּ נָא רַבּוֹתַי (דַּיָּנִים מֻמְחִים), כָּל נֶדֶר אוֹ שְׁבוּעָה אוֹ אִסָּר אוֹ קוֹנָם אוֹ חֵרֶם שֶׁנָּדַרְתִּי אוֹ נִשְׁבַּעְתִּי בְּהָקִיץ אוֹ בַחֲלוֹם, אוֹ נִשְׁבַּעְתִּי בְּשֵׁמוֹת הַקְּדוֹשִׁים שֶׁאֵינָם נִמְחָקִים וּבְשֵׁם הוי״ה בָּרוּךְ הוּא, וְכָל מִינֵי נְזִירוּת שֶׁקִּבַּלְתִּי עָלַי וַאֲפִלּוּ נְזִירוּת שִׁמְשׁוֹן, וְכָל שׁוּם אִסּוּר וַאֲפִלּוּ אִסּוּר הֲנָאָה שֶׁאָסַרְתִּי עָלַי אוֹ עַל אֲחֵרִים בְּכָל לָשׁוֹן שֶׁל אִסּוּר בֵּין בִּלְשׁוֹן אִסּוּר אוֹ חֵרֶם אוֹ קוֹנָם, וְכָל שׁוּם קַבָּלָה אֲפִלּוּ שֶׁל מִצְוָה שֶׁקִּבַּלְתִּי עָלַי בֵּין בִּלְשׁוֹן נֶדֶר בֵּין בִּלְשׁוֹן נְדָבָה בֵּין בִּלְשׁוֹן שְׁבוּעָה בֵּין בִּלְשׁוֹן נְזִירוּת בֵּין בְּכָל לָשׁוֹן, וְגַם הַנַּעֲשֶׂה בִּתְקִיעַת כָּף. בֵּין כָּל נֶדֶר וּבֵין כָּל נְדָבָה וּבֵין שׁוּם מִנְהַג שֶׁל מִצְוָה שֶׁנָּהַגְתִּי אֶת עַצְמִי, וְכָל מוֹצָא שְׂפָתַי שֶׁיָּצָא מִפִּי אוֹ שֶׁנָּדַרְתִּי וְגָמַרְתִּי בְלִבִּי לַעֲשׂוֹת שׁוּם מִצְוָה מֵהַמִּצְוֹת אוֹ אֵיזוֹ הַנְהָגָה טוֹבָה אוֹ אֵיזֶה דָבָר טוֹב שֶׁנָּהַגְתִּי שָׁלֹשׁ פְּעָמִים, וְלֹא הִתְנֵיתִי שֶׁיְּהֵא בְּלִי נֶדֶר. הֵן דָּבָר שֶׁעָשִׂיתִי, הֵן עַל עַצְמִי הֵן עַל אֲחֵרִים, הֵן אוֹתָן הַיְדוּעִים לִי הֵן אוֹתָן שֶׁכְּבָר שָׁכַחְתִּי. בְּכֻלְּהוֹן אִתְחֲרַטְנָא בְהוֹן מֵעִקָּרָא, וְשׁוֹאֵל וּמְבַקֵּשׁ אֲנִי מִמַּעֲלַתְכֶם הַתָּרָה עֲלֵיהֶם, כִּי יָרֵאתִי פֶּן אֶכָּשֵׁל וְנִלְכַּדְתִּי, חַס וְשָׁלוֹם, בַּעֲוֹן נְדָרִים וּשְׁבוּעוֹת וּנְזִירוּת וַחֲרָמוֹת וְאִסּוּרִין וְקוֹנָמוֹת וְהַסְכָּמוֹת. וְאֵין אֲנִי תוֹהֵא, חַס וְשָׁלוֹם, עַל קִיּוּם הַמַּעֲשִׂים הַטּוֹבִים הָהֵם שֶׁעָשִׂיתִי, רַק אֲנִי מִתְחָרֵט עַל קַבָּלַת הָעִנְיָנִים בִּלְשׁוֹן נֶדֶר אוֹ שְׁבוּעָה אוֹ נְזִירוּת אוֹ אִסּוּר אוֹ חֵרֶם אוֹ קוֹנָם אוֹ הַסְכָּמָה אוֹ קַבָּלָה בְלֵב, וּמִתְחָרֵט אֲנִי עַל זֶה שֶׁלֹּא אָמַרְתִּי הִנְנִי עוֹשֶׂה דָבָר זֶה בְּלִי נֶדֶר וּשְׁבוּעָה וּנְזִירוּת וְחֵרֶם וְאִסּוּר וְקוֹנָם וְקַבָּלָה בְלֵב.

לָכֵן אֲנִי שׁוֹאֵל הַתָּרָה בְּכֻלְּהוֹן.

---

ANNULMENT OF VOWS

To avoid entering the High Holy Days under the pressure of unfulfilled undertakings to God, our custom is to annul or "release" vows on the morning before Rosh HaShana. A related, though more solemn, ceremony takes place immediately prior to Yom Kippur in the form of *Kol Nidrei*.

I regret all these things I have mentioned, whether they related to monetary matters, or to the body or to the soul.

In relation to them all, I regret the language of vow, oath, naziriteship, prohibition, ban, penalty, and acceptance of the heart.

To be sure, according to the law, one who regrets and seeks annulment must specify the vow [from which he seeks release]. But please know, my masters, that it is impossible to specify them, for they are many. I do not seek release from vows that cannot be annulled. Therefore, may it be in your eyes as if I had specified them.

*The judges say the following three times:*

May all be permitted to you. May all be forgiven you. May all be allowed to you. There is now no vow, oath, naziriteship, ban, prohibition, penalty, ostracism, excommunication, or curse. There is now pardon, forgiveness and atonement. And just as the earthly court has granted permission, so may the heavenly court grant permission.

*The one seeking annulment of vows says:*

Behold I make a formal declaration before you that I cancel from now onward all vows and all oaths, naziriteships, prohibitions, penalties, bans, agreements and acceptances of the heart that I may accept upon myself, whether awake or in a dream, except a vow to fast that I undertake at the time of the afternoon prayer. If I forget the conditions of this declaration and make a vow from this day onward, as of now I retroactively regret them and declare them to be null and void, without effect or validity, and they shall have no force whatsoever. Regarding them all, I regret them from now and for ever.

---

The basis of release is regret: had one known what one knows now, one would not have undertaken the vow. The release is performed by three adult men sitting as a court, and its effect is retroactive: it is as if the vow had never been made. The entire process emphasizes the solemnity of verbal commitments. We must be true to our word and never lightly promise to do what we may not be able to fulfill.

Rabbi Joseph Soloveitchik explained that the annulment of vows is similar to the process of repentance itself. We express *ḥarata*, remorse, for our sins. We would not have committed them had we fully understood what the consequences would be, and had we been reflective rather than impulsive. Thus repentance has the power, as does the annulment of vows, to undo the past, at least insofar as sins between us and God.

אֲנִי מִתְחָרֵט עַל כָּל הַנִּזְכָּר, בֵּין אִם הָיוּ הַמַּעֲשִׂים מִדְּבָרִים הַנּוֹגְעִים בְּמָמוֹן, בֵּין מֵהַדְּבָרִים הַנּוֹגְעִים בְּגוּף, בֵּין מֵהַדְּבָרִים הַנּוֹגְעִים אֶל הַנְּשָׁמָה.

בְּכֻלְּהוֹן אֲנִי מִתְחָרֵט עַל לְשׁוֹן נֶדֶר וּשְׁבוּעָה וּנְזִירוּת וְאִסּוּר וְחֵרֶם וְקוֹנָם וְקַבָּלָה בְלֵב.

וְהִנֵּה מִצַּד הַדִּין הַמִּתְחָרֵט וְהַמְבַקֵּשׁ הַתָּרָה צָרִיךְ לִפְרֹט הַנֶּדֶר, אַךְ דְּעוּ נָא רַבּוֹתַי, כִּי אִי אֶפְשָׁר לְפָרְטָם, כִּי רַבִּים הֵם. וְאֵין אֲנִי מְבַקֵּשׁ הַתָּרָה עַל אוֹתָם הַנְּדָרִים שֶׁאֵין לְהַתִּיר אוֹתָם, עַל כֵּן יִהְיוּ נָא בְעֵינֵיכֶם כְּאִלּוּ הָיִיתִי פוֹרְטָם.

*The judges say the following three times:*

הַכֹּל יִהְיוּ מֻתָּרִים לָךְ, הַכֹּל מְחוּלִים לָךְ, הַכֹּל שְׁרוּיִים לָךְ. אֵין כָּאן לֹא נֶדֶר וְלֹא שְׁבוּעָה וְלֹא נְזִירוּת וְלֹא חֵרֶם וְלֹא אִסּוּר וְלֹא קוֹנָם וְלֹא נִדּוּי וְלֹא שַׁמְתָּא וְלֹא אָרוּר. אֲבָל יֵשׁ כָּאן מְחִילָה וּסְלִיחָה וְכַפָּרָה. וּכְשֵׁם שֶׁמַּתִּירִים בְּבֵית דִּין שֶׁל מַטָּה, כָּךְ יִהְיוּ מֻתָּרִים מִבֵּית דִּין שֶׁל מַעְלָה.

*The one seeking annulment of vows says:*

הֲרֵי אֲנִי מוֹסֵר מוֹדָעָה לִפְנֵיכֶם, וַאֲנִי מְבַטֵּל מִכָּאן וּלְהַבָּא כָּל הַנְּדָרִים וְכָל שְׁבוּעוֹת וּנְזִירוּת וְאִסּוּרִין וְקוֹנָמוֹת וַחֲרָמוֹת וְהַסְכָּמוֹת וְקַבָּלָה בְלֵב שֶׁאֲקַבֵּל עָלַי בְּעַצְמִי, הֵן בְּהָקִיץ הֵן בַּחֲלוֹם, חוּץ מִנִּדְרֵי תַעֲנִית בִּשְׁעַת מִנְחָה. וּבְאִם אֶשְׁכַּח לִתְנַאי מוֹדָעָה הַזֹּאת וְאֶדֹּר מֵהַיּוֹם עוֹד, מֵעַתָּה אֲנִי מִתְחָרֵט עֲלֵיהֶם וּמַתְנֶה עֲלֵיהֶם שֶׁיִּהְיוּ כֻּלָּן בְּטֵלִין וּמְבֻטָּלִין, לָא שְׁרִירִין וְלָא קַיָּמִין, וְלָא יְהוֹן חָלִין כְּלָל וּכְלָל. בְּכֻלָּן אִתְחֲרַטְנָא בְהוֹן מֵעַתָּה וְעַד עוֹלָם.

---

The undertakings involved here relate to vows made to God in respect of behavior not categorically demanded or forbidden by Jewish law. The declaration covers a range of such commitments. A *neder* is a vow forbidding something to oneself. An *isar* is a more general category of self-imposed prohibition. A *shevua* is an oath relating to an action rather than an object. It is a promise to do, or not do, a certain act. A *ḥerem* renders an object forbidden by designating it as sacred property. A *konam* designates it as if it were a sacrifice. *Nezirut,* the acceptance, usually for a period of thirty days, of the status of a nazirite (Num. 6:1–21), involves abstaining from wine or grapes, cutting one's hair, or contact with a corpse.

# Prozbul

*On the last day of a Shemitta year, all debts which one Jew owes another are annulled. One who wishes to collect his debts nonetheless must give a court of three judges a prozbul – a transfer of the debts to the court – after which he might collect the debts as the court's representative. This form, and other variations, may be found on the Koren website. See law 4.*

*After the creditor says the declaration marked by quotation marks, the judges sign the following form, and give it to the creditor:*

We three were sitting as a Beit Din, and (*name*) son of (*father's name*) came before us and said:

> "As this year is the seventh year, and I am owed money, in debts that are documented or orally agreed upon, by individuals and/or by companies, I hereby present this Prozbul and transfer every debt owed me to you, the judges before whom I make my declaration, and thus authorize you to exact payment of every debt I am owed. Henceforth you will be my executors and may exact repayment in my name. If you do not exact repayment, then I myself, having presented this Prozbul, may henceforth exact repayment of every debt that is owed me at this time, from any debtor, at any time that I choose."

This being in order we, the Beit Din undersigned – having seen that this person has presented this Prozbul in accordance with the procedure laid out by Hillel and the sages – decree that the seventh year will not cancel the debts owed him, and that he will thus be entitled to exact their repayment at any time he chooses. We undersign this on the (*insert date*) day of the month of Elul in the year (*insert Hebrew year*), here in (*insert location*).

Signed: (*signature of judge*)

Signed: (*signature of judge*)

Signed: (*signature of judge*)

---

ing that they might be unable to reclaim their money. This was in direct contravention of the Torah (see Deut. 15:9). Seeing that the poor were suffering, Hillel devised the prozbul, a legal agreement by which the lender transfers his loan to the Beit Din, thus circumscribing the release of debts (Mishna, *Gittin* 34b). A prozbul is usually written on the last day of a sabbatical year.

# פרוזבול

*On the last day of a* שמיטה *year, all debts which one Jew owes another are annulled. One who wishes to collect his debts nonetheless must give a court of three judges a* פרוזבול *– a transfer of the debts to the court – after which he might collect the debts as the court's representative. This form, and other variations, may be found on the Koren website. See law 4.*

*After the creditor says the declaration marked by quotation marks, the judges sign the following form, and give it to the creditor:*

בְּמוֹתַב תְּלָתָא בֵּי דִינָא כַּחֲדָא הֲוֵינָא, וּבָא לְפָנֵינוּ (פלוני בֶּן פלוני) וְאָמַר לָנוּ:

"הֵן שָׁנָה זוֹ הִיא שְׁנַת הַשְּׁבִיעִית, וְיֵשׁ לִי חוֹבוֹת בִּשְׁטָר וּבְעַל פֶּה עַל אֵיזֶה אֲנָשִׁים וְ/אוֹ חֲבָרוֹת, וַהֲרֵינִי מוֹסֵר בִּפְנֵיכֶם פְּרוֹזְבּוֹל זֶה וְכָל חוֹב שֶׁיֵּשׁ לִי לָכֶם, הַדַּיָּנִים שֶׁבִּפְנֵיהֶם אֲנִי מַצְהִיר, וַהֲרֵינִי מַרְשֶׁה אֶתְכֶם לִגְבּוֹת כָּל חוֹב שֶׁיֵּשׁ לִי, וּמֵעַתָּה הֱיוּ אַתֶּם דַּיָּנִים וּגְבוּ אוֹתוֹ בִּשְׁבִילִי; וְאִם לֹא תִגְבּוּהוּ אַתֶּם, מֵעַתָּה כֵּיוָן שֶׁמָּסַרְתִּי פְּרוֹזְבּוֹל זֶה, אֶגְבֶּה אֲנִי כָּל חוֹב שֶׁיֵּשׁ לִי עַד הַיּוֹם אֵצֶל כָּל אָדָם כָּל זְמַן שֶׁאֶרְצֶה".

וְאָנוּ, בֵּית הַדִּין הַחֲתוּמִים מַטָּה, כֵּיוָן שֶׁרָאִינוּ דְּבָרָיו נְכוֹנִים, וְהוֹאִיל וּמָסַר לְפָנֵינוּ דִּבְרֵי פְּרוֹזְבּוֹל כְּתַקָּנַת הִלֵּל וַחֲזָ"ל, קָבַעְנוּ שֶׁלֹּא תְשַׁמֵּט שְׁבִיעִית חוֹבוֹתָיו וְיוּכַל לִגְבּוֹתָם כָּל עֵת שֶׁיִּרְצֶה. וּבָאנוּ עַל הֶחָתוּם, יוֹם *(insert day of month)* לְחֹדֶשׁ אֱלוּל שְׁנַת *(insert year)*, פֹּה בּ*(insert location)*.

נְאֻם: *(signature of judge)*

נְאֻם: *(signature of judge)*

נְאֻם: *(signature of judge)*

---

PROZBUL

The Torah (Deut. 15:2) prescribes that all debts be canceled in the seventh year. In the late Second Temple period, however, Hillel noted that the wealthy were refusing to give loans to the poor as the seventh year approached, know-

## EIRUV TEḤUMIN

*On Shabbat and Yom Tov it is forbidden to walk more than 2000 cubits (about 3000 feet) beyond the boundary (teḥum) of the town where you live or are staying when the day begins. By placing food sufficient for two meals, before nightfall, at a point within 2000 cubits from the town limits, you confer on that place the status of a dwelling for the next day, and are then permitted to walk 2000 cubits from there.*

בָּרוּךְ Blessed are You, Lord our God, King of the Universe,
who has made us holy through His commandments,
and has commanded us about the mitzva of Eiruv.

By this Eiruv may we be permitted to walk from this place, two thousand cubits in any direction.

## EIRUV ḤATZEROT

*On Shabbat it is forbidden to carry objects from one private domain to another, or from a private domain into space shared by others, such as a communal staircase, corridor or courtyard. If the first day of Rosh HaShana falls on Shabbat an Eiruv Ḥatzerot is created when each of the Jewish households in a court or apartment block, before Shabbat, places a loaf of bread or matza in one of the homes. The entire court or block then becomes a single private domain within which it is permitted to carry.*

בָּרוּךְ Blessed are You, Lord our God, King of the Universe,
who has made us holy through His commandments,
and has commanded us about the mitzva of Eiruv.

By this Eiruv may we be permitted to move, carry out and carry in from the houses to the courtyard, or from the courtyard to the houses, or from house to house, for all the houses within the courtyard.

## EIRUV TAVSHILIN

*It is not permitted to cook for Shabbat when the first day of Rosh HaShana falls on a Thursday unless an Eiruv Tavshilin has been made prior to Rosh HaShana. This is done by taking a loaf or piece of matza together with a boiled egg, or a piece of cooked fish or meat to be used on Shabbat. While holding them, say the following:*

בָּרוּךְ Blessed are You, Lord our God, King of the Universe,
who has made us holy through His commandments,
and has commanded us about the mitzva of Eiruv.

By this Eiruv may we be permitted to bake, cook, insulate food, light a flame and do everything necessary on the festival for the sake of Shabbat, for us and for all Jews living in this city.

---

the same root as *erev*, "evening," the time that joins day and night; *arev*, a "guarantor," who joins another in a bond of shared responsibility; and *arev*, "pleasant," the mood that prevails when people join in friendship. An *Eiruv* softens the sharp divides of boundaries.

## עירוב תחומין

*On שבת and יום טוב it is forbidden to walk more than 2000 cubits (about 3000 feet) beyond the boundary (תחום) of the town where you live or are staying when the day begins. By placing food sufficient for two meals, before nightfall, at a point within 2000 cubits from the town limits, you confer on that place the status of a dwelling for the next day, and are then permitted to walk 2000 cubits from there.*

**בָּרוּךְ אַתָּה יהוה אֱלֹהֵינוּ מֶלֶךְ הָעוֹלָם**
**אֲשֶׁר קִדְּשָׁנוּ בְּמִצְוֹתָיו וְצִוָּנוּ עַל מִצְוַת עֵרוּב.**

בְּדֵין עֵרוּבָא יְהֵא שְׁרֵא לִי לְמֵיזַל מֵאַתְרָא הָדֵין תְּרֵין אַלְפִין אַמִּין לְכָל רוּחָא.

## עירוב חצרות

*On שבת it is forbidden to carry objects from one private domain to another, or from a private domain into space shared by others, such as a communal staircase, corridor or courtyard. If the first day of ראש השנה falls on שבת, an עירוב חצרות is created when each of the Jewish households in a court or apartment block, before שבת, places a loaf of bread or matza in one of the homes. The entire court or block then becomes a single private domain within which it is permitted to carry.*

**בָּרוּךְ אַתָּה יהוה אֱלֹהֵינוּ מֶלֶךְ הָעוֹלָם**
**אֲשֶׁר קִדְּשָׁנוּ בְּמִצְוֹתָיו וְצִוָּנוּ עַל מִצְוַת עֵרוּב.**

בְּדֵין עֵרוּבָא יְהֵא שְׁרֵא לַנָא לְטַלְטוּלֵי וּלְאַפּוּקֵי וּלְעַיּוּלֵי מִן הַבָּתִּים לֶחָצֵר וּמִן הֶחָצֵר לַבָּתִּים וּמִבַּיִת לְבַיִת לְכָל הַבָּתִּים שֶׁבֶּחָצֵר.

## עירוב תבשילין

*It is not permitted to cook for שבת when the first day of ראש השנה falls on Thursday unless an עירוב תבשילין has been made prior to ראש השנה. This is done by taking a loaf or piece of matza together with a boiled egg, or a piece of cooked fish or meat to be used on שבת. While holding them, say the following:*

**בָּרוּךְ אַתָּה יהוה אֱלֹהֵינוּ מֶלֶךְ הָעוֹלָם**
**אֲשֶׁר קִדְּשָׁנוּ בְּמִצְוֹתָיו וְצִוָּנוּ עַל מִצְוַת עֵרוּב.**

בְּדֵין עֵרוּבָא יְהֵא שְׁרֵא לַנָא לְמֵיפָא וּלְבַשָּׁלָא וּלְאַטְמָנָא וּלְאַדְלָקָא שְׁרָגָא וּלְמֶעְבַּד כָּל צָרְכַּנָא מִיּוֹמָא טָבָא לְשַׁבְּתָא, לָנוּ וּלְכָל יִשְׂרָאֵל הַדָּרִים בָּעִיר הַזֹּאת.

---

EIRUVIN

*Eiruvin* are halakhic devices relating to Shabbat and Yom Tov by which the sages "joined" different domains of space and time. *Eiruv* comes from

## CANDLE LIGHTING

*On both nights, say the following blessing and then light the candles.*
*On the second night, the candles must be lit from an existing flame.*
*If the first day of Rosh HaShana is Shabbat, cover the eyes with the hands after lighting the candles and say the following blessing, adding the words in parentheses.*

בָּרוּךְ Blessed are You, Lord our God, King of the Universe,
who has made us holy through His commandments,
and has commanded us to light
(the Sabbath light and) the festival light.

*The blessing "Sheheḥeyanu" ("Who has given us life") is said on both evenings.*

בָּרוּךְ Blessed are You, Lord our God, King of the Universe,
who has given us life, sustained us,
and brought us to this time.

*Prayer after candlelighting (add the words in parentheses as appropriate):*

יְהִי May it be Your will, Lord my God and God of my forebears, that You give me grace – me (and my husband/and my father/and my mother/and my sons and my daughters) and all those close to me, and give us and all Israel good and long lives. And remember us with a memory that brings goodness and blessing; come to us with compassion and bless us with great blessings. Build our homes until they are complete, and allow Your Presence to live among us. And may I merit to raise children and grandchildren, each one wise and understanding, loving the Lord and in awe of God, people of truth, holy children, who will cling on to the Lord and light up the world with Torah and with good actions, and with all the kinds of work that serve the Creator. Please, hear my pleading at this time, by the merit of Sarah and Rebecca, Rachel and Leah our mothers, and light our candle that it should never go out, and light up Your face, so that we shall be saved, Amen.

---

wife, parent and child, sustained and strengthened by the love of God. In the soft luster of this holy light we see the pristine beauty of the familiar and recover a sense of the sacred, the immanence of transcendence, as it bathes the faces of those we love with its radiance.

# הדלקת נרות

*On both nights, say the following blessing and then light the candles.*
*On the second night, the candles must be lit from an existing flame.*
*If the first day of* ראש השנה *is* שבת*, cover the eyes with the hands after lighting the candles and say the following blessing, adding the words in parentheses.*

בָּרוּךְ אַתָּה יהוה אֱלֹהֵינוּ מֶלֶךְ הָעוֹלָם
אֲשֶׁר קִדְּשָׁנוּ בְּמִצְוֹתָיו
וְצִוָּנוּ לְהַדְלִיק נֵר שֶׁל (שַׁבָּת וְשֶׁל) יוֹם טוֹב.

*The blessing* שֶׁהֶחֱיָנוּ *is said on both evenings.*

בָּרוּךְ אַתָּה יהוה אֱלֹהֵינוּ מֶלֶךְ הָעוֹלָם
שֶׁהֶחֱיָנוּ וְקִיְּמָנוּ, וְהִגִּיעָנוּ לַזְּמַן הַזֶּה.

*Prayer after candlelighting (add the words in parentheses as appropriate):*

יְהִי רָצוֹן מִלְּפָנֶיךָ יהוה אֱלֹהַי וֵאלֹהֵי אֲבוֹתַי, שֶׁתְּחוֹנֵן אוֹתִי (וְאֶת אִישִׁי / וְאֶת אָבִי / וְאֶת אִמִּי / וְאֶת בָּנַי וְאֶת בְּנוֹתַי) וְאֶת כָּל קְרוֹבַי, וְתִתֶּן לָנוּ וּלְכָל יִשְׂרָאֵל חַיִּים טוֹבִים וַאֲרֻכִּים, וְתִזְכְּרֵנוּ בְּזִכְרוֹן טוֹבָה וּבְרָכָה, וְתִפְקְדֵנוּ בִּפְקֻדַּת יְשׁוּעָה וְרַחֲמִים, וּתְבָרְכֵנוּ בְּרָכוֹת גְּדוֹלוֹת, וְתַשְׁלִים בָּתֵּינוּ וְתַשְׁכֵּן שְׁכִינָתְךָ בֵּינֵינוּ. וְזַכֵּנִי לְגַדֵּל בָּנִים וּבְנֵי בָנִים חֲכָמִים וּנְבוֹנִים, אוֹהֲבֵי יהוה יִרְאֵי אֱלֹהִים, אַנְשֵׁי אֱמֶת זֶרַע קֹדֶשׁ, בַּיהוה דְּבֵקִים וּמְאִירִים אֶת הָעוֹלָם בַּתּוֹרָה וּבְמַעֲשִׂים טוֹבִים וּבְכָל מְלֶאכֶת עֲבוֹדַת הַבּוֹרֵא. אָנָּא שְׁמַע אֶת תְּחִנָּתִי בָּעֵת הַזֹּאת בִּזְכוּת שָׂרָה וְרִבְקָה וְרָחֵל וְלֵאָה אִמּוֹתֵינוּ, וְהָאֵר נֵרֵנוּ שֶׁלֹּא יִכְבֶּה לְעוֹלָם וָעֶד, וְהָאֵר פָּנֶיךָ וְנִוָּשֵׁעָה. אָמֵן.

---

HADLAKAT NEROT – CANDLE LIGHTING

The lights kindled before Shabbat and Yom Tov symbolize the Divine Presence ("The Lord is my light," Ps. 27:1), as well as *shalom bayit*, the domestic peace that prevails when a home is filled with the love between husband and

# Minḥa for Erev Rosh HaShana

*If the first day of Rosh HaShana falls on a Shabbat, in some congregations the following psalm is said before Minḥa on Friday afternoon. On other days the service starts with "Happy are those" on page 14.*

הֹדוּ Thank the LORD for He is good; His loving-kindness is for ever. Let those the LORD redeemed say this – those He redeemed from the enemy's hand, those He gathered from the lands, from east and west, from north and south. Some lost their way in desert wastelands, finding no way to a city where they could live. They were hungry and thirsty, and their spirit grew faint. Then they cried out to the LORD in their trouble, and He rescued them from their distress. He led them by a straight path to a city where they could live. Let them thank the LORD for His loving-kindness and His wondrous deeds for humankind, for He satisfies the thirsty and fills the hungry with good. Some sat in darkness and the shadow of death, cruelly bound in iron chains, for they had rebelled against God's words and despised the counsel of the Most High. He humbled their hearts with hard labor; they stumbled, and there was none to help. Then they cried to the LORD in their trouble, and He saved them from their distress. He brought them out from darkness and the shadow of death and broke open their chains. Let them thank the LORD for His loving-kindness and His wondrous deeds for humankind, for He shattered gates of bronze and broke their iron bars. Some were fools with sinful ways, and suffered affliction because of their iniquities. They found all food repulsive, and came close to the gates of death. Then they cried to the LORD in their trouble, and He saved them from their distress. He sent His word and healed them; He rescued them from their destruction. Let them thank the LORD for His loving-kindness and His wondrous deeds for humankind. Let them sacrifice thanksgiving-offerings and tell His deeds with songs of joy. Those who go to sea in ships, plying their trade in the mighty waters, have seen the works of the LORD, His wondrous deeds in the deep. He spoke and stirred up a tempest that lifted high the waves. They rose to the heavens and plunged down to the depths; their souls melted in misery. They reeled and staggered like drunkards; all their skill was to no avail. Then they cried to the LORD in their trouble, and He brought them out of their distress. He stilled the storm to a whisper, and the waves of the sea grew calm. They rejoiced when all was quiet, then He guided them to

# מנחה לערב ראש השנה

*If the first day of* ראש השנה *falls on a* שבת*, in some congregations the following psalm is said before* מנחה *on Friday afternoon. On other days the service starts with* אַשְׁרֵי *on page 15.*

תהלים קז

הֹדוּ לַיהוה כִּי־טוֹב, כִּי לְעוֹלָם חַסְדּוֹ: יֹאמְרוּ גְּאוּלֵי יהוה, אֲשֶׁר גְּאָלָם
מִיַּד־צָר: וּמֵאֲרָצוֹת קִבְּצָם, מִמִּזְרָח וּמִמַּעֲרָב, מִצָּפוֹן וּמִיָּם: תָּעוּ בַמִּדְבָּר,
בִּישִׁימוֹן דָּרֶךְ, עִיר מוֹשָׁב לֹא מָצָאוּ: רְעֵבִים גַּם־צְמֵאִים, נַפְשָׁם בָּהֶם
תִּתְעַטָּף: וַיִּצְעֲקוּ אֶל־יהוה בַּצַּר לָהֶם, מִמְּצוּקוֹתֵיהֶם יַצִּילֵם: וַיַּדְרִיכֵם
בְּדֶרֶךְ יְשָׁרָה, לָלֶכֶת אֶל־עִיר מוֹשָׁב: יוֹדוּ לַיהוה חַסְדּוֹ, וְנִפְלְאוֹתָיו
לִבְנֵי אָדָם: כִּי־הִשְׂבִּיעַ נֶפֶשׁ שֹׁקֵקָה, וְנֶפֶשׁ רְעֵבָה מִלֵּא־טוֹב: יֹשְׁבֵי
חֹשֶׁךְ וְצַלְמָוֶת, אֲסִירֵי עֳנִי וּבַרְזֶל: כִּי־הִמְרוּ אִמְרֵי־אֵל, וַעֲצַת עֶלְיוֹן
נָאָצוּ: וַיַּכְנַע בֶּעָמָל לִבָּם, כָּשְׁלוּ וְאֵין עֹזֵר: וַיִּזְעֲקוּ אֶל־יהוה בַּצַּר לָהֶם,
מִמְּצֻקוֹתֵיהֶם יוֹשִׁיעֵם: יוֹצִיאֵם מֵחֹשֶׁךְ וְצַלְמָוֶת, וּמוֹסְרוֹתֵיהֶם יְנַתֵּק:
יוֹדוּ לַיהוה חַסְדּוֹ, וְנִפְלְאוֹתָיו לִבְנֵי אָדָם: כִּי־שִׁבַּר דַּלְתוֹת נְחֹשֶׁת,
וּבְרִיחֵי בַרְזֶל גִּדֵּעַ: אֱוִלִים מִדֶּרֶךְ פִּשְׁעָם, וּמֵעֲוֹנֹתֵיהֶם יִתְעַנּוּ: כָּל־אֹכֶל
תְּתַעֵב נַפְשָׁם, וַיַּגִּיעוּ עַד־שַׁעֲרֵי מָוֶת: וַיִּזְעֲקוּ אֶל־יהוה בַּצַּר לָהֶם,
מִמְּצֻקוֹתֵיהֶם יוֹשִׁיעֵם: יִשְׁלַח דְּבָרוֹ וְיִרְפָּאֵם, וִימַלֵּט מִשְּׁחִיתוֹתָם: יוֹדוּ
לַיהוה חַסְדּוֹ, וְנִפְלְאוֹתָיו לִבְנֵי אָדָם: וְיִזְבְּחוּ זִבְחֵי תוֹדָה וִיסַפְּרוּ מַעֲשָׂיו
בְּרִנָּה: יוֹרְדֵי הַיָּם בָּאֳנִיּוֹת, עֹשֵׂי מְלָאכָה בְּמַיִם רַבִּים: הֵמָּה רָאוּ מַעֲשֵׂי
יהוה, וְנִפְלְאוֹתָיו בִּמְצוּלָה: וַיֹּאמֶר, וַיַּעֲמֵד רוּחַ סְעָרָה, וַתְּרוֹמֵם גַּלָּיו:
יַעֲלוּ שָׁמַיִם, יֵרְדוּ תְהוֹמוֹת, נַפְשָׁם בְּרָעָה תִתְמוֹגָג: יָחוֹגּוּ וְיָנוּעוּ כַּשִּׁכּוֹר,
וְכָל־חָכְמָתָם תִּתְבַּלָּע: וַיִּצְעֲקוּ אֶל־יהוה בַּצַּר לָהֶם, וּמִמְּצוּקֹתֵיהֶם
יוֹצִיאֵם: יָקֵם סְעָרָה לִדְמָמָה, וַיֶּחֱשׁוּ גַּלֵּיהֶם: וַיִּשְׂמְחוּ כִי־יִשְׁתֹּקוּ, וַיַּנְחֵם
אֶל־מְחוֹז חֶפְצָם: יוֹדוּ לַיהוה חַסְדּוֹ, וְנִפְלְאוֹתָיו לִבְנֵי אָדָם: וִירֹמְמוּהוּ
בִּקְהַל־עָם, וּבְמוֹשַׁב זְקֵנִים יְהַלְלוּהוּ: יָשֵׂם נְהָרוֹת לְמִדְבָּר, וּמֹצָאֵי מַיִם
לְצִמָּאוֹן: אֶרֶץ פְּרִי לִמְלֵחָה, מֵרָעַת יוֹשְׁבֵי בָהּ: יָשֵׂם מִדְבָּר לַאֲגַם־מַיִם,

their destination. Let them thank the LORD for His loving-kindness and His wondrous deeds for humankind. Let them exalt Him in the assembly of the people and praise Him in the council of the elders. He turns rivers into a desert, springs of water into parched land, fruitful land into a salt marsh, because of the wickedness of its inhabitants. He turns the desert into pools of water, parched land into flowing springs; He brings the hungry to live there, they build themselves a town in which to live. They sow fields and plant vineyards that yield a fruitful harvest; He blesses them, and they increase greatly, their herds do not decrease, though they had been few and brought low by oppression, adversity and sorrow. He pours contempt on nobles and makes them wander in a pathless waste. ▸ He lifts the destitute from poverty and enlarges their families like flocks. The upright see and rejoice, but the mouth of all wrongdoers is stopped. Whoever is wise, let him lay these things to heart, and reflect on the loving-kindness of the LORD.

*Some have the custom to recite before Minḥa the Daily Sacrifice (page 240) or the Korbanot/Offerings (pages 238–244), omitting the Taking of the Ashes and the Order of the Priestly Functions.*

אַשְׁרֵי Happy are those who dwell in Your House; *Ps. 84*
they shall continue to praise You, Selah!
Happy are the people for whom this is so; *Ps. 144*
happy are the people whose God is the LORD.
A song of praise by David. *Ps. 145*
I will exalt You, my God, the King, and bless Your name for ever and all time. Every day I will bless You, and praise Your name for

---

through many streets and across the marketplace throughout the day. He almost forgets that there is a Maker of the world. Only when the time for the afternoon prayer comes, does he remember, "I must pray." And then, from the bottom of his heart, he heaves a sigh of regret that he has spent his day on idle matters, and he runs into a side street and stands there and prays. God holds him dear, very dear, and his prayer pierces the heavens.

ASHREI

*Ashrei*, at the beginning of Minḥa, is an abridged form of the more extended *Pesukei DeZimra*, the Verses of Praise, of the morning service. It is a medita-

וְאֶרֶץ צִיָּה לְמֹצָאֵי מָיִם: וַיּוֹשֶׁב שָׁם רְעֵבִים, וַיְכוֹנְנוּ עִיר מוֹשָׁב: וַיִּזְרְעוּ שָׂדוֹת, וַיִּטְּעוּ כְרָמִים, וַיַּעֲשׂוּ פְּרִי תְבוּאָה: וַיְבָרְכֵם וַיִּרְבּוּ מְאֹד, וּבְהֶמְתָּם לֹא יַמְעִיט: וַיִּמְעֲטוּ וַיָּשֹׁחוּ, מֵעֹצֶר רָעָה וְיָגוֹן: שֹׁפֵךְ בּוּז עַל־נְדִיבִים, וַיַּתְעֵם בְּתֹהוּ לֹא־דָרֶךְ: ◂ וַיְשַׂגֵּב אֶבְיוֹן מֵעוֹנִי, וַיָּשֶׂם כַּצֹּאן מִשְׁפָּחוֹת: יִרְאוּ יְשָׁרִים וְיִשְׂמָחוּ, וְכָל־עַוְלָה קָפְצָה פִּיהָ: מִי־חָכָם וְיִשְׁמָר־אֵלֶּה, וְיִתְבּוֹנְנוּ חַסְדֵי יהוה:

*Some have the custom to recite before* מנחה, פרשת קרבן התמיד *(page 241) or* סדר הקרבנות *(pages 239–245), omitting* פרשת תרומת הדשן *and* סדר המערכה.

תהלים פד אַשְׁרֵי יוֹשְׁבֵי בֵיתֶךָ, עוֹד יְהַלְלוּךָ סֶּלָה:

תהלים קמד אַשְׁרֵי הָעָם שֶׁכָּכָה לּוֹ, אַשְׁרֵי הָעָם שֶׁיהוה אֱלֹהָיו:

תהלים קמה תְּהִלָּה לְדָוִד

אֲרוֹמִמְךָ אֱלוֹהַי הַמֶּלֶךְ, וַאֲבָרְכָה שִׁמְךָ לְעוֹלָם וָעֶד:

בְּכָל־יוֹם אֲבָרְכֶךָּ, וַאֲהַלְלָה שִׁמְךָ לְעוֹלָם וָעֶד:

---

MINḤA – AFTERNOON SERVICE

The Afternoon Service corresponds to the daily afternoon sacrifice (Num. 28:8). Minḥa, literally "meal offering," was not unique to the afternoon sacrifice. The afternoon service may have become known as Minḥa because of the verse in Psalms (141:2), "May my prayer be like incense before You, the lifting up of my hands like the afternoon offering [*minḥat arev*]."

The sages attached special significance to the afternoon prayer, noting that Elijah's prayer was answered at this time (1 Kings 18:36). It is easier to pray in the morning and evening as we are about to begin or end our engagement with the world for the day. Minḥa is more demanding. It means that we are turning to God in the midst of all our distractions. We are bringing Him into our life when it is maximally preoccupied with other things. Minḥa is the triumph of the important over the urgent, of what matters ultimately over what matters immediately. That is why prayer in the midst of the day has a special transformative power.

The Ba'al Shem Tov said: Imagine a man whose business hounds him

ever and all time. Great is the LORD and greatly to be praised; His greatness is unfathomable. One generation will praise Your works to the next, and tell of Your mighty deeds. On the glorious splendor of Your majesty I will meditate, and on the acts of Your wonders. They shall talk of the power of Your awesome deeds, and I will tell of Your greatness. They shall recite the record of Your great goodness, and sing with joy of Your righteousness. The LORD is gracious and compassionate, slow to anger and great in loving-kindness. The LORD is good to all, and His compassion extends to all His works. All Your works shall thank You, LORD, and Your devoted ones shall bless You. They shall talk of the glory of Your kingship, and speak of Your might. To make known to mankind His mighty deeds and the glorious majesty of His kingship. Your kingdom is an everlasting kingdom, and Your reign is for all generations. The LORD supports all who fall, and raises all who are bowed down. All raise their eyes to You in hope, and You give them their food in due season. You open Your hand, and satisfy every living thing with favor. The LORD is righteous in all His ways, and kind in all He

---

(2) It contains the verse, "You open Your hand, and satisfy every living thing with favor," regarded by the sages as one of the essential features of prayer, namely recognition of our complete dependence on God (*Berakhot* 4b). Psalm 145 is also the only one of the 150 psalms to be called a psalm (*tehilla*) in its superscription.

To it have been added two verses at the beginning and one at the end. The verses at the beginning use the word *Ashrei* – the first word of the book of Psalms – three times. The concluding verse ends with the word "Halleluya," the last word of the book of Psalms. Thus *Ashrei* is a miniature version of the book of Psalms as a whole.

*Ashrei* means "happy, blessed, fruitful, flourishing." It refers not to a temporary emotional state but to a life as a whole. One who is *ashrei* does well and fares well, living uprightly and honestly, respected by those worthy of respect. The word is in the plural construct, literally "the *happinesses* of," as if to say that happiness is not one thing but a harmonious blend of many things that

גָּדוֹל יהוה וּמְהֻלָּל מְאֹד, וְלִגְדֻלָּתוֹ אֵין חֵקֶר:
דּוֹר לְדוֹר יְשַׁבַּח מַעֲשֶׂיךָ, וּגְבוּרֹתֶיךָ יַגִּידוּ:
הֲדַר כְּבוֹד הוֹדֶךָ, וְדִבְרֵי נִפְלְאֹתֶיךָ אָשִׂיחָה:
וֶעֱזוּז נוֹרְאֹתֶיךָ יֹאמֵרוּ, וּגְדוּלָּתְךָ אֲסַפְּרֶנָּה:
זֵכֶר רַב־טוּבְךָ יַבִּיעוּ, וְצִדְקָתְךָ יְרַנֵּנוּ:
חַנּוּן וְרַחוּם יהוה, אֶרֶךְ אַפַּיִם וּגְדָל־חָסֶד:
טוֹב־יהוה לַכֹּל, וְרַחֲמָיו עַל־כָּל־מַעֲשָׂיו:
יוֹדוּךָ יהוה כָּל־מַעֲשֶׂיךָ, וַחֲסִידֶיךָ יְבָרְכוּכָה:
כְּבוֹד מַלְכוּתְךָ יֹאמֵרוּ, וּגְבוּרָתְךָ יְדַבֵּרוּ:
לְהוֹדִיעַ לִבְנֵי הָאָדָם גְּבוּרֹתָיו, וּכְבוֹד הֲדַר מַלְכוּתוֹ:
מַלְכוּתְךָ מַלְכוּת כָּל־עֹלָמִים, וּמֶמְשַׁלְתְּךָ בְּכָל־דּוֹר וָדֹר:
סוֹמֵךְ יהוה לְכָל־הַנֹּפְלִים, וְזוֹקֵף לְכָל־הַכְּפוּפִים:
עֵינֵי־כֹל אֵלֶיךָ יְשַׂבֵּרוּ, וְאַתָּה נוֹתֵן־לָהֶם אֶת־אָכְלָם בְּעִתּוֹ:
פּוֹתֵחַ אֶת־יָדֶךָ, וּמַשְׂבִּיעַ לְכָל־חַי רָצוֹן:
צַדִּיק יהוה בְּכָל־דְּרָכָיו, וְחָסִיד בְּכָל־מַעֲשָׂיו:

---

tion prior to the Amida. The Amida is prayer in its purest form, and it requires *kavana,* a direction of the mind, a focusing of our thoughts. *Kavana* involves "clearing your mind of all extraneous thoughts, and seeing yourself as if you are standing before the Divine Presence. Therefore it is necessary to sit for a while before prayer in order to direct your mind, and then pray gently and pleadingly, not like one who prays as if he were carrying a burden which he is keen to unload and leave" (Maimonides, Laws of Prayer 4:16). *Ashrei* is the way we "sit for a while before prayer" in order to direct our mind (*Berakhot* 32b). Therefore, though it may be said standing or sitting, the custom is to say it sitting.

It consists of Psalm 145, chosen for two reasons: (1) It is an alphabetical acrostic, praising God with every letter of the alphabet (except the *nun,* missing lest it refer to a verse that speaks about the fall, *nefila,* of Israel);

does. The LORD is close to all who call on Him, to all who call on Him in truth. He fulfills the will of those who revere Him; He hears their cry and saves them. The LORD guards all who love Him, but all the wicked He will destroy. ▸ My mouth shall speak the praise of the LORD, and all creatures shall bless His holy name for ever and all time.

We will bless the LORD now and for ever. Halleluya! *Ps. 115*

HALF KADDISH

*Leader:* יִתְגַּדַּל Magnified and sanctified may His great name be,
in the world He created by His will.
May He establish His kingdom,
make His salvation flourish,
and hasten His messiah,
in your lifetime and in your days,
and in the lifetime of all the house of Israel,
swiftly and soon –
and say: Amen.

*All:* May His great name be blessed for ever and all time.

*Leader:* Blessed and praised,
glorified and exalted,
raised and honored,
uplifted and lauded
be the name of the Holy One, blessed be He,
beyond any blessing,
song, praise and consolation
uttered in the world –
and say: Amen.

---

of the LORD, and who meditates on His Torah day and night. He is like a tree planted by streams of water that yields its fruit in season and whose leaf does not wither – whatever he does prospers" (Psalm 1:1–3).

קָרוֹב יהוה לְכָל־קֹרְאָיו, לְכֹל אֲשֶׁר יִקְרָאֻהוּ בֶאֱמֶת:
רְצוֹן־יְרֵאָיו יַעֲשֶׂה, וְאֶת־שַׁוְעָתָם יִשְׁמַע, וְיוֹשִׁיעֵם:
שׁוֹמֵר יהוה אֶת־כָּל־אֹהֲבָיו, וְאֵת כָּל־הָרְשָׁעִים יַשְׁמִיד:
‹ תְּהִלַּת יהוה יְדַבֶּר פִּי, וִיבָרֵךְ כָּל־בָּשָׂר שֵׁם קָדְשׁוֹ לְעוֹלָם וָעֶד:
וַאֲנַחְנוּ נְבָרֵךְ יָהּ מֵעַתָּה וְעַד־עוֹלָם, הַלְלוּיָהּ: תהלים קטו

## חצי קדיש

ש״ץ: יִתְגַּדַּל וְיִתְקַדַּשׁ שְׁמֵהּ רַבָּא (קהל: אָמֵן)
בְּעָלְמָא דִּי בְרָא כִרְעוּתֵהּ
וְיַמְלִיךְ מַלְכוּתֵהּ
וְיַצְמַח פֻּרְקָנֵהּ וִיקָרֵב מְשִׁיחֵהּ (קהל: אָמֵן)
בְּחַיֵּיכוֹן וּבְיוֹמֵיכוֹן וּבְחַיֵּי דְכָל בֵּית יִשְׂרָאֵל
בַּעֲגָלָא וּבִזְמַן קָרִיב
וְאִמְרוּ אָמֵן. (קהל: אָמֵן)

קהל וש״ץ: יְהֵא שְׁמֵהּ רַבָּא מְבָרַךְ לְעָלַם וּלְעָלְמֵי עָלְמַיָּא.

ש״ץ: יִתְבָּרַךְ וְיִשְׁתַּבַּח וְיִתְפָּאַר וְיִתְרוֹמַם וְיִתְנַשֵּׂא
וְיִתְהַדָּר וְיִתְעַלֶּה וְיִתְהַלָּל
שְׁמֵהּ דְּקֻדְשָׁא בְּרִיךְ הוּא (קהל: אָמֵן)
לְעֵלָּא מִן כָּל בִּרְכָתָא וְשִׁירָתָא, תֻּשְׁבְּחָתָא וְנֶחֱמָתָא
דַּאֲמִירָן בְּעָלְמָא
וְאִמְרוּ אָמֵן. (קהל: אָמֵן)

---

add up to make a good life. Psalm 1 gives a vivid picture of such a life: "Happy is one who does not walk in step with the wicked, or stand in the place of sinners, or sit in the company of mockers, but whose delight is in the Torah

## THE AMIDA

*The following prayer, until "in former years" on page 36, is said silently, standing with feet together. If there is a minyan, the Amida is repeated aloud by the Leader. Take three steps forward and at the points indicated by ▾, bend the knees at the first word, bow at the second, and stand straight before saying God's name.*

When I proclaim the LORD's name, give glory to our God. *Deut. 32*
O LORD, open my lips, so that my mouth may declare Your praise. *Ps. 51*

### PATRIARCHS

▾בָּרוּךְ Blessed are You, LORD our God and God of our fathers,
God of Abraham, God of Isaac and God of Jacob;
the great, mighty and awesome God, God Most High,
who bestows acts of loving-kindness and creates all,
who remembers the loving-kindness of the fathers
and will bring a Redeemer to their children's children
for the sake of His name, in love.
King, Helper, Savior, Shield:
▾Blessed are You,
LORD, Shield of Abraham.

### DIVINE MIGHT

אַתָּה גִּבּוֹר You are eternally mighty, LORD.
You give life to the dead and have great power to save.

*In Israel:* He causes the dew to fall.

---

of our ancestors, guardians of our children's future, remembering God in the midst of time and placing our destiny in His hands.

*The central blessings.* There are thirteen central blessings in the weekday Amida and they are grouped into four sets of three: (1) personal spiritual requests: for knowledge, repentance and forgiveness; (2) personal material requests: for redemption, healing and prosperity; (3) collective material-political requests: for the ingathering of exiles, the restoration of sovereignty, and the removal of enemies; and (4) collective spiritual requests: for the righteous,

# עמידה

*The following prayer, until* קַדְמֹנִיּוֹת *on page 37, is said silently, standing with feet together. If there is a* מנין*, the* עמידה *is repeated aloud by the* שליח ציבור*. Take three steps forward and at the points indicated by* ˚*, bend the knees at the first word, bow at the second, and stand straight before saying God's name.*

דברים לב כִּי שֵׁם יהוה אֶקְרָא, הָבוּ גֹדֶל לֵאלֹהֵינוּ:
תהלים נא אֲדֹנָי, שְׂפָתַי תִּפְתָּח, וּפִי יַגִּיד תְּהִלָּתֶךָ:

אבות

˚בָּרוּךְ אַתָּה יהוה, אֱלֹהֵינוּ וֵאלֹהֵי אֲבוֹתֵינוּ
אֱלֹהֵי אַבְרָהָם, אֱלֹהֵי יִצְחָק, וֵאלֹהֵי יַעֲקֹב
הָאֵל הַגָּדוֹל הַגִּבּוֹר וְהַנּוֹרָא, אֵל עֶלְיוֹן
גּוֹמֵל חֲסָדִים טוֹבִים, קוֹנֵה הַכֹּל
וְזוֹכֵר חַסְדֵי אָבוֹת
וּמֵבִיא גוֹאֵל לִבְנֵי בְנֵיהֶם לְמַעַן שְׁמוֹ בְּאַהֲבָה.
מֶלֶךְ עוֹזֵר וּמוֹשִׁיעַ וּמָגֵן.
˚בָּרוּךְ אַתָּה יהוה, מָגֵן אַבְרָהָם.

גבורות

אַתָּה גִּבּוֹר לְעוֹלָם, אֲדֹנָי
מְחַיֵּה מֵתִים אַתָּה, רַב לְהוֹשִׁיעַ
בארץ ישראל: מוֹרִיד הַטָּל

---

THE AFTERNOON AMIDA

The sages (*Berakhot* 26b) associated the afternoon Amida with Isaac, who "went out to meditate in the field toward evening" (Gen. 24:63). If Abraham represents the dawn of Jewish faith, and Jacob the nighttime of exile, Isaac represents the afternoon joining of past and future, the unspectacular heroism of Jewish continuity. We are each a link in the chain of generations, heirs

He sustains the living with loving-kindness,
and with great compassion revives the dead.
He supports the fallen,
heals the sick,
sets captives free,
and keeps His faith with those who sleep in the dust.
Who is like You, Master of might,
and to whom can You be compared,
O King who brings death and gives life,
and makes salvation grow?
Faithful are You to revive the dead.
Blessed are You, LORD,
who revives the dead.

*When saying the Amida silently, continue with "You are holy" on the next page.*

---

KEDUSHA

*During the Leader's Repetition, the following is said standing with feet together, rising on the toes at the words indicated by ▴.*

*Cong. then Leader:* נְקַדֵּשׁ We will sanctify and revere You
with the song sung by the holy Seraphim,
who speak the threefold declaration of Your holiness,
as is written by Your prophet,
"And they [the angels] call to one another saying: *Is. 6*

*Cong. then Leader:* ▴Holy, ▴holy, ▴holy is the LORD of hosts;
the whole world is filled with His glory."
Those facing them praise You and say:

*Cong. then Leader:* ▴"Blessed is the LORD's glory from His place." *Ezek. 3*
And in Your holy Writings it is written thus:

*Cong. then Leader:* ▴"The LORD shall reign for ever. *Ps. 146*
He is your God, Zion,
from generation to generation, Halleluya!"

*The Leader continues with "You are holy" on the next page.*

---

מְכַלְכֵּל חַיִּים בְּחֶסֶד
מְחַיֵּה מֵתִים בְּרַחֲמִים רַבִּים
סוֹמֵךְ נוֹפְלִים, וְרוֹפֵא חוֹלִים, וּמַתִּיר אֲסוּרִים
וּמְקַיֵּם אֱמוּנָתוֹ לִישֵׁנֵי עָפָר.
מִי כָמְוֹךָ, בַּעַל גְּבוּרוֹת
וּמִי דּוֹמֶה לָּךְ
מֶלֶךְ, מֵמִית וּמְחַיֶּה וּמַצְמִיחַ יְשׁוּעָה.
וְנֶאֱמָן אַתָּה לְהַחֲיוֹת מֵתִים.
בָּרוּךְ אַתָּה יהוה, מְחַיֵּה הַמֵּתִים.

*When saying the* עמידה *silently, continue with* אַתָּה קָדוֹשׁ *on the next page.*

---

קדושה

*During the* חזרת הש״ץ, *the following is said standing with feet together, rising on the toes at the words indicated by* ˄.

קהל *then* ש״ץ: נַקְדִּישָׁךְ וְנַעֲרִיצָךְ כְּנְעַם שִׂיחַ סוֹד שַׂרְפֵי קֹדֶשׁ,
הַמְשַׁלְּשִׁים לְךָ קְדֻשָּׁה
ישעיה ו כַּכָּתוּב עַל יַד נְבִיאֶךָ, וְקָרָא זֶה אֶל־זֶה וְאָמַר

קהל *then* ש״ץ: ˄קָדוֹשׁ, ˄קָדוֹשׁ, ˄קָדוֹשׁ, יהוה צְבָאוֹת, מְלֹא כָל־הָאָרֶץ כְּבוֹדוֹ:
לְעֻמָּתָם מְשַׁבְּחִים וְאוֹמְרִים

יחזקאל ג קהל *then* ש״ץ: ˄בָּרוּךְ כְּבוֹד־יהוה מִמְּקוֹמוֹ:
וּבְדִבְרֵי קָדְשְׁךָ כָּתוּב לֵאמֹר

תהלים קמו קהל *then* ש״ץ: ˄יִמְלֹךְ יהוה לְעוֹלָם, אֱלֹהַיִךְ צִיּוֹן לְדֹר וָדֹר, הַלְלוּיָהּ:

*The* שליח ציבור *continues with* אַתָּה קָדוֹשׁ *on the next page.*

---

the rebuilding of Jerusalem, and the restoration of the kingdom of David. The thirteenth blessing is all-embracing, asking God to hear and heed our prayer.

HOLINESS

אַתָּה קָדוֹשׁ You are holy and Your name is holy,
and holy ones praise You daily, Selah!
For You, God, are a great and holy King.
Blessed are You, Lord,
the holy God.

KNOWLEDGE

אַתָּה חוֹנֵן You grace humanity with knowledge
and teach mortals understanding.
Grace us with the wisdom, understanding
and knowledge that come from You.
Blessed are You, Lord,
who graciously grants knowledge.

REPENTANCE

הֲשִׁיבֵנוּ Bring us back, our Father, to Your Torah.
Draw us near, our King, to Your service.
Lead us back to You in perfect repentance.
Blessed are You, Lord,
who desires repentance.

FORGIVENESS

*Strike the left side of the chest at °.*

סְלַח לָנוּ Forgive us, our Father, for we have °sinned.
Pardon us, our King, for we have °transgressed;
for You are the good and forgiving God.
Blessed are You, Lord,
the gracious One who repeatedly forgives.

---

Knowing how we should live, we come to realize how we fall short, and this brings us to repentance. Only then do we ask for forgiveness. We must put in the work of self-understanding and self-judgment before we can ask God to excuse our lapses.

קדושת השם

אַתָּה קָדוֹשׁ וְשִׁמְךָ קָדוֹשׁ
וּקְדוֹשִׁים בְּכָל יוֹם יְהַלְלוּךָ סֶּלָה
כִּי אֵל מֶלֶךְ גָּדוֹל וְקָדוֹשׁ אָתָּה.
בָּרוּךְ אַתָּה יהוה, הָאֵל הַקָּדוֹשׁ.

דעת

אַתָּה חוֹנֵן לְאָדָם דַּעַת
וּמְלַמֵּד לֶאֱנוֹשׁ בִּינָה.
חָנֵּנוּ מֵאִתְּךָ חָכְמָה בִּינָה וָדָעַת.
בָּרוּךְ אַתָּה יהוה, חוֹנֵן הַדָּעַת.

תשובה

הֲשִׁיבֵנוּ אָבִינוּ לְתוֹרָתֶךָ, וְקָרְבֵנוּ מַלְכֵּנוּ לַעֲבוֹדָתֶךָ
וְהַחֲזִירֵנוּ בִּתְשׁוּבָה שְׁלֵמָה לְפָנֶיךָ.
בָּרוּךְ אַתָּה יהוה, הָרוֹצֶה בִּתְשׁוּבָה.

סליחה

*Strike the left side of the chest at °.*

סְלַח לָנוּ אָבִינוּ כִּי °חָטָאנוּ
מְחַל לָנוּ מַלְכֵּנוּ כִּי °פָשָׁעְנוּ
כִּי אֵל טוֹב וְסַלָּח אָתָּה.
בָּרוּךְ אַתָּה יהוה, חַנּוּן הַמַּרְבֶּה לִסְלֹחַ.

---

*Knowledge, Repentance and Forgiveness.* Note the sequence. First we pray for knowledge and understanding. Without these it is as if we travel blind. Judaism is a religion of emotion, but emotion instructed by the mind. Second, understanding should lead us not to intellectual arrogance but humility.

REDEMPTION

רְאֵה Look, please, on our affliction, plead our cause,
and redeem us with a complete redemption, soon,
for Your name's sake,
for You are a powerful God and Redeemer.
Blessed are You, LORD,
the Redeemer of Israel.

HEALING

רְפָאֵנוּ Heal us, LORD, and we shall be healed.
Save us and we shall be saved, for You are our praise.
Bring remedy and healing to all our illnesses and pains,
complete recovery for all our ailments,

---

*The following prayer for a sick person may be said here:*

May it be Your will, O LORD my God and God of my ancestors, that You speedily send a complete recovery from heaven, a healing of both soul and body, to the patient (*name*), son/daughter of (*mother's name*) among the other afflicted of Israel.

---

for You, God, King, are a faithful and compassionate Healer.
Blessed are You, LORD,
Healer of the sick of His people Israel.

PROSPERITY

בָּרֵךְ Bless this year for us, LORD our God,
and all its types of produce for good.
Grant blessing on the face of the earth,
and from its goodness satisfy us,
and grace our year as the best of years, as a blessing,
for You are the good and beneficent God,
who gives the years their blessing.
Blessed are You, LORD,
who blesses the years.

גאולה

רְאֵה נָא בְעָנְיֵנוּ, וְרִיבָה רִיבֵנוּ
וּגְאָלֵנוּ גְאֻלָּה שְׁלֵמָה מְהֵרָה לְמַעַן שְׁמֶךָ
כִּי אֵל גּוֹאֵל חָזָק אָתָּה.
בָּרוּךְ אַתָּה יהוה, גּוֹאֵל יִשְׂרָאֵל.

רפואה

רְפָאֵנוּ יהוה וְנֵרָפֵא, הוֹשִׁיעֵנוּ וְנִוָּשֵׁעָה, כִּי תְהִלָּתֵנוּ אָתָּה
וְהַעֲלֵה אֲרוּכָה וּמַרְפֵּא לְכָל תַּחֲלוּאֵינוּ וּלְכָל מַכְאוֹבֵינוּ
וּרְפוּאָה שְׁלֵמָה לְכָל מַכּוֹתֵינוּ

---

*The following prayer for a sick person may be said here:*

יְהִי רָצוֹן מִלְּפָנֶיךָ יהוה אֱלֹהַי וֵאלֹהֵי אֲבוֹתַי, שֶׁתִּשְׁלַח מְהֵרָה רְפוּאָה שְׁלֵמָה
מִן הַשָּׁמַיִם רְפוּאַת הַנֶּפֶשׁ וּרְפוּאַת הַגּוּף לַחוֹלֶה/לַחוֹלָה *name of patient*
בֶּן/בַּת *mother's name* בְּתוֹךְ שְׁאָר חוֹלֵי יִשְׂרָאֵל.

---

כִּי אֵל מֶלֶךְ רוֹפֵא נֶאֱמָן וְרַחֲמָן אָתָּה.
בָּרוּךְ אַתָּה יהוה, רוֹפֵא חוֹלֵי עַמּוֹ יִשְׂרָאֵל.

ברכת השנים

בָּרֵךְ עָלֵינוּ יהוה אֱלֹהֵינוּ אֶת הַשָּׁנָה הַזֹּאת
וְאֶת כָּל מִינֵי תְבוּאָתָהּ, לְטוֹבָה
וְתֵן בְּרָכָה עַל פְּנֵי הָאֲדָמָה
וְשַׂבְּעֵנוּ מִטּוּבָהּ
וּבָרֵךְ שְׁנָתֵנוּ כַּשָּׁנִים הַטּוֹבוֹת לִבְרָכָה
כִּי אֵל טוֹב וּמֵטִיב אַתָּה וּמְבָרֵךְ הַשָּׁנִים.
בָּרוּךְ אַתָּה יהוה, מְבָרֵךְ הַשָּׁנִים.

INGATHERING OF EXILES

תְּקַע Sound the great shofar for our freedom,
raise high the banner to gather our exiles,
and gather us together speedily,
from the four quarters of the earth back to our land.
Blessed are You, LORD,
who gathers the dispersed of His people Israel.

JUSTICE

הָשִׁיבָה Restore our judges as at first,
and our counselors as at the beginning,
and remove from us sorrow and sighing.
May You alone, LORD, reign over us soon
with loving-kindness and compassion,
with righteousness and justice.
Blessed are You, LORD,
the King who loves righteousness and justice.

AGAINST INFORMERS

וְלַמַּלְשִׁינִים For the slanderers
let there be no hope,
and may all heretics perish in an instant.
May all Your people's enemies swiftly be cut down.
May You swiftly uproot, crush, cast down the arrogant,
and obliterate and bring them low and humble them
swiftly in our days.
Blessed are You, LORD,
who destroys enemies and humbles the arrogant.

THE RIGHTEOUS

עַל הַצַּדִּיקִים To the righteous, the pious,
the elders of the remnant of Your people the house of Israel,
the survivors among their scholars,
the righteous converts, and to us,
may Your compassion be aroused, please, LORD our God.

קבוץ גלויות

תְּקַע בְּשׁוֹפָר גָּדוֹל לְחֵרוּתֵנוּ
וְשָׂא נֵס לְקַבֵּץ גָּלֻיּוֹתֵינוּ
וְקַבְּצֵנוּ יַחַד מְהֵרָה מֵאַרְבַּע כַּנְפוֹת הָאָרֶץ לְאַרְצֵנוּ.
בָּרוּךְ אַתָּה יהוה, מְקַבֵּץ נִדְחֵי עַמּוֹ יִשְׂרָאֵל.

השבת המשפט

הָשִׁיבָה שׁוֹפְטֵינוּ כְּבָרִאשׁוֹנָה וְיוֹעֲצֵינוּ כְּבַתְּחִלָּה
וְהָסֵר מִמֶּנּוּ יָגוֹן וַאֲנָחָה
וּמְלֹךְ עָלֵינוּ מְהֵרָה אַתָּה יהוה לְבַדְּךָ בְּחֶסֶד וּבְרַחֲמִים
בְּצֶדֶק וּבְמִשְׁפָּט.
בָּרוּךְ אַתָּה יהוה, מֶלֶךְ אוֹהֵב צְדָקָה וּמִשְׁפָּט.

ברכת המינים

וְלַמַּלְשִׁינִים אַל תְּהִי תִקְוָה
וְכָל הַמִּינִים כְּרֶגַע יֹאבֵדוּ
וְכָל אוֹיְבֵי עַמְּךָ מְהֵרָה יִכָּרֵתוּ
וְהַזֵּדִים מְהֵרָה תְעַקֵּר וּתְשַׁבֵּר וּתְמַגֵּר
וּתְכַלֵּם וְתַשְׁפִּילֵם וְתַכְנִיעֵם בִּמְהֵרָה בְיָמֵינוּ.
בָּרוּךְ אַתָּה יהוה, שׁוֹבֵר אוֹיְבִים וּמַכְנִיעַ זֵדִים.

על הצדיקים

עַל הַצַּדִּיקִים וְעַל הַחֲסִידִים
וְעַל זִקְנֵי שְׁאֵרִית עַמְּךָ בֵּית יִשְׂרָאֵל
וְעַל פְּלֵיטַת בֵּית סוֹפְרֵיהֶם
וְעַל גֵּרֵי הַצֶּדֶק, וְעָלֵינוּ
יֶהֱמוּ נָא רַחֲמֶיךָ, יהוה אֱלֹהֵינוּ

Grant a good reward to all who sincerely trust in Your name.
Set our lot with them,
so that we may never be ashamed,
for in You we trust,
and upon Your great loving-kindness we truly depend.
Blessed are You, Lord,
who is the support and trust of the righteous.

REBUILDING JERUSALEM

וְלִירוּשָׁלַיִם To Jerusalem, Your city, may You return in compassion,
and may You dwell in it as You promised.
May You rebuild it rapidly in our days as an everlasting structure,
and install within it soon the throne of David, Your servant.
Blessed are You, Lord,
who builds Jerusalem.

KINGDOM OF DAVID

אֶת צֶמַח May the offshoot of Your servant David soon flower,
and may his pride be raised high by Your salvation,
for we wait for Your salvation all day.
Blessed are You, Lord,
who makes the glory of salvation flourish.

RESPONSE TO PRAYER

אָב הָרַחֲמָן Compassionate Father,
listen to our voice, Lord our God.
Spare us and have compassion on us,
and in compassion and favor accept our prayer,
for You, God, listen to prayers and pleas.
Do not turn us away, O our King,
empty-handed from Your presence,
be gracious to us, answer us and listen to our prayer.
For You listen to the prayer of every mouth.
Blessed are You,
Lord, who listens to prayer.

וְתֵן שָׂכָר טוֹב לְכָל הַבּוֹטְחִים בְּשִׁמְךָ בֶּאֱמֶת
וְשִׂים חֶלְקֵנוּ עִמָּהֶם
וּלְעוֹלָם לֹא נֵבוֹשׁ, כִּי בְךָ בָּטָחְנוּ
וְעַל חַסְדְּךָ הַגָּדוֹל בֶּאֱמֶת נִשְׁעָנְנוּ.
בָּרוּךְ אַתָּה יהוה, מִשְׁעָן וּמִבְטָח לַצַּדִּיקִים.

בניין ירושלים

וְלִירוּשָׁלַיִם עִירְךָ בְּרַחֲמִים תָּשׁוּב
וְתִשְׁכֹּן בְּתוֹכָהּ כַּאֲשֶׁר דִּבַּרְתָּ
וּבְנֵה אוֹתָהּ בְּקָרוֹב בְּיָמֵינוּ בִּנְיַן עוֹלָם
וְכִסֵּא דָוִד עַבְדְּךָ מְהֵרָה לְתוֹכָהּ תָּכִין.
בָּרוּךְ אַתָּה יהוה, בּוֹנֵה יְרוּשָׁלָיִם.

מלכות בית דוד

אֶת צֶמַח דָּוִד עַבְדְּךָ מְהֵרָה תַצְמִיחַ, וְקַרְנוֹ תָּרוּם בִּישׁוּעָתֶךָ
כִּי לִישׁוּעָתְךָ קִוִּינוּ כָּל הַיּוֹם.
בָּרוּךְ אַתָּה יהוה, מַצְמִיחַ קֶרֶן יְשׁוּעָה.

שומע תפלה

אָב הָרַחֲמָן, שְׁמַע קוֹלֵנוּ יהוה אֱלֹהֵינוּ
חוּס וְרַחֵם עָלֵינוּ
וְקַבֵּל בְּרַחֲמִים וּבְרָצוֹן אֶת תְּפִלָּתֵנוּ
כִּי אֵל שׁוֹמֵעַ תְּפִלּוֹת וְתַחֲנוּנִים אָתָּה
וּמִלְּפָנֶיךָ מַלְכֵּנוּ רֵיקָם אַל תְּשִׁיבֵנוּ
חָנֵּנוּ וַעֲנֵנוּ וּשְׁמַע תְּפִלָּתֵנוּ
כִּי אַתָּה שׁוֹמֵעַ תְּפִלַּת כָּל פֶּה.
בָּרוּךְ אַתָּה יהוה, שׁוֹמֵעַ תְּפִלָּה.

TEMPLE SERVICE

רְצֵה Find favor, LORD our God,
in Your people Israel, and heed their prayer.
Restore the service to Your most holy House,
and accept soon, in love and favor,
the fire-offerings of Israel and their prayer.
May the service of Your people Israel always find favor with You.
And may our eyes witness Your return to Zion in compassion.
Blessed are You, LORD, who restores His Presence to Zion.

THANKSGIVING

*Bow at the first nine words.*

מוֹדִים We give thanks to You,
for You are the LORD our God
and God of our ancestors
for ever and all time.
You are the Rock of our lives,
Shield of our salvation
from generation to generation.
We will thank You and
declare Your praise for our lives,
which are entrusted into Your hand;
for our souls,
which are placed in Your charge;
for Your miracles
which are with us every day;
and for Your wonders and favors
at all times, evening,
morning and midday.
You are good –
for Your compassion never fails.
You are compassionate –
for Your loving-kindnesses never cease;
for we have always placed our hope in You.

*During the Leader's Repetition, the congregation says quietly:*

מוֹדִים We give thanks to You,
for You are the LORD our God
and God of our ancestors,
God of all flesh,
who formed us
and formed the universe.
Blessings and thanks
are due to Your great
and holy name for giving us
life and sustaining us.
May You continue
to give us life and sustain us;
and may You gather our
exiles to Your holy courts,
to keep Your decrees,
do Your will and serve You
with a perfect heart,
for it is for us
to give You thanks.
Blessed be God to whom
thanksgiving is due.

---

Warsaw, Vilna or New York. He is suddenly transported to Jerusalem, and his prayer is transformed into an offering in the Temple. Rabbi Judah HaLevi

עבודה

רְצֵה יהוה אֱלֹהֵינוּ בְּעַמְּךָ יִשְׂרָאֵל, וְלִתְפִלָּתָם שְׁעֵה
וְהָשֵׁב אֶת הָעֲבוֹדָה לִדְבִיר בֵּיתֶךָ
וְאִשֵּׁי יִשְׂרָאֵל וּתְפִלָּתָם, מְהֵרָה בְּאַהֲבָה תְקַבֵּל בְּרָצוֹן
וּתְהִי לְרָצוֹן תָּמִיד עֲבוֹדַת יִשְׂרָאֵל עַמֶּךָ.
וְתֶחֱזֶינָה עֵינֵינוּ בְּשׁוּבְךָ לְצִיּוֹן בְּרַחֲמִים.
בָּרוּךְ אַתָּה יהוה, הַמַּחֲזִיר שְׁכִינָתוֹ לְצִיּוֹן.

הודאה

*Bow at the first five words.*

מוֹדִים אֲנַחְנוּ לָךְ
שָׁאַתָּה הוּא יהוה אֱלֹהֵינוּ
וֵאלֹהֵי אֲבוֹתֵינוּ לְעוֹלָם וָעֶד.
צוּר חַיֵּינוּ, מָגֵן יִשְׁעֵנוּ
אַתָּה הוּא לְדוֹר וָדוֹר.
נוֹדֶה לְּךָ וּנְסַפֵּר תְּהִלָּתֶךָ
עַל חַיֵּינוּ הַמְּסוּרִים בְּיָדֶךָ
וְעַל נִשְׁמוֹתֵינוּ הַפְּקוּדוֹת לָךְ
וְעַל נִסֶּיךָ שֶׁבְּכָל יוֹם עִמָּנוּ
וְעַל נִפְלְאוֹתֶיךָ וְטוֹבוֹתֶיךָ
שֶׁבְּכָל עֵת, עֶרֶב וָבֹקֶר וְצָהֳרָיִם.
הַטּוֹב, כִּי לֹא כָלוּ רַחֲמֶיךָ
וְהַמְרַחֵם, כִּי לֹא תַמּוּ חֲסָדֶיךָ
כִּי מֵעוֹלָם קִוִּינוּ לָךְ.

*During the* חזרת הש״ץ, *the* קהל *says quietly:*

מוֹדִים אֲנַחְנוּ לָךְ
שָׁאַתָּה הוּא יהוה אֱלֹהֵינוּ
וֵאלֹהֵי אֲבוֹתֵינוּ
אֱלֹהֵי כָל בָּשָׂר
יוֹצְרֵנוּ, יוֹצֵר בְּרֵאשִׁית.
בְּרָכוֹת וְהוֹדָאוֹת
לְשִׁמְךָ הַגָּדוֹל וְהַקָּדוֹשׁ
עַל שֶׁהֶחֱיִיתָנוּ וְקִיַּמְתָּנוּ.
כֵּן תְּחַיֵּנוּ וּתְקַיְּמֵנוּ
וְתֶאֱסֹף גָּלֻיּוֹתֵינוּ
לְחַצְרוֹת קָדְשֶׁךָ
לִשְׁמֹר חֻקֶּיךָ וְלַעֲשׂוֹת רְצוֹנֶךָ
וּלְעָבְדְּךָ בְּלֵבָב שָׁלֵם
עַל שֶׁאֲנַחְנוּ מוֹדִים לָךְ.
בָּרוּךְ אֵל הַהוֹדָאוֹת.

---

*Temple Service and Thanksgiving.* “As the Jew recites *Retzeh* and beseeches God to accept his sacrifices, he is no longer praying in his local synagogue in

וְעַל כֻּלָּם For all these things
may Your name be blessed and exalted,
and raised up our King, continually, for ever and all time.
Let all that lives thank You, Selah!
and praise and bless Your great name in truth, always,
because it is good,
God, our Savior and Help, Selah! the beneficent God.
▾Blessed are You, Lord,
whose name is "the Good"
and to whom thanks are due.

TEMPLE SERVICE

שִׂים שָׁלוֹם Grant peace, goodness and blessing,
life, grace, loving-kindness and compassion
to us and all Israel Your people.
Bless us, our Father, all as one,
with the light of Your face,
for by the light of Your face You have given us, Lord our God,
the Torah of life and love of kindness,
righteousness, blessing, compassion, life and peace.
May it be good in Your eyes
to bless us and all Your people Israel
at every time, in every hour, with Your peace.
Blessed are You, Lord,
who blesses His people Israel with peace.

*The following verse concludes the Leader's Repetition of the Amida.*
*Some also say it here as part of the silent Amida.*

May the words of my mouth and the meditation of my heart *Ps. 19*
find favor before You, Lord, my Rock and Redeemer.

---

we were standing in the presence of the restored *Shekhina*." (Rabbi Joseph Soloveitchik)

וְעַל כֻּלָּם
יִתְבָּרַךְ וְיִתְרוֹמַם וְיִתְנַשֵּׂא שִׁמְךָ מַלְכֵּנוּ תָּמִיד לְעוֹלָם וָעֶד.
וְכֹל הַחַיִּים יוֹדְוּךָ סֶּלָה
וִיהַלְלוּ וִיבָרְכוּ אֶת שִׁמְךָ הַגָּדוֹל בֶּאֱמֶת לְעוֹלָם כִּי טוֹב
הָאֵל יְשׁוּעָתֵנוּ וְעֶזְרָתֵנוּ סֶלָה, הָאֵל הַטּוֹב.
ׄבָּרוּךְ אַתָּה יהוה, הַטּוֹב שִׁמְךָ וּלְךָ נָאֶה לְהוֹדוֹת.

ברכת שלום

שִׂים שָׁלוֹם טוֹבָה וּבְרָכָה
חַיִּים חֵן וָחֶסֶד וְרַחֲמִים
עָלֵינוּ וְעַל כָּל יִשְׂרָאֵל עַמֶּךָ.
בָּרְכֵנוּ אָבִינוּ כֻּלָּנוּ כְּאֶחָד בְּאוֹר פָּנֶיךָ
כִּי בְאוֹר פָּנֶיךָ נָתַתָּ לָּנוּ יהוה אֱלֹהֵינוּ
תּוֹרַת חַיִּים וְאַהֲבַת חֶסֶד
וּצְדָקָה וּבְרָכָה וְרַחֲמִים וְחַיִּים וְשָׁלוֹם.
וְטוֹב יִהְיֶה בְעֵינֶיךָ לְבָרְכֵנוּ וּלְבָרֵךְ אֶת כָּל עַמְּךָ יִשְׂרָאֵל
בְּכָל עֵת וּבְכָל שָׁעָה בִּשְׁלוֹמֶךָ
בָּרוּךְ אַתָּה יהוה, הַמְבָרֵךְ אֶת עַמּוֹ יִשְׂרָאֵל בַּשָּׁלוֹם.

*The following verse concludes the* חזרת הש״ץ.
*Some also say it here as part of the silent* עמידה.

תהלים יט יִהְיוּ לְרָצוֹן אִמְרֵי־פִי וְהֶגְיוֹן לִבִּי לְפָנֶיךָ, יהוה צוּרִי וְגֹאֲלִי:

---

(*Kuzari* 3:19) highlights that at this juncture in the Amida we are praying for the *Shekhina* to return to Jerusalem. We must therefore bow at *Modim* as if

אֱלֹהַי My God, *Berakhot 17a*
guard my tongue from evil and my lips from deceitful speech.
To those who curse me, let my soul be silent;
may my soul be to all like the dust.
Open my heart to Your Torah
and let my soul pursue Your commandments.
As for all who rise up or plan evil against me,
swiftly thwart their counsel and frustrate their plans.

*Some add this prayer:*

יְהִי רָצוֹן May it be Your will, LORD my God, God of my ancestors,
that envy of no man may rise up in me, nor envy of me in any other;
that I will not be angry today, nor make You angry;
and save me from my evil impulse,
placing humility and modesty into my heart.
Our King and God, make Your name One in Your world;
build up Your city, establish Your House and complete Your Sanctuary,
gather in the exiles, redeem Your flock, and have Your congregation rejoice.

Act for the sake of Your name;
act for the sake of Your right hand;
act for the sake of Your Torah;
act for the sake of Your holiness.
That Your beloved ones may be delivered, *Ps. 60*
save with Your right hand and answer me.
May the words of my mouth and the meditation of my heart *Ps. 19*
find favor before You, LORD, my Rock and Redeemer.

*Bow, take three steps back, then bow, first left, then right, then center, while saying:*

May He who makes peace in His high places,
make peace for us and all Israel –
and say: Amen.

יְהִי רָצוֹן May it be Your will, LORD our God and God of our ancestors,
that the Temple be rebuilt speedily in our days,
and grant us a share in Your Torah.
And there we will serve You with reverence,
as in the days of old and as in former years.
Then the offering of Judah and Jerusalem will be pleasing to the LORD *Mal. 3*
as in the days of old and as in former years.

ברכות יז.

אֱלֹהַי

נְצֹר לְשׁוֹנִי מֵרָע וּשְׂפָתַי מִדַּבֵּר מִרְמָה

וְלִמְקַלְלַי נַפְשִׁי תִדֹּם, וְנַפְשִׁי כֶּעָפָר לַכֹּל תִּהְיֶה.

פְּתַח לִבִּי בְּתוֹרָתֶךָ, וְאַחֲרֵי מִצְוֹתֶיךָ תִּרְדֹּף נַפְשִׁי.

וְכָל הַקָּמִים וְהַחוֹשְׁבִים עָלַי רָעָה

מְהֵרָה הָפֵר עֲצָתָם וְקַלְקֵל מַחֲשַׁבְתָּם.

*Some add this prayer:*

יְהִי רָצוֹן מִלְּפָנֶיךָ יהוה אֱלֹהַי וֵאלֹהֵי אֲבוֹתַי

שֶׁלֹּא תַעֲלֶה קִנְאַת אָדָם עָלַי, וְלֹא קִנְאָתִי עַל אֲחֵרִים

וְשֶׁלֹּא אֶכְעֹס הַיּוֹם, וְשֶׁלֹּא אַכְעִיסֶךָ

וְתַצִּילֵנִי מִיֵּצֶר הָרָע, וְתֵן בְּלִבִּי הַכְנָעָה וַעֲנָוָה.

מַלְכֵּנוּ וֵאלֹהֵינוּ, יַחֵד שִׁמְךָ בְּעוֹלָמֶךָ

בְּנֵה עִירָךְ, יַסֵּד בֵּיתָךְ וְשַׁכְלֵל הֵיכָלָךְ

וְקַבֵּץ קִבּוּץ גָּלֻיּוֹת, וּפְדֵה צֹאנָךְ וְשַׂמַּח עֲדָתָךְ.

עֲשֵׂה לְמַעַן שְׁמֶךָ, עֲשֵׂה לְמַעַן יְמִינֶךָ

עֲשֵׂה לְמַעַן תּוֹרָתֶךָ, עֲשֵׂה לְמַעַן קְדֻשָּׁתֶךָ.

תהלים ס לְמַעַן יֵחָלְצוּן יְדִידֶיךָ, הוֹשִׁיעָה יְמִינְךָ וַעֲנֵנִי:

תהלים יט יִהְיוּ לְרָצוֹן אִמְרֵי־פִי וְהֶגְיוֹן לִבִּי לְפָנֶיךָ, יהוה צוּרִי וְגֹאֲלִי:

*Bow, take three steps back, then bow, first left, then right, then center, while saying:*

עֹשֶׂה שָׁלוֹם בִּמְרוֹמָיו

הוּא יַעֲשֶׂה שָׁלוֹם עָלֵינוּ וְעַל כָּל יִשְׂרָאֵל

וְאִמְרוּ אָמֵן.

יְהִי רָצוֹן מִלְּפָנֶיךָ יהוה אֱלֹהֵינוּ וֵאלֹהֵי אֲבוֹתֵינוּ

שֶׁיִּבָּנֶה בֵּית הַמִּקְדָּשׁ בִּמְהֵרָה בְיָמֵינוּ

וְתֵן חֶלְקֵנוּ בְּתוֹרָתֶךָ

וְשָׁם נַעֲבָדְךָ בְּיִרְאָה כִּימֵי עוֹלָם וּכְשָׁנִים קַדְמֹנִיּוֹת.

מלאכי ג וְעָרְבָה לַיהוה מִנְחַת יְהוּדָה וִירוּשָׁלָםִ כִּימֵי עוֹלָם וּכְשָׁנִים קַדְמֹנִיּוֹת:

## FULL KADDISH

*Leader:* יִתְגַּדַּל Magnified and sanctified
may His great name be,
in the world He created by His will.
May He establish His kingdom,
make His salvation flourish,
and hasten His messiah,
in your lifetime and in your days,
and in the lifetime of all the house of Israel,
swiftly and soon –
and say: Amen.

*All:* May His great name be blessed for ever and all time.

*Leader:* Blessed and praised,
glorified and exalted,
raised and honored,
uplifted and lauded be
the name of the Holy One, blessed be He,
beyond any blessing,
song, praise and consolation
uttered in the world –
and say: Amen.

May the prayers and pleas of all the house of Israel
be accepted by their Father in heaven –
and say: Amen.

May there be great peace from heaven,
and a good life for us and all Israel –
and say: Amen.

*Bow, take three steps back, as if taking leave of the Divine Presence, then bow, first left, then right, then center, while saying:*

May He who makes peace in His high places,
make peace for us and all Israel –
and say: Amen.

## קדיש שלם

ש״ץ: יִתְגַּדַּל וְיִתְקַדַּשׁ שְׁמֵהּ רַבָּא (קהל: אָמֵן)
בְּעָלְמָא דִּי בְרָא כִרְעוּתֵהּ
וְיַמְלִיךְ מַלְכוּתֵהּ וְיַצְמַח פֻּרְקָנֵהּ וִיקָרֵב מְשִׁיחֵהּ (קהל: אָמֵן)
בְּחַיֵּיכוֹן וּבְיוֹמֵיכוֹן וּבְחַיֵּי דְכָל בֵּית יִשְׂרָאֵל
בַּעֲגָלָא וּבִזְמַן קָרִיב
וְאִמְרוּ אָמֵן. (קהל: אָמֵן)

קהל וש״ץ: יְהֵא שְׁמֵהּ רַבָּא מְבָרַךְ לְעָלַם וּלְעָלְמֵי עָלְמַיָּא.

ש״ץ: יִתְבָּרַךְ וְיִשְׁתַּבַּח וְיִתְפָּאַר
וְיִתְרוֹמַם וְיִתְנַשֵּׂא וְיִתְהַדָּר וְיִתְעַלֶּה וְיִתְהַלָּל
שְׁמֵהּ דְּקֻדְשָׁא בְּרִיךְ הוּא (קהל: אָמֵן)
לְעֵלָּא מִן כָּל בִּרְכָתָא וְשִׁירָתָא, תֻּשְׁבְּחָתָא וְנֶחֱמָתָא
דַּאֲמִירָן בְּעָלְמָא
וְאִמְרוּ אָמֵן. (קהל: אָמֵן)

תִּתְקַבַּל צְלוֹתְהוֹן וּבָעוּתְהוֹן דְּכָל בֵּית יִשְׂרָאֵל
קֳדָם אֲבוּהוֹן דִּי בִשְׁמַיָּא
וְאִמְרוּ אָמֵן. (קהל: אָמֵן)

יְהֵא שְׁלָמָא רַבָּא מִן שְׁמַיָּא
וְחַיִּים טוֹבִים עָלֵינוּ וְעַל כָּל יִשְׂרָאֵל
וְאִמְרוּ אָמֵן. (קהל: אָמֵן)

*Bow, take three steps back, as if taking leave of the Divine Presence, then bow, first left, then right, then center, while saying:*

עֹשֶׂה שָׁלוֹם בִּמְרוֹמָיו
הוּא יַעֲשֶׂה שָׁלוֹם עָלֵינוּ וְעַל כָּל יִשְׂרָאֵל
וְאִמְרוּ אָמֵן. (קהל: אָמֵן)

*Stand while saying Aleinu. Bow at* ▾.

עָלֵינוּ It is our duty to praise the Master of all,
and ascribe greatness
to the Author of creation,
who has not made us
like the nations of the lands
nor placed us like the families of the earth;
who has not made our portion like theirs,
nor our destiny like all their multitudes.
For they worship vanity and emptiness,
and pray to a god who cannot save.
▾ But we bow in worship
and thank the Supreme King of kings,
the Holy One, blessed be He,
who extends the heavens and establishes the earth,
whose throne of glory is in the heavens above,
and whose power's Presence is in the highest of heights.
He is our God; there is no other.
Truly He is our King, there is none else,
as it is written in His Torah:
"You shall know and take to heart this day *Deut. 4*
that the Lord is God,
in the heavens above and on the earth below.
There is no other."

---

uniqueness of the Jewish people and its vocation. We are different. It is not our highest aspiration to be like everyone else. We have been singled out for a sacred mission, to be God's ambassadors, His witnesses, part of a nation that in itself testifies to something larger than itself, to a divine presence in history.

But Judaism is not just inward-turning particularity. The second paragraph is a no less emphatic prayer for universality, for the day when all humanity will recognize the sovereignty of God. All humans are in God's image, part

*Stand while saying* עָלֵינוּ. *Bow at* ᵛ.

עָלֵינוּ לְשַׁבֵּחַ לַאֲדוֹן הַכֹּל
לָתֵת גְּדֻלָּה לְיוֹצֵר בְּרֵאשִׁית
שֶׁלֹּא עָשָׂנוּ כְּגוֹיֵי הָאֲרָצוֹת
וְלֹא שָׂמָנוּ כְּמִשְׁפְּחוֹת הָאֲדָמָה
שֶׁלֹּא שָׂם חֶלְקֵנוּ כָּהֶם וְגוֹרָלֵנוּ כְּכָל הֲמוֹנָם.
שֶׁהֵם מִשְׁתַּחֲוִים לְהֶבֶל וָרִיק וּמִתְפַּלְלִים אֶל אֵל לֹא יוֹשִׁיעַ.
ᵛוַאֲנַחְנוּ כּוֹרְעִים וּמִשְׁתַּחֲוִים וּמוֹדִים
לִפְנֵי מֶלֶךְ מַלְכֵי הַמְּלָכִים, הַקָּדוֹשׁ בָּרוּךְ הוּא
שֶׁהוּא נוֹטֶה שָׁמַיִם וְיוֹסֵד אָרֶץ
וּמוֹשַׁב יְקָרוֹ בַּשָּׁמַיִם מִמַּעַל
וּשְׁכִינַת עֻזּוֹ בְּגָבְהֵי מְרוֹמִים.
הוּא אֱלֹהֵינוּ, אֵין עוֹד.
אֱמֶת מַלְכֵּנוּ, אֶפֶס זוּלָתוֹ
כַּכָּתוּב בְּתוֹרָתוֹ
דברים ד וְיָדַעְתָּ הַיּוֹם וַהֲשֵׁבֹתָ אֶל־לְבָבֶךָ
כִּי יהוה הוּא הָאֱלֹהִים בַּשָּׁמַיִם מִמַּעַל וְעַל־הָאָרֶץ מִתָּחַת
אֵין עוֹד:

---

ALEINU

This prayer has a special association with Rosh HaShana since it was first used as the prelude to *Malkhiyot*, the verses relating to God's kingship, that are central to the Musaf Amida of Rosh HaShana. Only in the thirteenth century did it begin to be said daily at the conclusion of each service.

Note the contrast between the first and second paragraphs. The first is a quintessential statement of Jewish particularity. We thank God for the

Therefore, we place our hope in You, LORD our God,
that we may soon see the glory of Your power,
when You will remove abominations from the earth,
and idols will be utterly destroyed,
when the world will be perfected
under the sovereignty of the Almighty,
when all humanity will call on Your name,
to turn all the earth's wicked toward You.
All the world's inhabitants will realize and know
that to You every knee must bow
and every tongue swear loyalty.
Before You, LORD our God,
they will kneel and bow down
and give honor to Your glorious name.
They will all accept the yoke of Your kingdom,
and You will reign over them soon and for ever.
For the kingdom is Yours,
and to all eternity You will reign in glory,
as it is written in Your Torah:
"The LORD will reign for ever and ever." *Ex. 15*
▸ And it is said:
"Then the LORD shall be King over all the earth; *Zech. 14*
on that day the LORD shall be One and His name One."

*Some add:*
Have no fear of sudden terror or of the ruin when it overtakes the wicked. *Prov. 3*
Devise your strategy, but it will be thwarted; propose your plan, *Is. 8*
but it will not stand, for God is with us.
When you grow old, I will still be the same. *Is. 46*
When your hair turns gray, I will still carry you.
I made you, I will bear you,
I will carry you, and I will rescue you.

---

being what we uniquely are, do we contribute to humanity as a whole what only we can give.

וְעַל כֵּן נְקַוֶּה לְּךָ יהוה אֱלֹהֵינוּ
לִרְאוֹת מְהֵרָה בְּתִפְאֶרֶת עֻזֶּךָ
לְהַעֲבִיר גִּלּוּלִים מִן הָאָרֶץ
וְהָאֱלִילִים כָּרוֹת יִכָּרֵתוּן
לְתַקֵּן עוֹלָם בְּמַלְכוּת שַׁדַּי.
וְכָל בְּנֵי בָשָׂר יִקְרְאוּ בִשְׁמֶךָ לְהַפְנוֹת אֵלֶיךָ כָּל רִשְׁעֵי אָרֶץ.
יַכִּירוּ וְיֵדְעוּ כָּל יוֹשְׁבֵי תֵבֵל
כִּי לְךָ תִּכְרַע כָּל בֶּרֶךְ, תִּשָּׁבַע כָּל לָשׁוֹן.
לְפָנֶיךָ יהוה אֱלֹהֵינוּ יִכְרְעוּ וְיִפֹּלוּ, וְלִכְבוֹד שִׁמְךָ יְקָר יִתֵּנוּ
וִיקַבְּלוּ כֻלָּם אֶת עֹל מַלְכוּתֶךָ
וְתִמְלֹךְ עֲלֵיהֶם מְהֵרָה לְעוֹלָם וָעֶד.
כִּי הַמַּלְכוּת שֶׁלְּךָ הִיא וּלְעוֹלְמֵי עַד תִּמְלֹךְ בְּכָבוֹד
כַּכָּתוּב בְּתוֹרָתֶךָ,
יהוה יִמְלֹךְ לְעֹלָם וָעֶד: שמות טו
◂ וְנֶאֱמַר, וְהָיָה יהוה לְמֶלֶךְ עַל־כָּל־הָאָרֶץ זכריה יד
בַּיּוֹם הַהוּא יִהְיֶה יהוה אֶחָד וּשְׁמוֹ אֶחָד:

*Some add:*

אַל־תִּירָא מִפַּחַד פִּתְאֹם וּמִשֹּׁאַת רְשָׁעִים כִּי תָבֹא: משלי ג
עֻצוּ עֵצָה וְתֻפָר, דַּבְּרוּ דָבָר וְלֹא יָקוּם, כִּי עִמָּנוּ אֵל: ישעיה ח
וְעַד־זִקְנָה אֲנִי הוּא, וְעַד־שֵׂיבָה אֲנִי אֶסְבֹּל ישעיה מו
אֲנִי עָשִׂיתִי וַאֲנִי אֶשָּׂא וַאֲנִי אֶסְבֹּל וַאֲמַלֵּט:

---

of God's world, heirs to God's covenant with Noah, and in the future, as polytheism and atheism reveal themselves to be empty creeds, all humanity will turn to the One God.

There is no contradiction between particularity and universality. Only by

## MOURNER'S KADDISH

*The following prayer, said by mourners, requires the presence of a minyan.*
*A transliteration can be found on page 1095.*

*Mourner:* יִתְגַּדַּל Magnified and sanctified
may His great name be,
in the world He created by His will.
May He establish His kingdom,
make His salvation flourish,
and hasten His messiah,
in your lifetime and in your days,
and in the lifetime of all the house of Israel,
swiftly and soon –
and say: Amen.

*All:* May His great name be blessed for ever and all time.

*Mourner:* Blessed and praised, glorified and exalted,
raised and honored, uplifted and lauded
be the name of the Holy One,
blessed be He,
beyond any blessing, song, praise and consolation
uttered in the world –
and say: Amen.

May there be great peace from heaven,
and a good life for us and all Israel –
and say: Amen.

*Bow, take three steps back, as if taking leave of the Divine Presence,*
*then bow, first left, then right, then center, while saying:*

May He who makes peace in His high places,
make peace for us and all Israel –
and say: Amen.

---

the congregation to praise God by saying, "May His great name be blessed for ever and all time." According to the Talmud, whenever Jews enter a synagogue or a house of study and say "May His great name be blessed," the

## קדיש יתום

*The following prayer, said by mourners, requires the presence of a* מנין*.*
*A transliteration can be found on page 1095.*

אבל: יִתְגַּדַּל וְיִתְקַדַּשׁ שְׁמֵהּ רַבָּא (קהל: אָמֵן)
בְּעָלְמָא דִּי בְרָא כִרְעוּתֵהּ
וְיַמְלִיךְ מַלְכוּתֵהּ וְיַצְמַח פֻּרְקָנֵהּ וִיקָרֵב מְשִׁיחֵהּ (קהל: אָמֵן)
בְּחַיֵּיכוֹן וּבְיוֹמֵיכוֹן וּבְחַיֵּי דְכָל בֵּית יִשְׂרָאֵל
בַּעֲגָלָא וּבִזְמַן קָרִיב וְאִמְרוּ אָמֵן. (קהל: אָמֵן)

קהל ואבל: יְהֵא שְׁמֵהּ רַבָּא מְבָרַךְ לְעָלַם וּלְעָלְמֵי עָלְמַיָּא.

אבל: יִתְבָּרַךְ וְיִשְׁתַּבַּח וְיִתְפָּאַר
וְיִתְרוֹמַם וְיִתְנַשֵּׂא וְיִתְהַדָּר וְיִתְעַלֶּה וְיִתְהַלָּל
שְׁמֵהּ דְּקֻדְשָׁא בְּרִיךְ הוּא (קהל: אָמֵן)
לְעֵלָּא מִן כָּל בִּרְכָתָא
וְשִׁירָתָא, תֻּשְׁבְּחָתָא וְנֶחֱמָתָא
דַּאֲמִירָן בְּעָלְמָא, וְאִמְרוּ אָמֵן. (קהל: אָמֵן)

יְהֵא שְׁלָמָא רַבָּא מִן שְׁמַיָּא
וְחַיִּים טוֹבִים עָלֵינוּ וְעַל כָּל יִשְׂרָאֵל, וְאִמְרוּ אָמֵן. (קהל: אָמֵן)

*Bow, take three steps back, as if taking leave of the Divine Presence,*
*then bow, first left, then right, then center, while saying:*

עֹשֶׂה שָׁלוֹם בִּמְרוֹמָיו
הוּא יַעֲשֶׂה שָׁלוֹם
עָלֵינוּ וְעַל כָּל יִשְׂרָאֵל, וְאִמְרוּ אָמֵן. (קהל: אָמֵן)

---

MOURNERS' KADDISH

We bring credit to the memory of the dead by doing acts that confer merit on the living. This especially applies to the saying of Kaddish, since it causes

לְדָוִד By David. The Lord is my light and my salvation – whom then shall I fear? The Lord is the stronghold of my life – of whom shall I be afraid? When evil men close in on me to devour my flesh, it is they, my enemies and foes, who stumble and fall. Should an army besiege me, my heart would not fear. Should war break out against me, still I would be confident. One thing I ask of the Lord, only this do I seek: to live in the House of the Lord all the days of my life, to gaze on the beauty of the Lord and worship in His Temple. For He will keep me safe in His pavilion on the day of trouble. He will hide me under the cover of His tent. He will set me high upon a rock. Now my head is high above my enemies who surround me. I will sacrifice in His tent with shouts of joy. I will sing and chant praises to the Lord. Lord, hear my voice when I call. Be gracious to me and answer me. On Your behalf my heart says, "Seek My face." Your face, Lord, will I seek. Do not hide Your face from me. Do not turn Your servant away in anger. You have been my help. Do not reject or forsake me, God, my Savior. Were my father and my mother to forsake me, the Lord would take me in. Teach me Your way, Lord, and lead me on a level path, because of my oppressors. Do not abandon me to the will of my foes, for false witnesses have risen against me, breathing violence. ▸ Were it not for my faith that I shall see the Lord's goodness in the land of the living. Hope in the Lord. Be strong and of good courage, and hope in the Lord! *Ps. 27*

*Mourner's Kaddish, see previous page.*

---

The psalm is said morning and evening from the beginning of Elul until Shemini Atzeret. Its connection with this time of the year is based on the rabbinic interpretation: *The Lord is my light* on Rosh HaShana, *and my salvation* on Yom Kippur. *He will keep me safe in His pavilion* [*besukko*] – this refers to Sukkot (*Vayikra Raba*).

לְךָ אָמַר לִבִּי *On Your behalf my heart says.* A striking statement of the voice of faith within the human heart. We may feel far from God but we can sometimes hear in the silence of the soul God's call summoning us to seek Him.

לְדָוִד, יהוה אוֹרִי וְיִשְׁעִי, מִמִּי אִירָא, יהוה מָעוֹז־חַיַּי, מִמִּי אֶפְחָד: תהלים כז
בִּקְרֹב עָלַי מְרֵעִים לֶאֱכֹל אֶת־בְּשָׂרִי, צָרַי וְאֹיְבַי לִי, הֵמָּה כָשְׁלוּ וְנָפָלוּ:
אִם־תַּחֲנֶה עָלַי מַחֲנֶה, לֹא־יִירָא לִבִּי, אִם־תָּקוּם עָלַי מִלְחָמָה, בְּזֹאת
אֲנִי בוֹטֵחַ: אַחַת שָׁאַלְתִּי מֵאֵת־יהוה, אוֹתָהּ אֲבַקֵּשׁ, שִׁבְתִּי בְּבֵית־
יהוה כָּל־יְמֵי חַיַּי, לַחֲזוֹת בְּנֹעַם־יהוה, וּלְבַקֵּר בְּהֵיכָלוֹ: כִּי יִצְפְּנֵנִי
בְּסֻכֹּה בְּיוֹם רָעָה, יַסְתִּרֵנִי בְּסֵתֶר אָהֳלוֹ, בְּצוּר יְרוֹמְמֵנִי: וְעַתָּה יָרוּם
רֹאשִׁי עַל אֹיְבַי סְבִיבוֹתַי, וְאֶזְבְּחָה בְאָהֳלוֹ זִבְחֵי תְרוּעָה, אָשִׁירָה
וַאֲזַמְּרָה לַיהוה: שְׁמַע־יהוה קוֹלִי אֶקְרָא, וְחָנֵּנִי וַעֲנֵנִי: לְךָ אָמַר לִבִּי
בַּקְּשׁוּ פָנָי, אֶת־פָּנֶיךָ יהוה אֲבַקֵּשׁ: אַל־תַּסְתֵּר פָּנֶיךָ מִמֶּנִּי, אַל תַּט־
בְּאַף עַבְדֶּךָ, עֶזְרָתִי הָיִיתָ, אַל־תִּטְּשֵׁנִי וְאַל־תַּעַזְבֵנִי, אֱלֹהֵי יִשְׁעִי:
כִּי־אָבִי וְאִמִּי עֲזָבוּנִי, וַיהוה יַאַסְפֵנִי: הוֹרֵנִי יהוה דַּרְכֶּךָ, וּנְחֵנִי בְּאֹרַח
מִישׁוֹר, לְמַעַן שׁוֹרְרָי: אַל־תִּתְּנֵנִי בְּנֶפֶשׁ צָרָי, כִּי קָמוּ־בִי עֵדֵי־שֶׁקֶר,
וִיפֵחַ חָמָס: ‹ לוּלֵא הֶאֱמַנְתִּי לִרְאוֹת בְּטוּב־יהוה בְּאֶרֶץ חַיִּים: קַוֵּה
אֶל־יהוה, חֲזַק וְיַאֲמֵץ לִבֶּךָ, וְקַוֵּה אֶל־יהוה:

*קדיש יתום, see previous page.*

---

Holy One, blessed be He, nods His head and says: "Happy is the King who is thus praised in this house" (*Berakhot* 3a). Note that Kaddish speaks neither of death nor of the past. It speaks about the future and about peace. We honor the dead by the way we live. We honor the past by the future we create.

לְדָוִד *Psalm 27.* A magnificent statement of trust in God who is with us at all times if we are with Him, who will never reject us even were our own parents to do so, who gives us confidence in hard times and the courage to face our enemies without fear. The words, "The Lord is my light," in their Latin translation, *Dominus illuminatio mea*, form the motto of Oxford University and appear on its coat of arms.

לדוד, יהוה אורי וישעי, ממי אירא, יהוה מעוז־חיי, ממי אפחד: בקרב עלי מרעים לאכל את־בשרי, צרי ואיבי לי, המה כשלו ונפלו: אם־תחנה עלי מחנה, לא־יירא לבי, אם־תקום עלי מלחמה, בזאת אני בוטח: אחת שאלתי מאת־יהוה, אותה אבקש, שבתי בבית־יהוה כל־ימי חיי, לחזות בנעם־יהוה, ולבקר בהיכלו: כי יצפנני בסכה ביום רעה, יסתרני בסתר אהלו, בצור ירוממני: ועתה ירום ראשי על איבי סביבותי, ואזבחה באהלו זבחי תרועה, אשירה ואזמרה ליהוה: שמע־יהוה קולי אקרא, וחנני וענני: לך אמר לבי בקשו פני, את־פניך יהוה אבקש: אל־תסתר פניך ממני, אל תט־באף עבדך, עזרתי היית, אל־תטשני ואל־תעזבני, אלהי ישעי: כי־אבי ואמי עזבוני, ויהוה יאספני: הורני יהוה דרכך, ונחני בארח מישור, למען שוררי: אל־תתנני בנפש צרי, כי קמו־בי עדי־שקר, ויפח חמס: לולא האמנתי לראות בטוב־יהוה בארץ חיים: קוה אל־יהוה, חזק ויאמץ לבך, וקוה אל־יהוה:

תהלים כז

Holy One, blessed be He, nods His head and says: "Happy is the King who is thus praised in this house" (Berakhot 3a). Note that Kaddish speaks neither of death nor of the past. It speaks about the future and about peace. We honor the dead by the way we live. We honor the past by the future we

לדוד Psalm 27. A magnificent statement of trust in God who is with us at all times if we are with Him, who will never reject us even if our own parents forsake us, who gives us confidence in hard times and the courage to face our enemies without fear. The words, "The LORD is my light," in their Latin translation, Dominus illuminatio mea, form the motto of Oxford University and appear on its coat of arms.

וּבַחֹ֨דֶשׁ הַשְּׁבִיעִ֜י

בְּאֶחָ֣ד לַחֹ֗דֶשׁ

מִֽקְרָא־קֹ֙דֶשׁ֙ יִהְיֶ֣ה לָכֶ֔ם

כָּל־מְלֶ֥אכֶת עֲבֹדָ֖ה

לֹ֣א תַעֲשׂ֑וּ

# י֥וֹם תְּרוּעָ֖ה

יִהְיֶ֥ה לָכֶֽם׃

במדבר כט

תִּקְע֣וּ בַחֹ֣דֶשׁ שׁוֹפָ֑ר בַּ֝כֵּ֗סֶה לְי֣וֹם חַגֵּֽנוּ׃
כִּ֤י חֹ֣ק לְיִשְׂרָאֵ֣ל ה֑וּא מִ֝שְׁפָּ֗ט לֵאלֹהֵ֥י יַעֲקֹֽב׃

תהלים פא

*Some say the following poem after Minḥa.*
*Its author is Rabbi Avraham Ḥazan, a student of Nahmanides.*

אָחוֹת קְטַנָּה Little Sister – she prepares
her prayers, and declaims her praise for You.
God, please heal her maladies.
Bring an end to the year
and its curses.

She calls upon You with pleasant words,
in song and festive joy, as befits You.
Why do You turn a blind eye when You see
strangers consuming the land of her inheritance?
Bring an end to the year
and its curses.

Tend to Your flock that the lions scattered round,
and pour out Your wrath
upon those who cry "Raze it to the ground!"
They tore at the stem Your right hand planted,
pulled it out,
and left her not a single fruit.
Bring an end to the year
and its curses.

Raise her from subjugation to the highest sovereignty,
for in the pit of exile her soul melts away.
And as vileness is exalted she pours out her heart,
making her home among the poorest of the poor.
Bring an end to the year
and its curses.

---

the way both in Europe and in Jerusalem itself. The poem, composed in the thirteenth century by Rabbi Abraham Ḥazan of Gerona, is a plea for Rosh HaShana to mark a turning point in the fate of Jewry. *Little Sister*: a phrase taken from Song of Songs (8:8), here meaning the Jewish people.

*Some say the following poem after* מנחה.
*Its author is Rabbi Avraham Ḥazan, a student of Nahmanides.*

אָחוֹת קְטַנָּה, תְּפִלּוֹתֶיהָ
עוֹרְכָה וְעוֹנָה תְּהִלּוֹתֶיהָ
אֵל נָא רְפָא נָא לְמַחֲלוֹתֶיהָ. תִּכְלֶה שָׁנָה וְקִלְלוֹתֶיהָ.

בְּנֹעַם מִלִּים לְךָ תִּקְרָאֶה
וְשִׁיר וְהִלּוּלִים, כִּי לְךָ נָאֶה
עַל מָה תַּעְלִים עֵינְךָ, וְתִרְאֶה
זָרִים אוֹכְלִים נַחֲלוֹתֶיהָ. תִּכְלֶה שָׁנָה וְקִלְלוֹתֶיהָ.

רְעֵה אֶת צֹאנְךָ אֲרָיוֹת זֵרוּ
וּשְׁפֹךְ חֲרוֹנְךָ בְּאוֹמְרִים עָרוּ
וְכַנַּת יְמִינְךָ פָּרְצוּ וְאָרוּ
לֹא הִשְׁאִירוּ עוֹלְלוֹתֶיהָ. תִּכְלֶה שָׁנָה וְקִלְלוֹתֶיהָ.

הָקֵם מִשְׁפְּלוּת לְרֹאשׁ מַמְלֶכֶת
כִּי בְּבוֹר גָּלוּת נַפְשָׁהּ נִתֶּכֶת
וּכְרֻם זְלוּת לִבָּהּ שׁוֹפֶכֶת
בְּדַלֵּי דַלּוּת מִשְׁכְּנוֹתֶיהָ. תִּכְלֶה שָׁנָה וְקִלְלוֹתֶיהָ.

---

AḤOT KETANA – LITTLE SISTER
A cry from the heart of Spanish Jewry during the age of the Crusades, as Christians fought Muslims for control of the Holy Land, massacring Jews on

When will You raise Your daughter from the pit,
and shatter the yoke of the prison she is in?
Working wonders as You ride forth like a hero
to quash and bring an end to those who destroy her.
Bring an end to the year
and its curses.

All her wealth has been taken by the nations,
and they gorged themselves
and each plundered her bounty.
And though they tore her heart, nevertheless
her steps did not stray from Your path.
Bring an end to the year
and its curses.

Her song has ceased; please, increase her desire
to yearn the proximity of her Beloved, as You remove
all suffering from her heart and turn again
to seek out the love of her bridal days.
Bring an end to the year
and its curses.

Guide her gently to a pasture where she might rest;
too long is she neglected by her yearned-for Beloved.
She is like a budding blossom, her shoots blooming,
though her fruit has not ripened yet in its clusters.
Bring an end to the year
and its curses.

Take strength and rejoice, for the plundering has ended.
Raise your hopes to your Rock
for He has safeguarded His covenant
with you; and go up to Zion where it shall be declared:
"Pave her path, pave her path anew!"
Begin the year
and its blessings.

מָתַי תַּעֲלֶה בְּתֹךְ מִבּוֹר
מִבֵּית כֶּלֶא עֻלָּהּ תִּשְׁבֹּר
וְהַפְלֵא פֶלֶא בְּצֵאתְךָ כְּגִבּוֹר
לְהָתֵם וְכַלֵּה מְכַלּוֹתֶיהָ. תִּכְלֶה שָׁנָה וְקִלְלוֹתֶיהָ.

חֵילָהּ קָבְעוּ הַגּוֹי כֻּלּוֹ
וְטוּבָהּ שָׁבְעוּ, וּבָזְזוּ אִישׁ לוֹ
וְלִבָּהּ קָרְעוּ, וּבְכָל זֹאת, לֹא
מִמְּךָ נָעוּ מַעְגְּלוֹתֶיהָ. תִּכְלֶה שָׁנָה וְקִלְלוֹתֶיהָ.

זְמִירָהּ שָׁבַת, וְחֶשְׁקָהּ תַּגְבִּיר
לַחְפֹּץ קִרְבַת דּוֹדָהּ, וְתַעֲבִיר
מִלֵּב דַּאֲבַת נַפְשָׁהּ וְתָסִיר
לְבַקֵּשׁ אַהֲבַת כְּלוּלוֹתֶיהָ. תִּכְלֶה שָׁנָה וְקִלְלוֹתֶיהָ.

נְחֶהָ בְּנַחַת לִנְוֵה וּבְצָהּ
רַב נִזְנַחַת מִדּוֹד חֶפְצָהּ
וְהִוא כְּפֹרַחַת עָלְתָה נִצָּהּ
לֹא הִבְשִׁילוּ אַשְׁכְּלוֹתֶיהָ. תִּכְלֶה שָׁנָה וְקִלְלוֹתֶיהָ.

חִזְקוּ וְגִילוּ כִּי שֹׁד גָּמַר
לְצוּר הוֹחִילוּ, בְּרִיתוֹ שָׁמַר
לָכֶם, וְתַעֲלוּ לְצִיּוֹן, וְאָמַר
סֹלּוּ סֹלּוּ מְסִלּוֹתֶיהָ. תָּחֵל שָׁנָה וּבִרְכוֹתֶיהָ.

*When Rosh HaShana falls on a weekday, Ma'ariv begins on page 64.*
*When Rosh HaShana falls on Shabbat, most congregations begin with Psalm 29 on the next page; some congregations sing "Beloved of the soul" at this point before the Kabbalat Shabbat service.*

יְדִיד Beloved of the soul, Father of compassion,
draw Your servant close to Your will.
Like a deer will Your servant run
and fall prostrate before Your beauty.
To him Your love is sweeter
than honey from the comb, than any taste.

הָדוּר Glorious, beautiful, radiance of the world,
my soul is sick with love for You.
Please, God, heal her now
by showing her Your tender radiance.
Then she will recover her strength and be healed,
Be Your servant for eternity.

וָתִיק Ancient of Days, let Your mercy be aroused;
please have pity on Your beloved child.
How long have I yearned
to see the glory of Your strength.
Please, my God, my heart's desire –
hasten; do not hide Yourself.

הִגָּלֵה Reveal Yourself, beloved, and spread over me
the tabernacle of Your peace.
Let the earth shine with Your glory,
let us be overjoyed and rejoice in You.
Hurry, beloved, for the appointed time has come,
and be gracious to me as in the times of old.

*When* ראש השנה *falls on a weekday,* מעריב *begins on page 65.*
*When* ראש השנה *falls on* שבת*, most congregations begin with* מִזְמוֹר לְדָוִד *on the next page;*
*some congregations sing* יְדִיד נֶפֶשׁ *at this point before the* קבלת שבת *service.*

יְדִיד נֶפֶשׁ, אָב הָרַחֲמָן, מְשֹׁךְ עַבְדָּךְ אֶל רְצוֹנָךְ
יָרוּץ עַבְדָּךְ כְּמוֹ אַיָּל, יִשְׁתַּחֲוֶה מוּל הֲדָרָךְ
כִּי יֶעֱרַב לוֹ יְדִידוּתָךְ, מִנֹּפֶת צוּף וְכָל טָעַם.

הָדוּר, נָאֶה, זִיו הָעוֹלָם, נַפְשִׁי חוֹלַת אַהֲבָתָךְ
אָנָּא, אֵל נָא, רְפָא נָא לָהּ, בְּהַרְאוֹת לָהּ נֹעַם זִיוָךְ
אָז תִּתְחַזֵּק וְתִתְרַפֵּא, וְהָיְתָה לָּךְ שִׁפְחַת עוֹלָם.

וָתִיק, יֶהֱמוּ רַחֲמֶיךָ, וְחוּס נָא עַל בֵּן אוֹהֲבָךְ
כִּי זֶה כַּמֶּה נִכְסֹף נִכְסַף לִרְאוֹת בְּתִפְאֶרֶת עֻזָּךְ
אָנָּא, אֵלִי, מַחְמַד לִבִּי, חוּשָׁה נָּא, וְאַל תִּתְעַלָּם.

הִגָּלֶה נָא וּפְרֹשׂ, חָבִיב, עָלַי אֶת סֻכַּת שְׁלוֹמָךְ
תָּאִיר אֶרֶץ מִכְּבוֹדָךְ, נָגִילָה וְנִשְׂמְחָה בָּךְ.
מַהֵר, אָהוּב, כִּי בָא מוֹעֵד, וְחָנֵּנִי כִּימֵי עוֹלָם.

*The following psalm is said standing:*

מִזְמוֹר לְדָוִד A psalm of David. Render to the Lord, you angelic powers, *Ps. 29*
render to the Lord glory and might.
Render to the Lord the glory due to His name.
Bow to the Lord in the beauty of holiness.
The Lord's voice echoes over the waters; the God of glory thunders;
the Lord is over the mighty waters.
The Lord's voice in power, the Lord's voice in beauty,
the Lord's voice breaks cedars,
the Lord shatters the cedars of Lebanon.
He makes Lebanon skip like a calf, Sirion like a young wild ox.
The Lord's voice cleaves flames of fire.
The Lord's voice makes the desert quake,
the Lord shakes the desert of Kadesh.
▸ The Lord's voice makes hinds calve and strips the forests bare,
and in His temple all say: "Glory!"
The Lord sat enthroned at the Flood,
the Lord sits enthroned as King for ever.
The Lord will give strength to His people;
the Lord will bless His people with peace.

*The following is said in some congregations:*

Please, by the power of Your great right hand,
set the captive nation free.
Accept Your people's prayer. Strengthen us, purify us,
You who are revered.
Please, Mighty One, guard like the pupil of the eye
those who seek Your unity.
Bless them, cleanse them,
grant them the compassion of Your righteousness always.
Mighty One, Holy One, in Your great goodness
guide Your congregation.
Only One, Exalted One, turn to Your people,
who proclaim Your holiness.
Accept our plea and heed our cry, You who know all secret thoughts.

Blessed be the name of His glorious kingdom for ever and all time.

*The following psalm is said standing:*

מִזְמוֹר לְדָוִד, הָבוּ לַיהוה בְּנֵי אֵלִים, הָבוּ לַיהוה כָּבוֹד וָעֹז: תהלים כט
הָבוּ לַיהוה כְּבוֹד שְׁמוֹ, הִשְׁתַּחֲווּ לַיהוה בְּהַדְרַת־קֹדֶשׁ:
קוֹל יהוה עַל־הַמָּיִם, אֵל־הַכָּבוֹד הִרְעִים
יהוה עַל־מַיִם רַבִּים:
קוֹל־יהוה בַּכֹּחַ, קוֹל יהוה בֶּהָדָר:
קוֹל יהוה שֹׁבֵר אֲרָזִים, וַיְשַׁבֵּר יהוה אֶת־אַרְזֵי הַלְּבָנוֹן:
וַיַּרְקִידֵם כְּמוֹ־עֵגֶל, לְבָנוֹן וְשִׂרְיוֹן כְּמוֹ בֶן־רְאֵמִים:
קוֹל־יהוה חֹצֵב לַהֲבוֹת אֵשׁ:
קוֹל יהוה יָחִיל מִדְבָּר, יָחִיל יהוה מִדְבַּר קָדֵשׁ:
◂ קוֹל יהוה יְחוֹלֵל אַיָּלוֹת וַיֶּחֱשֹׂף יְעָרוֹת
וּבְהֵיכָלוֹ, כֻּלּוֹ אֹמֵר כָּבוֹד:
יהוה לַמַּבּוּל יָשָׁב, וַיֵּשֶׁב יהוה מֶלֶךְ לְעוֹלָם:
יהוה עֹז לְעַמּוֹ יִתֵּן, יהוה יְבָרֵךְ אֶת־עַמּוֹ בַשָּׁלוֹם:

*The following is said in some congregations:*

אָנָּא, בְּכֹחַ גְּדֻלַּת יְמִינְךָ, תַּתִּיר צְרוּרָה.
קַבֵּל רִנַּת עַמְּךָ, שַׂגְּבֵנוּ, טַהֲרֵנוּ, נוֹרָא.
נָא גִבּוֹר, דּוֹרְשֵׁי יִחוּדְךָ כְּבָבַת שָׁמְרֵם.
בָּרְכֵם, טַהֲרֵם, רַחֲמֵי צִדְקָתְךָ תָּמִיד גָּמְלֵם.
חֲסִין קָדוֹשׁ, בְּרֹב טוּבְךָ נַהֵל עֲדָתֶךָ.
יָחִיד גֵּאֶה, לְעַמְּךָ פְּנֵה, זוֹכְרֵי קְדֻשָּׁתֶךָ.
שַׁוְעָתֵנוּ קַבֵּל וּשְׁמַע צַעֲקָתֵנוּ, יוֹדֵעַ תַּעֲלוּמוֹת.
בָּרוּךְ שֵׁם כְּבוֹד מַלְכוּתוֹ לְעוֹלָם וָעֶד.

לְכָה דוֹדִי Come, my Beloved, to greet the bride;
let us welcome the Sabbath.

Come, my Beloved,
to greet the bride;
let us welcome the Sabbath.

שָׁמוֹר "Observe" and "Remember" in one act of speech,
the One and Only God made us hear.
The LORD is One and His name is One,
for renown, for splendor, and for praise.

Come, my Beloved,
to greet the bride;
let us welcome the Sabbath.

יָמִין Right and left you shall spread out,
and God you will revere.
Through the descendant of Peretz,
we shall rejoice and we shall be glad.

Come, my Beloved,
to greet the bride;
let us welcome the Sabbath.

*Stand and turn to face the door or the rear (usually western side) of the synagogue, as if to greet the incoming bride, bowing at the words "Enter, O bride!," then turn back.*

בּוֹאִי Come in peace, O crown of her husband;
come with joy and jubilation,
among the faithful
of the treasured people.
Enter, O bride! Enter, O bride!
Enter, O bride, Shabbat the queen!

Come, my Beloved,
to greet the bride;
let us welcome the Sabbath.

לְכָה דוֹדִי לִקְרַאת כַּלָּה, פְּנֵי שַׁבָּת נְקַבְּלָה.

לְכָה דוֹדִי לִקְרַאת כַּלָּה, פְּנֵי שַׁבָּת נְקַבְּלָה.

שָׁמוֹר וְזָכוֹר בְּדִבּוּר אֶחָד
הִשְׁמִיעָנוּ אֵל הַמְיֻחָד
יהוה אֶחָד וּשְׁמוֹ אֶחָד
לְשֵׁם וּלְתִפְאֶרֶת וְלִתְהִלָּה.

לְכָה דוֹדִי לִקְרַאת כַּלָּה, פְּנֵי שַׁבָּת נְקַבְּלָה.

לִקְרַאת שַׁבָּת לְכוּ וְנֵלְכָה
כִּי הִיא מְקוֹר הַבְּרָכָה
מֵרֹאשׁ מִקֶּדֶם נְסוּכָה
סוֹף מַעֲשֶׂה בְּמַחֲשָׁבָה תְּחִלָּה.

לְכָה דוֹדִי לִקְרַאת כַּלָּה, פְּנֵי שַׁבָּת נְקַבְּלָה.

יָמִין וּשְׂמֹאל תִּפְרֹצִי
וְאֶת יהוה תַּעֲרִיצִי
עַל יַד אִישׁ בֶּן פַּרְצִי
וְנִשְׂמְחָה וְנָגִילָה.

לְכָה דוֹדִי לִקְרַאת כַּלָּה, פְּנֵי שַׁבָּת נְקַבְּלָה.

*Stand and turn to face the door or the rear (usually western side) of the* בית כנסת*, as if to greet the incoming bride, bowing at the words* בּוֹאִי כַלָּה*, then turn back.*

בּוֹאִי בְשָׁלוֹם עֲטֶרֶת בַּעְלָהּ
גַּם בְּשִׂמְחָה וּבְצָהֳלָה
תּוֹךְ אֱמוּנֵי עַם סְגֻלָּה
בּוֹאִי כַלָּה, בּוֹאִי כַלָּה
בּוֹאִי כַלָּה, שַׁבָּת מַלְכְּתָא.

לְכָה דוֹדִי לִקְרַאת כַּלָּה, פְּנֵי שַׁבָּת נְקַבְּלָה.

מִזְמוֹר A psalm. A song for the Sabbath day. *Ps. 92*
It is good to thank the Lord
and sing psalms to Your name, Most High –
to tell of Your loving-kindness in the morning
and Your faithfulness at night,
to the music of the ten-stringed lyre and the melody of the harp.
For You have made me rejoice by Your work, O Lord;
I sing for joy at the deeds of Your hands.
How great are Your deeds, Lord, and how very deep Your thoughts.
A boor cannot know, nor can a fool understand,
that though the wicked spring up like grass and all evildoers flourish,
it is only that they may be destroyed for ever.
But You, Lord, are eternally exalted.
For behold Your enemies, Lord, behold Your enemies will perish;
all evildoers will be scattered.
You have raised my pride like that of a wild ox;
I am anointed with fresh oil.
My eyes shall look in triumph on my adversaries,
my ears shall hear the downfall of the wicked who rise against me.
▸ The righteous will flourish like a palm tree
and grow tall like a cedar in Lebanon.
Planted in the Lord's House, blossoming in our God's courtyards,
they will still bear fruit in old age, and stay vigorous and fresh,
proclaiming that the Lord is upright:
He is my Rock, in whom there is no wrong.

יהוה מָלָךְ The Lord reigns. He is robed in majesty. *Ps. 93*
The Lord is robed, girded with strength.
The world is firmly established; it cannot be moved.
Your throne stands firm as of old; You are eternal.
Rivers lift up, Lord, rivers lift up their voice,
rivers lift up their crashing waves.
▸ Mightier than the noise of many waters,
than the mighty waves of the sea is the Lord on high.
Your testimonies are very sure;
holiness adorns Your House, Lord, for evermore.

תהלים צב

מִזְמוֹר שִׁיר לְיוֹם הַשַּׁבָּת:
טוֹב לְהֹדוֹת לַיהוה, וּלְזַמֵּר לְשִׁמְךָ עֶלְיוֹן:
לְהַגִּיד בַּבֹּקֶר חַסְדֶּךָ, וֶאֱמוּנָתְךָ בַּלֵּילוֹת:
עֲלֵי־עָשׂוֹר וַעֲלֵי־נָבֶל, עֲלֵי הִגָּיוֹן בְּכִנּוֹר:
כִּי שִׂמַּחְתַּנִי יהוה בְּפָעֳלֶךָ, בְּמַעֲשֵׂי יָדֶיךָ אֲרַנֵּן:
מַה־גָּדְלוּ מַעֲשֶׂיךָ יהוה, מְאֹד עָמְקוּ מַחְשְׁבֹתֶיךָ:
אִישׁ־בַּעַר לֹא יֵדָע, וּכְסִיל לֹא־יָבִין אֶת־זֹאת:
בִּפְרֹחַ רְשָׁעִים כְּמוֹ עֵשֶׂב, וַיָּצִיצוּ כָּל־פֹּעֲלֵי אָוֶן
לְהִשָּׁמְדָם עֲדֵי־עַד:
וְאַתָּה מָרוֹם לְעֹלָם יהוה:
כִּי הִנֵּה אֹיְבֶיךָ יהוה, כִּי־הִנֵּה אֹיְבֶיךָ יֹאבֵדוּ
יִתְפָּרְדוּ כָּל־פֹּעֲלֵי אָוֶן:
וַתָּרֶם כִּרְאֵים קַרְנִי, בַּלֹּתִי בְּשֶׁמֶן רַעֲנָן:
וַתַּבֵּט עֵינִי בְּשׁוּרָי, בַּקָּמִים עָלַי מְרֵעִים תִּשְׁמַעְנָה אָזְנָי:
◂ צַדִּיק כַּתָּמָר יִפְרָח, כְּאֶרֶז בַּלְּבָנוֹן יִשְׂגֶּה:
שְׁתוּלִים בְּבֵית יהוה, בְּחַצְרוֹת אֱלֹהֵינוּ יַפְרִיחוּ:
עוֹד יְנוּבוּן בְּשֵׂיבָה, דְּשֵׁנִים וְרַעֲנַנִּים יִהְיוּ:
לְהַגִּיד כִּי־יָשָׁר יהוה, צוּרִי, וְלֹא־עַוְלָתָה בּוֹ:

תהלים צג

יהוה מָלָךְ, גֵּאוּת לָבֵשׁ
לָבֵשׁ יהוה עֹז הִתְאַזָּר, אַף־תִּכּוֹן תֵּבֵל בַּל־תִּמּוֹט:
נָכוֹן כִּסְאֲךָ מֵאָז, מֵעוֹלָם אָתָּה:
נָשְׂאוּ נְהָרוֹת יהוה, נָשְׂאוּ נְהָרוֹת קוֹלָם, יִשְׂאוּ נְהָרוֹת דָּכְיָם:
◂ מִקֹּלוֹת מַיִם רַבִּים, אַדִּירִים מִשְׁבְּרֵי־יָם, אַדִּיר בַּמָּרוֹם יהוה:
עֵדֹתֶיךָ נֶאֶמְנוּ מְאֹד, לְבֵיתְךָ נַאֲוָה־קֹדֶשׁ, יהוה לְאֹרֶךְ יָמִים:

## MOURNER'S KADDISH

*The following prayer, said by mourners, requires the presence of a minyan.*
*A transliteration can be found on page 1095.*

*Mourner:* יִתְגַּדַּל Magnified and sanctified
may His great name be,
in the world He created by His will.
May He establish His kingdom,
make His salvation flourish,
and hasten His messiah,
in your lifetime and in your days,
and in the lifetime of all the house of Israel,
swiftly and soon –
and say: Amen.

*All:* May His great name be blessed for ever and all time.

*Mourner:* Blessed and praised,
glorified and exalted,
raised and honored, uplifted and lauded
be the name of the Holy One,
blessed be He,
beyond any blessing,
song, praise and consolation
uttered in the world –
and say: Amen.

May there be great peace from heaven,
and a good life for us and all Israel –
and say: Amen.

*Bow, take three steps back, as if taking leave of the Divine Presence,*
*then bow, first left, then right, then center, while saying:*

May He who makes peace in His high places,
make peace for us and all Israel –
and say: Amen.

## קדיש יתום

*The following prayer, said by mourners, requires the presence of a* מנין.
*A transliteration can be found on page 1095.*

אבל: יִתְגַּדַּל וְיִתְקַדַּשׁ שְׁמֵהּ רַבָּא (קהל: אָמֵן)
בְּעָלְמָא דִּי בְרָא כִרְעוּתֵהּ
וְיַמְלִיךְ מַלְכוּתֵהּ וְיַצְמַח פֻּרְקָנֵהּ וִיקָרֵב מְשִׁיחֵהּ (קהל: אָמֵן)
בְּחַיֵּיכוֹן וּבְיוֹמֵיכוֹן וּבְחַיֵּי דְכָל בֵּית יִשְׂרָאֵל
בַּעֲגָלָא וּבִזְמַן קָרִיב
וְאִמְרוּ אָמֵן. (קהל: אָמֵן)

קהל ואבל: יְהֵא שְׁמֵהּ רַבָּא מְבָרַךְ לְעָלַם וּלְעָלְמֵי עָלְמַיָּא.

אבל: יִתְבָּרַךְ וְיִשְׁתַּבַּח וְיִתְפָּאַר
וְיִתְרוֹמַם וְיִתְנַשֵּׂא וְיִתְהַדָּר וְיִתְעַלֶּה וְיִתְהַלָּל
שְׁמֵהּ דְּקֻדְשָׁא בְּרִיךְ הוּא (קהל: אָמֵן)
לְעֵלָּא לְעֵלָּא מִכָּל בִּרְכָתָא וְשִׁירָתָא, תֻּשְׁבְּחָתָא וְנֶחֱמָתָא
דַּאֲמִירָן בְּעָלְמָא
וְאִמְרוּ אָמֵן. (קהל: אָמֵן)

יְהֵא שְׁלָמָא רַבָּא מִן שְׁמַיָּא
וְחַיִּים טוֹבִים עָלֵינוּ וְעַל כָּל יִשְׂרָאֵל
וְאִמְרוּ אָמֵן. (קהל: אָמֵן)

*Bow, take three steps back, as if taking leave of the Divine Presence, then bow, first left, then right, then center, while saying:*

עֹשֶׂה הַשָּׁלוֹם בִּמְרוֹמָיו
הוּא יַעֲשֶׂה שָׁלוֹם עָלֵינוּ וְעַל כָּל יִשְׂרָאֵל
וְאִמְרוּ אָמֵן. (קהל: אָמֵן)

# Ma'ariv for Rosh HaShana

## BLESSINGS OF THE SHEMA

*The Leader says the following, bowing at "Bless," standing straight at "the Lord." The congregation, followed by the Leader, responds, bowing at "Bless," standing straight at "the Lord."*

*Leader:* **BLESS**
the LORD, the blessed One.

*Congregation:* Bless the LORD, the blessed One,
for ever and all time.

*Leader:* Bless the LORD, the blessed One,
for ever and all time.

בָּרוּךְ Blessed are You, LORD our God, King of the Universe,
who by His word brings on evenings,
by His wisdom opens the gates of heaven,
with understanding makes time change and the seasons rotate,
and by His will orders the stars in their constellations in the sky.
He creates day and night,
rolling away the light before the darkness,
and darkness before the light.
▸ He makes the day pass and brings on night,
distinguishing day from night:
the LORD of hosts is His name.
May the living and forever enduring God rule over us for all time.
Blessed are You, LORD, who brings on evenings.

---

of a ladder stretching from earth to heaven. Awakening from that vision he gave the most profound description of the effect of prayer: "Surely God was in this place and I did not know it" (Gen. 28:16). At night he wrestled with an angel and was given the name Israel, one who "struggles with God and with men and prevails" (Gen. 32:28).

# מעריב לראש השנה

## קריאת שמע וברכותיה

*The* שליח ציבור *says the following, bowing at* בָּרְכוּ*, standing straight at* ה׳.
*The* קהל*, followed by the* שליח ציבור*, responds, bowing at* בָּרוּךְ*, standing straight at* ה׳.

ש״ץ: בָּרְכוּ

אֶת יהוה הַמְבֹרָךְ.

קהל: בָּרוּךְ יהוה הַמְבֹרָךְ לְעוֹלָם וָעֶד.

ש״ץ: בָּרוּךְ יהוה הַמְבֹרָךְ לְעוֹלָם וָעֶד.

בָּרוּךְ אַתָּה יהוה אֱלֹהֵינוּ מֶלֶךְ הָעוֹלָם
אֲשֶׁר בִּדְבָרוֹ מַעֲרִיב עֲרָבִים בְּחָכְמָה פּוֹתֵחַ שְׁעָרִים
וּבִתְבוּנָה מְשַׁנֶּה עִתִּים וּמַחֲלִיף אֶת הַזְּמַנִּים
וּמְסַדֵּר אֶת הַכּוֹכָבִים בְּמִשְׁמְרוֹתֵיהֶם בָּרָקִיעַ כִּרְצוֹנוֹ.
בּוֹרֵא יוֹם וָלַיְלָה, גּוֹלֵל אוֹר מִפְּנֵי חֹשֶׁךְ וְחֹשֶׁךְ מִפְּנֵי אוֹר
◂ וּמַעֲבִיר יוֹם וּמֵבִיא לָיְלָה
וּמַבְדִּיל בֵּין יוֹם וּבֵין לָיְלָה
יהוה צְבָאוֹת שְׁמוֹ.
אֵל חַי וְקַיָּם תָּמִיד, יִמְלֹךְ עָלֵינוּ לְעוֹלָם וָעֶד.
בָּרוּךְ אַתָּה יהוה, הַמַּעֲרִיב עֲרָבִים.

---

EVENING SERVICE

Ma'ariv is the prayer associated with Jacob, the man whose greatest encounters with God were at night. At night he had a vision, symbolic of prayer itself,

אַהֲבַת עוֹלָם With everlasting love
have You loved Your people, the house of Israel.
You have taught us Torah and commandments,
decrees and laws of justice.
Therefore, LORD our God, when we lie down and when we rise up
we will speak of Your decrees,
rejoicing in the words of the study of Your Torah
and Your commandments for ever.
▸ For they are our life and the length of our days;
on them will we meditate day and night.
May You never take away Your love from us.
Blessed are You, LORD, who loves His people Israel.

---

אַהֲבַת עוֹלָם *With everlasting love.* This short but intensely moving paragraph refutes the calumny directed against Judaism that it is a religion of law, not love. In Judaism law and love go together, for when we obey God's command we are united with Him at the level of deed, and when we study God's word we are united at the level of mind. Law brings us close to God. It is a supreme expression of love. When we love someone we seek to do their will. That is what happens when a Jew observes the Torah, keeping its laws.

וּבָהֶם נֶהְגֶּה יוֹמָם וָלָיְלָה *On them we will meditate day and night.* No religion has placed greater emphasis on lifelong study than Judaism. Joshua, Moses' successor, was told by God, "Keep this Book of the Torah always on your lips; meditate on it day and night" (Joshua 1:8). Kings of Israel were commanded to write their own *Sefer Torah* and keep it with them: "He is to read it all the days of his life" (Deut. 17:19). The first psalm says, "Happy is the one …whose delight is in the Torah of the LORD, and who meditates on His Torah day and night" (Ps. 1:1–2). Theophrastus, a disciple of Aristotle, spoke about the Jews as "a nation of philosophers." Josephus, in the first century, wrote, "Should any one of our nation be asked about our laws, he will repeat them as readily as his own name. The result of our thorough education in our laws from the very dawn of intelligence is that they are, as it were, engraved on our souls." The house of study was no less holy than the house of prayer. Jews were the people whose citadels were schools, whose heroes were teachers, and whose passion was learning and the life of the mind.

אַהֲבַת עוֹלָם בֵּית יִשְׂרָאֵל עַמְּךָ אָהָבְתָּ
תּוֹרָה וּמִצְוֹת, חֻקִּים וּמִשְׁפָּטִים, אוֹתָנוּ לִמַּדְתָּ
עַל כֵּן יהוה אֱלֹהֵינוּ בְּשָׁכְבֵנוּ וּבְקוּמֵנוּ נָשִׂיחַ בְּחֻקֶּיךָ
וְנִשְׂמַח בְּדִבְרֵי תַלְמוּד תּוֹרָתֶךָ וּבְמִצְוֹתֶיךָ לְעוֹלָם וָעֶד
◂ כִּי הֵם חַיֵּינוּ וְאֹרֶךְ יָמֵינוּ, וּבָהֶם נֶהְגֶּה יוֹמָם וָלָיְלָה.
וְאַהֲבָתְךָ אַל תָּסִיר מִמֶּנּוּ לְעוֹלָמִים.
בָּרוּךְ אַתָּה יהוה, אוֹהֵב עַמּוֹ יִשְׂרָאֵל.

---

Judaism has known its dawns, its ages of new hope, associated with Abraham. It has known the full brightness of day, its ages of peace and continuity, associated with Isaac's life after the binding. But it has also known its nights. Night is when we take with us the spirit of Jacob, a man who knew fear but was never defeated by it.

NIGHT AND ROSH HASHANA

There are two cycles of time in Judaism: *religious-historical time,* which begins in spring with Pesaḥ and the month of Nisan, and *natural time* which begins in the autumn with Tishrei and Rosh HaShana. Nisan is the anniversary of the birth of Jewish history; Tishrei is the anniversary of the creation of the universe. These correspond to the two concepts of day in Judaism: the *natural day,* which begins with night ("And it was evening and it was morning, one day," Genesis 1:5), and the *daily cycle of prayer* – Shaḥarit, Minḥa, Ma'ariv, corresponding to Abraham, Isaac and Jacob – which begins with morning. Nature begins in and returns to darkness. Faith begins in and returns to light. (Rabbi Samson Raphael Hirsch)

THE BLESSINGS OF THE SHEMA

The blessings that surround the Shema, evening and morning, are a precisely articulated summary of the three basic elements of Jewish faith: (1) creation – the existence and unity of God, Author and Architect of all; (2) revelation – God's word to us through Moses and the prophets; and (3) redemption – God's interventions into history, especially the exodus from Egypt.

The Siddur and Maḥzor are the supreme expressions of Jewish faith. For the most part Jews did not write books of theology; they wrote prayers. In Judaism we do not speak *about* God; we speak *to* God. We do not *discuss* faith; we *express* faith. Faith is our relationship with God made articulate in the words of prayer.

*The Shema must be said with intense concentration. See laws 10–14.*

*When not with a minyan, say:*

God, faithful King!

*The following verse should be said aloud, while covering the eyes with the right hand:*

# Listen, Israel: the LORD is our God, the LORD is One.

*Deut. 6*

*Quietly:* Blessed be the name of His glorious kingdom for ever and all time.

וְאָהַבְתָּ Love the LORD your God with all your heart, with all your soul, and with all your might. These words which I command you today shall be on your heart. Teach them repeatedly to your children, speaking of them when you sit at home and when you travel on the way, when you lie down and when you rise. Bind them as a sign on your hand, and they shall be an emblem between your eyes. Write them on the doorposts of your house and gates. *Deut. 6*

---

וְאָהַבְתָּ אֵת יהוה אֱלֹהֶיךָ *Love the LORD your God.* Judaism is the supreme example of a moral system based on (personal, not impersonal) love. Almost all moral systems have a principle of justice – act toward others as you would wish them to act toward you. None, except for Judaism and the monotheisms that borrowed from it, regards love (of God, of the neighbor and the stranger) as a moral imperative. This was and remains a revolutionary, transformative idea.

וְשִׁנַּנְתָּם לְבָנֶיךָ *Teach them repeatedly to your children.* In Judaism to be a parent is to be an educator. In the sole place in which God explains why He chose Abraham to be the founder of a new faith, He said: "For I have chosen him, *so that he will direct his children and his household after him* to keep the way of the LORD by doing what is right and just" (Gen. 18:19). Abraham was chosen, not as a saint or hero, but as a parent who would teach his children. Indeed, the *Ab* in Abraham's name means "father." The highest duty we have as parents is to hand on our beliefs, ideals and way of life to our children. Education, in Judaism, happens primarily at home within the matrix of the family, and only secondarily in the school and house of study, sacred though these institutions are.

*The* שמע *must be said with intense concentration. See laws 10–14.*
*When not with a* מנין*, say:*

אֵל מֶלֶךְ נֶאֱמָן

*The following verse should be said aloud, while covering the eyes with the right hand:*

**שְׁמַע יִשְׂרָאֵל, יהוה אֱלֹהֵינוּ, יהוה | אֶחָד׃** דברים ו

*Quietly* בָּרוּךְ שֵׁם כְּבוֹד מַלְכוּתוֹ לְעוֹלָם וָעֶד.

וְאָהַבְתָּ אֵת יהוה אֱלֹהֶיךָ, בְּכָל־לְבָבְךָ וּבְכָל־נַפְשְׁךָ וּבְכָל־ דברים ו
מְאֹדֶךָ׃ וְהָיוּ הַדְּבָרִים הָאֵלֶּה, אֲשֶׁר אָנֹכִי מְצַוְּךָ הַיּוֹם, עַל־לְבָבֶךָ׃
וְשִׁנַּנְתָּם לְבָנֶיךָ וְדִבַּרְתָּ בָּם, בְּשִׁבְתְּךָ בְּבֵיתֶךָ וּבְלֶכְתְּךָ בַדֶּרֶךְ,
וּבְשָׁכְבְּךָ וּבְקוּמֶךָ׃ וּקְשַׁרְתָּם לְאוֹת עַל־יָדֶךָ וְהָיוּ לְטֹטָפֹת בֵּין
עֵינֶיךָ׃ וּכְתַבְתָּם עַל־מְזֻזוֹת בֵּיתֶךָ וּבִשְׁעָרֶיךָ׃

---

SHEMA

The first line of the Shema is among the first we learn as children and among the last we say at the end of life. Rabbi Akiva pronounced it as he went to a martyr's death (*Berakhot* 61b) as did countless others over the centuries, especially during the Holocaust. It is the supreme declaration of Jewish faith. Metaphysically it tells us that there is only one God, that unity is at the heart of the cosmos and that conflict is not written into the fabric of the universe. The diversity of the created world points to the unity of its Creator. Existentially it says that God is our only ultimate Sovereign, our only focus of worship, and that by these words we pledge our loyalty to Him. This is what the sages meant when they called the first paragraph of the Shema, "acceptance of the yoke of the kingdom of heaven." (Mishna, *Berakhot* 13a) It is our twice-daily oath of allegiance, our declaration of commitment and love.

בָּרוּךְ שֵׁם *Blessed be the name.* This was the response said in the Temple after blessings (*Ta'anit* 16b), and most dramatically, the response of the people after the High Priest's declarations on Yom Kippur (Mishna, *Yoma* 35b). It is said quietly because it is not part of the biblical text (*Pesaḥim* 56a).

וְהָיָה If you indeed heed My commandments with which I charge you today, to love the LORD your God and worship Him with all your heart and with all your soul, I will give rain in your land in its season, the early and late rain; and you shall gather in your grain, wine and oil. I will give grass in your field for your cattle, and you shall eat and be satisfied. Be careful lest your heart be tempted and you go astray and worship other gods, bowing down to them. Then the LORD's anger will flare against you and He will close the heavens so that there will be no rain. The land will not yield its crops, and you will perish swiftly from the good land that the LORD is giving you. Therefore, set these, My words, on your heart and soul. Bind them as a sign on your hand, and they shall be an emblem between your eyes. Teach them to your children, speaking of them when you sit at home and when you travel on the way, when you lie down and when you rise. Write them on the doorposts of your house and gates, so that you and your children may live long in the land that the LORD swore to your ancestors to give them, for as long as the heavens are above the earth. *Deut. 11*

וַיֹּאמֶר The LORD spoke to Moses, saying: Speak to the Israelites and tell them to make tassels on the corners of their garments for all generations. They shall attach to the tassel at each corner a thread of blue. This shall be your tassel, and you shall see it *Num. 15*

---

the Nile Delta, the water supply of the land of Israel is limited and unpredictable, subject to periodic droughts, as happened in the days of the patriarchs and still happens today. It is therefore a land that encourages its inhabitants to look up toward the heavens, one that constantly reminds them that their destiny is dependent on God.

פְּתִיל תְּכֵלֶת *A thread of blue. Tekhelet* and *lavan*, blue and white, represent two approaches of man to himself and to the world. In Hebrew, *lavan* signifies not only the color white but also clarity, rationality and openness. The Torah wants us to understand the world, exploring natural phenomena with the methods of science, not to live in ignorance and obscurity. *Tekhelet* represents

דברים יא וְהָיָה אִם־שָׁמֹעַ תִּשְׁמְעוּ אֶל־מִצְוֺתַי אֲשֶׁר אָנֹכִי מְצַוֶּה אֶתְכֶם
הַיּוֹם, לְאַהֲבָה אֶת־יהוה אֱלֹהֵיכֶם וּלְעָבְדוֹ, בְּכָל־לְבַבְכֶם וּבְכָל־
נַפְשְׁכֶם: וְנָתַתִּי מְטַר־אַרְצְכֶם בְּעִתּוֹ, יוֹרֶה וּמַלְקוֹשׁ, וְאָסַפְתָּ
דְגָנֶךָ וְתִירֹשְׁךָ וְיִצְהָרֶךָ: וְנָתַתִּי עֵשֶׂב בְּשָׂדְךָ לִבְהֶמְתֶּךָ, וְאָכַלְתָּ
וְשָׂבָעְתָּ: הִשָּׁמְרוּ לָכֶם פֶּן־יִפְתֶּה לְבַבְכֶם, וְסַרְתֶּם וַעֲבַדְתֶּם
אֱלֹהִים אֲחֵרִים וְהִשְׁתַּחֲוִיתֶם לָהֶם: וְחָרָה אַף־יהוה בָּכֶם, וְעָצַר
אֶת־הַשָּׁמַיִם וְלֹא־יִהְיֶה מָטָר, וְהָאֲדָמָה לֹא תִתֵּן אֶת־יְבוּלָהּ,
וַאֲבַדְתֶּם מְהֵרָה מֵעַל הָאָרֶץ הַטֹּבָה אֲשֶׁר יהוה נֹתֵן לָכֶם:
וְשַׂמְתֶּם אֶת־דְּבָרַי אֵלֶּה עַל־לְבַבְכֶם וְעַל־נַפְשְׁכֶם, וּקְשַׁרְתֶּם
אֹתָם לְאוֹת עַל־יֶדְכֶם, וְהָיוּ לְטוֹטָפֹת בֵּין עֵינֵיכֶם: וְלִמַּדְתֶּם
אֹתָם אֶת־בְּנֵיכֶם לְדַבֵּר בָּם, בְּשִׁבְתְּךָ בְּבֵיתֶךָ וּבְלֶכְתְּךָ בַדֶּרֶךְ,
וּבְשָׁכְבְּךָ וּבְקוּמֶךָ: וּכְתַבְתָּם עַל־מְזוּזוֹת בֵּיתֶךָ וּבִשְׁעָרֶיךָ: לְמַעַן
יִרְבּוּ יְמֵיכֶם וִימֵי בְנֵיכֶם עַל הָאֲדָמָה אֲשֶׁר נִשְׁבַּע יהוה לַאֲבֹתֵיכֶם
לָתֵת לָהֶם, כִּימֵי הַשָּׁמַיִם עַל־הָאָרֶץ:

במדבר טו וַיֹּאמֶר יהוה אֶל־מֹשֶׁה לֵּאמֹר: דַּבֵּר אֶל־בְּנֵי יִשְׂרָאֵל וְאָמַרְתָּ
אֲלֵהֶם, וְעָשׂוּ לָהֶם צִיצִת עַל־כַּנְפֵי בִגְדֵיהֶם לְדֹרֹתָם, וְנָתְנוּ
עַל־צִיצִת הַכָּנָף פְּתִיל תְּכֵלֶת: וְהָיָה לָכֶם לְצִיצִת, וּרְאִיתֶם אֹתוֹ

---

וְנָתַתִּי מְטַר־אַרְצְכֶם בְּעִתּוֹ *I will give rain in your land in its season.* At the end of his life Moses spoke to the next generation about the special character, the geography and climate, of the land of Israel. "The land you are entering to inherit is not like the land of Egypt, from which you have come, where you planted your seed and irrigated it by foot as in a vegetable garden. The land you are crossing the Jordan to take possession of is a land of mountains and valleys that drinks rain from heaven. It is a land the Lord your God cares for; the eyes of the Lord your God are continually on it from the beginning of the year to its end" (Deut. 11:10–12). Unlike the Tigris-Euphrates Valley and

and remember all of the LORD's commandments and keep them, not straying after your heart and after your eyes, following your own sinful desires. Thus you will be reminded to keep all My commandments, and be holy to your God. I am the LORD your God, who brought you out of the land of Egypt to be your God. I am the LORD your God.

True –

*The Leader repeats:*

‣ The LORD your God is true –

וֶאֱמוּנָה – and faithful is all this,
and firmly established for us
that He is the LORD our God,
and there is none beside Him,
and that we, Israel, are His people.
He is our King, who redeems us from the hand of kings
and delivers us from the grasp of all tyrants.
He is our God,
who on our behalf repays our foes
and brings just retribution on our mortal enemies;
who performs great deeds beyond understanding;
miracles and wonders beyond number;
who kept us alive, not letting our foot slip;
who led us on the high places of our enemies,
raising our pride above all our foes;
who did miracles for us
and brought vengeance against Pharaoh;
who performed signs and wonders
in the land of Ham's children;

---

inapproachability, the ineffable. There are elements of reality beyond our rational understanding and control and these are symbolized by *tekhelet*, which represents the numinous and awe-inspiring. We seek to understand

וּזְכַרְתֶּם֙ אֶת־כׇּל־מִצְוֺ֣ת יהוה וַעֲשִׂיתֶ֖ם אֹתָ֑ם, וְלֹֽא־תָת֜וּרוּ אַחֲרֵ֤י לְבַבְכֶם֙ וְאַחֲרֵ֣י עֵֽינֵיכֶ֔ם, אֲשֶׁר־אַתֶּ֥ם זֹנִ֖ים אַחֲרֵיהֶֽם: לְמַ֣עַן תִּזְכְּר֔וּ וַעֲשִׂיתֶ֖ם אֶת־כׇּל־מִצְוֺתָ֑י, וִהְיִיתֶ֥ם קְדֹשִׁ֖ים לֵאלֹהֵיכֶֽם: אֲנִ֞י יהוה אֱלֹהֵיכֶ֗ם, אֲשֶׁ֨ר הוֹצֵ֤אתִי אֶתְכֶם֙ מֵאֶ֣רֶץ מִצְרַ֔יִם, לִהְי֥וֹת לָכֶ֖ם לֵאלֹהִ֑ים, אֲנִ֖י יהוה אֱלֹהֵיכֶֽם:

# אֱמֶת

*The* שליח ציבור *repeats:*

‹ יהוה אֱלֹהֵיכֶם אֱמֶת

וֶאֱמוּנָה כׇּל זֹאת וְקַיָּם עָלֵינוּ
כִּי הוּא יהוה אֱלֹהֵינוּ וְאֵין זוּלָתוֹ
וַאֲנַחְנוּ יִשְׂרָאֵל עַמּוֹ.
הַפּוֹדֵנוּ מִיַּד מְלָכִים
מַלְכֵּנוּ הַגּוֹאֲלֵנוּ מִכַּף כׇּל הֶעָרִיצִים.
הָאֵל הַנִּפְרָע לָנוּ מִצָּרֵינוּ
וְהַמְשַׁלֵּם גְּמוּל לְכׇל אוֹיְבֵי נַפְשֵׁנוּ.
הָעוֹשֶׂה גְדוֹלוֹת עַד אֵין חֵקֶר
נִסִּים וְנִפְלָאוֹת עַד אֵין מִסְפָּר
הַשָּׂם נַפְשֵׁנוּ בַּחַיִּים, וְלֹא נָתַן לַמּוֹט רַגְלֵנוּ
הַמַּדְרִיכֵנוּ עַל בָּמוֹת אוֹיְבֵינוּ
וַיָּרֶם קַרְנֵנוּ עַל כׇּל שׂוֹנְאֵינוּ.
הָעוֹשֶׂה לָּנוּ נִסִּים וּנְקָמָה בְּפַרְעֹה
אוֹתוֹת וּמוֹפְתִים בְּאַדְמַת בְּנֵי חָם.

---

the opposite. The sages said that it resembles the sea, which is like the sky, which represents the celestial throne (*Sota* 17a). Blue represents distance,

who smote in His wrath all the firstborn of Egypt,
and brought out His people Israel from their midst
into everlasting freedom;
who led His children through the divided Reed Sea,
plunging their pursuers and enemies into the depths.
When His children saw His might,
they gave praise and thanks to His name,
▸ and willingly accepted His Sovereignty.
Moses and the children of Israel
then sang a song to You with great joy, and they all exclaimed:

> "Who is like You, LORD, among the mighty? *Ex. 15*
> Who is like You, majestic in holiness,
> awesome in praises, doing wonders?"

▸ Your children beheld Your majesty
as You parted the sea before Moses.
"This is my God!" they responded, and then said:

> "The LORD shall reign for ever and ever." *Ibid.*

▸ And it is said,

> "For the LORD has redeemed Jacob *Jer. 31*
> and rescued him from a power stronger than his own."

Blessed are You, LORD, who redeemed Israel.

הַשְׁכִּיבֵנוּ Help us lie down, O LORD our God, in peace,
and rise up, O our King, to good lives and to peace.
Spread over us Your canopy of peace.
Direct us with Your good counsel,
and save us quickly for the sake of Your name.

---

Your hands I commit my spirit." (Ps. 31:6). As long as there is daylight, we feel ourselves masters of our situation. We become what Rabbi Soloveitchik called "majestic." But as the day nears its end we become "covenantal." We recognize our vulnerability. We place ourselves in God's hands.

On the face of it, the presence of this prayer here breaks the rule that there

הַמַּכֶּה בְעֶבְרָתוֹ כָּל בְּכוֹרֵי מִצְרָיִם
וַיּוֹצֵא אֶת עַמּוֹ יִשְׂרָאֵל מִתּוֹכָם לְחֵרוּת עוֹלָם.
הַמַּעֲבִיר בָּנָיו בֵּין גִּזְרֵי יַם סוּף
אֶת רוֹדְפֵיהֶם וְאֶת שׂוֹנְאֵיהֶם בִּתְהוֹמוֹת טִבַּע
וְרָאוּ בָנָיו גְּבוּרָתוֹ, שִׁבְּחוּ וְהוֹדוּ לִשְׁמוֹ
◂ וּמַלְכוּתוֹ בְּרָצוֹן קִבְּלוּ עֲלֵיהֶם.
מֹשֶׁה וּבְנֵי יִשְׂרָאֵל, לְךָ עָנוּ שִׁירָה בְּשִׂמְחָה רַבָּה
וְאָמְרוּ כֻלָּם

שמות טו
מִי־כָמֹכָה בָּאֵלִם יהוה
מִי כָּמֹכָה נֶאְדָּר בַּקֹּדֶשׁ
נוֹרָא תְהִלֹּת עֹשֵׂה פֶלֶא:

◂ מַלְכוּתְךָ רָאוּ בָנֶיךָ, בּוֹקֵעַ יָם לִפְנֵי מֹשֶׁה
זֶה אֵלִי עָנוּ, וְאָמְרוּ

שם
יהוה יִמְלֹךְ לְעֹלָם וָעֶד:

◂ וְנֶאֱמַר

ירמיהו לא
כִּי־פָדָה יהוה אֶת־יַעֲקֹב, וּגְאָלוֹ מִיַּד חָזָק מִמֶּנּוּ:
בָּרוּךְ אַתָּה יהוה, גָּאַל יִשְׂרָאֵל.

הַשְׁכִּיבֵנוּ יהוה אֱלֹהֵינוּ לְשָׁלוֹם
וְהַעֲמִידֵנוּ מַלְכֵּנוּ לְחַיִּים טוֹבִים וּלְשָׁלוֹם
וּפְרֹשׂ עָלֵינוּ סֻכַּת שְׁלוֹמֶךָ, וְתַקְּנֵנוּ בְּעֵצָה טוֹבָה מִלְּפָנֶיךָ
וְהוֹשִׁיעֵנוּ מְהֵרָה לְמַעַן שְׁמֶךָ.

---

what can be understood, but also to interpret through an act of faith what lies beyond the horizon of human understanding. (Rabbi Joseph Soloveitchik)

הַשְׁכִּיבֵנוּ...לְשָׁלוֹם *Help us lie down … in peace.* A sublime expression of trust as we prepare for sleep. It recalls the line, incorporated into *Adon Olam,* "Into

Shield us and remove from us every enemy,
plague, sword, famine and sorrow.
Remove the adversary from before and behind us.
Shelter us in the shadow of Your wings,
for You, God, are our Guardian and Deliverer;
You, God, are a gracious and compassionate King.
▸ Guard our going out and our coming in,
for life and peace, from now and for ever.
Spread a canopy of compassion, life and peace over us.
Blessed are You, LORD, who spreads a canopy of peace over us,
over all His people Israel, and over Jerusalem.

*The congregation stands.*

---

*On Shabbat, the congregation, together with the Leader, adds:*

וְשָׁמְרוּ The children of Israel must keep the Sabbath, *Ex. 31*
observing the Sabbath in every generation
as an everlasting covenant.
It is a sign between Me and the children of Israel for ever,
for in six days the LORD made the heavens and the earth,
but on the seventh day He ceased work and refreshed Himself.

---

*The congregation, then Leader:*

תִּקְעוּ Sound the shofar on the new moon, *Ps. 81*
on our feast day when the moon is hidden.
For it is a statute for Israel, an ordinance of the God of Jacob.

---

God the Redeemer is not only present in the great miracles of our people's past but also in the simple trust with which we go to sleep at night. God's everlasting arms continue to embrace us. Redemption does not have to be miraculous or public to be redemption.

תִּקְעוּ בַחֹדֶשׁ שׁוֹפָר... *Sound the shofar… on our feast day when the moon is hidden.* Rosh HaShana is the only biblical festival that takes place on Rosh Ḥodesh, the New Moon, so it became known as *Keseh*, "Hidden" (*Vayikra Raba* 29:6). Some relate the word *keseh* to *kiseh*, "a throne," and thus to Rosh HaShana when God is enthroned as King (*Meshekh Ḥokhma* to Num. 29:1).

וְהָגֵן בַּעֲדֵנוּ, וְהָסֵר מֵעָלֵינוּ אוֹיֵב, דֶּבֶר וְחֶרֶב וְרָעָב וְיָגוֹן
וְהָסֵר שָׂטָן מִלְּפָנֵינוּ וּמֵאַחֲרֵינוּ, וּבְצֵל כְּנָפֶיךָ תַּסְתִּירֵנוּ
כִּי אֵל שׁוֹמְרֵנוּ וּמַצִּילֵנוּ אָתָּה
כִּי אֵל מֶלֶךְ חַנּוּן וְרַחוּם אָתָּה.
‹ וּשְׁמֹר צֵאתֵנוּ וּבוֹאֵנוּ לְחַיִּים וּלְשָׁלוֹם מֵעַתָּה וְעַד עוֹלָם.
וּפְרֹשׂ עָלֵינוּ סֻכַּת רַחֲמִים וְחַיִּים וְשָׁלוֹם.
בָּרוּךְ אַתָּה יהוה
הַפּוֹרֵשׂ סֻכַּת שָׁלוֹם עָלֵינוּ וְעַל כָּל עַמּוֹ יִשְׂרָאֵל וְעַל יְרוּשָׁלָיִם.

*The* קהל *stands.*

---

*On* שבת*, the* קהל*, together with the* שליח ציבור*, adds:*

שמות לא
וְשָׁמְרוּ בְנֵי־יִשְׂרָאֵל אֶת־הַשַּׁבָּת
לַעֲשׂוֹת אֶת־הַשַּׁבָּת לְדֹרֹתָם בְּרִית עוֹלָם:
בֵּינִי וּבֵין בְּנֵי יִשְׂרָאֵל, אוֹת הִוא לְעֹלָם
כִּי־שֵׁשֶׁת יָמִים עָשָׂה יהוה אֶת־הַשָּׁמַיִם וְאֶת־הָאָרֶץ
וּבַיּוֹם הַשְּׁבִיעִי שָׁבַת וַיִּנָּפַשׁ:

---

*The* קהל*, then* שליח ציבור*:*

תהלים פא
תִּקְעוּ בַחֹדֶשׁ שׁוֹפָר, בַּכֶּסֶה לְיוֹם חַגֵּנוּ:
כִּי חֹק לְיִשְׂרָאֵל הוּא, מִשְׁפָּט לֵאלֹהֵי יַעֲקֹב:

---

should be no interruption between *ge'ula,* "redemption" (the end of the previous blessing) and the Amida itself (*Berakhot* 30a). However, the sages ruled that it, too, deals with the subject of redemption and therefore does not constitute an interruption (*Berakhot* 4b). There is, nevertheless, a significant difference between the subject matter of the two paragraphs. The first deals with the historic redemption of the nation as they stood trapped between the chariots of the Egyptian army and the Sea of Reeds, which miraculously parted so that the Israelites were able to cross to safety. The second is a simple, intimate personal prayer about lying down in peace and rising up in peace.

### HALF KADDISH

*Leader:* יִתְגַּדַּל Magnified and sanctified may His great name be,
in the world He created by His will.
May He establish His kingdom,
make His salvation flourish,
and hasten His messiah, in your lifetime and in your days,
and in the lifetime of all the house of Israel,
swiftly and soon – and say: Amen.

*All:* May His great name be blessed for ever and all time.

*Leader:* Blessed and praised, glorified and exalted,
raised and honored, uplifted and lauded
be the name of the Holy One, blessed be He,
beyond any blessing,
song, praise and consolation
uttered in the world – and say: Amen.

## THE AMIDA

*The following prayer, until "in former years" on page 94, is said silently, standing with feet together. Take three steps forward and at the points indicated by ▾, bend the knees at the first word, bow at the second, and stand straight before saying God's name.*

O Lord, open my lips, *Ps. 51*
so that my mouth may declare Your praise.

### PATRIARCHS

▾בָּרוּךְ Blessed are You, Lord our God and God of our fathers,
God of Abraham, God of Isaac and God of Jacob;
the great, mighty and awesome God, God Most High,
who bestows acts of loving-kindness and creates all,
who remembers the loving-kindness of the fathers and will bring
and will bring a Redeemer to their children's children
for the sake of His name, in love.

---

distant than at other times; more distant than the most distant star, closer to us than we are to ourselves. How can the Creator of a hundred billion galaxies, each of a hundred billion stars, care for us individually? Yet He does. He knows us, loves us, believes in us, and if we are honest in our turning to Him, He forgives us all the sins we committed against Him.

חצי קדיש

ש״ץ: יִתְגַּדַּל וְיִתְקַדַּשׁ שְׁמֵהּ רַבָּא (קהל: אָמֵן)
בְּעָלְמָא דִּי בְרָא כִרְעוּתֵהּ
וְיַמְלִיךְ מַלְכוּתֵהּ וְיַצְמַח פֻּרְקָנֵהּ וִיקָרֵב מְשִׁיחֵהּ (קהל: אָמֵן)
בְּחַיֵּיכוֹן וּבְיוֹמֵיכוֹן וּבְחַיֵּי דְכָל בֵּית יִשְׂרָאֵל
בַּעֲגָלָא וּבִזְמַן קָרִיב, וְאִמְרוּ אָמֵן. (קהל: אָמֵן)

קהל וש״ץ: יְהֵא שְׁמֵהּ רַבָּא מְבָרַךְ לְעָלַם וּלְעָלְמֵי עָלְמַיָּא.

ש״ץ: יִתְבָּרַךְ וְיִשְׁתַּבַּח וְיִתְפָּאַר וְיִתְרוֹמַם וְיִתְנַשֵּׂא
וְיִתְהַדָּר וְיִתְעַלֶּה וְיִתְהַלָּל
שְׁמֵהּ דְּקֻדְשָׁא בְּרִיךְ הוּא (קהל: אָמֵן)
לְעֵלָּא לְעֵלָּא מִכָּל בִּרְכָתָא וְשִׁירָתָא, תֻּשְׁבְּחָתָא וְנֶחֱמָתָא
דַּאֲמִירָן בְּעָלְמָא, וְאִמְרוּ אָמֵן. (קהל: אָמֵן)

## עמידה

*The following prayer, until* קַדְמֹנִיּוֹת *on page 95, is said silently, standing with feet together. Take three steps forward and at the points indicated by* ▾*, bend the knees at the first word, bow at the second, and stand straight before saying God's name.*

תהלים נא — אֲדֹנָי, שְׂפָתַי תִּפְתָּח, וּפִי יַגִּיד תְּהִלָּתֶךָ:

אבות

▾בָּרוּךְ אַתָּה יהוה, אֱלֹהֵינוּ וֵאלֹהֵי אֲבוֹתֵינוּ
אֱלֹהֵי אַבְרָהָם, אֱלֹהֵי יִצְחָק, וֵאלֹהֵי יַעֲקֹב
הָאֵל הַגָּדוֹל הַגִּבּוֹר וְהַנּוֹרָא, אֵל עֶלְיוֹן
גּוֹמֵל חֲסָדִים טוֹבִים, קוֹנֵה הַכֹּל
וְזוֹכֵר חַסְדֵי אָבוֹת
וּמֵבִיא גוֹאֵל לִבְנֵי בְנֵיהֶם לְמַעַן שְׁמוֹ בְּאַהֲבָה.

---

KADDISH

During the Ten Days of Repentance the word לְעֵלָּא, "beyond," is repeated, as if to say that God is doubly beyond the reach of human understanding. Such is the paradox of these holy days that God is closer and at the same time more

זׇכְרֵנוּ לְחַיִּים Remember us for life, O King who desires life,
and write us in the book of life –
for Your sake, O God of life.

King, Helper, Savior, Shield:
▾Blessed are You, LORD, Shield of Abraham.

DIVINE MIGHT

אַתָּה גִּבּוֹר You are eternally mighty, LORD.
You give life to the dead and have great power to save.

*In Israel:* He causes the dew to fall.

He sustains the living with loving-kindness,
and with great compassion revives the dead.
He supports the fallen, heals the sick, sets captives free,
and keeps His faith with those who sleep in the dust.
Who is like You, Master of might, and to whom can You be compared,
O King who brings death and gives life, and makes salvation grow?

מִי כָמוֹךָ Who is like You, compassionate Father,
who remembers His creatures in compassion, for life?

Faithful are You to revive the dead.
Blessed are You, LORD, who revives the dead.

---

וְכׇתְבֵנוּ בְּסֵפֶר הַחַיִּים *Write us in the book of life.* "Rabbi Kruspedai said in the name of Rabbi Yoḥanan: Three books are opened on Rosh HaShana, one for the wholly righteous, one for the wholly wicked and one for the intermediates. The wholly righteous are immediately inscribed and sealed in the book of life. The wholly wicked are immediately inscribed and sealed in the book of death. The judgment of the intermediates is suspended from Rosh HaShana to Yom Kippur. If they are found worthy, they are inscribed for life; if unworthy, they are inscribed for death" (*Rosh HaShana* 16b). The idea that our lives are written in a book by God goes back to the prayer of Moses at the time of the sin of the Golden Calf. Moses prayed: "But now, please forgive their sin – but if not, then blot me out of the book You have written" (Ex. 32:32). When Jews – the People of the Book – think of life, they think of a book. Our lives are each a chapter in the book of Jewish life, of which we, with God, are the co-authors.

זָכְרֵנוּ לְחַיִּים, מֶלֶךְ חָפֵץ בַּחַיִּים
וְכָתְבֵנוּ בְּסֵפֶר הַחַיִּים, לְמַעַנְךָ אֱלֹהִים חַיִּים.

מֶלֶךְ עוֹזֵר וּמוֹשִׁיעַ וּמָגֵן.
בָּרוּךְ אַתָּה יהוה, מָגֵן אַבְרָהָם.

גבורות

אַתָּה גִּבּוֹר לְעוֹלָם, אֲדֹנָי
מְחַיֵּה מֵתִים אַתָּה, רַב לְהוֹשִׁיעַ

בארץ ישראל: מוֹרִיד הַטָּל

מְכַלְכֵּל חַיִּים בְּחֶסֶד, מְחַיֵּה מֵתִים בְּרַחֲמִים רַבִּים
סוֹמֵךְ נוֹפְלִים, וְרוֹפֵא חוֹלִים, וּמַתִּיר אֲסוּרִים
וּמְקַיֵּם אֱמוּנָתוֹ לִישֵׁנֵי עָפָר.
מִי כָמְוֹךָ, בַּעַל גְּבוּרוֹת, וּמִי דּוֹמֶה לָּךְ
מֶלֶךְ, מֵמִית וּמְחַיֶּה וּמַצְמִיחַ יְשׁוּעָה.

מִי כָמְוֹךָ אַב הָרַחֲמָן
זוֹכֵר יְצוּרָיו לְחַיִּים בְּרַחֲמִים.

וְנֶאֱמָן אַתָּה לְהַחֲיוֹת מֵתִים.
בָּרוּךְ אַתָּה יהוה, מְחַיֵּה הַמֵּתִים.

---

זָכְרֵנוּ לְחַיִּים *Remember us for life.* This is one of four additions made to the first two and last two blessings of the Amida during the Ten Days of Repentance. There was initial opposition to their inclusion, since we do not normally make requests during the first and last three blessings, whose themes are, respectively, praise and thanksgiving. Nor do we make requests on Shabbat or Yom Tov. However, since these were deemed to be collective, not individual, requests they were eventually permitted (Abudarham). They lend to the prayers a tone of entreaty distinctive to this time.

HOLINESS

אַתָּה קָדוֹשׁ You are holy and Your name is holy,
and holy ones praise You daily, Selah!
For You, God, are a great and holy King.

לְדוֹר וָדוֹר From generation to generation declare God King,
for He alone is lofty and holy.

וּבְכֵן יִתְקַדַּשׁ And so may Your name be sanctified, Lord our God,
through Israel Your nation and Jerusalem, Your city,
and Zion, the dwelling place of Your honor
and through the royal house of David Your anointed,
and Your Sanctuary and Your Temple.

וּבְכֵן תֵּן פַּחְדְּךָ And so place the fear of You, Lord our God,
over all that You have made,
and the terror of You over all You have created,
and all who were made will stand in awe of You,
and all of creation will worship You,
and they will be bound all together as one
to carry out Your will with an undivided heart;
for we know, Lord our God,
that all dominion is laid out before You,
strength is in Your palm, and might in Your right hand,
Your name spreading awe over all You have created.

---

Used here it sets up an association with the binding of Isaac which, according to the Talmud, is why we blow the shofar on Rosh HaShana, in memory of the ram that was caught in a thicket by its horns.

עַל כָּל מַעֲשֶׂיךָ *Over all that You have made.* The prayers of Rosh HaShana have a universality unlike those of Pesaḥ, Shavuot and Sukkot. They refer not just to the Jewish people but to all humanity, for on Rosh HaShana "All who walk on earth pass before [God]" in judgment, like sheep before a shepherd (Mishna, *Rosh HaShana* 1:2). Rosh HaShana is the anniversary of creation and of the birth of humanity. The God of Israel is the God of all.

קדושת השם

אַתָּה קָדוֹשׁ וְשִׁמְךָ קָדוֹשׁ, וּקְדוֹשִׁים בְּכָל יוֹם יְהַלְלְוּךָ סֶּלָה.
כִּי אֵל מֶלֶךְ גָּדוֹל וְקָדוֹשׁ אָתָּה.

לְדוֹר וָדוֹר הַמְלִיכוּ לָאֵל
כִּי הוּא לְבַדּוֹ מָרוֹם וְקָדוֹשׁ.

וּבְכֵן יִתְקַדַּשׁ שִׁמְךָ יהוה אֱלֹהֵינוּ
עַל יִשְׂרָאֵל עַמֶּךָ וְעַל יְרוּשָׁלַיִם עִירֶךָ
וְעַל צִיּוֹן מִשְׁכַּן כְּבוֹדֶךָ וְעַל מַלְכוּת בֵּית דָּוִד מְשִׁיחֶךָ
וְעַל מְכוֹנְךָ וְהֵיכָלֶךָ.

וּבְכֵן תֵּן פַּחְדְּךָ יהוה אֱלֹהֵינוּ עַל כָּל מַעֲשֶׂיךָ
וְאֵימָתְךָ עַל כָּל מַה שֶּׁבָּרָאתָ
וְיִירָאוּךָ כָּל הַמַּעֲשִׂים, וְיִשְׁתַּחֲווּ לְפָנֶיךָ כָּל הַבְּרוּאִים
וְיֵעָשׂוּ כֻלָּם אֲגֻדָּה אַחַת לַעֲשׂוֹת רְצוֹנְךָ בְּלֵבָב שָׁלֵם
כְּמוֹ שֶׁיָּדַעְנוּ יהוה אֱלֹהֵינוּ שֶׁהַשָּׁלְטָן לְפָנֶיךָ
עֹז בְּיָדְךָ וּגְבוּרָה בִּימִינֶךָ
וְשִׁמְךָ נוֹרָא עַל כָּל מַה שֶּׁבָּרָאתָ.

---

וּבְכֵן *And so…* The repetition of the word *uvkhen* in this blessing, a distinctive feature of the *Amidot* of Rosh HaShana and Yom Kippur, recalls the words of Esther to Mordekhai: "Go, gather together all the Jews who are in Shushan and fast for me. Do not eat or drink for three days, night or day. I and my attendants will fast as you do. And so [*uvkhen*], I will go to the king, even though it is against the law. And if I perish, I perish" (Esther 4:16). So here the word evokes the fear and trembling we feel as we stand before not a human ruler but the divine King. (Abudarham)

וּבְכֵן תֵּן פַּחְדְּךָ *And so place the fear of You.* The word *paḥad* is associated in the Torah with Isaac (Gen. 31:42) and with the binding (Radak, Nahmanides).

וּבְכֵן תֵּן כָּבוֹד And so place honor, LORD, upon Your people,
praise on those who fear You
and hope into those who seek You,
the confidence to speak into all who long for You,
gladness to Your land and joy to Your city,
the flourishing of pride to David Your servant,
and a lamp laid out for his descendant, Your anointed,
soon, in our days.

וּבְכֵן צַדִּיקִים And then righteous people will see and rejoice,
and the upright will exult,
and the pious revel in joy,
and injustice will have nothing more to say,
and all wickedness will fade away like smoke
as You sweep the rule of arrogance from the earth.

וְתִמְלֹךְ And You, who are the LORD our God,
will rule alone over all those You have made,
in Mount Zion, the dwelling of Your glory,
and in Jerusalem, Your holy city,
as it is written in Your holy Writings:
"The LORD shall reign for ever. *Ps. 146*
He is your God, Zion, from generation to generation, Halleluya!"

קָדוֹשׁ אַתָּה You are holy, Your name is awesome,
and there is no god but You,
as it is written,
"The LORD of hosts shall be raised up through His judgment, *Is. 5*
the Holy God, made holy in righteousness."
Blessed are You, LORD, the holy King.

---

is characteristic of Jewish thought. Similarly in the Torah we move from all humanity (Adam, Noah) to Abraham and his descendants, not all of whom are part of His covenant (Ishmael, Esau), then to the bearers of the covenant, the children of Jacob. So, too, in Grace after Meals we move from the world

וּבְכֵן תֵּן כָּבוֹד יהוה לְעַמֶּךָ
תְּהִלָּה לִירֵאֶיךָ וְתִקְוָה טוֹבָה לְדוֹרְשֶׁיךָ
וּפִתְחוֹן פֶּה לַמְיַחֲלִים לָךְ
שִׂמְחָה לְאַרְצֶךָ, וְשָׂשׂוֹן לְעִירֶךָ
וּצְמִיחַת קֶרֶן לְדָוִד עַבְדֶּךָ
וַעֲרִיכַת נֵר לְבֶן יִשַׁי מְשִׁיחֶךָ בִּמְהֵרָה בְיָמֵינוּ.

וּבְכֵן צַדִּיקִים יִרְאוּ וְיִשְׂמָחוּ, וִישָׁרִים יַעֲלֹזוּ
וַחֲסִידִים בְּרִנָּה יָגִילוּ, וְעוֹלָתָה תִּקְפָּץ פִּיהָ
וְכָל הָרִשְׁעָה כֻּלָּהּ כְּעָשָׁן תִּכְלֶה
כִּי תַעֲבִיר מֶמְשֶׁלֶת זָדוֹן מִן הָאָרֶץ.

וְתִמְלֹךְ אַתָּה הוּא יהוה אֱלֹהֵינוּ
מְהֵרָה לְבַדֶּךָ עַל כָּל מַעֲשֶׂיךָ
בְּהַר צִיּוֹן מִשְׁכַּן כְּבוֹדֶךָ
וּבִירוּשָׁלַיִם עִיר קָדְשֶׁךָ
כַּכָּתוּב בְּדִבְרֵי קָדְשֶׁךָ
יִמְלֹךְ יהוה לְעוֹלָם, אֱלֹהַיִךְ צִיּוֹן לְדֹר וָדֹר, הַלְלוּיָהּ: תהלים קמו

קָדוֹשׁ אַתָּה וְנוֹרָא שְׁמֶךָ, וְאֵין אֱלוֹהַּ מִבַּלְעָדֶיךָ
כַּכָּתוּב, וַיִּגְבַּהּ יהוה צְבָאוֹת בַּמִּשְׁפָּט ישעיה ה
וְהָאֵל הַקָּדוֹשׁ נִקְדַּשׁ בִּצְדָקָה:
בָּרוּךְ אַתָּה יהוה, הַמֶּלֶךְ הַקָּדוֹשׁ.

---

**וּבְכֵן תֵּן כָּבוֹד** *And so place honor.* Note how the three paragraphs beginning with *uvkhen* move from the universal to the particular: first all humanity, then Your people, then the righteous and upright. This direction, beginning with the universal and progressively narrowing the focus to the particular,

HOLINESS OF THE DAY

אַתָּה בְחַרְתָּנוּ You have chosen us from among all peoples.
You have loved and favored us.
You have raised us above all tongues.
You have made us holy through Your commandments.
You have brought us near, our King, to Your service,
and have called us by Your great and holy name.

---

*On Motza'ei Shabbat:*

וַתּוֹדִיעֵנוּ You have made known to us, LORD our God, Your righteous laws, and have taught us to perform Your will's decrees. You have given us, LORD our God, just laws and true teachings, good precepts and commandments. You have given us as our heritage seasons of joy, holy festivals, and occasions for presenting our freewill offerings. You have given us as our heritage the holiness of the Sabbath, the glory of the festival, and the festive offerings of the pilgrimage days. You have distinguished, LORD our God, between sacred and secular, between light and darkness, between Israel and the nations, between the seventh day and the six days of work. You have distinguished between the holiness of the Sabbath and the holiness of the festival, and have made the seventh day holy above the six days of work. You have distinguished and sanctified Your people Israel with Your holiness.

---

*On Shabbat, add the words in parentheses:*

וַתִּתֶּן לָנוּ And You, LORD our God, have given us in love
(this Sabbath day and) this Day of Remembrance,
a day of (recalling) blowing the shofar,
(with love,) a holy assembly
in memory of the exodus from Egypt.

---

Plato especially, which moves from the particular to the universal. In Judaism, what is precious to God is our particularity, our uniqueness.

קדושת היום

אַתָּה בְחַרְתָּנוּ מִכָּל הָעַמִּים
אָהַבְתָּ אוֹתָנוּ וְרָצִיתָ בָּנוּ
וְרוֹמַמְתָּנוּ מִכָּל הַלְּשׁוֹנוֹת
וְקִדַּשְׁתָּנוּ בְּמִצְוֹתֶיךָ
וְקֵרַבְתָּנוּ מַלְכֵּנוּ לַעֲבוֹדָתֶךָ
וְשִׁמְךָ הַגָּדוֹל וְהַקָּדוֹשׁ עָלֵינוּ קָרָאתָ.

---

*On* מוצאי שבת:

וַתּוֹדִיעֵנוּ יהוה אֱלֹהֵינוּ אֶת מִשְׁפְּטֵי צִדְקֶךָ, וַתְּלַמְּדֵנוּ לַעֲשׂוֹת חֻקֵּי רְצוֹנֶךָ, וַתִּתֶּן לָנוּ יהוה אֱלֹהֵינוּ מִשְׁפָּטִים יְשָׁרִים וְתוֹרוֹת אֱמֶת, חֻקִּים וּמִצְוֹת טוֹבִים, וַתַּנְחִילֵנוּ זְמַנֵּי שָׂשׂוֹן וּמוֹעֲדֵי קֹדֶשׁ וְחַגֵּי נְדָבָה, וַתּוֹרִישֵׁנוּ קְדֻשַּׁת שַׁבָּת וּכְבוֹד מוֹעֵד וַחֲגִיגַת הָרֶגֶל. וַתַּבְדֵּל יהוה אֱלֹהֵינוּ בֵּין קֹדֶשׁ לְחֹל, בֵּין אוֹר לְחֹשֶׁךְ, בֵּין יִשְׂרָאֵל לָעַמִּים, בֵּין יוֹם הַשְּׁבִיעִי לְשֵׁשֶׁת יְמֵי הַמַּעֲשֶׂה. בֵּין קְדֻשַּׁת שַׁבָּת לִקְדֻשַּׁת יוֹם טוֹב הִבְדַּלְתָּ, וְאֶת יוֹם הַשְּׁבִיעִי מִשֵּׁשֶׁת יְמֵי הַמַּעֲשֶׂה קִדַּשְׁתָּ, הִבְדַּלְתָּ וְקִדַּשְׁתָּ אֶת עַמְּךָ יִשְׂרָאֵל בִּקְדֻשָּׁתֶךָ.

---

*On* שבת*, add the words in parentheses:*

וַתִּתֶּן לָנוּ יהוה אֱלֹהֵינוּ בְּאַהֲבָה
אֶת יוֹם (הַשַּׁבָּת הַזֶּה וְאֶת יוֹם) הַזִּכָּרוֹן הַזֶּה
יוֹם (זִכְרוֹן) תְּרוּעָה
(בְּאַהֲבָה) מִקְרָא קֹדֶשׁ, זֵכֶר לִיצִיאַת מִצְרָיִם.

---

(first blessing) to the land of Israel (second blessing), and then to Jerusalem (third blessing). This is the opposite of the Greek way of thinking, that of

אֱלֹהֵינוּ Our God and God of our ancestors,
may there rise, come, reach, appear, be favored, heard,
regarded and remembered before You,
our recollection and remembrance,
as well as the remembrance of our ancestors,
and of the Messiah, son of David Your servant,
and of Jerusalem Your holy city,
and of all Your people the house of Israel –
for deliverance and well-being,
grace, loving-kindness and compassion,
life and peace, on this Day of Remembrance.
On it remember us, LORD our God, for good;
recollect us for blessing,
and deliver us for a good life.
In accord with Your promise of salvation and compassion,
spare us and be gracious to us;
have compassion on us and deliver us,
for our eyes are turned to You
because You, God, are a gracious and compassionate King.

אֱלֹהֵינוּ Our God and God of our ancestors,
rule over all the world in Your honor,
and be raised above all the earth in Your glory,
and appear, in the splendor of Your great might
before all those who live in this world, Your domain.
And all who were made will know that You made them,
and all who were formed will know that You formed them,
and all that have breath in their mouths will declare:
The LORD, God of Israel is King,
and His kingship has dominion over all.

---

the blessings of Your festivals," is not said on Rosh HaShana and Yom Kippur because it refers to "joy and gladness," which are not the primary mood of the Days of Awe (see the discussion in *Tur* and *Shulḥan Arukh, Oraḥ Ḥayyim* 582).

אֱלֹהֵינוּ וֵאלֹהֵי אֲבוֹתֵינוּ
יַעֲלֶה וְיָבוֹא וְיַגִּיעַ, וְיֵרָאֶה וְיֵרָצֶה וְיִשָּׁמַע
וְיִפָּקֵד וְיִזָּכֵר זִכְרוֹנֵנוּ וּפִקְדוֹנֵנוּ וְזִכְרוֹן אֲבוֹתֵינוּ
וְזִכְרוֹן מָשִׁיחַ בֶּן דָּוִד עַבְדֶּךָ
וְזִכְרוֹן יְרוּשָׁלַיִם עִיר קָדְשֶׁךָ
וְזִכְרוֹן כָּל עַמְּךָ בֵּית יִשְׂרָאֵל, לְפָנֶיךָ
לִפְלֵיטָה לְטוֹבָה, לְחֵן וּלְחֶסֶד וּלְרַחֲמִים, לְחַיִּים וּלְשָׁלוֹם
בְּיוֹם הַזִּכָּרוֹן הַזֶּה.
זָכְרֵנוּ יהוה אֱלֹהֵינוּ בּוֹ לְטוֹבָה
וּפָקְדֵנוּ בוֹ לִבְרָכָה
וְהוֹשִׁיעֵנוּ בוֹ לְחַיִּים טוֹבִים.
וּבִדְבַר יְשׁוּעָה וְרַחֲמִים חוּס וְחָנֵּנוּ, וְרַחֵם עָלֵינוּ וְהוֹשִׁיעֵנוּ
כִּי אֵלֶיךָ עֵינֵינוּ, כִּי אֵל מֶלֶךְ חַנּוּן וְרַחוּם אָתָּה.

אֱלֹהֵינוּ וֵאלֹהֵי אֲבוֹתֵינוּ
מְלֹךְ עַל כָּל הָעוֹלָם כֻּלּוֹ בִּכְבוֹדֶךָ
וְהִנָּשֵׂא עַל כָּל הָאָרֶץ בִּיקָרֶךָ
וְהוֹפַע בַּהֲדַר גְּאוֹן עֻזֶּךָ עַל כָּל יוֹשְׁבֵי תֵבֵל אַרְצֶךָ.
וְיֵדַע כָּל פָּעוּל כִּי אַתָּה פְעַלְתּוֹ, וְיָבִין כָּל יָצוּר כִּי אַתָּה יְצַרְתּוֹ
וְיֹאמַר כֹּל אֲשֶׁר נְשָׁמָה בְאַפּוֹ
יהוה אֱלֹהֵי יִשְׂרָאֵל מֶלֶךְ וּמַלְכוּתוֹ בַּכֹּל מָשָׁלָה.

---

אֱלֹהֵינוּ וֵאלֹהֵי אֲבוֹתֵינוּ *Our God and God of our ancestors.* This prayer, originally said in the land of Israel on all festivals, was deemed especially appropriate to Rosh HaShana and Yom Kippur, because of its universality. The corresponding prayer said on other festivals, *"Vehasi'enu,* Bestow on us, Lord our God,

*On Shabbat, add the words in parentheses:*

(Our God and God of our ancestors, find favor, please, in our rest.)
Make us holy through Your commandments
and grant us our share in Your Torah.
Satisfy us with Your goodness, grant our souls joy in Your salvation
(in love and favor, Lord our God,
grant us as our heritage Your holy Sabbath,
so that all Israel, who sanctify Your name may find rest on it),
and purify our hearts to serve You in truth.
For You, Lord, are truth, and Your word is truth
and holds true forever.
Blessed are You, Lord, King over all the earth,
who sanctifies (the Sabbath,) Israel and the Day of Remembrance.

TEMPLE SERVICE

רְצֵה Find favor, Lord our God,
in Your people Israel, and heed their prayer.
Restore the service to Your most holy House,
and accept soon, in love and favor,
the fire-offerings of Israel and their prayer.
May the service of Your people Israel always find favor with You.
And may our eyes witness Your return to Zion in compassion.
Blessed are You, Lord, who restores His Presence to Zion.

THANKSGIVING

*Bow at the first nine words.*

מוֹדִים We give thanks to You,
for You are the Lord our God and God of our ancestors
for ever and all time.
You are the Rock of our lives,
Shield of our salvation from generation to generation.

---

he would die (Gen. 2:16). Yet, though he ate, he did not die immediately. He lived a long life. It follows that Adam and Eve were forgiven their sin. Rosh HaShana is the anniversary of the day the first humans were created, sinned, and were forgiven. So may it be a day of forgiveness for us.

*On* שבת*, add the words in parentheses:*

(אֱלֹהֵינוּ וֵאלֹהֵי אֲבוֹתֵינוּ, רְצֵה נָא בִמְנוּחָתֵנוּ)
קַדְּשֵׁנוּ בְּמִצְוֹתֶיךָ וְתֵן חֶלְקֵנוּ בְּתוֹרָתֶךָ
שַׂבְּעֵנוּ מִטּוּבֶךָ, וְשַׂמַּח נַפְשֵׁנוּ בִּישׁוּעָתֶךָ
(וְהַנְחִילֵנוּ יהוה אֱלֹהֵינוּ בְּאַהֲבָה וּבְרָצוֹן שַׁבַּת קָדְשֶׁךָ
וְיָנוּחוּ בָהּ כָּל יִשְׂרָאֵל מְקַדְּשֵׁי שְׁמֶךָ)
וְטַהֵר לִבֵּנוּ לְעָבְדְּךָ בֶּאֱמֶת
כִּי אַתָּה אֱלֹהִים אֱמֶת, וּדְבָרְךָ אֱמֶת וְקַיָּם לָעַד.
בָּרוּךְ אַתָּה יהוה, מֶלֶךְ עַל כָּל הָאָרֶץ
מְקַדֵּשׁ (הַשַּׁבָּת וְ) יִשְׂרָאֵל וְיוֹם הַזִּכָּרוֹן.

עבודה

רְצֵה יהוה אֱלֹהֵינוּ בְּעַמְּךָ יִשְׂרָאֵל, וְלִתְפִלָּתָם שְׁעֵה
וְהָשֵׁב אֶת הָעֲבוֹדָה לִדְבִיר בֵּיתֶךָ
וְאִשֵּׁי יִשְׂרָאֵל וּתְפִלָּתָם, מְהֵרָה בְּאַהֲבָה תְקַבֵּל בְּרָצוֹן
וּתְהִי לְרָצוֹן תָּמִיד עֲבוֹדַת יִשְׂרָאֵל עַמֶּךָ.
וְתֶחֱזֶינָה עֵינֵינוּ בְּשׁוּבְךָ לְצִיּוֹן בְּרַחֲמִים.
בָּרוּךְ אַתָּה יהוה, הַמַּחֲזִיר שְׁכִינָתוֹ לְצִיּוֹן.

הודאה

*Bow at the first five words.*

מוֹדִים אֲנַחְנוּ לָךְ
שָׁאַתָּה הוּא יהוה אֱלֹהֵינוּ וֵאלֹהֵי אֲבוֹתֵינוּ לְעוֹלָם וָעֶד.
צוּר חַיֵּינוּ, מָגֵן יִשְׁעֵנוּ, אַתָּה הוּא לְדוֹר וָדוֹר.

---

**וּדְבָרְךָ אֱמֶת וְקַיָּם לָעַד** *Your word is truth and holds true forever.* Based on Psalms 119:89, "Your word, Lord, is eternal; it stands firm in the heavens." Even as You judged Adam, the first human, with compassion, so judge us with compassion (*Mordekhai*). Adam was told that if he ate of the Tree of Knowledge

We will thank You and declare Your praise for our lives,
which are entrusted into Your hand;
for our souls, which are placed in Your charge;
for Your miracles which are with us every day;
and for Your wonders and favors at all times,
evening, morning and midday.
You are good – for Your compassion never fails.
You are compassionate – for Your loving-kindnesses never cease;
for we have always placed our hope in You.
For all these things may Your name be blessed and exalted,
and raised up our King, continually, for ever and all time.

וּכְתֹב And write, for a good life, all the children of Your covenant.

Let all that lives thank You, Selah!
and praise and bless Your great name in truth, always,
because it is good,
God, our Savior and Help, Selah! the beneficent God.
▾Blessed are You, LORD, whose name is "the Good"
and to whom thanks are due.

PEACE

שָׁלוֹם רָב Grant great peace to Your people Israel for ever,
for You are the sovereign LORD of all peace;
and may it be good in Your eyes to bless us
and all Your people Israel
at every time, in every hour, with Your peace.

בְּסֵפֶר חַיִּים In the book of life, blessing, peace and prosperity,
and good decrees, salvations and consolations,
may we and all Your people the house of Israel
be remembered and written before You
for a good life, and for peace.

Blessed are You, LORD, who blesses His people Israel with peace.

*Some say the following verse:*

May the words of my mouth and the meditation of my heart *Ps. 19*
find favor before You, LORD, my Rock and Redeemer.

נוֹדֶה לְּךָ וּנְסַפֵּר תְּהִלָּתֶךָ עַל חַיֵּינוּ הַמְּסוּרִים בְּיָדֶךָ
וְעַל נִשְׁמוֹתֵינוּ הַפְּקוּדוֹת לָךְ
וְעַל נִסֶּיךָ שֶׁבְּכָל יוֹם עִמָּנוּ
וְעַל נִפְלְאוֹתֶיךָ וְטוֹבוֹתֶיךָ שֶׁבְּכָל עֵת, עֶרֶב וָבֹקֶר וְצָהֳרָיִם.
הַטּוֹב, כִּי לֹא כָלוּ רַחֲמֶיךָ, וְהַמְרַחֵם, כִּי לֹא תַמּוּ חֲסָדֶיךָ
כִּי מֵעוֹלָם קִוִּינוּ לָךְ.
וְעַל כֻּלָּם
יִתְבָּרַךְ וְיִתְרוֹמַם וְיִתְנַשֵּׂא שִׁמְךָ מַלְכֵּנוּ תָּמִיד לְעוֹלָם וָעֶד.

וּכְתֹב לְחַיִּים טוֹבִים כָּל בְּנֵי בְרִיתֶךָ.

וְכֹל הַחַיִּים יוֹדוּךָ סֶּלָה
וִיהַלְלוּ וִיבָרְכוּ אֶת שִׁמְךָ הַגָּדוֹל בֶּאֱמֶת לְעוֹלָם כִּי טוֹב
הָאֵל יְשׁוּעָתֵנוּ וְעֶזְרָתֵנוּ סֶלָה, הָאֵל הַטּוֹב.
בָּרוּךְ אַתָּה יהוה, הַטּוֹב שִׁמְךָ וּלְךָ נָאֶה לְהוֹדוֹת.

ברכת שלום

שָׁלוֹם רָב עַל יִשְׂרָאֵל עַמְּךָ תָּשִׂים לְעוֹלָם
כִּי אַתָּה הוּא מֶלֶךְ אָדוֹן לְכָל הַשָּׁלוֹם.
וְטוֹב יִהְיֶה בְעֵינֶיךָ לְבָרְכֵנוּ, וּלְבָרֵךְ אֶת כָּל עַמְּךָ יִשְׂרָאֵל
בְּכָל עֵת וּבְכָל שָׁעָה בִּשְׁלוֹמֶךָ.

בְּסֵפֶר חַיִּים, בְּרָכָה וְשָׁלוֹם, וּפַרְנָסָה טוֹבָה
וּגְזֵרוֹת טוֹבוֹת, יְשׁוּעוֹת וְנֶחָמוֹת נִזָּכֵר וְנִכָּתֵב לְפָנֶיךָ
אֲנַחְנוּ וְכָל עַמְּךָ בֵּית יִשְׂרָאֵל לְחַיִּים טוֹבִים וּלְשָׁלוֹם.

בָּרוּךְ אַתָּה יהוה, הַמְבָרֵךְ אֶת עַמּוֹ יִשְׂרָאֵל בַּשָּׁלוֹם.

*Some say the following verse:*

יִהְיוּ לְרָצוֹן אִמְרֵי־פִי וְהֶגְיוֹן לִבִּי לְפָנֶיךָ, יהוה צוּרִי וְגֹאֲלִי: תהלים יט

אֱלֹהַי My God, *Berakhot 17a*
guard my tongue from evil and my lips from deceitful speech.
To those who curse me, let my soul be silent;
may my soul be to all like the dust.
Open my heart to Your Torah
and let my soul pursue Your commandments.
As for all who rise up or plan evil against me,
swiftly thwart their counsel and frustrate their plans.

*Some add this prayer:*
יְהִי רָצוֹן May it be Your will, LORD my God, God of my ancestors,
that envy of no man may rise up in me, nor envy of me in any other;
that I will not be angry today, nor make You angry;
and save me from my evil impulse,
placing humility and modesty into my heart.
Our King and God, make Your name One in Your world;
build up Your city, establish Your House and complete Your Sanctuary,
gather in the exiles, redeem Your flock,
and have Your congregation rejoice.

Act for the sake of Your name;
act for the sake of Your right hand;
act for the sake of Your Torah; act for the sake of Your holiness.
That Your beloved ones may be delivered, *Ps. 60*
save with Your right hand and answer me.
May the words of my mouth and the meditation of my heart *Ps. 19*
find favor before You, LORD, my Rock and Redeemer.

*Bow, take three steps back, then bow, first left, then right, then center, while saying:*
May He who makes peace in His high places,
make peace for us and all Israel – and say: Amen.

יְהִי רָצוֹן May it be Your will, LORD our God and God of our ancestors,
that the Temple be rebuilt speedily in our days, and grant us a share in Your Torah.
And there we will serve You with reverence,
as in the days of old and as in former years.
Then the offering of Judah and Jerusalem *Mal. 3*
will be pleasing to the LORD as in the days of old and as in former years.

אֱלֹהַי ברכות יז.
נְצֹר לְשׁוֹנִי מֵרָע וּשְׂפָתַי מִדַּבֵּר מִרְמָה
וְלִמְקַלְלַי נַפְשִׁי תִדֹּם, וְנַפְשִׁי כֶּעָפָר לַכֹּל תִּהְיֶה.
פְּתַח לִבִּי בְּתוֹרָתֶךָ, וְאַחֲרֵי מִצְוֹתֶיךָ תִּרְדֹּף נַפְשִׁי.
וְכָל הַקָּמִים וְהַחוֹשְׁבִים עָלַי רָעָה
מְהֵרָה הָפֵר עֲצָתָם וְקַלְקֵל מַחֲשַׁבְתָּם.

*Some add this prayer:*

יְהִי רָצוֹן מִלְּפָנֶיךָ יהוה אֱלֹהַי וֵאלֹהֵי אֲבוֹתַי
שֶׁלֹּא תַעֲלֶה קִנְאַת אָדָם עָלַי, וְלֹא קִנְאָתִי עַל אֲחֵרִים
וְשֶׁלֹּא אֶכְעֹס הַיּוֹם, וְשֶׁלֹּא אַכְעִיסֶךָ
וְתַצִּילֵנִי מִיֵּצֶר הָרָע, וְתֵן בְּלִבִּי הַכְנָעָה וַעֲנָוָה.
מַלְכֵּנוּ וֵאלֹהֵינוּ, יַחֵד שִׁמְךָ בְּעוֹלָמֶךָ
בְּנֵה עִירָךְ, יַסֵּד בֵּיתְךָ וְשַׁכְלֵל הֵיכָלֶךָ
וְקַבֵּץ קִבּוּץ גָּלֻיּוֹת, וּפְדֵה צֹאנֶךָ וְשַׂמַּח עֲדָתֶךָ.

עֲשֵׂה לְמַעַן שְׁמֶךָ, עֲשֵׂה לְמַעַן יְמִינֶךָ
עֲשֵׂה לְמַעַן תּוֹרָתֶךָ, עֲשֵׂה לְמַעַן קְדֻשָּׁתֶךָ.
לְמַעַן יֵחָלְצוּן יְדִידֶיךָ, הוֹשִׁיעָה יְמִינְךָ וַעֲנֵנִי: תהלים ס
יִהְיוּ לְרָצוֹן אִמְרֵי־פִי וְהֶגְיוֹן לִבִּי לְפָנֶיךָ, יהוה צוּרִי וְגֹאֲלִי: תהלים יט

*Bow, take three steps back, then bow, first left, then right, then center, while saying:*

עֹשֶׂה הַשָּׁלוֹם בִּמְרוֹמָיו
הוּא יַעֲשֶׂה שָׁלוֹם עָלֵינוּ וְעַל כָּל יִשְׂרָאֵל, וְאִמְרוּ אָמֵן.

יְהִי רָצוֹן מִלְּפָנֶיךָ יהוה אֱלֹהֵינוּ וֵאלֹהֵי אֲבוֹתֵינוּ
שֶׁיִּבָּנֶה בֵּית הַמִּקְדָּשׁ בִּמְהֵרָה בְיָמֵינוּ, וְתֵן חֶלְקֵנוּ בְּתוֹרָתֶךָ
וְשָׁם נַעֲבָדְךָ בְּיִרְאָה כִּימֵי עוֹלָם וּכְשָׁנִים קַדְמֹנִיּוֹת.
וְעָרְבָה לַיהוה מִנְחַת יְהוּדָה וִירוּשָׁלָםִ כִּימֵי עוֹלָם וּכְשָׁנִים קַדְמֹנִיּוֹת: מלאכי ג

*When Rosh HaShana falls on Shabbat continue below.*
*On all other days continue with Psalm 24 on the next page.*

*All stand and say:*

וַיְכֻלּוּ Then the heavens and the earth were completed, Gen. 2
and all their array.
With the seventh day, God completed the work He had done.
He ceased on the seventh day from all the work He had done.
God blessed the seventh day and declared it holy,
because on it He ceased from all His work He had created to do.

*The Leader continues:*

בָּרוּךְ Blessed are You, Lord our God and God of our fathers,
God of Abraham, God of Isaac and God of Jacob,
the great, mighty and awesome God,
God Most High, Creator of heaven and earth.

*The congregation then the Leader:*

מָגֵן אָבוֹת By His word, He was the Shield of our ancestors.
By His promise, He will revive the dead.
There is none like the holy King
who gives rest to His people on His holy Sabbath day,
for He found them worthy of His favor to give them rest.
Before Him we will come in worship with reverence and awe,
giving thanks to His name daily, continually, with due blessings.
He is God to whom thanks are due, the Lord of peace
who sanctifies the Sabbath and blesses the seventh day,
and in holiness gives rest to a people filled with delight,
in remembrance of the work of creation.

*The Leader continues:*

אֱלֹהֵינוּ Our God and God of our ancestors,
find favor, please, in our rest.
Make us holy through Your commandments
and grant us our share in Your Torah.
Satisfy us with Your goodness,
grant our souls joy in Your salvation,
and purify our hearts to serve You in truth.

*When ראש השנה falls on שבת continue below.*
*On all other days continue with לְדָוִד מִזְמוֹר on the next page.*

*All stand and say:*

וַיְכֻלּוּ הַשָּׁמַיִם וְהָאָרֶץ וְכָל־צְבָאָם: בראשית ב
וַיְכַל אֱלֹהִים בַּיּוֹם הַשְּׁבִיעִי מְלַאכְתּוֹ אֲשֶׁר עָשָׂה
וַיִּשְׁבֹּת בַּיּוֹם הַשְּׁבִיעִי מִכָּל־מְלַאכְתּוֹ אֲשֶׁר עָשָׂה:
וַיְבָרֶךְ אֱלֹהִים אֶת־יוֹם הַשְּׁבִיעִי, וַיְקַדֵּשׁ אֹתוֹ
כִּי בוֹ שָׁבַת מִכָּל־מְלַאכְתּוֹ, אֲשֶׁר־בָּרָא אֱלֹהִים, לַעֲשׂוֹת:

*The שליח ציבור continues:*

בָּרוּךְ אַתָּה יהוה, אֱלֹהֵינוּ וֵאלֹהֵי אֲבוֹתֵינוּ
אֱלֹהֵי אַבְרָהָם, אֱלֹהֵי יִצְחָק, וֵאלֹהֵי יַעֲקֹב
הָאֵל הַגָּדוֹל הַגִּבּוֹר וְהַנּוֹרָא, אֵל עֶלְיוֹן, קֹנֵה שָׁמַיִם וָאָרֶץ.

*The קהל then the שליח ציבור:*

מָגֵן אָבוֹת בִּדְבָרוֹ, מְחַיֵּה מֵתִים בְּמַאֲמָרוֹ
הַמֶּלֶךְ הַקָּדוֹשׁ שֶׁאֵין כָּמְוֹהוּ
הַמֵּנִיחַ לְעַמּוֹ בְּיוֹם שַׁבַּת קָדְשׁוֹ, כִּי בָם רָצָה לְהָנִיחַ לָהֶם
לְפָנָיו נַעֲבֹד בְּיִרְאָה וָפַחַד
וְנוֹדֶה לִשְׁמוֹ בְּכָל יוֹם תָּמִיד, מֵעֵין הַבְּרָכוֹת
אֵל הַהוֹדָאוֹת, אֲדוֹן הַשָּׁלוֹם
מְקַדֵּשׁ הַשַּׁבָּת וּמְבָרֵךְ שְׁבִיעִי
וּמֵנִיחַ בִּקְדֻשָּׁה לְעַם מְדֻשְּׁנֵי עֹנֶג
זֵכֶר לְמַעֲשֵׂה בְרֵאשִׁית.

*The שליח ציבור continues:*

אֱלֹהֵינוּ וֵאלֹהֵי אֲבוֹתֵינוּ, רְצֵה נָא בִמְנוּחָתֵנוּ.
קַדְּשֵׁנוּ בְּמִצְוֹתֶיךָ וְתֵן חֶלְקֵנוּ בְּתוֹרָתֶךָ
שַׂבְּעֵנוּ מִטּוּבֶךָ וְשַׂמַּח נַפְשֵׁנוּ בִּישׁוּעָתֶךָ
וְטַהֵר לִבֵּנוּ לְעָבְדְּךָ בֶּאֱמֶת.

In love and favor, LORD our God,
grant us as our heritage Your holy Sabbath,
so that all Israel who sanctify Your name may find rest on it.
Blessed are You, LORD, who sanctifies the Sabbath.

## PRAYER FOR SUSTENANCE

*The Ark is opened and the following psalm is said responsively:*

לְדָוִד מִזְמוֹר A psalm of David. The earth is the LORD's Ps. 24
and all it contains, the world and all who live in it.
For He founded it on the seas and established it on the streams.
Who may climb the mountain of the LORD?
Who may stand in His holy place?
He who has clean hands and a pure heart,
who has not taken My name in vain, or sworn deceitfully.
He shall receive blessing from the LORD,
and just reward from God, his salvation.
This is a generation of those who seek Him,
the descendants of Jacob who seek Your presence, Selah!
Lift up your heads, O gates; be uplifted, eternal doors,
so that the King of glory may enter.
Who is the King of glory?
It is the LORD, strong and mighty, the LORD mighty in battle.
Lift up your heads, O gates; lift them up, eternal doors,
so that the King of glory may enter.
Who is He, the King of glory? The LORD of hosts,
He is the King of glory, Selah!

*Some add silently the following Kabbalistic prayer:*

May it be Your will, LORD our God, God of our ancestors, the great, mighty and awesome God, that You be filled with compassion, and are gracious to us, for Your own sake and for the holiness of this psalm [we have said], and the holy names mentioned in it, and for the holiness of its verses and words and letters and notes, and its secrets, and the holiness of the Holy Name [דיקרנוסא] that arises from the verse "I shall rain down upon you blessing without bounds" – and from the verse "Turn the light of Your face toward us, LORD." And write us in the book of good sustenance, this year and for every year after – write us there, and all the people of our households, all the days of our lives, [that we may sustain ourselves] fully, with all that is needed and more, in permissible ways and not forbidden ones, in serenity, without suffering, and without hard labor and struggle, in tranquility and peace and security, with no

Mal. 3
Ps. 4

וְהַנְחִילֵנוּ יהוה אֱלֹהֵינוּ בְּאַהֲבָה וּבְרָצוֹן שַׁבַּת קָדְשֶׁךָ
וְיָנוּחוּ בָהּ כָּל יִשְׂרָאֵל מְקַדְּשֵׁי שְׁמֶךָ.
בָּרוּךְ אַתָּה יהוה, מְקַדֵּשׁ הַשַּׁבָּת.

### תפילה לפרנסה

*The* ארון קודש *is opened and the following psalm is said responsively:*

תהלים כד
לְדָוִד מִזְמוֹר, לַיהוה הָאָרֶץ וּמְלוֹאָהּ, תֵּבֵל וְיֹשְׁבֵי בָהּ:
כִּי־הוּא עַל־יַמִּים יְסָדָהּ, וְעַל־נְהָרוֹת יְכוֹנְנֶהָ:
מִי־יַעֲלֶה בְהַר־יהוה, וּמִי־יָקוּם בִּמְקוֹם קָדְשׁוֹ:
נְקִי כַפַּיִם וּבַר־לֵבָב, אֲשֶׁר לֹא־נָשָׂא לַשָּׁוְא נַפְשִׁי
וְלֹא נִשְׁבַּע לְמִרְמָה:
יִשָּׂא בְרָכָה מֵאֵת יהוה, וּצְדָקָה מֵאֱלֹהֵי יִשְׁעוֹ:
זֶה דּוֹר דֹּרְשָׁו, מְבַקְשֵׁי פָנֶיךָ יַעֲקֹב סֶלָה:
שְׂאוּ שְׁעָרִים רָאשֵׁיכֶם, וְהִנָּשְׂאוּ פִּתְחֵי עוֹלָם
וְיָבוֹא מֶלֶךְ הַכָּבוֹד:
מִי זֶה מֶלֶךְ הַכָּבוֹד, יהוה עִזּוּז וְגִבּוֹר, יהוה גִּבּוֹר מִלְחָמָה:
שְׂאוּ שְׁעָרִים רָאשֵׁיכֶם, וּשְׂאוּ פִּתְחֵי עוֹלָם, וְיָבֹא מֶלֶךְ הַכָּבוֹד:
מִי הוּא זֶה מֶלֶךְ הַכָּבוֹד, יהוה צְבָאוֹת הוּא מֶלֶךְ הַכָּבוֹד סֶלָה:

*Some add silently the following Kabbalistic prayer:*

יְהִי רָצוֹן מִלְּפָנֶיךָ, יהוה אֱלֹהֵינוּ, הָאֵל הַגָּדוֹל הַגִּבּוֹר וְהַנּוֹרָא, שֶׁתִּתְמַלֵּא רַחֲמִים,
וְתָחֹן עָלֵינוּ לְמַעַנְךָ וּלְמַעַן קְדֻשַּׁת הַמִּזְמוֹר הַזֶּה, וְהַשֵּׁמוֹת הַקְּדוֹשִׁים הַנִּזְכָּרִים
בּוֹ, וּקְדֻשַּׁת פְּסוּקָיו וְתֵבוֹתָיו וְאוֹתִיּוֹתָיו וּטְעָמָיו וְסוֹדוֹתָיו, וּקְדֻשַּׁת הַשֵּׁם הַקָּדוֹשׁ
מלאכי ג [דיקרנוסא] הַיּוֹצֵא מִפָּסוּק: וַהֲרִיקֹתִי לָכֶם בְּרָכָה עַד־בְּלִי־דָי: וּמִפָּסוּק: נְסָה־עָלֵינוּ
תהלים ד אוֹר פָּנֶיךָ יהוה: וְכָתְבֵנוּ בְּסֵפֶר פַּרְנָסָה טוֹבָה וְכַלְכָּלָה שָׁנָה זוֹ וְכָל שָׁנָה וְשָׁנָה, לָנוּ
וּלְכָל בְּנֵי בֵיתֵנוּ כָּל יְמֵי חַיֵּינוּ, בִּמְלוּי וּבְרֶוַח, בְּהֶתֵּר וְלֹא בְּאִסּוּר, בְּנַחַת וְלֹא בְּצַעַר,
וְלֹא בְּעָמָל וָטֹרַח, בְּשַׁלְוָה וְהַשְׁקֵט וָבֶטַח, בְּלִי שׁוּם עַיִן הָרָע. וּתְזַכֵּנוּ לַעֲבֹד עֲבוֹדַת
הַקֹּדֶשׁ בְּלִי שׁוּם טִרְדָּה. וּתְפַרְנְסֵנוּ פַּרְנָסָה שֶׁלֹּא יִהְיֶה בָהּ שׁוּם בּוּשָׁה וּכְלִמָּה. וְלֹא

evil eye upon us. Allow us the merit of carrying out our holy service untroubled. And sustain us with a living that comes without any shame or humiliation; let us never be dependent on the gifts of other people, but always receive from Your full, broad hand. Let us be successful and let us profit from all our study and in all the works of our hands and our dealings. May our houses be full of the LORD's blessing, and let us have bread enough to satisfy us, let us be well. Compassionate and gracious, Protector, Supporter, Savior, Upright One, Redeemer [רח״ש תמי״ך], have compassion for us and listen to our prayer, for You listen to the prayers that each mouth speaks. Blessed is the One who listens to prayers [ארארית״א כוז״ו אזבוגא].

## FULL KADDISH

*Leader:* יִתְגַּדַּל Magnified and sanctified may His great name be,
in the world He created by His will.
May He establish His kingdom,
make His salvation flourish,
and hasten His messiah,
in your lifetime and in your days,
and in the lifetime of all the house of Israel,
swiftly and soon – and say: Amen.

*All:* May His great name be blessed for ever and all time.

*Leader:* Blessed and praised, glorified and exalted,
raised and honored, uplifted and lauded be
the name of the Holy One, blessed be He,
beyond any blessing,
song, praise and consolation
uttered in the world – and say: Amen.

May the prayers and pleas of all the house of Israel
be accepted by their Father in heaven – and say: Amen.

May there be great peace from heaven,
and a good life for us and all Israel – and say: Amen.

*Bow, take three steps back, as if taking leave of the Divine Presence, then bow, first left, then right, then center, while saying:*

May He who makes peace in His high places,
make peace for us and all Israel – and say: Amen.

נִצְטָרֵךְ לְמַתְּנַת בָּשָׂר וָדָם, כִּי אִם מִיָּדְךָ הַמְּלֵאָה וְהָרְחָבָה. וְתַצְלִיחֵנוּ וְתַרְוִיחֵנוּ בְּכָל לִמּוּדֵנוּ וּבְכָל מַעֲשֵׂה יָדֵינוּ וַעֲסָקֵינוּ. וִיהְיֶה בֵּיתֵנוּ מָלֵא בִּרְכַּת יהוה. וְנִשְׂבַּע לֶחֶם וְנִהְיֶה טוֹבִים. רַחוּם חַנּוּן שׁוֹמֵר תּוֹמֵךְ מַצִּיל יָשָׁר פּוֹדֶה [רח״ש תמי״ף] רַחֵם עָלֵינוּ וּשְׁמַע תְּפִלָּתֵנוּ, כִּי אַתָּה שׁוֹמֵעַ תְּפִלַּת כָּל פֶּה. בָּרוּךְ שׁוֹמֵעַ תְּפִלָּה [אוכף אראריתי״א כוז״ו אזבוגא].

## קדיש שלם

ש״ץ: יִתְגַּדַּל וְיִתְקַדַּשׁ שְׁמֵהּ רַבָּא (קהל: אָמֵן)
בְּעָלְמָא דִּי בְרָא כִרְעוּתֵהּ
וְיַמְלִיךְ מַלְכוּתֵהּ וְיַצְמַח פֻּרְקָנֵהּ וִיקָרֵב מְשִׁיחֵהּ (קהל: אָמֵן)
בְּחַיֵּיכוֹן וּבְיוֹמֵיכוֹן וּבְחַיֵּי דְכָל בֵּית יִשְׂרָאֵל
בַּעֲגָלָא וּבִזְמַן קָרִיב, וְאִמְרוּ אָמֵן. (קהל: אָמֵן)

קהל וש״ץ: יְהֵא שְׁמֵהּ רַבָּא מְבָרַךְ לְעָלַם וּלְעָלְמֵי עָלְמַיָּא.

ש״ץ: יִתְבָּרַךְ וְיִשְׁתַּבַּח וְיִתְפָּאַר וְיִתְרוֹמַם וְיִתְנַשֵּׂא
וְיִתְהַדָּר וְיִתְעַלֶּה וְיִתְהַלָּל
שְׁמֵהּ דְּקֻדְשָׁא בְּרִיךְ הוּא (קהל: אָמֵן)
לְעֵלָּא לְעֵלָּא מִכָּל בִּרְכָתָא
וְשִׁירָתָא, תֻּשְׁבְּחָתָא וְנֶחֱמָתָא
דַּאֲמִירָן בְּעָלְמָא, וְאִמְרוּ אָמֵן. (קהל: אָמֵן)

תִּתְקַבַּל צְלוֹתְהוֹן וּבָעוּתְהוֹן דְּכָל בֵּית יִשְׂרָאֵל
קֳדָם אֲבוּהוֹן דִּי בִשְׁמַיָּא, וְאִמְרוּ אָמֵן. (קהל: אָמֵן)

יְהֵא שְׁלָמָא רַבָּא מִן שְׁמַיָּא
וְחַיִּים טוֹבִים עָלֵינוּ וְעַל כָּל יִשְׂרָאֵל, וְאִמְרוּ אָמֵן. (קהל: אָמֵן)

*Bow, take three steps back, as if taking leave of the Divine Presence, then bow, first left, then right, then center, while saying:*

עֹשֶׂה הַשָּׁלוֹם בִּמְרוֹמָיו
הוּא יַעֲשֶׂה שָׁלוֹם עָלֵינוּ וְעַל כָּל יִשְׂרָאֵל, וְאִמְרוּ אָמֵן. (קהל: אָמֵן)

# Kiddush in the Synagogue

*The Leader raises a cup of wine and says:*

Please pay attention, my masters.
Blessed are You, LORD our God, King of the Universe,
who creates the fruit of the vine.

*On Shabbat, add the words in parentheses:*

בָּרוּךְ Blessed are You, LORD our God,
King of the Universe,
who has chosen us from among all peoples,
raised us above all tongues,
and made us holy through His commandments.
You have given us, LORD our God, in love,
this (Sabbath and this) Day of Remembrance,
a day of (recalling) blowing the shofar,
(with love,) a holy assembly in memory of the exodus from Egypt,
for You have chosen us and sanctified us above all peoples,
and Your word is true and endures for ever.
Blessed are You, LORD, King over all the earth,
who sanctifies (the Sabbath,) Israel and the Day of Remembrance.

*On Motza'ei Shabbat, the following Havdala is added:*

בָּרוּךְ Blessed are You, LORD our God, King of the Universe,
who creates the lights of fire.

Blessed are You, LORD our God, King of the Universe, who distinguishes between sacred and secular, between light and darkness, between Israel and the nations, between the seventh day and the six days of work. You have made a distinction between the holiness of the Sabbath and the holiness of festivals, and have sanctified the seventh day above the six days of work. You have distinguished and sanctified Your people Israel with Your holiness. Blessed are You, LORD, who distinguishes between sacred and sacred.

*The following is said on both evenings:*

בָּרוּךְ Blessed are You, LORD our God, King of the Universe,
who has given us life, sustained us, and brought us to this time.

*The wine should be drunk by children under the age of Bar/Bat Mitzva or, if there are none, by the Leader.*

# קידוש בבית הכנסת

*The* שליח ציבור *raises a cup of wine and says:*

סַבְרִי מָרָנָן

בָּרוּךְ אַתָּה יהוה אֱלֹהֵינוּ מֶלֶךְ הָעוֹלָם, בּוֹרֵא פְּרִי הַגָּפֶן.

*On* שבת*, add the words in parentheses:*

בָּרוּךְ אַתָּה יהוה אֱלֹהֵינוּ מֶלֶךְ הָעוֹלָם
אֲשֶׁר בָּחַר בָּנוּ מִכָּל עָם
וְרוֹמְמָנוּ מִכָּל לָשׁוֹן, וְקִדְּשָׁנוּ בְּמִצְוֹתָיו
וַתִּתֶּן לָנוּ יהוה אֱלֹהֵינוּ בְּאַהֲבָה
אֶת יוֹם (הַשַּׁבָּת הַזֶּה וְאֶת יוֹם)
הַזִּכָּרוֹן הַזֶּה, יוֹם (זִכְרוֹן) תְּרוּעָה
(בְּאַהֲבָה) מִקְרָא קֹדֶשׁ, זֵכֶר לִיצִיאַת מִצְרָיִם
כִּי בָנוּ בָחַרְתָּ וְאוֹתָנוּ קִדַּשְׁתָּ מִכָּל הָעַמִּים
וּדְבָרְךָ אֱמֶת וְקַיָּם לָעַד.
בָּרוּךְ אַתָּה יהוה, מֶלֶךְ עַל כָּל הָאָרֶץ
מְקַדֵּשׁ (הַשַּׁבָּת וְ) יִשְׂרָאֵל וְיוֹם הַזִּכָּרוֹן.

*On* מוצאי שבת*, the following* הבדלה *is added:*

בָּרוּךְ אַתָּה יהוה אֱלֹהֵינוּ מֶלֶךְ הָעוֹלָם, בּוֹרֵא מְאוֹרֵי הָאֵשׁ.

בָּרוּךְ אַתָּה יהוה אֱלֹהֵינוּ מֶלֶךְ הָעוֹלָם, הַמַּבְדִּיל בֵּין קֹדֶשׁ לְחֹל, בֵּין אוֹר לְחֹשֶׁךְ, בֵּין יִשְׂרָאֵל לָעַמִּים, בֵּין יוֹם הַשְּׁבִיעִי לְשֵׁשֶׁת יְמֵי הַמַּעֲשֶׂה. בֵּין קְדֻשַּׁת שַׁבָּת לִקְדֻשַּׁת יוֹם טוֹב הִבְדַּלְתָּ, וְאֶת יוֹם הַשְּׁבִיעִי מִשֵּׁשֶׁת יְמֵי הַמַּעֲשֶׂה קִדַּשְׁתָּ, הִבְדַּלְתָּ וְקִדַּשְׁתָּ אֶת עַמְּךָ יִשְׂרָאֵל בִּקְדֻשָּׁתֶךָ. בָּרוּךְ אַתָּה יהוה, הַמַּבְדִּיל בֵּין קֹדֶשׁ לְקֹדֶשׁ.

*The following is said on both evenings:*

בָּרוּךְ אַתָּה יהוה אֱלֹהֵינוּ מֶלֶךְ הָעוֹלָם
שֶׁהֶחֱיָנוּ וְקִיְּמָנוּ וְהִגִּיעָנוּ לַזְּמַן הַזֶּה.

*The wine should be drunk by children under the age of* בר מצווה *or* בת מצווה *or, if there are none, by the* שליח ציבור*.*

*Stand while saying Aleinu. Bow at* ▾.

עָלֵינוּ It is our duty to praise the Master of all,
and ascribe greatness to the Author of creation,
who has not made us like the nations of the lands
nor placed us like the families of the earth;
who has not made our portion like theirs,
nor our destiny like all their multitudes.
(For they worship vanity and emptiness,
and pray to a god who cannot save.)
▾But we bow in worship
and thank the Supreme King of kings, the Holy One, blessed be He,
who extends the heavens and establishes the earth,
whose throne of glory is in the heavens above,
and whose power's Presence is in the highest of heights.
He is our God; there is no other.
Truly He is our King, there is none else, as it is written in His Torah:
"You shall know and take to heart this day *Deut. 4*
that the LORD is God, in the heavens above and on the earth below.
There is no other."

Therefore, we place our hope in You, LORD our God,
that we may soon see the glory of Your power,
when You will remove abominations from the earth,
and idols will be utterly destroyed,
when the world will be perfected under the sovereignty of the Almighty,
when all humanity will call on Your name,
to turn all the earth's wicked toward You.
All the world's inhabitants will realize and know
that to You every knee must bow and every tongue swear loyalty.
Before You, LORD our God, they will kneel and bow down
and give honor to Your glorious name.
They will all accept the yoke of Your kingdom,
and You will reign over them soon and for ever.
For the kingdom is Yours, and to all eternity You will reign in glory,
as it is written in Your Torah: "The LORD will reign for ever and ever." *Ex. 15*
▸ And it is said: "Then the LORD shall be King over all the earth; *Zech. 14*
on that day the LORD shall be One and His name One."

*Stand while saying* עָלֵינוּ. *Bow at* ▾.

עָלֵינוּ לְשַׁבֵּחַ לַאֲדוֹן הַכֹּל, לָתֵת גְּדֻלָּה לְיוֹצֵר בְּרֵאשִׁית
שֶׁלֹּא עָשָׂנוּ כְּגוֹיֵי הָאֲרָצוֹת, וְלֹא שָׂמָנוּ כְּמִשְׁפְּחוֹת הָאֲדָמָה
שֶׁלֹּא שָׂם חֶלְקֵנוּ כָּהֶם וְגוֹרָלֵנוּ כְּכָל הֲמוֹנָם.
(שֶׁהֵם מִשְׁתַּחֲוִים לְהֶבֶל וָרִיק וּמִתְפַּלְלִים אֶל אֵל לֹא יוֹשִׁיעַ.)
▾וַאֲנַחְנוּ כּוֹרְעִים וּמִשְׁתַּחֲוִים וּמוֹדִים
לִפְנֵי מֶלֶךְ מַלְכֵי הַמְּלָכִים, הַקָּדוֹשׁ בָּרוּךְ הוּא
שֶׁהוּא נוֹטֶה שָׁמַיִם וְיוֹסֵד אָרֶץ, וּמוֹשַׁב יְקָרוֹ בַּשָּׁמַיִם מִמַּעַל
וּשְׁכִינַת עֻזּוֹ בְּגָבְהֵי מְרוֹמִים.
הוּא אֱלֹהֵינוּ, אֵין עוֹד.
אֱמֶת מַלְכֵּנוּ, אֶפֶס זוּלָתוֹ כַּכָּתוּב בְּתוֹרָתוֹ
וְיָדַעְתָּ הַיּוֹם וַהֲשֵׁבֹתָ אֶל־לְבָבֶךָ דברים ד
כִּי יהוה הוּא הָאֱלֹהִים בַּשָּׁמַיִם מִמַּעַל וְעַל־הָאָרֶץ מִתָּחַת, אֵין עוֹד:

וְעַל כֵּן נְקַוֶּה לְּךָ יהוה אֱלֹהֵינוּ, לִרְאוֹת מְהֵרָה בְּתִפְאֶרֶת עֻזֶּךָ
לְהַעֲבִיר גִּלּוּלִים מִן הָאָרֶץ, וְהָאֱלִילִים כָּרוֹת יִכָּרֵתוּן
לְתַקֵּן עוֹלָם בְּמַלְכוּת שַׁדַּי.
וְכָל בְּנֵי בָשָׂר יִקְרְאוּ בִשְׁמֶךָ לְהַפְנוֹת אֵלֶיךָ כָּל רִשְׁעֵי אָרֶץ.
יַכִּירוּ וְיֵדְעוּ כָּל יוֹשְׁבֵי תֵבֵל
כִּי לְךָ תִּכְרַע כָּל בֶּרֶךְ, תִּשָּׁבַע כָּל לָשׁוֹן.
לְפָנֶיךָ יהוה אֱלֹהֵינוּ יִכְרְעוּ וְיִפֹּלוּ, וְלִכְבוֹד שִׁמְךָ יְקָר יִתֵּנוּ
וִיקַבְּלוּ כֻלָּם אֶת עֹל מַלְכוּתֶךָ
וְתִמְלֹךְ עֲלֵיהֶם מְהֵרָה לְעוֹלָם וָעֶד.
כִּי הַמַּלְכוּת שֶׁלְּךָ הִיא וּלְעוֹלְמֵי עַד תִּמְלֹךְ בְּכָבוֹד
כַּכָּתוּב בְּתוֹרָתֶךָ, יהוה יִמְלֹךְ לְעֹלָם וָעֶד: שמות טו
◂ וְנֶאֱמַר, וְהָיָה יהוה לְמֶלֶךְ עַל־כָּל־הָאָרֶץ זכריה יד
בַּיּוֹם הַהוּא יִהְיֶה יהוה אֶחָד וּשְׁמוֹ אֶחָד:

*Some add:*

Have no fear of sudden terror or of the ruin when it overtakes the wicked. *Prov. 3*
Devise your strategy, but it will be thwarted; *Is. 8*
propose your plan, but it will not stand, for God is with us.
When you grow old, I will still be the same. *Is. 46*
When your hair turns gray, I will still carry you.
I made you, I will bear you, I will carry you, and I will rescue you.

## MOURNER'S KADDISH

*The following prayer, said by mourners, requires the presence of a minyan. A transliteration can be found on page 1095.*

*Mourner:* יִתְגַּדַּל Magnified and sanctified
may His great name be,
in the world He created by His will.
May He establish His kingdom,
make His salvation flourish,
and hasten His messiah,
in your lifetime and in your days,
and in the lifetime of all the house of Israel,
swiftly and soon – and say: Amen.

*All:* May His great name be blessed for ever and all time.

*Mourner:* Blessed and praised, glorified and exalted,
raised and honored, uplifted and lauded
be the name of the Holy One, blessed be He,
beyond any blessing,
song, praise and consolation
uttered in the world – and say: Amen.

May there be great peace from heaven,
and a good life for us and all Israel – and say: Amen.

*Bow, take three steps back, as if taking leave of the Divine Presence, then bow, first left, then right, then center, while saying:*

May He who makes peace in His high places,
make peace for us and all Israel – and say: Amen.

*Some add:*

אַל־תִּירָא מִפַּחַד פִּתְאֹם וּמִשֹּׁאַת רְשָׁעִים כִּי תָבֹא: משלי ג
עֻצוּ עֵצָה וְתֻפָר, דַּבְּרוּ דָבָר וְלֹא יָקוּם, כִּי עִמָּנוּ אֵל: ישעיה ח
וְעַד־זִקְנָה אֲנִי הוּא, וְעַד־שֵׂיבָה אֲנִי אֶסְבֹּל ישעיה מו
אֲנִי עָשִׂיתִי וַאֲנִי אֶשָּׂא וַאֲנִי אֶסְבֹּל וַאֲמַלֵּט:

## קדיש יתום

*The following prayer, said by mourners, requires the presence of a* מנין*.*
*A transliteration can be found on page 1095.*

אבל: יִתְגַּדַּל וְיִתְקַדַּשׁ שְׁמֵהּ רַבָּא (קהל: אָמֵן)
בְּעָלְמָא דִּי בְרָא כִרְעוּתֵהּ
וְיַמְלִיךְ מַלְכוּתֵהּ וְיַצְמַח פֻּרְקָנֵהּ וִיקָרֵב מְשִׁיחֵהּ (קהל: אָמֵן)
בְּחַיֵּיכוֹן וּבְיוֹמֵיכוֹן וּבְחַיֵּי דְכָל בֵּית יִשְׂרָאֵל
בַּעֲגָלָא וּבִזְמַן קָרִיב, וְאִמְרוּ אָמֵן. (קהל: אָמֵן)

קהל ואבל: יְהֵא שְׁמֵהּ רַבָּא מְבָרַךְ לְעָלַם וּלְעָלְמֵי עָלְמַיָּא.

אבל: יִתְבָּרַךְ וְיִשְׁתַּבַּח וְיִתְפָּאַר
וְיִתְרוֹמַם וְיִתְנַשֵּׂא וְיִתְהַדָּר וְיִתְעַלֶּה וְיִתְהַלָּל
שְׁמֵהּ דְּקֻדְשָׁא בְּרִיךְ הוּא (קהל: אָמֵן)
לְעֵלָּא לְעֵלָּא מִכָּל בִּרְכָתָא
וְשִׁירָתָא, תֻּשְׁבְּחָתָא וְנֶחֱמָתָא
דַּאֲמִירָן בְּעָלְמָא, וְאִמְרוּ אָמֵן. (קהל: אָמֵן)

יְהֵא שְׁלָמָא רַבָּא מִן שְׁמַיָּא
וְחַיִּים טוֹבִים עָלֵינוּ וְעַל כָּל יִשְׂרָאֵל, וְאִמְרוּ אָמֵן. (קהל: אָמֵן)

*Bow, take three steps back, as if taking leave of the Divine Presence,*
*then bow, first left, then right, then center, while saying:*

עֹשֶׂה הַשָּׁלוֹם בִּמְרוֹמָיו
הוּא יַעֲשֶׂה שָׁלוֹם עָלֵינוּ וְעַל כָּל יִשְׂרָאֵל, וְאִמְרוּ אָמֵן. (קהל: אָמֵן)

Lord of the universe,
who reigned before the birth of any thing –

When by His will all things were made
then was His name proclaimed King.

And when all things shall cease to be
He alone will reign in awe.

He was, He is, and He shall be
glorious for evermore.

He is One, there is none else,
alone, unique, beyond compare;

Without beginning, without end,
His might, His rule are everywhere.

He is my God; my Redeemer lives.
He is the Rock on whom I rely –

My banner and my safe retreat,
my cup, my portion when I cry.

Into His hand my soul I place,
when I awake and when I sleep.

The Lord is with me, I shall not fear;
body and soul from harm will He keep.

# אֲדוֹן עוֹלָם

אֲשֶׁר מָלַךְ בְּטֶרֶם כָּל־יְצִיר נִבְרָא.
לְעֵת נַעֲשָׂה בְחֶפְצוֹ כֹּל אֲזַי מֶלֶךְ שְׁמוֹ נִקְרָא.
וְאַחֲרֵי כִּכְלוֹת הַכֹּל לְבַדּוֹ יִמְלֹךְ נוֹרָא.
וְהוּא הָיָה וְהוּא הֹוֶה וְהוּא יִהְיֶה בְּתִפְאָרָה.
וְהוּא אֶחָד וְאֵין שֵׁנִי לְהַמְשִׁיל לוֹ לְהַחְבִּירָה.
בְּלִי רֵאשִׁית בְּלִי תַכְלִית וְלוֹ הָעֹז וְהַמִּשְׂרָה.
וְהוּא אֵלִי וְחַי גֹּאֲלִי וְצוּר חֶבְלִי בְּעֵת צָרָה.
וְהוּא נִסִּי וּמָנוֹס לִי מְנָת כּוֹסִי בְּיוֹם אֶקְרָא.
בְּיָדוֹ אַפְקִיד רוּחִי בְּעֵת אִישַׁן וְאָעִירָה.
וְעִם רוּחִי גְּוִיָּתִי יהוה לִי וְלֹא אִירָא.

**GREAT**
is the living God and praised.
He exists, and His existence is beyond time.

He is One, and there is no unity like His.
Unfathomable, His Oneness is infinite.

He has neither bodily form nor substance;
His holiness is beyond compare.

He preceded all that was created.
He was first: there was no beginning to His beginning.

Behold He is Master of the Universe; every creature
shows His greatness and majesty.

The rich flow of His prophecy He gave
to His treasured people in whom He gloried.

Never in Israel has there arisen another like Moses,
a prophet who beheld God's image.

God gave His people a Torah of truth
by the hand of His prophet, most faithful of His House.

God will not alter or change His law
for any other, for eternity.

He sees and knows our secret thoughts;
as soon as something is begun, He foresees its end.

He rewards people with loving-kindness according to their deeds;
He punishes the wicked according to his wickedness.

At the end of days He will send our Messiah,
to redeem those who await His final salvation.

God will revive the dead in His great loving-kindness.
Blessed for evermore is His glorious name!

# יִגְדַּל

אֱלֹהִים חַי וְיִשְׁתַּבַּח, נִמְצָא וְאֵין עֵת אֶל מְצִיאוּתוֹ.

אֶחָד וְאֵין יָחִיד כְּיִחוּדוֹ, נֶעְלָם וְגַם אֵין סוֹף לְאַחְדּוּתוֹ.

אֵין לוֹ דְּמוּת הַגּוּף וְאֵינוֹ גוּף, לֹא נַעֲרֹךְ אֵלָיו קְדֻשָּׁתוֹ.

קַדְמוֹן לְכָל דָּבָר אֲשֶׁר נִבְרָא, רִאשׁוֹן וְאֵין רֵאשִׁית לְרֵאשִׁיתוֹ.

הִנּוֹ אֲדוֹן עוֹלָם, וְכָל נוֹצָר יוֹרֶה גְדֻלָּתוֹ וּמַלְכוּתוֹ.

שֶׁפַע נְבוּאָתוֹ נְתָנוֹ אֶל־אַנְשֵׁי סְגֻלָּתוֹ וְתִפְאַרְתּוֹ.

לֹא קָם בְּיִשְׂרָאֵל כְּמֹשֶׁה עוֹד נָבִיא וּמַבִּיט אֶת תְּמוּנָתוֹ.

תּוֹרַת אֱמֶת נָתַן לְעַמּוֹ אֵל עַל יַד נְבִיאוֹ נֶאֱמַן בֵּיתוֹ.

לֹא יַחֲלִיף הָאֵל וְלֹא יָמִיר דָּתוֹ לְעוֹלָמִים לְזוּלָתוֹ.

צוֹפֶה וְיוֹדֵעַ סְתָרֵינוּ, מַבִּיט לְסוֹף דָּבָר בְּקַדְמָתוֹ.

גּוֹמֵל לְאִישׁ חֱסֶד כְּמִפְעָלוֹ, נוֹתֵן לְרָשָׁע רָע כְּרִשְׁעָתוֹ.

יִשְׁלַח לְקֵץ יָמִין מְשִׁיחֵנוּ לִפְדּוֹת מְחַכֵּי קֵץ יְשׁוּעָתוֹ.

מֵתִים יְחַיֶּה אֵל בְּרֹב חַסְדּוֹ, בָּרוּךְ עֲדֵי עַד שֵׁם תְּהִלָּתוֹ.

*On the first night of Rosh HaShana*
*it is customary to greet people as follows:*

לְשָׁנָה טוֹבָה May your name be written and sealed
for a good year.

# Rosh HaShana Evening

## BLESSING THE CHILDREN

*On the evenings of Shabbat and Yom Tov,*
*many have the custom to bless their children.*

*To sons, say:*
יְשִׂמְךָ May God
make you like Ephraim
and Manasseh.

*To daughters, say:*
יְשִׂימֵךְ May God
make you like Sarah, Rebecca,
Rachel and Leah.

*Gen. 48*

יְבָרֶכְךָ May the Lord bless you and protect you.
May the Lord make His face shine on you
and be gracious to you.
May the Lord turn His face toward you
and grant you peace.

*Num. 6*

---

לְשָׁנָה טוֹבָה תִּכָּתֵב וְתֵחָתֵם *May your name be written and sealed for a good year.* According to the Talmud, only the perfectly righteous are immediately written and sealed in the book of life. By giving this greeting, we therefore pray that those around us be considered perfectly righteous – for as we judge others, so are we judged. Those who judge others harshly are judged harshly. Those who judge others favorably are judged favorably.

*On the first night of* ראש השנה *it is customary to greet people as follows:*

*To a man:*

לְשָׁנָה טוֹבָה תִּכָּתֵב וְתֵחָתֵם.

*To a woman:*

לְשָׁנָה טוֹבָה תִּכָּתְבִי וְתֵחָתֵמִי.

*To men:*

לְשָׁנָה טוֹבָה תִּכָּתְבוּ וְתֵחָתֵמוּ.

*To women:*

לְשָׁנָה טוֹבָה תִּכָּתַבְנָה וְתֵחָתַמְנָה.

# סדר ליל ראש השנה

## ברכת הבנים

*On* ליל שבת *and* ערב יום טוב*,*
*many have the custom to bless their children.*

*To sons, say:*

יְשִׂמְךָ אֱלֹהִים
כְּאֶפְרַיִם וְכִמְנַשֶּׁה:

*To daughters, say:*

בראשית מח

יְשִׂימֵךְ אֱלֹהִים
כְּשָׂרָה רִבְקָה רָחֵל וְלֵאָה.

במדבר ו

יְבָרֶכְךָ יהוה וְיִשְׁמְרֶךָ:
יָאֵר יהוה פָּנָיו אֵלֶיךָ וִיחֻנֶּךָּ:
יִשָּׂא יהוה פָּנָיו אֵלֶיךָ וְיָשֵׂם לְךָ שָׁלוֹם:

*On Friday night the following is said before Kiddush.*
*Many people sing each of the four verses of the following song three times:*

שָׁלוֹם עֲלֵיכֶם Welcome, ministering angels, angels of the Most High,
from the Supreme King of kings, the Holy One, blessed be He.

Enter in peace, angels of peace, angels of the Most High,
from the Supreme King of kings, the Holy One, blessed be He.

Bless me with peace, angels of peace, angels of the Most High,
from the Supreme King of kings, the Holy One, blessed be He.

Go in peace, angels of peace, angels of the Most High,
from the Supreme King of kings, the Holy One, blessed be He.

כִּי מַלְאָכָיו He will command His angels about you, *Ps. 91*
to guard you in all your ways.
May the LORD guard your going out and your return, *Ps. 121*
from now and for all time.

אֵשֶׁת־חַיִל A woman of strength, who can find? Her worth is far beyond pearls. *Prov. 31* Her husband's heart trusts in her, and he has no lack of gain. She brings him good, not harm, all the days of her life. She seeks wool and linen, and works with willing hands. She is like a ship laden with merchandise, bringing her food from afar. She rises while it is still night, providing food for her household, portions for her maids. She considers a field and buys it; from her earnings she plants a vineyard. She girds herself with strength, and braces her arms for her tasks. She sees that her business goes well; her lamp does not go out at night. She holds the distaff in her hand, and grasps the spindle with her palms. She reaches out her palm to the poor, and extends her hand to the needy. She has no fear for her family when it snows, for all her household is clothed in crimson wool. She makes elegant coverings; her clothing is fine linen and purple wool. Her husband is well known in the gates, where he sits with the elders of the land. She makes linen garments and sells them, and supplies merchants with sashes. She is clothed with strength and dignity; she can laugh at the days to come. She opens her mouth with wisdom, and the law of kindness is on her tongue. She watches over the ways of her household, and never eats the bread of idleness. Her children rise and call her happy; her husband also praises her: "Many women have excelled, but you surpass them all." Charm is deceptive and beauty vain: it is the God-fearing woman who deserves praise. Give her the reward she has earned; let her deeds bring her praise in the gates.

*On Friday night the following is said before* קידוש*:*
*Many people sing each of the four verses of the following song three times:*

שָׁלוֹם עֲלֵיכֶם, מַלְאֲכֵי הַשָּׁרֵת, מַלְאֲכֵי עֶלְיוֹן
מִמֶּלֶךְ מַלְכֵי הַמְּלָכִים, הַקָּדוֹשׁ בָּרוּךְ הוּא.

בּוֹאֲכֶם לְשָׁלוֹם, מַלְאֲכֵי הַשָּׁלוֹם, מַלְאֲכֵי עֶלְיוֹן
מִמֶּלֶךְ מַלְכֵי הַמְּלָכִים, הַקָּדוֹשׁ בָּרוּךְ הוּא.

בָּרְכוּנִי לְשָׁלוֹם, מַלְאֲכֵי הַשָּׁלוֹם, מַלְאֲכֵי עֶלְיוֹן
מִמֶּלֶךְ מַלְכֵי הַמְּלָכִים, הַקָּדוֹשׁ בָּרוּךְ הוּא.

צֵאתְכֶם לְשָׁלוֹם, מַלְאֲכֵי הַשָּׁלוֹם, מַלְאֲכֵי עֶלְיוֹן
מִמֶּלֶךְ מַלְכֵי הַמְּלָכִים, הַקָּדוֹשׁ בָּרוּךְ הוּא.

כִּי מַלְאָכָיו יְצַוֶּה־לָּךְ, לִשְׁמָרְךָ בְּכָל־דְּרָכֶיךָ: תהלים צא
יהוה יִשְׁמָר־צֵאתְךָ וּבוֹאֶךָ, מֵעַתָּה וְעַד־עוֹלָם: תהלים קכא

אֵשֶׁת־חַיִל מִי יִמְצָא, וְרָחֹק מִפְּנִינִים מִכְרָהּ: בָּטַח בָּהּ לֵב בַּעְלָהּ, וְשָׁלָל משלי לא
לֹא יֶחְסָר: גְּמָלַתְהוּ טוֹב וְלֹא־רָע, כֹּל יְמֵי חַיֶּיהָ: דָּרְשָׁה צֶמֶר וּפִשְׁתִּים,
וַתַּעַשׂ בְּחֵפֶץ כַּפֶּיהָ: הָיְתָה כָּאֳנִיּוֹת סוֹחֵר, מִמֶּרְחָק תָּבִיא לַחְמָהּ: וַתָּקָם
בְּעוֹד לַיְלָה, וַתִּתֵּן טֶרֶף לְבֵיתָהּ, וְחֹק לְנַעֲרֹתֶיהָ: זָמְמָה שָׂדֶה וַתִּקָּחֵהוּ,
מִפְּרִי כַפֶּיהָ נָטְעָה כָּרֶם: חָגְרָה בְעוֹז מָתְנֶיהָ, וַתְּאַמֵּץ זְרוֹעֹתֶיהָ: טָעֲמָה
כִּי־טוֹב סַחְרָהּ, לֹא־יִכְבֶּה בַלַּיְלָה נֵרָהּ: יָדֶיהָ שִׁלְּחָה בַכִּישׁוֹר, וְכַפֶּיהָ תָּמְכוּ
פָלֶךְ: כַּפָּהּ פָּרְשָׂה לֶעָנִי, וְיָדֶיהָ שִׁלְּחָה לָאֶבְיוֹן: לֹא־תִירָא לְבֵיתָהּ מִשָּׁלֶג,
כִּי כָל־בֵּיתָהּ לָבֻשׁ שָׁנִים: מַרְבַדִּים עָשְׂתָה־לָּהּ, שֵׁשׁ וְאַרְגָּמָן לְבוּשָׁהּ:
נוֹדָע בַּשְּׁעָרִים בַּעְלָהּ, בְּשִׁבְתּוֹ עִם־זִקְנֵי־אָרֶץ: סָדִין עָשְׂתָה וַתִּמְכֹּר,
וַחֲגוֹר נָתְנָה לַכְּנַעֲנִי: עוֹז־וְהָדָר לְבוּשָׁהּ, וַתִּשְׂחַק לְיוֹם אַחֲרוֹן: פִּיהָ
פָּתְחָה בְחָכְמָה, וְתוֹרַת־חֶסֶד עַל־לְשׁוֹנָהּ: צוֹפִיָּה הֲלִיכוֹת בֵּיתָהּ, וְלֶחֶם
עַצְלוּת לֹא תֹאכֵל: קָמוּ בָנֶיהָ וַיְאַשְּׁרוּהָ, בַּעְלָהּ וַיְהַלְלָהּ: רַבּוֹת בָּנוֹת
עָשׂוּ חָיִל, וְאַתְּ עָלִית עַל־כֻּלָּנָה: שֶׁקֶר הַחֵן וְהֶבֶל הַיֹּפִי, אִשָּׁה יִרְאַת־
יהוה הִיא תִתְהַלָּל: תְּנוּ־לָהּ מִפְּרִי יָדֶיהָ, וִיהַלְלוּהָ בַשְּׁעָרִים מַעֲשֶׂיהָ:

# Kiddush for Rosh HaShana Evening

*On Shabbat add:*

*quietly:* And it was evening, and it was morning – *Gen. 1*

יוֹם הַשִּׁשִּׁי the sixth day.

Then the heavens and the earth were completed, and all their array. *Gen. 2*
With the seventh day, God completed the work He had done. He ceased on the seventh day from all the work He had done. God blessed the seventh day and declared it holy, because on it He ceased from all His work He had created to do.

*On other evenings start Kiddush here:*

*When saying Kiddush for others:* Please pay attention, my masters.

Blessed are You, Lord our God, King of the Universe,
who creates the fruit of the vine.

*On Shabbat, add the words in parentheses.*

בָּרוּךְ Blessed are You, Lord our God, King of the Universe,
who has chosen us from among all peoples,
raised us above all tongues,
and made us holy through His commandments.
You have given us, Lord our God, in love,
this (Sabbath and this) Day of Remembrance,
a day of (recalling) blowing the shofar,
(with love,) a holy assembly in memory of the exodus from Egypt,
for You have chosen us and sanctified us above all peoples,
and Your word is true and endures for ever.
Blessed are You, Lord, King over all the earth,
who sanctifies (the Sabbath,) Israel and the Day of Remembrance.

---

which we proclaim the holiness of the day. We do this in two ways, first by declaring the holiness of the day in the central blessing of the evening Amida, then at home by making a similar declaration over a cup of wine. Holiness in Judaism lives in these two environments: the community and the family.

מְקַדֵּשׁ יִשְׂרָאֵל וְיוֹם הַזִּכָּרוֹן *Who sanctifies Israel and the Day of Remembrance.* The order here is precise. It was God who sanctified the Sabbath, but the Israelites

# קידוש לליל ראש השנה

*On* שבת *add:*

*quietly* וַיְהִי־עֶרֶב וַיְהִי־בֹקֶר בראשית א
יוֹם הַשִּׁשִּׁי:

וַיְכֻלּוּ הַשָּׁמַיִם וְהָאָרֶץ וְכָל־צְבָאָם: וַיְכַל אֱלֹהִים בַּיּוֹם הַשְּׁבִיעִי בראשית ב
מְלַאכְתּוֹ אֲשֶׁר עָשָׂה, וַיִּשְׁבֹּת בַּיּוֹם הַשְּׁבִיעִי מִכָּל־מְלַאכְתּוֹ אֲשֶׁר
עָשָׂה: וַיְבָרֶךְ אֱלֹהִים אֶת־יוֹם הַשְּׁבִיעִי, וַיְקַדֵּשׁ אֹתוֹ, כִּי בוֹ שָׁבַת
מִכָּל־מְלַאכְתּוֹ, אֲשֶׁר־בָּרָא אֱלֹהִים, לַעֲשׂוֹת:

*On other evenings start* קידוש *here:*

*When saying* קידוש *for others* סַבְרִי מָרָנָן

בָּרוּךְ אַתָּה יהוה אֱלֹהֵינוּ מֶלֶךְ הָעוֹלָם, בּוֹרֵא פְּרִי הַגָּפֶן.

*On* שבת*, add the words in parentheses.*

בָּרוּךְ אַתָּה יהוה אֱלֹהֵינוּ מֶלֶךְ הָעוֹלָם
אֲשֶׁר בָּחַר בָּנוּ מִכָּל עָם
וְרוֹמְמָנוּ מִכָּל לָשׁוֹן, וְקִדְּשָׁנוּ בְּמִצְוֹתָיו
וַתִּתֶּן לָנוּ יהוה אֱלֹהֵינוּ בְּאַהֲבָה
אֶת יוֹם (הַשַּׁבָּת הַזֶּה וְאֶת יוֹם)
הַזִּכָּרוֹן הַזֶּה, יוֹם (זִכְרוֹן) תְּרוּעָה
(בְּאַהֲבָה) מִקְרָא קֹדֶשׁ, זֵכֶר לִיצִיאַת מִצְרָיִם
כִּי בָנוּ בָחַרְתָּ וְאוֹתָנוּ קִדַּשְׁתָּ מִכָּל הָעַמִּים
וּדְבָרְךָ אֱמֶת וְקַיָּם לָעַד.
בָּרוּךְ אַתָּה יהוה, מֶלֶךְ עַל כָּל הָאָרֶץ
מְקַדֵּשׁ (הַשַּׁבָּת וְ) יִשְׂרָאֵל וְיוֹם הַזִּכָּרוֹן.

---

KIDDUSH

The first thing declared holy in the Torah is not a place but a time. God "blessed the seventh day and made it holy." Kiddush is a performative act in

*On Motza'ei Shabbat, the following Havdala is added:*

בָּרוּךְ Blessed are You, Lord our God, King of the Universe, who creates the lights of fire.

Blessed are You, Lord our God, King of the Universe, who distinguishes between sacred and secular, between light and darkness, between Israel and the nations, between the seventh day and the six days of work. You have made a distinction between the holiness of the Sabbath and the holiness of festivals, and have sanctified the seventh day above the six days of work. You have distinguished and sanctified Your people Israel with Your holiness. Blessed are You, Lord, who distinguishes between sacred and sacred.

*The following blessing is said on both nights of Rosh HaShana. On the second night, new fruit is placed on the table, and one should have in mind that the blessing is also on the new fruit.*

בָּרוּךְ Blessed are You, Lord our God, King of the Universe, who has given us life, sustained us, and brought us to this time.

*It is customary for all present to drink of the wine.*

*On the first night, following Kiddush and "HaMotzi," an apple is dipped in honey and the following is said:*

בָּרוּךְ Blessed are You, Lord our God, King of the Universe, who creates the fruit of the tree.

*After eating some of the apple and honey, say:*

יְהִי רָצוֹן May it be Your will, Lord our God and God of our ancestors, that You renew for us a good and sweet year.

---

we cease merely to exist. We feel vividly alive. We are aware of the power of now. Life is God's gift. The breath we breathe is His. To be a Jew is to make a blessing over life.

CUSTOMS AT THE TABLE ON THE NIGHT OF ROSH HASHANA

The hands are washed, and the blessing "Who brings forth bread" is made over two loaves. It is customary on Rosh HaShana to dip the bread in honey as a sign that the coming year will be sweet.

Likewise it is a custom on the night of Rosh HaShana to eat an apple dipped in honey and say over it, first the blessing "Who creates the fruit of the tree" and then, "May it be Your will… that You renew for us a good and sweet year." Eating food that tastes sweet is in memory of Nehemiah's instruction to the people on Rosh HaShana to enjoy sweet food and drink (Neh. 8:10).

*On* מוצאי שבת*, the following* הבדלה *is added:*

בָּרוּךְ אַתָּה יהוה אֱלֹהֵינוּ מֶלֶךְ הָעוֹלָם, בּוֹרֵא מְאוֹרֵי הָאֵשׁ.

בָּרוּךְ אַתָּה יהוה אֱלֹהֵינוּ מֶלֶךְ הָעוֹלָם, הַמַּבְדִּיל בֵּין קֹדֶשׁ לְחֹל, בֵּין אוֹר לְחֹשֶׁךְ, בֵּין יִשְׂרָאֵל לָעַמִּים, בֵּין יוֹם הַשְּׁבִיעִי לְשֵׁשֶׁת יְמֵי הַמַּעֲשֶׂה. בֵּין קְדֻשַּׁת שַׁבָּת לִקְדֻשַּׁת יוֹם טוֹב הִבְדַּלְתָּ, וְאֶת יוֹם הַשְּׁבִיעִי מִשֵּׁשֶׁת יְמֵי הַמַּעֲשֶׂה קִדַּשְׁתָּ, הִבְדַּלְתָּ וְקִדַּשְׁתָּ אֶת עַמְּךָ יִשְׂרָאֵל בִּקְדֻשָּׁתֶךָ. בָּרוּךְ אַתָּה יהוה, הַמַּבְדִּיל בֵּין קֹדֶשׁ לְקֹדֶשׁ.

*The following blessing is said on both nights of* ראש השנה*. On the second night, new fruit is placed on the table, and one should have in mind that the blessing is also on the new fruit.*

בָּרוּךְ אַתָּה יהוה אֱלֹהֵינוּ מֶלֶךְ הָעוֹלָם
שֶׁהֶחֱיָנוּ וְקִיְּמָנוּ וְהִגִּיעָנוּ לַזְּמַן הַזֶּה.

*It is customary for all present to drink of the wine.*

*On the first night, following* קידוש *and* המוציא*, an apple is dipped in honey and the following is said:*

בָּרוּךְ אַתָּה יהוה אֱלֹהֵינוּ מֶלֶךְ הָעוֹלָם, בּוֹרֵא פְּרִי הָעֵץ.

*After eating some of the apple and honey, say:*

יְהִי רָצוֹן מִלְּפָנֶיךָ יהוה אֱלֹהֵינוּ וֵאלֹהֵי אֲבוֹתֵינוּ
שֶׁתְּחַדֵּשׁ עָלֵינוּ שָׁנָה טוֹבָה וּמְתוּקָה.

---

who were charged – in the first mitzva given to them while they were still in Egypt – to sanctify the months, regulate the calendar and thus determine on which day the festival would fall. Hence the sanctity of the people of Israel takes precedence over the sanctity of the day, but the sanctity of the Sabbath precedes both. This is evident in both the concluding blessing and in the structure of the passage as a whole. On Shabbat, Kiddush begins with the sanctity of the day and only then speaks of Israel as the chosen people. On festivals, Kiddush begins with God's choice of Israel and only then speaks of the holiness of the day.

שֶׁהֶחֱיָנוּ *Who has given us life.* A blessing over the passage of time at moments when we are specifically aware of the passage of time, like festivals, or memorable events like buying a new house. It is at such moments that

## SIMANIM

*Many have the custom to eat the following symbolic foods on Rosh HaShana and to say the accompanying blessings.*

ON DATES

יְהִי רָצוֹן May it be Your will,
Lord our God and God of our ancestors,
that our enemies meet their end.

ON POMEGRANATE

יְהִי רָצוֹן May it be Your will,
Lord our God and God of our ancestors,
that we produce as much merit
as the pomegranate produces seeds.

ON FENUGREEK

יְהִי רָצוֹן Blessed are You, Lord our God, King of the Universe,
who creates fruit of the ground.
May it be Your will,
Lord our God and God of our ancestors,
that our merits grow abundant.

---

family, without giving anything to eat and drink to the poor and bitter in soul – his meal is not a rejoicing in a divine commandment but a rejoicing in his own stomach. (Maimonides, Laws of Festival Rest 6:18)

SOLEMNITY AND JOY

There is an emotional duality peculiar to Rosh HaShana. It is a time of fear and awe, a day of judgment. That is the reason we do not say Hallel.

The ministering angels said before the Holy One, blessed be He: Why do not the Israelites sing a song before You on the New Year and on the Day of Atonement? He answered them: Would that be possible? The King sits on the throne of Judgment, with the books of those destined to live and destined to die before Him. Can Israel sing a song at such a time? (*Rosh HaShana* 32b)

# סימנים

*Many have the custom to eat the following symbolic foods on* ראש השנה *and to say the accompanying blessings.*

תמרים

יְהִי רָצוֹן מִלְּפָנֶיךָ יהוה אֱלֹהֵינוּ וֵאלֹהֵי אֲבוֹתֵינוּ
שֶׁיִּתַּמּוּ שׂוֹנְאֵינוּ.

רימון

יְהִי רָצוֹן מִלְּפָנֶיךָ יהוה אֱלֹהֵינוּ וֵאלֹהֵי אֲבוֹתֵינוּ
שֶׁנִּרְבֶּה זְכֻיּוֹת כְּרִמּוֹן.

רוביא (חילבה)

בָּרוּךְ אַתָּה יהוה אֱלֹהֵינוּ מֶלֶךְ הָעוֹלָם, בּוֹרֵא פְּרִי הָאֲדָמָה.
יְהִי רָצוֹן מִלְּפָנֶיךָ יהוה אֱלֹהֵינוּ וֵאלֹהֵי אֲבוֹתֵינוּ
שֶׁיִּרְבּוּ זְכֻיּוֹתֵינוּ.

---

Abaye said: Since omens are significant, one should make a habit, at the beginning of the year, to eat pumpkin, fenugreek, leek, beet and dates [since they grow in profusion and are a symbol of prosperity]. (*Horayot* 12a)

There are many other customs and local traditions. In France in the twelfth century the custom was to eat red apples; in Provence it was grapes, figs, a calf's head, and anything new, easily digested, and tasty (*Maḥzor Vitry*). Many have the custom not to eat nuts on Rosh HaShana.

CARE FOR THE POOR

One should invite to one's table the poor and the lonely so that they too may enjoy the festive occasion. One should send gifts to the poor, as it is written: "Go and enjoy choice food and sweet drinks, and send some to those who have nothing prepared" (Neh. 8:10).

While one eats and drinks oneself, it is his duty to feed the stranger, the orphan, the widow and other poor and unfortunate people, for he who locks the doors of his courtyard and eats and drinks with his wife and

ON LEEK

יְהִי רָצוֹן May it be Your will,
LORD our God and God of our ancestors,
that our enemies be cut off.

ON BEET

יְהִי רָצוֹן May it be Your will,
LORD our God and God of our ancestors,
that our enemies vanish.

ON SQUASH

יְהִי רָצוֹן May it be Your will,
LORD our God and God of our ancestors,
that the evil decree against us be torn apart,
and our merit be read out before You.

ON THE HEAD OF A SHEEP, OR A FISH

יְהִי רָצוֹן May it be Your will,
LORD our God and God of our ancestors,
that we be the head, not the tail.

ON FISH

יְהִי רָצוֹן May it be Your will,
LORD our God and God of our ancestors,
that we multiply like fish.

---

For this reason it is fit that we celebrate Rosh HaShana as a festive day, but since it is a day of judgment for all living things it is also fit that we observe Rosh HaShana with greater fear and awe than other festive days. (*Sefer HaḤinukh*, 311)

Usually, a person who has a judgment pending against him dresses in black and neglects his appearance in worry of the outcome. Israel however is different. They dress in white, they eat, drink and rejoice in the knowledge that God will perform miracles on their behalf [and forgive them]. (Talmud Yerushalmi, *Rosh HaShana* 1:3)

כרתי (כרישה)

יְהִי רָצוֹן מִלְּפָנֶיךָ יהוה אֱלֹהֵינוּ וֵאלֹהֵי אֲבוֹתֵינוּ
שֶׁיִּכָּרְתוּ שׂוֹנְאֵינוּ.

סלק

יְהִי רָצוֹן מִלְּפָנֶיךָ יהוה אֱלֹהֵינוּ וֵאלֹהֵי אֲבוֹתֵינוּ
שֶׁיִּסְתַּלְּקוּ שׂוֹנְאֵינוּ.

קרא (דלעת קטנה)

יְהִי רָצוֹן מִלְּפָנֶיךָ יהוה אֱלֹהֵינוּ וֵאלֹהֵי אֲבוֹתֵינוּ
שֶׁתִּקְרַע רֹעַ גְּזַר דִּינֵנוּ, וְיִקָּרְאוּ לְפָנֶיךָ זְכֻיּוֹתֵינוּ.

ראש כבש, או דג

יְהִי רָצוֹן מִלְּפָנֶיךָ יהוה אֱלֹהֵינוּ וֵאלֹהֵי אֲבוֹתֵינוּ
שֶׁנִּהְיֶה לְרֹאשׁ וְלֹא לְזָנָב.

דגים

יְהִי רָצוֹן מִלְּפָנֶיךָ יהוה אֱלֹהֵינוּ וֵאלֹהֵי אֲבוֹתֵינוּ
שֶׁנִּפְרֶה וְנִרְבֶּה כְּדָגִים.

---

Yet it is also a day of joy. When Ezra and Nehemiah convened a national assembly on the first of Tishrei and Ezra read the Torah to the people, the crowd, realizing how far it had drifted from God's law, began to weep. Nehemiah told them not to weep, "For the joy of the Lord is your strength" (Neh. 8:10).

It is out of kindness toward His creatures that the Lord remembers them and reviews their deeds year after year on Rosh HaShana, that their sins may not grow too numerous, that there may be room for forgiveness, and being few, He may forgive them. For if He were not to remember them for a long time, their sins would multiply to such an extent as to doom the world, God forbid. So this revered day assures the world of survival.

# Birkat HaMazon / Grace after Meals

שִׁיר הַמַּעֲלוֹת A song of ascents. When the LORD brought back the exiles of Zion we were like people who dream. Then were our mouths filled with laughter, and our tongues with songs of joy. Then was it said among the nations, "The LORD has done great things for them." The LORD did do great things for us and we rejoiced. Bring back our exiles, LORD, like streams in a dry land. May those who sowed in tears, reap in joy. May one who goes out weeping, carrying a bag of seed, come back with songs of joy, carrying his sheaves. *Ps. 126*

*Some say:*

תְּהִלַּת My mouth shall speak the praise of God, and all creatures shall bless His holy name for ever and all time. *Ps. 145*
We will bless God now and for ever. *Ps. 115*
Halleluya! Thank the LORD for He is good; His loving-kindness is for ever. *Ps. 136*
Who can tell of the LORD's mighty acts and make all His praise be heard? *Ps. 106*

## ZIMMUN / INVITATION

*When three or more men say Birkat HaMazon together, the following zimmun is said. When three or more women say Birkat HaMazon, substitute "Friends" for "Gentlemen." The leader should ask permission from those with precedence to lead the Birkat HaMazon.*

*Leader* Gentlemen, let us say grace.

*Others* May the name of the LORD be blessed from now and for ever. *Ps. 113*

*Leader* May the name of the LORD be blessed from now and for ever.
With your permission, (my father and teacher / my mother and teacher / the Kohanim present / our teacher the Rabbi / the master of this house / the mistress of this house)
my masters and teachers,
let us bless (*in a minyan:* our God,)
the One from whose food we have eaten.

*Others* Blessed be (*in a minyan:* our God,) the One from whose food we have eaten, and by whose goodness we live.

**People present who have not taken part in the meal say:*
*Blessed be (*in a minyan:* our God,) the One whose name is continually blessed for ever and all time.

*Leader* Blessed be (*in a minyan:* our God,) the One from whose food we have eaten, and by whose goodness we live.
Blessed be He, and blessed be His name.

# ברכת המזון

תהלים קכו שִׁיר הַמַּעֲלוֹת, בְּשׁוּב יהוה אֶת־שִׁיבַת צִיּוֹן, הָיִינוּ כְּחֹלְמִים: אָז יִמָּלֵא
שְׂחוֹק פִּינוּ וּלְשׁוֹנֵנוּ רִנָּה, אָז יֹאמְרוּ בַגּוֹיִם הִגְדִּיל יהוה לַעֲשׂוֹת
עִם־אֵלֶּה: הִגְדִּיל יהוה לַעֲשׂוֹת עִמָּנוּ, הָיִינוּ שְׂמֵחִים: שׁוּבָה יהוה
אֶת־שְׁבִיתֵנוּ, כַּאֲפִיקִים בַּנֶּגֶב: הַזֹּרְעִים בְּדִמְעָה בְּרִנָּה יִקְצֹרוּ: הָלוֹךְ
יֵלֵךְ וּבָכֹה נֹשֵׂא מֶשֶׁךְ־הַזָּרַע, בֹּא־יָבֹא בְרִנָּה נֹשֵׂא אֲלֻמֹּתָיו:

*Some say:*

תהלים קמה תהלים קטו תְּהִלַּת יהוה יְדַבֶּר פִּי, וִיבָרֵךְ כָּל־בָּשָׂר שֵׁם קָדְשׁוֹ לְעוֹלָם וָעֶד: וַאֲנַחְנוּ
תהלים קלו נְבָרֵךְ יָהּ מֵעַתָּה וְעַד־עוֹלָם, הַלְלוּיָהּ: הוֹדוּ לַיהוה כִּי־טוֹב, כִּי לְעוֹלָם
תהלים קו חַסְדּוֹ: מִי יְמַלֵּל גְּבוּרוֹת יהוה, יַשְׁמִיעַ כָּל־תְּהִלָּתוֹ:

## סדר הזימון

*When three or more men say* ברכת המזון *together, the following* זימון *is said.*
*When three or more women say* ברכת המזון*, substitute* חֲבֵרוֹתַי *for* רַבּוֹתַי*.*
*The leader should ask permission from those with precedence to lead the* ברכת המזון*.*

*Leader* רַבּוֹתַי, נְבָרֵךְ.

תהלים קיג *Others* יְהִי שֵׁם יהוה מְבֹרָךְ מֵעַתָּה וְעַד־עוֹלָם:

*Leader* יְהִי שֵׁם יהוה מְבֹרָךְ מֵעַתָּה וְעַד־עוֹלָם:
בִּרְשׁוּת (אָבִי מוֹרִי / אִמִּי מוֹרָתִי / כֹּהֲנִים / מוֹרֵנוּ הָרַב /
בַּעַל הַבַּיִת הַזֶּה / בַּעֲלַת הַבַּיִת הַזֶּה)
מָרָנָן וְרַבָּנָן וְרַבּוֹתַי
נְבָרֵךְ (במנין: אֱלֹהֵינוּ) שֶׁאָכַלְנוּ מִשֶּׁלּוֹ.

*Others* בָּרוּךְ (במנין: אֱלֹהֵינוּ) שֶׁאָכַלְנוּ מִשֶּׁלּוֹ וּבְטוּבוֹ חָיִינוּ.

**People present who have not taken part in the meal say:*

*בָּרוּךְ (במנין: אֱלֹהֵינוּ) וּמְבֹרָךְ שְׁמוֹ תָּמִיד לְעוֹלָם וָעֶד.

*Leader* בָּרוּךְ (במנין: אֱלֹהֵינוּ) שֶׁאָכַלְנוּ מִשֶּׁלּוֹ וּבְטוּבוֹ חָיִינוּ.
בָּרוּךְ הוּא וּבָרוּךְ שְׁמוֹ.

BLESSING OF NOURISHMENT

בָּרוּךְ Blessed are You, Lord our God,
King of the Universe,
who in His goodness feeds the whole world
with grace, kindness and compassion.
He gives food to all living things,
for His kindness is for ever.
Because of His continual great goodness,
we have never lacked food,
nor may we ever lack it,
for the sake of His great name.
For He is God who feeds and sustains all,
does good to all,
and prepares food for all creatures He has created.
As it is said:
"You open Your hand, *Ps. 145*
and satisfy every living thing with favor."
Blessed are You, Lord, who feeds all.

BLESSING OF LAND

נוֹדֶה We thank You, Lord our God,
for having granted as a heritage to our ancestors
a desirable, good and spacious land;
for bringing us out, Lord our God, from the land of Egypt,
freeing us from the house of slavery;
for Your covenant which You sealed in our flesh;
for Your Torah which You taught us;
for Your laws which You made known to us;
for the life, grace and kindness
You have bestowed on us;
and for the food
by which You continually feed and sustain us,
every day, every season, every hour.

ברכת הזן

בָּרוּךְ אַתָּה יהוה אֱלֹהֵינוּ מֶלֶךְ הָעוֹלָם
הַזָּן אֶת הָעוֹלָם כֻּלּוֹ בְּטוּבוֹ
בְּחֵן בְּחֶסֶד וּבְרַחֲמִים
הוּא נוֹתֵן לֶחֶם לְכָל בָּשָׂר כִּי לְעוֹלָם חַסְדּוֹ.
וּבְטוּבוֹ הַגָּדוֹל, תָּמִיד לֹא חָסַר לָנוּ
וְאַל יֶחְסַר לָנוּ מָזוֹן לְעוֹלָם וָעֶד
בַּעֲבוּר שְׁמוֹ הַגָּדוֹל.
כִּי הוּא אֵל זָן וּמְפַרְנֵס לַכֹּל
וּמֵטִיב לַכֹּל, וּמֵכִין מָזוֹן לְכָל בְּרִיּוֹתָיו אֲשֶׁר בָּרָא.
כָּאָמוּר: פּוֹתֵחַ אֶת־יָדֶךָ וּמַשְׂבִּיעַ לְכָל־חַי רָצוֹן: תהלים קמה
בָּרוּךְ אַתָּה יהוה, הַזָּן אֶת הַכֹּל.

ברכת הארץ

נוֹדֶה לְּךָ, יהוה אֱלֹהֵינוּ
עַל שֶׁהִנְחַלְתָּ לַאֲבוֹתֵינוּ אֶרֶץ חֶמְדָּה טוֹבָה וּרְחָבָה
וְעַל שֶׁהוֹצֵאתָנוּ יהוה אֱלֹהֵינוּ מֵאֶרֶץ מִצְרַיִם
וּפְדִיתָנוּ מִבֵּית עֲבָדִים
וְעַל בְּרִיתְךָ שֶׁחָתַמְתָּ בִּבְשָׂרֵנוּ
וְעַל תּוֹרָתְךָ שֶׁלִּמַּדְתָּנוּ
וְעַל חֻקֶּיךָ שֶׁהוֹדַעְתָּנוּ
וְעַל חַיִּים חֵן וָחֶסֶד שֶׁחוֹנַנְתָּנוּ
וְעַל אֲכִילַת מָזוֹן שָׁאַתָּה זָן וּמְפַרְנֵס אוֹתָנוּ תָּמִיד
בְּכָל יוֹם וּבְכָל עֵת וּבְכָל שָׁעָה.

וְעַל הַכֹּל For all this, LORD our God,
we thank and bless You.
May Your name be blessed continually
by the mouth of all that lives, for ever and all time –
for so it is written:
"You will eat and be satisfied, *Deut. 8*
then you shall bless the LORD your God
for the good land He has given you."
Blessed are You, LORD,
for the land and for the food.

BLESSING FOR JERUSALEM

רַחֵם נָא Have compassion, please,
LORD our God,
on Israel Your people,
on Jerusalem Your city,
on Zion the dwelling place of Your glory,
on the royal house of David Your anointed,
and on the great and holy House that bears Your name.
Our God, our Father,
tend us, feed us,
sustain us and support us,
relieve us and send us relief,
LORD our God,
swiftly from all our troubles.
Please, LORD our God,
do not make us dependent
on the gifts or loans of other people,
but only on Your full, open, holy and generous hand
so that we may suffer
neither shame nor humiliation
for ever and all time.

וְעַל הַכֹּל, יהוה אֱלֹהֵינוּ
אֲנַחְנוּ מוֹדִים לָךְ וּמְבָרְכִים אוֹתָךְ
יִתְבָּרַךְ שִׁמְךָ בְּפִי כָּל חַי תָּמִיד לְעוֹלָם וָעֶד
כַּכָּתוּב:
וְאָכַלְתָּ וְשָׂבָעְתָּ, וּבֵרַכְתָּ אֶת־יהוה אֱלֹהֶיךָ דברים ח
עַל־הָאָרֶץ הַטֹּבָה אֲשֶׁר נָתַן־לָךְ:
בָּרוּךְ אַתָּה יהוה
עַל הָאָרֶץ וְעַל הַמָּזוֹן.

ברכת ירושלים

רַחֵם נָא, יהוה אֱלֹהֵינוּ
עַל יִשְׂרָאֵל עַמֶּךָ
וְעַל יְרוּשָׁלַיִם עִירֶךָ
וְעַל צִיּוֹן מִשְׁכַּן כְּבוֹדֶךָ
וְעַל מַלְכוּת בֵּית דָּוִד מְשִׁיחֶךָ
וְעַל הַבַּיִת הַגָּדוֹל וְהַקָּדוֹשׁ שֶׁנִּקְרָא שִׁמְךָ עָלָיו.
אֱלֹהֵינוּ, אָבִינוּ
רְעֵנוּ, זוּנֵנוּ, פַּרְנְסֵנוּ וְכַלְכְּלֵנוּ
וְהַרְוִיחֵנוּ, וְהַרְוַח לָנוּ יהוה אֱלֹהֵינוּ מְהֵרָה מִכָּל צָרוֹתֵינוּ.
וְנָא אַל תַּצְרִיכֵנוּ, יהוה אֱלֹהֵינוּ
לֹא לִידֵי מַתְּנַת בָּשָׂר וָדָם
וְלֹא לִידֵי הַלְוָאָתָם
כִּי אִם לְיָדְךָ הַמְּלֵאָה, הַפְּתוּחָה, הַקְּדוֹשָׁה וְהָרְחָבָה
שֶׁלֹּא נֵבוֹשׁ וְלֹא נִכָּלֵם לְעוֹלָם וָעֶד.

*On Shabbat, say:*

רְצֵה Favor and strengthen us, LORD our God,
through Your commandments,
especially through the commandment of the seventh day,
this great and holy Sabbath.
For it is, for You, a great and holy day.
On it we cease work and rest in love
in accord with Your will's commandment.
May it be Your will, LORD our God,
to grant us rest without distress,
grief, or lament on our day of rest.
May You show us the consolation of Zion Your city,
and the rebuilding of Jerusalem Your holy city,
for You are the Master of salvation and consolation.

אֱלֹהֵינוּ Our God and God of our ancestors,
may there rise, come, reach, appear, be favored, heard,
regarded and remembered before You,
our recollection and remembrance,
as well as the remembrance of our ancestors,
and of the Messiah, son of David Your servant,
and of Jerusalem Your holy city,
and of all Your people the house of Israel –
for deliverance and well-being,
grace, loving-kindness and compassion,
life and peace, on this day of Remembrance.
On it remember us, LORD our God, for good;
recollect us for blessing,
and deliver us for good lives.
In accord with Your promise of salvation and compassion,
spare us and be gracious to us;
have compassion on us and deliver us,
for our eyes are turned to You because You are God,
gracious and compassionate King.

*On* שבת*, say:*

רְצֵה וְהַחֲלִיצֵנוּ, יהוה אֱלֹהֵינוּ, בְּמִצְוֹתֶיךָ
וּבְמִצְוַת יוֹם הַשְּׁבִיעִי הַשַּׁבָּת הַגָּדוֹל וְהַקָּדוֹשׁ הַזֶּה
כִּי יוֹם זֶה גָּדוֹל וְקָדוֹשׁ הוּא לְפָנֶיךָ
לִשְׁבָּת בּוֹ, וְלָנוּחַ בּוֹ בְּאַהֲבָה כְּמִצְוַת רְצוֹנֶךָ
וּבִרְצוֹנְךָ הָנִיחַ לָנוּ, יהוה אֱלֹהֵינוּ
שֶׁלֹּא תְהֵא צָרָה וְיָגוֹן וַאֲנָחָה בְּיוֹם מְנוּחָתֵנוּ
וְהַרְאֵנוּ, יהוה אֱלֹהֵינוּ, בְּנֶחָמַת צִיּוֹן עִירֶךָ
וּבְבִנְיַן יְרוּשָׁלַיִם עִיר קָדְשֶׁךָ
כִּי אַתָּה הוּא בַּעַל הַיְשׁוּעוֹת וּבַעַל הַנֶּחָמוֹת.

אֱלֹהֵינוּ וֵאלֹהֵי אֲבוֹתֵינוּ
יַעֲלֶה וְיָבוֹא וְיַגִּיעַ, וְיֵרָאֶה וְיֵרָצֶה וְיִשָּׁמַע
וְיִפָּקֵד וְיִזָּכֵר זִכְרוֹנֵנוּ וּפִקְדוֹנֵנוּ, וְזִכְרוֹן אֲבוֹתֵינוּ
וְזִכְרוֹן מָשִׁיחַ בֶּן דָּוִד עַבְדֶּךָ
וְזִכְרוֹן יְרוּשָׁלַיִם עִיר קָדְשֶׁךָ
וְזִכְרוֹן כָּל עַמְּךָ בֵּית יִשְׂרָאֵל
לְפָנֶיךָ, לִפְלֵיטָה לְטוֹבָה, לְחֵן וּלְחֶסֶד וּלְרַחֲמִים
לְחַיִּים וּלְשָׁלוֹם בְּיוֹם הַזִּכָּרוֹן הַזֶּה.
זָכְרֵנוּ יהוה אֱלֹהֵינוּ בּוֹ לְטוֹבָה
וּפָקְדֵנוּ בוֹ לִבְרָכָה
וְהוֹשִׁיעֵנוּ בוֹ לְחַיִּים טוֹבִים.
וּבִדְבַר יְשׁוּעָה וְרַחֲמִים, חוּס וְחָנֵּנוּ וְרַחֵם עָלֵינוּ, וְהוֹשִׁיעֵנוּ
כִּי אֵלֶיךָ עֵינֵינוּ, כִּי אֵל מֶלֶךְ חַנּוּן וְרַחוּם אָתָּה.

וּבְנֵה And may Jerusalem the holy city be rebuilt soon, in our time.
Blessed are You, LORD, who in His compassion
will rebuild Jerusalem. Amen.

BLESSING OF GOD'S GOODNESS

בָּרוּךְ Blessed are You, LORD our God, King of the Universe –
God our Father, our King, our Sovereign,
our Creator, our Redeemer, our Maker,
our Holy One, the Holy One of Jacob.
He is our Shepherd, Israel's Shepherd,
the good King who does good to all.
Every day He has done, is doing, and will do good to us.
He has acted, is acting, and will always act kindly toward us for ever,
granting us grace, kindness and compassion, relief and rescue,
prosperity, blessing, redemption and comfort,
sustenance and support, compassion, life, peace and all good things,
and of all good things may He never let us lack.

ADDITIONAL REQUESTS

הָרַחֲמָן May the Compassionate One reign over us
for ever and all time.
May the Compassionate One be blessed
in heaven and on earth.
May the Compassionate One be praised
from generation to generation,
be glorified by us to all eternity,
and honored among us for ever and all time.
May the Compassionate One
grant us an honorable livelihood.
May the Compassionate One break the yoke from our neck
and lead us upright to our land.
May the Compassionate One send us many blessings to this house
and this table at which we have eaten.
May the Compassionate One send us Elijah the prophet –
may he be remembered for good –
to bring us good tidings of salvation and consolation.

וּבְנֵה יְרוּשָׁלַיִם עִיר הַקֹּדֶשׁ בִּמְהֵרָה בְיָמֵינוּ.
בָּרוּךְ אַתָּה יהוה, בּוֹנֵה בְרַחֲמָיו יְרוּשָׁלָיִם, אָמֵן.

ברכת הטוב והמטיב

בָּרוּךְ אַתָּה יהוה אֱלֹהֵינוּ מֶלֶךְ הָעוֹלָם
הָאֵל אָבִינוּ, מַלְכֵּנוּ, אַדִּירֵנוּ
בּוֹרְאֵנוּ, גּוֹאֲלֵנוּ, יוֹצְרֵנוּ, קְדוֹשֵׁנוּ, קְדוֹשׁ יַעֲקֹב
רוֹעֵנוּ, רוֹעֵה יִשְׂרָאֵל, הַמֶּלֶךְ הַטּוֹב וְהַמֵּיטִיב לַכֹּל, שֶׁבְּכָל יוֹם וָיוֹם
הוּא הֵיטִיב, הוּא מֵיטִיב, הוּא יֵיטִיב לָנוּ
הוּא גְמָלָנוּ, הוּא גוֹמְלֵנוּ, הוּא יִגְמְלֵנוּ לָעַד
לְחֵן וּלְחֶסֶד וּלְרַחֲמִים, וּלְרֶוַח, הַצָּלָה וְהַצְלָחָה
בְּרָכָה וִישׁוּעָה, נֶחָמָה, פַּרְנָסָה וְכַלְכָּלָה
וְרַחֲמִים וְחַיִּים וְשָׁלוֹם וְכָל טוֹב, וּמִכָּל טוּב לְעוֹלָם אַל יְחַסְּרֵנוּ.

בקשות נוספות

הָרַחֲמָן הוּא יִמְלֹךְ עָלֵינוּ לְעוֹלָם וָעֶד.
הָרַחֲמָן הוּא יִתְבָּרַךְ בַּשָּׁמַיִם וּבָאָרֶץ.
הָרַחֲמָן הוּא יִשְׁתַּבַּח לְדוֹר דּוֹרִים, וְיִתְפָּאַר בָּנוּ לָעַד וּלְנֵצַח נְצָחִים
וְיִתְהַדַּר בָּנוּ לָעַד וּלְעוֹלְמֵי עוֹלָמִים.
הָרַחֲמָן הוּא יְפַרְנְסֵנוּ בְּכָבוֹד.
הָרַחֲמָן הוּא יִשְׁבֹּר עֻלֵּנוּ מֵעַל צַוָּארֵנוּ
וְהוּא יוֹלִיכֵנוּ קוֹמְמִיּוּת לְאַרְצֵנוּ.
הָרַחֲמָן הוּא יִשְׁלַח לָנוּ בְּרָכָה מְרֻבָּה בַּבַּיִת הַזֶּה
וְעַל שֻׁלְחָן זֶה שֶׁאָכַלְנוּ עָלָיו.
הָרַחֲמָן הוּא יִשְׁלַח לָנוּ אֶת אֵלִיָּהוּ הַנָּבִיא זָכוּר לַטּוֹב
וִיבַשֶּׂר לָנוּ בְּשׂוֹרוֹת טוֹבוֹת יְשׁוּעוֹת וְנֶחָמוֹת.

May the Compassionate One bless
the state of Israel,
first flowering of our redemption.
May the Compassionate One bless
the members of Israel's Defense Forces,
who stand guard over our land.

*A guest says:*

יְהִי רָצוֹן May it be Your will that the master of this house shall not suffer shame in this world, nor humiliation in the World to Come. May all he owns prosper greatly, and may his and our possessions be successful and close to hand. Let not the Accuser hold sway over his deeds or ours, and may no thought of sin, iniquity or transgression enter him or us from now and for evermore.

הָרַחֲמָן May the Compassionate One bless –

*When eating at one's own table, say (include the words in parentheses that apply):*
me (my wife/husband, / my father, my teacher / my mother,
my teacher/ my children,) and all that is mine,

*A guest at someone else's table says (include the words in parentheses that apply):*
the master of this house, him (and his wife,
the mistress of this house / and his children,) and all that is his,

*Children at their parents' table say (include the words in parentheses that apply):*
my father, my teacher, (master of this house,) and my mother,
my teacher, (mistress of this house,) them, their household,
their children, and all that is theirs.

*For all other guests, add:*
and all the diners here,

together with us and all that is ours.
Just as our forefathers
Abraham, Isaac and Jacob were blessed in all, from all, with all,
so may He bless all of us together
with a complete blessing,
and let us say: Amen.

הָרַחֲמָן הוּא יְבָרֵךְ אֶת מְדִינַת יִשְׂרָאֵל
רֵאשִׁית צְמִיחַת גְּאֻלָּתֵנוּ.
הָרַחֲמָן הוּא יְבָרֵךְ אֶת חַיָּלֵי צְבָא הַהֲגָנָה לְיִשְׂרָאֵל
הָעוֹמְדִים עַל מִשְׁמַר אַרְצֵנוּ.

*A guest says:*

יְהִי רָצוֹן שֶׁלֹּא יֵבוֹשׁ בַּעַל הַבַּיִת בָּעוֹלָם הַזֶּה, וְלֹא יִכָּלֵם לָעוֹלָם הַבָּא, וְיַצְלִיחַ מְאֹד בְּכָל נְכָסָיו, וְיִהְיוּ נְכָסָיו וּנְכָסֵינוּ מֻצְלָחִים וּקְרוֹבִים לָעִיר, וְאַל יִשְׁלֹט שָׂטָן לֹא בְּמַעֲשֵׂה יָדָיו וְלֹא בְּמַעֲשֵׂה יָדֵינוּ. וְאַל יִזְדַּקֵּק לֹא לְפָנָיו וְלֹא לְפָנֵינוּ שׁוּם דְּבַר הִרְהוּר חֵטְא, עֲבֵירָה וְעָוֹן, מֵעַתָּה וְעַד עוֹלָם.

הָרַחֲמָן הוּא יְבָרֵךְ

*When eating at one's own table, say (include the words in parentheses that apply):*

אוֹתִי (וְאֶת אִשְׁתִּי / וְאֶת בַּעְלִי / וְאֶת אָבִי מוֹרִי / וְאֶת אִמִּי מוֹרָתִי / וְאֶת זַרְעִי) וְאֶת כָּל אֲשֶׁר לִי.

*A guest at someone else's table says (include the words in parentheses that apply):*

אֶת בַּעַל הַבַּיִת הַזֶּה, אוֹתוֹ (וְאֶת אִשְׁתּוֹ בַּעֲלַת הַבַּיִת הַזֶּה / וְאֶת זַרְעוֹ) וְאֶת כָּל אֲשֶׁר לוֹ.

*Children at their parents' table say (include the words in parentheses that apply):*

אֶת אָבִי מוֹרִי (בַּעַל הַבַּיִת הַזֶּה), וְאֶת אִמִּי מוֹרָתִי (בַּעֲלַת הַבַּיִת הַזֶּה), אוֹתָם וְאֶת בֵּיתָם וְאֶת זַרְעָם וְאֶת כָּל אֲשֶׁר לָהֶם

*For all other guests, add:*

וְאֶת כָּל הַמְסֻבִּין כָּאן

אוֹתָנוּ וְאֶת כָּל אֲשֶׁר לָנוּ
כְּמוֹ שֶׁנִּתְבָּרְכוּ אֲבוֹתֵינוּ
אַבְרָהָם יִצְחָק וְיַעֲקֹב, בַּכֹּל, מִכֹּל, כֹּל
כֵּן יְבָרֵךְ אוֹתָנוּ כֻּלָּנוּ יַחַד בִּבְרָכָה שְׁלֵמָה, וְנֹאמַר אָמֵן.

בַּמָּרוֹם On high, may grace be invoked for them and for us,
as a safeguard of peace.
May we receive a blessing from the LORD
and a just reward from the God of our salvation,
and may we find grace and good favor in the eyes of God and man.

*On Shabbat:* May the Compassionate One let us inherit
the time, that will be entirely Shabbat
and rest for life everlasting.

May the Compassionate One renew for us this year,
for good and blessing.

הָרַחֲמָן May the Compassionate One make us worthy
of the Messianic Age and life in the World to Come.
He is a tower of salvation to His king, *II Sam. 22*
showing kindness to His anointed,
to David and his descendants for ever.
He who makes peace in His high places,
may He make peace for us and all Israel,
and let us say: Amen.

יְראוּ Fear the LORD, you His holy ones; *Ps. 34*
those who fear Him lack nothing.
Young lions may grow weak and hungry,
but those who seek the LORD lack no good thing.
Thank the LORD for He is good; *Ps. 118*
His loving-kindness is for ever.
You open Your hand, and satisfy every living thing with favor. *Ps. 145*
Blessed is the person who trusts in the LORD, *Jer. 17*
whose trust is in the LORD alone.
Once I was young, and now I am old, *Ps. 37*
yet I have never watched a righteous man forsaken
or his children begging for bread.
The LORD will give His people strength. *Ps. 29*
The LORD will bless His people with peace.

בַּמָּרוֹם יְלַמְּדוּ עֲלֵיהֶם וְעָלֵינוּ זְכוּת שֶׁתְּהֵא לְמִשְׁמֶרֶת שָׁלוֹם
וְנִשָּׂא בְרָכָה מֵאֵת יהוה וּצְדָקָה מֵאֱלֹהֵי יִשְׁעֵנוּ
וְנִמְצָא חֵן וְשֵׂכֶל טוֹב בְּעֵינֵי אֱלֹהִים וְאָדָם.

בשבת: הָרַחֲמָן הוּא יַנְחִילֵנוּ
יוֹם שֶׁכֻּלּוֹ שַׁבָּת וּמְנוּחָה לְחַיֵּי הָעוֹלָמִים.

הָרַחֲמָן הוּא יְחַדֵּשׁ עָלֵינוּ
אֶת הַשָּׁנָה הַזֹּאת לְטוֹבָה וְלִבְרָכָה.

הָרַחֲמָן הוּא יְזַכֵּנוּ לִימוֹת הַמָּשִׁיחַ וּלְחַיֵּי הָעוֹלָם הַבָּא
מִגְדּוֹל יְשׁוּעוֹת מַלְכּוֹ שמואל ב׳ כב
וְעֹשֶׂה־חֶסֶד לִמְשִׁיחוֹ, לְדָוִד וּלְזַרְעוֹ עַד־עוֹלָם:
עֹשֶׂה שָׁלוֹם בִּמְרוֹמָיו
הוּא יַעֲשֶׂה שָׁלוֹם עָלֵינוּ וְעַל כָּל יִשְׂרָאֵל
וְאִמְרוּ אָמֵן.

יְראוּ אֶת־יהוה קְדֹשָׁיו, כִּי־אֵין מַחְסוֹר לִירֵאָיו: תהלים לד
כְּפִירִים רָשׁוּ וְרָעֵבוּ, וְדֹרְשֵׁי יהוה לֹא־יַחְסְרוּ כָל־טוֹב:
הוֹדוּ לַיהוה כִּי־טוֹב, כִּי לְעוֹלָם חַסְדּוֹ: תהלים קיח
פּוֹתֵחַ אֶת־יָדֶךָ, וּמַשְׂבִּיעַ לְכָל־חַי רָצוֹן: תהלים קמה
בָּרוּךְ הַגֶּבֶר אֲשֶׁר יִבְטַח בַּיהוה, וְהָיָה יהוה מִבְטַחוֹ: ירמיה יז
נַעַר הָיִיתִי גַּם־זָקַנְתִּי תהלים לז
וְלֹא־רָאִיתִי צַדִּיק נֶעֱזָב וְזַרְעוֹ מְבַקֶּשׁ־לָחֶם:
יהוה עֹז לְעַמּוֹ יִתֵּן תהלים כט
יהוה יְבָרֵךְ אֶת־עַמּוֹ בַשָּׁלוֹם:

# משנה ראש השנה

# MISHNA ROSH HASHANA

## NOTE TO COMMENTARY ON THE MISHNAYOT

References to the Mishna are often confusing, as the division of each chapter into individual mishnayot changes from edition to edition. Therefore, we have reluctantly adopted the policy of referencing mishnayot according to the page number of the Babylonian Talmud where the mishna appears, such as: Mishna, *Menaḥot* 65a. Mishnayot which have no Talmud tractate are also referenced according to the Vilna edition, such as: Mishna, *Bikkurim* 1:10. One obvious exception is the references within *Rosh HaShana*, where cross-references to the mishna, translation and notes appear according to the order we have followed here.

Likewise, references to the *Tosefta* are according to the Vilna edition. (Despite some other editions being considered more reliable, the Vilna Talmud edition is still more accessible, and in none of the references does the edition make any substantial difference.)

References to the Jerusalem Talmud have the chapter and mishna according to the Venice 1523 edition, which is the cornerstone for most printed editions. We have used the Hebrew name Yerushalmi, for example, "Yerushalmi, *Ḥagiga* 2:2."

Unless otherwise specified, a citation of the Talmud refers to the Babylonian Talmud, and a citation of a page or a commentary refers to *Massekhet Rosh HaShana*.

Citations of the Rif and his commentators are according to the pages of *Hilkhot Rav Alfas* printed at the back of the Vilna edition – for example, "*Nimukei Yosef, Sanhedrin* 4b," does not refer to page 4b of the Talmud, but rather to the page numbering of the *Hilkhot Rav Alfas* section in the back of the book (which, in this case, corresponds to page 25a in the Talmud).

In the commentary to the Maḥzor, the names Maimonides and Nahmanides are used; in these notes, we have used the Hebrew acronyms Rambam and Ramban.

The *Tur, Shulḥan Arukh* and commentaries around them are written in longhand; however, we have abbreviated the names of their components, such as, "*Shulḥan Arukh*, ḤM 34:16." OḤ stands for *Oraḥ Ḥayyim*, YD for *Yoreh De'ah*, and ḤM for *Ḥoshen Mishpat* (*Even HaEzer* is not referred to in these notes). Some commentaries only wrote on one of the components, and those we have left unspecified, such as "*Magen Avraham* 131:16," omitting OḤ.

Rabbi David Fuchs

# Massekhet Rosh HaShana

## CHAPTER ONE

1 There are four new years:

The first of Nisan is New Year for kings and festivals.

---

the children of Israel were come out of the land of Egypt, *in the fourth year of Solomon's reign over Israel*, in the month *Ziv* [literally, the month of glory], which is the second month…" (1 Kings, 6:1). The sages identified the month Ziv with Iyar (see Rashi ad loc., Yerushalmi *Rosh HaShana* 1:1 and the *Zohar* on *Parashat Bemidbar* for explanations of this identification), concluding that the years of the reign of all Jewish kings begin in Nisan. Even if a king was crowned in Adar he would only reign a month before entering his second year. Both Talmuds (*Rosh HaShana* 2b; Yerushalmi ad loc.) deduce this from the fact that the exodus from Egypt was mentioned in the verse. The Talmud also established that while the New Year for Jewish kings begins in Nisan, the New Year for Gentile monarchs begins in Tishrei.

The existence of a fixed method of counting the years is especially significant in dating legal documents. In the Second Temple period, when Judea had no king, a similar method of counting the years was employed in dating documents. The Talmud calls that system *"minyan shetarot,"* the tally of the documents, beginning one thousand years after the exodus (*Avoda Zara* 10a).

וְלָרְגָלִים *And festivals.* When the calendar is discussed in the Torah, the three pilgramage festivals are always listed chronologically, beginning with Pesaḥ (Ex. 23 and 34; Lev. 22–23; Num. 28–29; Deut. 16).

The Talmud (4a) suggests that this order has ramifications significant beyond establishing the relative importance of the festivals. The Torah (Deut. 23:22) prohibits delaying the fulfillment of one's vows, and the sages interpreted this to prohibit postponement for one year at most. According to Rabbi Shimon, this year is a cycle of pilgrimage festivals, in the order that they appear in the verse. One who vows shortly after Pesaḥ will not violate the prohibition unless he postpones fulfilling his vow for five pilgrimage festivals, i.e. until Sukkot passes a second time. Rabbi Eliezer ben Yaakov agrees that the order of the festivals as they appear in the verse is crucial, though he adopts a much stricter approach. Since Sukkot is the last of the festivals, if one vowed on the eve of Sukkot, he must fulfill that vow by the end of Sukkot,

# מסכת ראש השנה

## פרק ראשון

א אַרְבָּעָה רָאשֵׁי שָׁנִים הֵם:
בְּאֶחָד בְּנִיסָן, רֹאשׁ הַשָּׁנָה לַמְּלָכִים וְלָרְגָלִים

---

CHAPTER ONE

The term "Rosh HaShana" appears only once in the Bible – not in the Torah but in the book of Ezekiel (40:1): "On Rosh HaShana, on the tenth of the month." Rosh HaShana clearly refers here, not to a day, but to the first month of the year. The only month in which the tenth day has special significance is Tishrei. Indeed, the sages taught that the verse is referring to the Yom Kippur of a Jubilee year (*Arakhin* 12a).

If, however, Rosh HaShana indicates "the first month," then it should not refer to Tishrei, but to Nisan, since prior to leaving Egypt the Israelites were explicitly instructed: "This month [Nisan] shall be to you the first of the months" (Ex. 12:2), and the Torah consistently numbers months "the first," "the second," "the third month" etc. on this basis.

The sages resolved this apparent contradiction by distinguishing between four functionally different years. They designated four dates to serve as Rosh HaShana for each of those years – as well as four different times when the world is judged.

The Talmud (20a) reads the word "month" (*Ḥodesh*) in the aforementioned command "This month shall be to you…" as referring to the new moon. This verse is understood to have been spoken as God shows Moses and Aaron the new moon, commanding them to declare a new month only when the new moon is seen. The procedure became known as *Kiddush HaḤodesh* – the consecration of the month.

The mishna does not articulate this logical segue; it moves seamlessly into treatment of the details of the consecration of the month, concentrating on two areas: When is consecration of the month considered so crucial that the laws of Shabbat may be suspended for that purpose; and upon whose testimony can the court rely in order to declare a new month.

רֹאשׁ הַשָּׁנָה לַמְּלָכִים *New Year for kings… Years are numbered in the Bible in relation to the reign of a given king* – "In the four hundred and eightieth year after

The first of Elul is New Year for animal tithes –
Rabbi Elazar and Rabbi Shimon say: This is the first of Tishrei.
The first of Tishrei is New Year for years, and Sabbatical years and Jubilees,
and also for tree-planting and vegetables.
The first of Shevat is New Year for trees – thus Beit Shammai.
Beit Hillel say: This is the fifteenth.

---

on Rosh HaShana in the Remembrances blessing: "This day is the opening of all Your works, a remembrance of the very first day" (page 508), as well as several times in the Rosh HaShana liturgy.

וְלַשְּׁמִטִּין וְלַיּוֹבְלוֹת *Sabbatical years and Jubilees.* The Sabbatical year, with its various laws, begins and ends in Tishrei (see Deut. 31:10). The same is true of the Jubilee year (Lev. 25:9), which tragically, was no longer in practice in the Mishnaic period.

לַנְּטִיעָה וְלַיְּרָקוֹת *Tree-planting and vegetables.* One may not eat the fruits a tree produces during the three years after it was planted, and the fruits that grow in the fourth year must be eaten in Jerusalem. These years are counted from Tishrei, such that a tree planted in Elul completes its first year within a month. Vegetables are tithed immediately after their harvest. Just as Elul distinguishes the calves and lambs of one year from those of the next, so the first of Tishrei is the cut-off date for the vegetables of a given year, and those harvested afterwards are tithed with the produce of the following season.

ראש הַשָּׁנָה לָאִילָן *New Year for trees.* Unlike vegetables, tithed at harvest, the determination of the year to which fruits belong for purposes of tithing takes place while the fruits are still in the early stages of their development. Shevat falls late in winter, when most trees are dormant or blossoming. That year's produce, in terms of both tithes and the Sabbatical year, will develop only in the following months. Beit Shammai rule that every New Year should coincide with a new moon; Beit Hillel, however, hold the critical date to be mid-month, when most of the winter's rain has already fallen (*Rosh HaShana* 14a). The Meiri points out that this marks the midpoint between Tevet, when winter begins in earnest, and Nisan, which opens the spring. The custom to

בְּאֶחָד בֶּאֱלוּל, רֹאשׁ הַשָּׁנָה לְמַעְשַׂר בְּהֵמָה
רַבִּי אֶלְעָזָר וְרַבִּי שִׁמְעוֹן אוֹמְרִים: בְּאֶחָד בְּתִשְׁרֵי
בְּאֶחָד בְּתִשְׁרֵי, רֹאשׁ הַשָּׁנָה לַשָּׁנִים וְלַשְּׁמִטִּין וְלַיּוֹבְלוֹת,
לַנְּטִיעָה וְלַיְּרָקוֹת
בְּאֶחָד בִּשְׁבָט רֹאשׁ הַשָּׁנָה לָאִילָן, כְּדִבְרֵי בֵית שַׁמַּאי
בֵּית הִלֵּל אוֹמְרִים: בַּחֲמִשָּׁה עָשָׂר בּוֹ.

---

eight days later. (Both views were eventually rejected; one who dedicates an offering has a complete cycle of three pilgrimage festivals in which to fulfill his vow, beginning from the time he makes the vow. See Rambam, *Hilkhot Ma'aseh HaKorbanot* 14:13).

רֹאשׁ הַשָּׁנָה לְמַעְשַׂר בְּהֵמָה *New Year for animal tithes.* In Temple times, all livestock were required to be tithed. When the newborn calves and lambs were counted, the tenth animal of each species was designated to be slaughtered and eaten in Jerusalem (Lev. 27:32). If only nine young of a particular species were born on a farm in a given year, no tithe was required, even if a tenth was born in the following year. If nineteen young were born in a given year, only one was designated as an animal tithe, and so on. "New Year for animal tithes," then, was the cut-off point. Any animal born thereafter was attributed to the flock of the following year. Rabbi Elazar and Rabbi Shimon postpone this date by one month, to align the New Years of cattle and of arable produce; however, the majority of the sages rule that the New Year for cattle be the first of Elul, as it is the end of the calving season (*Rosh HaShana* 8a), and enables one to complete his tithing before the Tishrei holidays (*Bekhorot* 57b–58b). The debate remains unresolved: The Rambam rules in accordance with the opinion of Rabbi Elazar and Rabbi Shimon (*Hilkhot Bekhorot* 7:6), and *Sefer Mitzvot Gadol* rules in accordance with the opinion of the first *tanna* cited in the mishna (Positive Commandment 212).

רֹאשׁ הַשָּׁנָה לַשָּׁנִים *New Year for years.* The date of creation is debated in the Talmud (10b–12a); Rabbi Yehoshua suggests the first of Nisan, while Rabbi Eliezer holds that it is the first of Tishrei. This dispute is not decided in the Talmud (10b–12a), but the consensus among later sages was that the world was created in Tishrei. This opinion is also reflected in the additional prayer

2 There are four times when the world is judged:
At Pesaḥ, for the crops;
at Shavuot, for tree fruits;
at Rosh HaShana, all who have come into this world
pass before Him like sheep,
as it is said, "He forms the hearts of all, Ps. 33
and discerns all their deeds";
and at Sukkot they are judged for the water.

---

itself. The interpretation of the term as referring to "sheep," while similar, is a more sympathetic one as it evokes the image of a caring shepherd (cf. Ps. 23:1).

הַיֹּצֵר יַחַד לִבָּם, הַמֵּבִין אֶל־כָּל־מַעֲשֵׂיהֶם *"He forms the hearts of all, and discerns all their deeds."* This verse is understood in the context of the one it immediately follows – "He looks down from the place of His dwelling, at all the inhabitants of earth" – evoking the image of God viewing all the world at a glance (*Rosh HaShana* 18a). The parallelism in the verse moves us from "hearts" to "deeds" and from God's creation to His knowledge of all. While judging the world as a whole, God is aware of our many different actions, an awareness stemming from His intimate knowledge of the "heart." Taken in the context of our mishna, this verse reflects the paradox of divine knowledge, which is simultaneously general and particular (*Tosefot Yom Tov*).

וּבֶחָג, נִדּוֹנִין עַל הַמַּיִם *And at Sukkot they are judged for the water.* By Sukkot, at the threshold of autumn, the wells and reservoirs are empty; the *Hoshanot* recited on Sukkot are requests for rain, and the Four Species of plants represent the world's need for water (*Shibolei HaLeket* 366). This cycle of rain prayers peaks on Hoshana Raba, the last day of the festival, and the final day of judgment for rainfall (Rashi, *Yoma* 21b). The Kabbalists considered Hoshana Raba the culmination of the process of judgment which opened on Rosh HaShana (*Zohar, Parashat Tzav*). The Mishna does not use the names, "Shavuot" and "Sukkot," that we use today. Shavuot is called *Atzeret*, "an Assembley," recalling the day the nation stood as one to receive the Torah (Ramban, Lev. 23:36), while Sukkot, "the time of our rejoicing," is simply called *Ḥag* – "the Festival."

ב בְּאַרְבָּעָה פְרָקִים הָעוֹלָם נִדּוֹן:
בְּפֶסַח, עַל הַתְּבוּאָה
בָּעֲצֶרֶת, עַל פֵּרוֹת הָאִילָן
בְּרֹאשׁ הַשָּׁנָה, כָּל בָּאֵי הָעוֹלָם עוֹבְרִין לְפָנָיו כִּבְנֵי מָרוֹן
שֶׁנֶּאֱמַר: הַיֹּצֵר יַחַד לִבָּם, הַמֵּבִין אֶל־כָּל־מַעֲשֵׂיהֶם: תהלים לג
וּבֶחָג, נִדּוֹנִין עַל הַמַּיִם.

---

eat fruits of the land of Israel on *Tu BiShvat* stems from this mishna (*Magen Avraham* 131:16).

בְּאַרְבָּעָה פְּרָקִים הָעוֹלָם נִדּוֹן *There are four times when the world is judged.* The sages understood that judgment for a given year must take place adjacent to the implementation of that reward or punishment. Failure to do so could lead to a situation where an individual who repented is punished for past crimes. According to this approach, until the consequences of one's actions have been visited upon the world, one can still repent. Consequently, in the spring, judgment for the spring crops is rendered; in the autumn for the autumn rainfall, etc.

בַּפֶּסַח, עַל הַתְּבוּאָה *At Pesaḥ for the crops.* The first grain harvest (that of the barley) begins on the first day of Ḥol HaMo'ed Pesaḥ (Mishna, *Menaḥot* 65a; cf. Deut. 16:8–9 and Rashi ad loc.).

בָּעֲצֶרֶת, עַל פֵּרוֹת הָאִילָן *At Shavuot for fruit trees.* First fruits are brought to the Temple only from Shavuot until Sukkot (Rashi, *Rosh HaShana* 16a, based on Mishna *Bikkurim* 1:10).

כִּבְנֵי מָרוֹן *Like sheep.* The meaning of the term כבני מרון is unclear. Rav Sa'adia Gaon (*Sefer HaEgron*) translates it as "on parade." The Talmud (18a) cites three possible explanations: "sheep," used here, is reflected in the ancient prayer *Untaneh Tokef* – "As a shepherd's searching gaze meets his flock…" (page 546). Another reading, suggested by Shmuel, "Like David's battalions," is an apt metaphor for the judgment that we undergo on Rosh HaShana. Just as soldiers are reviewed and counted before entering battle, but not all of those who set out will return, on Rosh HaShana we are judged for life

3 There are six months for which the messengers go out:
for Nisan because of Pesaḥ,
for Av because of the fast,
for Elul because of Rosh HaShana,
for Tishrei to set the festivals,
for Kislev because of Ḥanukka,
and for Adar because of Purim.
When the Temple stood
they would go out for Iyar also, because of Pesaḥ Katan.

4 There are two months for which one breaks Shabbat:
for Nisan and for Tishrei.
For on these the messengers would go out to Syria,
and by these the dates of the festivals are set.

---

Diaspora communities kept Rosh HaShana on the thirtieth and thirty-first days from the first of Elul. Messengers would set out from Jerusalem immediately after the festival, however, so that the hearts of Diaspora Jews "need not beat [in terror] on Yom Kippur" (Rashi, *Rosh HaShana* 18a).

וּכְשֶׁהָיָה בֵית הַמִּקְדָּשׁ קַיָּם *When the Temple stood.* One who was ritually impure on Pesaḥ could not bring the Paschal lamb then, but had the opportunity to bring it instead a month later. "Pesaḥ Katan" lost its practical significance with the loss of the Temple service. Some commentators point out that, as the Fast of Av was not instituted until this loss, the messengers were dispatched for only six months when the Temple stood as well (Meiri, *Tiferet Yisrael*).

עַל שְׁנֵי חֳדָשִׁים *There are two months.* For these two months, the Shabbat prohibitions were suspended for witnesses to the new moon to enable them to travel to Jerusalem and testify. The messengers could then start out for the Diaspora immediately after Shabbat, avoiding an extra day's delay.

שֶׁבָּהֶן הַשְּׁלוּחִין יוֹצְאִין *For on these the messengers would go out.* The previous mishna listed six months when the messengers would set out to the Diaspora; but Shabbat prohibitions were suspended only for these two months. The commandment to celebrate the festivals "in their due times" (Lev. 23:37) both delays the messengers until the date of Rosh Ḥodesh has been officially declared and affords their mission a special urgency (*Rosh HaShana* 21b, and Rashi ad loc.).

וּבָהֶן מְתַקְּנִין אֶת הַמּוֹעֲדוֹת *By these the dates of the festivals are set.* Not only the timing of Pesaḥ, but also that of Shavuot, is determined by Rosh Ḥodesh

ג עַל שִׁשָּׁה חֳדָשִׁים הַשְּׁלוּחִים יוֹצְאִין:
עַל נִיסָן מִפְּנֵי הַפֶּסַח
עַל אָב מִפְּנֵי הַתַּעֲנִית
עַל אֱלוּל מִפְּנֵי רֹאשׁ הַשָּׁנָה
עַל תִּשְׁרֵי מִפְּנֵי תַקָּנַת הַמּוֹעֲדוֹת
עַל כִּסְלֵו מִפְּנֵי הַחֲנֻכָּה
וְעַל אֲדָר מִפְּנֵי הַפּוּרִים.
וּכְשֶׁהָיָה בֵּית הַמִּקְדָּשׁ קַיָּם
יוֹצְאִין אַף עַל אִיָּר מִפְּנֵי פֶּסַח קָטָן.

ד עַל שְׁנֵי חֳדָשִׁים מְחַלְּלִין אֶת הַשַּׁבָּת:
עַל נִיסָן וְעַל תִּשְׁרֵי
שֶׁבָּהֶן הַשְּׁלוּחִין יוֹצְאִין לְסוּרְיָא
וּבָהֶן מְתַקְּנִין אֶת הַמּוֹעֲדוֹת.

---

הַשְּׁלוּחִים יוֹצְאִין *The messengers go out.* Chapter two describes two systems by which the communities of the Diaspora were informed of the new month declared in Jerusalem. The more reliable system involved dispatching messengers; members of the rabbinic community would travel to the various communities in the Diaspora. These journeys were taxing – six hundred kilometers, for instance, from Jerusalem to the Jewish centers of Babylonia – and unless there was a festival in a given month, informing the Diaspora of the precise date of the first of the month was not of critical importance.

עַל אֱלוּל מִפְּנֵי רֹאשׁ הַשָּׁנָה *For Elul because of Rosh HaShana.* By Torah law, Rosh HaShana is a single day. It became a two-day festival because even in Jerusalem, it was not until the middle of the thirtieth day of Elul that it could be determined whether that day would be the first of Tishrei or not. The message, in any case, could not be conveyed beyond the city until the festival was over – and so a second day of the festival would be kept, as is practiced today even in Israel (Rif, *Beitza* 3a; Tosafot, *Rosh HaShana* 18a).

מִפְּנֵי תַקָּנַת הַמּוֹעֲדוֹת *To set the festivals.* Regardless of the new moon, the

When the Temple stood, they would break Shabbat for any month,
to set the offerings.

5 Whether the new moon is clearly seen or not,
one breaks Shabbat to testify.
Rabbi Yose said, if it is clearly seen,
one does not break Shabbat.

6 Once, more than forty pairs of witnesses passed by,
and Rabbi Akiva stopped them when they came to Lod.
Rabban Gamliel sent to tell him,
"If you prevent the public coming,
you mislead them for the future."

---

that, if it is so clearly visible, someone closer to Jerusalem must surely have seen it as well. Rabbi Yose holds that, in that case, the Shabbat prohibitions are not suspended; but the Rabbis hold that one should not assume that others will testify. The new moon appears only briefly and is extremely narrow; few people see it in any given month, and it is always possible that there are clouds obscuring it from view over Jerusalem.

**אִם מְעַכֵּב אַתָּה אֶת הָרַבִּים** *If you prevent the public coming.* This case deals with a different dilemma. Only one pair of witnesses is needed to consecrate the new moon, meaning that technically, all those who arrive after the first pair have wasted an arduous journey. However, the sages sought to encourage witnesses to go and testify (see mishna 2:6) rather than feel that their journey so far had been wasted, so that they and others would be keen to come in future months. The mishna states that Rabbi Akiva prevented forty pairs of witnesses from proceeding to Jerusalem. According to Rabbi Yehuda (*Rosh HaShana* 22a), Rabbi Akiva would never have done this, and he substitutes one Zepher of Gader who was sanctioned by Rabban Gamliel and demoted from his leadership position (but see note to 4:4). According to the Meiri, this took place on Shabbat. Even in that case, the Rabbis preferred to allow the witnesses to proceed with their journey, rather than being frustrated and so refraining from coming in the future.

וּכְשֶׁהָיָה בֵּית הַמִּקְדָּשׁ קַיָּם, מְחַלְּלִין אַף עַל כֻּלָּן
מִפְּנֵי תַקָּנַת הַקָּרְבָּן.

ה בֵּין שֶׁנִּרְאָה בַעֲלִיל, בֵּין שֶׁלֹּא נִרְאָה בַעֲלִיל
מְחַלְּלִין עָלָיו אֶת הַשַּׁבָּת.
רַבִּי יוֹסֵי אוֹמֵר: אִם נִרְאָה בַעֲלִיל
אֵין מְחַלְּלִין עָלָיו אֶת הַשַּׁבָּת.

ו מַעֲשֶׂה שֶׁעָבְרוּ יוֹתֵר מֵאַרְבָּעִים זוּג
וְעִכְּבָן רַבִּי עֲקִיבָא בְּלוּד.
שָׁלַח לוֹ רַבָּן גַּמְלִיאֵל:
אִם מְעַכֵּב אַתָּה אֶת הָרַבִּים
נִמְצֵאתָ מַכְשִׁילָן לֶעָתִיד לָבֹא.

---

Nisan (Shavuot begins at the close of the forty-nine-day count from the second day of Pesaḥ). However, Shabbat prohibitions were not suspended for Elul, as the uncertainty whether Rosh HaShana was established on the thirtieth or thirty-first day of Elul remained (*Tosafot Yom Tov*).

מִפְּנֵי תַקָּנַת הַקָּרְבָּן *To set the offerings.* When the Temple was standing, an additional (*"musaf"*) offering was sacrificed on the new moon, making it essential that the declaration of the new moon coincide with its appearance. Therefore, testifying about the new moon does justify desecrating the Shabbat in itself; however, after the Temple was destroyed, Rabban Yoḥanan ben Zakkai decreed that the Shabbat prohibitions would no longer be suspended for the other months (ibid.).

נִרְאָה בַעֲלִיל *Clearly seen.* The meaning of the word *ba'alil* is not certain; in his commentary on Psalm 12:7, Rashi cites no less than four possibilities. The Talmud (21b) understands the word to mean "clearly," but the suggestion "high in the sky" may also be appropriate (Bartenura). The mishna addresses the dilemma of a witness who sees the moon on Friday night but assumes

7 If a father and son both see the new moon they should come;
they cannot testify together,
but if one becomes invalid,
then the other one can join with somebody else.
Rabbi Shimon says: A father and son and all other kin,
are able to testify together to the moon.
Rabbi Yose said: Once, Tuvia the doctor
saw the new moon in Jerusalem,
he and his son and his liberated slave.
The priests accepted testimony from him and from his son,
but declared his slave an invalid witness.
And when they came to court,
they took testimony from him and from his slave
but declared his son invalid.

---

Some restrictions, however, related to the concept of *yiḥus* (lineage), still apply to him – for instance, a priest may not marry a former maidservant (Mishna, *Kiddushin* 69a). The Talmud (*Sanhedrin* 36b) rules that while a person of less than optimal lineage may testify – and, indeed, judge – monetary disputes, he may not judge capital cases.

וְקִבְּלוּ הַכֹּהֲנִים *The priests accepted.* The Mishna (*Ketubot* 12a) mentions a court of priests, in parallel with, but tolerated by, the Sanhedrin. The priests traditionally emphasized lineage, and, in this case, presumably held the view (later expressed by Rabbi Shimon), that relatives are eligible to testify, and liberated slaves are ineligible to testify as to the sighting of the new moon because it has the legal status of capital cases (see *Tosafot,* 22a). It may be that the Sanhedrin overruled the priests' autonomous court in this case, or possibly the priests simply heard the witnesses first, to give them time to prepare the Musaf offering for Rosh Ḥodesh.

ז אָב וּבְנוֹ שֶׁרָאוּ אֶת הַחֹדֶשׁ, יֵלְכוּ
לֹא שֶׁמִּצְטָרְפִין זֶה עִם זֶה
אֶלָּא שֶׁאִם יִפָּסֵל אֶחָד מֵהֶן
יִצְטָרֵף הַשֵּׁנִי עִם אַחֵר.
רַבִּי שִׁמְעוֹן אוֹמֵר: אָב וּבְנוֹ וְכָל הַקְּרוֹבִין
כְּשֵׁרִין לְעֵדוּת הַחֹדֶשׁ.
אָמַר רַבִּי יוֹסֵי: מַעֲשֶׂה בְטוֹבִיָּה הָרוֹפֵא
שֶׁרָאָה אֶת הַחֹדֶשׁ בִּירוּשָׁלַיִם, הוּא וּבְנוֹ וְעַבְדּוֹ הַמְשֻׁחְרָר
וְקִבְּלוּ הַכֹּהֲנִים אוֹתוֹ וְאֶת בְּנוֹ, וּפָסְלוּ אֶת עַבְדּוֹ.
וּכְשֶׁבָּאוּ לִפְנֵי בֵית דִּין
קִבְּלוּ אוֹתוֹ וְאֶת עַבְדּוֹ, וּפָסְלוּ אֶת בְּנוֹ.

---

לֹא שֶׁמִּצְטָרְפִין זֶה עִם זֶה *They cannot testify together.* In principle, valid testimony can only be provided by two legally eligible, unrelated men, who witnessed the event about which they are testifying together. Testimony regarding sighting of the moon is valid even from two witnesses who witnessed it individually.

רַבִּי שִׁמְעוֹן אוֹמֵר *Rabbi Shimon says.* Rabbi Shimon's argument is based on the Biblical source of the rules of calendar testimony: the command "This month shall be for you..." (Ex. 12:2–3) was addressed to two brothers, Moses and Aaron – surely showing that related witnesses are acceptable for this unique kind of testimony. However, the rabbis read the verse differently; for them, Moses and Aaron are archetypal of the judges charged with accepting the testimony and establishing the new moon (Rashi, 22a).

וְעַבְדּוֹ הַמְשֻׁחְרָר *His liberated slave.* A non-Jewish slave who is liberated is Jewish.

8 These are invalid witnesses:
One who plays with dice,
one who lends on interest,
one who sends out pigeons,
one who trades the produce of the Sabbatical year,
and slaves.
This is the rule:
for any testimony women cannot give,
these men too are invalid.

---

Perhaps, lending with interest is not really theft, but rather a violation of the value of charity, exploiting another person's neediness (*Pnei Yehoshua, Bava Metzia* 62a). The standard explanation is that the mishna refers to people who engage in "*avak ribit*" ("dust," or taint, of usury) – legitimate transactions in which the creditor has an unfair advantage, easy profit without risk; these transactions are only rabbinically forbidden (*Nimukei Yosef, Sanhedrin* 4b).

וּמַפְרִיחֵי יוֹנִים *One who sends out pigeons.* The Talmud (*Sanhedrin* 25a) classes the professional pigeon racer together with the dice player – this is another form of gambling. The Rambam suggests that dove-keepers were known for trying to attract their neighbors' birds back to their own dovecotes (*Hilkhot Edut* 10:4).

וְסוֹחֲרֵי שְׁבִיעִית *One who trades the produce of the Sabbatical year.* Produce that grows in the *shemitta* year may not be gathered for commercial purposes (Mishna, *Shevi'it* 7:3), as during that year the fruits are designated for eating, and not for any other purpose (*Bekhorot* 12b). This is a biblical prohibition, but it is not articulated in the Torah, which is why even usually scrupulous people may rationalize transgressing it (Meiri, *Rosh HaShana* 22a).

The common thread among all of the activities listed is a willingness to stretch or transgress the law for financial gain; someone who is willing to compromise his morals for profit is liable to bear false witness for a bribe (Rashi ad loc.).

וַעֲבָדִים *Slaves.* A non-Jew who was purchased by a Jew as a slave must undergo partial conversion to Judaism. The conversion process is only completed when the slave is liberated, as was the case in Tuvia's household (see mishna seven). A slave, then, is not yet Jewish, and cannot serve as a witness.

הָאִשָּׁה *Women.* Women are not eligible to testify in formal courts (*Shevuot* 30a), but are considered trustworthy (Tosafot, *Gittin* 2b). The four categories

ח אֵלּוּ הֵן הַפְּסוּלִין:
הַמְשַׂחֵק בַּקֻּבְיָא
וּמַלְוֵי בְּרִבִּית
וּמַפְרִיחֵי יוֹנִים
וְסוֹחֲרֵי שְׁבִיעִית
וַעֲבָדִים.
זֶה הַכְּלָל:
כָּל עֵדוּת שֶׁאֵין הָאִשָּׁה כְּשֵׁרָה לָהּ
אַף הֵן אֵינָן כְּשֵׁרִים לָהּ.

---

אֵלּוּ הֵן הַפְּסוּלִין *These are invalid witnesses.* The types of witnesses whose testimony is inherently suspect are discussed at length in tractate *Sanhedrin* (24b–27b). While convicted criminals who violated Torah law are clearly ineligible, the ones listed here are "borderline" cases. The Talmud understands them to be either sophisticated forms of thieves – or social outcasts, who do not contribute to the common good. (This debate continued among the early commentaries, see Tosafot, *Sanhedrin* 24b–25a.)

הַמְשַׂחֵק בַּקֻּבְיָא *One who plays with dice.* A gambler. One view, maintained by Rashi, is that any payment of a gambling debt is made under duress, as the loser had never really believed that he would lose and consequently never believed he would have to pay, so his commitment to pay if he lost was not made on good faith. Therefore, one who gambles and forces others to pay when they lose is a thief by rabbinic law. Rabbeinu Tam and others argue that gambling payments are made in good faith and are valid; a person, however, who makes his living in this way is opting out of the productive life of society, making him an untrustworthy figure within it. This view considers recreational gambling a deplorable pastime, but does not invalidate the gambler as a witness if he also does productive work. This more lenient view was accepted by later decisors of halakha (*Shulḥan Arukh,* ḤM 34:16).

וּמַלְוֵי בְּרִבִּית *One who lends on interest.* Usury is a heinous crime, prohibited three times in the Torah (Ex. 22:24–6; Lev. 25:35–7; Deut. 23:20–1), and harshly condemned by the Prophets (see Ezek. 18:13). The question is then, why is it mentioned in the mishna which deals with thieves by rabbinic law?

9 One who sees the new moon but cannot walk,
he is taken on a donkey,
or even on his bed.
If there is danger they take sticks,
and if the way is long, they take food,
because for a distance a night and a day in length,
one breaks Shabbat and goes
to bear witness to the moon,
as it is said: "These are the appointed times of the LORD… *Lev. 23*
which you shall announce in their due seasons."

---

וְאִם צוֹדָה לָהֶם *If there is danger.* Literally "if there is an ambush awaiting them." Possible dangers include wild animals and violent people, including the sectarians discussed in chapter two, who may wish to target witnesses (Rashi).

אֵלֶּה מוֹעֲדֵי ה׳ *"These are the appointed times of the LORD."* Leviticus 23:4 introduces a list of the "sacred assemblies" that Israel is commanded to convene throughout the year. The mishna here underscores complexity in the verse: On the one hand, these are "the appointed times of the LORD"; on the other, it is Israel who are commanded to "convene them." The courts play a genuine role in investing these times with sanctity. The command is to do this, literally translated, "in *their* [the festivals'] appointed times," and this overrides the prohibitions of Shabbat. The same command is understood to mean that the new month cannot be consecrated retroactively, such that if the court cannot declare it in time, it is postponed until the next day (mishna 3:1; however, see note to mishna 2:8). A journey to testify on Shabbat, then, should only be undertaken if the witnesses will arrive within that night and day (Ritva).

ט מִי שֶׁרָאָה אֶת הַחֹדֶשׁ וְאֵינוֹ יָכוֹל לְהַלֵּךְ
מוֹלִיכִין אוֹתוֹ עַל הַחֲמוֹר, אֲפִלּוּ בְּמִטָּה
וְאִם צוֹדֶה לָהֶם, לוֹקְחִין בְּיָדָם מַקְלוֹת
וְאִם הָיְתָה דֶּרֶךְ רְחוֹקָה, לוֹקְחִין בְּיָדָם מְזוֹנוֹת.
שֶׁעַל מַהֲלַךְ לַיְלָה וָיוֹם
מְחַלְּלִין אֶת הַשַּׁבָּת וְיוֹצְאִין לְעֵדוּת הַחֹדֶשׁ
שֶׁנֶּאֱמַר: אֵלֶּה מוֹעֲדֵי ה'... אֲשֶׁר־תִּקְרְאוּ אֹתָם בְּמוֹעֲדָם: ויקרא כג

---

listed above (prior to the slaves) who are considered suspect, are disqualified from any testimony that a woman may not give. However, a woman's testimony is valid in certain cases, such as that of an *aguna* (literally, "anchored"), a woman whose husband is missing and requires evidence of his death in order to remarry. For this important need, many of the rules of evidence are suspended (*Yevamot* 122a). In the Talmud, Rav Ashi deduces that those who fall into the categories listed in this mishna are eligible for this important testimony (22a).

**מִי שֶׁרָאָה** *One who sees.* At the chapter's close we return to the dilemma of one who sights the new moon on Shabbat. His testimony is so important that the prohibitions of Shabbat are suspended for him and others in order to facilitate it. A disabled person who cannot walk must be carried, and the witness and his escort may carry weapons for defense and food for the journey. These allowances apply only if they are able to reach the court and testify on the same day.

# CHAPTER TWO

1 If they do not know him,
then another is sent with him to vouch for his character.
At first they would accept testimony to the new moon from any man,
but when the sects began to sabotage,
the court enacted
that they accept it only from those they knew.

---

that sort was liable to develop was probably the driving force behind Rabban Gamliel's vigorous assertion of his authority as Nasi, which we encountered already in mishna 1:6.

אִם אֵינָן מַכִּירִין אוֹתוֹ *If they do not know him.* If the judges on the court were not personally familiar with witnesses who came to testify that they saw the moon, then the authorities of their home settlements were responsible for their credibility. The language of the mishna implies that only one witness was sent, but once establishing the witnesses' character became the issue, a formal testimony was required, and the Talmud concludes that two character witnesses were necessary (22b).

מִשֶּׁקִּלְקְלוּ הַמִּינִין *When the sects began to sabotage.* The term *minim* means "heretics," referring to any of the numerous sects that proliferated during the late Second Temple period. The term later became identified with the early Christians, and after Christianity's rise to power, many texts that included a reference to the *minim* were censored, often by the Jews themselves. Some variant readings of this mishna substituted *Apikorsim*, "non-believers," while the Talmud cites it as "the Boethusians." Censorship issues aside, this ascription is very likely accurate. The Boethusians were a sect ideologically opposed to rabbinic traditions regarding, among other things, the timing of Shavuot. Arguing that the Omer should be counted from the Shabbat of Pesaḥ, rather than the second day of the festival, their Shavuot always fell on a Sunday (Mishna, *Menaḥot* 65a). The *Tosefta* (1:14; also Talmud 22b) relates an incident in which a system of bribing false witnesses to manipulate the rabbinic calendar to bring it in line with the Boethusian system was exposed.

To manipulate the calendar so that the first day of Pesaḥ would fall on Shabbat, the Boethusians would need to find people willing to desecrate the Shabbat two weeks earlier and falsely testify that Rosh Ḥodesh Nisan was on Shabbat. Had their testimony stood, the Paschal offering would have

# פרק שני

א אִם אֵינָן מַכִּירִין אוֹתוֹ
מְשַׁלְּחִין אַחֵר עִמּוֹ לַהֲעִידוֹ.
בָּרִאשׁוֹנָה הָיוּ מְקַבְּלִין עֵדוּת הַחֹדֶשׁ מִכָּל אָדָם
מִשֶּׁקִּלְקְלוּ הַמִּינִין, הִתְקִינוּ
שֶׁלֹּא יְהוּ מְקַבְּלִין אֶלָּא מִן הַמַּכִּירִים.

---

CHAPTER TWO

Chapter one dealt with the process of consecrating the new moon from the witnesses' perspective; this chapter turns to the court. Even the first mishna of chapter two, which still describes the witnesses' setting out, is concerned with the ordinances instituted by the Sanhedrin in order to ensure witnesses' credibility.

Chronologically, the fifth mishna, which describes measures instituted by the court to preserve the integrity of the calendar process, should immediately follow the first, as it describes the witnesses' arrival in Jerusalem. The second, third and fourth mishnayot, which describe the flares, seem tangential. The fifth, sixth and seventh mishnayot detail the court's examination of the witnesses, and declaration of the new month.

The closing two mishnayot reflect the first two, in describing the Sanhedrin's effort to preserve the integrity of the calendar process. However, while the first two describe measures instituted to counter external sabotage efforts, the last two mishnayot deal with a different challenge: dissent among the sages themselves.

There are many advantages to the rabbinic culture of debate along with the existence of different customs and traditions. They do, however, have the potential to cause schism and even collapse. The Torah strongly condemns one who flouts the accepted authority (Deut. 17:8–13). It was only a few generations prior to the destruction of the Second Temple that rabbinic Judaism contained serious halakhic disputes (Yerushalmi, *Ḥagiga* 2:2). A famous Geonic-era dispute between the rabbis of Eretz Yisrael, headed by Rabbi Aharon ben Meir and the Rabbis of Babylonia, whose arguments were eloquently articulated by Rav Sa'adia Gaon, centered around the day that Rosh HaShana 4682 occurred. That led to Pesaḥ being celebrated on different dates during the years 4682–4683 (922–923 CE). Concern that a dispute of

2 At first they would light flares,
but when the Samaritans began to sabotage,
the court enacted
that the messengers be sent out.

3 How would they light the flares?
They would bring long poles of cedar
and reeds and pine and flax fibres,
and bind them with a rope,
and a man would take them up to the top of the mountain and set them alight,
and he would wave them this way and that,
raise them and lower them,
until he could see his fellow
doing the same from the top of the next mountain,
and so too on the third.

---

מִשֶּׁקִּלְקְלוּ הַכּוּתִים *When the Samaritans began to sabotage.* The Samaritans were termed *kutim* in rabbinic literature, after one of the places (possibly the modern town of al-Kut, Iraq) from which the kings of Assyria have exiled them, sending them to the vanquished Northern Kingdom and the ten tribes of Israel to their lands (II Kings 17:24). They converted en masse; originally the sages were uncertain how to relate to their conversion (*Kiddushin* 75b–76a), but ultimately they disqualified their conversion altogether (*Ḥullin* 6a). According to the Yerushalmi (ad loc.), that decree was issued by Rabbi Yehuda HaNasi, more than a century after the Temple's destruction, by which time the Samaritans constituted a majority of the population in the mountains north of Judea.

כְּלֻנְסָאוֹת שֶׁלְּאֶרֶז אֲרֻכִּין *Long poles of cedar.* The flares were constructed of long cedar poles, wrapped in incendiary materials. The "oil tree" is identified with the stone pine (Felix, *The World of Biblical Botany* p. 88); reeds and fibers peeled from flax stems would quickly have produced a bright flame.

וּמוֹלִיךְ וּמֵבִיא *And he would wave them this way and that.* Waving was part of the Temple service: meal-offerings were waved, as were some of the sacrifices (Mishna, *Menaḥot* 61a). This waving is still practiced on Sukkot, when reciting the blessing on the Four Species and in certain passages of Hallel (*Sukka*

ב בָּרִאשׁוֹנָה הָיוּ מַשִּׂיאִין מַשּׂוּאוֹת
מִשֶּׁקִּלְקְלוּ הַכּוּתִים, הִתְקִינוּ
שֶׁיְּהוּ שְׁלוּחִין יוֹצְאִין.

ג כֵּיצַד הָיוּ מַשִּׂיאִין מַשּׂוּאוֹת?
מְבִיאִין כְּלֻנְסָאוֹת שֶׁלְּאֶרֶז אֲרֻכִּין
וְקָנִים וַעֲצֵי שֶׁמֶן וּנְעֹרֶת שֶׁלְּפִשְׁתָּן
וְכוֹרֵךְ בִּמְשִׁיחָה.
וְעוֹלֶה לְרֹאשׁ הָהָר וּמַצִּית בָּהֶן אֶת הָאוּר
וּמוֹלִיךְ וּמֵבִיא וּמַעֲלֶה וּמוֹרִיד
עַד שֶׁהוּא רוֹאֶה אֶת חֲבֵרוֹ
שֶׁהוּא עוֹשֶׂה כֵן בְּרֹאשׁ הָהָר הַשֵּׁנִי
וְכֵן בְּרֹאשׁ הָהָר הַשְּׁלִישִׁי.

---

been brought on Friday, with Pesaḥ falling on Shabbat, two weeks later. The counting of the Omer would then have begun, as the Boethusians advocated, on Motza'ei Shabbat. The plot was foiled when the witness – who had taken the money and desecrated Shabbat himself to ensure that others would not do so – informed the Sanhedrin of the plot. The new month was then duly consecrated on Sunday. Coincidentally or not, a debate in *Pesaḥim* 66a brings up the fact that, in Hillel's living memory, the Paschal offering was never once offered on Shabbat; this may obliquely suggest that the testimony-fixing incident that was exposed was not the first of its kind, and that sectarians really had sometimes succeeded in manipulating the beginning of Nisan in some years.

מַשּׂוּאוֹת *Flares.* In the system described by the Talmud (22b), the flares were lit only in months when the new moon had been seen on the thirtieth night; in other months, seeing no flares on the thirty-first, the communities outside Israel knew that the new month would begin the following day. An exception to this practice was when the thirty-first night was the eve of Shabbat; in this case, the flares were lit on the following night, when Shabbat was over.

4 Where would they light the flares?
From the Oil Mount to Sarteva,
and from Sarteva to Gripina,
from Gripina to Ḥavran,
and from Ḥavran to Beit Biltin,
and from Beit Biltin – the man would not move:
he would wave the flares this way and that,
raise them and lower them,
until he saw all the Diaspora ablaze before him
like one fire.

5 There was a large courtyard in Jerusalem,
and its name was Beit Yaazek,
and there all the witnesses would gather,
and the court would examine them there.
They would make great meals for the witnesses,
to encourage them to come.
At first
they would not move from there all day,
but Rabban Gamliel the Elder enacted
that they could walk two thousand cubits in each direction.

---

כָּל הַגּוֹלָה *All the Diaspora.* The Talmud (23b) reads this to be the Babylonian city of Pumbedita, where Jews would climb onto their roofs with torches to celebrate the arrival of the message from Jerusalem.

וּבֵית יַעְזֵק *Beit Yaazek.* The Talmud (23b) associates this name with Isaiah 5:2, understanding it to mean "a stone wall." The "great banquets" were made to encourage potential witnesses to come. According to Rambam, these banquets were held on each day that could potentially be the new moon (*Hilkhot Kiddush HaḤodesh* 2:7). However, Rashi explains that these meals were served specifically on Shabbat, when food would be more of a concern for the travelers. In this case, the court meeting in Beit Yaazek, outside its usual setting, would be a special courtesy to the Shabbat witnesses.

בָּרִאשׁוֹנָה לֹא הָיוּ זָזִין מִשָּׁם *At first they would not move from there.* On Shabbat, one may not leave his place of residence (Ex. 16:29). However, the Shabbat

ד וּמֵאַיִן הָיוּ מַשִּׂיאִין מַשּׂוּאוֹת?
מֵהַר הַמִּשְׁחָה לְסַרְטְבָא
וּמִסַּרְטְבָא לִגְרוֹפִינָא
וּמִגְּרוֹפִינָא לְחַוְרָן
וּמֵחַוְרָן לְבֵית בִּלְתִּין
וּמִבֵּית בִּלְתִּין לֹא זָזוּ מִשָּׁם
אֶלָּא מוֹלִיךְ וּמֵבִיא וּמַעֲלֶה וּמוֹרִיד
עַד שֶׁהָיָה רוֹאֶה כָּל הַגּוֹלָה לְפָנָיו
כִּמְדוּרַת הָאֵשׁ.

ה חָצֵר גְּדוֹלָה הָיְתָה בִירוּשָׁלַיִם
וּבֵית יַעְזֵק הָיְתָה נִקְרֵאת
וּלְשָׁם כָּל הָעֵדִים מִתְכַּנְּסִים
וּבֵית דִּין בּוֹדְקִין אוֹתָם שָׁם.
וּסְעוּדוֹת גְּדוֹלוֹת עוֹשִׂין לָהֶם
בִּשְׁבִיל שֶׁיְּהוּ רְגִילִין לָבֹא.
בָּרִאשׁוֹנָה
לֹא הָיוּ זָזִין מִשָּׁם כָּל הַיּוֹם
הִתְקִין רַבָּן גַּמְלִיאֵל הַזָּקֵן
שֶׁיְּהוּ מְהַלְּכִין אַלְפַּיִם אַמָּה לְכָל רוּחַ.

---

37b). In the case of the flares, this deliberate, ritualized movement underscored the distant light as the flares of the new moon, and not a shooting star (Tosafot).

מֵהַר הַמִּשְׁחָה *From the Oil Mount.* The route described carried the message from the Mount of Olives in Jerusalem, northwards and eastwards to Babylonia.

And not only these –
midwives coming to birth as well,
and those who came to save someone from fire,
or militias, or a river, or an earthquake –
all these are considered like people of the city,
and have two thousand cubits to walk in each direction.

6 How would they examine the witnesses?
They would examine first, the first pair to come.
Bringing in first the elder of the pair, they would say to him:
"Tell us, how did you see the moon –
before the sun or after?
North of it or south?
How high was it and which way was it turned?
How broad did it appear?"

---

these were also included in the enactment of Rabban Gamliel; however, the mishna in *Eiruvin* 44b accords them an even greater incentive: there "all those who come to save may return to their places." Indeed, the version that appears in the Rif is "since all those who come to save…" indicating that the ordinance allowing those people to return home was the precedent for the leniency accorded those who come to testify. The ruling has contemporary relevance, particularly for medics, ambulance drivers, and even doctors on a hospital staff whose shifts fall on Shabbat. The *Shulḥan Arukh* (OḤ 407:3) rules that returning home is permitted only if it is dangerous to stay where one is, but recent halakha decisiors extend this leniency to anyone engaged in saving lives who might be needed again (*BeTzel HaḤokhma* 4:94; *Shemirat Shabbat KeHilkhata* 40:66–71).

הַגָּדוֹל *The elder.* Literally "the greater" – the one who demands more respect (generally the older) of the first pair of witnesses to arrive.

כֵּיצַד רָאִיתָ אֶת הַלְּבָנָה *How did you see the moon?* The witnesses are asked for details of the moon's position when they saw it: Was it before the sun, did the tips of the crescent point west, as if the moon precedes the sun or after (with the tips facing east), as if it follows the sun? On which side of the horizon did it appear; was it north of the point where the sun rises or south of that point? How high did it appear in the sky? At what angle? How wide was the crescent?

וְלֹא אֵלּוּ בִּלְבַד
אֶלָּא אַף הַחֲכָמָה הַבָּאָה לְיַלֵּד
וְהַבָּא לְהַצִּיל מִן הַדְּלֵקָה
וּמִן הַגַּיִס וּמִן הַנָּהָר, וּמִן הַמַּפֹּלֶת
הֲרֵי אֵלּוּ כְּאַנְשֵׁי הָעִיר
וְיֵשׁ לָהֶם אַלְפַּיִם אַמָּה לְכָל רוּחַ.

ו כֵּיצַד בּוֹדְקִין אֶת הָעֵדִים?
זוּג שֶׁבָּא רִאשׁוֹן, בּוֹדְקִין אוֹתוֹ רִאשׁוֹן
וּמַכְנִיסִין אֶת הַגָּדוֹל שֶׁבָּהֶן, וְאוֹמְרִים לוֹ:
אֱמֹר, כֵּיצַד רָאִיתָ אֶת הַלְּבָנָה
לִפְנֵי הַחַמָּה אוֹ לְאַחַר הַחַמָּה?
לִצְפוֹנָהּ אוֹ לִדְרוֹמָהּ?
כַּמָּה הָיָה גָּבוֹהַּ וּלְאַיִן הָיָה נוֹטֶה?
וְכַמָּה הָיָה רָחָב?

---

boundary of each city, which is the point until which the residents of the city may walk, extends two-thousand cubits beyond the city limits (*Eiruvin* 51a). One who goes beyond the Shabbat boundary during Shabbat, even if dragged against his will, loses this extension (Mishna, *Eiruvin* 41b). Beit Yaazek would have provided the Shabbat witnesses with some space, and may have been chosen for this purpose (*Pnei Yehoshua*), but it would still be restrictive; Rabban Gamliel the Elder therefore instituted that witnesses for a new moon are considered residents of Jerusalem, enabling them to walk throughout the city.

הַחֲכָמָה הַבָּאָה לְיַלֵּד *Midwives coming to birth.* The mishna goes on to list other groups who, having left their Shabbat boundary to save lives, were accorded the status of residents of the city to which they traveled while performing the intended task (only as far as the Shabbat boundary is concerned), to encourage the decision to come. The phrasing of the mishna implies that

If he said "before the sun,"
it meant nothing.
Afterwards they would bring the second in, and test him.
If their words were aligned,
their testimony stood.
All the other pairs would be asked for the main points,
not because they were needed,
but so that they would not leave disappointed –
and so to encourage them to come.

7 Then the head of the court would say,
"Consecrated!"
and all the people after him:
"Consecrated, consecrated!"
Whether it was seen in its time or not – they would consecrate it.
Rabbi Elazar bar Tzadok says:
If it is seen not in its time,
they need not consecrate the month,
for Heaven has already consecrated it.

8 Rabban Gamliel had pictures of the moon in different shapes
on a board and on the wall in his upper room,

---

long. If the new moon appears "in its time," on the thirtieth day, then the new month must be announced. By the thirty-first day, however, it is clear that the new month has arrived and the announcement is unnecessary (see the note to mishna two, regarding the flare system). The Talmud (24a) rules in accordance with Rabbi Elazar bar Tzadok.

לְרַבָּן גַּמְלִיאֵל *Rabban Gamliel.* Nasi in the first generation after the destruction of Jerusalem, Rabban Gamliel was the grandson of Rabban Gamliel the Elder, mentioned above. He received witnesses in the upper room of his house in the new seat of the Sanhedrin in Yavne.

בַּטַּבְלָא וּבַכֹּתֶל *On a board and on the wall.* Some manuscript versions of the mishna have "on a board on the wall." In our reading Rabban Gamliel has two sets of images, one on his table (the common usage of the word *tabla* in the Talmud), and one on the wall (*Tiferet Yisrael*).

אִם אָמַר 'לִפְנֵי הַחַמָּה', לֹא אָמַר כְּלוּם.
וְאַחַר כָּךְ הָיוּ מַכְנִיסִים אֶת הַשֵּׁנִי וּבוֹדְקִין אוֹתוֹ.
אִם נִמְצְאוּ דִבְרֵיהֶם מְכֻוָּנִים, עֵדוּתָן קַיֶּמֶת.
וּשְׁאָר כָּל הַזּוּגוֹת שׁוֹאֲלִין אוֹתָם רָאשֵׁי דְבָרִים
לֹא שֶׁהָיוּ צְרִיכִין לָהֶן
אֶלָּא כְּדֵי שֶׁלֹּא יֵצְאוּ בְּפַחֵי נֶפֶשׁ
בִּשְׁבִיל שֶׁיְּהוּ רְגִילִים לָבֹא.

ז רֹאשׁ בֵּית דִּין אוֹמֵר: מְקֻדָּשׁ!
וְכָל הָעָם עוֹנִין אַחֲרָיו: מְקֻדָּשׁ, מְקֻדָּשׁ!
בֵּין שֶׁנִּרְאָה בִזְמַנּוֹ בֵּין שֶׁלֹּא נִרְאָה בִזְמַנּוֹ
מְקַדְּשִׁין אוֹתוֹ.
רַבִּי אֶלְעָזָר בַּר צָדוֹק אוֹמֵר: אִם לֹא נִרְאָה בִזְמַנּוֹ
אֵין מְקַדְּשִׁין אוֹתוֹ
שֶׁכְּבָר קִדְּשׁוּהוּ שָׁמַיִם.

ח דְּמוּת צוּרוֹת לְבָנוֹת הָיוּ לוֹ לְרַבָּן גַּמְלִיאֵל
בַּטַּבְלָא וּבַכֹּתֶל בַּעֲלִיָּתוֹ

---

**אִם אָמַר 'לִפְנֵי הַחַמָּה'** *If he said "Before the sun."* Since the moon has no light of its own, only reflected light of the sun, the side facing the sun is always illuminated, and the tips of the crescent face away from the sun. If the witness answered incorrectly, he is deemed unreliable and rejected. His answers to the other questions were similarly assessed based on their plausibility.

**וְכָל הָעָם עוֹנִין אַחֲרָיו** *And all the people after him.* The consecration of the month was a ceremonial public occasion. Blessings and prayers composed to accompany the declaration "consecrated" appear in later sources (see *Massekhet Soferim* 19:9). Today this declaration is familiar from the marriage ceremony.

**בִּזְמַנּוֹ** *In its time.* A lunar month is always either twenty-nine or thirty days

and he would show these to laymen who would come,
and say: "Did you see it this way or like this?"
Once, a pair of witnesses came and said,
"We saw it at dawn in the east
and at night in the west."
Rabbi Yoḥanan ben Nuri said,
"These are false witnesses!"
But when they came to Yavneh,
Rabban Gamliel accepted them.
Then again, a pair of witnesses came and said,
"We saw it in its time,"
but on the next night it could not be seen.
Rabban Gamliel accepted them.
Rabbi Dosa ben Harkinas said,
"These are false witnesses!
How can one testify that a woman gave birth,
when the next day her belly is between her teeth?!"
Rabbi Yehoshua said, "I see your words."

---

on the thirtieth night ("in its time"), leading the court to sanctify the new moon on the thirtieth day. On the following night ("its intercalated day"), when the moon should have visible even longer, the judges could not see it, despite the clear sky (Rashi). This led them to doubt, in retrospect, the reliability of the witnesses' testimony, and the accuracy of the date that had been fixed. Rabbi Dosa expressed this doubt by an analogy: If a woman is visibly pregnant today, it is unlikely that she gave birth yesterday. In both cases, the Rambam (based on the Talmud, 25a) argues that Rabban Gamliel trusted the oral tradition of his fathers, who taught him how to calculate when the new moon should be seen, and viewed the witnesses' testimony as a formality rather than as proof. Most commentators dispute this approach; but as the authority of the Sanhedrin waned, Hillel, the penultimate Nasi, established a fixed calendar according to his family's tradition. (According to a letter by Rav Hai Gaon, this was done in the year 4119, or 359 BCE). That is the calendar still in use today.

רוֹאֶה אֲנִי אֶת דְּבָרֶיךָ *I see your words.* Translated literally here, the phrase means "I agree," or "I accept what you say." It will be echoed at the story's close, when Rabban Gamliel thanks Rabbi Yehoshua "for accepting my words."

שֶׁבָּהֶן מַרְאֶה אֶת הַהֶדְיוֹטוֹת
וְאוֹמֵר: הֲכָזֶה רָאִיתָ אוֹ כָזֶה?
מַעֲשֶׂה שֶׁבָּאוּ שְׁנַיִם וְאָמְרוּ:
רְאִינוּהוּ שַׁחֲרִית בַּמִּזְרָח, וְעַרְבִית בַּמַּעֲרָב.
אָמַר רַבִּי יוֹחָנָן בֶּן נוּרִי: עֵדֵי שֶׁקֶר הֵם!
כְּשֶׁבָּאוּ לְיַבְנֶה, קִבְּלָן רַבָּן גַּמְלִיאֵל.
וְעוֹד בָּאוּ שְׁנַיִם וְאָמְרוּ:
רְאִינוּהוּ בִּזְמַנּוֹ
וּבְלֵיל עִבּוּרוֹ לֹא נִרְאָה
וְקִבְּלָן רַבָּן גַּמְלִיאֵל.
אָמַר רַבִּי דוֹסָא בֶּן הַרְכִּינַס: עֵדֵי שֶׁקֶר הֵן!
הֵיאַךְ מְעִידִים עַל הָאִשָּׁה שֶׁיָּלְדָה
וּלְמָחָר כְּרֵסָהּ בֵּין שִׁנֶּיהָ?
אָמַר לוֹ רַבִּי יְהוֹשֻׁעַ: רוֹאֶה אֲנִי אֶת דְּבָרֶיךָ.

---

רְאִינוּהוּ שַׁחֲרִית בַּמִּזְרָח *We saw it at dawn in the east.* The witnesses claim to have seen the remnant of last month's moon in the morning of the day before they saw the new moon at night. As this is impossible, Rabbi Yoḥanan ben Nuri disqualified their entire testimony. However, Rabban Gamliel accepted the part relating to the new moon, even though the earlier part must be mistaken (Rambam, Bartenura).

רְאִינוּהוּ בִּזְמַנּוֹ *We saw it in its time.* The suspect claim may be read in two ways. Some commentators understand the entire phrase as spoken in the voice of the witnesses: "We saw it in its time [that is, on the thirtieth night], but on the next night [the month's "added day"] it could not be seen" (Rambam, Bartenura). This would indicate that, in Rabban Gamliel's time, it was possible to consecrate the new moon retroactively – the witnesses have come on the thirty-first day to describe what they saw two nights previously, and indeed, that is Rambam's ruling (*Hilkhot Kiddush HaḤodesh* 3:16). Most commentaries, however, prefer Rashi's explanation, which we followed in our translation. In that scenario, the witnesses claimed to have seen the moon

9 Rabban Gamliel sent to him saying,
"You must come to me with your staff and your money,
on Yom Kippur as it falls by your counting."
Rabbi Akiva sought out Rabbi Yehoshua, and found him distressed.
Rabbi Akiva said,
"I can show that whatever Rabban Gamliel rules, is fixed –
as it is said: 'These are the appointed times of the LORD… Lev. 23
which you shall announce' –
whether 'in their due seasons' or not,
I have no appointed times but these."
Rabbi Yehoshua went to Rabbi Dosa ben Harkinas.
He said,
"If you challenge the court of Rabban Gamliel,
then we must challenge every single court that has been
from the time of Moses until now,

---

The Talmud (25a) records the full form of the conversation – Rabbi Yehoshua was embittered, so Rabbi Akiva opened with: "Rabbi, may I mention one thing you have taught me?"

אֵין לִי מוֹעֲדוֹת אֶלָּא אֵלּוּ *I have no appointed times but these.* Rabbi Akiva cites the same verse, Leviticus 23:4, at the end of chapter one. There it was to underscore the importance of declaring the new month on the correct day, "at their appointed times," an importance great enough to override the prohibitions of Shabbat for the witnesses. Rabbi Akiva, however, stresses the other side of this coin: Although it is important for the court to rule accurately, even if they fail to do so, their ruling remains intact. "Even if you do so unwittingly, even if you do so intentionally, even if you are misled – once you declare them, these are My appointed times; if not, they are not My appointed times" (*Sifra, Emor* 9:9:3) The word *otam,* spelt three times without a vav in the biblical passage, is interpreted as an emphatically repeated "you" (*atem*) – "that you shall call" (Bartenura, based on *Smag,* Positive Commandment 46). Quoting the verse: "These are My appointed times" (Lev. 23:2), Rabbi Akiva reassures Rabbi Yehoshua that the dates set by Rabban Gamliel's court are, by definition, the correct ones. According to the Talmud, Rabbi Yehoshua answered him with "Akiva, you have consoled me" (see *Makkot* 24b, for another famous example

ט שָׁלַח לוֹ רַבָּן גַּמְלִיאֵל:
גּוֹזְרַנִי עָלֶיךָ שֶׁתָּבֹא אֶצְלִי בְּמַקֶּלְךָ וּבִמְעוֹתֶיךָ
בְּיוֹם הַכִּפּוּרִים שֶׁחָל לִהְיוֹת בְּחֶשְׁבּוֹנְךָ.
הָלַךְ וּמְצָאוֹ רַבִּי עֲקִיבָא מֵצֵר
אָמַר לוֹ: יֵשׁ לִי לִלְמוֹד
שֶׁכָּל מַה שֶּׁעָשָׂה רַבָּן גַּמְלִיאֵל עָשׂוּי
שֶׁנֶּאֱמַר: אֵלֶּה מוֹעֲדֵי ה׳ מִקְרָאֵי קֹדֶשׁ, אֲשֶׁר תִּקְרְאוּ אֹתָם: ויקרא כג
בֵּין בִּזְמַנָּן בֵּין שֶׁלֹּא בִזְמַנָּן
אֵין לִי מוֹעֲדוֹת אֶלָּא אֵלּוּ.
בָּא לוֹ אֵצֶל רַבִּי דוֹסָא בֶּן הַרְכִּינַס
אָמַר לוֹ: אִם בָּאִין אָנוּ לָדוּן
אַחַר בֵּית דִּינוֹ שֶׁלְּרַבָּן גַּמְלִיאֵל
צְרִיכִין אָנוּ לָדוּן
אַחַר כָּל בֵּית דִּין וּבֵית דִּין שֶׁעָמַד
מִימוֹת מֹשֶׁה וְעַד עַכְשָׁיו

---

**שָׁלַח לוֹ רַבָּן גַּמְלִיאֵל** *Rabban Gamliel sent to him.* The doubtful testimony was given, apparently, on Rosh HaShana. While subservient to the Nasi, Rabbi Yehoshua was the *Av Beit Din* ("head of the court"), the most revered and influential member of the Sanhedrin. Rabbi Dosa ben Harkinas may also have expressed his doubts, but the endorsement of Rabbi Yehoshua created an actual threat of Yom Kippur being observed on different days. Rabban Gamliel acted decisively, placing Rabbi Yehoshua between a rock and a hard place: if he counted the days to Yom Kippur from Rosh HaShana according to his own calculation, then obeying Rabban Gamliel's command would have meant desecrating the holiest day of the year. Failing to do so, however, would amount to a statement that the court has led the entire nation to desecrate it.

**הָלַךְ וּמְצָאוֹ רַבִּי עֲקִיבָא** *Rabbi Akiva sought out… and found him.* Rabbi Akiva was Rabbi Yehoshua's foremost student, and keenly felt the need to console him.

as it is said: 'Moses and Aaron, Nadav and Avihu Ex. 24
and seventy of the elders of Israel went up.'
Why were the names of those elders not specified?
To teach us that
any three men who stand up to act as a court for Israel
have the same authority as the court of Moses."
Rabbi Yehoshua took his staff and his money in his hand,
and went to Yavneh, to Rabban Gamliel,
on the day that fell to be Yom Kippur by his counting.
Rabban Gamliel stood and kissed him on his head.
He said, "Come in peace, my master and student;
my master in wisdom,
and my student for accepting my words."

---

רַבִּי בְּחָכְמָה *"My master in wisdom..."* Rabban Gamliel tried to mollify Rabbi Yehoshua, calling him his master. The Talmud ends this conversation with Rabban Gamliel's words "Happy is the generation, wherein the great obey the lesser." However, this was not the last time these two giants clashed (see *Berakhot* 27b).

Rabban Gamliel's statement to Rabbi Yehoshua seems to be an admission that he erred. Could it be that he realized that he was wrong, but once the flares were lit, the necessity to have the entire Jewish world observe Yom Kippur on the same day dictated that the original declaration remain intact? Rabbi Akiva's statement to Rabbi Yehoshua seems to support that. That is how Rabbi Zeraḥya HaLevi understood the mishna in *Sefer HaMaor* (5b). Most commentators rejected his opinion, which is certainly not consistent with the opinion of the Rambam cited above (note to mishna 8).

The authority delegated to Moshe and inherited by the Sanhedrin is not merely that of establishing an astronomic truth (important as that is, see *Shabbat* 75a); it is the power to consecrate time. The Midrash describes God and the Heavenly Host as waiting on Rosh HaShana Eve for the Sanhedrin to declare the new moon, and with it, the Universal day of Judgment (*Yalkut Shimoni* 190). This is reflected by the blessings in the prayers and Kiddush of the Festivals: "Blessed are You ... who sanctifies Israel and the seasons." He sanctifies Israel, and through them, He sanctifies the seasons.

שֶׁנֶּאֱמַר: וַיַּעַל מֹשֶׁה וְאַהֲרֹן, נָדָב וַאֲבִיהוּא שמות כד
וְשִׁבְעִים מִזִּקְנֵי יִשְׂרָאֵל:
וְלָמָּה לֹא נִתְפָּרְשׁוּ שְׁמוֹתָן שֶׁלַּזְּקֵנִים?
אֶלָּא לְלַמֵּד
שֶׁכָּל שְׁלֹשָׁה וּשְׁלֹשָׁה שֶׁעָמְדוּ בֵּית דִּין עַל יִשְׂרָאֵל
הֲרֵי הֵם כְּבֵית דִּינוֹ שֶׁלְּמֹשֶׁה.
נָטַל מַקְלוֹ וּמָעוֹתָיו בְּיָדוֹ
וְהָלַךְ לְיַבְנֶה אֵצֶל רַבָּן גַּמְלִיאֵל
בְּיוֹם שֶׁחָל יוֹם הַכִּפּוּרִים לִהְיוֹת בְּחֶשְׁבּוֹנוֹ.
עָמַד רַבָּן גַּמְלִיאֵל וּנְשָׁקוֹ עַל רֹאשׁוֹ
אָמַר לוֹ: בּוֹא בְשָׁלוֹם, רַבִּי וְתַלְמִידִי!
רַבִּי בְחָכְמָה
וְתַלְמִידִי שֶׁקִּבַּלְתָּ אֶת דְּבָרַי.

---

of Rabbi Akiva's tact). Nonetheless, Rabbi Yehoshua still went to consult with Rabbi Dosa ben Harkinas, who was first to question the witnesses' credibility.

מֹשֶׁה וְאַהֲרֹן *Moses and Aaron.* When Moses first taught Israel the commandments, and Israel accepted, "We shall do and obey," (Ex. 24:7), seventy elders were invited to the foot of Mount Sinai, where "they saw the God of Israel" (ibid. 10). As Moses ascended the mountain, he left these elders to deal with any legal questions that might arise in his absence. Given the immensity of this event, the anonymity of the "seventy elders of Israel" is noteworthy. Rabbi Dosa ben Harkinas' emphasis is slightly different from Rabbi Akiva's. Rabbi Akiva argues that the New Year declared on earth is of necessity the correct one. Rabbi Dosa ben Harkinas, who has already declared his disapproval of the court's decision, stresses the importance of following it nonetheless. Any halakhic court, regardless of who its judges are, is invested with the authority that Moses transferred to the anonymous elders when he left them at the foot of Mount Sinai. Accepting that authority is both a practical necessity, and a mitzva in its own right.

## CHAPTER THREE

1 If the court and all Israel saw the moon,
and witnesses were examined,
but night fell before they had time to say "Consecrated" –
the month is lengthened.
If only the court saw it,
then two must stand and testify before the other judges,
and they say "Consecrated, consecrated!"
If only three saw it and they are the court,

---

emphasize this point; perhaps it understood the division of the chapters of the Mishna as highlighting both the reconciliation between Rabban Gamliel and Rabbi Yehoshua and the reinforcement of the court's authority that it suggests.

From the second mishna onwards, in any case, the chapter deals with the laws of sounding the shofar, the essence of the festival that is "a day of the blowing of the shofar for you" (Num. 29:1). The Mishna identifies the species from which a shofar may be taken (mishna 2), describes its sounding in the Temple (mishna 3), compares it to other ritual soundings of the shofar (mishnayot 4 and 5), discusses what might render a shofar flawed (mishna 6), describes the concept of *kavana* in relation to the shofar (mishna 7), and mentions which people might sound the shofar to fulfill the obligations of others (mishna 8). Before elucidating this point, mishna eight cites two proofs from the Torah regarding the importance of *kavana* – directing, or attuning, one's consiousness to fulfilling mitzvot.

**רָאוּהוּ בֵּית דִּין וְכָל יִשְׂרָאֵל** *If the court and all Israel saw.* This need not be understood literally that everyone saw the new moon, but rather enough people saw it to make it quite clear that the new month could be declared. This empirical fact – or even the examination and authentication of witnesses and their testimony – is not enough to fix the calendar, and if the court does not complete the process of consecrating the month before the day has ended, then it is the following day that becomes the first of the month.

**רָאוּהוּ בֵּית דִּין בִּלְבַד** *If only the court saw it.* A witness may not serve as a judge in the same case in which he testified. In the absence of other witnesses, two of the judges may testify before three other judges, who would render their decision based on the testimony and not based on their own sighting

# פרק שלישי

א רָאוּהוּ בֵּית דִּין וְכָל יִשְׂרָאֵל
נֶחְקְרוּ הָעֵדִים
וְלֹא הִסְפִּיקוּ לוֹמַר: מְקֻדָּשׁ, עַד שֶׁחָשֵׁכָה
הֲרֵי זֶה מְעֻבָּר.
רָאוּהוּ בֵּית דִּין בִּלְבַד
יַעַמְדוּ שְׁנַיִם וְיָעִידוּ בִּפְנֵיהֶם
וְיֹאמְרוּ: מְקֻדָּשׁ, מְקֻדָּשׁ!
רָאוּהוּ שְׁלֹשָׁה, וְהֵן בֵּית דִּין

---

CHAPTER THREE

Chapter three sees a change of tack in the Mishna; moving on from the calendar we turn to the laws of Rosh HaShana itself, and in particular of the shofar. This change in theme does not take place, however, until after the first Mishna, once again raising the question of why the break between these chapters, as between chapters one and two, does not align with their content.

One answer, offered by the *Melekhet Shlomo,* is based upon the reading of the Mishna in the Yerushalmi ad loc., which has "If the court *or* all of Israel," alluding to the fact that in this chapter the Mishna is moving from the Sanhedrin to the masses, leading to the individual's obligations at Rosh HaShana. The *Tiferet Yisrael,* based on a comment by Rashi on chapter four (30b), points out that in the case described in the first mishna – when Rosh HaShana cannot be consecrated in its time – a second day of the festival is kept even in the court itself. Therefore, the actions described in this mishna are no longer preparations for Rosh HaShana, but part of the holiday itself.

The *Tosefta* may indicate a third answer. The *Tosefta* for Rosh HaShana has only two chapters, also seemingly split in a similar way: the first chapter and the first verse of the second chapter discuss *Kiddush HaḤodesh,* and the rest of the second chapter is about the shofar and the Rosh HaShana prayers. The second chapter opens with "If the new moon was consecrated on the thirtieth day, and the witnesses were found to be false, it is still consecrated…," while the first ended with Rabbi Dosa ben Harkinas' argument brought above regarding the legitimacy of the court. It appears that the *Tosefta* wanted to

two must stand,
and two others are appointed to sit with the one,
and they testify before them,
and the court says "Consecrated, consecrated!"
For an individual cannot judge alone.

2 All shofarot are kosher, except for a cow's,
for that is a horn.
Rabbi Yose said: Are not all shofarot called horns?
as it is said: "When they sound a long note on the horn of a ram..." Josh. 6

3 The shofar of Rosh HaShana was that of an ibex –
straight, and plated with gold at the mouth,
and to its sides there were two trumpets.

---

referred to as a *keren* in the Torah, but is paralleled to the horn of an oryx antelope (Deut. 33:17; Tosafot point out that this should disqualify the oryx's horn as well). In Modern Hebrew, *keren* is a generic term, while *shofar* is ceremonial.

וַהֲלֹא כָל הַשּׁוֹפָרוֹת נִקְרְאוּ קֶרֶן *Are not all shofarot called horns?* Rabbi Yose dissented, pointing out that in the verse quoted, the two terms are used interchangeably (the continuation, not quoted, is "when you hear the sound of the *shofar*").

The Talmud (26a) suggests two other reasons for the distinction: a cow's horn is not hollow (the Ramban, in his sermon for Rosh HaShana, disqualified all horns that are not hollow); and "An accuser cannot turn advocate" – the cow's horn evokes the golden calf, the first sin Israel committed after receiving the Torah (see Rashi, Ex. 32:34: "There is no calamity that befalls Israel that does not include punishment for the sin of the calf").

שׁוֹפָר שֶׁלְּרֹאשׁ הַשָּׁנָה *The shofar of Rosh HaShana.* This and the following two mishnayot discuss the type of shofar preferable for each occasion. The *yael* is mentioned twice in the Bible (Ps. 104:18 and Job 39:1) as living in the mountains or on rocky terrain. Today it is usually identified with the ibex, a species of wild goat indigenous to the Ein Gedi region of Israel, which is indeed called *yael* in modern Hebrew (see, however, the note on mishna five).

מְצֻפֶּה זָהָב *Plated with gold.* This describes the shofar sounded in the Temple (Bartenura). The Talmud disqualifies a shofar with a plated mouthpiece, but

יַעַמְדוּ שְׁנַיִם
וְיוֹשִׁיבוּ מֵחַבְרֵיהֶם אֵצֶל הַיָּחִיד, וְיָעִידוּ בִפְנֵיהֶם
וְיֹאמְרוּ: מְקֻדָּשׁ, מְקֻדָּשׁ!
שֶׁאֵין הַיָּחִיד נֶאֱמָן עַל יְדֵי עַצְמוֹ.

ב כָּל הַשּׁוֹפָרוֹת כְּשֵׁרִין
חוּץ מִשֶּׁלַּפָּרָה
מִפְּנֵי שֶׁהוּא קֶרֶן.
אָמַר רַבִּי יוֹסֵי: וַהֲלֹא כָל הַשּׁוֹפָרוֹת נִקְרְאוּ קֶרֶן
שֶׁנֶּאֱמַר: בִּמְשֹׁךְ בְּקֶרֶן הַיּוֹבֵל: יהושע ו

ג שׁוֹפָר שֶׁלְּרֹאשׁ הַשָּׁנָה
שֶׁלַּיָּעֵל, פָּשׁוּט וּפִיו מְצֻפֶּה זָהָב
וּשְׁתֵּי חֲצוֹצְרוֹת מִן הַצְּדָדִין.

---

of the moon. The Talmud (25b–26a) debates whether this rule applies to criminal law as well: Rabbi Akiva argued that in matters of life and death, judges cannot achieve the necessary detachment from what they have seen and hence would not be allowed to preside, even if their testimony was not required.Rabbi Tarfon, on the other hand, believed that they can maintain objectivity. Here, however, even Rabbi Akiva would agree that one who did not deliberately go out looking for the moon can act as judge in this case (see Rashbam, *Bava Batra* 114a).

וְיוֹשִׁיבוּ מֵחַבְרֵיהֶם *Two others are appointed.* The issue here is not the reliability of the judges, but the need for a formal court to declare the month consecrated (Rashi). The model for *Kiddush HaḤodesh*, according to the Talmud, is the commandment given to Moses and Aaron in Egypt and therefore a single judge is insufficient (25b). Two are also insufficient, since a court must consist of an odd number of judges, to enable a majority decision in cases of disagreement (Tosafot, based on *Sanhedrin* 3b).

כָּל הַשּׁוֹפָרוֹת *All shofarot.* The Mishna distinguishes here between two words (*shofar* and *keren*) for the horn of an animal. A cow's horn is not explicitly

A long note sounded from the shofar,
and short notes from the trumpets,
for the commandment of the day was the shofar.

4 On fast days they would blow the shofarot of rams –
curved, and plated with silver at the mouth,
and in between the shofarot were two trumpets.
Short notes sounded from the shofarot,
and long notes from the trumpets,
for the commandment of the day was the trumpets.

5 The Jubilee is like Rosh HaShana
with respect to the shofar and to the blessings.
Rabbi Yehuda says,
"On Rosh HaShana one blows the shofar of a ram,
and for the Jubilee, that of an ibex."

---

הַיּוֹבֵל *The Jubilee.* To herald the start of a Jubilee year a shofar was sounded on Yom Kippur (Lev. 25:9), and the three blessings that constitute the heart of the Rosh HaShana Musaf prayer were added to the Yom Kippur Musaf prayer as well (see mishna 4:5).

Rabbi Yehuda disagreed with the opinion cited in mishna three, holding that the ram's horn is preferable to an ibex's for Rosh HaShana. As well as symbolizing humility, the ram's horn evokes the binding of Isaac (see commentary, page 476). As the shofar of the Jubilee sounds in the liberation of the slaves and the return of the land to its owners, the long, straight horn of the ibex is an appropriate symbol (Tosafot). It is Rabbi Yehuda's view that was codified in halakha, although some halakhic decisors ruled in accordance with the opinion of Levi (*Rosh HaShana* 26a) that a ram's horn was sounded on both occasions. The Rambam took a radical approach, and ruled that only a ram's horn is valid (*Hilkhot Shofar* 1:1). His approach was rejected by other authorities. The Yemenite community, whose general practice corresponds to the Rambam's rulings, do not use a ram's horn, but rather they use the horn of the Kudu – an African antelope – possibly based on a tradition identifying this animal with the *yael* mentioned in the Mishna.

שׁוֹפָר מַאֲרִיךְ וַחֲצוֹצְרוֹת מְקַצְּרוֹת
שֶׁמִּצְוַת הַיּוֹם בַּשּׁוֹפָר.

ד בַּתַּעֲנִיּוֹת
בְּשֶׁלַּזְּכָרִים, כְּפוּפִין וּפִיהֶן מְצֻפֶּה כֶסֶף
וּשְׁתֵּי חֲצוֹצְרוֹת בָּאֶמְצַע.
שׁוֹפָר מְקַצֵּר וַחֲצוֹצְרוֹת מַאֲרִיכוֹת
שֶׁמִּצְוַת הַיּוֹם בַּחֲצוֹצְרוֹת.

ה שָׁוֶה הַיּוֹבֵל לְרֹאשׁ הַשָּׁנָה, לַתְּקִיעָה וְלַבְּרָכוֹת.
רַבִּי יְהוּדָה אוֹמֵר:
בְּרֹאשׁ הַשָּׁנָה תּוֹקְעִין בְּשֶׁלַּזְּכָרִים
וּבַיּוֹבְלוֹת בְּשֶׁלַּיְּעֵלִים.

---

allows gilding the body of the shofar (27b). This shofar was plated at the point where it began narrowing, but not at the mouthpiece itself (27a). The *Tiferet Yisrael* points out that the use of gold is problematic in and of itself, as it evokes the golden calf, but mere plating is acceptable. The longer note of the shofar ensured that it could be heard, and would not be drowned out by the trumpets.

**בַּתַּעֲנִיּוֹת** *On fast days.* Silver trumpets, used in the Torah to gather the people for travel and war (Num. 10:1–10), were later sounded on the fast days decreed due to droughts and other communal hardships as "one of the practices of repentance… When trouble comes, and they cry out and sound the trumpets, everyone will know that their evil actions caused their misfortune" (Rambam, *Hilkhot Ta'aniyot* 1:2).

**כְּפוּפִין** *Curved.* The ibex has a long horn shaped in a wide arc, straighter than a ram's, which is twisted. The Talmud explains that the shapes of the different horns symbolize different ways of standing before God in prayer – on Rosh HaShana we should look straight up toward heaven; on fast days we should humble ourselves (Rashi).

6 A shofar which was cracked and glued together
is unfit for the commandment.
Shards of a shofar stuck together
are unfit.
If it had a hole in it and was mended,
if the hole had interfered with the sound –
it is unfit for the commandment.
If not – then it is fit.

7 If one blows the shofar into a pit or a cellar or a barrel,
one who hears the sound of the shofar –
has fulfilled his obligation;
one who hears the echo – has not.
So, too, one who walks behind a synagogue,
or whose house adjoins the synagogue,
and who hears the sound of the shofar or the sound of the megilla,

---

into the floor of a house. The word may derive from Greek (*Arukh*). Some editions read *pitam*, with the same meaning, derived from the Hebrew root meaning "fattened."

קוֹל שׁוֹפָר *The sound of the shofar.* This mishna is referring to times when the Romans prohibited certain Jewish practices, including the sounding of the shofar, and Jews sought sound-proofed venues to do so (Rav Hai Gaon). In any case, the general principle is that the sound of the shofar must be heard directly, not through an echo.

וְכֵן *So, too.* The connection is surprising, as the two cases do not seem similar. The first addresses the quality of the sound that one must hear, while the second addresses the case of a passer-by who hears a valid sound. The Talmud brings the two cases closer by pointing out that people sitting in the pit or barrel into which the shofar was blown have clearly heard its sound and fulfilled their obligation. The Mishna, then, must be discussing the status of those standing outside the pit who hear the sound of the shofar. The second case cites an additional requirement for fulfilling the mitzva: the sound must be both sufficiently clear, and consciously listened to.

ו שׁוֹפָר שֶׁנִּסְדַּק וְדִבְּקוֹ, פָּסוּל
דִּבֵּק שִׁבְרֵי שׁוֹפָרוֹת, פָּסוּל
נִקַּב וּסְתָמוֹ:
אִם מְעַכֵּב אֶת הַתְּקִיעָה - פָּסוּל
וְאִם לָאו - כָּשֵׁר.

ז הַתּוֹקֵעַ לְתוֹךְ הַבּוֹר אוֹ לְתוֹךְ הַדּוּת אוֹ לְתוֹךְ הַפִּיטָס:
אִם קוֹל שׁוֹפָר שָׁמַע - יָצָא
וְאִם קוֹל הֲבָרָה שָׁמַע - לֹא יָצָא.
וְכֵן מִי שֶׁהָיָה עוֹבֵר אֲחוֹרֵי בֵית הַכְּנֶסֶת
אוֹ שֶׁהָיָה בֵיתוֹ סָמוּךְ לְבֵית הַכְּנֶסֶת
וְשָׁמַע קוֹל שׁוֹפָר אוֹ קוֹל מְגִלָּה:

---

**שׁוֹפָר שֶׁנִּסְדַּק...שִׁבְרֵי שׁוֹפָרוֹת** *A shofar which was cracked... Shards of a shofar.* The sound emerging from the *shofar* must be natural. Therefore, if it was produced by a cracked or broken *shofar* that was repaired, it is disqualified from use. However, the Talmud (27b) states that a crack across the shofar's width (as opposed to its length) may be repaired, as long as the distance from the crack to the mouth of the shofar is at least the minimum length of a shofar.

**נִקַּב** *If it had a hole in it.* If the shofar was not cracked along its length, and the hole in it has been repaired without using any non-shofar material, providing that the shofar could have produced an acceptable sound before the repair, it retains its fitness. The Ramban required the repair to have been done by heating and reshaping the shofar; Rashi and the Rosh allowed plugging the hole with glue.

**לְתוֹךְ הַבּוֹר אוֹ לְתוֹךְ הַדּוּת** *Into a pit or a cellar.* The two words are close in meaning, but while the first is dug out of the ground, the second is part of the house, built underground or into a wall.

**הַפִּיטָס** *Or a barrel.* A *pitas* is a large, clay earthenware receptacle used for storage (see *Beitza* 15b). These either stood independently or were built

if he attunes his heart to it –
he has fulfilled his obligation,
and if he does not – he has not.
Even though both heard it, one attuned his heart,
and the other did not.

8 "When Moses raised his hand, Israel prevailed..." *Ex. 17*
Could it be that Moses' hands won or lost the war?
No, rather this is to tell you,
that when Israel raised their eyes above
and submitted their hearts to their Father in heaven –
they prevailed,

---

5. To remind us of the Temple's destruction and prompt us to pray for its restoration
6. To evoke the binding of Isaac (see commentary to 3:5)
7. To make us humble ourselves before God (see commentary to 3:4)
8. To raise awareness of the impending Day of Judgment
9. To prepare for the miraculous ingathering of the exiles
10. To affirm our belief in the future resurrection.

The kabbalists have composed elaborate prayers to facilitate having the proper intent (see pages 467–475). There were those who objected to laymen reciting them, as they do not understand what they are saying (*Magen Avraham* 98:1). Others considered them independent prayers, which have nothing to do with the mitzva of shofar (*Derekh HaḤayyim*).

**וְהָיָה כַּאֲשֶׁר יָרִים מֹשֶׁה יָדוֹ** *"When Moses raised his hand..."* This "submission of the heart" goes beyond the simple *kavana* required to fulfill a mitzva. The Israelites prevailed when they directed their hearts, not to the technical fulfillment of a mitzva, but in a fuller, more existential sense, they transcended their immediate predicament and looked to God.

**אוֹ שׁוֹבְרוֹת מִלְחָמָה** *Or lost the war.* The Hebrew phrase (literally, "or break the war") is difficult – the *Mekhilta* reads "or break down the Amalekites." The phrase, however, could anticipate the later moment when Moses stands between holding up, and breaking, the tablets of the Law (see *Tanḥuma, BeShalaḥ* 27).

אִם כִּוֵּן לִבּוֹ – יָצָא
וְאִם לָאו – לֹא יָצָא.
אַף עַל פִּי שֶׁזֶּה שָׁמַע וְזֶה שָׁמַע
זֶה כִּוֵּן לִבּוֹ וְזֶה לֹא כִּוֵּן לִבּוֹ.

ח וְהָיָה כַּאֲשֶׁר יָרִים מֹשֶׁה יָדוֹ וְגָבַר יִשְׂרָאֵל: וְגוֹמֵר. שמות יז
וְכִי יָדָיו שֶׁלְּמֹשֶׁה עוֹשׂוֹת מִלְחָמָה אוֹ שׁוֹבְרוֹת מִלְחָמָה?
אֶלָּא לוֹמַר לָךְ:
כָּל זְמַן שֶׁהָיוּ יִשְׂרָאֵל מִסְתַּכְּלִים כְּלַפֵּי מַעְלָה
וּמְשַׁעְבְּדִין אֶת לִבָּם לַאֲבִיהֶם שֶׁבַּשָּׁמַיִם
הָיוּ מִתְגַּבְּרִים

---

אִם כִּוֵּן לִבּוֹ *If he attunes his heart.* Both one hearing the sound of the shofar and one sounding the shofar must have in mind the intention to fulfill the mitzva. The congregation in the synagogue gathered specifically for that purpose. Consequently, even if one of them forgets to "attune his heart" at the moment of the sounding, his *kavana* is considered sufficient (*Mishna Berura* 589:16, following Radbaz). On the other hand, one who happens to pass by the synagogue and hears the shofar incidentally, does not fulfill his obligation unless he makes a conscious decision to listen. The debate whether or not mitzvot require *kavana* is developed in the Talmud (28a–29a), and continues among the Geonim and Rishonim (early commentaries). It was concluded that *kavana* is necessary for the fulfillment of a mitzva, but only in the minimalist sense of a general intention to carry out the command (*Tur, OḤ* 589).

Rav Sa'adia Gaon compiled a list of ten reasons for the mitzva to sound the shofar (cited by Abudarham):

1. To remember the creation
2. To call us to repent before Yom Kippur (this is the primary reason cited by the Rambam, *Hilkhot Teshuva* 3:4)
3. To echo the revelation at Sinai (see commentary on 4:6)
4. To symbolize the words of the prophets (see Ezek. 32:2–3)

and when they did not –
they fell.
In the same way you could say,
"Make a serpent of fire and place it on a standard, *Num. 21*
and anyone who was bitten but sees that, will live."
Could it be that the serpent kills or that the serpent gives life?
No –
but when Israel raised their eyes above
and submitted their hearts to their Father in heaven –
they lived,
and when did not –
they died.
A deaf man, an imbecile, and a child
cannot fulfill an obligation for others.
This is the rule:
one who is not obliged by a command
cannot fulfill it for others.

---

is not one who is intellectually or emotionally impaired, but rather one whose conduct is bizarre, i.e. one "who strolls at night, who sleeps in a cemetery, or who tears his clothes."

In recent generations, when more and more people with severe hearing impairments are able to communicate intelligibly, contemporary halakhic decisors have debated the appropriate status to ascribe to these people in Jewish Law. Rabbi E.Y. Waldenberg ruled that under those circumstances, they are considered fully competent and obligated to fulfill the mitzvot (*Tzitz Eliezer* 15:46:3). Rabbi Moshe Feinstein holds that they are still considered halakhically deaf (*Iggerot Moshe*, YD 4:17). In any case, the mitzva of the shofar specifically requires the sense of hearing, making any deaf person exempt, and therefore unable to sound it for others to fulfill their obligation (*Shulḥan Arukh*, OḤ 589:2, following the *Kol Bo*).

וְאִם לָאו
הָיוּ נוֹפְלִין.
כַּיּוֹצֵא בַדָּבָר אַתָּה אוֹמֵר:
עֲשֵׂה לְךָ שָׂרָף וְשִׂים אֹתוֹ עַל־נֵס במדבר כא
וְהָיָה כָּל־הַנָּשׁוּךְ וְרָאָה אֹתוֹ וָחָי:
וְכִי נָחָשׁ מֵמִית, אוֹ נָחָשׁ מְחַיֶּה?
אֶלָּא בִּזְמַן שֶׁיִּשְׂרָאֵל מִסְתַּכְּלִין כְּלַפֵּי מַעְלָה
וּמְשַׁעְבְּדִין אֶת לִבָּם לַאֲבִיהֶן שֶׁבַּשָּׁמַיִם
הָיוּ מִתְרַפְּאִים
וְאִם לָאו
הָיוּ נִמּוֹקִים.
חֵרֵשׁ, שׁוֹטֶה וְקָטָן
אֵין מוֹצִיאִין אֶת הָרַבִּים יְדֵי חוֹבָתָן.
זֶה הַכְּלָל: כָּל שֶׁאֵינוֹ מְחֻיָּב בַּדָּבָר
אֵינוֹ מוֹצִיא אֶת הָרַבִּים יְדֵי חוֹבָתָן.

---

וְכִי נָחָשׁ *Could it be that the serpent…* The misconception, indeed, ultimately took hold. There were those who actually worshiped the copper serpent, as the means of divine salvation (*Tosefta, Avoda Zara* 4:3) until King Hezekiah destroyed it (II Kings 18:4).

חֵרֵשׁ *A deaf man.* One who is both deaf and mute (Mishna, *Terumot* 1:2); a deaf person who can speak is considered fully accountable for his or her actions, and is obligated to fulfill all the mitzvot, unlike a child or imbecile. Likewise, the imbecile whom the mishna exempts from the mitzva of shofar

# CHAPTER FOUR

1 When Rosh HaShana fell on Shabbat,

---

music on Shabbat (Rambam, *Hilkhot Shabbat* 23:4 – extrapolating *Beitza* 36b), music was played, even on Shabbat, as a part of the service in the Temple (*Sukka* 55a). If the Torah explicitly commands the sounding of the shofar on Yom Tov, this mitzva should be permitted on Shabbat.

Consequently, the problematic part of the mishna is not that the shofar was sounded in the Temple on Shabbat, but that it was prohibited "in the provinces" (see below). The Talmud Yerushalmi discusses this at length and offers three explanations for the differentiation between the Temple and the rest of the country.

As part of the sacrificial service of the day, the sounding of the shofar in the Temple is qualitatively different from that outside (see Rambam, *Hilkhot Shofar* 1:2, who rules that only in the Temple the shofar was accompanied by trumpets). What is more, it is only in the Temple, where the new moon was consecrated, that it was known for sure if the day was indeed Rosh HaShana. Thirdly, the Yerushalmi compares the verse that calls Rosh HaShana "a day of blowing the shofar" (Num. 29:1), with the one that calls it "a day of recalling blowing the shofar" (Lev. 23:24). On weekdays, Rosh HaShana is a day of sounding, but on Shabbat it is a day of recalling the sounding – except in the Temple, where it is part of the sacrificial service. This last distinction is manifest in our prayer service for the day: There is a different formula for the *Amida* prayer when Rosh HaShana occurs on a weekday: "And You… have given us in love this Day of Remembrance, a day of blowing the shofar…," while when it occurs on Shabbat the formula is: "… a day of recalling blowing the shofar" (Raaviya, 537). Similarly, when the first day of Rosh HaShana falls on Shabbat, the *piyutim* that refer to the shofar are postponed until the second day, with *piyutim* from the second day service moved forward to replace them (see pages 367–385; 663–677). The Talmud Bavli (29b) rejects the Yerushalmi's reasons, offering a technical one instead: The sages decreed that the shofar may not be sounded on Shabbat lest one will carry his shofar in the public domain in order to enlist the aid of an expert in fulfilling his obligation, just as they decreed that the four species may not be taken on Shabbat of Sukkot, and the megilla may not be read on Shabbat (this last ruling now applies only in Jerusalem, where the megilla is normally read on *Shushan Purim*, Adar 15th; Adar 14th never falls

# פרק רביעי

## א יוֹם טוֹב שֶׁלְּרֹאשׁ הַשָּׁנָה שֶׁחָל לִהְיוֹת בַּשַּׁבָּת

CHAPTER FOUR

The closing chapter of the Mishna deals with the sounding of the shofar itself. First noting the differences in the observance of the mitzva in Jerusalem (or the Temple – see note to mishna one) and outside it, the chapter moves from Rabban Yoḥanan ben Zakkai's ordinance on this subject to four other ordinances of his regarding the festivals; the final two relating to consecrating the new month, which was the primary subject of the first two chapters of the tractate.

Mishnayot five to seven discuss the formula of the Musaf prayer on Rosh HaShana. The sages understood that the mitzva of the shofar is fulfilled in the context of prayer: "Recite before Me… Kingship, so that you crown Me as your King; Remembrances, so that your memory will come before Me favorably; and how? Through the shofar" (*Rosh HaShana* 16a and 34b). As Rav Hutner explains (*Paḥad Yitzḥak, Rosh HaShana* 25:1) the sounding of the shofar serves a double purpose, both affirming God as our king and beseeching Him to remember us with kindness. Rosh HaShana is the only day on which we are commanded to pray: "a day of recalling blowing the shofar, a holy assembly" (Lev. 23:24).

The last two mishnayot of the tractate return to the sounding itself. Mishna eight enumerates laws one may not break in order to fulfill the mitzva, while mishna nine discusses the three different notes that are sounded, concluding with the question of whether an individual need recite all nine blessings, or whether one may rely on the shali'aḥ tzibbur to fulfill the obligation on the congregation's behalf. This relates to the mitzva of shofar – Rav Soloveitchik (*Yemei Zikaron* p. 143) explained that fulfilling the mitzva is an interaction between two parties – the one sounding the shofar, and the community hearing those sounds. The same can be said regarding prayer as well; the Repetition of the Amida affords us the opportunity to engage in communal prayer after having addressed God as individuals.

**יוֹם טוֹב שֶׁלְּרֹאשׁ הַשָּׁנָה שֶׁחָל לִהְיוֹת בַּשַּׁבָּת** *When Rosh HaShana fell on Shabbat.* Blowing the shofar is not considered a *melakha*, labor forbidden on Shabbat and Yom Tov, but rather a *ḥokhma*, a skill (*Rosh HaShana* 29b et al.). While we might expect it to be subject to the rabbinic prohibition against playing

in the Temple they would sound the shofar,
but in the provinces, they would not.
After the Temple was destroyed,
Rabban Yoḥanan ben Zakkai enacted
that they sound it in every place with a court.
Rabbi Elazar said,
Rabban Yoḥanan ben Zakkai only enacted this for Yavneh.
They said to him –
Yavneh is the same for this
as any other place where the court may be.

---

Rabbi Akiva Yosef Schlesinger did, indeed, blow the shofar there on Shabbat Rosh HaShana 5666 (1905).

מִשֶּׁחָרַב בֵּית הַמִּקְדָּשׁ *After the Temple was destroyed.* Rabban Yoḥanan ben Zakkai, one of the disciples of Hillel (*Sukka* 28a), had the foresight to leave Jerusalem before the destruction of the Temple, and gained Roman agreement to reinstitute the Sanhedrin in Yavne, thus keeping the world of Torah alive (*Gittin* 56b). The Talmud enumerates nine ordinances instituted by Rabban Yoḥanan (*Rosh HaShana* 31b). Under his leadership, the new center at Yavne took over the role of consecrating the month, and Rabban Yoḥanan ben Zakkai instituted, just as in the Temple, that the shofar would be sounded on Shabbat before the Sanhedrin in Yavne. The Talmud alludes to the fact that initially this ordinance encountered serious internal opposition (29b).

בְּכָל מָקוֹם שֶׁיֵּשׁ בּוֹ בֵית דִּין *In every place with a court.* According to the Rambam (*Hilkhot Shofar* 2:9), this applies only to the seat of the Sanhedrin, as the shofar was only sounded on Shabbat before the court which consecrated the new month. Rashi held that it applies every place where there is a regular, authoritative court of twenty-three members, a "lesser Sanhedrin" (see *Sanhedrin* 2a). The Rif ruled in accordance with Rashi's understanding, and sounded the shofar before his court on Shabbat, as he considered it the preeminent court of his time (Rosh, *Rosh HaShana* 4:1; see Ran, 8a for a different explanation). Other Rishonim disagreed with his ruling, and the *Shulḥan Arukh* ruled that today the shofar may not be sounded anywhere on Shabbat, without exception (*OḤ* 558:5).

בַּמִּקְדָּשׁ הָיוּ תוֹקְעִים
אֲבָל לֹא בַמְּדִינָה.
מִשֶּׁחָרַב בֵּית הַמִּקְדָּשׁ
הִתְקִין רַבָּן יוֹחָנָן בֶּן זַכַּאי
שֶׁיְּהוּ תוֹקְעִין בְּכָל מָקוֹם שֶׁיֵּשׁ בּוֹ בֵית דִּין.
אָמַר רַבִּי אֶלְעָזָר:
לֹא הִתְקִין רַבָּן יוֹחָנָן בֶּן זַכַּאי
אֶלָּא בְיַבְנֶה בִּלְבַד.
אָמְרוּ לוֹ:
אֶחָד יַבְנֶה, וְאֶחָד כָּל מָקוֹם שֶׁיֵּשׁ בּוֹ בֵית דִּין.

---

on Shabbat). In any case, none of these precautionary Shabbat prohibitions were in effect in the Temple (Rashi).

**וּבַמְּדִינָה** *In the provinces.* The final chapter of tractate *Eiruvin* cites a list of rabbinic decrees that were in effect in the *Medina* but not in the *Mikdash*. In modern Hebrew, the term *Medina* means "state," and in Biblical Hebrew it means "province" (see Esther 1:1). As Radak points out (*Sefer HaShorashim*), the word is often used to denote "town," which corresponds to its meaning in related languages (Aramaic, Arabic). The question is, what does it mean in this mishna?

Rashi (here and in *Eiruvin*) understood the term *baMedina* to include Jerusalem: it is only in the Temple itself – in his reading – that rabbinic enactments did not apply, if implementing them might interfere with the service. Within the Temple precincts preventive rulings were unnecessary, as neither priests nor worshipers were likely to desecrate Shabbat while there. Rambam, on the other hand, writes (commentary to the Mishna, and in *Hilkhot Shofar* 2:8) that the shofar was sounded on Shabbat throughout Jerusalem, the whole city being included in the term *Mikdash*.

On the basis of this view, some have suggested that even today, one may blow the shofar on Shabbat in Jerusalem, at least within the Old City walls.

2 Jerusalem had another advantage over Yavneh:
each settlement where one saw it and heard it
and was close by and could come,
sounded the shofar.
But in Yavneh
they could only sound within the court itself.

3 At first,
one would take the lulav seven days in the Temple,
but in the provinces, one day only.
After the Temple was destroyed,
Rabban Yoḥanan ben Zakkai enacted
that one takes the lulav seven days in the provinces,
in remembrance of the Temple;
and that all the day of waving, new produce be forbidden.

---

festivals, during which people came "before the Lord" (Deut. 16:15; see ibid., 11). The first day was the only day on which this mitzva was performed in the provinces. Taking the four species, like the sounding of the shofar, is forbidden on Shabbat as a precaution against people carrying in the public domain.

זֵכֶר לַמִּקְדָּשׁ *In remembrance of the Temple.* "They called you an outcast, saying: this is Zion, for whom no one cares [Jer. 30:17]. Therefore, she must be cared for" (*Rosh HaShana* 30a; *Sukka* 41a). The Talmud cites this verse as a source for all the ordinances instituted "in rememberance of the Temple." Rabbi Yosef Rozin of Rogachev (*Mikhtevei Torah* 154) understands these as a way of reenactment of the festival as celebrated in the Temple, preparing us for when it will be restored. Rabbi Meir Simḥa of Dvinsk (*Or Same'aḥ, Hilkhot Lulav* 7:15) argued that the memory of the Temple was merely the rationale for the ordinance, and it will continue to be in effect even after the Redemption.

וְשֶׁיְּהֵא יוֹם הֶנֵף *And that all the day of waving.* The Torah prohibits one to partake of the harvest of the new crop until a communal meal-offering is sacrificed (Lev. 23:14). The waving of this offering (the *omer* offering, named after the volume unit mentioned in Ex. 16:36) was the culmination of a ceremonial process, which began with the public reaping of the first sheaves of barley, which were then threshed, toasted, ground and sifted thirteen times,

ב וְעוֹד זֹאת הָיְתָה יְרוּשָׁלַיִם יְתֵרָה עַל יַבְנֶה
שֶׁכָּל עִיר שֶׁהִיא רוֹאָה וְשׁוֹמַעַת וּקְרוֹבָה וִיכוֹלָה לָבֹא
תּוֹקְעִין
וּבְיַבְנֶה
לֹא הָיוּ תוֹקְעִין, אֶלָּא בְּבֵית דִּין בִּלְבַד.

ג בָּרִאשׁוֹנָה
הָיָה הַלּוּלָב נִטָּל בַּמִּקְדָּשׁ שִׁבְעָה
וּבַמְּדִינָה יוֹם אֶחָד.
מִשֶּׁחָרַב בֵּית הַמִּקְדָּשׁ
הִתְקִין רַבָּן יוֹחָנָן בֶּן זַכַּאי
שֶׁיְּהֵא הַלּוּלָב נִטָּל בַּמְּדִינָה שִׁבְעָה
זֵכֶר לַמִּקְדָּשׁ
וְשֶׁיְּהֵא יוֹם הֶנֵף כֻּלּוֹ אָסוּר.

---

שֶׁכָּל עִיר *Each settlement.* Residents of the farms and villages surrounding Jerusalem would come to the city to participate in the Temple service. People who could see Jerusalem, and hear the shofar sounded there from their houses, and who could walk there on Shabbat unobstructed, were considered residents of Jerusalem in this sense (cf. *Megilla* 3b, regarding the date of Purim). This appears to support the ruling of the Rambam cited in the note to the previous mishna, but some understand that it refers to the final forty years that the Temple was standing, after the Sanhedrin left the Chamber of Hewn Stone (Ritva, Meiri; the exile of the Sanhedrin is mentioned in *Sanhedrin* 41a and *Avoda Zara* 8b).

הָיָה הַלּוּלָב נִטָּל *One would take the lulav.* The Torah instructs us to take the four species on the first day of Sukkot, and to rejoice "before the LORD" for seven days (Lev. 23:40). The sages understood this verse as a mitzva for each individual to take the four species on the first day (Ramban, Lev. 23:15), and a separate mitzva to rejoice with the four species in the Temple all seven days (*Sifra*, cited in Rashi, *Sukka* 41a), as Sukkot is one of the three pilgrim

4 At first,
they would accept testimony to the new moon all day long.
Once,
the witnesses' arrival was delayed,
and the Levites mistook their song.
Then they enacted,
that they would only accept testimony until the hour of Minḥa.
If witnesses came from Minḥa onwards,
they would treat that day as holy and the next, too, as holy.

---

only to crops grown by Jews. This lenient opinion was almost universally accepted. In recent generations, due to improved refrigeration techniques, it is more feasible to avoid new produce.

וְנִתְקַלְקְלוּ הַלְוִיִּם בַּשִּׁיר *And the Levites mistook their song.* The new month can begin on either the thirtieth or the thirty-first day of the previous month. Since the court could only receive testimony during the day (*Rosh HaShana* 25b), the thirtieth morning always began with uncertainty. While the Temple stood, the Levites would sing the psalm for each weekday twice (31a), once accompanying the morning Daily Offering and once accompanying the afternoon Daily Offering. On the thirtieth day, then, they would sing the regular weekday song in the morning; and if the month was consecrated before the afternoon offering, they would accompany it with the psalm for Rosh Ḥodesh. The delayed arrival of witnesses on this occasion caused the Levites either to sing the usual weekday song a second time, or to fail to sing at all (30b). An alternative reading is suggested by the Rambam (*Hilkhot Kiddush HaḤodesh* 3:6), who writes that the problem was that the Musaf offering was not sacrificed on time.

מִן הַמִּנְחָה וּלְמַעְלָה *From Minḥa onwards.* If the witnesses arrived after the afternoon offering had been sacrificed, and the additional offering had not been sacrificed, and the special psalm of Rosh Ḥodesh or Rosh HaShana had not been recited, the remainder of the day was treated as sacred, i.e. if it was Rosh HaShana they would refrain from performing labor throughout the day, but the following day would also be observed as Rosh Ḥodesh, when they would perform the appropriate service and refrain from performing labor if it was Rosh HaShana (Rashi).

ד בָּרִאשׁוֹנָה
הָיוּ מְקַבְּלִין עֵדוּת הַחֹדֶשׁ כָּל הַיּוֹם.
פַּעַם אַחַת
נִשְׁתָּהוּ הָעֵדִים מִלָּבוֹא
וְנִתְקַלְקְלוּ הַלְוִיִּם בַּשִּׁיר
הִתְקִינוּ
שֶׁלֹּא יְהוּ מְקַבְּלִין אֶלָּא עַד הַמִּנְחָה
וְאִם בָּאוּ עֵדִים מִן הַמִּנְחָה וּלְמַעְלָה
נוֹהֲגִין אוֹתוֹ הַיּוֹם קֹדֶשׁ וּלְמָחָר קֹדֶשׁ.

---

in preparation for its offering (as described in the sixth chapter of *Menaḥot*). This ceremony was performed on the second day of Pesaḥ, despite the objection of some sectarians (see mishna 2:1 and note). "The *omer* having been offered, they left the Temple and found the streetmarkets of Jerusalem replete with flour and toast…" (*Menaḥot* 67b). Residents of the provinces could begin partaking of the new produce in the middle of the day, confident that the Omer had already been offered (ibid. 68a). After the destruction of the Temple, Rabban Yoḥanan ben Zakkai instituted that partaking of the new produce would be prohibited the entire day (see *Menaḥot* 68b for a discussion of his sources and motives).

The Mishna in *Kiddushin* 37a relates a debate as to whether this prohibition of "*ḥadash*" (new produce) applies in the Diaspora as well as in the land of Israel. In *Menaḥot* 68b the Talmud states that even according to the lenient opinion there is a rabbinic prohibition against *ḥadash* abroad. This is not a great inconvenience around the Mediterranean, but in Northern Europe, where the crops are only sown after the end of winter, this has caused a severe problem – crops are planted before Pesaḥ but reaped after it, defining them as new produce until the following Pesaḥ. Rabbi Yoel Sirkis (Baḥ, YD 293) ruled in the seventeenth century that when no *yashan* (old produce) is available, one may eat *ḥadash*, based on the *Or Zarua* (1:328) who ruled that *ḥadash* in the Diaspora was only a rabbinic prohibition, and Rabbi Yitzḥak ben Asher (Tosafot, *Kiddushin* 36b), who ruled that the restriction applies

After the Temple was destroyed,
Rabban Yoḥanan ben Zakkai enacted
that they would accept testimony to the new moon all day long.

Rabbi Yehoshua ben Korḥa said:
Rabban Yoḥanan ben Zakkai had another enactment:
Even if the head of the court is in some other place,
the witnesses need go nowhere else but to its meeting-place.

5 The order of the blessings:
One says "Patriarchs" and "Divine Might" and "Holiness of the Name,"
and includes "Kingship" with them,
and does not sound the shofar;
one says "Holiness of the Day"
and sounds;
"Remembrances"
and sounds;
"Shofarot"
and sounds;
and says "Temple Service" and "Thanksgiving" and "the Priestly Blessing" –

---

Rabban Yoḥanan ben Zakkai chose to make the institution, rather than the leading figure of the Nasi, the center of authority. Consequently, testimony to the moon could be accepted in his absence.

סֵדֶר בְּרָכוֹת *The order of the blessings.* Every Amida prayer opens and closes with the same blessings; "Patriarchs" (*Magen Avraham*), "Divine Might" (*Meḥayyeh HaMetim*) and "Holiness" (*Ata Kadosh*) at the beginning and "Temple Service" (*Retzeh*), "Thanksgiving" (*Modim*) and "the Priestly Blessing" (*Sim Shalom*) at the end. On Shabbat and festivals the thirteen petitioning blessings that constitute the heart of the Amida prayer on weekdays are replaced by the respective "Holiness of the Day" blessings. On Musaf of Rosh HaShana, they are replaced by three blessings, corresponding to the three central themes of the day, "Kingship," "Remembrance" and "Shofarot." "Kingship" is combined with the regular middle blessing of the Amida prayer.

וּבִרְכַּת כֹּהֲנִים *The Priestly Blessing.* The language of *Sim Shalom* ("Grant peace...") – "Bless us," "by the light of Your face," "peace" – mirrors the

מִשֶּׁחָרַב בֵּית הַמִּקְדָּשׁ
הִתְקִין רַבָּן יוֹחָנָן בֶּן זַכַּאי
שֶׁיְּהוּ מְקַבְּלִין עֵדוּת הַחֹדֶשׁ כָּל הַיּוֹם.
אָמַר רַבִּי יְהוֹשֻׁעַ בֶּן קָרְחָה:
וְעוֹד זֹאת הִתְקִין רַבָּן יוֹחָנָן בֶּן זַכַּאי
שֶׁאֲפִלּוּ רֹאשׁ בֵּית דִּין בְּכָל מָקוֹם
שֶׁלֹּא יְהוּא הָעֵדִים הוֹלְכִין
אֶלָּא לִמְקוֹם הַוַּעַד.

ה סֵדֶר בְּרָכוֹת:
אוֹמֵר אָבוֹת וּגְבוּרוֹת וּקְדֻשַּׁת הַשֵּׁם
וְכוֹלֵל מַלְכִיּוֹת עִמָּהֶן, וְאֵינוֹ תוֹקֵעַ
קְדֻשַּׁת הַיּוֹם, וְתוֹקֵעַ
זִכְרוֹנוֹת, וְתוֹקֵעַ
שׁוֹפָרוֹת, וְתוֹקֵעַ
וְאוֹמֵר עֲבוֹדָה וְהוֹדָאָה וּבִרְכַּת כֹּהֲנִים

---

מִשֶּׁחָרַב בֵּית הַמִּקְדָּשׁ *After the Temple was destroyed.* In mishna two, Rabban Yoḥanan ben Zakkai instituted a stringency "in remembrance of the Temple." Here he abrogated a stringency that applied when the Temple stood, but ceased to be relevant after its destruction. Once the Temple services were stopped, late-arriving witnesses caused no problems.

Unlike the ordinance of sounding the shofar on Shabbat in Yavne, which encountered serious opposition (see note to mishna one), none is recorded to this one, although it overturned an enactment from the time of the Temple. Possibly the dwindling population in the wake of the destruction made such an ordinance necessary; but still one might expect a debate, especially by Rabbi Akiva, who is often quoted as trusting in the imminent Redemption (Yerushalmi, *Taanit* 4:5; *Tanḥuma, Ekev* 7). This might be the background to the stopping of the witnesses mentioned in mishna 1:6.

לִמְקוֹם הַוַּעַד *Its meeting-place.* When founding the new Sanhedrin at Yavne,

thus Rabbi Yoḥanan ben Nuri.
Rabbi Akiva said to him:
If one does not sound the shofar in "Kingship,"
then why does he mention it there?
Rather, one says "Fathers," "Might" and "Holiness of the Name,"
includes "Kingship" with "Holiness of the Day"
and sounds;
"Remembrances"
and sounds;
"Shofarot"
and sounds;
and says "Temple Service" and "Thanksgiving"
and "the Priestly Blessing."

---

Days of Repentance, one who ends the blessing as usual with "the holy God" must repeat the Amida (*Shulḥan Arukh*, OḤ 582:2, following the Rashba).

**אִם אֵינוֹ תוֹקֵעַ** *If one does not sound.* The shofar must be sounded together with three consecutive blessings (*Tiferet Yisrael*).

**לָמָּה הוּא מַזְכִּיר** *Why does he mention it there?* The Kingship verses (Rabbeinu Ḥananel); this may refer to the phrase: "King over all the earth" at the conclusion of the fourth blessing. According to the Meiri, Rabbi Yoḥanan ben Nuri really did not recite this section – which entails omitting it from all the Rosh HaShana and Yom Kippur prayers.

**אֶלָּא אוֹמֵר** *Rather, one says…* The three blessings deal respectively with (1) God as Creator and Ruler over all creation; (2) God as intimate, omniscient Judge; (3) God as He was revealed to man at Sinai and will be in the future redemption. In the Tanakh, the shofar has a similar broad range of symbolisms. Shofarot are sounded to evoke the merit of the binding of Isaac. They were sounded at the revelation at Sinai and to mark the coronation of kings, and will be sounded to herald the final redemption. In Musaf, then, the shofar punctuates the meditations on these three major aspects of God's judgment. The Talmud (32a) cites a third opinion – that of Rabban Shimon ben Gamliel (who succeeded his father, Rabban Gamliel, who appeared in chapter two) – who agrees with Rabbi Akiva's ordering of the blessings, except, unlike Rabbi Akiva, he combines "Holiness of the Day" with "Remembrances" to make it the fifth blessing.

דִּבְרֵי רַבִּי יוֹחָנָן בֶּן נוּרִי.
אָמַר לוֹ רַבִּי עֲקִיבָא:
אִם אֵינוֹ תּוֹקֵעַ לַמַּלְכִיּוֹת, לָמָּה הוּא מַזְכִּיר?
אֶלָּא אוֹמֵר אָבוֹת וּגְבוּרוֹת וּקְדֻשַּׁת הַשֵּׁם
וְכוֹלֵל מַלְכִיּוֹת עִם קְדֻשַּׁת הַיּוֹם, וְתוֹקֵעַ
זִכְרוֹנוֹת, וְתוֹקֵעַ
שׁוֹפָרוֹת, וְתוֹקֵעַ
וְאוֹמֵר עֲבוֹדָה וְהוֹדָאָה וּבִרְכַּת כֹּהֲנִים.

---

words of the Priestly Blessing. For this reason the Ashkenazi custom is to say *Sim Shalom* only at times when the Priestly Blessing or its alternative "Our God and God of our fathers" is said. When the Priestly Blessing is not recited, *Shalom Rav* ("Grant great peace"), a simpler formulation of the prayer for peace, is said. Customs differ regarding the appropriate blessing for Minḥa on Shabbat; there is no Priestly Blessing at Minḥa; but, on the other hand, the Torah, which is certainly a blessing of no less significance, is read (Rama, *OḤ* 127:2).

רַבִּי יוֹחָנָן בֶּן נוּרִי *Rabbi Yoḥanan ben Nuri.* "On the days of your rejoicing – your festivals and New Moon celebrations – you shall sound a note on the trumpets… and they will be a rememberance for you before your God. I am the LORD your God" (Num. 10:10). The sages understood this apparently redundant conclusion: "I am the LORD your God" to be a declaration acknowledging His rule over us (*Sifrei* 77; see Rashi, 32a); this verse thus becomes a source for the interlacing of the three themes of Kingship, Rememberance and the Shofar. Although Kingship appears last in the verse, it is a prerequisite to the others, and so it is the first of the three in the order of the Amida (*Tosafot Yom Tov*). According to Rabbi Yoḥanan ben Nuri, the logical place to mention God's Kingship is in the blessing sanctifying His name, as on Rosh HaShana the two are connected. Although this opinion was ultimately rejected, the idea finds expression at the end of the expanded version of the third blessing said on the Days of Awe: "And You, LORD, will rule alone over those You have made… Blessed are you, LORD, the holy King." The substitution of the word "King" for "God" is key, and throughout the Ten

6 One should say no less than
ten verses of Kingship, ten of Remembrance,
and ten of Shofarot.
Rabbi Yoḥanan ben Nuri says:
If one says three of each, he has fulfilled his obligation.
One should never say a verse of Rembembrance, Kingship or Shofarot,
which deals with calamity.
One begins with Torah
and closes with the Prophets.
Rabbi Yose says:
If one closes with Torah,
he has fulfilled his obligation.

---

**מַתְחִיל בַּתּוֹרָה וּמַשְׁלִים בַּנָּבִיא** *One begins with Torah and closes with the Prophets.* Concluding with the Prophets rather than the Writings seems counterintuitive. Ramban cites a Geonic tradition that the Writings preceded the Prophets; however, as the Tosafot point out, the Talmud (*Megilla* 31a) discusses ideas "written in the Torah, repeated in the Prophets, and stated a third time in the Writings" – indicating the order we are familiar with today. Tosafot respond by noting that all the verses we quote from the Writings in these blessings derive from the book of Psalms. Attributed to King David, these belong chronologically before the Prophets. Another answer may lie in the content of the chosen verses; in each blessing the Torah verses cover a variety of themes (with the exception of Shofarot, in which all three verses speak of the revelation at Sinai), the verses from the Writings (with one exception) glorify God in the present, while those from the Prophets concern the redemption, directing us from praise toward a prayer for the future.

**יָצָא** *He has fulfilled his obligation.* The Talmud explains what Rabbi Yose meant: that one should conclude with a verse from the Torah, but that this is not imperative. Today we open with three Torah verses, followed by three verses from the Writings, and then three from the Prophets. The tenth, concluding verse is from the Torah. In the Remembrance and Shofarot blessings this concluding verse is postponed to the very end of the blessing. The Kingship blessing is said with the Holiness of the Day, so after the tenth verse of Kingship we return to the formula with which we end the fourth blessing in all the day's prayers. The tenth verse of Kingship is the first verse of the Shema

ו אֵין פּוֹחֲתִין
מֵעֶשֶׂר מַלְכִיּוֹת, מֵעֲשָׂרָה זִכְרוֹנוֹת, מֵעֲשָׂרָה שׁוֹפָרוֹת.
רַבִּי יוֹחָנָן בֶּן נוּרִי אוֹמֵר:
אִם אָמַר שָׁלֹשׁ שָׁלֹשׁ מִכֻּלָּן, יָצָא.
אֵין מַזְכִּירִין זִכְרוֹן מַלְכוּת וְשׁוֹפָר שֶׁלְּפֻרְעָנוּת.
מַתְחִיל בַּתּוֹרָה וּמַשְׁלִים בַּנָּבִיא.
רַבִּי יוֹסֵי אוֹמֵר:
אִם הִשְׁלִים בַּתּוֹרָה, יָצָא.

---

When the issue was raised in Usha (the Galilean town that housed the Sanhedrin after Yavne), Rabban Shimon ben Gamliel testified that the custom in Yavne followed Rabbi Akiva's teaching, which resulted in its being accepted as the halakha. Until that point, the custom in Judea was in accordance with the opinion of Rabbi Akiva, while in the Galilee it was in accordance with the opinion of Rabbi Yoḥanan ben Nuri (Yerushalmi), which we still follow. Our fourth blessing, however, does not interweave the two topics of Holiness of the Day and Kingship; it is constructed of two parts, the first ending with the verses of the Additional Offering (as in any Musaf prayer), and the second beginning with *Aleinu*. This internal division between the usual "Holiness of the Day" passage and the special liturgy of Rosh HaShana is highlighted in the Leader's Repetition, where prefatory *piyutim* are said in the middle of *Aleinu* (pages 575–579).

**אֵין פּוֹחֲתִין מֵעֶשֶׂר מַלְכִיּוֹת** *One should say no less than ten verses of Kingship.* The three blessings are accompanied by relevant verses from the Torah, Prophets and Writings. There are many possible verses in the Tanakh appropriate for this purpose and, at the time of the Mishna, the liturgy had not been fixed and there was room for personal preference in the selection of material within the accepted framework of prayer. The Talmud (32a) cites sources for the different opinions regarding the number of verses which should be recited.

**שֶׁלְּפֻרְעָנוּת** *Which deals with calamity.* The verses of Kingship, Remembrance and Shofarot should not be negative ones, such as Ezekiel 20:33: "With a strong hand and an outstretched arm and with fury poured out shall I rule over you" (32b).

7 When one passes before the Ark
to lead the service at Rosh HaShana,
it is the second who calls for the sounding.
But on days when Hallel is said,
it is the first man who leads Hallel.

8 The shofar of Rosh HaShana –
One may not leave the Sabbath boundary to fetch it,
or clear debris off it,
or climb a tree,
or ride an animal,
or set sail to fetch it,

---

אֵין מַעֲבִירִין עָלָיו אֶת הַתְּחוּם *One may not leave the Sabbath boundary.* Either to hear the shofar (Rashi) or to fetch it (Bartenura; based on Rambam, *Hilkhot Shofar* 1:4). Carrying is permitted on festivals, but stepping beyond the two-thousand-cubit Shabbat boundary is not. The Rishonim, with the exception of Rav Aḥai Gaon, (*She'ilta* 48), held this to be a rabbinic prohibition. The Rif (*Eiruvin* 5a) ruled that going beyond twelve Talmudic miles (twelve to fourteen kilometers) on Shabbat or a festival is prohibited by the Torah; but most halakhic decisors ruled that that too is only rabbinic (see *Beit Yosef*, OḤ 397). The Talmud (32b) connects this to the question of whether a positive commandment overrides a prohibition where they conflict with one another. In *Yevamot* 3b–4a it is shown that it does, if they arise simultaneously (Rashi, *Shabbat* 132a; see Ramban, Ex. 20:7). However, in this case, the positive commandment to hear the shofar cannot override the positive commandment to rest on Shabbat (Lev. 23:24), even if the actual violation is only of a rabbinic prohibition (see Ran, *Rosh HaShana* 9b).

וְאֵין מְפַקְּחִין עָלָיו אֶת הַגַּל *Or clear debris off it.* Fallen debris is *muktzeh*, and clearing it is rabbinically prohibited (most Rishonim, following Rashi; Rabbeinu Ḥananel sees it is a Torah prohibition – see *Eiruvin* 35a). This is used (*Yoma* 83a) as the classical case of descerating Shabbat to save a person's life – "*pikuaḥ nefesh*" literally means "removing debris from atop a soul."

לֹא עוֹלִין בָּאִילָן וְלֹא רוֹכְבִין עַל גַּבֵּי בְהֵמָה וְלֹא שָׁטִין עַל פְּנֵי הַמַּיִם *Climb a tree, ride an animal, set sail.* All three activities are rabbinically prohibited, lest one come to perform labor prohibited by Torah law (*Beitza* 36b).

ז הָעוֹבֵר לִפְנֵי הַתֵּבָה
בְּיוֹם טוֹב שֶׁלְּרֹאשׁ הַשָּׁנָה
הַשֵּׁנִי מַתְקִיעַ
וּבְשָׁעַת הַהַלֵּל
הָרִאשׁוֹן מַקְרֵא אֶת הַהַלֵּל.

ח שׁוֹפָר שֶׁלְּרֹאשׁ הַשָּׁנָה
אֵין מַעֲבִירִין עָלָיו אֶת הַתְּחוּם
וְאֵין מְפַקְּחִין עָלָיו אֶת הַגַּל
לֹא עוֹלִין בָּאִילָן
וְלֹא רוֹכְבִין עַל גַּבֵּי בְהֵמָה
וְלֹא שָׁטִין עַל פְּנֵי הַמַּיִם

(32b), because the ultimate expression of God's kingship is Israel uniting together in accepting Him (Maharal, *Netiv HaAvoda* 7).

הַשֵּׁנִי *It is the second.* In the ancient synagogue, different members of the praying congregation would stand and "pass before the Ark" to lead the different services; "the second" is the one who leads Musaf. The Talmud (32b) cites two reasons for only sounding the shofar in Musaf. First, the delay allows many people to come and fulfill the mitzva, and second, during the time when the Romans clamped down on different areas of Jewish practice, sounding the shofar well into an organized prayer service rather than at its opening was less likely to be interpreted as threatening (see commentary on 3:7). Rav Hai Gaon (quoted by the Rosh, 4:4) noted the word *Matki'a* – literally, one who causes another to blow – understanding from it that the second Leader does not sound the shofar himself, but rather that his recitation of the blessings sets the timing for the sounding of the shofar.

וּבְשָׁעַת הַהַלֵּל *Days when Hallel is said.* On the three pilgrimage festivals and on Rosh Ḥodesh, Hallel is recited as part of Shaḥarit, because "the eager will fulfill a mitzva early" (32b). This mishna indicates that Hallel is not recited on Rosh HaShana – see commentary on page 413.

and one may not cut it,
whether the reason is the rabbinic rules for resting,
or whether the mode of cutting is forbidden by the Torah.
But if one wishes to pour water or wine over a shofar,
he may.
One need not prevent children from sounding the shofar,
but may join them in blowing it until they have learnt.
One who plays it without purpose
has not fulfilled his obligation,
and neither has one who hears that man.

9 The order of the shofar notes –
Three,
where in each three there are three.

---

שָׁלֹשׁ שֶׁל שָׁלֹשׁ שָׁלֹשׁ *Three, where in each three there are three.* The Talmud (34a) derives the number from the three times that sounding the shofar is mentioned in the Torah (Lev. 23:24; 25:9; Num. 29:1). Each shofar blowing consists of three sounds – *tekia, terua, tekia* (based on Num. 10:5–6). The Talmud debates what kind of sound the *terua* mentioned in the Torah is. It is understood to represent a crying sound, but it is not clear whether it is: (a) short, defined, sobs (*shevarim*); (b) a long, gasping wail (*terua*); or (c) sobs which break down into a wail (*shevarim-terua*). Because of this doubt, we perform all three possibilities, in a set of thirty separate sounds, and, according to the custom recorded in the Talmud (16a), blow two sets – one before Musaf and one while saying the blessings. The *Arukh* (quoted in Tosafot, 33b) mentions a Babylonian custom of sounding the shofar a hundred times: thirty sounds before Musaf, thirty during the silent Amida, thirty during the Leader's Repetition, and ten more afterwards. This custom is not mentioned in Geonic sources, and the *Arukh* himself is not a proponent of it – but it was adopted by Rabbi Yitzḥak Luria (the Ari) and his disciples, with many Sephardic and Hasidic congregations in their wake. Most Ashkenazi congregations adopted the custom of the *Shenei Luḥot HaBerit* (Shela), of blowing forty sounds at the end of Musaf instead of in the middle of the silent Amida, to avoid distracting those who pray at a different pace from the one who sounds the shofar (*Mishna Berura,* 596:4).

וְאֵין חוֹתְכִין אוֹתוֹ
בֵּין בְּדָבָר שֶׁהוּא מִשּׁוּם שְׁבוּת
וּבֵין בְּדָבָר שֶׁהוּא מִשּׁוּם לֹא תַעֲשֶׂה.
אֲבָל אִם רָצָה לִתֵּן לְתוֹכוֹ מַיִם אוֹ יַיִן, יִתֵּן.
אֵין מְעַכְּבִין אֶת הַתִּינוֹקוֹת מִלִּתְקוֹעַ
אֲבָל מִתְעַסְּקִין עִמָּהֶן עַד שֶׁיִּלְמְדוּ
וְהַמִּתְעַסֵּק לֹא יָצָא
וְהַשּׁוֹמֵעַ מִן הַמִּתְעַסֵּק לֹא יָצָא.

ט סֵדֶר תְּקִיעוֹת
שָׁלֹשׁ שֶׁלְּשָׁלֹשׁ שָׁלֹשׁ.

---

וְאֵין חוֹתְכִין אוֹתוֹ *One may not cut it.* Cutting the shofar from an animal's head is prohibited on the festival by Torah law only if he uses a tool normally used for that purpose; any less conventional methods are prohibited by the sages.

מַיִם אוֹ יַיִן *Water or wine.* Wetting the shofar to enhance its sound is not prohibited, as it does not permanently change it, only temporarily makes the sound clearer (*Or Zaru'a* 2:265).

אֵין מְעַכְּבִין *One need not prevent.* According to the Talmud (33a), even on Shabbat.

וְהַמִּתְעַסֵּק *One who plays it without purpose.* As mentioned above (3:7), the mitzva of the shofar requires *kavana,* the intention to fulfill the command. Some have held that intent to perform the mitzva is unnecessary, and therefore one who sounds the shofar for music, for example, fulfills his obligation. All agree, however, that one who did not intend to sound the shofar at all, for example if he blows into it to clean it and a sound emerges, does not fulfill his obligation (33b), and if another person listened to it, even with full *kavana,* he has not fulfilled the mitzva. The halakha decisors have concluded that the shofar requires specific *kavana* to fulfill the obligation, and blowing the shofar for music cannot fulfill the mitzva either (*Shulḥan Arukh,* OḤ 589:8).

A tekia is the length of three teruot.
A terua is the length of three staccato notes.
If one sounds a tekia the first time,
but afterwards draws one out the length of two –
it counts for him only as one.
One who says the blessings, and only then finds a shofar,
sounds tekia-shevarim-tekia
three times.
Just as the leader of the service is obliged to say the blessings,
so is every individual also.
Rabban Gamliel says:
The leader of the service
fulfills the command for them all.

---

the Leader is to serve those members of the community who are unable to pray themselves (34b). Even if everyone in a given congregation is capable of praying himself (as is often the case today, when printed siddurim and maḥzorim are readily available), since people who might be less literate occasionally attend the synagogue, the custom should still be maintained in all congregations (*Ḥazon Ish*, OḤ 19:6).

שְׁלִיחַ צִבּוּר מוֹצִיא אֶת הָרַבִּים יְדֵי חוֹבָתָן *The leader of the service fulfills the command for them all.* The silent Amida, in this view, merely provides the Leader with the opportunity to review his prayer before saying it out loud (ibid.). Rabban Gamliel's view was ultimately accepted as halakha, at least in the context of the High Holy Days (35a). This is the source for the custom of the Yemenites, who do not recite a silent prayer at all, and fulfill their obligation by listening to the Leader's prayer; and for the Babylonian *Geonic* period custom, that the congregation recited a standard Musaf of seven blessings, with only the Leader reciting the Kingship, Remembrances and Shofarot blessings. This approach was rejected by the Rosh (4:14), giving everyone the opportunity to pray Kingship, Remembrances and Shofarot twice – both as individuals, and as a part of the community.

שִׁעוּר תְּקִיעָה כְּשָׁלֹשׁ תְּרוּעוֹת.
שִׁעוּר תְּרוּעָה כְּשָׁלֹשׁ יַבָּבוֹת.
תָּקַע בָּרִאשׁוֹנָה, וּמָשַׁךְ בַּשְּׁנִיָּה כִּשְׁתַּיִם
אֵין בְּיָדוֹ אֶלָּא אַחַת.
מִי שֶׁבֵּרַךְ וְאַחַר כָּךְ נִתְמַנָּה לוֹ שׁוֹפָר
תּוֹקֵעַ וּמֵרִיעַ וְתוֹקֵעַ שָׁלֹשׁ פְּעָמִים.
כְּשֵׁם שֶׁשְּׁלִיחַ צִבּוּר חַיָּב, כָּךְ כָּל יָחִיד וְיָחִיד חַיָּב.
רַבָּן גַּמְלִיאֵל אוֹמֵר:
שְׁלִיחַ צִבּוּר מוֹצִיא אֶת הָרַבִּים יְדֵי חוֹבָתָן.

---

**שִׁעוּר תְּקִיעָה כְּשָׁלֹשׁ תְּרוּעוֹת** *A tekia is the length of three teruot.* The use of the term *terua* is confusing. In the Torah, it refers to the crying sound between the straight *tekiot*. In the maḥzor, the word refers to the wailing note, as distinct from the *shevarim*. Here, the word means "sob," synonymous with our *shevarim* – while our *terua*, as called and blown in the synagogue, is made up of nine staccato notes.

**וּמָשַׁךְ בַּשְּׁנִיָּה כִּשְׁתַּיִם** *Draws one out the length of two.* One cannot merge two sets of notes by drawing the closing *tekia* of one set out to include the opening *tekia* of the next. This elongated *tekia* is considered the closing note of the first set only; a new note must be sounded to open the second (*Tur*, OḤ 590, following 34b. The Yerushalmi suggests that the long *tekia* might not count at all).

**מִי שֶׁבֵּרַךְ** *One who says the blessings.* The Talmud (34b) distinguishes between communal prayer, in which the shofar must be integrated with the Amida, and the prayer of an individual. However, even an individual is obligated to sound three sets of three sounds, corresponding to the Kingship, Remembrances and Shofarot blessings (Rashi).

**כְּשֵׁם שֶׁשְּׁלִיחַ צִבּוּר חַיָּב** *Just as the leader of the service is obliged.* To recite the Amida, at Rosh HaShana and in general (Bartenura). In this view, the role of

# שחרית

## SHAḤARIT


| | | |
|---|---|---|
| השכמת הבוקר | 209 | ON WAKING |
| ברכות התורה | 213 | BLESSINGS OVER THE TORAH |
| עטיפת טלית | 217 | TALLIT |
| הכנה לתפילה | 219 | PREPARATION FOR PRAYER |
| ברכות השחר | 225 | MORNING BLESSINGS |
| תפילות השחר | 257 | MORNING PRAYERS |
| פסוקי דזמרה | 283 | PESUKEI DEZIMRA |
| נשמת | 305 | NISHMAT |
| המלך | 309 | HAMELEKH |
| ברכו | 315 | BAREKHU |
| קריאת שמע | 333 | THE SHEMA |
| עמידה | 343 | THE AMIDA |

# Shaḥarit

*The following order of prayers and blessings, which departs from that of most prayer books, is based on the consensus of recent halakhic authorities. See laws 33–35.*

## ON WAKING

*On waking, our first thought should be that we are in the presence of God. Since we are forbidden to speak God's name until we have washed our hands, the following prayer is said, which, without mentioning God's name, acknowledges His presence and gives thanks for a new day and for the gift of life. See law 27.*

מוֹדֶה I thank You, living and eternal King,
for giving me back my soul in mercy.
Great is Your faithfulness.

*Wash hands and say the following blessings.*
*Some have the custom to say "Wisdom begins" on page 214 at this point.*

בָּרוּךְ Blessed are You, LORD our God, King of the Universe,
who has made us holy through His commandments,
and has commanded us about washing hands.

בָּרוּךְ Blessed are You, LORD our God, King of the Universe,
who formed man in wisdom
and created in him many orifices and cavities.
It is revealed and known before the throne of Your glory
that were one of them to be ruptured or blocked,
it would be impossible to survive
and stand before You, even for a moment.
Blessed are You, LORD,
Healer of all flesh who does wondrous deeds.

# שחרית

*The following order of prayers and blessings, which departs from that of most prayer books, is based on the consensus of recent halakhic authorities. See laws 33–35.*

## השכמת הבוקר

*On waking, our first thought should be that we are in the presence of God. Since we are forbidden to speak God's name until we have washed our hands, the following prayer is said, which, without mentioning God's name, acknowledges His presence and gives thanks for a new day and for the gift of life. See law 27.*

מוֹדֶה/ *women* מוֹדָה/ אֲנִי לְפָנֶיךָ מֶלֶךְ חַי וְקַיָּם
שֶׁהֶחֱזַרְתָּ בִּי נִשְׁמָתִי בְּחֶמְלָה
רַבָּה אֱמוּנָתֶךָ.

*Wash hands and say the following blessings.*
*Some have the custom to say* רֵאשִׁית חָכְמָה *on page 215 at this point.*

בָּרוּךְ אַתָּה יהוה אֱלֹהֵינוּ מֶלֶךְ הָעוֹלָם
אֲשֶׁר קִדְּשָׁנוּ בְּמִצְוֹתָיו וְצִוָּנוּ עַל נְטִילַת יָדָיִם.

בָּרוּךְ אַתָּה יהוה אֱלֹהֵינוּ מֶלֶךְ הָעוֹלָם
אֲשֶׁר יָצַר אֶת הָאָדָם בְּחָכְמָה
וּבָרָא בוֹ נְקָבִים נְקָבִים, חֲלוּלִים חֲלוּלִים.
גָּלוּי וְיָדוּעַ לִפְנֵי כִסֵּא כְבוֹדֶךָ
שֶׁאִם יִפָּתֵחַ אֶחָד מֵהֶם אוֹ יִסָּתֵם אֶחָד מֵהֶם
אִי אֶפְשַׁר לְהִתְקַיֵּם וְלַעֲמֹד לְפָנֶיךָ אֲפִלּוּ שָׁעָה אֶחָת.
בָּרוּךְ אַתָּה יהוה, רוֹפֵא כָל בָּשָׂר וּמַפְלִיא לַעֲשׂוֹת.

אֱלֹהַי My God,
the soul You placed within me is pure.
You created it,
You formed it,
You breathed it into me,
and You guard it while it is within me.
One day You will take it from me,
and restore it to me in the time to come.
As long as the soul is within me,
I will thank You,
LORD my God and God of my ancestors,
Master of all works, LORD of all souls.
Blessed are You, LORD,
who restores souls to lifeless bodies.

## TZITZIT

*The following blessing is said before putting on tzitzit. Neither it nor the subsequent prayer is said by those who wear a tallit. The blessing over the latter exempts the former. See laws 36–39.*

בָּרוּךְ Blessed are You, LORD our God, King of the Universe,
who has made us holy through His commandments,
and has commanded us
about the command of tasseled garments.

*After putting on tzitzit, say:*

יְהִי רָצוֹן May it be Your will, LORD my God and God of my ancestors,
that the commandment of the tasseled garment be considered before You
as if I had fulfilled it in all its specifics, details and intentions,
as well as the 613 commandments dependent on it,
Amen, Selah.

אֱלֹהַי
נְשָׁמָה שֶׁנָּתַתָּ בִּי טְהוֹרָה הִיא.
אַתָּה בְרָאתָהּ
אַתָּה יְצַרְתָּהּ
אַתָּה נְפַחְתָּהּ בִּי
וְאַתָּה מְשַׁמְּרָהּ בְּקִרְבִּי, וְאַתָּה עָתִיד לִטְּלָהּ מִמֶּנִּי
וּלְהַחֲזִירָהּ בִּי לֶעָתִיד לָבוֹא.
כָּל זְמַן שֶׁהַנְּשָׁמָה בְקִרְבִּי, מוֹדֶה/*women* מוֹדָה/ אֲנִי לְפָנֶיךָ
יהוה אֱלֹהַי וֵאלֹהֵי אֲבוֹתַי
רִבּוֹן כָּל הַמַּעֲשִׂים, אֲדוֹן כָּל הַנְּשָׁמוֹת.
בָּרוּךְ אַתָּה יהוה, הַמַּחֲזִיר נְשָׁמוֹת לִפְגָרִים מֵתִים.

### לבישת ציצית

*The following blessing is said before putting on a* טלית קטן.
*Neither it nor* יְהִי רָצוֹן *is said by those who wear a* טלית. *The blessing over the latter exempts the former. See laws 36–39.*

בָּרוּךְ אַתָּה יהוה אֱלֹהֵינוּ מֶלֶךְ הָעוֹלָם
אֲשֶׁר קִדְּשָׁנוּ בְּמִצְוֹתָיו וְצִוָּנוּ עַל מִצְוַת צִיצִית.

*After putting on the* טלית קטן, *say:*

יְהִי רָצוֹן מִלְּפָנֶיךָ, יהוה אֱלֹהַי וֵאלֹהֵי אֲבוֹתַי
שֶׁתְּהֵא חֲשׁוּבָה מִצְוַת צִיצִית לְפָנֶיךָ
כְּאִלּוּ קִיַּמְתִּיהָ בְּכָל פְּרָטֶיהָ וְדִקְדּוּקֶיהָ וְכַוָּנוֹתֶיהָ
וְתַרְיַ״ג מִצְוֹת הַתְּלוּיוֹת בָּהּ
אָמֵן סֶלָה.

## BLESSINGS OVER THE TORAH

*In Judaism, study is greater even than prayer. So, before beginning to pray, we engage in a miniature act of study, preceded by the appropriate blessings. The blessings are followed by brief selections from Scripture, Mishna and Gemara, the three foundational texts of Judaism.*

בָּרוּךְ Blessed are You, LORD our God, King of the Universe,
who has made us holy through His commandments,
and has commanded us to engage in study
of the words of Torah.
Please, LORD our God, make the words of Your Torah
sweet in our mouths and in the mouths of Your people,
the house of Israel,
so that we, our descendants and their descendants
and the descendants of Your people,
the house of Israel,
may all know Your name and study Your Torah for its own sake.
Blessed are You, LORD, who teaches Torah to His people Israel.

בָּרוּךְ Blessed are You, LORD our God, King of the Universe,
who has chosen us from all the peoples and given us His Torah.
Blessed are You, LORD, Giver of the Torah.

וַיְדַבֵּר The LORD spoke to Moses, saying: *Num.*
Speak to Aaron and his sons, and tell them,
You shall bless the Israelites like this; say to them:
May the LORD bless you and protect you.
May the LORD make His face shine on you
and be gracious to you.
May the LORD turn His face toward you and grant you peace.
And so they shall place My name over the Israelites,
and I will bless them.

---

BIRKOT HATORAH – BLESSINGS OVER THE TORAH

In Judaism learning is an even higher religious experience than prayer (*Shabbat* 10a), for in prayer we speak to God, but in studying the divine

# ברכות התורה

*In Judaism, study is greater even than prayer. So, before beginning to pray, we engage in a miniature act of study, preceded by the appropriate blessings. The blessings are followed by brief selections from* תנ״ך, משנה *and* גמרא*, the three foundational texts of Judaism.*

בָּרוּךְ אַתָּה יהוה אֱלֹהֵינוּ מֶלֶךְ הָעוֹלָם
אֲשֶׁר קִדְּשָׁנוּ בְּמִצְוֹתָיו
וְצִוָּנוּ לַעֲסֹק בְּדִבְרֵי תוֹרָה.
וְהַעֲרֶב נָא יהוה אֱלֹהֵינוּ אֶת דִּבְרֵי תוֹרָתְךָ
בְּפִינוּ וּבְפִיּוֹת עַמְּךָ בֵּית יִשְׂרָאֵל
וְנִהְיֶה אֲנַחְנוּ וְצֶאֱצָאֵינוּ וְצֶאֱצָאֵי צֶאֱצָאֵינוּ
וְצֶאֱצָאֵי עַמְּךָ בֵּית יִשְׂרָאֵל
כֻּלָּנוּ יוֹדְעֵי שְׁמֶךָ וְלוֹמְדֵי תוֹרָתְךָ לִשְׁמָהּ.
בָּרוּךְ אַתָּה יהוה, הַמְלַמֵּד תּוֹרָה לְעַמּוֹ יִשְׂרָאֵל.

בָּרוּךְ אַתָּה יהוה אֱלֹהֵינוּ מֶלֶךְ הָעוֹלָם
אֲשֶׁר בָּחַר בָּנוּ מִכָּל הָעַמִּים וְנָתַן לָנוּ אֶת תּוֹרָתוֹ.
בָּרוּךְ אַתָּה יהוה, נוֹתֵן הַתּוֹרָה.

וַיְדַבֵּר יהוה אֶל־מֹשֶׁה לֵּאמֹר: במדבר ו
דַּבֵּר אֶל־אַהֲרֹן וְאֶל־בָּנָיו לֵאמֹר
כֹּה תְבָרְכוּ אֶת־בְּנֵי יִשְׂרָאֵל
אָמוֹר לָהֶם:
יְבָרֶכְךָ יהוה וְיִשְׁמְרֶךָ:
יָאֵר יהוה פָּנָיו אֵלֶיךָ וִיחֻנֶּךָּ:
יִשָּׂא יהוה פָּנָיו אֵלֶיךָ וְיָשֵׂם לְךָ שָׁלוֹם:
וְשָׂמוּ אֶת־שְׁמִי עַל־בְּנֵי יִשְׂרָאֵל, וַאֲנִי אֲבָרְכֵם:

אֵלּוּ These are the things for which there is no fixed measure: *Mishna Pe'ah 1:1*
the corner of the field, first-fruits,
appearances before the LORD
[on festivals, with offerings],
acts of kindness and the study of Torah.

אֵלּוּ These are the things *Shabbat 127a*
whose fruits we eat in this world
but whose full reward awaits us
in the World to Come:
honoring parents; acts of kindness;
arriving early at the house of study
morning and evening;
hospitality to strangers; visiting the sick;
helping the needy bride; attending to the dead;
devotion in prayer;
and bringing peace between neighbors,
and between husband and wife –
but the study of Torah is equal to them all.

*Some say:*
רֵאשִׁית חָכְמָה Wisdom begins in awe of the LORD; *Ps. 111*
all who fulfill [His commandments] gain good understanding;
His praise is ever-lasting.
The Torah Moses commanded us *Deut. 33*
is the heritage of the congregation of Jacob.
Listen, my son, to your father's instruction, *Prov. 1*
and do not forsake your mother's teaching.
May the Torah be my faith and Almighty God my help.
Blessed be the name of His glorious kingdom for ever and all time.

---

a third for Talmud (*Kiddushin* 30a). That is the structure of the three passages that follow: first a passage from the Torah; then from the Mishna, tractate *Pe'ah*; then a passage from the Talmud, tractate *Shabbat*.

משנה פאה א:א

אֵלּוּ דְבָרִים שֶׁאֵין לָהֶם שִׁעוּר
הַפֵּאָה וְהַבִּכּוּרִים וְהָרֵאָיוֹן
וּגְמִילוּת חֲסָדִים וְתַלְמוּד תּוֹרָה.

שבת קכז.

אֵלּוּ דְבָרִים שֶׁאָדָם אוֹכֵל פֵּרוֹתֵיהֶם בָּעוֹלָם הַזֶּה
וְהַקֶּרֶן קַיֶּמֶת לוֹ לָעוֹלָם הַבָּא
וְאֵלּוּ הֵן
כִּבּוּד אָב וָאֵם, וּגְמִילוּת חֲסָדִים
וְהַשְׁכָּמַת בֵּית הַמִּדְרָשׁ שַׁחֲרִית וְעַרְבִית
וְהַכְנָסַת אוֹרְחִים, וּבִקּוּר חוֹלִים
וְהַכְנָסַת כַּלָּה, וּלְוָיַת הַמֵּת
וְעִיּוּן תְּפִלָּה
וַהֲבָאַת שָׁלוֹם בֵּין אָדָם לַחֲבֵרוֹ וּבֵין אִישׁ לְאִשְׁתּוֹ
וְתַלְמוּד תּוֹרָה כְּנֶגֶד כֻּלָּם.

*Some say:*

תהלים קיא

רֵאשִׁית חָכְמָה יִרְאַת יהוה
שֵׂכֶל טוֹב לְכָל־עֹשֵׂיהֶם, תְּהִלָּתוֹ עֹמֶדֶת לָעַד:

דברים לג

תּוֹרָה צִוָּה־לָנוּ מֹשֶׁה, מוֹרָשָׁה קְהִלַּת יַעֲקֹב:

משלי א

שְׁמַע בְּנִי מוּסַר אָבִיךָ וְאַל־תִּטֹּשׁ תּוֹרַת אִמֶּךָ:
תּוֹרָה תְּהֵא אֱמוּנָתִי, וְאֵל שַׁדַּי בְּעֶזְרָתִי.
בָּרוּךְ שֵׁם כְּבוֹד מַלְכוּתוֹ לְעוֹלָם וָעֶד.

---

word we hear God speak to us. So we preface the act of prayer with an act of learning. The basic structure of learning is to divide one's time into three: a third to study *Mikra*, the Written Torah, a third for the study of Mishna, and

## TALLIT

*Say the following meditation before putting on the tallit. Meditations before the fulfillment of mitzvot are to ensure that we do so with the requisite intention (kavana). This particularly applies to mitzvot whose purpose is to induce in us certain states of mind, as is the case with tallit and tefillin, both of which are external symbols of inward commitment to the life of observance of the mitzvot.*

בָּרְכִי נַפְשִׁי Bless the LORD, my soul. LORD, my God, You are very great, clothed in majesty and splendor, wrapped in a robe of light, spreading out the heavens like a tent. *Ps. 104*

*Some say:*

For the sake of the unification of the Holy One, blessed be He, and His Divine Presence, in reverence and love, to unify the name *Yod-Heh* with *Vav-Heh* in perfect unity in the name of all Israel.

I am about to wrap myself in this tasseled garment (tallit). So may my soul, my 248 limbs and 365 sinews be wrapped in the light of the tassel (*hatzitzit*) which amounts to 613 [commandments]. And just as I cover myself with a tasseled garment in this world, so may I be worthy of rabbinical dress and a fine garment in the World to Come in the Garden of Eden. Through the commandment of tassels may my life's-breath, spirit, soul and prayer be delivered from external impediments, and may the tallit spread its wings over them like an eagle stirring up its nest, hovering over its young. May the *Deut. 32* commandment of the tasseled garment be considered before the Holy One, blessed be He, as if I had fulfilled it in all its specifics, details and intentions, as well as the 613 commandments dependent on it, Amen, Selah.

*Before wrapping oneself in the tallit, say:*

בָּרוּךְ Blessed are You, LORD our God, King of the Universe,
who has made us holy through His commandments,
and has commanded us to wrap ourselves in the tasseled garment.

*According to the Shela (R. Isaiah Horowitz), one should say these verses after wrapping oneself in the tallit:*

מַה־יָּקָר How precious is Your loving-kindness, O God, and the children of men find refuge under the shadow of Your wings. They are filled with the rich plenty of Your House. You give them drink from Your river of delights. For with You is the fountain of life; in Your light, we see light. Continue Your loving-kindness to those who know You, and Your righteousness to the upright in heart. *Ps. 36*

---

29:1). The Torah says that as they left Eden, God made them "garments of skin" (Gen. 3:21). However, in the school of Rabbi Meir they read this phrase to mean "garments of light" (*Bereshit Raba* 20:12). Thus the first penitents were wrapped in a robe of light, as God Himself is in Psalm 104. For a penitent stands even higher than the righteous (*Berakhot* 34b).

# עטיפת טלית

*Say the following meditation before putting on the* טלית*. Meditations before the fulfillment of* מצוות *are to ensure that we do so with the requisite intention (*כוונה*). This particularly applies to* מצוות *whose purpose is to induce in us certain states of mind, as is the case with* טלית *and* תפילין*, both of which are external symbols of inward commitment to the life of observance of the* מצוות*.*

תהלים קד בָּרְכִי נַפְשִׁי אֶת־יהוה, יהוה אֱלֹהַי גָּדַלְתָּ מְּאֹד, הוֹד וְהָדָר לָבָשְׁתָּ:
עֹטֶה־אוֹר כַּשַּׂלְמָה, נוֹטֶה שָׁמַיִם כַּיְרִיעָה:

*Some say:*

לְשֵׁם יִחוּד קֻדְשָׁא בְּרִיךְ הוּא וּשְׁכִינְתֵּהּ בִּדְחִילוּ וּרְחִימוּ, לְיַחֵד שֵׁם י״ה בו״ה בְּיִחוּדָא שְׁלִים בְּשֵׁם כָּל יִשְׂרָאֵל.

הֲרֵינִי מִתְעַטֵּף בַּצִּיצִית. כֵּן תִּתְעַטֵּף נִשְׁמָתִי וּרְמַ״ח אֵבָרַי וּשְׁסָ״ה גִידַי בְּאוֹר הַצִּיצִית הָעוֹלָה תַּרְיַ״ג. וּכְשֵׁם שֶׁאֲנִי מִתְכַּסֶּה בְּטַלִּית בָּעוֹלָם הַזֶּה, כָּךְ אֶזְכֶּה לַחֲלוּקָא דְרַבָּנָן וּלְטַלִּית נָאָה לָעוֹלָם הַבָּא בְּגַן עֵדֶן. וְעַל יְדֵי מִצְוַת צִיצִית תִּנָּצֵל נַפְשִׁי רוּחִי וְנִשְׁמָתִי וּתְפִלָּתִי מִן הַחִיצוֹנִים. וְהַטַּלִּית תִּפְרֹשׂ כְּנָפֶיהָ עֲלֵיהֶם וְתַצִּילֵם, כְּנֶשֶׁר יָעִיר קִנּוֹ עַל־גּוֹזָלָיו יְרַחֵף: (דברים לב) וּתְהֵא חֲשׁוּבָה מִצְוַת צִיצִית לִפְנֵי הַקָּדוֹשׁ בָּרוּךְ הוּא, כְּאִלּוּ קִיַּמְתִּיהָ בְּכָל פְּרָטֶיהָ וְדִקְדּוּקֶיהָ וְכַוָּנוֹתֶיהָ וְתַרְיַ״ג מִצְוֹת הַתְּלוּיוֹת בָּהּ, אָמֵן סֶלָה.

*Before wrapping oneself in the* טלית*, say:*

בָּרוּךְ אַתָּה יהוה אֱלֹהֵינוּ מֶלֶךְ הָעוֹלָם
אֲשֶׁר קִדְּשָׁנוּ בְּמִצְוֹתָיו וְצִוָּנוּ לְהִתְעַטֵּף בַּצִּיצִית.

*According to the Shela (R. Isaiah Horowitz), one should say these verses after wrapping oneself in the* טלית*:*

תהלים לו מַה־יָּקָר חַסְדְּךָ אֱלֹהִים, וּבְנֵי אָדָם בְּצֵל כְּנָפֶיךָ יֶחֱסָיוּן: יִרְוְיֻן מִדֶּשֶׁן בֵּיתֶךָ, וְנַחַל עֲדָנֶיךָ תַשְׁקֵם: כִּי־עִמְּךָ מְקוֹר חַיִּים, בְּאוֹרְךָ נִרְאֶה־אוֹר: מְשֹׁךְ חַסְדְּךָ לְיֹדְעֶיךָ, וְצִדְקָתְךָ לְיִשְׁרֵי־לֵב:

---

בָּרְכִי נַפְשִׁי אֶת־יהוה *Bless the* Lord*, my soul.* These words, from Psalm 104, are said every day before putting on the tallit, but they have a special resonance on Rosh HaShana. This was the day on which, according to tradition, the first humans were created. That same day they sinned, eating the forbidden fruit. Initially God had said, "On the day you eat from it, you will surely die" (Gen. 2:17), yet they did not die; they were pardoned. So Rosh HaShana is the anniversary of the first sin and the first act of divine forgiveness (*Vayikra Raba*

## PREPARATION FOR PRAYER

*On entering the synagogue:*

# HOW GOODLY *Num. 24*

are your tents, Jacob, your dwelling places, Israel.
As for me, *Ps. 5*
in Your great loving-kindness,
I will come into Your House.
I will bow down to Your holy Temple
in awe of You.
LORD, I love the habitation of Your House, *Ps. 26*
the place where Your glory dwells.

As for me,
I will bow in worship;
I will bend the knee
before the LORD my Maker.

As for me, *Ps. 69*
may my prayer come to You, LORD,
at a time of favor.
God, in Your great loving-kindness,
answer me with Your faithful salvation.

# הכנה לתפילה

*On entering the* בית כנסת*:*

במדבר כד

מַה־טֹּבוּ

אֹהָלֶיךָ יַעֲקֹב, מִשְׁכְּנֹתֶיךָ יִשְׂרָאֵל:

תהלים ה

וַאֲנִי בְּרֹב חַסְדְּךָ אָבוֹא בֵיתֶךָ

אֶשְׁתַּחֲוֶה אֶל־הֵיכַל־קָדְשְׁךָ

בְּיִרְאָתֶךָ:

תהלים כו

יהוה אָהַבְתִּי מְעוֹן בֵּיתֶךָ

וּמְקוֹם מִשְׁכַּן כְּבוֹדֶךָ:

וַאֲנִי אֶשְׁתַּחֲוֶה

וְאֶכְרָעָה

אֶבְרְכָה לִפְנֵי יהוה עֹשִׂי.

תהלים סט

וַאֲנִי תְפִלָּתִי־לְךָ יהוה

עֵת רָצוֹן

אֱלֹהִים בְּרָב־חַסְדֶּךָ

עֲנֵנִי בֶּאֱמֶת יִשְׁעֶךָ:

*The following poems, on this page and the next, both from the Middle Ages, are summary statements of Jewish faith, orienting us to the spiritual contours of the world that we actualize in the mind by the act of prayer.*

LORD OF THE UNIVERSE,
who reigned before the birth of any thing –

When by His will all things were made
then was His name proclaimed King.

And when all things shall cease to be
He alone will reign in awe.

He was, He is, and He shall be
glorious for evermore.

He is One, there is none else,
alone, unique, beyond compare;

Without beginning, without end,
His might, His rule are everywhere.

He is my God; my Redeemer lives.
He is the Rock on whom I rely –

My banner and my safe retreat,
my cup, my portion when I cry.

Into His hand my soul I place,
when I awake and when I sleep.

The LORD is with me, I shall not fear;
body and soul from harm will He keep.

*The following poems, on this page and the next, both from the Middle Ages, are summary statements of Jewish faith, orienting us to the spiritual contours of the world that we actualize in the mind by the act of prayer.*

# אֲדוֹן עוֹלָם

אֲשֶׁר מָלַךְ בְּטֶרֶם כָּל־יְצִיר נִבְרָא.
לְעֵת נַעֲשָׂה בְחֶפְצוֹ כֹּל אֲזַי מֶלֶךְ שְׁמוֹ נִקְרָא.
וְאַחֲרֵי כִּכְלוֹת הַכֹּל לְבַדּוֹ יִמְלֹךְ נוֹרָא.
וְהוּא הָיָה וְהוּא הֹוֶה וְהוּא יִהְיֶה בְּתִפְאָרָה.
וְהוּא אֶחָד וְאֵין שֵׁנִי לְהַמְשִׁיל לוֹ לְהַחְבִּירָה.
בְּלִי רֵאשִׁית בְּלִי תַכְלִית וְלוֹ הָעֹז וְהַמִּשְׂרָה.
וְהוּא אֵלִי וְחַי גֹּאֲלִי וְצוּר חֶבְלִי בְּעֵת צָרָה.
וְהוּא נִסִּי וּמָנוֹס לִי מְנָת כּוֹסִי בְּיוֹם אֶקְרָא.
בְּיָדוֹ אַפְקִיד רוּחִי בְּעֵת אִישַׁן וְאָעִירָה.
וְעִם רוּחִי גְּוִיָּתִי יהוה לִי וְלֹא אִירָא.

**GREAT**
is the living God and praised.
He exists, and His existence is beyond time.

He is One, and there is no unity like His.
Unfathomable, His Oneness is infinite.

He has neither bodily form nor substance;
His holiness is beyond compare.

He preceded all that was created.
He was first: there was no beginning to His beginning.

Behold He is Master of the Universe; and every creature
shows His greatness and majesty.

The rich flow of His prophecy He gave
to His treasured people in whom He gloried.

Never in Israel has there arisen another like Moses,
a prophet who beheld God's image.

God gave His people a Torah of truth
by the hand of His prophet, most faithful of His House.

God will not alter or change His law
for any other, for eternity.

He sees and knows our secret thoughts;
as soon as something is begun, He foresees its end.

He rewards people with loving-kindness according to their deeds;
He punishes the wicked according to his wickedness.

At the end of days He will send our Messiah
to redeem those who await His final salvation.

God will revive the dead in His great loving-kindness.
Blessed for evermore is His glorious name!

# יִגְדַּל

אֱלֹהִים חַי וְיִשְׁתַּבַּח, נִמְצָא וְאֵין עֵת אֶל מְצִיאוּתוֹ.

אֶחָד וְאֵין יָחִיד כְּיִחוּדוֹ, נֶעְלָם וְגַם אֵין סוֹף לְאַחְדוּתוֹ.

אֵין לוֹ דְמוּת הַגּוּף וְאֵינוֹ גוּף, לֹא נַעֲרֹךְ אֵלָיו קְדֻשָּׁתוֹ.

קַדְמוֹן לְכָל דָּבָר אֲשֶׁר נִבְרָא, רִאשׁוֹן וְאֵין רֵאשִׁית לְרֵאשִׁיתוֹ.

הִנּוֹ אֲדוֹן עוֹלָם, וְכָל נוֹצָר יוֹרֶה גְדֻלָּתוֹ וּמַלְכוּתוֹ.

שֶׁפַע נְבוּאָתוֹ נְתָנוֹ אֶל־אַנְשֵׁי סְגֻלָּתוֹ וְתִפְאַרְתּוֹ.

לֹא קָם בְּיִשְׂרָאֵל כְּמֹשֶׁה עוֹד נָבִיא וּמַבִּיט אֶת תְּמוּנָתוֹ.

תּוֹרַת אֱמֶת נָתַן לְעַמּוֹ אֵל עַל יַד נְבִיאוֹ נֶאֱמַן בֵּיתוֹ.

לֹא יַחֲלִיף הָאֵל וְלֹא יָמִיר דָּתוֹ לְעוֹלָמִים לְזוּלָתוֹ.

צוֹפֶה וְיוֹדֵעַ סְתָרֵינוּ, מַבִּיט לְסוֹף דָּבָר בְּקַדְמָתוֹ.

גּוֹמֵל לְאִישׁ חֶסֶד כְּמִפְעָלוֹ, נוֹתֵן לְרָשָׁע רָע כְּרִשְׁעָתוֹ.

יִשְׁלַח לְקֵץ יָמִין מְשִׁיחֵנוּ לִפְדּוֹת מְחַכֵּי קֵץ יְשׁוּעָתוֹ.

מֵתִים יְחַיֶּה אֵל בְּרֹב חַסְדּוֹ, בָּרוּךְ עֲדֵי עַד שֵׁם תְּהִלָּתוֹ.

## MORNING BLESSINGS

*The following blessings are said aloud by the Leader, but each individual should say them quietly as well. It is our custom to say them standing.*

בָּרוּךְ Blessed are You, LORD our God, King of the Universe,
who gives the heart understanding
to distinguish day from night.

Blessed are You, LORD our God, King of the Universe,
who has not made me a heathen.

Blessed are You, LORD our God, King of the Universe,
who has not made me a slave.

Blessed are You, LORD our God, King of the Universe,
*men:* who has not made me a woman.
*women:* who has made me according to His will.

Blessed are You, LORD our God, King of the Universe,
who gives sight to the blind.

Blessed are You, LORD our God, King of the Universe,
who clothes the naked.

Blessed are You, LORD our God, King of the Universe,
who sets captives free.

Blessed are You, LORD our God, King of the Universe,
who raises those bowed down.

Blessed are You, LORD our God, King of the Universe,
who spreads the earth above the waters.

---

בָּרוּךְ אַתָּה...אֲשֶׁר נָתַן לַשֶּׂכְוִי בִינָה *Blessed are You... who gives the heart understanding.* These blessings, itemized in the Talmud (*Berakhot* 60b), were originally said at home to accompany the various stages of waking and rising. Several medieval authorities took the view that they should be said in the synagogue.

To bless God means to thank Him for His blessings. Every act of acknowledgment opens us to the presence of God in all that surrounds us. "The world is full of the light of God, but to see it we must learn to open our eyes" (Rabbi Naḥman of Bratslav).

# ברכות השחר

*The following blessings are said aloud by the* שליח ציבור*, but each individual should say them quietly as well. It is our custom to say them standing.*

בָּרוּךְ אַתָּה יהוה אֱלֹהֵינוּ מֶלֶךְ הָעוֹלָם
אֲשֶׁר נָתַן לַשֶּׂכְוִי בִינָה
לְהַבְחִין בֵּין יוֹם וּבֵין לָיְלָה.

בָּרוּךְ אַתָּה יהוה אֱלֹהֵינוּ מֶלֶךְ הָעוֹלָם
שֶׁלֹּא עָשַׂנִי גּוֹי.

בָּרוּךְ אַתָּה יהוה אֱלֹהֵינוּ מֶלֶךְ הָעוֹלָם
שֶׁלֹּא עָשַׂנִי עָבֶד.

בָּרוּךְ אַתָּה יהוה אֱלֹהֵינוּ מֶלֶךְ הָעוֹלָם
*men* שֶׁלֹּא עָשַׂנִי אִשָּׁה. / *women* שֶׁעָשַׂנִי כִּרְצוֹנוֹ.

בָּרוּךְ אַתָּה יהוה אֱלֹהֵינוּ מֶלֶךְ הָעוֹלָם
פּוֹקֵחַ עִוְרִים.

בָּרוּךְ אַתָּה יהוה אֱלֹהֵינוּ מֶלֶךְ הָעוֹלָם
מַלְבִּישׁ עֲרֻמִּים.

בָּרוּךְ אַתָּה יהוה אֱלֹהֵינוּ מֶלֶךְ הָעוֹלָם
מַתִּיר אֲסוּרִים.

בָּרוּךְ אַתָּה יהוה אֱלֹהֵינוּ מֶלֶךְ הָעוֹלָם
זוֹקֵף כְּפוּפִים.

בָּרוּךְ אַתָּה יהוה אֱלֹהֵינוּ מֶלֶךְ הָעוֹלָם
רוֹקַע הָאָרֶץ עַל הַמָּיִם.

Blessed are You, Lord our God, King of the Universe,
who makes firm the steps of man.
Blessed are You, Lord our God, King of the Universe,
who has provided me with all I need.
Blessed are You, Lord our God, King of the Universe,
who girds Israel with strength.
Blessed are You, Lord our God, King of the Universe,
who crowns Israel with glory.
Blessed are You, Lord our God, King of the Universe,
who gives strength to the weary.

בָּרוּךְ Blessed are You, Lord our God, King of the Universe, who removes sleep from my eyes and slumber from my eyelids. And may it be Your will, Lord our God and God of our ancestors, to accustom us to Your Torah, and make us attached to Your commandments. Lead us not into error, transgression, iniquity, temptation or disgrace. Do not let the evil instinct dominate us. Keep us far from a bad man and a bad companion. Help us attach ourselves to the good instinct and to good deeds and bend our instincts to be subservient to You. Grant us, this day and every day, grace, loving-kindness and compassion in Your eyes and in the eyes of all who see us, and bestow loving-kindness upon us. Blessed are You, Lord, who bestows loving-kindness on His people Israel.

יְהִי רָצוֹן May it be Your will, Lord my God and God of my ancestors, to save me today and every day, from the arrogant and from arrogance itself, from a bad man, a bad instinct, a bad friend, a bad neighbor, a bad mishap, from an evil eye, an evil tongue, from slander, lies, hatred of others, libelous plots, unnatural death, severe illness, pernicious events, a destructive adversary, a harsh trial and a harsh opponent, whether or not he is a son of the covenant, and from the judgment of Gehinnom. *Berakhot 16b*

---

וְהַרְחִיקֵנוּ מֵאָדָם רָע וּמֵחָבֵר רָע *Keep us far from a bad man and a bad companion.* It is natural for a person to be influenced in his beliefs and deeds by his neighbors and friends, and to act according to the custom of his fellow citizens. Therefore one should associate with the righteous and frequent the company of the wise so as to learn from their behavior, keeping far from the benighted wicked so as not to be corrupted by their example. (Maimonides, Laws of Temperaments 6:1)

בָּרוּךְ אַתָּה יהוה אֱלֹהֵינוּ מֶלֶךְ הָעוֹלָם
הַמֵּכִין מִצְעֲדֵי גָבֶר.

בָּרוּךְ אַתָּה יהוה אֱלֹהֵינוּ מֶלֶךְ הָעוֹלָם
שֶׁעָשָׂה לִי כָּל צָרְכִּי.

בָּרוּךְ אַתָּה יהוה אֱלֹהֵינוּ מֶלֶךְ הָעוֹלָם
אוֹזֵר יִשְׂרָאֵל בִּגְבוּרָה.

בָּרוּךְ אַתָּה יהוה אֱלֹהֵינוּ מֶלֶךְ הָעוֹלָם
עוֹטֵר יִשְׂרָאֵל בְּתִפְאָרָה.

בָּרוּךְ אַתָּה יהוה אֱלֹהֵינוּ מֶלֶךְ הָעוֹלָם
הַנּוֹתֵן לַיָּעֵף כֹּחַ.

בָּרוּךְ אַתָּה יהוה אֱלֹהֵינוּ מֶלֶךְ הָעוֹלָם, הַמַּעֲבִיר שֵׁנָה מֵעֵינַי וּתְנוּמָה מֵעַפְעַפָּי. וִיהִי רָצוֹן מִלְּפָנֶיךָ יהוה אֱלֹהֵינוּ וֵאלֹהֵי אֲבוֹתֵינוּ שֶׁתַּרְגִּילֵנוּ בְּתוֹרָתֶךָ, וְדַבְּקֵנוּ בְּמִצְוֹתֶיךָ, וְאַל תְּבִיאֵנוּ לֹא לִידֵי חֵטְא, וְלֹא לִידֵי עֲבֵרָה וְעָוֹן, וְלֹא לִידֵי נִסָּיוֹן וְלֹא לִידֵי בִזָּיוֹן, וְאַל תַּשְׁלֶט בָּנוּ יֵצֶר הָרָע, וְהַרְחִיקֵנוּ מֵאָדָם רָע וּמֵחָבֵר רָע, וְדַבְּקֵנוּ בְּיֵצֶר הַטּוֹב וּבְמַעֲשִׂים טוֹבִים, וְכֹף אֶת יִצְרֵנוּ לְהִשְׁתַּעְבֶּד לָךְ, וּתְנֵנוּ הַיּוֹם וּבְכָל יוֹם לְחֵן וּלְחֶסֶד וּלְרַחֲמִים, בְּעֵינֶיךָ, וּבְעֵינֵי כָל רוֹאֵינוּ, וְתִגְמְלֵנוּ חֲסָדִים טוֹבִים. בָּרוּךְ אַתָּה יהוה, גּוֹמֵל חֲסָדִים טוֹבִים לְעַמּוֹ יִשְׂרָאֵל.

יְהִי רָצוֹן מִלְּפָנֶיךָ יהוה אֱלֹהַי וֵאלֹהֵי אֲבוֹתַי, שֶׁתַּצִּילֵנִי הַיּוֹם וּבְכָל יוֹם מֵעַזֵּי פָנִים וּמֵעַזּוּת פָּנִים, מֵאָדָם רָע, מִיֵּצֶר רָע, וּמֵחָבֵר רָע, וּמִשָּׁכֵן רָע, וּמִפֶּגַע רָע, מֵעַיִן הָרָע, מִלָּשׁוֹן הָרָע, מִמַּלְשִׁינוּת, מֵעֵדוּת שֶׁקֶר, מִשִּׂנְאַת הַבְּרִיּוֹת, מֵעֲלִילָה, מִמִּיתָה מְשֻׁנָּה, מֵחֳלָיִים רָעִים, מִמִּקְרִים רָעִים, וּמִשָּׂטָן הַמַּשְׁחִית, מִדִּין קָשֶׁה, וּמִבַּעַל דִּין קָשֶׁה בֵּין שֶׁהוּא בֶן בְּרִית וּבֵין שֶׁאֵינוֹ בֶן בְּרִית, וּמִדִּינָהּ שֶׁל גֵּיהִנֹּם. ברכות טז:

# THE BINDING OF ISAAC

*On the basis of Jewish mystical tradition, some have the custom of saying daily the biblical passage recounting the Binding of Isaac, the supreme trial of faith in which Abraham demonstrated his love of God above all other loves. Most omit the introductory and concluding prayers, "Our God and God of our ancestors" and "Master of the Universe." Others skip to "A person should" on page 232.*

Our God and God of our ancestors, remember us with a favorable memory, and recall us with a remembrance of salvation and compassion from the highest of high heavens. Remember, LORD our God, on our behalf, the love of the ancients, Abraham, Isaac and Yisrael Your servants; the covenant, the loving-kindness, and the oath You swore to Abraham our father on Mount Moriah, and the Binding, when he bound Isaac his son on the altar, as is written in Your Torah:

It happened after these things that God tested Abraham. He said to him, *Gen. 22*
"Abraham!" "Here I am," he replied. He said, "Take your son, your only son, Isaac, whom you love, and go to the land of Moriah and offer him there as a burnt-offering on one of the mountains which I shall say to you." Early the next morning Abraham rose and saddled his donkey and took his two lads with him, and Isaac his son, and he cut wood for the burnt-offering, and he set out for the place of which God had told him. On the third day Abraham looked up and saw the place from afar. Abraham said to his lads, "Stay here with the donkey while I and the boy go on ahead. We will worship and we will return to you." Abraham took the wood for the burnt-offering and placed it on Isaac his son, and he took in his hand the fire and the knife, and the two of them went together. Isaac said to Abraham his father, "Father?" and he said "Here I am, my son." And he said, "Here are the fire and the wood, but where is the sheep for the burnt-offering?" Abraham said, "God will see to the sheep for the burnt-offering, my son." And the two of them went together. They came to the place God had told him about, and Abraham built there an altar and arranged the wood and bound Isaac his son and laid him on the altar on top of the wood. He reached out his hand and took the knife to slay his son. Then an angel of the LORD called out to him from heaven, "Abraham! Abraham!" He said, "Here I am." He said, "Do not reach out your hand against the boy; do not do anything to him, for now I know that you fear God, because you have not held back your son, your only son, from Me." Abraham looked up and there he saw a ram caught in a thicket by its horns, and Abraham went and took the ram and offered it as a burnt-offering instead of his son. Abraham called that place "The LORD will see," as is said to this day, "On the mountain of the LORD He will be seen." The angel of the LORD called to Abraham a second time from heaven, and said, "By Myself I swear,

# פרשת העקדה

*On the basis of Jewish mystical tradition, some have the custom of saying daily the biblical passage recounting the Binding of Isaac, the supreme trial of faith in which Abraham demonstrated his love of God above all other loves. Most omit the introductory and concluding prayers,* אֱלֹהֵֽינוּ וֵאלֹהֵי אֲבוֹתֵֽינוּ *and* רִבּוֹנוֹ שֶׁל עוֹלָם*. Others skip to* לְעוֹלָם יְהֵא אָדָם *on page 233.*

אֱלֹהֵֽינוּ וֵאלֹהֵי אֲבוֹתֵֽינוּ, זׇכְרֵֽנוּ בְּזִכְרוֹן טוֹב לְפָנֶֽיךָ, וּפׇקְדֵֽנוּ בִּפְקֻדַּת יְשׁוּעָה וְרַחֲמִים מִשְּׁמֵי שְׁמֵי קֶֽדֶם, וּזְכׇר לָֽנוּ יהוה אֱלֹהֵֽינוּ, אַהֲבַת הַקַּדְמוֹנִים אַבְרָהָם יִצְחָק וְיִשְׂרָאֵל עֲבָדֶֽיךָ, אֶת הַבְּרִית וְאֶת הַחֶֽסֶד וְאֶת הַשְּׁבוּעָה שֶׁנִּשְׁבַּֽעְתָּ לְאַבְרָהָם אָבִֽינוּ בְּהַר הַמּוֹרִיָּה, וְאֶת הָעֲקֵדָה שֶׁעָקַד אֶת יִצְחָק בְּנוֹ עַל גַּבֵּי הַמִּזְבֵּֽחַ, כַּכָּתוּב בְּתוֹרָתֶֽךָ:

וַיְהִי אַחַר הַדְּבָרִים הָאֵֽלֶּה, וְהָאֱלֹהִים נִסָּה אֶת־אַבְרָהָם, וַיֹּֽאמֶר אֵלָיו בראשית כב
אַבְרָהָם, וַיֹּֽאמֶר הִנֵּֽנִי: וַיֹּֽאמֶר קַח־נָא אֶת־בִּנְךָ אֶת־יְחִידְךָ אֲשֶׁר־אָהַֽבְתָּ, אֶת־יִצְחָק, וְלֶךְ־לְךָ אֶל־אֶֽרֶץ הַמֹּרִיָּה, וְהַעֲלֵֽהוּ שָׁם לְעֹלָה עַל אַחַד הֶהָרִים אֲשֶׁר אֹמַר אֵלֶֽיךָ: וַיַּשְׁכֵּם אַבְרָהָם בַּבֹּֽקֶר, וַיַּחֲבֹשׁ אֶת־חֲמֹרוֹ, וַיִּקַּח אֶת־שְׁנֵי נְעָרָיו אִתּוֹ וְאֵת יִצְחָק בְּנוֹ, וַיְבַקַּע עֲצֵי עֹלָה, וַיָּֽקׇם וַיֵּֽלֶךְ אֶל־הַמָּקוֹם אֲשֶׁר־אָמַר־לוֹ הָאֱלֹהִים: בַּיּוֹם הַשְּׁלִישִׁי וַיִּשָּׂא אַבְרָהָם אֶת־עֵינָיו וַיַּרְא אֶת־הַמָּקוֹם מֵרָחֹק: וַיֹּֽאמֶר אַבְרָהָם אֶל־נְעָרָיו, שְׁבוּ־לָכֶם פֹּה עִם־הַחֲמוֹר, וַאֲנִי וְהַנַּֽעַר נֵלְכָה עַד־כֹּה, וְנִשְׁתַּחֲוֶה וְנָשֽׁוּבָה אֲלֵיכֶם: וַיִּקַּח אַבְרָהָם אֶת־עֲצֵי הָעֹלָה וַיָּֽשֶׂם עַל־יִצְחָק בְּנוֹ, וַיִּקַּח בְּיָדוֹ אֶת־הָאֵשׁ וְאֶת־הַמַּאֲכֶֽלֶת, וַיֵּלְכוּ שְׁנֵיהֶם יַחְדָּו: וַיֹּֽאמֶר יִצְחָק אֶל־אַבְרָהָם אָבִיו, וַיֹּֽאמֶר אָבִי, וַיֹּֽאמֶר הִנֶּֽנִּי בְנִי, וַיֹּֽאמֶר, הִנֵּה הָאֵשׁ וְהָעֵצִים, וְאַיֵּה הַשֶּׂה לְעֹלָה: וַיֹּֽאמֶר אַבְרָהָם, אֱלֹהִים יִרְאֶה־לּוֹ הַשֶּׂה לְעֹלָה, בְּנִי, וַיֵּלְכוּ שְׁנֵיהֶם יַחְדָּו: וַיָּבֹֽאוּ אֶל־הַמָּקוֹם אֲשֶׁר אָמַר־לוֹ הָאֱלֹהִים, וַיִּֽבֶן שָׁם אַבְרָהָם אֶת־הַמִּזְבֵּֽחַ וַיַּעֲרֹךְ אֶת־הָעֵצִים, וַיַּעֲקֹד אֶת־יִצְחָק בְּנוֹ, וַיָּֽשֶׂם אֹתוֹ עַל־הַמִּזְבֵּֽחַ מִמַּֽעַל לָעֵצִים: וַיִּשְׁלַח אַבְרָהָם אֶת־יָדוֹ, וַיִּקַּח אֶת־הַמַּאֲכֶֽלֶת, לִשְׁחֹט אֶת־בְּנוֹ: וַיִּקְרָא אֵלָיו מַלְאַךְ יהוה מִן־הַשָּׁמַֽיִם, וַיֹּֽאמֶר אַבְרָהָם אַבְרָהָם, וַיֹּֽאמֶר הִנֵּֽנִי: וַיֹּֽאמֶר אַל־תִּשְׁלַח יָדְךָ אֶל־הַנַּֽעַר, וְאַל־תַּֽעַשׂ לוֹ מְאֽוּמָה, כִּי עַתָּה יָדַֽעְתִּי כִּי־יְרֵא אֱלֹהִים אַתָּה, וְלֹא חָשַֽׂכְתָּ אֶת־בִּנְךָ אֶת־יְחִידְךָ מִמֶּֽנִּי: וַיִּשָּׂא אַבְרָהָם אֶת־עֵינָיו, וַיַּרְא וְהִנֵּה־אַֽיִל, אַחַר נֶאֱחַז בַּסְּבַךְ בְּקַרְנָיו, וַיֵּֽלֶךְ אַבְרָהָם וַיִּקַּח אֶת־הָאַֽיִל, וַיַּעֲלֵֽהוּ לְעֹלָה תַּֽחַת

declares the LORD, that because you have done this and have not held back your son, your only son, I will greatly bless you and greatly multiply your descendants, as the stars of heaven and the sand of the seashore, and your descendants shall take possession of the gates of their enemies. Through your descendants, all the nations of the earth will be blessed, because you have heeded My voice." Then Abraham returned to his lads, and they rose and went together to Beersheba, and Abraham stayed in Beersheba.

*Most omit.*

Master of the Universe, just as Abraham our father suppressed his compassion to do Your will wholeheartedly, so may Your compassion suppress Your anger from us and may Your compassion prevail over Your other attributes. Deal with us, LORD our God, with the attributes of loving-kindness and compassion, and in Your great goodness may Your anger be turned away from Your people, Your city, Your land and Your inheritance. Fulfill in us, LORD our God, the promise You made in Your Torah
through the hand of Moses Your servant, as it is said: "I will remember My covenant *Lev. 26*
with Jacob, and also My covenant with Isaac, and also My covenant with Abraham
I will remember, and the land I will remember." And it is said: "Even so, when they *Ibid.*
are in the land of their enemies I shall not reject them and shall not detest them to the point of destruction, to the point of breaking My covenant with them, for I am the LORD their God." And it is said: "I shall remember for them the covenant of the early ones, those I took out of the land of Egypt before the eyes of the nations, in
order to be their God: I am the LORD." And it is said: "And the LORD your God shall *Deut. 30*
restore your fortunes and have compassion for you, and shall return and gather you in from all the nations among whom the LORD your God has scattered you. If your distanced ones are at the the very ends of the heavens, from there shall the LORD your God gather you; from there shall He bring you." And it is said: "Then the LORD your God will bring you to the land your ancestors possessed and you will possess it; and He will make you more prosperous and numerous than your ancestors." It
has been said by Your prophets, "LORD, be gracious to us, we have waited for You, *Is. 33*
be their strength by morning, our salvation in times of trouble." It is said, "This is *Jer. 30*
a time of trouble for Jacob, but he will be saved from it." And it is said: "In all their *Is. 63*
troubles He too was troubled, and the angel in His presence saved them; in His love and His mercy He redeemed them, took them up and carried them all those
days of long ago." And it is said, "Who is a God like You, who pardons iniquity and *Mic. 7*
forgives the transgression of the remnant of His heritage? He does not stay angry for ever, but delights in loving-kindness. He will again have compassion on us, suppress our iniquities, and cast into the depths of the sea all their sins. Grant truth to Jacob, kindness to Abraham, as You promised our fathers in days long ago." And it
is said, "I shall bring them to My holy mountain, and I shall make them rejoice in *Is. 56*
My House of prayer; their offerings and their sacrifices will be accepted, desired on My altar, for My House will be called a house of prayer for all peoples."

בְּנוֹ: וַיִּקְרָא אַבְרָהָם שֵׁם־הַמָּקוֹם הַהוּא יהוה יִרְאֶה, אֲשֶׁר יֵאָמֵר הַיּוֹם בְּהַר יהוה יֵרָאֶה: וַיִּקְרָא מַלְאַךְ יהוה אֶל־אַבְרָהָם שֵׁנִית מִן־הַשָּׁמָיִם: וַיֹּאמֶר, בִּי נִשְׁבַּעְתִּי נְאֻם־יהוה, כִּי יַעַן אֲשֶׁר עָשִׂיתָ אֶת־הַדָּבָר הַזֶּה, וְלֹא חָשַׂכְתָּ אֶת־בִּנְךָ אֶת־יְחִידֶךָ: כִּי־בָרֵךְ אֲבָרֶכְךָ, וְהַרְבָּה אַרְבֶּה אֶת־זַרְעֲךָ כְּכוֹכְבֵי הַשָּׁמַיִם, וְכַחוֹל אֲשֶׁר עַל־שְׂפַת הַיָּם, וְיִרַשׁ זַרְעֲךָ אֵת שַׁעַר אֹיְבָיו: וְהִתְבָּרְכוּ בְזַרְעֲךָ כֹּל גּוֹיֵי הָאָרֶץ, עֵקֶב אֲשֶׁר שָׁמַעְתָּ בְּקֹלִי: וַיָּשָׁב אַבְרָהָם אֶל־נְעָרָיו, וַיָּקֻמוּ וַיֵּלְכוּ יַחְדָּו אֶל־בְּאֵר שָׁבַע, וַיֵּשֶׁב אַבְרָהָם בִּבְאֵר שָׁבַע:

*Most omit.*

רִבּוֹנוֹ שֶׁל עוֹלָם, כְּמוֹ שֶׁכָּבַשׁ אַבְרָהָם אָבִינוּ אֶת רַחֲמָיו לַעֲשׂוֹת רְצוֹנְךָ בְּלֵבָב
שָׁלֵם, כֵּן יִכְבְּשׁוּ רַחֲמֶיךָ אֶת כַּעַסְךָ מֵעָלֵינוּ וְיִגֹּלּוּ רַחֲמֶיךָ עַל מִדּוֹתֶיךָ. וְתִתְנַהֵג
עִמָּנוּ יהוה אֱלֹהֵינוּ בְּמִדַּת הַחֶסֶד וּבְמִדַּת הָרַחֲמִים, וּבְטוּבְךָ הַגָּדוֹל יָשׁוּב חֲרוֹן
אַפְּךָ מֵעַמְּךָ וּמֵעִירְךָ וּמֵאַרְצְךָ וּמִנַּחֲלָתֶךָ. וְקַיֶּם לָנוּ יהוה אֱלֹהֵינוּ אֶת הַדָּבָר
שֶׁהִבְטַחְתָּנוּ בְתוֹרָתֶךָ עַל יְדֵי מֹשֶׁה עַבְדֶּךָ, כָּאָמוּר: וְזָכַרְתִּי אֶת־בְּרִיתִי יַעֲקוֹב ויקרא כו
וְאַף אֶת־בְּרִיתִי יִצְחָק, וְאַף אֶת־בְּרִיתִי אַבְרָהָם אֶזְכֹּר, וְהָאָרֶץ אֶזְכֹּר: וְנֶאֱמַר: וְאַף שם
גַּם־זֹאת בִּהְיוֹתָם בְּאֶרֶץ אֹיְבֵיהֶם, לֹא־מְאַסְתִּים וְלֹא־גְעַלְתִּים לְכַלֹּתָם, לְהָפֵר
בְּרִיתִי אִתָּם, כִּי אֲנִי יהוה אֱלֹהֵיהֶם: וְנֶאֱמַר: וְזָכַרְתִּי לָהֶם בְּרִית רִאשֹׁנִים, אֲשֶׁר
הוֹצֵאתִי־אֹתָם מֵאֶרֶץ מִצְרַיִם לְעֵינֵי הַגּוֹיִם, לִהְיוֹת לָהֶם לֵאלֹהִים, אֲנִי יהוה:
וְנֶאֱמַר: וְשָׁב יהוה אֱלֹהֶיךָ אֶת־שְׁבוּתְךָ וְרִחֲמֶךָ, וְשָׁב וְקִבֶּצְךָ מִכָּל־הָעַמִּים, דברים ל
אֲשֶׁר הֱפִיצְךָ יהוה אֱלֹהֶיךָ שָׁמָּה: אִם־יִהְיֶה נִדַּחֲךָ בִּקְצֵה הַשָּׁמָיִם, מִשָּׁם יְקַבֶּצְךָ
יהוה אֱלֹהֶיךָ, וּמִשָּׁם יִקָּחֶךָ: וְנֶאֱמַר: וֶהֱבִיאֲךָ יהוה אֱלֹהֶיךָ אֶל־הָאָרֶץ אֲשֶׁר־
יָרְשׁוּ אֲבֹתֶיךָ וִירִשְׁתָּהּ, וְהֵיטִבְךָ וְהִרְבְּךָ מֵאֲבֹתֶיךָ: וְנֶאֱמַר עַל יְדֵי נְבִיאֶךָ: יהוה ישעיה לג
חָנֵּנוּ, לְךָ קִוִּינוּ, הֱיֵה זְרֹעָם לַבְּקָרִים אַף־יְשׁוּעָתֵנוּ בְּעֵת צָרָה: וְנֶאֱמַר: וְעֵת־צָרָה ירמיה ל
הִיא לְיַעֲקֹב וּמִמֶּנָּה יִוָּשֵׁעַ: וְנֶאֱמַר: בְּכָל־צָרָתָם לוֹ צָר, וּמַלְאַךְ פָּנָיו הוֹשִׁיעָם, ישעיה סג
בְּאַהֲבָתוֹ וּבְחֶמְלָתוֹ הוּא גְאָלָם, וַיְנַטְּלֵם וַיְנַשְּׂאֵם כָּל־יְמֵי עוֹלָם: וְנֶאֱמַר: מִי־אֵל מיכה ז
כָּמוֹךָ נֹשֵׂא עָוֹן וְעֹבֵר עַל־פֶּשַׁע לִשְׁאֵרִית נַחֲלָתוֹ, לֹא־הֶחֱזִיק לָעַד אַפּוֹ, כִּי־חָפֵץ
חֶסֶד הוּא: יָשׁוּב יְרַחֲמֵנוּ יִכְבֹּשׁ עֲוֹנֹתֵינוּ, וְתַשְׁלִיךְ בִּמְצֻלוֹת יָם כָּל־חַטֹּאתָם:
תִּתֵּן אֱמֶת לְיַעֲקֹב, חֶסֶד לְאַבְרָהָם, אֲשֶׁר־נִשְׁבַּעְתָּ לַאֲבֹתֵינוּ מִימֵי קֶדֶם: וְנֶאֱמַר:
וַהֲבִיאוֹתִים אֶל־הַר קָדְשִׁי, וְשִׂמַּחְתִּים בְּבֵית תְּפִלָּתִי, עוֹלֹתֵיהֶם וְזִבְחֵיהֶם לְרָצוֹן ישעיה נו
עַל־מִזְבְּחִי, כִּי בֵיתִי בֵּית־תְּפִלָּה יִקָּרֵא לְכָל־הָעַמִּים:

## ACCEPTING THE SOVEREIGNTY OF HEAVEN

לְעוֹלָם A person should always be God-fearing, privately and publicly, acknowledging the truth and speaking it in his heart. *Tanna DeVei Eliyahu, ch. 21*
He should rise early and say:

Master of all worlds, LORD of lords,
not because of our righteousness *Dan. 9*
do we lay our pleas before You,
but because of Your great compassion.

What are we? What are our lives?
What is our loving-kindness?
What is our righteousness?
What is our salvation?
What is our strength?
What is our might?
What shall we say before You,
LORD our God and God of our ancestors?
Are not all the mighty like nothing before You,
the men of renown as if they had never been,
the wise as if they know nothing,
and the understanding as if they lack intelligence?
For their many works are in vain,
and the days of their lives like a fleeting breath before You.
The pre-eminence of man over the animals is nothing, *Eccl. 3*
for all is but a fleeting breath,
apart from the pure soul
that will one day give report before Your glorious throne.
And all the nations are as nothing before You,
as it is said:
"Nations are as a drop in the bucket, *Is. 40*
considered as the dust left on the scales;
He lifts up the islands like fine sand."

---

countless generations of people who, with heroic and understated courage, kept faith with faith itself.

# קבלת עול מלכות שמים

תנא דבי אליהו, פרק כא

לְעוֹלָם יְהֵא אָדָם יְרֵא שָׁמַיִם בְּסֵתֶר וּבְגָלוּי
וּמוֹדֶה עַל הָאֱמֶת, וְדוֹבֵר אֱמֶת בִּלְבָבוֹ
וְיַשְׁכֵּם וְיֹאמַר
רִבּוֹן כָּל הָעוֹלָמִים וַאֲדוֹנֵי הָאֲדוֹנִים
דניאל ט לֹא עַל־צִדְקוֹתֵינוּ אֲנַחְנוּ מַפִּילִים תַּחֲנוּנֵינוּ לְפָנֶיךָ
כִּי עַל־רַחֲמֶיךָ הָרַבִּים:

מָה אָנוּ, מֶה חַיֵּינוּ, מֶה חַסְדֵּנוּ, מַה צִּדְקוֹתֵינוּ
מַה יְשׁוּעָתֵנוּ, מַה כֹּחֵנוּ, מַה גְּבוּרָתֵנוּ
מַה נֹּאמַר לְפָנֶיךָ, יהוה אֱלֹהֵינוּ וֵאלֹהֵי אֲבוֹתֵינוּ
הֲלֹא כָּל הַגִּבּוֹרִים כְּאַיִן לְפָנֶיךָ
וְאַנְשֵׁי הַשֵּׁם כְּלֹא הָיוּ
וַחֲכָמִים כִּבְלִי מַדָּע, וּנְבוֹנִים כִּבְלִי הַשְׂכֵּל
כִּי רֹב מַעֲשֵׂיהֶם תֹּהוּ, וִימֵי חַיֵּיהֶם הֶבֶל לְפָנֶיךָ
קהלת ג וּמוֹתַר הָאָדָם מִן־הַבְּהֵמָה אָיִן
כִּי הַכֹּל הָבֶל:

לְבַד הַנְּשָׁמָה הַטְּהוֹרָה
שֶׁהִיא עֲתִידָה לִתֵּן דִּין וְחֶשְׁבּוֹן לִפְנֵי כִסֵּא כְבוֹדֶךָ.
וְכָל הַגּוֹיִם כְּאַיִן נֶגְדֶּךָ
שֶׁנֶּאֱמַר
ישעיה מ הֵן גּוֹיִם כְּמַר מִדְּלִי, וּכְשַׁחַק מֹאזְנַיִם נֶחְשָׁבוּ
הֵן אִיִּים כַּדַּק יִטּוֹל:

---

מָה אָנוּ... אֲבָל אֲנַחְנוּ עַמְּךָ *What are we?... Yet we are Your people.* Individually we may be small, but collectively we are heirs to greatness. For we are part of God's people, heirs to His covenant, descendants of the patriarchs and of

אֲבָל But we are Your people,
the children of Your covenant,
the children of Abraham, Your beloved,
to whom You made a promise on Mount Moriah;
the offspring of Isaac his only one
who was bound on the altar;
the congregation of Jacob Your firstborn son
whom – because of the love with which You loved him
and the joy with which You rejoiced in him –
You called Yisrael and Yeshurun.

לְפִיכָךְ Therefore it is our duty
to thank You, and to praise, glorify, bless, sanctify
and give praise and thanks to Your name.
Happy are we, how good is our portion,
how lovely our fate, how beautiful our heritage.

► אַשְׁרֵינוּ Happy are we who come early and late
to synagogues and study houses,
and proclaim the unity of Your name
every day, continually, and twice recite with love –

Listen, Israel: the LORD is our God, the LORD is One. *Deut. 6*

*Quietly:* Blessed be the name of His glorious kingdom for ever and all time.

*If there is a concern that the Shema will not be recited within the prescribed time, then all three paragraphs should be said. See law 44.*

Love the LORD your God with all your heart, with all your soul, and with all your might. These words which I command you today shall be on your heart. Teach them repeatedly to your children, speaking of them when you sit at home and when you travel on the way, when you lie down and when you rise. Bind them as a sign on your hand, and they shall be an emblem between your eyes. Write them on the doorposts of your house and gates.

---

The English historian A.L. Rowse, at the end of his life, wrote: "If there is any honor in all the world that I should like, it would be to be an honorary Jewish citizen."

אֲבָל אֲנַחְנוּ עַמְּךָ בְּנֵי בְרִיתֶךָ
בְּנֵי אַבְרָהָם אֹהַבְךָ שֶׁנִּשְׁבַּעְתָּ לּוֹ בְּהַר הַמּוֹרִיָּה
זֶרַע יִצְחָק יְחִידוֹ שֶׁנֶּעֱקַד עַל גַּבֵּי הַמִּזְבֵּחַ
עֲדַת יַעֲקֹב בִּנְךָ בְכוֹרֶךָ
שֶׁמֵּאַהֲבָתְךָ שֶׁאָהַבְתָּ אוֹתוֹ, וּמִשִּׂמְחָתְךָ שֶׁשָּׂמַחְתָּ בּוֹ
קָרָאתָ אֶת שְׁמוֹ יִשְׂרָאֵל וִישֻׁרוּן.

לְפִיכָךְ אֲנַחְנוּ חַיָּבִים
לְהוֹדוֹת לְךָ וּלְשַׁבֵּחֲךָ וּלְפָאֶרְךָ
וּלְבָרֵךְ וּלְקַדֵּשׁ וְלִתֵּן שֶׁבַח וְהוֹדָיָה לִשְׁמֶךָ.
אַשְׁרֵינוּ, מַה טּוֹב חֶלְקֵנוּ, וּמַה נָּעִים גּוֹרָלֵנוּ, וּמַה יָּפָה יְרֻשָּׁתֵנוּ.

אַשְׁרֵינוּ, שֶׁאֲנוּ מַשְׁכִּימִים וּמַעֲרִיבִים
בְּבָתֵּי כְנֵסִיּוֹת וּבְבָתֵּי מִדְרָשׁוֹת
וּמְיַחֲדִים שִׁמְךָ בְּכָל יוֹם תָּמִיד וְאוֹמְרִים פַּעֲמַיִם בְּאַהֲבָה

דברים ו

**שְׁמַע יִשְׂרָאֵל, יהוה אֱלֹהֵינוּ, יהוה אֶחָד:**

*Quietly* בָּרוּךְ שֵׁם כְּבוֹד מַלְכוּתוֹ לְעוֹלָם וָעֶד.

*If there is a concern that the שמע will not be recited within the prescribed time, then all three paragraphs should be said. See law 44.*

וְאָהַבְתָּ אֵת יהוה אֱלֹהֶיךָ, בְּכָל־לְבָבְךָ, וּבְכָל־נַפְשְׁךָ, וּבְכָל־מְאֹדֶךָ: וְהָיוּ הַדְּבָרִים הָאֵלֶּה, אֲשֶׁר אָנֹכִי מְצַוְּךָ הַיּוֹם, עַל־לְבָבֶךָ: וְשִׁנַּנְתָּם לְבָנֶיךָ, וְדִבַּרְתָּ בָּם, בְּשִׁבְתְּךָ בְּבֵיתֶךָ, וּבְלֶכְתְּךָ בַדֶּרֶךְ, וּבְשָׁכְבְּךָ וּבְקוּמֶךָ: וּקְשַׁרְתָּם לְאוֹת עַל־יָדֶךָ וְהָיוּ לְטֹטָפֹת בֵּין עֵינֶיךָ: וּכְתַבְתָּם עַל־מְזֻזוֹת בֵּיתֶךָ וּבִשְׁעָרֶיךָ:

---

אַשְׁרֵינוּ *Happy are we.* There is something momentous in this declaration, after all the suffering the Jewish people have undergone. For we have been summoned to be God's witnesses, His ambassadors to an often godless world.

אַתָּה הוּא It was You who existed before the world was created,
it is You now that the world has been created.
It is You in this world and You in the World to Come.
Sanctify Your name through those who sanctify Your name,
and sanctify Your name throughout Your world.
By Your salvation may our pride be exalted;
raise our pride high above,
and save us soon for the sake of Your name.
Blessed is He who sanctifies His name among the multitudes.

אַתָּה הוּא You are the Lord our God
in heaven and on earth, and in the highest heaven of heavens.
Truly, You are the first and You are the last,
and besides You there is no god.
Gather the scattered ones, those who hope in You,
from the four quarters of the earth.
May all mankind recognize and know that You are God alone,
Most High over all the kingdoms on earth.

You made the heavens and the earth,
the sea and all they contain.
Who among all the works of Your hands, above and below,
can tell You what to do or how to act?

Heavenly Father, living and forever enduring,
deal righteously and kindly with us
for the sake of Your great, mighty and awesome name
by which we are called,
and fulfill for us, Lord our God, that which You have promised us
through Your seer, Zephaniah,
as it is said:

> "At that time I will bring you home, *Zeph. 3*
> and at that time I will gather you,
> for I will give you renown and praise among all the
> peoples of the earth when I bring back your exiles
> before your eyes, says the Lord."

אַתָּה הוּא עַד שֶׁלֹּא נִבְרָא הָעוֹלָם, אַתָּה הוּא מִשֶּׁנִּבְרָא הָעוֹלָם.
אַתָּה הוּא בָּעוֹלָם הַזֶּה, וְאַתָּה הוּא לָעוֹלָם הַבָּא.
קַדֵּשׁ אֶת שִׁמְךָ עַל מַקְדִּישֵׁי שְׁמֶךָ, וְקַדֵּשׁ אֶת שִׁמְךָ בְּעוֹלָמֶךָ
וּבִישׁוּעָתְךָ תָּרוּם וְתַגְבִּיהַּ קַרְנֵנוּ לְמַעְלָה
וְהוֹשִׁיעֵנוּ בְּקָרוֹב לְמַעַן שְׁמֶךָ.
בָּרוּךְ הַמְקַדֵּשׁ שְׁמוֹ בָּרַבִּים.

אַתָּה הוּא יהוה אֱלֹהֵינוּ
בַּשָּׁמַיִם וּבָאָרֶץ וּבִשְׁמֵי הַשָּׁמַיִם הָעֶלְיוֹנִים.
אֱמֶת, אַתָּה הוּא רִאשׁוֹן, וְאַתָּה הוּא אַחֲרוֹן
וּמִבַּלְעָדֶיךָ אֵין אֱלֹהִים.
קַבֵּץ נְפוּצוֹת קֹוֶיךָ מֵאַרְבַּע כַּנְפוֹת הָאָרֶץ.
יַכִּירוּ וְיֵדְעוּ כָּל בָּאֵי עוֹלָם
כִּי אַתָּה הוּא הָאֱלֹהִים לְבַדֶּךָ, עֶלְיוֹן לְכֹל מַמְלְכוֹת הָאָרֶץ.

אַתָּה עָשִׂיתָ אֶת הַשָּׁמַיִם וְאֶת הָאָרֶץ
אֶת הַיָּם וְאֶת כָּל אֲשֶׁר בָּם
וּמִי בְּכָל מַעֲשֵׂי יָדֶיךָ בָּעֶלְיוֹנִים וּבַתַּחְתּוֹנִים
שֶׁיֹּאמַר לְךָ מַה תַּעֲשֶׂה וּמַה תִּפְעָל.

אָבִינוּ שֶׁבַּשָּׁמַיִם, חַי וְקַיָּם
עֲשֵׂה עִמָּנוּ צְדָקָה וָחֶסֶד
בַּעֲבוּר שִׁמְךָ הַגָּדוֹל הַגִּבּוֹר וְהַנּוֹרָא שֶׁנִּקְרָא עָלֵינוּ
וְקַיֶּם לָנוּ יהוה אֱלֹהֵינוּ אֶת הַדָּבָר
שֶׁהִבְטַחְתָּנוּ עַל יְדֵי צְפַנְיָה חוֹזָךְ, כָּאָמוּר
בָּעֵת הַהִיא אָבִיא אֶתְכֶם, וּבָעֵת קַבְּצִי אֶתְכֶם צפניה ג
כִּי־אֶתֵּן אֶתְכֶם לְשֵׁם וְלִתְהִלָּה בְּכֹל עַמֵּי הָאָרֶץ
בְּשׁוּבִי אֶת־שְׁבוּתֵיכֶם לְעֵינֵיכֶם, אָמַר יהוה:

# OFFERINGS

*The sages held that, in the absence of the Temple, studying the laws of sacrifices is the equivalent of offering them. Hence the following texts. There are different customs as to how many passages are to be said, and one should follow the custom of one's congregation. The minimum requirement is to say the verses relating to The Daily Sacrifice on the next page.*

## THE BASIN

The LORD spoke to Moses, saying: Make a bronze basin, with its bronze stand for washing, and place it between the Tent of Meeting and the altar, and put water in it. From it, Aaron and his sons are to wash their hands and feet. When they enter the Tent of Meeting, they shall wash with water so that they will not die; likewise when they approach the altar to minister, presenting a fire-offering to the LORD. They must wash their hands and feet so that they will not die. This shall be an everlasting ordinance for Aaron and his descendants throughout their generations. *Ex. 30*

## TAKING OF THE ASHES

The LORD spoke to Moses, saying: Instruct Aaron and his sons, saying, This is the law of the burnt-offering. The burnt-offering shall remain on the altar hearth throughout the night until morning, and the altar fire shall be kept burning on it. The priest shall then put on his linen garments, and linen breeches next to his body, and shall remove the ashes of the burnt-offering that the fire has consumed on the altar and place them beside the altar. Then he shall take off these clothes and put on others, and carry the ashes outside the camp to a clean place. The fire on the altar must be kept burning; it must not go out. Each morning the priest shall burn wood on it, and prepare on it the burnt-offering and burn the fat of the peace-offerings. A perpetual fire must be kept burning on the altar; it must not go out. *Lev. 6*

May it be Your will, LORD our God and God of our ancestors, that You have compassion on us and pardon us all our sins, grant atonement for all our iniquities and forgive all our transgressions. May the Temple be rebuilt swiftly in our days so that we may offer You the continual-offering that it may atone for us as You have prescribed for us in Your Torah through Moses Your servant, from the mouthpiece of Your glory, as it is said:

---

sacrifices of praise instead of bulls" (Hos. 14:3), the sages said that learning about the sacrifices was like offering them. "Whoever reads the order of

# סדר הקרבנות

*חז״ל held that, in the absence of the Temple, studying the laws of sacrifices is the equivalent of offering them. Hence the following texts. There are different customs as to how many passages are to be said, and one should follow the custom of one's congregation. The minimum requirement is to say the verses relating to the קרבן תמיד on the next page.*

### פרשת הכיור

וַיְדַבֵּר יהוה אֶל־מֹשֶׁה לֵּאמֹר: וְעָשִׂיתָ כִּיּוֹר נְחֹשֶׁת וְכַנּוֹ נְחֹשֶׁת לְרָחְצָה, שמות ל
וְנָתַתָּ אֹתוֹ בֵּין־אֹהֶל מוֹעֵד וּבֵין הַמִּזְבֵּחַ, וְנָתַתָּ שָׁמָּה מָיִם: וְרָחֲצוּ אַהֲרֹן
וּבָנָיו מִמֶּנּוּ אֶת־יְדֵיהֶם וְאֶת־רַגְלֵיהֶם: בְּבֹאָם אֶל־אֹהֶל מוֹעֵד יִרְחֲצוּ־
מַיִם, וְלֹא יָמֻתוּ, אוֹ בְגִשְׁתָּם אֶל־הַמִּזְבֵּחַ לְשָׁרֵת, לְהַקְטִיר אִשֶּׁה לַיהוה:
וְרָחֲצוּ יְדֵיהֶם וְרַגְלֵיהֶם וְלֹא יָמֻתוּ, וְהָיְתָה לָהֶם חָק־עוֹלָם, לוֹ וּלְזַרְעוֹ
לְדֹרֹתָם:

### פרשת תרומת הדשן

וַיְדַבֵּר יהוה אֶל־מֹשֶׁה לֵּאמֹר: צַו אֶת־אַהֲרֹן וְאֶת־בָּנָיו לֵאמֹר, זֹאת ויקרא ו
תּוֹרַת הָעֹלָה, הִוא הָעֹלָה עַל מוֹקְדָה עַל־הַמִּזְבֵּחַ כָּל־הַלַּיְלָה עַד־הַבֹּקֶר,
וְאֵשׁ הַמִּזְבֵּחַ תּוּקַד בּוֹ: וְלָבַשׁ הַכֹּהֵן מִדּוֹ בַד, וּמִכְנְסֵי־בַד יִלְבַּשׁ עַל־
בְּשָׂרוֹ, וְהֵרִים אֶת־הַדֶּשֶׁן אֲשֶׁר תֹּאכַל הָאֵשׁ אֶת־הָעֹלָה, עַל־הַמִּזְבֵּחַ,
וְשָׂמוֹ אֵצֶל הַמִּזְבֵּחַ: וּפָשַׁט אֶת־בְּגָדָיו, וְלָבַשׁ בְּגָדִים אֲחֵרִים, וְהוֹצִיא
אֶת־הַדֶּשֶׁן אֶל־מִחוּץ לַמַּחֲנֶה, אֶל־מָקוֹם טָהוֹר: וְהָאֵשׁ עַל־הַמִּזְבֵּחַ
תּוּקַד־בּוֹ, לֹא תִכְבֶּה, וּבִעֵר עָלֶיהָ הַכֹּהֵן עֵצִים בַּבֹּקֶר בַּבֹּקֶר, וְעָרַךְ עָלֶיהָ
הָעֹלָה, וְהִקְטִיר עָלֶיהָ חֶלְבֵי הַשְּׁלָמִים: אֵשׁ, תָּמִיד תּוּקַד עַל־הַמִּזְבֵּחַ,
לֹא תִכְבֶּה:

יְהִי רָצוֹן מִלְּפָנֶיךָ יהוה אֱלֹהֵינוּ וֵאלֹהֵי אֲבוֹתֵינוּ, שֶׁתְּרַחֵם עָלֵינוּ, וְתִמְחָל לָנוּ עַל כָּל חַטֹּאתֵינוּ וּתְכַפֶּר לָנוּ עַל כָּל עֲוֹנוֹתֵינוּ וְתִסְלַח לָנוּ עַל כָּל פְּשָׁעֵינוּ, וְשֶׁיִּבָּנֶה בֵּית הַמִּקְדָּשׁ בִּמְהֵרָה בְיָמֵינוּ, וְנַקְרִיב לְפָנֶיךָ קָרְבַּן הַתָּמִיד שֶׁיְּכַפֵּר בַּעֲדֵנוּ, כְּמוֹ שֶׁכָּתַבְתָּ עָלֵינוּ בְּתוֹרָתֶךָ עַל יְדֵי מֹשֶׁה עַבְדֶּךָ מִפִּי כְבוֹדֶךָ, כָּאָמוּר

---

SEDER KORBANOT – OFFERINGS

When the Temple was destroyed, sacrifices ceased. Yet in a momentous leap of the spirit, following the prophet Hosea who said, "Accept our good

THE DAILY SACRIFICE

וַיְדַבֵּר The Lord said to Moses, "Command the Israelites and tell them: 'Be careful to offer to Me at the appointed time My food-offering consumed by fire, as an aroma pleasing to Me.' Tell them: 'This is the fire-offering you shall offer to the Lord – two lambs a year old without blemish, as a regular burnt-offering each day. Prepare one lamb in the morning and the other toward evening, together with a meal-offering of a tenth of an ephah of fine flour mixed with a quarter of a hin of oil from pressed olives. This is the regular burnt-offering instituted at Mount Sinai as a pleasing aroma, a fire-offering made to the Lord. Its libation is to be a quarter of a hin [of wine] with each lamb, poured in the Sanctuary as a libation of strong drink to the Lord. Prepare the second lamb in the afternoon, along with the same meal-offering and libation as in the morning. This is a fire-offering, an aroma pleasing to the Lord.'" *Num. 28*

וְשָׁחַט He shall slaughter it at the north side of the altar before the Lord, and Aaron's sons the priests shall sprinkle its blood against the altar on all sides. *Lev. 1*

May it be Your will, Lord our God and God of our ancestors,
that this recitation be considered accepted and favored before You
as if we had offered the daily sacrifice at its appointed time and place, according to its laws.

It is You, Lord our God, to whom our ancestors offered fragrant incense when the Temple stood, as You commanded them through Moses Your prophet, as is written in Your Torah:

THE INCENSE

The Lord said to Moses: Take fragrant spices – balsam, onycha, galbanum and pure frankincense, all in equal amounts – and make a fragrant blend of incense, the work of a perfumer, well mixed, pure and holy. Grind it very finely and place it in front of the [Ark of] Testimony in the Tent of Meeting, where I will meet with you. It shall be most holy to you. *Ex. 30*

---

There are many different customs as to which passages to say. Those in large print constitute the original order of prayer as found in the siddurim

פרשת קרבן התמיד

במדבר כח וַיְדַבֵּר יהוה אֶל־מֹשֶׁה לֵּאמֹר: צַו אֶת־בְּנֵי יִשְׂרָאֵל וְאָמַרְתָּ אֲלֵהֶם, אֶת־קָרְבָּנִי לַחְמִי לְאִשַּׁי, רֵיחַ נִיחֹחִי, תִּשְׁמְרוּ לְהַקְרִיב לִי בְּמוֹעֲדוֹ: וְאָמַרְתָּ לָהֶם, זֶה הָאִשֶּׁה אֲשֶׁר תַּקְרִיבוּ לַיהוה, כְּבָשִׂים בְּנֵי־שָׁנָה תְמִימִם שְׁנַיִם לַיּוֹם, עֹלָה תָמִיד: אֶת־הַכֶּבֶשׂ אֶחָד תַּעֲשֶׂה בַבֹּקֶר, וְאֵת הַכֶּבֶשׂ הַשֵּׁנִי תַּעֲשֶׂה בֵּין הָעַרְבָּיִם: וַעֲשִׂירִית הָאֵיפָה סֹלֶת לְמִנְחָה, בְּלוּלָה בְּשֶׁמֶן כָּתִית רְבִיעִת הַהִין: עֹלַת תָּמִיד, הָעֲשֻׂיָה בְּהַר סִינַי, לְרֵיחַ נִיחֹחַ אִשֶּׁה לַיהוה: וְנִסְכּוֹ רְבִיעִת הַהִין לַכֶּבֶשׂ הָאֶחָד, בַּקֹּדֶשׁ הַסֵּךְ נֶסֶךְ שֵׁכָר לַיהוה: וְאֵת הַכֶּבֶשׂ הַשֵּׁנִי תַּעֲשֶׂה בֵּין הָעַרְבָּיִם, כְּמִנְחַת הַבֹּקֶר וּכְנִסְכּוֹ תַּעֲשֶׂה, אִשֵּׁה רֵיחַ נִיחֹחַ לַיהוה:

ויקרא א וְשָׁחַט אֹתוֹ עַל יֶרֶךְ הַמִּזְבֵּחַ צָפֹנָה לִפְנֵי יהוה, וְזָרְקוּ בְּנֵי אַהֲרֹן הַכֹּהֲנִים אֶת־דָּמוֹ עַל־הַמִּזְבֵּחַ, סָבִיב:

יְהִי רָצוֹן מִלְּפָנֶיךָ, יהוה אֱלֹהֵינוּ וֵאלֹהֵי אֲבוֹתֵינוּ
שֶׁתְּהֵא אֲמִירָה זוֹ חֲשׁוּבָה וּמְקֻבֶּלֶת וּמְרֻצָּה לְפָנֶיךָ
כְּאִלּוּ הִקְרַבְנוּ קָרְבַּן הַתָּמִיד בְּמוֹעֲדוֹ וּבִמְקוֹמוֹ וּכְהִלְכָתוֹ.

אַתָּה הוּא יהוה אֱלֹהֵינוּ שֶׁהִקְטִירוּ אֲבוֹתֵינוּ לְפָנֶיךָ אֶת קְטֹרֶת הַסַּמִּים בִּזְמַן שֶׁבֵּית הַמִּקְדָּשׁ הָיָה קַיָּם, כַּאֲשֶׁר צִוִּיתָ אוֹתָם עַל יְדֵי מֹשֶׁה נְבִיאֶךָ, כַּכָּתוּב בְּתוֹרָתֶךָ:

פרשת הקטורת

שמות ל וַיֹּאמֶר יהוה אֶל־מֹשֶׁה, קַח־לְךָ סַמִּים נָטָף וּשְׁחֵלֶת וְחֶלְבְּנָה, סַמִּים וּלְבֹנָה זַכָּה, בַּד בְּבַד יִהְיֶה: וְעָשִׂיתָ אֹתָהּ קְטֹרֶת, רֹקַח מַעֲשֵׂה רוֹקֵחַ, מְמֻלָּח, טָהוֹר קֹדֶשׁ: וְשָׁחַקְתָּ מִמֶּנָּה הָדֵק, וְנָתַתָּה מִמֶּנָּה לִפְנֵי הָעֵדֻת בְּאֹהֶל מוֹעֵד אֲשֶׁר אִוָּעֵד לְךָ שָׁמָּה, קֹדֶשׁ קָדָשִׁים תִּהְיֶה לָכֶם:

---

sacrifices, I will deem it as if they had offered them before Me and I will grant them pardon for all their iniquities" (*Ta'anit* 27b).

And it is said:

> Aaron shall burn fragrant incense on the altar every morning when he cleans the lamps. He shall burn incense again when he lights the lamps toward evening so that there will be incense before the LORD at all times, throughout your generations.

The rabbis taught: How was the incense prepared? It weighed 368 manehs, 365 corresponding to the number of days in a solar year, a maneh for each day, half to be offered in the morning and half in the afternoon, and three additional manehs from which the High Priest took two handfuls on Yom Kippur. These were put back into the mortar on the day before Yom Kippur and ground again very thoroughly so as to be extremely fine. The incense contained eleven kinds of spices: balsam, onycha, galbanum and frankincense, each weighing seventy manehs; myrrh, cassia, spikenard and saffron, each weighing sixteen manehs; twelve manehs of costus, three of aromatic bark; nine of cinnamon; nine kabs of Carsina lye; three seahs and three kabs of Cyprus wine. If Cyprus wine was not available, old white wine might be used. A quarter of a kab of Sodom salt, and a minute amount of a smoke-raising herb. Rabbi Nathan the Babylonian says: also a minute amount of Jordan amber. If one added honey to the mixture, he rendered it unfit for sacred use. If he omitted any one of its ingredients, he is guilty of a capital offense. *Keritot 6a*

Rabban Simeon ben Gamliel says: "Balsam" refers to the sap that drips from the balsam tree. The Carsina lye was used for bleaching the onycha to improve it. The Cyprus wine was used to soak the onycha in it to make it pungent. Though urine is suitable for this purpose, it is not brought into the Temple out of respect.

It was taught, Rabbi Nathan says: While it was being ground, another would say, "Grind well, well grind," because the [rhythmic] sound is good for spices. If it was mixed in half-quantities, it is fit for use, but we have not heard whether this applies to a third or a quarter. Rabbi Judah said: The general rule is that if it was made in the correct proportions, it is fit for use even if made in half-quantity, but if he omitted any one of its ingredients, he is guilty of a capital offense.

It was taught, Bar Kappara says: Once every sixty or seventy years, the accumulated surpluses amounted to half the yearly quantity. Bar Kappara also taught: If a minute quantity of honey had been mixed into the incense, no one could have resisted the scent. Why did they not put honey into it? Because the Torah says, "For you are not to burn any leaven or honey in a fire-offering made to the LORD." *JT Yoma 4:5* *Lev. 2*

---

Yishma'el – considered as Talmud in the broad sense defined by Maimonides as "deducing conclusions from premises, developing implications of statements, comparing dicta, and studying the hermeneutical principles by which the Torah is interpreted" (Laws of Torah Study 1:11).

וְנֶאֱמַר
וְהִקְטִיר עָלָיו אַהֲרֹן קְטֹרֶת סַמִּים, בַּבֹּקֶר בַּבֹּקֶר בְּהֵיטִיבוֹ אֶת־הַנֵּרֹת יַקְטִירֶנָּה: וּבְהַעֲלֹת אַהֲרֹן אֶת־הַנֵּרֹת בֵּין הָעַרְבַּיִם יַקְטִירֶנָּה, קְטֹרֶת תָּמִיד לִפְנֵי יהוה לְדֹרֹתֵיכֶם:

כריתות ו. תָּנוּ רַבָּנָן: פִּטּוּם הַקְּטֹרֶת כֵּיצַד, שְׁלֹשׁ מֵאוֹת וְשִׁשִּׁים וּשְׁמוֹנָה מָנִים הָיוּ בָהּ. שְׁלֹשׁ מֵאוֹת וְשִׁשִּׁים וַחֲמִשָּׁה כְּמִנְיַן יְמוֹת הַחַמָּה, מָנֶה לְכָל יוֹם, פְּרַס בְּשַׁחֲרִית וּפְרַס בֵּין הָעַרְבַּיִם, וּשְׁלֹשָׁה מָנִים יְתֵרִים שֶׁמֵּהֶם מַכְנִיס כֹּהֵן גָּדוֹל מְלֹא חָפְנָיו בְּיוֹם הַכִּפּוּרִים, וּמַחֲזִירָן לְמַכְתֶּשֶׁת בְּעֶרֶב יוֹם הַכִּפּוּרִים וְשׁוֹחֲקָן יָפֶה יָפֶה, כְּדֵי שֶׁתְּהֵא דַקָּה מִן הַדַּקָּה. וְאַחַד עָשָׂר סַמָּנִים הָיוּ בָהּ, וְאֵלּוּ הֵן: הַצֳּרִי, וְהַצִּפֹּרֶן, וְהַחֶלְבְּנָה, וְהַלְּבוֹנָה מִשְׁקַל שִׁבְעִים שִׁבְעִים מָנֶה, מֹר, וּקְצִיעָה, שִׁבֹּלֶת נֵרְדְּ, וְכַרְכֹּם מִשְׁקַל שִׁשָּׁה עָשָׂר שִׁשָּׁה עָשָׂר מָנֶה, הַקֹּשְׁטְ שְׁנֵים עָשָׂר, קִלּוּפָה שְׁלֹשָׁה, קִנָּמוֹן תִּשְׁעָה, בֹּרִית כַּרְשִׁינָה תִּשְׁעָה קַבִּין, יֵין קַפְרִיסִין סְאִין תְּלָת וְקַבִּין תְּלָתָא, וְאִם לֹא מָצָא יֵין קַפְרִיסִין, מֵבִיא חֲמַר חִוַּרְיָן עַתִּיק. מֶלַח סְדוֹמִית רֹבַע, מַעֲלֶה עָשָׁן כָּל שֶׁהוּא. רַבִּי נָתָן הַבַּבְלִי אוֹמֵר: אַף כִּפַּת הַיַּרְדֵּן כָּל שֶׁהוּא, וְאִם נָתַן בָּהּ דְּבַשׁ פְּסָלָהּ, וְאִם חִסַּר אֶחָד מִכָּל סַמָּנֶיהָ, חַיָּב מִיתָה.

רַבָּן שִׁמְעוֹן בֶּן גַּמְלִיאֵל אוֹמֵר: הַצֳּרִי אֵינוֹ אֶלָּא שְׂרָף הַנּוֹטֵף מֵעֲצֵי הַקְּטָף. בֹּרִית כַּרְשִׁינָה שֶׁשָּׁפִין בָּהּ אֶת הַצִּפֹּרֶן כְּדֵי שֶׁתְּהֵא נָאָה, יֵין קַפְרִיסִין שֶׁשּׁוֹרִין בּוֹ אֶת הַצִּפֹּרֶן כְּדֵי שֶׁתְּהֵא עַזָּה, וַהֲלֹא מֵי רַגְלַיִם יָפִין לָהּ, אֶלָּא שֶׁאֵין מַכְנִיסִין מֵי רַגְלַיִם בַּמִּקְדָּשׁ מִפְּנֵי הַכָּבוֹד.

תַּנְיָא, רַבִּי נָתָן אוֹמֵר: כְּשֶׁהוּא שׁוֹחֵק אוֹמֵר, הָדֵק הֵיטֵב הֵיטֵב הָדֵק, מִפְּנֵי שֶׁהַקּוֹל יָפֶה לַבְּשָׂמִים. פִּטְּמָהּ לַחֲצָאִין כְּשֵׁרָה, לִשְׁלִישׁ וְלִרְבִיעַ לֹא שָׁמַעְנוּ. אָמַר רַבִּי יְהוּדָה: זֶה הַכְּלָל, אִם כְּמִדָּתָהּ כְּשֵׁרָה לַחֲצָאִין, וְאִם חִסַּר אֶחָד מִכָּל סַמָּנֶיהָ חַיָּב מִיתָה.

ירושלמי יומא ד, הלכה ה תַּנְיָא, בַּר קַפָּרָא אוֹמֵר: אַחַת לְשִׁשִּׁים אוֹ לְשִׁבְעִים שָׁנָה הָיְתָה בָאָה שֶׁל שִׁירַיִם לַחֲצָאִין. וְעוֹד תָּנֵי בַּר קַפָּרָא: אִלּוּ הָיָה נוֹתֵן בָּהּ קוֹרְטוֹב שֶׁל דְּבַשׁ אֵין אָדָם יָכוֹל
ויקרא ב לַעֲמֹד מִפְּנֵי רֵיחָהּ, וְלָמָּה אֵין מְעָרְבִין בָּהּ דְּבַשׁ, מִפְּנֵי שֶׁהַתּוֹרָה אָמְרָה: כִּי כָל־שְׂאֹר וְכָל־דְּבַשׁ לֹא־תַקְטִירוּ מִמֶּנּוּ אִשֶּׁה לַיהוה:

---

of Rav Amram Gaon and Rav Sa'adia Gaon. The texts follow the threefold structure of (1) a passage from the Torah, (2) a section of the Mishna, and (3) a passage of Talmud, in this case the Interpretive Principles of Rabbi

*The following three verses are each said three times:*

The LORD of hosts is with us; the God of Jacob is our stronghold, Selah. *Ps. 46*
LORD of hosts, happy is the one who trusts in You. *Ps. 84*
LORD, save! May the King answer us on the day we call. *Ps. 20*

You are my hiding place; You will protect me from distress *Ps. 32*
and surround me with songs of salvation, Selah.
Then the offering of Judah and Jerusalem will be pleasing to the LORD *Mal. 3*
as in the days of old and as in former years.

## THE ORDER OF THE PRIESTLY FUNCTIONS

Abaye related the order of the daily priestly functions in the name of tradition *Yoma 33a* and in accordance with Abba Shaul: The large pile [of wood] comes before the second pile for the incense; the second pile for the incense precedes the laying in order of the two logs of wood; the laying in order of the two logs of wood comes before the removing of ashes from the inner altar; the removing of ashes from the inner altar precedes the cleaning of the five lamps; the cleaning of the five lamps comes before the blood of the daily offering; the blood of the daily offering precedes the cleaning of the [other] two lamps; the cleaning of the two lamps comes before the incense-offering; the incense-offering precedes the burning of the limbs; the burning of the limbs comes before the meal-offering; the meal-offering precedes the pancakes; the pancakes come before the wine-libations; the wine-libations precede the additional offerings; the additional offerings come before the [frankincense] censers; the censers precede the daily afternoon offering; as it is said, "On it he shall arrange burnt- *Lev. 6* offerings, and on it he shall burn the fat of the peace-offerings" – "on it" [the daily offering] all the offerings were completed.

Please, by the power of Your great right hand, set the captive nation free.
Accept Your people's prayer. Strengthen us, purify us, You who are revered.
Please, Mighty One, guard like the pupil of the eye those who seek Your unity.
Bless them, cleanse them,
grant them the compassion of Your righteousness always.
Mighty One, Holy One, in Your great goodness guide Your congregation.
Only One, Exalted One, turn to Your people, who proclaim Your holiness.
Accept our plea and heed our cry, You who know all secret thoughts.
Blessed be the name of His glorious kingdom for ever and all time.

*Some omit:*

Master of the Universe, You have commanded us to offer the daily sacrifice at its appointed time with the priests at their service, the Levites on their platform, and the Israelites at their post. Now, because of our sins, the Temple is destroyed and the daily sacrifice discontinued, and we have no priest at his service, no Levite on his platform, no Israelite at his post. But You said: "We will offer in place of bullocks *Hos. 14*

*The following three verses are each said three times:*

יהוה צְבָאוֹת עִמָּנוּ, מִשְׂגָּב לָנוּ אֱלֹהֵי יַעֲקֹב סֶלָה: תהלים מו

יהוה צְבָאוֹת, אַשְׁרֵי אָדָם בֹּטֵחַ בָּךְ: תהלים פד

יהוה הוֹשִׁיעָה, הַמֶּלֶךְ יַעֲנֵנוּ בְיוֹם־קָרְאֵנוּ: תהלים כ

אַתָּה סֵתֶר לִי, מִצַּר תִּצְּרֵנִי, רָנֵּי פַלֵּט תְּסוֹבְבֵנִי סֶלָה: תהלים לב

וְעָרְבָה לַיהוה מִנְחַת יְהוּדָה וִירוּשָׁלָםִ מלאכי ג

כִּימֵי עוֹלָם וּכְשָׁנִים קַדְמֹנִיּוֹת:

## סדר המערכה

אַבַּיֵּי הֲוָה מְסַדֵּר סֵדֶר הַמַּעֲרָכָה מִשְּׁמָא דִּגְמָרָא, וְאַלִּבָּא דְאַבָּא שָׁאוּל: יומא לג.
מַעֲרָכָה גְדוֹלָה קוֹדֶמֶת לְמַעֲרָכָה שְׁנִיָּה שֶׁל קְטֹרֶת, וּמַעֲרָכָה שְׁנִיָּה שֶׁל קְטֹרֶת
קוֹדֶמֶת לְסִדּוּר שְׁנֵי גִזְרֵי עֵצִים, וְסִדּוּר שְׁנֵי גִזְרֵי עֵצִים קוֹדֵם לְדִשּׁוּן מִזְבֵּחַ
הַפְּנִימִי, וְדִשּׁוּן מִזְבֵּחַ הַפְּנִימִי קוֹדֵם לַהֲטָבַת חָמֵשׁ נֵרוֹת, וַהֲטָבַת חָמֵשׁ נֵרוֹת
קוֹדֶמֶת לְדַם הַתָּמִיד, וְדַם הַתָּמִיד קוֹדֵם לַהֲטָבַת שְׁתֵּי נֵרוֹת, וַהֲטָבַת שְׁתֵּי
נֵרוֹת קוֹדֶמֶת לִקְטֹרֶת, וּקְטֹרֶת קוֹדֶמֶת לְאֵבָרִים, וְאֵבָרִים לְמִנְחָה, וּמִנְחָה
לַחֲבִתִּין, וַחֲבִתִּין לִנְסָכִין, וּנְסָכִין לְמוּסָפִין, וּמוּסָפִין לְבָזִיכִין, וּבָזִיכִין קוֹדְמִין
לְתָמִיד שֶׁל בֵּין הָעַרְבָּיִם. שֶׁנֶּאֱמַר: וְעָרַךְ עָלֶיהָ הָעֹלָה, וְהִקְטִיר עָלֶיהָ חֶלְבֵי ויקרא ו
הַשְּׁלָמִים: עָלֶיהָ הַשְׁלֵם כָּל הַקָּרְבָּנוֹת כֻּלָּם.

אָנָּא, בְּכֹחַ גְּדֻלַּת יְמִינְךָ, תַּתִּיר צְרוּרָה.\
קַבֵּל רִנַּת עַמְּךָ, שַׂגְּבֵנוּ, טַהֲרֵנוּ, נוֹרָא.\
נָא גִבּוֹר, דּוֹרְשֵׁי יִחוּדְךָ כְּבָבַת שָׁמְרֵם.\
בָּרְכֵם, טַהֲרֵם, רַחֲמֵי צִדְקָתְךָ תָּמִיד גָּמְלֵם.\
חֲסִין קָדוֹשׁ, בְּרֹב טוּבְךָ נַהֵל עֲדָתֶךָ.\
יָחִיד גֵּאֶה, לְעַמְּךָ פְּנֵה, זוֹכְרֵי קְדֻשָּׁתֶךָ.\
שַׁוְעָתֵנוּ קַבֵּל וּשְׁמַע צַעֲקָתֵנוּ, יוֹדֵעַ תַּעֲלוּמוֹת.\
בָּרוּךְ שֵׁם כְּבוֹד מַלְכוּתוֹ לְעוֹלָם וָעֶד.

*Some omit:*

רִבּוֹן הָעוֹלָמִים, אַתָּה צִוִּיתָנוּ לְהַקְרִיב קָרְבַּן הַתָּמִיד בְּמוֹעֲדוֹ וְלִהְיוֹת כֹּהֲנִים בַּעֲבוֹדָתָם וּלְוִיִּם בְּדוּכָנָם וְיִשְׂרָאֵל בְּמַעֲמָדָם, וְעַתָּה בַּעֲוֹנוֹתֵינוּ חָרַב בֵּית הַמִּקְדָּשׁ וּבָטַל הַתָּמִיד וְאֵין לָנוּ לֹא כֹהֵן בַּעֲבוֹדָתוֹ וְלֹא לֵוִי בְּדוּכָנוֹ וְלֹא יִשְׂרָאֵל

[the prayer of] our lips." Therefore may it be Your will, LORD our God and God of our ancestors, that the prayer of our lips be considered, accepted and favored before You as if we had offered the daily sacrifice at its appointed time and place, according to its laws, and had gathered in our divisions. And it is said: "This is the law of the burnt-offering, of the meal-offering, of the sin-offering, of the guilt-offering, of the inauguration-offering and of the peace-offering." *Lev. 7*

*On Shabbat:*

וּבְיוֹם הַשַּׁבָּת On the Shabbat day, make an offering of two lambs a year old, without blemish, together with two-tenths of an ephah of fine flour mixed with oil as a meal-offering, and its appropriate libation. *Num. 28*
This is the burnt-offering for every Shabbat,
in addition to the regular daily burnt-offering and its libation.

## LAWS OF OFFERINGS, MISHNA ZEVAḤIM

אֵיזֶהוּ מְקוֹמָן What is the location for sacrifices? The holiest offerings were slaughtered on the north side. The bull and he-goat of Yom Kippur were slaughtered on the north side. Their blood was received in a sacred vessel on the north side, and had to be sprinkled between the poles [of the Ark], toward the veil [screening the Holy of Holies], and on the golden altar. [The omission of] one of these sprinklings invalidated [the atonement ceremony]. The leftover blood was to be poured onto the western base of the outer altar. If this was not done, however, the omission did not invalidate [the ceremony]. *Zevaḥim Ch. 5*

The bulls and he-goats that were completely burnt were slaughtered on the north side, their blood was received in a sacred vessel on the north side, and had to be sprinkled toward the veil and on the golden altar. [The omission of] one of these sprinklings invalidated [the ceremony]. The leftover blood was to be poured onto the western base of the outer altar. If this was not done, however, the omission did not invalidate [the ceremony]. All these offerings were burnt where the altar ashes were deposited.

The communal and individual sin-offerings – these are the communal sin-offerings: the he-goats offered on Rosh Ḥodesh and festivals were slaughtered on the north side, their blood was received in a sacred vessel on the north side, and required four sprinklings, one on each of the four corners of the altar. How was this done? The priest ascended the ramp and turned [right] onto the surrounding ledge. He came to the southeast corner, then went to the northeast, then to the northwest, then to the southwest. The leftover blood he poured onto the southern base. [The meat of these offerings], prepared in any manner, was eaten within the [courtyard] curtains, by males of the priest-hood, on that day and the following night, until midnight.

בְּמַעֲמָדוֹ, וְאַתָּה אָמַרְתָּ: וּנְשַׁלְּמָה פָרִים שְׂפָתֵינוּ: לָכֵן יְהִי רָצוֹן מִלְּפָנֶיךָ יהוה הושע יד
אֱלֹהֵינוּ וֵאלֹהֵי אֲבוֹתֵינוּ, שֶׁיְּהֵא שִׂיחַ שִׂפְתוֹתֵינוּ חָשׁוּב וּמְקֻבָּל וּמְרֻצֶּה לְפָנֶיךָ
כְּאִלּוּ הִקְרַבְנוּ קָרְבַּן הַתָּמִיד בְּמוֹעֲדוֹ וְעָמַדְנוּ עַל מַעֲמָדוֹ. וְנֶאֱמַר: זֹאת הַתּוֹרָה ויקרא ז
לָעֹלָה לַמִּנְחָה וְלַחַטָּאת וְלָאָשָׁם וְלַמִּלּוּאִים וּלְזֶבַח הַשְּׁלָמִים:

בשבת:

וּבְיוֹם הַשַּׁבָּת שְׁנֵי־כְבָשִׂים בְּנֵי־שָׁנָה תְּמִימִם במדבר כח
וּשְׁנֵי עֶשְׂרֹנִים סֹלֶת מִנְחָה בְּלוּלָה בַשֶּׁמֶן, וְנִסְכּוֹ:
עֹלַת שַׁבַּת בְּשַׁבַּתּוֹ, עַל־עֹלַת הַתָּמִיד וְנִסְכָּהּ:

דיני זבחים

אֵיזֶהוּ מְקוֹמָן שֶׁל זְבָחִים. קָדְשֵׁי קָדָשִׁים שְׁחִיטָתָן בַּצָּפוֹן. פַּר וְשָׂעִיר זבחים פרק ה
שֶׁל יוֹם הַכִּפּוּרִים, שְׁחִיטָתָן בַּצָּפוֹן, וְקִבּוּל דָּמָן בִּכְלִי שָׁרֵת בַּצָּפוֹן, וְדָמָן טָעוּן הַזָּיָה עַל בֵּין הַבַּדִּים, וְעַל הַפָּרֹכֶת, וְעַל מִזְבַּח הַזָּהָב. מַתָּנָה אַחַת מֵהֶן מְעַכָּבֶת. שְׁיָרֵי הַדָּם הָיָה שׁוֹפֵךְ עַל יְסוֹד מַעֲרָבִי שֶׁל מִזְבֵּחַ הַחִיצוֹן, אִם לֹא נָתַן לֹא עִכֵּב.

פָּרִים הַנִּשְׂרָפִים וּשְׂעִירִים הַנִּשְׂרָפִים, שְׁחִיטָתָן בַּצָּפוֹן, וְקִבּוּל דָּמָן בִּכְלִי שָׁרֵת בַּצָּפוֹן, וְדָמָן טָעוּן הַזָּיָה עַל הַפָּרֹכֶת וְעַל מִזְבַּח הַזָּהָב. מַתָּנָה אַחַת מֵהֶן מְעַכָּבֶת. שְׁיָרֵי הַדָּם הָיָה שׁוֹפֵךְ עַל יְסוֹד מַעֲרָבִי שֶׁל מִזְבֵּחַ הַחִיצוֹן, אִם לֹא נָתַן לֹא עִכֵּב. אֵלּוּ וָאֵלּוּ נִשְׂרָפִין בְּבֵית הַדֶּשֶׁן.

חַטֹּאת הַצִּבּוּר וְהַיָּחִיד. אֵלּוּ הֵן חַטֹּאת הַצִּבּוּר: שְׂעִירֵי רָאשֵׁי חֳדָשִׁים וְשֶׁל מוֹעֲדוֹת. שְׁחִיטָתָן בַּצָּפוֹן, וְקִבּוּל דָּמָן בִּכְלִי שָׁרֵת בַּצָּפוֹן, וְדָמָן טָעוּן אַרְבַּע מַתָּנוֹת עַל אַרְבַּע קְרָנוֹת. כֵּיצַד, עָלָה בַכֶּבֶשׁ, וּפָנָה לַסּוֹבֵב, וּבָא לוֹ לְקֶרֶן דְּרוֹמִית מִזְרָחִית, מִזְרָחִית צְפוֹנִית, צְפוֹנִית מַעֲרָבִית, מַעֲרָבִית דְּרוֹמִית. שְׁיָרֵי הַדָּם הָיָה שׁוֹפֵךְ עַל יְסוֹד דְּרוֹמִי. וְנֶאֱכָלִין לִפְנִים מִן הַקְּלָעִים, לְזִכְרֵי כְהֻנָּה, בְּכָל מַאֲכָל, לְיוֹם וָלַיְלָה עַד חֲצוֹת.

The burnt-offering was among the holiest of sacrifices. It was slaughtered on the north side, its blood was received in a sacred vessel on the north side, and required two sprinklings [at opposite corners of the altar], making four in all. The offering had to be flayed, dismembered and wholly consumed by fire.

The communal peace-offerings and the guilt-offerings – these are the guilt-offerings: the guilt-offering for robbery; the guilt-offering for profane use of a sacred object; the guilt-offering [for violating] a betrothed maidservant; the guilt-offering of a Nazirite [who had become defiled by a corpse]; the guilt-offering of a leper [at his cleansing]; and the guilt-offering in case of doubt. All these were slaughtered on the north side, their blood was received in a sacred vessel on the north side, and required two sprinklings [at opposite corners of the altar], making four in all. [The meat of these offerings], prepared in any manner, was eaten within the [courtyard] curtains, by males of the priesthood, on that day and the following night, until midnight.

The thanksgiving-offering and the ram of a Nazirite were offerings of lesser holiness. They could be slaughtered anywhere in the Temple court, and their blood required two sprinklings [at opposite corners of the altar], making four in all. The meat of these offerings, prepared in any manner, was eaten anywhere within the city [Jerusalem], by anyone during that day and the following night until midnight. This also applied to the portion of these sacrifices [given to the priests], except that the priests' portion was only to be eaten by the priests, their wives, children and servants.

Peace-offerings were [also] of lesser holiness. They could be slaughtered anywhere in the Temple court, and their blood required two sprinklings [at opposite corners of the altar], making four in all. The meat of these offerings, prepared in any manner, was eaten anywhere within the city [Jerusalem], by anyone, for two days and one night. This also applied to the portion of these sacrifices [given to the priests], except that the priests' portion was only to be eaten by the priests, their wives, children and servants.

The firstborn and tithe of cattle and the Pesaḥ lamb were sacrifices of lesser holiness. They could be slaughtered anywhere in the Temple court, and their blood required only one sprinkling, which had to be done at the base of the altar. They differed in their consumption: the firstborn was eaten only by priests, while the tithe could be eaten by anyone. Both could be eaten anywhere within the city, prepared in any manner, during two days and one night. The Pesaḥ lamb had to be eaten that night until midnight. It could only be eaten by those who had been numbered for it, and eaten only roasted.

הָעוֹלָה קֹדֶשׁ קָדָשִׁים. שְׁחִיטָתָהּ בַּצָּפוֹן, וְקִבּוּל דָּמָהּ בִּכְלִי שָׁרֵת בַּצָּפוֹן, וְדָמָהּ טָעוּן שְׁתֵּי מַתָּנוֹת שֶׁהֵן אַרְבַּע, וּטְעוּנָה הֶפְשֵׁט וְנִתּוּחַ, וְכָלִיל לָאִשִּׁים.

זִבְחֵי שַׁלְמֵי צִבּוּר וַאֲשָׁמוֹת. אֵלּוּ הֵן אֲשָׁמוֹת: אֲשַׁם גְּזֵלוֹת, אֲשַׁם מְעִילוֹת, אֲשַׁם שִׁפְחָה חֲרוּפָה, אֲשַׁם נָזִיר, אֲשַׁם מְצֹרָע, אָשָׁם תָּלוּי. שְׁחִיטָתָן בַּצָּפוֹן, וְקִבּוּל דָּמָן בִּכְלִי שָׁרֵת בַּצָּפוֹן, וְדָמָן טָעוּן שְׁתֵּי מַתָּנוֹת שֶׁהֵן אַרְבַּע. וְנֶאֱכָלִין לִפְנִים מִן הַקְּלָעִים, לְזִכְרֵי כְהֻנָּה, בְּכָל מַאֲכָל, לְיוֹם וָלַיְלָה עַד חֲצוֹת.

הַתּוֹדָה וְאֵיל נָזִיר קָדָשִׁים קַלִּים. שְׁחִיטָתָן בְּכָל מָקוֹם בָּעֲזָרָה, וְדָמָן טָעוּן שְׁתֵּי מַתָּנוֹת שֶׁהֵן אַרְבַּע, וְנֶאֱכָלִין בְּכָל הָעִיר, לְכָל אָדָם, בְּכָל מַאֲכָל, לְיוֹם וָלַיְלָה עַד חֲצוֹת. הַמּוּרָם מֵהֶם כַּיּוֹצֵא בָהֶם, אֶלָּא שֶׁהַמּוּרָם נֶאֱכָל לַכֹּהֲנִים, לִנְשֵׁיהֶם, וְלִבְנֵיהֶם וּלְעַבְדֵיהֶם.

שְׁלָמִים קָדָשִׁים קַלִּים. שְׁחִיטָתָן בְּכָל מָקוֹם בָּעֲזָרָה, וְדָמָן טָעוּן שְׁתֵּי מַתָּנוֹת שֶׁהֵן אַרְבַּע, וְנֶאֱכָלִין בְּכָל הָעִיר, לְכָל אָדָם, בְּכָל מַאֲכָל, לִשְׁנֵי יָמִים וְלַיְלָה אֶחָד. הַמּוּרָם מֵהֶם כַּיּוֹצֵא בָהֶם, אֶלָּא שֶׁהַמּוּרָם נֶאֱכָל לַכֹּהֲנִים, לִנְשֵׁיהֶם, וְלִבְנֵיהֶם וּלְעַבְדֵיהֶם.

הַבְּכוֹר וְהַמַּעֲשֵׂר וְהַפֶּסַח קָדָשִׁים קַלִּים. שְׁחִיטָתָן בְּכָל מָקוֹם בָּעֲזָרָה, וְדָמָן טָעוּן מַתָּנָה אֶחָת, וּבִלְבָד שֶׁיִּתֵּן כְּנֶגֶד הַיְסוֹד. שִׁנָּה בַאֲכִילָתָן, הַבְּכוֹר נֶאֱכָל לַכֹּהֲנִים וְהַמַּעֲשֵׂר לְכָל אָדָם, וְנֶאֱכָלִין בְּכָל הָעִיר, בְּכָל מַאֲכָל, לִשְׁנֵי יָמִים וְלַיְלָה אֶחָד. הַפֶּסַח אֵינוֹ נֶאֱכָל אֶלָּא בַלַּיְלָה, וְאֵינוֹ נֶאֱכָל אֶלָּא עַד חֲצוֹת, וְאֵינוֹ נֶאֱכָל אֶלָּא לִמְנוּיָיו, וְאֵינוֹ נֶאֱכָל אֶלָּא צָלִי.

## THE INTERPRETIVE PRINCIPLES OF RABBI YISHMAEL

רַבִּי יִשְׁמָעֵאל Rabbi Yishmael says:
The Torah is expounded by thirteen principles:

1. An inference from a lenient law to a strict one, and vice versa.
2. An inference drawn from identical words in two passages.
3. A general principle derived from one text or two related texts.
4. A general law followed by specific examples
 [where the law applies exclusively to those examples].
5. A specific example followed by a general law
 [where the law applies to everything implied in the general statement].
6. A general law followed by specific examples and concluding with a general law: here you may infer only cases similar to the examples.
7. When a general statement requires clarification by a specific example, or a specific example requires clarification by a general statement [then rules 4 and 5 do not apply].
8. When a particular case, already included in the general statement, is expressly mentioned to teach something new, that special provision applies to all other cases included in the general statement.
9. When a particular case, though included in the general statement, is expressly mentioned with a provision similar to the general law, such a case is singled out to lessen the severity of the law, not to increase it.
10. When a particular case, though included in the general statement, is explicitly mentioned with a provision differing from the general law, it is singled out to lessen in some respects, and in others to increase, the severity of the law.
11. When a particular case, though included in the general statement, is explicitly mentioned with a new provision, the terms of the general statement no longer apply to it, unless Scripture indicates explicitly that they do apply.
12. A matter elucidated from its context, or from the following passage.
13. Also, when two passages [seem to] contradict each other, [they are to be elucidated by] a third passage that reconciles them.

May it be Your will, Lord our God and God of our ancestors, that the Temple be speedily rebuilt in our days, and grant us our share in Your Torah. And may we serve You there in reverence, as in the days of old and as in former years.

---

the second century CE, was a contemporary of Rabbi Akiva. As a child he lived through the destruction of the Second Temple; he was taken as a captive to Rome but was ransomed and rescued by Rabbi Yehoshua. He and Rabbi Akiva both formulated interpretive principles to show how the Oral Torah was derived from the Written Torah. Known for his love of humanity and especially of every Jew, he taught that "All Israel are to be regarded as princes."

## ברייתא דרבי ישמעאל

רַבִּי יִשְׁמָעֵאל אוֹמֵר: בִּשְׁלֹשׁ עֶשְׂרֵה מִדּוֹת הַתּוֹרָה נִדְרֶשֶׁת

א מִקַּל וָחֹמֶר

ב וּמִגְּזֵרָה שָׁוָה

ג מִבִּנְיַן אָב מִכָּתוּב אֶחָד, וּמִבִּנְיַן אָב מִשְּׁנֵי כְתוּבִים

ד מִכְּלָל וּפְרָט

ה מִפְּרָט וּכְלָל

ו כְּלָל וּפְרָט וּכְלָל, אִי אַתָּה דָן אֶלָּא כְּעֵין הַפְּרָט

ז מִכְּלָל שֶׁהוּא צָרִיךְ לִפְרָט, וּמִפְּרָט שֶׁהוּא צָרִיךְ לִכְלָל

ח כָּל דָּבָר שֶׁהָיָה בִּכְלָל, וְיָצָא מִן הַכְּלָל לְלַמֵּד
לֹא לְלַמֵּד עַל עַצְמוֹ יָצָא, אֶלָּא לְלַמֵּד עַל הַכְּלָל כֻּלּוֹ יָצָא

ט כָּל דָּבָר שֶׁהָיָה בִּכְלָל, וְיָצָא לִטְעֹן טֹעַן אֶחָד שֶׁהוּא כְעִנְיָנוֹ
יָצָא לְהָקֵל וְלֹא לְהַחֲמִיר

י כָּל דָּבָר שֶׁהָיָה בִּכְלָל, וְיָצָא לִטְעֹן טֹעַן אַחֵר שֶׁלֹּא כְעִנְיָנוֹ
יָצָא לְהָקֵל וּלְהַחֲמִיר

יא כָּל דָּבָר שֶׁהָיָה בִּכְלָל, וְיָצָא לִדּוֹן בַּדָּבָר הֶחָדָשׁ
אִי אַתָּה יָכוֹל לְהַחֲזִירוֹ לִכְלָלוֹ
עַד שֶׁיַּחֲזִירֶנּוּ הַכָּתוּב לִכְלָלוֹ בְּפֵרוּשׁ

יב דָּבָר הַלָּמֵד מֵעִנְיָנוֹ, וְדָבָר הַלָּמֵד מִסּוֹפוֹ

יג וְכֵן שְׁנֵי כְתוּבִים הַמַּכְחִישִׁים זֶה אֶת זֶה
עַד שֶׁיָּבוֹא הַכָּתוּב הַשְּׁלִישִׁי וְיַכְרִיעַ בֵּינֵיהֶם.

יְהִי רָצוֹן מִלְּפָנֶיךָ, יהוה אֱלֹהֵינוּ וֵאלֹהֵי אֲבוֹתֵינוּ, שֶׁיִּבָּנֶה בֵּית הַמִּקְדָּשׁ בִּמְהֵרָה בְיָמֵינוּ, וְתֵן חֶלְקֵנוּ בְּתוֹרָתֶךָ, וְשָׁם נַעֲבָדְךָ בְּיִרְאָה כִּימֵי עוֹלָם וּכְשָׁנִים קַדְמוֹנִיּוֹת.

---

THE INTERPRETIVE PRINCIPLES OF RABBI YISHMA'EL

This passage was chosen because it appears at the beginning of *Sifra,* the halakhic commentary to Leviticus, the book where most of the laws relating to sacrifices appear. Rabbi Yishma'el ben Elisha, who lived in the first half of

## THE RABBIS' KADDISH

*The following prayer requires the presence of a minyan.*
*A transliteration can be found on page 1094.*

*Mourner:* יִתְגַּדַּל Magnified and sanctified
may His great name be,
in the world He created by His will.
May He establish His kingdom,
make His salvation flourish,
and hasten His messiah,
in your lifetime
and in your days,
and in the lifetime of all the house of Israel,
swiftly and soon –
and say: Amen.

*All:* May His great name be blessed
for ever and all time.

*Mourner:* Blessed and praised,
glorified and exalted,
raised and honored,
uplifted and lauded
be the name of the Holy One,
blessed be He,
beyond any blessing,
song, praise and consolation
uttered in the world –
and say: Amen.

---

The sages attached deep significance to the congregational response, "May His great name be blessed…"

Whenever Jews enter a synagogue or house of study and say: "May His great name be blessed," the Holy One, blessed be He, nods His head and says, "Happy is the King who is thus praised in His house." (*Berakhot* 3a)

## קדיש דרבנן

*The following prayer requires the presence of a* מנין.
*A transliteration can be found on page 1094.*

אבל: יִתְגַּדַּל וְיִתְקַדַּשׁ שְׁמֵהּ רַבָּא (קהל: אָמֵן)
בְּעָלְמָא דִּי בְרָא כִרְעוּתֵהּ
וְיַמְלִיךְ מַלְכוּתֵהּ
וְיַצְמַח פֻּרְקָנֵהּ וִיקָרֵב מְשִׁיחֵהּ (קהל: אָמֵן)
בְּחַיֵּיכוֹן וּבְיוֹמֵיכוֹן וּבְחַיֵּי דְכָל בֵּית יִשְׂרָאֵל
בַּעֲגָלָא וּבִזְמַן קָרִיב
וְאִמְרוּ אָמֵן. (קהל: אָמֵן)

קהל ואבל: יְהֵא שְׁמֵהּ רַבָּא מְבָרַךְ לְעָלַם וּלְעָלְמֵי עָלְמַיָּא.

אבל: יִתְבָּרַךְ וְיִשְׁתַּבַּח וְיִתְפָּאַר וְיִתְרוֹמַם וְיִתְנַשֵּׂא
וְיִתְהַדָּר וְיִתְעַלֶּה וְיִתְהַלָּל
שְׁמֵהּ דְּקֻדְשָׁא בְּרִיךְ הוּא (קהל: אָמֵן)
לְעֵלָּא לְעֵלָּא מִכָּל בִּרְכָתָא וְשִׁירָתָא
תֻּשְׁבְּחָתָא וְנֶחֱמָתָא
דַּאֲמִירָן בְּעָלְמָא
וְאִמְרוּ אָמֵן. (קהל: אָמֵן)

---

THE RABBIS' KADDISH
The Kaddish had its origin not in the synagogue but in the house of study. It grew out of the custom, still widely practiced, of ending each discourse or sermon with the hope that we may speedily see the coming of the Messianic Age when the sovereignty of God will be recognized by all the dwellers on earth. It is written mainly in Aramaic, the language most widely spoken by Jews in the first centuries of the Common Era.

To Israel, to the teachers,
their disciples
and their disciples' disciples,
and to all who engage
in the study of Torah,
in this (*in Israel add:* holy) place
or elsewhere,
may there come to them
and you great peace,
grace, kindness and compassion,
long life, ample sustenance
and deliverance,
from their Father
who is in heaven and on earth –
and say: Amen.

May there be great peace from heaven,
and a good life for us and all Israel –
and say: Amen.

*Bow, take three steps back, as if taking leave of the Divine Presence, then bow, first left, then right, then center, while saying:*

May He who makes peace in His high places,
in His compassion make peace
for us and all Israel –
and say: Amen.

עַל יִשְׂרָאֵל וְעַל רַבָּנָן
וְעַל תַּלְמִידֵיהוֹן וְעַל כָּל תַּלְמִידֵי תַלְמִידֵיהוֹן
וְעַל כָּל מָאן דְּעָסְקִין בְּאוֹרַיְתָא
דִּי בְּאַתְרָא (בארץ ישראל: קַדִּישָׁא) הָדֵין, וְדִי בְּכָל אֲתַר וַאֲתַר
יְהֵא לְהוֹן וּלְכוֹן שְׁלָמָא רַבָּא
חִנָּא וְחִסְדָּא, וְרַחֲמֵי, וְחַיֵּי אֲרִיכֵי, וּמְזוֹנֵי רְוִיחֵי
וּפֻרְקָנָא מִן קֳדָם אֲבוּהוֹן
דִּי בִשְׁמַיָּא וְאַרְעָא
וְאִמְרוּ אָמֵן. (קהל: אָמֵן)

יְהֵא שְׁלָמָא רַבָּא מִן שְׁמַיָּא
וְחַיִּים טוֹבִים עָלֵינוּ וְעַל כָּל יִשְׂרָאֵל
וְאִמְרוּ אָמֵן. (קהל: אָמֵן)

*Bow, take three steps back, as if taking leave of the Divine Presence, then bow, first left, then right, then center, while saying:*

עֹשֶׂה הַשָּׁלוֹם בִּמְרוֹמָיו
הוּא בְּרַחֲמָיו יַעֲשֶׂה שָׁלוֹם
עָלֵינוּ וְעַל כָּל יִשְׂרָאֵל
וְאִמְרוּ אָמֵן. (קהל: אָמֵן)

## MORNING PRAYERS

הודו Thank the LORD, call on His name, make His acts known among the peoples. Sing to Him, make music to Him, tell of all His wonders. Glory in His holy name; let the hearts of those who seek the LORD rejoice. Search out the LORD and His strength; seek His presence at all times. Remember the wonders He has done, His miracles, and the judgments He pronounced. Descendants of Yisrael His servant, sons of Jacob His chosen ones: He is the LORD our God. His judgments are throughout the earth. Remember His covenant for ever, the word He commanded for a thousand generations. He made it with Abraham, vowed it to Isaac, and confirmed it to Jacob as a statute and to Israel as an everlasting covenant, saying, "To you I will give the land of Canaan as your allotted heritage." You were then small in number, few, strangers there, wandering from nation to nation, from one kingdom to another, but He let no man oppress them, and for their sake He rebuked kings: "Do not touch My anointed ones, and do My prophets no harm." Sing to the LORD, all the earth; proclaim His salvation daily. Declare His glory among the nations, His marvels among all the peoples. For great is the LORD and greatly to be praised; He is awesome beyond all heavenly powers. ▸ For all the gods of the peoples are mere idols; it was the LORD who made the heavens. *1 Chr. 16*

Before Him are majesty and splendor; there is strength and beauty in His holy place. Render to the LORD, families of the peoples, render to the LORD honor and might. Render to the LORD the glory due to His name; bring an offering and come before Him; bow down to the LORD in the splendor of holiness. Tremble before Him, all the earth;

---

the nation, and its dependence on divine providence. He recalls all that had happened to the Israelites in the long years of wandering and insecurity, culminating in this moment when they had become a nation in their own land, with Jerusalem as their capital, and the Divine Presence, symbolized by the Ark, come to rest in their midst. The passage ends with the response of the people: "And all the people said 'Amen' and 'Praise the LORD.'" According to *Seder Olam*, this passage was recited daily (in two halves, one in the morning,

# תפילות השחר

דברי הימים א׳ טז

הוֹדוּ לַיהוה קִרְאוּ בִשְׁמוֹ, הוֹדִיעוּ בָעַמִּים עֲלִילֹתָיו: שִׁירוּ לוֹ,
זַמְּרוּ־לוֹ, שִׂיחוּ בְּכָל־נִפְלְאוֹתָיו: הִתְהַלְלוּ בְּשֵׁם קָדְשׁוֹ, יִשְׂמַח לֵב
מְבַקְשֵׁי יהוה: דִּרְשׁוּ יהוה וְעֻזּוֹ, בַּקְּשׁוּ פָנָיו תָּמִיד: זִכְרוּ נִפְלְאֹתָיו
אֲשֶׁר עָשָׂה, מֹפְתָיו וּמִשְׁפְּטֵי־פִיהוּ: זֶרַע יִשְׂרָאֵל עַבְדּוֹ, בְּנֵי יַעֲקֹב
בְּחִירָיו: הוּא יהוה אֱלֹהֵינוּ בְּכָל־הָאָרֶץ מִשְׁפָּטָיו: זִכְרוּ לְעוֹלָם
בְּרִיתוֹ, דָּבָר צִוָּה לְאֶלֶף דּוֹר: אֲשֶׁר כָּרַת אֶת־אַבְרָהָם, וּשְׁבוּעָתוֹ
לְיִצְחָק: וַיַּעֲמִידֶהָ לְיַעֲקֹב לְחֹק, לְיִשְׂרָאֵל בְּרִית עוֹלָם: לֵאמֹר, לְךָ
אֶתֵּן אֶרֶץ־כְּנָעַן, חֶבֶל נַחֲלַתְכֶם: בִּהְיוֹתְכֶם מְתֵי מִסְפָּר, כִּמְעַט
וְגָרִים בָּהּ: וַיִּתְהַלְּכוּ מִגּוֹי אֶל־גּוֹי, וּמִמַּמְלָכָה אֶל־עַם אַחֵר: לֹא־
הִנִּיחַ לְאִישׁ לְעָשְׁקָם, וַיּוֹכַח עֲלֵיהֶם מְלָכִים: אַל־תִּגְּעוּ בִּמְשִׁיחָי,
וּבִנְבִיאַי אַל־תָּרֵעוּ: שִׁירוּ לַיהוה כָּל־הָאָרֶץ, בַּשְּׂרוּ מִיּוֹם־אֶל־יוֹם
יְשׁוּעָתוֹ: סַפְּרוּ בַגּוֹיִם אֶת־כְּבוֹדוֹ, בְּכָל־הָעַמִּים נִפְלְאֹתָיו: כִּי גָדוֹל
יהוה וּמְהֻלָּל מְאֹד, וְנוֹרָא הוּא עַל־כָּל־אֱלֹהִים: ‹ כִּי כָּל־אֱלֹהֵי
הָעַמִּים אֱלִילִים, וַיהוה שָׁמַיִם עָשָׂה:

הוֹד וְהָדָר לְפָנָיו, עֹז וְחֶדְוָה בִּמְקֹמוֹ: הָבוּ לַיהוה מִשְׁפְּחוֹת
עַמִּים, הָבוּ לַיהוה כָּבוֹד וָעֹז: הָבוּ לַיהוה כְּבוֹד שְׁמוֹ, שְׂאוּ מִנְחָה
וּבֹאוּ לְפָנָיו, הִשְׁתַּחֲווּ לַיהוה בְּהַדְרַת־קֹדֶשׁ: חִילוּ מִלְּפָנָיו כָּל־

---

הודו לַיהוה *Thank the Lord.* The Bible gives us a vivid account of the moment when this passage was first recited: when King David brought the Ark of the Covenant to Jerusalem, newly established as the capital of the Jewish state. The Ark, which had been captured by the Philistines, was brought back by David to a temporary resting-place. Later it was carried into Jerusalem to scenes of great jubilation. As on other momentous occasions in the life of biblical Israel, the leader (here David) reminds the people of the history of

the world stands firm, it will not be shaken. Let the heavens rejoice and the earth be glad; let them declare among the nations, "The LORD is King." Let the sea roar, and all that is in it; let the fields be jubilant, and all they contain. Then the trees of the forest will sing for joy before the LORD, for He is coming to judge the earth. Thank the LORD for He is good; His loving-kindness is for ever. Say: "Save us, God of our salvation; gather us and rescue us from the nations, to acknowledge Your holy name and glory in praise of You. Blessed is the LORD, God of Israel, from this world to eternity." And let all the people say "Amen" and "Praise the LORD."

Exalt the LORD our God and bow before His footstool: He is holy. *Ps. 99*
Exalt the LORD our God and bow at His holy mountain; for holy is the
LORD our God.

He is compassionate. He forgives iniquity and does not destroy. *Ps. 78*
Repeatedly He suppresses His anger, not rousing His full wrath. You, *Ps. 40*
LORD: do not withhold Your compassion from me. May Your loving-
kindness and truth always guard me. Remember, LORD, Your acts of *Ps. 25*
compassion and love, for they have existed for ever. Ascribe power *Ps. 68*
to God, whose majesty is over Israel and whose might is in the skies.
You are awesome, God, in Your holy places. It is the God of Israel who
gives might and strength to the people, may God be blessed. God of *Ps. 94*
retribution, LORD, God of retribution, appear. Arise, Judge of the earth,
to repay the arrogant their just deserts. Salvation belongs to the LORD; *Ps. 3*
may Your blessing rest upon Your people, Selah! ▸ The LORD of hosts *Ps. 46*
is with us, the God of Jacob is our stronghold, Selah! LORD of hosts, *Ps. 84*
happy is the one who trusts in You. LORD, save! May the King answer *Ps. 20*
us on the day we call.

Save Your people and bless Your heritage; tend them and carry them *Ps. 28*
for ever. Our soul longs for the LORD; He is our Help and Shield. For *Ps. 33*
in Him our hearts rejoice, for in His holy name we have trusted. May
Your loving-kindness, LORD, be upon us, as we have put our hope in

---

רוֹמְמוּ יהוה אֱלֹהֵינוּ *Exalt the LORD our God.* A selection of verses from the book of Psalms, expressing hope and trust in God. As so often in Psalms, the voice in these verses modulates from people to person, from nation to individual.

הָאָרֶץ, אַף־תִּכּוֹן תֵּבֵל בַּל־תִּמּוֹט: יִשְׂמְחוּ הַשָּׁמַיִם וְתָגֵל הָאָרֶץ,
וְיֹאמְרוּ בַגּוֹיִם יהוה מָלָךְ: יִרְעַם הַיָּם וּמְלוֹאוֹ, יַעֲלֹץ הַשָּׂדֶה וְכָל־
אֲשֶׁר־בּוֹ: אָז יְרַנְּנוּ עֲצֵי הַיָּעַר, מִלִּפְנֵי יהוה, כִּי־בָא לִשְׁפּוֹט אֶת־
הָאָרֶץ: הוֹדוּ לַיהוה כִּי טוֹב, כִּי לְעוֹלָם חַסְדּוֹ: וְאִמְרוּ, הוֹשִׁיעֵנוּ
אֱלֹהֵי יִשְׁעֵנוּ, וְקַבְּצֵנוּ וְהַצִּילֵנוּ מִן־הַגּוֹיִם, לְהֹדוֹת לְשֵׁם קׇדְשֶׁךָ,
לְהִשְׁתַּבֵּחַ בִּתְהִלָּתֶךָ: בָּרוּךְ יהוה אֱלֹהֵי יִשְׂרָאֵל מִן־הָעוֹלָם וְעַד־
הָעֹלָם, וַיֹּאמְרוּ כׇל־הָעָם אָמֵן, וְהַלֵּל לַיהוה:

רוֹמְמוּ יהוה אֱלֹהֵינוּ וְהִשְׁתַּחֲווּ לַהֲדֹם רַגְלָיו, קָדוֹשׁ הוּא: תהלים צט
רוֹמְמוּ יהוה אֱלֹהֵינוּ וְהִשְׁתַּחֲווּ לְהַר קׇדְשׁוֹ, כִּי־קָדוֹשׁ יהוה אֱלֹהֵינוּ:

וְהוּא רַחוּם, יְכַפֵּר עָוֹן וְלֹא־יַשְׁחִית, וְהִרְבָּה לְהָשִׁיב אַפּוֹ, תהלים עח
וְלֹא־יָעִיר כׇּל־חֲמָתוֹ: אַתָּה יהוה לֹא־תִכְלָא רַחֲמֶיךָ מִמֶּנִּי, חַסְדְּךָ תהלים מ
וַאֲמִתְּךָ תָּמִיד יִצְּרוּנִי: זְכֹר־רַחֲמֶיךָ יהוה וַחֲסָדֶיךָ, כִּי מֵעוֹלָם תהלים כה
הֵמָּה: תְּנוּ עֹז לֵאלֹהִים, עַל־יִשְׂרָאֵל גַּאֲוָתוֹ, וְעֻזּוֹ בַּשְּׁחָקִים: נוֹרָא תהלים סח
אֱלֹהִים מִמִּקְדָּשֶׁיךָ, אֵל יִשְׂרָאֵל הוּא נֹתֵן עֹז וְתַעֲצֻמוֹת לָעָם,
בָּרוּךְ אֱלֹהִים: אֵל־נְקָמוֹת יהוה, אֵל נְקָמוֹת הוֹפִיעַ: הִנָּשֵׂא שֹׁפֵט תהלים צד
הָאָרֶץ, הָשֵׁב גְּמוּל עַל־גֵּאִים: לַיהוה הַיְשׁוּעָה, עַל־עַמְּךָ בִרְכָתֶךָ תהלים ג
סֶּלָה: ◂ יהוה צְבָאוֹת עִמָּנוּ, מִשְׂגָּב לָנוּ אֱלֹהֵי יַעֲקֹב סֶלָה: יהוה תהלים פד תהלים מו
צְבָאוֹת, אַשְׁרֵי אָדָם בֹּטֵחַ בָּךְ: יהוה הוֹשִׁיעָה, הַמֶּלֶךְ יַעֲנֵנוּ תהלים כ
בְיוֹם־קׇרְאֵנוּ:

הוֹשִׁיעָה אֶת־עַמֶּךָ, וּבָרֵךְ אֶת־נַחֲלָתֶךָ, וּרְעֵם וְנַשְּׂאֵם עַד־ תהלים כח
הָעוֹלָם: נַפְשֵׁנוּ חִכְּתָה לַיהוה, עֶזְרֵנוּ וּמָגִנֵּנוּ הוּא: כִּי־בוֹ יִשְׂמַח תהלים לג
לִבֵּנוּ, כִּי בְשֵׁם קׇדְשׁוֹ בָטָחְנוּ: יְהִי־חַסְדְּךָ יהוה עָלֵינוּ, כַּאֲשֶׁר

---

the other in the afternoon) as an accompaniment to the sacrifices, from that day until the inauguration of the Temple in the time of Solomon.

You. Show us, LORD, Your loving-kindness and grant us Your salvation. Ps. 85
Arise, help us and redeem us for the sake of Your love. I am the LORD Ps. 44 Ps. 81
your God who brought you up from the land of Egypt: open your
mouth wide and I will fill it. Happy is the people for whom this is so; Ps. 144
happy is the people whose God is the LORD. ▸ As for me, I trust in Your Ps. 13
loving-kindness; my heart rejoices in Your salvation. I will sing to the
LORD for He has been good to me.

מִזְמוֹר שִׁיר A psalm of David. A song for the dedication of the House. I Ps. 30
will exalt You, LORD, for You have lifted me up, and not let my enemies rejoice over me. LORD, my God, I cried to You for help and You healed me. LORD, You lifted my soul from the grave; You spared me from going down to the pit. Sing to the LORD, you His devoted ones, and give thanks to His holy name. For His anger is for a moment, but His favor for a lifetime. At night there may be weeping, but in the morning there is joy. When I felt secure, I said, "I shall never be shaken." LORD, when You favored me, You made me stand firm as a mountain, but when You hid Your face, I was terrified. To You, LORD, I called; I pleaded with my LORD: "What gain would there be if I died and went down to the grave? Can dust thank You? Can it declare Your truth? Hear, LORD, and be gracious to me; LORD, be my help." You have turned my sorrow into dancing. ▸ You have removed my sackcloth and clothed me with joy, so that my soul may sing to You and not be silent. LORD my God, for ever will I thank You.

---

Verses of Praise. The connecting theme is the sense of life restored as a reason for giving praise. The Psalmist recalls a crisis when his life, hitherto secure, was suddenly in danger. It was then that he prayed to God, "What gain would there be if I died... Can dust thank You?" So, we, waking to the life of a new day, express our sense of joy "so that my soul may sing to You and not be silent."

כִּי דִלִּיתָנִי *For You have lifted me up.* The Hebrew verb is used to refer to the act of drawing water from a well. Just as a bucket is lowered to bring up fresh water, so sometimes we experience distress and from it gain new strength (*Sefat Emet*).

תהלים פה תהלים מד יַחֲלְנוּ לָךְ: הַרְאֵנוּ יהוה חַסְדֶּךָ, וְיֶשְׁעֲךָ תִּתֶּן־לָנוּ: קוּמָה עֶזְרָתָה
תהלים פא לָּנוּ, וּפְדֵנוּ לְמַעַן חַסְדֶּךָ: אָנֹכִי יהוה אֱלֹהֶיךָ הַמַּעַלְךָ מֵאֶרֶץ
תהלים קמד מִצְרָיִם, הַרְחֶב־פִּיךָ וַאֲמַלְאֵהוּ: אַשְׁרֵי הָעָם שֶׁכָּכָה לּוֹ, אַשְׁרֵי
תהלים יג הָעָם שֶׁיהוה אֱלֹהָיו: ◄ וַאֲנִי בְּחַסְדְּךָ בָטַחְתִּי, יָגֵל לִבִּי בִּישׁוּעָתֶךָ,
אָשִׁירָה לַיהוה, כִּי גָמַל עָלָי:

תהלים ל מִזְמוֹר שִׁיר־חֲנֻכַּת הַבַּיִת לְדָוִד: אֲרוֹמִמְךָ יהוה כִּי דִלִּיתָנִי, וְלֹא־
שִׂמַּחְתָּ אֹיְבַי לִי: יהוה אֱלֹהָי, שִׁוַּעְתִּי אֵלֶיךָ וַתִּרְפָּאֵנִי: יהוה,
הֶעֱלִיתָ מִן־שְׁאוֹל נַפְשִׁי, חִיִּיתַנִי מִיָּרְדִי־בוֹר: זַמְּרוּ לַיהוה חֲסִידָיו,
וְהוֹדוּ לְזֵכֶר קָדְשׁוֹ: כִּי רֶגַע בְּאַפּוֹ, חַיִּים בִּרְצוֹנוֹ, בָּעֶרֶב יָלִין בֶּכִי
וְלַבֹּקֶר רִנָּה: וַאֲנִי אָמַרְתִּי בְשַׁלְוִי, בַּל־אֶמּוֹט לְעוֹלָם: יהוה,
בִּרְצוֹנְךָ הֶעֱמַדְתָּה לְהַרְרִי עֹז, הִסְתַּרְתָּ פָנֶיךָ הָיִיתִי נִבְהָל: אֵלֶיךָ
יהוה אֶקְרָא, וְאֶל־אֲדֹנָי אֶתְחַנָּן: מַה־בֶּצַע בְּדָמִי, בְּרִדְתִּי אֶל
שָׁחַת, הֲיוֹדְךָ עָפָר, הֲיַגִּיד אֲמִתֶּךָ: שְׁמַע־יהוה וְחָנֵּנִי, יהוה הֱיֵה־
עֹזֵר לִי: ◄ הָפַכְתָּ מִסְפְּדִי לְמָחוֹל לִי, פִּתַּחְתָּ שַׂקִּי, וַתְּאַזְּרֵנִי שִׂמְחָה:
לְמַעַן יְזַמֶּרְךָ כָבוֹד וְלֹא יִדֹּם, יהוה אֱלֹהַי, לְעוֹלָם אוֹדֶךָּ:

---

On the one hand, "It is the God of Israel who gives power and strength to His people"; on the other, "As for me [as an individual], I will trust in Your loving-kindness." This frequent shift from public to private and back again is one of the most distinctive features of Jewish sensibility. We speak to God from the innermost depths of our being, yet we are also members of an extended family, a people, a nation, whose fate and destiny we share, and on whose behalf we pray.

מִזְמוֹר שִׁיר־חֲנֻכַּת הַבַּיִת *A song for the dedication of the House.* According to Rashi, King David wrote this psalm to be sung at the inauguration of the Temple, though he knew it would only take place in the lifetime of his son Solomon. The psalm was added to the daily prayers in the seventeenth century. It is beautifully suited to be a bridge between the Morning Blessings and the

*Stand until just before Psalm 19 below.*

יהוה The Lord is King, the Lord was King,
the Lord will be King for ever and all time.
The Lord is King, the Lord was King,
the Lord will be King for ever and all time.

וְהָיָה Then the Lord shall be King over all the earth; *Zech. 14*
on that day the Lord shall be One and His name One.

הוֹשִׁיעֵנוּ Save us, Lord our God, gather us from the nations, *Ps. 106*
to thank Your holy name, and glory in praise of You.
Blessed is the Lord, God of Israel, from this world to eternity.
And let all the people say "Amen, Halleluya!"
Let all that breathes praise the Lord. Halleluya! *Ps. 150*

לַמְנַצֵּחַ For the conductor of music. A psalm of David. *Ps. 19*
The heavens declare the glory of God;
the skies proclaim the work of His hands.
Day to day they pour forth speech;
night to night they communicate knowledge.
There is no speech, there are no words,
their voice is not heard.
Yet their music carries throughout the earth,
their words to the end of the world.
In them He has set a tent for the sun.
It emerges like a groom from his marriage chamber,
rejoicing like a champion about to run a race.

---

a song begun softly and continued with ever-increasing volume. The extra psalms begin, in Psalm 19, with the universe singing a silent song ("their voice is not heard") and end (after the angels' song, "Majesty and faithfulness…" and the opening of *Pesukei DeZimra*), in Psalm 93, in a magnificent crescendo ("mightier than the noise of many waters" [page 286]).

לַמְנַצֵּחַ *Psalm 19.* A hymn of glory to the universe as God's work and the Torah as God's word. In the first half of the poem, the Psalmist speaks metaphori-

*Stand until just before* למנצח *below.*

יהוה מֶלֶךְ, יהוה מָלָךְ, יהוה יִמְלֹךְ לְעֹלָם וָעֶד.
יהוה מֶלֶךְ, יהוה מָלָךְ, יהוה יִמְלֹךְ לְעֹלָם וָעֶד.

זכריה יד
וְהָיָה יהוה לְמֶלֶךְ עַל־כָּל־הָאָרֶץ
בַּיּוֹם הַהוּא יִהְיֶה יהוה אֶחָד וּשְׁמוֹ אֶחָד:

תהלים קו
הוֹשִׁיעֵנוּ יהוה אֱלֹהֵינוּ, וְקַבְּצֵנוּ מִן־הַגּוֹיִם
לְהוֹדוֹת לְשֵׁם קָדְשֶׁךָ, לְהִשְׁתַּבֵּחַ בִּתְהִלָּתֶךָ:
בָּרוּךְ יהוה אֱלֹהֵי יִשְׂרָאֵל מִן־הָעוֹלָם וְעַד הָעוֹלָם
וְאָמַר כָּל־הָעָם אָמֵן, הַלְלוּיָהּ:
תהלים קנ
כֹּל הַנְּשָׁמָה תְּהַלֵּל יָהּ, הַלְלוּיָהּ:

תהלים יט
לַמְנַצֵּחַ מִזְמוֹר לְדָוִד:
הַשָּׁמַיִם מְסַפְּרִים כְּבוֹד־אֵל, וּמַעֲשֵׂה יָדָיו מַגִּיד הָרָקִיעַ:
יוֹם לְיוֹם יַבִּיעַ אֹמֶר, וְלַיְלָה לְּלַיְלָה יְחַוֶּה־דָּעַת:
אֵין־אֹמֶר וְאֵין דְּבָרִים, בְּלִי נִשְׁמָע קוֹלָם:
בְּכָל־הָאָרֶץ יָצָא קַוָּם, וּבִקְצֵה תֵבֵל מִלֵּיהֶם
לַשֶּׁמֶשׁ שָׂם־אֹהֶל בָּהֶם:
וְהוּא כְּחָתָן יֹצֵא מֵחֻפָּתוֹ, יָשִׂישׂ כְּגִבּוֹר לָרוּץ אֹרַח:

---

EXTRA PSALMS FOR SHABBAT AND FESTIVALS

In the earliest siddurim, those of Rav Amram Gaon and Sa'adia Gaon in the ninth and tenth centuries, we already find well established the custom of saying extra psalms on Shabbat and festivals. This is because, work being forbidden, we have more time to pray, and also because on Shabbat we reflect on God's creation, and the psalms we say are meditations on this theme.

There is a striking feature of the beginning and end of this sequence. According to one interpretation (Meiri), the phrase "a song of ascents" means

It rises at one end of the heaven
and makes its circuit to the other:
nothing is hidden from its heat.
The LORD's Torah is perfect, refreshing the soul.
The LORD's testimony is faithful, making the simple wise.
The LORD's precepts are just, gladdening the heart.
The LORD's commandment is radiant, giving light to the eyes.
The fear of the LORD is pure, enduring for ever.
The LORD's judgments are true, altogether righteous.
More precious than gold, than much fine gold.
They are sweeter than honey, than honey from the comb.
Your servant, too, is careful of them,
for in observing them there is great reward.
Yet who can discern his errors?
Cleanse me of hidden faults.
Keep Your servant also from willful sins;
let them not have dominion over me.
Then shall I be blameless,
and innocent of grave sin.
▸ May the words of my mouth and the meditation of my heart
find favor before You, LORD, my Rock and my Redeemer.

רַנְּנוּ Sing joyfully to the LORD, you righteous, for praise from the *Ps. 33*
upright is seemly. Give thanks to the LORD with the harp; make music
to Him on the ten-stringed lute. Sing Him a new song, play skillfully
with shouts of joy. For the LORD's word is right, and all His deeds are
done in faith. He loves righteousness and justice; the earth is full of the

---

רַנְּנוּ *Psalm 33.* This hymn, celebrating God the Creator and Redeemer, opens with seven expressions of praise – sing joyfully, praise, give thanks, make music, sing, play, shout – and ends with seven collective identifications with God: He is our soul, our help, our shield, our hearts, our trust, our love, our hope. *And all His deeds are done in faith.* "God had faith in the world and created it" (*Sifrei* to Deut. 32:4). More than we have faith in God, God has faith in us. *No king is saved by the size of his army* (see next page)*:* A constant

מִקְצֵה הַשָּׁמַיִם מוֹצָאוֹ, וּתְקוּפָתוֹ עַל־קְצוֹתָם
וְאֵין נִסְתָּר מֵחַמָּתוֹ:
תּוֹרַת יהוה תְּמִימָה, מְשִׁיבַת נָפֶשׁ
עֵדוּת יהוה נֶאֱמָנָה, מַחְכִּימַת פֶּתִי:
פִּקּוּדֵי יהוה יְשָׁרִים, מְשַׂמְּחֵי־לֵב
מִצְוַת יהוה בָּרָה, מְאִירַת עֵינָיִם:
יִרְאַת יהוה טְהוֹרָה, עוֹמֶדֶת לָעַד
מִשְׁפְּטֵי־יהוה אֱמֶת, צָדְקוּ יַחְדָּו:
הַנֶּחֱמָדִים מִזָּהָב וּמִפַּז רָב, וּמְתוּקִים מִדְּבַשׁ וְנֹפֶת צוּפִים:
גַּם־עַבְדְּךָ נִזְהָר בָּהֶם, בְּשָׁמְרָם עֵקֶב רָב:
שְׁגִיאוֹת מִי־יָבִין, מִנִּסְתָּרוֹת נַקֵּנִי:
גַּם מִזֵּדִים חֲשֹׂךְ עַבְדֶּךָ, אַל־יִמְשְׁלוּ־בִי אָז אֵיתָם
וְנִקֵּיתִי מִפֶּשַׁע רָב:
◂ יִהְיוּ לְרָצוֹן אִמְרֵי־פִי וְהֶגְיוֹן לִבִּי לְפָנֶיךָ, יהוה, צוּרִי וְגוֹאֲלִי:

רַנְּנוּ צַדִּיקִים בַּיהוה, לַיְשָׁרִים נָאוָה תְהִלָּה: הוֹדוּ לַיהוה בְּכִנּוֹר, תהלים לג
בְּנֵבֶל עָשׂוֹר זַמְּרוּ־לוֹ: שִׁירוּ־לוֹ שִׁיר חָדָשׁ, הֵיטִיבוּ נַגֵּן בִּתְרוּעָה:
כִּי־יָשָׁר דְּבַר־יהוה, וְכָל־מַעֲשֵׂהוּ בֶּאֱמוּנָה: אֹהֵב צְדָקָה וּמִשְׁפָּט,

---

cally of creation singing a song of praise to its Creator, a silent song yet one that can be heard by those whose ears are attuned to wonder. But God's word not only gives life to the natural universe: it instructs the human universe, the world we make by our actions and reactions. The Psalmist celebrates God's creation of the world-that-is, and His revelation of the world-that-ought-to-be.

Two things fill the mind with ever-increasing wonder and awe, the more often and the more intensely the mind of thought is drawn to them: the starry heavens above me and the moral law within me. (Immanuel Kant)

LORD's loving-kindness. By the LORD's word the heavens were made, and all their starry host by the breath of His mouth. He gathers the sea waters as a heap, and places the deep in storehouses. Let all the earth fear the LORD, and all the world's inhabitants stand in awe of Him. For He spoke, and it was; He commanded, and it stood firm. The LORD foils the plans of nations; He thwarts the intentions of peoples. The LORD's plans stand for ever, His heart's intents for all generations. Happy is the nation whose God is the LORD, the people He has chosen as His own. From heaven the LORD looks down and sees all mankind; from His dwelling place He oversees all who live on earth. He forms the hearts of all, and discerns all their deeds. No king is saved by the size of his army; no warrior is delivered by great strength. A horse is a vain hope for deliverance; despite its great strength, it cannot save. The eye of the LORD is on those who fear Him, on those who place their hope in His unfailing love, to rescue their soul from death, and keep them alive in famine. Our soul waits for the LORD; He is our Help and Shield. ▸ In Him our hearts rejoice, for we trust in His holy name. Let Your unfailing love be upon us, LORD, as we have put our hope in You.

לְדָוִד Of David. When he pretended to be insane before Abimelech, who drove him away, and he left. *Ps. 34*

I will bless the LORD at all times;
His praise will be always on my lips.
My soul will glory in the LORD;
let the lowly hear this and rejoice.
Magnify the LORD with me;
let us exalt His name together.
I sought the LORD, and He answered me;
He saved me from all my fears.
Those who look to Him are radiant;
their faces are never downcast.

---

psalm of thanksgiving that follows is constructed as an alphabetical acrostic. An extra verse has been added at the end to avoid closing on a negative note.

*Magnify the LORD with me*: This verse is taken by the sages as the source

חֶסֶד יהוה מָלְאָה הָאָרֶץ: בִּדְבַר יהוה שָׁמַיִם נַעֲשׂוּ, וּבְרוּחַ פִּיו כָּל־צְבָאָם: כֹּנֵס כַּנֵּד מֵי הַיָּם, נֹתֵן בְּאוֹצָרוֹת תְּהוֹמוֹת: יִירְאוּ מֵיהוה כָּל־הָאָרֶץ, מִמֶּנּוּ יָגוּרוּ כָּל־יֹשְׁבֵי תֵבֵל: כִּי הוּא אָמַר וַיֶּהִי, הוּא־צִוָּה וַיַּעֲמֹד: יהוה הֵפִיר עֲצַת־גּוֹיִם, הֵנִיא מַחְשְׁבוֹת עַמִּים: עֲצַת יהוה לְעוֹלָם תַּעֲמֹד, מַחְשְׁבוֹת לִבּוֹ לְדֹר וָדֹר: אַשְׁרֵי הַגּוֹי אֲשֶׁר־יהוה אֱלֹהָיו, הָעָם בָּחַר לְנַחֲלָה לוֹ: מִשָּׁמַיִם הִבִּיט יהוה, רָאָה אֶת־כָּל־בְּנֵי הָאָדָם: מִמְּכוֹן־שִׁבְתּוֹ הִשְׁגִּיחַ, אֶל כָּל־יֹשְׁבֵי הָאָרֶץ: הַיֹּצֵר יַחַד לִבָּם, הַמֵּבִין אֶל־כָּל־מַעֲשֵׂיהֶם: אֵין־הַמֶּלֶךְ נוֹשָׁע בְּרָב־חָיִל, גִּבּוֹר לֹא־יִנָּצֵל בְּרָב־כֹּחַ: שֶׁקֶר הַסּוּס לִתְשׁוּעָה, וּבְרֹב חֵילוֹ לֹא יְמַלֵּט: הִנֵּה עֵין יהוה אֶל־יְרֵאָיו, לַמְיַחֲלִים לְחַסְדּוֹ: לְהַצִּיל מִמָּוֶת נַפְשָׁם, וּלְחַיּוֹתָם בָּרָעָב: נַפְשֵׁנוּ חִכְּתָה לַיהוה, עֶזְרֵנוּ וּמָגִנֵּנוּ הוּא: › כִּי־בוֹ יִשְׂמַח לִבֵּנוּ, כִּי בְשֵׁם קָדְשׁוֹ בָטָחְנוּ: יְהִי־חַסְדְּךָ יהוה עָלֵינוּ, כַּאֲשֶׁר יִחַלְנוּ לָךְ:

לְדָוִד, בְּשַׁנּוֹתוֹ אֶת־טַעְמוֹ לִפְנֵי אֲבִימֶלֶךְ, וַיְגָרְשֵׁהוּ וַיֵּלַךְ: תהלים לד

אֲבָרְכָה אֶת־יהוה בְּכָל־עֵת, תָּמִיד תְּהִלָּתוֹ בְּפִי:
בַּיהוה תִּתְהַלֵּל נַפְשִׁי, יִשְׁמְעוּ עֲנָוִים וְיִשְׂמָחוּ:
גַּדְּלוּ לַיהוה אִתִּי, וּנְרוֹמְמָה שְׁמוֹ יַחְדָּו:
דָּרַשְׁתִּי אֶת־יהוה וְעָנָנִי, וּמִכָּל־מְגוּרוֹתַי הִצִּילָנִי:
הִבִּיטוּ אֵלָיו וְנָהָרוּ, וּפְנֵיהֶם אַל־יֶחְפָּרוּ:

---

theme of Tanakh. It is moral strength, not military strength, that wins battles in the long run.

לְדָוִד *Psalm 34.* During the period that David was fleeing from King Saul, he took refuge in the Philistine city of Gath. There, however, he was recognized and his life was again in danger. Feigning insanity in order to appear harmless, he was dismissed by the king and was able to escape (1 Samuel 21:11–16). The

This poor man called, and the LORD heard;
He saved him from all his troubles.
The LORD's angel encamps around those who fear Him,
and He rescues them.
Taste and see that the LORD is good;
happy is the man who takes refuge in Him.
Fear the LORD, you His holy ones,
for those who fear Him lack nothing.
Young lions may grow weak and hungry,
but those who seek the LORD lack no good thing.
Come, my children, listen to me;
I will teach you the fear of the LORD.
Who desires life,
loving each day to see good?
Then guard your tongue from evil
and your lips from speaking deceit.
Turn from evil and do good;
seek peace and pursue it.
The eyes of the LORD are on the righteous
and His ears attentive to their cry;
The LORD's face is set against those who do evil,
to erase their memory from the earth.
The righteous cry out, and the LORD hears them;
delivering them from all their troubles.
The LORD is close to the brokenhearted,
and saves those who are crushed in spirit.
Many troubles may befall the righteous,
but the LORD delivers him from them all;
He protects all his bones,
so that none of them will be broken.
Evil will slay the wicked;
the enemies of the righteous will be condemned.
‣ The LORD redeems His servants;
those who take refuge in Him shall not be condemned.

זֶה עָנִי קָרָא, וַיהוה שָׁמֵעַ, וּמִכָּל־צָרוֹתָיו הוֹשִׁיעוֹ:
חֹנֶה מַלְאַךְ־יהוה סָבִיב לִירֵאָיו, וַיְחַלְּצֵם:
טַעֲמוּ וּרְאוּ כִּי־טוֹב יהוה, אַשְׁרֵי הַגֶּבֶר יֶחֱסֶה־בּוֹ:
יְראוּ אֶת־יהוה קְדֹשָׁיו, כִּי־אֵין מַחְסוֹר לִירֵאָיו:
כְּפִירִים רָשׁוּ וְרָעֵבוּ, וְדֹרְשֵׁי יהוה לֹא־יַחְסְרוּ כָל־טוֹב:
לְכוּ־בָנִים שִׁמְעוּ־לִי, יִרְאַת יהוה אֲלַמֶּדְכֶם:
מִי־הָאִישׁ הֶחָפֵץ חַיִּים, אֹהֵב יָמִים לִרְאוֹת טוֹב:
נְצֹר לְשׁוֹנְךָ מֵרָע, וּשְׂפָתֶיךָ מִדַּבֵּר מִרְמָה:
סוּר מֵרָע וַעֲשֵׂה־טוֹב, בַּקֵּשׁ שָׁלוֹם וְרָדְפֵהוּ:
עֵינֵי יהוה אֶל־צַדִּיקִים, וְאָזְנָיו אֶל־שַׁוְעָתָם:
פְּנֵי יהוה בְּעֹשֵׂי רָע, לְהַכְרִית מֵאֶרֶץ זִכְרָם:
צָעֲקוּ וַיהוה שָׁמֵעַ, וּמִכָּל־צָרוֹתָם הִצִּילָם:
קָרוֹב יהוה לְנִשְׁבְּרֵי־לֵב, וְאֶת־דַּכְּאֵי־רוּחַ יוֹשִׁיעַ:
רַבּוֹת רָעוֹת צַדִּיק, וּמִכֻּלָּם יַצִּילֶנּוּ יהוה:
שֹׁמֵר כָּל־עַצְמוֹתָיו, אַחַת מֵהֵנָּה לֹא נִשְׁבָּרָה:
תְּמוֹתֵת רָשָׁע רָעָה, וְשֹׂנְאֵי צַדִּיק יֶאְשָׁמוּ:
◂ פּוֹדֶה יהוה נֶפֶשׁ עֲבָדָיו, וְלֹא יֶאְשְׁמוּ כָּל־הַחֹסִים בּוֹ:

---

of the institution of summoning to prayer, as in the Grace after Meals. It is also said on taking the Torah scroll out of the Ark. *Taste and see:* Religious experience precedes religious understanding. God's goodness has to be felt before it can be thought. *Guard your tongue from evil*: The sages said about *lashon hara,* evil speech, that it harms the one who says it, the one it is said about, and the one who gives credence to it. *Seek peace and pursue it:* "Seek peace where you are, and pursue it elsewhere" (*Avot deRabbi Natan*).

תְּפִלָּה לְמֹשֶׁה A prayer of Moses, the man of God. LORD, You have been our shelter in every generation. Before the mountains were born, before You brought forth the earth and the world, from everlasting to everlasting You are God. You turn men back to dust, saying, "Return, you children of men." For a thousand years in Your sight are like yesterday when it has passed, like a watch in the night. You sweep men away; they sleep. In the morning they are like grass newly grown: in the morning it flourishes and is new, but by evening it withers and dries up. For we are consumed by Your anger, terrified by Your fury. You have set our iniquities before You, our secret sins in the light of Your presence. All our days pass away in Your wrath, we spend our years like a sigh. The span of our life is seventy years, or if we are strong, eighty years; but the best of them is trouble and sorrow, for they quickly pass, and we fly away. Who can know the force of Your anger? Your wrath matches the fear due to You. Teach us rightly to number our days, that we may gain a heart of wisdom. Relent, O LORD! How much longer? Be sorry for Your servants. Satisfy us in the morning with Your loving-kindness, that we may sing and rejoice all our days. Grant us joy for as many days as You have afflicted us, for as many years as we saw trouble. Let Your deeds be seen by Your servants, and Your glory by their children. ▸ May the pleasantness of the LORD our God be upon us. Establish for us the work of our hands, O establish the work of our hands. *Ps. 90*

יֹשֵׁב בְּסֵתֶר He who lives in the shelter of the Most High dwells in the shadow of the Almighty. I say of the LORD, my Refuge and Stronghold, my God in whom I trust, that He will save you from the fowler's snare and the deadly pestilence. With His pinions He will cover you, *Ps. 91*

---

the sages, this is the blessing Moses gave the Israelites when they finished constructing the Tabernacle, adding, "May the Divine Presence rest in the work of your hands" (Rashi to Ex. 39:43).

יֹשֵׁב בְּסֵתֶר *Psalm 91.* A prayer for protection from danger and harm. The psalm uses many images for God's protection. To those who trust in Him, He is shelter, shadow, refuge and stronghold. He protects us beneath His wings, and encircles us like a shield. When we are in distress, He is with us. When we are in danger, we are not alone. Trust defeats terror, and faith conquers fear. The first speaker in the psalm is human; the second, God Himself (*Sanhedrin* 103a).

תהלים צ
תְּפִלָּה לְמֹשֶׁה אִישׁ־הָאֱלֹהִים, אֲדֹנָי, מָעוֹן אַתָּה הָיִיתָ לָּנוּ בְּדֹר וָדֹר: בְּטֶרֶם הָרִים יֻלָּדוּ, וַתְּחוֹלֵל אֶרֶץ וְתֵבֵל, וּמֵעוֹלָם עַד־עוֹלָם אַתָּה אֵל: תָּשֵׁב אֱנוֹשׁ עַד־דַּכָּא, וַתֹּאמֶר שׁוּבוּ בְנֵי־אָדָם: כִּי אֶלֶף שָׁנִים בְּעֵינֶיךָ, כְּיוֹם אֶתְמוֹל כִּי יַעֲבֹר, וְאַשְׁמוּרָה בַלָּיְלָה: זְרַמְתָּם, שֵׁנָה יִהְיוּ, בַּבֹּקֶר כֶּחָצִיר יַחֲלֹף: בַּבֹּקֶר יָצִיץ וְחָלָף, לָעֶרֶב יְמוֹלֵל וְיָבֵשׁ: כִּי־כָלִינוּ בְאַפֶּךָ, וּבַחֲמָתְךָ נִבְהָלְנוּ: שַׁתָּ עֲוֹנֹתֵינוּ לְנֶגְדֶּךָ, עֲלֻמֵנוּ לִמְאוֹר פָּנֶיךָ: כִּי כָל־יָמֵינוּ פָּנוּ בְעֶבְרָתֶךָ, כִּלִּינוּ שָׁנֵינוּ כְמוֹ־הֶגֶה: יְמֵי־שְׁנוֹתֵינוּ בָהֶם שִׁבְעִים שָׁנָה, וְאִם בִּגְבוּרֹת שְׁמוֹנִים שָׁנָה, וְרָהְבָּם עָמָל וָאָוֶן, כִּי־גָז חִישׁ וַנָּעֻפָה: מִי־יוֹדֵעַ עֹז אַפֶּךָ, וּכְיִרְאָתְךָ עֶבְרָתֶךָ: לִמְנוֹת יָמֵינוּ כֵּן הוֹדַע, וְנָבִא לְבַב חָכְמָה: שׁוּבָה יהוה עַד־מָתָי, וְהִנָּחֵם עַל־עֲבָדֶיךָ: שַׂבְּעֵנוּ בַבֹּקֶר חַסְדֶּךָ, וּנְרַנְּנָה וְנִשְׂמְחָה בְּכָל־יָמֵינוּ: שַׂמְּחֵנוּ כִּימוֹת עִנִּיתָנוּ, שְׁנוֹת רָאִינוּ רָעָה: יֵרָאֶה אֶל־עֲבָדֶיךָ פָעֳלֶךָ, וַהֲדָרְךָ עַל־בְּנֵיהֶם: ◂ וִיהִי נֹעַם אֲדֹנָי אֱלֹהֵינוּ עָלֵינוּ, וּמַעֲשֵׂה יָדֵינוּ כּוֹנְנָה עָלֵינוּ, וּמַעֲשֵׂה יָדֵינוּ כּוֹנְנֵהוּ:

תהלים צא
יֹשֵׁב בְּסֵתֶר עֶלְיוֹן, בְּצֵל שַׁדַּי יִתְלוֹנָן: אֹמַר לַיהוה מַחְסִי וּמְצוּדָתִי, אֱלֹהַי אֶבְטַח־בּוֹ: כִּי הוּא יַצִּילְךָ מִפַּח יָקוּשׁ, מִדֶּבֶר הַוּוֹת: בְּאֶבְרָתוֹ יָסֶךְ לָךְ, וְתַחַת־כְּנָפָיו תֶּחְסֶה, צִנָּה וְסֹחֵרָה אֲמִתּוֹ:

---

תְּפִלָּה לְמֹשֶׁה *Psalm 90.* A moving meditation on the eternity of God and the shortness of our lives. *You sweep men away:* A succession of poetic images conveying the brevity of human life: it flows as fast as a swollen river; as quickly as a sleep or a dream; it is like grass in a parched land that withers by the end of the day; it is like a sigh, a mere breath, like a bird that briefly lands then flies away. The speed with which these metaphors succeed one another mirrors the rapidity with which the days and years pass. *Teach us rightly to number our days:* The moral at the heart of this psalm, especially relevant on Rosh HaShana as we ask to be written in the book of life, is: teach us to remember how short life is, that we may spend our time on the things that endure. *May the pleasantness of the Lord our God be upon us:* According to

and beneath His wings you will find shelter; His faithfulness is an encircling shield. You need not fear terror by night, nor the arrow that flies by day; not the pestilence that stalks in darkness, nor the plague that ravages at noon. A thousand may fall at your side, ten thousand at your right hand, but it will not come near you. You will only look with your eyes and see the punishment of the wicked. Because you said "The LORD is my Refuge," taking the Most High as your shelter, no harm will befall you, no plague will come near your tent, for He will command His angels about you, to guard you in all your ways. They will lift you in their hands, lest your foot stumble on a stone. You will tread on lions and vipers, you will trample on young lions and snakes. [God says] "Because he loves Me, I will rescue him; I will protect him, because he acknowledges My name. When he calls on Me, I will answer him, I will be with him in distress, I will deliver him and bring him honor. ▸ With long life I will satisfy him, and show him My salvation. With long life I will satisfy him, and show him My salvation."

מִזְמוֹר A Psalm. Sing a new song to the LORD, for He has done wondrous things; He has saved by His right hand and His holy arm. The LORD has made His salvation known; He has displayed His righteousness in the sight of the nations. He remembered His loving-kindness and faithfulness to the house of Israel; all the ends of the earth have seen the victory of our LORD. Shout for joy to the LORD, all the earth; burst into song, sing with joy, play music. Play music to the LORD on the harp – on the harp with the sound of singing. With trumpets and the sound of the shofar, shout for joy before the LORD, the King. ▸ Let the sea and all that is in it thunder, the world and all who live in it. Let the rivers clap their hands, the mountains sing together for joy – before the LORD, for He is coming to judge the earth. He will judge the world with justice, and the peoples with equity. *Ps. 98*

שִׁיר לַמַּעֲלוֹת A song of ascents. I lift my eyes up to the hills; from where will my help come? My help comes from the LORD, Maker of heaven *Ps. 121*

---

All herald His coming with joy, for they know that when He sits in judgment He will resolve all disputes with equity.

שִׁיר לַמַּעֲלוֹת *Psalm 121:* One of the great expressions of trust in God's pro-

לֹא־תִירָא מִפַּחַד לָיְלָה, מֵחֵץ יָעוּף יוֹמָם: מִדֶּבֶר בָּאֹפֶל יַהֲלֹךְ, מִקֶּטֶב יָשׁוּד צָהֳרָיִם: יִפֹּל מִצִּדְּךָ אֶלֶף, וּרְבָבָה מִימִינֶךָ, אֵלֶיךָ לֹא יִגָּשׁ: רַק בְּעֵינֶיךָ תַבִּיט, וְשִׁלֻּמַת רְשָׁעִים תִּרְאֶה: כִּי־אַתָּה יהוה מַחְסִי, עֶלְיוֹן שַׂמְתָּ מְעוֹנֶךָ: לֹא־תְאֻנֶּה אֵלֶיךָ רָעָה, וְנֶגַע לֹא־יִקְרַב בְּאָהֳלֶךָ: כִּי מַלְאָכָיו יְצַוֶּה־לָּךְ, לִשְׁמָרְךָ בְּכָל־דְּרָכֶיךָ: עַל־כַּפַּיִם יִשָּׂאוּנְךָ, פֶּן־תִּגֹּף בָּאֶבֶן רַגְלֶךָ: עַל־שַׁחַל וָפֶתֶן תִּדְרֹךְ, תִּרְמֹס כְּפִיר וְתַנִּין: כִּי בִי חָשַׁק וַאֲפַלְּטֵהוּ, אֲשַׂגְּבֵהוּ כִּי־יָדַע שְׁמִי: יִקְרָאֵנִי וְאֶעֱנֵהוּ, עִמּוֹ אָנֹכִי בְצָרָה, אֲחַלְּצֵהוּ וַאֲכַבְּדֵהוּ:
◂ אֹרֶךְ יָמִים אַשְׂבִּיעֵהוּ, וְאַרְאֵהוּ בִּישׁוּעָתִי:
אֹרֶךְ יָמִים אַשְׂבִּיעֵהוּ, וְאַרְאֵהוּ בִּישׁוּעָתִי:

תהלים צח
מִזְמוֹר, שִׁירוּ לַיהוה שִׁיר חָדָשׁ כִּי־נִפְלָאוֹת עָשָׂה, הוֹשִׁיעָה־לּוֹ יְמִינוֹ וּזְרוֹעַ קָדְשׁוֹ: הוֹדִיעַ יהוה יְשׁוּעָתוֹ, לְעֵינֵי הַגּוֹיִם גִּלָּה צִדְקָתוֹ: זָכַר חַסְדּוֹ וֶאֱמוּנָתוֹ לְבֵית יִשְׂרָאֵל, רָאוּ כָל־אַפְסֵי־אָרֶץ אֵת יְשׁוּעַת אֱלֹהֵינוּ: הָרִיעוּ לַיהוה כָּל־הָאָרֶץ, פִּצְחוּ וְרַנְּנוּ וְזַמֵּרוּ: זַמְּרוּ לַיהוה בְּכִנּוֹר, בְּכִנּוֹר וְקוֹל זִמְרָה: בַּחֲצֹצְרוֹת וְקוֹל שׁוֹפָר, הָרִיעוּ לִפְנֵי הַמֶּלֶךְ יהוה: יִרְעַם הַיָּם וּמְלֹאוֹ, תֵּבֵל וְיֹשְׁבֵי בָהּ:
◂ נְהָרוֹת יִמְחֲאוּ־כָף, יַחַד הָרִים יְרַנֵּנוּ: לִפְנֵי יהוה כִּי בָא לִשְׁפֹּט הָאָרֶץ, יִשְׁפֹּט־תֵּבֵל בְּצֶדֶק, וְעַמִּים בְּמֵישָׁרִים:

תהלים קכא
שִׁיר לַמַּעֲלוֹת, אֶשָּׂא עֵינַי אֶל־הֶהָרִים, מֵאַיִן יָבֹא עֶזְרִי: עֶזְרִי מֵעִם יהוה, עֹשֵׂה שָׁמַיִם וָאָרֶץ: אַל־יִתֵּן לַמּוֹט רַגְלֶךָ, אַל־יָנוּם שֹׁמְרֶךָ:

---

מִזְמוֹר *Psalm 98. A Psalm. Sing a new song to the* *Lord:* In this celebratory song, the Psalmist describes redemption in the vivid image of a royal arrival. The King who is also Judge and Deliverer is about to come. The trumpets sound a clarion to announce His entrance. A roar is heard, not just from the assembled people but from the universe itself: the sea, the earth, rivers and mountains.

and earth. He will not let your foot stumble; He who guards you does not slumber. See: the Guardian of Israel neither slumbers nor sleeps. The LORD is your Guardian; the LORD is your Shade at your right hand. The sun will not strike you by day, nor the moon by night. ▸ The LORD will guard you from all harm; He will guard your life. The LORD will guard your going and coming, now and for evermore.

שִׁיר הַמַּעֲלוֹת A song of ascents. Of David. I rejoiced when they said to me, "Let us go to the House of the LORD." Our feet stood within your gates, Jerusalem: Jerusalem built as a city joined together. There the tribes went up, the tribes of the LORD – as a testimony to Israel – to give thanks to the name of the LORD. For there the thrones of justice are set, the thrones of the house of David. Pray for the peace of Jerusalem: "May those who love you prosper. May there be peace within your ramparts, tranquility in your citadels." ▸ For the sake of my brothers and my friends, I shall say, "Peace be within you." For the sake of the House of the LORD our God, I shall seek your good. *Ps. 122*

שִׁיר הַמַּעֲלוֹת A song of ascents. To You, enthroned in heaven, I lift my eyes. As the eyes of slaves turn to their master's hand, or the eyes of a slave-girl to the hand of her mistress, so our eyes are turned to the LORD our God, awaiting His favor. ▸ Show us favor, LORD, show us favor, for we have suffered more than enough contempt. Too long have we suffered the scorn of the complacent, the contempt of arrogant men. *Ps. 123*

שִׁיר הַמַּעֲלוֹת A song of ascents. Of David. Had the LORD not been on our side – let Israel say it – had the LORD not been on our side when men rose up against us, they would have swallowed us alive when their anger raged against us. The waters would have engulfed us; the torrent would have swept over us; over us would have swept the raging waters. Blessed be the LORD who did not leave us as a prey for their teeth. *Ps. 124*

---

שִׁיר הַמַּעֲלוֹת *Psalm 124:* A psalm of thanksgiving for deliverance, using – as often in Psalms – a rapid succession of different images: the people have been in danger of being swallowed, swept away as if in a flood, a prey to the enemy's teeth, captured in a hunter's trap. The images do not coalesce into a single metaphor. Rather, they combine to express a mood; in this case, the sense of sudden release from danger.

הִנֵּה לֹא־יָנוּם וְלֹא יִישָׁן שׁוֹמֵר יִשְׂרָאֵל: יהוה שֹׁמְרֶךָ, יהוה צִלְּךָ
עַל־יַד יְמִינֶךָ: יוֹמָם הַשֶּׁמֶשׁ לֹא־יַכֶּכָּה, וְיָרֵחַ בַּלָּיְלָה: • יהוה יִשְׁמָרְךָ
מִכָּל־רָע, יִשְׁמֹר אֶת־נַפְשֶׁךָ: יהוה יִשְׁמָר־צֵאתְךָ וּבוֹאֶךָ, מֵעַתָּה
וְעַד־עוֹלָם:

שִׁיר הַמַּעֲלוֹת לְדָוִד, שָׂמַחְתִּי בְּאֹמְרִים לִי בֵּית יהוה נֵלֵךְ: עֹמְדוֹת תהלים קכב
הָיוּ רַגְלֵינוּ, בִּשְׁעָרַיִךְ יְרוּשָׁלָםִ: יְרוּשָׁלַםִ הַבְּנוּיָה, כְּעִיר שֶׁחֻבְּרָה־
לָּהּ יַחְדָּו: שֶׁשָּׁם עָלוּ שְׁבָטִים שִׁבְטֵי־יָהּ, עֵדוּת לְיִשְׂרָאֵל, לְהֹדוֹת
לְשֵׁם יהוה: כִּי שָׁמָּה יָשְׁבוּ כִסְאוֹת לְמִשְׁפָּט, כִּסְאוֹת לְבֵית דָּוִד:
שַׁאֲלוּ שְׁלוֹם יְרוּשָׁלָםִ, יִשְׁלָיוּ אֹהֲבָיִךְ: יְהִי־שָׁלוֹם בְּחֵילֵךְ, שַׁלְוָה
בְּאַרְמְנוֹתָיִךְ: • לְמַעַן אַחַי וְרֵעָי, אֲדַבְּרָה־נָּא שָׁלוֹם בָּךְ: לְמַעַן
בֵּית־יהוה אֱלֹהֵינוּ, אֲבַקְשָׁה טוֹב לָךְ:

שִׁיר הַמַּעֲלוֹת, אֵלֶיךָ נָשָׂאתִי אֶת־עֵינַי, הַיֹּשְׁבִי בַּשָּׁמָיִם: הִנֵּה כְעֵינֵי תהלים קכג
עֲבָדִים אֶל־יַד אֲדוֹנֵיהֶם, כְּעֵינֵי שִׁפְחָה אֶל־יַד גְּבִרְתָּהּ, כֵּן עֵינֵינוּ
אֶל־יהוה אֱלֹהֵינוּ, עַד שֶׁיְּחָנֵּנוּ: • חָנֵּנוּ יהוה חָנֵּנוּ, כִּי־רַב שָׂבַעְנוּ
בוּז: רַבַּת שָׂבְעָה־לָּהּ נַפְשֵׁנוּ, הַלַּעַג הַשַּׁאֲנַנִּים, הַבּוּז לִגְאֵי יוֹנִים:

שִׁיר הַמַּעֲלוֹת לְדָוִד, לוּלֵי יהוה שֶׁהָיָה לָנוּ, יֹאמַר־נָא יִשְׂרָאֵל: לוּלֵי תהלים קכד
יהוה שֶׁהָיָה לָנוּ, בְּקוּם עָלֵינוּ אָדָם: אֲזַי חַיִּים בְּלָעוּנוּ, בַּחֲרוֹת אַפָּם
בָּנוּ: אֲזַי הַמַּיִם שְׁטָפוּנוּ, נַחְלָה עָבַר עַל־נַפְשֵׁנוּ: אֲזַי עָבַר עַל־
נַפְשֵׁנוּ, הַמַּיִם הַזֵּידוֹנִים: בָּרוּךְ יהוה, שֶׁלֹּא נְתָנָנוּ טֶרֶף לְשִׁנֵּיהֶם:

---

tection, often recited in times of trouble. The Hebrew root *sh-m-r*, "guard, protect," appears six times in this short psalm.

שִׁיר הַמַּעֲלוֹת *Psalm 122:* A song sung by pilgrims on the way to Jerusalem. The Hebrew is awash with alliterations on the *sh* sound – as in *sha'alu shelom Yerushalayim yishlayu* – echoing the sound of the second half of the name "Jerusalem," *shalayim*, related to *shalom*, "peace." Here, literary style mirrors substance: the gentle, soothing sounds evoke Jerusalem at peace.

▸ We escaped like a bird from the fowler's trap; the trap broke and we escaped. Our help is in the name of the Lord, Maker of heaven and earth.

הַלְלוּיָהּ Halleluya! Praise the name of the Lord. Praise Him, you servants of the Lord who stand in the Lord's House, in the courtyards of the House of our God. Praise the Lord, for the Lord is good; sing praises to His name, for it is lovely. For the Lord has chosen Jacob as His own, Israel as His treasure. For I know that the Lord is great, that our Lord is above all heavenly powers. Whatever pleases the Lord, He does, in heaven and on earth, in the seas and all the depths. He raises clouds from the ends of the earth; He sends lightning with the rain; He brings out the wind from His storehouses. He struck down the firstborn of Egypt, of both man and animals. He sent signs and wonders into your midst, Egypt – against Pharaoh and all his servants. He struck down many nations and slew mighty kings: Siḥon, King of the Amorites, Og, King of Bashan, and all the kingdoms of Canaan, giving their land as a heritage, a heritage for His people Israel. Your name, Lord, endures for ever; Your renown, Lord, for all generations. For the Lord will bring justice to His people, and have compassion on His servants. The idols of the nations are silver and gold, the work of human hands. They have mouths, but cannot speak; eyes, but cannot see; ears, but cannot hear; there is no breath in their mouths. Those who make them will become like them: so will all who trust in them. ▸ House of Israel, bless the Lord. House of Aaron, bless the Lord. House of Levi, bless the Lord. You who fear the Lord, bless the Lord. Blessed is the Lord from Zion, He who dwells in Jerusalem. Halleluya! *Ps. 135*

---

congregational responses are set out in full, line by line. In Psalm 135 the responses are likely to have been, for the first section, "Halleluya" ("Praise the Lord"), and for the last, "Blessed be the Lord." Psalm 135 is structured in three parts: the first and last speak about the truth of God and the falsity of idols; the second about God's power over nature and history. The first part is five verses long; the second, seven; the third, nine. *He struck down the firstborn of Egypt*: These lines are paralleled in the next psalm. *The idols of the nations are silver and gold… You who fear the Lord, bless the Lord:* almost exactly paralleled in Hallel (Psalm 115:4–13).

◂ נַפְשֵׁנוּ כְּצִפּוֹר נִמְלְטָה מִפַּח יוֹקְשִׁים, הַפַּח נִשְׁבָּר וַאֲנַחְנוּ נִמְלָטְנוּ:
עֶזְרֵנוּ בְּשֵׁם יהוה, עֹשֵׂה שָׁמַיִם וָאָרֶץ:

תהלים קלה

הַלְלוּיָהּ, הַלְלוּ אֶת־שֵׁם יהוה, הַלְלוּ עַבְדֵי יהוה: שֶׁעֹמְדִים בְּבֵית
יהוה, בְּחַצְרוֹת בֵּית אֱלֹהֵינוּ: הַלְלוּיָהּ כִּי־טוֹב יהוה, זַמְּרוּ לִשְׁמוֹ
כִּי נָעִים: כִּי־יַעֲקֹב בָּחַר לוֹ יָהּ, יִשְׂרָאֵל לִסְגֻלָּתוֹ: כִּי אֲנִי יָדַעְתִּי
כִּי־גָדוֹל יהוה, וַאֲדֹנֵינוּ מִכָּל־אֱלֹהִים: כֹּל אֲשֶׁר־חָפֵץ יהוה עָשָׂה,
בַּשָּׁמַיִם וּבָאָרֶץ, בַּיַּמִּים וְכָל־תְּהֹמוֹת: מַעֲלֶה נְשִׂאִים מִקְצֵה הָאָרֶץ,
בְּרָקִים לַמָּטָר עָשָׂה, מוֹצֵא־רוּחַ מֵאוֹצְרוֹתָיו: שֶׁהִכָּה בְּכוֹרֵי מִצְרָיִם,
מֵאָדָם עַד־בְּהֵמָה: שָׁלַח אוֹתֹת וּמֹפְתִים בְּתוֹכֵכִי מִצְרָיִם, בְּפַרְעֹה
וּבְכָל־עֲבָדָיו: שֶׁהִכָּה גּוֹיִם רַבִּים, וְהָרַג מְלָכִים עֲצוּמִים: לְסִיחוֹן
מֶלֶךְ הָאֱמֹרִי, וּלְעוֹג מֶלֶךְ הַבָּשָׁן, וּלְכֹל מַמְלְכוֹת כְּנָעַן: וְנָתַן אַרְצָם
נַחֲלָה, נַחֲלָה לְיִשְׂרָאֵל עַמּוֹ: יהוה שִׁמְךָ לְעוֹלָם, יהוה זִכְרְךָ לְדֹר־
וָדֹר: כִּי־יָדִין יהוה עַמּוֹ, וְעַל־עֲבָדָיו יִתְנֶחָם: עֲצַבֵּי הַגּוֹיִם כֶּסֶף
וְזָהָב, מַעֲשֵׂה יְדֵי אָדָם: פֶּה־לָהֶם וְלֹא יְדַבֵּרוּ, עֵינַיִם לָהֶם וְלֹא
יִרְאוּ: אָזְנַיִם לָהֶם וְלֹא יַאֲזִינוּ, אַף אֵין־יֶשׁ־רוּחַ בְּפִיהֶם: כְּמוֹהֶם
יִהְיוּ עֹשֵׂיהֶם, כֹּל אֲשֶׁר־בֹּטֵחַ בָּהֶם: ◂ בֵּית יִשְׂרָאֵל בָּרְכוּ אֶת־יהוה,
בֵּית אַהֲרֹן בָּרְכוּ אֶת־יהוה: בֵּית הַלֵּוִי בָּרְכוּ אֶת־יהוה, יִרְאֵי יהוה
בָּרְכוּ אֶת־יהוה: בָּרוּךְ יהוה מִצִּיּוֹן, שֹׁכֵן יְרוּשָׁלָםִ, הַלְלוּיָהּ:

---

הַלְלוּיָהּ *Psalms 135–136.* Two psalms forming a single composite unit, similar in tone, vocabulary and literary structure to the group of Psalms 113–118, known as Hallel. Some sages called these two psalms "The Great Hallel" to distinguish them from Psalms 113–118 which they called "The Egyptian Hallel" since it contains a reference to the exodus from Egypt (others confined the description to Psalm 136 alone). It is likely that both were written for public worship in the Temple, and both are litanies: a series of invocations said by a leader of prayer, together with congregational responses. Psalm 136, with its refrain "His loving-kindness is for ever," is the only psalm in which the

*The custom is to stand for the following psalm.*

| | | |
|---|---|---|
| הודו Thank the Lord for He is good; | His loving-kindness is for ever. | *Ps. 136* |
| Thank the God of gods, | His loving-kindness is for ever. | |
| Thank the Lord of lords, | His loving-kindness is for ever. | |
| To the One who alone works great wonders, | His loving-kindness is for ever. | |
| Who made the heavens with wisdom, | His loving-kindness is for ever. | |
| Who spread the earth upon the waters, | His loving-kindness is for ever. | |
| Who made the great lights, | His loving-kindness is for ever. | |
| The sun to rule by day, | His loving-kindness is for ever. | |
| The moon and the stars to rule by night, | His loving-kindness is for ever. | |
| Who struck Egypt through their firstborn, | His loving-kindness is for ever. | |
| And brought out Israel from their midst, | His loving-kindness is for ever. | |
| With a strong hand and outstretched arm, | His loving-kindness is for ever. | |
| Who split the Reed Sea into parts, | His loving-kindness is for ever. | |
| And made Israel pass through it, | His loving-kindness is for ever. | |
| Casting Pharaoh and his army into the Reed Sea; | His loving-kindness is for ever. | |
| Who led His people through the wilderness; | His loving-kindness is for ever. | |
| Who struck down great kings, | His loving-kindness is for ever. | |
| And slew mighty kings, | His loving-kindness is for ever. | |
| Siḥon, King of the Amorites, | His loving-kindness is for ever. | |
| And Og, King of Bashan, | His loving-kindness is for ever. | |
| And gave their land as a heritage, | His loving-kindness is for ever. | |
| A heritage for His servant Israel; | His loving-kindness is for ever. | |
| Who remembered us in our lowly state, | His loving-kindness is for ever. | |
| And rescued us from our tormentors, | His loving-kindness is for ever. | |

---

הודו *Psalm 136.* Originally in the Temple, the leader of prayer said the first half of each verse, to which the congregation responded with the second

*The custom is to stand for the following psalm.*

תהלים קלו

הוֹדוּ לַיהוה כִּי־טוֹב כִּי לְעוֹלָם חַסְדּוֹ:
הוֹדוּ לֵאלֹהֵי הָאֱלֹהִים כִּי לְעוֹלָם חַסְדּוֹ:
הוֹדוּ לַאֲדֹנֵי הָאֲדֹנִים כִּי לְעוֹלָם חַסְדּוֹ:
לְעֹשֵׂה נִפְלָאוֹת גְּדֹלוֹת לְבַדּוֹ כִּי לְעוֹלָם חַסְדּוֹ:
לְעֹשֵׂה הַשָּׁמַיִם בִּתְבוּנָה כִּי לְעוֹלָם חַסְדּוֹ:
לְרֹקַע הָאָרֶץ עַל־הַמָּיִם כִּי לְעוֹלָם חַסְדּוֹ:
לְעֹשֵׂה אוֹרִים גְּדֹלִים כִּי לְעוֹלָם חַסְדּוֹ:
אֶת־הַשֶּׁמֶשׁ לְמֶמְשֶׁלֶת בַּיּוֹם כִּי לְעוֹלָם חַסְדּוֹ:
אֶת־הַיָּרֵחַ וְכוֹכָבִים לְמֶמְשְׁלוֹת בַּלָּיְלָה כִּי לְעוֹלָם חַסְדּוֹ:
לְמַכֵּה מִצְרַיִם בִּבְכוֹרֵיהֶם כִּי לְעוֹלָם חַסְדּוֹ:
וַיּוֹצֵא יִשְׂרָאֵל מִתּוֹכָם כִּי לְעוֹלָם חַסְדּוֹ:
בְּיָד חֲזָקָה וּבִזְרוֹעַ נְטוּיָה כִּי לְעוֹלָם חַסְדּוֹ:
לְגֹזֵר יַם־סוּף לִגְזָרִים כִּי לְעוֹלָם חַסְדּוֹ:
וְהֶעֱבִיר יִשְׂרָאֵל בְּתוֹכוֹ כִּי לְעוֹלָם חַסְדּוֹ:
וְנִעֵר פַּרְעֹה וְחֵילוֹ בְיַם־סוּף כִּי לְעוֹלָם חַסְדּוֹ:
לְמוֹלִיךְ עַמּוֹ בַּמִּדְבָּר כִּי לְעוֹלָם חַסְדּוֹ:
לְמַכֵּה מְלָכִים גְּדֹלִים כִּי לְעוֹלָם חַסְדּוֹ:
וַיַּהֲרֹג מְלָכִים אַדִּירִים כִּי לְעוֹלָם חַסְדּוֹ:
לְסִיחוֹן מֶלֶךְ הָאֱמֹרִי כִּי לְעוֹלָם חַסְדּוֹ:
וּלְעוֹג מֶלֶךְ הַבָּשָׁן כִּי לְעוֹלָם חַסְדּוֹ:
וְנָתַן אַרְצָם לְנַחֲלָה כִּי לְעוֹלָם חַסְדּוֹ:
נַחֲלָה לְיִשְׂרָאֵל עַבְדּוֹ כִּי לְעוֹלָם חַסְדּוֹ:
שֶׁבְּשִׁפְלֵנוּ זָכַר לָנוּ כִּי לְעוֹלָם חַסְדּוֹ:
וַיִּפְרְקֵנוּ מִצָּרֵינוּ כִּי לְעוֹלָם חַסְדּוֹ:

▸ Who gives food to all flesh, His loving-kindness is for ever.
Give thanks to the God of heaven. His loving-kindness is for ever.

הָאַדֶּרֶת Majesty and faithfulness are His who lives forever.
Understanding and blessing are His who lives forever.
Loftiness and greatness are His who lives forever.
Knowing and speech are His who lives forever.
Splendor and honor are His who lives forever.
Destiny and antiquity are His who lives forever.
Clarity and light are His who lives forever.
Power and intense might are His who lives forever.
Ceremony and purity are His who lives forever.
Unity and awe are His who lives forever
The crown and the honor are His who lives forever.
Teaching and learning are His who lives forever.
The realm and the rule are His who lives forever.
Beauty and eternity are His who lives forever.
Greatness and transcendence are His who lives forever.
Strength and humility are His who lives forever.
Salvation and glory are His who lives forever.
Radiance and righteousness are His who lives forever.
Declaration and sanctity are His who lives forever.
Fanfare and sublimity are His who lives forever.
▸ The song and the celebration are His who lives forever.
Praise and adoration are His who lives forever.

---

half. As in several other psalms, the poem opens with cosmology and ends with history; it begins with God as Creator, and continues with God as Redeemer. The sages related the twenty-six verses of the psalm to the twenty-six generations between Adam and the Giving of the Torah – from creation to revelation. Because of its summary of the events of the exodus, it forms part of the Haggada on Pesaḥ.

◂ נֹתֵן לֶחֶם לְכָל־בָּשָׂר כִּי לְעוֹלָם חַסְדּוֹ:
הוֹדוּ לְאֵל הַשָּׁמָיִם כִּי לְעוֹלָם חַסְדּוֹ:

הָאַדֶּרֶת וְהָאֱמוּנָה לְחַי עוֹלָמִים
הַבִּינָה וְהַבְּרָכָה לְחַי עוֹלָמִים
הַגַּאֲוָה וְהַגְּדֻלָּה לְחַי עוֹלָמִים
הַדֵּעָה וְהַדִּבּוּר לְחַי עוֹלָמִים
הַהוֹד וְהֶהָדָר לְחַי עוֹלָמִים
הַוַּעַד וְהַוָּתִיקוּת לְחַי עוֹלָמִים
הַזִּיו וְהַזֹּהַר לְחַי עוֹלָמִים
הַחַיִל וְהַחֹסֶן לְחַי עוֹלָמִים
הַטֶּכֶס וְהַטֹּהַר לְחַי עוֹלָמִים
הַיִּחוּד וְהַיִּרְאָה לְחַי עוֹלָמִים
הַכֶּתֶר וְהַכָּבוֹד לְחַי עוֹלָמִים
הַלֶּקַח וְהַלִּבּוּב לְחַי עוֹלָמִים
הַמְּלוּכָה וְהַמֶּמְשָׁלָה לְחַי עוֹלָמִים
הַנּוֹי וְהַנֵּצַח לְחַי עוֹלָמִים
הַסִּגּוּי וְהַשֶּׂגֶב לְחַי עוֹלָמִים
הָעֹז וְהָעֲנָוָה לְחַי עוֹלָמִים
הַפְּדוּת וְהַפְּאֵר לְחַי עוֹלָמִים
הַצְּבִי וְהַצֶּדֶק לְחַי עוֹלָמִים
הַקְּרִיאָה וְהַקְּדֻשָּׁה לְחַי עוֹלָמִים
הָרֹן וְהָרוֹמֵמוּת לְחַי עוֹלָמִים
◂ הַשִּׁיר וְהַשֶּׁבַח לְחַי עוֹלָמִים
הַתְּהִלָּה וְהַתִּפְאֶרֶת לְחַי עוֹלָמִים

## PESUKEI DEZIMRA

*The following introductory blessing to the Pesukei DeZimra (Verses of Praise) is said standing, while holding the two front tzitziot of the tallit. They are kissed and released at the end of the blessing at "songs of praise" (on the next page). From the beginning of this prayer to the end of the Amida, conversation is forbidden.*

*Some say:*

I hereby prepare my mouth to thank, praise and laud my Creator, for the sake of the unification of the Holy One, blessed be He, and His Divine Presence, through that which is hidden and concealed, in the name of all Israel.

# BLESSED IS HE WHO SPOKE

and the world came into being, blessed is He.
Blessed is He who speaks and acts.
Blessed is He who decrees and fulfills.
Blessed is He who creates the universe.
Blessed is He who shows compassion to the earth.
Blessed is He who shows compassion to all creatures.
Blessed is He who gives a good reward
to those who fear Him.
Blessed is He who lives for ever and exists to eternity.
Blessed is He who redeems and saves.
Blessed is His name.

---

afterward. It is impossible to move directly from worldly concerns to the intense concentration required for genuine prayer, and vice versa. The verse cited as proof of this practice is Psalms 84:5 – "Happy are they that dwell in Your House" – and this verse occupies a prominent place at the heart of the "Verses of Praise."

The basic theme of the Verses of Praise is God as architect and creator of a universe of splendor and diversity, whose orderliness testifies to the single creative will which underlies all that is. The psalms tell this story not in scientific prose but majestic poetry, not *proving* but *proclaiming* the One at the heart of all. Its mood is captured in a phrase from Isaiah (40:26): "Lift your eyes on high, and see who has created these things."

בָּרוּךְ שֶׁאָמַר *Blessed is He who spoke.* An introductory blessing to the Verses

# פסוקי דזמרה

*The following introductory blessing to the* פסוקי דזמרה *is said standing, while holding the two front* ציציות *of the* טלית*. They are kissed and released at the end of the blessing at* בַּתִּשְׁבָּחוֹת *(on the next page). From the beginning of this prayer to the end of the* עמידה*, conversation is forbidden.*

*Some say:*

הֲרֵינִי מְזַמֵּן אֶת פִּי לְהוֹדוֹת וּלְהַלֵּל וּלְשַׁבֵּחַ אֶת בּוֹרְאִי, לְשֵׁם יִחוּד קֻדְשָׁא בְּרִיךְ הוּא וּשְׁכִינְתֵּהּ עַל יְדֵי הַהוּא טָמִיר וְנֶעְלָם בְּשֵׁם כָּל יִשְׂרָאֵל.

בָּרוּךְ שֶׁאָמַר וְהָיָה הָעוֹלָם, בָּרוּךְ הוּא.
בָּרוּךְ אוֹמֵר וְעוֹשֶׂה
בָּרוּךְ גּוֹזֵר וּמְקַיֵּם
בָּרוּךְ עוֹשֶׂה בְרֵאשִׁית
בָּרוּךְ מְרַחֵם עַל הָאָרֶץ
בָּרוּךְ מְרַחֵם עַל הַבְּרִיּוֹת
בָּרוּךְ מְשַׁלֵּם שָׂכָר טוֹב לִירֵאָיו
בָּרוּךְ חַי לָעַד וְקַיָּם לָנֶצַח
בָּרוּךְ פּוֹדֶה וּמַצִּיל
בָּרוּךְ שְׁמוֹ

---

PESUKEI DEZIMRA – VERSES OF PRAISE

This section of the prayers is based on the Talmudic teaching (*Berakhot* 32b) that "The pious men of old used to wait for an hour [before they prayed], then they prayed for an hour, and then they would wait again for an hour." Prayer requires mental preparation beforehand, as well as a gradual leave-taking

Blessed are You, LORD our God,
King of the Universe,
God, compassionate Father,
extolled by the mouth of His people,
praised and glorified by the tongue of His devoted ones
and those who serve Him.
With the songs of Your servant David
we will praise You, O LORD our God.
With praises and psalms
we will magnify and praise You, glorify You,
proclaim Your kingship and speak Your name, our King, our God,
▸ the only One, Giver of life to the worlds,
the King whose great name is praised
and glorified to all eternity.
Blessed are You, LORD, the King extolled with songs of praise.

מִזְמוֹר שִׁיר A psalm. A song for the Sabbath day. It is good to thank *Ps. 92*
the LORD and sing psalms to Your name, Most High – to tell of Your loving-kindness in the morning and Your faithfulness at night, to the music of the ten-stringed lyre and the melody of the harp. For You have made me rejoice by Your work, O LORD; I sing for joy at the deeds of Your hands. How great are Your deeds, LORD, and how very deep Your thoughts. A boor cannot know, nor can a fool understand,

---

("With the songs [psalms] of your servant David we will praise You") but also from the books of Chronicles and Nehemiah ("extolled by the mouth of His people"). To emphasize the significance of this declaration, it is our custom to recite it standing and, at the end, kiss the two front fringes of the tallit.

מִזְמוֹר שִׁיר *Psalm 92.* The sages said about this psalm that it was "a song for the time to come, for the day which will be entirely Sabbath and rest for life everlasting." There are three forms of Shabbat. The first was the Sabbath of creation when the world was still in a state of harmony. The last is the Sabbath of redemption in the time to come, when humanity will have learned to live in harmony. Between them is the Sabbath of the present, a mere temporary respite from a world still riven by strife. The poet places his trust in God's

בָּרוּךְ אַתָּה יהוה אֱלֹהֵינוּ מֶלֶךְ הָעוֹלָם
הָאֵל הָאָב הָרַחֲמָן הַמְהֻלָּל בְּפֶה עַמּוֹ
מְשֻׁבָּח וּמְפֹאָר בִּלְשׁוֹן חֲסִידָיו וַעֲבָדָיו
וּבְשִׁירֵי דָוִד עַבְדֶּךָ
נְהַלֶּלְךָ יהוה אֱלֹהֵינוּ.
בִּשְׁבָחוֹת וּבִזְמִירוֹת
נְגַדֶּלְךָ וּנְשַׁבֵּחֲךָ וּנְפָאֶרְךָ וְנַמְלִיכְךָ
וְנַזְכִּיר שִׁמְךָ, מַלְכֵּנוּ אֱלֹהֵינוּ
◂ יָחִיד חֵי הָעוֹלָמִים
מֶלֶךְ, מְשֻׁבָּח וּמְפֹאָר עֲדֵי עַד שְׁמוֹ הַגָּדוֹל
בָּרוּךְ אַתָּה יהוה, מֶלֶךְ מְהֻלָּל בַּתִּשְׁבָּחוֹת.

מִזְמוֹר שִׁיר לְיוֹם הַשַּׁבָּת: טוֹב לְהֹדוֹת לַיהוה, וּלְזַמֵּר לְשִׁמְךָ עֶלְיוֹן: תהלים צב
לְהַגִּיד בַּבֹּקֶר חַסְדֶּךָ, וֶאֱמוּנָתְךָ בַּלֵּילוֹת: עֲלֵי־עָשׂוֹר וַעֲלֵי־נָבֶל,
עֲלֵי הִגָּיוֹן בְּכִנּוֹר: כִּי שִׂמַּחְתַּנִי יהוה בְּפָעֳלֶךָ, בְּמַעֲשֵׂי יָדֶיךָ אֲרַנֵּן:
מַה־גָּדְלוּ מַעֲשֶׂיךָ יהוה, מְאֹד עָמְקוּ מַחְשְׁבֹתֶיךָ: אִישׁ־בַּעַר לֹא

---

of Praise, in two parts. The first is a ten-part litany of praise to God as Creator, each phrase introduced with the word "Blessed" (the second phrase, "בָּרוּךְ הוּא, Blessed is He," is not a separate verse but originally a congregational response). The first line summarizes with utmost brevity – "Blessed is He who spoke and the world came into being" – the essential point of Genesis 1, that creation took place without a struggle between contending elements. It was the result of a single creative will. The blessing also emphasizes that within the universe there are moral as well as scientific laws. The tenfold blessing reflects the rabbinic saying that "With ten utterances the world was created."

בָּרוּךְ אַתָּה יהוה אֱלֹהֵינוּ *Blessed are You, Lord our God.* The second half of the blessing is a prelude to the biblical verses that follow, mainly from Psalms

that though the wicked spring up like grass and all evildoers flourish, it is only that they may be destroyed for ever. But You, LORD, are eternally exalted. For behold Your enemies, LORD, behold Your enemies will perish; all evildoers will be scattered. You have raised my pride like that of a wild ox; I am anointed with fresh oil. My eyes shall look in triumph on my adversaries, my ears shall hear the downfall of the wicked who rise against me. ▸ The righteous will flourish like a palm tree and grow tall like a cedar in Lebanon. Planted in the LORD's House, blossoming in our God's courtyards, they will still bear fruit in old age, and stay vigorous and fresh, proclaiming that the LORD is upright: He is my Rock, in whom there is no wrong.

יהוה מָלָךְ The LORD reigns. He is robed in majesty. The LORD is robed, *Ps. 93*
girded with strength. The world is firmly established; it cannot be moved. Your throne stands firm as of old; You are eternal. Rivers lift up, LORD, rivers lift up their voice, rivers lift up their crashing waves. ▸ Mightier than the noise of many waters, than the mighty waves of the sea is the LORD on high. Your testimonies are very sure; holiness adorns Your House, LORD, for evermore.

יְהִי כְבוֹד May the LORD's glory be for ever; may the LORD rejoice in *Ps. 104*
His works. May the LORD's name be blessed, now and for ever. From *Ps. 113*
the rising of the sun to its setting, may the LORD's name be praised.
The LORD is high above all nations; His glory is above the heavens.
LORD, Your name is for ever. Your renown, LORD, is for all generations. *Ps. 135*

---

three-phrase rhythm evokes the power of ocean waves as they rise, yet high above them is the grandeur and glory of God.

יְהִי כְבוֹד יהוה *May the LORD's glory.* An anthology of verses, mainly from Psalms, but also from Chronicles and Proverbs. One verse, "The LORD is King, the LORD was King, the LORD will be King for ever and all time," does not appear in this form in the Bible – it is a combination of three biblical phrases, two from Psalms, one from Exodus (at the end of the Song at the Sea). It will figure later as the refrain of one of the poems said in the Repetition of the Shaḥarit Amida. The verses take us through the following sequence

יֵדָע, וּכְסִיל לֹא־יָבִין אֶת־זֹאת: בִּפְרֹחַ רְשָׁעִים כְּמוֹ עֵשֶׂב, וַיָּצִיצוּ
כָּל־פֹּעֲלֵי אָוֶן, לְהִשָּׁמְדָם עֲדֵי־עַד: וְאַתָּה מָרוֹם לְעֹלָם יהוה:
כִּי הִנֵּה אֹיְבֶיךָ יהוה, כִּי־הִנֵּה אֹיְבֶיךָ יֹאבֵדוּ, יִתְפָּרְדוּ כָּל־פֹּעֲלֵי
אָוֶן: וַתָּרֶם כִּרְאֵים קַרְנִי, בַּלֹּתִי בְּשֶׁמֶן רַעֲנָן: וַתַּבֵּט עֵינִי בְּשׁוּרָי,
בַּקָּמִים עָלַי מְרֵעִים תִּשְׁמַעְנָה אָזְנָי: › צַדִּיק כַּתָּמָר יִפְרָח, כְּאֶרֶז
בַּלְּבָנוֹן יִשְׂגֶּה: שְׁתוּלִים בְּבֵית יהוה, בְּחַצְרוֹת אֱלֹהֵינוּ יַפְרִיחוּ:
עוֹד יְנוּבוּן בְּשֵׂיבָה, דְּשֵׁנִים וְרַעֲנַנִּים יִהְיוּ: לְהַגִּיד כִּי־יָשָׁר יהוה,
צוּרִי, וְלֹא־עַוְלָתָה בּוֹ:

יהוה מָלָךְ, גֵּאוּת לָבֵשׁ, לָבֵשׁ יהוה עֹז הִתְאַזָּר, אַף־תִּכּוֹן תֵּבֵל תהלים צג
בַּל־תִּמּוֹט: נָכוֹן כִּסְאֲךָ מֵאָז, מֵעוֹלָם אָתָּה: נָשְׂאוּ נְהָרוֹת יהוה,
נָשְׂאוּ נְהָרוֹת קוֹלָם, יִשְׂאוּ נְהָרוֹת דָּכְיָם: › מִקֹּלוֹת מַיִם רַבִּים,
אַדִּירִים מִשְׁבְּרֵי־יָם, אַדִּיר בַּמָּרוֹם יהוה: עֵדֹתֶיךָ נֶאֶמְנוּ מְאֹד
לְבֵיתְךָ נַאֲוָה־קֹדֶשׁ, יהוה לְאֹרֶךְ יָמִים:

יְהִי כְבוֹד יהוה לְעוֹלָם, יִשְׂמַח יהוה בְּמַעֲשָׂיו: יְהִי שֵׁם יהוה מְבֹרָךְ, תהלים קד תהלים קיג
מֵעַתָּה וְעַד־עוֹלָם: מִמִּזְרַח־שֶׁמֶשׁ עַד־מְבוֹאוֹ, מְהֻלָּל שֵׁם יהוה:
רָם עַל־כָּל־גּוֹיִם יהוה, עַל הַשָּׁמַיִם כְּבוֹדוֹ: יהוה שִׁמְךָ לְעוֹלָם, תהלים קלה

---

"faithfulness at night" – the night of history where the wicked seem to flourish and the righteous to suffer. That, he says, is only in the short term. Ultimately, evil is self-destructive; righteousness will win the final battle. There will be a Sabbath of redemption when the world regains the harmony it first had, when humans learn to live at peace with the world and with one another.

יהוה מָלָךְ *Psalm 93.* A declaration of God's majesty, with many verbal allusions to the Song at the Sea (Ex. 15). In many ancient cultures the sea was a metaphor for the powers of chaos. The psalm dismisses this entire mindset. God's power is supreme. "The sea is His, for He made it" (Ps. 95:5). The surging movement of the phrases in the middle verses with their cumulative

The LORD has established His throne in heaven; His kingdom rules *Ps. 103*
all. Let the heavens rejoice and the earth be glad. Let them say among *1 Chr. 16*
the nations, "The LORD is King." The LORD is King, the LORD was
King, the LORD will be King for ever and all time. The LORD is King *Ps. 10*
for ever and all time; nations will perish from His land. The LORD foils *Ps. 33*
the plans of nations; He frustrates the intentions of peoples. Many are *Prov. 19*
the intentions in a person's mind, but the LORD's plan prevails. The *Ps. 33*
LORD's plan shall stand for ever, His mind's intent for all generations.
For He spoke and it was; He commanded and it stood firm. For the *Ps. 132*
LORD has chosen Zion; He desired it for His dwelling. For the LORD *Ps. 135*
has chosen Jacob, Israel as His special treasure. For the LORD will not *Ps. 94*
abandon His people; nor will He forsake His heritage. ▸ He is com- *Ps. 78*
passionate. He forgives iniquity and does not destroy. Repeatedly He
suppresses His anger, not rousing His full wrath. LORD, save! May the *Ps. 20*
King answer us on the day we call.

*The line beginning with "You open Your hand" should be said with special concentration, representing as it does the key idea of this psalm, and of Pesukei DeZimra as a whole, that God is the creator and sustainer of all.*

אַשְׁרֵי Happy are those who dwell in Your House; *Ps. 84*
they shall continue to praise You, Selah!
Happy are the people for whom this is so; *Ps. 144*
happy are the people whose God is the LORD.
A song of praise by David. *Ps. 145*
I will exalt You, my God, the King, and bless Your name for ever and all time. Every day I will bless You, and praise Your name for ever and all time. Great is the LORD and greatly to be

---

אַשְׁרֵי *Happy are those.* Psalm 145 is the single most important passage in the Verses of Praise. The sages saw it as the paradigm of praise, firstly because it is constructed as an alphabetic acrostic (with the exception of the letter *nun*), thus praising God with all the letters of the alphabet; second, because it contains the verse "You open Your hand, and satisfy every living thing," encapsulating the idea that God not merely created the universe in the beginning, but also daily sustains it and the life it contains. The sages ruled

יהוה זִכְרְךָ לְדֹר־וָדֹר: יהוה בַּשָּׁמַיִם הֵכִין כִּסְאוֹ, וּמַלְכוּתוֹ בַּכֹּל תהלים קג
מָשָׁלָה: יִשְׂמְחוּ הַשָּׁמַיִם וְתָגֵל הָאָרֶץ, וְיֹאמְרוּ בַגּוֹיִם יהוה מָלָךְ: דברי הימים א׳ טז
יהוה מֶלֶךְ, יהוה מָלָךְ, יהוה יִמְלֹךְ לְעוֹלָם וָעֶד. יהוה מֶלֶךְ עוֹלָם תהלים י
וָעֶד, אָבְדוּ גוֹיִם מֵאַרְצוֹ: יהוה הֵפִיר עֲצַת־גּוֹיִם, הֵנִיא מַחְשְׁבוֹת תהלים לג
עַמִּים: רַבּוֹת מַחֲשָׁבוֹת בְּלֶב־אִישׁ, וַעֲצַת יהוה הִיא תָקוּם: עֲצַת משלי יט תהלים לג
יהוה לְעוֹלָם תַּעֲמֹד, מַחְשְׁבוֹת לִבּוֹ לְדֹר וָדֹר: כִּי הוּא אָמַר וַיֶּהִי,
הוּא־צִוָּה וַיַּעֲמֹד: כִּי־בָחַר יהוה בְּצִיּוֹן, אִוָּהּ לְמוֹשָׁב לוֹ: כִּי־יַעֲקֹב תהלים קלב תהלים קלה
בָּחַר לוֹ יָהּ, יִשְׂרָאֵל לִסְגֻלָּתוֹ: כִּי לֹא־יִטֹּשׁ יהוה עַמּוֹ, וְנַחֲלָתוֹ לֹא תהלים צד
יַעֲזֹב: ◂ וְהוּא רַחוּם, יְכַפֵּר עָוֹן וְלֹא־יַשְׁחִית, וְהִרְבָּה לְהָשִׁיב אַפּוֹ, תהלים עח
וְלֹא־יָעִיר כָּל־חֲמָתוֹ: יהוה הוֹשִׁיעָה, הַמֶּלֶךְ יַעֲנֵנוּ בְיוֹם־קָרְאֵנוּ: תהלים כ

*The line beginning with* פּוֹתֵחַ אֶת יָדֶךָ *should be said with special concentration, representing as it does the key idea of this psalm, and of* פסוקי דזמרה *as a whole, that God is the creator and sustainer of all.*

אַשְׁרֵי יוֹשְׁבֵי בֵיתֶךָ, עוֹד יְהַלְלוּךָ סֶּלָה: תהלים פד
אַשְׁרֵי הָעָם שֶׁכָּכָה לּוֹ, אַשְׁרֵי הָעָם שֶׁיהוה אֱלֹהָיו: תהלים קמד
תְּהִלָּה לְדָוִד תהלים קמה
אֲרוֹמִמְךָ אֱלוֹהַי הַמֶּלֶךְ, וַאֲבָרְכָה שִׁמְךָ לְעוֹלָם וָעֶד:
בְּכָל־יוֹם אֲבָרְכֶךָּ, וַאֲהַלְלָה שִׁמְךָ לְעוֹלָם וָעֶד:
גָּדוֹל יהוה וּמְהֻלָּל מְאֹד, וְלִגְדֻלָּתוֹ אֵין חֵקֶר:

---

of thought: God created the universe; therefore God is sovereign over the universe. In the short term it may seem that human beings determine their own fate even against the will of heaven. However, it is not so: "The LORD's plan prevails." God has chosen a particular people (Zion, Jacob) to exemplify this truth, for Israel is the only nation whose very existence is dependent on its covenant with God. Because Israel recognizes no ultimate king other than God, it turns to Him in prayer.

praised; His greatness is unfathomable. One generation will praise Your works to the next, and tell of Your mighty deeds. On the glorious splendor of Your majesty I will meditate, and on the acts of Your wonders. They shall talk of the power of Your awesome deeds, and I will tell of Your greatness. They shall recite the record of Your great goodness, and sing with joy of Your righteousness. The LORD is gracious and compassionate, slow to anger and great in loving-kindness. The LORD is good to all, and His compassion extends to all His works. All Your works shall thank You, LORD, and Your devoted ones shall bless You. They shall talk of the glory of Your kingship, and speak of Your might. To make known to mankind His mighty deeds and the glorious majesty of His kingship. Your kingdom is an everlasting kingdom, and Your reign is for all generations. The LORD supports all who fall, and raises all who are bowed down. All raise their eyes to You in hope, and You give them their food in due season. You open Your hand, and satisfy every living thing with favor. The LORD is righteous in all His ways, and kind in all He does. The LORD is close to all who call on Him, to all who call on Him in truth. He fulfills the will of those who revere Him; He hears their cry and saves them. The LORD guards all who love Him, but all the wicked He will destroy. ▸ My mouth shall speak the praise of the LORD, and all creatures shall bless His holy name for ever and all time.

We will bless the LORD now and for ever. Halleluya! *Ps. 115*

---

about God's praise throughout the generations; 8–14 depict God's kingship and compassion; 15–21 are about how God heeds prayer. The psalm is built on numerical structures (3, 7, 10) that closely resemble the creation narrative in Genesis 1:1–2:3.

Added to Psalm 145 are verses from other psalms: two at the beginning, which include the word *Ashrei* ("happy") three times; and one at the end, which ends with *Halleluya*. It thus epitomizes the book of Psalms as a whole, which begins with the word *Ashrei* and ends with the word *Halleluya*.

דּוֹר לְדוֹר יְשַׁבַּח מַעֲשֶׂיךָ, וּגְבוּרֹתֶיךָ יַגִּידוּ:
הֲדַר כְּבוֹד הוֹדֶךָ, וְדִבְרֵי נִפְלְאֹתֶיךָ אָשִׂיחָה:
וֶעֱזוּז נוֹרְאֹתֶיךָ יֹאמֵרוּ, וּגְדוּלָּתְךָ אֲסַפְּרֶנָּה:
זֵכֶר רַב־טוּבְךָ יַבִּיעוּ, וְצִדְקָתְךָ יְרַנֵּנוּ:
חַנּוּן וְרַחוּם יהוה, אֶרֶךְ אַפַּיִם וּגְדׇל־חָסֶד:
טוֹב־יהוה לַכֹּל, וְרַחֲמָיו עַל־כׇּל־מַעֲשָׂיו:
יוֹדוּךָ יהוה כׇּל־מַעֲשֶׂיךָ, וַחֲסִידֶיךָ יְבָרְכוּכָה:
כְּבוֹד מַלְכוּתְךָ יֹאמֵרוּ, וּגְבוּרָתְךָ יְדַבֵּרוּ:
לְהוֹדִיעַ לִבְנֵי הָאָדָם גְּבוּרֹתָיו, וּכְבוֹד הֲדַר מַלְכוּתוֹ:
מַלְכוּתְךָ מַלְכוּת כׇּל־עֹלָמִים, וּמֶמְשַׁלְתְּךָ בְּכׇל־דּוֹר וָדֹר:
סוֹמֵךְ יהוה לְכׇל־הַנֹּפְלִים, וְזוֹקֵף לְכׇל־הַכְּפוּפִים:
עֵינֵי־כֹל אֵלֶיךָ יְשַׂבֵּרוּ, וְאַתָּה נוֹתֵן־לָהֶם אֶת־אׇכְלָם בְּעִתּוֹ:
פּוֹתֵחַ אֶת־יָדֶךָ, וּמַשְׂבִּיעַ לְכׇל־חַי רָצוֹן:
צַדִּיק יהוה בְּכׇל־דְּרָכָיו, וְחָסִיד בְּכׇל־מַעֲשָׂיו:
קָרוֹב יהוה לְכׇל־קֹרְאָיו, לְכֹל אֲשֶׁר יִקְרָאֻהוּ בֶאֱמֶת:
רְצוֹן־יְרֵאָיו יַעֲשֶׂה, וְאֶת־שַׁוְעָתָם יִשְׁמַע, וְיוֹשִׁיעֵם:
שׁוֹמֵר יהוה אֶת־כׇּל־אֹהֲבָיו, וְאֵת כׇּל־הָרְשָׁעִים יַשְׁמִיד:
◂ תְּהִלַּת יהוה יְדַבֶּר פִּי, וִיבָרֵךְ כׇּל־בָּשָׂר שֵׁם קׇדְשׁוֹ לְעוֹלָם וָעֶד:
וַאֲנַחְנוּ נְבָרֵךְ יָהּ מֵעַתָּה וְעַד־עוֹלָם, הַלְלוּיָהּ: תהלים קטו

---

that it be said three times daily (twice in the morning service, once in the afternoon).

There are other reasons for its prominence. It is the only one of the 150 psalms to be called *Tehilla LeDavid*, "A Song of Praise by David." It contains the phrase, "Every day I will bless You," suggesting that it be said daily. Its twenty-one lines are constructed in three groups of seven verses: 1–7 are

הַלְלוּיָהּ Halleluya! Praise the LORD, my soul. I will praise the LORD all my life; I will sing to my God as long as I live. Put not your trust in princes, or in mortal man who cannot save. His breath expires, he returns to the earth; on that day his plans come to an end. Happy is he whose help is the God of Jacob, whose hope is in the LORD his God who made heaven and earth, the sea and all they contain; He who keeps faith for ever. He secures justice for the oppressed. He gives food to the hungry. The LORD sets captives free. The LORD gives sight to the blind. The LORD raises those bowed down. The LORD loves the righteous. The LORD protects the stranger. He gives courage to the orphan and widow. He thwarts the way of the wicked. ▸ The LORD shall reign for ever. He is your God, Zion, for all generations. Halleluya! Ps. 146

הַלְלוּיָהּ Halleluya! How good it is to sing songs to our God; how pleasant and fitting to praise Him. The LORD rebuilds Jerusalem. He gathers the scattered exiles of Israel. He heals the brokenhearted and binds up their wounds. He counts the number of the stars, calling each by name. Great is our LORD and mighty in power; His understanding has no limit. The LORD gives courage to the humble, but casts the wicked to the ground. Sing to the LORD in thanks; make music to our God on the harp. He covers the sky with clouds. He provides the earth with rain and makes grass grow on the hills. He gives food to the cattle and to the ravens when they cry. He does not take delight in the strength of horses nor pleasure in the fleetness of man. The LORD takes pleasure in those who fear Him, who put their hope in His loving care. Praise the LORD, Jerusalem; sing Ps. 147

---

salem and who has given Israel what He has given no other nation: His laws.

*The LORD rebuilds Jerusalem:* Note the moving and unexpected juxtaposition in these three verses: between God as the LORD of history ("gathers the scattered exiles") and God as Master of the cosmos ("counts the number of the stars") comes God the Healer of shattered souls ("heals the brokenhearted and binds up their wounds"). Bringing comfort to the distressed is as important to God as the great events of history or the vastness of space.

תהלים קמו
הַלְלוּיָהּ, הַלְלִי נַפְשִׁי אֶת־יהוה: אֲהַלְלָה יהוה בְּחַיָּי, אֲזַמְּרָה
לֵאלֹהַי בְּעוֹדִי: אַל־תִּבְטְחוּ בִנְדִיבִים, בְּבֶן־אָדָם שֶׁאֵין לוֹ
תְשׁוּעָה: תֵּצֵא רוּחוֹ, יָשֻׁב לְאַדְמָתוֹ, בַּיּוֹם הַהוּא אָבְדוּ עֶשְׁתֹּנֹתָיו:
אַשְׁרֵי שֶׁאֵל יַעֲקֹב בְּעֶזְרוֹ, שִׂבְרוֹ עַל־יהוה אֱלֹהָיו: עֹשֶׂה שָׁמַיִם
וָאָרֶץ, אֶת־הַיָּם וְאֶת־כָּל־אֲשֶׁר־בָּם, הַשֹּׁמֵר אֱמֶת לְעוֹלָם: עֹשֶׂה
מִשְׁפָּט לָעֲשׁוּקִים, נֹתֵן לֶחֶם לָרְעֵבִים, יהוה מַתִּיר אֲסוּרִים: יהוה
פֹּקֵחַ עִוְרִים, יהוה זֹקֵף כְּפוּפִים, יהוה אֹהֵב צַדִּיקִים: יהוה שֹׁמֵר
אֶת־גֵּרִים, יָתוֹם וְאַלְמָנָה יְעוֹדֵד, וְדֶרֶךְ רְשָׁעִים יְעַוֵּת: ‹ יִמְלֹךְ
יהוה לְעוֹלָם, אֱלֹהַיִךְ צִיּוֹן לְדֹר וָדֹר, הַלְלוּיָהּ:

תהלים קמז
הַלְלוּיָהּ, כִּי־טוֹב זַמְּרָה אֱלֹהֵינוּ, כִּי־נָעִים נָאוָה תְהִלָּה: בּוֹנֵה
יְרוּשָׁלַםִ יהוה, נִדְחֵי יִשְׂרָאֵל יְכַנֵּס: הָרוֹפֵא לִשְׁבוּרֵי לֵב, וּמְחַבֵּשׁ
לְעַצְּבוֹתָם: מוֹנֶה מִסְפָּר לַכּוֹכָבִים, לְכֻלָּם שֵׁמוֹת יִקְרָא: גָּדוֹל
אֲדוֹנֵינוּ וְרַב־כֹּחַ, לִתְבוּנָתוֹ אֵין מִסְפָּר: מְעוֹדֵד עֲנָוִים יהוה,
מַשְׁפִּיל רְשָׁעִים עֲדֵי־אָרֶץ: עֱנוּ לַיהוה בְּתוֹדָה, זַמְּרוּ לֵאלֹהֵינוּ
בְכִנּוֹר: הַמְכַסֶּה שָׁמַיִם בְּעָבִים, הַמֵּכִין לָאָרֶץ מָטָר, הַמַּצְמִיחַ
הָרִים חָצִיר: נוֹתֵן לִבְהֵמָה לַחְמָהּ, לִבְנֵי עֹרֵב אֲשֶׁר יִקְרָאוּ:
לֹא בִגְבוּרַת הַסּוּס יֶחְפָּץ, לֹא־בְשׁוֹקֵי הָאִישׁ יִרְצֶה: רוֹצֶה
יהוה אֶת־יְרֵאָיו, אֶת־הַמְיַחֲלִים לְחַסְדּוֹ: שַׁבְּחִי יְרוּשָׁלַםִ אֶת־

---

הַלְלוּיָהּ *Psalm 146.* A song of praise contrasting divine justice with its human counterpart. Humans are mortal. Their rule does not last. God is the only ultimate source of justice, especially to the vulnerable and those at the margins of society: the oppressed, the hungry, the captives, the blind, the stranger, the orphan and the widow. God, the supreme power, cares for the powerless.

הַלְלוּיָהּ *Psalm 147.* A symphonic celebration of universality and particularity: the God of the universe who knows each star by name, who makes the wind blow and scatters snow like fleece, is the God who cares for Zion and Jeruto your God, Zion, for He has strengthened the bars of your gates and blessed your children in your midst. He has brought peace to your borders, and satisfied you with the finest wheat. He sends His commandment to earth; swiftly runs His word. He spreads snow like fleece, sprinkles frost like ashes, scatters hail like crumbs. Who can stand His cold? He sends His word and melts them; He makes the wind blow and the waters flow. ▸ He has declared His words to Jacob, His statutes and laws to Israel. He has done this for no other nation; such laws they do not know. Halleluya!

הַלְלוּיָהּ Halleluya! Praise the Lord from the heavens, praise Him in the heights. Praise Him, all His angels; praise Him, all His hosts. Praise Him, sun and moon; praise Him, all shining stars. Praise Him, highest heavens and the waters above the heavens. Let them praise the name of the Lord, for He commanded and they were created. He established them for ever and all time, issuing a decree that will never change. Praise the Lord from the earth: sea monsters and all the deep seas; fire and hail, snow and mist, storm winds that obey His word; mountains and all hills, fruit trees and all cedars; wild animals and all cattle, creeping things and winged birds; kings of the earth and all nations, princes and all judges on earth; youths and maidens, old and young. ▸ Let them praise the name of the Lord, for His name alone is sublime; His majesty is above earth and heaven. He has raised the pride of His people, for the glory of all His devoted ones, the children of Israel, the people close to Him. Halleluya! *Ps. 148*

---

they are different in style. The first contains seven phrases, each beginning with the word "praise." The second opens with a single call to praise, and then enumerates twenty-four earthly bodies, beginning with those found in water, wind and fire, then moving to the earth, plants and animals, and culminating in humans. Each half ends with an invocation beginning, "Let them praise the name of the Lord." The psalm begins and ends, as do all the last five, with "Halleluya."

יהוה, הַלְלִי אֱלֹהַיִךְ צִיּוֹן: כִּי־חִזַּק בְּרִיחֵי שְׁעָרָיִךְ, בֵּרַךְ בָּנַיִךְ
בְּקִרְבֵּךְ: הַשָּׂם־גְּבוּלֵךְ שָׁלוֹם, חֵלֶב חִטִּים יַשְׂבִּיעֵךְ: הַשֹּׁלֵחַ
אִמְרָתוֹ אָרֶץ, עַד־מְהֵרָה יָרוּץ דְּבָרוֹ: הַנֹּתֵן שֶׁלֶג כַּצָּמֶר, כְּפוֹר
כָּאֵפֶר יְפַזֵּר: מַשְׁלִיךְ קַרְחוֹ כְפִתִּים, לִפְנֵי קָרָתוֹ מִי יַעֲמֹד: יִשְׁלַח
דְּבָרוֹ וְיַמְסֵם, יַשֵּׁב רוּחוֹ יִזְּלוּ־מָיִם: ‹ מַגִּיד דְּבָרָו לְיַעֲקֹב, חֻקָּיו
וּמִשְׁפָּטָיו לְיִשְׂרָאֵל: לֹא עָשָׂה כֵן לְכָל־גּוֹי, וּמִשְׁפָּטִים בַּל־יְדָעוּם,
הַלְלוּיָהּ:

תהלים קמח הַלְלוּיָהּ, הַלְלוּ אֶת־יהוה מִן־הַשָּׁמַיִם, הַלְלוּהוּ בַּמְּרוֹמִים:
הַלְלוּהוּ כָל־מַלְאָכָיו, הַלְלוּהוּ כָּל־צְבָאָו: הַלְלוּהוּ שֶׁמֶשׁ וְיָרֵחַ,
הַלְלוּהוּ כָּל־כּוֹכְבֵי אוֹר: הַלְלוּהוּ שְׁמֵי הַשָּׁמָיִם, וְהַמַּיִם אֲשֶׁר
מֵעַל הַשָּׁמָיִם: יְהַלְלוּ אֶת־שֵׁם יהוה, כִּי הוּא צִוָּה וְנִבְרָאוּ:
וַיַּעֲמִידֵם לָעַד לְעוֹלָם, חָק־נָתַן וְלֹא יַעֲבוֹר: הַלְלוּ אֶת־יהוה
מִן־הָאָרֶץ, תַּנִּינִים וְכָל־תְּהֹמוֹת: אֵשׁ וּבָרָד שֶׁלֶג וְקִיטוֹר, רוּחַ
סְעָרָה עֹשָׂה דְבָרוֹ: הֶהָרִים וְכָל־גְּבָעוֹת, עֵץ פְּרִי וְכָל־אֲרָזִים:
הַחַיָּה וְכָל־בְּהֵמָה, רֶמֶשׂ וְצִפּוֹר כָּנָף: מַלְכֵי־אֶרֶץ וְכָל־לְאֻמִּים,
שָׂרִים וְכָל־שֹׁפְטֵי אָרֶץ: בַּחוּרִים וְגַם־בְּתוּלוֹת, זְקֵנִים עִם־נְעָרִים:
‹ יְהַלְלוּ אֶת־שֵׁם יהוה, כִּי־נִשְׂגָּב שְׁמוֹ לְבַדּוֹ, הוֹדוֹ עַל־אֶרֶץ
וְשָׁמָיִם: וַיָּרֶם קֶרֶן לְעַמּוֹ, תְּהִלָּה לְכָל־חֲסִידָיו, לִבְנֵי יִשְׂרָאֵל עַם
קְרֹבוֹ, הַלְלוּיָהּ:

---

הַלְלוּיָהּ *Psalm 148.* A jubilant call to the universe and all it contains – described here in its vast panoply – to praise God. The verb "praise" appears ten times within the body of the psalm, corresponding to the ten creative utterances with which God created the world, (the ten times the phrase "And God said" appears in Genesis 1). The psalm is divided into two parts. The first is about the heavens and all they contain, the second is about the earth – and

הַלְלוּיָהּ Halleluya! Sing to the Lord a new song, His praise in the assembly of the devoted. Let Israel rejoice in its Maker; let the children of Zion exult in their King. Let them praise His name with dancing; sing praises to Him with timbrel and harp. For the Lord delights in His people; He adorns the humble with salvation. Let the devoted revel in glory; let them sing for joy on their beds. Let high praises of God be in their throats, and a two-edged sword in their hand: to impose retribution on the nations, punishment on the peoples, ▸ binding their kings with chains, their nobles with iron fetters, carrying out the judgment written against them. This is the glory of all His devoted ones. Halleluya! *Ps. 149*

הַלְלוּיָהּ Halleluya! *Ps. 150*
Praise God in His holy place;
praise Him in the heavens of His power.
Praise Him for His mighty deeds;
praise Him for His surpassing greatness.
Praise Him with blasts of the shofar;
praise Him with the harp and lyre.
Praise Him with timbrel and dance;
praise Him with strings and flute.
▸ Praise Him with clashing cymbals;
praise Him with resounding cymbals.
Let all that breathes praise the Lord. Halleluya!
Let all that breathes praise the Lord. Halleluya!

---

Mount (Maimonides, Laws of First Fruits [*Bikkurim*] 4:17). In it we hear the word "praise" thirteen times – fifteen if we count the repeated final verse. Eight musical instruments are mentioned, four of which – strings, flute, and the two kinds of cymbals – are not mentioned elsewhere in Psalms. The book of Psalms, which contains some of the most moving of all religious expressions of anguish and grief, dejection and loneliness, nonetheless begins with happiness and ends in joy. It begins with the individual living by the word and will of God and ends with all creation singing the praises of its Creator. Such religious poetry has never been surpassed.

הַלְלוּיָהּ, שִׁירוּ לַיהוה שִׁיר חָדָשׁ, תְּהִלָּתוֹ בִּקְהַל חֲסִידִים: יִשְׂמַח תהלים קמט
יִשְׂרָאֵל בְּעֹשָׂיו, בְּנֵי־צִיּוֹן יָגִילוּ בְמַלְכָּם: יְהַלְלוּ שְׁמוֹ בְמָחוֹל, בְּתֹף
וְכִנּוֹר יְזַמְּרוּ־לוֹ: כִּי־רוֹצֶה יהוה בְּעַמּוֹ, יְפָאֵר עֲנָוִים בִּישׁוּעָה:
יַעְלְזוּ חֲסִידִים בְּכָבוֹד, יְרַנְּנוּ עַל־מִשְׁכְּבוֹתָם: רוֹמְמוֹת אֵל
בִּגְרוֹנָם, וְחֶרֶב פִּיפִיּוֹת בְּיָדָם: לַעֲשׂוֹת נְקָמָה בַּגּוֹיִם, תּוֹכֵחוֹת
בַּלְאֻמִּים: ‹ לֶאְסֹר מַלְכֵיהֶם בְּזִקִּים, וְנִכְבְּדֵיהֶם בְּכַבְלֵי בַרְזֶל:
לַעֲשׂוֹת בָּהֶם מִשְׁפָּט כָּתוּב, הָדָר הוּא לְכָל־חֲסִידָיו, הַלְלוּיָהּ:

הַלְלוּיָהּ תהלים קנ
הַלְלוּ־אֵל בְּקָדְשׁוֹ, הַלְלוּהוּ בִּרְקִיעַ עֻזּוֹ:
הַלְלוּהוּ בִגְבוּרֹתָיו, הַלְלוּהוּ כְּרֹב גֻּדְלוֹ:
הַלְלוּהוּ בְּתֵקַע שׁוֹפָר, הַלְלוּהוּ בְּנֵבֶל וְכִנּוֹר:
הַלְלוּהוּ בְּתֹף וּמָחוֹל, הַלְלוּהוּ בְּמִנִּים וְעֻגָב:
הַלְלוּהוּ בְצִלְצְלֵי־שָׁמַע, הַלְלוּהוּ בְּצִלְצְלֵי תְרוּעָה: ◄
כֹּל הַנְּשָׁמָה תְּהַלֵּל יָהּ, הַלְלוּיָהּ:
כֹּל הַנְּשָׁמָה תְּהַלֵּל יָהּ, הַלְלוּיָהּ:

---

הַלְלוּיָהּ *Psalm 149.* For the most part Psalms 145–150 are about God in creation. This psalm speaks about God in history. It is a song celebrating a military victory. The people describe themselves not as soldiers but as *ḥasidim*, God's "devoted" ones (the word appears three times in the psalm), and the song is the corollary of the verse in Psalm 147, which says that God "does not take delight in the strength of horses nor pleasure in the fleetness of man." This, the second-from-last psalm, also mirrors the second psalm, which speaks about the hubris of kings who believe they can defeat God. This psalm testifies to the opposite: it is "the humble" who are "adorned with salvation."

הַלְלוּיָהּ *Psalm 150.* A sustained shout for joy that brings the book of Psalms to a close on a musical crescendo. In ancient times this psalm was said by pilgrims bringing first fruits to Jerusalem, when they reached the Temple

בָּרוּךְ Blessed be the LORD for ever. Amen and Amen. Ps. 89
Blessed from Zion be the LORD who dwells in Jerusalem. Halleluya! Ps. 135
Blessed be the LORD, God of Israel, who alone does wonders. Ps. 72
▸ Blessed be His glorious name for ever,
and may all the earth be filled with His glory.
Amen and Amen.

*Stand until "The soul" on page 304.*

וַיְבָרֶךְ David blessed the LORD in front of the entire assembly. David said, "Blessed are You, LORD, God of our father Yisrael, for ever and ever. Yours, LORD, are the greatness and the power, the glory, majesty and splendor, for everything in heaven and earth is Yours. Yours, LORD, is the kingdom; You are exalted as Head over all. Both riches and honor are in Your gift and You reign over all things. In Your hand are strength and might. It is in Your power to make great and give strength to all. Therefore, our God, we thank You and praise Your glorious name." *1 Chr. 29* Let them bless Your revered name, exalted above all blessing and praise. You alone are the LORD. You made the heavens, even the highest heavens, and all their hosts, the earth and all that is on it, the seas and all they contain. You give life to them all, and the hosts of heaven worship You. ▸ You are the LORD God who chose Abram and brought him out of Ur of the Chaldees, changing his name to Abraham. You found his heart faithful toward You, ◂ and You made a covenant with him to give to his descendants *Neh. 9*

---

the Ark to it. Now at the end of his life he assembled the people and charged them with the sacred task of building the Temple. In the second, after the Babylonian exile, Ezra and Nehemiah summoned the people to reaffirm their historic covenant with God. The third, after the Israelites had crossed the Sea of Reeds, was the moment when they left the land over which Pharaoh ruled. They were now God's people, under His sole domain. Common to all three passages is that they were said at historic moments when the people pledged themselves to be defined as a nation bound together by a sacred task.

Instead of simply moving from individual to communal worship, the Siddur takes us through three transformative moments in Jewish history when the people constituted themselves as a nation dedicated to the service of God. They were no longer mere individuals (returning exiles, escaping slaves) but a group, a nation, a community of faith.

בָּרוּךְ יהוה לְעוֹלָם, אָמֵן וְאָמֵן: תהלים פט

בָּרוּךְ יהוה מִצִּיּוֹן, שֹׁכֵן יְרוּשָׁלָםִ, הַלְלוּיָהּ: תהלים קלה

בָּרוּךְ יהוה אֱלֹהִים אֱלֹהֵי יִשְׂרָאֵל, עֹשֵׂה נִפְלָאוֹת לְבַדּוֹ: תהלים עב

וּבָרוּךְ שֵׁם כְּבוֹדוֹ לְעוֹלָם

וְיִמָּלֵא כְבוֹדוֹ אֶת־כׇּל־הָאָרֶץ, אָמֵן וְאָמֵן:

*Stand until* נִשְׁמַת *on page 305.*

דברי הימים א׳ כט וַיְבָרֶךְ דָּוִיד אֶת־יהוה לְעֵינֵי כׇּל־הַקָּהָל, וַיֹּאמֶר דָּוִיד, בָּרוּךְ אַתָּה
יהוה, אֱלֹהֵי יִשְׂרָאֵל אָבִינוּ, מֵעוֹלָם וְעַד־עוֹלָם: לְךָ יהוה הַגְּדֻלָּה
וְהַגְּבוּרָה וְהַתִּפְאֶרֶת וְהַנֵּצַח וְהַהוֹד, כִּי־כֹל בַּשָּׁמַיִם וּבָאָרֶץ,
לְךָ יהוה הַמַּמְלָכָה וְהַמִּתְנַשֵּׂא לְכֹל לְרֹאשׁ: וְהָעֹשֶׁר וְהַכָּבוֹד
מִלְּפָנֶיךָ, וְאַתָּה מוֹשֵׁל בַּכֹּל, וּבְיָדְךָ כֹּחַ וּגְבוּרָה, וּבְיָדְךָ לְגַדֵּל
וּלְחַזֵּק לַכֹּל: וְעַתָּה אֱלֹהֵינוּ מוֹדִים אֲנַחְנוּ לָךְ, וּמְהַלְלִים לְשֵׁם
נחמיה ט תִּפְאַרְתֶּךָ: וִיבָרְכוּ שֵׁם כְּבֹדֶךָ, וּמְרוֹמַם עַל־כׇּל־בְּרָכָה
וּתְהִלָּה: אַתָּה־הוּא יהוה לְבַדֶּךָ, אַתָּ עָשִׂיתָ אֶת־הַשָּׁמַיִם, שְׁמֵי
הַשָּׁמַיִם וְכׇל־צְבָאָם, הָאָרֶץ וְכׇל־אֲשֶׁר עָלֶיהָ, הַיַּמִּים וְכׇל־אֲשֶׁר
בָּהֶם, וְאַתָּה מְחַיֶּה אֶת־כֻּלָּם, וּצְבָא הַשָּׁמַיִם לְךָ מִשְׁתַּחֲוִים:
◂ אַתָּה הוּא יהוה הָאֱלֹהִים אֲשֶׁר בָּחַרְתָּ בְּאַבְרָם, וְהוֹצֵאתוֹ מֵאוּר
כַּשְׂדִּים, וְשַׂמְתָּ שְּׁמוֹ אַבְרָהָם: וּמָצָאתָ אֶת־לְבָבוֹ נֶאֱמָן לְפָנֶיךָ, ◂

---

וַיְבָרֶךְ דָּוִיד *David blessed.* The first of three passages marking historic transitions in the history of Israel: (1) King David's prayer for the building of the Temple, (2) the prayer said at the gathering convened by Ezra after the return from the Babylonian exile (Neh. 9), and (3) the song Moses and the Israelites sang at the Sea of Reeds, after the waters had miraculously divided, allowing them to cross to safety.

One reason for their presence here is that thus far we have prayed as individuals. Communal prayer is about to begin. The three historic passages are about the constitution of a *community* of prayer.

In the first, David had made Jerusalem the capital of the nation and brought

the land of the Canaanites, Hittites, Amorites, Perizzites, Jebusites and Girgashites. You fulfilled Your promise for You are righteous. You saw the suffering of our ancestors in Egypt. You heard their cry at the Sea of Reeds. You sent signs and wonders against Pharaoh, all his servants and all the people of his land, because You knew how arrogantly the Egyptians treated them. You created for Yourself renown that remains to this day. ▸ You divided the sea before them, so that they passed through the sea on dry land, but You cast their pursuers into the depths, like a stone into mighty waters.

וַיּֽוֹשַׁע That day the Lord saved Israel from the hands of the Egyptians, and Israel saw the Egyptians lying dead on the seashore. ▸ When Israel saw the great power the Lord had displayed against the Egyptians, the people feared the Lord, and believed in the Lord and in His servant, Moses. *Ex. 14*

אָז יָשִׁיר־מֹשֶׁה Then Moses and the Israelites sang this song to the *Ex. 15*
Lord, saying:
I will sing to the Lord, for He has triumphed gloriously;
horse and rider He has hurled into the sea.
The Lord is my strength and song; He has become my salvation.
This is my God, and I will beautify Him,
my father's God, and I will exalt Him.
The Lord is a Master of war; Lord is His name.
Pharaoh's chariots and army He cast into the sea;
the best of his officers drowned in the Sea of Reeds.
The deep waters covered them;
they went down to the depths like a stone.
Your right hand, Lord, is majestic in power.
Your right hand, Lord, shatters the enemy.
In the greatness of Your majesty, You overthrew those who rose against You.
You sent out Your fury; it consumed them like stubble.
By the blast of Your nostrils the waters piled up.
The surging waters stood straight like a wall;
the deeps congealed in the heart of the sea.
The enemy said, "I will pursue. I will overtake. I will divide the spoil.

וְכָרוֹת עִמּוֹ הַבְּרִית לָתֵת אֶת־אֶרֶץ הַכְּנַעֲנִי הַחִתִּי הָאֱמֹרִי וְהַפְּרִזִּי
וְהַיְבוּסִי וְהַגִּרְגָּשִׁי, לָתֵת לְזַרְעוֹ, וַתָּקֶם אֶת־דְּבָרֶיךָ, כִּי צַדִּיק אָתָּה:
וַתֵּרֶא אֶת־עֳנִי אֲבֹתֵינוּ בְּמִצְרָיִם, וְאֶת־זַעֲקָתָם שָׁמַעְתָּ עַל־יַם־
סוּף: וַתִּתֵּן אֹתֹת וּמֹפְתִים בְּפַרְעֹה וּבְכָל־עֲבָדָיו וּבְכָל־עַם אַרְצוֹ, כִּי
יָדַעְתָּ כִּי הֵזִידוּ עֲלֵיהֶם, וַתַּעַשׂ־לְךָ שֵׁם כְּהַיּוֹם הַזֶּה: ◂ וְהַיָּם בָּקַעְתָּ
לִפְנֵיהֶם, וַיַּעַבְרוּ בְתוֹךְ־הַיָּם בַּיַּבָּשָׁה, וְאֶת־רֹדְפֵיהֶם הִשְׁלַכְתָּ
בִמְצוֹלֹת כְּמוֹ־אֶבֶן, בְּמַיִם עַזִּים:

וַיּוֹשַׁע יהוה בַּיּוֹם הַהוּא אֶת־יִשְׂרָאֵל מִיַּד מִצְרָיִם, וַיַּרְא יִשְׂרָאֵל שמות יד
אֶת־מִצְרַיִם מֵת עַל־שְׂפַת הַיָּם: ◂ וַיַּרְא יִשְׂרָאֵל אֶת־הַיָּד הַגְּדֹלָה
אֲשֶׁר עָשָׂה יהוה בְּמִצְרַיִם, וַיִּירְאוּ הָעָם אֶת־יהוה, וַיַּאֲמִינוּ בַּיהוה
וּבְמֹשֶׁה עַבְדּוֹ:

אָז יָשִׁיר־מֹשֶׁה וּבְנֵי יִשְׂרָאֵל אֶת־הַשִּׁירָה הַזֹּאת לַיהוה, וַיֹּאמְרוּ שמות טו
לֵאמֹר, אָשִׁירָה לַיהוה כִּי־גָאֹה גָּאָה, סוּס
וְרֹכְבוֹ רָמָה בַיָּם: עָזִּי וְזִמְרָת יָהּ וַיְהִי־לִי
לִישׁוּעָה, זֶה אֵלִי וְאַנְוֵהוּ, אֱלֹהֵי
אָבִי וַאֲרֹמְמֶנְהוּ: יהוה אִישׁ מִלְחָמָה, יהוה
שְׁמוֹ: מַרְכְּבֹת פַּרְעֹה וְחֵילוֹ יָרָה בַיָּם, וּמִבְחַר
שָׁלִשָׁיו טֻבְּעוּ בְיַם־סוּף: תְּהֹמֹת יְכַסְיֻמוּ, יָרְדוּ בִמְצוֹלֹת כְּמוֹ־
אָבֶן: יְמִינְךָ יהוה נֶאְדָּרִי בַּכֹּחַ, יְמִינְךָ
יהוה תִּרְעַץ אוֹיֵב: וּבְרֹב גְּאוֹנְךָ תַּהֲרֹס
קָמֶיךָ, תְּשַׁלַּח חֲרֹנְךָ יֹאכְלֵמוֹ כַּקַּשׁ: וּבְרוּחַ
אַפֶּיךָ נֶעֶרְמוּ מַיִם, נִצְּבוּ כְמוֹ־נֵד
נֹזְלִים, קָפְאוּ תְהֹמֹת בְּלֶב־יָם: אָמַר
אוֹיֵב אֶרְדֹּף, אַשִּׂיג, אֲחַלֵּק שָׁלָל, תִּמְלָאֵמוֹ

My desire shall have its fill of them.
I will draw my sword. My hand will destroy them."
You blew with Your wind; the sea covered them.
They sank in the mighty waters like lead.
Who is like You, LORD, among the mighty?
Who is like You – majestic in holiness, awesome in glory,
working wonders?
You stretched out Your right hand,
the earth swallowed them.
In Your loving-kindness, You led the people You redeemed.
In Your strength, You guided them to Your holy abode.
Nations heard and trembled;
terror gripped Philistia's inhabitants.
The chiefs of Edom were dismayed,
Moab's leaders were seized with trembling,
the people of Canaan melted away.
Fear and dread fell upon them.
By the power of Your arm, they were still as stone –
until Your people crossed, LORD,
until the people You acquired crossed over.
You will bring them and plant them on the mountain of Your heritage –
the place, LORD, You made for Your dwelling,
the Sanctuary, LORD, Your hands established.
The LORD will reign for ever and all time.
The LORD will reign for ever and all time.
The LORD's kingship is established
for ever and to all eternity.

When Pharaoh's horses, chariots and riders went into the sea,
the LORD brought the waters of the sea back over them,
but the Israelites walked on dry land through the sea.

▸ For kingship is the LORD's and He rules over the nations. *Ps. 22*
Saviors shall go up to Mount Zion to judge Mount Esau, *Ob. 1*
and the LORD's shall be the kingdom.
Then the LORD shall be King over all the earth; *Zech. 14*
on that day the LORD shall be One and His name One,

נַפְשִׁי, אָרִיק חַרְבִּי תּוֹרִישֵׁמוֹ יָדִי: נָשַׁפְתָּ
בְרוּחֲךָ כִּסָּמוֹ יָם, צָלֲלוּ כַּעוֹפֶרֶת בְּמַיִם
אַדִּירִים: מִי־כָמֹכָה בָּאֵלִם יהוה, מִי
כָּמֹכָה נֶאְדָּר בַּקֹּדֶשׁ, נוֹרָא תְהִלֹּת עֹשֵׂה
פֶלֶא: נָטִיתָ יְמִינְךָ תִּבְלָעֵמוֹ אָרֶץ: נָחִיתָ
בְחַסְדְּךָ עַם־זוּ גָּאָלְתָּ, נֵהַלְתָּ בְעָזְּךָ אֶל־נְוֵה
קָדְשֶׁךָ: שָׁמְעוּ עַמִּים יִרְגָּזוּן, חִיל
אָחַז יֹשְׁבֵי פְּלָשֶׁת: אָז נִבְהֲלוּ אַלּוּפֵי
אֱדוֹם, אֵילֵי מוֹאָב יֹאחֲזֵמוֹ רָעַד, נָמֹגוּ
כֹּל יֹשְׁבֵי כְנָעַן: תִּפֹּל עֲלֵיהֶם אֵימָתָה
וָפַחַד, בִּגְדֹל זְרוֹעֲךָ יִדְּמוּ כָּאָבֶן, עַד־
יַעֲבֹר עַמְּךָ יהוה, עַד־יַעֲבֹר עַם־זוּ
קָנִיתָ: תְּבִאֵמוֹ וְתִטָּעֵמוֹ בְּהַר נַחֲלָתְךָ, מָכוֹן
לְשִׁבְתְּךָ פָּעַלְתָּ יהוה, מִקְּדָשׁ אֲדֹנָי כּוֹנְנוּ
יָדֶיךָ: יהוה יִמְלֹךְ לְעֹלָם וָעֶד:

יהוה יִמְלֹךְ לְעֹלָם וָעֶד.
יהוה מַלְכוּתֵהּ קָאֵם לְעָלַם וּלְעָלְמֵי עָלְמַיָּא.

כִּי
בָא סוּס פַּרְעֹה בְּרִכְבּוֹ וּבְפָרָשָׁיו בַּיָּם, וַיָּשֶׁב יהוה עֲלֵהֶם אֶת־מֵי
הַיָּם, וּבְנֵי יִשְׂרָאֵל הָלְכוּ בַיַּבָּשָׁה בְּתוֹךְ הַיָּם:

▸ כִּי לַיהוה הַמְּלוּכָה וּמֹשֵׁל בַּגּוֹיִם: תהלים כב
וְעָלוּ מוֹשִׁעִים בְּהַר צִיּוֹן לִשְׁפֹּט אֶת־הַר עֵשָׂו עובדיה א
וְהָיְתָה לַיהוה הַמְּלוּכָה:
וְהָיָה יהוה לְמֶלֶךְ עַל־כָּל־הָאָרֶץ זכריה יד
בַּיּוֹם הַהוּא יִהְיֶה יהוה אֶחָד וּשְׁמוֹ אֶחָד:

# THE SOUL

of all that lives shall bless Your name, LORD our God,
and the spirit of all flesh shall always glorify
and exalt Your remembrance, our King.
From eternity to eternity You are God.
Without You, we have no King, Redeemer or Savior,
who liberates, rescues, sustains, responds
and shows compassion in every time of trouble and distress.
We have no King to help and support us but You,
God of the first and last, God of all creatures, Master of all ages,
extolled by a multitude of praises,
who guides His world with loving-kindness
and His creatures with compassion.
The LORD is awake; He neither slumbers nor sleeps. *Ps. 121*
He rouses the sleepers and wakens the slumberers.
He makes the dumb speak, sets the bound free,
supports the fallen, raises those bowed down
and reveals what is hidden.
To You alone we give thanks;
and if our mouths were as full of song as the sea,
and our tongue with jubilation as its myriad waves,
if our lips were full of praise like the spacious heavens,
and our eyes shone like the sun and moon,
if our hands were outstretched like eagles of the sky,
and our feet as swift as hinds – still we could not thank You enough,
LORD our God and God of our ancestors,
or bless Your name, our King,
for even one of the thousand thousands
and myriad myriads of favors, miracles and wonders
You have done for our ancestors and us.

---

to the recitation of Psalms. The second part, beginning "To You alone we give thanks," is mentioned in the Talmud (*Berakhot* 59b) as a thanksgiving prayer for rain.

The first section is an extended meditation on the last words of the book of Psalms: "Let all that breathes praise the LORD." Hebrew has many words for

# נִשְׁמַת

כָּל חַי תְּבָרֵךְ אֶת שִׁמְךָ, יהוה אֱלֹהֵינוּ
וְרוּחַ כָּל בָּשָׂר תְּפָאֵר וּתְרוֹמֵם זִכְרְךָ מַלְכֵּנוּ תָּמִיד.
מִן הָעוֹלָם וְעַד הָעוֹלָם אַתָּה אֵל
וּמִבַּלְעָדֶיךָ אֵין לָנוּ מֶלֶךְ גּוֹאֵל וּמוֹשִׁיעַ
פּוֹדֶה וּמַצִּיל וּמְפַרְנֵס וְעוֹנֶה וּמְרַחֵם
בְּכָל עֵת צָרָה וְצוּקָה אֵין לָנוּ מֶלֶךְ עוֹזֵר וְסוֹמֵךְ אֶלָּא אָתָּה.
אֱלֹהֵי הָרִאשׁוֹנִים וְהָאַחֲרוֹנִים, אֱלוֹהַּ כָּל בְּרִיּוֹת
אֲדוֹן כָּל תּוֹלָדוֹת, הַמְהֻלָּל בְּרֹב הַתִּשְׁבָּחוֹת
הַמְנַהֵג עוֹלָמוֹ בְּחֶסֶד וּבְרִיּוֹתָיו בְּרַחֲמִים.
וַיהוה עֵר, הִנֵּה לֹא־יָנוּם וְלֹא יִישָׁן: תהלים קכא
הַמְעוֹרֵר יְשֵׁנִים וְהַמֵּקִיץ נִרְדָּמִים
וְהַמֵּשִׂיחַ אִלְּמִים וְהַמַּתִּיר אֲסוּרִים
וְהַסּוֹמֵךְ נוֹפְלִים וְהַזּוֹקֵף כְּפוּפִים וְהַמְפַעְנֵחַ נֶעְלָמִים
וּלְךָ לְבַדְּךָ אֲנַחְנוּ מוֹדִים
וְאִלּוּ פִינוּ מָלֵא שִׁירָה כַּיָּם, וּלְשׁוֹנֵנוּ רִנָּה כַּהֲמוֹן גַּלָּיו
וְשִׂפְתוֹתֵינוּ שֶׁבַח כְּמֶרְחֲבֵי רָקִיעַ, וְעֵינֵינוּ מְאִירוֹת כַּשֶּׁמֶשׁ וְכַיָּרֵחַ
וְיָדֵינוּ פְרוּשׂוֹת כְּנִשְׁרֵי שָׁמָיִם, וְרַגְלֵינוּ קַלּוֹת כָּאַיָּלוֹת
אֵין אֲנַחְנוּ מַסְפִּיקִים לְהוֹדוֹת לְךָ יהוה אֱלֹהֵינוּ וֵאלֹהֵי אֲבוֹתֵינוּ
וּלְבָרֵךְ אֶת שִׁמְךָ, מַלְכֵּנוּ
עַל אַחַת מֵאֶלֶף אֶלֶף אַלְפֵי אֲלָפִים, וְרִבֵּי רְבָבוֹת פְּעָמִים הַטּוֹבוֹת
נִסִּים וְנִפְלָאוֹת שֶׁעָשִׂיתָ עִם אֲבוֹתֵינוּ וְעִמָּנוּ.

---

נִשְׁמַת *The soul of all that lives.* This magnificent poem is composed of two parts. The first, according to Rabbi Yoḥanan, is the "blessing of the song" mentioned in the Mishna as a conclusion to saying Hallel in the Seder service on Pesaḥ (*Pesaḥim* 118a). Just as there, so here, it stands as a conclusion

You redeemed us from Egypt long ago, LORD our God,
and freed us from the house of bondage.
In famine You nourished us; in times of plenty You sustained us.
You delivered us from the sword, saved us from the plague,
and spared us from many serious, lasting illnesses.
Until now Your mercies have helped us.
Your love has not forsaken us, LORD our God.
May You, LORD our God, never abandon us.
Therefore the limbs You formed within us,
the spirit and soul You breathed into our nostrils,
and the tongue You placed in our mouth –
they will thank and bless, praise, glorify and sing, exalt and esteem,
hallow and do homage to Your name, O our King, always.
For every mouth shall give thanks to You,
every tongue vow allegiance to You, every eye shall watch for You,
every knee shall bend to You, every upright body shall bow to You,
all hearts shall fear You, and our innermost being
sing praises to Your name, as is written:

"All my bones shall say: LORD, who is like You? *Ps. 35*
You save the poor from one stronger than him,
the poor and needy from one who would rob him."

It is You who hear the pleading of the poor;
You will listen to the cries of the destitute and save them.
Who is like You? Who is equal to You? Who can be compared to You?
O great, mighty and awesome God, God Most High,
Maker of heaven and earth.
▸ We will laud, praise and glorify You and bless Your holy name,
as it is said:

"Of David. Bless the LORD, O my soul, *Ps. 103*
and all that is within me bless His holy name."

God – in Your absolute power, Great – in the glory of Your name,
Mighty – for ever, Awesome – in Your awe-inspiring deeds,

---

do in a state of rest. In the still silence of the turning world it is as if we hear all that lives singing a song of praise to God who brought the universe into being, sustains it, and guides the destinies of all things.

מִלְּפָנִים מִמִּצְרַיִם גְּאַלְתָּנוּ, יהוה אֱלֹהֵינוּ, וּמִבֵּית עֲבָדִים פְּדִיתָנוּ
בְּרָעָב זַנְתָּנוּ וּבְשָׂבָע כִּלְכַּלְתָּנוּ, מֵחֶרֶב הִצַּלְתָּנוּ וּמִדֶּבֶר מִלַּטְתָּנוּ
וּמֵחֳלָיִים רָעִים וְרַבִּים וְנֶאֱמָנִים דִּלִּיתָנוּ.
עַד הֵנָּה עֲזָרוּנוּ רַחֲמֶיךָ, וְלֹא עֲזָבוּנוּ חֲסָדֶיךָ, יהוה אֱלֹהֵינוּ
וְאַל תִּטְּשֵׁנוּ, יהוה אֱלֹהֵינוּ, לָנֶצַח.
עַל כֵּן אֵבָרִים שֶׁפִּלַּגְתָּ בָּנוּ
וְרוּחַ וּנְשָׁמָה שֶׁנָּפַחְתָּ בְּאַפֵּינוּ, וְלָשׁוֹן אֲשֶׁר שַׂמְתָּ בְּפִינוּ
הֵן הֵם יוֹדוּ וִיבָרְכוּ וִישַׁבְּחוּ וִיפָאֲרוּ וִישׁוֹרְרוּ
וִירוֹמְמוּ וְיַעֲרִיצוּ וְיַקְדִּישׁוּ וְיַמְלִיכוּ אֶת שִׁמְךָ מַלְכֵּנוּ תָּמִיד
כִּי כָל פֶּה לְךָ יוֹדֶה וְכָל לָשׁוֹן לְךָ תִשָּׁבַע וְכָל עַיִן לְךָ תְצַפֶּה
וְכָל בֶּרֶךְ לְךָ תִכְרַע וְכָל קוֹמָה לְפָנֶיךָ תִשְׁתַּחֲוֶה
וְכָל הַלְּבָבוֹת יִירָאוּךָ וְכָל קֶרֶב וּכְלָיוֹת יְזַמְּרוּ לִשְׁמֶךָ
כַּדָּבָר שֶׁכָּתוּב

תהלים לה כָּל עַצְמֹתַי תֹּאמַרְנָה יהוה מִי כָמוֹךָ
מַצִּיל עָנִי מֵחָזָק מִמֶּנּוּ, וְעָנִי וְאֶבְיוֹן מִגֹּזְלוֹ:

שַׁוְעַת עֲנִיִּים אַתָּה תִשְׁמַע, צַעֲקַת הַדַּל תַּקְשִׁיב וְתוֹשִׁיעַ.
מִי יִדְמֶה לָּךְ וּמִי יִשְׁוֶה לָּךְ וּמִי יַעֲרָךְ לָךְ.
הָאֵל הַגָּדוֹל, הַגִּבּוֹר וְהַנּוֹרָא, אֵל עֶלְיוֹן, קוֹנֵה שָׁמַיִם וָאָרֶץ.
נְהַלֶּלְךָ וּנְשַׁבֵּחֲךָ וּנְפָאֶרְךָ וּנְבָרֵךְ אֶת שֵׁם קָדְשֶׁךָ
כָּאָמוּר

תהלים קג לְדָוִד, בָּרְכִי נַפְשִׁי אֶת־יהוה, וְכָל־קְרָבַי אֶת־שֵׁם קָדְשׁוֹ:

הָאֵל בְּתַעֲצוּמוֹת עֻזֶּךָ
הַגָּדוֹל בִּכְבוֹד שְׁמֶךָ
הַגִּבּוֹר לָנֶצַח וְהַנּוֹרָא בְּנוֹרְאוֹתֶיךָ

---

soul, all deriving from verbs related to breathing. *Neshama* – the word linking this passage to the end of Psalms, means to breathe deeply, as we are able to

*The Leader for Shaharit begins here:*

# THE KING –

who sits on a throne, high and lofty
He inhabits eternity; exalted and holy is His name.
And it is written:
Sing joyfully to the LORD, you righteous, *Ps. 33*
for praise from the upright is seemly.

| | | |
|---|---|---|
| ▸ By the mouth | of the upright | You shall be extolled. |
| By the lips | of the righteous | You shall be blessed. |
| By the tongue | of the devout | You shall be sanctified, |
| And in the midst | of the holy | You shall be praised. |

וּבְמַקְהֲלוֹת And in the assemblies
of tens of thousands of Your people, the house of Israel,
with joyous song shall Your name, our King,
be glorified in every generation.
▸ For this is the duty of all creatures before You,
LORD our God and God of our ancestors:
to thank, praise, laud, glorify, exalt,
honor, celebrate, bless, raise high and acclaim –
even beyond all the words of song and praise
of David, son of Jesse, Your servant, Your anointed.

---

הַמֶּלֶךְ *The King.* In a brilliant stroke, without changing a word of the usual Shabbat and festival prayers at this point, the overarching theme of Rosh HaShana – God's kingship – is signaled by the emphasis placed on this one word, *HaMelekh*, "the King," often by the main *shaliah tzibbur* taking over at this point, sometimes singing the word as he ascends the *bima*, and by the music itself which begins softly in a minor key and rises to a triumphant major. This practice dates back to Rabbi Meir of Rothenburg in the thirteenth century.

וּבְמַקְהֲלוֹת *And in the assemblies.* The list of nine words for praise corresponds to the nine additional psalms we say on Sabbaths and festivals. The word "assemblies" refers to the large congregations present in synagogues on holy days, reminding us of the Temple, full at such times.

*The* שליח ציבור *for* שחרית *begins here:*

# הַמֶּֽלֶךְ

יוֹשֵׁב עַל כִּסֵּא, רָם וְנִשָּׂא

שׁוֹכֵן עַד, מָרוֹם וְקָדוֹשׁ שְׁמוֹ

וְכָתוּב

רַנְּנוּ צַדִּיקִים בַּיהוה, לַיְשָׁרִים נָאוָה תְהִלָּה: תהלים לג

| | | |
|---|---|---|
| ◂ בְּפִי | יְשָׁרִים | תִּתְרוֹמָם |
| וּבְשִׂפְתֵי | צַדִּיקִים | תִּתְבָּרַךְ |
| וּבִלְשׁוֹן | חֲסִידִים | תִּתְקַדָּשׁ |
| וּבְקֶרֶב | קְדוֹשִׁים | תִּתְהַלָּל |

וּבְמַקְהֲלוֹת רִבְבוֹת עַמְּךָ בֵּית יִשְׂרָאֵל

בְּרִנָּה יִתְפָּאַר שִׁמְךָ מַלְכֵּנוּ בְּכָל דּוֹר וָדוֹר

◂ שֶׁכֵּן חוֹבַת כָּל הַיְצוּרִים

לְפָנֶיךָ יהוה אֱלֹהֵינוּ וֵאלֹהֵי אֲבוֹתֵינוּ

לְהוֹדוֹת, לְהַלֵּל, לְשַׁבֵּחַ, לְפָאֵר, לְרוֹמֵם

לְהַדֵּר וּלְנַצֵּחַ, לְבָרֵךְ לְעַלֵּה וּלְקַלֵּס

עַל כָּל דִּבְרֵי שִׁירוֹת וְתִשְׁבְּחוֹת

דָּוִד בֶּן יִשַׁי, עַבְדְּךָ מְשִׁיחֶךָ.

---

The second section is composed around a phrase from Psalms: "All my bones shall say, LORD, who is like You?" – thus ingeniously linking the psalms of praise with the Song at the Sea, which contains the same phrase "Who is like You?" Through a fine series of images, the poet expresses the human inability to adequately thank God, itemizing how the various limbs ("All my bones") may praise Him.

*Stand until after "Barekhu" on page 314.*

וּבְכֵן יִשְׁתַּבַּח May Your name, then, be praised for ever, our King,
the great and holy God, King in heaven and on earth.
For to You, LORD our God and God of our ancestors,
it is right to offer song and praise, hymn and psalm,
strength and dominion, eternity, greatness and power,
song of praise and glory, holiness and kingship,
▸ blessings and thanks to Your great and holy name,
and for all eternities You are God.
Blessed are You, LORD, God and King, exalted and acclaimed in praises,
God of thanksgivings, Master of wonders,
Creator of all souls, Ruler over all that He has made,
He who delights in hymns of song,
King, Only One, God, Giver of life to the worlds.

*The Ark is opened and this psalm is said responsively, verse by verse.*

שִׁיר הַמַּעֲלוֹת A song of ascents. *Ps. 130*
From the depths I have called to You, LORD.
LORD, hear my voice; let Your ears be attentive to my plea.
If You, LORD, should keep account of sins: O LORD, who could stand?
But with You there is forgiveness, that You may be held in awe.

---

In one of his sermons, Rabbi Joseph Soloveitchik spoke about a Jewish doctor, an atheist, who wrote about his experiences in a concentration camp in Latvia. The labor was backbreaking, the conditions unbearable. Few survived. Among the prisoners was a group of yeshiva students together with their teacher, followers of the *Musar* school of Novardok. Each night, returning to the barracks the rabbi and his students would sit on the ground and recite Psalm 130, *From the depths I have called to You, LORD*. The doctor wrote that he would have given his life to have the faith to recite psalms under such circumstances (*Derashot HaRav*, pp. 120–21*).

מִמַּעֲמַקִּים *From the depths:* the Psalmist, in the midst of despair, compares himself to a drowning man crying out for rescue from the depths of the sea. כִּי־עִמְּךָ הַסְּלִיחָה, לְמַעַן תִּוָּרֵא *But with You there is forgiveness, that You may be held in awe.* Who inspires deeper fear: One who rejects us, or One who refuses to reject us? One who rejects us makes no more demands on us. We go our

* Arnold Lustiger, *Derashot HaRav* (Edison, NJ: Ohr Publishers, 2003).

*Stand until after* בָּרְכוּ *on page 315.*

וּבְכֵן יִשְׁתַּבַּח שִׁמְךָ לָעַד, מַלְכֵּנוּ
הָאֵל, הַמֶּלֶךְ, הַגָּדוֹל וְהַקָּדוֹשׁ בַּשָּׁמַיִם וּבָאָרֶץ
כִּי לְךָ נָאֶה, יהוה אֱלֹהֵינוּ וֵאלֹהֵי אֲבוֹתֵינוּ
שִׁיר וּשְׁבָחָה, הַלֵּל וְזִמְרָה
עֹז וּמֶמְשָׁלָה, נֶצַח, גְּדֻלָּה וּגְבוּרָה
תְּהִלָּה וְתִפְאֶרֶת, קְדֻשָּׁה וּמַלְכוּת
בְּרָכוֹת וְהוֹדָאוֹת לְשִׁמְךָ הַגָּדוֹל וְהַקָּדוֹשׁ
וּמֵעוֹלָם וְעַד עוֹלָם אַתָּה אֵל.
בָּרוּךְ אַתָּה יהוה, אֵל מֶלֶךְ גָּדוֹל וּמְהֻלָּל בַּתִּשְׁבָּחוֹת
אֵל הַהוֹדָאוֹת, אֲדוֹן הַנִּפְלָאוֹת
בּוֹרֵא כָּל הַנְּשָׁמוֹת, רִבּוֹן כָּל הַמַּעֲשִׂים
הַבּוֹחֵר בְּשִׁירֵי זִמְרָה, מֶלֶךְ, יָחִיד, אֵל, חֵי הָעוֹלָמִים.

*The* ארון קודש *is opened and this psalm is said responsively, verse by verse.*

שִׁיר הַמַּעֲלוֹת, מִמַּעֲמַקִּים קְרָאתִיךָ יהוה: תהלים קל
אֲדֹנָי שִׁמְעָה בְקוֹלִי, תִּהְיֶינָה אָזְנֶיךָ קַשֻּׁבוֹת לְקוֹל תַּחֲנוּנָי:
אִם־עֲוֹנוֹת תִּשְׁמָר־יָהּ, אֲדֹנָי מִי יַעֲמֹד:
כִּי־עִמְּךָ הַסְּלִיחָה, לְמַעַן תִּוָּרֵא:

---

**וּבְכֵן יִשְׁתַּבַּח שִׁמְךָ לָעַד** *May Your name, then, be praised for ever.* The concluding blessing over the Verses of Praise which, like the introductory blessing, is said standing. The fifteen terms of glorification equal the number of "Songs of Ascents."

**שִׁיר הַמַּעֲלוֹת** *Psalm 130.* It is customary to say this psalm responsively. The connection with the Days of Awe is obvious: this is one of the supreme penitential psalms, known outside Judaism by the Latin translation, *De Profundis,* "from the depths." In Israel in early times it was this prayer, rather than *Kol Nidrei,* with which the evening service of Yom Kippur began.

I wait for the Lord, my soul waits, and in His word I put my hope.
My soul waits for the Lord more than watchmen wait for the morning,
more than watchmen wait for the morning.
Israel, put your hope in the Lord,
for with the Lord there is loving-kindness,
and great is His power to redeem.
It is He who will redeem Israel from all their sins.

*The Ark is closed.*

### HALF KADDISH

*Leader:* יִתְגַּדַּל Magnified and sanctified may His great name be,
in the world He created by His will.
May He establish His kingdom,
make His salvation flourish, and hasten His messiah,
in your lifetime and in your days,
and in the lifetime of all the house of Israel,
swiftly and soon – and say: Amen.

*All:* May His great name be blessed for ever and all time.

*Leader:* Blessed and praised, glorified and exalted,
raised and honored, uplifted and lauded
be the name of the Holy One, blessed be He,
beyond any blessing, song, praise and consolation
uttered in the world – and say: Amen.

---

Good morning, Master of the Universe. I, Levi Yitzḥak son of Sarah from Berditchev, approach You with a grievance on behalf of Your people, Israel.

What do You have against Israel? Why have You imposed Yourself on Israel? In everything it is, "Command the children of Israel," "Speak to the children of Israel."

Merciful Father, there are many nations in the world: Persians, Babylonians, Romans. What do the Russians say? Their ruler is the Czar. What do the Germans say? Their ruler is the Kaiser. What do the English say? Their ruler is the king.

But I, Levi Yitzḥak son of Sarah from Berditchev, say: You are *HaMelekh yoshev al kiseh ram venisa*, "The King who sits on a throne, high and lofty," and I will not leave this place until there is an end to the Exile.

*Yitgadal veyitkadash shemeh raba*, "Magnified and sanctified may His great name be…"

קִוִּיתִי יהוה קִוְּתָה נַפְשִׁי, וְלִדְבָרוֹ הוֹחָלְתִּי:
נַפְשִׁי לַאדֹנָי, מִשֹּׁמְרִים לַבֹּקֶר, שֹׁמְרִים לַבֹּקֶר:
יַחֵל יִשְׂרָאֵל אֶל־יהוה, כִּי־עִם־יהוה הַחֶסֶד, וְהַרְבֵּה עִמּוֹ פְדוּת:
וְהוּא יִפְדֶּה אֶת־יִשְׂרָאֵל, מִכֹּל עֲוֹנוֹתָיו:

*The* ארון קודש *is closed.*

### חצי קדיש

ש״ץ: יִתְגַּדַּל וְיִתְקַדַּשׁ שְׁמֵהּ רַבָּא (קהל: אָמֵן)
בְּעָלְמָא דִּי בְרָא כִרְעוּתֵהּ
וְיַמְלִיךְ מַלְכוּתֵהּ וְיַצְמַח פֻּרְקָנֵהּ וִיקָרֵב מְשִׁיחֵהּ (קהל: אָמֵן)
בְּחַיֵּיכוֹן וּבְיוֹמֵיכוֹן וּבְחַיֵּי דְכָל בֵּית יִשְׂרָאֵל
בַּעֲגָלָא וּבִזְמַן קָרִיב, וְאִמְרוּ אָמֵן. (קהל: אָמֵן)

קהל וש״ץ: יְהֵא שְׁמֵהּ רַבָּא מְבָרַךְ לְעָלַם וּלְעָלְמֵי עָלְמַיָּא.

ש״ץ: יִתְבָּרַךְ וְיִשְׁתַּבַּח וְיִתְפָּאַר וְיִתְרוֹמַם וְיִתְנַשֵּׂא
וְיִתְהַדָּר וְיִתְעַלֶּה וְיִתְהַלָּל שְׁמֵהּ דְּקֻדְשָׁא בְּרִיךְ הוּא (קהל: אָמֵן)
לְעֵלָּא לְעֵלָּא מִכָּל בִּרְכָתָא וְשִׁירָתָא, תֻּשְׁבְּחָתָא וְנֶחֱמָתָא
דַּאֲמִירָן בְּעָלְמָא, וְאִמְרוּ אָמֵן. (קהל: אָמֵן)

---

separate ways. But One who refuses to reject us, never losing faith in us, and refusing to let go – that is the One we fear, not because we fear Him, but because ultimately we fear ourselves. We fear greatness. We fear the effort it demands. There are times we would rather be left alone. That is one of the sources of disbelief. It is easy to live in a universe that makes no demands on us. God's forgiveness makes demands on us, for God believes in us more than we believe in ourselves. מִשֹּׁמְרִים לַבֹּקֶר *More than watchmen wait for the morning.* More than watchmen wait for the first light of dawn, so I wait for the light of God's forgiveness in the dark night of the soul.

HALF KADDISH
Rabbi Levi Yitzḥak of Berditchev, the Hasidic master, was known for his daring prayers on behalf of the Jewish people. One Rosh HaShana morning he uttered the following prayer before Kaddish:

## BLESSINGS OF THE SHEMA

*The following blessing and response are said only in the presence of a minyan. They represent a formal summons to the congregation to engage in an act of collective prayer. The custom of bowing at this point is based on 1 Chronicles 29:20, "David said to the whole assembly, 'Now bless the Lord your God.' All the assembly blessed the Lord God of their fathers and bowed their heads low to the Lord and the King."*

*The Leader says the following, bowing at "Bless," standing straight at "the Lord." The congregation, followed by the Leader, responds, bowing at "Bless," standing straight at "the Lord."*

*Leader:* **BLESS**
the Lord, the blessed One.

*Congregation:* Bless the Lord, the blessed One,
for ever and all time.

*Leader:* Bless the Lord, the blessed One,
for ever and all time.

*The custom is to sit from this point until the Amida, since the predominant emotion of this section of the prayers is love rather than awe. Conversation is forbidden until after the Amida.*

בָּרוּךְ Blessed are You, Lord our God,
King of the Universe,
who forms light and creates darkness, *Is. 45*
makes peace and creates all.

---

of the entire Jewish people. Since then, though Jews have been scattered and dispersed, wherever ten gather in prayer it is as if the whole Jewish people were present. The community is a microcosm of the nation.

בָּרוּךְ אַתָּה...יוֹצֵר אוֹר וּבוֹרֵא חֹשֶׁךְ *Blessed are You... who forms light and creates darkness.* This line, adapted from a verse in Isaiah, was placed at the beginning of communal prayer as a protest against dualism: the idea that there are two forces at work in the universe, the God of good, and an independent force of evil, known variously as the demiurge, the devil, Satan, Belial, Lucifer, or the power of darkness. Dualism entered the West through Persian Man-

# קריאת שמע וברכותיה

*The following blessing and response are said only in the presence of a מנין.*
*They represent a formal summons to the קהל to engage in an act of collective prayer.*
*The custom of bowing at this point is based on דברי הימים א׳ כט, כ, "David said to the whole assembly, 'Now bless the Lord your God.' All the assembly blessed the Lord God of their fathers and bowed their heads low to the Lord and the King."*
*The שליח ציבור says the following, bowing at בָּרְכוּ, standing straight at ה׳.*
*The קהל, followed by the שליח ציבור, responds, bowing at בָּרוּךְ, standing straight at ה׳.*

ש״ץ: **בָּרְכוּ**
אֶת יהוה הַמְבֹרָךְ.

קהל: בָּרוּךְ יהוה הַמְבֹרָךְ לְעוֹלָם וָעֶד.

ש״ץ: בָּרוּךְ יהוה הַמְבֹרָךְ לְעוֹלָם וָעֶד.

*The custom is to sit from this point until the עמידה, since the predominant emotion of this section of the prayers is love rather than awe.*
*Conversation is forbidden until after the עמידה.*

בָּרוּךְ אַתָּה יהוה אֱלֹהֵינוּ מֶלֶךְ הָעוֹלָם
יוֹצֵר אוֹר וּבוֹרֵא חֹשֶׁךְ ישעיה מה
עֹשֶׂה שָׁלוֹם וּבוֹרֵא אֶת הַכֹּל.

---

SUMMONS TO PRAYER

**בָּרְכוּ אֶת יהוה** *Bless the Lord.* An ancient formula (see Neh. 9:5) for summoning the congregation to prayer. From this point onward, communal prayer begins. Prayers of special sanctity require a *minyan*, a quorum of ten adult males. The ten spies who brought back a negative report about the land were called a "congregation." In response to Abraham's prayer about Sodom (Gen. 18), God assured him that if it contained ten righteous individuals, their merits would save the city. Ten is thus the minimum number to constitute a community. When the Temple stood, sacrifices were offered daily on behalf

אוֹר עוֹלָם Endless light in a treasure-house of life.
Lights from obscurity – He spoke and they became.

*On the first day, some congregations say the piyut,*
*"O King girded with strength" (page 1006) at this point.*
*On the second day, some congregations say the piyut,*
*"O King, Your words are true" (page 1040) at this point.*

*On Shabbat continue with "All will thank You" on the next page.*
*On a weekday continue here:*

הַמֵּאִיר In compassion He gives light to the earth and its inhabitants,
and in His goodness continually renews the work of creation,
day after day.
How numerous are Your works LORD; Ps. 104
You made them all in wisdom.
The earth is full of Your creations.
He is the King exalted alone since the beginning of time –
praised, glorified and elevated since the world began.
Eternal God,
in Your great compassion, have compassion on us,
LORD of our strength, Rock of our refuge,
Shield of our salvation, You are our stronghold.

---

other. God feared that the wicked would make use of it. What did He do? He hid it for the righteous in the World to Come (*Ḥagiga* 12a). Rav Kook said that from time to time there are great men whom God blesses with a vision of that hidden light. They see the world filled with the radiance of God. He believed great artists were sometimes able to convey this in their work.

וּבְטוּבוֹ מְחַדֵּשׁ בְּכָל יוֹם תָּמִיד מַעֲשֵׂה בְרֵאשִׁית *And in His goodness continually renews the work of creation, day after day.* Rabbi Judah HaLevi pointed out the difference between divine creation (something from nothing) and human creation (something from something). A human creation, once made, continues to exist. A divine creation, since it is made from nothing, would lapse back into nothingness were God to cease continually to recreate it. Thus, at the deepest level, all things are daily, constantly, made new again. One of the powers of prayer – as with great art – is to allow us to see the world with new eyes and sense the miracle of existence. "Not how the world is, but that it is, is the mystical."

# אוֹר עוֹלָם בְּאוֹצַר חַיִּים, אוֹרוֹת מֵאֹפֶל אָמַר וַיֶּהִי.

*On the first day, some congregations say the piyut,* מֶלֶךְ אָזוּר גְּבוּרָה *(page 1007) at this point.*
*On the second day, some congregations say the piyut,* מֶלֶךְ אָמוֹן מַאֲמָרְךָ *(page 1041) at this point.*

*On* שבת *continue with* הַכֹּל יוֹדְוּךָ *on the next page.*
*On a weekday continue here:*

הַמֵּאִיר לָאָרֶץ וְלַדָּרִים עָלֶיהָ בְּרַחֲמִים
וּבְטוּבוֹ מְחַדֵּשׁ בְּכָל יוֹם תָּמִיד מַעֲשֵׂה בְרֵאשִׁית.
תהלים קד מָה־רַבּוּ מַעֲשֶׂיךָ יהוה, כֻּלָּם בְּחָכְמָה עָשִׂיתָ
מָלְאָה הָאָרֶץ קִנְיָנֶךָ:
הַמֶּלֶךְ הַמְרוֹמָם לְבַדּוֹ מֵאָז
הַמְשֻׁבָּח וְהַמְפֹאָר וְהַמִּתְנַשֵּׂא מִימוֹת עוֹלָם.
אֱלֹהֵי עוֹלָם
בְּרַחֲמֶיךָ הָרַבִּים רַחֵם עָלֵינוּ
אֲדוֹן עֻזֵּנוּ, צוּר מִשְׂגַּבֵּנוּ
מָגֵן יִשְׁעֵנוּ, מִשְׂגָּב בַּעֲדֵנוּ.

---

ichaeism and Greek Gnosticism and is a constant temptation to those who seek to locate the source of evil in some inhuman or antihuman force – some externalized Other – rather than within ourselves. Those unable to acknowledge the good and evil within themselves sometimes project the evil onto others. That is the root of such myths as the Blood Libel and the Protocols of the Elders of Zion, and it survives today. Not only is dualism incompatible with monotheism; it is also responsible for some of the great hatreds of history.'

**אוֹר עוֹלָם** *Endless light.* A fragment of a prayer composed by the earliest known composer of *piyut* (liturgical poetry), Yose ben Yose, who lived in the land of Israel, probably in the fifth century. It refers to the light of the first day of creation – not physical light, since the sun was not created until the fourth day, but spiritual light.

According to tradition, the light of the first day of creation was so strong and luminous that it was possible to see from one end of the world to the

The blessed God, great in knowledge,
prepared and made the rays of the sun.
He who is good formed glory for His name,
surrounding His power with radiant stars.
The leaders of His hosts,
the holy ones, exalt the Almighty, constantly proclaiming God's glory and holiness.
▸ May You be blessed, LORD our God,
in the heavens above and on the earth below,
for all the magnificence of Your handiwork
and for the radiant lights You have formed;
all these will glorify You, Selah!

*On a weekday continue with "May You be forever blessed, our Rock" on page 324. On Shabbat continue here:*

All will thank You. All will praise You.
All will declare: Nothing is as holy as the LORD.
All will exalt You, Selah, You who form all –
the God who daily opens the doors of the gates of the East
and cleaves the windows of the sky,
who brings out the sun from its place and the moon from its abode,
giving light to the whole world and its inhabitants
whom He created by the attribute of compassion.
In compassion He gives light to the earth and its inhabitants,
and in His goodness daily, continually, renews the work of creation.
How numerous are Your works LORD; You made them all in wisdom; *Ps. 104*
the earth is full of Your creations.
He is the King who alone was exalted since time began,
praised, glorified and raised high from days of old.
Eternal God, in Your great compassion, have compassion on us,
LORD of our strength, Rock of our refuge,
Shield of our salvation, Stronghold of our safety.

---

הַכֹּל יוֹדוּךָ *All will thank You.* This passage is far longer than its weekday equivalent since Shabbat is a memorial of creation (Roke'aḥ). Thus we devote extra attention to this, the first blessing before Shema, whose subject is creation.

אֵל בָּרוּךְ גְּדוֹל דֵּעָה
הֵכִין וּפָעַל זָהֳרֵי חַמָּה
טוֹב יָצַר כָּבוֹד לִשְׁמוֹ
מְאוֹרוֹת נָתַן סְבִיבוֹת עֻזּוֹ
פִּנּוֹת צְבָאָיו קְדוֹשִׁים, רוֹמְמֵי שַׁדַּי
תָּמִיד מְסַפְּרִים כְּבוֹד אֵל וּקְדֻשָּׁתוֹ.
תִּתְבָּרַךְ יהוה אֱלֹהֵינוּ בַּשָּׁמַיִם מִמַּעַל וְעַל הָאָרֶץ מִתָּחַת
עַל כָּל שֶׁבַח מַעֲשֵׂה יָדֶיךָ, וְעַל מְאוֹרֵי אוֹר שֶׁיָּצַרְתָּ
הֵמָּה יְפָאֲרוּךָ סֶּלָה.

*On a weekday continue with* תִּתְבָּרַךְ לָנֶצַח, צוּרֵנוּ *on page 325. On* שבת *continue here:*

הַכֹּל יוֹדוּךָ וְהַכֹּל יְשַׁבְּחוּךָ
וְהַכֹּל יֹאמְרוּ אֵין קָדוֹשׁ כַּיהוה
הַכֹּל יְרוֹמְמוּךָ סֶּלָה, יוֹצֵר הַכֹּל.
הָאֵל הַפּוֹתֵחַ בְּכָל יוֹם דַּלְתוֹת שַׁעֲרֵי מִזְרָח
וּבוֹקֵעַ חַלּוֹנֵי רָקִיעַ
מוֹצִיא חַמָּה מִמְּקוֹמָהּ וּלְבָנָה מִמְּכוֹן שִׁבְתָּהּ
וּמֵאִיר לָעוֹלָם כֻּלּוֹ וּלְיוֹשְׁבָיו שֶׁבָּרָא בְּמִדַּת הָרַחֲמִים.
הַמֵּאִיר לָאָרֶץ וְלַדָּרִים עָלֶיהָ בְּרַחֲמִים
וּבְטוּבוֹ מְחַדֵּשׁ בְּכָל יוֹם תָּמִיד מַעֲשֵׂה בְרֵאשִׁית.
תהלים קד מָה־רַבּוּ מַעֲשֶׂיךָ, יהוה, כֻּלָּם בְּחָכְמָה עָשִׂיתָ
מָלְאָה הָאָרֶץ קִנְיָנֶךָ:
הַמֶּלֶךְ הַמְרוֹמָם לְבַדּוֹ מֵאָז
הַמְשֻׁבָּח וְהַמְפֹאָר וְהַמִּתְנַשֵּׂא מִימוֹת עוֹלָם.
אֱלֹהֵי עוֹלָם, בְּרַחֲמֶיךָ הָרַבִּים רַחֵם עָלֵינוּ
אֲדוֹן עֻזֵּנוּ, צוּר מִשְׂגַּבֵּנוּ, מָגֵן יִשְׁעֵנוּ, מִשְׂגָּב בַּעֲדֵנוּ.

אֵין עֲרֹךְ לְךָ None can be compared to You, there is none besides You;
None without You. Who is like You?

▸ None can be compared to You,
Lord our God – in this world.
There is none besides You, our King –
in the life of the World to Come.
There is none but You, our Redeemer –
in the days of the Messiah.
There is none like You, our Savior –
at the resurrection of the dead.

אֵל אָדוֹן God, Lord of all creation,
the Blessed, is blessed by every soul.
His greatness and goodness fill the world;
knowledge and wisdom surround His splendor.

Exalted above the holy Ḥayyot,
adorned in glory on the Chariot;
merit and right are before His throne,
His glory infused with kindness and compassion.

Good are the radiant stars our God created;
He formed them with knowledge,
understanding and deliberation.
He gave them strength and might
to rule throughout the world.

---

justice prevail in the affairs of mankind; and (4) the resurrection of the dead, the final denouement of history, when those who have died will live again.

אֵל אָדוֹן עַל כָּל הַמַּעֲשִׂים *God, Lord of all creation.* An ancient prayer, influenced by *merkava* mysticism, envisioning God surrounded by the angels and the myriad stars. *Merkava* or "Chariot" mysticism was based on the vision seen by Ezekiel and described by him in the first chapter of the book that bears his name. כָּל צְבָא מָרוֹם *All the hosts on high*: Having mentioned the sun and moon, the Hebrew hints at the other planets of the Ptolemaic system: שֶֽׁבַח נוֹתְנִים לוֹ כָּל צְבָא מָרוֹם – the *shin* of *shevaḥ* signaling Saturn (*Shabbetai*), and so on for Venus (נ for *Noga*), Mercury (כ for *Kokhav*), Jupiter (צ for *Tzedek*) and Mars (מ for *Maadim*).

אֵין עֲרוֹךְ לְךָ
וְאֵין זוּלָתֶךָ
אֶפֶס בִּלְתֶּךָ
וּמִי דּוֹמֶה לָּךְ.

› אֵין עֲרוֹךְ לְךָ, יהוה אֱלֹהֵינוּ, בָּעוֹלָם הַזֶּה
וְאֵין זוּלָתְךָ, מַלְכֵּנוּ, לְחַיֵּי הָעוֹלָם הַבָּא
אֶפֶס בִּלְתְּךָ, גּוֹאֲלֵנוּ, לִימוֹת הַמָּשִׁיחַ
וְאֵין דּוֹמֶה לְּךָ, מוֹשִׁיעֵנוּ, לִתְחִיַּת הַמֵּתִים.

אֵל אָדוֹן עַל כָּל הַמַּעֲשִׂים
בָּרוּךְ וּמְבֹרָךְ בְּפִי כָּל הַנְּשָׁמָה
גָּדְלוֹ וְטוּבוֹ מָלֵא עוֹלָם
דַּעַת וּתְבוּנָה סוֹבְבִים הוֹדוֹ.

הַמִּתְגָּאֶה עַל חַיּוֹת הַקֹּדֶשׁ
וְנֶהְדָּר בְּכָבוֹד עַל הַמֶּרְכָּבָה
זְכוּת וּמִישׁוֹר לִפְנֵי כִסְאוֹ
חֶסֶד וְרַחֲמִים מָלֵא כְבוֹדוֹ.

טוֹבִים מְאוֹרוֹת שֶׁבָּרָא אֱלֹהֵינוּ
יְצָרָם בְּדַעַת בְּבִינָה וּבְהַשְׂכֵּל
כֹּחַ וּגְבוּרָה נָתַן בָּהֶם
לִהְיוֹת מוֹשְׁלִים בְּקֶרֶב תֵּבֵל.

---

**בָּעוֹלָם הַזֶּה...לְחַיֵּי הָעוֹלָם הַבָּא** *In this world... in the life of the World to Come.* The prayer sets out the four time-zones of existence: (1) this world that we inhabit now; (2) the World to Come – according to Maimonides (Laws of Repentance 8:1), the realm of the soul after death; (3) the days of the Messiah, when the Temple will be rebuilt, the rule of David restored, and peace and

Full of splendor, radiating light,
beautiful is their splendor throughout the world.
Glad as they go forth, joyous as they return,
they fulfill with awe their Creator's will.

Glory and honor they give to His name,
jubilation and song at the mention of His majesty.
He called the sun into being and it shone with light.
He looked and fashioned the form of the moon.

All the hosts on high give Him praise;
the Seraphim, Ḥayyot and holy Ophanim
ascribe glory and greatness –

לָאֵל To God who rested from all works,
and on the seventh day ascended and sat on His throne of glory.
He robed the day of rest in glory
and called the Sabbath day a delight.
This is the seventh day's song of praise,
that on it God rested from all His work.
The seventh day itself gives praise, saying,
"A psalm, a song for the Sabbath day. *Ps. 92*
It is good to give thanks to the Lord."
Therefore let all He has formed glorify and bless God.
Let them give praise and honor, grandeur and glory to God,
the King, who formed all things,
and in His holiness gave a heritage of rest
to His people Israel on the holy Sabbath day.
May Your name, O Lord our God, be sanctified,
and Your renown, O our King, be glorified
in the heavens above and on the earth below.
May You be blessed, our Deliverer,
for all the magnificence of Your handiwork
and for the radiant lights You have formed;
all these will glorify You, Selah!

---

**וְיוֹם הַשְּׁבִיעִי מְשַׁבֵּחַ** *The seventh day itself gives praise.* A midrashic idea, based on the phrase that opens Psalm 92: "A Psalm, a song of the Sabbath day," here

מְלֵאִים זִיו וּמְפִיקִים נֹגַהּ
נָאֶה זִיוָם בְּכָל הָעוֹלָם
שְׂמֵחִים בְּצֵאתָם וְשָׂשִׂים בְּבוֹאָם
עוֹשִׂים בְּאֵימָה רְצוֹן קוֹנָם.

פְּאֵר וְכָבוֹד נוֹתְנִים לִשְׁמוֹ
צָהֳלָה וְרִנָּה לְזֵכֶר מַלְכוּתוֹ
קָרָא לַשֶּׁמֶשׁ וַיִּזְרַח אוֹר
רָאָה וְהִתְקִין צוּרַת הַלְּבָנָה.

שֶׁבַח נוֹתְנִים לוֹ כָּל צְבָא מָרוֹם
תִּפְאֶרֶת וּגְדֻלָּה, שְׂרָפִים וְחַיּוֹת וְאוֹפַנֵּי הַקֹּדֶשׁ.

לָאֵל אֲשֶׁר שָׁבַת מִכָּל הַמַּעֲשִׂים
בַּיּוֹם הַשְּׁבִיעִי נִתְעַלָּה וְיָשַׁב עַל כִּסֵּא כְבוֹדוֹ.
תִּפְאֶרֶת עָטָה לְיוֹם הַמְּנוּחָה
עֹנֶג קָרָא לְיוֹם הַשַּׁבָּת.
זֶה שִׁיר שֶׁבַח שֶׁל יוֹם הַשְּׁבִיעִי
שֶׁבּוֹ שָׁבַת אֵל מִכָּל מְלַאכְתּוֹ
וְיוֹם הַשְּׁבִיעִי מְשַׁבֵּחַ וְאוֹמֵר
מִזְמוֹר שִׁיר לְיוֹם הַשַּׁבָּת, טוֹב לְהֹדוֹת לַיהוה: תהלים צב
לְפִיכָךְ יְפָאֲרוּ וִיבָרְכוּ לָאֵל כָּל יְצוּרָיו
שֶׁבַח יְקָר וּגְדֻלָּה וְכָבוֹד יִתְּנוּ לָאֵל מֶלֶךְ יוֹצֵר כֹּל
הַמַּנְחִיל מְנוּחָה לְעַמּוֹ יִשְׂרָאֵל בִּקְדֻשָּׁתוֹ בְּיוֹם שַׁבַּת קֹדֶשׁ.
שִׁמְךָ יהוה אֱלֹהֵינוּ יִתְקַדַּשׁ, וְזִכְרְךָ מַלְכֵּנוּ יִתְפָּאַר
בַּשָּׁמַיִם מִמַּעַל וְעַל הָאָרֶץ מִתָּחַת.
תִּתְבָּרַךְ מוֹשִׁיעֵנוּ עַל כָּל שֶׁבַח מַעֲשֵׂה יָדֶיךָ
וְעַל מְאוֹרֵי אוֹר שֶׁיָּצַרְתָּ, הֵמָּה יְפָאֲרוּךָ סֶּלָה.

*On all days continue here:*

תִּתְבָּרַךְ לָנֶצַח May You be forever blessed,
our Rock, King and Redeemer,
Creator of holy beings.
May Your name be praised for ever,
our King, Creator of the ministering angels,
all of whom stand in the universe's heights,
proclaiming together,
in awe, aloud,
the words of the living God,
the eternal King.
They are all beloved,
all pure,
all mighty,
all holy,
and all perform in awe and reverence
the will of their Maker.
▸ All open their mouths in holiness and purity,
with song and psalm,
and bless, praise, glorify,
revere, sanctify and declare the sovereignty of –
the name of the great, mighty
and awesome God and King,
holy is He.

---

three times in the morning prayers: (1) before the Shema, (2) during the Leader's Repetition of the Amida, and (3) toward the end of prayer, except on Shabbat and festivals, when the third is transferred to the afternoon.

This section of the prayers – the vision of the heavenly throne and the angels – is part of the mystical tradition in Judaism. Prayer is Jacob's ladder, stretching from earth to heaven, with "angels of the Lord" ascending and descending (*Zohar*). The three *kedushot* represent, respectively, the ascent, the summit, and the descent: the journey of the soul from earth to heaven and back again, transformed by our experience of the Divine.

*On all days continue here:*

תִּתְבָּרַךְ לָנֶצַח
צוּרֵנוּ מַלְכֵּנוּ וְגוֹאֲלֵנוּ, בּוֹרֵא קְדוֹשִׁים
יִשְׁתַּבַּח שִׁמְךָ לָעַד
מַלְכֵּנוּ, יוֹצֵר מְשָׁרְתִים
וַאֲשֶׁר מְשָׁרְתָיו כֻּלָּם עוֹמְדִים בְּרוּם עוֹלָם
וּמַשְׁמִיעִים בְּיִרְאָה יַחַד בְּקוֹל
דִּבְרֵי אֱלֹהִים חַיִּים וּמֶלֶךְ עוֹלָם.
כֻּלָּם אֲהוּבִים, כֻּלָּם בְּרוּרִים
כֻּלָּם גִּבּוֹרִים, כֻּלָּם קְדוֹשִׁים
וְכֻלָּם עוֹשִׂים בְּאֵימָה וּבְיִרְאָה רְצוֹן קוֹנָם
◂ וְכֻלָּם פּוֹתְחִים אֶת פִּיהֶם
בִּקְדֻשָּׁה וּבְטָהֳרָה
בְּשִׁירָה וּבְזִמְרָה
וּמְבָרְכִין וּמְשַׁבְּחִין וּמְפָאֲרִין
וּמַעֲרִיצִין וּמַקְדִּישִׁין וּמַמְלִיכִין
אֶת שֵׁם הָאֵל הַמֶּלֶךְ הַגָּדוֹל, הַגִּבּוֹר וְהַנּוֹרָא
קָדוֹשׁ הוּא.

---

understood not as a song *for* the Sabbath, but *by* the Sabbath. It is as if, in the silence of Shabbat, we hear the song Creation sings to its Creator, the "music of the spheres."

תִּתְבָּרַךְ לָנֶצַח *May You be forever blessed.* Two prophets, Isaiah and Ezekiel, saw mystical visions of God among His heavenly host, the choir of angels. These visions, together with the words the prophets heard the angels sing ("Holy, holy, holy" in Isaiah's vision; "Blessed is the LORD's glory from His place" in Ezekiel's), form the heart of *Kedusha*, the "Holiness" prayer. This is recited

All accept on themselves, one from another,
the yoke of the kingdom of heaven,
granting permission to one another with love,
to sanctify the One who formed them, in serene spirit,
pure speech and sweet melody.
All, as one, proclaim His holiness in awe,
saying in reverence:

*All say aloud:*

Holy, holy, holy is the LORD of hosts; *Is. 6*
the whole world is filled with His glory.

*Some congregations say the piyut, "His glory He canopied" on page 1010.*

*The congregation, followed by the Leader, recites one of the following versions according to their custom. Some hold that a congregation which doesn't say Yotzerot (the piyutim added to the blessing of Yotzer) should say "Then the Ophanim."*

The Ḥayyot sing out, / and the Cherubim glorify, / and the Seraphim pray, / and the Erelim bless, / with the face of each Ḥayya and Ophan and Cherub / turned toward the Seraphim. / Facing these, they give praise, saying:

Then the Ophanim and the Holy Ḥayyot, / with a roar of noise, / raise themselves toward the Seraphim and, / facing them, give praise, saying:

*All say aloud:*

Blessed is the LORD's glory from His place. *Ezek. 3*

---

sion in honor of the day. Others recite the usual text said daily: "Then the Ophanim…"

וְהַחַיּוֹת...וּכְרוּבִים...וּשְׂרָפִים...וְאֶרְאֶלִּים...וְאוֹפָן *Hayyot… Cherubim… Seraphim… Erelim…* [*each*] *Ophan.* Five kinds of angels seen by Isaiah and Ezekiel in their visions. Ḥayyot are "living beings" surrounded by fire. Cherubim are guardian angels, mentioned in the story of the Garden of Eden (Gen. 3:24). Representations of them were above the Ark in the Tabernacle and later the Temple. Seraphim are angels of fire. Erelim are described by Isaiah (33:7) as angels of peace. Ophanim are angels described as "wheels within wheels."

וְכֻלָּם מְקַבְּלִים עֲלֵיהֶם עֹל מַלְכוּת שָׁמַיִם זֶה מִזֶּה
וְנוֹתְנִים בְּאַהֲבָה רְשׁוּת זֶה לָזֶה
לְהַקְדִּישׁ לְיוֹצְרָם בְּנַחַת רוּחַ
בְּשָׂפָה בְרוּרָה וּבִנְעִימָה
קְדֻשָּׁה כֻּלָּם כְּאֶחָד
עוֹנִים בְּאֵימָה וְאוֹמְרִים בְּיִרְאָה

*All say aloud:*

ישעיה ו
קָדוֹשׁ, קָדוֹשׁ, קָדוֹשׁ יהוה צְבָאוֹת
מְלֹא כָל־הָאָרֶץ כְּבוֹדוֹ:

*Some congregations say the piyut,* כְּבוֹדוֹ אִהֵל *on page 1011.*

*The* קהל*, followed by the* שליח ציבור*, recites one of the following versions according to their custom.*
*Some hold that a congregation which doesn't say* יוצרות *should say* וְהָאוֹפַנִּים.

וְהַחַיּוֹת יְשׁוֹרֵרוּ / וּכְרוּבִים יְפָאֵרוּ
וּשְׂרָפִים יָרֹנּוּ / וְאֶרְאֶלִּים יְבָרֵכוּ
פְּנֵי כָל חַיָּה וְאוֹפָן וּכְרוּב לְעֻמַּת שְׂרָפִים
לְעֻמָּתָם מְשַׁבְּחִים וְאוֹמְרִים

וְהָאוֹפַנִּים וְחַיּוֹת הַקֹּדֶשׁ
בְּרַעַשׁ גָּדוֹל
מִתְנַשְּׂאִים לְעֻמַּת שְׂרָפִים
לְעֻמָּתָם מְשַׁבְּחִים וְאוֹמְרִים

*All say aloud:*

יחזקאל ג
בָּרוּךְ כְּבוֹד־יהוה מִמְּקוֹמוֹ:

---

וּבִנְעִימָה *Sweet melody.* The angel's praise has three elements, and by implication so should ours: serene spirit (*naḥat ruaḥ*), pure speech (*safa berura*), and sweet melody (*ne'ima*). They summarize the ideal elements of prayer: spiritual *tranquility*, cognitive *clarity*, and aesthetic *beauty*.

וְהַחַיּוֹת יְשׁוֹרֵרוּ *The Ḥayyot sing out.* An extended version of the passage linking the angelic praise in Isaiah's vision with that in Ezekiel's. Rosh HaShana is the anniversary of creation, and since this entire section of the prayers is about creation, most have the custom of saying this more elaborate ver-

לָאֵל To the blessed God they offer melodies.
To the King,
living and eternal God,
they say psalms and proclaim praises.
For it is He alone, exalted and holy,
who does mighty deeds
and creates new things,
who is Master of battles
and sows righteousness,
who makes salvation grow
and creates cures,
who is is revered in praises,
the LORD of wonders,
who in His goodness,
continually renews the work of creation, day after day,
as it is said:
"[Praise] Him who made the great lights, *Ps. 136*
for His love endures for ever."
▸ May You make a new light shine over Zion,
and may we all soon be worthy of its light.
Blessed are You, LORD, who forms the radiant lights.

---

כִּי הוּא לְבַדּוֹ *For it is He alone.* There follows a veiled reference to the seven heavenly bodies: פּוֹעֵל גְּבוּרוֹת *Does mighty deeds* is a reference to the sun spoken of in Psalm 19 as "rejoicing like a champion [*gibor*]." עוֹשֶׂה חֲדָשׁוֹת *Creates new things* refers to the moon which renews itself each month. בַּעַל מִלְחָמוֹת *Master of battles* refers to Mars, the planet symbolizing war. זוֹרֵעַ צְדָקוֹת *Sows righteousness* is a reference to Jupiter, called *Tzedek*, righteousness, in Hebrew. מַצְמִיחַ יְשׁוּעוֹת *Makes salvation grow* refers to Mercury – *Kokhav* in Hebrew – since Bilaam predicts the Messiah will "step forth as a star [*kokhav*] from Jacob" (Num. 24:17). בּוֹרֵא רְפוּאוֹת *Creates cures* refers to Venus, *Noga* in Hebrew, the "brightness" which brings healing in its wings (Mal. 3:20). נוֹרָא תְהִלּוֹת *Revered in praises* is Saturn, whose name *Shabbetai* is like praise, *shevaḥ*. (Rabbi Jacob Emden)

לָאֵל בָּרוּךְ נְעִימוֹת יִתֵּנוּ
לַמֶּלֶךְ אֵל חַי וְקַיָּם
זְמִירוֹת יֹאמֵרוּ וְתִשְׁבָּחוֹת יַשְׁמִיעוּ
כִּי הוּא לְבַדּוֹ מָרוֹם וְקָדוֹשׁ
פּוֹעֵל גְּבוּרוֹת, עוֹשֶׂה חֲדָשׁוֹת
בַּעַל מִלְחָמוֹת, זוֹרֵעַ צְדָקוֹת
מַצְמִיחַ יְשׁוּעוֹת, בּוֹרֵא רְפוּאוֹת
נוֹרָא תְהִלּוֹת, אֲדוֹן הַנִּפְלָאוֹת
הַמְחַדֵּשׁ בְּטוּבוֹ בְּכָל יוֹם תָּמִיד מַעֲשֵׂה בְרֵאשִׁית
כָּאָמוּר
תהלים קלו לְעֹשֵׂה אוֹרִים גְּדֹלִים
כִּי לְעוֹלָם חַסְדּוֹ:
◂ אוֹר חָדָשׁ עַל צִיּוֹן תָּאִיר
וְנִזְכֶּה כֻלָּנוּ בִּמְהֵרָה לְאוֹרוֹ.
בָּרוּךְ אַתָּה יהוה, יוֹצֵר הַמְּאוֹרוֹת.

---

Together they form a heavenly retinue surrounding the divine throne, an angelic choir singing God's praises.

In Tanakh, angels appear on earth as divine emissaries, but here we speak of them mystically as the prophets saw them in heaven, singing God's song. The point the poet is making is that, at the height of prayer, we too should aspire to become like angels, leaving our worldly concerns behind, thinking not of ourselves but of God, opening our eyes to the radiance of Being, hearing the music of creation, becoming a voice in the choral symphony of the universe as it sings to its Creator.

Song is essential to understanding the difference between science and faith. Science describes creation in speech, faith evokes it in song. Science is prose, faith is poetry. Science explains, faith celebrates. Faith sings, because music is the language of the soul.

אַהֲבַת עוֹלָם With everlasting love have You loved us, Lord our God,
and with surpassing compassion have You had compassion on us.
Our Father, our King, for the sake of Your great name,
and for the sake of our ancestors who trusted in You,
and to whom You taught the laws of life,
to perform Your will wholeheartedly, be gracious also to us and teach us.
Our Father, compassionate Father, ever compassionate,
please, have compassion on us.
Instill in our hearts the wisdom to understand and discern,
to listen, learn and teach, to observe, perform and fulfill
all the teachings of Your Torah in love.
Enlighten our eyes in Your Torah
and let our hearts cling to Your commandments.
Unite our hearts to love and revere Your name,
so that we may never be ashamed or humiliated or fall.
And because we have trusted in Your holy, great, mighty and revered name,
may we be glad and rejoice in Your salvation.

*At this point, gather the four tzitziot of the tallit, holding them in the left hand.*

Let Your compassion, Lord our God, and Your great kindness
never leave us, Selah, for all eternity.
Quickly, bring us blessing and peace,
speedily from the four quarters of the earth,
break the yoke from our neck and lead us quickly, upright, to our land.
▸ For You are a God who performs acts of salvation,
and You chose us from all peoples and tongues,
bringing us close, our King, to Your great name for ever, in truth and in love,
that we may thank You, and proclaim Your Oneness in love,
and love Your name.
Blessed are You, Lord, who chooses His people Israel in love.

---

grandeur to spiritual intimacy. The phrase "Our Father, compassionate Father, ever compassionate, please, have compassion on us," with its twofold repetition of "father" and threefold mention of compassion in the space of six Hebrew words, is one of the most concentrated expressions of the love and trust we feel for God – the God who said, "My child, My firstborn, Israel" (Ex. 4:22). The channel through which this love flows is the Torah, God's covenant with His people. This contains "the laws of life" in a double sense: laws that *guide* us in life, and laws that *give* us life.

אַהֲבַת עוֹלָם אֲהַבְתָּנוּ, יהוה אֱלֹהֵינוּ
חֶמְלָה גְדוֹלָה וִיתֵרָה חָמַלְתָּ עָלֵינוּ.
אָבִינוּ מַלְכֵּנוּ
בַּעֲבוּר שִׁמְךָ הַגָּדוֹל, וּבַעֲבוּר אֲבוֹתֵינוּ שֶׁבָּטְחוּ בְךָ
וַתְּלַמְּדֵם חֻקֵּי חַיִּים, לַעֲשׂוֹת רְצוֹנְךָ בְּלֵבָב שָׁלֵם
כֵּן תְּחָנֵּנוּ וּתְלַמְּדֵנוּ.
אָבִינוּ, אָב הָרַחֲמָן, הַמְרַחֵם, רַחֵם נָא עָלֵינוּ
וְתֵן בְּלִבֵּנוּ בִּינָה לְהָבִין וּלְהַשְׂכִּיל
לִשְׁמֹעַ, לִלְמֹד וּלְלַמֵּד, לִשְׁמֹר וְלַעֲשׂוֹת, וּלְקַיֵּם
אֶת כָּל דִּבְרֵי תַלְמוּד תּוֹרָתֶךָ בְּאַהֲבָה.
וְהָאֵר עֵינֵינוּ בְּתוֹרָתֶךָ, וְדַבֵּק לִבֵּנוּ בְּמִצְוֹתֶיךָ
וְיַחֵד לְבָבֵנוּ לְאַהֲבָה וּלְיִרְאָה אֶת שְׁמֶךָ
לְמַעַן לֹא נֵבוֹשׁ וְלֹא נִכָּלֵם וְלֹא נִכָּשֵׁל לְעוֹלָם וָעֶד.
כִּי בְשֵׁם קָדְשְׁךָ הַגָּדוֹל הַגִּבּוֹר וְהַנּוֹרָא בָּטָחְנוּ
נָגִילָה וְנִשְׂמְחָה בִּישׁוּעָתֶךָ.

*At this point, gather the four* ציציות *of the* טלית*, holding them in the left hand.*

וְרַחֲמֶיךָ יהוה אֱלֹהֵינוּ וַחֲסָדֶיךָ הָרַבִּים, אַל יַעַזְבוּנוּ נֶצַח סֶלָה וָעֶד.
מַהֵר וְהָבֵא עָלֵינוּ בְּרָכָה וְשָׁלוֹם, מְהֵרָה מֵאַרְבַּע כַּנְפוֹת כָּל הָאָרֶץ
וּשְׁבֹר עֻלֵּנוּ מֵעַל צַוָּארֵנוּ וְתוֹלִיכֵנוּ מְהֵרָה קוֹמְמִיּוּת לְאַרְצֵנוּ.
◂ כִּי אֵל פּוֹעֵל יְשׁוּעוֹת אָתָּה, וּבָנוּ בָחַרְתָּ מִכָּל עַם וְלָשׁוֹן
וְקֵרַבְתָּנוּ מַלְכֵּנוּ לְשִׁמְךָ הַגָּדוֹל סֶלָה, בֶּאֱמֶת בְּאַהֲבָה
לְהוֹדוֹת לְךָ וּלְיַחֶדְךָ בְּאַהֲבָה, וּלְאַהֲבָה אֶת שְׁמֶךָ.
בָּרוּךְ אַתָּה יהוה, הַבּוֹחֵר בְּעַמּוֹ יִשְׂרָאֵל בְּאַהֲבָה.

---

**אַהֲבַת עוֹלָם אֲהַבְתָּנוּ** *With everlasting love have You loved us.* One of the supreme expressions of love in the liturgy. Having spoken of God's relationship to the universe, we now speak of His relationship to us, moving from cosmic

*The Shema must be said with intense concentration. In the first paragraph one should accept, with love, the sovereignty of God; in the second, the mitzvot as the will of God. The end of the third paragraph constitutes fulfillment of the mitzva to remember, morning and evening, the exodus from Egypt. See laws 10–14.*

*When not praying with a minyan, say:*

God, faithful King!

*The following verse should be said aloud, while covering the eyes with the right hand:*

# Listen, Israel: the LORD is our God, the LORD is One.

*Deut. 6*

*Quietly:* Blessed be the name of His glorious kingdom for ever and all time.

וְאָהַבְתָּ Love the LORD your God with all your heart, with all your soul, and with all your might. These words which I command you today shall be on your heart. Teach them repeatedly to your children, speaking of them when you sit at home and when you travel on the way, when you lie down and when you rise. Bind them as a sign on your hand, and they shall be an emblem between your eyes. Write them on the doorposts of your house and gates. *Deut. 6*

---

only ultimate reality; (4) God is One despite the many ways in which He reveals Himself, through creation, revelation and redemption; (5) God is One despite the different ways He has revealed Himself in history, in war, in peace, in tragedy and triumph; (6) God is One despite the different ways He relates to us, sometimes in judgment, sometimes in compassion, mercy, grace and forgiveness; (7) God alone is our King and our only object of worship. According to the Ba'al Shem Tov the meaning is: The universe is filled with God's glory, and there is nothing devoid of His presence.

וְשִׁנַּנְתָּם...וּקְשַׁרְתָּם...וּכְתַבְתָּם *Teach them... bind them... write them.* Judaism is supremely a religion of words. By words, God created the natural universe. By words we create the human universe. By words, the prophets transformed the horizon of human hope. It is through words that we relate to one another, words that express, inform, thank, encourage, inspire. Conversation is the defeat of existential loneliness. Through honest words, words that come from the heart, we cross the abyss between soul and soul. Words are the vehicles of meaning, and because Judaism is the world's greatest statement

*The* שמע *must be said with intense concentration. In the first paragraph one should accept, with love, the sovereignty of God; in the second, the* מצוות *as the will of God. The end of the third paragraph constitutes fulfillment of the* מצווה *to remember, morning and evening, the exodus from Egypt. See laws 10–14.*

*When not praying with a* מנין*, say:*

אֵל מֶלֶךְ נֶאֱמָן

*The following verse should be said aloud, while covering the eyes with the right hand:*

דברים ו שְׁמַע יִשְׂרָאֵל, יְהוָה אֱלֹהֵינוּ, יְהוָה ׀ אֶחָד׃

*Quietly* בָּרוּךְ שֵׁם כְּבוֹד מַלְכוּתוֹ לְעוֹלָם וָעֶד.

דברים ו וְאָהַבְתָּ אֵת יְהוָה אֱלֹהֶיךָ, בְּכָל־לְבָבְךָ וּבְכָל־נַפְשְׁךָ וּבְכָל־
מְאֹדֶךָ׃ וְהָיוּ הַדְּבָרִים הָאֵלֶּה, אֲשֶׁר אָנֹכִי מְצַוְּךָ הַיּוֹם, עַל־לְבָבֶךָ׃
וְשִׁנַּנְתָּם לְבָנֶיךָ וְדִבַּרְתָּ בָּם, בְּשִׁבְתְּךָ בְּבֵיתֶךָ וּבְלֶכְתְּךָ בַדֶּרֶךְ,
וּבְשָׁכְבְּךָ וּבְקוּמֶךָ׃ וּקְשַׁרְתָּם לְאוֹת עַל־יָדֶךָ וְהָיוּ לְטֹטָפֹת בֵּין
עֵינֶיךָ׃ וּכְתַבְתָּם עַל־מְזֻזוֹת בֵּיתֶךָ וּבִשְׁעָרֶיךָ׃

---

שְׁמַע יִשְׂרָאֵל *Listen, Israel.* The greatest, simplest, briefest statement of Jewish faith: the faith that God is One. For those who believed that there were many gods, there was no meaning to history. The gods clashed. They were at worst actively hostile, at best indifferent to humanity. "As flies to wanton boys, are we to the gods; they kill us for their sport."

For those who believe there is no god, equally there is no meaning to history. The universe is the result of blind forces. It and we came into being for no reason; for no reason we exist, for no reason we will die, and it will be as if we had never been.

We believe, to the contrary, that the God of love created the universe and us in love, and calls on us to live a life suffused with love: love of God, love of neighbor and of stranger, the love of husband and wife, parent and child. There have been many civilizations in history and many systems of ethics but none has placed love – personal love – at the heart of its values and at the epicentre of being.

יהוה אֶחָד *The Lord is One.* This has many meanings, depending on context: (1) There is only one God; (2) God is a unity, indivisible; (3) God is the

וְהָיָה If you indeed heed My commandments with which I charge you today, to love the LORD your God and worship Him with all your heart and with all your soul, I will give rain in your land in its season, the early and late rain; and you shall gather in your grain, wine and oil. I will give grass in your field for your cattle, and you shall eat and be satisfied. Be careful lest your heart be tempted and you go astray and worship other gods, bowing down to them. Then the LORD's anger will flare against you and He will close the heavens so that there will be no rain. The land will not yield its crops, and you will perish swiftly from the good land that the LORD is giving you. Therefore, set these, My words, on your heart and soul. Bind them as a sign on your hand, and they shall be an emblem between your eyes. Teach them to your children, speaking of them when you sit at home and when you travel on the way, when you lie down and when you rise. Write them on the doorposts of your house and gates, so that you and your children may live long in the land that the LORD swore to your ancestors to give them, for as long as the heavens are above the earth. *Deut. 11*

*Transfer the tzitziot to the right hand, kissing them at °.*

וַיֹּאמֶר The LORD spoke to Moses, saying: Speak to the Israelites and tell them to make °tassels on the corners of their garments for all generations. They shall attach to the °tassel at each corner a thread of blue. This shall be your °tassel, and you shall see it and remember all of the LORD's commandments and keep them, not straying after your heart and after your eyes, following your own sinful desires. Thus you will be reminded to keep all My *Num. 15*

---

sation between the generations. In Jewish law, the obligation to learn is subordinate to the obligation to teach (Maimonides, Laws of Torah Study 1:1–5).

לְמַעַן יִרְבּוּ יְמֵיכֶם וִימֵי בְנֵיכֶם *So that you and your children may live long.* Strong nations are impossible without strong families. "Those who plan for one year, plant crops. Those who plan for ten years, plant trees. Those who plan for centuries, educate children."

וְהָיָה אִם־שָׁמֹעַ תִּשְׁמְעוּ אֶל־מִצְוֺתַי אֲשֶׁר אָנֹכִי מְצַוֶּה אֶתְכֶם דברים יא
הַיּוֹם, לְאַהֲבָה אֶת־יהוה אֱלֹהֵיכֶם וּלְעָבְדוֹ, בְּכָל־לְבַבְכֶם וּבְכָל־
נַפְשְׁכֶם: וְנָתַתִּי מְטַר־אַרְצְכֶם בְּעִתּוֹ, יוֹרֶה וּמַלְקוֹשׁ, וְאָסַפְתָּ
דְגָנֶךָ וְתִירֹשְׁךָ וְיִצְהָרֶךָ: וְנָתַתִּי עֵשֶׂב בְּשָׂדְךָ לִבְהֶמְתֶּךָ, וְאָכַלְתָּ
וְשָׂבָעְתָּ: הִשָּׁמְרוּ לָכֶם פֶּן־יִפְתֶּה לְבַבְכֶם, וְסַרְתֶּם וַעֲבַדְתֶּם
אֱלֹהִים אֲחֵרִים וְהִשְׁתַּחֲוִיתֶם לָהֶם: וְחָרָה אַף־יהוה בָּכֶם, וְעָצַר
אֶת־הַשָּׁמַיִם וְלֹא־יִהְיֶה מָטָר, וְהָאֲדָמָה לֹא תִתֵּן אֶת־יְבוּלָהּ,
וַאֲבַדְתֶּם מְהֵרָה מֵעַל הָאָרֶץ הַטֹּבָה אֲשֶׁר יהוה נֹתֵן לָכֶם:
וְשַׂמְתֶּם אֶת־דְּבָרַי אֵלֶּה עַל־לְבַבְכֶם וְעַל־נַפְשְׁכֶם, וּקְשַׁרְתֶּם
אֹתָם לְאוֹת עַל־יֶדְכֶם, וְהָיוּ לְטוֹטָפֹת בֵּין עֵינֵיכֶם: וְלִמַּדְתֶּם
אֹתָם אֶת־בְּנֵיכֶם לְדַבֵּר בָּם, בְּשִׁבְתְּךָ בְּבֵיתֶךָ וּבְלֶכְתְּךָ בַדֶּרֶךְ,
וּבְשָׁכְבְּךָ וּבְקוּמֶךָ: וּכְתַבְתָּם עַל־מְזוּזוֹת בֵּיתֶךָ וּבִשְׁעָרֶיךָ: לְמַעַן
יִרְבּוּ יְמֵיכֶם וִימֵי בְנֵיכֶם עַל הָאֲדָמָה אֲשֶׁר נִשְׁבַּע יהוה לַאֲבֹתֵיכֶם
לָתֵת לָהֶם, כִּימֵי הַשָּׁמַיִם עַל־הָאָרֶץ:

*Transfer the* ציציות *to the right hand, kissing them at* °.

וַיֹּאמֶר יהוה אֶל־מֹשֶׁה לֵּאמֹר: דַּבֵּר אֶל־בְּנֵי יִשְׂרָאֵל וְאָמַרְתָּ במדבר טו
אֲלֵהֶם, וְעָשׂוּ לָהֶם °צִיצִת עַל־כַּנְפֵי בִגְדֵיהֶם לְדֹרֹתָם, וְנָתְנוּ
°עַל־צִיצִת הַכָּנָף פְּתִיל תְּכֵלֶת: וְהָיָה לָכֶם °לְצִיצִת, וּרְאִיתֶם
אֹתוֹ וּזְכַרְתֶּם אֶת־כָּל־מִצְוֺת יהוה וַעֲשִׂיתֶם אֹתָם, וְלֹא תָתוּרוּ

---

that life has meaning, we have enthroned words at the heart of our faith. More than a religion of holy places and holy objects, Judaism is a religion of holy words.

וְשִׁנַּנְתָּם לְבָנֶיךָ *Teach them repeatedly to your children* (previous page). In Judaism, a parent is, first and foremost, a teacher, and education itself the conver-

commandments, and be holy to your God. I am the LORD your God, who brought you out of the land of Egypt to be your God. I am the LORD your God.

°True –

*The Leader repeats:*

▸ The LORD your God is true –

וְיַצִּיב And firm, established and enduring, right, faithful,
beloved, cherished, delightful, pleasant,
awesome, mighty, perfect, accepted,
good and beautiful
is this faith for us for ever.

True is the eternal God, our King, Rock of Jacob,
Shield of our salvation.
He exists and His name exists through all generations.
His throne is established,
His kingship and faithfulness endure for ever.

*At °, kiss the tzitziot and release them.*

His words live and persist, faithful and desirable
°for ever and all time.
▸ So they were for our ancestors, so they are for us,
and so they will be for our children
and all our generations and for all future generations
of the seed of Israel, Your servants.

---

**יהוה אֱלֹהֵיכֶם אֱמֶת** *The LORD your God is true.* The linking of the last words of the Shema with the word "true," as in Jeremiah 10:10, constitutes an affirmation of everything we have said in the Shema, which is less a prayer than a declaration of faith. According to the *Zohar* (*VaYera* 101a), these three words are repeated to bring the total of words in the three paragraphs to 248, the number associated in tradition with the organs of the body, as if to say that our faith in God suffuses every fibre of our being. Faith has an effect not only on the soul but also the body.

אַחֲרֵי לְבַבְכֶם֙ וְאַחֲרֵ֣י עֵֽינֵיכֶ֔ם, אֲשֶׁר־אַתֶּ֥ם זֹנִ֖ים אַחֲרֵיהֶֽם: לְמַ֣עַן
תִּזְכְּר֔וּ וַעֲשִׂיתֶ֖ם אֶת־כׇּל־מִצְוֺתָ֑י, וִהְיִיתֶ֥ם קְדֹשִׁ֖ים לֵאלֹהֵיכֶֽם: אֲנִ֞י
יְהֹוָ֣ה אֱלֹהֵיכֶ֗ם, אֲשֶׁ֨ר הוֹצֵ֤אתִי אֶתְכֶם֙ מֵאֶ֣רֶץ מִצְרַ֔יִם, לִהְי֥וֹת לָכֶ֖ם
לֵאלֹהִ֑ים, אֲנִ֖י יְהֹוָ֥ה אֱלֹהֵיכֶֽם:

°אֱמֶת

*The* שליח ציבור *repeats:*

◂ יהוה אֱלֹהֵיכֶם אֱמֶת

וְיַצִּיב, וְנָכוֹן וְקַיָּם, וְיָשָׁר וְנֶאֱמָן
וְאָהוּב וְחָבִיב, וְנֶחְמָד וְנָעִים
וְנוֹרָא וְאַדִּיר, וּמְתֻקָּן וּמְקֻבָּל
וְטוֹב וְיָפֶה
הַדָּבָר הַזֶּה עָלֵינוּ לְעוֹלָם וָעֶד.

אֱמֶת אֱלֹהֵי עוֹלָם מַלְכֵּנוּ
צוּר יַעֲקֹב מָגֵן יִשְׁעֵנוּ
לְדוֹר וָדוֹר הוּא קַיָּם וּשְׁמוֹ קַיָּם
וְכִסְאוֹ נָכוֹן
וּמַלְכוּתוֹ וֶאֱמוּנָתוֹ לָעַד קַיֶּמֶת.

*At °, kiss the* ציציות *and release them.*

וּדְבָרָיו חָיִים וְקַיָּמִים
נֶאֱמָנִים וְנֶחֱמָדִים
°לָעַד וּלְעוֹלְמֵי עוֹלָמִים
◂ עַל אֲבוֹתֵינוּ וְעָלֵינוּ
עַל בָּנֵינוּ וְעַל דּוֹרוֹתֵינוּ
וְעַל כׇּל דּוֹרוֹת זֶרַע יִשְׂרָאֵל עֲבָדֶיךָ.

For the early and the later generations
this faith has proved good and enduring for ever –
True and faithful, an irrevocable law.
True You are the LORD: our God and God of our ancestors,
▸ our King and King of our ancestors,
our Redeemer and Redeemer of our ancestors,
our Maker, Rock of our salvation,
our Deliverer and Rescuer:
this has ever been Your name,
and we have no other God but You, Selah!

עֶזְרַת You have always been the help of our ancestors,
their Shield and Savior,
and that of their children
after them in every generation.
Your dwelling is in the heights of the universe,
and Your judgments and righteousness
reach to the ends of the earth.
True Happy is the one who obeys Your commandments
and takes to heart Your teaching and Your word.
True You are the Master of Your people, and a mighty King
who pleads the cause of old and young alike.
True You are the first and You are the last.
Besides You, we have no king, redeemer or savior.
True From Egypt You redeemed us, LORD our God,
and from the slave-house You delivered us.
All their firstborn You killed,
but Your firstborn of Israel You redeemed.
You split the Sea of Reeds for them,
and drowned the arrogant.
You brought Your beloved ones across.
The water covered their foes; *Ps. 106*
not one of them was left.

עַל הָרִאשׁוֹנִים וְעַל הָאַחֲרוֹנִים
דָּבָר טוֹב וְקַיָּם לְעוֹלָם וָעֶד
אֱמֶת וֶאֱמוּנָה, חֹק וְלֹא יַעֲבֹר.
אֱמֶת שָׁאַתָּה הוּא יהוה אֱלֹהֵינוּ וֵאלֹהֵי אֲבוֹתֵינוּ
‹ מַלְכֵּנוּ מֶלֶךְ אֲבוֹתֵינוּ
גּוֹאֲלֵנוּ גּוֹאֵל אֲבוֹתֵינוּ
יוֹצְרֵנוּ צוּר יְשׁוּעָתֵנוּ
פּוֹדֵנוּ וּמַצִּילֵנוּ מֵעוֹלָם הוּא שְׁמֶךָ
וְאֵין לָנוּ עוֹד אֱלֹהִים זוּלָתֶךָ סֶלָה.

עֶזְרַת אֲבוֹתֵינוּ אַתָּה הוּא מֵעוֹלָם
מָגֵן וּמוֹשִׁיעַ לָהֶם וְלִבְנֵיהֶם אַחֲרֵיהֶם בְּכָל דּוֹר וָדוֹר.
בְּרוּם עוֹלָם מוֹשָׁבֶךָ
וּמִשְׁפָּטֶיךָ וְצִדְקָתְךָ עַד אַפְסֵי אָרֶץ.
אֱמֶת אַשְׁרֵי אִישׁ שֶׁיִּשְׁמַע לְמִצְוֹתֶיךָ
וְתוֹרָתְךָ וּדְבָרְךָ יָשִׂים עַל לִבּוֹ.
אֱמֶת אַתָּה הוּא אָדוֹן לְעַמֶּךָ
וּמֶלֶךְ גִּבּוֹר לָרִיב רִיבָם לְאָבוֹת וּבָנִים.
אֱמֶת אַתָּה הוּא רִאשׁוֹן וְאַתָּה הוּא אַחֲרוֹן
וּמִבַּלְעָדֶיךָ אֵין לָנוּ מֶלֶךְ גּוֹאֵל וּמוֹשִׁיעַ.
אֱמֶת מִמִּצְרַיִם גְּאַלְתָּנוּ, יהוה אֱלֹהֵינוּ
וּמִבֵּית עֲבָדִים פְּדִיתָנוּ
כָּל בְּכוֹרֵיהֶם הָרַגְתָּ, וּבְכוֹרְךָ יִשְׂרָאֵל גָּאָלְתָּ
וְיַם סוּף לָהֶם בָּקַעְתָּ
וְזֵדִים טִבַּעְתָּ וִידִידִים הֶעֱבַרְתָּ
וַיְכַסּוּ מַיִם צָרֵיהֶם, אֶחָד מֵהֶם לֹא נוֹתָר. תהלים קו

For this, the beloved ones praised and exalted God,
the cherished ones sang psalms, songs and praises,
blessings and thanksgivings to the King,
the living and enduring God.
High and exalted, great and awesome,
He brings the haughty down to earth
and raises the lowly to the heights,
freeing captives and redeeming those in need, helping the poor
and answering His people Israel when they cry out to Him.

*Stand in preparation for the Amida. Take three steps back before beginning the Amida.*

▸ Praises to God Most High, their Redeemer,
the Blessed One who is blessed.
Moses and the children of Israel
recited to You a song with great joy, and they all exclaimed:
"Who is like You, LORD, among the mighty? *Ex. 15*
Who is like You, majestic in holiness,
awesome in praises, doing wonders?"

▸ With a new song, the redeemed people praised
Your great name at the seashore.
Together they all gave thanks,
proclaimed Your kingship, and declared:
"The LORD shall reign for ever and ever." *Ibid.*

*Congregants should end the following blessing together with the Leader so as to be able to move directly from the words "redeemed Israel" to the Amida, without the interruption of saying Amen.*

▸ צוּר יִשְׂרָאֵל Rock of Israel! Arise to the help of Israel.
Deliver, as You promised, Judah and Israel. It is said:
"Our Redeemer, the LORD of hosts is His name, *Is. 47*
the Holy One of Israel."
Blessed are You, LORD, who redeemed Israel.

---

An analogy: imagine visiting a historic building without knowing its history. The experience will be flat and vague. You may know that something happened here long ago, but not what or when or how. Now imagine visiting it having read its history. You now know that great people once stood here

עַל זֹאת שִׁבְּחוּ אֲהוּבִים, וְרוֹמְמוּ לָאֵל
וְנָתְנוּ יְדִידִים זְמִירוֹת, שִׁירוֹת וְתִשְׁבָּחוֹת
בְּרָכוֹת וְהוֹדָאוֹת לַמֶּלֶךְ אֵל חַי וְקַיָּם
רָם וְנִשָּׂא, גָּדוֹל וְנוֹרָא
מַשְׁפִּיל גֵּאִים עֲדֵי אָרֶץ, וּמַגְבִּיהַּ שְׁפָלִים עֲדֵי מָרוֹם
מוֹצִיא אֲסִירִים, וּפוֹדֶה עֲנָוִים וְעוֹזֵר דַּלִּים
וְעוֹנֶה לְעַמּוֹ יִשְׂרָאֵל בְּעֵת שַׁוְּעָם אֵלָיו.

*Stand in preparation for the* עמידה*. Take three steps back before beginning the* עמידה*.*

◂ תְּהִלּוֹת לְאֵל עֶלְיוֹן גּוֹאֲלָם, בָּרוּךְ הוּא וּמְבֹרָךְ
מֹשֶׁה וּבְנֵי יִשְׂרָאֵל, לְךָ עָנוּ שִׁירָה בְּשִׂמְחָה רַבָּה, וְאָמְרוּ כֻלָּם
שמות טו מִי־כָמֹכָה בָּאֵלִם, יהוה
מִי כָּמֹכָה נֶאְדָּר בַּקֹּדֶשׁ, נוֹרָא תְהִלֹּת, עֹשֵׂה פֶלֶא:

◂ שִׁירָה חֲדָשָׁה שִׁבְּחוּ גְאוּלִים
לְשִׁמְךָ הַגָּדוֹל עַל שְׂפַת הַיָּם
יַחַד כֻּלָּם הוֹדוּ וְהִמְלִיכוּ, וְאָמְרוּ
שם יהוה יִמְלֹךְ לְעֹלָם וָעֶד:

*The* קהל *should end the following blessing together with the* שליח ציבור *so as to be able to move directly from the words* גָּאַל יִשְׂרָאֵל *to the* עמידה*, without the interruption of saying* אמן*.*

◂ צוּר יִשְׂרָאֵל, קוּמָה בְּעֶזְרַת יִשְׂרָאֵל
וּפְדֵה כִנְאֻמֶךָ יְהוּדָה וְיִשְׂרָאֵל. וְנֶאֱמַר
ישעיה מז גֹּאֲלֵנוּ יהוה צְבָאוֹת שְׁמוֹ, קְדוֹשׁ יִשְׂרָאֵל:
בָּרוּךְ אַתָּה יהוה, גָּאַל יִשְׂרָאֵל.

---

גָּאַל יִשְׂרָאֵל *Who redeemed Israel.* The sages placed great emphasis on there being no interruption between redemption (the conclusion of this blessing) and prayer (*Berakhot* 4b; 9b). We move directly from God's presence in history to His presence in our lives.

## THE AMIDA

*The following prayer, until "in former years" on page 356, is said silently, standing with feet together. If there is a minyan, the Amida is repeated aloud by the Leader. Take three steps forward and at the points indicated by ˇ, bend the knees at the first word, bow at the second, and stand straight before saying God's name.*

O Lord, open my lips, so that my mouth may declare Your praise. *Ps. 51*

PATRIARCHS

ˇבָּרוּךְ Blessed are You, Lord our God and God of our fathers,
God of Abraham, God of Isaac and God of Jacob;
the great, mighty and awesome God, God Most High,
who bestows acts of loving-kindness, who creates all,
who remembers the loving-kindness of the fathers
and will bring a Redeemer to their children's children
for the sake of His name, in love.

זָכְרֵנוּ לְחַיִּים Remember us for life, O King who desires life,
and write us in the book of life – for Your sake, O God of life.

King, Helper, Savior, Shield:
ˇBlessed are You, Lord, Shield of Abraham.

---

אֱלֹהֵי אַבְרָהָם, אֱלֹהֵי יִצְחָק, וֵאלֹהֵי יַעֲקֹב *God of Abraham, God of Isaac and God of Jacob.* Though there is only one God, we do not say, "God of Abraham, Isaac and Jacob." Instead we emphasize the fact that each of the fathers served God in their own way; Abraham teaching us to pioneer, Isaac to fear and revere, Jacob to persevere.

מָגֵן אַבְרָהָם *Shield of Abraham.* This, the opening paragraph of prayer, implicitly asks the ultimate question of prayer: by what right do we stand before the Author of the universe, Creator of all, and ask Him to listen to us? The answer lies in the fact that, beginning with Abraham, our ancestors listened to God. It was Abraham who, in response to God's call, left his land, birthplace and father's house to travel to an unknown destination, there to become God's covenantal partner, His witness and ambassador to the world. In the merit of Abraham's listening to God, we ask God to listen to us.

זָכְרֵנוּ לְחַיִּים *Remember us for life.* The first of four additions made in the opening and closing paragraphs of prayer during the Ten Days that begin on Rosh

# עמידה

*The following prayer, until* קַדְמֹנִיּוֹת *on page 357, is said silently, standing with feet together. If there is a* מנין*, the* עמידה *is repeated aloud by the* שליח ציבור*. Take three steps forward and at the points indicated by* ˚*, bend the knees at the first word, bow at the second, and stand straight before saying God's name.*

אֲדֹנָי, שְׂפָתַי תִּפְתָּח, וּפִי יַגִּיד תְּהִלָּתֶךָ: תהלים נא

אבות

˚בָּרוּךְ אַתָּה יהוה, אֱלֹהֵינוּ וֵאלֹהֵי אֲבוֹתֵינוּ
אֱלֹהֵי אַבְרָהָם, אֱלֹהֵי יִצְחָק, וֵאלֹהֵי יַעֲקֹב
הָאֵל הַגָּדוֹל הַגִּבּוֹר וְהַנּוֹרָא, אֵל עֶלְיוֹן
גּוֹמֵל חֲסָדִים טוֹבִים, קוֹנֵה הַכֹּל
וְזוֹכֵר חַסְדֵי אָבוֹת
וּמֵבִיא גוֹאֵל לִבְנֵי בְנֵיהֶם לְמַעַן שְׁמוֹ בְּאַהֲבָה.

זָכְרֵנוּ לְחַיִּים, מֶלֶךְ חָפֵץ בַּחַיִּים
וְכָתְבֵנוּ בְּסֵפֶר הַחַיִּים, לְמַעַנְךָ אֱלֹהִים חַיִּים.

מֶלֶךְ עוֹזֵר וּמוֹשִׁיעַ וּמָגֵן.
˚בָּרוּךְ אַתָּה יהוה, מָגֵן אַבְרָהָם.

---

and epic events took place within its walls. You feel the strong, indefinable thrill of being linked with the past, a past that shaped the world in which you now live. So it is with God. You are about to enter the presence of a Presence that is not a mere abstraction, but the One who delivered our ancestors from danger, divided the sea, brought them through on dry land, and led them across the desert to the Promised Land. It is this Presence to whom we draw close when we pray, and prayer should never be devoid of a sense of awe.

אֱלֹהֵינוּ וֵאלֹהֵי אֲבוֹתֵינוּ *Our God and God of our fathers.* Our ancestors were the first to believe that God is One, and that He can be addressed in prayer: not prayer as ritual and rite, but prayer as a conversation between I and Thou. When we pray, we continue this tradition, guided by their precedent, empowered by the knowledge of the love God had for them.

DIVINE MIGHT

אַתָּה גִּבּוֹר You are eternally mighty, LORD.
You give life to the dead and have great power to save.

*In Israel:* He causes the dew to fall.

He sustains the living with loving-kindness,
and with great compassion revives the dead.
He supports the fallen, heals the sick, sets captives free,
and keeps His faith with those who sleep in the dust.
Who is like You, Master of might, and to whom can You be compared,
O King who brings death and gives life, and makes salvation grow?

מִי כָמְוֹךָ Who is like You, compassionate Father,
who remembers His creatures in compassion, for life?

Faithful are You to revive the dead.
Blessed are You, LORD, who revives the dead.

---

30:19). "Can the dead praise You, can they proclaim Your truth?" asked David in Psalms (30:10). God is the God of life, and it is in life itself that we find God. We may be dust of the earth, but within us is the breath of God. To be a Jew is to take hold of life and say a blessing over it. Judaism is a supremely life-affirming faith.

אַתָּה גִּבּוֹר *You are eternally mighty.* The second paragraph of the Amida is known as *Gevurot*, a blessing praising God's power and might. The specific structure of the prayer goes back to an ancient controversy between the sages and the Sadducees in Second Temple times, about belief in the resurrection of the dead. The sages held this to be a fundamental of Jewish faith, and signaled its centrality by including five references to it in this one paragraph alone. How it will be, we do not know, but that it will be, this we believe: that death is not the end. Loss is not final. Those who died will one day live again.

מִי כָמְוֹךָ אַב הָרַחֲמָן *Who is like You, compassionate Father?* This, the second of the special prayers for life, echoes two phrases in the blessing itself: "Who is like You" and "compassion," thus weaving the request into the text and context of the Amida.

גבורות

אַתָּה גִּבּוֹר לְעוֹלָם, אֲדֹנָי
מְחַיֵּה מֵתִים אַתָּה, רַב לְהוֹשִׁיעַ
בארץ ישראל: מוֹרִיד הַטָּל
מְכַלְכֵּל חַיִּים בְּחֶסֶד, מְחַיֵּה מֵתִים בְּרַחֲמִים רַבִּים
סוֹמֵךְ נוֹפְלִים, וְרוֹפֵא חוֹלִים, וּמַתִּיר אֲסוּרִים
וּמְקַיֵּם אֱמוּנָתוֹ לִישֵׁנֵי עָפָר.
מִי כָמְוֹךָ, בַּעַל גְּבוּרוֹת, וּמִי דּוֹמֶה לָּךְ
מֶלֶךְ, מֵמִית וּמְחַיֶּה וּמַצְמִיחַ יְשׁוּעָה.

מִי כָמְוֹךָ אַב הָרַחֲמָן
זוֹכֵר יְצוּרָיו לְחַיִּים בְּרַחֲמִים.

וְנֶאֱמָן אַתָּה לְהַחֲיוֹת מֵתִים.
בָּרוּךְ אַתָּה יהוה, מְחַיֵּה הַמֵּתִים.

---

HaShana and end on Yom Kippur. There was an initial resistance to the inclusion of these prayers since they are requests, *bakashot*, and we do not usually include requests in the opening and closing paragraphs of the Amida which are dedicated to praise, *shevaḥ*, and thanks, *hoda'a*. Eventually they were admitted on the grounds that the requests are not personal ("Remember me") but collective ("Remember us"). When praising and thanking God we may not ask for our individual needs but we may speak on behalf of the Jewish people, and humanity, as a whole.

This particular prayer with its fourfold repetition of the word "life," reminds of the centrality in Judaism of this life, this world; of finding God in the here-and-now of existence, not just in the World to Come. In many other religions, God is primarily to be found elsewhere: in heaven, life after death, the world of the soul and of eternity. Judaism, while believing in life after death, focuses relentlessly and gloriously on the presence of God here-where-we-are. Faith in God is faith in life. "Choose life" said Moses (Deut.

HOLINESS

אַתָּה קָדוֹשׁ You are holy and Your name is holy,
and holy ones praise You daily, Selah!
For You, God, are a great and holy King.

לְדוֹר וָדוֹר From generation to generation declare God King,
for He alone is lofty and holy.

וּבְכֵן יִתְקַדַּשׁ And so may Your name be sanctified, LORD our God,
through Israel Your nation
and Jerusalem, Your city,
and Zion, the dwelling place of Your honor
and through the royal house of David Your anointed,
and Your Sanctuary and Your Temple.

וּבְכֵן תֵּן פַּחְדְּךָ And so place the fear of You, LORD our God,
over all that You have made,
and the terror of You over all You have created,
and all who were made will stand in awe of You,
and all of creation will worship You,
and they will be bound all together as one
to carry out Your will with an undivided heart;
for we know, LORD our God,
that all dominion is laid out before You,
strength is in Your palm,
and might in Your right hand,
Your name spreading awe
over all You have created.

---

The three pilgrimage festivals – Pesaḥ, Shavuot and Sukkot – are about God as He has shaped the history of our people. They represent particularity: God and His relationship to the children of Israel. But on the Days of Awe we speak of God the Creator, Sovereign of the universe, the God who made all humankind – hence the universalism of this paragraph. All humanity, not just the Jewish people, is judged on these days, for our God is the God of everyone and everywhere, the God of humanity as such.

קדושת השם

אַתָּה קָדוֹשׁ וְשִׁמְךָ קָדוֹשׁ
וּקְדוֹשִׁים בְּכָל יוֹם יְהַלְלוּךָ סֶּלָה
כִּי אֵל מֶלֶךְ גָּדוֹל וְקָדוֹשׁ אָתָּה.

לְדוֹר וָדוֹר הַמְלִיכוּ לָאֵל
כִּי הוּא לְבַדּוֹ מָרוֹם וְקָדוֹשׁ.

וּבְכֵן יִתְקַדַּשׁ שִׁמְךָ יהוה אֱלֹהֵינוּ
עַל יִשְׂרָאֵל עַמֶּךָ וְעַל יְרוּשָׁלַיִם עִירֶךָ
וְעַל צִיּוֹן מִשְׁכַּן כְּבוֹדֶךָ וְעַל מַלְכוּת בֵּית דָּוִד מְשִׁיחֶךָ
וְעַל מְכוֹנְךָ וְהֵיכָלֶךָ.

וּבְכֵן תֵּן פַּחְדְּךָ יהוה אֱלֹהֵינוּ עַל כָּל מַעֲשֶׂיךָ
וְאֵימָתְךָ עַל כָּל מַה שֶּׁבָּרָאתָ
וְיִירָאוּךָ כָּל הַמַּעֲשִׂים
וְיִשְׁתַּחֲווּ לְפָנֶיךָ כָּל הַבְּרוּאִים
וְיֵעָשׂוּ כֻלָּם אֲגֻדָּה אֶחָת לַעֲשׂוֹת רְצוֹנְךָ בְּלֵבָב שָׁלֵם
כְּמוֹ שֶׁיָּדַעְנוּ יהוה אֱלֹהֵינוּ שֶׁהַשָּׁלְטָן לְפָנֶיךָ
עֹז בְּיָדְךָ וּגְבוּרָה בִּימִינֶךָ
וְשִׁמְךָ נוֹרָא עַל כָּל מַה שֶּׁבָּרָאתָ.

---

וּבְכֵן תֵּן פַּחְדְּךָ ...עַל כָּל מַעֲשֶׂיךָ *And so place the fear of You… over all that You have made.* Note the universality of this prayer that speaks not just of the Jewish people but of *all You have made, all You have created, all who were made, all of creation.* "On the High Festivals the Jew thinks not only of himself, but of peace and blessedness for all mankind," praying for the time "when the mighty shall be just and the just mighty; when all the children of men shall form one band of brotherhood; when national arrogance and oppression shall have passed away, like so much smoke from the earth" (J.H. Hertz).

וּבְכֵן תֵּן כָּבוֹד And so place honor, LORD, upon Your people,
praise on those who fear You
and hope into those who seek You,
the confidence to speak into all who long for You,
gladness to Your land and joy to Your city,
the flourishing of pride to David Your servant,
and a lamp laid out for his descendant, Your anointed,
soon, in our days.

וּבְכֵן צַדִּיקִים And then righteous people will see and rejoice,
and the upright will exult, and the pious revel in joy,
and injustice will have nothing more to say,
and all wickedness will fade away like smoke
as You sweep the rule of arrogance from the earth.

וְתִמְלֹךְ And You, who are the LORD our God,
will rule alone over all those You have made,
in Mount Zion, the dwelling of Your glory,
and in Jerusalem, Your holy city,
as it is written in Your holy Writings:
"The LORD shall reign for ever. *Ps. 146*
He is your God, Zion, from generation to generation, Halleluya!"

קָדוֹשׁ אַתָּה You are holy, Your name is awesome,
and there is no god but You,
as it is written,
"The LORD of hosts shall be raised up through His judgment, *Is. 5*
the Holy God, made holy in righteousness."
Blessed are You, LORD, the holy King.

HOLINESS OF THE DAY

אַתָּה בְחַרְתָּנוּ You have chosen us from among all peoples.
You have loved and favored us.
You have raised us above all tongues.
You have made us holy through Your commandments.
You have brought us near, our King, to Your service,
and have called us by Your great and holy name.

וּבְכֵן תֵּן כָּבוֹד יהוה לְעַמֶּךָ
תְּהִלָּה לִירֵאֶיךָ וְתִקְוָה טוֹבָה לְדוֹרְשֶׁיךָ
וּפִתְחוֹן פֶּה לַמְיַחֲלִים לָךְ
שִׂמְחָה לְאַרְצֶךָ, וְשָׂשׂוֹן לְעִירֶךָ
וּצְמִיחַת קֶרֶן לְדָוִד עַבְדֶּךָ
וַעֲרִיכַת נֵר לְבֶן יִשַׁי מְשִׁיחֶךָ בִּמְהֵרָה בְיָמֵינוּ.

וּבְכֵן צַדִּיקִים יִרְאוּ וְיִשְׂמָחוּ, וִישָׁרִים יַעֲלֹזוּ
וַחֲסִידִים בְּרִנָּה יָגִילוּ, וְעוֹלָתָה תִּקְפָּץ פִּיהָ
וְכָל הָרִשְׁעָה כֻּלָּהּ כְּעָשָׁן תִּכְלֶה
כִּי תַעֲבִיר מֶמְשֶׁלֶת זָדוֹן מִן הָאָרֶץ.

וְתִמְלֹךְ אַתָּה הוּא יהוה אֱלֹהֵינוּ
מְהֵרָה לְבַדֶּךָ עַל כָּל מַעֲשֶׂיךָ
בְּהַר צִיּוֹן מִשְׁכַּן כְּבוֹדֶךָ, וּבִירוּשָׁלַיִם עִיר קָדְשֶׁךָ
כַּכָּתוּב בְּדִבְרֵי קָדְשֶׁךָ
יִמְלֹךְ יהוה לְעוֹלָם, אֱלֹהַיִךְ צִיּוֹן לְדֹר וָדֹר, הַלְלוּיָהּ: תהלים קמו

קָדוֹשׁ אַתָּה וְנוֹרָא שְׁמֶךָ, וְאֵין אֱלוֹהַּ מִבַּלְעָדֶיךָ
כַּכָּתוּב, וַיִּגְבַּהּ יהוה צְבָאוֹת בַּמִּשְׁפָּט ישעיה ה
וְהָאֵל הַקָּדוֹשׁ נִקְדַּשׁ בִּצְדָקָה:
בָּרוּךְ אַתָּה יהוה, הַמֶּלֶךְ הַקָּדוֹשׁ.

קדושת היום

אַתָּה בְחַרְתָּנוּ מִכָּל הָעַמִּים
אָהַבְתָּ אוֹתָנוּ וְרָצִיתָ בָּנוּ, וְרוֹמַמְתָּנוּ מִכָּל הַלְּשׁוֹנוֹת
וְקִדַּשְׁתָּנוּ בְּמִצְוֹתֶיךָ, וְקֵרַבְתָּנוּ מַלְכֵּנוּ לַעֲבוֹדָתֶךָ
וְשִׁמְךָ הַגָּדוֹל וְהַקָּדוֹשׁ עָלֵינוּ קָרָאתָ.

*On Shabbat, add the words in parentheses:*

וַתִּתֶּן לָנוּ And You, LORD our God, have given us in love
(this Sabbath day and) this Day of Remembrance,
a day of (recalling) blowing the shofar,
(with love,) a holy assembly in memory of the exodus from Egypt.

אֱלֹהֵינוּ Our God and God of our ancestors,
may there rise, come, reach, appear, be favored, heard,
regarded and remembered before You,
our recollection and remembrance,
as well as the remembrance of our ancestors,
and of the Messiah, son of David Your servant,
and of Jerusalem Your holy city,
and of all Your people the house of Israel –
for deliverance and well-being,
grace, loving-kindness and compassion,
life and peace, on this Day of Remembrance.
On it remember us, LORD our God, for good;
recollect us for blessing,
and deliver us for a good life.
In accord with Your promise of salvation and compassion,
spare us and be gracious to us;
have compassion on us and deliver us,
for our eyes are turned to You
because You, God, are a gracious and compassionate King.

אֱלֹהֵינוּ Our God and God of our ancestors,
rule over all the world in Your honor,
and be raised above all the earth in Your glory,
and appear, in the splendor of Your great might
before all those who live in this world, Your domain.
And all who were made will know that You made them,
and all who were formed will know that You formed them,
and all that have breath in their mouths will declare:
The LORD, God of Israel is King,
and His kingship has dominion over all.

*On* שבת*, add the words in parentheses:*

וַתִּתֶּן לָנוּ יהוה אֱלֹהֵינוּ בְּאַהֲבָה
אֶת יוֹם (הַשַּׁבָּת הַזֶּה וְאֶת יוֹם) הַזִּכָּרוֹן הַזֶּה
יוֹם (זִכְרוֹן) תְּרוּעָה (בְּאַהֲבָה) מִקְרָא קֹדֶשׁ, זֵכֶר לִיצִיאַת מִצְרָיִם.

אֱלֹהֵינוּ וֵאלֹהֵי אֲבוֹתֵינוּ
יַעֲלֶה וְיָבוֹא וְיַגִּיעַ, וְיֵרָאֶה וְיֵרָצֶה וְיִשָּׁמַע
וְיִפָּקֵד וְיִזָּכֵר זִכְרוֹנֵנוּ וּפִקְדוֹנֵנוּ וְזִכְרוֹן אֲבוֹתֵינוּ
וְזִכְרוֹן מָשִׁיחַ בֶּן דָּוִד עַבְדֶּךָ, וְזִכְרוֹן יְרוּשָׁלַיִם עִיר קָדְשֶׁךָ
וְזִכְרוֹן כָּל עַמְּךָ בֵּית יִשְׂרָאֵל, לְפָנֶיךָ
לִפְלֵיטָה לְטוֹבָה, לְחֵן וּלְחֶסֶד וּלְרַחֲמִים, לְחַיִּים וּלְשָׁלוֹם
בְּיוֹם הַזִּכָּרוֹן הַזֶּה.
זָכְרֵנוּ יהוה אֱלֹהֵינוּ בּוֹ לְטוֹבָה, וּפָקְדֵנוּ בוֹ לִבְרָכָה
וְהוֹשִׁיעֵנוּ בוֹ לְחַיִּים טוֹבִים.
וּבִדְבַר יְשׁוּעָה וְרַחֲמִים חוּס וְחָנֵּנוּ, וְרַחֵם עָלֵינוּ וְהוֹשִׁיעֵנוּ
כִּי אֵלֶיךָ עֵינֵינוּ, כִּי אֵל מֶלֶךְ חַנּוּן וְרַחוּם אָתָּה.

אֱלֹהֵינוּ וֵאלֹהֵי אֲבוֹתֵינוּ
מְלֹךְ עַל כָּל הָעוֹלָם כֻּלּוֹ בִּכְבוֹדֶךָ, וְהִנָּשֵׂא עַל כָּל הָאָרֶץ בִּיקָרֶךָ
וְהוֹפַע בַּהֲדַר גְּאוֹן עֻזֶּךָ עַל כָּל יוֹשְׁבֵי תֵבֵל אַרְצֶךָ.
וְיֵדַע כָּל פָּעוּל כִּי אַתָּה פְעַלְתּוֹ, וְיָבִין כָּל יָצוּר כִּי אַתָּה יְצַרְתּוֹ
וְיֹאמַר כֹּל אֲשֶׁר נְשָׁמָה בְאַפּוֹ
יהוה אֱלֹהֵי יִשְׂרָאֵל מֶלֶךְ וּמַלְכוּתוֹ בַּכֹּל מָשָׁלָה.

---

מְלֹךְ עַל כָּל הָעוֹלָם *Rule over all the world.* This prayer is specific to the Days of Awe because of their emphasis on kingship and creation. It mirrors the universality of these days, in which we think not only of God's relationship to the Jewish people but also to humanity as a whole.

*On Shabbat, add the words in parentheses:*

(Our God and God of our ancestors, find favor, please, in our rest.)
Make us holy through Your commandments
and grant us our share in Your Torah.
Satisfy us with Your goodness, grant our souls joy in Your salvation
(in love and favor, LORD our God,
grant us as our heritage Your holy Sabbath,
so that all Israel who sanctify Your name may find rest on it),
and purify our hearts to serve You in truth.
For You, LORD, are truth, and Your word is truth
and holds true forever.
Blessed are You, LORD, King over all the earth,
who sanctifies (the Sabbath,) Israel and the Day of Remembrance.

TEMPLE SERVICE

רְצֵה Find favor, LORD our God, in Your people Israel,
and heed their prayer.
Restore the service to Your most holy House,
and accept soon, in love and favor,
the fire-offerings of Israel and their prayer.
May the service of Your people Israel always find favor with You.
And may our eyes witness Your return to Zion in compassion.
Blessed are You, LORD, who restores His Presence to Zion.

THANKSGIVING

*Bow at the first nine words.*

מוֹדִים We give thanks to You,
for You are the LORD our God and God of our ancestors
for ever and all time.
You are the Rock of our lives,
Shield of our salvation from generation to generation.
We will thank You and declare Your praise for our lives,
which are entrusted into Your hand;
for our souls, which are placed in Your charge;
for Your miracles which are with us every day;
and for Your wonders and favors
at all times, evening, morning and midday.

*On שבת, add the words in parentheses:*

(אֱלֹהֵינוּ וֵאלֹהֵי אֲבוֹתֵינוּ, רְצֵה נָא בִמְנוּחָתֵנוּ)
קַדְּשֵׁנוּ בְּמִצְוֹתֶיךָ וְתֵן חֶלְקֵנוּ בְּתוֹרָתֶךָ
שַׂבְּעֵנוּ מִטּוּבֶךָ, וְשַׂמַּח נַפְשֵׁנוּ בִּישׁוּעָתֶךָ
(וְהַנְחִילֵנוּ יהוה אֱלֹהֵינוּ בְּאַהֲבָה וּבְרָצוֹן שַׁבַּת קָדְשֶׁךָ
וְיָנוּחוּ בוֹ כָּל יִשְׂרָאֵל מְקַדְּשֵׁי שְׁמֶךָ)
וְטַהֵר לִבֵּנוּ לְעָבְדְּךָ בֶּאֱמֶת
כִּי אַתָּה אֱלֹהִים אֱמֶת, וּדְבָרְךָ אֱמֶת וְקַיָּם לָעַד.
בָּרוּךְ אַתָּה יהוה, מֶלֶךְ עַל כָּל הָאָרֶץ
מְקַדֵּשׁ (הַשַּׁבָּת וְ) יִשְׂרָאֵל וְיוֹם הַזִּכָּרוֹן.

עבודה

רְצֵה יהוה אֱלֹהֵינוּ בְּעַמְּךָ יִשְׂרָאֵל, וְלִתְפִלָּתָם שְׁעֵה
וְהָשֵׁב אֶת הָעֲבוֹדָה לִדְבִיר בֵּיתֶךָ
וְאִשֵּׁי יִשְׂרָאֵל וּתְפִלָּתָם, מְהֵרָה בְּאַהֲבָה תְקַבֵּל בְּרָצוֹן
וּתְהִי לְרָצוֹן תָּמִיד עֲבוֹדַת יִשְׂרָאֵל עַמֶּךָ.
וְתֶחֱזֶינָה עֵינֵינוּ בְּשׁוּבְךָ לְצִיּוֹן בְּרַחֲמִים.
בָּרוּךְ אַתָּה יהוה, הַמַּחֲזִיר שְׁכִינָתוֹ לְצִיּוֹן.

הודאה

*Bow at the first five words.*

מוֹדִים אֲנַחְנוּ לָךְ
שָׁאַתָּה הוּא יהוה אֱלֹהֵינוּ וֵאלֹהֵי אֲבוֹתֵינוּ לְעוֹלָם וָעֶד.
צוּר חַיֵּינוּ, מָגֵן יִשְׁעֵנוּ, אַתָּה הוּא לְדוֹר וָדוֹר.
נוֹדֶה לְּךָ וּנְסַפֵּר תְּהִלָּתֶךָ
עַל חַיֵּינוּ הַמְּסוּרִים בְּיָדֶךָ, וְעַל נִשְׁמוֹתֵינוּ הַפְּקוּדוֹת לָךְ
וְעַל נִסֶּיךָ שֶׁבְּכָל יוֹם עִמָּנוּ
וְעַל נִפְלְאוֹתֶיךָ וְטוֹבוֹתֶיךָ שֶׁבְּכָל עֵת, עֶרֶב וָבֹקֶר וְצָהֳרָיִם.

You are good – for Your compassion never fails.
You are compassionate – for Your loving-kindnesses never cease;
for we have always placed our hope in You.
For all these things
may Your name be blessed and exalted and raised up, our King,
continually, for ever and all time.

וּכְתֹב And write, for a good life, all the children of Your covenant.

Let all that lives thank You, Selah! and praise and bless
Your great name in truth, always, because it is good,
God, our Savior and Help, Selah! the beneficent God.
▾Blessed are You, Lord, whose name is "the Good"
and to whom thanks are due.

PEACE

שִׂים שָׁלוֹם Grant peace, goodness and blessing,
life, grace, loving-kindness and compassion
to us and all Israel Your people.
Bless us, our Father, all as one, with the light of Your face,
for by the light of Your face You have given us, Lord our God,
the Torah of life and love of kindness,
righteousness, blessing, compassion, life and peace.
May it be good in Your eyes
to bless us and all Your people Israel
at every time, in every hour, with Your peace.

בְּסֵפֶר חַיִּים In the book of life, blessing, peace and prosperity,
and good decrees, salvations and consolations
may we and all Your people the house of Israel
be remembered and written before You
for a good life, and for peace.

Blessed are You, Lord, who blesses His people Israel with peace.

*The following verse concludes the Leader's Repetition of the Amida.*
*Some also say it here as part of the silent Amida. See law 64.*

May the words of my mouth and the meditation of my heart *Ps. 19*
find favor before You, Lord, my Rock and Redeemer.

הַטּוֹב, כִּי לֹא כָלוּ רַחֲמֶיךָ וְהַמְרַחֵם, כִּי לֹא תַמּוּ חֲסָדֶיךָ
כִּי מֵעוֹלָם קִוִּינוּ לָךְ.
וְעַל כֻּלָּם
יִתְבָּרַךְ וְיִתְרוֹמַם וְיִתְנַשֵּׂא שִׁמְךָ מַלְכֵּנוּ תָּמִיד לְעוֹלָם וָעֶד.

וּכְתֹב לְחַיִּים טוֹבִים כָּל בְּנֵי בְרִיתֶךָ.

וְכֹל הַחַיִּים יוֹדְוּךָ סֶּלָה
וִיהַלְלוּ וִיבָרְכוּ אֶת שִׁמְךָ הַגָּדוֹל בֶּאֱמֶת לְעוֹלָם כִּי טוֹב
הָאֵל יְשׁוּעָתֵנוּ וְעֶזְרָתֵנוּ סֶלָה, הָאֵל הַטּוֹב.
ּבָּרוּךְ אַתָּה יהוה, הַטּוֹב שִׁמְךָ וּלְךָ נָאֶה לְהוֹדוֹת.

ברכת שלום

שִׂים שָׁלוֹם טוֹבָה וּבְרָכָה, חַיִּים חֵן וָחֶסֶד וְרַחֲמִים
עָלֵינוּ וְעַל כָּל יִשְׂרָאֵל עַמֶּךָ.
בָּרְכֵנוּ אָבִינוּ כֻּלָּנוּ כְּאֶחָד בְּאוֹר פָּנֶיךָ
כִּי בְאוֹר פָּנֶיךָ נָתַתָּ לָּנוּ יהוה אֱלֹהֵינוּ
תּוֹרַת חַיִּים וְאַהֲבַת חֶסֶד
וּצְדָקָה וּבְרָכָה וְרַחֲמִים וְחַיִּים וְשָׁלוֹם.
וְטוֹב יִהְיֶה בְּעֵינֶיךָ לְבָרְכֵנוּ וּלְבָרֵךְ אֶת כָּל עַמְּךָ יִשְׂרָאֵל
בְּכָל עֵת וּבְכָל שָׁעָה בִּשְׁלוֹמֶךָ.

בְּסֵפֶר חַיִּים, בְּרָכָה וְשָׁלוֹם, וּפַרְנָסָה טוֹבָה
וּגְזֵרוֹת טוֹבוֹת, יְשׁוּעוֹת וְנֶחָמוֹת נִזָּכֵר וְנִכָּתֵב לְפָנֶיךָ
אֲנַחְנוּ וְכָל עַמְּךָ בֵּית יִשְׂרָאֵל לְחַיִּים טוֹבִים וּלְשָׁלוֹם.

בָּרוּךְ אַתָּה יהוה, הַמְבָרֵךְ אֶת עַמּוֹ יִשְׂרָאֵל בַּשָּׁלוֹם.

*The following verse concludes the* חזרת הש״ץ.
*Some also say it here as part of the silent* עמידה. *See law 64.*

תהלים יט יִהְיוּ לְרָצוֹן אִמְרֵי־פִי וְהֶגְיוֹן לִבִּי לְפָנֶיךָ, יהוה צוּרִי וְגֹאֲלִי:

אֱלֹהַי My God, *Berakhot 17a*
guard my tongue from evil and my lips from deceitful speech.
To those who curse me, let my soul be silent;
may my soul be to all like the dust.
Open my heart to Your Torah
and let my soul pursue Your commandments.
As for all who rise up or plan evil against me,
swiftly thwart their counsel and frustrate their plans.

*Some add this prayer:*

יְהִי רָצוֹן May it be Your will, Lord my God, God of my ancestors,
that envy of no man may rise up in me, nor envy of me in any other;
that I will not be angry today, nor make You angry;
and save me from my evil impulse,
placing humility and modesty into my heart.
Our King and God, make Your name One in Your world;
build up Your city, establish Your House and complete Your Sanctuary,
gather in the exiles, redeem Your flock, and have Your congregation rejoice.

Act for the sake of Your name; act for the sake of Your right hand;
act for the sake of Your Torah; act for the sake of Your holiness.
That Your beloved ones may be delivered, *Ps. 60*
save with Your right hand and answer me.
May the words of my mouth and the meditation of my heart *Ps. 19*
find favor before You, Lord, my Rock and Redeemer.

*Bow, take three steps back, then bow, first left, then right, then center, while saying:*

May He who makes peace in His high places,
make peace for us and all Israel – and say: Amen.

יְהִי רָצוֹן May it be Your will, Lord our God and God of our ancestors,
that the Temple be rebuilt speedily in our days, and grant us a share in Your Torah.
And there we will serve You with reverence,
as in the days of old and as in former years.
Then the offering of Judah and Jerusalem *Mal. 3*
will be pleasing to the Lord as in the days of old and as in former years.

*The Leader's Repetition for the first day starts on page 360;
for the second day, on page 644.*

ברכות יז.

אֱלֹהַי
נְצֹר לְשׁוֹנִי מֵרָע וּשְׂפָתַי מִדַּבֵּר מִרְמָה
וְלִמְקַלְלַי נַפְשִׁי תִדֹּם, וְנַפְשִׁי כֶּעָפָר לַכֹּל תִּהְיֶה.
פְּתַח לִבִּי בְּתוֹרָתֶךָ, וְאַחֲרֵי מִצְוֹתֶיךָ תִּרְדֹּף נַפְשִׁי.
וְכָל הַקָּמִים וְהַחוֹשְׁבִים עָלַי רָעָה
מְהֵרָה הָפֵר עֲצָתָם וְקַלְקֵל מַחֲשַׁבְתָּם.

*Some add this prayer:*

יְהִי רָצוֹן מִלְּפָנֶיךָ יהוה אֱלֹהַי וֵאלֹהֵי אֲבוֹתַי
שֶׁלֹּא תַעֲלֶה קִנְאַת אָדָם עָלַי, וְלֹא קִנְאָתִי עַל אֲחֵרִים
וְשֶׁלֹּא אֶכְעֹס הַיּוֹם, וְשֶׁלֹּא אַכְעִיסֶךָ
וְתַצִּילֵנִי מִיֵּצֶר הָרָע, וְתֵן בְּלִבִּי הַכְנָעָה וַעֲנָוָה.
מַלְכֵּנוּ וֵאלֹהֵינוּ, יַחֵד שִׁמְךָ בְּעוֹלָמֶךָ
בְּנֵה עִירָךְ, יַסֵּד בֵּיתְךָ וְשַׁכְלֵל הֵיכָלֶךָ
וְקַבֵּץ קִבּוּץ גָּלֻיּוֹת, וּפְדֵה צֹאנְךָ וְשַׂמַּח עֲדָתֶךָ.

עֲשֵׂה לְמַעַן שְׁמֶךָ, עֲשֵׂה לְמַעַן יְמִינֶךָ
עֲשֵׂה לְמַעַן תּוֹרָתֶךָ, עֲשֵׂה לְמַעַן קְדֻשָּׁתֶךָ.
תהלים ס לְמַעַן יֵחָלְצוּן יְדִידֶיךָ, הוֹשִׁיעָה יְמִינְךָ וַעֲנֵנִי:
תהלים יט יִהְיוּ לְרָצוֹן אִמְרֵי־פִי וְהֶגְיוֹן לִבִּי לְפָנֶיךָ, יהוה צוּרִי וְגֹאֲלִי:

*Bow, take three steps back, then bow, first left, then right, then center, while saying:*

עֹשֶׂה הַשָּׁלוֹם בִּמְרוֹמָיו
הוּא יַעֲשֶׂה שָׁלוֹם עָלֵינוּ וְעַל כָּל יִשְׂרָאֵל, וְאִמְרוּ אָמֵן.

יְהִי רָצוֹן מִלְּפָנֶיךָ יהוה אֱלֹהֵינוּ וֵאלֹהֵי אֲבוֹתֵינוּ
שֶׁיִּבָּנֶה בֵּית הַמִּקְדָּשׁ בִּמְהֵרָה בְיָמֵינוּ, וְתֵן חֶלְקֵנוּ בְּתוֹרָתֶךָ
וְשָׁם נַעֲבָדְךָ בְּיִרְאָה כִּימֵי עוֹלָם וּכְשָׁנִים קַדְמֹנִיּוֹת.
מלאכי ג וְעָרְבָה לַיהוה מִנְחַת יְהוּדָה וִירוּשָׁלָםִ כִּימֵי עוֹלָם וּכְשָׁנִים קַדְמֹנִיּוֹת:

*The* חזרת חש״ץ *for the first day starts on page 361;*
*for the second day, on page 645.*

# סדר ליום א׳

## ORDER FOR THE FIRST DAY


| | | |
|---|---|---|
| חזרת הש״ץ לשחרית | 399 | LEADER'S REPETITION FOR SHAḤARIT |
| קדושה | 437 | KEDUSHA |
| אבינו מלכנו | 449 | AVINU MALKENU |
| הוצאת ספר תורה | 457 | REMOVING THE TORAH FROM THE ARK |
| סדר תקיעת שופר | 493 | THE BLOWING OF THE SHOFAR |
| הכנסת ספר תורה | 507 | RETURNING THE TORAH TO THE ARK |
| הנני העני ממעש | 510 | LEADER'S PRAYER |
| מוסף | 515 | MUSAF |
| חזרת הש״ץ למוסף | 551 | LEADER'S REPETITION FOR MUSAF |
| ונתנה תוקף / קדושה | 565 | UNTANEH TOKEF / KEDUSHA |
| קידושא רבה | 655 | KIDDUSH FOR ROSH HASHANA DAY |
| ברכה מעין שלוש | 655 | AL HAMIḤYA |

## THE AMIDA

*The Ark is opened.*

*The Leader takes three steps forward and at the points indicated by ▾, bends the knees at the first word, bows at the second, and stands straight before saying God's name.*

O LORD, open my lips, so that my mouth may declare Your praise. Ps. 51

### PATRIARCHS

▾בָּרוּךְ Blessed are You, LORD our God and God of our fathers,
God of Abraham, God of Isaac and God of Jacob;
the great, mighty and awesome God, God Most High,
who bestows acts of loving-kindness, who creates all,
who remembers the loving-kindness of the fathers
and will bring a Redeemer to their children's children
for the sake of His name, in love.

*Before each cycle (kerova) of piyutim, the Leader says a prefatory prayer, asking permission (reshut) to commence. The reshut consists of a standard opening "Drawing from the counsel of wise and knowing men…," and a short introductory piyut. Once, these piyutim would vary across different communities; today, the prefatory prayer of the eastern European nusaḥ is almost universally said among Ashkenazim.*

מִסּוֹד Drawing from the counsel of wise and knowing men,
from the teachings born of insight among those who understand,
I open my mouth now in prayer and pleading,
to implore and to plead before the King,
King of kings and LORD of lords.

---

additional liturgical poems added to the prayers on Sabbaths and festivals. There were vast numbers of these poetical compositions. Some 35,000 of them have been collected. There were times and places where each leader of prayer would compose his own. Some authorities, among them Sa'adia Gaon and Maimonides, had marked reservations about them. They felt they were unnecessary, at times their theology was questionable, and sometimes their Hebrew grammar was at fault.

Only with the invention of printing did the text become more standardized. The *piyutim* were sifted; relatively few gained general acceptance. But the ancient custom of assuring the congregation beforehand was kept in place.

# עמידה

*The* ארון קודש *is opened.*
*The* שליח ציבור *takes three steps forward and at the points indicated by* ᐩ*, bends the knees at the first word, bows at the second, and stands straight before saying God's name.*

תהלים נא — אֲדֹנָי, שְׂפָתַי תִּפְתָּח, וּפִי יַגִּיד תְּהִלָּתֶךָ:

אבות

ᐩבָּרוּךְ אַתָּה יהוה, אֱלֹהֵינוּ וֵאלֹהֵי אֲבוֹתֵינוּ
אֱלֹהֵי אַבְרָהָם, אֱלֹהֵי יִצְחָק, וֵאלֹהֵי יַעֲקֹב
הָאֵל הַגָּדוֹל הַגִּבּוֹר וְהַנּוֹרָא, אֵל עֶלְיוֹן
גּוֹמֵל חֲסָדִים טוֹבִים, קוֹנֵה הַכֹּל
וְזוֹכֵר חַסְדֵי אָבוֹת
וּמֵבִיא גוֹאֵל לִבְנֵי בְנֵיהֶם לְמַעַן שְׁמוֹ בְּאַהֲבָה.

*Before each cycle (*קרובה*) of piyutim, the* שליח ציבור *says a prefatory prayer, asking permission (*רשות*) to commence. The* רשות *consists of a standard opening "*...מִסּוֹד חֲכָמִים וּנְבוֹנִים*," and a short introductory piyut. Once, these piyutim would vary across different communities; today, the prefatory prayer of the eastern European* נוסח *is almost universally said among Ashkenazim.*

מִסּוֹד חֲכָמִים וּנְבוֹנִים
וּמִלֶּמֶד דַּעַת מְבִינִים
אֶפְתְּחָה פִּי בִּתְפִלָּה וּבְתַחֲנוּנִים
לְחַלּוֹת וּלְחַנֵּן פְּנֵי מֶלֶךְ מַלְכֵי הַמְּלָכִים וַאֲדוֹנֵי הָאֲדוֹנִים.

---

LEADER'S REPETITION

**מִסּוֹד חֲכָמִים וּנְבוֹנִים** *Drawing from the counsel of wise and knowing men.* This type of prayer is known as a *reshut*, an "asking of permission." The leader of prayer asks permission of the congregation to represent them in prayer. He assures them that the additional prayers he will be saying in the course of the Repetition were composed with the advice and approval of the learned and the wise.

The reason for making this point is that, during the Middle Ages there was considerable debate about the legitimacy of many of the *piyutim*, the

יָרֵאתִי I am afraid as I open my mouth to weave my prayer / as I rise to entreat the One who inspires awe and terror;

My good deeds are few, so I tremble in fear / I lack understanding, so how might I appease You?

O my Creator, grant me the understanding for handing down Your legacy; / strengthen and fortify me in the face of frailty and trembling.

May my whispered plea be received like the offerings of Ketoret incense; / May my utterances be sweet like the nectar of bees.

Receive me in my honesty, not as a hypocrite, / to obtain ransom and atonement on behalf of those who sent me.

May my cry be pleasing and not jarring, undeserving; / give heed to those who approach as if they were trembling with fear.

O gracious One, as You promised the one whom you passed over in the crevice of the rock, / hearken to my cry as I begin.

My insides are agitated when You examine my inner thoughts and intrigues, / and out of fear of judgment my soul grows weary.

If I am to be judged as I deserve then my heart shall tremble, / and the wellsprings of my eyelids shall run with tears like a drain of water.

I hope for righteousness from You and I pray: / remember the uprightness of our ancestors and let them intercede on our behalf.

My heart burns within me as I speak, like embers; / it stirs up within me as the trembling comes.

*The Ark is closed.*

---

as a prelude to the next *piyut* which begins with the words "*At ḥil,* The trembling comes."

It is only in profound humility that we approach God in prayer. Abraham called himself "dust and ashes" when praying for the cities of the plain (Gen. 18:27). Moses asked (Ex. 3:11), "Who am I" that I should lead? The Torah later calls him "the humblest man on the face of the earth" (Num. 12:3). In the life of the spirit, humility is greatness.

יָרֵאתִי בִּפְצוֹתִי שִׂיחַ לְהַשְׂחִיל / קוּמִי לְחַלּוֹת פְּנֵי נוֹרָא וְדָחִיל
וְקָטֹנְתִּי מֵעַשׂ לָכֵן אַזְחִיל / תְּבוּנָה חָסַרְתִּי וְאֵיךְ אוֹחִיל
יוֹצְרִי הֲבִינֵנִי מוֹרָשָׁה לְהַנְחִיל / אַיְּלֵנִי וְאַמְּצֵנִי מֵרִפְיוֹן וְחִיל
לַחֲשִׁי יֵרָצֶה כְּמַנְטִיף וּמַשְׁחִיל / בִּטּוּיַי יְמֻתַּק כְּצוּף נָחִיל
רָצוּי בְּיֹשֶׁר וְלֹא כְּמַכְחִיל / מְשַׁלְּחַי לְהַמְצִיא כֹּפֶר וּלְהַמְחִיל
שַׁאֲגִי יֶעֱרַב וְלֹא כְּמַשְׁחִיל / הֵעָתֵר לְנִגָּשִׁים וְנֶחְשָׁבִים כְּזָחִיל
חַנּוּן כְּהַבְטִיחֲךָ לְבִנְקֶרֶת מְחִיל / זַעֲקִי קְשֹׁב בְּעֵת אַתְחִיל
קְרָבַי יֶחְמְרוּ בְּחָקְרְךָ חַלְחִיל / וּמֵאֵימַת הַדִּין נַפְשִׁי תַבְחִיל
אִם כִּגְמוּל הַלֵּב יָחִיל / מְקוֹרֵי עַפְעַפַּי אַזִּיל כְּמַזְחִיל
צְדָקָה אֲקַוֶּה מִמְּךָ וְאוֹחִיל / יֹשֶׁר הוֹרַי זָכְרָה לְהַאֲחִיל
חַם לִבִּי בַּהֲגִיגִי יַגְחִיל / יִסְתָּעֵר בְּקִרְבִּי בְּעֵת אָת חִיל.

*The* ארון קודש *is closed.*

---

יָרֵאתִי בִּפְצוֹתִי *I am afraid as I open my mouth.* A continuation of the *reshut,* now addressed not to the congregation but to God. The initial letters of each verse spell out the name of the composer, Rabbi Yekutiel ben Moshe, who lived in Speyer in the eleventh century. The leader confesses his inadequacy and prays for God's help as he presents the pleas of those who have delegated him to represent them.

The leader of prayer on the High Holy Days was often a person of great spiritual stature. Sometimes it was the rabbi of the congregation. The sight of such a person publicly confessing his failings, together with the plaintive chant associated with *reshut* prayers, had great impact on the worshipers, moving them to a sense of humility and awe.

Each line of this prayer ends with the syllable *ḥil,* because it was written

*Most of the piyutim for First Day Shaḥarit were composed by Rabbi Elazar HaKalir. As part of the Leader's Repetition, they should ideally be said by the Leader alone. However, the prevailing custom is for the congregation to participate, and some of the piyutim are said together, with the Leader raising his voice only toward the end.*

*All:*

אָת חִיל The trembling comes on this day of judgment, / torturing every creature with its attendant terror.

They approach to kneel down on this day, / making straight their thoughts like the upright smoke of the Ketoret incense.

He who fashions all their hearts shall judge them, / and the wealthy and destitute shall be judged and weighed equally.

As memory of Abraham's cry: "Shall the Judge of all not act justly?" / may the worthiness of his pleas be recalled in our judgment.

Before He had fashioned any creature, / God had planned in His mind to create Abraham, the rock from which Israel was to be quarried.

He was created as worthy as Adam and placed among generations, / so that God might heap upon him the burden of the entire quarry.

It was on this day that his destined partner was given an abundance of strength; / the fruit of her womb began to blossom at the age of ninety.

And this was taken as a sign for our people, likened to a rose, / that we would pass before God with favor on Rosh HaShana.

Her offshoots are frightened as the shofar service of the day is observed; / as they stand to represent themselves before the throne of the most fearful One.

On this day they shall whisperingly offer up the sound of their speech, / gathering to sound the shofar in the hope of finding redemption.

They rely on the merit of Sarah so they might also be visited with grace, / and they roar as one while watching alertly at the gates of the LORD.

▸ Relying upon the ashes of the ram that replaced Isaac, / in the month of Tishrei when Sarah conceived.

*Cong.:* O LORD who ascends with stern judgment, may You rise in compassion at the sound of the shofar, / rather than destroying the valley and all the inhabitants therein.

▸ I shall sway Him with the shofar (*On Shabbat substitute*: the remembrance of the shofar) and my bended knee as I bow, / and I shall find companionship in the shelter of God's garden, among His beloved nation.

*Most of the piyutim for* שחרית ליום א׳ *were composed by Rabbi Elazar HaKalir. As part of the* חזרת הש״ץ*, they should ideally be said by the* שליח ציבור *alone. However, the prevailing custom is for the* קהל *to participate, and some of the piyutim are said together, with the* שליח ציבור *raising his voice only toward the end.*

*All:*

אָת חִיל יוֹם פְּקֻדָּה / בְּאֵימָיו כָּל לָחוּם לְשָׁקְדָה
גָּשִׁים בּוֹ בֶּרֶךְ לִקְוֹדָה / דֵּעַם לְיַשֵּׁר כְּעַל מוֹקְדָה.

הַיּוֹצֵר יַחַד כֶּסֶל נִשְׁפָּט / וְשׁוֹעַ וָדַל בְּפִלּוּס יִשְׁפָּט
זֶכֶר לֹא יַעֲשֶׂה מִשְׁפָּט / חִין עֶרְכּוֹ יִזְכַּר בַּמִּשְׁפָּט.

טֶרֶם כָּל מִפְעָל חָצַב / יָזַם בְּמַחֲשֶׁבֶת צוּר חָצַב
כְּאָחוֹר וָקֶדֶם בַּתָּוֶךְ נֶחְצַב / לְיַהֵב עָלָיו כָּל הַמַּחְצָב.

מְנָתוֹ כְּהַיּוֹם כְּחַ דְּשָׁנָה / נֵצֶר לְהַחֲנִיט לְתִשְׁעִים שָׁנָה
סִימָה אוֹת הֱיוֹת לְשׁוֹשַׁנָּה / עֻבַּר לְפָנָיו בְּרֹאשׁ הַשָּׁנָה.

פִּלְּצוּ פְרָחֶיהָ בְּחֹק יוֹם / צִיגָתָם פְּנֵי כֵס אָיֹם
קוֹל דִּבְבָם יַרְחִישׁוּ כְּהַיּוֹם / רוֹגְשִׁים לְהָרִיעַ לִמְצֹא פִּדְיוֹם.

שְׁעוּנִים עָלֶיהָ בָּהּ לְהִפָּקְדָה / שׁוֹאֲגִים בְּלַהַק דְּלָתוֹת לְשָׁקְדָה
◂ תְּמוּכִים בְּדֶשֶׁן שֶׂה עֲקֵדָה / תֶּשֶׁר אֲשֶׁר בּוֹ נִפְקָדָה.

A נַעֲלָה בְּדִין עֲלוֹת בִּתְרוּעָה / גֵּיא עִם דָּרֶיהָ לְרוֹעֲעָה
◂ בְּשׁוֹפָר (*On* שבת *substitute* בְּזִכְרוֹן שׁוֹפָר) אֲפַתֶּנּוּ, וּבְבֶרֶךְ כְּרִיעָה
בְּמְגִנַּת רֵעִים בְּגַנּוֹ אֶתְרוֹעֲעָה.

---

אָת חִיל *The trembling comes.* A poem by Elazar HaKalir, based on the tradition that Isaac was born, and bound, on this day. The poem focuses on the fact that God had already foreseen the birth of Abraham before He created humankind. It asks God to forgive us in the merits of Abraham and Sarah and their son.

*The Leader continues:*

זָכְרֵנוּ לְחַיִּים Remember us for life, O King who desires life,
and write us in the book of life – for Your sake, O God of life.
King, Helper, Savior, Shield:
▾Blessed are You, LORD, Shield of Abraham.

DIVINE MIGHT

אַתָּה גִּבּוֹר You are eternally mighty, LORD.
You give life to the dead and have great power to save.

*In Israel:* He causes the dew to fall.

He sustains the living with loving-kindness,
and with great compassion revives the dead.
He supports the fallen, heals the sick, sets captives free,
and keeps His faith with those who sleep in the dust.
Who is like You, Master of might, and to whom can You be compared,
O King who brings death and gives life, and makes salvation grow?

*The first three piyutim of each cycle, known as "Magen," "Meḥayeh," and "Meshalesh" (corresponding to the sections of the Amida in which they are inserted: the blessings of Patriarchs, Divine Might, and Kedusha respectively), recall God's hearkening to the prayers of three childless women in the Bible, which is also the subject matter of the Torah Reading and the Haftara for the first day of Rosh HaShana. The custom is for the congregation to say them with the Leader, who raises his voice in the last line, and then an extra stanza is added, with one line said by all and one by the Leader alone.*

*All:*

תַּאֲלַת זוּ When God desired to heal His nation's curse, / He taught them to arrange prayers that would avail them:
The healing song of the ancient mountains – their ancestors, / that they might cry aloud and purge the trap that is the evil inclination.

Their righteousness should float to the surface as they utter their cry, / and their good deeds throughout the years should be heeded.
It should be a time of acceptance and a day of salvation, / honoring the covenant-oath that was made when the ram's horn caught in the thicket.

---

saying that it was God who taught His people how to pray. It speaks of the nine blessings of the Musaf prayer and relates them to the nine mentions of God's name in Hannah's prayer for a child (cf. *Berakhot* 29a).

*The* שליח ציבור *continues:*

זָכְרֵנוּ לְחַיִּים, מֶלֶךְ חָפֵץ בַּחַיִּים
וְכָתְבֵנוּ בְּסֵפֶר הַחַיִּים, לְמַעַנְךָ אֱלֹהִים חַיִּים.
מֶלֶךְ עוֹזֵר וּמוֹשִׁיעַ וּמָגֵן.
ּבָּרוּךְ אַתָּה יהוה, מָגֵן אַבְרָהָם.

גבורות

אַתָּה גִּבּוֹר לְעוֹלָם, אֲדֹנָי
מְחַיֵּה מֵתִים אַתָּה, רַב לְהוֹשִׁיעַ
בארץ ישראל: מוֹרִיד הַטָּל
מְכַלְכֵּל חַיִּים בְּחֶסֶד, מְחַיֵּה מֵתִים בְּרַחֲמִים רַבִּים
סוֹמֵךְ נוֹפְלִים, וְרוֹפֵא חוֹלִים, וּמַתִּיר אֲסוּרִים
וּמְקַיֵּם אֱמוּנָתוֹ לִישֵׁנֵי עָפָר.
מִי כָמְוֹךָ, בַּעַל גְּבוּרוֹת, וּמִי דּוֹמֶה לָּךְ
מֶלֶךְ, מֵמִית וּמְחַיֶּה וּמַצְמִיחַ יְשׁוּעָה.

*The first three piyutim of each* קרובה*, known as "*מגן*," "*מחיה*," and "*משלש*" (corresponding to the sections of the* עמידה *in which they are inserted: the blessings of* אבות*,* גבורות*, and* קדושה *respectively), recall God's hearkening to the prayers of three childless women in the Bible, which is also the subject matter of the* קריאת התורה *and the* הפטרה *for the first day of* ראש השנה*. The custom is for the* קהל *to say them with the* שליח ציבור*, who raises his voice in the last line, and then an extra stanza is added, with one line said by all and one by the* שליח ציבור *alone.*

*All:*

תַּאֲלַת זוּ כְּחָפֵץ לְהַתְעִיל / שׁוּעַ עֵרֶךְ לְמִדָּם לְהוֹעִיל
רוֹן הַרְרֵי קֶדֶם הַמּוֹעִיל / קְרֹא בְגָרוֹן מוֹקֵשׁ לְהַגְעִיל.

צִדְקָם לְהַקְפּוֹת בְּנִיב שַׁוְעָה / פְּעָלָם בְּקֶרֶב שָׁנִים לְשַׁמְּעָה
עֵת רָצוֹן וְיוֹם יְשׁוּעָה / סְבִיכַת קֶרֶן וּבְרִית שְׁבוּעָה.

---

תַּאֲלַת זוּ כְּחָפֵץ לְהַתְעִיל *When God desired to heal His nation's curse.* A poem by HaKalir structured as a reverse acrostic, each line beginning with a letter of the alphabet and progressing backwards, from *tav* to *alef*. The poet begins by

They approach uttering nine blessings – / as the number of the Musaf paragraphs and blessings.
In accordance with God's name mentioned nine times / in the answered prayer of the barren mother Hannah who gave birth to seven children.

They shall utter God's royal might in the ten coronation verses, / in memory of Abraham and the ten tests he was given.
They shall recite the prescribed ten verses of Remembrance and of the Shofar, / in memory of Isaac who gave Jacob ten blessings of mastery.

And let God turn to the beloved child of the one from Naharayim, / he who was bound on Mount Moriah with his arms behind him.
May God espy the ashes of his sacrifice and show favor to the remnant of His nation / who approach Him morning and evening.

It was at this time of year when Isaac beseeched God / that his wife be released from barren bondage.
▸ The groan of that sufferer was heard as if crowned; / may You heed my call just as You heeded his prayer.

l: O awesome King on high, / may You bring forth our judgment into the light.
▸ I hope to place a crown upon Him / and, in His kindness, I shall be adorned with the reviving dew of life.

*The Leader continues:*

מִי כָמוֹךָ Who is like You, compassionate Father,
who remembers His creatures in compassion, for life?
Faithful are You to revive the dead.
Blessed are You, LORD, who revives the dead.

---

have a child, and the birth itself (Gen. 18:10) – it follows that Isaac prayed for a child the previous Rosh HaShana.

אֵיחֲלֶנּוּ כֶּתֶר לְעַטְּרָה *I hope to place a crown upon Him.* "There is no King without a people" (*Rabbeinu Bahye*, Gen. 38:30). Therefore, it is our recognition of God's sovereignty that makes this fact real in human consciousness.

נוֹבְבִים בְּגִישַׁת חוֹתָמוֹת תִּשְׁעָה /
מִסְפַּר שָׁתוֹת וְחוֹתְמֵיהֶן תִּשְׁעָה
לְמִנְיַן פִּלּוּל שֵׁמוֹת תִּשְׁעָה / כְּחַנָּה עֲקָרָה יָלְדָה שִׁבְעָה.

יְאַמִּירוּ עֹז מַלְכִיּוֹת עֶשֶׂר / טְבוּעוֹת לְשֵׁם בְּחַן עֶשֶׂר
חֹק זִכְרוֹנוֹת וְקוֹלוֹת עֶשֶׂר / זֵכֶר מְבֹרֵךְ גְּבִירוֹ בְּעֶשֶׂר.

וַיִּפֶן בְּאָהוּב אֲתוּיֵ נְהָרַיִם / הֶעָקוּד בְּהַר מוֹר אֲחוֹרַיִם
דִּשְּׁנוּ יְרֵא לָחוֹן שִׁירַיִם / גָּשִׁים עָדָיו בֹּקֶר וְצָהֳרָיִם.

בְּזֶה פֶּרֶק חִנֵּן עֲתִירָה / בְּעַד אֲסוּרָה עַד הֻתָּרָה
◂ אֶנְקַת אָסִיר אָז כְּהֻכְתָּרָה / אֵלַי לְהֵעָתֵר כְּמוֹ נֶעְתָּרָה.

מֶלֶךְ עֶלְיוֹן וְנוֹרָא / מִשְׁפָּטֵנוּ יוֹצִיא כָאוֹרָה
◂ אִיחֲלֵנוּ כֶּתֶר לַעֲטָרָה / בְּטַלְלֵי תֶחִי בְּחַסְדּוֹ אֶתְפָּאֳרָה.

*The* שליח ציבור *continues:*

מִי כָמְוֹךָ אַב הָרַחֲמָן, זוֹכֵר יְצוּרָיו לְחַיִּים בְּרַחֲמִים.
וְנֶאֱמָן אַתָּה לְהַחֲיוֹת מֵתִים.
בָּרוּךְ אַתָּה יהוה, מְחַיֵּה הַמֵּתִים.

---

יָלְדָה שִׁבְעָה *Who gave birth to seven children.* 1 Samuel 2:5 states that "the barren [i.e. Hannah] has borne seven [children]," yet 1 Samuel 2:21 says that she had "three sons and two daughters." The rabbis resolved the apparent contradiction by saying that she lived to see Samuel's two sons and that "grandchildren are like children" (*Pesikta Rabati* 43:6).

עֹז מַלְכִיּוֹת עֶשֶׂר *The ten coronation verses.* The poet links the ten verses of Kingship in Musaf with the ten trials of Abraham; and the ten verses of Remembrance and Shofar to the ten blessings Isaac gave to Jacob (Gen. 27:28–29).

בְּזֶה פֶּרֶק חִנֵּן *It was at this time of year when Isaac beseeched God.* Jacob and Esau were born on Rosh HaShana (*Rosh HaShana* 10b). By analogy with Sarah and the birth of Isaac – it was a year between Sarah being told that she would

*The "Meshalesh," completing the first group of piyutim.*

*All:*

אֶבֶן The stone of the earth and the pillars of darkness on which it rests, / the deep abyss and the barren depths,
were fit with the cornerstone of Jacob who serves as the foundation of the ancestral threesome, / that the people might rely on him in their prayer for redemption.

The original ancestral hill that is Rachel, who was despised for being barren, / was squared away on this day as the fourth stone in the edifice of Jacob.
As she cried tears for the children she had not yet birthed, / she heard from on high that she need not cry for she would yet be mother of many sons.

When ruddy Esau saw that she had not been visited with birth pangs, / he desired to take her as wife and she was alarmed.
She addressed many prayers to God that her hope might be realized; / redeeming her from the wicked one – she remained undefiled.

God recalled the righteousness of her ways / when He changed the child in her sister's womb from a boy to a girl.
He planned that on this day, she would be remembered as one of the mothers, / and arranged the switch of Dina for Joseph.

God changed the gender of the child the way an artisan changes a vessel, / strengthening and augmenting the banners of the hosts of Israel's tribes.
As God listened to the groans of Jacob, the master, / He gave him hope by providing his wife with two tribes.
Just as she was estranged at the start for being barren, / in the end her firstborn came to be like the first fruit of all the sons.
▸ Let her merit stand on behalf of her offshoots on the Day of Remembrance, / that God might recall us kindly just as her prayer was answered.

---

parents that we begin to understand the love and longing, as well as the tensions, between God, our Parent, and us, His children.

*The "משלש," completing the first group of piyutim.*

*All:*

אֶבֶן חוּג מְצוּק נְשִׁיָּה / תְּהוֹם רַבָּה צוּל שְׁאִיָּה
בְּפִנַּת רֹאשׁ יְסוֹד שְׁלִישִׁיָּה / שְׁתִּתוֹ שְׁעוֹן בָּהּ לְשַׁעְיָה.

גִּבְעַת שֹׁרֶשׁ מְאוּסַת בּוֹנִים / רִבְעָה הַיּוֹם מֵאַרְבַּע אֲבָנִים
דִּמְעוֹת מְבַכָּה עַל בָּנִים / קָשְׁבָה, מִנְעִי אֵם הַבָּנִים.

הָאַדְמוֹן, כְּבַט שֶׁלֹּא חָלָה / צָבָה לְקַחְתָּהּ לוֹ, וְנִתְבַּהֲלָה
וּפִלְּלָה רַבִּים בְּעַד הַתּוֹחֵלָה / פְּדוּתָהּ מִזֵּד, וְלֹא חֻלְּלָה.

זָכַר לָהּ יֹשֶׁר אֳרָחוֹת / עָבַר לְהָמִיר בְּבֶטֶן אָחוֹת
חִשְּׁבָהּ הַיּוֹם זִכְרָהּ לְהֵאָחוֹת / סִלּוּף דִּינָה בִּיהוֹסֵף לְהַנְחוֹת.

טֶבַע כְּלִי יוֹצֵר הֶעֱבִיר / נִסֵּי חֲיָלִים לְהַעֲצִים וּלְהַגְבִּיר
יָהּ כְּסֻכַּת אֶנְקַת גְּבִיר / מַטּוֹת שְׁנַיִם מְנֵה הַסְבִּיר.

כַּעֲקֶרֶת בַּיִת בְּתֶחַל נִכְּרָה / כְּבִכּוּר רֵאשִׁית בְּתֶכֶל בִּכְּרָה
לְבַדֶּיהָ תַּעֲמֹד בְּיוֹם זְכִירָה / לְהִזָּכֵר לָמוֹ כְּמוֹ נִזְכְּרָה.

---

אֶבֶן חוּג *The stone of the earth.* A poem constructed on the pattern known as *at-bash*: an ascending acrostic for the first phrase and a descending one for the second, so that the first letter of the alphabet, *alef*, is paired with the last, *tav*, and so on. According to tradition (*Rosh HaShana* 10b), three barren women, Sarah, Rachel and Hannah, were remembered on Rosh HaShana and granted a child. This poem is about Rachel.

סִלּוּף דִּינָה בִּיהוֹסֵף *The switch of Dina for Joseph.* A tradition tells that Rachel initially conceived a girl while Leah, in her seventh pregnancy, conceived a boy, but that by a miracle the children were transposed so that Rachel was able to give birth to Joseph while Leah gave birth to Dina (*Berakhot* 60a).

Rachel's tears at the fate of her children are mentioned in the Haftara for the second day of Rosh HaShana. It is striking how often our thoughts turn on these holy days to the relationship between parents and children and to the prayers of childless women. It is through our experience as children and

*The congregation says the next two verses aloud, followed by the Leader:*

The LORD shall reign for ever. Ps. 146
He is your God, Zion, from generation to generation, Halleluya!

You are the Holy One, enthroned on the praises of Israel. Ps. 22

*There follows an ancient piyut, author unknown, which most congregations add after the Meshalesh. In recent generations, the custom to say it responsively has spread; many congregations are accustomed to saying the second stich of each couplet together with the first of the next one. However, traditionally this piyut is said only by the Leader, with the congregation joining in at "He is alive and everlasting."*

*The Ark is opened.*

God, please.

You are our God, in heaven and on earth.
Mighty and revered, encircled with myriads.
He spoke and it was, commanded and it came into being.
His memory is forever, His life is everlasting.
Pure of eye, He sits concealed.
His crown is salvation, His garment is righteousness.
His cloak is jealousy, His coat is vengeance.
His counsel is candor, His wisdom is faith.
His deeds are truth, He is righteous and upright.
He is close to those
who call upon Him in truth, He is sublime and lofty.
He resides in the heavens, and hangs the earth over emptiness.

*All:*

He is alive and everlasting, awesome, lofty and holy.

*The Ark is closed.*

---

descriptions of God, all but two of which are biblical. The exceptions are "His life is everlasting" (Yerushalmi, *Berakhot* 2:3) and "His counsel is candor" (found only here).

מַעֲטֵהוּ קִנְאָה *His cloak is jealousy.* At the heart of Judaism is the faith that God loves. God's gaze is turned outward. By contrast, the gods of myth were egoistic, concerned about themselves, and the philosopher's god was passionless. Jealousy, when attributed to God, is the prophet's way of describing the pain of love betrayed.

נְאפָּד נְקָמָה *His coat is vengeance.* When Judaism speaks about the "vengeance" of God, it means two things: (1) vengeance belongs to God, not man (see Lev. 19:18); (2) ultimately there is justice in history. The great crimes do not go unpunished.

*The* קהל *says the next two verses aloud, followed by the* שליח ציבור*:*

תהלים קמו יִמְלֹךְ יהוה לְעוֹלָם, אֱלֹהַיִךְ צִיּוֹן לְדֹר וָדֹר, הַלְלוּיָהּ:

תהלים כב וְאַתָּה קָדוֹשׁ, יוֹשֵׁב תְּהִלּוֹת יִשְׂרָאֵל:

*There follows an ancient piyut, author unknown, which most congregations add after the* משלש*. In recent generations, the custom to say it responsively has spread; many congregations are accustomed to saying the second stich of each couplet together with the first of the next one. However, traditionally this piyut is said only by the* שליח ציבור*, with the congregation joining in at "*חַי וְקַיָּם*."*

*The* ארון קודש *is opened.*

אֵל נָא.

אַתָּה הוּא אֱלֹהֵינוּ בַּשָּׁמַיִם וּבָאָרֶץ.

גִּבּוֹר וְנַעֲרָץ דָּגוּל מֵרְבָבָה.

הוּא שָׂח וַיֶּהִי וְצִוָּה וְנִבְרָאוּ.

זִכְרוֹ לָנֶצַח חַי עוֹלָמִים.

טְהוֹר עֵינַיִם יוֹשֵׁב סֵתֶר.

כִּתְרוֹ יְשׁוּעָה לְבוּשׁוֹ צְדָקָה.

מַעֲטֵהוּ קִנְאָה נֶאְפַּד נְקָמָה.

סִתְרוֹ יֹשֶׁר עֲצָתוֹ אֱמוּנָה.

פְּעֻלָּתוֹ אֱמֶת צַדִּיק וְיָשָׁר.

קָרוֹב לְקוֹרְאָיו בֶּאֱמֶת רָם וּמִתְנַשֵּׂא.

שׁוֹכֵן שְׁחָקִים תּוֹלֶה אֶרֶץ עַל בְּלִימָה.

*All:*

חַי וְקַיָּם, נוֹרָא וּמָרוֹם וְקָדוֹשׁ.

*The* ארון קודש *is closed.*

---

וְאַתָּה קָדוֹשׁ, יוֹשֵׁב תְּהִלּוֹת יִשְׂרָאֵל *You are the Holy One, enthroned on the praises of Israel.* This stunning line, taken from Psalms 22:4, speaks of God's throne woven out of the words of His people as they sing His praise. This is the paradox: God is everywhere, but only when we recognize this fact does He live in the hearts and minds of humanity.

אַתָּה הוּא אֱלֹהֵינוּ *You are our God.* An alphabetical hymn composed out of

*On Shabbat the following is omitted and the service continues with "And so – The LORD remembered" on page 380.*

*The following piyutim, until "The LORD is King" on page 392, share a common triplet structure ending with the word "Holy" – in some this structure is a frame, said before and after the piyut; in others it features as a refrain. Some congregations omit these piyutim, saying responsively only these "Holy" triplets; this is the prevailing custom in Israel.*

*This piyut is recited by the Leader and the congregation together, with the Leader raising his voice only toward the end, and then adding the frame "Awaken and sound." If the first day of Yom Tov falls on Shabbat, the shofar is not blown and therefore the recitation of this piyut (which speaks of blowing the shofar) is postponed to the second day (page 670).*

*The Leader, then the congregation:*

תָּעִיר Awaken and sound the shofar, cut down all evildoers,
and be sanctified by those who know to observe
the sounding of the shofar. O Holy One.

*All (some congregations omit and continue with "And so – The LORD remembered" on the next page):*

אַדֶּרֶת The glorious mantle of our royalty – / why was it torn from us?/
And we have not returned to rule since
the Babylonian idol Bel was crowned king. / All followed it, so willing, /
in contrast to the laws of our religion.
A foreign power has reigned in mastery / over all of our people, who will not be free / until the kingdom of the LORD shall appear.

They burned my Temple, / they broke the backs of my innocent ones in slavery / and they have been given allowance to do as they please.
They spread throughout the length and breadth of the land / and drew back their bows, / extending the yoke of their oppression,
frightening the soft nation of Israel, / which now lies there trampled / while still the foreigners rule.

The foundations of the Sanctuary, which sustained the heaps of tithes, / were stripped and confiscated by the enemy horde, / and the Temple was laid bare to its foundation.
They raised their haughty heads in evil / and took crafty counsel against Your people; / they wielded the upper hand.
They burned with evil intentions; / their arrogance extended as far as the heavens / while they girded themselves with Your royal vestments.

---

pleads with God to end Israel's oppression so that they can return to serving God alone. The poem is written as an acrostic whose initial letters spell out the name of its author, Elazar bei-Rabbi Kalir.

*On* שבת *the following is omitted and the service continues with* וּבְכֵן, וַיהוה פָּקַד *on page 381.*

*The following piyutim, until "*יהוה מֶלֶךְ*" on page 393, share a common triplet structure ending with the word "*קָדוֹשׁ*" – in some this structure is a frame, said before and after the piyut; in others it features as a refrain. Some congregations omit these piyutim, saying responsively only these "*קָדוֹשׁ*" triplets; this is the prevailing custom in* ארץ ישראל.

*This piyut is recited by the* שליח ציבור *and the* קהל *together, with the* שליח ציבור *raising his voice only toward the end, and then adding the frame "*תָּעִיר וְתָרִיעַ*." If the first day of* יום טוב *falls on* שבת*, the* שופר *is not blown and therefore the recitation of this piyut (which speaks of blowing the* שופר*) is postponed to the second day (page 671).*

*The* שליח ציבור*, then the* קהל:

תָּעִיר וְתָרִיעַ, לְהַכְרִית כָּל מֵרִיעַ
וְתִקְדַּשׁ בְּיוֹדְעֵי לְהָרִיעַ. קָדוֹשׁ.

*All (some congregations omit and continue with* וּבְכֵן, וַיהוה פָּקַד *on the next page):*

אַדֶּרֶת מַמְלָכָה / עַל מָה הֻשְׁלְכָה / וְעוֹד לֹא מָלְכָה
לַבֵּל הִמְלִיכָה / וְאַחֲרָיו הָלְכָה / שֶׁלֹּא כַּהֲלָכָה
עָלֶיהָ הִמְלְכָה / גְּבֶרֶת מַמְלָכָה / עַד תּוֹפִיעַ מְלוּכָה.

זְבוּלִי חָרְבָה / מַתְמִימֵי פָּרְכָה / וְנִתַּן לָהּ אַרְכָּה
רָחֲבָה וְאָרְכָה / וְקֶשֶׁת דָּרְכָה / וְעֹל הֶאֱרִיכָה
בְּעֵתָה בְּרַכָּה / וְהִנֵּה דְרוּכָה / וְעַד עַתָּה מוֹלְכָה.

יְסוֹדוֹת עֲרֵמָה / עֵרָה וְהֶחֱרִימָה / וְעַד יְסוֹד עָרְמָה
רֹאשׁ הֵרִימָה / וְסוֹד הֶעֱרִימָה / וְיָדָהּ רָמָה
בָּעֲרָה מֵעָרְמָה / וְעַד שַׁחַק רוֹמָה / וְתֶאְפַּד מְלוּכָה.

---

תָּעִיר וְתָרִיעַ *Awaken and sound the shofar.* A conclusion of the previous poem. Most of these fragments, ending one poem and heralding the next, end with the word *Kadosh*, "holy," since all these poems have been inserted into the third paragraph of the Amida whose keyword and theme is holiness.

אַדֶּרֶת מַמְלָכָה *The glorious mantle of our royalty.* A powerful testament to the pathos of the Jewish people during their centuries of exile. On Rosh HaShana they proclaim the sovereignty of God. Yet they have lost their own sovereignty. Their enemies have desecrated their holy places, oppressed God's people, and arrogantly declared themselves, not God, the rulers of earth. The poet

They shred my curtains clear away / and plundered my Sanctuary, / turning over the earth till it was plowed clear.
They spread their rule / and adopted royal garb, / angering Your nation.
They plotted and conspired to rebel against God, / and labored to sway Your people to worship strange gods / as they defiled the reign of our LORD.

They oppressed the children of the King, / and before His eyes they uttered the words: / "What king do we have in heaven?"
They spoke arrogantly of the King's throne, / saying, "There is no other king but me; / no other king but I alone."
▸ O You who are loftier than any earthly king, / remove them and they shall no longer rule, / and reclaim the reign for Yourself alone.

*The Leader then the congregation:*

תָּעִיר Awaken and sound the shofar, cut down all evildoers,
and be sanctified by those who know to observe
the sounding of the shofar.
O Holy One.

*All:*

וּבְכֵן And so – The LORD remembered Sarah, just as He had said. *Gen. 21*

*The Leader then the congregation:*

צֶאֱצָאֶיהָ So may He remember her offspring favorably on this day.
O Holy One.

*All (some congregations omit and continue with "O King who offers deliverance from evil" on the next page):*

אֵם O matriarch who aged in righteousness, / though she had lost hope, she was finally granted fecundity,
when He who brought her forth, remembered her on Rosh HaShana.

It was this very day when she said, "Behold I am condemned / to remain wretched as my youth comes to an end."
You sealed her judgment righteously so she would not resort to reclusion.

Just as she was informed by Your messengers, so did it come to pass. / She made haste to entreat the Pure One,
but her request was granted before she began her prayer.

All who heard of her joy laughed and rejoiced, / for all childless women did bloom, though their time had passed,
and all called out to her, "The mother of sons is joyous." *Ps. 113*

יְרִיעוֹתַי גְּדוּדָה / אָהֳלִי שֻׁדְּדָה / וְחָרְשָׁה וְשׁוּדְּדָה
קְצִינוּת רְפָדָה / וּמַלְכוּת אֲפֻדָּה / וְזֹאת הַקְּפִידָה
יְזָמָה וּמָרָדָה / עֶבֶד לְזָר חָרָדָה / וְחִלְּלָה מְלוּכָה.

לְחָצָה בְּנֵי מֶלֶךְ / וּפָצָה לְעֵין מֶלֶךְ / מִי לִי בְּדוֹק מֶלֶךְ
יְהָרָה בְּכֵס מֶלֶךְ / זוּלָתִי אֵין מֶלֶךְ / אֲנִי וְאַפְסִי מֶלֶךְ
◂ רָם עַל כָּל מֶלֶךְ / תַּגְעִילֶנָּה מִמֶּלֶךְ / וּלְךָ תָּשִׁיב מְלוּכָה.

*The* שליח ציבור *then the* קהל*:*

תָּעִיר וְתָרִיעַ, לְהַכְרִית כָּל מֵרִיעַ
וְתִקְדַּשׁ בְּיוֹדְעֵי לְהָרִיעַ. קָדוֹשׁ.

*All:*

וּבְכֵן, וַיהוה פָּקַד אֶת שָׂרָה כַּאֲשֶׁר אָמָר בראשית כא

*The* שליח ציבור *then the* קהל*:*

צֶאֱצָאֶיהָ כֵּן פְּקֹד לְטוֹב הַיּוֹם. קָדוֹשׁ.

*All (some congregations omit and continue with* מֶלֶךְ מְמַלֵּט מֵרָעָה *on the next page):*

אֵם אֲשֶׁר בְּצֶדֶק נִתְיַשְּׁנָה / כְּמוֹ נִתְיָאֲשָׁה בְּתֶכֶל דְּשֵׁנָה
גּוּחָהּ, פְּקָדָהּ, בְּרֹאשׁ הַשָּׁנָה.

דִּכְּבָה, הַיּוֹם אֲנִי נִדּוֹנָה / הִנְנִי עֲגוּמָה כִּכְלוֹת עֶדְנָה
וַתְּחַתֵּם בְּצֶדֶק לְבַל הֱיוֹת עֲגוּנָה.

זֹאת כְּהִתְבַּשְּׂרָה הֶשְׁקְדָה / חַלּוֹת פְּנֵי צַח שָׁקְדָה
טֶרֶם קָרְאָה מִיָּד נִפְקְדָה.

יִצְחַק כָּל שֹׁמֵעַ זֹאת, שְׂמֵחָה / כִּי גַלְמוּדָה לְלֹא עֵת צָמֵחָה
תהלים קיג לָהּ הַכֹּל שִׁמְעוּ, אֵם הַבָּנִים שְׂמֵחָה.

---

אֵם אֲשֶׁר בְּצֶדֶק נִתְיַשְּׁנָה *O matriarch who aged in righteousness.* Another poem about one of the four hitherto infertile women who were granted children on Rosh HaShana, in this case Sarah. Written as an alphabetic acrostic, it speaks of her story and the birth of Isaac. It is a narrative of hope, about a woman who had almost given up hope, on this day of hope.

She found her peace though she had already begun to lose the freshness of youth, / and her beauty was renewed like an eagle,
as women of noble birth rejoiced in her company.

Exult and rejoice, they cried to her, / and shouted, "Sing joyfully, you who were formerly barren." *Is. 54*
And when the milk of their breasts ceased, her value rose in their eyes even more.

The woman of bitter spirit who had been childless, / was healed after ninety years when God rewarded her,
and she sent forth shoots that neither disappointed nor deceived.

▸ Turn Your eyes to the offspring – our ancestors – who were born on this day, /
and recall the three barren women [Sarah, Rachel and Hannah] whose prayers were answered this day, /
and by their merit may those who await You be vindicated, O Awesome One.

*Some add:*

So may He remember her offspring favorably on this day. O Holy One.

*The Leader then the congregation:*

מֶלֶךְ O King who offers deliverance from evil,
to those who observe the sounding of the shofar.
O Holy God.

*The Leader then the congregation:*

מֶלֶךְ O King, recall the ram caught by its horns in the thicket,
on behalf of those who sound the ram's horn on this day.
O Awesome and Holy One.

*All (some congregations omit and continue with "The LORD is King" on page 392):*

**אַאְפִּיד** I shall crown the Awesome One / by proclaiming His holiness threefold in the Kedusha on this day.

Mighty angelic heroes of strength and greatness, / gallop forward to receive Him in the house where His banner is raised!

The angelic camp that raises its voice in rousing sound, / exalts Him with fine words of praise!

For the One who forever recalls the merits of His creatures, / sing a new song of angelic praise!

The Good One bears our burdens for us; / declare His unity as the new moon comes!

מָצְאָה הַשְׁקֵט אַחֲרֵי בְלוֹתָהּ / נִתְחַדְּשָׁה כַּנֶּשֶׁר בִּנְוֹתָהּ
שָׂשׂוּ שָׂרוֹת לְלַוּוֹתָהּ.

עָלְזִי וְשִׂישִׂי עֲבוּרָהּ נִקְרָא / פִּצְוּ עָדֶיהָ, רָנִּי עֲקָרָה
צָמְקוּ שָׁדֶיהָ וְעוֹד בָּם יְקָרָה. ישעיה נד

קָשַׁת רְוּחַ אֲשֶׁר הָעֲקָרָה / וְרָפְאָה לְקֵץ תִּשְׁעִים, כְּנִתְבַּקְּרָה
שִׁלְּחָה פֵאָרוֹת וְלֹא שִׁקְּרָה.

תֵּפֶן בַּנְּצָרִים אֲשֶׁר חוֹלְלוּ כְּהַיּוֹם / וְשָׁלֹשׁ עֲקָרוֹת שֶׁהָפְקְדוּ בְּזֶה יוֹם
תַּצְדִּיק בְּצִדְקָתָם מְיַחֲלֶיךָ, אָיוֹם.

*Some add:*

צֶאֱצָאֶיהָ כֵּן פְּקֹד לְטוֹב הַיּוֹם. קָדוֹשׁ.

*The* שליח ציבור *then the* קהל*:*

מֶלֶךְ מְמַלֵּט מֵרָעָה, לְיוֹדְעֵי תְרוּעָה. הָאֵל קָדוֹשׁ.

*The* שליח ציבור *then the* קהל*:*

מֶלֶךְ זְכֹר אֲחוּז קֶרֶן, לְתוֹקְעֵי לְךָ הַיּוֹם בְּקֶרֶן. נוֹרָא וְקָדוֹשׁ.

*All (some congregations omit and continue with* יהוה מֶלֶךְ *on page 393):*

אַאְפִּיד נֵזֶר אָיוֹם / בְּשִׁלּוּשׁ קְדֻשָּׁה בַּיּוֹם.
גִּבּוֹרֵי כֹחַ גְּדֻלָּה / דַּהֲרוּהוּ בְּבֵית דְּגִילָה.
הוֹגֵי הֶגֶה הַמִּלָּה / וַתִּקּוּהוּ בְּהַלֵּל וּמִלָּה.
זוֹכֵר לָעַד זְכִיּוֹת / חַדְּשׁוּהוּ זֶמֶר חַיּוֹת.
טוֹב עוֹמֵס טֹרַח / יַחֲדוּהוּ בְּחִדּוּשׁ יָרֵחַ.

---

**אַאְפִּיד** *I shall crown.* On Rosh HaShana, the anniversary of God's coronation, it is as if we placed the crown on His head. The poet vividly describes the scene in heaven – the host of angels who form, as it were, God's retinue – as Israel proclaims God's sovereignty on earth. The first and third words in each stich form a double alphabetic acrostic.

He suppresses all sentiments of anger / so as not to implement the issue of His ire.
The angelic servants in His retinue of awe / offer awesome words of praise in the presence of Israel!
Seraphim, who swirl in the stormy ether: / call out to the One who removes His anger!
Wondrous angels, open your mouths to sing / in praise of the One who sees all things!
Congregations of this holy nation: / noisily clamor in your multitudes to elevate Him!
May You listen to the sounding of the call of the shofar, / and cause all guilt to be annulled.
▸ Please, sound the shofar thrice on Your holy mount, / and I shall now proclaim Your threefold holiness in full sanctity.
O King recall the ram caught by its horns in the thicket, on behalf of those who sound the ram's horn on this day. O Awesome and Holy One.

*On a weekday, the service continues with "The Lord is King" on page 392.*

*On Shabbat the service continues:*

*All:*

וּבְכֵן And so – The Lord remembered Sarah, just as He had said. *Gen. 21*

*The Leader then the congregation:*

צֶאֱצָאֶיהָ So may He remember her offspring favorably on this day. O Holy One.

*Another addition to the original cycle, this piyut originally had the line "So may He remember her offspring" as a refrain, switching to "their offspring" in the last line. Nowadays, this verse is often only recited at the beginning and end, if not omitted altogether. Some congregations omit this piyut entirely, continuing with "His name is glorified" on the next page.*

*All:*

אֵם O matriarch who aged in righteousness,
though she had lost hope, she was finally granted fecundity,
when He who brought her forth, remembered her on Rosh HaShana.

It was this very day when she said, "Behold I am condemned
to remain wretched as my youth comes to an end."
You sealed her judgment righteously so she would not resort to reclusion.

Just as she was informed by Your messengers, so did it come to pass.
She made haste to entreat the Pure One,
but her request was granted before she began her prayer.

All who heard of her joy laughed and rejoiced,
for all childless women did bloom, though their time had passed,
and all called out to her, "The mother of sons is joyous." *Ps. 113*

כּוֹבֵשׁ כָּל כְּעָסִים / לְבַל אַף לְהָשִׂים.
מְשָׁרְתֵי בְּחִיל מוֹרָא / נָכְחָם הַלְלוּ נוֹרָא.
שַׂרְפֵי סְבִיב סְעָרָה / עָנוּ לְמַעֲבִיר עֶבְרָה.
פְּלִיאִים פִּצְחוּ פֶה / צַלְצְלוּ הַכֹּל צוֹפֶה.
קְהִלּוֹת עַם קְדוֹשִׁים / רוֹמְמוּהוּ וְרִבְבוֹת רוֹעֲשִׁים.
שֵׁמַע קוֹל שׁוֹפָר / תַּאֲזִין, וְאַשְׁמָה תּוֹפָר.
◂ תְּשַׁלֵּשׁ שׁוֹפָרוֹת בְּהַר הַקֹּדֶשׁ / וַאֲשַׁלֵּשׁ קְדֻשָּׁה בַּקֹּדֶשׁ.
מֶלֶךְ זְכֹר אֲחוּז קֶרֶן, לְתוֹקְעֵי לְךָ הַיּוֹם בְּקֶרֶן. נוֹרָא וְקָדוֹשׁ.

*On a weekday, the service continues with* יהוה מֶלֶךְ *on page 393.*

*On* שבת *the service continues:*

*All:*

וּבְכֵן, וַיהוה פָּקַד אֶת שָׂרָה כַּאֲשֶׁר אָמָר בראשית כא

*The* שליח ציבור *then the* קהל*:*

צְאֶצָאֶיהָ כֵּן פְּקֹד לְטוֹב הַיּוֹם. קָדוֹשׁ.

*Another addition to the original cycle, this piyut originally had the line "*צְאֶצָאֶיהָ כֵּן פְּקֹד...*" as a refrain, switching to "*צְאֶצָאֵיהֶם*" in the last line. Nowadays, this verse is often only recited at the beginning and end, if not omitted altogether. Some congregations omit this piyut entirely, continuing with* שְׁמוֹ מְפָאֲרִים *on the next page.*

*All:*

אֵם אֲשֶׁר בְּצֶדֶק נִתְיַשְּׁנָה / בְּמוֹ נִתְיָאֲשָׁה בְּתֵבֵל דְּשֵׁנָה
גּוֹחָהּ, פְּקָדָהּ, בְּרֹאשׁ הַשָּׁנָה.

דִּבְּבָה, הַיּוֹם אֲנִי נְדוֹנָה / הִנְנִי עֲגוּמָה כִּכְלוֹת עֶדְנָה
וַתְּחַתֵּם בְּצֶדֶק לְבַל הֱיוֹת עֲגוּנָה.

זֹאת כְּהִתְבַּשְּׂרָה הָשְׁקְדָה / חִלּוֹת פְּנֵי צַח שָׁקְדָה
טֶרֶם קָרְאָה מִיַּד נִפְקָדָה.

יִצְחַק כָּל שֹׁמֵעַ זֹאת, שָׂמֵחָה / כִּי גַלְמוּדָה לְלֹא עֵת צָמֵחָה
לָהּ הַכֹּל שִׁמְעוּ, אֵם הַבָּנִים שְׂמֵחָה. תהלים קיג

She found her peace though she had already begun to lose the freshness of youth,
and her beauty was renewed like an eagle,
as women of noble birth rejoiced in her company.
Exult and rejoice, they cried to her,
and shouted, "Sing joyfully, you who were formerly barren." *Is. 54*
And when the milk of their breasts ceased, her value rose in their eyes even more.
The woman of bitter spirit who had been childless,
was healed after ninety years when God rewarded her,
and she sent forth shoots that neither disappointed nor deceived.
▸ Turn Your eyes to the offspring – our ancestors – who were born on this day,
and recall the three barren women [Sarah, Rachel and Hannah]
whose prayers were answered this day,
and by their merit may those who await You be vindicated, O Awesome One.

*Some add:*

So may He remember her offspring favorably on this day. O Holy One.

*Each of the next six stanzas is first said by the Leader, then the congregation:*

שְׁמוֹ His name is glorified by His rightful congregation,
and revered in songs of praise by the angels.
And in His Sanctuary His glory is spoken of by everyone. /
O Holy One.

The keepers of His commandments will yet return to their fortified haven;
His faithful followers converse with one another with much skill and wisdom:
And the LORD hearkened and listened and a book of remembrance was written. / O Holy One. *Mal. 3*

Refine your deeds so that the covenant may endure.
He who adorns the heavens shall heed your groans,
and your prayers shall be more pleasing to the LORD than an ox or bullock. / O Holy One. *Ps. 69*

---

it was composed by Rabbi Shimon HaGadol, who has encoded his name in the first five stanzas. A paean to God's majesty and to Rosh HaShana as the annual Day of Judgment.

מָצְאָה הַשֶּׁקֶט אַחֲרֵי בְלוֹתָהּ / נִתְחַדְּשָׁה כַּנֶּשֶׁר בְּנִוּוֹתָהּ
שָׂשׂוּ שָׂרוֹת לְלַוּוֹתָהּ.

ישעיה נד עַלְזִי וְשִׂישִׂי עֲבוּרָה נִקְרָא / פִּצְוּ עָדֶיהָ, רָנִּי עֲקָרָה
צָמְקוּ שָׁדֶיהָן וְעוֹד בָּם יְקָרָה.

קֶשֶׁת רְוַח אֲשֶׁר הָעֲקָרָה / וְרִפְאָה לְקֵץ תִּשְׁעִים, כְּנִתְבַּקְּרָה
שִׂלְחָה פֹּארוֹת וְלֹא שִׁקְּרָה.

תֵּפֶן בַּנְּצָרִים אֲשֶׁר חוֹלְלוּ כְּהַיּוֹם / וְשָׁלֹשׁ עֲקָרוֹת שֶׁהֻפְקְדוּ בְּזֶה יוֹם
תַּצְדִּיק בְּצִדְקָתָם מְיַחֲלֶיךָ, אָיוֹם.

*Some add:*

צֶאֱצָאֶיהָ כֵּן פְּקֹד לְטוֹב הַיּוֹם. קָדוֹשׁ.

*Each of the next six stanzas is first said by the* שליח ציבור*, then the* קהל*:*

שְׁמוֹ מְפָאֲרִים עֲדַת חֶבְלוֹ
וְנַעֲרָץ בְּאֶרְאֶלֵּי קֹדֶשׁ הִלּוּלוֹ
וּבְהֵיכָלוֹ כָּבוֹד אֹמֵר כֻּלּוֹ / קָדוֹשׁ.

שׁוֹמְרֵי מִצְוֹתָיו עוֹד יָשׁוּבוּן לְבִצָּרוֹן
נִדְבָּרִים יֵרָאוּ בְּהַכְשֵׁר וְיִתְרוֹן
מלאכי ג וַיַּקְשֵׁב יהוה וַיִּשְׁמָע, וַיִּכָּתֵב סֵפֶר זִכָּרוֹן: / קָדוֹשׁ.

שַׁפְּרוּ מַעֲשֵׂיכֶם, וּבְרִית לֹא תוּפַר
נַאֲקַתְכֶם יַאֲזִין, שְׁחָקִים שִׁפַּר
תהלים סט וְתִיטַב לַיהוה מִשּׁוֹר פָּר: / קָדוֹשׁ.

---

שְׁמוֹ מְפָאֲרִים *His name is glorified.* Said when the first day of Rosh HaShana falls on Shabbat, since the alternative first-day poem mentions the shofar, not blown on Shabbat. Adapted from a poem originally written for the second day,

Raise up the tribes that call upon You and let them rule,
as the outstretched branches of their oppressors are cut down and removed,
for the kingdom belongs to the LORD and He rules. / O Holy One. *Ps. 22*

May He return our captives from afar to His holy mount,
that we might glorify Him always in His holy Sanctuary,
for He has remembered His holy vow. / O Holy One. *Ps. 105*

All inhabitants of the world and those who reside on the earth, *Is. 18*
shall forever say that the LORD has done great things in the world,
and the LORD shall reign as King over the entire world. / *Zech. 14*
O Holy One.

*This complex piyut reprises six of the previous piyut's seven stanzas (only six are said on Shabbat, the seventh is recited on the second day of Yom Tov). Some congregations omit this piyut altogether, continuing with "He judges the world" on page 390.*

*Leader:* Splendor and glory I willingly give, / I lay out my prayer in thought and utterance.
*Cong:* I shall call upon God Most High. *Ps. 57*

*Leader:* On the day chosen in heaven, / when the LORD judges righteously that His sanctity might be revered,
*Cong:* For the LORD reigns; the earth shall rejoice. *Ps. 97*

*Leader:* His greatness has grown beyond what the world can contain; / who possesses the strength to tell of the fullness of His power?
*Cong:* God is King of all the earth; sing a psalm! *Ps. 47*

His name is glorified by His rightful congregation, / and revered in songs of praise by the angels. / And in His Sanctuary His glory is spoken of by everyone. / O Holy One.

*Leader:* All His creatures shall take note / and know that His mighty deeds are immense,
*Cong:* For He has made wondrous works to be remembered. *Ps. 111*

*Leader:* He established His cornerstone / His Torah legacy, so that His nation might revel in it,
*Cong:* He remembers His covenant forever. *Ps. 105*

שִׁבְטֵי מְקֹרָאֶיךָ עַלֵּה וְהַמְשֵׁל
נְטִישׁוֹת צָרִים בַּהֲתִיזְךָ לְנַשֵּׁל
כִּי לַיהוה הַמְּלוּכָה, וּמשֵׁל: / קָדוֹשׁ. תהלים כב

שְׁבוּתֵנוּ מִמֶּרְחָק, עֲלוֹת לְהַר קָדְשׁוֹ
וּנְפָאֲרֶנּוּ תָּמִיד בִּדְבִיר מִקְדָּשׁוֹ
כִּי־זָכַר אֶת־דְּבַר קָדְשׁוֹ: / קָדוֹשׁ. תהלים קה

כָּל־יֹשְׁבֵי תֵבֵל וְשֹׁכְנֵי אָרֶץ: ישעיה יח
יֹאמְרוּ תָמִיד, הִגְדִּיל יהוה לַעֲשׂוֹת בָּאָרֶץ
וְהָיָה יהוה לְמֶלֶךְ עַל־כָּל־הָאָרֶץ: / קָדוֹשׁ. זכריה יד

*This complex piyut reprises six of the previous piyut's seven stanzas (only six are said on* שבת*, the seventh is recited on the second day of* יום טוב*). Some congregations omit this piyut altogether, continuing with "*יִשְׁפֹּט תֵּבֵל*" on page 391.*

ש״ץ: אֶדֶר וָהוֹד אֶתֵּן בְּצִבְיוֹן / שֶׁוַע אֶעֱרֹךְ בְּנִיב וְהִגָּיוֹן
קהל: אֶקְרָא לֵאלֹהִים עֶלְיוֹן: תהלים נז

ש״ץ: בַּיּוֹם הַנִּבְחָר מִשְּׁמֵי עֶרֶץ / מֵישָׁרִים לִשְׁפֹּט, קֶדְשָׁתוֹ לְהַעֲרֵץ
קהל: יהוה מָלָךְ תָּגֵל הָאָרֶץ: תהלים צז

ש״ץ: גַּאֲוָתוֹ גָּדְלָה עוֹלָם מֵהָכִיל / עֱזוּזוֹ לְסַפֵּר כֹּחַ מִי יָכִיל
קהל: מֶלֶךְ כָּל־הָאָרֶץ אֱלֹהִים, זַמְּרוּ מַשְׂכִּיל: תהלים מז

שְׁמוֹ מְפָאֲרִים עֲדַת חֶבְלוֹ / וְנַעֲרָץ בְּאֶרְאֶלֵּי קֹדֶשׁ הִלּוּלוֹ
וּבְהֵיכָלוֹ כָּבוֹד אֹמֵר כֻּלּוֹ / קָדוֹשׁ.

ש״ץ: דֵּעַ יָשִׂימוּ כָּל בְּרִיּוֹתָיו / וְיֵדְעוּ כִּי גָדְלוּ גְּבוּרוֹתָיו
קהל: זֵכֶר עָשָׂה לְנִפְלְאֹתָיו: תהלים קיא

ש״ץ: הִצִּיב וְיָרָה אֶבֶן פִּנָּתוֹ / נַחֲלִיאֵל עָבוּר לְשַׁעְשֵׁעַ בַּאֲמִתּוֹ
קהל: זָכַר לְעוֹלָם בְּרִיתוֹ: תהלים קה

*Leader:* And the Lord inscribed in the law-book that I shall utter / the verses of remembrance, so that He might recall my remembrance every year,
*Cong:* As a testament in the Sanctuary of the Lord. *Zech. 6*

The keepers of His commandments will yet return to their fortified haven; / His faithful followers converse with one another with much skill and wisdom. / And the Lord hearkened and listened *Mal. 3*
and a book of remembrance was written. / O Holy One.

*Leader:* That holy sacrifice of Isaac which seemed fitting in His eyes, / He arranged for its exchange in the form of a ram to be offered before Him.
*Cong:* After it was caught in the thicket by its horns. *Gen. 22*

*Leader:* He taught [Isaac's] offshoots to sound the shofar at the start of this month, / and if the holy Sabbath should happen to fall upon this day,
*Cong:* Then the remembrance of the sound of the shofar shall serve to sanctify it. *Lev. 23*

*Leader:* Yet should its arrival for a scheduled weekday be announced, / then the command should go out that in all your borders the shofar shall sound,
*Cong:* For it shall be a day for you on which the shofar shall resound. *Num. 29*

Refine your deeds so that the covenant may endure. / He who adorns the heavens shall heed your groans, / and your prayers shall be more *Ps. 69*
pleasing to the Lord than an ox or bullock. / O Holy One.

*Leader:* May the Rock of my salvation be exalted in the mouth of every nation. / Reveal Your mighty arm to save Your people from those who rise against them.
*Cong:* For Your kingdom is an everlasting kingdom. *Ps. 145*

*Leader:* When You will reveal Yourself to the eyes of all and appear within Your Sanctuary, / congregations and multitudes will come forth to bear testimony:
*Cong:* The Lord shall reign forever and ever. *Ex. 15*

*Leader:* Strength and honor are fitting for You, uttered by / all the world, its inhabitants and all the islands.
*Cong:* Who shall not fear You, O King of all nations? *Jer. 10*

Raise up the tribes that call upon You and let them rule, / as the outstretched branches of their oppressors are cut down and removed, / for the kingdom belongs to the Lord and He rules. / O Holy One. *Ps. 22*

ש״ץ: וְרַשָּׁם בְּחֹק דָּת הֶגְיוֹנִי / בְּכָל שָׁנָה וְשָׁנָה לִזְכֹּר זִכְרוֹנִי

קהל: **לְזִכָּרוֹן בְּהֵיכַל יהוה:** זכריה ו

שׁוֹמְרֵי מִצְוֹתָיו עוֹד יָשׁוּבוּן לְבִצָּרוֹן / נִדְבָּרִים יְרֵאָיו בְּהֶכְשֵׁר וְיִתְרוֹן

וַיַּקְשֵׁב יהוה וַיִּשְׁמָע, וַיִּכָּתֵב סֵפֶר זִכָּרוֹן: / קָדוֹשׁ. מלאכי ג

ש״ץ: זֶבַח קֹדֶשׁ כְּהָכְשַׁר אָז בְּעֵינָיו / רֶגֶל תְּמוּרָתוֹ אַיִל לְהַקְרִיב לְפָנָיו

קהל: **אַחַר נֶאֱחַז בַּסְּבַךְ בְּקַרְנָיו:** בראשית כב

ש״ץ: חִכֵּם חֲנִיטָיו לִתְקֹעַ בְּזֶה חֹדֶשׁ / יוֹם זֶה אִם יִקְרֶה בְּשַׁבַּת קוֹדֶשׁ

קהל: **זִכְרוֹן תְּרוּעָה מִקְרָא־קֹדֶשׁ:** ויקרא כג

ש״ץ: טִבְעוּ אִם בְּחוֹל יְבוֹאֲכֶם / צַוּוּ לִתְקֹעַ בְּכָל גְּבוּלְכֶם

קהל: **יוֹם תְּרוּעָה יִהְיֶה לָכֶם:** במדבר כט

שַׁפְּרוּ מַעֲשֵׂיכֶם, וּבְרִית לֹא תוּפַר / נַאֲקַתְכֶם יַאֲזִין, שְׁחָקִים שִׁפֵּר

וְתִיטַב לַיהוה מִשּׁוֹר פָּר: / קָדוֹשׁ. תהלים סט

ש״ץ: יָרוּם צוּר יִשְׁעִי בְּפִי כָּל אֻמִּים / חָשַׂף זְרוֹעֲךָ לְהוֹשִׁיעַ מִמִּתְקוֹמְמִים

קהל: **מַלְכוּתְךָ מַלְכוּת כָּל־עֹלָמִים:** תהלים קמה

ש״ץ: כְּהִגָּלוֹתְךָ לְעֵין כֹּל שִׁכְנְךָ לְהִוָּעֵד / קְהִלּוֹת וּרְבָבוֹת בְּפִימוֹ לְהָעֵד

קהל: **יהוה יִמְלֹךְ לְעֹלָם וָעֶד:** שמות טו

ש״ץ: לְךָ יָאֲתָה כָּבוֹד וָעֹז הַגּוֹיִם / חֶלֶד וְשׁוֹכְנֶיהָ וְכָל הָאִיִּים

קהל: **מִי לֹא יִרָאֲךָ מֶלֶךְ הַגּוֹיִם:** ירמיה י

שִׁבְטֵי מִקְרָאֲךָ עֲלֵה וְהַמְשֵׁל / נְטִישׁוֹת צָרִים בְּהִתַּזְךָ לְנַשֵּׁל

כִּי לַיהוה הַמְּלוּכָה, וּמֹשֵׁל: / קָדוֹשׁ. תהלים כב

---

חִכֵּם חֲנִיטָיו לִתְקֹעַ *He taught His offshoots to sound the shofar.* A reference to the fact that Rosh HaShana is described in the Torah as both *Yom Terua,* "a day when the horn is sounded" (Num. 29:1) and *Zikhron Terua,* "a remembrance

*Leader:* Shatter and destroy the beams placed upon us by our oppressors, / gather Your scattered exiles and freely offer them redemption.

*Cong:* Remember the congregation You acquired long ago. *Ps. 74*

*Leader:* The noblest of nations shall be comforted doubly; / those who rise against them shall be exposed in humiliation.

*Cong:* May the LORD recall the day of Jerusalem's defeat and visit retribution upon the descendants of Edom. *Ps. 137*

*Leader:* Pave a straight road for us that we might stride, / and do not allow the ankles of Your precious child to falter.

*Cong:* As You have spoken: "I will remember him always." *Jer. 31*

May He return our captives from afar to His holy mount, /
that we might glorify Him always in His holy Sanctuary, /
for He has remembered His holy vow. / O Holy One. *Ps. 105*

*Leader:* May there be joy in the city, in the Sanctuary and hall. / May He restore the altar and all the attendant vessels.

*Cong:* The LORD shall reign forever. *Ex. 15*

*Leader:* The heavens and earth shall sing in His honor. / The forests shall clap hands to offer pleasant sounds to Him,

*Cong:* For the LORD has finally appointed His people. *Ruth 1*

*Leader:* The splendor of angels and the morning stars / shall offer praise and pleasant song.

*Cong:* Praise Him with the sounding of the shofar. *Ps. 150*

All inhabitants of the world and those who reside on the earth / *Is. 18*
shall forever say that the LORD has done great things in the world, /
and the LORD shall reign as King over the entire world. / O Holy One. *Zech. 14*

---

essential harmony between cosmos and ethos. Just as the universe is governed by physical laws, uncovered by science, so it is governed by moral laws, revealed in the Torah. The angels and the stars, heavenly beings and the lights of heaven, rejoice in the moral harmony of justice. Creation is completed by redemption, physics by ethics.

ש״ץ: מוֹטֹת צָרִים שַׁבֵּר וְהַכְחִידֵם / זְרוּיֶיךָ קַבֵּץ וְחִנָּם תִּפְדֵּם
קהל: זְכֹר עֲדָתְךָ קָנִיתָ קֶּדֶם: תהלים עד

ש״ץ: נְדִיבֵי עַמִּים יְנַחֲמוּ בְּכִפְלַיִם / קָמֵיהֶם עַל פָּנֵימוֹ גַּלֵּה שׁוּלַיִם
קהל: זְכֹר יהוה לִבְנֵי אֱדוֹם אֵת יוֹם יְרוּשָׁלָיִם: תהלים קלז

ש״ץ: סִלּוּל מְסִלָּתֵנוּ יַשֵּׁר לְצַעַד / וּבֵן יַקִּירְךָ קַרְסֹל לֹא יִמְעַד
קהל: כְּנַמְתָּ, זָכֹר אֶזְכְּרֶנּוּ עוֹד: ירמיה לא

שְׁבוּתֵנוּ מִמֶּרְחָק, עֲלוֹת לְהַר קָדְשׁוֹ / וּנְפָאֲרֶנּוּ תָּמִיד בִּדְבִיר מִקְדָּשׁוֹ
כִּי־זָכַר אֶת־דְּבַר קָדְשׁוֹ: / קָדוֹשׁ. תהלים קה

ש״ץ: קִרְיַת מָשׂוֹשׂ, הֵיכָל וְאוּלָם / מִזְבֵּחַ יָשִׁיב, וּכְלֵי שָׁרֵת כֻּלָּם
קהל: יהוה יִמְלֹךְ לְעֹלָם: שמות טו

ש״ץ: שָׁמַיִם וָאָרֶץ יְרַנְּנוּ לִשְׁמוֹ / יְעָרוֹת יִמְחֲאוּ כַף לְהַנְעִימוֹ
קהל: כִּי־פָקַד יהוה אֶת־עַמּוֹ: רות א

ש״ץ: תְּקֶף אֶרְאֶלִּים וְכוֹכְבֵי צֶפֶר / תְּהִלּוֹת יִתְּנוּ שֶׁבַח לְהַשְׁפֵּר
קהל: הַלְלוּהוּ בְּתֵקַע שׁוֹפָר: תהלים קנ

ישעיה יח כָּל־יֹשְׁבֵי תֵבֵל וְשֹׁכְנֵי אָרֶץ: / יֹאמְרוּ תָמִיד, הִגְדִּיל יהוה לַעֲשׂוֹת בָּאָרֶץ
זכריה יד וְהָיָה יהוה לְמֶלֶךְ עַל־כָּל־הָאָרֶץ: / קָדוֹשׁ.

---

of the sounding of the horn" (Lev. 23:24). The sages reconciled these two different descriptions by saying that the first refers to a weekday, when the shofar is sounded, the second to Shabbat, when the horn is merely remembered (*Rosh HaShana* 29b). Even though the decision not to blow the shofar on Shabbat was rabbinic, it was hinted at in the Torah.

תְּקֶף אֶרְאֶלִּים וְכוֹכְבֵי צֶפֶר *The splendor of angels and the morning stars.* It is impossible to understand the basic worldview of Judaism without the idea of the

*The next two verses are said first by the Leader, then by the congregation. Originally, these two verses were said by the congregation as alternating refrains after the verses of the following piyut. In recent generations, the custom is to say them only here at the start.*

יִשְׁפֹּט He judges the world with righteousness
and all nations with equity. / O Holy God.

וְהוּא For He alone is LORD – who can refuse Him? Job 23
What His soul desires, He performs. / O Awesome and Holy One.

*Like the previous piyut, this one is from the cycle said on the second day. The refrains "He judges" and "For He alone" alternate after each couplet.*

*All (some congregations omit and continue with "The LORD is King" on the next page):*

אֶתֵּן I shall ascribe righteousness to my Maker / on the day chosen for all deeds to be examined.
His majesty has greatly flourished, / but His humility is equal to His grandeur.
He is Master of the world entire; / who ever hardened his heart against Him and remained whole? Job 9
He recalls those who walk innocently, / He has compassion and takes up the orphan's cause.
He is pure, lofty and sublime, / He made all things becomingly at the proper time.
The Mighty One does not despise / anyone who is lowly in his own eyes.
Glorious, He rides the heavens, / fiery flames and bright light shine before Him.
He cuts down the evil with sharpened swords / on behalf of the orphans and the widows.
He offers man recompense for all his deeds, / He creates mouths to speak and renders speakers dumb.
He created all with compassion, / He is lofty, and lays lofty ones low.
He pardons His creatures with grace, / the works of the true God are perfect.
The earthly judges are vacant in His presence, / astounded and affrighted in their awe of Him. Is. 40
He takes up the cause of His nation, / judging them first to spare them His wrath.
The righteous tremble under His close scrutiny, / though they performed His laws faithfully.
He sees all hidden things, / residing in the lofty heavens.
He foresees events before they occur / and hastens the occurrences of the future.
He proclaims the future of all generations before they come to pass, / searching and examining the inner workings of hearts. Is. 41
▸ He who remembers His covenant with our ancestors, / may He fulfill His oath toward their descendants.

---

majesty on the one hand, His humility and concern for the powerless and poor on the other. So should we too be humble: "The Mighty One does not despise / anyone who is lowly in his own eyes."

*The next two verses are said first by the* שליח ציבור*, then by the* קהל*. Originally, these two verses were said by the* קהל *as alternating refrains after the verses of the following piyut. In recent generations, the custom is to say them only here at the start.*

**יִשְׁפֹּט תֵּבֵל בְּצֶדֶק, וּלְאֻמִּים בְּמֵישָׁרִים / הָאֵל קָדוֹשׁ.**

איוב כג **וְהוּא בְאֶחָד וּמִי יְשִׁיבֶנּוּ, וְנַפְשׁוֹ אִוְּתָה וַיָּעַשׂ: / נוֹרָא וְקָדוֹשׁ.**

*Like the previous piyut, this one is from the cycle said on the second day. The refrains "*יִשְׁפֹּט תֵּבֵל*" and "*וְהוּא בְאֶחָד*" alternate after each couplet.*
*All (some congregations omit and continue with* יהוה מֶלֶךְ *on the next page):*

אֶתֵּן לְפֹעֲלִי צֶדֶק / בַּיּוֹם הַנִּבְחָר מַעַשׂ לְהִבָּדֵק.
גַּאֲוָתוֹ מְאֹד גָּדְלָה / דֶּרֶךְ עֲנָוְתוֹ לְפִי הַגְּדֻלָּה.
איוב ט הוּא אֲדוֹן הָעוֹלָם / וּמִי הִקְשָׁה אֵלָיו וַיִּשְׁלָם.
זוֹכֵר הוֹלֵךְ בְּתֹם / חוֹנֵן וְעֹשֶׂה דִּין יָתוֹם.
טָהוֹר מָרוֹם וְנִשָּׂא / יָפֶה בְעִתּוֹ הַכֹּל עָשָׂה.
כַּבִּיר לֹא יִמְאַס / לְנִבְזֶה בְּעֵינָיו, נִמְאָס.
מְפֹאָר רֹכֵב עֲרָבוֹת / נֹגַהּ נֶגְדּוֹ, וְאֵשׁ לֶהָבוֹת.
סוֹעֵף בַּחֲרָבוֹת שְׁנוּנוֹת / עֲבוּר יְתוֹמִים וְאַלְמָנוֹת.
פֹּעַל אָדָם יְשַׁלֵּם / צָר פֶּה וּמֵשִׂים אִלֵּם.
קֹנֵה הַכֹּל בְּרַחֲמִים / רָם וּמַשְׁפִּיל רָמִים.
שׁוֹפֵט יְצוּרָיו בַּחֲנִינָה / תְּמִים פֹּעַל, אֵל אֱמוּנָה.
ישעיה מ שׁוֹפְטֵי אֶרֶץ כַּתֹּהוּ / מִפַּחְדּוֹ יִבָּהֲלוּ וְיִתְמָהוּ.
עוֹשֶׂה מִשְׁפַּט עַמּוֹ / וּתְחִלָּה מְקַדְּמָם מִפְּנֵי זַעְמוֹ.
נְדִיבִים בְּדִקְדּוּקָם יָחִילוּ / בַּאֲשֶׁר מִשְׁפָּטוֹ פָּעֳלוּ.
רוֹאֶה כָּל תַּעֲלוּמוֹת / יוֹשֵׁב בְּגָבְהֵי מְרוֹמוֹת.
צוֹפֶה כָּל נוֹלָדוֹת / חוֹפֵשׂ כָּל הָעֲתִידוֹת.
ישעיה מא קֹרֵא הַדֹּרוֹת מֵרֹאשׁ / חִקְרֵי לֵב לָתוּר וְלִדְרוֹשׁ.
◂ זוֹכֵר בְּרִית רִאשׁוֹנִים / קַיֵּם שְׁבוּעָה לָאַחֲרוֹנִים.

---

אֶתֵּן לְפֹעֲלִי צֶדֶק *I shall ascribe righteousness to my Maker.* Written by Rabbi Shimon bar Yitzḥak, the poem begins with a quotation from the book of Job, and is largely woven from biblical quotations attesting to God's power and

*The Ark is opened.*

*This piyut has a complex form in which the refrain has a double function. After each line, the congregation responds with one of the refrain's three phrases "The Lord is King," "The Lord was King" and "The Lord shall be King," and after each three-line stanza, the whole refrain is said. In many congregations, the Leader says the verses and the congregation only the refrains; in others, the Leader recites the two first lines and the congregation follows with the third. There are also congregations in which the entire piyut is sung by all.*

The Lord is King, The Lord was King,
and The Lord shall be King forever and ever.

The mighty among this awe-inspiring nation shall mightily proclaim aloud,
The Lord is King.
The angels formed from lightning shall bless aloud,
The Lord was King.
The angelic heroes on high shall forcefully proclaim aloud,
The Lord shall be King.

The Lord is King, the Lord was King,
and the Lord shall be King forever and ever.

The angels scattering flames as they gallop shall speak aloud,
The Lord is King.
The tumultuous camp of angels shall praise aloud,
The Lord was King.
The hosts and angelic creatures shall gather and proclaim aloud,
The Lord shall be King.

The Lord is King, the Lord was King,
and the Lord shall be King forever and ever.

Those who recall the songs of praise shall sing aloud,
The Lord is King.
The wise who resolve the Torah's riddles shall firmly proclaim aloud,
The Lord was King.
The angelic officers in the heavenly ether shall praise aloud,
The Lord shall be King.

The Lord is King, the Lord was King,
and the Lord shall be King forever and ever.

---

line containing a triple alphabetical acrostic, and followed by the threefold refrain that The Lord was, is, and always will be King. Its theme is the harmony between the praises we sing on earth and those the angels sing in heaven.

*The* ארון קודש *is opened.*

*This piyut has a complex form in which the refrain has a double function. After each line, the* קהל *responds with one of the refrain's three phrases "*יהוה מֶלֶךְ*," "*יהוה מָלָךְ*," and "*יהוה יִמְלֹךְ*," and after each three-line stanza, the whole refrain is said. In many congregations, the* שליח ציבור *says the verses and the* קהל *only the refrains; in others, the* שליח ציבור *recites the two first lines and the congregation follows with the third. There are also congregations in which the entire piyut is sung by all.*

יהוה מֶלֶךְ, יהוה מָלָךְ, יהוה יִמְלֹךְ לְעֹלָם וָעֶד.

אַדִּירֵי אֲיֻמָּה יַאְדִּירוּ בְקוֹל. יהוה מֶלֶךְ.
בְּרוּאֵי בָרָק יְבָרְכוּ בְקוֹל. יהוה מָלָךְ.
גִּבּוֹרֵי גְּבַהּ יַגְבִּירוּ בְקוֹל. יהוה יִמְלֹךְ.

יהוה מֶלֶךְ, יהוה מָלָךְ, יהוה יִמְלֹךְ לְעֹלָם וָעֶד.

דּוֹהֲרֵי דוֹלְקִים יְדוֹבְבוּ בְקוֹל. יהוה מֶלֶךְ.
הֲמוֹנֵי הֲמֻלָּה יְהַלְלוּ בְקוֹל. יהוה מָלָךְ.
וַחֲיָלִים וְחַיּוֹת יְוַעֲדוּ בְקוֹל. יהוה יִמְלֹךְ.

יהוה מֶלֶךְ, יהוה מָלָךְ, יהוה יִמְלֹךְ לְעֹלָם וָעֶד.

זוֹכְרֵי זְמִירוֹת יְזַמְּרוּ בְקוֹל. יהוה מֶלֶךְ.
חַכְמֵי חִידוֹת יְחַסְּנוּ בְקוֹל. יהוה מָלָךְ.
טַפְסְרֵי טְפוּחִים יְטַכְּסוּ בְקוֹל. יהוה יִמְלֹךְ.

יהוה מֶלֶךְ, יהוה מָלָךְ, יהוה יִמְלֹךְ לְעֹלָם וָעֶד.

---

יהוה מֶלֶךְ *The* Lord *is King.* The line "The Lord is King, The Lord was King, The Lord shall be King forever and ever," though it appears in our daily prayers, is not biblical. It is the joining of three biblical fragments. The poet, HaKalir, has here based himself on two themes. First is the threefold angelic sanctification of God that Isaiah heard in his vision of heaven: "Holy, holy, holy is the Lord of hosts." The second is the idea that when we say the *Kedusha,* we too are like the angels. So the poem is written in three lines, with each

The heirs of the precious Torah shall rightfully sing aloud,
The LORD is King.
The mighty angels of valor shall crown Him aloud, The LORD was King.
The angels robed in flames shall heartily reinforce aloud,
The LORD shall be King.

The LORD is King, the LORD was King,
and the LORD shall be King forever and ever.

Those who sing sweet words to God shall utter aloud, The LORD is King.
The angels of flashing light shall musically proclaim aloud,
The LORD was King.
The swirling Seraphim shall cantillate aloud, The LORD shall be King.

The LORD is King, the LORD was King,
and the LORD shall be King forever and ever.

Those who elaborate the Torah's might shall proclaim aloud,
The LORD is King.
Those who fear Your wondrous works shall burst out aloud,
The LORD was King.
Your hosts of servants, faithful as sheep, shall ring out aloud,
The LORD shall be King.

The LORD is King, the LORD was King,
and the LORD shall be King forever and ever.

The sacred congregations shall sanctify aloud, The LORD is King.
The myriads of Your multitudes shall sing mellifluously aloud,
The LORD was King.
The angels of fiery sparks shall repeat aloud, The LORD shall be King.

The LORD is King, the LORD was King,
and the LORD shall be King forever and ever.

Those who uphold God's praise shall steadfastly proclaim aloud,
The LORD is King.
Those who assert Your glory shall innocently proclaim aloud,
The LORD was King.
Those who fulfill the Torah faithfully shall recount aloud,
The LORD shall be King.

The LORD is King, the LORD was King,
and the LORD shall be King forever and ever.

יוֹרְשֵׁי יְקָרָה יְיַשְּׁרוּ בְקוֹל. יהוה מֶלֶךְ.
כַּבִּירֵי כֹחַ יַכְתִּירוּ בְקוֹל. יהוה מָלָךְ.
לְבוּשֵׁי לֶהָבוֹת יְלַבְּבוּ בְקוֹל. יהוה יִמְלֹךְ.

יהוה מֶלֶךְ, יהוה מָלָךְ, יהוה יִמְלֹךְ לְעֹלָם וָעֶד.

מַנְעִימֵי מֶלֶל יְמַלְּלוּ בְקוֹל. יהוה מֶלֶךְ.
נוֹצְצֵי נֹגַהּ יְנַצְּחוּ בְקוֹל. יהוה מָלָךְ.
שְׂרָפִים סוֹבְבִים יְסַלְסְלוּ בְקוֹל. יהוה יִמְלֹךְ.

יהוה מֶלֶךְ, יהוה מָלָךְ, יהוה יִמְלֹךְ לְעֹלָם וָעֶד.

עוֹרְכֵי עֹז יַעֲנוּ בְקוֹל. יהוה מֶלֶךְ.
פְּחוּדֵי פִלְאֲךָ יִפְצְחוּ בְקוֹל. יהוה מָלָךְ.
צִבְאוֹת צְאנֶךָ יְצַלְצְלוּ בְקוֹל. יהוה יִמְלֹךְ.

יהוה מֶלֶךְ, יהוה מָלָךְ, יהוה יִמְלֹךְ לְעֹלָם וָעֶד.

קְהִלּוֹת קֹדֶשׁ יַקְדִּישׁוּ בְקוֹל. יהוה מֶלֶךְ.
רִבְבוֹת רְבָבָה יְרַנְּנוּ בְקוֹל. יהוה מָלָךְ.
שְׁבִיבֵי שַׁלְהָבוֹת יְשַׁנְּנוּ בְקוֹל. יהוה יִמְלֹךְ.

יהוה מֶלֶךְ, יהוה מָלָךְ, יהוה יִמְלֹךְ לְעֹלָם וָעֶד.

תּוֹמְכֵי תְהִלּוֹת יַתְמִידוּ בְקוֹל. יהוה מֶלֶךְ.
תּוֹקְפֵי תִפְאַרְתֶּךָ יַתְמִימוּ בְקוֹל. יהוה מָלָךְ.
תְּמִימֵי תְעוּדָה יְתַנּוּ בְקוֹל. יהוה יִמְלֹךְ.

יהוה מֶלֶךְ, יהוה מָלָךְ, יהוה יִמְלֹךְ לְעֹלָם וָעֶד.

*There follows an ancient piyut, author unknown, which most congregations add before Kedusha. In recent generations the custom to say it responsively has spread; many congregations are accustomed to saying the second stich of each couplet together with the first of the next one. Some sing the entire piyut collectively. However, traditionally this piyut is said only by the Leader, with the congregation joining in at "And so, sanctity will rise up to You" on the next page.*

And so, all shall crown You.

The God who renders judgment.
The One who examines hearts on the Day of Judgment.
The One who reveals deep secrets in judgment.
The One who speaks candidly on the Day of Judgment.
The One who voices His wisdom in judgment.
The One who is diligent and performs kindness
on the Day of Judgment.
The One who recalls His covenant in judgment.
The One who shows compassion toward His creations
on the Day of Judgment.
The One who purifies those who rely on Him in judgment.
The One who knows all inner thoughts on the Day of Judgment.
The One who suppresses His anger in judgment.
The One who clothes Himself with righteousness
on the Day of Judgment.
The One who forgives sins in judgment.
The awesome and praiseworthy One
on the Day of Judgment.
The One who forgives those He bears in judgment.
The One who answers those who call on Him
on the Day of Judgment.
The One who exercises His compassion in judgment.
The One who sees all hidden secrets on the Day of Judgment.
The One who acquires His servants in judgment.
The One who takes pity on His nation on the Day of Judgment.
The One who guards those who love Him in judgment.
The One who supports His innocent ones
on the Day of Judgment.

*The Ark is closed.*

*There follows an ancient piyut, author unknown, which most congregations add before* השודך*. In recent generations the custom to say it responsively has spread; many congregations are accustomed to saying the second stich of each couplet together with the first of the next one. Some sing the entire piyut collectively. However, traditionally this piyut is said only by the* שליח ציבור*, with the congregation joining in at "*וּבְכֵן לְךָ תַעֲלֶה קְדֻשָּׁה*" on the next page.*

# וּבְכֵן לְךָ הַכֹּל יַכְתִּירוּ.

לְאֵל עוֹרֵךְ דִּין לְבוֹחֵן לְבָבוֹת בְּיוֹם דִּין.
לְגוֹלֶה עֲמֻקּוֹת בַּדִּין לְדוֹבֵר מֵישָׁרִים בְּיוֹם דִּין.
לְהוֹגֶה דֵעוֹת בַּדִּין לְוָתִיק וְעוֹשֶׂה חֶסֶד בְּיוֹם דִּין.
לְזוֹכֵר בְּרִיתוֹ בַּדִּין לְחוֹמֵל מַעֲשָׂיו בְּיוֹם דִּין.
לְטַהֵר חוֹסָיו בַּדִּין לְיוֹדֵעַ מַחֲשָׁבוֹת בְּיוֹם דִּין
לְכוֹבֵשׁ כַּעְסוֹ בַּדִּין לְלוֹבֵשׁ צְדָקוֹת בְּיוֹם דִּין.
לְמוֹחֵל עֲוֹנוֹת בַּדִּין לְנוֹרָא תְהִלּוֹת בְּיוֹם דִּין.
לְסוֹלֵחַ לַעֲמוּסָיו בַּדִּין לְעוֹנֶה לְקוֹרְאָיו בְּיוֹם דִּין.
לְפוֹעֵל רַחֲמָיו בַּדִּין לְצוֹפֶה נִסְתָּרוֹת בְּיוֹם דִּין.
לְקוֹנֶה עֲבָדָיו בַּדִּין לְרַחֵם עַמּוֹ בְּיוֹם דִּין.
לְשׁוֹמֵר אֹהֲבָיו בַּדִּין לְתוֹמֵךְ תְּמִימָיו בְּיוֹם דִּין.

*The* ארון קודש *is closed.*

---

וּבְכֵן לְךָ הַכֹּל יַכְתִּירוּ *And so, all shall crown You.* A powerful fugue, affirming both the awesome mood and nature of the day – God sitting in judgment on the Day of Judgment – yet also God's compassion and forgiveness. Without both, the human world could not survive. Without justice and judgment there would be anarchy, a war of all against all. But without compassion and forgiveness we would all be condemned, since "There is none on earth so righteous as to do only good and never sin" (Eccl. 7:20). The prayer is much loved because of its plaintive melody. Though said in Shaḥarit on the first day, it is often moved to Musaf on the second day.

*All:*

וּבְכֵן לְךָ And so, sanctity will rise up to You; for You, our God, are King.

*Some congregations say the piyut "Melekh BeMishpat" on page 1014 before the Kedusha.*

KEDUSHA

*The following is said standing with feet together, rising on the toes at the words indicated by ▴.*

*The congregation then the Leader:*

נְקַדֵּשָׁךְ We will sanctify and revere You
with the song sung by the holy Seraphim,
who speak the threefold declaration of Your holiness,
as is written by Your prophet,
"And they [the angels] call to one another saying: Is. 6

*The congregation then the Leader:*

▴Holy, ▴holy, ▴holy is the LORD of hosts;
the whole world is filled with His glory."
Then with a sound of mighty noise, majestic and strong,
they make their voice heard, raising themselves
toward the Seraphim, and facing them praise You and say:

*The congregation then the Leader:*

▴"Blessed is the LORD's glory from His place." Ezek. 3
Reveal Yourself from Your place, O our King, and reign over us,
for we are waiting for You. When will You reign in Zion?
May it be soon in our days, and may You dwell there for ever and all time.
May You be exalted and sanctified in the midst of Jerusalem, Your city,
from generation to generation for evermore.
May our eyes see Your kingdom,
as is said in the songs of Your splendor,
written by David Your righteous anointed one:

*The congregation then the Leader:*

▴"The LORD shall reign for ever. He is your God, Zion, Ps. 146
from generation to generation, Halleluya!"

---

them singing "Holy, holy, holy is the LORD of hosts; the whole world is filled with His glory." Ezekiel heard them singing, "Blessed is the LORD's glory from

*All:*

וּבְכֵן לְךָ תַעֲלֶה קְדֻשָּׁה, כִּי אַתָּה אֱלֹהֵינוּ מֶלֶךְ.

*Some congregations say the piyut* מֶלֶךְ בְּמִשְׁפָּט *on page 1014 before* קדושה.

## קדושה

*The following is said standing with feet together, rising on the toes at the words indicated by* ˄.

*The* קהל *then the* שליח ציבור*:*

נַקְדִּישְׁךָ וְנַעֲרִיצְךָ כְּנֹעַם שִׂיחַ סוֹד שַׂרְפֵי קֹדֶשׁ
הַמְשַׁלְּשִׁים לְךָ קְדֻשָּׁה
כַּכָּתוּב עַל יַד נְבִיאֶךָ, וְקָרָא זֶה אֶל־זֶה וְאָמַר ישעיה ו

*The* קהל *then the* שליח ציבור*:*

˄קָדוֹשׁ, ˄קָדוֹשׁ, ˄קָדוֹשׁ, יהוה צְבָאוֹת, מְלֹא כָל־הָאָרֶץ כְּבוֹדוֹ:
אָז בְּקוֹל רַעַשׁ גָּדוֹל אַדִּיר וְחָזָק מַשְׁמִיעִים קוֹל
מִתְנַשְּׂאִים לְעֻמַּת שְׂרָפִים, לְעֻמָּתָם מְשַׁבְּחִים וְאוֹמְרִים

*The* קהל *then the* שליח ציבור*:*

˄בָּרוּךְ כְּבוֹד־יהוה מִמְּקוֹמוֹ: יחזקאל ג
מִמְּקוֹמְךָ מַלְכֵּנוּ תוֹפִיעַ וְתִמְלֹךְ עָלֵינוּ, כִּי מְחַכִּים אֲנַחְנוּ לָךְ
מָתַי תִּמְלֹךְ בְּצִיּוֹן, בְּקָרוֹב בְּיָמֵינוּ לְעוֹלָם וָעֶד תִּשְׁכֹּן
תִּתְגַּדַּל וְתִתְקַדַּשׁ בְּתוֹךְ יְרוּשָׁלַיִם עִירְךָ לְדוֹר וָדוֹר וּלְנֵצַח נְצָחִים.
וְעֵינֵינוּ תִרְאֶינָה מַלְכוּתֶךָ
כַּדָּבָר הָאָמוּר בְּשִׁירֵי עֻזֶּךָ, עַל יְדֵי דָוִד מְשִׁיחַ צִדְקֶךָ

*The* קהל *then the* שליח ציבור*:*

˄יִמְלֹךְ יהוה לְעוֹלָם, אֱלֹהַיִךְ צִיּוֹן לְדֹר וָדֹר, הַלְלוּיָהּ: תהלים קמו

---

KEDUSHA

The Kedusha is one of the holiest as well as the most audacious of prayers. It is based on the visions of Isaiah and Ezekiel who saw God enthroned in heaven surrounded by a retinue of angels singing His praises. Isaiah heard

HOLINESS

אַתָּה קָדוֹשׁ You are holy and Your name is holy,
and holy ones praise You daily, Selah!
For You, God, are a great and holy King.

לְדוֹר וָדוֹר From generation to generation declare God King,
for He alone is lofty and holy.

וּבְכֵן יִתְקַדַּשׁ And so may Your name be sanctified, Lord our God,
through Israel Your nation and Jerusalem, Your city,
and Zion, the dwelling place of Your honor
and through the royal house of David Your anointed,
and Your Sanctuary and Your Temple.

וּבְכֵן תֵּן פַּחְדְּךָ And so place the fear of You, LORD our God,
over all that You have made,
and the terror of You over all You have created,
and all who were made will stand in awe of You,
and all of creation will worship You,
and they will be bound all together as one
to carry out Your will with an undivided heart;
for we know, LORD our God,
that all dominion is laid out before You,
strength is in Your palm,
and might in Your right hand,
Your name spreading awe
over all You have created.

---

and the Amida itself – it is as if we now stand in the innermost court of the King, joining our voices to the angelic choir. We have climbed the ladder of prayer stretching from earth to heaven, and we now stand on its uppermost rung. This is prayer's supreme mystical moment. We have left planet Earth far behind and we become part of the music of infinity.

קדושת השם

אַתָּה קָדוֹשׁ וְשִׁמְךָ קָדוֹשׁ
וּקְדוֹשִׁים בְּכָל יוֹם יְהַלְלוּךָ סֶּלָה
כִּי אֵל מֶלֶךְ גָּדוֹל וְקָדוֹשׁ אָתָּה.

לְדוֹר וָדוֹר הַמְלִיכוּ לָאֵל
כִּי הוּא לְבַדּוֹ מָרוֹם וְקָדוֹשׁ.

וּבְכֵן יִתְקַדַּשׁ שִׁמְךָ יהוה אֱלֹהֵינוּ
עַל יִשְׂרָאֵל עַמֶּךָ וְעַל יְרוּשָׁלַיִם עִירֶךָ
וְעַל צִיּוֹן מִשְׁכַּן כְּבוֹדֶךָ
וְעַל מַלְכוּת בֵּית דָּוִד מְשִׁיחֶךָ
וְעַל מְכוֹנְךָ וְהֵיכָלֶךָ.

וּבְכֵן תֵּן פַּחְדְּךָ יהוה אֱלֹהֵינוּ עַל כָּל מַעֲשֶׂיךָ
וְאֵימָתְךָ עַל כָּל מַה שֶּׁבָּרָאתָ
וְיִירָאוּךָ כָּל הַמַּעֲשִׂים
וְיִשְׁתַּחֲווּ לְפָנֶיךָ כָּל הַבְּרוּאִים
וְיֵעָשׂוּ כֻלָּם אֲגֻדָּה אֶחָת לַעֲשׂוֹת רְצוֹנְךָ בְּלֵבָב שָׁלֵם
כְּמוֹ שֶׁיָּדַעְנוּ יהוה אֱלֹהֵינוּ שֶׁהַשָּׁלְטָן לְפָנֶיךָ
עֹז בְּיָדְךָ וּגְבוּרָה בִּימִינֶךָ
וְשִׁמְךָ נוֹרָא עַל כָּל מַה שֶּׁבָּרָאתָ.

---

His place." These two lines, plus a third taken from Psalms, form the core of the *Kedusha*. What is daring is the idea that having come thus far in prayer – through the dawn blessings, the verses of praise, Shema and its blessings,

וּבְכֵן תֵּן כָּבוֹד And so place honor, LORD, upon Your people,
praise on those who fear You
and hope into those who seek You,
the confidence to speak into all who long for You,
gladness to Your land and joy to Your city,
the flourishing of pride to David Your servant,
and a lamp laid out for his descendant, Your anointed,
soon, in our days.

וּבְכֵן צַדִּיקִים And then righteous people
will see and rejoice,
and the upright will exult,
and the pious revel in joy,
and injustice will have nothing more to say,
and all wickedness will fade away like smoke
as You sweep the rule of arrogance from the earth.

וְתִמְלֹךְ And You, who are the Lord our God,
will rule alone over all those You have made,
in Mount Zion, the dwelling of Your glory,
and in Jerusalem, Your holy city,
as it is written in Your holy Writings:
"The LORD shall reign for ever. *Ps. 146*
He is your God, Zion, from generation to generation, Halleluya!"

קָדוֹשׁ אַתָּה You are holy,
Your name is awesome,
and there is no god but You,
as it is written,
"The LORD of hosts shall be raised up through His judgment, *Is. 5*
the Holy God, made holy in righteousness."
Blessed are You, LORD,
the holy King.

וּבְכֵן תֵּן כָּבוֹד יהוה לְעַמֶּךָ
תְּהִלָּה לִירֵאֶיךָ וְתִקְוָה טוֹבָה לְדוֹרְשֶׁיךָ
וּפִתְחוֹן פֶּה לַמְיַחֲלִים לָךְ
שִׂמְחָה לְאַרְצֶךָ, וְשָׂשׂוֹן לְעִירֶךָ
וּצְמִיחַת קֶרֶן לְדָוִד עַבְדֶּךָ
וַעֲרִיכַת נֵר לְבֶן יִשַׁי מְשִׁיחֶךָ בִּמְהֵרָה בְיָמֵינוּ.

וּבְכֵן צַדִּיקִים יִרְאוּ וְיִשְׂמָחוּ, וִישָׁרִים יַעֲלֹזוּ
וַחֲסִידִים בְּרִנָּה יָגִילוּ
וְעוֹלָתָה תִּקְפָּץ פִּיהָ
וְכָל הָרִשְׁעָה כֻּלָּהּ כְּעָשָׁן תִּכְלֶה
כִּי תַעֲבִיר מֶמְשֶׁלֶת זָדוֹן מִן הָאָרֶץ.

וְתִמְלֹךְ אַתָּה הוּא יהוה אֱלֹהֵינוּ
מְהֵרָה לְבַדֶּךָ עַל כָּל מַעֲשֶׂיךָ
בְּהַר צִיּוֹן מִשְׁכַּן כְּבוֹדֶךָ
וּבִירוּשָׁלַיִם עִיר קָדְשֶׁךָ
כַּכָּתוּב בְּדִבְרֵי קָדְשֶׁךָ
תהלים קמו יִמְלֹךְ יהוה לְעוֹלָם, אֱלֹהַיִךְ צִיּוֹן לְדֹר וָדֹר, הַלְלוּיָהּ:

קָדוֹשׁ אַתָּה וְנוֹרָא שְׁמֶךָ
וְאֵין אֱלוֹהַּ מִבַּלְעָדֶיךָ
ישעיה ה כַּכָּתוּב, וַיִּגְבַּהּ יהוה צְבָאוֹת בַּמִּשְׁפָּט
וְהָאֵל הַקָּדוֹשׁ נִקְדַּשׁ בִּצְדָקָה:
בָּרוּךְ אַתָּה יהוה, הַמֶּלֶךְ הַקָּדוֹשׁ.

HOLINESS OF THE DAY

אַתָּה בְחַרְתָּנוּ You have chosen us from among all peoples.
You have loved and favored us.
You have raised us above all tongues.
You have made us holy through Your commandments.
You have brought us near, our King, to Your service,
and have called us by Your great and holy name.

*On Shabbat, add the words in parentheses:*

וַתִּתֶּן לָנוּ And You, LORD our God, have given us in love
(this Sabbath day and)
this Day of Remembrance,
a day of (recalling) blowing the shofar,
(with love,) a holy assembly in memory of the exodus from Egypt.

אֱלֹהֵינוּ Our God and God of our ancestors,
may there rise, come, reach, appear, be favored, heard,
regarded and remembered before You,
our recollection and remembrance,
as well as the remembrance of our ancestors,
and of the Messiah, son of David Your servant,
and of Jerusalem Your holy city,
and of all Your people the house of Israel –
for deliverance and well-being,
grace, loving-kindness and compassion, life and peace,
on this Day of Remembrance.
On it remember us, LORD our God, for good;
recollect us for blessing,
and deliver us for a good life.
In accord with Your promise of salvation and compassion,
spare us and be gracious to us;
have compassion on us and deliver us,
for our eyes are turned to You
because You, God, are a gracious and compassionate King.

קדושת היום

אַתָּה בְחַרְתָּנוּ מִכָּל הָעַמִּים
אָהַבְתָּ אוֹתָנוּ וְרָצִיתָ בָּנוּ
וְרוֹמַמְתָּנוּ מִכָּל הַלְּשׁוֹנוֹת
וְקִדַּשְׁתָּנוּ בְּמִצְוֹתֶיךָ
וְקֵרַבְתָּנוּ מַלְכֵּנוּ לַעֲבוֹדָתֶךָ
וְשִׁמְךָ הַגָּדוֹל וְהַקָּדוֹשׁ עָלֵינוּ קָרָאתָ.

*On* שבת*, add the words in parentheses:*

וַתִּתֶּן לָנוּ יהוה אֱלֹהֵינוּ בְּאַהֲבָה
אֶת יוֹם (הַשַּׁבָּת הַזֶּה וְאֶת יוֹם) הַזִּכָּרוֹן הַזֶּה
יוֹם (זִכְרוֹן) תְּרוּעָה (בְּאַהֲבָה) מִקְרָא קֹדֶשׁ
זֵכֶר לִיצִיאַת מִצְרָיִם.

אֱלֹהֵינוּ וֵאלֹהֵי אֲבוֹתֵינוּ
יַעֲלֶה וְיָבוֹא וְיַגִּיעַ, וְיֵרָאֶה וְיֵרָצֶה וְיִשָּׁמַע
וְיִפָּקֵד וְיִזָּכֵר זִכְרוֹנֵנוּ וּפִקְדוֹנֵנוּ וְזִכְרוֹן אֲבוֹתֵינוּ
וְזִכְרוֹן מָשִׁיחַ בֶּן דָּוִד עַבְדֶּךָ
וְזִכְרוֹן יְרוּשָׁלַיִם עִיר קָדְשֶׁךָ
וְזִכְרוֹן כָּל עַמְּךָ בֵּית יִשְׂרָאֵל, לְפָנֶיךָ
לִפְלֵיטָה לְטוֹבָה, לְחֵן וּלְחֶסֶד וּלְרַחֲמִים, לְחַיִּים וּלְשָׁלוֹם
בְּיוֹם הַזִּכָּרוֹן הַזֶּה.
זָכְרֵנוּ יהוה אֱלֹהֵינוּ בּוֹ לְטוֹבָה, וּפָקְדֵנוּ בוֹ לִבְרָכָה
וְהוֹשִׁיעֵנוּ בוֹ לְחַיִּים טוֹבִים.
וּבִדְבַר יְשׁוּעָה וְרַחֲמִים חוּס וְחָנֵּנוּ, וְרַחֵם עָלֵינוּ וְהוֹשִׁיעֵנוּ
כִּי אֵלֶיךָ עֵינֵינוּ, כִּי אֵל מֶלֶךְ חַנּוּן וְרַחוּם אָתָּה.

*On Shabbat, add the words in parentheses:*

אֱלֹהֵינוּ Our God and God of our ancestors,
rule over all the world in Your honor,
and be raised above all the earth in Your glory,
and appear, in the splendor of Your great might
before all those who live in this world, Your domain.
And all who were made will know that You made them,
and all who were formed will know that You formed them,
and all that have breath in their mouths will declare:
The LORD, God of Israel is King,
and His kingship has dominion over all.
(Our God and God of our ancestors,
find favor, please, in our rest.)
Make us holy through Your commandments
and grant us our share in Your Torah.
Satisfy us with Your goodness, grant our souls joy in Your salvation
(in love and favor, LORD our God,
grant us as our heritage Your holy Sabbath,
so that all Israel who sanctify Your name may find rest on it),
and purify our hearts to serve You in truth.
For You, LORD, are truth,
and Your word is truth and holds true forever.
Blessed are You, LORD, King over all the earth,
who sanctifies (the Sabbath,) Israel and the Day of Remembrance.

TEMPLE SERVICE

רְצֵה Find favor, LORD our God, in Your people Israel,
and heed their prayer.
Restore the service to Your most holy House,
and accept soon, in love and favor,
the fire-offerings of Israel and their prayer.
May the service of Your people Israel always find favor with You.
And may our eyes witness Your return to Zion in compassion.
Blessed are You, LORD, who restores His Presence to Zion.

*On שבת, add the words in parentheses:*

אֱלֹהֵינוּ וֵאלֹהֵי אֲבוֹתֵינוּ
מְלֹךְ עַל כָּל הָעוֹלָם כֻּלּוֹ בִּכְבוֹדֶךָ
וְהִנָּשֵׂא עַל כָּל הָאָרֶץ בִּיקָרֶךָ
וְהוֹפַע בַּהֲדַר גְּאוֹן עֻזֶּךָ עַל כָּל יוֹשְׁבֵי תֵבֵל אַרְצֶךָ.
וְיֵדַע כָּל פָּעוּל כִּי אַתָּה פְעַלְתּוֹ, וְיָבִין כָּל יָצוּר כִּי אַתָּה יְצַרְתּוֹ
וְיֹאמַר כֹּל אֲשֶׁר נְשָׁמָה בְאַפּוֹ
יהוה אֱלֹהֵי יִשְׂרָאֵל מֶלֶךְ וּמַלְכוּתוֹ בַּכֹּל מָשָׁלָה.
(אֱלֹהֵינוּ וֵאלֹהֵי אֲבוֹתֵינוּ, רְצֵה נָא בִמְנוּחָתֵנוּ)
קַדְּשֵׁנוּ בְּמִצְוֹתֶיךָ וְתֵן חֶלְקֵנוּ בְּתוֹרָתֶךָ
שַׂבְּעֵנוּ מִטּוּבֶךָ, וְשַׂמַּח נַפְשֵׁנוּ בִּישׁוּעָתֶךָ
(וְהַנְחִילֵנוּ יהוה אֱלֹהֵינוּ בְּאַהֲבָה וּבְרָצוֹן שַׁבַּת קָדְשֶׁךָ
וְיָנוּחוּ בוֹ כָּל יִשְׂרָאֵל מְקַדְּשֵׁי שְׁמֶךָ)
וְטַהֵר לִבֵּנוּ לְעָבְדְּךָ בֶּאֱמֶת
כִּי אַתָּה אֱלֹהִים אֱמֶת, וּדְבָרְךָ אֱמֶת וְקַיָּם לָעַד.
בָּרוּךְ אַתָּה יהוה, מֶלֶךְ עַל כָּל הָאָרֶץ
מְקַדֵּשׁ (הַשַּׁבָּת וְ) יִשְׂרָאֵל וְיוֹם הַזִּכָּרוֹן.

עבודה

רְצֵה יהוה אֱלֹהֵינוּ בְּעַמְּךָ יִשְׂרָאֵל, וְלִתְפִלָּתָם שְׁעֵה
וְהָשֵׁב אֶת הָעֲבוֹדָה לִדְבִיר בֵּיתֶךָ
וְאִשֵּׁי יִשְׂרָאֵל וּתְפִלָּתָם, מְהֵרָה בְּאַהֲבָה תְקַבֵּל בְּרָצוֹן
וּתְהִי לְרָצוֹן תָּמִיד עֲבוֹדַת יִשְׂרָאֵל עַמֶּךָ.
וְתֶחֱזֶינָה עֵינֵינוּ בְּשׁוּבְךָ לְצִיּוֹן בְּרַחֲמִים.
בָּרוּךְ אַתָּה יהוה, הַמַּחֲזִיר שְׁכִינָתוֹ לְצִיּוֹן.

THANKSGIVING

*Bow at the first nine words.*

מוֹדִים We give thanks to You,
for You are the LORD our God
and God of our ancestors
for ever and all time.
You are the Rock of our lives,
Shield of our salvation
from generation to generation.
We will thank You and
declare Your praise for our lives,
which are entrusted into Your hand;
for our souls,
which are placed in Your charge;
for Your miracles
which are with us every day;
and for Your wonders and favors
at all times, evening,
morning and midday.
You are good –
for Your compassion never fails.
You are compassionate –
for Your loving-kindnesses never cease;
for we have always
placed our hope in You.

*During the Leader's Repetition, the congregation says quietly:*

מוֹדִים We give thanks to You,
for You are the LORD our God
and God of our ancestors,
God of all flesh,
who formed us
and formed the universe.
Blessings and thanks
are due to Your great
and holy name for giving us
life and sustaining us.
May You continue
to give us life
and sustain us;
and may You gather our
exiles to Your holy courts,
to keep Your decrees,
do Your will
and serve You
with a perfect heart,
for it is for us
to give You thanks.
Blessed be God to whom
thanksgiving is due.

וְעַל כֻּלָּם For all these things may Your name be blessed and exalted and raised up, our King, continually, for ever and all time.

וּכְתֹב And write, for a good life, all the children of Your covenant.

Let all that lives thank You, Selah! and praise and bless
Your great name in truth, always, because it is good,
God, our Savior and Help, Selah! the beneficent God.
Blessed are You, LORD, whose name is "the Good"
and to whom thanks are due.

הודאה

*Bow at the first five words.*

| | *During the* חזרת הש״ץ*, the* קהל *says quietly:* |
|---|---|
| ׳מוֹדִים אֲנַחְנוּ לָךְ | ׳מוֹדִים אֲנַחְנוּ לָךְ |
| שָׁאַתָּה הוּא יהוה אֱלֹהֵינוּ | שָׁאַתָּה הוּא יהוה אֱלֹהֵינוּ |
| וֵאלֹהֵי אֲבוֹתֵינוּ לְעוֹלָם וָעֶד. | וֵאלֹהֵי אֲבוֹתֵינוּ |
| צוּר חַיֵּינוּ, מָגֵן יִשְׁעֵנוּ | אֱלֹהֵי כָל בָּשָׂר |
| אַתָּה הוּא לְדוֹר וָדוֹר. | יוֹצְרֵנוּ, יוֹצֵר בְּרֵאשִׁית. |
| נוֹדֶה לְּךָ וּנְסַפֵּר תְּהִלָּתֶךָ | בְּרָכוֹת וְהוֹדָאוֹת |
| עַל חַיֵּינוּ הַמְּסוּרִים בְּיָדֶךָ | לְשִׁמְךָ הַגָּדוֹל וְהַקָּדוֹשׁ |
| וְעַל נִשְׁמוֹתֵינוּ הַפְּקוּדוֹת לָךְ | עַל שֶׁהֶחֱיִיתָנוּ וְקִיַּמְתָּנוּ. |
| וְעַל נִסֶּיךָ שֶׁבְּכָל יוֹם עִמָּנוּ | כֵּן תְּחַיֵּנוּ וּתְקַיְּמֵנוּ |
| וְעַל נִפְלְאוֹתֶיךָ וְטוֹבוֹתֶיךָ | וְתֶאֱסֹף גָּלֻיּוֹתֵינוּ |
| שֶׁבְּכָל עֵת, עֶרֶב וָבֹקֶר וְצָהֳרָיִם. | לְחַצְרוֹת קָדְשֶׁךָ |
| הַטּוֹב, כִּי לֹא כָלוּ רַחֲמֶיךָ | לִשְׁמֹר חֻקֶּיךָ וְלַעֲשׂוֹת רְצוֹנֶךָ |
| וְהַמְרַחֵם, כִּי לֹא תַמּוּ חֲסָדֶיךָ | וּלְעָבְדְּךָ בְּלֵבָב שָׁלֵם |
| כִּי מֵעוֹלָם קִוִּינוּ לָךְ. | עַל שֶׁאֲנַחְנוּ מוֹדִים לָךְ. |
| | בָּרוּךְ אֵל הַהוֹדָאוֹת. |

וְעַל כֻּלָּם
יִתְבָּרַךְ וְיִתְרוֹמַם וְיִתְנַשֵּׂא שִׁמְךָ מַלְכֵּנוּ תָּמִיד לְעוֹלָם וָעֶד.

וּכְתֹב לְחַיִּים טוֹבִים כָּל בְּנֵי בְרִיתֶךָ.

וְכֹל הַחַיִּים יוֹדוּךָ סֶּלָה
וִיהַלְלוּ וִיבָרְכוּ אֶת שִׁמְךָ הַגָּדוֹל בֶּאֱמֶת לְעוֹלָם כִּי טוֹב
הָאֵל יְשׁוּעָתֵנוּ וְעֶזְרָתֵנוּ סֶלָה, הָאֵל הַטּוֹב.
׳בָּרוּךְ אַתָּה יהוה, הַטּוֹב שִׁמְךָ וּלְךָ נָאֶה לְהוֹדוֹת.

*In Israel, if Kohanim bless the congregation, turn to page 1002. See laws 91–96.*

אֱלֹהֵינוּ Our God and God of our fathers, bless us with the threefold blessing in the Torah, written by the hand of Moses Your servant and pronounced by Aaron and his sons the priests, Your holy people, as it is said:

May the Lord bless you and protect you. *Num. 6*
*Cong:* May it be Your will.
May the Lord make His face shine on you
and be gracious to you. *Cong:* May it be Your will.
May the Lord turn His face toward you,
and grant you peace. *Cong:* May it be Your will.

PEACE

שִׂים שָׁלוֹם Grant peace, goodness and blessing,
life, grace, loving-kindness and compassion
to us and all Israel Your people.
Bless us, our Father, all as one, with the light of Your face,
for by the light of Your face You have given us, Lord our God,
the Torah of life and love of kindness,
righteousness, blessing, compassion, life and peace.
May it be good in Your eyes to bless us and all Your people Israel
at every time, in every hour, with Your peace.

*The congregation then the Leader:*

בְּסֵפֶר חַיִּים In the book of life, blessing, peace and prosperity,
and good decrees, salvations and consolations
may we and all Your people the house of Israel
be remembered and written before You
for a good life, and for peace.

Blessed are You, Lord, who blesses His people Israel with peace.

*The following verse concludes the Leader's Repetition of the Amida.*
*Some also say it here as part of the silent Amida. See law 64.*

May the words of my mouth and the meditation of my heart *Ps. 19*
find favor before You, Lord, my Rock and Redeemer.

*In* ארץ ישראל*, if* כהנים *say* ברכת כהנים*, turn to page 1003. See laws 91–96.*

אֱלֹהֵינוּ וֵאלֹהֵי אֲבוֹתֵינוּ, בָּרְכֵנוּ בַּבְּרָכָה הַמְשֻׁלֶּשֶׁת בַּתּוֹרָה הַכְּתוּבָה עַל יְדֵי מֹשֶׁה עַבְדֶּךָ, הָאֲמוּרָה מִפִּי אַהֲרֹן וּבָנָיו כֹּהֲנִים עַם קְדוֹשֶׁיךָ, כָּאָמוּר

יְבָרֶכְךָ יהוה וְיִשְׁמְרֶךָ: קהל: כֵּן יְהִי רָצוֹן במדבר ו

יָאֵר יהוה פָּנָיו אֵלֶיךָ וִיחֻנֶּךָּ: קהל: כֵּן יְהִי רָצוֹן

יִשָּׂא יהוה פָּנָיו אֵלֶיךָ וְיָשֵׂם לְךָ שָׁלוֹם: קהל: כֵּן יְהִי רָצוֹן

ברכת שלום

שִׂים שָׁלוֹם טוֹבָה וּבְרָכָה, חַיִּים חֵן וָחֶסֶד וְרַחֲמִים
עָלֵינוּ וְעַל כָּל יִשְׂרָאֵל עַמֶּךָ.
בָּרְכֵנוּ אָבִינוּ כֻּלָּנוּ כְּאֶחָד בְּאוֹר פָּנֶיךָ
כִּי בְאוֹר פָּנֶיךָ נָתַתָּ לָּנוּ יהוה אֱלֹהֵינוּ
תּוֹרַת חַיִּים וְאַהֲבַת חֶסֶד
וּצְדָקָה וּבְרָכָה וְרַחֲמִים וְחַיִּים וְשָׁלוֹם.
וְטוֹב יִהְיֶה בְּעֵינֶיךָ לְבָרְכֵנוּ וּלְבָרֵךְ אֶת כָּל עַמְּךָ יִשְׂרָאֵל
בְּכָל עֵת וּבְכָל שָׁעָה בִּשְׁלוֹמֶךָ.

*The* קהל *then the* שליח ציבור*:*

בְּסֵפֶר חַיִּים, בְּרָכָה וְשָׁלוֹם, וּפַרְנָסָה טוֹבָה
וּגְזֵרוֹת טוֹבוֹת, יְשׁוּעוֹת וְנֶחָמוֹת, נִזָּכֵר וְנִכָּתֵב לְפָנֶיךָ
אֲנַחְנוּ וְכָל עַמְּךָ בֵּית יִשְׂרָאֵל לְחַיִּים טוֹבִים וּלְשָׁלוֹם.

בָּרוּךְ אַתָּה יהוה, הַמְבָרֵךְ אֶת עַמּוֹ יִשְׂרָאֵל בַּשָּׁלוֹם.

*The following verse concludes the* חזרת הש״ץ.
*Some also say it here as part of the silent* עמידה*. See law 64.*

יִהְיוּ לְרָצוֹן אִמְרֵי־פִי וְהֶגְיוֹן לִבִּי לְפָנֶיךָ, יהוה צוּרִי וְגֹאֲלִי: תהלים יט

*On Shabbat, Avinu Malkenu is not said,*
*and the service continues with Full Kaddish on page 418.*
*Some omit the first line, "We have sinned before You," in order to avoid calling attention to our sins on Rosh HaShana.*

*The Ark is opened.*

אָבִינוּ מַלְכֵּנוּ Our Father, our King, we have sinned before You.
Our Father, our King, we have no king but You.
Our Father, our King, deal kindly with us for the sake of Your name.
Our Father our King, renew for us a good year.
Our Father, our King, nullify all harsh decrees against us.
Our Father, our King, nullify the plans of those who hate us.

---

than the other man, but because he is always forbearing and the other is not." (*Ta'anit* 25b)

It was the genius of Rabbi Akiva to juxtapose two ideas – God is our King and we are His subjects, yet God is also our Father and we are His children – and with utter simplicity pray that God see us with the love of a parent before considering our lives with the detachment of a king.

The Nobel Prize–winning physicist Niels Bohr who devised complementarity theory in quantum physics – the principle that you cannot chart simultaneously the position and the velocity of a particle – said that the idea came to him when his son confessed to having stolen an item from a local shop. He found that he could think of him with love as a father, and with justice as a judge, but not both at the same time.

Rabbi Akiva's formula was used as the basis of this longer prayer, which exists in different forms among different rites, some as short as twenty-nine verses long. Ours has forty-four verses. The prayer bears the marks of having been added to at various times. Its basic structure mirrors the central requests of the weekday Amida. Other verses were added during periods of persecution and martyrdom, poverty and plague. The five-fold reference to the "books" of good life, and so on, are peculiar to the Ten Days of Repentance. *Avinu Malkenu* is not said on Shabbat since it was first said on a public fast day, and no public fast can be ordained on Shabbat.

חָטָאנוּ לְפָנֶיךָ *We have sinned before You.* Even though we knew we were before You, and that You see all we do, still we sinned (Rabbi Isaiah Horowitz, Shela).

*On* שבת*,* אָבִינוּ מַלְכֵּנוּ *is not said,*
*and the service continues with* קדיש שלם *on page 419.*
*Some omit the first line,* חָטָאנוּ לְפָנֶיךָ*, in order to avoid calling attention to our sins on* ראש השנה*.*

*The* ארון קודש *is opened.*

אָבִינוּ מַלְכֵּנוּ, חָטָאנוּ לְפָנֶיךָ.
אָבִינוּ מַלְכֵּנוּ, אֵין לָנוּ מֶלֶךְ אֶלָּא אָתָּה.
אָבִינוּ מַלְכֵּנוּ, עֲשֵׂה עִמָּנוּ לְמַעַן שְׁמֶךָ.
אָבִינוּ מַלְכֵּנוּ, חַדֵּשׁ עָלֵינוּ שָׁנָה טוֹבָה.
אָבִינוּ מַלְכֵּנוּ, בַּטֵּל מֵעָלֵינוּ כָּל גְּזֵרוֹת קָשׁוֹת.
אָבִינוּ מַלְכֵּנוּ, בַּטֵּל מַחְשְׁבוֹת שׂוֹנְאֵינוּ.

---

NO HALLEL ON ROSH HASHANA

Rabbi Abahu said: The ministering angels asked the Holy One, blessed be He, why Israel does not sing songs of praise [Hallel] on Rosh HaShana and Yom Kippur. He replied, "Can a King sit on the throne of judgment with the books of life and death open before Him, and Israel sing songs of praise?" (*Rosh HaShana* 32b)

Another reason: Hallel is a response to God in history: the exodus on Pesaḥ, the giving of the Torah on Shavuot and the forty years in the wilderness on Sukkot. Rosh HaShana and Yom Kippur are not festivals of history. They are about the eternal questions of life and death, good and evil, sin and atonement, judgment and forgiveness.

Some say that *Avinu Malkenu* stands in place of Hallel.

AVINU MALKENU – OUR FATHER, OUR KING

Once, during a drought, Rabbi Eliezer stood before the Ark and recited the twenty-four blessings for fast days but his prayer was not answered. Rabbi Akiva stood before the Ark and said: "Our Father, our King, we have no king but You; our Father, our King, for Your sake have mercy upon us," and rain fell. The rabbis suspected Rabbi Eliezer of being a lesser figure than Rabbi Akiva, but a Heavenly Voice was heard proclaiming, "The prayer of this man, Rabbi Akiva, was answered not because he is greater

Our Father, our King, thwart the counsel of our enemies.
Our Father, our King, rid us of every oppressor and adversary.
Our Father, our King, close the mouths of our adversaries and accusers.
Our Father, our King, eradicate pestilence, sword, famine,
captivity and destruction, iniquity and
annihilation
from the people of Your covenant.
Our Father, our King, withhold the plague from Your heritage.
Our Father, our King, forgive and pardon all our iniquities.
Our Father, our King, wipe away and remove our transgressions and
sins from Your sight.
Our Father, our King, erase in Your abundant mercy all records of our
sins.

*The following nine verses are said responsively, first by the Leader, then by the congregation:*

Our Father, our King, bring us back to You in perfect repentance.
Our Father, our King, send a complete healing to the sick of Your
people.
Our Father, our King, tear up the evil decree against us.
Our Father, our King, remember us with a memory of favorable deeds
before You.
Our Father, our King, write us in the book of good life.
Our Father, our King, write us in the book of redemption and salvation.
Our Father, our King, write us in the book of livelihood and sustenance.
Our Father, our King, write us in the book of merit.
Our Father, our King, write us in the book of pardon and forgiveness.

*End of responsive reading.*

---

Anti-Semitism, the "oldest hatred," is ultimately dislike of the unlike – the fear, mutating into hate, of the stranger. It is for this reason that the Torah commands us thirty-six times to love the stranger. Anti-Semitism, though it begins with Jews, never ends with Jews. It is the paradigm case of the hatred of difference. And since difference is constitutive of our humanity, a society that has no room for Jews has no room for humanity. It must be fought in the name, and for the sake, of our shared humanity.

אָבִינוּ מַלְכֵּנוּ, הָפֵר עֲצַת אוֹיְבֵינוּ.
אָבִינוּ מַלְכֵּנוּ, כַּלֵּה כָּל צַר וּמַשְׂטִין מֵעָלֵינוּ.
אָבִינוּ מַלְכֵּנוּ, סְתֹם פִּיּוֹת מַשְׂטִינֵנוּ וּמְקַטְרְגֵנוּ.
אָבִינוּ מַלְכֵּנוּ, כַּלֵּה דֶּבֶר וְחֶרֶב וְרָעָב וּשְׁבִי וּמַשְׁחִית וְעָוֹן וּשְׁמַד מִבְּנֵי בְרִיתֶךָ.
אָבִינוּ מַלְכֵּנוּ, מְנַע מַגֵּפָה מִנַּחֲלָתֶךָ.
אָבִינוּ מַלְכֵּנוּ, סְלַח וּמְחַל לְכָל עֲוֹנוֹתֵינוּ.
אָבִינוּ מַלְכֵּנוּ, מְחֵה וְהַעֲבֵר פְּשָׁעֵינוּ וְחַטֹּאתֵינוּ מִנֶּגֶד עֵינֶיךָ.
אָבִינוּ מַלְכֵּנוּ, מְחֹק בְּרַחֲמֶיךָ הָרַבִּים כָּל שִׁטְרֵי חוֹבוֹתֵינוּ.

*The following nine verses are said responsively, first by the* שליח ציבור*, then by the* קהל*:*

אָבִינוּ מַלְכֵּנוּ, הַחֲזִירֵנוּ בִּתְשׁוּבָה שְׁלֵמָה לְפָנֶיךָ.
אָבִינוּ מַלְכֵּנוּ, שְׁלַח רְפוּאָה שְׁלֵמָה לְחוֹלֵי עַמֶּךָ.
אָבִינוּ מַלְכֵּנוּ, קְרַע רֹעַ גְּזַר דִּינֵנוּ.
אָבִינוּ מַלְכֵּנוּ, זָכְרֵנוּ בְּזִכָּרוֹן טוֹב לְפָנֶיךָ.
אָבִינוּ מַלְכֵּנוּ, כָּתְבֵנוּ בְּסֵפֶר חַיִּים טוֹבִים.
אָבִינוּ מַלְכֵּנוּ, כָּתְבֵנוּ בְּסֵפֶר גְּאֻלָּה וִישׁוּעָה.
אָבִינוּ מַלְכֵּנוּ, כָּתְבֵנוּ בְּסֵפֶר פַּרְנָסָה וְכַלְכָּלָה.
אָבִינוּ מַלְכֵּנוּ, כָּתְבֵנוּ בְּסֵפֶר זְכֻיּוֹת.
אָבִינוּ מַלְכֵּנוּ, כָּתְבֵנוּ בְּסֵפֶר סְלִיחָה וּמְחִילָה.

*End of responsive reading.*

---

סְתֹם פִּיּוֹת מַשְׂטִינֵנוּ וּמְקַטְרְגֵנוּ *Close the mouths of our adversaries and accusers.* A reference to the multitude of false accusations leveled against Jews: the Blood Libel, charges of poisoning wells, spreading the plague, and so on throughout centuries of hate. Some anti-Semitic myths survive to this day.

Our Father, our King, let salvation soon flourish for us.

Our Father, our King, raise the honor of Your people Israel.

Our Father, our King, raise the honor of Your anointed.

Our Father, our King, fill our hands with Your blessings.

Our Father, our King, fill our storehouses with abundance.

Our Father, our King, hear our voice, pity and be compassionate to us.

Our Father, our King, accept, with compassion and favor, our prayer.

Our Father, our King, open the gates of heaven to our prayer.

Our Father, our King, remember that we are dust.

Our Father, our King, please do not turn us away from You empty-handed.

Our Father, our King, may this moment be a moment of compassion and a time of favor before You.

Our Father, our King, have pity on us, our children and our infants.

Our Father, our King, act for the sake of those who were killed for Your holy name.

Our Father, our King, act for the sake of those who were slaughtered for proclaiming Your Unity.

Our Father, our King, act for the sake of those
who went through fire and water
to sanctify Your name.

Our Father, our King, avenge before our eyes
the spilt blood of Your servants.

Our Father, our King, act for Your sake, if not for ours.

Our Father, our King, act for Your sake, and save us.

Our Father, our King, act for the sake of Your abundant compassion.

Our Father, our King, act for the sake of Your great, mighty and awesome name by which we are called.

▸ Our Father, our King, be gracious to us and answer us, though we have no worthy deeds; act with us in charity and loving-kindness and save us.

*The Ark is closed.*

אָבִינוּ מַלְכֵּנוּ, הַצְמַח לָנוּ יְשׁוּעָה בְּקָרוֹב.
אָבִינוּ מַלְכֵּנוּ, הָרֵם קֶרֶן יִשְׂרָאֵל עַמֶּךָ.
אָבִינוּ מַלְכֵּנוּ, הָרֵם קֶרֶן מְשִׁיחֶךָ.
אָבִינוּ מַלְכֵּנוּ, מַלֵּא יָדֵינוּ מִבִּרְכוֹתֶיךָ.
אָבִינוּ מַלְכֵּנוּ, מַלֵּא אֲסָמֵינוּ שָׂבָע.
אָבִינוּ מַלְכֵּנוּ, שְׁמַע קוֹלֵנוּ, חוּס וְרַחֵם עָלֵינוּ.
אָבִינוּ מַלְכֵּנוּ, קַבֵּל בְּרַחֲמִים וּבְרָצוֹן אֶת תְּפִלָּתֵנוּ.
אָבִינוּ מַלְכֵּנוּ, פְּתַח שַׁעֲרֵי שָׁמַיִם לִתְפִלָּתֵנוּ.
אָבִינוּ מַלְכֵּנוּ, זְכֹר כִּי עָפָר אֲנָחְנוּ.
אָבִינוּ מַלְכֵּנוּ, נָא אַל תְּשִׁיבֵנוּ רֵיקָם מִלְּפָנֶיךָ.
אָבִינוּ מַלְכֵּנוּ, תְּהֵא הַשָּׁעָה הַזֹּאת שְׁעַת רַחֲמִים
וְעֵת רָצוֹן מִלְּפָנֶיךָ.
אָבִינוּ מַלְכֵּנוּ, חֲמֹל עָלֵינוּ וְעַל עוֹלָלֵינוּ וְטַפֵּנוּ.
אָבִינוּ מַלְכֵּנוּ, עֲשֵׂה לְמַעַן הֲרוּגִים עַל שֵׁם קָדְשֶׁךָ.
אָבִינוּ מַלְכֵּנוּ, עֲשֵׂה לְמַעַן טְבוּחִים עַל יִחוּדֶךָ.
אָבִינוּ מַלְכֵּנוּ, עֲשֵׂה לְמַעַן בָּאֵי בָאֵשׁ וּבַמַּיִם עַל קִדּוּשׁ שְׁמֶךָ.
אָבִינוּ מַלְכֵּנוּ, נְקֹם לְעֵינֵינוּ נִקְמַת דַּם עֲבָדֶיךָ הַשָּׁפוּךְ.
אָבִינוּ מַלְכֵּנוּ, עֲשֵׂה לְמַעַנְךָ אִם לֹא לְמַעֲנֵנוּ.
אָבִינוּ מַלְכֵּנוּ, עֲשֵׂה לְמַעַנְךָ וְהוֹשִׁיעֵנוּ.
אָבִינוּ מַלְכֵּנוּ, עֲשֵׂה לְמַעַן רַחֲמֶיךָ הָרַבִּים.
אָבִינוּ מַלְכֵּנוּ, עֲשֵׂה לְמַעַן שִׁמְךָ הַגָּדוֹל הַגִּבּוֹר וְהַנּוֹרָא
שֶׁנִּקְרָא עָלֵינוּ.
◂ אָבִינוּ מַלְכֵּנוּ, חָנֵּנוּ וַעֲנֵנוּ, כִּי אֵין בָּנוּ מַעֲשִׂים
עֲשֵׂה עִמָּנוּ צְדָקָה וָחֶסֶד וְהוֹשִׁיעֵנוּ.

*The* ארון קודש *is closed.*

FULL KADDISH

*Leader:* יִתְגַּדַּל Magnified and sanctified may His great name be,
in the world He created by His will.
May He establish His kingdom,
make His salvation flourish,
and hasten His messiah,
in your lifetime and in your days,
and in the lifetime of all the house of Israel,
swiftly and soon – and say: Amen.

*All:* May His great name be blessed for ever and all time.

*Leader:* Blessed and praised, glorified and exalted,
raised and honored,
uplifted and lauded be
the name of the Holy One,
blessed be He, beyond any blessing,
song, praise and consolation
uttered in the world – and say: Amen.

May the prayers and pleas of all the house of Israel
be accepted by their Father in heaven – and say: Amen.

May there be great peace from heaven,
and a good life for us and all Israel – and say: Amen.

*Bow, take three steps back, as if taking leave of the Divine Presence, then bow, first left, then right, then center, while saying:*

May He who makes peace in His high places,
make peace for us and all Israel – and say: Amen.

---

he made peace between the warring parties. "What do you do," he asked his questioner, "when you say the words *Oseh shalom bimromav*?" "I take three steps backward," the man replied. "That," said Rabbi Salant, "is how peace is made. Each party has to take three steps backward." To make peace we must sacrifice a little of our desire for the sake of someone else's desire. Those who are unable to step back are unable to make peace.

## קדיש שלם

ש״ץ: יִתְגַּדַּל וְיִתְקַדַּשׁ שְׁמֵהּ רַבָּא (קהל: אָמֵן)
בְּעָלְמָא דִּי בְרָא כִרְעוּתֵהּ
וְיַמְלִיךְ מַלְכוּתֵהּ וְיַצְמַח פֻּרְקָנֵהּ וִיקָרֵב מְשִׁיחֵהּ (קהל: אָמֵן)
בְּחַיֵּיכוֹן וּבְיוֹמֵיכוֹן וּבְחַיֵּי דְכָל בֵּית יִשְׂרָאֵל
בַּעֲגָלָא וּבִזְמַן קָרִיב, וְאִמְרוּ אָמֵן. (קהל: אָמֵן)

קהל וש״ץ: יְהֵא שְׁמֵהּ רַבָּא מְבָרַךְ לְעָלַם וּלְעָלְמֵי עָלְמַיָּא.

ש״ץ: יִתְבָּרַךְ וְיִשְׁתַּבַּח וְיִתְפָּאַר וְיִתְרוֹמַם וְיִתְנַשֵּׂא
וְיִתְהַדָּר וְיִתְעַלֶּה וְיִתְהַלָּל
שְׁמֵהּ דְּקֻדְשָׁא בְּרִיךְ הוּא (קהל: אָמֵן)
לְעֵלָּא לְעֵלָּא מִכָּל בִּרְכָתָא
וְשִׁירָתָא, תֻּשְׁבְּחָתָא וְנֶחֱמָתָא
דַּאֲמִירָן בְּעָלְמָא, וְאִמְרוּ אָמֵן. (קהל: אָמֵן)

תִּתְקַבַּל צְלוֹתְהוֹן וּבָעוּתְהוֹן דְּכָל בֵּית יִשְׂרָאֵל
קֳדָם אֲבוּהוֹן דִּי בִשְׁמַיָּא, וְאִמְרוּ אָמֵן. (קהל: אָמֵן)

יְהֵא שְׁלָמָא רַבָּא מִן שְׁמַיָּא
וְחַיִּים טוֹבִים עָלֵינוּ וְעַל כָּל יִשְׂרָאֵל, וְאִמְרוּ אָמֵן. (קהל: אָמֵן)

*Bow, take three steps back, as if taking leave of the Divine Presence, then bow, first left, then right, then center, while saying:*

עֹשֶׂה הַשָּׁלוֹם בִּמְרוֹמָיו
הוּא יַעֲשֶׂה שָׁלוֹם עָלֵינוּ
וְעַל כָּל יִשְׂרָאֵל, וְאִמְרוּ אָמֵן. (קהל: אָמֵן)

---

עֹשֶׂה הַשָּׁלוֹם בִּמְרוֹמָיו *He who makes peace in His high places.* Rabbi Shmuel Salant, who often spent time resolving family disputes, was once asked how

## THE DAILY PSALM

*One of the following psalms is said on the appropriate day of the week as indicated. After the psalm, the Mourner's Kaddish is said.*

*Monday:* Today is the second day of the week,
on which the Levites used to say this psalm in the Temple:

שִׁיר מִזְמוֹר A song. A psalm of the sons of Koraḥ. Great is the LORD and greatly to be praised in the city of God, on His holy mountain – beautiful in its heights, joy of all the earth, Mount Zion on its northern side, city of the great King. In its citadels God is known as a stronghold. See how the kings joined forces, advancing together. They saw, they were astounded, they panicked, they fled. There fear seized them, like the pains of a woman giving birth, like ships of Tarshish wrecked by an eastern wind. What we had heard, now we have seen, in the city of the LORD of hosts, in the city of our God. May God preserve it for ever, Selah! In the midst of Your Temple, God, we meditate on Your love. As is Your name, God, so is Your praise: it reaches to the ends of the earth. Your right hand is filled with righteousness. Let Mount Zion rejoice, let the towns of Judah be glad, because of Your judgments. Walk around Zion and encircle it. Count its towers, note its strong walls, view its citadels, so that you may tell a future generation ▸ that this is God, our God, for ever and ever. He will guide us for evermore. *Ps. 48*

*Mourner's Kaddish (page 426)*

*Tuesday:* Today is the third day of the week,
on which the Levites used to say this psalm in the Temple:

מִזְמוֹר לְאָסָף A psalm of Asaph. God stands in the divine assembly. Among the judges He delivers judgment. How long will you judge unjustly, showing favor to the wicked? Selah. Do justice to the weak and the orphaned. Vindicate the poor and destitute. Rescue the weak and needy. Save them from the hand of the wicked. They do not know nor do they understand. They walk about in darkness while all the earth's foundations shake. I once said, "You are like gods, all of you are sons of the Most High." But you shall die like mere men, you will fall like any prince. ▸ Arise, O LORD, judge the earth, for all the nations are Your possession. *Ps. 82*

*Mourner's Kaddish (page 426)*

## שיר של יום

*One of the following psalms is said on the appropriate day of the week as indicated. After the psalm,* קדיש יתום *is said.*

*Monday* הַיּוֹם יוֹם שֵׁנִי בְּשַׁבָּת, שֶׁבּוֹ הָיוּ הַלְוִיִּם אוֹמְרִים בְּבֵית הַמִּקְדָּשׁ:

תהלים מח

שִׁיר מִזְמוֹר לִבְנֵי־קֹרַח: גָּדוֹל יהוה וּמְהֻלָּל מְאֹד, בְּעִיר אֱלֹהֵינוּ, הַר־קָדְשׁוֹ: יְפֵה נוֹף מְשׂוֹשׂ כָּל־הָאָרֶץ, הַר־צִיּוֹן יַרְכְּתֵי צָפוֹן, קִרְיַת מֶלֶךְ רָב: אֱלֹהִים בְּאַרְמְנוֹתֶיהָ נוֹדַע לְמִשְׂגָּב: כִּי־הִנֵּה הַמְּלָכִים נוֹעֲדוּ, עָבְרוּ יַחְדָּו: הֵמָּה רָאוּ כֵּן תָּמָהוּ, נִבְהֲלוּ נֶחְפָּזוּ: רְעָדָה אֲחָזָתַם שָׁם, חִיל כַּיּוֹלֵדָה: בְּרוּחַ קָדִים תְּשַׁבֵּר אֳנִיּוֹת תַּרְשִׁישׁ: כַּאֲשֶׁר שָׁמַעְנוּ כֵּן רָאִינוּ, בְּעִיר־יהוה צְבָאוֹת, בְּעִיר אֱלֹהֵינוּ, אֱלֹהִים יְכוֹנְנֶהָ עַד־עוֹלָם סֶלָה: דִּמִּינוּ אֱלֹהִים חַסְדֶּךָ, בְּקֶרֶב הֵיכָלֶךָ: כְּשִׁמְךָ אֱלֹהִים כֵּן תְּהִלָּתְךָ עַל־קַצְוֵי־אֶרֶץ, צֶדֶק מָלְאָה יְמִינֶךָ: יִשְׂמַח הַר־צִיּוֹן, תָּגֵלְנָה בְּנוֹת יְהוּדָה, לְמַעַן מִשְׁפָּטֶיךָ: סֹבּוּ צִיּוֹן וְהַקִּיפוּהָ, סִפְרוּ מִגְדָּלֶיהָ: שִׁיתוּ לִבְּכֶם לְחֵילָה, פַּסְּגוּ אַרְמְנוֹתֶיהָ, לְמַעַן תְּסַפְּרוּ לְדוֹר אַחֲרוֹן: ◂ כִּי זֶה אֱלֹהִים אֱלֹהֵינוּ עוֹלָם וָעֶד, הוּא יְנַהֲגֵנוּ עַל־מוּת:

קדיש יתום (*page 427*)

*Tuesday* הַיּוֹם יוֹם שְׁלִישִׁי בְּשַׁבָּת, שֶׁבּוֹ הָיוּ הַלְוִיִּם אוֹמְרִים בְּבֵית הַמִּקְדָּשׁ:

תהלים פב

מִזְמוֹר לְאָסָף, אֱלֹהִים נִצָּב בַּעֲדַת־אֵל, בְּקֶרֶב אֱלֹהִים יִשְׁפֹּט: עַד־מָתַי תִּשְׁפְּטוּ־עָוֶל, וּפְנֵי רְשָׁעִים תִּשְׂאוּ־סֶלָה: שִׁפְטוּ־דַל וְיָתוֹם, עָנִי וָרָשׁ הַצְדִּיקוּ: פַּלְּטוּ־דַל וְאֶבְיוֹן, מִיַּד רְשָׁעִים הַצִּילוּ: לֹא יָדְעוּ וְלֹא יָבִינוּ, בַּחֲשֵׁכָה יִתְהַלָּכוּ, יִמּוֹטוּ כָּל־מוֹסְדֵי אָרֶץ: אֲנִי־אָמַרְתִּי אֱלֹהִים אַתֶּם, וּבְנֵי עֶלְיוֹן כֻּלְּכֶם: אָכֵן כְּאָדָם תְּמוּתוּן, וּכְאַחַד הַשָּׂרִים תִּפֹּלוּ: ◂ קוּמָה אֱלֹהִים שָׁפְטָה הָאָרֶץ, כִּי־אַתָּה תִנְחַל בְּכָל־הַגּוֹיִם:

קדיש יתום (*page 427*)

*Thursday:* Today is the fifth day of the week,
on which the Levites used to say this psalm in the Temple:

לַמְנַצֵּחַ For the conductor of music. On the Gittit. By Asaph. Sing for joy *Ps. 81*
to God, our strength. Shout aloud to the God of Jacob. Raise a song, beat the drum, play the sweet harp and lyre. Sound the shofar on the new moon, on our feast day when the moon is hidden. For it is a statute for Israel, an ordinance of the God of Jacob. He established it as a testimony for Joseph when He went forth against the land of Egypt, where I heard a language that I did not know. I relieved his shoulder of the burden. His hands were freed from the builder's basket. In distress you called and I rescued you. I answered you from the secret place of thunder; I tested you at the waters of Meribah, Selah! Hear, My people, and I will warn you. Israel, if you would only listen to Me! Let there be no strange god among you. Do not bow down to an alien god. I am the LORD your God who brought you out of the land of Egypt. Open your mouth wide and I will fill it. But My people would not listen to Me. Israel would have none of Me. So I left them to their stubborn hearts, letting them follow their own devices. If only My people would listen to Me, if Israel would walk in My ways, I would soon subdue their enemies, and turn My hand against their foes. Those who hate the LORD would cower before Him and their doom would last for ever. ▸ He would feed Israel with the finest wheat – with honey from the rock I would satisfy you.

*Mourner's Kaddish (page 426)*

*Shabbat:* Today is the holy Sabbath,
on which the Levites used to say this psalm in the Temple:

מִזְמוֹר A psalm. A song for the Sabbath day. It is good to thank the LORD *Ps. 92*
and sing psalms to Your name, Most High – to tell of Your loving-kindness in the morning and Your faithfulness at night, to the music of the ten-stringed lyre and the melody of the harp. For You have made me rejoice by Your work, O LORD; I sing for joy at the deeds of Your hands. How great are Your deeds, LORD, and how very deep Your thoughts. A boor cannot know, nor can a fool understand, that though the wicked spring up like grass and all evildoers flourish, it is only that they may be destroyed for ever. But You, LORD, are eternally exalted. For behold Your enemies, LORD, behold Your enemies will perish; all evildoers will be

*Thursday* הַיּוֹם יוֹם חֲמִישִׁי בְּשַׁבָּת, שֶׁבּוֹ הָיוּ הַלְוִיִּם אוֹמְרִים בְּבֵית הַמִּקְדָּשׁ:

תהלים פא

לַמְנַצֵּחַ עַל־הַגִּתִּית לְאָסָף: הַרְנִינוּ לֵאלֹהִים עוּזֵּנוּ, הָרִיעוּ לֵאלֹהֵי יַעֲקֹב: שְׂאוּ־זִמְרָה וּתְנוּ־תֹף, כִּנּוֹר נָעִים עִם־נָבֶל: תִּקְעוּ בַחֹדֶשׁ שׁוֹפָר, בַּכֶּסֶה לְיוֹם חַגֵּנוּ: כִּי חֹק לְיִשְׂרָאֵל הוּא, מִשְׁפָּט לֵאלֹהֵי יַעֲקֹב: עֵדוּת בִּיהוֹסֵף שָׂמוֹ, בְּצֵאתוֹ עַל־אֶרֶץ מִצְרָיִם, שְׂפַת לֹא־יָדַעְתִּי אֶשְׁמָע: הֲסִירוֹתִי מִסֵּבֶל שִׁכְמוֹ, כַּפָּיו מִדּוּד תַּעֲבֹרְנָה: בַּצָּרָה קָרָאתָ וָאֲחַלְּצֶךָּ, אֶעֶנְךָ בְּסֵתֶר רַעַם, אֶבְחָנְךָ עַל־מֵי מְרִיבָה סֶלָה: שְׁמַע עַמִּי וְאָעִידָה בָּךְ, יִשְׂרָאֵל אִם־תִּשְׁמַע־לִי: לֹא־יִהְיֶה בְךָ אֵל זָר, וְלֹא תִשְׁתַּחֲוֶה לְאֵל נֵכָר: אָנֹכִי יהוה אֱלֹהֶיךָ, הַמַּעַלְךָ מֵאֶרֶץ מִצְרָיִם, הַרְחֶב־פִּיךָ וַאֲמַלְאֵהוּ: וְלֹא־שָׁמַע עַמִּי לְקוֹלִי, וְיִשְׂרָאֵל לֹא־אָבָה לִי: וָאֲשַׁלְּחֵהוּ בִּשְׁרִירוּת לִבָּם, יֵלְכוּ בְּמוֹעֲצוֹתֵיהֶם: לוּ עַמִּי שֹׁמֵעַ לִי, יִשְׂרָאֵל בִּדְרָכַי יְהַלֵּכוּ: כִּמְעַט אוֹיְבֵיהֶם אַכְנִיעַ, וְעַל־צָרֵיהֶם אָשִׁיב יָדִי: מְשַׂנְאֵי יהוה יְכַחֲשׁוּ־לוֹ, וִיהִי עִתָּם לְעוֹלָם: ◁ וַיַּאֲכִילֵהוּ מֵחֵלֶב חִטָּה, וּמִצּוּר, דְּבַשׁ אַשְׂבִּיעֶךָ:

קדיש יתום (*page 427*)

שבת הַיּוֹם יוֹם שַׁבַּת קֹדֶשׁ, שֶׁבּוֹ הָיוּ הַלְוִיִּם אוֹמְרִים בְּבֵית הַמִּקְדָּשׁ:

תהלים צב

מִזְמוֹר שִׁיר לְיוֹם הַשַּׁבָּת: טוֹב לְהֹדוֹת לַיהוה, וּלְזַמֵּר לְשִׁמְךָ עֶלְיוֹן: לְהַגִּיד בַּבֹּקֶר חַסְדֶּךָ, וֶאֱמוּנָתְךָ בַּלֵּילוֹת: עֲלֵי־עָשׂוֹר וַעֲלֵי־נָבֶל, עֲלֵי הִגָּיוֹן בְּכִנּוֹר: כִּי שִׂמַּחְתַּנִי יהוה בְּפָעֳלֶךָ, בְּמַעֲשֵׂי יָדֶיךָ אֲרַנֵּן: מַה־גָּדְלוּ מַעֲשֶׂיךָ יהוה, מְאֹד עָמְקוּ מַחְשְׁבֹתֶיךָ: אִישׁ־בַּעַר לֹא יֵדָע, וּכְסִיל לֹא־יָבִין אֶת־זֹאת: בִּפְרֹחַ רְשָׁעִים כְּמוֹ־עֵשֶׂב, וַיָּצִיצוּ כָּל־פֹּעֲלֵי אָוֶן, לְהִשָּׁמְדָם עֲדֵי־עַד: וְאַתָּה מָרוֹם לְעֹלָם יהוה: כִּי הִנֵּה אֹיְבֶיךָ יהוה, כִּי־הִנֵּה אֹיְבֶיךָ יֹאבֵדוּ,

scattered. You have raised my pride like that of a wild ox; I am anointed with fresh oil. My eyes shall look in triumph on my adversaries; my ears shall hear the downfall of the wicked who rise against me. The righteous will flourish like a palm tree and grow tall like a cedar in Lebanon. Planted in the LORD's House, blossoming in our God's courtyards, ▸ they will still bear fruit in old age, and stay vigorous and fresh, proclaiming that the LORD is upright: He is my Rock, in whom there is no wrong.

*Mourner's Kaddish (on the next page)*

*The following psalm is said on all days.*
*Some congregations recite it at the end of Musaf.*

לְדָוִד By David. The LORD is my light and my salvation – whom then shall I fear? The LORD is the stronghold of my life – of whom shall I be afraid? When evil men close in on me to devour my flesh, it is they, my enemies and foes, who stumble and fall. Should an army besiege me, my heart would not fear. Should war break out against me, still I would be confident. One thing I ask of the LORD, only this do I seek: to live in the House of the LORD all the days of my life, to gaze on the beauty of the LORD and worship in His Temple. For He will keep me safe in His pavilion on the day of trouble. He will hide me under the cover of His tent. He will set me high upon a rock. Now my head is high above my enemies who surround me. I will sacrifice in His tent with shouts of joy. I will sing and chant praises to the LORD. LORD, hear my voice when I call. Be gracious to me and answer me. On Your behalf my heart says, "Seek My face." Your face, LORD, will I seek. Do not hide Your face from me. Do not turn Your servant away in anger. You have been my help. Do not reject or forsake me, God, my Savior. Were my father and my mother to forsake me, the LORD would take me in. Teach me Your way, LORD, and lead me on a level path, because of my oppressors. Do not abandon me to the will of my foes, for false witnesses have risen against me, breathing violence. ▸ Were it not for my faith that I shall see the LORD's goodness in the land of the living. Hope in the LORD. Be strong and of good courage, and hope in the LORD! *Ps. 27*

*Mourner's Kaddish (on the next page)*

*In some congregations, the Song of Glory (page 632) is recited here.*

יִתְפָּרְדוּ כָּל־פֹּעֲלֵי אָוֶן: וַתָּרֶם כִּרְאֵים קַרְנִי, בַּלֹּתִי בְּשֶׁמֶן רַעֲנָן: וַתַּבֵּט עֵינִי בְּשׁוּרָי, בַּקָּמִים עָלַי מְרֵעִים תִּשְׁמַעְנָה אָזְנָי: צַדִּיק כַּתָּמָר יִפְרָח, כְּאֶרֶז בַּלְּבָנוֹן יִשְׂגֶּה: שְׁתוּלִים בְּבֵית יהוה, בְּחַצְרוֹת אֱלֹהֵינוּ יַפְרִיחוּ: › עוֹד יְנוּבוּן בְּשֵׂיבָה, דְּשֵׁנִים וְרַעֲנַנִּים יִהְיוּ: לְהַגִּיד כִּי־יָשָׁר יהוה, צוּרִי, וְלֹא־עַוְלָתָה בּוֹ:

קדיש יתום (*on the next page*)

*The following psalm is said on all days.*
*Some congregations recite it at the end of* מוסף.

לְדָוִד, יהוה אוֹרִי וְיִשְׁעִי, מִמִּי אִירָא, יהוה מָעוֹז־חַיַּי, מִמִּי אֶפְחָד: תהלים כז
בִּקְרֹב עָלַי מְרֵעִים לֶאֱכֹל אֶת־בְּשָׂרִי, צָרַי וְאֹיְבַי לִי, הֵמָּה כָּשְׁלוּ וְנָפָלוּ: אִם־תַּחֲנֶה עָלַי מַחֲנֶה, לֹא־יִירָא לִבִּי, אִם־תָּקוּם עָלַי מִלְחָמָה, בְּזֹאת אֲנִי בוֹטֵחַ: אַחַת שָׁאַלְתִּי מֵאֵת־יהוה, אוֹתָהּ אֲבַקֵּשׁ, שִׁבְתִּי בְּבֵית־יהוה כָּל־יְמֵי חַיַּי, לַחֲזוֹת בְּנֹעַם־יהוה, וּלְבַקֵּר בְּהֵיכָלוֹ: כִּי יִצְפְּנֵנִי בְּסֻכֹּה בְּיוֹם רָעָה, יַסְתִּרֵנִי בְּסֵתֶר אָהֳלוֹ, בְּצוּר יְרוֹמְמֵנִי: וְעַתָּה יָרוּם רֹאשִׁי עַל אֹיְבַי סְבִיבוֹתַי, וְאֶזְבְּחָה בְאָהֳלוֹ זִבְחֵי תְרוּעָה, אָשִׁירָה וַאֲזַמְּרָה לַיהוה: שְׁמַע־יהוה קוֹלִי אֶקְרָא, וְחָנֵּנִי וַעֲנֵנִי: לְךָ אָמַר לִבִּי בַּקְּשׁוּ פָנָי, אֶת־פָּנֶיךָ יהוה אֲבַקֵּשׁ: אַל־תַּסְתֵּר פָּנֶיךָ מִמֶּנִּי, אַל תַּט־בְּאַף עַבְדֶּךָ, עֶזְרָתִי הָיִיתָ, אַל־תִּטְּשֵׁנִי וְאַל־תַּעַזְבֵנִי, אֱלֹהֵי יִשְׁעִי: כִּי־אָבִי וְאִמִּי עֲזָבוּנִי, וַיהוה יַאַסְפֵנִי: הוֹרֵנִי יהוה דַּרְכֶּךָ, וּנְחֵנִי בְּאֹרַח מִישׁוֹר, לְמַעַן שׁוֹרְרָי: אַל־תִּתְּנֵנִי בְּנֶפֶשׁ צָרָי, כִּי קָמוּ־בִי עֵדֵי־שֶׁקֶר, וִיפֵחַ חָמָס: › לוּלֵא הֶאֱמַנְתִּי לִרְאוֹת בְּטוּב־יהוה בְּאֶרֶץ חַיִּים: קַוֵּה אֶל־יהוה, חֲזַק וְיַאֲמֵץ לִבֶּךָ, וְקַוֵּה אֶל־יהוה:

קדיש יתום (*on the next page*)

*In some congregations,* אַנְעִים זְמִירוֹת *(page 633) is recited here.*

## MOURNER'S KADDISH

*The following prayer, said by mourners, requires the presence of a minyan. A transliteration can be found on page 1095.*

*Mourner:* יִתְגַּדַּל Magnified and sanctified
may His great name be,
in the world He created by His will.
May He establish His kingdom,
make His salvation flourish,
and hasten His messiah,
in your lifetime and in your days,
and in the lifetime of all the house of Israel,
swiftly and soon –
and say: Amen.

*All:* May His great name be blessed for ever and all time.

*Mourner:* Blessed and praised, glorified and exalted,
raised and honored,
uplifted and lauded
be the name of the Holy One,
blessed be He,
beyond any blessing,
song, praise and consolation
uttered in the world –
and say: Amen.

May there be great peace from heaven,
and a good life for us and all Israel –
and say: Amen.

*Bow, take three steps back, as if taking leave of the Divine Presence, then bow, first left, then right, then center, while saying:*

May He who makes peace in His high places,
make peace for us and all Israel –
and say: Amen.

## קדיש יתום

*The following prayer, said by mourners, requires the presence of a* מנין.
*A transliteration can be found on page 1095.*

אבל: יִתְגַּדַּל וְיִתְקַדַּשׁ שְׁמֵהּ רַבָּא (קהל: אָמֵן)
בְּעָלְמָא דִּי בְרָא כִרְעוּתֵהּ
וְיַמְלִיךְ מַלְכוּתֵהּ
וְיַצְמַח פֻּרְקָנֵהּ וִיקָרֵב מְשִׁיחֵהּ (קהל: אָמֵן)
בְּחַיֵּיכוֹן וּבְיוֹמֵיכוֹן וּבְחַיֵּי דְכָל בֵּית יִשְׂרָאֵל
בַּעֲגָלָא וּבִזְמַן קָרִיב
וְאִמְרוּ אָמֵן. (קהל: אָמֵן)

קהל ואבל: יְהֵא שְׁמֵהּ רַבָּא מְבָרַךְ לְעָלַם וּלְעָלְמֵי עָלְמַיָּא.

אבל: יִתְבָּרַךְ וְיִשְׁתַּבַּח וְיִתְפָּאַר
וְיִתְרוֹמַם וְיִתְנַשֵּׂא וְיִתְהַדָּר וְיִתְעַלֶּה וְיִתְהַלָּל
שְׁמֵהּ דְּקֻדְשָׁא בְּרִיךְ הוּא (קהל: אָמֵן)
לְעֵלָּא לְעֵלָּא מִכָּל בִּרְכָתָא
וְשִׁירָתָא, תֻּשְׁבְּחָתָא וְנֶחֱמָתָא
דַּאֲמִירָן בְּעָלְמָא
וְאִמְרוּ אָמֵן. (קהל: אָמֵן)

יְהֵא שְׁלָמָא רַבָּא מִן שְׁמַיָּא
וְחַיִּים טוֹבִים עָלֵינוּ וְעַל כָּל יִשְׂרָאֵל
וְאִמְרוּ אָמֵן. (קהל: אָמֵן)

*Bow, take three steps back, as if taking leave of the Divine Presence, then bow, first left, then right, then center, while saying:*

עֹשֶׂה הַשָּׁלוֹם בִּמְרוֹמָיו
הוּא יַעֲשֶׂה שָׁלוֹם עָלֵינוּ וְעַל כָּל יִשְׂרָאֵל
וְאִמְרוּ אָמֵן. (קהל: אָמֵן)

## REMOVING THE TORAH FROM THE ARK

אַתָּה הָרְאֵתָ You have been shown [these things] so that you may know that the LORD is God; besides Him there is no other. Deut. 4
There is none like You among the heavenly powers, LORD, Ps. 86
and there are no works like Yours.
Your kingdom is an eternal kingdom, Ps. 145
and Your dominion is for all generations.

The LORD is King, the LORD was King,
the LORD shall be King for ever and all time.
The LORD will give strength to His people; Ps. 29
the LORD will bless His people with peace.

Father of compassion,
favor Zion with Your goodness; rebuild the walls of Jerusalem. Ps. 51
For we trust in You alone, King, God,
high and exalted, Master of worlds.

*The Ark is opened and the congregation stands. All say:*

וַיְהִי בִּנְסֹעַ Whenever the Ark set out, Moses would say, Num. 10
"Arise, LORD, and may Your enemies be scattered.
May those who hate You flee before You."
For the Torah shall come forth from Zion, Is. 2
and the word of the LORD from Jerusalem.
Blessed is He who, in His holiness, gave the Torah to His people Israel.

---

famously in the days of King Josiah (II Kings 23) and Ezra (Neh. 8). According to tradition, Moses ordained that the Torah be read regularly and publicly: a long reading on Shabbat morning and shorter readings on Mondays and Thursdays. Ezra, reinstituting this practice, added the reading on Shabbat afternoon. Thus from its earliest days, the synagogue was a place of study as well as prayer. During the Second Temple and later eras, the reading was accompanied by verse-by-verse translation into the vernacular, mainly Aramaic. In the course of time the act of taking the Torah from, and returning it to, the Ark became ceremonial moments in their own right.

# הוצאת ספר תורה

דברים ד אַתָּה הָרְאֵתָ לָדַעַת, כִּי יהוה הוּא הָאֱלֹהִים, אֵין עוֹד מִלְּבַדּוֹ:
תהלים פו אֵין־כָּמוֹךָ בָאֱלֹהִים, אֲדֹנָי, וְאֵין כְּמַעֲשֶׂיךָ:
תהלים קמה מַלְכוּתְךָ מַלְכוּת כָּל־עֹלָמִים, וּמֶמְשַׁלְתְּךָ בְּכָל־דּוֹר וָדֹר:

יהוה מֶלֶךְ, יהוה מָלָךְ, יהוה יִמְלֹךְ לְעֹלָם וָעֶד.
תהלים כט יהוה עֹז לְעַמּוֹ יִתֵּן, יהוה יְבָרֵךְ אֶת־עַמּוֹ בַשָּׁלוֹם:

תהלים נא אַב הָרַחֲמִים, הֵיטִיבָה בִרְצוֹנְךָ אֶת־צִיּוֹן תִּבְנֶה חוֹמוֹת יְרוּשָׁלָםִ:
כִּי בְךָ לְבַד בָּטָחְנוּ, מֶלֶךְ אֵל רָם וְנִשָּׂא, אֲדוֹן עוֹלָמִים.

*The* ארון קודש *is opened and the* קהל *stands. All say:*

במדבר י וַיְהִי בִּנְסֹעַ הָאָרֹן וַיֹּאמֶר מֹשֶׁה
קוּמָה יהוה וְיָפֻצוּ אֹיְבֶיךָ וְיָנֻסוּ מְשַׂנְאֶיךָ מִפָּנֶיךָ:
ישעיה ב כִּי מִצִּיּוֹן תֵּצֵא תוֹרָה וּדְבַר־יהוה מִירוּשָׁלָםִ:
בָּרוּךְ שֶׁנָּתַן תּוֹרָה לְעַמּוֹ יִשְׂרָאֵל בִּקְדֻשָּׁתוֹ.

---

READING OF THE TORAH

Since the revelation at Mount Sinai, the Jewish people has been a nation defined by a book: the Torah. The Mosaic books are more than sacred literature. They are the written constitution of the house of Israel as a nation under the sovereignty of God, the basis of its collective memory, the record of its covenant with God, the template of its existence as "a kingdom of priests and a holy nation" (Ex. 19:6), and the detailed specification of the task it is called on to perform – to construct a society on the basis of justice and compassion and the inalienable dignity of the human person as the image of God. Just as the Torah is central to Jewish life, so the reading of the Torah is central to the synagogue service.

The Tanakh records several key moments in Jewish history when national rededication was accompanied by a public reading of the Torah, most

*On Shabbat, the following prayers are omitted and the service continues with "Blessed is the name" below.*

*The following (The Thirteen Attributes of Mercy) is said three times:*

יהוה The LORD, the LORD, compassionate and gracious God, slow to anger, abounding in loving-kindness and truth, extending loving-kindness to a thousand generations, forgiving iniquity, rebellion and sin, and absolving [the guilty who repent]. *Ex. 34*

רִבּוֹנוֹ Master of the Universe, fulfill my requests for good. Satisfy my desire, grant my request, and pardon me for all my iniquities and all iniquities of the members of my household, with the pardon of loving-kindness and compassion. Purify us from our sins, our iniquities and our transgressions; remember us with a memory of favorable deeds before You and be mindful of us in salvation and compassion. Remember us for a good life, for peace, for livelihood and sustenance, for bread to eat and clothes to wear, for wealth, honor and length of days dedicated to Your Torah and its commandments. Grant us discernment and understanding that we may understand and discern its deep secrets. Send healing for all our pain, and bless all the work of our hands. Ordain for us decrees of good, salvation and consolation, and nullify all hard and harsh decrees against us. And may the hearts of the government, its advisers and ministers / *In Israel:* And may the hearts of our ministers and their advisers, / be favorable toward us. Amen. May this be Your will. May the words of my mouth and the meditation of my heart find favor before You, LORD, my Rock and Redeemer. *Ps. 19*

*Say the following verse three times:*

וַאֲנִי As for me, may my prayer come to You, LORD, at a time of favor. O God, in Your great love, answer me with Your faithful salvation. *Ps. 69*

*On all days continue:*

בְּרִיךְ Blessed is the name of the Master of the Universe. Blessed is Your crown and Your place. May Your favor always be with Your people Israel. Show Your people the salvation of Your right hand in Your Temple. Grant us the gift of Your good light, and accept our prayers in mercy. May it be Your will to prolong our life in goodness. May I be counted among the righteous, so that You will have compassion on me and protect me and all that is mine and all that is Your people Israel's. You feed all; You sustain all; You rule over all; You rule over kings, for sovereignty is Yours. I am a servant of the Holy One, blessed be He, before whom and before whose glorious Torah I bow at all times. Not in man do I trust, nor on any angel do I rely, but on the God of heaven who is the God of truth, whose Torah is truth, whose prophets speak truth, and who abounds in acts of love and truth. ▸ In Him I trust, and to His holy and glorious name I offer praises. May it be Your will to open my heart to the Torah, and to fulfill the wishes of my heart and of the hearts of all Your people Israel for good, for life, and for peace. *Zohar, Vayak-hel*

*On* שבת*, the following prayers are omitted and the service continues with* בְּרִיךְ שְׁמֵהּ *below.*

*The following* (י״ג מידות הרחמים) *is said three times:*

שמות לד

**יהוה, יהוה, אֵל רַחוּם וְחַנּוּן, אֶרֶךְ אַפַּיִם וְרַב־חֶסֶד וֶאֱמֶת: נֹצֵר חֶסֶד לָאֲלָפִים, נֹשֵׂא עָוֹן וָפֶשַׁע וְחַטָּאָה, וְנַקֵּה:**

רִבּוֹנוֹ שֶׁל עוֹלָם, מַלֵּא מִשְׁאֲלוֹתַי לְטוֹבָה, וְהָפֵק רְצוֹנִי וְתֵן שְׁאֵלָתִי, וּמְחֹל לִי עַל כָּל עֲוֹנוֹתַי וְעַל כָּל עֲוֹנוֹת אַנְשֵׁי בֵיתִי, מְחִילָה בְּחֶסֶד מְחִילָה בְּרַחֲמִים, וְטַהֲרֵנוּ מֵחֲטָאֵינוּ וּמֵעֲוֹנוֹתֵינוּ וּמִפְּשָׁעֵינוּ, וְזָכְרֵנוּ בְּזִכָּרוֹן טוֹב לְפָנֶיךָ, וּפָקְדֵנוּ בִּפְקֻדַּת יְשׁוּעָה וְרַחֲמִים. וְזָכְרֵנוּ לְחַיִּים טוֹבִים וּלְשָׁלוֹם, וּפַרְנָסָה וְכַלְכָּלָה, וְלֶחֶם לֶאֱכֹל וּבֶגֶד לִלְבֹּשׁ, וְעֹשֶׁר וְכָבוֹד, וְאֹרֶךְ יָמִים לַהֲגוֹת בְּתוֹרָתֶךָ וּלְקַיֵּם מִצְוֹתֶיהָ, וְשֵׂכֶל וּבִינָה לְהָבִין וּלְהַשְׂכִּיל עִמְקֵי סוֹדוֹתֶיהָ. וְהָפֵק רְפוּאָה לְכָל מַכְאוֹבֵינוּ, וּבָרֵךְ כָּל מַעֲשֵׂה יָדֵינוּ, וּגְזֹר עָלֵינוּ גְּזֵרוֹת טוֹבוֹת יְשׁוּעוֹת וְנֶחָמוֹת, וּבַטֵּל מֵעָלֵינוּ כָּל גְּזֵרוֹת קָשׁוֹת וְרָעוֹת, וְתֵן בְּלֵב הַמַּלְכוּת וְיוֹעֲצֶיהָ וְשָׂרֶיהָ
תהלים יט / בארץ ישראל: וְתֵן בְּלֵב שָׂרֵינוּ וְיוֹעֲצֵיהֶם/ עָלֵינוּ לְטוֹבָה. אָמֵן וְכֵן יְהִי רָצוֹן. יִהְיוּ לְרָצוֹן אִמְרֵי־פִי וְהֶגְיוֹן לִבִּי לְפָנֶיךָ, יהוה צוּרִי וְגוֹאֲלִי:

*Say the following verse three times:*

תהלים סט

**וַאֲנִי תְפִלָּתִי־לְךָ יהוה, עֵת רָצוֹן, אֱלֹהִים בְּרָב־חַסְדֶּךָ עֲנֵנִי בֶּאֱמֶת יִשְׁעֶךָ:**

*On all days continue:*

זוהר ויקהל

בְּרִיךְ שְׁמֵהּ דְּמָרֵא עָלְמָא, בְּרִיךְ כִּתְרָךְ וְאַתְרָךְ. יְהֵא רְעוּתָךְ עִם עַמָּךְ יִשְׂרָאֵל לְעָלַם, וּפֻרְקַן יְמִינָךְ אַחֲזֵי לְעַמָּךְ בְּבֵית מַקְדְּשָׁךְ, וּלְאַמְטוֹיֵי לָנָא מִטּוּב נְהוֹרָךְ, וּלְקַבֵּל צְלוֹתַנָא בְּרַחֲמִין. יְהֵא רַעֲוָא קֳדָמָךְ דְּתוֹרִיךְ לָן חַיִּין בְּטִיבוּ, וְלֶהֱוֵי אֲנָא פְּקִידָא בְּגוֹ צַדִּיקַיָּא, לְמִרְחַם עָלַי וּלְמִנְטַר יָתִי וְיַת כָּל דִּי לִי וְדִי לְעַמָּךְ יִשְׂרָאֵל. אַנְתְּ הוּא זָן לְכֹלָּא וּמְפַרְנֵס לְכֹלָּא, אַנְתְּ הוּא שַׁלִּיט עַל כֹּלָּא, אַנְתְּ הוּא דְּשַׁלִּיט עַל מַלְכַיָּא, וּמַלְכוּתָא דִּילָךְ הִיא. אֲנָא עַבְדָּא דְקֻדְשָׁא בְּרִיךְ הוּא, דְּסָגֵדְנָא קַמֵּהּ וּמִקַּמֵּי דִּיקַר אוֹרַיְתֵהּ בְּכָל עִדָּן וְעִדָּן. לָא עַל אֱנָשׁ רְחִיצְנָא וְלָא עַל בַּר אֱלָהִין סָמִיכְנָא, אֶלָּא בֶּאֱלָהָא דִשְׁמַיָּא, דְּהוּא אֱלָהָא קְשׁוֹט, וְאוֹרַיְתֵהּ קְשׁוֹט, וּנְבִיאוֹהִי קְשׁוֹט, וּמַסְגֵּא לְמֶעְבַּד טַבְוָן וּקְשׁוֹט. ◄ בֵּהּ אֲנָא רָחִיץ, וְלִשְׁמֵהּ קַדִּישָׁא יַקִּירָא אֲנָא אֵמַר תֻּשְׁבְּחָן. יְהֵא רַעֲוָא קֳדָמָךְ דְּתִפְתַּח לִבָּאִי בְּאוֹרַיְתָא, וְתַשְׁלִים מִשְׁאֲלִין דְּלִבָּאִי וְלִבָּא דְכָל עַמָּךְ יִשְׂרָאֵל לְטַב וּלְחַיִּין וְלִשְׁלָם.

*Two Torah scrolls are removed from the Ark. The Leader takes one in his right arm and, followed by the congregation, says:*

Listen, Israel: the LORD is our God, the LORD is One. *Deut. 6*

*Leader then congregation:*

One is our God; great is our Master;
holy and awesome is His name.

*The Leader turns to face the Ark, bows and says:*

Magnify the LORD with me, and let us exalt His name together. *Ps. 34*

*The Ark is closed. The Leader carries the Torah scroll to the bima and the congregation says:*

לְךָ Yours, LORD, are the greatness and the power, the glory and the majesty and splendor, for everything in heaven and earth is Yours. Yours, LORD, is the kingdom; You are exalted as Head over all. *1 Chr. 29*

רוֹמְמוּ Exalt the LORD our God and bow to His footstool; He is holy. *Ps. 99*
Exalt the LORD our God, and bow at His holy mountain, for holy is the LORD our God.

Over all may the name of the Supreme King of kings, the Holy One blessed be He, be magnified and sanctified, praised and glorified, exalted and extolled, in the worlds that He has created – this world and the World to Come – in accordance with His will, and the will of those who fear Him, and the will of the whole house of Israel. He is the Rock of worlds, LORD of all creatures, God of all souls, who dwells in the spacious heights and inhabits the high heavens of old. His holiness is over the Ḥayyot and over the throne of glory. Therefore may Your name, LORD our God, be sanctified among us in the sight of all that
lives. Let us sing before Him a new song, as it is written: "Sing to God, make *Ps. 68*
music for His name, extol Him who rides the clouds – the LORD is His name – and exult before Him." And may we see Him eye to eye when He returns to
His abode as it is written: "For they shall see eye to eye when the LORD returns *Is. 52*
to Zion." And it is said: "Then will the glory of the LORD be revealed, and all *Is. 40*
mankind together shall see that the mouth of the LORD has spoken."

Father of mercy, have compassion on the people borne by Him. May He remember the covenant with the mighty (patriarchs), and deliver us from evil times. May He reproach the evil instinct in the people by Him, and graciously grant that we be an eternal remnant. May He fulfill in good measure our requests for salvation and compassion.

*Two* ספרי תורה *are removed from the* ארון קודש*. The* שליח ציבור *takes one in his right arm and, followed by the* קהל*, says:*

דברים ו שְׁמַע יִשְׂרָאֵל, יהוה אֱלֹהֵינוּ, יהוה אֶחָד:

קהל *then* שליח ציבור*:*

אֶחָד אֱלֹהֵינוּ, גָּדוֹל אֲדוֹנֵינוּ, קָדוֹשׁ וְנוֹרָא שְׁמוֹ.

*The* שליח ציבור *turns to face the* ארון קודש*, bows and says:*

תהלים לד גַּדְּלוּ לַיהוה אִתִּי וּנְרוֹמְמָה שְׁמוֹ יַחְדָּו:

*The* ארון קודש *is closed. The* שליח ציבור *carries the* ספר תורה *to the* בימה *and the* קהל *says:*

דברי הימים א׳ כט לְךָ יהוה הַגְּדֻלָּה וְהַגְּבוּרָה וְהַתִּפְאֶרֶת וְהַנֵּצַח וְהַהוֹד, כִּי־כֹל
בַּשָּׁמַיִם וּבָאָרֶץ, לְךָ יהוה הַמַּמְלָכָה וְהַמִּתְנַשֵּׂא לְכֹל לְרֹאשׁ:

תהלים צט רוֹמְמוּ יהוה אֱלֹהֵינוּ וְהִשְׁתַּחֲווּ לַהֲדֹם רַגְלָיו, קָדוֹשׁ הוּא: רוֹמְמוּ
יהוה אֱלֹהֵינוּ וְהִשְׁתַּחֲווּ לְהַר קָדְשׁוֹ, כִּי־קָדוֹשׁ יהוה אֱלֹהֵינוּ:

עַל הַכֹּל יִתְגַּדַּל וְיִתְקַדַּשׁ וְיִשְׁתַּבַּח וְיִתְפָּאַר וְיִתְרוֹמַם וְיִתְנַשֵּׂא שְׁמוֹ
שֶׁל מֶלֶךְ מַלְכֵי הַמְּלָכִים הַקָּדוֹשׁ בָּרוּךְ הוּא בָּעוֹלָמוֹת שֶׁבָּרָא, הָעוֹלָם
הַזֶּה וְהָעוֹלָם הַבָּא, כִּרְצוֹנוֹ וְכִרְצוֹן יְרֵאָיו וְכִרְצוֹן כָּל בֵּית יִשְׂרָאֵל. צוּר
הָעוֹלָמִים, אֲדוֹן כָּל הַבְּרִיּוֹת, אֱלוֹהַּ כָּל הַנְּפָשׁוֹת, הַיּוֹשֵׁב בְּמֶרְחֲבֵי
מָרוֹם, הַשּׁוֹכֵן בִּשְׁמֵי שְׁמֵי קֶדֶם, קְדֻשָּׁתוֹ עַל הַחַיּוֹת, וּקְדֻשָּׁתוֹ עַל כִּסֵּא
הַכָּבוֹד. וּבְכֵן יִתְקַדַּשׁ שִׁמְךָ בָּנוּ יהוה אֱלֹהֵינוּ לְעֵינֵי כָּל חָי, וְנֹאמַר לְפָנָיו
תהלים סח שִׁיר חָדָשׁ, כַּכָּתוּב: שִׁירוּ לֵאלֹהִים זַמְּרוּ שְׁמוֹ, סֹלּוּ לָרֹכֵב בָּעֲרָבוֹת, בְּיָהּ
ישעיה נב שְׁמוֹ, וְעִלְזוּ לְפָנָיו: וְנִרְאֵהוּ עַיִן בְּעַיִן בְּשׁוּבוֹ אֶל נָוֵהוּ, כַּכָּתוּב: כִּי עַיִן
ישעיה מ בְּעַיִן יִרְאוּ בְּשׁוּב יהוה צִיּוֹן: וְנֶאֱמַר: וְנִגְלָה כְּבוֹד יהוה, וְרָאוּ כָל־בָּשָׂר
יַחְדָּו כִּי פִּי יהוה דִּבֵּר:

אַב הָרַחֲמִים הוּא יְרַחֵם עַם עֲמוּסִים, וְיִזְכֹּר בְּרִית אֵיתָנִים, וְיַצִּיל
נַפְשׁוֹתֵינוּ מִן הַשָּׁעוֹת הָרָעוֹת, וְיִגְעַר בְּיֵצֶר הָרָע מִן הַנְּשׂוּאִים, וְיָחֹן אוֹתָנוּ
לִפְלֵיטַת עוֹלָמִים, וִימַלֵּא מִשְׁאֲלוֹתֵינוּ בְּמִדָּה טוֹבָה יְשׁוּעָה וְרַחֲמִים.

*The Torah scroll is placed on the bima and the Gabbai calls a Kohen to the Torah. See law 68.*

וְיַעֲזֹר May He help, shield and save all who seek refuge in Him, and let us say: Amen. Let us all render greatness to our God and give honor to the Torah. *Let the Kohen come forward. Arise (*name* son of *father's name*), the Kohen.

**If no Kohen is present, a Levi or Yisrael is called up as follows:*

/As there is no Kohen, arise (*name* son of *father's name*) in place of a Kohen./

Blessed is He who, in His holiness, gave the Torah to His people Israel.

*The congregation followed by the Gabbai:*

You who cling to the LORD your God are all alive today. *Deut. 4*

*The Reader shows the oleh the section to be read. The oleh touches the scroll at that place with the tzitzit of his tallit, which he then kisses. Holding the handles of the scroll, he says:*

*Oleh:* Bless the LORD, the blessed One.

*Cong:* Bless the LORD, the blessed One, for ever and all time.

*Oleh:* Bless the LORD, the blessed One, for ever and all time.

Blessed are You, LORD our God, King of the Universe,
who has chosen us from all peoples
and has given us His Torah.
Blessed are You, LORD, Giver of the Torah.

*After the reading, the oleh says:*

*Oleh:* Blessed are You, LORD our God, King of the Universe,
who has given us the Torah of truth,
planting everlasting life in our midst.
Blessed are You, LORD, Giver of the Torah.

---

matically, known as the *ba'al koreh*), "so as not to shame those who do not know how to read" (Rabbeinu Tam, in Tosafot *Bava Batra* 15a). Instead, the *oleh* says the blessings before and after the portion, and recites the text silently along with the reader.

*The* ספר תורה *is placed on the* שולחן *and the* גבאי *calls a* כהן *to the* תורה. *See law 68.*

**וְיַעֲזֹר וְיָגֵן וְיוֹשִׁיעַ לְכָל הַחוֹסִים בּוֹ, וְנֹאמַר אָמֵן. הַכֹּל הָבוּ גֹדֶל לֵאלֹהֵינוּ וּתְנוּ כָבוֹד לַתּוֹרָה. *כֹּהֵן קְרַב, יַעֲמֹד (פלוני בֶּן פלוני) הַכֹּהֵן.**

**If no* כהן *is present, a* לוי *or* ישראל *is called up as follows:*

/אֵין כָּאן כֹּהֵן, יַעֲמֹד (פלוני בֶּן פלוני) בִּמְקוֹם כֹּהֵן./

**בָּרוּךְ שֶׁנָּתַן תּוֹרָה לְעַמּוֹ יִשְׂרָאֵל בִּקְדֻשָּׁתוֹ.**

*The* קהל *followed by the* גבאי:

דברים ד **וְאַתֶּם הַדְּבֵקִים בַּיהוה אֱלֹהֵיכֶם חַיִּים כֻּלְּכֶם הַיּוֹם:**

*The* קורא *shows the* עולה *the section to be read. The* עולה *touches the scroll at that place with the* ציצית *of his* טלית*, which he then kisses. Holding the handles of the scroll, he says:*

עולה: **בָּרְכוּ אֶת יהוה הַמְבֹרָךְ.**

קהל: בָּרוּךְ יהוה הַמְבֹרָךְ לְעוֹלָם וָעֶד.

עולה: **בָּרוּךְ יהוה הַמְבֹרָךְ לְעוֹלָם וָעֶד.**

**בָּרוּךְ אַתָּה יהוה, אֱלֹהֵינוּ מֶלֶךְ הָעוֹלָם**
**אֲשֶׁר בָּחַר בָּנוּ מִכָּל הָעַמִּים וְנָתַן לָנוּ אֶת תּוֹרָתוֹ.**
**בָּרוּךְ אַתָּה יהוה, נוֹתֵן הַתּוֹרָה.**

*After the* קריאת התורה*, the* עולה *says:*

עולה: **בָּרוּךְ אַתָּה יהוה אֱלֹהֵינוּ מֶלֶךְ הָעוֹלָם**
**אֲשֶׁר נָתַן לָנוּ תּוֹרַת אֱמֶת וְחַיֵּי עוֹלָם נָטַע בְּתוֹכֵנוּ.**
**בָּרוּךְ אַתָּה יהוה, נוֹתֵן הַתּוֹרָה.**

---

ASCENT TO THE TORAH

The original custom was that each *oleh*, one called to the Torah, would read his own portion. Not everyone was able to do this, so the practice developed of entrusting the reading to one with expertise (commonly, though ungram-

*One who has survived a situation of danger (see commentary) says:*

Blessed are You, LORD our God, King of the Universe, who bestows good on the unworthy, who has bestowed on me much good.

*The congregation responds:*

Amen. May He who bestowed much good on you continue to bestow on you much good, Selah.

FOR AN OLEH

May He who blessed our fathers, Abraham, Isaac and Jacob, bless (*name*, son of *father's name*) who has been called up in honor of the All-Present, in honor of the Torah, (*On Shabbat:* in honor of the Shabbat) and in honor of the Day of Judgment. As a reward for this, may the Holy One, blessed be He, protect and deliver him from all trouble and distress, all infection and illness, and send blessing and success to all the work of his hands, and write him and seal him for a good life on this Day of Judgment, together with all Israel, his brethren, and let us say: Amen.

FOR A SICK MAN

May He who blessed our fathers, Abraham, Isaac and Jacob, Moses and Aaron, David and Solomon, bless and heal one who is ill, (*sick person's name*, son of *mother's name*), on whose behalf (*name of the one making the offering*) is making a contribution to charity. As a reward for this, may the Holy One, blessed be He, be filled with compassion for him, to restore his health, cure him, strengthen and revive him, sending him a swift and full recovery from heaven to all his 248 organs and 365 sinews, amongst the other sick ones in Israel, a healing of the spirit and a healing of the body – may healing be quick to come – now, swiftly and soon, and let us say: Amen.

FOR A SICK WOMAN

May He who blessed our fathers, Abraham, Isaac and Jacob, Moses and Aaron, David and Solomon, bless and heal one who is ill, (*sick person's name*, daughter of *mother's name*), on whose behalf (*name of the one making the offering*) is making a contribution to charity. As a reward for this, may the

---

not necessarily at the time of the reading of the Torah, and within three days of the event.

הַגּוֹמֵל לְחַיָּבִים טוֹבוֹת *Who bestows good on the unworthy.* Reminiscent of Jacob's prayer (Genesis 32:10), "I am unworthy of all the kindness and faithfulness You have shown Your servant."

*One who has survived a situation of danger (see commentary) says:*

בָּרוּךְ אַתָּה יהוה אֱלֹהֵינוּ מֶלֶךְ הָעוֹלָם הַגּוֹמֵל לְחַיָּבִים טוֹבוֹת שֶׁגְּמָלַנִי כָּל טוֹב.

*The* קהל *responds:*

אָמֵן. מִי שֶׁגְּמָלְךָ כָּל טוֹב הוּא יִגְמָלְךָ כָּל טוֹב, סֶלָה.

## מי שברך לעולה לתורה

מִי שֶׁבֵּרַךְ אֲבוֹתֵינוּ אַבְרָהָם יִצְחָק וְיַעֲקֹב, הוּא יְבָרֵךְ אֶת (פלוני בֶּן פלוני), בַּעֲבוּר שֶׁעָלָה לִכְבוֹד הַמָּקוֹם וְלִכְבוֹד הַתּוֹרָה (בשבת: וְלִכְבוֹד הַשַּׁבָּת) וְלִכְבוֹד יוֹם הַדִּין. בִּשְׂכַר זֶה הַקָּדוֹשׁ בָּרוּךְ הוּא יִשְׁמְרֵהוּ וְיַצִּילֵהוּ מִכָּל צָרָה וְצוּקָה וּמִכָּל נֶגַע וּמַחֲלָה, וְיִשְׁלַח בְּרָכָה וְהַצְלָחָה בְּכָל מַעֲשֵׂה יָדָיו, וְיִכְתְּבֵהוּ וְיַחְתְּמֵהוּ לְחַיִּים טוֹבִים בְּיוֹם הַדִּין הַזֶּה עִם כָּל יִשְׂרָאֵל אֶחָיו, וְנֹאמַר אָמֵן.

## מי שברך לחולֶה

מִי שֶׁבֵּרַךְ אֲבוֹתֵינוּ אַבְרָהָם יִצְחָק וְיַעֲקֹב, מֹשֶׁה וְאַהֲרֹן דָּוִד וּשְׁלֹמֹה הוּא יְבָרֵךְ וִירַפֵּא אֶת הַחוֹלֶה (פלוני בֶּן פלונית) בַּעֲבוּר שֶׁ(פלוני בֶּן פלוני) נוֹדֵר צְדָקָה בַּעֲבוּרוֹ. בִּשְׂכַר זֶה הַקָּדוֹשׁ בָּרוּךְ הוּא יִמָּלֵא רַחֲמִים עָלָיו לְהַחֲלִימוֹ וּלְרַפֹּאתוֹ וּלְהַחֲזִיקוֹ וּלְהַחֲיוֹתוֹ וְיִשְׁלַח לוֹ מְהֵרָה רְפוּאָה שְׁלֵמָה מִן הַשָּׁמַיִם לִרְמַ״ח אֵבָרָיו וּשְׁסָ״ה גִּידָיו בְּתוֹךְ שְׁאָר חוֹלֵי יִשְׂרָאֵל, רְפוּאַת הַנֶּפֶשׁ וּרְפוּאַת הַגּוּף. הַשְׁתָּא בַּעֲגָלָא וּבִזְמַן קָרִיב, וְנֹאמַר אָמֵן.

## מי שברך לחולָה

מִי שֶׁבֵּרַךְ אֲבוֹתֵינוּ אַבְרָהָם יִצְחָק וְיַעֲקֹב, מֹשֶׁה וְאַהֲרֹן דָּוִד וּשְׁלֹמֹה הוּא יְבָרֵךְ וִירַפֵּא אֶת הַחוֹלָה (פלונית בַּת פלונית) בַּעֲבוּר שֶׁ(פלוני בֶּן פלוני) נוֹדֵר צְדָקָה בַּעֲבוּרָהּ. בִּשְׂכַר זֶה הַקָּדוֹשׁ בָּרוּךְ הוּא יִמָּלֵא רַחֲמִים עָלֶיהָ לְהַחֲלִימָהּ

---

BIRKAT HAGOMEL

This blessing, "Who bestows," is mentioned in the Talmud (*Berakhot* 54b). It is to be said after the following four circumstances: (1) release from captivity, (2) recovery from a potentially life-threatening illness, (3) a dangerous journey, and (4) a sea-crossing (nowadays, many also say it after an air flight). It is said in the presence of a *minyan* (at least ten adult males), usually, though

Holy One, blessed be He, be filled with compassion for her, to restore her health, cure her, strengthen and revive her, sending her a swift and full recovery from heaven to all her organs and sinews, amongst the other sick ones in Israel, a healing of the spirit and a healing of the body – may healing be quick to come – now, swiftly and soon, and let us say: Amen.

## TORAH READING FOR THE FIRST DAY

The LORD remembered Sarah just as He had said, and just as He had *Gen. 21*
spoken then, so He did for her. So Sarah conceived, and she bore
Abraham a son in his old age, at the time that God had mentioned.
Abraham named the son who was born to him, the son whom Sarah

---

On the brink of the exodus, Moses gathers the people and addresses them (Ex. 12–13). He speaks about none of the things we would expect – freedom, the journey, the land of milk and honey. Instead he speaks three times about children: "And you shall tell your child on that day…"

Children have been the casualties of our age. In the West they have suffered from the breakdown of marriage and the exploitations of a consumer culture. In some parts of the world they have been used as labor, in others they have become the victims of terror or even trained as terrorists, taught to hate. The protests have been too few.

There are cultures that live in the present. Eventually, inevitably, they lose their way. There are cultures that live in the past. Nursing grievances, they seek revenge. Judaism is a supreme example of a culture that, while celebrating the present and honoring the past, lives for the future – for its children.

The stories of Sarah and Hannah and their joy at the birth of their children are two of the enduring symbols of Judaism. There is no gift like the gift of a child, no responsibility greater than the responsibility of a parent, no miracle more profound than the way love brings new life into the world, and no question a better guide to life than to ask: Will my next act make the world a little better for our children?

**וַיהוה פָּקַד אֶת־שָׂרָה** *The LORD remembered Sarah.* According to the sages, Isaac was born on Rosh HaShana. The stories of Sarah and Hannah, two infertile women who longed for and were granted a child, teach us the power of prayer. Even though prayer is not immediately answered, we should not lose hope.

**וַיִּקְרָא אַבְרָהָם אֶת־שֶׁם־בְּנוֹ** *Abraham named the son.* The name Isaac means, "He will laugh." Isaac, the first Jewish child, hints at the fact that though we

וּלְרַפְּאתָהּ וּלְהַחֲזִיקָהּ וּלְהַחֲיוֹתָהּ וְיִשְׁלַח לָהּ מְהֵרָה רְפוּאָה שְׁלֵמָה מִן הַשָּׁמַיִם לְכָל אֵבָרֶיהָ וּלְכָל גִּידֶיהָ בְּתוֹךְ שְׁאָר חוֹלֵי יִשְׂרָאֵל, רְפוּאַת הַנֶּפֶשׁ וּרְפוּאַת הַגּוּף. הַשְׁתָּא בַּעֲגָלָא וּבִזְמַן קָרִיב, וְנֹאמַר אָמֵן.

קריאת התורה ליום א׳

בראשית כא

וַיהֹוָה פָּקַד אֶת־שָׂרָה כַּאֲשֶׁר אָמָר וַיַּעַשׂ יְהֹוָה לְשָׂרָה כַּאֲשֶׁר דִּבֵּר: וַתַּהַר וַתֵּלֶד שָׂרָה לְאַבְרָהָם בֵּן לִזְקֻנָיו לַמּוֹעֵד אֲשֶׁר־דִּבֶּר אֹתוֹ אֱלֹהִים: וַיִּקְרָא אַבְרָהָם אֶת־שֶׁם־בְּנוֹ הַנּוֹלַד־לוֹ אֲשֶׁר־יָלְדָה־לּוֹ

TORAH READING – FIRST DAY: THE BIRTH OF ISAAC

The Torah and Haftara readings for the first day of Rosh HaShana form an eloquent pair of witnesses to Jewish values. Rosh HaShana is the anniversary of creation. *Hayom harat olam,* we say in our prayers: "Today the world was born." We would surely have expected the Torah reading to be from the opening of Genesis, "In the beginning, God created." And the Haftara? What better than the great hymn of Isaiah, "This is what God the Lord says – the Creator of the heavens, who stretches them out, who spreads out the earth with all that springs from it, who gives breath to its people, and life to those who walk on it" (Is. 42:5).

Logical but wrong. Instead, both readings are about the birth of a child to an infertile woman. In the Torah we read the story of the birth of Isaac to Sarah. In the Haftara we read about the birth of Samuel to Hannah. This counterintuitive choice tells us much about the humane vision at the heart of Jewish life. A single life, said the sages, is like a universe (Mishna, *Sanhedrin* 37a). *If you seek to understand the meaning of creation, think about the birth of a child.*

Faith in Judaism is not a form of science. It is a form of love. To understand the universe as God's creation, we do not need advanced degrees in cosmology. We need to understand what it is to be a parent, bringing new life into being through an act of love. Judaism was the first moral system to place love – for God, for our neighbor, and for the stranger – at the heart of its values. Its supreme expression is the selfless, sacrificing, unconditional love of a parent for a child.

Throughout the centuries, Judaism has been the great child-centered civilization. Only once does the Torah tell us why Abraham was chosen: "So that he will instruct his children and his household after him to keep the way of the Lord" (Gen. 18:19).

bore – Isaac. And he circumcised Isaac, his son, when the child was eight days old, just as God had commanded him to do. LEVI Abraham was a hundred years old when his son Isaac was born to him. "God," said Sarah, "has made laughter for me; all those who hear of this will laugh with me." She said, "Who would ever have said to Abraham, 'Sarah will one day nurse children?' And yet I have borne him a son in his old age." The baby grew, and he was weaned; Abraham laid out a great feast on the day when Isaac was weaned. (*Shabbat:* SHELISHI) And Sarah saw the son of Hagar the Egyptian – the son she had borne Abraham – making sport. She said to Abraham, "Send away that slave and her son, for the slave's son cannot inherit you alongside Isaac." This distressed Abraham deeply, because of his son. But God said to him, "Do not think this wrong, because of the boy or because of your slave; listen to Sarah, to whatever she says, for it is Isaac who will keep your name alive; and I shall build a nation from the maid's son also, because he too is your descendant." SHELISHI (*Shabbat:* REVI'I) Early the next morning Abraham rose, and he took bread and a flask of water, and gave them to Hagar; he placed them over her shoulder, and the child also, and he sent her away. Hagar left, and she went astray in the desert of Be'er Sheva. The water in the flask was exhausted, and she threw the boy down beneath one of the bushes. And Hagar went off and sat herself beyond, a bowshot's distance away, for she said, "Just let me not see it, when the child dies." She sat down there at a distance beyond, and then she raised up her voice and wept. And God heard the voice of the boy. An angel called out to Hagar from the heavens and said to her, "What is wrong, Hagar? Do not be frightened; for God

---

וַיֹּאמֶר אֱלֹהִים אֶל־אַבְרָהָם אַל־יֵרַע בְּעֵינֶיךָ *But God said to him, "Do not think this is wrong."* Isaac was to be Abraham's heir. Ishmael was also Abraham's son and would be blessed by God, but Sarah wanted there to be no argument over the inheritance. (J.H. Hertz)

וַיִּשְׁמַע אֱלֹהִים אֶת־קוֹל הַנַּעַר *And God heard the voice of the boy.* Though neither Hagar nor Ishmael were part of the special covenant with Abraham, God heard their tears and answered their cry, for God is the God of all humanity and is close to all who truly call on Him.

שָׂרָה יִצְחָק׃ וַיָּמׇל אַבְרָהָם אֶת־יִצְחָק בְּנוֹ בֶּן־שְׁמֹנַת יָמִים כַּאֲשֶׁר
צִוָּה אֹתוֹ אֱלֹהִים׃ וְאַבְרָהָם בֶּן־מְאַת שָׁנָה בְּהִוָּלֶד לוֹ אֵת יִצְחָק לוי
בְּנוֹ׃ וַתֹּאמֶר שָׂרָה צְחֹק עָשָׂה לִי אֱלֹהִים כׇּל־הַשֹּׁמֵעַ יִצְחַק־לִי׃
וַתֹּאמֶר מִי מִלֵּל לְאַבְרָהָם הֵינִיקָה בָנִים שָׂרָה כִּי־יָלַדְתִּי בֵן לִזְקֻנָיו׃
וַיִּגְדַּל הַיֶּלֶד וַיִּגָּמַל וַיַּעַשׂ אַבְרָהָם מִשְׁתֶּה גָדוֹל בְּיוֹם הִגָּמֵל אֶת־
יִצְחָק׃ וַתֵּרֶא שָׂרָה אֶת־בֶּן־הָגָר הַמִּצְרִית אֲשֶׁר־יָלְדָה לְאַבְרָהָם (בשבת שלישי)
מְצַחֵק׃ וַתֹּאמֶר לְאַבְרָהָם גָּרֵשׁ הָאָמָה הַזֹּאת וְאֶת־בְּנָהּ כִּי לֹא
יִירַשׁ בֶּן־הָאָמָה הַזֹּאת עִם־בְּנִי עִם־יִצְחָק׃ וַיֵּרַע הַדָּבָר מְאֹד
בְּעֵינֵי אַבְרָהָם עַל אוֹדֹת בְּנוֹ׃ וַיֹּאמֶר אֱלֹהִים אֶל־אַבְרָהָם אַל־יֵרַע
בְּעֵינֶיךָ עַל־הַנַּעַר וְעַל־אֲמָתֶךָ כֹּל אֲשֶׁר תֹּאמַר אֵלֶיךָ שָׂרָה שְׁמַע
בְּקֹלָהּ כִּי בְיִצְחָק יִקָּרֵא לְךָ זָרַע׃ וְגַם אֶת־בֶּן־הָאָמָה לְגוֹי אֲשִׂימֶנּוּ שלישי (בשבת
כִּי זַרְעֲךָ הוּא׃ וַיַּשְׁכֵּם אַבְרָהָם ׀ בַּבֹּקֶר וַיִּקַּח־לֶחֶם וְחֵמַת מַיִם וַיִּתֵּן רביעי)
אֶל־הָגָר שָׂם עַל־שִׁכְמָהּ וְאֶת־הַיֶּלֶד וַיְשַׁלְּחֶהָ וַתֵּלֶךְ וַתֵּתַע בְּמִדְבַּר
בְּאֵר שָׁבַע׃ וַיִּכְלוּ הַמַּיִם מִן־הַחֵמֶת וַתַּשְׁלֵךְ אֶת־הַיֶּלֶד תַּחַת אַחַד
הַשִּׂיחִם׃ וַתֵּלֶךְ וַתֵּשֶׁב לָהּ מִנֶּגֶד הַרְחֵק כִּמְטַחֲוֵי קֶשֶׁת כִּי אָמְרָה
אַל־אֶרְאֶה בְּמוֹת הַיָּלֶד וַתֵּשֶׁב מִנֶּגֶד וַתִּשָּׂא אֶת־קֹלָהּ וַתֵּבְךְּ׃
וַיִּשְׁמַע אֱלֹהִים אֶת־קוֹל הַנַּעַר וַיִּקְרָא מַלְאַךְ אֱלֹהִים ׀ אֶל־הָגָר
מִן־הַשָּׁמַיִם וַיֹּאמֶר לָהּ מַה־לָּךְ הָגָר אַל־תִּירְאִי כִּי־שָׁמַע אֱלֹהִים

---

may suffer many trials, we will eventually know the laughter of joy. Jewish history has often been written in tears, but that is neither its essence nor its destiny. The festivals of the seventh month begin, on Rosh HaShana and Yom Kippur, in awe and fear – but end, on Sukkot and Simḥat Torah, in joy. So does Jewish life as a whole. There may be tribulation, but in the end, there is celebration.

עַל אוֹדֹת בְּנוֹ *Because of his son.* Ishmael was Abraham's son but not Sarah's. This is the first intimation that Jewish identity follows the mother, not the father.

has heard the boy's voice, there in the place where he is. Get up; lift up the boy and keep your hand firmly on him, for I am going to build him up into a great nation." God opened her eyes and she saw a well, and she went and filled the flask with water, and helped the boy to drink. God was with the boy, and he grew, and there in the desert he lived, and became a bowman. He settled in the Paran desert, and his mother brought him a wife from the land of Egypt. (*Shabbat:* ḤAMISHI)

REVI'I (*Shabbat:* SHISHI) It was at that time that Avimelekh and his chief of staff, Pikhol, said to Abraham, "God is with you in all that you do. Now swear to me by your God, that you will not deceive me or my son or my grandson; treat me and all the land you have lived in with the same kindness I have shown toward you." Abraham said, "I swear." And then he reproached Avimelekh for the well of water that Avimelekh's slaves had stolen. "I do not know who did this," Avimelekh said, "and you did not tell me before, I have never heard of all this until today!" Abraham took sheep and cattle and gave them to Avimelekh, and the two forged a covenant together. And Abraham then set the seven sheep from the flock apart.

ḤAMISHI (*Shabbat:* SHEVI'I) Avimelekh asked him, "What are these seven sheep that you have set apart by themselves?" And he said, "These seven sheep are for you to take from me as witness to the fact that it was I who dug that well." And so it was that he named the place Be'er Sheva, because it was there that the two of them vowed. They forged their covenant in Be'er Sheva, and then Avimelekh and Pikhol, his chief of staff, stood up and returned to the land of the Philistines. Abraham planted a tamarisk tree at Be'er Sheva, and there he called out the name of the Lord, God of all the world. And Abraham lived on in the land of the Philistines for many years after.

---

he is in the present: there, where he is." (Rashi, following *Bereshit Raba* 53:14)

וַיִּפְקַח אֱלֹהִים אֶת־עֵינֶיהָ *God opened her eyes.* Sometimes blessings lie all around us, but we do not see them. "The world is full of the light of God, but to see it we have to learn to open our eyes" (Rabbi Naḥman of Bratslav).

וְהוֹכִחַ אַבְרָהָם אֶת־אֲבִימֶלֶךְ *And then he reproached Avimelekh.* Abraham reproved him for tolerating violence in his country (Seforno).

(בשבת חמישי) אֶל־ק֥וֹל הַנַּ֖עַר בַּאֲשֶׁ֥ר הוּא־שָֽׁם׃ ק֚וּמִי שְׂאִ֣י אֶת־הַנַּ֔עַר וְהַחֲזִ֥יקִי
אֶת־יָדֵ֖ךְ בּ֑וֹ כִּֽי־לְג֥וֹי גָּד֖וֹל אֲשִׂימֶֽנּוּ׃ וַיִּפְקַ֤ח אֱלֹהִים֙ אֶת־עֵינֶ֔יהָ וַתֵּ֖רֶא
בְּאֵ֣ר מָ֑יִם וַתֵּ֜לֶךְ וַתְּמַלֵּ֤א אֶת־הַחֵ֙מֶת֙ מַ֔יִם וַתַּ֖שְׁקְ אֶת־הַנָּֽעַר׃ וַיְהִ֧י
אֱלֹהִ֛ים אֶת־הַנַּ֖עַר וַיִּגְדָּ֑ל וַיֵּ֙שֶׁב֙ בַּמִּדְבָּ֔ר וַיְהִ֖י רֹבֶ֥ה קַשָּֽׁת׃ וַיֵּ֖שֶׁב
בְּמִדְבַּ֣ר פָּארָ֑ן וַתִּֽקַּֽח־ל֥וֹ אִמּ֛וֹ אִשָּׁ֖ה מֵאֶ֥רֶץ מִצְרָֽיִם׃

רביעי (בשבת ששי) וַיְהִי֙ בָּעֵ֣ת הַהִ֔וא וַיֹּ֣אמֶר אֲבִימֶ֗לֶךְ וּפִיכֹל֙ שַׂר־צְבָא֔וֹ אֶל־אַבְרָהָ֖ם
לֵאמֹ֑ר אֱלֹהִ֣ים עִמְּךָ֔ בְּכֹ֥ל אֲשֶׁר־אַתָּ֖ה עֹשֶֽׂה׃ וְעַתָּ֗ה הִשָּׁ֨בְעָה לִּ֤י
בֵֽאלֹהִים֙ הֵ֔נָּה אִם־תִּשְׁקֹ֣ר לִ֔י וּלְנִינִ֖י וּלְנֶכְדִּ֑י כַּחֶ֨סֶד אֲשֶׁר־עָשִׂ֤יתִי
עִמְּךָ֙ תַּעֲשֶׂ֣ה עִמָּדִ֔י וְעִם־הָאָ֖רֶץ אֲשֶׁר־גַּ֥רְתָּה בָּֽהּ׃ וַיֹּ֙אמֶר֙ אַבְרָהָ֔ם
אָנֹכִ֖י אִשָּׁבֵֽעַ׃ וְהוֹכִ֥חַ אַבְרָהָ֖ם אֶת־אֲבִימֶ֑לֶךְ עַל־אֹדוֹת֙ בְּאֵ֣ר הַמַּ֔יִם
אֲשֶׁ֥ר גָּזְל֖וּ עַבְדֵ֥י אֲבִימֶֽלֶךְ׃ וַיֹּ֣אמֶר אֲבִימֶ֔לֶךְ לֹ֣א יָדַ֔עְתִּי מִ֥י עָשָׂ֖ה
אֶת־הַדָּבָ֣ר הַזֶּ֑ה וְגַם־אַתָּ֞ה לֹא־הִגַּ֣דְתָּ לִּ֗י וְגַ֧ם אָנֹכִ֛י לֹ֥א שָׁמַ֖עְתִּי
בִּלְתִּ֥י הַיּֽוֹם׃ וַיִּקַּ֤ח אַבְרָהָם֙ צֹ֣אן וּבָקָ֔ר וַיִּתֵּ֖ן לַאֲבִימֶ֑לֶךְ וַיִּכְרְת֥וּ
חמישי (בשבת שביעי) שְׁנֵיהֶ֖ם בְּרִֽית׃ וַיַּצֵּ֣ב אַבְרָהָ֗ם אֶת־שֶׁ֛בַע כִּבְשֹׂ֥ת הַצֹּ֖אן לְבַדְּהֶֽן׃
וַיֹּ֥אמֶר אֲבִימֶ֖לֶךְ אֶל־אַבְרָהָ֑ם מָ֣ה הֵ֗נָּה שֶׁ֤בַע כְּבָשֹׂת֙ הָאֵ֔לֶּה אֲשֶׁ֥ר
הִצַּ֖בְתָּ לְבַדָּֽנָה׃ וַיֹּ֕אמֶר כִּ֚י אֶת־שֶׁ֣בַע כְּבָשֹׂ֔ת תִּקַּ֖ח מִיָּדִ֑י בַּעֲבוּר֙
תִּֽהְיֶה־לִּ֣י לְעֵדָ֔ה כִּ֥י חָפַ֖רְתִּי אֶת־הַבְּאֵ֥ר הַזֹּֽאת׃ עַל־כֵּ֗ן קָרָ֛א לַמָּק֥וֹם
הַה֖וּא בְּאֵ֣ר שָׁ֑בַע כִּ֛י שָׁ֥ם נִשְׁבְּע֖וּ שְׁנֵיהֶֽם׃ וַיִּכְרְת֥וּ בְרִ֖ית בִּבְאֵ֣ר
שָׁ֑בַע וַיָּ֣קָם אֲבִימֶ֗לֶךְ וּפִיכֹל֙ שַׂר־צְבָא֔וֹ וַיָּשֻׁ֖בוּ אֶל־אֶ֥רֶץ פְּלִשְׁתִּֽים׃
וַיִּטַּ֥ע אֶ֖שֶׁל בִּבְאֵ֣ר שָׁ֑בַע וַיִּקְרָא־שָׁ֔ם בְּשֵׁ֥ם יְהוָ֖ה אֵ֥ל עוֹלָֽם׃ וַיָּ֧גָר
אַבְרָהָ֛ם בְּאֶ֥רֶץ פְּלִשְׁתִּ֖ים יָמִ֥ים רַבִּֽים׃

---

בַּאֲשֶׁר הוּא־שָׁם *There in the place where he is.* The angels accused Ishmael, saying that his descendants would one day persecute the children of Israel. "What is he now?" asked God, "innocent or guilty?" "Innocent," replied the angels. God then said, "I judge a person only on the basis of where

## HALF KADDISH

*Before Maftir is read, the Reader says Half Kaddish:*

*Reader:* יִתְגַּדַּל Magnified and sanctified
may His great name be,
in the world He created by His will.
May He establish His kingdom,
make His salvation flourish,
and hasten His messiah,
in your lifetime and in your days,
and in the lifetime of all the house of Israel,
swiftly and soon – and say: Amen.

*All:* May His great name be blessed for ever and all time.

*Reader:* Blessed and praised,
glorified and exalted,
raised and honored,
uplifted and lauded
be the name of the Holy One, blessed be He,
above and beyond any blessing,
song, praise and consolation
uttered in the world –
and say: Amen.

## HAGBAHA AND GELILA

*The first Torah scroll is lifted and the congregation says:*

וְזֹאת הַתּוֹרָה This is the Torah *Deut. 4*
that Moses placed before the children of Israel,
at the Lord's commandment, by the hand of Moses. *Num. 9*

*Some add:* It is a tree of life to those who grasp it, and those who uphold it are happy. *Prov. 3*
Its ways are ways of pleasantness, and all its paths are peace.
Long life is in its right hand; in its left, riches and honor.
It pleased the Lord for the sake of [Israel's] righteousness, *Is. 42*
to make the Torah great and glorious.

*The first Torah scroll is bound and covered and the oleh for Maftir is called to the second Torah scroll.*

## חצי קדיש

*Before* מפטיר *is read, the* קורא *says* חצי קדיש:

קורא: יִתְגַּדַּל וְיִתְקַדַּשׁ שְׁמֵהּ רַבָּא (קהל: אָמֵן)
בְּעָלְמָא דִּי בְרָא כִרְעוּתֵהּ
וְיַמְלִיךְ מַלְכוּתֵהּ
וְיַצְמַח פֻּרְקָנֵהּ וִיקָרֵב מְשִׁיחֵהּ (קהל: אָמֵן)
בְּחַיֵּיכוֹן וּבְיוֹמֵיכוֹן וּבְחַיֵּי דְכָל בֵּית יִשְׂרָאֵל
בַּעֲגָלָא וּבִזְמַן קָרִיב
וְאִמְרוּ אָמֵן. (קהל: אָמֵן)

קהל וקורא: יְהֵא שְׁמֵהּ רַבָּא מְבָרַךְ לְעָלַם וּלְעָלְמֵי עָלְמַיָּא.

קורא: יִתְבָּרַךְ וְיִשְׁתַּבַּח וְיִתְפָּאַר וְיִתְרוֹמַם וְיִתְנַשֵּׂא
וְיִתְהַדָּר וְיִתְעַלֶּה וְיִתְהַלָּל
שְׁמֵהּ דְּקֻדְשָׁא בְּרִיךְ הוּא (קהל: אָמֵן)
לְעֵלָּא לְעֵלָּא מִכָּל בִּרְכָתָא וְשִׁירָתָא, תֻּשְׁבְּחָתָא וְנֶחֱמָתָא
דַּאֲמִירָן בְּעָלְמָא
וְאִמְרוּ אָמֵן. (קהל: אָמֵן)

## הגבהה וגלילה

*The first* ספר תורה *is lifted and the* קהל *says:*

וְזֹאת הַתּוֹרָה אֲשֶׁר־שָׂם מֹשֶׁה לִפְנֵי בְּנֵי יִשְׂרָאֵל: דברים ד
עַל־פִּי יהוה בְּיַד מֹשֶׁה: במדבר ט

*Some add* עֵץ־חַיִּים הִיא לַמַּחֲזִיקִים בָּהּ וְתֹמְכֶיהָ מְאֻשָּׁר: משלי ג
דְּרָכֶיהָ דַרְכֵי־נֹעַם וְכָל־נְתִיבֹתֶיהָ שָׁלוֹם:
אֹרֶךְ יָמִים בִּימִינָהּ, בִּשְׂמֹאולָהּ עֹשֶׁר וְכָבוֹד:
יהוה חָפֵץ לְמַעַן צִדְקוֹ יַגְדִּיל תּוֹרָה וְיַאְדִּיר: ישעיה מב

*The first* ספר תורה *is bound and covered and the* עולה *for* מפטיר *is called to the second* ספר תורה.

## MAFTIR

On the first day of the seventh month you shall hold a sacred assembly. You shall do no laborious work, and it shall be a day of the blowing of the shofar for you. You shall make a burnt-offering of pleasing aroma to the LORD: a young bullock, a ram, and seven yearling male lambs; they shall be without blemish. And their meal-offerings, fine flour mixed with oil, three-tenths of an ephah for the bull, two-tenths of an ephah for the ram, and one-tenth of an ephah for each of the seven lambs, one male goat for atonement. All this aside from the burnt-offering of the New Moon and its meal-offering, and the regular daily burnt-offering with its meal-offering, and their libations according to their ordinance, a burnt-offering of pleasing odor to the LORD. *Num. 29:1–6*

## HAGBAHA AND GELILA

*The second Torah scroll is lifted and the congregation says:*

וְזֹאת הַתּוֹרָה This is the Torah *Deut. 4*
that Moses placed before the children of Israel,
at the LORD's commandment, *Num. 9*
by the hand of Moses.

*Some add:* It is a tree of life to those who grasp it, and those who uphold it are happy. *Prov. 3*
Its ways are ways of pleasantness, and all its paths are peace.
Long life is in its right hand; in its left, riches and honor.
It pleased the LORD for the sake of [Israel's] righteousness, *Is. 42*
to make the Torah great and glorious.

*The second Torah scroll is bound and covered and the oleh for Maftir reads the Haftara.*

## BLESSING BEFORE READING THE HAFTARA

*Before reading the Haftara, the person called up for Maftir says:*

בָּרוּךְ Blessed are You, LORD our God, King of the Universe, who chose good prophets and was pleased with their words, spoken in truth. Blessed are You, LORD, who chose the Torah, His servant Moses, His people Israel, and the prophets of truth and righteousness.

## מפטיר

וּבַחֹ֨דֶשׁ הַשְּׁבִיעִ֜י בְּאֶחָ֣ד לַחֹ֗דֶשׁ מִֽקְרָא־קֹ֙דֶשׁ֙ יִהְיֶ֣ה לָכֶ֔ם כָּל־ במדבר כט: א–ו
מְלֶ֥אכֶת עֲבֹדָ֖ה לֹ֣א תַעֲשׂ֑וּ י֥וֹם תְּרוּעָ֖ה יִהְיֶ֥ה לָכֶֽם׃ וַעֲשִׂיתֶ֨ם עֹלָ֜ה
לְרֵ֤יחַ נִיחֹ֙חַ֙ לַֽיהוָ֔ה פַּ֧ר בֶּן־בָּקָ֛ר אֶחָ֖ד אַ֣יִל אֶחָ֑ד כְּבָשִׂ֧ים בְּנֵי־שָׁנָ֛ה
שִׁבְעָ֖ה תְּמִימִֽם׃ וּמִ֨נְחָתָ֔ם סֹ֖לֶת בְּלוּלָ֣ה בַשָּׁ֑מֶן שְׁלֹשָׁ֤ה עֶשְׂרֹנִים֙
לַפָּ֔ר שְׁנֵ֥י עֶשְׂרֹנִ֖ים לָאָֽיִל׃ וְעִשָּׂר֣וֹן אֶחָ֔ד לַכֶּ֖בֶשׂ הָאֶחָ֑ד לְשִׁבְעַ֖ת
הַכְּבָשִֽׂים׃ וּשְׂעִיר־עִזִּ֥ים אֶחָ֖ד חַטָּ֑את לְכַפֵּ֖ר עֲלֵיכֶֽם׃ מִלְּבַד֩ עֹלַ֨ת
הַחֹ֜דֶשׁ וּמִנְחָתָ֗הּ וְעֹלַ֤ת הַתָּמִיד֙ וּמִנְחָתָ֔הּ וְנִסְכֵּיהֶ֖ם כְּמִשְׁפָּטָ֑ם לְרֵ֣יחַ
נִיחֹ֔חַ אִשֶּׁ֖ה לַֽיהוָֽה׃

## הגבהה וגלילה

*The second* ספר תורה *is lifted and the* קהל *says:*

וְזֹאת הַתּוֹרָה אֲשֶׁר־שָׂם מֹשֶׁה לִפְנֵי בְּנֵי יִשְׂרָאֵל: דברים ד

עַל־פִּי יהוה בְּיַד מֹשֶׁה: במדבר ט

*Some add*

עֵץ־חַיִּים הִיא לַמַּחֲזִיקִים בָּהּ וְתֹמְכֶיהָ מְאֻשָּׁר: משלי ג
דְּרָכֶיהָ דַרְכֵי־נֹעַם וְכָל־נְתִיבוֹתֶיהָ שָׁלוֹם:
אֹרֶךְ יָמִים בִּימִינָהּ, בִּשְׂמֹאולָהּ עֹשֶׁר וְכָבוֹד:
יהוה חָפֵץ לְמַעַן צִדְקוֹ יַגְדִּיל תּוֹרָה וְיַאְדִּיר: ישעיה מב

*The second* ספר תורה *is bound and covered and the* עולה *for* מפטיר *reads the* הפטרה.

## ברכה קודם ההפטרה

*Before reading the* הפטרה*, the person called up for* מפטיר *says:*

בָּרוּךְ אַתָּה יהוה אֱלֹהֵינוּ מֶלֶךְ הָעוֹלָם אֲשֶׁר בָּחַר בִּנְבִיאִים טוֹבִים, וְרָצָה בְדִבְרֵיהֶם הַנֶּאֱמָרִים בֶּאֱמֶת. בָּרוּךְ אַתָּה יהוה, הַבּוֹחֵר בַּתּוֹרָה וּבְמֹשֶׁה עַבְדּוֹ וּבְיִשְׂרָאֵל עַמּוֹ וּבִנְבִיאֵי הָאֱמֶת וָצֶדֶק.

## HAFTARA FOR THE FIRST DAY

*1 Sam. 1:1–2:10*

Once there was a man from Ramatayim Tzofim, from Mount Ephraim, and his name was Elkana son of Yeroḥam son of Elihu son of Toḥu son of Tzuf, a resident of Ephraim. [The man] had two wives; the first was named Hannah and the second, Peninah; and while Peninah had children, Hannah had none. This man would go up from his city, year by year, to worship and to make offerings to the LORD of hosts in Shiloh, where Ḥofni and Pineḥas served as priests to the LORD. The day would come, and Elkanah would make his offering, and give portions of it to Peninah his wife and to all her sons and daughters. And to Hannah he would give the most generous portion, for it was Hannah that he loved, though the LORD had shut off her womb. And her rival would torment her, torment her to fill her with fury – because the LORD had shut off her womb. [Elkanah] did the same thing year after year, whenever [Hannah] went up to the LORD's House; and so [Peninah] would torment her, until she wept, and would not eat. "Why are you crying, Hannah," her husband, Elkanah, said, "why will you not eat, and why is your heart so pained? Am I not better to you than ten sons?" Hannah got up after they had eaten at Shiloh, and after they had drunk, and Eli the Priest was seated upon his chair at the doorway of the LORD's Sanctuary. And she was bitter within, and prayed to the LORD and wept – wept. And she made a vow, saying, "LORD of hosts,

---

it possible for the other partner to fulfill his or her desire for a child" (*Family Redeemed,** p. 52).

וְהִיא מָרַת נָפֶשׁ *And she was bitter within.* Hannah now knew that she was alone and had only God to whom to turn.

וּבָכֹה תִבְכֶּה *And wept – wept.* Even though all other gates of prayer may be closed, the gate of tears is never closed (*Bava Metzia* 59a). In an orphanage at night there are no tears. Children only cry when they know there will be someone to answer their cry. We are told that there is a gate of tears to teach

* Rabbi J.B. Soloveitchik, *Family Redeemed*, eds. D. Shatz and J.B. Wolowelsky (Jersey City, NJ: KTAV Publishing House, 2000).

## הפטרה ליום א׳

וַיְהִי אִישׁ אֶחָד מִן־הָרָמָתַיִם צוֹפִים מֵהַר אֶפְרָיִם וּשְׁמוֹ אֶלְקָנָה שמואל א׳ א,א–ב,י
בֶּן־יְרֹחָם בֶּן־אֱלִיהוּא בֶּן־תֹּחוּ בֶן־צוּף אֶפְרָתִי: וְלוֹ שְׁתֵּי נָשִׁים
שֵׁם אַחַת חַנָּה וְשֵׁם הַשֵּׁנִית פְּנִנָּה וַיְהִי לִפְנִנָּה יְלָדִים וּלְחַנָּה אֵין
יְלָדִים: וְעָלָה הָאִישׁ הַהוּא מֵעִירוֹ מִיָּמִים ׀ יָמִימָה לְהִשְׁתַּחֲוֺת
וְלִזְבֹּחַ לַיהוָה צְבָאוֹת בְּשִׁלֹה וְשָׁם שְׁנֵי בְנֵי־עֵלִי חָפְנִי וּפִנְחָס
כֹּהֲנִים לַיהוָה: וַיְהִי הַיּוֹם וַיִּזְבַּח אֶלְקָנָה וְנָתַן לִפְנִנָּה אִשְׁתּוֹ
וּלְכָל־בָּנֶיהָ וּבְנוֹתֶיהָ מָנוֹת: וּלְחַנָּה יִתֵּן מָנָה אַחַת אַפָּיִם כִּי אֶת־
חַנָּה אָהֵב וַיהוָה סָגַר רַחְמָהּ: וְכִעֲסַתָּה צָרָתָהּ גַּם־כַּעַס בַּעֲבוּר
הַרְּעִמָהּ כִּי־סָגַר יְהוָה בְּעַד רַחְמָהּ: וְכֵן יַעֲשֶׂה שָׁנָה בְשָׁנָה מִדֵּי
עֲלֹתָהּ בְּבֵית יְהוָה כֵּן תַּכְעִסֶנָּה וַתִּבְכֶּה וְלֹא תֹאכַל: וַיֹּאמֶר לָהּ
אֶלְקָנָה אִישָׁהּ חַנָּה לָמֶה תִבְכִּי וְלָמֶה לֹא תֹאכְלִי וְלָמֶה יֵרַע
לְבָבֵךְ הֲלוֹא אָנֹכִי טוֹב לָךְ מֵעֲשָׂרָה בָּנִים: וַתָּקָם חַנָּה אַחֲרֵי
אָכְלָה בְשִׁלֹה וְאַחֲרֵי שָׁתֹה וְעֵלִי הַכֹּהֵן יֹשֵׁב עַל־הַכִּסֵּא עַל־
מְזוּזַת הֵיכַל יְהוָה: וְהִיא מָרַת נָפֶשׁ וַתִּתְפַּלֵּל עַל־יְהוָה וּבָכֹה
תִבְכֶּה: וַתִּדֹּר נֶדֶר וַתֹּאמַר יְהוָה צְבָאוֹת אִם־רָאֹה תִרְאֶה ׀

---

HAFTARA – FIRST DAY: THE BIRTH OF SAMUEL
Hannah, childless, provoked, misunderstood, became an eternal symbol of Jewish prayer. To this day when we say the silent Amida, we do so in imitation of her: "She was speaking in her heart." From here we learn that one who prays must direct his heart. "Her lips were moving": one who prays must frame the words distinctly with his lips. "Her voice could not be heard": one must not raise one's voice (*Berakhot* 31a). Hannah's intimate, passionate prayer teaches us how to pray.

**הֲלוֹא אָנֹכִי טוֹב לָךְ מֵעֲשָׂרָה בָּנִים** *Am I not better to you than ten sons?* Elkana was wrong in not understanding Hannah's longing for a child. Marriage partners are required "not only to give to and accept from each other but also to make

if You see Your slave's agony, and remember me and do not forget Your slave, and if You give Your slave a son – I shall give him to the LORD all the days of his life, and no razor shall ever be lifted to his head." And as she continued to pray there, for a long time, before the LORD, Eli was watching her mouth. And Hannah, she was speaking in her heart: her lips were moving, her voice could not be heard, and Eli thought her drunk. And Eli said to her, "When will you stop acting the drunkard? Clear yourself of that wine." And Hannah said, "No, sir; I am a woman whose spirit has grown heavy, I have drunk neither new wine nor old; I have been pouring out my soul before the LORD. Do not look at your slave as if I were the lowest of the low; it is from the great burden of words on my mind and my torment that I spoke all this time." Then Eli said, "Go peacefully; and may the God of Israel grant you whatever it was you asked of Him." She said, "May your humble servant but deserve the grace you have shown her," and the woman went upon her way, and ate, and that expression she had worn, she wore no more. Early the next morning they got up and worshiped the LORD, and they went back, and came to their home at Ramah. And Elkana knew his wife Hannah – and the LORD remembered her. And in the fullness of time, Hannah conceived and gave birth to a son, and she named him Samuel, "because I asked him of the LORD." The man, Elkanah, and all his household, went up to make sacrifices to the LORD; the regular, yearly sacrifice and the offering he had vowed. But Hannah did not go up, for she said to her husband, "Not until the boy is weaned; then I shall bring him; he will appear before the LORD and he will stay there forever." "Do as you see fit," said Elkanah, her husband. "Stay until you have weaned him; and may the LORD but fulfill His own words." So the woman stayed there and she nursed her son, until she had weaned him. And when she had weaned him she brought him up with her, with three bulls, an *ephah* of flour and a flask of wine, and took him to the LORD's house in Shiloh; and the boy was yet young. They slaughtered

---

וַתִּקְרָא אֶת־שְׁמוֹ שְׁמוּאֵל כִּי מֵיהוה שְׁאִלְתִּיו *And she named him Samuel, "because I asked him of the LORD."* The phrase can also be translated as "I borrowed

בְּעֳנִ֣י אֲמָתֶ֗ךָ וּזְכַרְתַּ֙נִי֙ וְלֹא־תִשְׁכַּ֣ח אֶת־אֲמָתֶ֔ךָ וְנָתַתָּ֥ה לַאֲמָתְךָ֖
זֶ֣רַע אֲנָשִׁ֑ים וּנְתַתִּ֤יו לַֽיהוָה֙ כׇּל־יְמֵ֣י חַיָּ֔יו וּמוֹרָ֖ה לֹא־יַעֲלֶ֥ה עַל־
רֹאשֽׁוֹ׃ וְהָיָה֙ כִּ֣י הִרְבְּתָ֔ה לְהִתְפַּלֵּ֖ל לִפְנֵ֣י יְהוָ֑ה וְעֵלִ֖י שֹׁמֵ֥ר אֶת־
פִּֽיהָ׃ וְחַנָּ֗ה הִ֚יא מְדַבֶּ֣רֶת עַל־לִבָּ֔הּ רַ֚ק שְׂפָתֶ֣יהָ נָּע֔וֹת וְקוֹלָ֖הּ
לֹ֣א יִשָּׁמֵ֑עַ וַיַּחְשְׁבֶ֥הָ עֵלִ֖י לְשִׁכֹּרָֽה׃ וַיֹּ֤אמֶר אֵלֶ֙יהָ֙ עֵלִ֔י עַד־מָתַ֖י
תִּשְׁתַּכָּרִ֑ין הָסִ֥ירִי אֶת־יֵינֵ֖ךְ מֵעָלָֽיִךְ׃ וַתַּ֨עַן חַנָּ֤ה וַתֹּ֙אמֶר֙ לֹ֣א אֲדֹנִ֔י
אִשָּׁ֤ה קְשַׁת־ר֙וּחַ֙ אָנֹ֔כִי וְיַ֥יִן וְשֵׁכָ֖ר לֹ֣א שָׁתִ֑יתִי וָאֶשְׁפֹּ֥ךְ אֶת־נַפְשִׁ֖י
לִפְנֵ֥י יְהוָֽה׃ אַל־תִּתֵּן֙ אֶת־אֲמָ֣תְךָ֔ לִפְנֵ֖י בַּת־בְּלִיָּ֑עַל כִּֽי־מֵרֹ֥ב
שִׂיחִ֛י וְכַעְסִ֖י דִּבַּ֥רְתִּי עַד־הֵֽנָּה׃ וַיַּ֧עַן עֵלִ֛י וַיֹּ֖אמֶר לְכִ֣י לְשָׁל֑וֹם
וֵאלֹהֵ֣י יִשְׂרָאֵ֗ל יִתֵּן֙ אֶת־שֵׁ֣לָתֵ֔ךְ אֲשֶׁ֥ר שָׁאַ֖לְתְּ מֵעִמּֽוֹ׃ וַתֹּ֕אמֶר
תִּמְצָ֧א שִׁפְחָתְךָ֛ חֵ֖ן בְּעֵינֶ֑יךָ וַתֵּ֨לֶךְ הָאִשָּׁ֤ה לְדַרְכָּהּ֙ וַתֹּאכַ֔ל וּפָנֶ֥יהָ
לֹא־הָיוּ־לָ֖הּ עֽוֹד׃ וַיַּשְׁכִּ֣מוּ בַבֹּ֗קֶר וַיִּֽשְׁתַּחֲווּ֙ לִפְנֵ֣י יְהוָ֔ה וַיָּשֻׁ֕בוּ
וַיָּבֹ֥אוּ אֶל־בֵּיתָ֖ם הָרָמָ֑תָה וַיֵּ֤דַע אֶלְקָנָה֙ אֶת־חַנָּ֣ה אִשְׁתּ֔וֹ וַֽיִּזְכְּרֶ֖הָ
יְהוָֽה׃ וַיְהִי֙ לִתְקֻפ֣וֹת הַיָּמִ֔ים וַתַּ֥הַר חַנָּ֖ה וַתֵּ֣לֶד בֵּ֑ן וַתִּקְרָ֤א אֶת־
שְׁמוֹ֙ שְׁמוּאֵ֔ל כִּ֥י מֵיְהוָ֖ה שְׁאִלְתִּֽיו׃ וַיַּ֛עַל הָאִ֥ישׁ אֶלְקָנָ֖ה וְכׇל־
בֵּית֑וֹ לִזְבֹּ֧חַ לַֽיהוָ֛ה אֶת־זֶ֥בַח הַיָּמִ֖ים וְאֶת־נִדְרֽוֹ׃ וְחַנָּ֖ה לֹ֣א עָלָ֑תָה
כִּֽי־אָמְרָ֣ה לְאִישָׁ֗הּ עַ֣ד יִגָּמֵ֤ל הַנַּ֙עַר֙ וַהֲבִאֹתִ֗יו וְנִרְאָה֙ אֶת־פְּנֵ֣י
יְהוָ֔ה וְיָ֥שַׁב שָׁ֖ם עַד־עוֹלָֽם׃ וַיֹּ֣אמֶר לָהּ֩ אֶלְקָנָ֨ה אִישָׁ֜הּ עֲשִׂ֧י הַטּ֣וֹב
בְּעֵינַ֗יִךְ שְׁבִי֙ עַד־גׇּמְלֵ֣ךְ אֹת֔וֹ אַ֛ךְ יָקֵ֥ם יְהוָ֖ה אֶת־דְּבָר֑וֹ וַתֵּ֤שֶׁב
הָאִשָּׁה֙ וַתֵּ֣ינֶק אֶת־בְּנָ֔הּ עַד־גׇמְלָ֖הּ אֹתֽוֹ׃ וַתַּעֲלֵ֨הוּ עִמָּ֜הּ כַּאֲשֶׁ֣ר

---

us that our tears are heard and to give us the strength to cry (Rabbi Menaḥem Mendel of Kotzk).

לֹא אֲדֹנִי *No, Sir.* From this we learn that if we are wrongly suspected, we should clear our name (*Berakhot* 31b).

a bull and brought the boy to Eli. And she said, "Please, sir – sir, as you live, I am that woman who stood here with you and prayed to the Lord. It was for this boy that I prayed, and the Lord gave me what I asked of Him. Now I too give him over, to the Lord, forever: he is given over to the Lord" – and there he worshiped the Lord.

And Hannah prayed. She said:
My heart glories in the Lord, / my horns raised in pride by the Lord,
my mouth wide in scorn for my foes: / for my joy is in Your salvation.
There is none so holy as the Lord,
for there is none but You, / there is no Rock like our God.
Stop speaking high and mighty, on and on,
these swollen words that leave your mouths –
for the Lord is the God of knowledge, / His acts precisely measured;
the bows of strong heroes are broken,
while those who once stumbled gird greatness.
Those who were once full of bread go to hire, / while the hungry rest;
while the childless woman births seven children,
the mother of so many sons falls desolate.
The Lord kills, and He brings life,
He throws us down to hell and He lifts us.
The Lord makes destitute, enriches, / debases; He raises –
He lifts the poor out of the dust,
and raises abject men from the dunghills,
to seat them up there with princes, / to bequeath them chairs of honor,
for the earth's precipices are the Lord's
and upon them He balances all the world.
He will guard the steps of His followers,
while the evil are silenced in darkness,
for it is not by strength that men master.
The Lord – His opponents are broken,
He thunders the skies above them,
the Lord will judge to the ends of the earth,
will grant His own king strength,
He will raise proud the horns of His anointed.

גְּמָלַתּוּ בְּפָרִים שְׁלֹשָׁה וְאֵיפָה אַחַת קֶמַח וְנֵבֶל יַיִן וַתְּבִאֵהוּ
בֵית־יהוה שִׁלוֹ וְהַנַּעַר נָעַר: וַיִּשְׁחֲטוּ אֶת־הַפָּר וַיָּבִאוּ אֶת־הַנַּעַר
אֶל־עֵלִי: וַתֹּאמֶר בִּי אֲדֹנִי חֵי נַפְשְׁךָ אֲדֹנִי אֲנִי הָאִשָּׁה הַנִּצֶּבֶת
עִמְּכָה בָּזֶה לְהִתְפַּלֵּל אֶל־יהוה: אֶל־הַנַּעַר הַזֶּה הִתְפַּלָּלְתִּי
וַיִּתֵּן יהוה לִי אֶת־שְׁאֵלָתִי אֲשֶׁר שָׁאַלְתִּי מֵעִמּוֹ: וְגַם אָנֹכִי
הִשְׁאִלְתִּהוּ לַיהוה כָּל־הַיָּמִים אֲשֶׁר הָיָה הוּא שָׁאוּל לַיהוה
וַיִּשְׁתַּחוּ שָׁם לַיהוה: וַתִּתְפַּלֵּל חַנָּה וַתֹּאמַר עָלַץ
לִבִּי בַּיהוה רָמָה קַרְנִי בַּיהוה רָחַב פִּי עַל־אוֹיְבַי כִּי שָׂמַחְתִּי
בִּישׁוּעָתֶךָ: אֵין־קָדוֹשׁ כַּיהוה כִּי־אֵין בִּלְתֶּךָ וְאֵין צוּר כֵּאלֹהֵינוּ:
אַל־תַּרְבּוּ תְדַבְּרוּ גְּבֹהָה גְבֹהָה יֵצֵא עָתָק מִפִּיכֶם כִּי אֵל דֵּעוֹת
יהוה ולא נִתְכְּנוּ עֲלִלוֹת: קֶשֶׁת גִּבֹּרִים חַתִּים וְנִכְשָׁלִים אָזְרוּ וְלוֹ
חָיִל: שְׂבֵעִים בַּלֶּחֶם נִשְׂכָּרוּ וּרְעֵבִים חָדֵלּוּ עַד־עֲקָרָה יָלְדָה
שִׁבְעָה וְרַבַּת בָּנִים אֻמְלָלָה: יהוה מֵמִית וּמְחַיֶּה מוֹרִיד שְׁאוֹל
וַיָּעַל: יהוה מוֹרִישׁ וּמַעֲשִׁיר מַשְׁפִּיל אַף־מְרוֹמֵם: מֵקִים מֵעָפָר
דָּל מֵאַשְׁפֹּת יָרִים אֶבְיוֹן לְהוֹשִׁיב עִם־נְדִיבִים וְכִסֵּא כָבוֹד יַנְחִלֵם
כִּי לַיהוה מְצֻקֵי אֶרֶץ וַיָּשֶׁת עֲלֵיהֶם תֵּבֵל: רַגְלֵי חֲסִידָו יִשְׁמֹר
וּרְשָׁעִים בַּחֹשֶׁךְ יִדָּמּוּ כִּי־לֹא בְכֹחַ יִגְבַּר־אִישׁ: יהוה יֵחַתּוּ מְרִיבָו
עָלָו בַּשָּׁמַיִם יַרְעֵם יהוה יָדִין אַפְסֵי־אָרֶץ וְיִתֶּן־עֹז לְמַלְכּוֹ וְיָרֵם
קֶרֶן מְשִׁיחוֹ:

---

him from the LORD." Our children do not belong to us, but to God and to themselves. "In the covenantal community, the urge to love is purged of its egotistical, instinctual elements and turns into a need to serve, to sacrifice… [The mother] teaches, educates, trains, and consecrates the child to God" (*Family Redeemed*, p. 112).

## BLESSINGS AFTER THE HAFTARA

*After the Haftara, the person called up for Maftir says the following blessings:*

בָּרוּךְ Blessed are You, Lord our God, King of the Universe, Rock of all worlds, righteous for all generations, the faithful God who says and does, speaks and fulfills, all of whose words are truth and righteousness. You are faithful, Lord our God, and faithful are Your words, not one of which returns unfulfilled, for You, God, are a faithful and compassionate King. Blessed are You, Lord, faithful in all His words.

רַחֵם Have compassion on Zion for it is the source of our life, and save the one grieved in spirit swiftly in our days. Blessed are You, Lord, who makes Zion rejoice in her children.

שַׂמְּחֵנוּ Grant us joy, Lord our God, through Elijah the prophet Your servant, and through the kingdom of the house of David Your anointed – may he soon come and make our hearts glad. May no stranger sit on his throne, and may others not continue to inherit his glory, for You promised him by Your holy name that his light would never be extinguished. Blessed are You, Lord, Shield of David.

*On Shabbat, add the words in parentheses:*

עַל הַתּוֹרָה For the Torah, for Divine worship, for the prophets, (for this Sabbath day) and for this Day of Remembrance, which You, Lord our God, have given us (for holiness and rest), for honor and glory – for all these we thank and bless You, Lord our God, and may Your name be blessed by the mouth of all that lives, continually, for ever and all time, for Your word is true and endures for ever. Blessed are You, Lord, King over all the earth, who sanctifies (the Sabbath,) Israel and the Day of Remembrance.

*On a weekday, the service continues with the various prayers for government on page 458.*

*On Shabbat continue:*

יְקוּם פֻּרְקָן May deliverance arise from heaven, bringing grace, love and compassion, long life, ample sustenance and heavenly help, physical health and enlightenment of mind, living and thriving children who

---

and thus "mirror more faithfully than any other part of the Siddur the diversity and versatility of the Jewish experience."

יְקוּם פֻּרְקָן *May deliverance arise.* A prayer for the religious and lay leadership of Babylonian Jewry, dating from a period – the Talmudic and Geonic

## ברכות לאחר ההפטרה

*After the* הפטרה*, the person called up for* מפטיר *says the following blessings:*

בָּרוּךְ אַתָּה יהוה אֱלֹהֵינוּ מֶלֶךְ הָעוֹלָם, צוּר כָּל הָעוֹלָמִים, צַדִּיק בְּכָל הַדּוֹרוֹת, הָאֵל הַנֶּאֱמָן, הָאוֹמֵר וְעוֹשֶׂה, הַמְדַבֵּר וּמְקַיֵּם, שֶׁכָּל דְּבָרָיו אֱמֶת וָצֶדֶק. נֶאֱמָן אַתָּה הוּא יהוה אֱלֹהֵינוּ וְנֶאֱמָנִים דְּבָרֶיךָ, וְדָבָר אֶחָד מִדְּבָרֶיךָ אָחוֹר לֹא יָשׁוּב רֵיקָם, כִּי אֵל מֶלֶךְ נֶאֱמָן וְרַחֲמָן אָתָּה. בָּרוּךְ אַתָּה יהוה, הָאֵל הַנֶּאֱמָן בְּכָל דְּבָרָיו.

רַחֵם עַל צִיּוֹן כִּי הִיא בֵּית חַיֵּינוּ, וְלַעֲלוּבַת נֶפֶשׁ תּוֹשִׁיעַ בִּמְהֵרָה בְיָמֵינוּ. בָּרוּךְ אַתָּה יהוה, מְשַׂמֵּחַ צִיּוֹן בְּבָנֶיהָ.

שַׂמְּחֵנוּ יהוה אֱלֹהֵינוּ בְּאֵלִיָּהוּ הַנָּבִיא עַבְדֶּךָ, וּבְמַלְכוּת בֵּית דָּוִד מְשִׁיחֶךָ, בִּמְהֵרָה יָבוֹא וְיָגֵל לִבֵּנוּ. עַל כִּסְאוֹ לֹא יֵשֶׁב זָר, וְלֹא יִנְחֲלוּ עוֹד אֲחֵרִים אֶת כְּבוֹדוֹ, כִּי בְשֵׁם קָדְשְׁךָ נִשְׁבַּעְתָּ לּוֹ שֶׁלֹּא יִכְבֶּה נֵרוֹ לְעוֹלָם וָעֶד. בָּרוּךְ אַתָּה יהוה, מָגֵן דָּוִד.

*On* שבת*, add the words in parentheses:*

עַל הַתּוֹרָה וְעַל הָעֲבוֹדָה וְעַל הַנְּבִיאִים (וְעַל יוֹם הַשַּׁבָּת הַזֶּה) וְעַל יוֹם הַזִּכָּרוֹן הַזֶּה, שֶׁנָּתַתָּ לָּנוּ יהוה אֱלֹהֵינוּ (לִקְדֻשָּׁה וְלִמְנוּחָה) לְכָבוֹד וּלְתִפְאָרֶת. עַל הַכֹּל יהוה אֱלֹהֵינוּ אֲנַחְנוּ מוֹדִים לָךְ וּמְבָרְכִים אוֹתָךְ, יִתְבָּרַךְ שִׁמְךָ בְּפִי כָּל חַי תָּמִיד לְעוֹלָם וָעֶד, וּדְבָרְךָ אֱמֶת וְקַיָּם לָעַד. בָּרוּךְ אַתָּה יהוה, מֶלֶךְ עַל כָּל הָאָרֶץ, מְקַדֵּשׁ (הַשַּׁבָּת וְ) יִשְׂרָאֵל וְיוֹם הַזִּכָּרוֹן.

*On a weekday, the service continues with the various prayers for government on page 459.*
*On* שבת *continue:*

יְקוּם פֻּרְקָן מִן שְׁמַיָּא, חִנָּא וְחִסְדָּא וְרַחֲמֵי וְחַיֵּי אֲרִיכֵי וּמְזוֹנֵי רְוִיחֵי, וְסִיַּעְתָּא דִשְׁמַיָּא, וּבַרְיוּת גּוּפָא וּנְהוֹרָא מְעַלְּיָא, זַרְעָא חַיָּא וְקַיָּמָא,

---

*Special Prayers.* A series of prayers for Jewish communities and their leadership. As Lord Jakobovits pointed out, they originate from different centuries and locations, they use three languages, Aramaic, Hebrew and the vernacular,

will neither interrupt nor cease from the words of the Torah – to our masters and teachers of the holy communities in the land of Israel and Babylon; to the leaders of assemblies and the leaders of communities in exile; to the heads of academies and to the judges in the gates; to all their disciples and their disciples' disciples, and to all who occupy themselves in study of the Torah. May the King of the Universe bless them, prolonging their lives, increasing their days, and adding to their years. May they be redeemed and delivered from all distress and illness. May our Master in heaven be their help at all times and seasons; and let us say: Amen.

יְקוּם פֻּרְקָן May deliverance arise from heaven, bringing grace, love and compassion, long life, ample sustenance and heavenly help, physical health and enlightenment of mind, living and thriving children who will neither interrupt nor cease from the words of the Torah – to all this holy congregation, great and small, women and children. May the King of the Universe bless you, prolonging your lives, increasing your days, and adding to your years. May you be redeemed and delivered from all distress and illness. May our Master in heaven be your help at all times and seasons; and let us say: Amen.

מִי שֶׁבֵּרַךְ May He who blessed our fathers, Abraham, Isaac and Jacob, bless all this holy congregation, together with all other holy congregations: them, their wives, their sons and daughters, and all that is theirs. May He bless those who unite to form synagogues for prayer and those who come there to pray; those who provide lamps for light and wine for Kiddush and Havdala, food for visitors and charity for the poor, and all who faithfully occupy themselves with the needs of the community. May the Holy One, blessed be He, give them their reward; may He remove from them all illness, grant them complete healing, and forgive all their sins. May He send blessing and success to all the work of their hands, together with all Israel their brethren; and let us say: Amen.

---

eras – when Babylonia was a major center of Jewish life. The phrase "and all the lands of our dispersion" was added to make the prayer relevant to other centers. The next two blessings – one in Aramaic and based on the previous prayer, the other in Hebrew – are for all those who work for and sustain the congregation.

זַרְעָא דִּי לָא יִפְסֻק וְדִי לָא יִבְטֻל מִפִּתְגָּמֵי אוֹרַיְתָא, לְמָרָנָן וְרַבָּנָן חֲבוּרָתָא קַדִּישָׁתָא דִּי בְּאַרְעָא דְיִשְׂרָאֵל וְדִי בְּבָבֶל, לְרֵישֵׁי כַלָּה, וּלְרֵישֵׁי גָלְוָתָא, וּלְרֵישֵׁי מְתִיבָתָא, וּלְדַיָּנֵי דְבָבָא, לְכָל תַּלְמִידֵיהוֹן, וּלְכָל תַּלְמִידֵי תַלְמִידֵיהוֹן, וּלְכָל מָאן דְּעָסְקִין בְּאוֹרַיְתָא. מַלְכָּא דְעָלְמָא יְבָרֵךְ יָתְהוֹן, יַפֵּשׁ חַיֵּיהוֹן וְיַסְגֵּא יוֹמֵיהוֹן, וְיִתֵּן אַרְכָא לִשְׁנֵיהוֹן, וְיִתְפָּרְקוּן וְיִשְׁתֵּיזְבוּן מִן כָּל עָקָא וּמִן כָּל מַרְעִין בִּישִׁין. מָרַן דִּי בִשְׁמַיָּא יְהֵא בְסַעְדְּהוֹן כָּל זְמַן וְעִדָּן, וְנֹאמַר אָמֵן.

יְקוּם פֻּרְקָן מִן שְׁמַיָּא, חִנָּא וְחִסְדָּא וְרַחֲמֵי וְחַיֵּי אֲרִיכֵי וּמְזוֹנֵי רְוִיחֵי, וְסִיַּעְתָּא דִשְׁמַיָּא, וּבַרְיוּת גּוּפָא וּנְהוֹרָא מְעַלְיָא, זַרְעָא חַיָּא וְקַיָּמָא, זַרְעָא דִּי לָא יִפְסֻק וְדִי לָא יִבְטֻל מִפִּתְגָּמֵי אוֹרַיְתָא, לְכָל קְהָלָא קַדִּישָׁא הָדֵין, רַבְרְבַיָּא עִם זְעֵרַיָּא, טַפְלָא וּנְשַׁיָּא. מַלְכָּא דְעָלְמָא יְבָרֵךְ יָתְכוֹן, יַפֵּשׁ חַיֵּיכוֹן וְיַסְגֵּא יוֹמֵיכוֹן, וְיִתֵּן אַרְכָא לִשְׁנֵיכוֹן, וְתִתְפָּרְקוּן וְתִשְׁתֵּיזְבוּן מִן כָּל עָקָא וּמִן כָּל מַרְעִין בִּישִׁין. מָרַן דִּי בִשְׁמַיָּא יְהֵא בְסַעְדְּכוֹן כָּל זְמַן וְעִדָּן, וְנֹאמַר אָמֵן.

מִי שֶׁבֵּרַךְ אֲבוֹתֵינוּ אַבְרָהָם יִצְחָק וְיַעֲקֹב, הוּא יְבָרֵךְ אֶת כָּל הַקָּהָל הַקָּדוֹשׁ הַזֶּה עִם כָּל קְהִלּוֹת הַקֹּדֶשׁ, הֵם וּנְשֵׁיהֶם וּבְנֵיהֶם וּבְנוֹתֵיהֶם וְכָל אֲשֶׁר לָהֶם, וּמִי שֶׁמְּיַחֲדִים בָּתֵּי כְנֵסִיּוֹת לִתְפִלָּה, וּמִי שֶׁבָּאִים בְּתוֹכָם לְהִתְפַּלֵּל, וּמִי שֶׁנּוֹתְנִים נֵר לַמָּאוֹר וְיַיִן לְקִדּוּשׁ וּלְהַבְדָּלָה וּפַת לָאוֹרְחִים וּצְדָקָה לָעֲנִיִּים, וְכָל מִי שֶׁעוֹסְקִים בְּצָרְכֵי צִבּוּר בֶּאֱמוּנָה. הַקָּדוֹשׁ בָּרוּךְ הוּא יְשַׁלֵּם שְׂכָרָם, וְיָסִיר מֵהֶם כָּל מַחֲלָה, וְיִרְפָּא לְכָל גּוּפָם, וְיִסְלַח לְכָל עֲוֹנָם, וְיִשְׁלַח בְּרָכָה וְהַצְלָחָה בְּכָל מַעֲשֵׂי יְדֵיהֶם עִם כָּל יִשְׂרָאֵל אֲחֵיהֶם, וְנֹאמַר אָמֵן.

*The Prayer for the Welfare of the Canadian Government is on the next page.*

## PRAYER FOR THE WELFARE OF THE AMERICAN GOVERNMENT

*The Leader says the following:*

**הַנּוֹתֵן תְּשׁוּעָה** May He who gives salvation to kings and dominion to princes, whose kingdom is an everlasting kingdom, who delivers His servant David from the evil sword, who makes a way in the sea and a path through the mighty waters, bless and protect, guard and help, exalt, magnify and uplift the President, Vice President and all officials of this land. May the Supreme King of kings in His mercy put into their hearts and the hearts of all their counselors and officials, to deal kindly with us and all Israel. In their days and in ours, may Judah be saved and Israel dwell in safety, and may the Redeemer come to Zion. May this be His will, and let us say: Amen.

## PRAYER FOR THE SAFETY OF THE AMERICAN MILITARY FORCES

*The Leader says the following:*

**אַדִּיר בַּמָּרוֹם** God on high who dwells in might, the King to whom peace belongs, look down from Your holy habitation and bless the soldiers of the American military forces who risk their lives for the sake of peace on earth. Be their shelter and stronghold, and let them not falter. Give them the strength and courage to thwart the plans of the enemy and end the rule of evil. May their enemies be scattered and their foes flee before them, and may they rejoice in Your salvation. Bring them back safely to their homes, as is written: "The Lord *Ps. 121* will guard you from all harm, He will guard your life. The Lord will guard your going and coming, now and for evermore." And may there be fulfilled for us the verse: "Nation shall not lift up sword against *Is. 2* nation, nor shall they learn war any more." Let all the inhabitants on earth know that sovereignty is Yours and Your name inspires awe over all You have created – and let us say: Amen.

---

the Babylonian exile (sixth century BCE): "Seek the peace of the city to which I have carried you in exile. Pray to the Lord for it, because in its peace, you shall find peace." Similar guidance was given at a later period (first century CE)

*The Prayer for the Welfare of the Canadian Government is on the next page.*

תפילה לשלום המלכות

*The* שליח ציבור *says the following:*

הַנּוֹתֵן תְּשׁוּעָה לַמְּלָכִים וּמֶמְשָׁלָה לַנְּסִיכִים, מַלְכוּתוֹ מַלְכוּת כָּל עוֹלָמִים, הַפּוֹצֶה אֶת דָּוִד עַבְדּוֹ מֵחֶרֶב רָעָה, הַנּוֹתֵן בַּיָּם דֶּרֶךְ וּבְמַיִם עַזִּים נְתִיבָה, הוּא יְבָרֵךְ וְיִשְׁמֹר וְיִנְצֹר וְיַעֲזֹר וִירוֹמֵם וִיגַדֵּל וִינַשֵּׂא לְמַעְלָה אֶת הַנָּשִׂיא וְאֵת מִשְׁנֵהוּ וְאֶת כָּל שָׂרֵי הָאָרֶץ הַזֹּאת. מֶלֶךְ מַלְכֵי הַמְּלָכִים, בְּרַחֲמָיו יִתֵּן בְּלִבָּם וּבְלֵב כָּל יוֹעֲצֵיהֶם וְשָׂרֵיהֶם לַעֲשׂוֹת טוֹבָה עִמָּנוּ וְעִם כָּל יִשְׂרָאֵל. בִּימֵיהֶם וּבְיָמֵינוּ תִּוָּשַׁע יְהוּדָה, וְיִשְׂרָאֵל יִשְׁכֹּן לָבֶטַח, וּבָא לְצִיּוֹן גּוֹאֵל. וְכֵן יְהִי רָצוֹן, וְנֹאמַר אָמֵן.

תפילה לשלום חיילי צבא ארצות הברית

*The* שליח ציבור *says the following:*

אַדִּיר בַּמָּרוֹם שׁוֹכֵן בִּגְבוּרָה, מֶלֶךְ שֶׁהַשָּׁלוֹם שֶׁלּוֹ, הַשְׁקִיפָה מִמְּעוֹן קָדְשֶׁךָ, וּבָרֵךְ אֶת חַיָּלֵי צְבָא אַרְצוֹת הַבְּרִית, הַמְחָרְפִים נַפְשָׁם בְּלֶכְתָּם לָשִׂים שָׁלוֹם בָּאָרֶץ. הֱיֵה נָא לָהֶם מַחֲסֶה וּמָעוֹז, וְאַל תִּתֵּן לַמּוֹט רַגְלָם, חַזֵּק יְדֵיהֶם וְאַמֵּץ רוּחָם לְהָפֵר עֲצַת אוֹיֵב וּלְהַעֲבִיר מֶמְשֶׁלֶת זָדוֹן, יָפוּצוּ אוֹיְבֵיהֶם וְיָנוּסוּ מְשַׂנְאֵיהֶם מִפְּנֵיהֶם, וְיִשְׂמְחוּ בִּישׁוּעָתֶךָ. הֲשִׁיבֵם בְּשָׁלוֹם אֶל בֵּיתָם, כַּכָּתוּב בְּדִבְרֵי קָדְשֶׁךָ:
תהלים קכא יהוה יִשְׁמָרְךָ מִכָּל־רָע, יִשְׁמֹר אֶת־נַפְשֶׁךָ: יהוה יִשְׁמָר־צֵאתְךָ
ישעיה ב וּבוֹאֶךָ, מֵעַתָּה וְעַד־עוֹלָם: וְקַיֵּם בָּנוּ מִקְרָא שֶׁכָּתוּב: לֹא־יִשָּׂא גוֹי
אֶל־גּוֹי חֶרֶב, וְלֹא־יִלְמְדוּ עוֹד מִלְחָמָה: וְיֵדְעוּ כָּל יוֹשְׁבֵי תֵבֵל כִּי לְךָ מְלוּכָה יָאֲתָה, וְשִׁמְךָ נוֹרָא עַל כָּל מַה שֶּׁבָּרָאתָ. וְנֹאמַר אָמֵן.

---

תפילה לשלום המלכות *Prayer for the Welfare of the Government.* This prayer echoes the instruction of Jeremiah (29:7) to those dispersed at the time of

## PRAYER FOR THE WELFARE OF THE CANADIAN GOVERNMENT

*The Leader says the following:*

הַנּוֹתֵן תְּשׁוּעָה May He who gives salvation to kings and dominion to princes, whose kingdom is an everlasting kingdom, who delivers His servant David from the evil sword, who makes a way in the sea and a path through the mighty waters, bless and protect, guard and help, exalt, magnify and uplift the Prime Minister and all the elected and appointed officials of Canada. May the Supreme King of kings in His mercy put into their hearts and the hearts of all their counselors and officials, to deal kindly with us and all Israel. In their days and in ours, may Judah be saved and Israel dwell in safety, and may the Redeemer come to Zion. May this be His will, and let us say: Amen.

## PRAYER FOR THE SAFETY OF THE CANADIAN MILITARY FORCES

*The Leader says the following:*

אַדִּיר בַּמָּרוֹם God on high who dwells in might, the King to whom peace belongs, look down from Your holy habitation and bless the soldiers of the Canadian Forces who risk their lives for the sake of peace on earth. Be their shelter and stronghold, and let them not falter. Give them the strength and courage to thwart the plans of the enemy and end the rule of evil. May their enemies be scattered and their foes flee before them, and may they rejoice in Your salvation. Bring them back safely to their homes, as is written: "The LORD will guard you *Ps. 121* from all harm, He will guard your life. The LORD will guard your going and coming, now and for evermore." And may there be fulfilled for us the verse: "Nation shall not lift up sword against nation, nor shall *Is. 2* they learn war any more." Let all the inhabitants on earth know that sovereignty is Yours and Your name inspires awe over all You have created – and let us say: Amen.

---

it, people would swallow one another alive" (*Avot* 3:2). To be a Jew is to be loyal to the country in which we live, to work for the common good and for the good of all humankind, to care for the welfare of others, and to work for good relations between different groups.

## תפילה לשלום המלכות

*The* שליח ציבור *says the following:*

הַנּוֹתֵן תְּשׁוּעָה לַמְּלָכִים וּמֶמְשָׁלָה לַנְּסִיכִים, מַלְכוּתוֹ מַלְכוּת כָּל עוֹלָמִים, הַפּוֹצֶה אֶת דָּוִד עַבְדּוֹ מֵחֶרֶב רָעָה, הַנּוֹתֵן בַּיָּם דֶּרֶךְ וּבְמַיִם עַזִּים נְתִיבָה, הוּא יְבָרֵךְ וְיִשְׁמֹר וְיִנְצֹר וְיַעֲזֹר וִירוֹמֵם וִיגַדֵּל וִינַשֵּׂא לְמַעְלָה אֶת רֹאשׁ הַמֶּמְשָׁלָה וְאֶת כָּל שָׂרֵי הָאָרֶץ הַזֹּאת. מֶלֶךְ מַלְכֵי הַמְּלָכִים, בְּרַחֲמָיו יִתֵּן בְּלִבָּם וּבְלֵב כָּל יוֹעֲצֵיהֶם וְשָׂרֵיהֶם לַעֲשׂוֹת טוֹבָה עִמָּנוּ וְעִם כָּל יִשְׂרָאֵל. בִּימֵיהֶם וּבְיָמֵינוּ תִּוָּשַׁע יְהוּדָה, וְיִשְׂרָאֵל יִשְׁכֹּן לָבֶטַח, וּבָא לְצִיּוֹן גּוֹאֵל. וְכֵן יְהִי רָצוֹן, וְנֹאמַר אָמֵן.

## תפילה לשלום חיילי צבא קנדה

*The* שליח ציבור *says the following:*

אַדִּיר בַּמָּרוֹם שׁוֹכֵן בִּגְבוּרָה, מֶלֶךְ שֶׁהַשָּׁלוֹם שֶׁלּוֹ, הַשְׁקִיפָה מִמְּעוֹן קָדְשְׁךָ, וּבָרֵךְ אֶת חַיָּלֵי צְבָא קָנָדָה, הַמְחָרְפִים נַפְשָׁם בְּלֶכְתָּם לָשִׂים שָׁלוֹם בָּאָרֶץ. הֱיֵה נָא לָהֶם מַחֲסֶה וּמָעוֹז, וְאַל תִּתֵּן לַמּוֹט רַגְלָם, חַזֵּק יְדֵיהֶם וְאַמֵּץ רוּחָם לְהָפֵר עֲצַת אוֹיֵב וּלְהַעֲבִיר מֶמְשֶׁלֶת זָדוֹן, יָפוּצוּ אוֹיְבֵיהֶם וְיָנוּסוּ מְשַׂנְאֵיהֶם מִפְּנֵיהֶם, וְיִשְׂמְחוּ בִּישׁוּעָתֶךָ.
הֲשִׁיבֵם בְּשָׁלוֹם אֶל בֵּיתָם, כַּכָּתוּב בְּדִבְרֵי קָדְשֶׁךָ: יהוה יִשְׁמָרְךָ תהלים קכא
מִכָּל־רָע, יִשְׁמֹר אֶת־נַפְשֶׁךָ: יהוה יִשְׁמָר־צֵאתְךָ וּבוֹאֶךָ, מֵעַתָּה
וְעַד־עוֹלָם: וְקַיֵּם בָּנוּ מִקְרָא שֶׁכָּתוּב: לֹא־יִשָּׂא גוֹי אֶל־גּוֹי חֶרֶב, ישעיה ב
וְלֹא־יִלְמְדוּ עוֹד מִלְחָמָה: וְיֵדְעוּ כָּל יוֹשְׁבֵי תֵבֵל כִּי לְךָ מְלוּכָה יָאֲתָה, וְשִׁמְךָ נוֹרָא עַל כָּל מַה שֶּׁבָּרָאתָ. וְנֹאמַר אָמֵן.

---

after the Roman conquest of Jerusalem: "Rabbi Ḥanina, the deputy High Priest, said: Pray for the welfare of the government, for were it not for fear of

## PRAYER FOR THE STATE OF ISRAEL

*The Leader says the following prayer:*

אָבִינוּ שֶׁבַּשָּׁמַיִם Heavenly Father, Israel's Rock and Redeemer, bless the State of Israel, the first flowering of our redemption. Shield it under the wings of Your loving-kindness and spread over it the Tabernacle of Your peace. Send Your light and truth to its leaders, ministers and counselors, and direct them with good counsel before You.

Strengthen the hands of the defenders of our Holy Land; grant them deliverance, our God, and crown them with the crown of victory. Grant peace in the land and everlasting joy to its inhabitants.

As for our brothers, the whole house of Israel, remember them in all the lands of our (*In Israel:* their) dispersion, and swiftly lead us (*In Israel:* them) upright to Zion Your city, and Jerusalem Your dwelling place, as is written in the Torah of Moses Your servant: "Even if you are scattered to the furthermost lands under the heavens, from there the LORD your God will gather you and take you back. The LORD your God will bring you to the land your ancestors possessed and you will possess it; and He will make you more prosperous and numerous than your ancestors. Then the LORD your God will open up your heart and the heart of your descendants, to love the LORD your God with all your heart and with all your soul, that you may live." *Deut. 30*

Unite our hearts to love and revere Your name and observe all the words of Your Torah, and swiftly send us Your righteous anointed one of the house of David, to redeem those who long for Your salvation.

Appear in Your glorious majesty over all the dwellers on earth, and let all who breathe declare: The LORD God of Israel is King and His kingship has dominion over all. Amen, Selah.

---

flowering of our redemption," a spiritual event in religious time. The return of Jews to the land of their ancestors in fulfillment of the vision of the prophets, their recovery of independence as a sovereign nation after two thousand years of dispersion and powerlessness, and their reaffirmation of life after the Holocaust: these form a new and epoch-making chapter in the narrative begun in the book of Genesis, when Abraham and Sarah heeded God's call and set out on the journey "to the land that I will show you" (12:1).

## תפילה לשלום מדינת ישראל

*The* שליח ציבור *says the following prayer:*

אָבִינוּ שֶׁבַּשָּׁמַיִם, צוּר יִשְׂרָאֵל וְגוֹאֲלוֹ, בָּרֵךְ אֶת מְדִינַת יִשְׂרָאֵל, רֵאשִׁית צְמִיחַת גְּאֻלָּתֵנוּ. הָגֵן עָלֶיהָ בְּאֶבְרַת חַסְדֶּךָ וּפְרֹשׂ עָלֶיהָ סֻכַּת שְׁלוֹמֶךָ, וּשְׁלַח אוֹרְךָ וַאֲמִתְּךָ לְרָאשֶׁיהָ, שָׂרֶיהָ וְיוֹעֲצֶיהָ, וְתַקְּנֵם בְּעֵצָה טוֹבָה מִלְּפָנֶיךָ.

חַזֵּק אֶת יְדֵי מְגִנֵּי אֶרֶץ קָדְשֵׁנוּ, וְהַנְחִילֵם אֱלֹהֵינוּ יְשׁוּעָה וַעֲטֶרֶת נִצָּחוֹן תְּעַטְּרֵם, וְנָתַתָּ שָׁלוֹם בָּאָרֶץ וְשִׂמְחַת עוֹלָם לְיוֹשְׁבֶיהָ.

וְאֶת אַחֵינוּ כָּל בֵּית יִשְׂרָאֵל, פְּקָד נָא בְּכָל אַרְצוֹת פְּזוּרֵינוּ, וְתוֹלִיכֵנוּ
/בארץ ישראל: פְּזוּרֵיהֶם, וְתוֹלִיכֵם/ מְהֵרָה קוֹמְמִיּוּת לְצִיּוֹן עִירֶךָ וְלִירוּשָׁלַיִם
מִשְׁכַּן שְׁמֶךָ, כַּכָּתוּב בְּתוֹרַת מֹשֶׁה עַבְדֶּךָ: אִם־יִהְיֶה נִדַּחֲךָ בִּקְצֵה דברים ל
הַשָּׁמָיִם, מִשָּׁם יְקַבֶּצְךָ יהוה אֱלֹהֶיךָ וּמִשָּׁם יִקָּחֶךָ: וֶהֱבִיאֲךָ יהוה
אֱלֹהֶיךָ אֶל־הָאָרֶץ אֲשֶׁר־יָרְשׁוּ אֲבֹתֶיךָ וִירִשְׁתָּהּ, וְהֵיטִבְךָ וְהִרְבְּךָ
מֵאֲבֹתֶיךָ: וּמָל יהוה אֱלֹהֶיךָ אֶת־לְבָבְךָ וְאֶת־לְבַב זַרְעֶךָ, לְאַהֲבָה
אֶת־יהוה אֱלֹהֶיךָ בְּכָל־לְבָבְךָ וּבְכָל־נַפְשְׁךָ, לְמַעַן חַיֶּיךָ:

וְיַחֵד לְבָבֵנוּ לְאַהֲבָה וּלְיִרְאָה אֶת שְׁמֶךָ, וְלִשְׁמֹר אֶת כָּל דִּבְרֵי תּוֹרָתֶךָ, וּשְׁלַח לָנוּ מְהֵרָה בֶּן דָּוִד מְשִׁיחַ צִדְקֶךָ, לִפְדּוֹת מְחַכֵּי קֵץ יְשׁוּעָתֶךָ.

וְהוֹפַע בַּהֲדַר גְּאוֹן עֻזֶּךָ עַל כָּל יוֹשְׁבֵי תֵבֵל אַרְצֶךָ, וְיֹאמַר כֹּל אֲשֶׁר נְשָׁמָה בְאַפּוֹ, יהוה אֱלֹהֵי יִשְׂרָאֵל מֶלֶךְ וּמַלְכוּתוֹ בַּכֹּל מָשָׁלָה, אָמֵן סֶלָה.

---

PRAYER FOR THE STATE OF ISRAEL

Composed on the birth of the modern State of Israel by its then Chief Rabbi, Isaac HaLevy Herzog. The prayer is notable for its theological statement that the birth of the State was not just a political event in secular time, but "the first

## PRAYER FOR ISRAEL'S DEFENSE FORCES

*The Leader says the following prayer:*

מִי שֶׁבֵּרַךְ May He who blessed our ancestors, Abraham, Isaac and Jacob, bless the members of Israel's Defense Forces and its security services who stand guard over our land and the cities of our God, from the Lebanese border to the Egyptian desert, from the Mediterranean sea to the approach of the Aravah, and wherever else they are, on land, in air and at sea. May the Lord make the enemies who rise against us be struck down before them. May the Holy One, blessed be He, protect and deliver them from all trouble and distress, affliction and illness, and send blessing and success to all the work of their hands. May He subdue our enemies under them and crown them with deliverance and victory. And may there be fulfilled in them the verse, "It is the Lord your God *Deut. 20* who goes with you to fight for you against your enemies, to deliver you." And let us say: Amen.

## PRAYER FOR THOSE BEING HELD IN CAPTIVITY

*If Israeli soldiers or civilians are being held in captivity, the Leader says the following:*

מִי שֶׁבֵּרַךְ May He who blessed our ancestors, Abraham, Isaac and Jacob, Joseph, Moses and Aaron, David and Solomon, bless, protect and guard the members of Israel's Defense Forces missing in action or held captive, and other captives among our brethren, the whole house of Israel, who are in distress or captivity, as we, the members of this holy congregation, pray on their behalf. May the Holy One, blessed be He, have compassion on them and bring them out from darkness and the shadow of death; may He break their bonds, deliver them from their distress, and bring them swiftly back to their families' embrace. Give thanks to the Lord *Ps. 107* for His loving-kindness and for the wonders He does for the children of men; and may there be fulfilled in them the verse: "Those redeemed by *Is. 35* the Lord will return; they will enter Zion with singing, and everlasting joy will crown their heads. Gladness and joy will overtake them, and sorrow and sighing will flee away." And let us say: Amen.

---

Israel in modern times have known all too little peace. This prayer ends with the words said in biblical times by the priest "anointed for battle" (Deut. 20:3–4), reminding us that Israel's strength is its faith: "Not by might nor by power, but by My spirit, says the Lord of hosts" (Zech. 4:6).

## מי שברך לחיילי צה״ל

*The* שליח ציבור *says the following prayer:*

מִי שֶׁבֵּרַךְ אֲבוֹתֵינוּ אַבְרָהָם יִצְחָק וְיַעֲקֹב הוּא יְבָרֵךְ אֶת חַיָּלֵי
צְבָא הַהֲגָנָה לְיִשְׂרָאֵל וְאַנְשֵׁי כֹּחוֹת הַבִּטָּחוֹן, הָעוֹמְדִים עַל מִשְׁמַר
אַרְצֵנוּ וְעָרֵי אֱלֹהֵינוּ, מִגְּבוּל הַלְּבָנוֹן וְעַד מִדְבַּר מִצְרַיִם וּמִן הַיָּם
הַגָּדוֹל עַד לְבוֹא הָעֲרָבָה וּבְכָל מָקוֹם שֶׁהֵם, בַּיַּבָּשָׁה, בָּאֲוִיר וּבַיָּם.
יִתֵּן יהוה אֶת אוֹיְבֵינוּ הַקָּמִים עָלֵינוּ נִגָּפִים לִפְנֵיהֶם. הַקָּדוֹשׁ בָּרוּךְ
הוּא יִשְׁמֹר וְיַצִּיל אֶת חַיָּלֵינוּ מִכָּל צָרָה וְצוּקָה וּמִכָּל נֶגַע וּמַחֲלָה,
וְיִשְׁלַח בְּרָכָה וְהַצְלָחָה בְּכָל מַעֲשֵׂי יְדֵיהֶם. יַדְבֵּר שׂוֹנְאֵינוּ תַּחְתֵּיהֶם
וִיעַטְּרֵם בְּכֶתֶר יְשׁוּעָה וּבַעֲטֶרֶת נִצָּחוֹן. וִיקֻיַּם בָּהֶם הַכָּתוּב: כִּי דברים כ
יהוה אֱלֹהֵיכֶם הַהֹלֵךְ עִמָּכֶם לְהִלָּחֵם לָכֶם עִם־אֹיְבֵיכֶם לְהוֹשִׁיעַ
אֶתְכֶם: וְנֹאמַר אָמֵן.

## מי שברך לשבויים

*If Israeli soldiers or civilians are being held in captivity, the* שליח ציבור *says the following:*

מִי שֶׁבֵּרַךְ אֲבוֹתֵינוּ אַבְרָהָם יִצְחָק וְיַעֲקֹב, יוֹסֵף מֹשֶׁה וְאַהֲרֹן,
דָּוִד וּשְׁלֹמֹה, הוּא יְבָרֵךְ וְיִשְׁמֹר וְיִנְצֹר אֶת נֶעְדְּרֵי צְבָא הַהֲגָנָה
לְיִשְׂרָאֵל וּשְׁבוּיָו, וְאֶת כָּל אַחֵינוּ הַנְּתוּנִים בְּצָרָה וּבְשִׁבְיָה, בַּעֲבוּר
שֶׁכָּל הַקָּהָל הַקָּדוֹשׁ הַזֶּה מִתְפַּלֵּל בַּעֲבוּרָם. הַקָּדוֹשׁ בָּרוּךְ הוּא
יִמָּלֵא רַחֲמִים עֲלֵיהֶם, וְיוֹצִיאֵם מֵחֹשֶׁךְ וְצַלְמָוֶת, וּמוֹסְרוֹתֵיהֶם
יְנַתֵּק, וּמִמְּצוּקוֹתֵיהֶם יוֹשִׁיעֵם, וִישִׁיבֵם מְהֵרָה לְחֵיק מִשְׁפְּחוֹתֵיהֶם.
יוֹדוּ לַיהוה חַסְדּוֹ וְנִפְלְאוֹתָיו לִבְנֵי אָדָם: וִיקֻיַּם בָּהֶם מִקְרָא תהלים קז
שֶׁכָּתוּב: וּפְדוּיֵי יהוה יְשֻׁבוּן, וּבָאוּ צִיּוֹן בְּרִנָּה, וְשִׂמְחַת עוֹלָם ישעיה לה
עַל־רֹאשָׁם, שָׂשׂוֹן וְשִׂמְחָה יַשִּׂיגוּ, וְנָסוּ יָגוֹן וַאֲנָחָה: וְנֹאמַר אָמֵן.

---

PRAYER FOR ISRAEL'S DEFENSE FORCES

Though the prophets of Israel – Isaiah and Micah especially – were the first visionaries of peace, the Jewish people throughout history and the State of

*On Shabbat, the shofar is not sounded and the service continues with "Happy are those who dwell" on page 476.*
*If there is a Brit Mila, it takes place at this point, before he blowing of the shofar (see page 996).*

## THE BLOWING OF THE SHOFAR

*In most congregations, all say seven times:*

For the conductor of music. Of the sons of Koraḥ. A sacred song. *Ps. 47*
Sound your hands together, all peoples, make a voice of joy
resound to God,
for the LORD is most high, awesome, great King over all the earth.
It is He who subjugates peoples under us, nations beneath our feet.
He chooses our legacy for us: the pride of this Jacob He loves, Selah!
God is raised up in sound, raised, the LORD, in the voice of the shofar.
Sing out to God, sing! Sing out to our King, sing!
For God is King over all the earth – Sing out: a psalm.
God reigns over nations;
God takes His place on the throne of His holiness.
The noble men of peoples have gathered,
the people of Abraham's God.
For all the earth's defenses are of God, and He is raised high above.

### PRAYER FOR THE TOKE'A (SHOFAR BLOWER)

*In many congregations, the Toke'a recites the following prayer quietly:*

Master of all worlds, Your children, the children of Your beloved ones, have turned their faces toward You, placing their trust in Your vast loving-kindness, and have appointed me their emissary to blow the shofar before You, as You commanded us in Your Torah. Remember for their sake the merit of our forefather Abraham, who walked before You in innocence, and the merit of our forefather Isaac, and his binding upon the altar, and the merit of our forefather Jacob, an innocent man, dwelling in tents, and the merit of Moses and Aaron, David and Solomon, and all the righteous people of the world. Stand up from Your throne of judgment and sit upon Your throne of compassion, as it is said, "God has been raised up in sound, raised, the LORD, in the voice of the shofar." *Ps. 47* I know of myself that I am not worthy to ask anything of You, even for myself, to say nothing of other people, and certainly that I do not have the understanding or wisdom to hold the correct intentions, with the right holy names, while blowing the shofar – but I place my trust in Your compassion, and know that You will not turn me away empty-handed from Your presence. In Your goodness, awaken Your compassion, and may the pleasantness of the LORD our God be *Ps. 90*

*On* שבת*, the* שופר *is not sounded and the service continues with* אַשְׁרֵי יוֹשְׁבֵי בֵיתֶךָ *on page 477.* *If there is a* ברית מילה*, it takes place at this point, before* תקיעת שופר *(see page 997).*

# סדר תקיעת שופר

*In most congregations, all say seven times:*

תהלים מז

לַמְנַצֵּחַ לִבְנֵי־קֹרַח מִזְמוֹר:
כָּל־הָעַמִּים תִּקְעוּ־כָף, הָרִיעוּ לֵאלֹהִים בְּקוֹל רִנָּה:
כִּי־יהוה עֶלְיוֹן נוֹרָא, מֶלֶךְ גָּדוֹל עַל־כָּל־הָאָרֶץ:
יַדְבֵּר עַמִּים תַּחְתֵּינוּ, וּלְאֻמִּים תַּחַת רַגְלֵינוּ:
יִבְחַר־לָנוּ אֶת־נַחֲלָתֵנוּ, אֶת גְּאוֹן יַעֲקֹב אֲשֶׁר־אָהֵב סֶלָה:
עָלָה אֱלֹהִים בִּתְרוּעָה, יהוה בְּקוֹל שׁוֹפָר:
זַמְּרוּ אֱלֹהִים זַמֵּרוּ, זַמְּרוּ לְמַלְכֵּנוּ זַמֵּרוּ:
כִּי מֶלֶךְ כָּל־הָאָרֶץ אֱלֹהִים, זַמְּרוּ מַשְׂכִּיל:
מָלַךְ אֱלֹהִים עַל־גּוֹיִם, אֱלֹהִים יָשַׁב עַל־כִּסֵּא קָדְשׁוֹ:
נְדִיבֵי עַמִּים נֶאֱסָפוּ, עַם אֱלֹהֵי אַבְרָהָם
כִּי לֵאלֹהִים מָגִנֵּי־אֶרֶץ, מְאֹד נַעֲלָה:

### תחינה לתוקע

*In many congregations, the* תוקע *recites the following prayer quietly:*

רִבּוֹן הָעוֹלָמִים, בָּנֶיךָ בְּנֵי רְחוּמֶיךָ שָׂמוּ פְנֵיהֶם לְנֶגְדְּךָ וּבָטְחוּ עַל רֹב חֲסָדֶיךָ, וְשָׂמוּנִי שָׁלִיחַ לִתְקוֹעַ בְּשׁוֹפָר לְפָנֶיךָ כְּמוֹ שֶׁצִּוִּיתָנוּ בְּתוֹרָתֶךָ, וְאַתָּה תִּזְכֹּר לָהֶם זְכוּת אַבְרָהָם אָבִינוּ אֲשֶׁר הִתְהַלֵּךְ לְפָנֶיךָ וְהָיָה תָמִים, וּזְכוּת יִצְחָק אָבִינוּ וַעֲקֵדָתוֹ כְּשֶׁנֶּעֱקַד עַל גַּב הַמִּזְבֵּחַ, וּזְכוּת יַעֲקֹב אָבִינוּ אִישׁ תָּם יֹשֵׁב אֹהָלִים, וּזְכוּת שֶׁל מֹשֶׁה וְאַהֲרֹן דָּוִד וּשְׁלֹמֹה וְכָל צַדִּיקֵי עוֹלָם, וְתַעֲמֹד מִכִּסֵּא הַדִּין

---

לַמְנַצֵּחַ *Psalm 47.* A coronation psalm proclaiming God's majesty and kingship, making special reference to the sound of the shofar as the clarion celebrating His presence and majesty. The psalm contains seven mentions of the word *Elohim,* God in His attribute of judgment and justice, and many have the custom to say it seven times, thus ascending forty-nine rungs of the ladder to His presence at the fiftieth level.

upon us. Establish for us the work of our hands, O establish the work of our hands. And connect our good intentions to actual deeds, as if we had blown the shofar with all the correct intentions. May our shofar notes rise up to awaken Your compassion; show compassion for Your children, and turn judgment to kindness and compassion for them through these sounds, and step beyond the rule of law for their sake. Shut and seal the mouth of the Adversary, and do not let him accuse us. And when recriminations against us come before You, do not wipe our names out of Your book, and write for a good life, all the children of Your covenant. May the words of my mouth and the meditation of my heart find favor before You, LORD, my Rock and Redeemer. Amen. *Ps. 19*

*Some add:*

May it be Your will, LORD my God, the God of judgment, that now may be a time of favor before You. Please, in Your great compassion and vast loving-kindness, tear away all the partitions that separate You from Your people Israel on this day, and send away all adversaries and accusers of Your people Israel. Close the mouth of the Adversary, and do not let him accuse us, for our eyes are turned toward You. I will exalt You, my God, King, the God of judgment, who listens to the prayers and shofar notes of Your people Israel today, with compassion. Amen.

*The following is said responsively, Toke'a then congregation.*

מִן־הַמֵּצַר In my distress I called on the LORD. *Ps. 118*
The LORD answered me and set me free.
You have heard my voice, do not close Your ear *Lam. 3*
to my need, from my pleading.
Your first word is truth; *Ps. 119*
and each of Your righteous laws is eternal.
Be Your slave's guarantor for good; *Ibid.*
do not let the arrogant oppress me.
I revel in Your words *Ibid.*
as if discovering great spoils.
Teach me goodness of sense and insight, *Ibid.*
for I have faith in Your commands.
Desire the offerings of my mouth, please, LORD, *Ibid.*
and teach me Your laws.

---

of the book of Job, not as an independent force of evil (an idea incompatible with Jewish monotheism), but as the counsel for the prosecution in a trial when human lives are passing under divine judgment. In essence we ask

תהלים מז וְתֵשֵׁב עַל כִּסֵּא הָרַחֲמִים, כַּדָּבָר שֶׁנֶּאֱמַר: עָלָה אֱלֹהִים בִּתְרוּעָה, יהוה בְּקוֹל
שׁוֹפָר: וַאֲנִי יוֹדֵעַ בְּעַצְמִי שֶׁאֵינֶנִּי כְּדַאי לְבַקֵּשׁ עַל עַצְמִי, וְכָל שֶׁכֵּן עַל אֲחֵרִים,
וְכָל שֶׁכֵּן שֶׁאֵין בִּי לֹא דַעַת וְלֹא חָכְמָה לְכַוֵּן כַּוָּנוֹת הַתְּקִיעוֹת וְצֵרוּפֵי שְׁמוֹתֶיךָ
הַקְּדוֹשִׁים, אֲבָל בָּטַחְתִּי בְּרַחֲמֶיךָ הָרַבִּים וְיָדַעְתִּי כִּי לֹא תְשִׁיבֵנִי רֵיקָם מִלְּפָנֶיךָ,
תהלים צ וְאַתָּה בְּטוּבְךָ תְּעוֹרֵר רַחֲמֶיךָ, וִיהִי נֹעַם אֲדֹנָי אֱלֹהֵינוּ עָלֵינוּ, וּמַעֲשֵׂה יָדֵינוּ כּוֹנְנָה
עָלֵינוּ, וּמַעֲשֵׂה יָדֵינוּ כּוֹנְנֵהוּ: וְתִצָּרֵף מַחֲשַׁבְתֵּנוּ הַטּוֹבָה לְמַעֲשֶׂה, כְּאִלּוּ נִתְכַּוַּנּוּ
בְּכָל כַּוָּנוֹת הַתְּקִיעוֹת, וְיַעֲלוּ תְּקִיעוֹתֵינוּ לְעוֹרֵר רַחֲמֶיךָ, וּתְרַחֵם עַל בָּנֶיךָ, וְתַהֲפֹךְ
לָהֶם עַל יְדֵי תְקִיעוֹת אֵלֶּה מִדַּת הַדִּין לְמִדַּת הַחֶסֶד וְהָרַחֲמִים, וְתִכָּנֵס לָהֶם
לִפְנִים מִשּׁוּרַת הַדִּין. סְתֹם וַחֲתֹם פֶּה שָׂטָן וְאַל יַשְׂטִין עָלֵינוּ, וּבְבוֹא תוֹכֵחָה
תהלים יט לְנֶגְדֶּךָ שְׁמֵנוּ מִסִּפְרְךָ אַל תִּמַח, וּכְתֹב לְחַיִּים טוֹבִים כָּל בְּנֵי בְרִיתֶנוּ. יִהְיוּ לְרָצוֹן
אִמְרֵי־פִי וְהֶגְיוֹן לִבִּי לְפָנֶיךָ, יהוה צוּרִי וְגֹאֲלִי: אָמֵן.

*Some add:*

יְהִי רָצוֹן מִלְּפָנֶיךָ יהוה אֱלֹהַי אֱלֹהֵי הַמִּשְׁפָּט, שֶׁתְּהִי עַתָּה עֵת רָצוֹן לְפָנֶיךָ, וְתִקְרַע
בְּרַחֲמֶיךָ הָרַבִּים וַחֲסָדֶיךָ הַגְּדוֹלִים אֵת כָּל הַמָּסַכִים אֲשֶׁר הֵם מַבְדִּילִים בֵּינְךָ
וּבֵין עַמְּךָ יִשְׂרָאֵל הַיּוֹם הַזֶּה, וְהַעֲבֵר מִלְּפָנֶיךָ כָּל הַמַּשְׂטִינִים וְהַמְקַטְרְגִים עַל עַמְּךָ
יִשְׂרָאֵל, סְתֹם פֶּה שָׂטָן וְאַל יַשְׂטִין עָלֵינוּ, כִּי אֵלֶיךָ תְּלוּיוֹת עֵינֵינוּ. אֲרוֹמִמְךָ אֱלוֹהַי
הַמֶּלֶךְ אֱלֹהֵי הַמִּשְׁפָּט שְׁמַע קוֹל תְּפִלּוֹת וּתְרוּעוֹת עַמְּךָ יִשְׂרָאֵל הַיּוֹם בְּרַחֲמִים, אָמֵן.

*The following is said responsively,* תוקע *then* קהל.

תהלים קיח **מִן־הַמֵּצַר קָרָאתִי יָּהּ, עָנָנִי בַמֶּרְחָב יָהּ:**
איכה ג **קוֹלִי שָׁמָעְתָּ, אַל־תַּעְלֵם אָזְנְךָ לְרַוְחָתִי לְשַׁוְעָתִי:**
תהלים קיט **רֹאשׁ־דְּבָרְךָ אֱמֶת, וּלְעוֹלָם כָּל־מִשְׁפַּט צִדְקֶךָ:**
שם **עֲרֹב עַבְדְּךָ לְטוֹב, אַל־יַעַשְׁקֻנִי זֵדִים:**
שם **שָׂשׂ אָנֹכִי עַל־אִמְרָתֶךָ, כְּמוֹצֵא שָׁלָל רָב:**
שם **טוּב טַעַם וָדַעַת לַמְּדֵנִי, כִּי בְמִצְוֹתֶיךָ הֶאֱמָנְתִּי:**
שם **נִדְבוֹת פִּי רְצֵה־נָא יהוה, וּמִשְׁפָּטֶיךָ לַמְּדֵנִי:**

---

מִן־הַמֵּצַר *In my distress.* Seven verses calling on God's compassion. The initial letters of verses 2–7 spell out the words *Kera Satan*, "May Satan, the Adversary, be torn [confounded]." Satan appears in Tanakh, especially at the opening

*The Toke'a adds:*

עָלָה God has been raised up in sound, Ps. 47
raised, the LORD, in the voice of the shofar.

*The Toke'a says:*

I am prepared and ready to fulfill the commandment that our Creator has commanded us, to blow the shofar on this day, as is written in the Torah: "It shall be a day of the sounding of the shofar to you."

*The Toke'a recites the following blessings on behalf of the congregation. The blessings apply to all the shofar blasts sounded throughout Musaf, and for this reason, no unnecessary interruptions may be made until the final blasts are sounded at the end of Musaf.*

בָּרוּךְ Blessed are You, LORD our God, King of the Universe, who has made us holy through His commandments, and has commanded us to listen to the sound of the shofar.

בָּרוּךְ Blessed are You, LORD our God, King of the Universe, who has given us life, sustained us, and brought us to this time.

*The Makri calls out the shofar sounds one by one and the Toke'a blows the shofar.*

| | | |
|---|---|---|
| TEKIA | SHEVARIM TERUA | TEKIA |
| TEKIA | SHEVARIM TERUA | TEKIA |
| TEKIA | SHEVARIM TERUA | TEKIA |

*Some congregations say the following prayer (although many authorities rule that this constitutes an interruption and therefore should not be said). The angelic names that appear in parentheses should not be spoken.*

May it be Your will, LORD my God and God of my ancestors, that the sound of TaSHRaT [tekia-shevarim-terua-tekia] that we sound may be made into a crown for You by the angel (שרשי״ה) who is assigned to this role, and may rise up and rest upon Your head, my God; and make us a sign of good favor, and be filled with compassion for us. Blessed are You, Master of compassion.

---

degree Judaism emphasizes both individual and collective responsibility: on the one hand, "If I am not for myself who will be?," on the other, "If I am only for myself, what am I?" (*Avot* 1:14). We blow the shofar twice as if to say, "If I have failings as an individual, judge me favorably in the merits of the community. If we have failings as a community, consider our merits as individuals."

THE SHOFAR

The Torah calls Rosh HaShana "the day when the horn is sounded" and its central event is the sounding of the shofar – the sound that more than any

*The* תוקע *adds:*

תהלים מז

עָלָה אֱלֹהִים בִּתְרוּעָה, יהוה בְּקוֹל שׁוֹפָר:

*The* תוקע *says:*

הֲרֵי אֲנִי מוּכָן וּמְזֻמָּן לְקַיֵּם הַמִּצְוָה שֶׁצִּוָּנוּ בּוֹרְאֵנוּ לִתְקוֹעַ בְּשׁוֹפָר הַיּוֹם הַזֶּה כְּמוֹ שֶׁכָּתוּב בַּתּוֹרָה יוֹם תְּרוּעָה יִהְיֶה לָכֶם.

*The* תוקע *recites the following* ברכות *on behalf of the* קהל*. The* ברכות *apply to all the* שופר *blasts sounded throughout* מוסף*, and for this reason, no unnecessary interruptions may be made until the final blasts are sounded at the end of* מוסף*.*

בָּרוּךְ אַתָּה יהוה אֱלֹהֵינוּ מֶלֶךְ הָעוֹלָם
אֲשֶׁר קִדְּשָׁנוּ בְּמִצְוֹתָיו, וְצִוָּנוּ לִשְׁמֹעַ קוֹל שׁוֹפָר.

בָּרוּךְ אַתָּה יהוה אֱלֹהֵינוּ מֶלֶךְ הָעוֹלָם
שֶׁהֶחֱיָנוּ וְקִיְּמָנוּ, וְהִגִּיעָנוּ לַזְּמַן הַזֶּה.

*The* מקריא *calls out the* תקיעות *one by one and the* תוקע *blows the* שופר*.*

| | | |
|---|---|---|
| תקיעה | שברים תרועה | תקיעה |
| תקיעה | שברים תרועה | תקיעה |
| תקיעה | שברים תרועה | תקיעה |

*Some congregations say the following prayer (although many authorities rule that this constitutes an interruption and therefore should not be said). The angelic names that appear in parentheses should not be spoken.*

יְהִי רָצוֹן מִלְּפָנֶיךָ יהוה אֱלֹהַי וֵאלֹהֵי אֲבוֹתַי שֶׁתְּקִיעַת תשר״ת שֶׁאֲנַחְנוּ תוֹקְעִים הַיּוֹם תֵּעָשֶׂה מִמֶּנָּה עֲטָרָה עַל יַד הַמְמֻנֶּה (שרשי״ה) לִהְיוֹת עוֹלָה וְלֵישֵׁב בְּרֹאשְׁךָ אֱלֹהַי, וַעֲשֵׂה עִמָּנוּ אוֹת לְטוֹבָה וְהִמָּלֵא עָלֵינוּ רַחֲמִים. בָּרוּךְ אַתָּה בַּעַל הָרַחֲמִים.

---

God not to heed the accusations that may be brought against us, but to focus instead on the good we have done and on the merits of those who came before us.

The Talmud (*Rosh HaShana* 16b) says that we blow the shofar in two cycles, once before Musaf and once during it, "to confuse the Adversary." Several explanations have been given as to what this might mean. One interpretation is this: before Musaf we fulfill the command as individuals. During Musaf we do so as a community (Maimonides, Laws of Shofar 3:7). To a unique

*The Makri calls out the shofar sounds one by one and the Toke'a blows the shofar.*

| | | |
|---|---|---|
| TEKIA | SHEVARIM | TEKIA |
| TEKIA | SHEVARIM | TEKIA |
| TEKIA | SHEVARIM | TEKIA |

*Some congregations say the following prayer (although many authorities rule that this constitutes an interruption and therefore should not be said). The angelic names that appear in parentheses should not be spoken.*

May it be Your will, LORD my God and God of my ancestors, that the sound of TaSHaT [tekia-shevarim-tekia] that we sound today be stitched across the curtain before You by the angel (טרטיא״ל) who is assigned to this role, and be accepted by Elijah of blessed memory and (ישעיה״ה) the minister of the Face, the ministering angel (מטטרו״ן); and be filled with compassion for us. Blessed are You, Master of compassion.

---

companied the Israelites on their journeys (Num. 10:1–10). In the Temple on Rosh HaShana two trumpets were sounded as well as the shofar. Yet the shofar survived; the trumpets remain only as a memory. In Jewish history the simple has tended to prevail over the sophisticated, for God seeks the unadorned heart. The very naturalness of the shofar gives it its power.

The shofar is the wordless cry at the heart of a religion of words. Judaism is a profoundly verbal culture, a religion of holy texts, impassioned conversation and "argument for the sake of heaven." Yet there is a time for emotions that lie too deep for words. The sound of the shofar breaks through the carapace of the self-justifying mind and touches us directly, at the most primal level of our being.

On the meaning of the shofar of Rosh HaShana there are two radically different interpretations. The first is that of Rabbi Abahu in the Talmud: "The Holy One, blessed be He, said: Blow before Me a ram's horn that I may remember for you the binding of Isaac, son of Abraham, and I shall account it to you as if you had bound yourself before Me" (*Rosh HaShana* 16a). The shofar recalls the ram, caught in a thicket by its horns, sacrificed in Isaac's place.

In this view the shofar is a cry from earth to heaven, from us to God. It represents Jewish faithfulness and sacrifice. For millennia Jews suffered for their faith yet, for the most part, they did not abandon it. The shofar, Rabbi Abahu is suggesting, is a way of saying, "Master of the Universe, we may have faults and failings, but we stayed true to You and to our covenant with You. We come before You with a history that began with Abraham and Isaac's lonely ordeal. Forgive us for the sake of our ancestors' suffering, loyally and willingly endured."

Maimonides gives the opposite interpretation: "Even though the blowing

*The* מקריא *calls out the* תקיעות *one by one and the* תוקע *blows the* שופר*.*

| | | |
|---|---|---|
| תקיעה | שברים | תקיעה |
| תקיעה | שברים | תקיעה |
| תקיעה | שברים | תקיעה |

*Some congregations say the following prayer (although many authorities rule that this constitutes an interruption and therefore should not be said). The angelic names that appear in parentheses should not be spoken.*

יְהִי רָצוֹן לְפָנֶיךָ יהוה אֱלֹהַי וֵאלֹהֵי אֲבוֹתַי שֶׁתְּקִיעַת תשר״ת שֶׁאֲנַחְנוּ תוֹקְעִים הַיּוֹם תְּהֵי מְרֻקֶּמֶת עַל הַיְרִיעָה עַל יַד הַמְמֻנֶּה (טרטיא״ל) וּתְקַבְּלֶנָּה עַל יַד אֵלִיָּהוּ זָכוּר לַטּוֹב וְ(ישעיה״ה) שַׂר הַפָּנִים שַׂר (מטטרו״ן), וְהִמָּלֵא עָלֵינוּ רַחֲמִים. בָּרוּךְ אַתָּה בַּעַל הָרַחֲמִים.

---

other has been the signal of momentousness in Jewish history, italicizing time for special emphasis.

It sounded when the Israelites heard the voice of God and accepted the covenant at Mount Sinai: "There was the sound of the shofar growing louder and louder" (Ex. 19:19). It accompanied them into battle in the days of Joshua at Jericho: "When the people heard the sound of the shofar, they shouted with a great shout, and the wall fell down flat" (Josh. 6:20). In the jubilee year it became the sound of freedom: "On the tenth day of the seventh month, you shall make a proclamation with the shofar… You shall sanctify the fiftieth year, and proclaim liberty throughout the land to all its inhabitants: this is your jubilee and you shall return every man to his possession, and you shall return every man to his family" (Lev. 25:9–10). It was an alarm, warning of impending danger: "Shall the ram's horn be blown in a city and the people not tremble?" (Amos 3:6). It was, said Isaiah, the sound of the great shofar that would signal the ingathering of exiles when Israel returned to its land (Is. 27:13). It was sounded in 1967 during the Six Day War at that intensely emotional moment when Jews were again able to pray at the Western Wall in Jerusalem. It is the sound of judgment: "Lift up your voice like a horn and declare to My people their transgression" (Is. 58:1). And it is the sound of God's majesty: "With trumpets and the sound of the shofar shout before the King, the LORD" (Ps. 98:6).

Why the shofar? One reason is that it is simple, easily available, a natural product, not a manufactured one. The shofar was not the only instrument to serve as a clarion. The Torah speaks about two silver trumpets that ac-

*The Makri calls out the shofar sounds one by one and the Toke'a blows the shofar.*

| | | |
|---|---|---|
| TEKIA | TERUA | TEKIA |
| TEKIA | TERUA | TEKIA |
| TEKIA | TERUA | TEKIA GEDOLA |

*Some congregations say the following prayer (although many authorities rule that this constitutes an interruption and therefore should not be said).*

And so may it be Your will, LORD our God and God of our ancestors, that all the angels responsible for the shofar and for the tekia and for the shevarim and for the terua may rise up before the throne of Your glory, and may advocate for us before You, to atone for all our sins.

---

Originally the shofar was sounded in the morning service, on the principle that "the zealous perform commands at the earliest possible opportunity." However, a tragic event happened during the Mishnaic period. Roman soldiers heard the shofar being blown at daybreak and thought that Jews were being summoned to do battle. They mounted an attack and many Jews died. Thereafter it was ruled that the shofar be blown at a later stage in the day, during Musaf, by which time it would be clear that the gathering was only for prayer (*Rosh HaShana* 32b).

The shofar is sounded, during the Leader's Repetition, at each of the three central blessings of the Musaf Amida: the passages relating to Kingship, Remembrances and Shofar. A further complete cycle of thirty notes was introduced before Musaf, though it is the notes sounded in Musaf that constitute the main fulfillment of the command. Some (notably Hasidim) have the custom of blowing shofar during the silent Amida also. Many have the custom, at the conclusion of Musaf, of completing a hundred notes. The end of each cycle is marked by an extended blast, the *tekia gedola*.

There were differing views as to what constitutes the mitzva of shofar. Is it to blow (in which case the *toke'a* is fulfilling the command on our behalf) or is it to listen (in which case we all fulfill the command equally)? In the end, the consensus was that the command is to listen, and this is reflected in the blessing: "Who has commanded us to listen to the sound of the shofar" – meaning, to hear it with the intention of fulfilling the command.

If the primary command is *listening*, we can understand it more deeply. Fundamental to Judaism was its revolutionary insistence that God cannot be seen. The pagans worshiped things and events that were visible: the sun, the stars, the rain, the sea, the earth – events and objects in nature. Judaism

*The* מקריא *calls out the* תקיעות *one by one and the* תוקע *blows the* שופר*.*

| | | |
|---|---|---|
| תקיעה | תרועה | תקיעה |
| תקיעה | תרועה | תקיעה |
| תקיעה | תרועה | תקיעה גדולה |

*Some congregations say the following prayer (although many authorities rule that this constitutes an interruption and therefore should not be said).*

וּבְכֵן יְהִי רָצוֹן לְפָנֶיךָ יהוה אֱלֹהֵינוּ וֵאלֹהֵי אֲבוֹתֵינוּ שֶׁיַּעֲלוּ כָּל הַמַּלְאָכִים הַמְמֻנִּים עַל הַשּׁוֹפָר וְעַל הַתְּקִיעָה וְעַל הַשְּׁבָרִים וְעַל הַתְּרוּעָה לִפְנֵי כִּסֵּא כְבוֹדֶךָ וְיַמְלִיצוּ טוֹב בַּעֲדֵנוּ לְכַפֵּר עַל כָּל חַטֹּאתֵינוּ.

---

of the shofar on Rosh HaShana is a scriptural decree, nonetheless it contains an allusion, as if to say: Wake, sleepers, from your sleep, and slumberers wake from your slumbers. Examine your deeds and turn in *teshuva*. Remember your Creator, you who forget the truth in the vanities of time, spending the year in vanity and emptiness that neither helps nor saves. Look to your souls and improve your ways and deeds" (Maimonides, Laws of Repentance 3:4).

In this alternate view the shofar is not a cry from earth to heaven, but a call from heaven to earth, God's call to us to return to Him. Both views are true. In the *tekia*, the powerful clarion, we hear God's call to us. In the *terua*, the broken tones of weeping, we hear our ancestors' tears.

On Rosh HaShana the primary sound is the *terua*, for that is how the Torah names the day. It is "the day of the *terua*" (Num. 29:1) or "the remembrance of the *terua*" (Lev. 23:24). On the basis of Judges 5:28, the sages understood *terua* to be the sound of weeping, as the mother of Sisera wept when her son failed to return from battle.

There was a doubt as to whether this was a sigh (three broken notes, known as *shevarim*) or a sob (nine short notes, which we call *terua*) or both (*shevarim-terua*) combined. To avoid any possibility of error, we sound all three, each preceded and followed by the long, plain note called a *tekia*. Rav Hai Gaon explained that the practice arose not because of doubt but because different communities had different customs, and our current practice encompasses them all.

The Torah mentions *terua* three times, twice in connection with Rosh HaShana and once in the context of the Yom Kippur of the jubilee year (Lev. 25:9). For that reason we blow each combination of notes three times.

*The next three verses are recited responsively, Leader then congregation:*

אַשְׁרֵי Happy is the people who know this sound. Ps. 89
LORD, they shall walk by the light of Your face.
All day long they will rejoice in Your name,
and be raised up in Your righteousness.
For You are the splendor of their strength,
and our power is raised through Your desire.

*The Leader says the first verse of Ashrei aloud and all continue:*

אַשְׁרֵי Happy are those who dwell in Your House; Ps. 84
they shall continue to praise You, Selah!
Happy are the people for whom this is so; Ps. 144
happy are the people whose God is the LORD.
A song of praise by David. Ps. 145

I will exalt You, my God, the King, and bless Your name for ever and all time. Every day I will bless You, and praise Your name for ever and all time. Great is the LORD and greatly to be praised; His greatness is unfathomable. One generation will praise Your works to the next, and tell of Your mighty deeds. On the glorious

---

pure listening to the wordless cry of the shofar, our call to God, His call to us.

The ram's horn reminds us of the binding of Isaac, when a ram caught in a thicket by its horns was offered instead (Gen. 22:13). Rabbi Ḥanina ben Dosa said: no part of that ram went to waste. Its ashes became the base of the inner altar. Its sinews were made into the strings of David's harp. Its skin became the girdle of Elijah's loins. Of its horns, one was heard at Sinai. The other is destined to be heard when the exiles are gathered in to the land of Israel, to fulfill the words of the prophet, "It shall come to pass on that day that a great shofar will be blown" (Isaiah 27:13), (*Pirkei deRabbi Eliezer*, 30). To be a Jew is to live between these memories and that hope.

Rabbi Levi Yitzḥak of Berditchev told this story: Once a king was out hunting in a forest and became lost. He asked many people the way back to the palace but none could tell him. Finally he found a wise man who showed him the way and accompanied him. The king, wishing to reward the man, gave him high office and great wealth. Many years later the wise man sinned against the

*The next three verses are recited responsively,* שליח ציבור *then* קהל*:*

תהלים פט אַשְׁרֵי הָעָם יוֹדְעֵי תְרוּעָה, יהוה בְּאוֹר־פָּנֶיךָ יְהַלֵּכוּן:
בְּשִׁמְךָ יְגִילוּן כָּל־הַיּוֹם, וּבְצִדְקָתְךָ יָרוּמוּ:
כִּי־תִפְאֶרֶת עֻזָּמוֹ אָתָּה, וּבִרְצוֹנְךָ תָּרוּם קַרְנֵנוּ:

*The* שליח ציבור *says the first verse of* אשרי *aloud and all continue:*

תהלים פד אַשְׁרֵי יוֹשְׁבֵי בֵיתֶךָ, עוֹד יְהַלְלוּךָ סֶּלָה:
תהלים קמד אַשְׁרֵי הָעָם שֶׁכָּכָה לּוֹ, אַשְׁרֵי הָעָם שֶׁיהוה אֱלֹהָיו:
תהלים קמה תְּהִלָּה לְדָוִד
אֲרוֹמִמְךָ אֱלוֹהַי הַמֶּלֶךְ, וַאֲבָרְכָה שִׁמְךָ לְעוֹלָם וָעֶד:
בְּכָל־יוֹם אֲבָרְכֶךָּ, וַאֲהַלְלָה שִׁמְךָ לְעוֹלָם וָעֶד:
גָּדוֹל יהוה וּמְהֻלָּל מְאֹד, וְלִגְדֻלָּתוֹ אֵין חֵקֶר:
דּוֹר לְדוֹר יְשַׁבַּח מַעֲשֶׂיךָ, וּגְבוּרֹתֶיךָ יַגִּידוּ:

---

insisted that God transcends nature. God is invisible. Worshiping images is idolatry. Moses reminds the Israelites that at Sinai "You heard the sound of words, but saw no image; there was only a voice" (Deut. 4:12).

As a result, *listening* is a fundamental category in Judaism, most powerfully expressed in the opening words of our most famous prayer: *Shema Yisrael. Shema* has a range of senses in biblical Hebrew: it means to hear, to listen, to understand, to internalize, and to respond in action. There is no equivalent word in contemporary English: the closest is the verb "to hearken."

When we say the first verse of the Shema we cover our eyes, as if turning from the world of sight to that of sound, no longer distracted by what our eyes can see, instead listening to the word, the voice, of God. One of the most remarkable features of biblical Hebrew is that, though the Torah contains 613 commands, there is no Hebrew word that means "to obey." Modern Hebrew uses the word *letzayet,* which was originally Aramaic. Instead the Torah uses the word *shema,* meaning, to listen and respond.

It is thus no accident that at the beginning of a new year, at the start of a holy period when we are called on to return to God – the God who is not an image but a voice, a summons, a call – we should begin with an act of

splendor of Your majesty I will meditate, and on the acts of Your wonders. They shall talk of the power of Your awesome deeds, and I will tell of Your greatness. They shall recite the record of Your great goodness, and sing with joy of Your righteousness. The LORD is gracious and compassionate, slow to anger and great in loving-kindness. The LORD is good to all, and His compassion extends to all His works. All Your works shall thank You, LORD, and Your devoted ones shall bless You. They shall talk of the glory of Your kingship, and speak of Your might. To make known to mankind His mighty deeds and the glorious majesty of His kingship. Your kingdom is an everlasting kingdom, and Your reign is for all generations. The LORD supports all who fall, and raises all who are bowed down. All raise their eyes to You in hope, and You give them their food in due season. You open Your hand, and satisfy every living thing with favor. The LORD is righteous in all His ways, and kind in all He does. The LORD is close to all who

---

sound beseeching You to fulfill Your obligation of providing dowries for my daughters." The simple honesty of this man touched Levi Yitzḥak and he engaged him to blow the shofar.

Once it happened in the days of Rabbi Abraham Isaac HaKohen Kook that a group of workers, under pressure to complete a building in one of the neighborhoods of Jerusalem, worked on Rosh HaShana. People living in the area sent word to Rabbi Kook, expecting him to order them immediately to stop. Instead he sent an emissary to blow shofar for the workers. They stopped working to listen. Some began to cry. When the blowing was completed, they decided of their own accord not to continue working on the holy day. Some ran home, changed their clothes, and went with the emissary to pray with the Rabbi. (*Celebration of the Soul,** p. 41)

In his early years Rabbi Kook would himself blow shofar, but in his later years, when the effort was too great, he would read out the order of the blasts and Rabbi David Cohen, "the Nazirite," would blow. One year Zalman Shazar,

* See R. Moshe Zvi Neriah, *Celebration of the Soul: The Holidays in the Life and Thought of Rabbi Avraham Yitzchak Kook*, trans. Pesach Jaffe (Jerusalem: Genesis Jerusalem Press, 1992).

הֲדַר כְּבוֹד הוֹדֶךָ, וְדִבְרֵי נִפְלְאֹתֶיךָ אָשִׂיחָה:
וֶעֱזוּז נוֹרְאֹתֶיךָ יֹאמֵרוּ, וּגְדוּלָּתְךָ אֲסַפְּרֶנָּה:
זֵכֶר רַב־טוּבְךָ יַבִּיעוּ, וְצִדְקָתְךָ יְרַנֵּנוּ:
חַנּוּן וְרַחוּם יהוה, אֶרֶךְ אַפַּיִם וּגְדָל־חָסֶד:
טוֹב־יהוה לַכֹּל, וְרַחֲמָיו עַל־כָּל־מַעֲשָׂיו:
יוֹדוּךָ יהוה כָּל־מַעֲשֶׂיךָ, וַחֲסִידֶיךָ יְבָרְכוּכָה:
כְּבוֹד מַלְכוּתְךָ יֹאמֵרוּ, וּגְבוּרָתְךָ יְדַבֵּרוּ:
לְהוֹדִיעַ לִבְנֵי הָאָדָם גְּבוּרֹתָיו, וּכְבוֹד הֲדַר מַלְכוּתוֹ:
מַלְכוּתְךָ מַלְכוּת כָּל־עֹלָמִים, וּמֶמְשַׁלְתְּךָ בְּכָל־דּוֹר וָדֹר:
סוֹמֵךְ יהוה לְכָל־הַנֹּפְלִים, וְזוֹקֵף לְכָל־הַכְּפוּפִים:
עֵינֵי־כֹל אֵלֶיךָ יְשַׂבֵּרוּ, וְאַתָּה נוֹתֵן־לָהֶם אֶת־אָכְלָם בְּעִתּוֹ:
פּוֹתֵחַ אֶת־יָדֶךָ, וּמַשְׂבִּיעַ לְכָל־חַי רָצוֹן:
צַדִּיק יהוה בְּכָל־דְּרָכָיו, וְחָסִיד בְּכָל־מַעֲשָׂיו:

---

king, who became angry and threatened to send him for trial. The man knew that the judges would condemn him, so he begged to be allowed to come before the king in the clothes he wore on the day he first helped him. The king, seeing him in these clothes, remembered that day, his anger dissipated and he forgave him. So, said Levi Yitzḥak, are we on Rosh HaShana. We may have sinned before the King, but it was our ancestors who accepted the Torah. So we sound the shofar as it sounded on that day, as it is written "There was the sound of the shofar growing louder and louder" (Ex. 19:19), and we pray that God's anger may dissipate and He will forgive us. (*Kedushat Levi*)

One year, Rabbi Levi Yitzḥak of Berditchev interviewed a number of candidates for the blowing of the shofar for Rosh HaShana. "What will be your thoughts as you are blowing?" he asked each, but none of their answers satisfied him. Finally, one answered him thus: "Rabbi, I am a simple poor Jew. I have four daughters, none of whom is married, and I cannot afford dowries for them. When I blow the shofar I will be thinking, 'Merciful One, I am fulfilling the commandments You have ordained. Give ear to the shofar

call on Him, to all who call on Him in truth. He fulfills the will of those who revere Him; He hears their cry and saves them. The LORD guards all who love Him, but all the wicked He will destroy. ▸ My mouth shall speak the praise of the LORD, and all creatures shall bless His holy name for ever and all time.

We will bless the LORD now and for ever. Halleluya! *Ps. 115*

## RETURNING THE TORAH TO THE ARK

*The Ark is opened. All stand. The Leader takes one of the Torah scrolls and says:*

יְהַלְלוּ Let them praise the name of the LORD, *Ps. 148*
for His name alone is sublime.

*The congregation responds:*

הוֹדוֹ His majesty is above earth and heaven.
He has raised the horn of His people,
for the glory of all His devoted ones,
the children of Israel, the people close to Him.
Halleluya!

*While the Torah scrolls are being returned to the Ark, on a weekday the following is said. On Shabbat, Psalm 29, on the next page, is said.*

לְדָוִד מִזְמוֹר A psalm of David. The earth is the LORD's and all it contains, the world and all who live in it. For He founded it on the seas and established it on the streams. Who may climb the mountain of the LORD? Who may stand in His holy place? He who has clean hands and a pure heart, who has not taken My name in vain, or sworn deceitfully. He shall receive blessing from the LORD, and just *Ps. 24*

---

Cohen, Chief Rabbi of Haifa: "They both stood with closed eyes, Rav Kook reading out the sounds and Rabbi David blowing shofar. The blasts sounded as if they came from another world. I felt that I was hearing the shofar of redemption, the call of the shofar of *Mashiach*, which heralds the ingathering of the exiles. I was shaken to the roots of my soul, and will never forget that experience." (*Celebration of the Soul*, p. 38)

קָרוֹב יהוה לְכָל־קֹרְאָיו, לְכֹל אֲשֶׁר יִקְרָאֻהוּ בֶאֱמֶת:
רְצוֹן־יְרֵאָיו יַעֲשֶׂה, וְאֶת־שַׁוְעָתָם יִשְׁמַע, וְיוֹשִׁיעֵם:
שׁוֹמֵר יהוה אֶת־כָּל־אֹהֲבָיו, וְאֵת כָּל־הָרְשָׁעִים יַשְׁמִיד:
› תְּהִלַּת יהוה יְדַבֶּר פִּי, וִיבָרֵךְ כָּל־בָּשָׂר שֵׁם קָדְשׁוֹ לְעוֹלָם וָעֶד:
וַאֲנַחְנוּ נְבָרֵךְ יָהּ מֵעַתָּה וְעַד־עוֹלָם, הַלְלוּיָהּ: תהלים קטו

## הכנסת ספר תורה

*The* ארון קודש *is opened. All stand. The* שליח ציבור *takes one of the* ספרי תורה *and says:*

יְהַלְלוּ אֶת־שֵׁם יהוה, כִּי־נִשְׂגָּב שְׁמוֹ, לְבַדּוֹ תהלים קמח

*The* קהל *responds:*

הוֹדוֹ עַל־אֶרֶץ וְשָׁמָיִם:
וַיָּרֶם קֶרֶן לְעַמּוֹ
תְּהִלָּה לְכָל־חֲסִידָיו
לִבְנֵי יִשְׂרָאֵל עַם קְרֹבוֹ
הַלְלוּיָהּ:

*While the* ספרי תורה *are being returned to the* ארון קודש,
*on a weekday, the following is said. On* שבת, מִזְמוֹר לְדָוִד*, on the next page, is said.*

תהלים כד לְדָוִד מִזְמוֹר, לַיהוה הָאָרֶץ וּמְלוֹאָהּ, תֵּבֵל וְיֹשְׁבֵי בָהּ: כִּי־הוּא
עַל־יַמִּים יְסָדָהּ, וְעַל־נְהָרוֹת יְכוֹנְנֶהָ: מִי־יַעֲלֶה בְהַר־יהוה,
וּמִי־יָקוּם בִּמְקוֹם קָדְשׁוֹ: נְקִי כַפַּיִם וּבַר־לֵבָב, אֲשֶׁר לֹא־נָשָׂא
לַשָּׁוְא נַפְשִׁי וְלֹא נִשְׁבַּע לְמִרְמָה: יִשָּׂא בְרָכָה מֵאֵת יהוה, וּצְדָקָה

---

later to become President of the State of Israel, visited Rav Kook during Elul and found the Rav and Rabbi David rehearsing the blowing for Rosh HaShana, together with the *kavanot,* the mystical meditations, that silently accompanied them. Shazar later told Rabbi David's son, Rabbi She'ar Yashuv

reward from God, his salvation. This is a generation of those who seek Him, the descendants of Jacob who seek Your presence, Selah! Lift up your heads, O gates; be uplifted, eternal doors, so that the King of glory may enter. Who is the King of glory? It is the LORD, strong and mighty, the LORD mighty in battle. Lift up your heads, O gates; lift them up, eternal doors, so that the King of glory may enter. Who is He, the King of glory? The LORD of hosts, He is the King of glory, Selah!

*On Shabbat the following is said:*

מִזְמוֹר לְדָוִד A psalm of David. Render to the LORD, you angelic pow- *Ps. 29*
ers, render to the LORD glory and might. Render to the LORD the glory due to His name. Bow down to the LORD in the splendor of holiness. The LORD's voice echoes over the waters; the God of glory thunders; the LORD is over the mighty waters. The LORD's voice in power, the LORD's voice in beauty, the LORD's voice breaks cedars, the LORD shatters the cedars of Lebanon. He makes Lebanon skip like a calf, Sirion like a young wild ox. The LORD's voice cleaves flames of fire. The LORD's voice makes the desert quake, the LORD shakes the desert of Kadesh. The LORD's voice makes hinds calve and strips the forests bare, and in His temple all say: "Glory!" The LORD sat enthroned at the Flood, the LORD sits enthroned as King for ever. The LORD will give strength to His people; the LORD will bless His people with peace.

*As the Torah scrolls are placed into the Ark, all say:*

וּבְנֻחֹה יֹאמַר When the Ark came to rest, Moses would say: "Return, *Num. 10*
O LORD, to the myriad thousands of Israel." Advance, LORD, to Your *Ps. 132*
resting place, You and Your mighty Ark. Your priests are clothed in righteousness, and Your devoted ones sing in joy. For the sake of Your
servant David, do not reject Your anointed one. For I give you good *Prov. 4*
instruction; do not forsake My Torah. ▸ It is a tree of life to those *Prov. 3*
who grasp it, and those who uphold it are happy. Its ways are ways
of pleasantness, and all its paths are peace. Turn us back, O LORD, to *Lam. 5*
You, and we will return. Renew our days as of old.

*The Ark is closed.*

מֵאֱלֹהֵי יִשְׁעוֹ: זֶה דּוֹר דֹּרְשָׁו, מְבַקְשֵׁי פָנֶיךָ, יַעֲקֹב, סֶלָה: שְׂאוּ שְׁעָרִים רָאשֵׁיכֶם, וְהִנָּשְׂאוּ פִּתְחֵי עוֹלָם, וְיָבוֹא מֶלֶךְ הַכָּבוֹד: מִי זֶה מֶלֶךְ הַכָּבוֹד, יהוה עִזּוּז וְגִבּוֹר, יהוה גִּבּוֹר מִלְחָמָה: שְׂאוּ שְׁעָרִים רָאשֵׁיכֶם, וּשְׂאוּ פִּתְחֵי עוֹלָם, וְיָבֹא מֶלֶךְ הַכָּבוֹד: מִי הוּא זֶה מֶלֶךְ הַכָּבוֹד, יהוה צְבָאוֹת הוּא מֶלֶךְ הַכָּבוֹד, סֶלָה:

*On שבת the following is said:*

מִזְמוֹר לְדָוִד, הָבוּ לַיהוה בְּנֵי אֵלִים, הָבוּ לַיהוה כָּבוֹד וָעֹז: הָבוּ לַיהוה כְּבוֹד שְׁמוֹ, הִשְׁתַּחֲווּ לַיהוה בְּהַדְרַת־קֹדֶשׁ: קוֹל יהוה עַל־הַמָּיִם, אֵל־הַכָּבוֹד הִרְעִים, יהוה עַל־מַיִם רַבִּים: קוֹל־יהוה בַּכֹּחַ, קוֹל יהוה בֶּהָדָר: קוֹל יהוה שֹׁבֵר אֲרָזִים, וַיְשַׁבֵּר יהוה אֶת־אַרְזֵי הַלְּבָנוֹן: וַיַּרְקִידֵם כְּמוֹ־עֵגֶל, לְבָנוֹן וְשִׂרְיוֹן כְּמוֹ בֶן־רְאֵמִים: קוֹל־יהוה חֹצֵב לַהֲבוֹת אֵשׁ: קוֹל יהוה יָחִיל מִדְבָּר, יָחִיל יהוה מִדְבַּר קָדֵשׁ: קוֹל יהוה יְחוֹלֵל אַיָּלוֹת וַיֶּחֱשֹׂף יְעָרוֹת, וּבְהֵיכָלוֹ, כֻּלּוֹ אֹמֵר כָּבוֹד: יהוה לַמַּבּוּל יָשָׁב, וַיֵּשֶׁב יהוה מֶלֶךְ לְעוֹלָם: יהוה עֹז לְעַמּוֹ יִתֵּן, יהוה יְבָרֵךְ אֶת־עַמּוֹ בַשָּׁלוֹם: תהלים כט

*As the ספרי תורה are placed into the ארון קודש, all say:*

וּבְנֻחֹה יֹאמַר, שׁוּבָה יהוה רִבְבוֹת אַלְפֵי יִשְׂרָאֵל: קוּמָה יהוה לִמְנוּחָתֶךָ, אַתָּה וַאֲרוֹן עֻזֶּךָ: כֹּהֲנֶיךָ יִלְבְּשׁוּ־צֶדֶק, וַחֲסִידֶיךָ יְרַנֵּנוּ: בַּעֲבוּר דָּוִד עַבְדֶּךָ אַל־תָּשֵׁב פְּנֵי מְשִׁיחֶךָ: כִּי לֶקַח טוֹב נָתַתִּי לָכֶם, תּוֹרָתִי אַל־תַּעֲזֹבוּ: ‹ עֵץ־חַיִּים הִיא לַמַּחֲזִיקִים בָּהּ, וְתֹמְכֶיהָ מְאֻשָּׁר: דְּרָכֶיהָ דַרְכֵי־נֹעַם וְכָל־נְתִיבוֹתֶיהָ שָׁלוֹם: הֲשִׁיבֵנוּ יהוה אֵלֶיךָ וְנָשׁוּבָה, חַדֵּשׁ יָמֵינוּ כְּקֶדֶם:

במדבר י / תהלים קלב / משלי ד / משלי ג / איכה ה

*The ארון קודש is closed.*

*The Leader says the following before Musaf:*

הִנְנִי Here I am, empty of deeds, in turmoil, fearing the One who sits enthroned on the praises of Israel. I have come here to stand up and plead with You for Your people Israel who have sent me, even though I am not worthy or fitting to come. And so I ask of You, God of Abraham, God of Isaac and God of Jacob, the LORD, the LORD, compassionate and gracious God, my God, Almighty, fearful and awesome, please, give me success along the road that I tread, to stand and ask for compassion for me and for those who have sent me, and please, do not condemn them for my sins, do not hold them liable for my crimes, for I am a sinner, I do wrong, do not let them be disgraced by my sins, let them not be ashamed of me, nor me of them. Accept my prayer as if it were the prayer of an old man, experienced and fluent, one whose past is becoming and whose beard is long and his voice pleasant, and whose mind is involved with the concerns of others. Banish the Adversary, that he should not draw me aside. Let the banner that we fly for You be love, cover all our crimes over with love, and turn all our fast days and torments to happiness and joy – ours and those of all Israel – to life and to peace; [let us] love truth and peace, and let there be no obstacle to my prayer.

וִיהִי רָצוֹן And may it be Your will, LORD, God of Abraham, God of Isaac and God of Jacob, the great and mighty and awesome God, God Most High, "I shall be what I shall be," that all the angels who carry our prayers should bring my prayer before the throne of Your glory, and lay it out before You, for the sake of all the righteous and honest, innocent and upright people, and for the sake of the glory of Your great and mighty and awesome name. For You listen with compassion to the prayers of Your people Israel. Blessed are You, who listens to prayers.

---

congregation, but I alone cannot carry you on my shoulders. Each of you must exercise your own repentance, prayer and charity."

*The* שליח ציבור *says the following before* מוסף*:*

הִנְנִי הֶעָנִי מִמַּעַשׂ, נִרְעָשׁ וְנִפְחָד מִפַּחַד יוֹשֵׁב תְּהִלּוֹת יִשְׂרָאֵל, בָּאתִי לַעֲמֹד וּלְחַנֵּן לְפָנֶיךָ עַל עַמְּךָ יִשְׂרָאֵל אֲשֶׁר שְׁלָחוּנִי, וְאַף עַל פִּי שֶׁאֵינִי כְדַאי וְהָגוּן לְכָךְ. עַל כֵּן אֲבַקֶּשְׁךָ אֱלֹהֵי אַבְרָהָם אֱלֹהֵי יִצְחָק וֵאלֹהֵי יַעֲקֹב, יהוה יהוה, אֵל רַחוּם וְחַנּוּן, אֱלֹהִים, שַׁדַּי אָיוֹם וְנוֹרָא, הֱיֵה נָא מַצְלִיחַ דַּרְכִּי אֲשֶׁר אָנֹכִי הוֹלֵךְ לַעֲמֹד לְבַקֵּשׁ רַחֲמִים עָלַי וְעַל שׁוֹלְחַי. וְנָא אַל תַּפְשִׁיעֵם בְּחַטֹּאתַי וְאַל תְּחַיְּבֵם בַּעֲוֹנוֹתַי, כִּי חוֹטֵא וּפוֹשֵׁעַ אָנִי, וְאַל יִכָּלְמוּ בִּפְשָׁעַי, וְאַל יֵבֹשׁוּ בִּי וְאַל אֵבוֹשָׁה בָּהֶם. וְקַבֵּל תְּפִלָּתִי כִּתְפִלַּת זָקֵן וְרָגִיל, וּפִרְקוֹ נָאֶה וּזְקָנוֹ מְגֻדָּל וְקוֹלוֹ נָעִים, וּמְעֹרָב בְּדַעַת עִם הַבְּרִיּוֹת. וְתִגְעַר בְּשָּׂטָן לְבַל יַשְׂטִינֵנוּ, וִיהִי נָא דִּגְלֵנוּ עָלֶיךָ אַהֲבָה, לְכָל פְּשָׁעִים תְּכַסֶּה בְּאַהֲבָה, וְכָל צוֹמוֹתֵינוּ וְעִנּוּיֵינוּ הֲפָךְ לָנוּ וּלְכָל יִשְׂרָאֵל לְשָׂשׂוֹן וּלְשִׂמְחָה לְחַיִּים וּלְשָׁלוֹם, הָאֱמֶת וְהַשָּׁלוֹם אֱהָבוּ, וְאַל יְהִי שׁוּם מִכְשׁוֹל בִּתְפִלָּתִי.

וִיהִי רָצוֹן מִלְּפָנֶיךָ יהוה אֱלֹהֵי אַבְרָהָם אֱלֹהֵי יִצְחָק וֵאלֹהֵי יַעֲקֹב, הָאֵל הַגָּדוֹל הַגִּבּוֹר וְהַנּוֹרָא אֵל עֶלְיוֹן אֶהְיֶה אֲשֶׁר אֶהְיֶה, שֶׁכָּל הַמַּלְאָכִים שֶׁהֵם בַּעֲלֵי תְפִלּוֹת יָבִיאוּ תְפִלָּתִי לִפְנֵי כִסֵּא כְבוֹדֶךָ וְיָפִיצוּ אוֹתָהּ לְפָנֶיךָ, בַּעֲבוּר כָּל הַצַּדִּיקִים וְהַחֲסִידִים הַתְּמִימִים וְהַיְשָׁרִים, וּבַעֲבוּר כְּבוֹד שִׁמְךָ הַגָּדוֹל הַגִּבּוֹר וְהַנּוֹרָא. כִּי אַתָּה שׁוֹמֵעַ תְּפִלַּת עַמְּךָ יִשְׂרָאֵל בְּרַחֲמִים, בָּרוּךְ אַתָּה שׁוֹמֵעַ תְּפִלָּה.

---

PREPARING TO PRAY

One Rosh HaShana, Rabbi Menaḥem Mendel of Rimanov turned to the congregation who had come to pray with him, and said: "You are a beautiful

*Some add:*

I know, Lord, that Your laws are righteous; *Ps. 119*
that in faithfulness You gave me suffering.
Listen to me and answer me; I tremble as I speak, and I cry. *Ps. 55*
But my soul will rejoice in the Lord, will exult in His salvation; *Ps. 35*
He who gives salvation to kings, *Ps. 144*
who saved His servant David from the cruel sword.

## HALF KADDISH

*Leader:* יִתְגַּדַּל Magnified and sanctified
may His great name be,
in the world He created by His will.
May He establish His kingdom,
make His salvation flourish,
and hasten His messiah,
in your lifetime and in your days,
and in the lifetime of all the house of Israel,
swiftly and soon –
and say: Amen.

*All:* May His great name be blessed for ever and all time.

*Leader:* Blessed and praised, glorified and exalted,
raised and honored, uplifted and lauded
be the name of the Holy One,
blessed be He,
above and beyond any blessing,
song, praise and consolation
uttered in the world –
and say: Amen.

---

he is a great individual. If the king chose to hang his crown on a wooden peg in the wall, would the peg boast that its beauty drew the king's gaze to it? (Rabbi Moshe of Kobryn)

*Some add:*

יָדַעְתִּי יהוה כִּי־צֶדֶק מִשְׁפָּטֶיךָ, וֶאֱמוּנָה עִנִּיתָנִי: תהלים קיט

הַקְשִׁיבָה לִּי וַעֲנֵנִי, אָרִיד בְּשִׂיחִי וְאָהִימָה: תהלים נה

וְנַפְשִׁי תָּגִיל בַּיהוה, תָּשִׂישׂ בִּישׁוּעָתוֹ: תהלים לה

הַנּוֹתֵן תְּשׁוּעָה לַמְּלָכִים, הַפּוֹצֶה אֶת־דָּוִד עַבְדּוֹ מֵחֶרֶב רָעָה: תהלים קמד

## חצי קדיש

ש״ץ: יִתְגַּדַּל וְיִתְקַדַּשׁ שְׁמֵהּ רַבָּא (קהל: אָמֵן)

בְּעָלְמָא דִּי בְרָא כִרְעוּתֵהּ

וְיַמְלִיךְ מַלְכוּתֵהּ

וְיַצְמַח פֻּרְקָנֵהּ וִיקָרֵב מְשִׁיחֵהּ (קהל: אָמֵן)

בְּחַיֵּיכוֹן וּבְיוֹמֵיכוֹן וּבְחַיֵּי דְכָל בֵּית יִשְׂרָאֵל

בַּעֲגָלָא וּבִזְמַן קָרִיב, וְאִמְרוּ אָמֵן. (קהל: אָמֵן)

קהל וש״ץ: יְהֵא שְׁמֵהּ רַבָּא מְבָרַךְ לְעָלַם וּלְעָלְמֵי עָלְמַיָּא.

ש״ץ: יִתְבָּרַךְ וְיִשְׁתַּבַּח וְיִתְפָּאַר וְיִתְרוֹמַם וְיִתְנַשֵּׂא

וְיִתְהַדָּר וְיִתְעַלֶּה וְיִתְהַלָּל

שְׁמֵהּ דְּקֻדְשָׁא בְּרִיךְ הוּא (קהל: אָמֵן)

לְעֵלָּא לְעֵלָּא מִכָּל בִּרְכָתָא וְשִׁירָתָא

תֻּשְׁבְּחָתָא וְנֶחֱמָתָא

דַּאֲמִירָן בְּעָלְמָא, וְאִמְרוּ אָמֵן. (קהל: אָמֵן)

---

"I dwell… with the one who is of a contrite and humble spirit" (Isaiah 57:15). Repentance begins with humility (Rabbeinu Baḥye). No crown carries such royalty as humility (Rabbi Elazar ben Yehuda Roke'aḥ). One who is a leader in Israel should not think that the Lord of the universe chose him because

# Musaf for the First Day

## THE AMIDA

*The following prayer, until "in former years" on page 526, is said silently, standing with feet together. If there is a minyan, the Amida is repeated aloud by the Leader. Take three steps forward and at the points indicated by ▾, bend the knees at the first word, bow at the second, and stand straight before saying God's name.*

When I proclaim the LORD's name, give glory to our God. *Deut. 32*

O LORD, open my lips, so that my mouth may declare Your praise. *Ps. 51*

PATRIARCHS

▾בָּרוּךְ Blessed are You, LORD our God and God of our fathers,
God of Abraham, God of Isaac and God of Jacob;
the great, mighty and awesome God, God Most High,

---

Kingship, Remembrance and Shofar are the key ideas of Rosh HaShana. First it is the anniversary of the day when God created the universe and thus became its Sovereign. Second it is the day He remembers our lives and those of our ancestors, and we pray to be judged favorably, if not for our sake then for theirs. Third, it is the day of the shofar, the sound that has accompanied the children of Israel through the epic events of their history and will accompany them in the future: the sound of tears and hope, warning and celebration.

Each of the three prayers blends universality and particularity. *Malkhiyot* speaks of God as King of Israel but contains a plea that His majesty be recognized by all humanity. In *Zikhronot* we speak of God remembering the whole of creation as well as His chosen people. In *Shofarot,* alongside the shofar of Sinai we speak of the shofar that Isaiah said will one day be heard by "All the inhabitants of the world, all the dwellers on earth." That is the fugue of Rosh HaShana.

וֵאלֹהֵי אֲבוֹתֵינוּ *And God of our fathers.* The first paragraph speaks about the fathers, Abraham, Isaac and Jacob, for it is in their merit that we pray. Even Moses, when he prayed on behalf of the people, did so by invoking them (Ex. 32:13). We pray not as isolated individuals but as members of a family, whose history stretches over some four thousand years. And we pray to God not as a metaphysical abstraction but as the One who made a covenant with our ancestors that has shaped our history ever since.

# מוסף ליום א׳

## עמידה

*The following prayer, until* קַדְמֹנִיּוֹת *on page 527, is said silently, standing with feet together. If there is a* מנין*, the* עמידה *is repeated aloud by the* שליח ציבור*. Take three steps forward and at the points indicated by* ˅*, bend the knees at the first word, bow at the second, and stand straight before saying God's name.*

כִּי שֵׁם יהוה אֶקְרָא, הָבוּ גֹדֶל לֵאלֹהֵינוּ: דברים לב

אֲדֹנָי, שְׂפָתַי תִּפְתָּח, וּפִי יַגִּיד תְּהִלָּתֶךָ: תהלים נא

אבות

˅בָּרוּךְ ˅אַתָּה יהוה, אֱלֹהֵינוּ וֵאלֹהֵי אֲבוֹתֵינוּ
אֱלֹהֵי אַבְרָהָם, אֱלֹהֵי יִצְחָק, וֵאלֹהֵי יַעֲקֹב
הָאֵל הַגָּדוֹל הַגִּבּוֹר וְהַנּוֹרָא, אֵל עֶלְיוֹן

---

MUSAF

Musaf represents the "additional" sacrifice offered on special days: Shabbat, Festivals and Rosh Ḥodesh, and is said only on these days. Whereas the three daily prayers go back to the patriarchs (Shaḥarit to Abraham, Minḥa to Isaac, Ma'ariv to Jacob), Musaf is only connected to a sacrifice. Hence it has a more sacrificial feel than the other Amidot.

Musaf generally consists of the same opening three and closing three blessings as all other Amidot, plus a central blessing representing *kedushat hayom*, the special sanctity of the day. Rosh HaShana is an exception. In place of one central blessing it has three, representing the three central themes of the day: (1) *Malkhiyot*, referring to God's kingship; (2) *Zikhronot*, remembrances, in which we express our faith that God remembers our deeds and His covenant with our ancestors and us; and (3) *Shofarot*, references to the shofar and the part it plays in Jewish history and destiny.

All three central blessings have the same structure. They begin with an introductory prologue announcing the theme of the blessing. There then follow ten biblical verses, each referring to "King," "remembrance" or "shofar," the first three from the Torah, the second three from *Ketuvim*, the "Writings," and the third three from the prophetic books. The tenth verse returns to the Torah, the book of our beginnings. The blessing ends with a prayer.

who bestows acts of loving-kindness, who creates all,
who remembers the loving-kindness of the fathers
and will bring a Redeemer to their children's children
for the sake of His name, in love.

זָכְרֵנוּ לְחַיִּים Remember us for life, O King who desires life,
and write us in the book of life – for Your sake, O God of life.

King, Helper, Savior, Shield:
▾Blessed are You, LORD, Shield of Abraham.

DIVINE MIGHT

אַתָּה גִּבּוֹר You are eternally mighty, LORD.
You give life to the dead and have great power to save.

*In Israel:* He causes the dew to fall.

He sustains the living with loving-kindness,
and with great compassion revives the dead.
He supports the fallen, heals the sick, sets captives free,
and keeps His faith with those who sleep in the dust.
Who is like You, Master of might,
and to whom can You be compared,
O King who brings death and gives life,
and makes salvation grow?

מִי כָמְוֹךָ Who is like You, compassionate Father,
who remembers His creatures in compassion, for life?

Faithful are You to revive the dead.
Blessed are You, LORD, who revives the dead.

---

chimes with "who remembers the loving-kindness of the fathers." God remembers. Therefore the past is not lost. It exists in God's eternity.

מִי כָמְוֹךָ אַב הָרַחֲמָן *Who is like You, compassionate Father?* The second addition made throughout the Ten Days. The word "compassion" echoes the earlier phrase, "With great compassion revives the dead."

גּוֹמֵל חֲסָדִים טוֹבִים, קוֹנֵה הַכֹּל
וְזוֹכֵר חַסְדֵי אָבוֹת
וּמֵבִיא גוֹאֵל לִבְנֵי בְנֵיהֶם לְמַעַן שְׁמוֹ בְּאַהֲבָה.

זָכְרֵנוּ לְחַיִּים, מֶלֶךְ חָפֵץ בַּחַיִּים
וְכָתְבֵנוּ בְּסֵפֶר הַחַיִּים, לְמַעַנְךָ אֱלֹהִים חַיִּים.

מֶלֶךְ עוֹזֵר וּמוֹשִׁיעַ וּמָגֵן.
ּבָּרוּךְ אַתָּה יהוה, מָגֵן אַבְרָהָם.

גבורות

אַתָּה גִּבּוֹר לְעוֹלָם, אֲדֹנָי
מְחַיֵּה מֵתִים אַתָּה, רַב לְהוֹשִׁיעַ
בארץ ישראל: מוֹרִיד הַטָּל
מְכַלְכֵּל חַיִּים בְּחֶסֶד, מְחַיֵּה מֵתִים בְּרַחֲמִים רַבִּים
סוֹמֵךְ נוֹפְלִים, וְרוֹפֵא חוֹלִים, וּמַתִּיר אֲסוּרִים
וּמְקַיֵּם אֱמוּנָתוֹ לִישֵׁנֵי עָפָר.
מִי כָמְוֹךָ, בַּעַל גְּבוּרוֹת, וּמִי דּוֹמֶה לָּךְ
מֶלֶךְ, מֵמִית וּמְחַיֶּה וּמַצְמִיחַ יְשׁוּעָה.

מִי כָמְוֹךָ אַב הָרַחֲמָן
זוֹכֵר יְצוּרָיו לְחַיִּים בְּרַחֲמִים.

וְנֶאֱמָן אַתָּה לְהַחֲיוֹת מֵתִים.
בָּרוּךְ אַתָּה יהוה, מְחַיֵּה הַמֵּתִים.

---

זָכְרֵנוּ לְחַיִּים *Remember us for life.* One of the four additions said in the silent Amida throughout the Ten Days of Repentance. The word "remember"

HOLINESS

אַתָּה קָדוֹשׁ You are holy and Your name is holy,
and holy ones praise You daily, Selah!
For You, God, are a great and holy King.

לְדוֹר וָדוֹר From generation to generation declare God King,
for He alone is lofty and holy.

וּבְכֵן יִתְקַדַּשׁ And so may Your name be sanctified, Lord our God,
through Israel Your nation
and Jerusalem, Your city,
and Zion, the dwelling place of Your honor
and through the royal house of David Your anointed,
and Your Sanctuary and Your Temple.

וּבְכֵן תֵּן פַּחְדְּךָ And so place the fear of You, Lord our God,
over all that You have made,
and the terror of You over all You have created,
and all who were made will stand in awe of You,
and all of creation will worship You,
and they will be bound all together as one
to carry out Your will with an undivided heart;
for we know, Lord our God,
that all dominion is laid out before You,
strength is in Your palm,
and might in Your right hand,
Your name spreading awe
over all You have created.

---

in the fourth. As is often the case in Jewish prayer, we honor both views. Note again that it follows the normal structure of the Jewish imagination by moving from the universal to the particular: the first "And so" refers to all humanity, the second to "Your people," the third to the righteous, upright and pious.

קדושת השם

אַתָּה קָדוֹשׁ וְשִׁמְךָ קָדוֹשׁ
וּקְדוֹשִׁים בְּכָל יוֹם יְהַלְלוּךָ סֶּלָה
כִּי אֵל מֶלֶךְ גָּדוֹל וְקָדוֹשׁ אָתָּה.

לְדוֹר וָדוֹר הַמְלִיכוּ לָאֵל
כִּי הוּא לְבַדּוֹ מָרוֹם וְקָדוֹשׁ.

וּבְכֵן יִתְקַדַּשׁ שִׁמְךָ יהוה אֱלֹהֵינוּ
עַל יִשְׂרָאֵל עַמֶּךָ וְעַל יְרוּשָׁלַיִם עִירֶךָ
וְעַל צִיּוֹן מִשְׁכַּן כְּבוֹדֶךָ וְעַל מַלְכוּת בֵּית דָּוִד מְשִׁיחֶךָ
וְעַל מְכוֹנְךָ וְהֵיכָלֶךָ.

וּבְכֵן תֵּן פַּחְדְּךָ יהוה אֱלֹהֵינוּ עַל כָּל מַעֲשֶׂיךָ
וְאֵימָתְךָ עַל כָּל מַה שֶּׁבָּרָאתָ
וְיִירָאוּךָ כָּל הַמַּעֲשִׂים
וְיִשְׁתַּחֲווּ לְפָנֶיךָ כָּל הַבְּרוּאִים
וְיֵעָשׂוּ כֻלָּם אֲגֻדָּה אֶחָת לַעֲשׂוֹת רְצוֹנְךָ בְּלֵבָב שָׁלֵם
כְּמוֹ שֶׁיָּדַעְנוּ יהוה אֱלֹהֵינוּ שֶׁהַשָּׁלְטָן לְפָנֶיךָ
עֹז בְּיָדְךָ וּגְבוּרָה בִּימִינֶךָ
וְשִׁמְךָ נוֹרָא עַל כָּל מַה שֶּׁבָּרָאתָ.

---

וּבְכֵן תֵּן פַּחְדְּךָ *And so place the fear of You.* A special addition to the holiness blessing, a prayer about God's sovereignty over the universe. It follows the view of Rabbi Yoḥanan ben Nuri in the Mishna (*Rosh HaShana* 4:5) that the theme of Kingship (*Malkhiyot*) is to be inserted in the third blessing of the Amida, as opposed to Rabbi Akiva who held that it should be said

וּבְכֵן תֵּן כָּבוֹד And so place honor, Lord, upon Your people,
praise on those who fear You
and hope into those who seek You,
the confidence to speak
into all who long for You,
gladness to Your land and joy to Your city,
the flourishing of pride to David Your servant,
and a lamp laid out for his descendant, Your anointed,
soon, in our days.

וּבְכֵן צַדִּיקִים And then righteous people will see and rejoice,
and the upright will exult,
and the pious revel in joy,
and injustice will have nothing more to say,
and all wickedness will fade away like smoke
as You sweep the rule of arrogance from the earth.

וְתִמְלֹךְ And You, who are the Lord our God,
will rule alone over all those You have made,
in Mount Zion, the dwelling of Your glory,
and in Jerusalem, Your holy city,
as it is written in Your holy Writings:
"The Lord shall reign for ever. *Ps. 146*
He is your God, Zion,
from generation to generation, Halleluya!"

קָדוֹשׁ אַתָּה You are holy, Your name is awesome,
and there is no god but You,
as it is written,
"The Lord of hosts shall be raised up through His judgment, *Is. 5*
the Holy God, made holy in righteousness."
Blessed are You, Lord,
the holy King.

וּבְכֵן תֵּן כָּבוֹד יהוה לְעַמֶּךָ
תְּהִלָּה לִירֵאֶיךָ
וְתִקְוָה טוֹבָה לְדוֹרְשֶׁיךָ
וּפִתְחוֹן פֶּה לַמְיַחֲלִים לָךְ
שִׂמְחָה לְאַרְצֶךָ, וְשָׂשׂוֹן לְעִירֶךָ
וּצְמִיחַת קֶרֶן לְדָוִד עַבְדֶּךָ
וַעֲרִיכַת נֵר לְבֶן יִשַׁי מְשִׁיחֶךָ
בִּמְהֵרָה בְיָמֵינוּ.

וּבְכֵן צַדִּיקִים יִרְאוּ וְיִשְׂמָחוּ, וִישָׁרִים יַעֲלֹזוּ
וַחֲסִידִים בְּרִנָּה יָגִילוּ, וְעוֹלָתָה תִּקְפָּץ פִּיהָ
וְכָל הָרִשְׁעָה כֻּלָּהּ כְּעָשָׁן תִּכְלֶה
כִּי תַעֲבִיר מֶמְשֶׁלֶת זָדוֹן מִן הָאָרֶץ.

וְתִמְלֹךְ אַתָּה הוּא יהוה אֱלֹהֵינוּ
מְהֵרָה לְבַדֶּךָ עַל כָּל מַעֲשֶׂיךָ
בְּהַר צִיּוֹן מִשְׁכַּן כְּבוֹדֶךָ
וּבִירוּשָׁלַיִם עִיר קָדְשֶׁךָ
כַּכָּתוּב בְּדִבְרֵי קָדְשֶׁךָ
יִמְלֹךְ יהוה לְעוֹלָם, אֱלֹהַיִךְ צִיּוֹן לְדֹר וָדֹר, הַלְלוּיָהּ: תהלים קמו

קָדוֹשׁ אַתָּה וְנוֹרָא שְׁמֶךָ, וְאֵין אֱלוֹהַּ מִבַּלְעָדֶיךָ
כַּכָּתוּב, וַיִּגְבַּהּ יהוה צְבָאוֹת בַּמִּשְׁפָּט ישעיה ה
וְהָאֵל הַקָּדוֹשׁ נִקְדַּשׁ בִּצְדָקָה:
בָּרוּךְ אַתָּה יהוה, הַמֶּלֶךְ הַקָּדוֹשׁ.

HOLINESS OF THE DAY AND KINGSHIP

אַתָּה בְחַרְתָּנוּ You have chosen us from among all peoples.
You have loved and favored us.
You have raised us above all tongues.
You have made us holy through Your commandments.
You have brought us near, our King, to Your service,
and have called us by Your great and holy name.

*On Shabbat, add the words in parentheses:*

וַתִּתֶּן לָנוּ And You, LORD our God, have given us in love
(this Sabbath day and) this Day of Remembrance,
a day of (recalling) blowing the shofar,
(with love,) a holy assembly
in memory of the exodus from Egypt.

וּמִפְּנֵי חֲטָאֵינוּ But because of our sins we were exiled from our land
and driven far from our country.
We cannot perform our duties in Your chosen House,
the great and holy Temple that was called by Your name,
because of the hand that was stretched out
against Your Sanctuary.
May it be Your will, LORD our God and God of our ancestors,
merciful King,
that You in Your abounding compassion may once more
have mercy on us and on Your Sanctuary,
rebuilding it swiftly and adding to its glory.

---

we face God directly, addressing Him in the second person: "You." This one word differentiates Judaism from the philosophical tradition that sees God as an impersonal force, the First Cause, the Unmoved Mover, Necessary Being, and so on. In Judaism God is a "You," not an "It" – a Presence who relates to us as persons in all our particularity. This, said Judah HaLevi (*Kuzari*, IV:1–16), is the difference between the God of Abraham and the God of Aristotle. We can philosophize about the latter but we can talk only to the former.

קדושת היום ומלכויות

אַתָּה בְחַרְתָּנוּ מִכָּל הָעַמִּים
אָהַבְתָּ אוֹתָנוּ וְרָצִיתָ בָּנוּ
וְרוֹמַמְתָּנוּ מִכָּל הַלְּשׁוֹנוֹת
וְקִדַּשְׁתָּנוּ בְּמִצְוֹתֶיךָ
וְקֵרַבְתָּנוּ מַלְכֵּנוּ לַעֲבוֹדָתֶךָ
וְשִׁמְךָ הַגָּדוֹל וְהַקָּדוֹשׁ עָלֵינוּ קָרָאתָ.

*On* שבת*, add the words in parentheses:*

וַתִּתֶּן לָנוּ יהוה אֱלֹהֵינוּ בְּאַהֲבָה
אֶת יוֹם (הַשַּׁבָּת הַזֶּה וְאֶת יוֹם) הַזִּכָּרוֹן הַזֶּה
יוֹם (זִכְרוֹן) תְּרוּעָה (בְּאַהֲבָה)
מִקְרָא קֹדֶשׁ, זֵכֶר לִיצִיאַת מִצְרָיִם.

וּמִפְּנֵי חֲטָאֵינוּ גָּלִינוּ מֵאַרְצֵנוּ, וְנִתְרַחַקְנוּ מֵעַל אַדְמָתֵנוּ
וְאֵין אֲנוּ יְכוֹלִים לַעֲשׂוֹת חוֹבוֹתֵינוּ בְּבֵית בְּחִירָתֶךָ
בַּבַּיִת הַגָּדוֹל וְהַקָּדוֹשׁ שֶׁנִּקְרָא שִׁמְךָ עָלָיו
מִפְּנֵי הַיָּד שֶׁנִּשְׁתַּלְּחָה בְּמִקְדָּשֶׁךָ.
יְהִי רָצוֹן מִלְּפָנֶיךָ יהוה אֱלֹהֵינוּ וֵאלֹהֵי אֲבוֹתֵינוּ, מֶלֶךְ רַחֲמָן
שֶׁתָּשׁוּב וּתְרַחֵם עָלֵינוּ וְעַל מִקְדָּשְׁךָ בְּרַחֲמֶיךָ הָרַבִּים
וְתִבְנֵהוּ מְהֵרָה וּתְגַדֵּל כְּבוֹדוֹ.

---

אַתָּה בְחַרְתָּנוּ *You have chosen us.* The first of the central blessings, combining *kedushat hayom*, the special sanctity of the day, with *Malkhiyot*, the first of the three Rosh HaShana themes, God's kingship. The fourth paragraph of most, though not all, Amidot begins with the word "You," and it does so for a reason. Once the preliminary praise (the first three blessings) has been completed,

Our Father, our King, reveal the glory of Your kingdom to us swiftly.
Appear and be exalted over us in the sight of all that lives.
Bring back our scattered ones from among the nations,
and gather our dispersed people from the ends of the earth.

וַהֲבִיאֵנוּ לְצִיּוֹן Lead us to Zion, Your city, in jubilation,
and to Jerusalem, home of Your Temple, with everlasting joy.
There we will prepare for You our obligatory offerings:
the regular daily offerings in their order
and the additional offerings according to their law.
And the additional offerings (of this Sabbath day and) of this
Day of Remembrance we will prepare and offer before You in love,
in accord with Your will's commandment,
as You wrote for us in Your Torah
through Your servant Moses, by Your own word, as it is said:

*On Shabbat:* "וּבְיוֹם הַשַּׁבָּת On the Sabbath day, make an offering of two lambs a year old, without blemish, together with two-tenths of an ephah of fine flour mixed with oil as a meal-offering, and its appropriate libation. This is the burnt-offering for every Sabbath, in addition to the regular daily burnt-offering and its libation." *Num. 28*

וּבַחֹדֶשׁ הַשְּׁבִיעִי On the first day of the seventh month you shall hold a sacred assembly. You shall do no laborious work, and you shall mark a Day of the Blowing of the Shofar. You shall make a burnt-offering of pleasing aroma to the LORD: a young bullock, a ram, and seven yearling male lambs; they shall be without blemish. *Num. 29*

וּמִנְחָתָם וְנִסְכֵּיהֶם And their meal offerings and wine-libations as ordained: three-tenths of an ephah for the bull, two-tenths of an ephah for the ram, one-tenth of an ephah for each of the seven lambs, wine for the libations, two male goats for atonement, and two regular daily offerings according to their law.

מִלְּבַד All this aside from the burnt-offering of the New Moon and its meal-offering, and the regular daily burnt-offering with its meal-offering, and their libations according to their ordinance, a burnt-offering of pleasing odor to the LORD. *Ibid.*

אָבִינוּ מַלְכֵּנוּ, גַּלֵּה כְּבוֹד מַלְכוּתְךָ עָלֵינוּ מְהֵרָה
וְהוֹפַע וְהִנָּשֵׂא עָלֵינוּ לְעֵינֵי כָּל חָי
וְקָרֵב פְּזוּרֵינוּ מִבֵּין הַגּוֹיִם, וּנְפוּצוֹתֵינוּ כַּנֵּס מִיַּרְכְּתֵי אָרֶץ.

וַהֲבִיאֵנוּ לְצִיּוֹן עִירְךָ בְּרִנָּה
וְלִירוּשָׁלַיִם בֵּית מִקְדָּשְׁךָ בְּשִׂמְחַת עוֹלָם
וְשָׁם נַעֲשֶׂה לְפָנֶיךָ אֶת קָרְבְּנוֹת חוֹבוֹתֵינוּ
תְּמִידִים כְּסִדְרָם וּמוּסָפִים כְּהִלְכָתָם
וְאֶת מוּסְפֵי יוֹם (הַשַּׁבָּת הַזֶּה וְיוֹם) הַזִּכָּרוֹן הַזֶּה
נַעֲשֶׂה וְנַקְרִיב לְפָנֶיךָ בְּאַהֲבָה כְּמִצְוַת רְצוֹנֶךָ
כְּמוֹ שֶׁכָּתַבְתָּ עָלֵינוּ בְּתוֹרָתֶךָ
עַל יְדֵי מֹשֶׁה עַבְדֶּךָ מִפִּי כְבוֹדֶךָ, כָּאָמוּר

בשבת: וּבְיוֹם הַשַּׁבָּת, שְׁנֵי־כְבָשִׂים בְּנֵי־שָׁנָה תְּמִימִם, וּשְׁנֵי עֶשְׂרֹנִים סֹלֶת מִנְחָה בְּלוּלָה בַשֶּׁמֶן וְנִסְכּוֹ: עֹלַת שַׁבַּת בְּשַׁבַּתּוֹ, עַל־עֹלַת הַתָּמִיד וְנִסְכָּהּ: במדבר כח

וּבַחֹדֶשׁ הַשְּׁבִיעִי בְּאֶחָד לַחֹדֶשׁ מִקְרָא־קֹדֶשׁ יִהְיֶה לָכֶם, כָּל־מְלֶאכֶת עֲבֹדָה לֹא תַעֲשׂוּ, יוֹם תְּרוּעָה יִהְיֶה לָכֶם: וַעֲשִׂיתֶם עֹלָה לְרֵיחַ נִיחֹחַ לַיהוה, פַּר בֶּן־בָּקָר אֶחָד, אַיִל אֶחָד, כְּבָשִׂים בְּנֵי־שָׁנָה שִׁבְעָה תְּמִימִם: במדבר כט

וּמִנְחָתָם וְנִסְכֵּיהֶם כִּמְדֻבָּר, שְׁלֹשָׁה עֶשְׂרֹנִים לַפָּר וּשְׁנֵי עֶשְׂרֹנִים לָאָיִל, וְעִשָּׂרוֹן לַכֶּבֶשׂ, וְיַיִן כְּנִסְכּוֹ, וּשְׁנֵי שְׂעִירִים לְכַפֵּר, וּשְׁנֵי תְמִידִים כְּהִלְכָתָם.

מִלְּבַד עֹלַת הַחֹדֶשׁ וּמִנְחָתָהּ, וְעֹלַת הַתָּמִיד וּמִנְחָתָהּ, וְנִסְכֵּיהֶם כְּמִשְׁפָּטָם, לְרֵיחַ נִיחֹחַ, אִשֶּׁה לַיהוה: שם

*On Shabbat:* יִשְׂמְחוּ Those who keep the Sabbath and call it a delight shall rejoice in Your kingship. The people who sanctify the seventh day shall all be satisfied and take delight in Your goodness, for You favored the seventh day and declared it holy. You called it "most desirable of days" in remembrance of Creation.

עָלֵינוּ It is our duty to praise the Master of all,
and ascribe greatness to the Author of creation,
who has not made us like the nations of the lands,
nor placed us like the families of the earth;
who has not made our portion like theirs,
nor our destiny like all their multitudes.
(For they worship vanity and emptiness,
and pray to a god who cannot save.)
But we bow in worship
and thank the Supreme King of kings, the Holy One, blessed be He,
who extends the heavens and establishes the earth,
whose throne of glory is in the heavens above,
and whose power's Presence is in the highest of heights.
He is our God; there is no other.
Truly He is our King; there is none else,
as it is written in His Torah:
"You shall know and take to heart this day that the LORD is God, *Deut. 4*
in the heavens above and on the earth below. There is no other."

Therefore, we place our hope in You, LORD our God,
that we may soon see the glory of Your power,
when You will remove abominations from the earth,
and idols will be utterly destroyed,
when the world will be perfected
under the sovereignty of the Almighty,

---

that Jews are different in holding God as their only King, the only nation in the world constituted by a religious belief; and (2) the hope, expressed in the second paragraph, that one day all humanity will recognize the One God

בשבת: יִשְׂמְחוּ בְמַלְכוּתְךָ שׁוֹמְרֵי שַׁבָּת וְקוֹרְאֵי עֹנֶג. עַם מְקַדְּשֵׁי שְׁבִיעִי
כֻּלָּם יִשְׂבְּעוּ וְיִתְעַנְּגוּ מִטּוּבֶךָ, וּבַשְּׁבִיעִי רָצִיתָ בּוֹ וְקִדַּשְׁתּוֹ, חֶמְדַּת
יָמִים אוֹתוֹ קָרָאתָ, זֵכֶר לְמַעֲשֵׂה בְרֵאשִׁית.

עָלֵינוּ לְשַׁבֵּחַ לַאֲדוֹן הַכֹּל, לָתֵת גְּדֻלָּה לְיוֹצֵר בְּרֵאשִׁית
שֶׁלֹּא עָשָׂנוּ כְּגוֹיֵי הָאֲרָצוֹת, וְלֹא שָׂמָנוּ כְּמִשְׁפְּחוֹת הָאֲדָמָה
שֶׁלֹּא שָׂם חֶלְקֵנוּ כָּהֶם וְגוֹרָלֵנוּ כְּכָל הֲמוֹנָם.
(שֶׁהֵם מִשְׁתַּחֲוִים לְהֶבֶל וָרִיק וּמִתְפַּלְּלִים אֶל אֵל לֹא יוֹשִׁיעַ.)
וַאֲנַחְנוּ כּוֹרְעִים וּמִשְׁתַּחֲוִים וּמוֹדִים
לִפְנֵי מֶלֶךְ מַלְכֵי הַמְּלָכִים, הַקָּדוֹשׁ בָּרוּךְ הוּא
שֶׁהוּא נוֹטֶה שָׁמַיִם וְיוֹסֵד אָרֶץ, וּמוֹשַׁב יְקָרוֹ בַּשָּׁמַיִם מִמַּעַל
וּשְׁכִינַת עֻזּוֹ בְּגָבְהֵי מְרוֹמִים.
הוּא אֱלֹהֵינוּ, אֵין עוֹד.
אֱמֶת מַלְכֵּנוּ, אֶפֶס זוּלָתוֹ
כַּכָּתוּב בְּתוֹרָתוֹ
וְיָדַעְתָּ הַיּוֹם וַהֲשֵׁבֹתָ אֶל־לְבָבֶךָ דברים ד
כִּי יהוה הוּא הָאֱלֹהִים בַּשָּׁמַיִם מִמַּעַל וְעַל־הָאָרֶץ מִתָּחַת
אֵין עוֹד:

וְעַל כֵּן נְקַוֶּה לְּךָ יהוה אֱלֹהֵינוּ, לִרְאוֹת מְהֵרָה בְּתִפְאֶרֶת עֻזֶּךָ
לְהַעֲבִיר גִּלּוּלִים מִן הָאָרֶץ, וְהָאֱלִילִים כָּרוֹת יִכָּרֵתוּן
לְתַקֵּן עוֹלָם בְּמַלְכוּת שַׁדַּי.

---

עָלֵינוּ לְשַׁבֵּחַ *It is our duty to praise.* This is the original setting of the *Aleinu* prayer which only later – at least a thousand years after its composition – was adopted as the closing prayer for each of the three daily services. Structured in two paragraphs, it contrasts present reality with future hope: (1) the reality

when all humanity will call on Your name,
to turn all the earth's wicked toward You.
All the world's inhabitants will realize and know
that to You every knee must bow
and every tongue swear loyalty.
Before You, LORD our God, they will kneel and bow down
and give honor to Your glorious name.
They will all accept the yoke of Your kingdom,
and You will reign over them soon and for ever.
For the kingdom is Yours,
and to all eternity You will reign in glory,
as it is written in Your Torah:
"The LORD will reign for ever and ever." *Ex. 15*

And it is said:
He saw no injustice in Jacob, *Num. 23*
no deceit did He witness in Israel,
the LORD their God is with them,
and a King's adulation resounds among them.
And it is said:
[The LORD] became King in Yeshurun, *Deut. 33*
when the heads of the people gathered,
all the tribes of Israel together.

And in Your holy Writings it is said,
For kingship is the LORD's *Ps. 22*
and He rules over the nations.
And it is said:
The LORD reigns. *Ps. 93*
He is robed in majesty.
The LORD is robed, girded with strength.
The world is firmly established;
it cannot be moved.

וְכׇל בְּנֵי בָשָׂר יִקְרְאוּ בִשְׁמֶךָ לְהַפְנוֹת אֵלֶיךָ כׇּל רִשְׁעֵי אָרֶץ.
יַכִּירוּ וְיֵדְעוּ כׇּל יוֹשְׁבֵי תֵבֵל
כִּי לְךָ תִּכְרַע כׇּל בֶּרֶךְ, תִּשָּׁבַע כׇּל לָשׁוֹן.
לְפָנֶיךָ יהוה אֱלֹהֵינוּ יִכְרְעוּ וְיִפֹּלוּ
וְלִכְבוֹד שִׁמְךָ יְקָר יִתֵּנוּ
וִיקַבְּלוּ כֻלָּם אֶת עֹל מַלְכוּתֶךָ
וְתִמְלֹךְ עֲלֵיהֶם מְהֵרָה לְעוֹלָם וָעֶד.
כִּי הַמַּלְכוּת שֶׁלְּךָ הִיא וּלְעוֹלְמֵי עַד תִּמְלֹךְ בְּכָבוֹד
כַּכָּתוּב בְּתוֹרָתֶךָ

יהוה יִמְלֹךְ לְעֹלָם וָעֶד: שמות טו

וְנֶאֱמַר

לֹא־הִבִּיט אָוֶן בְּיַעֲקֹב, וְלֹא־רָאָה עָמָל בְּיִשְׂרָאֵל במדבר כג
יהוה אֱלֹהָיו עִמּוֹ, וּתְרוּעַת מֶלֶךְ בּוֹ:

וְנֶאֱמַר

וַיְהִי בִישֻׁרוּן מֶלֶךְ, בְּהִתְאַסֵּף רָאשֵׁי עָם דברים לג
יַחַד שִׁבְטֵי יִשְׂרָאֵל:

וּבְדִבְרֵי קׇדְשְׁךָ כָּתוּב לֵאמֹר

כִּי לַיהוה הַמְּלוּכָה וּמֹשֵׁל בַּגּוֹיִם: תהלים כב

וְנֶאֱמַר

יהוה מָלָךְ, גֵּאוּת לָבֵשׁ תהלים צג
לָבֵשׁ יהוה עֹז הִתְאַזָּר, אַף־תִּכּוֹן תֵּבֵל בַּל־תִּמּוֹט:

---

as their King. The prayer was edited by Rav, the third-century teacher who spanned the end of the Mishnaic era and the beginning of the period that produced the Babylonian Talmud. (Rav, also known as Abba Arikha, founded the academy at Sura.) In its earliest form, however, it may be much older.

And it is said:

Lift up your heads, O gates; *Ps. 24*
be uplifted, eternal doors,
so that the King of glory may enter.
Who is the King of glory?
It is the LORD, strong and mighty,
the LORD mighty in battle.
Lift up your heads, O gates;
lift them up, eternal doors,
so that the King of glory may enter.
Who is He, the King of glory?
The LORD of hosts, He is the King of glory, Selah!

And by Your servants the prophets it is written:

This is what the LORD, King of Israel and its Savior, *Is. 44*
the LORD of hosts has said:
"I am the first and I shall be the last,
and there is no other god but Me."

And it is said:

Saviors shall go up to Mount Zion *Ob. 1*
to judge Mount Esau,
and the LORD's shall be the kingdom.

And it is said:

Then shall the LORD be King over all the earth. *Zech. 14*
On that day the LORD shall be One
and His name One.

And in Your Torah it is written:

Listen, Israel: the LORD is our God, *Deut. 6*
the LORD is One.

אֱלֹהֵינוּ Our God and God of our ancestors,
rule over all the world in Your honor,
and be raised above all the earth in Your glory,
and appear, in the splendor of Your great might
before all those who live in this world, Your domain.

וְנֶאֱמַר

תהלים כד
שְׂאוּ שְׁעָרִים רָאשֵׁיכֶם, וְהִנָּשְׂאוּ פִּתְחֵי עוֹלָם
וְיָבוֹא מֶלֶךְ הַכָּבוֹד:
מִי זֶה מֶלֶךְ הַכָּבוֹד, יהוה עִזּוּז וְגִבּוֹר
יהוה גִּבּוֹר מִלְחָמָה:
שְׂאוּ שְׁעָרִים רָאשֵׁיכֶם, וּשְׂאוּ פִּתְחֵי עוֹלָם
וְיָבֹא מֶלֶךְ הַכָּבוֹד:
מִי הוּא זֶה מֶלֶךְ הַכָּבוֹד
יהוה צְבָאוֹת הוּא מֶלֶךְ הַכָּבוֹד סֶלָה:

וְעַל יְדֵי עֲבָדֶיךָ הַנְּבִיאִים כָּתוּב לֵאמֹר

ישעיה מד
כֹּה־אָמַר יהוה מֶלֶךְ־יִשְׂרָאֵל וְגֹאֲלוֹ, יהוה צְבָאוֹת
אֲנִי רִאשׁוֹן וַאֲנִי אַחֲרוֹן, וּמִבַּלְעָדַי אֵין אֱלֹהִים:

וְנֶאֱמַר

עובדיה א
וְעָלוּ מוֹשִׁעִים בְּהַר צִיּוֹן לִשְׁפֹּט אֶת־הַר עֵשָׂו
וְהָיְתָה לַיהוה הַמְּלוּכָה:

וְנֶאֱמַר

זכריה יד
וְהָיָה יהוה לְמֶלֶךְ עַל־כָּל־הָאָרֶץ
בַּיּוֹם הַהוּא יִהְיֶה יהוה אֶחָד וּשְׁמוֹ אֶחָד:

וּבְתוֹרָתְךָ כָּתוּב לֵאמֹר

דברים ו
שְׁמַע יִשְׂרָאֵל, יהוה אֱלֹהֵינוּ יהוה אֶחָד:

אֱלֹהֵינוּ וֵאלֹהֵי אֲבוֹתֵינוּ
מְלֹךְ עַל כָּל הָעוֹלָם כֻּלּוֹ בִּכְבוֹדֶךָ
וְהִנָּשֵׂא עַל כָּל הָאָרֶץ בִּיקָרֶךָ
וְהוֹפַע בַּהֲדַר גְּאוֹן עֻזֶּךָ עַל כָּל יוֹשְׁבֵי תֵבֵל אַרְצֶךָ.

And all who were made will know that You made them,
and all who were formed will know that You formed them,
and all that have breath in their mouths will declare:
The LORD, God of Israel is King,
and His kingship has dominion over all.

*On Shabbat, add the words in parentheses:*

(Our God and God of our ancestors,
find favor, please, in our rest.)
Make us holy through Your commandments
and grant us our share in Your Torah.
Satisfy us with Your goodness, grant our souls joy in Your salvation
(in love and favor, LORD our God,
grant us as our heritage Your holy Sabbath,
so that all Israel, who sanctify Your name may find rest on it),
and purify our hearts to serve You in truth.
For You, LORD, are truth, and Your word is truth
and holds true forever.
Blessed are You, LORD, King over all the earth,
who sanctifies (the Sabbath,) Israel
and the Day of Remembrance.

*In many congregations, the shofar is sounded (except on Shabbat).*

| | | |
|---|---|---|
| TEKIA | SHEVARIM TERUA | TEKIA |
| TEKIA | SHEVARIM | TEKIA |
| TEKIA | TERUA | TEKIA |

הַיּוֹם This day is the birth of the world.
This day stands all the world's creations up in judgment,
stands them as sons or as slaves –
If as sons, have compassion for us,
as a father has compassion for his sons.
And if as slaves, our eyes are raised and fixed on You
until You show us favor, and bring out our judgment like sunlight,
Awesome, Holy.

וְיֵדַע כָּל פָּעוּל כִּי אַתָּה פְעַלְתּוֹ
וְיָבִין כָּל יָצוּר כִּי אַתָּה יְצַרְתּוֹ
וְיֹאמַר כֹּל אֲשֶׁר נְשָׁמָה בְאַפּוֹ
יהוה אֱלֹהֵי יִשְׂרָאֵל מֶלֶךְ וּמַלְכוּתוֹ בַּכֹּל מָשָׁלָה.

*On* שבת*, add the words in parentheses:*

(אֱלֹהֵינוּ וֵאלֹהֵי אֲבוֹתֵינוּ, רְצֵה נָא בִמְנוּחָתֵנוּ)
קַדְּשֵׁנוּ בְּמִצְוֹתֶיךָ וְתֵן חֶלְקֵנוּ בְּתוֹרָתֶךָ
שַׂבְּעֵנוּ מִטּוּבֶךָ, וְשַׂמַּח נַפְשֵׁנוּ בִּישׁוּעָתֶךָ
(וְהַנְחִילֵנוּ יהוה אֱלֹהֵינוּ בְּאַהֲבָה וּבְרָצוֹן שַׁבַּת קָדְשֶׁךָ
וְיָנוּחוּ בוֹ כָּל יִשְׂרָאֵל מְקַדְּשֵׁי שְׁמֶךָ)
וְטַהֵר לִבֵּנוּ לְעָבְדְּךָ בֶּאֱמֶת
כִּי אַתָּה אֱלֹהִים אֱמֶת, וּדְבָרְךָ אֱמֶת וְקַיָּם לָעַד.
בָּרוּךְ אַתָּה יהוה, מֶלֶךְ עַל כָּל הָאָרֶץ
מְקַדֵּשׁ (הַשַּׁבָּת וְ) יִשְׂרָאֵל וְיוֹם הַזִּכָּרוֹן.

*In many congregations, the* שופר *is sounded (except on* שבת*).*

| | | |
|---|---|---|
| תקיעה | שברים תרועה | תקיעה |
| תקיעה | שברים | תקיעה |
| תקיעה | תרועה | תקיעה |

הַיּוֹם הֲרַת עוֹלָם, הַיּוֹם יַעֲמִיד בַּמִּשְׁפָּט כָּל יְצוּרֵי עוֹלָמִים
אִם כְּבָנִים אִם כַּעֲבָדִים.
אִם כְּבָנִים, רַחֲמֵנוּ כְּרַחֵם אָב עַל בָּנִים
וְאִם כַּעֲבָדִים, עֵינֵינוּ לְךָ תְלוּיוֹת עַד שֶׁתְּחָנֵּנוּ
וְתוֹצִיא כָאוֹר מִשְׁפָּטֵנוּ, אָיֹם קָדוֹשׁ.

REMEMBRANCES

אַתָּה זוֹכֵר You remember the making of the world;
You come to all those formed long ago.
Under Your gaze, all hidden things come to light,
all the many secrets buried since the Beginning.
For nothing is forgotten before the throne of Your glory,
and nothing is hidden from Your eyes.

You remember all of creation,
and all things that were formed – none is shrouded from You.
All is revealed and known before You, LORD our God,
who gazes and looks on to the last of all the ages.
For You bring a day decreed for remembrance
to come to each spirit and soul;
that Your many works be remembered,
Your numerous, endless creations.
From the very beginning You made it known,
long before this time You revealed it,
for this day is the opening of all Your works,
a remembrance of the very first day.
"For it is a decree for Israel, an ordinance of the God of Jacob." *Ps. 81*

And on it, it is said of every province,
which will come to the sword
and which to peace,
which will succumb to hunger
and which find plenty.
And all creations are regarded on this day;
remembered for life, or for death.

---

forget. Nor do Jews. More than any other people we preserve our memories. We recall every place where Jews once lived. We perpetuate the memory of those we have lost by giving their names to our children. We are the people of memory for whom those who died live on.

זכרונות

אַתָּה זוֹכֵר מַעֲשֵׂה עוֹלָם, וּפוֹקֵד כָּל יְצוּרֵי קֶדֶם
לְפָנֶיךָ נִגְלוּ כָּל תַּעֲלוּמוֹת וַהֲמוֹן נִסְתָּרוֹת שֶׁמִּבְּרֵאשִׁית
כִּי אֵין שִׁכְחָה לִפְנֵי כִסֵּא כְבוֹדֶךָ, וְאֵין נִסְתָּר מִנֶּגֶד עֵינֶיךָ.

אַתָּה זוֹכֵר אֶת כָּל הַמִּפְעָל, וְגַם כָּל הַיְצוּר לֹא נִכְחַד מִמֶּךָּ.
הַכֹּל גָּלוּי וְיָדְוּעַ לְפָנֶיךָ יהוה אֱלֹהֵינוּ
צוֹפֶה וּמַבִּיט עַד סוֹף כָּל הַדּוֹרוֹת
כִּי תָבִיא חֹק זִכָּרוֹן לְהִפָּקֵד כָּל רְוּחַ וָנֶפֶשׁ
לְהִזָּכֵר מַעֲשִׂים רַבִּים, וַהֲמוֹן בְּרִיּוֹת לְאֵין תַּכְלִית.
מֵרֵאשִׁית כָּזֹאת הוֹדָעְתָּ, וּמִלְּפָנִים אוֹתָהּ גִּלִּיתָ.
זֶה הַיּוֹם תְּחִלַּת מַעֲשֶׂיךָ, זִכָּרוֹן לְיוֹם רִאשׁוֹן
כִּי חֹק לְיִשְׂרָאֵל הוּא, מִשְׁפָּט לֵאלֹהֵי יַעֲקֹב: תהלים פא

וְעַל הַמְּדִינוֹת בּוֹ יֵאָמֵר
אֵיזוֹ לַחֶרֶב, וְאֵיזוֹ לַשָּׁלוֹם
אֵיזוֹ לָרָעָב, וְאֵיזוֹ לַשֹּׂבַע
וּבְרִיּוֹת בּוֹ יִפָּקֵדוּ, לְהַזְכִּירָם לַחַיִּים וְלַמָּוֶת.

---

אַתָּה זוֹכֵר *You remember.* The second Rosh HaShana theme: Remembrances. Judaism is a religion of memory. The root *zakhor,* "remember," appears 169 times in Tanakh. All ancient cultures saw gods in nature. Jews were the first people to see God in history, and to consider memory as a religious obligation. Time is structured in Judaism by the idea of covenant: a bond between God and the children of Israel, entered into in the past, binding us together in the present, and assuring us of a promised future. The deepest human fear, whether occasioned by distress or thoughts of our own mortality, is that we will be forgotten. We fear that we will live and die and it will be as if we had never been. Faith answers that fear by assuring us that God does not

מִי לֹא נִפְקַד Who may be overlooked on this day,
when the memory of every being formed comes before You? –
each person's works, his purpose,
the path that he chooses and follows,
the thoughts and the plans of all mankind,
and the impulses behind each person's acts?
Happy is the one who does not forget You,
the child of man who takes courage in You.
For one who seeks You will never stumble,
they need never be ashamed, who seek shelter in You.
For the memory of all that You have made passes before You,
You examine what each one does.
And Noah also, You remembered with love,
and You came to him with words of salvation, compassion,
when You brought on the waters of the great flood,
to destroy all creatures of flesh
because the practices they followed were corrupt.
And so let [Noah's] memory come to You, LORD our God,
that You multiply His children like the dust of the earth,
his descendants like sand of the sea.

As it is written in Your Torah:
"God remembered Noah and all the animals, *Gen. 8*
and all the cattle that were with him in the ark,
and God made a wind blow across the earth,
and the waters grew calm."

And it is said:
"God heard their groaning, *Ex. 2*
and God remembered His covenant
with Abraham, with Isaac and with Jacob."

And it is said:
"I will remember My covenant with Jacob, *Lev. 26*
and also My covenant with Isaac,
and also My covenant with Abraham I will remember,
and the land I will remember."

מִי לֹא נִפְקַד כְּהַיּוֹם הַזֶּה
כִּי זֵכֶר כָּל הַיְצוּר לְפָנֶיךָ בָּא
מַעֲשֵׂה אִישׁ וּפְקֻדָּתוֹ, וַעֲלִילוֹת מִצְעֲדֵי גָבֶר
מַחְשְׁבוֹת אָדָם וְתַחְבּוּלוֹתָיו, וְיִצְרֵי מַעַלְלֵי אִישׁ.
אַשְׁרֵי אִישׁ שֶׁלֹּא יִשְׁכָּחֶךָּ, וּבֶן אָדָם יִתְאַמֶּץ בָּךְ
כִּי דוֹרְשֶׁיךָ לְעוֹלָם לֹא יִכָּשֵׁלוּ
וְלֹא יִכָּלְמוּ לָנֶצַח כָּל הַחוֹסִים בָּךְ.
כִּי זֵכֶר כָּל הַמַּעֲשִׂים לְפָנֶיךָ בָּא, וְאַתָּה דוֹרֵשׁ מַעֲשֵׂה כֻלָּם.

וְגַם אֶת נֹחַ בְּאַהֲבָה זָכַרְתָּ, וַתִּפְקְדֵהוּ בִּדְבַר יְשׁוּעָה וְרַחֲמִים
בַּהֲבִיאֲךָ אֶת מֵי הַמַּבּוּל לְשַׁחֵת כָּל בָּשָׂר מִפְּנֵי רֹעַ מַעַלְלֵיהֶם
עַל כֵּן זִכְרוֹנוֹ בָּא לְפָנֶיךָ, יהוה אֱלֹהֵינוּ
לְהַרְבּוֹת זַרְעוֹ כְּעַפְרוֹת תֵּבֵל, וְצֶאֱצָאָיו כְּחוֹל הַיָּם.

כַּכָּתוּב בְּתוֹרָתֶךָ
וַיִּזְכֹּר אֱלֹהִים אֶת־נֹחַ בראשית ח
וְאֵת כָּל־הַחַיָּה וְאֶת־כָּל־הַבְּהֵמָה אֲשֶׁר אִתּוֹ בַּתֵּבָה
וַיַּעֲבֵר אֱלֹהִים רוּחַ עַל־הָאָרֶץ, וַיָּשֹׁכּוּ הַמָּיִם:

וְנֶאֱמַר
וַיִּשְׁמַע אֱלֹהִים אֶת־נַאֲקָתָם שמות ב
וַיִּזְכֹּר אֱלֹהִים אֶת־בְּרִיתוֹ
אֶת־אַבְרָהָם אֶת־יִצְחָק וְאֶת־יַעֲקֹב:

וְנֶאֱמַר
וְזָכַרְתִּי אֶת־בְּרִיתִי יַעֲקוֹב ויקרא כו
וְאַף אֶת־בְּרִיתִי יִצְחָק, וְאַף אֶת־בְּרִיתִי אַבְרָהָם אֶזְכֹּר
וְהָאָרֶץ אֶזְכֹּר:

And in Your holy Writings it is written thus:
“He has made remembrance for His wonders; *Ps. 111*
gracious and compassionate is the Lord.”
And it is said:
“He has given food to those who revere Him; *Ibid.*
He will remember His covenant forever.”
And it is said:
“He remembered His covenant for their sake, *Ps. 106*
and relented in His great love.”

And by Your servants the prophets it is written:
“Go and call out to Jerusalem, this is what the Lord has said: *Jer. 2*
‘I remember of you the kindness of your youth,
your love when you were a bride;
how you walked after Me in the desert, through a land not sown.’”
And it is said:
“I will remember the covenant I had with you *Ezek. 16*
in the days of your youth,
and I will establish with you an everlasting covenant.”
And it is said:
“Is Ephraim not a treasured son to Me, My child of delights? *Jer. 31*
As I speak of him, always, I remember him again.
And so it is that I long for him within,
I will tender him compassion, says the Lord.”

אֱלֹהֵינוּ Our God and God of our ancestors,
remember us with a favorable memory,
and recall us with a remembrance of salvation and compassion
from the highest ancient heaven.
Remember for our sake, Lord our God,
the covenant, the loving-kindness,
and the oath that You swore to Abraham our father on Mount Moriah.
And let the image of that binding,
when our father Abraham bound Isaac his son upon the altar,
be present before You;
when he suppressed his compassion, to do Your will wholeheartedly.

וּבְדִבְרֵי קָדְשְׁךָ כָּתוּב לֵאמֹר
זֵכֶר עָשָׂה לְנִפְלְאוֹתָיו, חַנּוּן וְרַחוּם יהוה: תהלים קיא
וְנֶאֱמַר
טֶרֶף נָתַן לִירֵאָיו, יִזְכֹּר לְעוֹלָם בְּרִיתוֹ: שם
וְנֶאֱמַר
וַיִּזְכֹּר לָהֶם בְּרִיתוֹ, וַיִּנָּחֵם כְּרֹב חֲסָדָו: תהלים קו

וְעַל יְדֵי עֲבָדֶיךָ הַנְּבִיאִים כָּתוּב לֵאמֹר
הָלֹךְ וְקָרָאתָ בְאָזְנֵי יְרוּשָׁלַ͏ִם לֵאמֹר, כֹּה אָמַר יהוה ירמיה ב
זָכַרְתִּי לָךְ חֶסֶד נְעוּרַיִךְ, אַהֲבַת כְּלוּלֹתָיִךְ
לֶכְתֵּךְ אַחֲרַי בַּמִּדְבָּר, בְּאֶרֶץ לֹא זְרוּעָה:
וְנֶאֱמַר
וְזָכַרְתִּי אֲנִי אֶת־בְּרִיתִי אוֹתָךְ בִּימֵי נְעוּרָיִךְ יחזקאל טז
וַהֲקִימוֹתִי לָךְ בְּרִית עוֹלָם:
וְנֶאֱמַר
הֲבֵן יַקִּיר לִי אֶפְרַיִם, אִם יֶלֶד שַׁעֲשֻׁעִים ירמיה לא
כִּי־מִדֵּי דַבְּרִי בּוֹ, זָכֹר אֶזְכְּרֶנּוּ עוֹד
עַל־כֵּן הָמוּ מֵעַי לוֹ, רַחֵם אֲרַחֲמֶנּוּ נְאֻם־יהוה:

אֱלֹהֵינוּ וֵאלֹהֵי אֲבוֹתֵינוּ, זָכְרֵנוּ בְּזִכָּרוֹן טוֹב לְפָנֶיךָ
וּפָקְדֵנוּ בִּפְקֻדַּת יְשׁוּעָה וְרַחֲמִים מִשְּׁמֵי שְׁמֵי קֶדֶם
וּזְכָר לָנוּ יהוה אֱלֹהֵינוּ
אֶת הַבְּרִית וְאֶת הַחֶסֶד וְאֶת הַשְּׁבוּעָה
אֲשֶׁר נִשְׁבַּעְתָּ לְאַבְרָהָם אָבִינוּ בְּהַר הַמּוֹרִיָּה
וְתֵרָאֶה לְפָנֶיךָ עֲקֵדָה
שֶׁעָקַד אַבְרָהָם אָבִינוּ אֶת יִצְחָק בְּנוֹ עַל גַּבֵּי הַמִּזְבֵּחַ
וְכָבַשׁ רַחֲמָיו, לַעֲשׂוֹת רְצוֹנְךָ בְּלֵבָב שָׁלֵם.

So, too, let Your compassion wrest Your anger from us,
and in Your great goodness may Your anger be turned away
from Your people, Your city, Your land and Your inheritance.
Fulfill for us, LORD our God, the promise You made in Your Torah,
at the hand of Moses Your servant and by Your own word,
as it is said:
"And I remembered, for their sake, *Lev. 26*
the covenant of the early ones,
whom I brought out of the land of Egypt
before the eyes of all nations,
to be God to them, I am the LORD."

כִּי זוֹכֵר For it has always been You
who remembered all forgotten things,
and there is no forgetfulness before the throne of Your glory,
and today in Your compassion, You remember
the binding of Isaac, for his descendants' sake.
Blessed are You, LORD,
who remembers the covenant.

*In many congregations, the shofar is sounded (except on Shabbat).*

TEKIA SHEVARIM TERUA TEKIA
TEKIA SHEVARIM TEKIA
TEKIA TERUA TEKIA

הַיּוֹם This day is the birth of the world.
This day stands all the world's creations up in judgment,
stands them as sons or as slaves –
If as sons, have compassion for us,
as a father has compassion for his sons.
And if as slaves, our eyes are raised and fixed on You
until You show us favor,
and bring out our judgment like sunlight,
Awesome, Holy.

כֵּן יִכְבְּשׁוּ רַחֲמֶיךָ אֶת כַּעַסְךָ מֵעָלֵינוּ
וּבְטוּבְךָ הַגָּדוֹל יָשׁוּב חֲרוֹן אַפְּךָ מֵעַמְּךָ
וּמֵעִירְךָ וּמֵאַרְצְךָ וּמִנַּחֲלָתֶךָ.
וְקַיֶּם לָנוּ יהוה אֱלֹהֵינוּ אֶת הַדָּבָר שֶׁהִבְטַחְתָּנוּ בְּתוֹרָתֶךָ
עַל יְדֵי מֹשֶׁה עַבְדֶּךָ, מִפִּי כְבוֹדֶךָ
כָּאָמוּר
וְזָכַרְתִּי לָהֶם בְּרִית רִאשֹׁנִים ויקרא כו
אֲשֶׁר הוֹצֵאתִי־אֹתָם מֵאֶרֶץ מִצְרַיִם לְעֵינֵי הַגּוֹיִם
לִהְיוֹת לָהֶם לֵאלֹהִים, אֲנִי יהוה:

כִּי זוֹכֵר כָּל הַנִּשְׁכָּחוֹת אַתָּה הוּא מֵעוֹלָם
וְאֵין שִׁכְחָה לִפְנֵי כִסֵּא כְבוֹדֶךָ
וַעֲקֵדַת יִצְחָק לְזַרְעוֹ הַיּוֹם בְּרַחֲמִים תִּזְכֹּר.
בָּרוּךְ אַתָּה יהוה, זוֹכֵר הַבְּרִית.

*In many congregations, the* שופר *is sounded (except on* שבת*).*

| תקיעה | שברים תרועה | תקיעה |
|---|---|---|
| תקיעה | שברים | תקיעה |
| תקיעה | תרועה | תקיעה |

הַיּוֹם הֲרַת עוֹלָם, הַיּוֹם יַעֲמִיד בַּמִּשְׁפָּט כָּל יְצוּרֵי עוֹלָמִים
אִם כְּבָנִים אִם כַּעֲבָדִים.
אִם כְּבָנִים, רַחֲמֵנוּ כְּרַחֵם אָב עַל בָּנִים
וְאִם כַּעֲבָדִים, עֵינֵינוּ לְךָ תְלוּיוֹת עַד שֶׁתְּחָנֵּנוּ
וְתוֹצִיא כָאוֹר מִשְׁפָּטֵנוּ, אָיֹם קָדוֹשׁ.

SHOFAROT

אַתָּה נִגְלֵיתָ You were revealed in a cloud of Your glory,
to Your holy nation, to speak with them.
Out of the heavens Your voice was heard;
You revealed Yourself in mists of purity.
And all the wide world quaked before You,
the works of creation shook in Your presence,
as You revealed Yourself, our King, on Mount Sinai,
to teach Your people Torah and the commandments,
to have them hear the majesty of Your voice –
Your sacred words amid flames of fire.
In thunder and lightning You revealed Yourself to them,
and amid the sound of the shofar You appeared.

As it is written in Your Torah:
"Then on the third day, in the morning – *Ex. 19*
thunder and lightning;
heavy cloud covered the mountain,
there was a very loud sound of the shofar,
and all of the people in the camp quaked."
And it is said:
"And the sound of the shofar grew ever louder – *Ibid.*
Moses spoke, and God answered him with a voice."
And it is said:
"And all the people saw the thunder and the flames, *Ex. 20*
and the sound of the shofar, and the mountain asmoke;
the people saw and they staggered, and stood far back."

And in Your holy Writings it is written thus:
"God has been raised up in sound: *Ps. 47*
raised, the Lord, in the voice of the shofar."
And it is said:
"With trumpets and the sound of the shofar, *Ps. 98*
shout for joy before the Lord, the King."

שופרות

אַתָּה נִגְלֵיתָ בַּעֲנַן כְּבוֹדֶךָ עַל עַם קָדְשְׁךָ לְדַבֵּר עִמָּם
מִן הַשָּׁמַיִם הִשְׁמַעְתָּם קוֹלֶךָ, וְנִגְלֵיתָ עֲלֵיהֶם בְּעַרְפִלֵּי טֹהַר.
גַּם כָּל הָעוֹלָם כֻּלּוֹ חָל מִפָּנֶיךָ, וּבְרִיּוֹת בְּרֵאשִׁית חָרְדוּ מִמֶּךָּ
בְּהִגָּלוֹתְךָ מַלְכֵּנוּ עַל הַר סִינַי, לְלַמֵּד לְעַמְּךָ תּוֹרָה וּמִצְוֹת
וַתַּשְׁמִיעֵם אֶת הוֹד קוֹלֶךָ, וְדִבְּרוֹת קָדְשְׁךָ מִלַּהֲבוֹת אֵשׁ.
בְּקוֹלוֹת וּבְרָקִים עֲלֵיהֶם נִגְלֵיתָ, וּבְקוֹל שׁוֹפָר עֲלֵיהֶם הוֹפָעְתָּ.

כַּכָּתוּב בְּתוֹרָתֶךָ

וַיְהִי בַיּוֹם הַשְּׁלִישִׁי בִּהְיֹת הַבֹּקֶר (שמות יט)
וַיְהִי קֹלֹת וּבְרָקִים וְעָנָן כָּבֵד עַל־הָהָר
וְקֹל שֹׁפָר חָזָק מְאֹד
וַיֶּחֱרַד כָּל־הָעָם אֲשֶׁר בַּמַּחֲנֶה:

וְנֶאֱמַר

וַיְהִי קוֹל הַשֹּׁפָר הוֹלֵךְ וְחָזֵק מְאֹד (שם)
מֹשֶׁה יְדַבֵּר, וְהָאֱלֹהִים יַעֲנֶנּוּ בְקוֹל:

וְנֶאֱמַר

וְכָל־הָעָם רֹאִים אֶת־הַקּוֹלֹת וְאֶת־הַלַּפִּידִם (שמות כ)
וְאֵת קוֹל הַשֹּׁפָר, וְאֶת־הָהָר עָשֵׁן
וַיַּרְא הָעָם וַיָּנֻעוּ, וַיַּעַמְדוּ מֵרָחֹק:

וּבְדִבְרֵי קָדְשְׁךָ כָּתוּב לֵאמֹר

עָלָה אֱלֹהִים בִּתְרוּעָה, יהוה בְּקוֹל שׁוֹפָר: (תהלים מז)

וְנֶאֱמַר

בַּחֲצֹצְרוֹת וְקוֹל שׁוֹפָר, הָרִיעוּ לִפְנֵי הַמֶּלֶךְ יהוה: (תהלים צח)

And it is said:

"Sound the shofar on the new moon, *Ps. 81*
on our feast day when the moon is hidden.
For it is a statute for Israel, an ordinance of the God of Jacob."

And it is said:

"Halleluya! Praise God in His holy place; *Ps. 150*
praise Him in the heavens of His power.
Praise Him for His mighty deeds;
praise Him for His surpassing greatness.
Praise Him with blasts of the shofar;
praise Him with the harp and lyre.
Praise Him with timbrel and dance;
praise Him with strings and flute.
Praise Him with clashing cymbals;
praise Him with resounding cymbals.
Let all that breathes praise the LORD.
Halleluya!"

And by Your servants the prophets it is written:

"All the inhabitants of the world, all the dwellers on this earth, *Is. 18*
when He lifts up a banner on the mountains, you will see it,
and when He sounds the shofar you shall hear."

And it is said:

"On that day a great shofar will be sounded, *Is. 27*
and those who are lost will come from the land of Assyria,
and those who were banished, from the land of Egypt,
and they will worship the LORD
at the holy mountain in Jerusalem."

And it is said:

"The LORD will appear to them, *Zech. 9*
His arrow will come out like lightning,
and the LORD God will sound the shofar,
and will move in stormwinds of the south.
The LORD of hosts will protect them –"
so, protect Your people Israel with Your peace.

וְנֶאֱמַר
תהלים פא
תִּקְעוּ בַחֹדֶשׁ שׁוֹפָר, בַּכֶּסֶה לְיוֹם חַגֵּנוּ:
כִּי חֹק לְיִשְׂרָאֵל הוּא, מִשְׁפָּט לֵאלֹהֵי יַעֲקֹב:

וְנֶאֱמַר
תהלים קנ
הַלְלוּיָהּ, הַלְלוּ־אֵל בְּקָדְשׁוֹ הַלְלוּהוּ בִּרְקִיעַ עֻזּוֹ:
הַלְלוּהוּ בִגְבוּרֹתָיו הַלְלוּהוּ כְּרֹב גֻּדְלוֹ:
הַלְלוּהוּ בְּתֵקַע שׁוֹפָר הַלְלוּהוּ בְּנֵבֶל וְכִנּוֹר:
הַלְלוּהוּ בְתֹף וּמָחוֹל הַלְלוּהוּ בְּמִנִּים וְעֻגָב:
הַלְלוּהוּ בְצִלְצְלֵי־שָׁמַע הַלְלוּהוּ בְּצִלְצְלֵי תְרוּעָה:
כֹּל הַנְּשָׁמָה תְּהַלֵּל יָהּ
הַלְלוּיָהּ:

וְעַל יְדֵי עֲבָדֶיךָ הַנְּבִיאִים כָּתוּב לֵאמֹר
ישעיה יח
כָּל־יֹשְׁבֵי תֵבֵל וְשֹׁכְנֵי אָרֶץ
כִּנְשֹׂא־נֵס הָרִים תִּרְאוּ, וְכִתְקֹעַ שׁוֹפָר תִּשְׁמָעוּ:

וְנֶאֱמַר
ישעיה כז
וְהָיָה בַּיּוֹם הַהוּא יִתָּקַע בְּשׁוֹפָר גָּדוֹל
וּבָאוּ הָאֹבְדִים בְּאֶרֶץ אַשּׁוּר, וְהַנִּדָּחִים בְּאֶרֶץ מִצְרָיִם
וְהִשְׁתַּחֲווּ לַיהוה בְּהַר הַקֹּדֶשׁ בִּירוּשָׁלָםִ:

וְנֶאֱמַר
זכריה ט
וַיהוה עֲלֵיהֶם יֵרָאֶה, וְיָצָא כַבָּרָק חִצּוֹ
וַאדֹנָי יֱהֹוִה בַּשּׁוֹפָר יִתְקָע
וְהָלַךְ בְּסַעֲרוֹת תֵּימָן:
יהוה צְבָאוֹת יָגֵן עֲלֵיהֶם:
כֵּן תָּגֵן עַל עַמְּךָ יִשְׂרָאֵל בִּשְׁלוֹמֶךָ.

אֱלֹהֵינוּ Our God and God of our ancestors,
sound the great shofar for our freedom,
raise high the banner to gather our exiles,
bring close our scattered ones from among the nations,
and gather our exiles from the very ends of the earth.
Bring us to Zion, Your city, in joy,
and to Jerusalem, Your Temple, in everlasting happiness.
There we will prepare for You our obligatory offerings,
as we were commanded in Your Torah,
at the hand of Your servant Moses and by Your own word,
as it is said:

On the days of your celebration, *Num. 10*
and at your times of gathering and at your New Moons,
sound the trumpets over your offerings
and over your peace-offerings,
and those days will be remembrance for you before your God,
I am the Lord your God.

כִּי אַתָּה שׁוֹמֵעַ For You hear the call of the shofar,
and listen to its sounding, and there is none to be compared to You.
Blessed are You, Lord, who listens to the sound of Your people
Israel's trumpet-blasts in compassion.

*In many congregations, the shofar is sounded (except on Shabbat).*

| | | |
|---|---|---|
| TEKIA | SHEVARIM TERUA | TEKIA |
| TEKIA | SHEVARIM | TEKIA |
| TEKIA | TERUA | TEKIA |

הַיּוֹם This day is the birth of the world.
This day stands all the world's creations up in judgment,
stands them as sons or as slaves –
If as sons, have compassion for us,
as a father has compassion for his sons.
And if as slaves, our eyes are raised and fixed on You
until You show us favor, and bring out our judgment like sunlight,
Awesome, Holy.

אֱלֹהֵינוּ וֵאלֹהֵי אֲבוֹתֵינוּ
תְּקַע בְּשׁוֹפָר גָּדוֹל לְחֵרוּתֵנוּ, וְשָׂא נֵס לְקַבֵּץ גָּלֻיּוֹתֵינוּ
וְקָרֵב פְּזוּרֵינוּ מִבֵּין הַגּוֹיִם, וּנְפוּצוֹתֵינוּ כַּנֵּס מִיַּרְכְּתֵי אָרֶץ.
וַהֲבִיאֵנוּ לְצִיּוֹן עִירְךָ בְּרִנָּה
וְלִירוּשָׁלַיִם בֵּית מִקְדָּשְׁךָ בְּשִׂמְחַת עוֹלָם
וְשָׁם נַעֲשֶׂה לְפָנֶיךָ אֶת קָרְבְּנוֹת חוֹבוֹתֵינוּ
כִּמְצֻוֶּה עָלֵינוּ בְּתוֹרָתֶךָ עַל יְדֵי מֹשֶׁה עַבְדֶּךָ, מִפִּי כְבוֹדֶךָ
כָּאָמוּר

וּבְיוֹם שִׂמְחַתְכֶם וּבְמוֹעֲדֵיכֶם וּבְרָאשֵׁי חָדְשֵׁכֶם במדבר י
וּתְקַעְתֶּם בַּחֲצֹצְרֹת עַל עֹלֹתֵיכֶם וְעַל זִבְחֵי שַׁלְמֵיכֶם
וְהָיוּ לָכֶם לְזִכָּרוֹן לִפְנֵי אֱלֹהֵיכֶם
אֲנִי יהוה אֱלֹהֵיכֶם:

כִּי אַתָּה שׁוֹמֵעַ קוֹל שׁוֹפָר וּמַאֲזִין תְּרוּעָה, וְאֵין דּוֹמֶה לָּךְ.
בָּרוּךְ אַתָּה יהוה, שׁוֹמֵעַ קוֹל תְּרוּעַת עַמּוֹ יִשְׂרָאֵל בְּרַחֲמִים.

*In many congregations, the* שופר *is sounded (except on* שבת*).*

| | | |
|---|---|---|
| תקיעה | שברים תרועה | תקיעה |
| תקיעה | שברים | תקיעה |
| תקיעה | תרועה | תקיעה |

הַיּוֹם הֲרַת עוֹלָם, הַיּוֹם יַעֲמִיד בַּמִּשְׁפָּט כָּל יְצוּרֵי עוֹלָמִים
אִם כְּבָנִים אִם כַּעֲבָדִים.
אִם כְּבָנִים, רַחֲמֵנוּ כְּרַחֵם אָב עַל בָּנִים
וְאִם כַּעֲבָדִים, עֵינֵינוּ לְךָ תְלוּיוֹת עַד שֶׁתְּחָנֵּנוּ
וְתוֹצִיא כָאוֹר מִשְׁפָּטֵנוּ, אָיֹם קָדוֹשׁ.

TEMPLE SERVICE

רְצֵה Find favor, LORD our God, in Your people Israel,
and heed their prayer.
Restore the service to Your most holy House,
and accept soon, in love and favor,
the fire-offerings of Israel and their prayer.
May the service of Your people Israel always find favor with You.
And may our eyes witness Your return to Zion in compassion.
Blessed are You, LORD, who restores His Presence to Zion.

THANKSGIVING

*Bow at the first nine words.*

מוֹדִים We give thanks to You,
for You are the LORD our God and God of our ancestors
for ever and all time.
You are the Rock of our lives,
Shield of our salvation from generation to generation.
We will thank You and declare Your praise for our lives,
which are entrusted into Your hand;
for our souls, which are placed in Your charge;
for Your miracles which are with us every day;
and for Your wonders and favors
at all times, evening, morning and midday.
You are good – for Your compassion never fails.
You are compassionate – for Your loving-kindnesses never cease;
for we have always placed our hope in You.
For all these things
may Your name be blessed and exalted and raised up, our King,
continually, for ever and all time.

וּכְתֹב And write, for a good life, all the children of Your covenant.

Let all that lives thank You, Selah! and praise and bless
Your great name in truth, always, because it is good,
God, our Savior and Help, Selah! the beneficent God.
Blessed are You, LORD, whose name is "the Good"
and to whom thanks are due.

---

וּכְתֹב לְחַיִּים טוֹבִים *And write for a good life.* The third of the extra prayers added during the Ten Days of Repentance. In the first, we asked to be written "for

עבודה

רְצֵה יהוה אֱלֹהֵינוּ בְּעַמְּךָ יִשְׂרָאֵל, וְלִתְפִלָּתָם שְׁעֵה
וְהָשֵׁב אֶת הָעֲבוֹדָה לִדְבִיר בֵּיתֶךָ
וְאִשֵּׁי יִשְׂרָאֵל וּתְפִלָּתָם, מְהֵרָה בְּאַהֲבָה תְקַבֵּל בְּרָצוֹן
וּתְהִי לְרָצוֹן תָּמִיד עֲבוֹדַת יִשְׂרָאֵל עַמֶּךָ.
וְתֶחֱזֶינָה עֵינֵינוּ בְּשׁוּבְךָ לְצִיּוֹן בְּרַחֲמִים.
בָּרוּךְ אַתָּה יהוה, הַמַּחֲזִיר שְׁכִינָתוֹ לְצִיּוֹן.

הודאה

*Bow at the first five words.*

ימוֹדִים אֲנַחְנוּ לָךְ
שָׁאַתָּה הוּא יהוה אֱלֹהֵינוּ וֵאלֹהֵי אֲבוֹתֵינוּ לְעוֹלָם וָעֶד.
צוּר חַיֵּינוּ, מָגֵן יִשְׁעֵנוּ, אַתָּה הוּא לְדוֹר וָדוֹר.
נוֹדֶה לְּךָ וּנְסַפֵּר תְּהִלָּתֶךָ
עַל חַיֵּינוּ הַמְּסוּרִים בְּיָדֶךָ, וְעַל נִשְׁמוֹתֵינוּ הַפְּקוּדוֹת לָךְ
וְעַל נִסֶּיךָ שֶׁבְּכָל יוֹם עִמָּנוּ
וְעַל נִפְלְאוֹתֶיךָ וְטוֹבוֹתֶיךָ שֶׁבְּכָל עֵת, עֶרֶב וָבֹקֶר וְצָהֳרָיִם.
הַטּוֹב, כִּי לֹא כָלוּ רַחֲמֶיךָ וְהַמְרַחֵם, כִּי לֹא תַמּוּ חֲסָדֶיךָ
כִּי מֵעוֹלָם קִוִּינוּ לָךְ.
וְעַל כֻּלָּם
יִתְבָּרַךְ וְיִתְרוֹמַם וְיִתְנַשֵּׂא שִׁמְךָ מַלְכֵּנוּ תָּמִיד לְעוֹלָם וָעֶד.
וּכְתֹב לְחַיִּים טוֹבִים כָּל בְּנֵי בְרִיתֶךָ.
וְכֹל הַחַיִּים יוֹדְוּךָ סֶּלָה
וִיהַלְלוּ וִיבָרְכוּ אֶת שִׁמְךָ הַגָּדוֹל בֶּאֱמֶת לְעוֹלָם כִּי טוֹב
הָאֵל יְשׁוּעָתֵנוּ וְעֶזְרָתֵנוּ סֶלָה, הָאֵל הַטּוֹב.
יבָּרוּךְ אַתָּה יהוה, הַטּוֹב שִׁמְךָ וּלְךָ נָאֶה לְהוֹדוֹת.

PEACE

שִׂים שָׁלוֹם Grant peace, goodness and blessing,
life, grace, loving-kindness and compassion
to us and all Israel Your people.
Bless us, our Father, all as one,
with the light of Your face,
for by the light of Your face
You have given us, LORD our God,
the Torah of life and love of kindness,
righteousness, blessing, compassion,
life and peace.
May it be good in Your eyes
to bless us and all Your people Israel
at every time, in every hour, with Your peace.

בְּסֵפֶר חַיִּים In the book of life,
blessing, peace and prosperity,
and good decrees, salvations and consolations
may we and all Your people the house of Israel
be remembered and written before You
for a good life, and for peace.

Blessed are You, LORD,
who blesses His people Israel with peace.

*The following verse concludes the Leader's Repetition of the Amida.*
*Some also say it here as part of the silent Amida. See law 64.*

May the words of my mouth and the meditation of my heart Ps. 19
find favor before You, LORD, my Rock and Redeemer.

---

charity to the poor, provides for the education of his children, buys a choice *etrog* for Sukkot, tasty food to honor Your Shabbat, and fulfills in a beautiful way Your other commands. Therefore, if You want the children of Israel to continue to obey Your commandments in the coming year, You must grant them an abundance of good fortune."

ברכת שלום

שִׂים שָׁלוֹם טוֹבָה וּבְרָכָה
חַיִּים חֵן וָחֶסֶד וְרַחֲמִים
עָלֵינוּ וְעַל כָּל יִשְׂרָאֵל עַמֶּךָ.
בָּרְכֵנוּ אָבִינוּ כֻּלָּנוּ כְּאֶחָד בְּאוֹר פָּנֶיךָ
כִּי בְאוֹר פָּנֶיךָ נָתַתָּ לָּנוּ יהוה אֱלֹהֵינוּ
תּוֹרַת חַיִּים וְאַהֲבַת חֶסֶד
וּצְדָקָה וּבְרָכָה וְרַחֲמִים וְחַיִּים וְשָׁלוֹם.
וְטוֹב יִהְיֶה בְעֵינֶיךָ לְבָרְכֵנוּ וּלְבָרֵךְ אֶת כָּל עַמְּךָ יִשְׂרָאֵל
בְּכָל עֵת וּבְכָל שָׁעָה בִּשְׁלוֹמֶךָ.

בְּסֵפֶר חַיִּים, בְּרָכָה וְשָׁלוֹם, וּפַרְנָסָה טוֹבָה
וּגְזֵרוֹת טוֹבוֹת, יְשׁוּעוֹת וְנֶחָמוֹת
נִזָּכֵר וְנִכָּתֵב לְפָנֶיךָ
אֲנַחְנוּ וְכָל עַמְּךָ בֵּית יִשְׂרָאֵל לְחַיִּים טוֹבִים וּלְשָׁלוֹם.

בָּרוּךְ אַתָּה יהוה, הַמְבָרֵךְ אֶת עַמּוֹ יִשְׂרָאֵל בַּשָּׁלוֹם.

*The following verse concludes the* חזרת הש״ץ.
*Some also say it here as part of the silent* עמידה. *See law 64.*

תהלים יט יִהְיוּ לְרָצוֹן אִמְרֵי־פִי וְהֶגְיוֹן לִבִּי לְפָנֶיךָ, יהוה צוּרִי וְגֹאֲלִי:

---

life." Now we ask to be written "for a good life." It is respectful to make the basic request first, and only afterward elaborate it.

בְּסֵפֶר חַיִּים *In the book of life.* The fourth of the extra prayers, and the fullest. *Prosperity.* On Rosh HaShana, Rabbi Levi Yitzḥak of Berditchev used to pray this prayer: "Master of the Universe: why does a Jew pray for a year of good sustenance? Why does a Jew need money? When he has the means, he gives

אֱלֹהַי My God, *Berakhot 17a*
guard my tongue from evil and my lips from deceitful speech.
To those who curse me, let my soul be silent;
may my soul be to all like the dust.
Open my heart to Your Torah
and let my soul pursue Your commandments.
As for all who rise up or plan evil against me,
swiftly thwart their counsel and frustrate their plans.

*Some add this prayer:*
יְהִי רָצוֹן May it be Your will, LORD my God, God of my ancestors,
that envy of no man may rise up in me, nor envy of me in any other;
that I will not be angry today, nor make You angry;
and save me from my evil impulse,
placing humility and modesty into my heart.
Our King and God, make Your name One in Your world;
build up Your city, establish Your House and complete Your Sanctuary,
gather in the exiles, redeem Your flock,
and have Your congregation rejoice.

Act for the sake of Your name; act for the sake of Your right hand;
act for the sake of Your Torah; act for the sake of Your holiness.
That Your beloved ones may be delivered, *Ps. 60*
save with Your right hand and answer me.
May the words of my mouth and the meditation of my heart *Ps. 19*
find favor before You, LORD, my Rock and Redeemer.

*Bow, take three steps back, then bow, first left, then right, then center, while saying:*

May He who makes peace in His high places,
make peace for us and all Israel – and say: Amen.

יְהִי רָצוֹן May it be Your will, LORD our God and God of our ancestors,
that the Temple be rebuilt speedily in our days,
and grant us a share in Your Torah.
And there we will serve You with reverence,
as in the days of old and as in former years.
Then the offering of Judah and Jerusalem *Mal. 3*
will be pleasing to the LORD as in the days of old and as in former years.

ברכות יז.

אֱלֹהַי
נְצֹר לְשׁוֹנִי מֵרָע וּשְׂפָתַי מִדַּבֵּר מִרְמָה
וְלִמְקַלְלַי נַפְשִׁי תִדֹּם, וְנַפְשִׁי כֶּעָפָר לַכֹּל תִּהְיֶה.
פְּתַח לִבִּי בְּתוֹרָתֶךָ, וְאַחֲרֵי מִצְוֹתֶיךָ תִּרְדֹּף נַפְשִׁי.
וְכָל הַקָּמִים וְהַחוֹשְׁבִים עָלַי רָעָה
מְהֵרָה הָפֵר עֲצָתָם וְקַלְקֵל מַחֲשַׁבְתָּם.

*Some add this prayer:*

יְהִי רָצוֹן מִלְּפָנֶיךָ יהוה אֱלֹהַי וֵאלֹהֵי אֲבוֹתַי
שֶׁלֹּא תַעֲלֶה קִנְאַת אָדָם עָלַי, וְלֹא קִנְאָתִי עַל אֲחֵרִים
וְשֶׁלֹּא אֶכְעֹס הַיּוֹם, וְשֶׁלֹּא אַכְעִיסֶךָ
וְתַצִּילֵנִי מִיֵּצֶר הָרָע, וְתֵן בְּלִבִּי הַכְנָעָה וַעֲנָוָה.
מַלְכֵּנוּ וֵאלֹהֵינוּ, יַחֵד שִׁמְךָ בְּעוֹלָמֶךָ
בְּנֵה עִירָךְ, יַסֵּד בֵּיתְךָ וְשַׁכְלֵל הֵיכָלֶךָ
וְקַבֵּץ קִבּוּץ גָּלֻיּוֹת, וּפְדֵה צֹאנְךָ וְשַׂמַּח עֲדָתֶךָ.

עֲשֵׂה לְמַעַן שְׁמֶךָ, עֲשֵׂה לְמַעַן יְמִינֶךָ
עֲשֵׂה לְמַעַן תּוֹרָתֶךָ, עֲשֵׂה לְמַעַן קְדֻשָּׁתֶךָ.
תהלים ס לְמַעַן יֵחָלְצוּן יְדִידֶיךָ, הוֹשִׁיעָה יְמִינְךָ וַעֲנֵנִי:
תהלים יט יִהְיוּ לְרָצוֹן אִמְרֵי־פִי וְהֶגְיוֹן לִבִּי לְפָנֶיךָ, יהוה צוּרִי וְגֹאֲלִי:

*Bow, take three steps back, then bow, first left, then right, then center, while saying:*

עֹשֶׂה הַשָּׁלוֹם בִּמְרוֹמָיו
הוּא יַעֲשֶׂה שָׁלוֹם עָלֵינוּ וְעַל כָּל יִשְׂרָאֵל, וְאִמְרוּ אָמֵן.

יְהִי רָצוֹן מִלְּפָנֶיךָ יהוה אֱלֹהֵינוּ וֵאלֹהֵי אֲבוֹתֵינוּ
שֶׁיִּבָּנֶה בֵּית הַמִּקְדָּשׁ בִּמְהֵרָה בְיָמֵינוּ
וְתֵן חֶלְקֵנוּ בְּתוֹרָתֶךָ
וְשָׁם נַעֲבָדְךָ בְּיִרְאָה כִּימֵי עוֹלָם וּכְשָׁנִים קַדְמֹנִיּוֹת.
מלאכי ג וְעָרְבָה לַיהוה מִנְחַת יְהוּדָה וִירוּשָׁלָםִ כִּימֵי עוֹלָם וּכְשָׁנִים קַדְמֹנִיּוֹת:

## LEADER'S REPETITION FOR THE FIRST DAY

*The Ark is opened.*

*The Leader takes three steps forward and at the points indicated by ▾, bends the knees at the first word, bows at the second, and stands straight before saying God's name.*

When I proclaim the LORD's name, give glory to our God. Deut. 32

O LORD, open my lips, so that my mouth may declare Your praise. Ps. 51

PATRIARCHS

▾בָּרוּךְ▾ Blessed are You, LORD our God and God of our fathers,
God of Abraham, God of Isaac and God of Jacob;
the great, mighty and awesome God, God Most High,
who bestows acts of loving-kindness, who creates all,
who remembers the loving-kindness of the fathers
and will bring a Redeemer to their children's children
for the sake of His name, in love.

*Before the cycle (kerova) of piyutim for Musaf, the Leader says only the standard opening "Drawing from the counsel of wise and knowing men…" as a Reshut (see page 360), as he has already said a Reshut before the silent Amida (page 484).*

מִסּוֹד Drawing from the counsel of wise and knowing men,
from the teachings born of insight among those who understand,
I open my mouth now in prayer and pleading,
to implore and to plead before the King,
King of kings and LORD of lords.

*The Ark is closed.*

---

silently to give time for the Leader silently to rehearse his prayer (*Rosh HaShana* 34b).

There is a third reason that encompasses the other two. We have two traditions of prayer in Judaism. One dates back to the spontaneous prayers offered by the patriarchs, matriarchs and prophets. The other sees prayer as a substitute for the communal sacrifices offered by the priests in the Temple (*Berakhot* 26b). When we pray silently we do so in the tradition of the prophets. When the Leader repeats the Amida aloud, he does so as if he were a priest in the Temple, offering words in place of a sacrifice on behalf of the people as a whole. In this striking parallelism we bring the two great spiritual traditions of Judaism together.

# חזרת הש״ץ למוסף ליום הראשון

*The* ארון קודש *is opened.*
*The* שליח ציבור *takes three steps forward and at the points indicated by* ׳, *bends the knees at the first word, bows at the second, and stands straight before saying God's name.*

דברים לב
כִּי שֵׁם יהוה אֶקְרָא, הָבוּ גֹדֶל לֵאלֹהֵינוּ:

תהלים נא
אֲדֹנָי, שְׂפָתַי תִּפְתָּח, וּפִי יַגִּיד תְּהִלָּתֶךָ:

אבות

׳בָּרוּךְ אַתָּה יהוה, אֱלֹהֵינוּ וֵאלֹהֵי אֲבוֹתֵינוּ
אֱלֹהֵי אַבְרָהָם, אֱלֹהֵי יִצְחָק, וֵאלֹהֵי יַעֲקֹב
הָאֵל הַגָּדוֹל הַגִּבּוֹר וְהַנּוֹרָא, אֵל עֶלְיוֹן
גּוֹמֵל חֲסָדִים טוֹבִים, קוֹנֵה הַכֹּל
וְזוֹכֵר חַסְדֵי אָבוֹת
וּמֵבִיא גוֹאֵל לִבְנֵי בְנֵיהֶם לְמַעַן שְׁמוֹ בְּאַהֲבָה.

*Before the cycle* (קרובה) *of piyutim for* מוסף, *the* שליח ציבור *says only the standard opening "*...מִסּוֹד חֲכָמִים וּנְבוֹנִים*" as a* רשות *(see page 361), as he has already said a* רשות *before the silent* עמידה *(page 485).*

מִסּוֹד חֲכָמִים וּנְבוֹנִים
וּמִלֶּמֶד דַּעַת מְבִינִים
אֶפְתְּחָה פִּי בִּתְפִלָּה וּבְתַחֲנוּנִים
לְחַלּוֹת וּלְחַנֵּן פְּנֵי מֶלֶךְ מַלְכֵי הַמְּלָכִים וַאֲדוֹנֵי הָאֲדוֹנִים.

*The* ארון קודש *is closed.*

---

MUSAF – LEADER'S REPETITION

There are two views as to why we repeat each Amida, with the exception of Ma'ariv. The sages held that the primary prayer was the silent Amida said by individuals. In their view, the Amida is repeated for the sake of those who are unable to pray for themselves, whether because they are unable to read, or – a more likely explanation – because in the days before printing, there were relatively few prayer books available and not everyone knew the prayers by heart.

According to Rabban Gamliel, the primary prayer is the Repetition said by the Leader on behalf of the whole congregation. We pray privately and

*Most of the piyutim for First Day Musaf were composed by Rabbi Elazar HaKalir. As in the kerova for Shaḥarit, the first three piyutim are structured in alphabetic acrostic – the Magen in a simple acrostic, the Meḥayeh in a reverse acrostic (תשר״ק), and the Meshalesh in a complex תב״ש. On Shabbat, since the shofar is not blown, references to its blowing are edited – the word "sounds" is changed to "recalls," and the "sound of the shofar" becomes the "remembrance of the shofar."*

אֳפֶד Day girded for judgment since the dawn of time, /
when every day's acts are examined,
as all beings come forth before the awesome face of the Divine, /
hoping that their judgment might be weighted toward redemption.

Day on which the first man, Adam, was created, /
and was given the commandment he failed to observe.
The LORD championed him, granting him relief; /
He set this day for judgment for all generations to observe.

The LORD who hews hills and boulders, planted His trees; / our forefathers, who were born on that day for Our Rock to rest His world upon. /
Those holy ancestors are as those who dwell in God's garden, His fellow creators, / where they speak on behalf of His confined, exiled nation.

This month of Tishrei is referred to as strength in their honor; /
You tested them as a banner for Your name both above and below. /
The books of life are open and tell of our actions, /
as all pass before You, providing an accounting.

It is a sentinel month, setting the dates of Your festivals, /
when Your flock passes beneath the rod as You bring them close. /
▸ As Your congregation sounds (*On Shabbat substitute*: recalls) their call to You on the ram's horn this day, / O Compassionate One, recall the oath You swore to Your servants, our ancestors.

*All:* May the sound (*On Shabbat*: the remembrance) of the shofar rise with our plea /
that the LORD God might be persuaded to grant us favor. /
▸ Return the flash of Your sharpened blade to its sheath; /
hold up Your shield, covering me with Your protection.

---

man and took the opportunity to ask him a question that had long puzzled him. "Rabbi," he said, "why does it say that God called to Adam, 'Where are you?' Surely God knows everything. He knew where Adam was." "Do you believe," said the rabbi, "that the Bible was given not just for one time but for all time?" "I do," said the warden. "Well then," said the rabbi, "God's question was not for Adam alone but for all of us. You who have lived for forty-eight years – to you, God is calling, 'Where are you?'" The warden, who had not told the rabbi his age, said, "Bravo!" But inwardly he trembled.

*Most of the piyutim for מוסף ליום א׳ were composed by Rabbi Elazar HaKalir. As in the קרובה for שחרית, the first three piyutim are structured in alphabetic acrostic – the מגן in a simple acrostic, the מחיה in a reverse acrostic (תשר״ק), and the משלש in a complex תב״ש. On שבת, since the שופר is not blown, references to its blowing are edited – the word בְּמָשְׁכָם is changed to בְּזָכְרָם, and נַעֲלָה שׁוֹפָר becomes נַעֲלָה זִכְרוֹן.*

אֶפֶּד מֵאָז לְשֶׁפֶט הַיּוֹם / בְּחוֹן מַעֲשֵׂה כָל יוֹם
גִּישַׁת יְקוּמִים פְּנֵי אָיֹם / דִּינָם בּוֹ לְפַלֵּס לְפִדְיוֹם.

הָרִאשׁוֹן אָדָם בּוֹ נוֹצָר / וְצֻוָּה חֹק וְלֹא נָצָר
זֶה מֵלִיץ כְּהִרְחִיב בַּצָּר / חֲקָקוֹ לַמִּשְׁפָּט וְלַדּוֹרוֹת מְנֻצָּר.

טִיעַת חוֹצֵב גְּבָעוֹת וְצוּרִים / יְלָדוּ בוֹ מֵרֹאשׁ צוּרִים
כְּיוֹשְׁבֵי נְטָעִים הֵמָּה הַיּוֹצְרִים / לְלַמֵּד בּוֹ צֶדֶק לַעֲצוּרִים.

מְיֻחָס שְׁמוֹ בְּשֵׁם אֵיתָנִים / נֵס לְהִתְנוֹסֵס עֶלְיוֹנִים וְתַחְתּוֹנִים
סְפָרִים נִפְתָּחִים וּמַעֲשִׂים מְתֻנִּים / עוֹבְרִים לְפָנֶיךָ וְחֶשְׁבּוֹן נוֹתְנִים.

פָּקִיד הוּכַן לְתִקּוּן מוֹעֲדֶיךָ / צֹאן לְהַעֲבִיר בַּשֵּׁבֶט עֲדֶיךָ
◂ קֶרֶן בְּמָשְׁכָם (On שבת substitute בְּזָכְרָם) הַיּוֹם, עֵדֶיךָ / רַחוּם זְכֹר שְׁבוּעַת עֲבָדֶיךָ.

A. נַעֲלָה (בשבת: זִכְרוֹן) שׁוֹפָר עִם תַּחֲנוּן / שַׁדַּי לְפַתּוֹתְךָ בָּם בְּחִנּוּן
◂ תָּשִׁיב לַנִּדָּן בְּרַק הַשָּׁנוּן / תַּחֲזִיק מָגֵן לְגוֹנְנִי בְּגִנּוּן.

---

אֶפֶּד מֵאָז לְשֶׁפֶט הַיּוֹם *Day girded for judgment since the dawn of time.* A poem based on the tradition that the first day of Tishrei is the anniversary of the creation of the first human beings. According to tradition, this was not only the day on which Adam and Eve were formed, but also the day they sinned and were sentenced to exile from Eden. But they were also forgiven. Initially God had said, "Do not eat from the Tree of Knowledge of good and evil, for on the day you eat from it, you will surely die" (Gen. 2:17), yet they ate and did not die. Thus Rosh HaShana has been, since the beginning of the human story, a day of forgiveness. It is the day when God calls to us, as He called to the first humans, "Where are you?"

When the first Lubavitcher Rebbe, Rabbi Shneur Zalman of Liadi, was imprisoned on false charges laid against him by his opponents, the warden of the prison, a man who often read the Bible, saw that his prisoner was a holy

*The Leader continues:*

זָכְרֵנוּ לְחַיִּים Remember us for life,
O King who desires life,
and write us in the book of life – for Your sake, O God of life.
King, Helper, Savior, Shield:
▾Blessed are You, LORD, Shield of Abraham.

DIVINE MIGHT

אַתָּה גִּבּוֹר You are eternally mighty, LORD.
You give life to the dead and have great power to save.

*In Israel:* He causes the dew to fall.

He sustains the living with loving-kindness,
and with great compassion revives the dead.
He supports the fallen,
heals the sick,
sets captives free,
and keeps His faith with those who sleep in the dust.
Who is like You, Master of might,
and to whom can You be compared,
O King who brings death and gives life,
and makes salvation grow?

---

hopes and fears? The answer is that it was Abraham who first heard the call of God summoning him to a journey and a mission, and it was with Abraham that God made the covenant in virtue of which we exist today as Jews. Abraham loved God; God loved Abraham, promising to be with his children and thus with us. We pray not on the basis of theological abstraction, but out of a sense of history, asking God to remember the lives of our ancestors who despite much suffering and persecution stayed loyal to God.

מְכַלְכֵּל חַיִּים *He sustains the living.* God cares for humanity. He gives us strength when we are weak, supports us when we fall and heals us when we are sick, giving us freedom and rescuing us from confinement. Most of all He gives us life. Even death is not the final word. There is a life beyond this, not only in heaven but one day on earth also. Those who died will live again. This we believe.

*The* שליח ציבור *continues:*

זָכְרֵנוּ לְחַיִּים, מֶלֶךְ חָפֵץ בַּחַיִּים
וְכָתְבֵנוּ בְּסֵפֶר הַחַיִּים, לְמַעַנְךָ אֱלֹהִים חַיִּים.
מֶלֶךְ עוֹזֵר וּמוֹשִׁיעַ וּמָגֵן.
ׂבָּרוּךְ אַתָּה יהוה, מָגֵן אַבְרָהָם.

גבורות

אַתָּה גִּבּוֹר לְעוֹלָם, אֲדֹנָי
מְחַיֵּה מֵתִים אַתָּה, רַב לְהוֹשִׁיעַ
בארץ ישראל: מוֹרִיד הַטָּל
מְכַלְכֵּל חַיִּים בְּחֶסֶד, מְחַיֵּה מֵתִים בְּרַחֲמִים רַבִּים
סוֹמֵךְ נוֹפְלִים, וְרוֹפֵא חוֹלִים, וּמַתִּיר אֲסוּרִים
וּמְקַיֵּם אֱמוּנָתוֹ לִישֵׁנֵי עָפָר.
מִי כָמְוֹךָ, בַּעַל גְּבוּרוֹת, וּמִי דּוֹמֶה לָּךְ
מֶלֶךְ, מֵמִית וּמְחַיֶּה וּמַצְמִיחַ יְשׁוּעָה.

---

וְכָתְבֵנוּ בְּסֵפֶר הַחַיִּים *And write us in the book of life.* Rabbi Levi Yitzḥak of Berditchev never failed to plead the cause of the Jewish people on the High Holy Days. Once, when Rosh HaShana fell on Shabbat, he prayed this prayer: "Master of the Universe, today is the New Year, when the books of life and its opposite lie open before You, and You inscribe the fate of every Jew. But Master of the Universe, today is Shabbat, and on Shabbat it is forbidden to write. There is only one exception: to save a life, for saving life overrides Shabbat. Therefore, Master of the Universe, You have no choice but to write them for life."

מָגֵן אַבְרָהָם *Shield of Abraham.* Every Amida begins with this prayer which refers back to the patriarchs and especially Abraham. It speaks to the most fundamental question: by what right do we pray? On what basis do we expect the Creator, vaster than the universe, older than time itself, to listen to us, our

*The Meḥayeh. The theme of the kerova for Musaf is judgment. Once again, on Shabbat the words "the sound of the shofar" are changed to "the remembrance of the shofar."*

*All:*

תֵּפֶן בְּמָכוֹן O Lord, turn on high toward the image of Jacob on Your throne, / as in Your mind, both support and rebuke are evoked.
O Lofty One, lend a listening ear; / turn to the sound (*On Shabbat substitute:* the remembrance) of the shofar as it rises from inhabited land.

May the distress You expressed before the Flood, that You would not contend with man, / not rise twice to bring destruction.
May this world, which is judged four times in different seasons, / be supported by Your kindness and truth, O Master.

Your faithful gather as on the day of battle, and wage war / against the stumbling block of the evil inclination they battle.
Turn to the sound of their shofar blasts from on high, / and exchange the seat of stern judgment for the throne of compassion.

For the special son who was judged as he lay bound on the altar, / may his offspring be graciously spared from judgment.
Far be it from You, O God of justice; / be reminded of Abraham's words: "Should [the Judge of all the earth] fail to judge righteously?"

And if, as humans do, Your people have transgressed Your covenant, / O Lord, in Your omnipotence, please adhere to Your promise.
▸ May the words of the Deuteronomic covenant that contain ill portents / be put off in remembrance of the threefold promise to our forefathers.

*All:* For the world that You inspect on Rosh HaShana, / may You rule the fate of our new year giving weight to our righteousness.
▸ A year of full harvest, dews, and rainfalls should the heat sear; / may those sealed in dust be brought to life by awakening dews.

*The Leader continues:*

מִי כָמוֹךָ Who is like You, compassionate Father,
who remembers His creatures in compassion, for life?
Faithful are You to revive the dead.
Blessed are You, Lord, who revives the dead.

---

made after the Flood, never again to destroy humankind (Gen. 9:9–17). Remember Isaac who was willing to be bound and sacrificed for Your sake. And since You will one day bring the dead back to life, then grant us, the living, life.

*The* מחיה*. The theme of the* קרובה *for* מוסף *is judgment.*
*Once again, on* שבת *the words* קוֹל שׁוֹפָר *are changed to* זִכְרוֹן שׁוֹפָר*.*

*All:*

**תֵּפֶן בְּמָכוֹן, לְכֵס שֶׁבֶת / שְׁעוֹן וּמוּסָר כְּעָלוּ בְּמַחֲשֶׁבֶת**
**רָם, תְּהִי נָא אָזְנְךָ קַשֶּׁבֶת /**
**קוֹל שׁוֹפָר** (*On* שבת *substitute* **זִכְרוֹן שׁוֹפָר**) **שְׁעוֹת מְנוּשֶּׁבֶת.**

**צָרַת אֹמֶר לֹא יָדוֹן / פַּעֲמַיִם לֹא תָקוּם לַאֲבַדּוֹן**
**עוֹלָם אֲשֶׁר בְּאַרְבָּעָה נִדּוֹן / סְמֹךְ בְּחַסְדְּךָ וּבַאֲמִתְּךָ, אָדוֹן.**

**נוֹעָדִים בְּיוֹם קְרָב וְנִלְחָמִים / מוּל אֶבֶן נֶגֶף מִתְלַחֲמִים**
**לְבוּב תְּרוּעָתָם שְׁעֵה מִמְּרוֹמִים / כִּסֵּא דִין לְהָמִיר בְּשֶׁל רַחֲמִים.**

**יָחִיד אֲשֶׁר בְּעֵקֶד נִשְׁפָּט / טְלָאָיו בּוֹ יְחֻנְּנוּ מִלְּהִשָּׁפֵט**
**חָלִילָה לְּךָ אֱלֹהֵי הַמִּשְׁפָּט / זְכוֹר לֹא יַעֲשֶׂה מִשְׁפָּט.**

**וְאִם כְּאָדָם עָבְרוּ בְרִית / הָאֵל כָּאֵל הַבֵּט בַּבְּרִית**
▸ **דִּבְרוֹת אֵלֶּה דִּבְרֵי הַבְּרִית / גַּלֵּה בְּזִכְרוֹן שְׁלוֹשׁ בְּרִית.**

A▸ **עוֹלָם בְּבַקָּרְךָ בְּרֹאשׁ הַשָּׁנָה / בְּהַכְרָעַת צֶדֶק תַּכְרִיעַ שָׁנָה**
▸ **אֲסוּמָה טְלוּלָה גְּשׁוּמָה אִם שְׁחוּנָה / אֲטוּמִים לְהַחֲיוֹת בְּטַלְלֵי שֵׁנָה.**

*The* שליח ציבור *continues:*

**מִי כָמְוֹךָ אַב הָרַחֲמָן**
**זוֹכֵר יְצוּרָיו לְחַיִּים בְּרַחֲמִים.**
**וְנֶאֱמָן אַתָּה לְהַחֲיוֹת מֵתִים.**
**בָּרוּךְ אַתָּה יהוה, מְחַיֵּה הַמֵּתִים.**

---

תֵּפֶן בְּמָכוֹן *O Lord, turn on high.* Another powerful poem by Elazar HaKalir, asking God to sit not on the Throne of Judgment but on that of "compassion and pity." And if, "as humans do," we sin, then remember the promise You

*The Meshalesh. The first group of each kerova often carries an additional theme that recurs in the penultimate stanza of the Magen and the Meḥayeh, and in the last line of the Meshalesh. Here the second, complementing theme is memory – we ask God to remember the merits of our fathers, as He sits in judgment.*

*All:*

אַף אֹרַח Even when You sit in judgment we raise our eyes to You;
in times of distress our souls' desire has been to reach out to You.
Already yesterday the pure of heart anticipated You,
before we had even sounded the shofar before You.

You issued the edict from the time of creation,
establishing repentance with Your first oration.
Before the start of judgment could be held,
You provided the errant with salvation from the scorching winds of Gehenna.

You created the twofold instincts in each of their hearts,
watching and looking upon their inner thoughts.
And if wickedness is seen concealed in their hearts,
You recall their ancestors for their sake.

In memory of the removal of the burden from the shoulder of Joseph,
as when a slave is freed from the affliction of the fetters of his bondage.
And if his offspring have erred in carnal sin,
His words will favor them with long life in the vain world below.

Hidden in Your heart is the vengeance at time's end,
when on this day, all the exiled will be gathered from the ends of the earth.
This day that is ordained as the time to awaken,
from time immemorial and year's end to year's end.

The throne shall be unveiled and the new moon of Tishrei shall be declared;
the evil thorns shall be scorched and wither in the day's fiery blaze.
▸ The stumbling block of evil shall be removed from insidious hearts,
that the memory of Abraham, Isaac and Jacob might be evoked.

*The* משלש*. The first group of each* קרובה *often carries an additional theme that recurs in the penultimate stanza of the* מגן *and the* מחיה*, and in the last line of the* משלש*. Here the second, complementing theme is memory – we ask God to remember the merits of our fathers, as He sits in judgment.*

*All:*

אַף אֹרַח מִשְׁפָּטֶיךָ קִוִּינוּךָ / תַּאֲוַת לֵב בַּצַּר פְּקַדְנוּךָ
בָּרֵי לֵבָב מֵאֶתְמוֹל קִדַּמְנוּךָ / שׁוֹפַר תְּרוּעָה טֶרֶם שִׁמַּעְנוּךָ.

גְּזֵרָה חֻקַּת מִיצִירַת בְּרֵאשִׁית / רֹאשׁ דְּבָרְךָ תְּשׁוּבָה לְהָשִׁית
דִּין טֶרֶם הֶעֱרַךְ מֵרֵאשִׁית / קָדְמָה לְמַלֵּט שׁוֹבָבִים מֵחֲרִישִׁית.

הַיּוֹצֵר יַחַד שְׁנֵי לְבָבֵיהֶם / צוֹפֶה וּמַבִּיט סַרְעַף קִרְבֵיהֶם
וְאִם אָוֶן נִרְאָה בְּמַחֲבוֹאֵיהֶם / פָּקוֹד תִּפְקֹד לָמוֹ קְרוֹבֵיהֶם.

זֶכֶר הֲסָרַת שֶׁכֶם מִסֵּבֶל / עֶבֶד כְּהָחְפַּשׁ מֵעִנּוּי כֶּבֶל
חֲנִיטָיו אִם תָּעְתְּעוּ בְּתֶבֶל / שִׂיחוֹ יְחוֹנְנֵם לְחַיֵּי הֶבֶל.

טְמִינַת לֵב וּנְקִימַת קֵץ / נִדָּחִים לֶאֱסֹף בּוֹ בְּקֵץ
יוֹם מוּכָן עִתִּים לְהָקֵץ / מִיָּמִים יָמִימָה וּמִקֵּץ לְקֵץ.

כֶּסֶא לְהַקְפּוֹת חֹדֶשׁ לִקּוֹב / כְּסוּחִים בְּלַהֲטוֹ לְהַבְהֵב לִרְקוֹב
◂ לְהָסִיר מִכְשׁוֹל מִלֵּב הֶעָקֹב / לְהִזָּכֵר לְאַבְרָהָם לְיִצְחָק וּלְיַעֲקֹב.

---

אַף אֹרַח מִשְׁפָּטֶיךָ *Even when You sit in judgment.* A complex acrostic by HaKalir. The first letter of the first phrase of each verse proceeds in alphabetical order, while the first letter of the second phrase runs in reverse alphabetical order, the two meeting in the middle in the last verse. Here form mirrors content, since the poem speaks both of the distant past and the distant future, whose memory and anticipation meet in us, here, now. The distant past: God created repentance even before the first humans. The distant future: one day the shofar will sound to gather in the scattered exiles of the Jewish people throughout the world. The reference to *the removal of the burden from the shoulder of Joseph* reflects the tradition that Joseph was released from prison on Rosh HaShana (*Rosh HaShana* 11a).

*The congregation says the next two verses aloud, then the Leader:*

The LORD shall reign for ever. Ps. 146
He is your God, Zion, from generation to generation, Halleluya!

You are the Holy One, enthroned on the praises of Israel. God, Please. Ps. 22

*The Leader, then the congregation:*

אֵל אֱמוּנָה O faithful God, as You prepare to pass judgment,
were You to press the letter of the law in judgment,
who would ever be found righteous before You and
acquitted by such judgment? / O Holy One.

*The Leader, then the congregation:*

אִם לֹא If He shall not do it on His own behalf
and remove all ire and wrath,
then no inquiry of man's actions will yield any merits. / O Holy One.

*Some congregations say the piyut, "The mighty representatives," on page 1018.*

*The Ark is opened. The full version of this piyut is on page 1024.*

וּבְכֵן And so – [The LORD] became King in Yeshurun.

The Supreme King
God who resides on high, / mighty on high,
may He lift the strength of His hand high –
He shall reign forever.

The Supreme King
Mighty in His assemblies, / He decrees and fulfills
and reveals hidden truths –
He shall reign forever.

The Supreme King
He speaks righteously, / garbed in righteousness,
He hearkens to our cries –
He shall reign forever.

---

destitute king, *melekh evyon*. Evidently this was considered disrespectful of the rulers of the countries in which Jews lived, and contrary to the principle, "Pray for the welfare of the government, for were it not for fear of it, people would swallow one another alive" (*Avot* 3:2).

Only the first and last of these verses are usually said, toward the end of

*The* קהל *says the next two verses aloud, then the* שליח ציבור*:*

תהלים קמו יִמְלֹךְ יהוה לְעוֹלָם, אֱלֹהַיִךְ צִיּוֹן לְדֹר וָדֹר, הַלְלוּיָהּ:

תהלים כב וְאַתָּה קָדוֹשׁ יוֹשֵׁב תְּהִלּוֹת יִשְׂרָאֵל: אֵל נָא.

*The* שליח ציבור*, then the* קהל*:*

אֵל אֱמוּנָה, בְּעָרְכְּךָ דִין / אִם תְּמַצֶּה עֹמֶק הַדִּין
מִי יִצְדַּק לְפָנֶיךָ בַּדִּין / קָדוֹשׁ.

*The* שליח ציבור*, then the* קהל*:*

אִם לֹא לְמַעֲנוֹ יַעַשׂ / וְיָסִיר חֲרוֹן אַף וָכַעַס
אֵין לְבַקֵּר וְלִמְצֹא מַעַשׂ / קָדוֹשׁ.

*Some congregations say the piyut,* אֹמֶץ אַדִּירֵי כָּל חֵפֶץ*, on page 1019.*

*The* ארון קודש *is opened. The full version of this piyut is on page 1025.*

וּבְכֵן, וַיְהִי בִישֻׁרוּן מֶלֶךְ

מֶלֶךְ עֶלְיוֹן
אֵל דָּר בַּמָּרוֹם / אַדִּיר בַּמָּרוֹם / אֹמֶץ יָדוֹ תָּרֹם
לַעֲדֵי עַד יִמְלֹךְ.

מֶלֶךְ עֶלְיוֹן
גִּבּוֹר לְהָקִים / גּוֹזֵר וּמֵקִים / גּוֹלֶה עֲמֻקִּים
לַעֲדֵי עַד יִמְלֹךְ.

מֶלֶךְ עֶלְיוֹן
הַמְדַבֵּר בִּצְדָקָה / הַלּוֹבֵשׁ צְדָקָה / הַמַּאֲזִין צְעָקָה
לַעֲדֵי עַד יִמְלֹךְ.

---

מֶלֶךְ עֶלְיוֹן *The Supreme King.* A glance at the first letter of each verse shows that this poem has been truncated: the verses beginning with even-numbered letters – *bet, dalet, vav* etc. – have been deleted. Initially each pair of verses contrasted God the sublime King, *Melekh elyon,* with a human ruler, the

The Supreme King
He recalls our ancestors / to vindicate His creatures,
wrathful to our oppressors –
He shall reign forever.

The Supreme King
Good is He who lives forever, / His kindness lasts forever, /
He laid out the eternal heavens –
He shall reign forever.

The Supreme King
Clothed in light like a garment, / all the luminaries of light,
He is mighty and luminous –
He shall reign forever.

The Supreme King
King who reigns forever, / He deciphers hidden mysteries
and puts speech in the mouth of the mute –
He shall reign forever.

The Supreme King
Bears all His creatures, / encompasses and consumes all, / looks upon all –
He shall reign forever.

The Supreme King
His glory is might, / the works of His right hand are mighty,
the Redeemer and Fortress –
He shall reign forever.

The Supreme King
His holy angels are like flames, / calling forth the waters of angelic name,
close to those who call upon Him in love –
He shall reign forever.

The Supreme King
He does not know sleep, / His closest angelic servants are at peace,
fine praise for the righteous fills His treasury –
He shall reign forever.

---

the poem. They are said in an undertone with the Ark closed. The poem as a whole has as its theme the central idea of Rosh HaShana itself: that God, Creator of the universe, is its supreme Sovereign. He is King, not only of the Jewish people, but of all humanity, of all that lives.

מֶלֶךְ עֶלְיוֹן
זוֹכֵר צוּרִים / זַכּוּת יְצוּרִים / זוֹעֵם צָרִים
לַעֲדֵי עַד יִמְלֹךְ.

מֶלֶךְ עֶלְיוֹן
טוֹב שׁוֹכֵן עַד / טוּבוֹ לָעַד / טִפַּח שְׁמֵי עַד
לַעֲדֵי עַד יִמְלֹךְ.

מֶלֶךְ עֶלְיוֹן
כַּשַּׂלְמָה עוֹטֶה אוֹר / כָּל מְאוֹרֵי אוֹר / כַּבִּיר וְנָאוֹר
לַעֲדֵי עַד יִמְלֹךְ.

מֶלֶךְ עֶלְיוֹן
מֶלֶךְ עוֹלָמִים / מְפַעֲנֵחַ נֶעֱלָמִים / מֵשִׂיחַ אִלְּמִים
לַעֲדֵי עַד יִמְלֹךְ.

מֶלֶךְ עֶלְיוֹן
סוֹבֵל כֹּל / סָב וּמְבַלֶּה כֹּל / סוֹקֵר בַּכֹּל
לַעֲדֵי עַד יִמְלֹךְ.

מֶלֶךְ עֶלְיוֹן
פְּאֵרוֹ עֹז / פֹּעַל יְמִינוֹ תָּעֹז / פּוֹדֶה וּמָעוֹז
לַעֲדֵי עַד יִמְלֹךְ.

מֶלֶךְ עֶלְיוֹן
קְדוֹשָׁיו לַהַב / קוֹרֵא מֵי רַהַב / קָרוֹב לְקוֹרְאָיו בְּאַהַב
לַעֲדֵי עַד יִמְלֹךְ.

מֶלֶךְ עֶלְיוֹן
שֵׁנָה אֵין לְפָנָיו / שֶׁקֶט בִּפְנִינָיו / שֶׁבַח טוֹב בְּמַצְפּוּנָיו
לַעֲדֵי עַד יִמְלֹךְ.

*The Ark is closed and the congregation says quietly:*

The destitute king
Worn and relegated to decay / in uppermost hell and beneath,
weary without rest –
till when shall he reign?

The destitute king
Sleep hovers over him, / deep sleep enfolds him,
confusion overwhelms him –
till when shall he reign?

*The Ark is opened.*

Yet the Supreme King
His vigor is eternal, / His glory forever and ever,
His praise stands eternally –
He shall reign forever.

*In some congregations the Ark is closed and opened by another honoree.*

*The following piyut, the Siluk, is the last of the piyutim before Kedusha.*

*All:*

**וּבְכֵן לְךָ** And so, sanctity will rise up to You;
for You, our God, are King.

*All:*

**וּנְתַנֶּה תֹּקֶף** Let us voice the power of this day's sanctity –
it is awesome, terrible;
on this day Your kingship is raised,
Your throne is founded upon love,
and You, with truth, sit upon it.
In truth, it is You: Judge and Accuser, Knowing One and Witness,
writing and sealing, counting, numbering,
remembering all forgotten things,
You open the book of memories –
it is read of itself, / and every man's name is signed there.

---

ings by Michelangelo or Rembrandt. The language is simple, the imagery strong, the rhythms insistent and the drama intense.

It is structured in four movements. The first sets the scene. The heavenly

*The* ארון קודש *is closed and the* קהל *says quietly:*

מֶלֶךְ אֶבְיוֹן
בָּלֶה וְיֹרֵד שַׁחַת / בִּשְׁאוֹל וּבְתַחַת / בְּלֵאוּת בְּלִי נַחַת
עַד מָתַי יִמְלֹךְ.

מֶלֶךְ אֶבְיוֹן
תְּנוּמָה תְעוּפֶנּוּ / תַּרְדֵּמָה תְּעוֹפְפֶנּוּ / תֹּהוּ יְשׁוּפֶנּוּ
עַד מָתַי יִמְלֹךְ.

*The* ארון קודש *is opened.*

אֲבָל מֶלֶךְ עֶלְיוֹן
תָּקְפּוֹ לָעַד / תִּפְאַרְתּוֹ עֲדֵי עַד / תְּהִלָּתוֹ עוֹמֶדֶת לָעַד
לַעֲדֵי עַד יִמְלֹךְ.

*In some congregations the* ארון קודש *is closed and opened by somebody else.*

*The following piyut, the* סילוק, *is the last of the piyutim before* קדושה.

*All:*

וּבְכֵן לְךָ תַעֲלֶה קְדֻשָּׁה, כִּי אַתָּה אֱלֹהֵינוּ מֶלֶךְ.

*All:*

וּנְתַנֶּה תֹּקֶף קְדֻשַּׁת הַיּוֹם / כִּי הוּא נוֹרָא וְאָיֹם
וּבוֹ תִנָּשֵׂא מַלְכוּתֶךָ / וְיִכּוֹן בְּחֶסֶד כִּסְאֶךָ / וְתֵשֵׁב עָלָיו בֶּאֱמֶת.
אֱמֶת, כִּי אַתָּה הוּא דַיָּן וּמוֹכִיחַ, וְיוֹדֵעַ וָעֵד
וְכוֹתֵב וְחוֹתֵם וְסוֹפֵר וּמוֹנֶה
וְתִזְכֹּר כָּל הַנִּשְׁכָּחוֹת / וְתִפְתַּח אֶת סֵפֶר הַזִּכְרוֹנוֹת
וּמֵאֵלָיו יִקָּרֵא / וְחוֹתַם יַד כָּל אָדָם בּוֹ.

---

UNTANEH TOKEF – LET US VOICE THE POWER

No prayer more powerfully defines the image of the Days of Awe than does *Untaneh Tokef*. It is the equivalent in words to one of the great religious paint-

**וּבְשׁוֹפָר גָּדוֹל** A great shofar sounds,
and a still small voice is heard,
angels rush forward / and are held by trembling, shaking;
they say, "Here is the Day of Judgment
visiting all the heavenly host for judgment –"
for they are not cleared in Your eyes in judgment.
And all who have come into this world pass before You like sheep.

---

The story of Rabbi Amnon may explain its adoption and adaptation by the Jewish communities of northern Europe. Whatever its origin, it is one of the masterpieces of Jewish prayer.

**וּבְשׁוֹפָר גָּדוֹל יִתָּקַע וְקוֹל דְּמָמָה דַקָּה יִשָּׁמַע** *A great shofar sounds, and a still small voice is heard.* In a brilliant linking of two famous biblical episodes, the prayer recalls two scenes on Mount Sinai. The first took place when the Torah was given to the Israelites in the days of Moses, when "the sound of the shofar grew louder and louder" (Ex. 19:19) and the people trembled. The second took place several centuries later when the prophet Elijah, after his confrontation with the false prophets of Baal, stood on the same mountain. There was a whirlwind, an earthquake and a fire, but God was not in any of these. Then came the *kol demama daka*, "a still small voice" (1 Kings 19:12). It is not the whirlwind, the earthquake or the fire that are truly terrifying but the still, small voice of God that tells us that we are in the presence of Infinity.

**כִּבְנֵי מָרוֹן** *Like sheep.* This phrase – in Hebrew, *kivnei maron* – appears in the Mishna (*Rosh HaShana* 1:2). The Talmud offers three interpretations. The first: like a flock of sheep being counted by a shepherd. We pass individually, one by one, before God's scrutiny. There are times when we are one of a crowd, but not today. Today God examines each of us individually.

The second: like the approach to Meron or Beit Ḥoron. This was a village approachable only by way of a steep path only wide enough for one person to pass at a time. Here too the idea is as in the previous interpretation: we are judged singly as individuals. But to it is added the idea of a steep ascent. We are climbing. The way is hard.

The third: like the army of King David. This reads the text as *kivenumeron*. *Numeron* is the Greek word for a host, an army. Here the emphasis is different. God is being crowned as King and we are His legions, His troops, the people who recognize His majesty and do battle on His behalf.

וּבְשׁוֹפָר גָּדוֹל יִתָּקַע / וְקוֹל דְּמָמָה דַקָּה יִשָּׁמַע
וּמַלְאָכִים יֵחָפֵזוּן / וְחִיל וּרְעָדָה יֹאחֵזוּן
וְיֹאמְרוּ, הִנֵּה יוֹם הַדִּין / לִפְקוֹד עַל צְבָא מָרוֹם בַּדִּין
כִּי לֹא יִזְכּוּ בְעֵינֶיךָ בַּדִּין
וְכָל בָּאֵי עוֹלָם יַעַבְרוּן לְפָנֶיךָ כִּבְנֵי מָרוֹן.

---

court is assembled. God sits in the seat of judgment. The angels tremble. Before Him is the book of all our deeds. In it our lives are written, bearing our signature, and we await the verdict.

The second defines what is at stake: Who will live, who will die? Who will flourish, who will suffer, who will be at ease, who will be in torment? Between now and Yom Kippur our fate is being decided on high.

Then comes the great outburst of faith that defines Judaism as a religion of hope. No fate is final. Repentance, prayer and charity can avert the evil decree. Life is not a script written by Aeschylus or Sophocles in which tragedy is inexorable. God forgives; God pardons; God exercises clemency – if we truly repent and pray and give to others.

Finally there is a moving reflection on the fragility of human life and the eternity of God. We are no more than a fragment of pottery, a blade of grass, a flower that fades, a shadow, a cloud, a breath of wind. Dust we are and to dust we return. But God is life forever. By attaching ourselves to Him we may "Hold Infinity in the palm of your hand / And Eternity in an hour" (William Blake).

We do not know exactly who composed *Untaneh Tokef* or when. A famous tradition dates it to the time when Jews in northern Europe were suffering brutal Christian persecution. It tells of Rabbi Amnon of Mainz, how he was pressured by the bishop, who was also mayor of the town, to convert. Eventually, after repeated prevarication, the bishop subjected him to cruel punishment, inflicting on him wounds from which he would die. On Rosh HaShana, sensing that he was on the verge of death, Rabbi Amnon asked to be carried to the synagogue. As he entered he found the congregation about to say the *Kedusha*, and asked for permission to say a prayer as his dying words. He then said *Untaneh Tokef*, and died (*Or Zarua* 2:276).

The discovery of ancient manuscripts in the Cairo Geniza suggests, however, that the prayer may be older than this. This and other factors suggest that, in its original form, it was composed in Israel several centuries before.

כְּבַקָּרַת רוֹעֶה As a shepherd's searching gaze meets his flock,
as he passes every sheep beneath his rod,
so You too pass Yours, count and number,
and regard the soul of every living thing;
and You rule off the limit of each creation's life,
and write down the verdict for each.

*In most congregations the following is said first by the congregation and then the Leader; in some by the Leader alone.*

בְּרֹאשׁ הַשָּׁנָה On Rosh HaShana it is written / and on Yom Kippur it is sealed: / how many will pass away and how many will be born; / who will live and who will die; / who in his due time and who before; / who by water and who by fire; / who by sword and who by beast; / who of hunger and who of thirst; / who by earthquake and who by plague; / who by strangling and who by stoning; / who will rest and who will wander; / who will be calm and who will be harassed; / who will be at ease and who will suffer; / who will become poor and who will grow rich; / who cast down and who raised high.

*In many editions of the maḥzor, the words "Repentance, Prayer and Charity" are accompanied by three corresponding words: fasting, crying, giving. The numerical value (gematria) of each Hebrew word being 136, these words indicate that the three modes of approaching God are equivalent (Minhagim of Rabbi Isaac Tirna, fifteenth century).*

*The congregation says aloud, followed by the Leader:*

*FASTING* *CRYING* *GIVING*

But **REPENTANCE, PRAYER** and **CHARITY**
avert the evil of the decree.

---

sides of what superficially looks like a contradiction. This dissonance is the source of our creative energy, our restless desire to heal a fractured world, as well as our intellectual honesty in refusing to simplify a complex faith.

We have just said, "On Rosh HaShana it is written and on Yom Kippur it is sealed...who will live and who will die," as if the future were determined on these days. Now we say the opposite: "But repentance, prayer and charity avert the evil of the decree." On this view, the future is not determined. No fate is final. There is always the possibility of an appeal, a plea for clemency, a royal or presidential pardon.

כְּבַקָּרַת רוֹעֶה עֶדְרוֹ / מַעֲבִיר צֹאנוֹ תַּחַת שִׁבְטוֹ
כֵּן תַּעֲבִיר וְתִסְפֹּר וְתִמְנֶה / וְתִפְקֹד נֶפֶשׁ כָּל חָי
וְתַחְתֹּךְ קִצְבָה לְכָל בְּרִיָּה / וְתִכְתֹּב אֶת גְּזַר דִּינָם.

*In most congregations the following is said first by the* קהל *and then the* שליח ציבור*; in some by the* שליח ציבור *alone.*

בְּרֹאשׁ הַשָּׁנָה יִכָּתֵבוּן / וּבְיוֹם צוֹם כִּפּוּר יֵחָתֵמוּן.
כַּמָּה יַעַבְרוּן וְכַמָּה יִבָּרֵאוּן
מִי יִחְיֶה וּמִי יָמוּת / מִי בְקִצּוֹ וּמִי לֹא בְקִצּוֹ
מִי בַמַּיִם וּמִי בָאֵשׁ / מִי בַחֶרֶב וּמִי בַחַיָּה / מִי בָרָעָב וּמִי בַצָּמָא
מִי בָרַעַשׁ וּמִי בַמַּגֵּפָה / מִי בַחֲנִיקָה וּמִי בַסְּקִילָה.
מִי יָנוּחַ וּמִי יָנוּעַ / מִי יַשְׁקִיט וּמִי יְטֹּרַף
מִי יִשָּׁלֵו וּמִי יִתְיַסָּר / מִי יֵעָנִי וּמִי יַעֲשִׁיר / מִי יֻשְׁפַּל וּמִי יָרוּם.

*In many editions of the* מחזור*, the words "*וּצְדָקָה וּתְפִלָּה וּתְשׁוּבָה*" are accompanied by three corresponding words:* צום, קול, ממון*. The numerical value (*גימטריה*) of each word being 136, these words indicate that the three modes of approaching God are equivalent (Minhagim of Rabbi Isaac Tirna, fifteenth century).*

*The* קהל *says aloud, followed by the* שליח ציבור*:*

צום קול ממון

וּתְשׁוּבָה וּתְפִלָּה וּצְדָקָה / מַעֲבִירִין אֶת רֹעַ הַגְּזֵרָה.

---

בְּרֹאשׁ הַשָּׁנָה יִכָּתֵבוּן *On Rosh HaShana it is written.* Rabbi Kruspedai said in the name of Rabbi Yoḥanan: On Rosh HaShana three books lie open in heaven: one for the completely wicked, one for the completely righteous, and one for the intermediate. The completely righteous are immediately inscribed in the book of life; the thoroughly wicked are immediately inscribed in the book of death; the verdict on the intermediate is suspended from New Year till the Day of Atonement. If they deserve well, they are inscribed in the book of life; if they do not deserve well, they are inscribed in the book of death. (*Rosh HaShana* 16b)

וּתְשׁוּבָה וּתְפִלָּה וּצְדָקָה מַעֲבִירִין אֶת רֹעַ הַגְּזֵרָה *But repentance, prayer and charity avert the evil of the decree.* Judaism lives in cognitive dissonance, believing both

*All:*

כִּי כְשִׁמְךָ For as Your name is, so is Your renown:
hard to anger, and readily appeased.
For You do not desire the condemned man's death,
but that he may come back from his ways, and live.
To the very day he dies, You wait for him;
and if he comes back: You welcome him at once.

---

Their degree is higher than those who have never sinned because they have had to struggle more fiercely to subdue their passions. (Maimonides, Laws of Repentance 7:4)

Rabbi Ḥayyim of Sanz told his followers this story. Once a man lost his way in a great forest. He searched for a way out, but each path he took only led him deeper into the woods. Eventually he heard the sound of someone approaching. His heart lifted. He waited till the other approached and asked him to show him the way out. "I do not know," said the other, "for I too am lost. But this I can tell you. Do not take the way I have been taking for it will lead you astray. And now let us search for a new way together." The rabbi lifted up his eyes to his followers, and they understood.

Said Rabbi Abraham Kook: Through penitence, all things are reunited with God; through the fact that penitence is operative in all worlds, all things are returned and reattached to the realm of divine perfection. (*The Lights of Penitence,** p. 49)

Penitence is the healthiest feeling of a person. A healthy soul in a healthy body must necessarily bring about the great happiness afforded by penitence, and the soul experiences therein the greatest natural delight. (Ibid., p. 53)

PRAYER

There are people who cannot understand prayer and its effect on the soul. The Ba'al Shem Tov explained this by way of a parable. He said: There was once a musician who played so beautifully that those who heard him stopped and began to dance. Once a deaf man came along. He saw all the people dancing but he could not hear the music. He thought they were all mad.

Rabbi Naḥman of Kosov taught that we should always have God in our thoughts. "But how," asked a disciple, "can we think of God while we are

* R. Abraham Isaac HaKohen Kook, *The Lights of Penitence*, trans. Ben Zion Bokser (Mahwah, NJ: Paulist Press, 1978).

*All:*

כִּי כְשִׁמְךָ כֵּן תְּהִלָּתֶךָ / קָשֶׁה לִכְעֹס וְנְוֹחַ לִרְצוֹת
כִּי לֹא תַחְפֹּץ בְּמוֹת הַמֵּת / כִּי אִם בְּשׁוּבוֹ מִדַּרְכּוֹ, וְחָיָה
וְעַד יוֹם מוֹתוֹ תְּחַכֶּה לוֹ / אִם יָשׁוּב, מִיַּד תְּקַבְּלוֹ.

---

There is a classic example of this in Tanakh.

> In those days Hezekiah became ill and was at the point of death. The prophet Isaiah son of Amotz went to him and said, "This is what the Lord says: Put your house in order, because you are going to die; you will not recover." Hezekiah turned his face to the wall and prayed to the Lord, "Remember, Lord, how I have walked before You faithfully and with wholehearted devotion and have done what is good in Your eyes." And Hezekiah wept bitterly. Before Isaiah had left the middle court, the word of the Lord came to him: "Go back and tell Hezekiah, the ruler of My people: This is what the Lord, God of your father David, says: I have heard your prayer and seen your tears; I will heal you." (II Kings 20:1–5; Isaiah 38:1–5)

Isaiah had told Hezekiah he would not recover, but he did. He lived for another fifteen years. God heard his prayer and granted him stay of execution. From this the Talmud infers, "Even if a sharp sword rests upon your neck you should not desist from prayer" (*Berakhot* 10a).

We pray for a good fate but we do not reconcile ourselves to fatalism.

וּתְשׁוּבָה וּתְפִלָּה וּצְדָקָה *Repentance, prayer and charity.* Repentance is our relationship to ourselves. Prayer is our relationship to God. *Tzedaka,* charity, is our relationship to others. We should be honest in our relationship with ourselves, humble in our relationship to God and generous in our relationship to others.

REPENTANCE

Once, shortly before Rosh HaShana, an itinerant shoemaker passed the house of Rabbi Levi Yitzḥak of Berditchev, crying, "Anything to mend?" When he heard these words the rabbi wept, saying, "Alas for my soul, for the Day of Judgment is almost at hand, and I have not yet mended myself."

Let not a repentant sinner imagine that he is far from the degree of the righteous because of his sins and misdeeds. That is not so, for he is beloved and precious to God as if he had never sinned. Indeed his reward is great, because he has tasted sin and yet separated from it, having conquered his evil inclination. It is written in the Talmud that "In the place where repentant sinners stand even the perfectly righteous cannot stand" (*Berakhot* 34b).

Truly, it was You who formed them,
You know the forces moving them: / they are but flesh and blood.

Man is founded in dust / and ends in dust.
He lays down his soul to bring home bread. / He is like a broken shard,
like grass dried up, like a faded flower,
like a fleeting shadow, like a passing cloud,
like a breath of wind, like whirling dust, like a dream that slips away.

---

duces no fruit, while I have stored away something that does produce fruit. My fathers stored away treasures of money, while I have stored away treasures of souls." (*Bava Batra* 11a)

Said the Rabbi of Kotzk: Take care of your own soul and another person's body, not of your own body and another person's soul.

The fifteenth-century Jewish diplomat and scholar Don Isaac Abrabanel (1437–1508), chancellor to King Ferdinand and Queen Isabella of Castile, was once asked by the king how much he owned. He named a certain sum. "But surely," the king said, "you own much more than that." "You asked me," Abrabanel replied, "how much I owned. The property I have, I do not own. Your majesty may seize it from me tomorrow. At best I am its temporary guardian. The sum I mentioned is what I have given away in charity. That merit alone, neither you nor any earthly power can take away from me." We own what we are willing to share.

אָדָם יְסוֹדוֹ מֵעָפָר וְסוֹפוֹ לֶעָפָר *Man is founded in dust and ends in dust.* It is said that when Shmuel Yosef Agnon won the Nobel Prize for literature he was besieged by reporters and photographers. One of them asked him to pose for a photograph by writing as if composing one of his novels. Agnon did. The photographer took the shot and left. One of those present, out of curiosity, looked at the piece of paper to see what Agnon had written at this moment of glory. Agnon had written the words, "Man is founded in dust and ends in dust." (Rabbi Jeffrey Cohen, *Prayer and Penitence**)

Rabbi Bunam of Pzhysha said to his disciples: Everyone should have two pockets, so that he can reach into one or the other according to his needs.

* Rabbi Jeffrey M. Cohen, *Prayer and Penitence: A Commentary on the High Holy Day Machzor* (Northvale, NJ: Jason Aronson, 1994), p. 83.

אֱמֶת, כִּי אַתָּה הוּא יוֹצְרָם / וְיוֹדֵעַ יִצְרָם / כִּי הֵם בָּשָׂר וָדָם.

אָדָם יְסוֹדוֹ מֵעָפָר / וְסוֹפוֹ לֶעָפָר
בְּנַפְשׁוֹ יָבִיא לַחְמוֹ / מָשׁוּל כַּחֶרֶס הַנִּשְׁבָּר
כְּחָצִיר יָבֵשׁ, וּכְצִיץ נוֹבֵל / כְּצֵל עוֹבֵר, וּכְעָנָן כָּלֶה
וּכְרְוּחַ נוֹשָׁבֶת, וּכְאָבָק פּוֹרֵחַ, וְכַחֲלוֹם יָעוּף.

---

engaged in business?" The rabbi replied, "If we can think of business when we are praying, then we can think of praying when we are doing business."

Is prayer answered? If God is changeless, how can we change Him by what we say? Even discounting this, why do we need to articulate our requests? Surely God, who sees the heart, knows our wishes even before we do, without our having to put them into words. What we wish to happen is either right or wrong in the eyes of God. If it is right, God will bring it about even if we do not pray. If it is wrong, God will not bring it about even if we do. So why pray?

The classic Jewish answer is simple but profound. Without a vessel to contain a blessing, there can be no blessing. If we have no receptacle to catch the rain, the rain may fall, but we will have none to drink. If we have no radio receiver, the sound-waves will flow, but we will be unable to convert them into sound. God's blessings flow continuously, but unless we make ourselves into a vessel for them, they will flow elsewhere. Prayer is the act of turning ourselves into a vehicle for the divine. Prayer changes the world because it changes us.

CHARITY

Our masters taught: it is related of King Monabaz [king of Adiabene in the first century CE who converted to Judaism] that during years of scarcity he spent all his own treasures and the treasures of his fathers on charity. His brothers and other members of his family reproached him: "Your fathers stored away treasures, adding to the treasures of their fathers, and you squander them!" He replied: "My fathers stored away for the world below, while I am storing away for the world above. My fathers stored away in a place where the hand of others can prevail, while I have stored away in a place where the hand of others cannot prevail. My fathers stored away something that pro-

*The congregation says aloud, followed by the Leader:*

**AND YOU ARE KING –**
**THE LIVING, EVERLASTING GOD.**

*The Ark is closed.*

*The congregation and then the Leader:*

אֵין קִצְבָה There is no end to Your years,
no limit to the days of Your life.
One cannot grasp the measure of Your glorious chariot;
one may not articulate Your most concealed name.
Your name is befitting to You
and You befit Your name.
By that name You have named us.
Act for Your name's sake.
Sanctify Your name
through those who sanctify Your name,
for the sake of the glory of Your name,
revered and sanctified,
with the words uttered by the holy Seraphim
who sanctify Your name in the Sanctuary,
those who live in heaven with those who live on earth
cry out and three times repeat
the threefold declaration of holiness to the Holy One,

---

time to time throughout our lives, we create a silence in the soul, we will hear it.

There is no life without a task, no person without a talent, no place without a fragment of God's light waiting to be discovered and redeemed, no situation without its possibility of sanctification, no moment without its call. It may take a lifetime to learn how to find these things, but once we learn, we realize in retrospect that all it ever took was the ability to listen. When God calls, He whispers our name – and the greatest reply, the reply of Abraham, is simply *Hineni*, "Here I am," ready to heed Your call, to mend a fragment of Your all-too-broken world.

*The* קהל *says aloud, followed by the* שליח ציבור*:*

וְאַתָּה הוּא מֶלֶךְ, אֵל חַי וְקַיָּם.

*The* ארון קודש *is closed.*

*The* קהל *and then the* שליח ציבור*:*

אֵין קִצְבָה לִשְׁנוֹתֶיךָ / וְאֵין קֵץ לְאֹרֶךְ יָמֶיךָ
וְאֵין לְשַׁעֵר מַרְכְּבוֹת כְּבוֹדֶךָ / וְאֵין לְפָרֵשׁ עֵילוּם שְׁמֶךָ.
שִׁמְךָ נָאֶה לְךָ / וְאַתָּה נָאֶה לִשְׁמֶךָ / וּשְׁמֵנוּ קָרָאתָ בִּשְׁמֶךָ.
עֲשֵׂה לְמַעַן שְׁמֶךָ, וְקַדֵּשׁ אֶת שִׁמְךָ עַל מַקְדִּישֵׁי שְׁמֶךָ
בַּעֲבוּר כְּבוֹד שִׁמְךָ הַנַּעֲרָץ וְהַנִּקְדָּשׁ
כְּסוֹד שִׂיחַ שַׂרְפֵי קֹדֶשׁ, הַמַּקְדִּישִׁים שִׁמְךָ בַּקֹּדֶשׁ
דָּרֵי מַעְלָה עִם דָּרֵי מַטָּה
קוֹרְאִים וּמְשַׁלְּשִׁים בְּשִׁלּוּשׁ קְדֻשָּׁה בַּקֹּדֶשׁ.

---

In his right pocket he should place the words, "For my sake was the world created." In his left pocket, he should place the words, "I am dust and ashes."

**וְכַחֲלוֹם יָעוּף** *Like a dream that slips away.* The greatest choice we will ever make is how we use the brief time we are given in this life. Shakespeare's Mark Antony was precisely, deliberately wrong. The good we do lives after us. The rest is oft interred with our bones. Will we, or will we not, discover our purpose in life and thus be etched with eternity?

God calls to us, each of us, here where we are, this person, in this situation, at this time, saying: there is an act only you can do, a situation only you can address, a moment that, if not seized, may never come again. God commands in generalities but calls in particulars. He knows our gifts and He knows the needs of the world. That is why we are here. There is an act only we can do, and only at this time, and that is our task. The sum of these tasks is the meaning of our life, the purpose of our existence, the story we are called on to write. God's call is almost inaudible. It speaks in "a still, small voice," meaning a voice we can only hear if we are listening. But it is there and if, from

## KEDUSHA

*During the Leader's Repetition, the following is said standing with feet together, rising on the toes at the words indicated by ▲.*

*Cong. then Leader:* כֶּתֶר They will crown You, Lord our God, the angels, the multitudes of heaven, together with Your nation Israel, gathering here below –

*Cong. then Leader:* Together all of them will speak the threefold declaration of Your holiness, as is said by Your prophet: "They call out to one another, saying: *Is. 6*

*Cong. then Leader:* ▲Holy, ▲holy, ▲holy is the Lord of hosts; the whole world is filled with His glory."

His glory fills the universe. His ministering angels ask each other: Where is the place of His glory, that we may revere Him there? Those facing them praise Him and say:

*Cong. then Leader:* ▲"Blessed is the Lord's glory from His place." *Ezek. 3*

From His place may He turn, in His compassion, to His nation, and be gracious to the people who proclaim the unity of His name, morning and evening, every day, continually, twice each day reciting in love the Shema:

*Cong. then Leader:* "Listen, Israel, the Lord is our God, the Lord is One." *Deut. 6*

He is our God, He is our Father, He is our King,
He is our Savior – and He will save us and redeem us again,
and, in His compassion He will let us hear Him say,
in the presence of all that lives: I have redeemed you again,
as I did at the beginning, "to be your God. *Num. 15*
I am the Lord your God."

*Cong. then Leader:* Glorious is our Glorious One, Lord our Master, *Ps. 8*
and glorious is Your name throughout the earth.
Then the Lord shall be King over all the earth; *Zech. 14*
on that day the Lord shall be One and His name One.

*Leader:* And in Your holy Writings it is written:

*Cong. then Leader:* ▲"The Lord shall reign for ever. *Ps. 146*
He is your God, Zion, from generation to generation, Halleluya!"

*Leader:* From generation to generation we will declare Your greatness,
and we will proclaim Your holiness for evermore.
Your praise, our God, shall not leave our mouth forever,
for You, God, are a great and holy King.

## קדושה

*During the* חורת הש״ץ*, the following is said standing with feet together, rising on the toes at the words indicated by* ˄.

*then* קהל ש״ץ: כֶּתֶר יִתְּנוּ לְךָ, יהוה אֱלֹהֵינוּ, מַלְאָכִים הֲמוֹנֵי מַעְלָה
עִם עַמְּךָ יִשְׂרָאֵל קְבוּצֵי מַטָּה

*then* קהל ש״ץ: יַחַד כֻּלָּם קְדֻשָּׁה לְךָ יְשַׁלֵּשׁוּ כַּדָּבָר הָאָמוּר עַל יַד נְבִיאֶךָ
ישעיה ו וְקָרָא זֶה אֶל־זֶה וְאָמַר

*then* קהל ש״ץ: ˄קָדוֹשׁ, ˄קָדוֹשׁ, ˄קָדוֹשׁ, יהוה צְבָאוֹת, מְלֹא כָל הָאָרֶץ כְּבוֹדוֹ:
כְּבוֹדוֹ מָלֵא עוֹלָם
מְשָׁרְתָיו שׁוֹאֲלִים זֶה לָזֶה, אַיֵּה מְקוֹם כְּבוֹדוֹ לְהַעֲרִיצוֹ
לְעֻמָּתָם מְשַׁבְּחִים וְאוֹמְרִים

*then* קהל ש״ץ: ˄בָּרוּךְ כְּבוֹד־יהוה מִמְּקוֹמוֹ: יחזקאל ג
מִמְּקוֹמוֹ הוּא יִפֶן בְּרַחֲמָיו לְעַמּוֹ
וְיָחֹן עַם הַמְיַחֲדִים שְׁמוֹ, עֶרֶב וָבֹקֶר בְּכָל יוֹם תָּמִיד
פַּעֲמַיִם בְּאַהֲבָה שְׁמַע אוֹמְרִים

*then* קהל ש״ץ: שְׁמַע יִשְׂרָאֵל, יהוה אֱלֹהֵינוּ, יהוה אֶחָד: דברים ו
הוּא אֱלֹהֵינוּ, הוּא אָבִינוּ, הוּא מַלְכֵּנוּ, הוּא מוֹשִׁיעֵנוּ
וְהוּא יוֹשִׁיעֵנוּ וְיִגְאָלֵנוּ שֵׁנִית, וְיַשְׁמִיעֵנוּ בְּרַחֲמָיו לְעֵינֵי כָּל חַי לֵאמֹר
הֵן גָּאַלְתִּי אֶתְכֶם אַחֲרִית כְּבְרֵאשִׁית לִהְיוֹת לָכֶם לֵאלֹהִים במדבר טו
אֲנִי יהוה אֱלֹהֵיכֶם:

*then* קהל ש״ץ: אַדִּיר אַדִּירֵנוּ, יהוה אֲדֹנֵינוּ, מָה־אַדִּיר שִׁמְךָ בְּכָל־הָאָרֶץ: תהלים ח
וְהָיָה יהוה לְמֶלֶךְ עַל־כָּל־הָאָרֶץ זכריה יד
בַּיּוֹם הַהוּא יִהְיֶה יהוה אֶחָד וּשְׁמוֹ אֶחָד:

ש״ץ: וּבְדִבְרֵי קָדְשְׁךָ כָּתוּב לֵאמֹר

*then* קהל ש״ץ: ˄יִמְלֹךְ יהוה לְעוֹלָם, אֱלֹהַיִךְ צִיּוֹן לְדֹר וָדֹר, הַלְלוּיָהּ: תהלים קמו

ש״ץ: לְדוֹר וָדוֹר נַגִּיד גָּדְלֶךָ, וּלְנֵצַח נְצָחִים קְדֻשָּׁתְךָ נַקְדִּישׁ
וְשִׁבְחֲךָ אֱלֹהֵינוּ מִפִּינוּ לֹא יָמוּשׁ לְעוֹלָם וָעֶד
כִּי אֵל מֶלֶךְ גָּדוֹל וְקָדוֹשׁ אָתָּה.

לְדוֹר וָדוֹר From generation to generation declare God King,
for He alone is lofty and holy.

*The following prayer originally began at "For with Your holiness." Nowadays, it is commonly sung as one stanza together with the later addition of the opening verse, "Have mercy on those You have made."*

חֲמֹל Have mercy on those You have made,
take joy in those You made,
and those who shelter in You will say,
as You absolve the ones You bear,
"Be sanctified, Lord, through all that You have made."

כִּי מַקְדִּישֶׁיךָ For with Your holiness You sanctify
all who affirm You holy;
it is fitting that the Holy One be glorified by holy ones.

*Leader:*

וּבְכֵן יִתְקַדַּשׁ And so may Your name be sanctified, Lord our God,
through Israel Your nation and Jerusalem, Your city,
and Zion, the dwelling place of Your honor
and through the royal house of David Your anointed,
and Your Sanctuary and Your Temple.

He, our Lord,
will yet remember for us the love of [Abraham] the steadfast one.
And for [Isaac] the son who was bound,
He will still the enmity against us,
and for the merit of [Jacob] the innocent man,
He will bring today our judgment out to the good,
for this day is holy to our Lord. *Neh. 8*

With no one to advocate for us against the accuser of sin,
speak words of law and of justice to Jacob;
and absolve us in the judgment, King of judgment.

---

בְּאֵין מֵלִיץ *With no one to advocate.* The poet, drawing on imagery from the book of Job, imagines a courtroom scene in which the accused has no defending counsel to answer the prosecuting attorney.

לְדוֹר וָדוֹר הַמְלִיכוּ לָאֵל, כִּי הוּא לְבַדּוֹ מָרוֹם וְקָדוֹשׁ.

*The following prayer originally began at "כִּי מַקְדִּישֶׁיךָ." Nowadays, it is commonly sung as one stanza together with the later addition of the opening verse, "חֲמֹל עַל מַעֲשֶׂיךָ."*

חֲמֹל עַל מַעֲשֶׂיךָ וְתִשְׂמַח בְּמַעֲשֶׂיךָ
וְיֹאמְרוּ לְךָ חוֹסֶיךָ בְּצַדֶּקְךָ עֲמוּסֶיךָ
תֻּקְדַּשׁ אָדוֹן עַל כָּל מַעֲשֶׂיךָ

כִּי מַקְדִּישֶׁיךָ בִּקְדֻשָּׁתְךָ קִדַּשְׁתָּ
נָאֶה לְקָדוֹשׁ פְּאֵר מִקְּדוֹשִׁים.

*The* שליח ציבור*:*

וּבְכֵן יִתְקַדַּשׁ שִׁמְךָ יהוה אֱלֹהֵינוּ
עַל יִשְׂרָאֵל עַמֶּךָ, וְעַל יְרוּשָׁלַיִם עִירֶךָ
וְעַל צִיּוֹן מִשְׁכַּן כְּבוֹדֶךָ, וְעַל מַלְכוּת בֵּית דָּוִד מְשִׁיחֶךָ
וְעַל מְכוֹנְךָ וְהֵיכָלֶךָ.

עוֹד יִזְכֹּר לָנוּ אַהֲבַת אֵיתָן, אֲדוֹנֵינוּ
וּבַבֵּן הַנֶּעֱקַד יַשְׁבִּית מְדַיְּנֵינוּ
וּבִזְכוּת הַתָּם יוֹצִיא הַיּוֹם לְצֶדֶק דִּינֵנוּ
נחמיה ח כִּי־קָדוֹשׁ הַיּוֹם לַאֲדֹנֵינוּ:

בְּאֵין מֵלִיץ יֹשֶׁר מוּל מַגִּיד פֶּשַׁע
תַּגִּיד לְיַעֲקֹב דָּבָר, חֹק וּמִשְׁפָּט
וְצַדְּקֵנוּ בַּמִּשְׁפָּט, הַמֶּלֶךְ הַמִּשְׁפָּט.

---

חֲמֹל עַל מַעֲשֶׂיךָ *Have mercy on those You have made.* A prayer woven out of several fragments from different places and times. Its theme is the mutual relationship between God's holiness and that of His people Israel. God made them holy; they declare Him holy.

*This piyut, with its double alphabetic acrostic, is attributed to Yannai (a poet who lived in Israel in the Byzantine era). In recent generations the custom to say it responsively has spread; many congregations are accustomed to saying the second stich of each couplet together with the first of the next one. Some sing the entire piyut collectively.*

*The Ark is opened.*

הָאוֹחֵז בְּיַד The One who holds in His hand the trait of stern judgment.
And all believe that He is the faithful God.

The One who examines and scrutinizes the hidden stores.
And all believe that He examines the conscience of all.

The One who redeems from death and ransoms from hell.
And all believe that He is a mighty Redeemer.

The sole Judge of all who enter the world.
And all believe that He is a truthful Judge.

The One whose name was pronounced "I will ever be what I am now."
And all believe that He was, is, and shall forever be.

The One whose praise is as affirmed as His name.
And all believe that He is One and there is no other.

The One who recalls kindly those who utter His name.
And all believe that He recalls His covenant.

The One who allots life to all the living.
And all believe that He lives and is everlasting.

---

from the heart of faith. Those who asked about the apparent injustices of the world were not doubters or sceptics. They were Judaism's supreme prophets. Moses asked, "O Lord, why have You brought trouble upon this people?" (Ex. 5:22). Jeremiah asked, "Why does the way of the wicked prosper? Why do all the faithless live at ease?" (Jer. 12:1). They did not ask because they did not believe. They asked because they *did* believe. If there were no Judge, there would be no justice and no question. There *is* a Judge. When then is justice? Above all else, Jewish thought through the centuries has been a sustained meditation on this question, never finding a final answer, realizing that here was a sacred mystery no human mind could penetrate. All other requests Moses made on behalf of the Jewish people, says the Talmud (*Berakhot* 7a), were granted except this: to understand why the righteous suffer.

*This piyut, with its double alphabetic acrostic, is attributed to Yannai (a poet who lived in ארץ ישראל in the Byzantine era). In recent generations the custom to say it responsively has spread; many congregations are accustomed to saying the second stich of each couplet together with the first of the next one. Some sing the entire piyut collectively.*

*The ארון קודש is opened.*

הָאוֹחֵז בְּיָד מִדַּת מִשְׁפָּט
וְכֹל מַאֲמִינִים שֶׁהוּא אֵל אֱמוּנָה.

הַבּוֹחֵן וּבוֹדֵק גִּנְזֵי נִסְתָּרוֹת
וְכֹל מַאֲמִינִים שֶׁהוּא בּוֹחֵן כְּלָיוֹת.

הַגּוֹאֵל מִמָּוֶת וּפוֹדֶה מִשַּׁחַת
וְכֹל מַאֲמִינִים שֶׁהוּא גּוֹאֵל חָזָק.

הַדָּן יְחִידִי לְבָאֵי עוֹלָם
וְכֹל מַאֲמִינִים שֶׁהוּא דַּיַּן אֱמֶת.

הֶהָגוּי בְּאֶהְיֶה אֲשֶׁר אֶהְיֶה
וְכֹל מַאֲמִינִים שֶׁהוּא הָיָה וְהֹוֶה וְיִהְיֶה.

הַוַּדַּאי, כִּשְׁמוֹ כֵּן תְּהִלָּתוֹ
וְכֹל מַאֲמִינִים שֶׁהוּא וְאֵין בִּלְתּוֹ.

הַזּוֹכֵר לְמַזְכִּירָיו טוֹבוֹת זִכְרוֹנוֹת
וְכֹל מַאֲמִינִים שֶׁהוּא זוֹכֵר הַבְּרִית.

הַחוֹתֵךְ חַיִּים לְכָל חָי
וְכֹל מַאֲמִינִים שֶׁהוּא חַי וְקַיָּם.

---

**וְכֹל מַאֲמִינִים** *And all believe.* A sustained declaration of faith in divine justice and compassion. Rosh HaShana, the Day of Judgment, is the living expression of Judaism's greatest leap of faith: the belief that the world is ruled by justice. No idea has been more revolutionary, and none more perplexing.

There are questions that challenge faith, and there are questions that come

The One who acts kindly with both the good and evil.
And all believe that He is kind to all.

The One who knows the devices of all creatures.
And all believe that He is the One who forms them in the womb.

The One who is omnipotent and formed the world at once.
And all believe that He is all-powerful.

The One who dwells concealed in His holy shade.
And all believe that He alone is God.

The One who crowns kings yet the reign is His alone.
And all believe that He is an everlasting King.

The One who acts kindly with each generation.
And all believe that He reserves kindness.

The One who acts patiently with evildoers
and turns a blind eye to the wayward.
And all believe that He is forgiving and exalted.

The lofty One whose eyes are turned to those who fear Him.
And all believe that He answers whispered prayers.

The One who opens the gates to those who come knocking penitently.
And all believe that His hand is ever open.

---

next, apparent or veiled behind a screen of mystery, but they are there. For without them life is a tale told by an idiot, full of sound and fury, signifying nothing. The faith of the Bible is neither optimistic nor naive. It contains no theodicies, no systematic answers, no easy consolations. At times, in the books of Job and Ecclesiastes and Lamentations, it comes close to the abyss of pain and despair. "I saw," says Ecclesiastes, "the tears of the oppressed – and they have no comforter" (4:1). "The Lord," says Lamentations, "has become like an enemy" (2:5). But the people of the Book refused to stop wrestling with the question. To believe was painful, but to disbelieve was too easy, too superficial, untrue.

The Rabbi of Klausenburg, Rabbi Yekutiel Yehuda Halberstam, who survived Auschwitz and lost his wife and eleven children in the Holocaust, once said: "The biggest miracle of all is that we, the survivors of the Holocaust, after all that we witnessed and lived through, still believe and have faith in

הַטּוֹב וּמֵיטִיב לָרָעִים וְלַטּוֹבִים
וְכֹל מַאֲמִינִים שֶׁהוּא טוֹב לַכֹּל.

הַיּוֹדֵעַ יֵצֶר כָּל יְצוּרִים
וְכֹל מַאֲמִינִים שֶׁהוּא יוֹצְרָם בַּבָּטֶן.

הַכֹּל יָכוֹל, וְכוֹלְלָם יַחַד
וְכֹל מַאֲמִינִים שֶׁהוּא כֹּל יָכוֹל.

הַלָּן בְּסֵתֶר בְּצֵל שַׁדַּי
וְכֹל מַאֲמִינִים שֶׁהוּא לְבַדּוֹ הוּא.

הַמַּמְלִיךְ מְלָכִים, וְלוֹ הַמְּלוּכָה
וְכֹל מַאֲמִינִים שֶׁהוּא מֶלֶךְ עוֹלָם.

הַנּוֹהֵג בְּחַסְדּוֹ עִם כָּל דּוֹר
וְכֹל מַאֲמִינִים שֶׁהוּא נוֹצֵר חֶסֶד.

הַסּוֹבֵל, וּמַעְלִים עַיִן מִסּוֹרְרִים
וְכֹל מַאֲמִינִים שֶׁהוּא סוֹלֵחַ סֶלָה.

הָעֶלְיוֹן, וְעֵינָיו עַל יְרֵאָיו
וְכֹל מַאֲמִינִים שֶׁהוּא עוֹנֶה לָחַשׁ.

הַפּוֹתֵחַ שַׁעַר לְדוֹפְקֵי בִתְשׁוּבָה
וְכֹל מַאֲמִינִים שֶׁהוּא פְּתוּחָה יָדוֹ.

---

As tenaciously as they asked, so they held firm to the faith without which there was no question: that there is a moral rule governing the universe and that what happens to us is in some way related to what we do. Good is rewarded and evil has no ultimate dominion. No Jewish belief is more central than this. It forms the core of the Hebrew Bible, the writings of the rabbis and the speculations of the Jewish mystics. Reward and punishment may be individual or collective, immediate or deferred, in this world or the

The One who espies the evildoer and wishes to justify him.
And all believe that He is righteous and upright.

The One who is slow to anger and defers wrath.
And all believe that His ire is hard to arouse.

The compassionate One who lets pity precede rage.
And all believe that He is easily appeased.

The constant One who considers great and small equally.
And all believe that He is a righteous Judge.

The perfect One who deals in integrity with the innocent.
And all believe that His works are perfect and complete.

*The Ark is closed (in some communities, the Ark remains open until the end of the next paragraph).*

תִּשְׂגַּב לְבַדֶּךָ You will be elevated, peerless,
and will rule over all that is, alone,
as is written by Your prophet,
"Then the LORD shall be King over all the earth; *Zech. 14*
on that day the LORD shall be One and His name One."

*The Leader continues:*

וּבְכֵן תֵּן פַּחְדְּךָ And so place the fear of You, LORD our God,
over all that You have made,
and the terror of You over all You have created,
and all who were made will stand in awe of You,
and all of creation will worship You,
and they will be bound all together as one
to carry out Your will with an undivided heart;
for we know, LORD our God,
that all dominion is laid out before You,
strength is in Your palm, and might in Your right hand,
Your name spreading awe over all You have created.

---

the Almighty God, may His name be blessed. This, my friends, is the miracle of miracles, the greatest miracle ever to have taken place." As he said these words, he wept. But still he believed.

הַצּוֹפֶה רָשָׁע, וְחָפֵץ לְהַצְדִּיקוֹ
וְכֹל מַאֲמִינִים שֶׁהוּא צַדִּיק וְיָשָׁר.

הַקָּצַר בְּזַעַם, וּמַאֲרִיךְ אַף
וְכֹל מַאֲמִינִים שֶׁהוּא קָשֶׁה לִכְעֹס.

הָרַחוּם, וּמַקְדִּים רַחֲמִים לְרֹגֶז
וְכֹל מַאֲמִינִים שֶׁהוּא רַךְ לִרְצוֹת.

הַשָּׁוֶה, וּמַשְׁוֶה קָטֹן וְגָדוֹל
וְכֹל מַאֲמִינִים שֶׁהוּא שׁוֹפֵט צֶדֶק.

הַתָּם, וּמִתַּמֵּם עִם תְּמִימִים
וְכֹל מַאֲמִינִים שֶׁהוּא תָּמִים פָּעֳלוֹ.

*The* ארון קודש *is closed (in some communities, the* ארון קודש *remains open until the end of the next paragraph).*

תִּשְׂגַּב לְבַדֶּךָ, וְתִמְלֹךְ עַל כֹּל בְּיִחוּד
כַּכָּתוּב עַל יַד נְבִיאֶךָ
זכריה יד וְהָיָה יהוה לְמֶלֶךְ עַל־כָּל־הָאָרֶץ
בַּיּוֹם הַהוּא יִהְיֶה יהוה אֶחָד וּשְׁמוֹ אֶחָד:

*The* שליח ציבור *continues:*

וּבְכֵן תֵּן פַּחְדְּךָ יהוה אֱלֹהֵינוּ עַל כָּל מַעֲשֶׂיךָ
וְאֵימָתְךָ עַל כָּל מַה שֶּׁבָּרָאתָ
וְיִירָאוּךָ כָּל הַמַּעֲשִׂים, וְיִשְׁתַּחֲווּ לְפָנֶיךָ כָּל הַבְּרוּאִים
וְיֵעָשׂוּ כֻלָּם אֲגֻדָּה אֶחָת לַעֲשׂוֹת רְצוֹנְךָ בְּלֵבָב שָׁלֵם
כְּמוֹ שֶׁיָּדַעְנוּ יהוה אֱלֹהֵינוּ שֶׁהַשָּׁלְטָן לְפָנֶיךָ
עֹז בְּיָדְךָ וּגְבוּרָה בִּימִינֶךָ
וְשִׁמְךָ נוֹרָא עַל כָּל מַה שֶּׁבָּרָאתָ.

וּבְכֵן תֵּן כָּבוֹד And so place honor, Lord, upon Your people,
praise on those who fear You and hope into those who seek You,
the confidence to speak into all who long for You,
gladness to Your land, and joy to Your city,
the flourishing of pride to David Your servant,
and a lamp laid out for his descendant, Your anointed,
soon, in our days.

וּבְכֵן צַדִּיקִים And then righteous people will see and rejoice,
and the upright will exult, and the pious revel in joy,
and injustice will have nothing more to say,
and all wickedness will fade away like smoke
as You sweep the rule of arrogance from the earth.

*This alphabetic piyut, author unknown, celebrates the future universal recognition of God by all the nations. It is usually sung collectively.*

וְיֶאֱתָיוּ And all shall come forth to worship You
and they shall bless Your honorable name.
And they shall tell of Your righteousness in the islands,
and nations that have not known You shall seek You out.
And all the ends of the earth shall praise You
and shall always say, "May the Lord forever be exalted."
And they shall spurn their idols
and be ashamed of their graven images.
And they shall turn their shoulder as one to worship You,
and those who seek Your presence
shall see You with the rising sun forever.

---

Rabbi Soloveitchik concluded:

I have given many sermons and written many discourses on the concept of Rosh HaShana, but nothing ever made me feel the true depth and power of the day as those words of my childhood teacher. Every year, when I recite in the Rosh HaShana prayers the words, "Rule over the whole world in Your glory," I remember my teacher in Chaslavitch.*

* Rabbi Joseph Soloveitchik's "Teshuva Derasha," lecture given on September 23, 1974 (Yiddish). Summarized and published in Soloveitchik's *Yemei Zikaron* [17:6], (Jerusalem: World Zionist Organization, 1986), pp. 149–150.

וּבְכֵן תֵּן כָּבוֹד יהוה לְעַמֶּךָ
תְּהִלָּה לִירֵאֶיךָ וְתִקְוָה טוֹבָה לְדוֹרְשֶׁיךָ
וּפִתְחוֹן פֶּה לַמְיַחֲלִים לָךְ, שִׂמְחָה לְאַרְצֶךָ, וְשָׂשׂוֹן לְעִירֶךָ
וּצְמִיחַת קֶרֶן לְדָוִד עַבְדֶּךָ, וַעֲרִיכַת נֵר לְבֶן יִשַׁי מְשִׁיחֶךָ
בִּמְהֵרָה בְיָמֵינוּ.

וּבְכֵן צַדִּיקִים יִרְאוּ וְיִשְׂמָחוּ, וִישָׁרִים יַעֲלֹזוּ
וַחֲסִידִים בְּרִנָּה יָגִילוּ, וְעוֹלָתָה תִּקְפָּץ פִּיהָ
וְכָל הָרִשְׁעָה כֻּלָּהּ כְּעָשָׁן תִּכְלֶה
כִּי תַעֲבִיר מֶמְשֶׁלֶת זָדוֹן מִן הָאָרֶץ.

*This alphabetic piyut, author unknown, celebrates the future universal recognition of God by all the nations. It is usually sung collectively.*

וְיֶאֱתָיוּ כֹּל לְעָבְדֶךָ / וִיבָרְכוּ שֵׁם כְּבוֹדֶךָ
וְיַגִּידוּ בָאִיִּים צִדְקֶךָ / וְיִדְרְשׁוּךָ עַמִּים לֹא יְדָעוּךָ
וִיהַלְלוּךָ כָּל אַפְסֵי אָרֶץ / וְיֹאמְרוּ תָמִיד יִגְדַּל יהוה
וְיִזְנְחוּ אֶת עֲצַבֵּיהֶם / וְיַחְפְּרוּ עִם פְּסִילֵיהֶם
וְיַטּוּ שְׁכֶם אֶחָד לְעָבְדֶךָ / וְיִירָאוּךָ עִם שֶׁמֶשׁ מְבַקְשֵׁי פָנֶיךָ

---

וְיֶאֱתָיוּ...וְיִתְּנוּ לְךָ כֶּתֶר מְלוּכָה *And all shall come… to offer You the royal crown.* Rabbi Joseph Soloveitchik used to speak about his childhood in Chaslavitch:

> Our teacher, who was a Chabad Hasid, said to us: "Do you know what Rosh HaShana is? The Rebbe, the Tzemaḥ Tzedek, would call the night of Rosh HaShana *Karanatzia Nacht* [Coronation Night]." Then he would ask the children, "Do you know whom we will be crowning?" Once I replied, "Czar Nicholas" [Nicholas II, the last Emperor of Russia]. The teacher responded: "Nicholas? He was crowned years ago. Why do we need to crown him again? Besides, he is not the real king. No, tonight, my dear children, we crown God.
>
> "And do you know who places the crown on his head?" the teacher continued. "Yankel the tailor, Berel the shoemaker, Zalman the water-carrier, Yossel the painter, Dovid the butcher…"

And they shall recognize Your majestic power,
and the errant ones shall learn to understand.
And they shall speak of Your might
and they shall exalt You who are exalted above all rulers.
And they shall leap back in fear in Your presence,
and they shall crown You with a diadem of glory.
And the mountains themselves shall break out in song,
and the islands shall joyfully shout as You are crowned.
And they shall accept the yoke of Your reign over them,
and You shall be exalted among assembled multitudes.
And they shall hear from far and wide and come
to offer You the royal crown.

וְתִמְלֹךְ And You, who are the LORD our God,
will rule alone over all those You have made,
in Mount Zion, the dwelling of Your glory,
and in Jerusalem, Your holy city,
as it is written in Your holy Writings:
"The LORD shall reign for ever. Ps. 146
He is your God, Zion, from generation to generation, Halleluya!"

קָדוֹשׁ אַתָּה You are holy, Your name is awesome,
and there is no god but You, as it is written,
"The LORD of hosts shall be raised up through His judgment, Is. 5
the Holy God, made holy in righteousness."
Blessed are You, LORD, the holy King.

HOLINESS OF THE DAY AND MALKHIYOT

אַתָּה בְחַרְתָּנוּ You have chosen us from among all peoples.
You have loved and favored us. You have raised us above all tongues.
You have made us holy through Your commandments.
You have brought us near, our King, to Your service,
and have called us by Your great and holy name.

---

remembrance; and *Shofarot,* verses relating to the shofar. In each case there are ten verses, the first three from the Mosaic books, the second three from *Ketuvim,* the Writings, and the third triad from the books of the prophets. The last verse in each case is from the Torah.

וְיַכִּירוּ כֹּחַ מַלְכוּתֶךָ / וְיִלְמְדוּ תוֹעִים בִּינָה
וִימַלְּלוּ אֶת גְּבוּרָתֶךָ / וִינַשְּׂאוּךָ, מִתְנַשֵּׂא לְכֹל לְרֹאשׁ
וִיסַלְּדוּ בְחִילָה פָּנֶיךָ / וִיעַטְּרוּךָ נֵזֶר תִּפְאָרָה
וְיִפְצְחוּ הָרִים רִנָּה / וְיִצְהֲלוּ אִיִּים בְּמָלְכֶךָ
וִיקַבְּלוּ עֹל מַלְכוּתְךָ עֲלֵיהֶם / וִירוֹמְמוּךָ בִּקְהַל עָם
וְיִשְׁמְעוּ רְחוֹקִים וְיָבוֹאוּ / וְיִתְּנוּ לְךָ כֶּתֶר מְלוּכָה.

וְתִמְלֹךְ אַתָּה הוּא יהוה אֱלֹהֵינוּ
מְהֵרָה לְבַדֶּךָ עַל כָּל מַעֲשֶׂיךָ
בְּהַר צִיּוֹן מִשְׁכַּן כְּבוֹדֶךָ
וּבִירוּשָׁלַיִם עִיר קָדְשֶׁךָ
כַּכָּתוּב בְּדִבְרֵי קָדְשֶׁךָ
יִמְלֹךְ יהוה לְעוֹלָם, אֱלֹהַיִךְ צִיּוֹן לְדֹר וָדֹר, הַלְלוּיָהּ: תהלים קמו

קָדוֹשׁ אַתָּה וְנוֹרָא שְׁמֶךָ, וְאֵין אֱלוֹהַּ מִבַּלְעָדֶיךָ
כַּכָּתוּב, וַיִּגְבַּהּ יהוה צְבָאוֹת בַּמִּשְׁפָּט ישעיה ה
וְהָאֵל הַקָּדוֹשׁ נִקְדַּשׁ בִּצְדָקָה:
בָּרוּךְ אַתָּה יהוה, הַמֶּלֶךְ הַקָּדוֹשׁ.

קדושת היום ומלכויות

אַתָּה בְחַרְתָּנוּ מִכָּל הָעַמִּים
אָהַבְתָּ אוֹתָנוּ וְרָצִיתָ בָּנוּ, וְרוֹמַמְתָּנוּ מִכָּל הַלְּשׁוֹנוֹת
וְקִדַּשְׁתָּנוּ בְּמִצְוֹתֶיךָ וְקֵרַבְתָּנוּ מַלְכֵּנוּ לַעֲבוֹדָתֶךָ
וְשִׁמְךָ הַגָּדוֹל וְהַקָּדוֹשׁ עָלֵינוּ קָרָאתָ.

---

MALKHIYOT: GOD'S KINGSHIP

We now begin the central drama of the Musaf Amida: three sections dealing respectively with *Malkhiyot,* God's kingship; *Zikhronot,* God's acts of

*On Shabbat, add the words in parentheses:*

וַתִּתֶּן לָנוּ And You, Lord our God, have given us in love
(this Sabbath day and) this Day of Remembrance,
a day of (recalling) blowing the shofar,
(with love,) a holy assembly in memory of the exodus from Egypt.

וּמִפְּנֵי חֲטָאֵינוּ But because of our sins
we were exiled from our land and driven far from our country.
We cannot perform our duties in Your chosen House,
the great and holy Temple that was called by Your name,
because of the hand that was stretched out against Your Sanctuary.
May it be Your will, Lord our God and God of our ancestors,
merciful King,
that You in Your abounding compassion may once more
have mercy on us and on Your Sanctuary,
rebuilding it swiftly and adding to its glory.

---

judgment of expediency… In this way the emancipated people of Athens became a tyrant." (Lord Acton*)

Without the constraint of the idea that above all human kings is the Divine King, all power tends to corrupt, and absolute power corrupts absolutely.

וּמִפְּנֵי חֲטָאֵינוּ גָּלִינוּ מֵאַרְצֵנוּ *But because of our sins we were exiled from our land.* This is a distinctively Jewish conception of sin and its consequences. A sin is an act that is not in the right place. The verb *ḥ-t-a,* "sin," comes from a verb that means "to miss the mark." The word *avera,* like its English translation, "transgression," means an act that oversteps the boundary. Justice is always "measure for measure." So the punishment for an *act* in the wrong place is exile, *being* in the wrong place. It was so from the beginning. For their sin, Adam and Eve were exiled from the Garden of Eden. For his sin, Cain was exiled and condemned to be a restless wanderer. The prophets saw Israel's exile as a national punishment for sin – for failure to stay faithful to God. Equally they saw *teshuva* as both a physical and spiritual return. Sin is displacement. *Teshuva* is homecoming.

* Sir John Dalberg-Acton, "The History of Freedom in Antiquity." An address given to the members of the Bridgnorth Institute on February 26, 1877. As cited in *Selected Writings of Lord Acton: Essays in the History of Liberty,* ed. J. Rufus Fears (Indianapolis, IN: Liberty Classics, 1985), pp. 13–14.

*On שבת, add the words in parentheses:*

וַתִּתֶּן לָנוּ יהוה אֱלֹהֵינוּ בְּאַהֲבָה
אֶת יוֹם (הַשַּׁבָּת הַזֶּה וְאֶת יוֹם) הַזִּכָּרוֹן הַזֶּה
יוֹם (זִכְרוֹן) תְּרוּעָה (בְּאַהֲבָה)
מִקְרָא קֹדֶשׁ, זֵכֶר לִיצִיאַת מִצְרָיִם.

וּמִפְּנֵי חֲטָאֵינוּ גָּלִינוּ מֵאַרְצֵנוּ, וְנִתְרַחַקְנוּ מֵעַל אַדְמָתֵנוּ
וְאֵין אֲנוּ יְכוֹלִים לַעֲשׂוֹת חוֹבוֹתֵינוּ בְּבֵית בְּחִירָתֶךָ
בַּבַּיִת הַגָּדוֹל וְהַקָּדוֹשׁ שֶׁנִּקְרָא שִׁמְךָ עָלָיו
מִפְּנֵי הַיָּד שֶׁנִּשְׁתַּלְּחָה בְּמִקְדָּשֶׁךָ.
יְהִי רָצוֹן מִלְּפָנֶיךָ יהוה אֱלֹהֵינוּ וֵאלֹהֵי אֲבוֹתֵינוּ
מֶלֶךְ רַחֲמָן
שֶׁתָּשׁוּב וּתְרַחֵם עָלֵינוּ וְעַל מִקְדָּשְׁךָ בְּרַחֲמֶיךָ הָרַבִּים
וְתִבְנֵהוּ מְהֵרָה וּתְגַדֵּל כְּבוֹדוֹ.

---

The idea of Divine Kingship has been historically one of Judaism's greatest contributions to Western civilization, though its implications were not fully understood until the sixteenth and seventeenth centuries when, under the influence of the Christian Hebraists, the foundations of modern freedom were laid in Europe and America.

The idea of God as the Supreme King entails that no human ruler or government has absolute authority. Every nation is "under God," meaning that God's command establishes the moral limits of power. Lacking this idea, the first and greatest democracy in ancient times, the Athens of Solon, descended into tyranny.

> The philosophy that was then in the ascendant taught them [the Athenians] that there is no law superior to that of the State – the lawgiver is above the law.
>
> It followed that the sovereign people had a right to do whatever was within its power, and was bound by no rule of right or wrong but its own

*On Shabbat, add the words in parentheses:*

Our Father, our King, reveal the glory of Your kingdom to us swiftly.
Appear and be exalted over us in the sight of all that lives.
Bring back our scattered ones from among the nations,
and gather our dispersed people from the ends of the earth.
Lead us to Zion, Your city, in jubilation,
and to Jerusalem, home of Your Temple, with everlasting joy.
There we will prepare for You our obligatory offerings:
the regular daily offerings in their order
and the additional offerings according to their law.
And the additional offerings (of this Sabbath day and) of this
Day of Remembrance we will prepare and offer before You in love,
in accord with Your will's commandment,
as You wrote for us in Your Torah
through Your servant Moses, by Your own word, as it is said:

*On Shabbat:* **וּבְיוֹם הַשַּׁבָּת** "On the Sabbath day, make an offering of two lambs a year old, without blemish, together with two-tenths of an ephah of fine flour mixed with oil as a meal-offering, and its appropriate libation. This is the burnt-offering for every Sabbath, in addition to the regular daily burnt-offering and its libation." *Num. 28*

**וּבַחֹדֶשׁ הַשְּׁבִיעִי** On the first day of the seventh month you shall hold a sacred assembly. You shall do no laborious work, and you shall mark a Day of the Blowing of the Shofar. You shall make a burnt-offering of pleasing aroma to the LORD: a young bullock, a ram, and seven yearling male lambs; they shall be without blemish. *Num. 29*

**וּמִנְחָתָם וְנִסְכֵּיהֶם** And their meal offerings and wine-libations as ordained: three-tenths of an ephah for the bull, two-tenths of an ephah for the ram, one-tenth of an ephah for each of the seven lambs, wine for the libations, two male goats for atonement, and two regular daily offerings according to their law.

**מִלְּבַד** All this aside from the burnt-offering of the New Moon and its meal-offering, and the regular daily burnt-offering with its meal-offering, and their libations according to their ordinance, a burnt-offering of pleasing odor to the LORD. *Num. 29*

*On* שבת*, add the words in parentheses:*

אָבִינוּ מַלְכֵּנוּ, גַּלֵּה כְּבוֹד מַלְכוּתְךָ עָלֵינוּ מְהֵרָה
וְהוֹפַע וְהִנָּשֵׂא עָלֵינוּ לְעֵינֵי כָּל חָי
וְקָרֵב פְּזוּרֵינוּ מִבֵּין הַגּוֹיִם, וּנְפוּצוֹתֵינוּ כַּנֵּס מִיַּרְכְּתֵי אָרֶץ.
וַהֲבִיאֵנוּ לְצִיּוֹן עִירְךָ בְּרִנָּה
וְלִירוּשָׁלַיִם בֵּית מִקְדָּשְׁךָ בְּשִׂמְחַת עוֹלָם
וְשָׁם נַעֲשֶׂה לְפָנֶיךָ אֶת קָרְבְּנוֹת חוֹבוֹתֵינוּ
תְּמִידִים כְּסִדְרָם וּמוּסָפִים כְּהִלְכָתָם
וְאֶת מוּסְפֵי יוֹם (הַשַּׁבָּת הַזֶּה וְיוֹם) הַזִּכָּרוֹן הַזֶּה
נַעֲשֶׂה וְנַקְרִיב לְפָנֶיךָ בְּאַהֲבָה כְּמִצְוַת רְצוֹנֶךָ
כְּמוֹ שֶׁכָּתַבְתָּ עָלֵינוּ בְּתוֹרָתֶךָ
עַל יְדֵי מֹשֶׁה עַבְדֶּךָ מִפִּי כְבוֹדֶךָ, כָּאָמוּר

בשבת: וּבְיוֹם הַשַּׁבָּת, שְׁנֵי־כְבָשִׂים בְּנֵי־שָׁנָה תְּמִימִם, וּשְׁנֵי עֶשְׂרֹנִים סֹלֶת מִנְחָה בְּלוּלָה בַשֶּׁמֶן וְנִסְכּוֹ: עֹלַת שַׁבַּת בְּשַׁבַּתּוֹ, עַל־עֹלַת הַתָּמִיד וְנִסְכָּהּ: במדבר כח

וּבַחֹדֶשׁ הַשְּׁבִיעִי בְּאֶחָד לַחֹדֶשׁ מִקְרָא־קֹדֶשׁ יִהְיֶה לָכֶם, כָּל־מְלֶאכֶת עֲבֹדָה לֹא תַעֲשׂוּ, יוֹם תְּרוּעָה יִהְיֶה לָכֶם: וַעֲשִׂיתֶם עֹלָה לְרֵיחַ נִיחֹחַ לַיהוה, פַּר בֶּן־בָּקָר אֶחָד, אַיִל אֶחָד, כְּבָשִׂים בְּנֵי־שָׁנָה שִׁבְעָה תְּמִימִם: במדבר כט

וּמִנְחָתָם וְנִסְכֵּיהֶם כִּמְדֻבָּר, שְׁלֹשָׁה עֶשְׂרֹנִים לַפָּר וּשְׁנֵי עֶשְׂרֹנִים לָאָיִל, וְעִשָּׂרוֹן לַכֶּבֶשׂ, וְיַיִן כְּנִסְכּוֹ, וּשְׁנֵי שְׂעִירִים לְכַפֵּר, וּשְׁנֵי תְמִידִים כְּהִלְכָתָם.

מִלְּבַד עֹלַת הַחֹדֶשׁ וּמִנְחָתָהּ, וְעֹלַת הַתָּמִיד וּמִנְחָתָהּ, וְנִסְכֵּיהֶם כְּמִשְׁפָּטָם, לְרֵיחַ נִיחֹחַ, אִשֶּׁה לַיהוה: במדבר כט

*On Shabbat:* יִשְׂמְחוּ Those who keep the Sabbath and call it a delight shall rejoice in Your kingship. The people who sanctify the seventh day shall all be satisfied and take delight in Your goodness, for You favored the seventh day and declared it holy. You called it "most desirable of days" in remembrance of Creation.

*The Ark is opened.*

עָלֵינוּ It is our duty to praise the Master of all,
and ascribe greatness to the Author of creation,
who has not made us like the nations of the lands,
nor placed us like the families of the earth;

*The Ark is closed.*

who has not made our portion like theirs,
nor our destiny like all their multitudes.
(For they worship vanity and emptiness,
and pray to a god who cannot save.)

*The Ark is opened and the congregation (in some congregations, only the Leader) kneels on the floor at "bow."*

▾But we bow in worship
and thank the Supreme King of kings, the Holy One, blessed be He,
who extends the heavens and establishes the earth,
whose throne of glory is in the heavens above,
and whose power's Presence is in the highest of heights.

---

Middle Ages, a Jew who had converted to Christianity cited this verse to make the false claim that Jews were criticizing or even ridiculing Christianity. In vain it was pointed out that the offending verse was taken from two verses in the book of Isaiah (30:7; 45:20). Isaiah lived at least seven centuries before the birth of Christianity and therefore could not have possibly had it in mind. Because of the fear of further animosity and persecution, many communities removed it from the prayer book, though some continue to say it.

וַאֲנַחְנוּ כּוֹרְעִים וּמִשְׁתַּחֲוִים *But we bow in worship.*
What distinguishes the Days of Awe from all other festivals is that here and only here does the Jew kneel. He does what he refused to do before the King of Persia, and no power on earth can compel him to do, and what he need not

בשבת: יִשְׂמְחוּ בְמַלְכוּתְךָ שׁוֹמְרֵי שַׁבָּת וְקוֹרְאֵי עֹנֶג. עַם מְקַדְּשֵׁי שְׁבִיעִי
כֻּלָּם יִשְׂבְּעוּ וְיִתְעַנְּגוּ מִטּוּבֶךָ, וּבַשְּׁבִיעִי רָצִיתָ בּוֹ וְקִדַּשְׁתּוֹ, חֶמְדַּת
יָמִים אוֹתוֹ קָרָאתָ, זֵכֶר לְמַעֲשֵׂה בְרֵאשִׁית.

*The* ארון קודש *is opened.*

עָלֵינוּ לְשַׁבֵּחַ לַאֲדוֹן הַכֹּל, לָתֵת גְּדֻלָּה לְיוֹצֵר בְּרֵאשִׁית
שֶׁלֹּא עָשָׂנוּ כְּגוֹיֵי הָאֲרָצוֹת, וְלֹא שָׂמָנוּ כְּמִשְׁפְּחוֹת הָאֲדָמָה

*The* ארון קודש *is closed.*

שֶׁלֹּא שָׂם חֶלְקֵנוּ כָּהֶם וְגוֹרָלֵנוּ כְּכָל הֲמוֹנָם.
(שֶׁהֵם מִשְׁתַּחֲוִים לְהֶבֶל וָרִיק וּמִתְפַּלְלִים אֶל אֵל לֹא יוֹשִׁיעַ.)

*The* ארון קודש *is opened and the* קהל *(in some congregations, only the* שליח ציבור*) kneels on the floor at* כּוֹרְעִים.

וַאֲנַחְנוּ כּוֹרְעִים וּמִשְׁתַּחֲוִים וּמוֹדִים
לִפְנֵי מֶלֶךְ מַלְכֵי הַמְּלָכִים, הַקָּדוֹשׁ בָּרוּךְ הוּא
שֶׁהוּא נוֹטֶה שָׁמַיִם וְיוֹסֵד אָרֶץ
וּמוֹשַׁב יְקָרוֹ בַּשָּׁמַיִם מִמַּעַל
וּשְׁכִינַת עֻזּוֹ בְּגָבְהֵי מְרוֹמִים.

---

ALEINU

*Aleinu* (which from the thirteenth century onwards was adopted as part of the daily prayers – it concludes each service) was originally written specifically for Rosh HaShana to serve as a prelude to the verses of *Malkhiyot* section about the kingship of God. It was edited by Rav, the great third-century rabbi who laid the foundations of Sura, one of the Babylonian academies from which emerged the Babylonian Talmud. Rav was one of the great architects of the Rosh HaShana prayers, he who ruled that instead of ending the third paragraph of the Amida with the phrase "the holy God," we should say "the holy King." The prayer in its earliest forms is very ancient.

One line from the original prayer – "For they worship vanity and emptiness and pray to a god who cannot save" – aroused controversy. During the

*In some congregations, the Leader says "You have been shown" while the congregation says "He is our God" below.*

He is our God; there is no other.
Truly He is our King; there is none else, as it is written in His Torah:
"You shall know and take to heart this day that the LORD is God, *Deut. 4*
in the heavens above and on the earth below.
There is no other."

---

*The Leader says the following while the congregation says "He is our God" above.*

אַתָּה הׇרְאֵתָ You have been shown, that you may know, that the LORD is our God: there is no other besides Him. You shall know and take to heart this day that the LORD is God, in the heavens above and on the earth below. There is no other. Listen, Israel: the LORD is our God, the LORD is One. For heaven, the highest heaven, the earth and all that it contains, belong to the LORD your God. For the LORD your God is the God of gods, the LORD of lords, the great, mighty and awesome God, God, who does not discriminate or accept any bribe. When I proclaim the LORD's name, give glory to our God. Blessed be the name of the LORD, now and for evermore.

*Deut. 4* *Deut. 6* *Deut. 10* *Ibid.* *Deut. 32* *Ps. 113*

---

*The Ark is closed.*

*A prefatory piyut before the verses of Malkhiyot, Zikhronot and Shofarot, the core of the day's service, in which the congregation asks that the prayers of the Leader will be accepted.*

אֱלֹהֵינוּ Our God and the God of our forefathers:
May You stand by the mouths of the emissaries of Your nation,
the house of Israel,
who stand before You to entreat You with prayer and supplication
on behalf of Your nation, the house of Israel.

---

On these Days of Awe the plea for bringing about such a future is already part of the Central Prayer, which – in solemn words – calls for the day when all creatures will prostrate themselves "that they may all form a single band to do God's will with a whole heart" [...] And what the congregation merely expresses in words in the course of the year, it here expresses in action: it prostrates itself before the King of Kings. (Franz Rosenzweig, *The Star of Redemption*)

הֱיֵה עִם פִּיפִיּוֹת *May You stand by the mouths.* This and the subsequent prayer, "I shall await the LORD" are *reshut* prayers, requesting permission to approach

*In some congregations, the* שליח ציבור *says* אַתָּה הָרְאֵתָ *while the* קהל *says* הוּא אֱלֹהֵינוּ *below.*

**הוּא אֱלֹהֵינוּ, אֵין עוֹד.**
**אֱמֶת מַלְכֵּנוּ, אֶפֶס זוּלָתוֹ, כַּכָּתוּב בְּתוֹרָתוֹ**
דברים ד **וְיָדַעְתָּ הַיּוֹם וַהֲשֵׁבֹתָ אֶל־לְבָבֶךָ**
**כִּי יהוה הוּא הָאֱלֹהִים בַּשָּׁמַיִם מִמַּעַל וְעַל־הָאָרֶץ מִתָּחַת**
**אֵין עוֹד:**

---

*The* שליח ציבור *says the following while the* קהל *says* הוּא אֱלֹהֵינוּ *above.*

דברים ד אַתָּה הָרְאֵתָ לָדַעַת, כִּי יהוה הוּא הָאֱלֹהִים, אֵין עוֹד מִלְּבַדּוֹ: וְיָדַעְתָּ
הַיּוֹם וַהֲשֵׁבֹתָ אֶל־לְבָבֶךָ, כִּי יהוה הוּא הָאֱלֹהִים בַּשָּׁמַיִם מִמַּעַל וְעַל־
דברים ו הָאָרֶץ מִתָּחַת, אֵין עוֹד: שְׁמַע יִשְׂרָאֵל, יהוה אֱלֹהֵינוּ, יהוה אֶחָד:
שם הֵן לַיהוה אֱלֹהֶיךָ הַשָּׁמַיִם וּשְׁמֵי הַשָּׁמָיִם, הָאָרֶץ וְכָל־אֲשֶׁר־בָּהּ: כִּי
דברים י יהוה אֱלֹהֵיכֶם הוּא אֱלֹהֵי הָאֱלֹהִים וַאֲדֹנֵי הָאֲדֹנִים, הָאֵל הַגָּדֹל
דברים לב הַגִּבֹּר וְהַנּוֹרָא אֲשֶׁר לֹא־יִשָּׂא פָנִים וְלֹא יִקַּח שֹׁחַד: כִּי שֵׁם יהוה
תהלים קיג אֶקְרָא, הָבוּ גֹדֶל לֵאלֹהֵינוּ: יְהִי שֵׁם יהוה מְבֹרָךְ, מֵעַתָּה וְעַד־עוֹלָם:

---

*The* ארון קודש *is closed.*

*A prefatory piyut before the verses of* מלכיות, זכרונות *and* שופרות, *the core of the day's service in which the* קהל *asks that the prayers of the* שליח ציבור *will be accepted.*

**אֱלֹהֵינוּ וֵאלֹהֵי אֲבוֹתֵינוּ**
**הֱיֵה עִם פִּיפִיּוֹת שְׁלוּחֵי עַמְּךָ בֵּית יִשְׂרָאֵל**
**הָעוֹמְדִים לְבַקֵּשׁ תְּפִלָּה וְתַחֲנוּנִים מִלְּפָנֶיךָ עַל עַמְּךָ בֵּית יִשְׂרָאֵל.**

---

do before God on any other day of the year, or in any other situation he may face during his lifetime. And he does not kneel to confess a fault or to pray for forgiveness of sins… He kneels only in beholding the immediate nearness of God, hence on an occasion which transcends the earthly needs of today…

The congregation participates directly in the feeling of God's nearness when it says the prayer that is bound up with the promise of a future time, "when every knee shall bow before God…" On the Days of Awe, this prayer mounts beyond the version of the Concluding Prayer of the everyday service.

Instruct them in what to say,
lend them understanding that they may know what to speak.
Let them know what they might ask You,
make known to them how they might glorify You.

May they walk in the light of Your countenance, *Ps. 89*
may they bend their knees before You.
May they bless Your nation with their speech,
and may they all receive blessing through Your uttered blessings.

May they pass Your nation before You,
while they stand in the midst of the congregation.
The eyes of Your nation hang on their word,
and their eyes await You in turn.

They approach the Holy Ark in fear,
trying to abate Your anger and wrath.
Your nation surrounds them as a wall,
and You on high, shall gaze upon them compassionately.

They raise their eyes heavenward to You,
and pour out their hearts like water before You.
And You shall hear them from the heavens. *II Chr. 6*

*In many congregations the following (until "O Lord of Israel") is said quietly by all.*

Please, do not allow their tongues to falter,
may their words not ensnare them.
And may they not be ashamed of their congregation, their support,
and may their congregation not be ashamed of them.
And may their mouths utter no words that negate Your will.
For those You show favor, Lord our God, are graced,
and it is those whom You teach who are learned.

---

Is Ḥanina greater than you are? He replied to her: No, but he is like a servant before the king, and I am like a nobleman before a king." (*Berakhot* 34b)

A servant, explains Rashi, needs no formal permission to enter the presence of a king, but a prince does. When we pray individually and silently we are like servants in God's presence. When the Leader prays aloud on behalf of the whole congregation, he is like a prince.

הוֹרֵם מַה שֶּׁיֹּאמְרוּ / הֲבִינֵם מַה שֶּׁיְּדַבֵּרוּ
הֲשִׁיבֵם מַה שֶּׁיִּשְׁאֲלוּ / יַדְּעֵם הֵיךְ יְפָאֵרוּ.

בְּאוֹר פָּנֶיךָ יְהַלֵּכוּן / בֶּרֶךְ לְךָ יִבְרְכוּן תהלים פט
עַמְּךָ בְּפִיהֶם יְבָרְכוּן / וּמִבִּרְכוֹת פִּיךָ כֻּלָּם יִתְבָּרְכוּן.

עַמְּךָ לְפָנֶיךָ יַעֲבִירוּן / וְהֵם בַּתָּוֶךְ יַעֲבֹרוּן
עֵינֵי עַמְּךָ בָּם תְּלוּיוֹת / וְעֵינֵיהֶם לְךָ מְיַחֲלוֹת.

גָּשִׁים מוּל אֲרוֹן הַקֹּדֶשׁ בְּאֵימָה / לְשַׁכֵּךְ כַּעַס וְחֵימָה
וְעַמְּךָ מַסְבִּיבִים אוֹתָם כַּחוֹמָה /
וְאַתָּה מִן הַשָּׁמַיִם תַּשְׁגִּיחַ, אוֹתָם לְרַחֲמָה.

עַיִן נוֹשְׂאִים לְךָ לַשָּׁמַיִם / לֵב שׁוֹפְכִים נִכְחֲךָ כַּמַּיִם
וְאַתָּה תִּשְׁמַע מִן הַשָּׁמַיִם. דברי הימים ב, ו

*In many congregations the following (until* אֱלֹהֵי יִשְׂרָאֵל*) is said quietly by all.*

שֶׁלֹּא יִכָּשְׁלוּ בִלְשׁוֹנָם / וְלֹא יִנָּקְשׁוּ בְשִׁנּוּנָם
וְלֹא יֵבֹשׁוּ בְּמַשְׁעֵנָם / וְלֹא יִכָּלְמוּ בָם שְׁאוֹנָם
וְאַל יֹאמַר פִּיהֶם דָּבָר שֶׁלֹּא כִרְצוֹנֶךָ.
כִּי חֲנוּנֶיךָ יהוה אֱלֹהֵינוּ הֵמָּה חֲנוּנִים /
וּמְלֻמָּדֶיךָ הֵמָּה מְלֻמָּדִים.

---

God in prayer, said by the Leader during the Repetition, though not by individuals in the silent Amida (*Tur, Oraḥ Ḥayyim* 591). The difference is explained by a passage in the Talmud.

Once it happened that Rabbi Ḥanina ben Dosa went to study Torah with Rabban Yoḥanan ben Zakkai. The son of Rabban Yoḥanan ben Zakkai fell ill. He said to him: Ḥanina my son, pray for him that he may live. He put his head between his knees and prayed for him and he lived. Said Rabban Yoḥanan ben Zakkai: If Ben Zakkai had put his head between his knees for the whole day, no notice would have been taken of him. Said his wife to him:

כְּמָה שֶׁיָּדַעְנוּ Just as we have known, O Lord,
that You show grace to those You favor and compassion
to those You deem deserving of compassion.
As it is written in Your Torah,
"And He said, I shall cause all My good to pass before you *Ex. 33*
and I shall call out the Tetragrammaton before you,
and I will show grace to those I favor
and compassion to those I deem deserving of compassion."
And it is written,
"May those who await You not be ashamed of me, *Ps. 69*
O God, Lord of hosts,
may those who seek You out not be humiliated through me,
O Lord of Israel."

*The Ark is opened.*

*A second prefatory piyut, said by the Leader:*

אוֹחִילָה I shall await the Lord, I shall entreat His favor,
I shall ask Him to grant my tongue eloquence.

In the midst of the congregated nation I shall sing of His strength;
I shall burst out in joyous melodies for His works.

The thoughts in man's heart are his to arrange, *Prov. 16*
but the tongue's eloquence comes from the Lord.

O Lord, open my lips, *Ps. 51*
so that my mouth may declare Your praise.

*In some congregations, the following verse is said quietly:*

May the words of my mouth and the meditation of my heart *Ps. 19*
find favor before You, Lord, my Rock and Redeemer.

*The Ark is closed.*

*Some congregations say a prefatory piyut before the Malkhiyot verses.*
*On weekdays, "Ansikha Malki" on page 1032; on Shabbat, "Ahalela" on page 1068.*

כְּמָה שֶׁיְּדַעְנוּ יהוה אֱלֹהֵינוּ
אֶת אֲשֶׁר תָּחֹן יוּחָן, וְאֶת אֲשֶׁר תְּרַחֵם יְרֻחָם.
כַּכָּתוּב בְּתוֹרָתֶךָ:

שמות לג
וַיֹּאמֶר, אֲנִי אַעֲבִיר כָּל־טוּבִי עַל־פָּנֶיךָ
וְקָרָאתִי בְשֵׁם יהוה לְפָנֶיךָ
וְחַנֹּתִי אֶת־אֲשֶׁר אָחֹן וְרִחַמְתִּי אֶת־אֲשֶׁר אֲרַחֵם:

וְנֶאֱמַר:

תהלים סט
אַל־יֵבֹשׁוּ בִי קֹוֶיךָ, אֲדֹנָי יֱהֹוִה צְבָאוֹת
אַל־יִכָּלְמוּ בִי מְבַקְשֶׁיךָ, אֱלֹהֵי יִשְׂרָאֵל:

*The ארון קודש is opened.*

*A second prefatory piyut, said by the שליח ציבור:*

אוֹחִילָה לָאֵל, אֲחַלֶּה פָנָיו
אֶשְׁאֲלָה מִמֶּנּוּ מַעֲנֵה לָשׁוֹן.

אֲשֶׁר בִּקְהַל עָם אָשִׁירָה עֻזּוֹ
אַבִּיעָה רְנָנוֹת בְּעַד מִפְעָלָיו.

משלי טז
לְאָדָם מַעַרְכֵי־לֵב וּמֵיהוה מַעֲנֵה לָשׁוֹן:

תהלים נא
אֲדֹנָי, שְׂפָתַי תִּפְתָּח, וּפִי יַגִּיד תְּהִלָּתֶךָ:

*In some congregations, the following verse is said quietly:*

תהלים יט
יִהְיוּ לְרָצוֹן אִמְרֵי־פִי וְהֶגְיוֹן לִבִּי לְפָנֶיךָ, יהוה צוּרִי וְגֹאֲלִי:

*The ארון קודש is closed.*

*Some congregations say a prefatory piyut before the מלכיות verses.*
*On weekdays, אַנְסִיכָה מַלְכִּי on page 1032; on שבת, אֲהַלְלָה on page 1068.*

וְעַל כֵּן Therefore, we place our hope in You, LORD our God,
that we may soon see the glory of Your power,
when You will remove abominations from the earth,
and idols will be utterly destroyed,
when the world will be perfected
under the sovereignty of the Almighty,
when all humanity will call on Your name,
to turn all the earth's wicked toward You.
All the world's inhabitants will realize and know
that to You every knee must bow and every tongue swear loyalty.
Before You, LORD our God, they will kneel and bow down
and give honor to Your glorious name.
They will all accept the yoke of Your kingdom,
and You will reign over them soon and for ever.

VERSES OF MALKHIYOT

For the kingdom is Yours,
and to all eternity You will reign in glory,
as it is written in Your Torah:
"The LORD will reign for ever and ever." *Ex. 15*

And it is said:
He saw no injustice in Jacob, *Num. 23*
no deceit did He witness in Israel,
the LORD their God is with them,
and a King's adulation resounds among them.

And it is said:
[The LORD] became King in Yeshurun, *Deut. 33*
when the heads of the people gathered,
all the tribes of Israel together.

And in Your holy Writings it is said,
For kingship is the LORD's *Ps. 22*
and He rules over the nations.

וְעַל כֵּן נְקַוֶּה לְּךָ יהוה אֱלֹהֵינוּ
לִרְאוֹת מְהֵרָה בְּתִפְאֶרֶת עֻזֶּךָ
לְהַעֲבִיר גִּלּוּלִים מִן הָאָרֶץ, וְהָאֱלִילִים כָּרוֹת יִכָּרֵתוּן
לְתַקֵּן עוֹלָם בְּמַלְכוּת שַׁדַּי.
וְכָל בְּנֵי בָשָׂר יִקְרְאוּ בִשְׁמֶךָ לְהַפְנוֹת אֵלֶיךָ כָּל רִשְׁעֵי אָרֶץ.
יַכִּירוּ וְיֵדְעוּ כָּל יוֹשְׁבֵי תֵבֵל
כִּי לְךָ תִּכְרַע כָּל בֶּרֶךְ, תִּשָּׁבַע כָּל לָשׁוֹן.
לְפָנֶיךָ יהוה אֱלֹהֵינוּ יִכְרְעוּ וְיִפֹּלוּ
וְלִכְבוֹד שִׁמְךָ יְקָר יִתֵּנוּ
וִיקַבְּלוּ כֻלָּם אֶת עֹל מַלְכוּתֶךָ
וְתִמְלֹךְ עֲלֵיהֶם מְהֵרָה לְעוֹלָם וָעֶד.

פסוקי מלכיות

כִּי הַמַּלְכוּת שֶׁלְּךָ הִיא וּלְעוֹלְמֵי עַד תִּמְלֹךְ בְּכָבוֹד
כַּכָּתוּב בְּתוֹרָתֶךָ
יהוה יִמְלֹךְ לְעֹלָם וָעֶד: שמות טו
וְנֶאֱמַר
לֹא־הִבִּיט אָוֶן בְּיַעֲקֹב, וְלֹא־רָאָה עָמָל בְּיִשְׂרָאֵל במדבר כג
יהוה אֱלֹהָיו עִמּוֹ, וּתְרוּעַת מֶלֶךְ בּוֹ:

וְנֶאֱמַר
וַיְהִי בִישֻׁרוּן מֶלֶךְ, בְּהִתְאַסֵּף רָאשֵׁי עָם דברים לג
יַחַד שִׁבְטֵי יִשְׂרָאֵל:

וּבְדִבְרֵי קָדְשְׁךָ כָּתוּב לֵאמֹר
כִּי לַיהוה הַמְּלוּכָה וּמֹשֵׁל בַּגּוֹיִם: תהלים כב

And it is said:

The LORD reigns. He is robed in majesty. *Ps. 93*
The LORD is robed, girded with strength.
The world is firmly established; it cannot be moved.

And it is said:

Lift up your heads, O gates; *Ps. 24*
be uplifted, eternal doors,
so that the King of glory may enter.
Who is the King of glory?
It is the LORD, strong and mighty,
the LORD mighty in battle.
Lift up your heads, O gates;
lift them up, eternal doors,
so that the King of glory may enter.
Who is He, the King of glory?
The LORD of hosts, He is the King of glory, Selah!

And by Your servants the prophets it is written:

This is what the LORD, King of Israel and its Savior, *Is. 44*
the LORD of hosts has said:
"I am the first and I shall be the last,
and there is no other god but Me."

And it is said:

Saviors shall go up to Mount Zion *Ob. 1*
to judge Mount Esau,
and the LORD's shall be the kingdom.

And it is said:

Then shall the LORD be King over all the earth. *Zech. 14*
On that day shall the LORD be One
and His name One.

And in Your Torah it is written:

Listen, Israel: the LORD is our God, *Deut. 6*
the LORD is One.

וְנֶאֱמַר

יהוה מָלָךְ, גֵּאוּת לָבֵשׁ תהלים צג
לָבֵשׁ יהוה עֹז הִתְאַזָּר, אַף־תִּכּוֹן תֵּבֵל בַּל־תִּמּוֹט:

וְנֶאֱמַר

שְׂאוּ שְׁעָרִים רָאשֵׁיכֶם, וְהִנָּשְׂאוּ פִּתְחֵי עוֹלָם תהלים כד
וְיָבוֹא מֶלֶךְ הַכָּבוֹד:
מִי זֶה מֶלֶךְ הַכָּבוֹד, יהוה עִזּוּז וְגִבּוֹר
יהוה גִּבּוֹר מִלְחָמָה:
שְׂאוּ שְׁעָרִים רָאשֵׁיכֶם, וּשְׂאוּ פִּתְחֵי עוֹלָם
וְיָבֹא מֶלֶךְ הַכָּבוֹד:
מִי הוּא זֶה מֶלֶךְ הַכָּבוֹד
יהוה צְבָאוֹת הוּא מֶלֶךְ הַכָּבוֹד סֶלָה:

וְעַל יְדֵי עֲבָדֶיךָ הַנְּבִיאִים כָּתוּב לֵאמֹר

כֹּה־אָמַר יהוה מֶלֶךְ־יִשְׂרָאֵל וְגֹאֲלוֹ, יהוה צְבָאוֹת ישעיה מד
אֲנִי רִאשׁוֹן וַאֲנִי אַחֲרוֹן, וּמִבַּלְעָדַי אֵין אֱלֹהִים:

וְנֶאֱמַר

וְעָלוּ מוֹשִׁעִים בְּהַר צִיּוֹן לִשְׁפֹּט אֶת־הַר עֵשָׂו עובדיה א
וְהָיְתָה לַיהוה הַמְּלוּכָה:

וְנֶאֱמַר

וְהָיָה יהוה לְמֶלֶךְ עַל־כָּל־הָאָרֶץ זכריה יד
בַּיּוֹם הַהוּא יִהְיֶה יהוה אֶחָד וּשְׁמוֹ אֶחָד:

וּבְתוֹרָתְךָ כָּתוּב לֵאמֹר

שְׁמַע יִשְׂרָאֵל, יהוה אֱלֹהֵינוּ יהוה אֶחָד: דברים ו

*On Shabbat, add the words in parentheses:*

אֱלֹהֵינוּ Our God and God of our ancestors,
rule over all the world in Your honor,
and be raised above all the earth in Your glory,
and appear, in the splendor of Your great might
before all those who live in this world, Your domain.
And all who were made will know that You made them,
and all who were formed will know that You formed them,
and all that have breath in their mouths will declare:
The LORD, God of Israel is King,
and His kingship has dominion over all.
(Our God and God of our ancestors, find favor, please, in our rest.)
Make us holy through Your commandments
and grant us our share in Your Torah.
Satisfy us with Your goodness, grant our souls joy in Your salvation
(in love and favor, LORD our God, grant us as our heritage Your holy Sabbath,
so that all Israel, who sanctify Your name may find rest on it),
and purify our hearts to serve You in truth.
For You, LORD, are truth, and Your word is truth
and holds true forever.
Blessed are You, LORD, King over all the earth,
who sanctifies (the Sabbath,) Israel and the Day of Remembrance.

*The congregation stands and the shofar is sounded (except on Shabbat).*

| | | |
|---|---|---|
| TEKIA | SHEVARIM TERUA | TEKIA |
| TEKIA | SHEVARIM | TEKIA |
| TEKIA | TERUA | TEKIA |

---

notes – *shevarim-terua, shevarim* and *terua* – represent the doubt (or some say, the variant customs) as to the nature of a *terua*, which according to everyone is a form of weeping, but which may be three sighs, nine sobs, or a combination of both. The *tekia* before and after is a clarion.

Rabbi Moshe Avigdor Amiel said that the sound of the shofar is a parable of life. It begins and ends with a *tekia*, the straightforwardness and simplicity of childhood and old age. Between them, though, life is a *terua*: complicated, convoluted, and fraught with tears.

*On* שבת*, add the words in parentheses:*

אֱלֹהֵינוּ וֵאלֹהֵי אֲבוֹתֵינוּ
מְלֹךְ עַל כָּל הָעוֹלָם כֻּלּוֹ בִּכְבוֹדֶךָ
וְהִנָּשֵׂא עַל כָּל הָאָרֶץ בִּיקָרֶךָ
וְהוֹפַע בַּהֲדַר גְּאוֹן עֻזֶּךָ עַל כָּל יוֹשְׁבֵי תֵבֵל אַרְצֶךָ.
וְיֵדַע כָּל פָּעוּל כִּי אַתָּה פְעַלְתּוֹ
וְיָבִין כָּל יָצוּר כִּי אַתָּה יְצַרְתּוֹ
וְיֹאמַר כֹּל אֲשֶׁר נְשָׁמָה בְאַפּוֹ
יהוה אֱלֹהֵי יִשְׂרָאֵל מֶלֶךְ וּמַלְכוּתוֹ בַּכֹּל מָשָׁלָה.
(אֱלֹהֵינוּ וֵאלֹהֵי אֲבוֹתֵינוּ, רְצֵה נָא בִמְנוּחָתֵנוּ)
קַדְּשֵׁנוּ בְּמִצְוֹתֶיךָ וְתֵן חֶלְקֵנוּ בְּתוֹרָתֶךָ
שַׂבְּעֵנוּ מִטּוּבֶךָ, וְשַׂמַּח נַפְשֵׁנוּ בִּישׁוּעָתֶךָ
(וְהַנְחִילֵנוּ יהוה אֱלֹהֵינוּ בְּאַהֲבָה וּבְרָצוֹן שַׁבַּת קָדְשֶׁךָ
וְיָנוּחוּ בוֹ כָּל יִשְׂרָאֵל מְקַדְּשֵׁי שְׁמֶךָ)
וְטַהֵר לִבֵּנוּ לְעָבְדְּךָ בֶּאֱמֶת
כִּי אַתָּה אֱלֹהִים אֱמֶת, וּדְבָרְךָ אֱמֶת וְקַיָּם לָעַד.
בָּרוּךְ אַתָּה יהוה, מֶלֶךְ עַל כָּל הָאָרֶץ
מְקַדֵּשׁ (הַשַּׁבָּת וְ) יִשְׂרָאֵל וְיוֹם הַזִּכָּרוֹן.

*The* קהל *stands and the* שופר *is sounded (except on* שבת*).*

| תקיעה | שברים תרועה | תקיעה |
|---|---|---|
| תקיעה | שברים | תקיעה |
| תקיעה | תרועה | תקיעה |

---

SHOFAR

The shofar blowing at this point – here and during the next two blessings – is the primary fulfillment of the command. The three variants of the middle

*The congregation, then the Leader (even on Shabbat):*

הַיּוֹם This day is the birth of the world.
This day stands all the world's creations up in judgment,
stands them as sons or as slaves –
If as sons, have compassion for us,
as a father has compassion for his sons.
And if as slaves, our eyes are raised and fixed on You
until You show us favor, and bring out our judgment like sunlight,
Awesome, Holy.

*On Shabbat omit:*

אֲרֶשֶׁת May our mouths' words rise beautiful before You,
most high and elevated God, who understands and heeds,
looks on and listens to the sounds of our shofar blasts.
Accept, with compassion and favor, our Order of the Kingship.

*Some congregations say a prefatory piyut before the Zikhronot. On weekdays, "Zekher Teḥillat kol Ma'as" on page 1034. On Shabbat, "Efḥad Bema'asei" on page 1070.*

REMEMBRANCES

אַתָּה זוֹכֵר You remember the making of the world;
You come to all those formed long ago.
Under Your gaze, all hidden things come to light,
all the many secrets buried since the Beginning.
For nothing is forgotten before the throne of Your glory,
and nothing is hidden from Your eyes.

You remember all of creation,
and all things that were formed – none is shrouded from You.
All is revealed and known before You, LORD our God,
who gazes and looks on to the last of all the ages.
For You bring a day decreed for remembrance
to come to each spirit and soul;
that Your many works shall be remembered,
Your numerous, endless creations.

---

the cities of the plain. "God remembered Rachel" and gave her a child. God remembers for the future. (Lord Jakobovits)

*The* קהל*, then the* שליח ציבור *(even on* שבת*):*

**הַיּוֹם הֲרַת עוֹלָם, הַיּוֹם יַעֲמִיד בַּמִּשְׁפָּט כָּל יְצוּרֵי עוֹלָמִים**
**אִם כְּבָנִים אִם כַּעֲבָדִים.**
**אִם כְּבָנִים, רַחֲמֵנוּ כְּרַחֵם אָב עַל בָּנִים**
**וְאִם כַּעֲבָדִים, עֵינֵינוּ לְךָ תְלוּיוֹת עַד שֶׁתְּחָנֵּנוּ**
**וְתוֹצִיא כָאוֹר מִשְׁפָּטֵנוּ, אָיֹם קָדוֹשׁ.**

*On* שבת *omit:*

**אֲרֶשֶׁת שְׂפָתֵינוּ יֶעֱרַב לְפָנֶיךָ**
**אֵל רָם וְנִשָּׂא, מֵבִין וּמַאֲזִין, מַבִּיט וּמַקְשִׁיב לְקוֹל תְּקִיעָתֵנוּ.**
**וּתְקַבֵּל בְּרַחֲמִים וּבְרָצוֹן סֵדֶר מַלְכִיּוֹתֵינוּ.**

*Some congregations say a prefatory piyut before the* זכרונות*.*
*On weekdays,* זֵכֶר תְּחִלַּת כָּל מַעַשׂ *on page 1034. On* שבת*,* אֶפְחַד בְּמַעֲשַׂי *on page 1070.*

זכרונות

**אַתָּה זוֹכֵר מַעֲשֵׂה עוֹלָם, וּפוֹקֵד כָּל יְצוּרֵי קֶדֶם**
**לְפָנֶיךָ נִגְלוּ כָּל תַּעֲלוּמוֹת וַהֲמוֹן נִסְתָּרוֹת שֶׁמִּבְּרֵאשִׁית**
**כִּי אֵין שִׁכְחָה לִפְנֵי כִסֵּא כְבוֹדֶךָ וְאֵין נִסְתָּר מִנֶּגֶד עֵינֶיךָ.**

**אַתָּה זוֹכֵר אֶת כָּל הַמִּפְעָל, וְגַם כָּל הַיְצוּר לֹא נִכְחַד מִמֶּךָּ.**
**הַכֹּל גָּלוּי וְיָדוּעַ לְפָנֶיךָ יהוה אֱלֹהֵינוּ**
**צוֹפֶה וּמַבִּיט עַד סוֹף כָּל הַדּוֹרוֹת**
**כִּי תָבִיא חֹק זִכָּרוֹן לְהִפָּקֵד כָּל רְוּחַ וָנָפֶשׁ**
**לְהִזָּכֵר מַעֲשִׂים רַבִּים, וַהֲמוֹן בְּרִיּוֹת לְאֵין תַּכְלִית.**

---

ZIKHRONOT: REMEMBRANCES

Remembering is usually a past-oriented process. But in Genesis we read three times of God remembering. "God remembered Noah" and brought him out on dry land. "God remembered Lot" and saved him from the destruction of

From the very beginning You made it known,
long before this time You revealed it,
for this day is the opening of all Your works,
a remembrance of the very first day.
"For it is a decree for Israel, *Ps. 81*
an ordinance of the God of Jacob."

And on it, it is said of every province
which will come to the sword and which to peace,
which will succumb to hunger and which find plenty.
And all creations are regarded on this day;
remembered for life, or for death.

מִי לֹא נִפְקַד Who may be overlooked on this day,
when the memory of every being formed comes before You;
each person's works, his purpose,
the path that he chooses and follows?
the thoughts and the plans of all mankind,
and the impulses behind each person's acts?
Happy the one who does not forget You,
the child of man who takes courage in You.
For one who seeks You will never stumble,
they need never be ashamed, who seek shelter in You.
For the memory of all that You have made passes before You,
You examine what each one does.

וְגַם And Noah also, You remembered with love,
and You came to him with words of salvation, compassion,
when You brought on the waters of the great flood,
to destroy all creatures of flesh
because the practices they followed were corrupt.
And so let [Noah's] memory come to You, LORD our God,
that You multiply His children like the dust of the earth,
his descendants like sand of the sea.

מֵרֵאשִׁית כָּזֹאת הוֹדַעְתָּ וּמִלְּפָנִים אוֹתָהּ גִּלִּיתָ.
זֶה הַיּוֹם תְּחִלַּת מַעֲשֶׂיךָ, זִכָּרוֹן לְיוֹם רִאשׁוֹן
כִּי חֹק לְיִשְׂרָאֵל הוּא, מִשְׁפָּט לֵאלֹהֵי יַעֲקֹב: תהלים פא

וְעַל הַמְּדִינוֹת בּוֹ יֵאָמֵר
אֵיזוֹ לַחֶרֶב, וְאֵיזוֹ לַשָּׁלוֹם
אֵיזוֹ לָרָעָב, וְאֵיזוֹ לַשֹּׂבַע
וּבְרִיּוֹת בּוֹ יִפָּקֵדוּ, לְהַזְכִּירָם לַחַיִּים וְלַמָּוֶת.

מִי לֹא נִפְקַד כְּהַיּוֹם הַזֶּה
כִּי זֵכֶר כָּל הַיְצוּר לְפָנֶיךָ בָּא
מַעֲשֵׂה אִישׁ וּפְקֻדָּתוֹ, וַעֲלִילוֹת מִצְעֲדֵי גָבֶר
מַחְשְׁבוֹת אָדָם וְתַחְבּוּלוֹתָיו, וְיִצְרֵי מַעַלְלֵי אִישׁ.
אַשְׁרֵי אִישׁ שֶׁלֹּא יִשְׁכָּחֶךָּ, וּבֶן אָדָם יִתְאַמֶּץ בָּךְ
כִּי דוֹרְשֶׁיךָ לְעוֹלָם לֹא יִכָּשֵׁלוּ
וְלֹא יִכָּלְמוּ לָנֶצַח כָּל הַחוֹסִים בָּךְ.
כִּי זֵכֶר כָּל הַמַּעֲשִׂים לְפָנֶיךָ בָּא,
וְאַתָּה דוֹרֵשׁ מַעֲשֵׂה כֻלָּם.

וְגַם אֶת נֹחַ בְּאַהֲבָה זָכַרְתָּ
וַתִּפְקְדֵהוּ בִּדְבַר יְשׁוּעָה וְרַחֲמִים
בַּהֲבִיאֲךָ אֶת מֵי הַמַּבּוּל לְשַׁחֵת כָּל בָּשָׂר מִפְּנֵי רֹעַ מַעַלְלֵיהֶם
עַל כֵּן זִכְרוֹנוֹ בָּא לְפָנֶיךָ, יהוה אֱלֹהֵינוּ
לְהַרְבּוֹת זַרְעוֹ כְּעַפְרוֹת תֵּבֵל, וְצֶאֱצָאָיו כְּחוֹל הַיָּם.

VERSES OF ZIKHRONOT

As it is written in Your Torah:
"God remembered Noah and all the animals *Gen. 8*
and all the cattle that were with him in the ark,
and God made a wind blow across the earth,
and the waters grew calm."

And it is said:
"God heard their groaning, *Ex. 2*
and God remembered His covenant
with Abraham, with Isaac and with Jacob."

And it is said:
"I will remember My covenant with Jacob, *Lev. 26*
and also My covenant with Isaac,
and also My covenant with Abraham I will remember,
and the land I will remember."

And in Your holy Writings it is written thus:
"He has made remembrance for His wonders; *Ps. 111*
gracious and compassionate is the LORD."

And it is said:
"He has given food to those who revere Him, *Ibid.*
He will remember His covenant forever."

And it is said:
"He remembered His covenant for their sake, *Ps. 106*
and relented in His great love."

---

of whose children remained faithful to Judaism. But perhaps we will not reach that level. So God promises that He will bring redemption for the sake of Isaac, remembering how Isaac was willing to be a sacrifice for the sake of his faith. But perhaps we will not reach that level. So God promises to bring redemption for the sake of Abraham, who was simply full of kindness. But even if we do not reach that level, then God will bring redemption for the sake of those who left exile and traveled to live in the land of Israel.

פסוקי זכרונות

כַּכָּתוּב בְּתוֹרָתֶךָ

בראשית ח וַיִּזְכֹּר אֱלֹהִים אֶת־נֹחַ
וְאֵת כׇּל־הַחַיָּה וְאֶת־כׇּל־הַבְּהֵמָה אֲשֶׁר אִתּוֹ בַּתֵּבָה
וַיַּעֲבֵר אֱלֹהִים רוּחַ עַל־הָאָרֶץ, וַיָּשֹׁכּוּ הַמָּיִם:

וְנֶאֱמַר

שמות ב וַיִּשְׁמַע אֱלֹהִים אֶת־נַאֲקָתָם
וַיִּזְכֹּר אֱלֹהִים אֶת־בְּרִיתוֹ
אֶת־אַבְרָהָם אֶת־יִצְחָק וְאֶת־יַעֲקֹב:

וְנֶאֱמַר

ויקרא כו וְזָכַרְתִּי אֶת־בְּרִיתִי יַעֲקוֹב
וְאַף אֶת־בְּרִיתִי יִצְחָק
וְאַף אֶת־בְּרִיתִי אַבְרָהָם אֶזְכֹּר
וְהָאָרֶץ אֶזְכֹּר:

וּבְדִבְרֵי קׇדְשְׁךָ כָּתוּב לֵאמֹר

תהלים קיא זֵכֶר עָשָׂה לְנִפְלְאוֹתָיו, חַנּוּן וְרַחוּם יהוה:

וְנֶאֱמַר

שם טֶרֶף נָתַן לִירֵאָיו, יִזְכֹּר לְעוֹלָם בְּרִיתוֹ:

וְנֶאֱמַר

תהלים קו וַיִּזְכֹּר לָהֶם בְּרִיתוֹ, וַיִּנָּחֵם כְּרֹב חֲסָדָו:

---

וְזָכַרְתִּי אֶת־בְּרִיתִי יַעֲקוֹב *I will remember My covenant with Jacob.* Rabbi Yaakov Moshe Charlap, a disciple of Rabbi Kook, explained the unusual sequence of this verse, which mentions the patriarchs in reverse order. God promises to bring redemption for the sake of Jacob, all twelve

And by Your servants the prophets it is written:
"Go and call out to Jerusalem, This is what the LORD has said. *Jer. 2*
'I remember of you the kindness of your youth,
your love when you were a bride;
how you walked after Me in the desert, through a land not sown.'"
And it is said:
"I will remember the covenant I had with you *Ezek. 16*
in the days of your youth,
and I will establish with you an everlasting covenant."
And it is said:
"'Is Ephraim not a treasured son to Me, My child of delights? *Jer. 31*
As I speak of him, always, I remember him again.
And so it is that I long for him within,
I will tender him compassion,' says the LORD."

אֱלֹהֵינוּ Our God and God of our ancestors,
remember us with a favorable memory,
and recall us with a remembrance of salvation and compassion
from the highest ancient heaven.
Remember for our sake, LORD our God,
the covenant, the loving-kindness,
and the oath that You swore to Abraham our father on Mount Moriah.
And let the image of that binding,
when our father Abraham bound Isaac his son upon the altar,
be present before You;
when he suppressed his compassion, to do Your will wholeheartedly.
So, too, let Your compassion wrest Your anger from us,
and in Your great goodness may Your anger be turned away
from Your people, Your city, Your land and Your inheritance.

---

in a line of the most melting beauty Jeremiah tells the other side of the story. The Israelites were willing to follow God into the desert through an unknown, unsown land, to a destination none of them had seen. Faith is the courage to take a risk and to begin a journey not knowing where it will lead, yet trusting God and following His call. Jews had that courage: it was the legacy of Abraham and Sarah who themselves set out on a journey, having heard the voice of God.

וְעַל יְדֵי עֲבָדֶיךָ הַנְּבִיאִים כָּתוּב לֵאמֹר

הָלֹךְ וְקָרָאתָ בְאׇזְנֵי יְרוּשָׁלַיִם לֵאמֹר ירמיה ב

כֹּה אָמַר יהוה, זָכַרְתִּי לָךְ חֶסֶד נְעוּרַיִךְ, אַהֲבַת כְּלוּלֹתָיִךְ

לֶכְתֵּךְ אַחֲרַי בַּמִּדְבָּר, בְּאֶרֶץ לֹא זְרוּעָה:

וְנֶאֱמַר

וְזָכַרְתִּי אֲנִי אֶת־בְּרִיתִי אוֹתָךְ בִּימֵי נְעוּרָיִךְ יחזקאל טז

וַהֲקִימוֹתִי לָךְ בְּרִית עוֹלָם:

וְנֶאֱמַר

הֲבֵן יַקִּיר לִי אֶפְרַיִם, אִם יֶלֶד שַׁעֲשֻׁעִים ירמיה לא

כִּי־מִדֵּי דַבְּרִי בּוֹ, זָכֹר אֶזְכְּרֶנּוּ עוֹד

עַל־כֵּן הָמוּ מֵעַי לוֹ, רַחֵם אֲרַחֲמֶנּוּ נְאֻם־יהוה:

אֱלֹהֵינוּ וֵאלֹהֵי אֲבוֹתֵינוּ

זָכְרֵנוּ בְּזִכָּרוֹן טוֹב לְפָנֶיךָ

וּפָקְדֵנוּ בִּפְקֻדַּת יְשׁוּעָה וְרַחֲמִים מִשְּׁמֵי שְׁמֵי קֶדֶם

וּזְכׇר לָנוּ יהוה אֱלֹהֵינוּ אֶת הַבְּרִית וְאֶת הַחֶסֶד וְאֶת הַשְּׁבוּעָה

אֲשֶׁר נִשְׁבַּעְתָּ לְאַבְרָהָם אָבִינוּ בְּהַר הַמּוֹרִיָּה

וְתֵרָאֶה לְפָנֶיךָ עֲקֵדָה

שֶׁעָקַד אַבְרָהָם אָבִינוּ אֶת יִצְחָק בְּנוֹ עַל גַּבֵּי הַמִּזְבֵּחַ

וְכָבַשׁ רַחֲמָיו, לַעֲשׂוֹת רְצוֹנְךָ בְּלֵבָב שָׁלֵם.

כֵּן יִכְבְּשׁוּ רַחֲמֶיךָ אֶת כַּעַסְךָ מֵעָלֵינוּ

וּבְטוּבְךָ הַגָּדוֹל יָשׁוּב חֲרוֹן אַפְּךָ

מֵעַמְּךָ וּמֵעִירְךָ וּמֵאַרְצְךָ וּמִנַּחֲלָתֶךָ.

---

זָכַרְתִּי לָךְ חֶסֶד נְעוּרַיִךְ *I remember of you the kindness of your youth.* One of the most moving lines in Tanakh. The Torah portrays the Israelites in the wilderness as querulous, ungrateful, fractious, rebellious, half-hearted and stiff-necked. Yet

Fulfill for us, LORD our God, the promise You made in Your Torah,
at the hand of Moses Your servant and by Your own word,
as it is said:

"And I remembered, for their sake, the covenant of the early ones, *Lev. 26*
whom I brought out of the land of Egypt
before the eyes of all nations,
to be God to them, I am the LORD."

כִּי זוֹכֵר For it has always been You
who remembered all forgotten things,
and there is no forgetfulness
before the throne of Your glory,
and today in Your compassion, You remember
the binding of Isaac, for his descendants' sake.
Blessed are You, LORD, who remembers the covenant.

*The congregation stands and the shofar is sounded (except on Shabbat).*

| | | |
|---|---|---|
| TEKIA | SHEVARIM TERUA | TEKIA |
| TEKIA | SHEVARIM | TEKIA |
| TEKIA | TERUA | TEKIA |

*The congregation, then the Leader (even on Shabbat):*

הַיּוֹם This day is the birth of the world.
This day stands all the world's creations up in judgment,
stands them as sons or as slaves –
If as sons, have compassion for us,
as a father has compassion for his sons.
And if as slaves, our eyes are raised and fixed on You
until You show us favor, and bring out our judgment like sunlight,
Awesome, Holy.

*On Shabbat omit:*

אֲרֶשֶׁת May our mouths' words rise beautiful before You,
most high and elevated God, who understands and heeds,
looks on and listens to the sounds of our shofar blasts.
Accept, with compassion and favor, our Order of the Remembrances.

וְקַיֶּם לָנוּ יהוה אֱלֹהֵינוּ אֶת הַדָּבָר שֶׁהִבְטַחְתָּנוּ בְּתוֹרָתֶךָ
עַל יְדֵי מֹשֶׁה עַבְדֶּךָ, מִפִּי כְבוֹדֶךָ
כָּאָמוּר
וְזָכַרְתִּי לָהֶם בְּרִית רִאשֹׁנִים ויקרא כו
אֲשֶׁר הוֹצֵאתִי־אֹתָם מֵאֶרֶץ מִצְרַיִם לְעֵינֵי הַגּוֹיִם
לִהְיוֹת לָהֶם לֵאלֹהִים, אֲנִי יהוה:

כִּי זוֹכֵר כָּל הַנִּשְׁכָּחוֹת אַתָּה הוּא מֵעוֹלָם
וְאֵין שִׁכְחָה לִפְנֵי כִסֵּא כְבוֹדֶךָ
וַעֲקֵדַת יִצְחָק לְזַרְעוֹ הַיּוֹם בְּרַחֲמִים תִּזְכֹּר.
בָּרוּךְ אַתָּה יהוה, זוֹכֵר הַבְּרִית.

*The* קהל *stands and the* שופר *is sounded (except on* שבת*).*

| תקיעה | שברים תרועה | תקיעה |
|---|---|---|
| תקיעה | שברים | תקיעה |
| תקיעה | תרועה | תקיעה |

*The* קהל*, then the* שליח ציבור *(even on* שבת*):*

הַיּוֹם הֲרַת עוֹלָם, הַיּוֹם יַעֲמִיד בַּמִּשְׁפָּט כָּל יְצוּרֵי עוֹלָמִים
אִם כְּבָנִים אִם כַּעֲבָדִים.
אִם כְּבָנִים, רַחֲמֵנוּ כְּרַחֵם אָב עַל בָּנִים
וְאִם כַּעֲבָדִים, עֵינֵינוּ לְךָ תְלוּיוֹת עַד שֶׁתְּחָנֵּנוּ
וְתוֹצִיא כָאוֹר מִשְׁפָּטֵנוּ, אָיֹם קָדוֹשׁ.

*On* שבת *omit:*

אֲרֶשֶׁת שְׂפָתֵינוּ יֶעֱרַב לְפָנֶיךָ
אֵל רָם וְנִשָּׂא, מֵבִין וּמַאֲזִין, מַבִּיט וּמַקְשִׁיב לְקוֹל תְּקִיעָתֵנוּ.
וּתְקַבֵּל בְּרַחֲמִים וּבְרָצוֹן סֵדֶר זִכְרוֹנוֹתֵינוּ.

*Some congregations say a prefatory piyut before the Shofarot.*
*On weekdays, "Esa De'i" on page 1037; on Shabbat, "Anusa LeEzra" on page 1072.*

SHOFAROT

אַתָּה נִגְלֵיתָ You were revealed in a cloud of Your glory,
to Your holy nation, to speak with them.
Out of the heavens Your voice was heard;
You revealed Yourself in mists of purity.
And all the wide world quaked before You,
the works of creation shook in Your presence,
as You revealed Yourself, our King, on Mount Sinai,
to teach Your people Torah and the commandments,
to have them hear the majesty of Your voice –
Your sacred words amid flames of fire.
In thunder and lightning You revealed Yourself to them,
and amid the sound of the shofar You appeared.

VERSES OF SHOFAROT

As it is written in Your Torah:
"Then on the third day, in the morning – *Ex. 19*
thunder and lightning; heavy cloud covered the mountain,
there was a very loud sound of the shofar,
and all of the people in the camp quaked."

And it is said:
"And the sound of the shofar grew ever louder – *Ibid.*
Moses spoke, and the LORD answered him with a voice."

And it is said:
"And all the people saw the thunder and the flames, *Ex. 20*
and the sound of the shofar, and the mountain asmoke;
the people saw and they staggered, and stood far back."

And by Your servants the prophets it is written:
"God has been raised up in sound: *Ps. 47*
raised, the LORD, in the voice of the shofar."

And it is said,
"With trumpets and the sound of the shofar, *Ps. 98*
shout for joy before the LORD, the King."

*Some congregations say a prefatory piyut before the* שופרות*.*
*On weekdays,* אֶשָּׂא דֵעִי *on page 1037; on* שבת*,* אָנוּסָה לְעֶזְרָה *on page 1072.*

שופרות

אַתָּה נִגְלֵיתָ בַּעֲנַן כְּבוֹדֶךָ עַל עַם קָדְשְׁךָ לְדַבֵּר עִמָּם
מִן הַשָּׁמַיִם הִשְׁמַעְתָּם קוֹלֶךָ, וְנִגְלֵיתָ עֲלֵיהֶם בְּעַרְפְלֵי טֹהַר.
גַּם כָּל הָעוֹלָם כֻּלּוֹ חָל מִפָּנֶיךָ, וּבְרִיּוֹת בְּרֵאשִׁית חָרְדוּ מִמֶּךָּ
בְּהִגָּלוֹתְךָ מַלְכֵּנוּ עַל הַר סִינַי, לְלַמֵּד לְעַמְּךָ תּוֹרָה וּמִצְוֹת
וַתַּשְׁמִיעֵם אֶת הוֹד קוֹלֶךָ, וְדִבְּרוֹת קָדְשְׁךָ מִלַּהֲבוֹת אֵשׁ.
בְּקוֹלוֹת וּבְרָקִים עֲלֵיהֶם נִגְלֵיתָ, וּבְקוֹל שׁוֹפָר עֲלֵיהֶם הוֹפָעְתָּ.

פסוקי שופרות

כַּכָּתוּב בְּתוֹרָתֶךָ
שמות יט וַיְהִי בַיּוֹם הַשְּׁלִישִׁי בִּהְיֹת הַבֹּקֶר
וַיְהִי קֹלֹת וּבְרָקִים וְעָנָן כָּבֵד עַל־הָהָר
וְקֹל שֹׁפָר חָזָק מְאֹד, וַיֶּחֱרַד כָּל־הָעָם אֲשֶׁר בַּמַּחֲנֶה:

וְנֶאֱמַר
שם וַיְהִי קוֹל הַשֹּׁפָר הוֹלֵךְ וְחָזֵק מְאֹד
מֹשֶׁה יְדַבֵּר, וְהָאֱלֹהִים יַעֲנֶנּוּ בְקוֹל:

וְנֶאֱמַר
שמות כ וְכָל־הָעָם רֹאִים אֶת־הַקּוֹלֹת וְאֶת־הַלַּפִּידִם
וְאֵת קוֹל הַשֹּׁפָר, וְאֶת־הָהָר עָשֵׁן
וַיַּרְא הָעָם וַיָּנֻעוּ, וַיַּעַמְדוּ מֵרָחֹק:

וּבְדִבְרֵי קָדְשְׁךָ כָּתוּב לֵאמֹר
תהלים מז עָלָה אֱלֹהִים בִּתְרוּעָה, יהוה בְּקוֹל שׁוֹפָר:

וְנֶאֱמַר
תהלים צח בַּחֲצֹצְרוֹת וְקוֹל שׁוֹפָר, הָרִיעוּ לִפְנֵי הַמֶּלֶךְ יהוה:

And it is said:
“Sound the shofar on the new moon, Ps. 81
on our feast day when the moon is hidden.
For it is a statute for Israel, an ordinance of the God of Jacob.”
And it is said:
“Halleluya! Praise God in His holy place; Ps. 150
praise Him in the heavens of His power.
Praise Him for His mighty deeds;
praise Him for His surpassing greatness.
Praise Him with blasts of the shofar;
praise Him with the harp and lyre.
Praise Him with timbrel and dance;
praise Him with strings and flute.
Praise Him with clashing cymbals;
praise Him with resounding cymbals.
Let all that breathes praise the Lord. Halleluya!”

And by Your servants the prophets it is written:
“All the inhabitants of the world, all the dwellers on this earth, Is. 18
when He lifts up a banner on the mountains, you will see it,
and when He sounds the shofar you shall hear.”
And it is said:
“On that day a great shofar will be sounded, Is. 27
and those who are lost will come from the land of Assyria,
and those who were banished, from the land of Egypt,
and they will worship the Lord at the holy mountain in Jerusalem.”
And it is said:
“The Lord will appear to them, Zech. 9
His arrow will come out like lightning,
and the Lord God will sound the shofar,
and will move in stormwinds of the south.
The Lord of hosts will protect them –”
so, protect Your people Israel with Your peace.

---

in our daily prayers we reverse the order. First we say, “Sound the great shofar for our freedom,” and only then “raise high the banner to gather our exiles.”

וְנֶאֱמַר

תהלים פא
תִּקְעוּ בַחֹדֶשׁ שׁוֹפָר, בַּכֵּסֶה לְיוֹם חַגֵּנוּ:
כִּי חֹק לְיִשְׂרָאֵל הוּא, מִשְׁפָּט לֵאלֹהֵי יַעֲקֹב:

וְנֶאֱמַר

תהלים קנ
הַלְלוּיָהּ, הַלְלוּ־אֵל בְּקָדְשׁוֹ הַלְלוּהוּ בִּרְקִיעַ עֻזּוֹ:
הַלְלוּהוּ בִגְבוּרֹתָיו הַלְלוּהוּ כְּרֹב גֻּדְלוֹ:
הַלְלוּהוּ בְּתֵקַע שׁוֹפָר הַלְלוּהוּ בְּנֵבֶל וְכִנּוֹר:
הַלְלוּהוּ בְתֹף וּמָחוֹל הַלְלוּהוּ בְּמִנִּים וְעֻגָב:
הַלְלוּהוּ בְצִלְצְלֵי־שָׁמַע הַלְלוּהוּ בְּצִלְצְלֵי תְרוּעָה:
כֹּל הַנְּשָׁמָה תְּהַלֵּל יָהּ, הַלְלוּיָהּ:

וְעַל יְדֵי עֲבָדֶיךָ הַנְּבִיאִים כָּתוּב לֵאמֹר

ישעיה יח
כָּל־יֹשְׁבֵי תֵבֵל וְשֹׁכְנֵי אָרֶץ
כִּנְשֹׂא־נֵס הָרִים תִּרְאוּ, וְכִתְקֹעַ שׁוֹפָר תִּשְׁמָעוּ:

וְנֶאֱמַר

ישעיה כז
וְהָיָה בַּיּוֹם הַהוּא יִתָּקַע בְּשׁוֹפָר גָּדוֹל
וּבָאוּ הָאֹבְדִים בְּאֶרֶץ אַשּׁוּר, וְהַנִּדָּחִים בְּאֶרֶץ מִצְרָיִם
וְהִשְׁתַּחֲווּ לַיהוה בְּהַר הַקֹּדֶשׁ בִּירוּשָׁלָםִ:

וְנֶאֱמַר

זכריה ט
וַיהוה עֲלֵיהֶם יֵרָאֶה, וְיָצָא כַבָּרָק חִצּוֹ
וַאדֹנָי יֱהוִה בַּשּׁוֹפָר יִתְקָע, וְהָלַךְ בְּסַעֲרוֹת תֵּימָן:
יהוה צְבָאוֹת יָגֵן עֲלֵיהֶם:
כֵּן תָּגֵן עַל עַמְּךָ יִשְׂרָאֵל בִּשְׁלוֹמֶךָ.

---

SHOFAROT – REFERENCES TO THE SHOFAR

**כִּנְשֹׂא־נֵס הָרִים תִּרְאוּ** *When He lifts up a banner on the mountains.* Here the prophet speaks first of a banner and then of the sound of a shofar, whereas

אֱלֹהֵינוּ Our God and God of our ancestors,
sound the great shofar for our freedom,
raise high the banner to gather our exiles,
bring close our scattered ones from among the nations,
and gather our exiles from the very ends of the earth.
Bring us to Zion, Your city, in joy,
and to Jerusalem, Your Temple, in everlasting happiness.
There we will prepare for You our obligatory offerings,
as we were commanded in Your Torah,
at the hand of Your servant Moses and by Your own word,
as it is said:

On the days of your celebration, *Num. 10*
and at your times of gathering and at your New Moons,
sound the trumpets over your offerings
and over your peace-offerings,
and those days will be remembrance for you before your God,
I am the LORD your God.

כִּי אַתָּה שׁוֹמֵעַ For You hear the call of the shofar,
and listen to its sounding, and there is none to be compared to You.
Blessed are You, LORD, who listens to the sound of Your people,
Israel's trumpet-blasts in compassion.

*The congregation stands and the shofar is sounded (except on Shabbat).*

| | | |
|---|---|---|
| TEKIA | SHEVARIM TERUA | TEKIA |
| TEKIA | SHEVARIM | TEKIA |
| TEKIA | TERUA | TEKIA |

---

those who were distant. But the prophet foresaw the actual events as they would transpire. It was those who were distant from Judaism (the secular Zionists) who saw the banner on the mountaintop before those who were close, the religious, heard the call of the shofar. (Rabbi Moshe Zvi Neriah, *Celebration of the Soul*)

אֱלֹהֵינוּ וֵאלֹהֵי אֲבוֹתֵינוּ
תְּקַע בְּשׁוֹפָר גָּדוֹל לְחֵרוּתֵנוּ, וְשָׂא נֵס לְקַבֵּץ גָּלֻיּוֹתֵינוּ
וְקָרֵב פְּזוּרֵינוּ מִבֵּין הַגּוֹיִם, וּנְפוּצוֹתֵינוּ כַּנֵּס מִיַּרְכְּתֵי אָרֶץ.
וַהֲבִיאֵנוּ לְצִיּוֹן עִירְךָ בְּרִנָּה
וְלִירוּשָׁלַיִם בֵּית מִקְדָּשְׁךָ בְּשִׂמְחַת עוֹלָם
וְשָׁם נַעֲשֶׂה לְפָנֶיךָ אֶת קָרְבְּנוֹת חוֹבוֹתֵינוּ
כַּמְצֻוֶּה עָלֵינוּ בְּתוֹרָתֶךָ עַל יְדֵי מֹשֶׁה עַבְדֶּךָ, מִפִּי כְבוֹדֶךָ
כָּאָמוּר

וּבְיוֹם שִׂמְחַתְכֶם וּבְמוֹעֲדֵיכֶם וּבְרָאשֵׁי חָדְשֵׁכֶם במדבר י
וּתְקַעְתֶּם בַּחֲצֹצְרֹת עַל עֹלֹתֵיכֶם וְעַל זִבְחֵי שַׁלְמֵיכֶם
וְהָיוּ לָכֶם לְזִכָּרוֹן לִפְנֵי אֱלֹהֵיכֶם
אֲנִי יהוה אֱלֹהֵיכֶם:

כִּי אַתָּה שׁוֹמֵעַ קוֹל שׁוֹפָר וּמַאֲזִין תְּרוּעָה, וְאֵין דּוֹמֶה לָּךְ.
בָּרוּךְ אַתָּה יהוה, שׁוֹמֵעַ קוֹל תְּרוּעַת עַמּוֹ יִשְׂרָאֵל בְּרַחֲמִים.

*The* קהל *stands and the* שופר *is sounded (except on* שבת*).*

| | | |
|---|---|---|
| תקיעה | שברים תרועה | תקיעה |
| תקיעה | שברים | תקיעה |
| תקיעה | תרועה | תקיעה |

---

On this, Rav Kook made a profound comment. The daily prayer, instituted by the sages of the Great Assembly, speaks of the logical sequence of events. The shofar calls those who are near, while a banner is raised for those too far away to hear. Logically, the ingathering of exiles to the land of Israel should first have moved those who were close to Judaism, and only later

*The congregation, then the Leader (even on Shabbat):*

הַיּוֹם This day is the birth of the world.
This day stands all the world's creations up in judgment,
stands them as sons or as slaves –
If as sons, have compassion for us, as a father has compassion for his sons.
And if as slaves, our eyes are raised and fixed on You
until You show us favor, and bring out our judgment like sunlight,
Awesome, Holy.

*On Shabbat omit:*

אֲרֶשֶׁת May our mouths' words rise beautiful before You,
most high and elevated God, who understands and heeds,
looks on and listens to the sounds of our shofar blasts.
Accept, with compassion and favor, our Order of the Shofarot.

TEMPLE SERVICE

רְצֵה Find favor, LORD our God, in Your people Israel,
and heed their prayer.
Restore the service to Your most holy House,
and accept soon, in love and favor,
the fire-offerings of Israel and their prayer.
May the service of Your people Israel always find favor with You.

*If Kohanim say the Priestly Blessing during the Leader's Repetition, the following is said (in Israel some use the formula on the next page); otherwise the Leader continues with "And may our eyes" on the next page.*

*All:* וְתֶעֱרַב May our entreaty be as pleasing to You as a burnt-offering and sacrifice. Please, Compassionate One, in Your abounding mercy restore Your Presence to Zion, Your city, and the order of the Temple service to Jerusalem. And may our eyes witness Your return to Zion in compassion, there we may serve You with reverence as in the days of old and as in former years.

*Leader:* Blessed are You, LORD, for You alone do we serve with reverence.

*The service continues with "We give thanks" on the next page.*

---

eyes witness," was said by Babylonian Jewry (Rav Amram Gaon). Because much of the additional poetry said on festivals was composed in Israel, this passage too was added to prayers in the Diaspora.

*The* קהל*, then the* שליח ציבור *(even on* שבת*):*

הַיּוֹם הֲרַת עוֹלָם, הַיּוֹם יַעֲמִיד בַּמִּשְׁפָּט כָּל יְצוּרֵי עוֹלָמִים
אִם כְּבָנִים אִם כַּעֲבָדִים.
אִם כְּבָנִים, רַחֲמֵנוּ כְּרַחֵם אָב עַל בָּנִים
וְאִם כַּעֲבָדִים, עֵינֵינוּ לְךָ תְלוּיוֹת עַד שֶׁתְּחָנֵּנוּ
וְתוֹצִיא כָאוֹר מִשְׁפָּטֵנוּ, אָיֹם קָדוֹשׁ.

*On* שבת *omit:*

אֲרֶשֶׁת שְׂפָתֵינוּ יֶעֱרַב לְפָנֶיךָ
אֵל רָם וְנִשָּׂא, מֵבִין וּמַאֲזִין, מַבִּיט וּמַקְשִׁיב לְקוֹל תְּקִיעָתֵנוּ.
וּתְקַבֵּל בְּרַחֲמִים וּבְרָצוֹן סֵדֶר שׁוֹפְרוֹתֵינוּ.

עבודה

רְצֵה יהוה אֱלֹהֵינוּ בְּעַמְּךָ יִשְׂרָאֵל, וְלִתְפִלָּתָם שְׁעֵה
וְהָשֵׁב אֶת הָעֲבוֹדָה לִדְבִיר בֵּיתֶךָ
וְאִשֵּׁי יִשְׂרָאֵל וּתְפִלָּתָם, מְהֵרָה בְּאַהֲבָה תְקַבֵּל בְּרָצוֹן
וּתְהִי לְרָצוֹן תָּמִיד עֲבוֹדַת יִשְׂרָאֵל עַמֶּךָ.

*If* כהנים *say* ברכת כהנים *during* חזרת הש״ץ*, the following is said (in* ארץ ישראל *some use the formula on the next page); otherwise the* שליח ציבור *continues with* וְתֶחֱזֶינָה *on the next page.*

קהל וש״ץ: וְתֶעֱרַב עָלֶיךָ עֲתִירָתֵנוּ כְּעוֹלָה וּכְקָרְבָּן. אָנָּא רַחוּם, בְּרַחֲמֶיךָ הָרַבִּים הָשֵׁב שְׁכִינָתְךָ לְצִיּוֹן עִירְךָ, וְסֵדֶר הָעֲבוֹדָה לִירוּשָׁלָיִם. וְתֶחֱזֶינָה עֵינֵינוּ בְּשׁוּבְךָ לְצִיּוֹן בְּרַחֲמִים. וְשָׁם נַעֲבָדְךָ בְּיִרְאָה כִּימֵי עוֹלָם וּכְשָׁנִים קַדְמוֹנִיּוֹת.

ש״ץ: בָּרוּךְ אַתָּה יהוה שֶׁאוֹתְךָ לְבַדְּךָ בְּיִרְאָה נַעֲבֹד.

*The service continues with* מוֹדִים *on the next page.*

---

וְתֶעֱרַב עָלֶיךָ עֲתִירָתֵנוּ *May our entreaty be as pleasing to You.* This text, said on festivals in one of its two variants, was originally said daily in Israel in Talmudic times (Yerushalmi, *Sota* 7:6), while the shorter form, "And may our

*In Israel some use the following formula instead:*

*All:* וְתֶעֱרַב May our entreaty be as pleasing to You as a burnt-offering and sacrifice. Please, Compassionate One, in Your abounding mercy restore Your Presence to Zion, Your city, and the order of the Temple service to Jerusalem. That there we may serve You with reverence as in the days of old and as in former years.

*Continue with "And may our eyes" (below).*

*When the Priestly Blessing is not said, the Leader continues:*

And may our eyes witness Your return to Zion in compassion.
Blessed are You, Lord, who restores His Presence to Zion.

THANKSGIVING

*Bow at the first nine words.*

מוֹדִים We give thanks to You,
for You are the Lord our God
and God of our ancestors
for ever and all time.
You are the Rock of our lives,
Shield of our salvation
from generation to generation.
We will thank You and
declare Your praise for our lives,
which are entrusted into Your hand;
for our souls,
which are placed in Your charge;
for Your miracles
which are with us every day;
and for Your wonders and favors
at all times, evening,
morning and midday.
You are good –
for Your compassion never fails.
You are compassionate –
for Your loving-kindnesses never cease,
for we have always placed our hope in You.

*As the Leader recites Modim, the congregation says quietly:*

מוֹדִים We give thanks to You,
for You are the Lord our God
and God of our ancestors,
God of all flesh,
who formed us
and formed the universe.
Blessings and thanks
are due to Your great
and holy name for giving us
life and sustaining us.
May You continue
to give us life and sustain us;
and may You gather our
exiles to Your holy courts,
to keep Your decrees,
do Your will and serve You
with a perfect heart,
for it is for us
to give You thanks.
Blessed be God to whom
thanksgiving is due.

וְעַל כֻּלָּם For all these things may Your name be blessed and exalted and raised up, our King, continually, for ever and all time.

*In* ארץ ישראל *some use the following formula instead:*

קהל וש״ץ: וְתֶעֱרַב עָלֶיךָ עֲתִירָתֵנוּ כְּעוֹלָה וּכְקָרְבָּן. אָנָּא רַחוּם, בְּרַחֲמֶיךָ הָרַבִּים הָשֵׁב שְׁכִינָתְךָ לְצִיּוֹן עִירְךָ, וְסֵדֶר הָעֲבוֹדָה לִירוּשָׁלָיִם. וְשָׁם נַעֲבָדְךָ בְּיִרְאָה כִּימֵי עוֹלָם וּכְשָׁנִים קַדְמוֹנִיּוֹת.

*Continue with* ותחזינה *(below).*

*When* ברכת כהנים *is not said, the* שליח ציבור *continues:*

וְתֶחֱזֶינָה עֵינֵינוּ בְּשׁוּבְךָ לְצִיּוֹן בְּרַחֲמִים.
בָּרוּךְ אַתָּה יהוה, הַמַּחֲזִיר שְׁכִינָתוֹ לְצִיּוֹן.

הודאה

*Bow at the first five words.*

מוֹדִים אֲנַחְנוּ לָךְ
שָׁאַתָּה הוּא יהוה אֱלֹהֵינוּ
וֵאלֹהֵי אֲבוֹתֵינוּ לְעוֹלָם וָעֶד.
צוּר חַיֵּינוּ, מָגֵן יִשְׁעֵנוּ
אַתָּה הוּא לְדוֹר וָדוֹר.
נוֹדֶה לְּךָ וּנְסַפֵּר תְּהִלָּתֶךָ
עַל חַיֵּינוּ הַמְּסוּרִים בְּיָדֶךָ
וְעַל נִשְׁמוֹתֵינוּ הַפְּקוּדוֹת לָךְ
וְעַל נִסֶּיךָ שֶׁבְּכָל יוֹם עִמָּנוּ
וְעַל נִפְלְאוֹתֶיךָ וְטוֹבוֹתֶיךָ
שֶׁבְּכָל עֵת, עֶרֶב וָבֹקֶר וְצָהֳרָיִם.
הַטּוֹב, כִּי לֹא כָלוּ רַחֲמֶיךָ
וְהַמְרַחֵם, כִּי לֹא תַמּוּ חֲסָדֶיךָ
כִּי מֵעוֹלָם קִוִּינוּ לָךְ.

*As the* שליח ציבור *recites* מודים, *the* קהל *says quietly:*

מוֹדִים אֲנַחְנוּ לָךְ
שָׁאַתָּה הוּא יהוה אֱלֹהֵינוּ
וֵאלֹהֵי אֲבוֹתֵינוּ
אֱלֹהֵי כָל בָּשָׂר
יוֹצְרֵנוּ, יוֹצֵר בְּרֵאשִׁית.
בְּרָכוֹת וְהוֹדָאוֹת
לְשִׁמְךָ הַגָּדוֹל וְהַקָּדוֹשׁ
עַל שֶׁהֶחֱיִיתָנוּ וְקִיַּמְתָּנוּ.
כֵּן תְּחַיֵּנוּ וּתְקַיְּמֵנוּ
וְתֶאֱסֹף גָּלֻיּוֹתֵינוּ
לְחַצְרוֹת קָדְשֶׁךָ
לִשְׁמֹר חֻקֶּיךָ וְלַעֲשׂוֹת רְצוֹנֶךָ
וּלְעָבְדְּךָ בְּלֵבָב שָׁלֵם
עַל שֶׁאֲנַחְנוּ מוֹדִים לָךְ.
בָּרוּךְ אֵל הַהוֹדָאוֹת.

וְעַל כֻּלָּם
יִתְבָּרַךְ וְיִתְרוֹמַם וְיִתְנַשֵּׂא שִׁמְךָ מַלְכֵּנוּ תָּמִיד לְעוֹלָם וָעֶד.

*The congregation, then the Leader:*

אָבִינוּ מַלְכֵּנוּ Our Father, our King,
remember Your compassion
and overcome Your anger,
and efface pestilence, sword, famine,
captivity and destruction,
iniquity and plague and bad mishap
and all illness, any harm or feud,
and all kinds of afflictions
and all harsh decrees and baseless hatred,
from us and from all the people of Your covenant.

*The congregation then the Leader:*

וּכְתֹב And write for a good life,
all the children of Your covenant.

Let all that lives thank You, Selah!
and praise and bless Your great name in truth,
always, because it is good,
God, our Savior and Help, Selah!
the beneficent God.
▾Blessed are You, LORD,
whose name is "the Good"
and to whom thanks are due.

*The following supplication is recited quietly while the Leader says "Let all that lives" above.*

*In some communities, the congregation says:*

יְהִי רָצוֹן May it be Your will, LORD our God and God of our ancestors, that this blessing which You have commanded to bless Your people Israel should be a complete blessing, with neither hindrance nor sin, now and forever.

*The Kohanim say:*

יְהִי רָצוֹן May it be Your will, LORD our God and God of our ancestors, that this blessing with which You have commanded us to bless Your people Israel should be a complete blessing, with neither hindrance nor sin, now and forever.

*In Israel the Priestly Blessing on page 1002 is said.*
*When the Priestly Blessing is not said, the Leader says the formula on page 612.*

*The* קהל*, then the* שליח ציבור*:*

אָבִינוּ מַלְכֵּנוּ
זְכֹר רַחֲמֶיךָ וּכְבֹשׁ כַּעַסְךָ
וְכַלֵּה דֶּבֶר, וְחֶרֶב, וְרָעָב
וּשְׁבִי, וּמַשְׁחִית, וְעָוֹן, וּמַגֵּפָה, וּפֶגַע רַע
וְכָל מַחֲלָה, וְכָל תַּקָּלָה, וְכָל קְטָטָה
וְכָל מִינֵי פֻרְעָנִיּוֹת, וְכָל גְּזֵרָה רָעָה, וְשִׂנְאַת חִנָּם
מֵעָלֵינוּ וּמֵעַל כָּל בְּנֵי בְרִיתֶךָ.

*The* קהל *then the* שליח ציבור*:*

וּכְתֹב לְחַיִּים טוֹבִים כָּל בְּנֵי בְרִיתֶךָ.

וְכֹל הַחַיִּים יוֹדְוּךָ סֶּלָה
וִיהַלְלוּ וִיבָרְכוּ אֶת שִׁמְךָ הַגָּדוֹל בֶּאֱמֶת לְעוֹלָם כִּי טוֹב
הָאֵל יְשׁוּעָתֵנוּ וְעֶזְרָתֵנוּ סֶלָה
הָאֵל הַטּוֹב.
׳בָּרוּךְ אַתָּה יהוה, הַטּוֹב שִׁמְךָ וּלְךָ נָאֶה לְהוֹדוֹת.

*The following supplication is recited quietly while the* שליח ציבור *says* וְכֹל הַחַיִּים *above.*

*The* כהנים *say:*

יְהִי רָצוֹן מִלְּפָנֶיךָ, יהוה אֱלֹהֵינוּ וֵאלֹהֵי אֲבוֹתֵינוּ, שֶׁתְּהֵא הַבְּרָכָה הַזֹּאת שֶׁצִּוִּיתָנוּ לְבָרֵךְ אֶת עַמְּךָ יִשְׂרָאֵל בְּרָכָה שְׁלֵמָה, וְלֹא יִהְיֶה בָּהּ שׁוּם מִכְשׁוֹל וְעָוֹן מֵעַתָּה וְעַד עוֹלָם.

*In some communities, the* קהל *says:*

יְהִי רָצוֹן מִלְּפָנֶיךָ, יהוה אֱלֹהֵינוּ וֵאלֹהֵי אֲבוֹתֵינוּ, שֶׁתְּהֵא הַבְּרָכָה הַזֹּאת שֶׁצִּוִּיתָ לְבָרֵךְ אֶת עַמְּךָ יִשְׂרָאֵל בְּרָכָה שְׁלֵמָה, וְלֹא יִהְיֶה בָּהּ שׁוּם מִכְשׁוֹל וְעָוֹן מֵעַתָּה וְעַד עוֹלָם.

*In* ארץ ישראל *the* ברכת כהנים *on page 1003 is said.*
*When* ברכת כהנים *is not said, the* שליח ציבור *says the formula on page 613.*

*The following is recited quietly by the Leader:*

אֱלֹהֵינוּ Our God and God of our fathers,
bless us with the threefold blessing in the Torah,
written by the hand of Moses Your servant
and pronounced by Aaron and his sons:

*The Leader says aloud:*

Kohanim!

*In most places, the congregation responds:*

Your holy people, as it said:

*The Kohanim say the following blessing in unison:*

בָּרוּךְ Blessed are You, LORD our God, King of the Universe, who has made us holy with the holiness of Aaron, and has commanded us to bless His people Israel with love.

*The first word in each sentence is said by the Leader, followed by the Kohanim. Some read silently the accompanying verses. One should remain silent and not look at the Kohanim while the blessings are being said.*

| | | |
|---|---|---|
| May [He] bless you | May the LORD, Maker of heaven and earth, bless you from Zion. | *Ps. 134* |
| The LORD | LORD, our LORD, how majestic is Your name throughout the earth. | *Ps. 8* |
| And protect you. | Protect me, God, for in You I take refuge. | *Ps. 16* |

*Read the following silently while the Kohanim chant. Omit on Shabbat.*

Master of the Universe, I am Yours and my dreams are Yours. I have dreamt a dream and I do not know what it means. May it be Your will, LORD my God and God of my fathers, that all my dreams be, for me and all Israel, for good, whether I have dreamt about myself, or about others, or others have dreamt about me. If they are good, strengthen and reinforce them, and may they be fulfilled in me and them like the dreams of the righteous Joseph. If, though, they need healing, heal them as You healed Hezekiah King of Judah from his illness, like Miriam the prophetess from her leprosy, like Na'aman from his leprosy, like the waters of Mara by Moses our teacher, and like the waters of Jericho by Elisha. And just as You turned the curses of Balaam the wicked from curse to blessing, so turn all my dreams about me and all Israel to good; protect me, be gracious to me and accept me. Amen.

*The following is recited quietly by the* שליח ציבור*:*

אֱלֹהֵינוּ וֵאלֹהֵי אֲבוֹתֵינוּ, בָּרְכֵנוּ בַּבְּרָכָה הַמְשֻׁלֶּשֶׁת בַּתּוֹרָה הַכְּתוּבָה עַל יְדֵי מֹשֶׁה עַבְדֶּךָ, הָאֲמוּרָה מִפִּי אַהֲרֹן וּבָנָיו

*The* שליח ציבור *says aloud:*

כֹּהֲנִים

*In most places, the* קהל *responds:*

עַם קְדוֹשֶׁךָ, כָּאָמוּר:

*The* כהנים *say the following blessing in unison:*

בָּרוּךְ אַתָּה יהוה אֱלֹהֵינוּ מֶלֶךְ הָעוֹלָם, אֲשֶׁר קִדְּשָׁנוּ בִּקְדֻשָּׁתוֹ שֶׁל אַהֲרֹן, וְצִוָּנוּ לְבָרֵךְ אֶת עַמּוֹ יִשְׂרָאֵל בְּאַהֲבָה.

*The first word in each sentence is said by the* שליח ציבור*, followed by the* כהנים*. Some read silently the accompanying verses. One should remain silent and not look at the* כהנים *while the blessings are being said.*

יְבָרֶכְךָ יְבָרֶכְךָ יהוה מִצִּיּוֹן, עֹשֵׂה שָׁמַיִם וָאָרֶץ: תהלים קלד

יהוה יהוה אֲדֹנֵינוּ, מָה־אַדִּיר שִׁמְךָ בְּכָל־הָאָרֶץ: תהלים ח

וְיִשְׁמְרֶךָ: שָׁמְרֵנִי אֵל, כִּי־חָסִיתִי בָךְ: תהלים טז

*Read the following silently while the* כהנים *chant. Omit on* שבת*.*

רִבּוֹנוֹ שֶׁל עוֹלָם, אֲנִי שֶׁלָּךְ וַחֲלוֹמוֹתַי שֶׁלָּךְ. חֲלוֹם חָלַמְתִּי וְאֵינִי יוֹדֵעַ מַה הוּא. יְהִי רָצוֹן מִלְּפָנֶיךָ, יהוה אֱלֹהַי וֵאלֹהֵי אֲבוֹתַי, שֶׁיִּהְיוּ כָּל חֲלוֹמוֹתַי עָלַי וְעַל כָּל יִשְׂרָאֵל לְטוֹבָה, בֵּין שֶׁחָלַמְתִּי עַל עַצְמִי, וּבֵין שֶׁחָלַמְתִּי עַל אֲחֵרִים, וּבֵין שֶׁחָלְמוּ אֲחֵרִים עָלָי. אִם טוֹבִים הֵם, חַזְּקֵם וְאַמְּצֵם, וְיִתְקַיְּמוּ בִי וּבָהֶם, כַּחֲלוֹמוֹתָיו שֶׁל יוֹסֵף הַצַּדִּיק. וְאִם צְרִיכִים רְפוּאָה, רְפָאֵם כְּחִזְקִיָּהוּ מֶלֶךְ יְהוּדָה מֵחָלְיוֹ, וּכְמִרְיָם הַנְּבִיאָה מִצָּרַעְתָּהּ, וּכְנַעֲמָן מִצָּרַעְתּוֹ, וּכְמֵי מָרָה עַל יְדֵי מֹשֶׁה רַבֵּנוּ, וּכְמֵי יְרִיחוֹ עַל יְדֵי אֱלִישָׁע. וּכְשֵׁם שֶׁהָפַכְתָּ אֶת קִלְלַת בִּלְעָם הָרָשָׁע מִקְּלָלָה לִבְרָכָה, כֵּן תַּהֲפֹךְ כָּל חֲלוֹמוֹתַי עָלַי וְעַל כָּל יִשְׂרָאֵל לְטוֹבָה, וְתִשְׁמְרֵנִי וּתְחָנֵּנִי וְתִרְצֵנִי. אָמֵן.

May [He] make shine — May God be gracious to us and bless us; may He make His face shine upon us, Selah. *Ps. 67*

The LORD — The LORD, the LORD, compassionate and gracious God, slow to anger, abounding in kindness and truth. *Ex. 34*

His face — Turn to me and be gracious to me, for I am alone and afflicted. *Ps. 25*

On you — To You, LORD, I lift up my soul. *Ibid.*

And be gracious to you. — As the eyes of slaves turn to their master's hand, or the eyes of a slave-girl to the hand of her mistress, so our eyes are turned to the LORD our God, awaiting His favor. *Ps. 123*

*Read the following silently while the Kohanim chant. Omit on Shabbat.*

Master of the Universe, I am Yours and my dreams are Yours. I have dreamt a dream and I do not know what it means. May it be Your will, LORD my God and God of my fathers, that all my dreams be, for me and all Israel, for good, whether I have dreamt about myself, or about others, or others have dreamt about me. If they are good, strengthen and reinforce them, and may they be fulfilled in me and them like the dreams of the righteous Joseph. If, though, they need healing, heal them as You healed Hezekiah King of Judah from his illness, like Miriam the prophetess from her leprosy, like Na'aman from his leprosy, like the waters of Mara by Moses our teacher, and like the waters of Jericho by Elisha. And just as You turned the curses of Balaam the wicked from curse to blessing, so turn all my dreams about me and all Israel to good; protect me, be gracious to me and accept me. Amen.

May [He] turn — May he receive a blessing from the LORD and a just reward from the God of his salvation. And he will win grace and good favor in the eyes of God and man. *Ps. 24* *Prov. 3*

The LORD — LORD, be gracious to us; we yearn for You. Be their strength every morning, our salvation in time of distress. *Is. 33*

His face — Do not hide Your face from me in the day of my distress. Turn Your ear to me; on the day I call, swiftly answer me. *Ps. 102*

Toward you — To You, enthroned in heaven, I lift my eyes. *Ps. 123*

And grant — They shall place My name on the children of Israel, and I will bless them. *Num. 6*

You — Yours, LORD, are the greatness and the power, the glory, majesty and splendor, for everything in heaven and earth is Yours. Yours, LORD, is the kingdom; You are exalted as Head over all. *1 Chr. 29*

Peace. — "Peace, peace, to those far and near," says the LORD, "and I will heal him." *Is. 57*

יְָאֵר אֱלֹהִים יְחָנֵּנוּ וִיבָרְכֵנוּ, יָאֵר פָּנָיו אִתָּנוּ סֶלָה: תהלים סז

יהוה יהוה, יהוה, אֵל רַחוּם וְחַנּוּן, אֶרֶךְ אַפַּיִם וְרַב־חֶסֶד וֶאֱמֶת: שמות לד

פָּנָיו פְּנֵה־אֵלַי וְחָנֵּנִי, כִּי־יָחִיד וְעָנִי אָנִי: תהלים כה

אֵלֶיךָ אֵלֶיךָ יהוה נַפְשִׁי אֶשָּׂא: שם

וִיחֻנֶּךָּ: הִנֵּה כְעֵינֵי עֲבָדִים אֶל־יַד אֲדוֹנֵיהֶם, כְּעֵינֵי שִׁפְחָה אֶל־יַד גְּבִרְתָּהּ תהלים קכג
כֵּן עֵינֵינוּ אֶל־יהוה אֱלֹהֵינוּ עַד שֶׁיְּחָנֵּנוּ:

*Read the following silently while the* כהנים *chant. Omit on* שבת*.*

רִבּוֹנוֹ שֶׁל עוֹלָם, אֲנִי שֶׁלָּךְ וַחֲלוֹמוֹתַי שֶׁלָּךְ. חֲלוֹם חָלַמְתִּי וְאֵינִי יוֹדֵעַ מַה הוּא. יְהִי רָצוֹן מִלְּפָנֶיךָ, יהוה אֱלֹהַי וֵאלֹהֵי אֲבוֹתַי, שֶׁיִּהְיוּ כָּל חֲלוֹמוֹתַי עָלַי וְעַל כָּל יִשְׂרָאֵל לְטוֹבָה, בֵּין שֶׁחָלַמְתִּי עַל עַצְמִי, וּבֵין שֶׁחָלַמְתִּי עַל אֲחֵרִים, וּבֵין שֶׁחָלְמוּ אֲחֵרִים עָלָי. אִם טוֹבִים הֵם, חַזְּקֵם וְאַמְּצֵם, וְיִתְקַיְּמוּ בִי וּבָהֶם, כַּחֲלוֹמוֹתָיו שֶׁל יוֹסֵף הַצַּדִּיק. וְאִם צְרִיכִים רְפוּאָה, רְפָאֵם כְּחִזְקִיָּהוּ מֶלֶךְ יְהוּדָה מֵחָלְיוֹ, וּכְמִרְיָם הַנְּבִיאָה מִצָּרַעְתָּהּ, וּכְנַעֲמָן מִצָּרַעְתּוֹ, וּכְמֵי מָרָה עַל יְדֵי מֹשֶׁה רַבֵּנוּ, וּכְמֵי יְרִיחוֹ עַל יְדֵי אֱלִישָׁע. וּכְשֵׁם שֶׁהָפַכְתָּ אֶת קִלְלַת בִּלְעָם הָרָשָׁע מִקְּלָלָה לִבְרָכָה, כֵּן תַּהֲפֹךְ כָּל חֲלוֹמוֹתַי עָלַי וְעַל כָּל יִשְׂרָאֵל לְטוֹבָה, וְתִשְׁמְרֵנִי וּתְחָנֵּנִי וְתִרְצֵנִי. אָמֵן.

יִשָּׂא יִשָּׂא בְרָכָה מֵאֵת יהוה, וּצְדָקָה מֵאֱלֹהֵי יִשְׁעוֹ: תהלים כד
וּמְצָא־חֵן וְשֵׂכֶל־טוֹב בְּעֵינֵי אֱלֹהִים וְאָדָם: משלי ג

יהוה יהוה חָנֵּנוּ, לְךָ קִוִּינוּ, הֱיֵה זְרֹעָם לַבְּקָרִים ישעיה לג
אַף־יְשׁוּעָתֵנוּ בְּעֵת צָרָה:

פָּנָיו אַל־תַּסְתֵּר פָּנֶיךָ מִמֶּנִּי בְּיוֹם צַר לִי, הַטֵּה־אֵלַי אָזְנֶךָ תהלים קב
בְּיוֹם אֶקְרָא מַהֵר עֲנֵנִי:

אֵלֶיךָ אֵלֶיךָ נָשָׂאתִי אֶת־עֵינַי, הַיֹּשְׁבִי בַּשָּׁמָיִם: תהלים קכג

וְיָשֵׂם וְשָׂמוּ אֶת־שְׁמִי עַל־בְּנֵי יִשְׂרָאֵל, וַאֲנִי אֲבָרְכֵם: במדבר ו

לְךָ לְךָ יהוה הַגְּדֻלָּה וְהַגְּבוּרָה וְהַתִּפְאֶרֶת וְהַנֵּצַח וְהַהוֹד דברי הימים א׳ כט
כִּי־כֹל בַּשָּׁמַיִם וּבָאָרֶץ, לְךָ יהוה הַמַּמְלָכָה
וְהַמִּתְנַשֵּׂא לְכֹל לְרֹאשׁ:

שָׁלוֹם: שָׁלוֹם שָׁלוֹם לָרָחוֹק וְלַקָּרוֹב, אָמַר יהוה, וּרְפָאתִיו: ישעיה נז

*Read the following silently while the Kohanim chant. Omit on Shabbat.*

May it be Your will, Lord my God and God of my fathers, that You act for the sake of Your simple, sacred kindness and great compassion, and for the purity of Your great, mighty and awesome name of twenty-two letters derived from the verses of the priestly blessing spoken by Aaron and his sons, Your holy people. May You be close to me when I call to You. May You hear my prayer, plea and cry as You did the cry of Jacob Your perfect one who was called "a plain man." May You grant me and all the members of my household our food and sustenance, generously not meagerly, honestly not otherwise, with satisfaction not pain, from Your generous hand, just as You gave a portion of bread to eat and clothes to wear to Jacob our father who was called "a plain man." May we find love, grace, kindness and compassion in Your sight and in the eyes of all who see us. May my words in service to You be heard, as You granted Joseph Your righteous one, at the time when he was robed by his father in a cloak of fine wool, that he find grace, kindness and compassion in Your sight and in the eyes of all who saw him. May You do wonders and miracles with me, and a sign for good. Grant me success in my paths, and set in my heart understanding that I may understand, discern and fulfill all the words of Your Torah's teachings and mysteries. Save me from errors and purify my thoughts and my heart to serve You and be in awe of You. Prolong my days (*add, where appropriate:* and those of my father, mother, wife, husband, son/s, and daughter/s) in joy and happiness, with much strength and peace. Amen, Selah.

*The Leader continues with "Grant peace" below.*

*The congregation says:*

אַדִּיר Majestic One on high who dwells in power: You are peace and Your name is peace. May it be Your will to bestow on us and on Your people the house of Israel, life and blessing as a safeguard for peace.

*The Kohanim say:*

רִבּוֹנוֹ Master of the Universe: we have done what You have decreed for us. So too may You deal with us as You have promised us. Look down from Your holy dwelling place, from heaven, and bless Your people Israel and the land You have given us as You promised on oath to our ancestors, a land flowing with milk and honey. *Deut. 26*

---

*If the Priestly Blessing is not said, the following is said by the Leader:*

Our God and God of our fathers, bless us with the threefold blessing in the Torah, written by the hand of Moses Your servant and pronounced by Aaron and his sons the priests, Your holy people, as it is said:

May the Lord bless you and protect you. *Num. 6*

*Cong:* May it be Your will.

May the Lord make His face shine on you and be gracious to you.

*Cong:* May it be Your will.

May the Lord turn His face toward you, and grant you peace.

*Cong:* May it be Your will.

---

*Read the following silently while the* כהנים *chant. Omit on* שבת.

יְהִי רָצוֹן מִלְּפָנֶיךָ, יהוה אֱלֹהַי וֵאלֹהֵי אֲבוֹתַי, שֶׁתַּעֲשֶׂה לְמַעַן קְדֻשַּׁת חֲסָדֶיךָ וְגֹדֶל רַחֲמֶיךָ הַפְּשׁוּטִים, וּלְמַעַן טָהֳרַת שִׁמְךָ הַגָּדוֹל הַגִּבּוֹר וְהַנּוֹרָא, בֶּן עֶשְׂרִים וּשְׁתַּיִם אוֹתִיּוֹת הַיּוֹצֵא מִפְּסוּקִים שֶׁל בִּרְכַּת כֹּהֲנִים הָאֲמוּרָה מִפִּי אַהֲרֹן וּבָנָיו עַם קְדוֹשֶׁךָ, שֶׁתִּהְיֶה קָרוֹב לִי בְּקָרְאִי לָךְ, וְתִשְׁמַע תְּפִלָּתִי נַאֲקָתִי וְאֶנְקָתִי תָּמִיד, כְּשֵׁם שֶׁשָּׁמַעְתָּ אֶנְקַת יַעֲקֹב תְּמִימֶךָ הַנִּקְרָא אִישׁ תָּם. וְתִתֶּן לִי וּלְכָל נַפְשׁוֹת בֵּיתִי מְזוֹנוֹתֵינוּ וּפַרְנָסָתֵנוּ בְּרֶוַח וְלֹא בְצִמְצוּם, בְּהֶתֵּר וְלֹא בְאִסּוּר, בְּנַחַת וְלֹא בְצַעַר, מִתַּחַת יָדְךָ הָרְחָבָה, כְּשֵׁם שֶׁנָּתַתָּ פִּסַּת לֶחֶם לֶאֱכֹל וּבֶגֶד לִלְבֹּשׁ לְיַעֲקֹב אָבִינוּ הַנִּקְרָא אִישׁ תָּם. וְתִתְּנֵנוּ לְאַהֲבָה, לְחֵן וּלְחֶסֶד וּלְרַחֲמִים בְּעֵינֶיךָ וּבְעֵינֵי כָל רוֹאֵינוּ, וְיִהְיוּ דְבָרַי נִשְׁמָעִים לַעֲבוֹדָתֶךָ, כְּשֵׁם שֶׁנָּתַתָּ אֶת יוֹסֵף צַדִּיקֶךָ בְּשָׁעָה שֶׁהִלְבִּישׁוֹ אָבִיו כְּתֹנֶת פַּסִּים לְחֵן וּלְחֶסֶד וּלְרַחֲמִים בְּעֵינֶיךָ וּבְעֵינֵי כָל רוֹאָיו. וְתַעֲשֶׂה עִמִּי נִפְלָאוֹת וְנִסִּים, וּלְטוֹבָה אוֹת, וְתַצְלִיחֵנִי בִּדְרָכַי, וְתֵן בְּלִבִּי בִּינָה לְהָבִין וּלְהַשְׂכִּיל וּלְקַיֵּם אֶת כָּל דִּבְרֵי תַלְמוּד תּוֹרָתֶךָ וְסוֹדוֹתֶיהָ, וְתַצִּילֵנִי מִשְּׁגִיאוֹת, וּתְטַהֵר רַעְיוֹנַי וְלִבִּי לַעֲבוֹדָתֶךָ, וְתַאֲרִיךְ יָמַי (וִימֵי אָבִי וְאִמִּי / וְאִשְׁתִּי / וּבַעְלִי / וּבָנַי וּבְנוֹתַי) בְּטוֹב וּבִנְעִימוֹת, בְּרֹב עֹז וְשָׁלוֹם, אָמֵן סֶלָה.

*The* שליח ציבור *continues with* שִׂים שָׁלוֹם *below.*

*The* קהל *says:*

אַדִּיר בַּמָּרוֹם שׁוֹכֵן בִּגְבוּרָה, אַתָּה שָׁלוֹם וְשִׁמְךָ שָׁלוֹם. יְהִי רָצוֹן שֶׁתָּשִׂים עָלֵינוּ וְעַל כָּל עַמְּךָ בֵּית יִשְׂרָאֵל חַיִּים וּבְרָכָה לְמִשְׁמֶרֶת שָׁלוֹם.

*The* כהנים *say:*

רִבּוֹנוֹ שֶׁל עוֹלָם, עָשִׂינוּ מַה שֶּׁגָּזַרְתָּ עָלֵינוּ, אַף אַתָּה עֲשֵׂה עִמָּנוּ כְּמוֹ שֶׁהִבְטַחְתָּנוּ. הַשְׁקִיפָה מִמְּעוֹן קָדְשְׁךָ מִן־הַשָּׁמַיִם, וּבָרֵךְ אֶת־עַמְּךָ אֶת־יִשְׂרָאֵל, וְאֵת הָאֲדָמָה אֲשֶׁר נָתַתָּה לָנוּ, כַּאֲשֶׁר נִשְׁבַּעְתָּ לַאֲבֹתֵינוּ, אֶרֶץ זָבַת חָלָב וּדְבָשׁ: דברים כו

*If* ברכת כהנים *is not said, the following is said by the* שליח ציבור*:*

אֱלֹהֵינוּ וֵאלֹהֵי אֲבוֹתֵינוּ, בָּרְכֵנוּ בַּבְּרָכָה הַמְשֻׁלֶּשֶׁת בַּתּוֹרָה, הַכְּתוּבָה עַל יְדֵי מֹשֶׁה עַבְדֶּךָ, הָאֲמוּרָה מִפִּי אַהֲרֹן וּבָנָיו כֹּהֲנִים עַם קְדוֹשֶׁיךָ, כָּאָמוּר

במדבר ו
יְבָרֶכְךָ יהוה וְיִשְׁמְרֶךָ: קהל: כֵּן יְהִי רָצוֹן
יָאֵר יהוה פָּנָיו אֵלֶיךָ וִיחֻנֶּךָּ: קהל: כֵּן יְהִי רָצוֹן
יִשָּׂא יהוה פָּנָיו אֵלֶיךָ וְיָשֵׂם לְךָ שָׁלוֹם: קהל: כֵּן יְהִי רָצוֹן

---

**יִשָּׂא יהוה פָּנָיו אֵלֶיךָ** *May the Lord turn His face toward you.* There is a strange and lovely detail in the construction of the Sanctuary. The holiest item of

PEACE

שִׂים שָׁלוֹם Grant peace, goodness and blessing,
life, grace, loving-kindness and compassion
to us and all Israel Your people.
Bless us, our Father, all as one,
with the light of Your face,
for by the light of Your face
You have given us, LORD our God,
the Torah of life and love of kindness,
righteousness, blessing, compassion, life and peace.
May it be good in Your eyes
to bless us and all Your people Israel
at every time, in every hour, with Your peace.

*The congregation then the Leader:*

בְּסֵפֶר חַיִּים In the book of life,
blessing, peace and prosperity,
and good decrees, salvations and consolations
may we and all Your people the house of Israel
be remembered and written before You
for a good life, and for peace.

*The congregation then the Leader:*

וְנֶאֱמַר It is said,
"Through Me your days will grow many, *Prov. 9*
and years of life will be added to your lot."

---

another interpretation, that they were intertwined like lovers (*Yoma* 54a). It was *between the two Cherubs* that God spoke to Moses. The message of this symbol was so significant that it was deemed by God Himself to be sufficient to outweigh the risk of misunderstanding. *God speaks where two persons turn their face to one another* in love, embrace, generosity and care. God's presence is everywhere. But not everywhere are we ready to receive it. When we open our "I" to another's "Thou" – that is where God lives. We discover God's image in ourselves by discerning it in another. God lives in *the between* that joins self to self through an act of covenantal love.

ברכת שלום

שִׂים שָׁלוֹם טוֹבָה וּבְרָכָה
חַיִּים חֵן וָחֶסֶד וְרַחֲמִים
עָלֵינוּ וְעַל כָּל יִשְׂרָאֵל עַמֶּךָ.
בָּרְכֵנוּ אָבִינוּ כֻּלָּנוּ כְּאֶחָד בְּאוֹר פָּנֶיךָ
כִּי בְאוֹר פָּנֶיךָ נָתַתָּ לָּנוּ יהוה אֱלֹהֵינוּ
תּוֹרַת חַיִּים וְאַהֲבַת חֶסֶד
וּצְדָקָה וּבְרָכָה וְרַחֲמִים וְחַיִּים וְשָׁלוֹם.
וְטוֹב יִהְיֶה בְּעֵינֶיךָ לְבָרְכֵנוּ וּלְבָרֵךְ אֶת כָּל עַמְּךָ יִשְׂרָאֵל
בְּכָל עֵת וּבְכָל שָׁעָה בִּשְׁלוֹמֶךָ.

*The* קהל *then the* שליח ציבור*:*

בְּסֵפֶר חַיִּים, בְּרָכָה וְשָׁלוֹם, וּפַרְנָסָה טוֹבָה
וּגְזֵרוֹת טוֹבוֹת, יְשׁוּעוֹת וְנֶחָמוֹת
נִזָּכֵר וְנִכָּתֵב לְפָנֶיךָ
אֲנַחְנוּ וְכָל עַמְּךָ בֵּית יִשְׂרָאֵל לְחַיִּים טוֹבִים וּלְשָׁלוֹם.

*The* קהל *then the* שליח ציבור*:*

וְנֶאֱמַר:
כִּי־בִי יִרְבּוּ יָמֶיךָ, וְיוֹסִיפוּ לְּךָ שְׁנוֹת חַיִּים: משלי ט

---

its furniture was the Ark. It contained the holiest of objects, the tablets on which were written God's word. Above the Ark were two figures, Cherubim. The Torah says that "their faces were turned to one another" (Ex. 25:20). Ostensibly this was a great risk. The Israelites had been told not to make any likeness that might be worshiped as a god, an idol. The Sanctuary itself was constructed in the aftermath of such an episode, the making of the Golden Calf. Why then were figures introduced into the Holy of Holies?

The sages say they were like children (Rashi, based on *Sukka* 5b), or, in

Write us down for good lives, O God of life,
and write us in the book of life.
As is written,
"You who cling to the LORD your God are all alive today." *Deut. 4*

*The Ark is opened by one of the Kohanim.*
*The Leader recites each phrase, and the congregation responds "Amen" and recites the next phrase. The full version of this piyut can be found on page 1074.*

הַיּוֹם This day, may You strengthen us. AMEN
This day, may You bless us. AMEN
This day, may You give us greatness. AMEN
This day, may You deal with us kindly. AMEN
This day, may You hear our cry. AMEN
This day, may You accept our prayers
compassionately and willingly. AMEN
This day, may You support us
with Your hand of righteousness. AMEN

*The Ark is closed.*

*The congregation then the Leader:*

כְּהַיּוֹם Bring us this day, happy, rejoicing, to a House restored,

as is written:
"I shall bring them to My holy mountain, *Is. 56*
and I shall have them rejoice in My house of prayer;
their offerings and their sacrifices
shall be accepted, desired on My altar,
for My House will be called a house of prayer for all peoples."

---

truth. A person who truly wants to repent must say, "It is true that I have sinned, but the past is the past. I will look only toward the future, and from now on I want to repent and return to God with all my heart." Our sages therefore teach us that the word "Now" – "this day" – alludes to repentance.

לְחַיִּים טוֹבִים תִּכְתְּבֵנוּ, אֱלֹהִים חַיִּים, כָּתְבֵנוּ בְּסֵפֶר הַחַיִּים.

כַּכָּתוּב:

וְאַתֶּם הַדְּבֵקִים בַּיהוה אֱלֹהֵיכֶם, חַיִּים כֻּלְּכֶם הַיּוֹם: דברים ד

*The* ארון קודש *is opened by one of the* כהנים.

*The* שליח ציבור *recites each phrase, and the* קהל *responds* אמן *and recites the next phrase.*

*The full version of this piyut can be found on page 1075.*

הַיּוֹם תְּאַמְּצֵנוּ. אָמֵן

הַיּוֹם תְּבָרְכֵנוּ. אָמֵן

הַיּוֹם תְּגַדְּלֵנוּ. אָמֵן

הַיּוֹם תִּדְרְשֵׁנוּ לְטוֹבָה. אָמֵן

הַיּוֹם תִּשְׁמַע שַׁוְעָתֵנוּ. אָמֵן

הַיּוֹם תְּקַבֵּל בְּרַחֲמִים וּבְרָצוֹן אֶת תְּפִלָּתֵנוּ. אָמֵן

הַיּוֹם תִּתְמְכֵנוּ בִּימִין צִדְקֶךָ. אָמֵן

*The* ארון קודש *is closed.*

*The* קהל *then the* שליח ציבור*:*

כְּהַיּוֹם הַזֶּה תְּבִיאֵנוּ, שָׂשִׂים וּשְׂמֵחִים בְּבִנְיַן שָׁלֵם.

כַּכָּתוּב

וַהֲבִיאוֹתִים אֶל־הַר קָדְשִׁי ישעיה נו

וְשִׂמַּחְתִּים בְּבֵית תְּפִלָּתִי

עוֹלֹתֵיהֶם וְזִבְחֵיהֶם לְרָצוֹן עַל־מִזְבְּחִי

כִּי בֵיתִי בֵּית־תְּפִלָּה יִקָּרֵא לְכָל־הָעַמִּים:

---

**הַיּוֹם** *This day.* Said the Maggid of Koznitz: The evil urge comes to a person and says: "How can you repent? You are so filled with sins." This is not the

And it is said,
"And the LORD commanded You Deut. 6
to perform all these statutes,
to fear the LORD our God,
that it may be good for us all our days;
to give us life as on this day."

And it is said,
"Righteousness will be in our hands, Ibid.
when we take care to fulfill all these commands
before the LORD our God,
as He has commanded."

Righteousness and blessing, compassion and life and peace –
may these be with us and with all Israel, forever.

*The Leader concludes:*
Blessed are You, LORD, who blesses His people Israel with peace.

*The following verse concludes the Leader's Repetition of the Amida. See law 64.*
May the words of my mouth and the meditation of my heart Ps. 19
find favor before You, LORD, my Rock and Redeemer.

---

to prosper our goal with hope and with future,
to appoint us a share in the garden of Eden,
to direct us in Your world
through good companions and good impulse,
that we may rise in the morning and find
our heart awake to fear Your name. (*Berakhot* 16b)

וְנֶאֱמַר
דברים ו
וַיְצַוֵּנוּ יהוה לַעֲשׂוֹת אֶת־כָּל־הַחֻקִּים הָאֵלֶּה
לְיִרְאָה אֶת־יהוה אֱלֹהֵינוּ
לְטוֹב לָנוּ כָּל־הַיָּמִים לְחַיֹּתֵנוּ כְּהַיּוֹם הַזֶּה:

וְנֶאֱמַר
שם
וּצְדָקָה תִּהְיֶה־לָּנוּ
כִּי־נִשְׁמֹר לַעֲשׂוֹת אֶת־כָּל־הַמִּצְוָה הַזֹּאת
לִפְנֵי יהוה אֱלֹהֵינוּ, כַּאֲשֶׁר צִוָּנוּ:

וּצְדָקָה וּבְרָכָה וְרַחֲמִים וְחַיִּים וְשָׁלוֹם
יִהְיֶה לָנוּ וּלְכָל יִשְׂרָאֵל עַד הָעוֹלָם.

*The* שליח ציבור *concludes:*

בָּרוּךְ אַתָּה יהוה, הַמְבָרֵךְ אֶת עַמּוֹ יִשְׂרָאֵל בַּשָּׁלוֹם.

*The following verse concludes the* חזרת הש״ץ. *See law 64.*

תהלים יט
יִהְיוּ לְרָצוֹן אִמְרֵי־פִי וְהֶגְיוֹן לִבִּי לְפָנֶיךָ, יהוה צוּרִי וְגֹאֲלִי:

---

הַמְבָרֵךְ אֶת עַמּוֹ יִשְׂרָאֵל בַּשָּׁלוֹם *who blesses His people Israel with peace.* Rabbi Elazar used to pray:

May it be Your will, O Lord our God,
to cause to dwell in our lot
love, fellowship, peace and friendship,
to widen our boundaries through disciples,

*The most common custom is to sound ten notes in the middle of Full Kaddish, before "May the prayers...", in order to complete one hundred notes (see law 81). Congregations who did not blew the shofar during the silent Amida ,blow forty additional notes; some sound all forty before "May the prayers...", and others sound thirty notes after ,Full Kaddish and ten more before the concluding Aleinu .*

*On Shabbat, the shofar is not sounded.*

## FULL KADDISH

*Leader:* יִתְגַּדַּל Magnified and sanctified may His great name be,
in the world He created by His will.
May He establish His kingdom,
make His salvation flourish,
and hasten His messiah,
in your lifetime and in your days,
and in the lifetime of all the house of Israel,
swiftly and soon – and say: Amen.

*All:* May His great name be blessed for ever and all time.

*Leader:* Blessed and praised, glorified and exalted,
raised and honored, uplifted and lauded be
the name of the Holy One,
blessed be He,
beyond any blessing, song, praise and consolation
uttered in the world – and say: Amen.

TEKIA SHEVARIM TERUA TEKIA

TEKIA SHEVARIM TEKIA

TEKIA TERUA TEKIA GEDOLA

May the prayers and pleas of all the house of Israel
be accepted by their Father in heaven – and say: Amen.

May there be great peace from heaven,
and a good life for us and all Israel – and say: Amen.

*Bow, take three steps back, as if taking leave of the Divine Presence, then bow, first left, then right, then center, while saying:*

May He who makes peace in His high places,
make peace for us and all Israel – and say: Amen.

*The most common custom is to sound ten notes in the middle of קדיש שלם, before תתקבל, in order to complete one hundred notes (see law 81).*

*Congregations who did not blew the שופר during the silent עמידה, blow forty additional notes; some sound all forty before תתקבל, and others sound thirty notes after קדיש שלם and ten more before the concluding עָלֵינוּ. On שבת, the שופר is not sounded.*

## קדיש שלם

ש״ץ: יִתְגַּדַּל וְיִתְקַדַּשׁ שְׁמֵהּ רַבָּא (קהל: אָמֵן)
בְּעָלְמָא דִּי בְרָא כִרְעוּתֵהּ
וְיַמְלִיךְ מַלְכוּתֵהּ וְיַצְמַח פֻּרְקָנֵהּ וִיקָרֵב מְשִׁיחֵהּ (קהל: אָמֵן)
בְּחַיֵּיכוֹן וּבְיוֹמֵיכוֹן וּבְחַיֵּי דְכָל בֵּית יִשְׂרָאֵל
בַּעֲגָלָא וּבִזְמַן קָרִיב, וְאִמְרוּ אָמֵן. (קהל: אָמֵן)

קהל וש״ץ: יְהֵא שְׁמֵהּ רַבָּא מְבָרַךְ לְעָלַם וּלְעָלְמֵי עָלְמַיָּא.

ש״ץ: יִתְבָּרַךְ וְיִשְׁתַּבַּח וְיִתְפָּאַר וְיִתְרוֹמַם וְיִתְנַשֵּׂא
וְיִתְהַדָּר וְיִתְעַלֶּה וְיִתְהַלָּל
שְׁמֵהּ דְּקֻדְשָׁא בְּרִיךְ הוּא (קהל: אָמֵן)
לְעֵלָּא לְעֵלָּא מִכָּל בִּרְכָתָא וְשִׁירָתָא, תֻּשְׁבְּחָתָא וְנֶחֱמָתָא
דַּאֲמִירָן בְּעָלְמָא, וְאִמְרוּ אָמֵן. (קהל: אָמֵן)

תקיעה שברים תרועה תקיעה
תקיעה שברים תקיעה
תקיעה תרועה תקיעה גדולה

תִּתְקַבַּל צְלוֹתְהוֹן וּבָעוּתְהוֹן דְּכָל בֵּית יִשְׂרָאֵל
קֳדָם אֲבוּהוֹן דִּי בִשְׁמַיָּא, וְאִמְרוּ אָמֵן. (קהל: אָמֵן)

יְהֵא שְׁלָמָא רַבָּא מִן שְׁמַיָּא
וְחַיִּים טוֹבִים עָלֵינוּ וְעַל כָּל יִשְׂרָאֵל, וְאִמְרוּ אָמֵן. (קהל: אָמֵן)

*Bow, take three steps back, as if taking leave of the Divine Presence, then bow, first left, then right, then center, while saying:*

עֹשֶׂה הַשָּׁלוֹם בִּמְרוֹמָיו, הוּא יַעֲשֶׂה שָׁלוֹם עָלֵינוּ
וְעַל כָּל יִשְׂרָאֵל, וְאִמְרוּ אָמֵן. (קהל: אָמֵן)

קַוֵּה Hope in the LORD. Be strong and of good courage, *Ps. 27*
and hope in the LORD!
There is no other one holy like the LORD, *I Sam. 2*
for there is none besides You, there is no Rock like our God.
For who but the LORD is God; who is a Rock apart from our God? *Ps. 18*

אֵין כֵּאלֹהֵינוּ There is none like our God, none like our LORD,
none like our King, none like our Savior.
Who is like our God? Who is like our LORD?
Who is like our King? Who is like our Savior?
We will thank our God, we will thank our LORD,
we will thank our King, we will thank our Savior.
Blessed is our God, blessed is our LORD,
blessed is our King, blessed is our Savior.
You are our God, You are our LORD,
You are our King, You are our Savior.
You are He to whom our ancestors offered the fragrant incense.

פִּטּוּם הַקְּטֹרֶת The incense mixture consisted of balsam, onycha, galbanum and frankincense, each weighing seventy manehs; myrrh, cassia, spikenard and saffron, each weighing sixteen manehs; twelve manehs of costus, three of aromatic bark; nine of cinnamon; nine kabs of Carsina lye; three seahs and three kabs of Cyprus wine. If Cyprus wine was not available, old white wine might be used. A quarter of a kab of Sodom salt, and a minute amount of a smoke-raising herb. Rabbi Nathan says: Also a minute amount of Jordan amber. If one added honey to the mixture, he rendered it unfit for sacred use. If he omitted any one of its ingredients, he is guilty of a capital offense. *Keritot 6a*

Rabban Shimon ben Gamliel says: "Balsam" refers to the sap that drips from the balsam tree. The Carsina lye was used for bleaching the onycha to improve it. The Cyprus wine was used to soak the onycha in it to make it pungent. Though urine is suitable for this purpose, it is not brought into the Temple out of respect.

These were the psalms which the Levites used to recite in the Temple: *Mishna, Tamid 7*
On the first day of the week they used to say: "The earth is the LORD's *Ps. 24*
and all it contains, the world and all who live in it."
On the second day they used to say: "Great is the LORD and *Ps. 48*
greatly to be praised in the city of God, on His holy mountain."

קַוֵּה אֶל־יהוה, חֲזַק וְיַאֲמֵץ לִבֶּךָ, וְקַוֵּה אֶל־יהוה: תהלים כז
אֵין־קָדוֹשׁ כַּיהוה, כִּי־אֵין בִּלְתֶּךָ, וְאֵין צוּר כֵּאלֹהֵינוּ: שמואל א׳ ב
כִּי מִי אֱלוֹהַּ מִבַּלְעֲדֵי יהוה, וּמִי צוּר זוּלָתִי אֱלֹהֵינוּ: תהלים יח

אֵין כֵּאלֹהֵינוּ, אֵין כַּאדוֹנֵינוּ, אֵין כְּמַלְכֵּנוּ, אֵין כְּמוֹשִׁיעֵנוּ.
מִי כֵאלֹהֵינוּ, מִי כַאדוֹנֵינוּ, מִי כְמַלְכֵּנוּ, מִי כְמוֹשִׁיעֵנוּ.
נוֹדֶה לֵאלֹהֵינוּ, נוֹדֶה לַאדוֹנֵינוּ, נוֹדֶה לְמַלְכֵּנוּ, נוֹדֶה לְמוֹשִׁיעֵנוּ.
בָּרוּךְ אֱלֹהֵינוּ, בָּרוּךְ אֲדוֹנֵינוּ, בָּרוּךְ מַלְכֵּנוּ, בָּרוּךְ מוֹשִׁיעֵנוּ.
אַתָּה הוּא אֱלֹהֵינוּ, אַתָּה הוּא אֲדוֹנֵינוּ
אַתָּה הוּא מַלְכֵּנוּ, אַתָּה הוּא מוֹשִׁיעֵנוּ.
אַתָּה הוּא שֶׁהִקְטִירוּ אֲבוֹתֵינוּ לְפָנֶיךָ אֶת קְטֹרֶת הַסַּמִּים.

כריתות ו. פִּטּוּם הַקְּטֹרֶת. הַצֳּרִי, וְהַצִּפֹּרֶן, וְהַחֶלְבְּנָה, וְהַלְּבוֹנָה מִשְׁקַל שִׁבְעִים שִׁבְעִים מָנֶה, מֹר, וּקְצִיעָה, שִׁבֹּלֶת נֵרְדְּ, וְכַרְכֹּם מִשְׁקַל שִׁשָּׁה עָשָׂר שִׁשָּׁה עָשָׂר מָנֶה, הַקֹּשְׁטְ שְׁנֵים עָשָׂר, קִלּוּפָה שְׁלֹשָׁה, וְקִנָּמוֹן תִּשְׁעָה, בֹּרִית כַּרְשִׁינָה תִּשְׁעָה קַבִּין, יֵין קַפְרִיסִין סְאִין תְּלָת וְקַבִּין תְּלָתָא וְאִם אֵין לוֹ יֵין קַפְרִיסִין, מֵבִיא חֲמַר חִוַּרְיָן עַתִּיק. מֶלַח סְדוֹמִית רֹבַע, מַעֲלֶה עָשָׁן כָּל שֶׁהוּא. רַבִּי נָתָן הַבַּבְלִי אוֹמֵר: אַף כִּפַּת הַיַּרְדֵּן כָּל שֶׁהוּא, וְאִם נָתַן בָּהּ דְּבַשׁ פְּסָלָהּ, וְאִם חִסַּר אֶחָד מִכָּל סַמָּנֶיהָ, חַיָּב מִיתָה.

רַבָּן שִׁמְעוֹן בֶּן גַּמְלִיאֵל אוֹמֵר: הַצֳּרִי אֵינוֹ אֶלָּא שְׂרָף הַנּוֹטֵף מֵעֲצֵי הַקְּטָף. בֹּרִית כַּרְשִׁינָה שֶׁשָּׁפִין בָּהּ אֶת הַצִּפֹּרֶן כְּדֵי שֶׁתְּהֵא נָאָה, יֵין קַפְרִיסִין שֶׁשּׁוֹרִין בּוֹ אֶת הַצִּפֹּרֶן כְּדֵי שֶׁתְּהֵא עַזָּה, וַהֲלֹא מֵי רַגְלַיִם יָפִין לָהּ, אֶלָּא שֶׁאֵין מַכְנִיסִין מֵי רַגְלַיִם בַּמִּקְדָּשׁ מִפְּנֵי הַכָּבוֹד.

משנה תמיד ז הַשִּׁיר שֶׁהַלְוִיִּם הָיוּ אוֹמְרִים בְּבֵית הַמִּקְדָּשׁ:
תהלים כד בַּיּוֹם הָרִאשׁוֹן הָיוּ אוֹמְרִים, לַיהוה הָאָרֶץ וּמְלוֹאָהּ, תֵּבֵל וְיֹשְׁבֵי בָהּ:
תהלים מח בַּשֵּׁנִי הָיוּ אוֹמְרִים, גָּדוֹל יהוה וּמְהֻלָּל מְאֹד, בְּעִיר אֱלֹהֵינוּ הַר־קָדְשׁוֹ:

On the third day they used to say: "God stands in the divine assembly. *Ps. 82*
Among the judges He delivers judgment."
On the fourth day they used to say: "God of retribution, LORD, *Ps. 94*
God of retribution, appear."
On the fifth day they used to say: "Sing for joy to God, our strength. *Ps. 81*
Shout aloud to the God of Jacob."
On the sixth day they used to say: "The LORD reigns: He is robed in majesty; *Ps. 93*
the LORD is robed, girded with strength;
the world is firmly established; it cannot be moved."
On the Sabbath they used to say: "A psalm, a song for the Sabbath day" – *Ps. 92*
[meaning] a psalm and song for the time to come,
for the day which will be entirely Sabbath and rest for life everlasting.

It was taught in the Academy of Elijah: Whoever studies [Torah] laws every day *Megilla 28b*
is assured that he will be destined for the World to Come, as it is said,
"The ways of the world are His" – read not, "ways" [*halikhot*] but "laws" [*halakhot*]. *Hab. 3*
Rabbi Elazar said in the name of Rabbi Ḥanina: The disciples of the sages increase *Berakhot 64a*
peace in the world, as it is said, "And all your children shall be taught of the LORD, *Is. 54*
and great shall be the peace of your children [*banayikh*]." Read not *banayikh*,
"your children," but *bonayikh*, "your builders." Those who love Your Torah have *Ps. 119*
great peace; there is no stumbling block for them. May there be peace within your *Ps. 122*
ramparts, prosperity in your palaces. For the sake of my brothers and friends, I
shall say, "Peace be within you." For the sake of the House of the LORD our God,
I will seek your good. ▸ May the LORD grant strength to His people; may the *Ps. 29*
LORD bless His people with peace.

## THE RABBIS' KADDISH

*The following prayer requires the presence of a minyan.*
*A transliteration can be found on page 1094.*

*Mourner:* יִתְגַּדַּל Magnified and sanctified may His great name be,
in the world He created by His will.
May He establish His kingdom,
make His salvation flourish,
and hasten His messiah,
in your lifetime and in your days,
and in the lifetime of all the house of Israel,
swiftly and soon – and say: Amen.

בִּשְׁלִישִׁי הָיוּ אוֹמְרִים, אֱלֹהִים נִצָּב בַּעֲדַת־אֵל, בְּקֶרֶב אֱלֹהִים יִשְׁפֹּט: תהלים פב
בָּרְבִיעִי הָיוּ אוֹמְרִים, אֵל־נְקָמוֹת יהוה, אֵל נְקָמוֹת הוֹפִיעַ: תהלים צד
בַּחֲמִישִׁי הָיוּ אוֹמְרִים, הַרְנִינוּ לֵאלֹהִים עוּזֵּנוּ, הָרִיעוּ לֵאלֹהֵי יַעֲקֹב: תהלים פא
בַּשִּׁשִּׁי הָיוּ אוֹמְרִים, יהוה מָלָךְ גֵּאוּת לָבֵשׁ, לָבֵשׁ יהוה עֹז הִתְאַזָּר תהלים צג
אַף־תִּכּוֹן תֵּבֵל בַּל־תִּמּוֹט:
בַּשַּׁבָּת הָיוּ אוֹמְרִים, מִזְמוֹר שִׁיר לְיוֹם הַשַּׁבָּת: תהלים צב
מִזְמוֹר שִׁיר לֶעָתִיד לָבוֹא, לְיוֹם שֶׁכֻּלּוֹ שַׁבָּת וּמְנוּחָה
לְחַיֵּי הָעוֹלָמִים.

תָּנָא דְבֵי אֵלִיָּהוּ: כָּל הַשּׁוֹנֶה הֲלָכוֹת בְּכָל יוֹם, מֻבְטָח לוֹ שֶׁהוּא בֶּן עוֹלָם מגילה כח:
הַבָּא, שֶׁנֶּאֱמַר, הֲלִיכוֹת עוֹלָם לוֹ: אַל תִּקְרֵי הֲלִיכוֹת אֶלָּא הֲלָכוֹת. חבקוק ג

אָמַר רַבִּי אֶלְעָזָר, אָמַר רַבִּי חֲנִינָא: תַּלְמִידֵי חֲכָמִים מַרְבִּים שָׁלוֹם בָּעוֹלָם, ברכות סד.
שֶׁנֶּאֱמַר, וְכָל־בָּנַיִךְ לִמּוּדֵי יהוה, וְרַב שְׁלוֹם בָּנָיִךְ: אַל תִּקְרֵי בָּנָיִךְ, אֶלָּא ישעיה נד
בּוֹנָיִךְ. שָׁלוֹם רָב לְאֹהֲבֵי תוֹרָתֶךָ, וְאֵין־לָמוֹ מִכְשׁוֹל: יְהִי־שָׁלוֹם בְּחֵילֵךְ, תהלים קיט תהלים קכב
שַׁלְוָה בְּאַרְמְנוֹתָיִךְ: לְמַעַן אַחַי וְרֵעָי אֲדַבְּרָה־נָּא שָׁלוֹם בָּךְ: לְמַעַן
בֵּית־יהוה אֱלֹהֵינוּ אֲבַקְשָׁה טוֹב לָךְ: ◂ יהוה עֹז לְעַמּוֹ יִתֵּן, יהוה יְבָרֵךְ תהלים כט
אֶת־עַמּוֹ בַשָּׁלוֹם:

## קדיש דרבנן

*The following prayer, said by mourners, requires the presence of a* מנין*.*
*A transliteration can be found on page 1094.*

יִתְגַּדַּל וְיִתְקַדַּשׁ שְׁמֵהּ רַבָּא (קהל: אָמֵן)
בְּעָלְמָא דִּי בְרָא כִרְעוּתֵהּ
וְיַמְלִיךְ מַלְכוּתֵהּ וְיַצְמַח פֻּרְקָנֵהּ וִיקָרֵב מְשִׁיחֵהּ (קהל: אָמֵן)
בְּחַיֵּיכוֹן וּבְיוֹמֵיכוֹן וּבְחַיֵּי דְכָל בֵּית יִשְׂרָאֵל
בַּעֲגָלָא וּבִזְמַן קָרִיב
וְאִמְרוּ אָמֵן. (קהל: אָמֵן)

קהל ואבל: יְהֵא שְׁמֵהּ רַבָּא מְבָרַךְ לְעָלַם וּלְעָלְמֵי עָלְמַיָּא.

אבל: יִתְבָּרַךְ וְיִשְׁתַּבַּח וְיִתְפָּאַר וְיִתְרוֹמַם וְיִתְנַשֵּׂא
וְיִתְהַדָּר וְיִתְעַלֶּה וְיִתְהַלָּל
שְׁמֵהּ דְּקֻדְשָׁא בְּרִיךְ הוּא (קהל: אָמֵן)
לְעֵלָּא לְעֵלָּא מִכָּל בִּרְכָתָא וְשִׁירָתָא, תֻּשְׁבְּחָתָא וְנֶחֱמָתָא
דַּאֲמִירָן בְּעָלְמָא
וְאִמְרוּ אָמֵן. (קהל: אָמֵן)

עַל יִשְׂרָאֵל וְעַל רַבָּנָן
וְעַל תַּלְמִידֵיהוֹן וְעַל כָּל תַּלְמִידֵי תַלְמִידֵיהוֹן
וְעַל כָּל מָאן דְּעָסְקִין בְּאוֹרַיְתָא
דִּי בְּאַתְרָא (בארץ ישראל: קַדִּישָׁא) הָדֵין, וְדִי בְּכָל אֲתַר וַאֲתַר
יְהֵא לְהוֹן וּלְכוֹן שְׁלָמָא רַבָּא
חִנָּא וְחִסְדָּא, וְרַחֲמֵי, וְחַיֵּי אֲרִיכֵי, וּמְזוֹנֵי רְוִיחֵי
וּפֻרְקָנָא מִן קֳדָם אֲבוּהוֹן
דִּי בִשְׁמַיָּא וְאַרְעָא
וְאִמְרוּ אָמֵן. (קהל: אָמֵן)

יְהֵא שְׁלָמָא רַבָּא מִן שְׁמַיָּא
וְחַיִּים טוֹבִים עָלֵינוּ וְעַל כָּל יִשְׂרָאֵל
וְאִמְרוּ אָמֵן. (קהל: אָמֵן)

*Bow, take three steps back, as if taking leave of the Divine Presence, then bow, first left, then right, then center, while saying:*

עֹשֶׂה הַשָּׁלוֹם בִּמְרוֹמָיו
הוּא בְּרַחֲמָיו יַעֲשֶׂה שָׁלוֹם עָלֵינוּ וְעַל כָּל יִשְׂרָאֵל
וְאִמְרוּ אָמֵן. (קהל: אָמֵן)

*Stand while saying Aleinu. Bow at ▼.*

עָלֵינוּ It is our duty to praise the Master of all,
and ascribe greatness to the Author of creation,
who has not made us like the nations of the lands
nor placed us like the families of the earth;
who has not made our portion like theirs,
nor our destiny like all their multitudes.
(For they worship vanity and emptiness,
and pray to a god who cannot save.)
▼But we bow in worship
and thank the Supreme King of kings, the Holy One, blessed be He,
who extends the heavens and establishes the earth,
whose throne of glory is in the heavens above,
and whose power's Presence is in the highest of heights.
He is our God; there is no other.
Truly He is our King, there is none else, as it is written in His Torah:
"You shall know and take to heart this day *Deut. 4*
that the LORD is God, in the heavens above and on the earth below.
There is no other."

Therefore, we place our hope in You, LORD our God,
that we may soon see the glory of Your power,
when You will remove abominations from the earth,
and idols will be utterly destroyed,
when the world will be perfected under the sovereignty of the Almighty,
when all humanity will call on Your name,
to turn all the earth's wicked toward You.
All the world's inhabitants will realize and know
that to You every knee must bow and every tongue swear loyalty.
Before You, LORD our God, they will kneel and bow down
and give honor to Your glorious name.
They will all accept the yoke of Your kingdom,
and You will reign over them soon and for ever.
For the kingdom is Yours, and to all eternity You will reign in glory,
as it is written in Your Torah: "The LORD will reign for ever and ever." *Ex. 15*
▸ And it is said: "Then the LORD shall be King over all the earth; *Zech. 14*
on that day the LORD shall be One and His name One."

*Stand while saying* עָלֵינוּ. *Bow at* ’.

עָלֵינוּ לְשַׁבֵּחַ לַאֲדוֹן הַכֹּל, לָתֵת גְּדֻלָּה לְיוֹצֵר בְּרֵאשִׁית
שֶׁלֹּא עָשָׂנוּ כְּגוֹיֵי הָאֲרָצוֹת, וְלֹא שָׂמָנוּ כְּמִשְׁפְּחוֹת הָאֲדָמָה
שֶׁלֹּא שָׂם חֶלְקֵנוּ כָּהֶם וְגוֹרָלֵנוּ כְּכָל הֲמוֹנָם.
(שֶׁהֵם מִשְׁתַּחֲוִים לְהֶבֶל וָרִיק וּמִתְפַּלְלִים אֶל אֵל לֹא יוֹשִׁיעַ.)
’וַאֲנַחְנוּ כּוֹרְעִים וּמִשְׁתַּחֲוִים וּמוֹדִים
לִפְנֵי מֶלֶךְ מַלְכֵי הַמְּלָכִים, הַקָּדוֹשׁ בָּרוּךְ הוּא
שֶׁהוּא נוֹטֶה שָׁמַיִם וְיוֹסֵד אָרֶץ, וּמוֹשַׁב יְקָרוֹ בַּשָּׁמַיִם מִמַּעַל
וּשְׁכִינַת עֻזּוֹ בְּגָבְהֵי מְרוֹמִים.
הוּא אֱלֹהֵינוּ, אֵין עוֹד.
אֱמֶת מַלְכֵּנוּ, אֶפֶס זוּלָתוֹ כַּכָּתוּב בְּתוֹרָתוֹ
וְיָדַעְתָּ הַיּוֹם וַהֲשֵׁבֹתָ אֶל־לְבָבֶךָ דברים ד
כִּי יהוה הוּא הָאֱלֹהִים בַּשָּׁמַיִם מִמַּעַל וְעַל־הָאָרֶץ מִתָּחַת, אֵין עוֹד:

וְעַל כֵּן נְקַוֶּה לְּךָ יהוה אֱלֹהֵינוּ, לִרְאוֹת מְהֵרָה בְּתִפְאֶרֶת עֻזֶּךָ
לְהַעֲבִיר גִּלּוּלִים מִן הָאָרֶץ, וְהָאֱלִילִים כָּרוֹת יִכָּרֵתוּן
לְתַקֵּן עוֹלָם בְּמַלְכוּת שַׁדַּי.
וְכָל בְּנֵי בָשָׂר יִקְרְאוּ בִשְׁמֶךָ לְהַפְנוֹת אֵלֶיךָ כָּל רִשְׁעֵי אָרֶץ.
יַכִּירוּ וְיֵדְעוּ כָּל יוֹשְׁבֵי תֵבֵל
כִּי לְךָ תִּכְרַע כָּל בֶּרֶךְ, תִּשָּׁבַע כָּל לָשׁוֹן.
לְפָנֶיךָ יהוה אֱלֹהֵינוּ יִכְרְעוּ וְיִפֹּלוּ, וְלִכְבוֹד שִׁמְךָ יְקָר יִתֵּנוּ
וִיקַבְּלוּ כֻלָּם אֶת עֹל מַלְכוּתֶךָ
וְתִמְלֹךְ עֲלֵיהֶם מְהֵרָה לְעוֹלָם וָעֶד.
כִּי הַמַּלְכוּת שֶׁלְּךָ הִיא וּלְעוֹלְמֵי עַד תִּמְלֹךְ בְּכָבוֹד
כַּכָּתוּב בְּתוֹרָתֶךָ, יהוה יִמְלֹךְ לְעֹלָם וָעֶד: שמות טו
◄ וְנֶאֱמַר, וְהָיָה יהוה לְמֶלֶךְ עַל־כָּל־הָאָרֶץ זכריה יד
בַּיּוֹם הַהוּא יִהְיֶה יהוה אֶחָד וּשְׁמוֹ אֶחָד:

*Some add:*

Have no fear of sudden terror or of the ruin when it overtakes the wicked. *Prov. 3*
Devise your strategy, but it will be thwarted; propose your plan, *Is. 8*
but it will not stand, for God is with us.
When you grow old, I will still be the same. *Is. 46*
When your hair turns gray, I will still carry you.
I made you, I will bear you, I will carry you, and I will rescue you.

## MOURNER'S KADDISH

*The following prayer, said by mourners, requires the presence of a minyan.*
*A transliteration can be found on page 1095.*

*Mourner:* יִתְגַּדַּל Magnified and sanctified may His great name be,
in the world He created by His will.
May He establish His kingdom,
make His salvation flourish, and hasten His messiah,
in your lifetime and in your days,
and in the lifetime of all the house of Israel,
swiftly and soon –
and say: Amen.

*All:* May His great name be blessed for ever and all time.

*Mourner:* Blessed and praised, glorified and exalted,
raised and honored, uplifted and lauded
be the name of the Holy One,
blessed be He,
beyond any blessing, song, praise and consolation
uttered in the world –
and say: Amen.

May there be great peace from heaven,
and a good life for us and all Israel –
and say: Amen.

*Bow, take three steps back, as if taking leave of the Divine Presence,*
*then bow, first left, then right, then center, while saying:*

May He who makes peace in His high places,
make peace for us and all Israel –
and say: Amen.

*Some add:*

משלי ג אַל־תִּירָא מִפַּחַד פִּתְאֹם וּמִשֹּׁאַת רְשָׁעִים כִּי תָבֹא:

ישעיה ח עֻצוּ עֵצָה וְתֻפָר, דַּבְּרוּ דָבָר וְלֹא יָקוּם, כִּי עִמָּנוּ אֵל:

ישעיה מו וְעַד־זִקְנָה אֲנִי הוּא, וְעַד־שֵׂיבָה אֲנִי אֶסְבֹּל
אֲנִי עָשִׂיתִי וַאֲנִי אֶשָּׂא וַאֲנִי אֶסְבֹּל וַאֲמַלֵּט:

## קדיש יתום

*The following prayer, said by mourners, requires the presence of a* מנין.
*A transliteration can be found on page 1095.*

אבל: יִתְגַּדַּל וְיִתְקַדַּשׁ שְׁמֵהּ רַבָּא (קהל: אָמֵן)
בְּעָלְמָא דִּי בְרָא כִרְעוּתֵהּ
וְיַמְלִיךְ מַלְכוּתֵהּ
וְיַצְמַח פֻּרְקָנֵהּ וִיקָרֵב מְשִׁיחֵהּ (קהל: אָמֵן)
בְּחַיֵּיכוֹן וּבְיוֹמֵיכוֹן וּבְחַיֵּי דְכָל בֵּית יִשְׂרָאֵל
בַּעֲגָלָא וּבִזְמַן קָרִיב, וְאִמְרוּ אָמֵן. (קהל: אָמֵן)

קהל ואבל: יְהֵא שְׁמֵהּ רַבָּא מְבָרַךְ לְעָלַם וּלְעָלְמֵי עָלְמַיָּא.

אבל: יִתְבָּרַךְ וְיִשְׁתַּבַּח וְיִתְפָּאַר
וְיִתְרוֹמַם וְיִתְנַשֵּׂא וְיִתְהַדָּר וְיִתְעַלֶּה וְיִתְהַלָּל
שְׁמֵהּ דְּקֻדְשָׁא בְּרִיךְ הוּא (קהל: אָמֵן)
לְעֵלָּא לְעֵלָּא מִכָּל בִּרְכָתָא
וְשִׁירָתָא, תֻּשְׁבְּחָתָא וְנֶחֱמָתָא
דַּאֲמִירָן בְּעָלְמָא, וְאִמְרוּ אָמֵן. (קהל: אָמֵן)

יְהֵא שְׁלָמָא רַבָּא מִן שְׁמַיָּא
וְחַיִּים טוֹבִים עָלֵינוּ וְעַל כָּל יִשְׂרָאֵל, וְאִמְרוּ אָמֵן. (קהל: אָמֵן)

*Bow, take three steps back, as if taking leave of the Divine Presence, then bow, first left, then right, then center, while saying:*

עֹשֶׂה הַשָּׁלוֹם בִּמְרוֹמָיו, הוּא יַעֲשֶׂה שָׁלוֹם עָלֵינוּ
וְעַל כָּל יִשְׂרָאֵל, וְאִמְרוּ אָמֵן. (קהל: אָמֵן)

## SONG OF GLORY

*The Ark is opened and all stand.*

*Leader:* I will sing sweet psalms and I will weave songs,
to You for whom my soul longs.

*Cong:* My soul yearns for the shelter of Your hand,
that all Your mystic secrets I might understand.

*Leader:* Whenever I speak of Your glory above,
my heart is yearning for Your love.

*Cong:* So Your glories I will proclaim,
and in songs of love give honor to Your name.

*Leader:* I will tell of Your glory though I have not seen You;
imagine and describe You, though I have not known You.

*Cong:* By the hand of Your prophets, through Your servants' mystery,
You gave a glimpse of Your wondrous majesty.

*Leader:* Recounting Your grandeur and Your glory,
of Your great deeds they told the story.

*Cong:* They depicted You, though not as You are,
but as You do: Your acts, Your power.

*Leader:* They represented You in many visions;
through them all You are One without divisions.

*Cong:* They saw You, now old, then young,
Your head with gray, with black hair hung.

*Leader:* Aged on the day of judgment, yet on the day of war,
a young warrior with mighty hands they saw.

*Cong:* Triumph like a helmet He wore on His head;
His right hand and holy arm to victory have led.

*Leader:* His curls are filled with dew drops of light,
His locks with fragments of the night.

*Cong:* He will glory in me, for He delights in me;
My diadem of beauty He shall be.

*Leader:* His head is like pure beaten gold;
Engraved on His brow, His sacred name behold.

*Cong:* For grace and glory, beauty and renown,
His people have adorned Him with a crown.

# שיר הכבוד

*The* ארון קודש *is opened and all stand.*

ש״ץ: אַנְעִים זְמִירוֹת וְשִׁירִים אֶאֱרֹג, כִּי אֵלֶיךָ נַפְשִׁי תַעֲרֹג.
קהל: נַפְשִׁי חָמְדָה בְּצֵל יָדֶךָ, לָדַעַת כָּל רָז סוֹדֶךָ.

ש״ץ: מִדֵּי דַבְּרִי בִּכְבוֹדֶךָ, הוֹמֶה לִבִּי אֶל דּוֹדֶיךָ.
קהל: עַל כֵּן אֲדַבֵּר בְּךָ נִכְבָּדוֹת, וְשִׁמְךָ אֲכַבֵּד בְּשִׁירֵי יְדִידוֹת.

ש״ץ: אֲסַפְּרָה כְבוֹדְךָ וְלֹא רְאִיתִיךָ, אֲדַמְּךָ אֲכַנְּךָ וְלֹא יְדַעְתִּיךָ.
קהל: בְּיַד נְבִיאֶיךָ בְּסוֹד עֲבָדֶיךָ, דִּמִּיתָ הֲדַר כְּבוֹד הוֹדֶךָ.

ש״ץ: גְּדֻלָּתְךָ וּגְבוּרָתֶךָ, כִּנּוּ לְתֹקֶף פְּעֻלָּתֶךָ.
קהל: דִּמּוּ אוֹתְךָ וְלֹא כְּפִי יֶשְׁךָ, וַיְשַׁוּוּךָ לְפִי מַעֲשֶׂיךָ.

ש״ץ: הִמְשִׁילוּךָ בְּרֹב חֶזְיוֹנוֹת, הִנְּךָ אֶחָד בְּכָל דִּמְיוֹנוֹת.
קהל: וַיֶּחֱזוּ בְךָ זִקְנָה וּבַחֲרוּת, וּשְׂעַר רֹאשְׁךָ בְּשֵׂיבָה וְשַׁחֲרוּת.

ש״ץ: זִקְנָה בְּיוֹם דִּין וּבַחֲרוּת בְּיוֹם קְרָב, כְּאִישׁ מִלְחָמוֹת יָדָיו לוֹ רָב.
קהל: חָבַשׁ כּוֹבַע יְשׁוּעָה בְּרֹאשׁוֹ, הוֹשִׁיעָה לּוֹ יְמִינוֹ וּזְרוֹעַ קָדְשׁוֹ.

ש״ץ: טַלְלֵי אוֹרוֹת רֹאשׁוֹ נִמְלָא, קְוֻצּוֹתָיו רְסִיסֵי לָיְלָה.
קהל: יִתְפָּאֵר בִּי כִּי חָפֵץ בִּי, וְהוּא יִהְיֶה לִּי לַעֲטֶרֶת צְבִי.

ש״ץ: כֶּתֶם טָהוֹר פָּז דְּמוּת רֹאשׁוֹ, וְחַק עַל מֵצַח כְּבוֹד שֵׁם קָדְשׁוֹ.
קהל: לְחֵן וּלְכָבוֹד צְבִי תִפְאָרָה, אֻמָּתוֹ לוֹ עִטְּרָה עֲטָרָה.

---

ANIM ZEMIROT – SONG OF GLORY

A mystical poem, attributed to Rabbi Yehuda HeḤasid (Germany, 1150–1217). Its theme is that God appears in many forms – the poet weaves together a long list of the metaphors and metonyms by which He is described by the prophets and poets of Tanakh – yet He remains One. Beyond the diversity of creation is the unity of the Creator. Beneath the noise of events is the music of Being. Behind the many ways in which we experience God – as Warrior,

ש״ץ: מַחְלְפוֹת רֹאשׁוֹ כְּבִימֵי בְחוּרוֹת, קְוֻצּוֹתָיו תַּלְתַּלִּים שְׁחוֹרוֹת.

קהל: נְוֵה הַצֶּדֶק צְבִי תִפְאַרְתּוֹ, יַעֲלֶה נָּא עַל רֹאשׁ שִׂמְחָתוֹ.

ש״ץ: סְגֻלָּתוֹ תְּהִי בְיָדוֹ עֲטֶרֶת, וּצְנִיף מְלוּכָה צְבִי תִפְאֶרֶת.

קהל: עֲמוּסִים נְשָׂאָם, עֲטֶרֶת עִנְּדָם, מֵאֲשֶׁר יָקְרוּ בְעֵינָיו כִּבְּדָם.

ש״ץ: פְּאֵרוֹ עָלַי וּפְאֵרִי עָלָיו, וְקָרוֹב אֵלַי בְּקָרְאִי אֵלָיו.

קהל: צַח וְאָדֹם לִלְבוּשׁוֹ אָדֹם, פּוּרָה בְדָרְכוֹ בְּבוֹאוֹ מֵאֱדוֹם.

ש״ץ: קֶשֶׁר תְּפִלִּין הֶרְאָה לֶעָנָו, תְּמוּנַת יהוה לְנֶגֶד עֵינָיו.

קהל: רוֹצֶה בְעַמּוֹ עֲנָוִים יְפָאֵר, יוֹשֵׁב תְּהִלּוֹת בָּם לְהִתְפָּאֵר.

ש״ץ: רֹאשׁ דְּבָרְךָ אֱמֶת קוֹרֵא מֵרֹאשׁ דּוֹר וָדוֹר, עַם דּוֹרֶשְׁךָ דְּרֹשׁ.

קהל: שִׁית הֲמוֹן שִׁירַי נָא עָלֶיךָ, וְרִנָּתִי תִּקְרַב אֵלֶיךָ.

ש״ץ: תְּהִלָּתִי תְּהִי לְרֹאשְׁךָ עֲטֶרֶת, וּתְפִלָּתִי תִּכּוֹן קְטֹרֶת.

קהל: תִּיקַר שִׁירַת רָשׁ בְּעֵינֶיךָ, כַּשִּׁיר יוּשַׁר עַל קָרְבָּנֶיךָ.

ש״ץ: בִּרְכָתִי תַעֲלֶה לְרֹאשׁ מַשְׁבִּיר, מְחוֹלֵל וּמוֹלִיד, צַדִּיק כַּבִּיר.

קהל: וּבְבִרְכָתִי תְנַעֲנַע לִי רֹאשׁ, וְאוֹתָהּ קַח לְךָ כִּבְשָׂמִים רֹאשׁ.

ש״ץ: יֶעֱרַב נָא שִׂיחִי עָלֶיךָ, כִּי נַפְשִׁי תַעֲרֹג אֵלֶיךָ.

*The* ארון קודש *is closed.*

לְךָ יהוה הַגְּדֻלָּה וְהַגְּבוּרָה וְהַתִּפְאֶרֶת וְהַנֵּצַח וְהַהוֹד, כִּי־כֹל בַּשָּׁמַיִם דברי הימים א׳ כט
וּבָאָרֶץ, לְךָ יהוה הַמַּמְלָכָה וְהַמִּתְנַשֵּׂא לְכֹל לְרֹאשׁ: ׳ מִי יְמַלֵּל גְּבוּרוֹת תהלים קו
יהוה, יַשְׁמִיעַ כָּל־תְּהִלָּתוֹ:

---

King, Father, Judge, in joy and grief, closeness and distance, intimacy and awe, penitence and praise – there is unity. Hence conflict is not written into the script of existence. As science is beginning to discover, the natural universe exhibits a precisely calibrated harmony of forces. Humans too will one day live in harmony when, together, they acknowledge the unity of God. This lovely poem with its daring imagery was considered by many to be too holy to be said daily. To mark its sanctity, the Ark is opened.

## MOURNER'S KADDISH

*The following prayer, said by mourners, requires the presence of a minyan.*
*A transliteration can be found on page 1095.*

*Mourner:* יִתְגַּדַּל Magnified and sanctified
may His great name be,
in the world He created by His will.
May He establish His kingdom,
make His salvation flourish,
and hasten His messiah,
in your lifetime and in your days,
and in the lifetime of all the house of Israel,
swiftly and soon –
and say: Amen.

*All:* May His great name be blessed for ever and all time.

*Mourner:* Blessed and praised, glorified and exalted,
raised and honored, uplifted and lauded
be the name of the Holy One,
blessed be He,
beyond any blessing,
song, praise and consolation
uttered in the world –
and say: Amen.

May there be great peace from heaven,
and a good life for us and all Israel –
and say: Amen.

*Bow, take three steps back, as if taking leave of the Divine Presence,*
*then bow, first left, then right, then center, while saying:*

May He who makes peace in His high places,
make peace for us and all Israel –
and say: Amen.

*Many congregations conclude the service*
*with Adon Olam (page 220) and/or Yigdal (page 222).*

## קדיש יתום

*The following prayer, said by mourners, requires the presence of a* מנין.
*A transliteration can be found on page 1095.*

אבל: יִתְגַּדַּל וְיִתְקַדַּשׁ שְׁמֵהּ רַבָּא (קהל: אָמֵן)
בְּעָלְמָא דִּי בְרָא כִרְעוּתֵהּ
וְיַמְלִיךְ מַלְכוּתֵהּ
וְיַצְמַח פֻּרְקָנֵהּ וִיקָרֵב מְשִׁיחֵהּ (קהל: אָמֵן)
בְּחַיֵּיכוֹן וּבְיוֹמֵיכוֹן וּבְחַיֵּי דְכָל בֵּית יִשְׂרָאֵל
בַּעֲגָלָא וּבִזְמַן קָרִיב, וְאִמְרוּ אָמֵן. (קהל: אָמֵן)

קהל ואבל: יְהֵא שְׁמֵהּ רַבָּא מְבָרַךְ לְעָלַם וּלְעָלְמֵי עָלְמַיָּא.

אבל: יִתְבָּרַךְ וְיִשְׁתַּבַּח וְיִתְפָּאַר
וְיִתְרוֹמַם וְיִתְנַשֵּׂא וְיִתְהַדָּר וְיִתְעַלֶּה וְיִתְהַלָּל
שְׁמֵהּ דְּקֻדְשָׁא בְּרִיךְ הוּא (קהל: אָמֵן)
לְעֵלָּא לְעֵלָּא מִכָּל בִּרְכָתָא
וְשִׁירָתָא, תֻּשְׁבְּחָתָא וְנֶחֱמָתָא
דַּאֲמִירָן בְּעָלְמָא, וְאִמְרוּ אָמֵן. (קהל: אָמֵן)

יְהֵא שְׁלָמָא רַבָּא מִן שְׁמַיָּא
וְחַיִּים טוֹבִים עָלֵינוּ וְעַל כָּל יִשְׂרָאֵל, וְאִמְרוּ אָמֵן. (קהל: אָמֵן)

*Bow, take three steps back, as if taking leave of the Divine Presence, then bow, first left, then right, then center, while saying:*

עֹשֶׂה הַשָּׁלוֹם בִּמְרוֹמָיו
הוּא יַעֲשֶׂה שָׁלוֹם עָלֵינוּ
וְעַל כָּל יִשְׂרָאֵל, וְאִמְרוּ אָמֵן. (קהל: אָמֵן)

*Many congregations conclude the service with* אֲדוֹן עוֹלָם *(page 221) and/or* יִגְדַּל *(page 223).*

## KIDDUSH FOR ROSH HASHANA DAY

*On Shabbat start here:*

וְשָׁמְרוּ The children of Israel must keep the Sabbath, observing the Sabbath in every generation as an everlasting covenant. It is a sign between Me and the children of Israel for ever, for in six days the LORD made the heavens and the earth, but on the seventh day He ceased work and refreshed Himself. *Ex. 31*

זָכוֹר Remember the Sabbath day to keep it holy. Six days you shall labor and do all your work, but the seventh day is a Sabbath of the LORD your God; on it you shall not do any work – you, your son or daughter, your male or female slave, or your cattle, or the stranger within your gates. For in six days the LORD made heaven and earth and sea and all that is in them, and rested on the seventh day; therefore the LORD blessed the Sabbath day and declared it holy. *Ex. 20*

*On Yom Tov that falls on a weekday, some start here:*

אֵלֶּה These are the appointed times of the LORD, sacred assemblies, which you shall announce in their due season. Thus Moses announced the LORD's appointed seasons to the children of Israel. *Lev. 23*

*On Yom Tov that falls on a weekday, start here:* *Ps. 81*

תִּקְעוּ Sound the shofar on the new moon,
on our feast day when the moon is hidden.
For it is a statute for Israel, an ordinance of the God of Jacob.

*When saying Kiddush for others:* Please pay attention, my masters.

בָּרוּךְ Blessed are You, LORD our God, King of the Universe,
who creates the fruit of the vine.

*Birkat HaMazon can be found on page 124.*

## BLESSING AFTER FOOD – AL HAMIḤYA

*Grace after eating from the "seven species" of produce with which Israel is blessed: food made from the five grains (but not bread); wine or grape juice; grapes, figs, pomegranates, olives, or dates.*

בָּרוּךְ Blessed are You, LORD our God, King of the Universe,

*After grain products (but not bread or matza):* for the nourishment and sustenance,

*After wine or grape juice:* for the vine and the fruit of the vine,

*After grapes, figs, olives, pomegranates or dates:* for the tree and the fruit of the tree,

*After grain products (but not bread or matza), and wine or grape juice:*

for the nourishment and sustenance and for the vine and the fruit of the vine,

# קידושא רבה לראש השנה

*On שבת start here:*

וְשָׁמְרוּ בְנֵי־יִשְׂרָאֵל אֶת־הַשַּׁבָּת, לַעֲשׂוֹת אֶת־הַשַּׁבָּת לְדֹרֹתָם בְּרִית שמות לא
עוֹלָם: בֵּינִי וּבֵין בְּנֵי יִשְׂרָאֵל אוֹת הִוא לְעֹלָם, כִּי־שֵׁשֶׁת יָמִים עָשָׂה יהוה
אֶת־הַשָּׁמַיִם וְאֶת־הָאָרֶץ וּבַיּוֹם הַשְּׁבִיעִי שָׁבַת וַיִּנָּפַשׁ:

זָכוֹר אֶת־יוֹם הַשַּׁבָּת לְקַדְּשׁוֹ: שֵׁשֶׁת יָמִים תַּעֲבֹד, וְעָשִׂיתָ כָּל־מְלַאכְתֶּךָ: שמות כ
וְיוֹם הַשְּׁבִיעִי שַׁבָּת לַיהוה אֱלֹהֶיךָ, לֹא־תַעֲשֶׂה כָל־מְלָאכָה אַתָּה וּבִנְךָ
וּבִתֶּךָ, עַבְדְּךָ וַאֲמָתְךָ וּבְהֶמְתֶּךָ, וְגֵרְךָ אֲשֶׁר בִּשְׁעָרֶיךָ: כִּי שֵׁשֶׁת־יָמִים עָשָׂה
יהוה אֶת־הַשָּׁמַיִם וְאֶת־הָאָרֶץ אֶת־הַיָּם וְאֶת־כָּל־אֲשֶׁר־בָּם, וַיָּנַח בַּיּוֹם
הַשְּׁבִיעִי, עַל־כֵּן בֵּרַךְ יהוה אֶת־יוֹם הַשַּׁבָּת וַיְקַדְּשֵׁהוּ:

*On יום טוב that falls on a weekday, some start here:*

אֵלֶּה מוֹעֲדֵי יהוה מִקְרָאֵי קֹדֶשׁ אֲשֶׁר־תִּקְרְאוּ אֹתָם בְּמוֹעֲדָם: ויקרא כג
וַיְדַבֵּר מֹשֶׁה אֶת־מֹעֲדֵי יהוה אֶל־בְּנֵי יִשְׂרָאֵל:

*On יום טוב that falls on a weekday, start here:*

תִּקְעוּ בַחֹדֶשׁ שׁוֹפָר, בַּכֶּסֶה לְיוֹם חַגֵּנוּ: תהלים פא
כִּי חֹק לְיִשְׂרָאֵל הוּא, מִשְׁפָּט לֵאלֹהֵי יַעֲקֹב:

*When saying קידוש for others* סַבְרִי מָרָנָן

בָּרוּךְ אַתָּה יהוה אֱלֹהֵינוּ מֶלֶךְ הָעוֹלָם, בּוֹרֵא פְּרִי הַגָּפֶן.

ברכת המזון *can be found on page 125.*

## ברכה מעין שלוש

*Grace after eating from the "seven species" of produce with which ארץ ישראל is blessed: food made from the five grains (but not bread); wine or grape juice; grapes, figs, pomegranates, olives, or dates.*

בָּרוּךְ אַתָּה יהוה אֱלֹהֵינוּ מֶלֶךְ הָעוֹלָם, עַל

*After grain products (but not bread or מצה):*
הַמִּחְיָה וְעַל הַכַּלְכָּלָה

*After wine or grape juice:*
הַגֶּפֶן וְעַל פְּרִי הַגֶּפֶן

*After grapes, figs, olives, pomegranates or dates:*
הָעֵץ וְעַל פְּרִי הָעֵץ

*After grain products (but not bread or מצה), and wine or grape juice:*

הַמִּחְיָה וְעַל הַכַּלְכָּלָה וְעַל הַגֶּפֶן וְעַל פְּרִי הַגֶּפֶן

and for the produce of the field; for the desirable, good and spacious land that You willingly gave as heritage to our ancestors, that they might eat of its fruit and be satisfied with its goodness. Have compassion, please, LORD our God, on Israel Your people, on Jerusalem, Your city, on Zion the home of Your glory, on Your altar and Your Temple. May You rebuild Jerusalem, the holy city swiftly in our time, and may You bring us back there, rejoicing in its rebuilding, eating from its fruit, satisfied by its goodness, and blessing You for it in holiness and purity.

*On Shabbat:* Be pleased to refresh us on this Sabbath Day and

Remember us for good on this Day of Remembrance. For You, God, are good and do good to all and we thank You for the land

*After grain products (but not bread or matza):*
and for the nourishment. Blessed are You, LORD, for the land and for the nourishment.

*After wine or grape juice:*
and for the fruit of the vine. Blessed are You, LORD, for the land and for the fruit of the vine.

*After grapes, figs, olives, pomegranates or dates:*
and for the fruit. Blessed are You, LORD, for the land and for the fruit.

*After grain products (but not bread or matza), and wine or grape juice:*
and for the nourishment and for the fruit of the vine.
Blessed are You, LORD,
for the land and for the nourishment
and the fruit of the vine.

## BLESSING AFTER FOOD – BOREH NEFASHOT

*After food or drink that does not require Birkat HaMazon or Al HaMiḥya – such as meat, fish, dairy products, vegetables, beverages, or fruit other than grapes, figs, pomegranates, olives or dates – say:*

בָּרוּךְ Blessed are You, LORD our God, King of the Universe,
who creates the many forms of life and their needs.
For all You have created to sustain the life of all that lives,
blessed be He, Giver of life to the worlds.

וְעַל תְּנוּבַת הַשָּׂדֶה וְעַל אֶרֶץ חֶמְדָּה טוֹבָה וּרְחָבָה, שֶׁרָצִיתָ וְהִנְחַלְתָּ לַאֲבוֹתֵינוּ לֶאֱכֹל מִפִּרְיָהּ וְלִשְׂבֹּעַ מִטּוּבָהּ. רַחֶם נָא יהוה אֱלֹהֵינוּ עַל יִשְׂרָאֵל עַמֶּךָ וְעַל יְרוּשָׁלַיִם עִירֶךָ וְעַל צִיּוֹן מִשְׁכַּן כְּבוֹדֶךָ וְעַל מִזְבְּחֶךָ וְעַל הֵיכָלֶךָ. וּבְנֵה יְרוּשָׁלַיִם עִיר הַקֹּדֶשׁ בִּמְהֵרָה בְיָמֵינוּ, וְהַעֲלֵנוּ לְתוֹכָהּ וְשַׂמְּחֵנוּ בְּבִנְיָנָהּ וְנֹאכַל מִפִּרְיָהּ וְנִשְׂבַּע מִטּוּבָהּ, וּנְבָרֶכְךָ עָלֶיהָ בִּקְדֻשָּׁה וּבְטָהֳרָה.

בשבת: וּרְצֵה וְהַחֲלִיצֵנוּ בְּיוֹם הַשַּׁבָּת הַזֶּה

וְזָכְרֵנוּ לְטוֹבָה בְּיוֹם הַזִּכָּרוֹן הַזֶּה, כִּי אַתָּה יהוה טוֹב וּמֵטִיב לַכֹּל, וְנוֹדֶה לְּךָ עַל הָאָרֶץ

*After grain products (but not bread or מצה):*

וְעַל הַמִּחְיָה.
בָּרוּךְ אַתָּה יהוה עַל הָאָרֶץ וְעַל הַמִּחְיָה.

*After wine or grape juice:*

וְעַל פְּרִי הַגָּפֶן.*
בָּרוּךְ אַתָּה יהוה עַל הָאָרֶץ וְעַל פְּרִי הַגָּפֶן.*

*After grapes, figs, olives, pomegranates or dates:*

וְעַל הַפֵּרוֹת.**
בָּרוּךְ אַתָּה יהוה עַל הָאָרֶץ וְעַל הַפֵּרוֹת.**

*After grain products (but not bread or מצה), and wine or grape juice:*

וְעַל הַמִּחְיָה וְעַל פְּרִי הַגָּפֶן.*
בָּרוּךְ אַתָּה יהוה, עַל הָאָרֶץ וְעַל הַמִּחְיָה וְעַל פְּרִי הַגָּפֶן.*

**If the wine is from ארץ ישראל, then substitute גַּפְנָהּ for הַגָּפֶן.*
***If the fruit is from ארץ ישראל, then substitute פֵּרוֹתֶיהָ for הַפֵּרוֹת.*

## בורא נפשות

*After food or drink that does not require ברכת המזון or מעין שלוש – such as meat, fish, dairy products, vegetables, beverages, or fruit other than grapes, figs, pomegranates, olives or dates – say:*

בָּרוּךְ אַתָּה יהוה אֱלֹהֵינוּ מֶלֶךְ הָעוֹלָם
בּוֹרֵא נְפָשׁוֹת רַבּוֹת וְחֶסְרוֹנָן
עַל כָּל מַה שֶּׁבָּרָאתָ לְהַחֲיוֹת בָּהֶם נֶפֶשׁ כָּל חָי.
בָּרוּךְ חֵי הָעוֹלָמִים.

# סדר ליום ב׳

## ORDER FOR THE SECOND DAY


| | | |
|---|---|---|
| חזרת הש״ץ לשחרית | 645 | LEADER'S REPETITION FOR SHAḤARIT |
| קדושה | 691 | KEDUSHA |
| אבינו מלכנו | 703 | AVINU MALKENU |
| הוצאת ספר תורה | 717 | REMOVING THE TORAH FROM THE ARK |
| הכנסת ספר תורה | 757 | RETURNING THE TORAH TO THE ARK |
| סדר תקיעת שופר | 749 | THE BLOWING OF THE SHOFAR |
| הנני העני ממעש | 761 | LEADER'S PRAYER |
| מוסף | 765 | MUSAF |
| חזרת הש״ץ למוסף | 803 | LEADER'S REPETITION FOR MUSAF |
| ונתנה תוקף / קדושה | 807 | UNTANEH TOKEF / KEDUSHA |
| קידושא רבה | 893 | KIDDUSH FOR ROSH HASHANA DAY |
| ברכה מעין שלוש | 893 | AL HAMIḤYA |

## LEADER'S REPETITION FOR THE SECOND DAY

*The Ark is opened.*

*The Leader takes three steps forward and at the points indicated by ▾, bends the knees at the first word, bows at the second, and stands straight before saying God's name.*

O Lord, open my lips, so that my mouth may declare Your praise. *Ps. 51*

PATRIARCHS

▾בָּרוּךְ▾ Blessed are You, Lord our God and God of our fathers,
God of Abraham, God of Isaac and God of Jacob;
the great, mighty and awesome God, God Most High,
who bestows acts of loving-kindness, who creates all,
who remembers the loving-kindness of the fathers
and will bring a Redeemer to their children's children
for the sake of His name, in love.

*Before each cycle (kerova) of piyutim, the Leader says a prefatory prayer, asking permission (Reshut) to commence. The Reshut consists of a standard opening "Drawing from the counsel of wise and knowing men…," and a short introductory piyut.*

מִסּוֹד Drawing from the counsel of wise and knowing men,
from the teachings born of insight among those who understand,
I open my mouth now in prayer and pleading,
to implore and to plead before the King,
King of kings and Lord of lords.

---

Rabbi Shimon was familiar with the work of the great poets who preceded him, especially Yannai and HaKalir, and his style was influenced by theirs. What makes his compositions distinctive is the note of tragedy they often strike. This was a period in which the position of Jews in Christian Europe began to worsen significantly. One historian has called it "the formation of a persecuting society." Jewish life in northern Europe from the tenth century onward had more than its share of persecutions and expulsions, and we hear in the literature they produced, beginning with Rabbi Shimon, the sound of tears and the language of lament.

As a young child in my grandfather's synagogue, I was haunted by the sadness of the melodies and only much later began to understand the centuries of suffering they expressed. Yet never before the modern age did Jews

# חזרת הש״ץ לשחרית ליום השני

*The* ארון קודש *is opened.*
*The* שליח ציבור *takes three steps forward and at the points indicated by* ˅*, bends the knees at the first word, bows at the second, and stands straight before saying God's name.*

אֲדֹנָי, שְׂפָתַי תִּפְתָּח, וּפִי יַגִּיד תְּהִלָּתֶךָ: תהלים נא

אבות

˅בָּרוּךְ אַתָּה יהוה, אֱלֹהֵינוּ וֵאלֹהֵי אֲבוֹתֵינוּ
אֱלֹהֵי אַבְרָהָם, אֱלֹהֵי יִצְחָק, וֵאלֹהֵי יַעֲקֹב
הָאֵל הַגָּדוֹל הַגִּבּוֹר וְהַנּוֹרָא, אֵל עֶלְיוֹן
גּוֹמֵל חֲסָדִים טוֹבִים, קוֹנֵה הַכֹּל
וְזוֹכֵר חַסְדֵי אָבוֹת
וּמֵבִיא גוֹאֵל לִבְנֵי בְנֵיהֶם לְמַעַן שְׁמוֹ בְּאַהֲבָה.

*Before each cycle* (קרובה) *of piyutim, the* שליח ציבור *says a prefatory prayer, asking permission* (רשות) *to commence. The* רשות *consists of a standard opening "*מִסּוֹד חֲכָמִים וּנְבוֹנִים...*" and a short introductory piyut.*

מִסּוֹד חֲכָמִים וּנְבוֹנִים
וּמִלֶּמֶד דַּעַת מְבִינִים
אֶפְתְּחָה פִּי בִּתְפִלָּה וּבְתַחֲנוּנִים
לְחַלּוֹת וּלְחַנֵּן פְּנֵי מֶלֶךְ מַלְכֵי הַמְּלָכִים וַאֲדוֹנֵי הָאֲדוֹנִים.

---

SECOND DAY

While pride of place is given on the first day to the poetry of Rabbi Elazar HaKalir who lived and worked in the land of Israel, much of the poetry said by Ashkenazi communities on the second day was written by Rabbi Shimon bar Yitzḥak, born in Mainz, c. 950. One of the first Ashkenazi liturgical poets, he was known as an outstanding Talmudic scholar, a colleague of the great Rabbeinu Gershom, and was held in high regard as one who "brought light to the exiles." Sometimes known as Rabbi Shimon HaGadol, it was said of him that in appearance he looked like "an angel of the Lord of hosts."

אָתִיתִי I have come forward in supplication with a torn and pained heart; / like a pauper in the doorway I have come to request Your compassion.

May You be stirred to compassion and not apply the law to its full extent. / O LORD please open my lips. *Ps. 51*

I have no words in my mouth and no speech on my tongue, / for, dear LORD, You already know all. *Ps. 139*

From the depths of my heart I shall entreat Your presence; / I shall seek shelter beneath Your wings for evermore. *Ps. 61*

Raging fever and trembling have taken hold of me with dread, / as I come to beseech the awesome LORD with serious consideration,

I lack discernment and wisdom and feel insufficient and wanting; / therefore I do cower before You in awe. *Job. 32*

I am weary with groaning, how can one stand before You? / For I have no good deeds worthy of merit in Your eyes.

Your multitudinous congregations have sent me to entreat You; / give their hearts the wisdom to speak, and cause Your ear to hear their pleas. *Ps. 10*

What am I and what is my life but worms and putrefaction? / I am an ignorant boor lacking all discretion.

I shall pitch my foundations in the book of Proverbs: / "A soft answer turns away anger." *Prov. 15*

My Strength, I wait upon You that You might support me. / May the unfolding of Your words give light, that I might speak.

Look upon me as if I were righteous, fortify my hands with strength, / for You are my Fortress, my God of kindness. *Ps. 59*

---

of the congregation "like a pauper in the doorway," begging for charity, or in this case, forgiveness.

כְּעָנִי בַפֶּתַח *Like a pauper in the doorway.* One midnight, when Rabbi Moshe Leib of Sasov was immersed in mystical teachings, a peasant started knocking at his door, demanding to be let in and be given a bed for the night. For a moment the rabbi was filled with anger. How dare the man make such demands in the middle of the night! But then he said to himself, "And what business does he have in God's world? But if God gets along with him, can I turn him away?" He opened the door immediately and prepared a bed.

אֲתִיתִי לְחַנְּנָךְ בְּלֵב קָרוּעַ וּמֻרְתָּח / בַּקֵּשׁ רַחֲמִים כְּעָנִי בַּפֶּתַח
גַּלְגֵּל רַחֲמֶיךָ וְדִין אַל תִּמְתַּח / אֲדֹנָי שְׂפָתַי תִּפְתָּח: תהלים נא

דָּבָר אֵין בְּפִי, וּבִלְשׁוֹנִי מִלָּה / הֵן יהוה יָדַעְתָּ כֻלָּהּ: תהלים קלט
וּמִמַּעֲמַקֵּי הַלֵּב לְפָנֶיךָ אוֹחִילָה / אֶחֱסֶה בְסֵתֶר כְּנָפֶיךָ סֶּלָה: תהלים סא

זַלְעָפָה וּפַלָּצוּת אֲחָזוּנִי בְּמוֹרָא / חַלּוֹת פְּנֵי נוֹרָא בְּנֶפֶשׁ יְקָרָה
טוּב טַעַם וָדַעַת, קָטֹנְתִּי לְחַסְּרָה / עַל־כֵּן זָחַלְתִּי וָאִירָא: איוב לב

יָגַעְתִּי בְּאַנְחָתִי אֵיךְ לַעֲמֹד לְפָנֶיךָ / כִּי אֵין מַעֲשִׂים לִזְכּוֹת בְּעֵינֶיךָ
לְחַלּוֹתָךְ שְׁלָחוּנִי מַקְהֵלוֹת הֲמוֹנֶיךָ / תָּכִין לִבָּם, תַּקְשִׁיב אָזְנֶךָ: תהלים י

מָה אֲנִי וּמֶה חַיַּי, תּוֹלֵעָה וְרִמָּה / נִבְעַר מִדַּעַת וּבְאֶפֶס מְזִמָּה
סָמַכְתִּי יְתֵדוֹתַי בְּסֵפֶר הַחָכְמָה / מַעֲנֶה־רַּךְ יָשִׁיב חֵמָה: משלי טו

עֻזִּי, אֵלֶיךָ אֶשְׁמֹרָה לְסַעֲדִי / פֶּתַח דְּבָרֶיךָ הָאֵר לְהַגִּידִי
צַדְּקֵנִי וְאַמְּצֵנִי, וְתֵן לְאֵל יָדִי / כִּי אַתָּה מִשְׂגַּבִּי, אֱלֹהֵי חַסְדִּי: תהלים נט

---

internalize the negative images projected on them by their neighbors, never did they give up hope of ultimate redemption, and despite many blandishments and threats, rarely did they forsake the faith of their ancestors. Theirs is a tale of loyalty and fidelity without parallel, and it is here, in the prayer book, that they expressed their faith. It is the often inspiring, sometimes heartbreaking, record of a people who never stopped speaking to God even when it seemed He had stopped speaking to them. It is the tale of a people who, though they walked more often than most through the valley of the shadow of death, never stopped believing in life and the God of life, and never stopped praying to be written in the book of life.

אֲתִיתִי לְחַנְּנָךְ *I have come forward in supplication.* A personal meditation said by the leader of prayer, distinguished by its extreme language of self-abasement: "What is my life but worms and putrefaction? I am an ignorant boor lacking all discretion." Rabbi Shimon, who wrote this prayer, also officiated as leader of prayer in Mainz, hence its deeply personal character. Its premise is that, whatever his inadequacies, the leader of prayer comes before God on behalf

Your congregations stand to ask Your forgiveness; / awaken Your mercy to have pity on them in Your compassion.
As they face You they pour out their hearts like water; / in Your dwelling place in heaven may You hear their prayer. *1 Kings 8*

Strengthen the weak hand of Your nation, / send forth succor and salvation.
May they grasp Your divine goodness so they might be strengthened and fortified: / "For every word of God is refined." *Prov. 30*

*The Ark is closed.*

*The Magen – recalling the righteousness of Abraham. As part of the Leader's Repetition, the piyutim should ideally be said by the Leader alone. However, the prevailing custom is for the congregation to participate, and some of the piyutim are said together, with the Leader raising his voice only toward the end.*

*All:*

**אִמְרָתְךָ צְרוּפָה** Your every word is refined and Your laws righteous, / please, do not be too meticulous in judgment with those who come before You;
as You approach to search out every secret and rupture, / seek to vindicate Your humble ones in judgment.

Behold, You have built Your world with kindness, / and as Master of kindness may You incline toward mercy.
May our good deeds outweigh the evil and may Your strength be founded; / have pity on the descendants of Abraham, the one brought out of Chaldea.

Please answer us before we even call out to You. / May we receive a kind response from You
on this day, as You recall and count Your creatures; / may Your angel camp round about us.

Cause Your trait of goodness to triumph for our sake, / cleanse us of all iniquity and remove all of our transgressions.
May Your arm fortify those who turn to You in hope expectantly, / and give them renewed strength and wings to fly.

---

or that of his generation. To be a Jew is to carry with us the merits of all those who stayed loyal to the covenant in good times and bad.

קְהָלֶיךָ עוֹמְדִים לְבַקֵּשׁ מְחִילָתֶךָ / רַחֲמֶיךָ יִכְמְרוּ, לְרַחֲמָם בְּחֶמְלָתֶךָ
מלכים א׳ ח שׁוֹפְכִים לֵב כַּמַּיִם לְעֻמָּתֶךָ / וְאַתָּה תִּשְׁמַע הַשָּׁמַיִם מְכוֹן שִׁבְתֶּךָ:

תְּחַזֵּק לְעַמְּךָ יָדַיִם הָרָפָה / שְׁלַח מֵאִתְּךָ עֵזֶר וּתְרוּפָה
משלי ל נַעֲמָךְ יַשִּׂיגוּ לְחַזֵּק וּלְתָקְפָּה / כָּל־אִמְרַת אֱלוֹהַּ צְרוּפָה:

*The* ארון קודש *is closed.*

*The* מגן *– recalling the righteousness of Abraham. As part of the* חזרת הש״ץ*, the piyutim should ideally be said by the* שליח ציבור *alone. However, the prevailing custom is for the* קהל *to participate, and some of the piyutim are said together, with the* שליח ציבור *raising his voice only toward the end.*

*All:*

אִמְרָתְךָ צְרוּפָה וְעֵדוֹתֶיךָ צֶדֶק / בָּאֵי עָדֶיךָ בְּרִיב, אַל תְּדַקְדֵּק
גִּשְׁתְּךָ לְחַפֵּשׂ כָּל תַּעֲלוּם וָבֶדֶק / דִּין עֲנִיֶּיךָ בְּמִשְׁפַּט הַצֶּדֶק.

הֵן עוֹלָמְךָ בָּנִיתָ בְּחֶסֶד / וְרַב חֶסֶד מַטֶּה כְּלַפֵּי חֶסֶד
זְכִיּוֹת הַכְרַע וְעֻזְּךָ תְּיַסֵּד / חֹן עַל נִינֵי מוֹצָא מִכֶּשֶׂד.

טֶרֶם נִקְרָא וְאַתָּה תַעֲנֶה / יִמָּצֵא לָנוּ חֶסֶד בְּמַעֲנֶה
כְּפָקְדְךָ הַיּוֹם יְצוּרֶיךָ לְהִמָּנֶה / לָנוּ מַלְאָכְךָ סָבִיב יַחֲנֶה.

מִדַּת טוּבְךָ עָלֵינוּ הַגְבֵּר / נַקֵּנוּ מֵעָוֹן וּפְשָׁעֵינוּ הַעֲבֵר
שַׂגֵּב בִּזְרוֹעַ לִמְקַוֶּיךָ בְּשֶׁבֶר / עֹז חֲלִיפַת כֹּחַ, וַעֲלִיַּת אֵבֶר.

---

אִמְרָתְךָ צְרוּפָה *Your every word is refined.* A plea to God to remember Abraham's faith and willingness to sacrifice, and to forgive us in his merit. Just as Abraham is associated with the attribute of *ḥesed*, loving kindness, may God act toward us with loving kindness. Recall that this poem is set in the first paragraph of the Amida, which ends with the words "shield of Abraham" – hence the poet's emphasis on Abraham. Even when Moses prayed, he asked God to forgive the Israelites in the merit of the patriarchs, not his own merit

פְּעֻלַּת אֶזְרָחִי לְפָנֶיךָ תִּזָּכֵר / צִדְקוֹ יָלִיץ כֹּשֶׁר, וּמַסְטִין יְסַכֵּר
קַבֵּל מוֹרָאֲךָ יִחוּדְךָ לְהַכֵּר / רָץ בְּפִקּוּדֶיךָ לְיַשֵּׁר וּלְיַקֵּר.

שָׁלֵם נִמְצָא בְּכָל אֲשֶׁר נִפְקָד / שָׁעֲשַׁע כְּהַיּוֹם בְּחֵטְא מְפַקֵּד
▸ תְּהִלָּה וָעֹז לִמְרַחֲמוֹ שָׁקַד / תַּמָּתוֹ בְּעֵת אֲשֶׁר פָּקָד.

A בּוֹ שְׁעָנְנוּ מֵעוֹלָם, וַיַּעֲנֵנוּ נוֹרָאוֹת / בִּרְצוּי חִנּוּנֵנוּ קַבֵּל כְּהַעֲלָאוֹת
▸ יְחַלְּצֵנוּ בְּמָגִנּוֹ מִתַּחֲלוּאֵי תוֹצָאוֹת / כְּצִפֳּרִים עָפוֹת כֵּן יָגֵן יהוה צְבָאוֹת: ישעיה לא

*The* שליח ציבור *continues:*

זָכְרֵנוּ לְחַיִּים, מֶלֶךְ חָפֵץ בַּחַיִּים
וְכָתְבֵנוּ בְּסֵפֶר הַחַיִּים, לְמַעַנְךָ אֱלֹהִים חַיִּים.
מֶלֶךְ עוֹזֵר וּמוֹשִׁיעַ וּמָגֵן.
ׁבָּרוּךְ אַתָּה יהוה, מָגֵן אַבְרָהָם.

גבורות

אַתָּה גִּבּוֹר לְעוֹלָם, אֲדֹנָי
מְחַיֵּה מֵתִים אַתָּה, רַב לְהוֹשִׁיעַ
בארץ ישראל: מוֹרִיד הַטָּל
מְכַלְכֵּל חַיִּים בְּחֶסֶד, מְחַיֵּה מֵתִים בְּרַחֲמִים רַבִּים
סוֹמֵךְ נוֹפְלִים, וְרוֹפֵא חוֹלִים, וּמַתִּיר אֲסוּרִים
וּמְקַיֵּם אֱמוּנָתוֹ לִישֵׁנֵי עָפָר.
מִי כָמוֹךָ, בַּעַל גְּבוּרוֹת, וּמִי דּוֹמֶה לָּךְ
מֶלֶךְ, מֵמִית וּמְחַיֶּה וּמַצְמִיחַ יְשׁוּעָה.

---

יְחַלְּצֵנוּ בְּמָגִנּוֹ מִתַּחֲלוּאֵי תוֹצָאוֹת *Deliver us from all deathly afflictions.* Sometimes translated as "from the 903 various deaths." The Talmud interprets the phrase

*The Meḥayeh, which reflects the Keriat HaTorah for the second day – the binding of Isaac.*

תָּמִים פָּעָלְךָ Your works are unblemished, O God of great counsel; / we have risen early to seek You out and observe Your righteousness.
Remove all filth and dissolve all accusations, / receive our groans and may our breached fences be repaired.

The flock we might have slaughtered to offer You has been destroyed – / young bulls and sheep which were once brought as peace- and burnt-offerings.
Now we set out our prayers before You instead; / may our speech be as pleasing to You as the incense and meal offerings.

Should the straight path become crooked as we walk, / as we turn away from the Torah You sent us and become lazy in our worship,
may the altar upon which Isaac was arranged stand before You in remembrance / of the knife that was raised over him, and the meat we have been allowed to eat ever since.

Father and son walked toward Mount Moriah as one, / to obey Your command by preparing a sacrifice.
Guard their offspring and may Your compassion be awakened; / may the remembrance of Your oath be as pleasing as the upright column of incense.

And as You sit this day in judgment over nations, / may You look upon their offspring and be filled with compassion.
May You clear us in judgment and may we not come away ashamed; / may the vine You planted in Your land flourish forever.

By virtue of the one who was bound on the altar may You listen from heaven / to those who call upon You out of hardship – the poor among Your nation.
▸ Inscribe our names for life in Your book, / and heed the words on our lips as when Isaac entreated You.

---

knife lifted against him his soul left his body. Then when word came from heaven, "Do not reach out your hand against the boy," he revived. Sensing that he had been restored from death to life, Isaac then recited the blessing, "Blessed are You, Lord, who revives the dead."

*The* מחיה*, which reflects the* קריאת התורה *for the second day – the* עקדת יצחק.

תָּמִים פָּעָלְךָ גְּדוֹל הָעֵצָה / שִׁחַרְנוּ פָּנֶיךָ וְצִדְקָתְךָ נִמְצָא
רַחֵץ טֶנֶף וְהָתֵם שִׁמְצָה / קַבֵּל אֶנֶק וּגְדֹר פִּרְצָה.

צֹאן לַטֶּבַח גָּזַר מִמִּכְלָה / פָּרִים וּכְבָשִׂים לִשְׁלָמִים וְעוֹלָה
עֲרִיכַת שָׂפָה נַעֲרֹךְ בִּתְפִלָּה / שִׂיחֵנוּ יְשֻׁפַּר כְּהֶקְטֵר וּבְלוּלָה.

נְתִיב יֹשֶׁר אִם נֶעֱקַל בְּלֶכֶת / מִשְׁלַחְתְּךָ לַעֲזֹב לְהִתְרַפּוֹת בִּמְלֶאכֶת
לְנֶגְדְּךָ יִפָּקֵד מִזְבֵּחַ מַעֲרֶכֶת / כְּמַאֲכֶלֶת הַמַּאֲכִילָה מֵאָז נֶעֱרֶכֶת.

יַחַד אָב וּבֵן בְּלֶכְתָּם לְהַר מוֹר / טֶבַח לְהָכִין, מִפְקָדְךָ לִשְׁמֹר
חֲנִיטָם נְצֹר רַחֲמִים לִכְמֹר / זֵכֶר שְׁבוּעָה כִּקְטֹרֶת לִתְמֹר.

וּבְשִׁבְתְּךָ הַיּוֹם לָדִין עַמִּים / הִמָּלֵא עַל צֶאֱצָאֵימוֹ רַחֲמִים
דִּינֵנוּ הַצְהֵר וְלֹא נֵצֵא נִכְלָמִים / גֶּפֶן מַטָּעֲתְךָ תָּכִין לְאֹרֶךְ יָמִים.

בִּזְכוּת נֶעֱקַד הַקְשִׁיבָה מִשַּׁחַק / אֶבְיוֹנֵי עַמְּךָ, קוֹרְאֶיךָ מִדֹּחַק
◂ שִׂמֵנוּ עַל סִפְרְךָ לְחַיִּים יֻחַק / וְנִיב שְׂפָתֵינוּ הַקְשֵׁב כְּוַיֵּעָתֵר יִצְחָק.

---

תָּמִים פָּעָלְךָ *Your works are unblemished.* Also written by Rabbi Shimon, the subject of this poem, set in the second paragraph of the Amida, is Isaac, the second of the patriarchs, who allowed himself to be bound on the altar in an act of supreme sacrifice that we will soon recall in the Torah reading for the second day. There is a midrashic tradition behind this poem. Recall that the first paragraph of the Amida ends with the phrase, "Shield of Abraham." Some sages accordingly inferred that the second paragraph, in which this poem is set, corresponds to the second of the patriarchs, Isaac. But the theme of the second paragraph is the resurrection of the dead. What is the connection between Isaac and the resurrection of the dead?

According to the Midrash (*Pirkei Rabbi Eliezer,* 30), when Isaac saw the

All: Our lips speak of Your strength and we shall live in Your righteousness; / vindicate us in Your compassion and be our arm of strength.
▸ God shall heal us after these two days [of Rosh HaShana], as He did before; / He shall raise us up on the third day [Yom Kippur], and we will live.

*The Leader continues:*

מִי כָמוֹךָ Who is like You, compassionate Father,
who remembers His creatures in compassion, for life?
Faithful are You to revive the dead.
Blessed are You, LORD, who revives the dead.

*Unlike the Kerovot of the first day – which were written by HaKalir – Rabbi Shimon bar Yitzhak's Meshalesh for the second day does not use an אתב״ש acrostic; instead, it spells the poet's name (a favored device of his). The theme of this piyut is the sentiment of the Leader as he begins to plead for the congregation. The first stanza was widely considered a Reshut, and therefore the prevailing custom is to open the Ark before reciting it.*

*The Ark is opened.*

שְׁלַחְתִּי I have been sent as emissary by Your chosen congregation, / those who guard Your faith and recognize Your Oneness in awe.
I have poured out my heart to be granted entreaty: / LORD, hear my voice when I cry out. *Ps. 27*

*The Ark is closed.*

You who speak righteousness, who grants favor and is willingly appeased, / let refuge and sanctuary be found by those who seek You.
If You were to carry out judgment to the full extent, none could withstand it. / May I be spared in judgment before You. *Ps. 17*

Accept the order of our shofar blasts without any reservations, / confuse our accusers and strengthen our defenders.
For Israel, Your matron, the congregation hewn from stone, / Your eyes behold all deeds justly. *Ibid.*

May the righteousness of the innocent Jacob be remembered before You, / he who dwelled in Your tents and whose image is engraved on Your throne.
Rescue me from evil and the blemish of iniquity; / I shall be innocent if they do not dominate me. *Ps. 19*

---

ally consisting of four words whose initial letters spell out the name of the poet, Shimon bar Yitzhak. The poem opens with a *reshut*: a request to be considered as the emissary of the congregation, in their merits not his own.

שְׂפָתֵינוּ מְדוֹבְבוֹת עֹז וּבְצִדְקָתוֹ נִחְיֶה / בְּרַחֲמִים יְצַדְּקֵנוּ וְזַרְעֵנוּ יִהְיֶה
יְחַיֵּינוּ כְּקֶדֶם מִיּוֹמַיִם, אֶהְיֶה / בַּיּוֹם הַשְּׁלִישִׁי יְקִימֵנוּ וְנִחְיֶה.

*The שליח ציבור continues:*

מִי כָמְוֹךָ אַב הָרַחֲמָן, זוֹכֵר יְצוּרָיו לְחַיִּים בְּרַחֲמִים.
וְנֶאֱמָן אַתָּה לְהַחֲיוֹת מֵתִים. בָּרוּךְ אַתָּה יהוה, מְחַיֵּה הַמֵּתִים.

*Unlike the קרובות of the first day – which were written by HaKalir – Rabbi Shimon bar Yitzḥak's משלש for the second day does not use an אתב״ש acrostic; instead, it spells the poet's name (a favored device of his). The theme of this piyut is the sentiment of the שליח ציבור as he begins to plead for the קהל. The first stanza was widely considered a רשות, and therefore the prevailing custom is to open the ארון קודש before reciting it.*

*The ארון קודש is opened.*

שְׁלַחְתִּי בְּמַלְאֲכוּת סֶגֶל חֲבוּרָה / שׁוֹמְרֵי אֱמוּנָתְךָ וּמְיַחֲדֶיךָ בְּמוֹרָא
תהלים כז שָׁפַכְתִּי שִׂיחַ לְבַקֵּשׁ עֲתִירָה / שְׁמַע־יהוה קוֹלִי אֶקְרָא:

*The ארון קודש is closed.*

מְדַבֵּר בִּצְדָקָה, חוֹנֵן וּמִתְרַצֶּה / מַחֲסֶה וּמִסְתּוֹר לְדוֹרְשֶׁיךָ הַמָּצֵא
תהלים יז מֵתַח דִּינְךָ אִם בִּיצוּרִים תְּמַצֶּה / מִלְּפָנֶיךָ מִשְׁפָּטִי יֵצֵא:

עֵרֶךְ תְּקִיעָתֵנוּ שְׁעֵה בְּבֵירוּרִים / עַרְבֵּב קַטֵּגוֹר וְאַמֵּץ סַנֵּגוֹרִים
שם עֲקֶרֶת בַּיִת וַחֲצוּבַת צוּרִים / עֵינֶיךָ תֶּחֱזֶינָה מֵישָׁרִים:

וְיִזָּכֵר לְפָנֶיךָ צִדְקַת הַתָּם / וְעֵד אֹהָלֶיךָ וּבְכִסְאֲךָ נֶחְתָּם
תהלים יט וְחַלְּצֵנִי מִפֶּשַׁע, וּמֵעָוֹן נִכְתָּם / אַל־יִמְשְׁלוּ־בִי אָז אֵיתָם:

---

בַּיּוֹם הַשְּׁלִישִׁי יְקִימֵנוּ *Raise us up on the third day.* A reference to the verse from Hosea, "In two days He will revive us, on the third day He will raise us up and we will endure in His presence" (Hosea 6:2). Rashi relates this to the two Temples that were destroyed, and the third that will endure forever. The poet plays on this idea, relating the two days to Rosh HaShana, and the third to Yom Kippur.

שְׁלַחְתִּי *I have been sent.* A poem written in four-line stanzas, each line usu-

O You who act kindly and remember the covenant, / cleanse us as with soap, that we may be pure of any hidden sins.
Guide us in Your truth and ensure that we prevail, / You who bear the iniquity and evil of the remnants of Your nation. *Mic. 7*

As You ascend to Your awesome, dreadful throne, / to judge the creatures of the earth this day,
in Your compassion toward us grant us redemption, / for we have praised God this entire day. *Ps. 44*

In Your compassion remove our evil inclinations, / desire us and shield us in the shelter of Your wings.
Crave our repentance and may Your forgiveness be abundant, / tend Your people with Your staff – the flock of Your heritage. *Mic. 7*

Teach us to forever walk in Your ways, / that the uprightness of Your commandments might be bound to our hearts.
May Your compassion be stirred to covet our forgiveness; / we know that we have sinned and there is no one who can withstand Your judgment.

Command salvation for Your beloved bride, Israel, / who thirsts for Your kindness and faints in longing for You.
Look and behold how she is in great pain; / Your righteousness is like the great mountains and Your judgments permeate the vast depths. *Ps. 36*

Desire our utterances and the sound of our shofar blasts, / cleanse us of our sins and cast away all our mistakes.
Utterly destroy the heads of our accusers. / Be gracious to us, O God, be gracious, for our souls take refuge in You. *Ps. 57*

Bring us closer to Your salvation on this day of our New Year; / gather all our exiles that they may dwell in our holy city.
May those who rise against me see that my salvation lies in You, / for I turn my hopes toward the Lord; He is the subject of all my hopes.

---

prosecuting counsel on this Day of Judgment. Jews in northern Europe in the Middle Ages would also have had in mind a different and human accuser, "those who hate and accuse" the Jews. The poet does not identify these two, the first mentioned toward the beginning of the poem, the second toward the end, but he asks God to protect His people from both.

נוֹהֵג בְּחֶסֶד, זוֹכֵר הַבְּרִית / נַקֵּנוּ מִנִּסְתָּרוֹת וְנִזְכֶּה כְּבוֹרִית
נְחֵנוּ בַּאֲמִתְּךָ, וּתְנֵנוּ לְאַחֲרִית / נֹשֵׂא עָוֹן וְעֹבֵר עַל־פֶּשַׁע לִשְׁאֵרִית: מיכה ז

בְּהִנָּשְׂאֲךָ לְכִסֵּא, נוֹרָא וְאָיֹם / בְּרוּאֵי חֶלֶד לְהִשָּׁפֵט כְּהַיּוֹם
בְּרַחֲמֶיךָ עָלֵינוּ הַמְצִיאֵנוּ פִּדְיוֹם / בֵּאלֹהִים הִלַּלְנוּ כָל־הַיּוֹם: תהלים מד

רֹעַ יִצְרֵנוּ הָסֵר בְּחֶמְלָתֶךָ / רְצֵנוּ וְסוֹכְכֵנוּ בְּמַחַס אֶבְרָתֶךָ
רְצֵה תְשׁוּבָתֵנוּ וְהַרְבֵּה מְחִילָתֶךָ / רְעֵה עַמְּךָ בְשִׁבְטֶךָ, צֹאן נַחֲלָתֶךָ: מיכה ז

יַדְעֵנוּ דְרָכֶיךָ וְאָרְחוֹתֶיךָ לִתְמֹד / יֹשֶׁר פִּקּוּדֶיךָ בְּלִבֵּנוּ לִצְמֹד
יִכְמְרוּ רַחֲמֶיךָ סְלִיחָתֵנוּ לַחְמֹד / יָדַעְנוּ כִּי חָטָאנוּ, וְאֵין מִי יַעֲמֹד.

צַוֵּה יְשׁוּעָתְךָ לְרַעְיָתְךָ הָאֲהוּבָה / צְמֵאָה לְחַסְדְּךָ, כְּמֵהָה וְתַאֵבָה
צְפֵה וְהַבֵּט כִּי מְאֹד נִכְאָבָה / צִדְקָתְךָ כְּהַרְרֵי־אֵל, מִשְׁפָּטֶיךָ תְּהוֹם רַבָּה: תהלים לו

חֲפֹץ בְּהֶגְיוֹנֵנוּ וּבְקוֹל תְּרוּעָתֵנוּ / חֲטָאֵינוּ הַלְבֵּן וְהַפְקֵר שִׁגְגֵנוּ
חַבֵּל וְהַצְמֵת קָדְקֹד מַשְׂטִינֵנוּ / חָנֵּנוּ אֱלֹהִים חָנֵּנוּ, כִּי בְךָ חָסְיָה נַפְשֵׁנוּ. תהלים נז

קָרְבֵנוּ לְיִשְׁעֲךָ בְּזֶה רֹאשׁ שְׁנָתִי / קַבֵּץ נְפוּצוֹתֵינוּ לְמִרְבַּץ קִרְיָתִי
קָמִים יֶחֱזוּ כִּי מֵאִתְּךָ תְּהִלָּתִי / קַוֵּה קִוִּיתִי יהוה תּוֹחַלְתִּי.

---

It looks forward to the sounding of the shofar, and is notable for the way it brings together two distinct ideas uppermost in the minds of the congregation in those times on this day. The Talmud says that we blow the shofar twice, once before Musaf, the other during the Leader's Repetition, "to confuse the Accuser" (*Rosh HaShana* 16b), the angel (HaSatan) charged with being the

*The* קהל *says the next two verses aloud, followed by the* שליח ציבור*:*

תהלים קמו
יִמְלֹךְ יהוה לְעוֹלָם
אֱלֹהַיִךְ צִיּוֹן לְדֹר וָדֹר
הַלְלוּיָהּ:

תהלים כב
וְאַתָּה קָדוֹשׁ, יוֹשֵׁב תְּהִלּוֹת יִשְׂרָאֵל:

*There follows an ancient piyut, author unknown, which most congregations add after the* משלש*. In recent generations the custom to say it responsively has spread; many congregations are accustomed to saying the second stich of each couplet together with the first of the next one. However, traditionally this piyut is said only by the* שליח ציבור*, with the congregation joining in at "*חַי וְקַיָּם*."*

*The* ארון קודש *is opened.*

אֵל נָא.

אַתָּה הוּא אֱלֹהֵינוּ בַּשָּׁמַיִם וּבָאָרֶץ.
גִּבּוֹר וְנַעֲרָץ דָּגוּל מֵרְבָבָה.
הוּא שָׂח וַיֶּהִי וְצִוָּה וְנִבְרָאוּ.
זִכְרוֹ לָנֶצַח חַי עוֹלָמִים.
טְהוֹר עֵינַיִם יוֹשֵׁב סֵתֶר.
כִּתְרוֹ יְשׁוּעָה לְבוּשׁוֹ צְדָקָה.
מַעֲטֵהוּ קִנְאָה נֶאְפַּד נְקָמָה.
סִתְרוֹ יֹשֶׁר עֲצָתוֹ אֱמוּנָה.
פְּעֻלָּתוֹ אֱמֶת צַדִּיק וְיָשָׁר.
קָרוֹב לְקוֹרְאָיו בֶּאֱמֶת רָם וּמִתְנַשֵּׂא.
שׁוֹכֵן שְׁחָקִים תּוֹלֶה אֶרֶץ עַל בְּלִימָה.

*All:*

חַי וְקַיָּם, נוֹרָא וּמָרוֹם וְקָדוֹשׁ.

*The* ארון קודש *is closed.*

*On a Sunday the service continues with "Awaken and sound" on page 670, on other days continue here:*

*Each of the next seven stanzas is first said by the Leader, then the congregation:*

שְׁמוֹ His name is glorified by His rightful congregation,
and revered in songs of praise by the angels.
And in His Sanctuary His glory is spoken of by everyone. / O Holy One.

The keepers of His commandments will yet return to their fortified haven;
His faithful followers converse with one another with much skill and wisdom:
And the LORD hearkened and listened and a book of remembrance was written. / O Holy One. *Mal. 3*

Refine your deeds so that the covenant may endure.
He who adorns the heavens shall heed your groans,
and your prayers shall be more pleasing to the LORD than an ox or bullock. / O Holy One. *Ps. 69*

Raise up the tribes that call upon You and let them rule,
as the outstretched branches of their oppressors are cut down and removed,
for the kingdom belongs to the LORD and He rules. / O Holy One. *Ps. 22*

May He return our captives from afar to His holy mount,
that we might glorify Him always in His holy Sanctuary,
for He has remembered His holy vow. / O Holy One. *Ps. 105*

His great name is praised as a tower of strength;
He shall eternally give His Messianic king strength and greatness.
On that day, a great shofar shall be sounded. O Holy One. *Is. 27*

All inhabitants of the world and those who reside on the earth, *Is. 18*
shall forever say that the LORD has done great things in the world,
and the LORD shall reign as King over the entire world. / O Holy One. *Zech. 14*

---

*Zikhronot,* God's remembrance; and *Shofarot,* references to the shofar. First the poet sets out these themes in six verses, each of three stichs, ending with the word "Holy," since this is the theme of the third paragraph of the Amida in which the poem is set. These then serve as refrains for a longer poem, constructed around three three-line verses, again continuing the theme of kingship, remembrance and shofar. The use of threefold structures at this point echoes the threefold "Holy, holy, holy" of the angels in Isaiah's vision, which we will shortly be reciting in the *Kedusha*. This elaborate structure is best thought of as verbal music, a theme played out in multiple variations interweaving with one another.

*On a Sunday the service continues with*
תָּעִיר וְתָרִיעַ *on page 671, on other days continue here:*

*Each of the next seven stanzas is first said by* שליח ציבור*, then the* קהל*:*

שְׁמוֹ מְפָאֲרִים עֲדַת חֶבְלוֹ
וְנַעֲרָץ בְּאֶרְאֶלֵּי קֹדֶשׁ הִלּוּלוֹ
וּבְהֵיכָלוֹ כָּבוֹד אֹמֵר כֻּלּוֹ / קָדוֹשׁ.

שׁוֹמְרֵי מִצְוֹתָיו עוֹד יְשׁוּבוּן לְבִצָּרוֹן
נִדְבָּרִים יְרֵאָיו בְּהַכְשֵׁר וְיִתְרוֹן
מלאכי ג וַיַּקְשֵׁב יהוה וַיִּשְׁמָע, וַיִּכָּתֵב סֵפֶר זִכָּרוֹן: / קָדוֹשׁ.

שַׁפְּרוּ מַעֲשֵׂיכֶם, וּבְרִית לֹא תוּפַר
נַאֲקַתְכֶם יַאֲזִין, שְׁחָקִים שִׁפֵּר
תהלים סט וְתִיטַב לַיהוה מִשּׁוֹר פָּר: / קָדוֹשׁ.

שִׁבְטֵי מְקֹרָאֶךָ עֲלֵה וְהַמְשֵׁל
נְטִישׁוֹת צָרִים בַּהֲתִזְּךָ לְנַשֵּׁל
תהלים כב כִּי לַיהוה הַמְּלוּכָה, וּמֹשֵׁל: / קָדוֹשׁ.

שְׁבוּתֵנוּ מִמֶּרְחָק, עֲלוֹת לְהַר קָדְשׁוֹ
וּנְפָאֲרֵנוּ תָמִיד בִּדְבִיר מִקְדָּשׁוֹ
תהלים קה כִּי־זָכַר אֶת־דְּבַר קָדְשׁוֹ: / קָדוֹשׁ.

שֶׁבַח מִגְדַּל עֹז, שֵׁם הַגָּדוֹל
נֶצַח בְּתִתּוֹ לְמַלְכּוֹ עֹז וּמִגְדּוֹל
ישעיה כז בַּיּוֹם הַהוּא יִתָּקַע בְּשׁוֹפָר גָּדוֹל: / קָדוֹשׁ.

ישעיה יח כָּל־יֹשְׁבֵי תֵבֵל וְשֹׁכְנֵי אָרֶץ:
יֹאמְרוּ תָמִיד, הִגְדִּיל יהוה לַעֲשׂוֹת בָּאָרֶץ
זכריה יד וְהָיָה יהוה לְמֶלֶךְ עַל־כָּל־הָאָרֶץ: / קָדוֹשׁ.

---

**שְׁמוֹ מְפָאֲרִים** *His name is glorified.* Another poem by Rabbi Shimon bar Yitzḥak, built around the three central themes of the day: *Malkhiyot,* God's kingship;

*This complex piyut reprises the previous piyut's seven stanzas. Some congregations omit this piyut altogether, continuing with "He judges the world" on page 668.*

*Leader:* אֶדֶר Splendor and glory I willingly give, / I lay out my prayer in thought and utterance.

*Cong:* I shall call upon the LORD Most High. *Ps. 57*

*Leader:* On the day chosen in heaven, / when the LORD judges righteously that His sanctity might be revered,

*Cong:* For the LORD reigns; the earth shall rejoice. *Ps. 97*

*Leader:* His greatness has grown beyond what the world can contain; who possesses the strength to tell of the fullness of His power?

*Cong:* God is King of all the earth; sing a psalm! *Ps. 47*

His name is glorified by His rightful congregation, / and revered in songs of praise by the angels. / And in His Sanctuary His glory is spoken of by everyone. / O Holy One.

*Leader:* All His creatures shall take note / and know that His mighty deeds are immense,

*Cong:* For He has made wondrous works to be remembered. *Ps. 111*

*Leader:* He established His cornerstone, / His Torah legacy, so that His nation might revel in it,

*Cong:* He remembers His covenant forever. *Ps. 105*

*Leader:* And the LORD inscribed in the law-book that I shall utter / the verses of remembrance, so that He might recall my remembrance every year,

*Cong:* As a testament in the Sanctuary of the LORD. *Zech. 6*

The keepers of His commandments will yet return to their fortified haven; / His faithful followers converse with one another with much skill and wisdom. / And the LORD hearkened and listened *Mal. 3*
and a book of remembrance was written. / O Holy One.

*Leader:* That holy sacrifice of Isaac which seemed fitting in His eyes, He arranged for its exchange in the form of a ram to be offered before Him.

*Cong:* After it was caught in the thicket by its horns. *Gen. 22*

---

הִצִּיב וִידָה אֶבֶן פִּנָּתוֹ *He established His cornerstone.* According to tradition, creation began with a stone core (*even shetia*) from which the earth gradually expanded (*Yoma* 54b). The Temple was built on this spot, which was also the

*This complex piyut reprises the previous piyut's seven stanzas. Some congregations omit this piyut altogether, continuing with "יִשְׁפֹּט תֵּבֵל" on page 669.*

ש״ץ: אֶדֶר וָהוֹד אֶתֵּן בְּצִבְיוֹן / שֶׁוַע אֶעֱרֹךְ בְּנִיב וְהִגָּיוֹן

קהל: אֶקְרָא לֵאלֹהִים עֶלְיוֹן: תהלים נז

ש״ץ: בַּיּוֹם הַנִּבְחָר מִשְּׁמֵי עֶרֶץ / מֵישָׁרִים לִשְׁפֹּט, קְדֻשָּׁתוֹ לְהַעֲרֵץ

קהל: יהוה מָלָךְ תָּגֵל הָאָרֶץ: תהלים צז

ש״ץ: גַּאֲוָתוֹ גָּדְלָה עוֹלָם מֵהָכִיל / עֱזוּזוֹ לְסַפֵּר כֹּחַ מִי יָכִיל

קהל: מֶלֶךְ כָּל־הָאָרֶץ אֱלֹהִים, זַמְּרוּ מַשְׂכִּיל: תהלים מז

שְׁמוֹ מְפָאֲרִים עֲדַת חֶבְלוֹ / וְנַעֲרָץ בְּאֶרְאֶלֵּי קֹדֶשׁ הִלּוּלוֹ
וּבְהֵיכָלוֹ כָּבוֹד אֹמֵר כֻּלּוֹ / קָדוֹשׁ.

ש״ץ: דֵּעַ יָשִׂימוּ כָּל בְּרִיּוֹתָיו / וְיֵדְעוּ כִּי גָּדְלוּ גְּבוּרוֹתָיו

קהל: זֵכֶר עָשָׂה לְנִפְלְאוֹתָיו: תהלים קיא

ש״ץ: הִצִּיב וְיָרָה אֶבֶן פִּנָּתוֹ / נַחֲלִיאֵל עֲבוּר לְשַׁעֲשֵׁעַ בָּאֲמָתוֹ

קהל: זָכַר לְעוֹלָם בְּרִיתוֹ: תהלים קה

ש״ץ: וְרַשַׁם בְּחֹק דָּת הֶגְיוֹנַי / בְּכָל שָׁנָה וְשָׁנָה לִזְכֹּר זִכְרוֹנַי

קהל: לְזִכָּרוֹן בְּהֵיכַל יהוה: זכריה ו

שׁוֹמְרֵי מִצְוֹתָיו עוֹד יָשׁוּבוּן לְבִצָּרוֹן / נִדְבָּרִים יֵרָאוּ בְּהַכְשֵׁר וְיִתְרוֹן
וַיַּקְשֵׁב יהוה וַיִּשְׁמָע, וַיִּכָּתֵב סֵפֶר זִכָּרוֹן: / קָדוֹשׁ. מלאכי ג

ש״ץ: זֶבַח קֹדֶשׁ כְּהֶכְשֵׁר אָז בְּעֵינָיו
רֶגֶל תְּמוּרָתוֹ אַיִל לְהַקְרִיב לְפָנָיו

קהל: אַחַר נֶאֱחַז בַּסְּבַךְ בְּקַרְנָיו: בראשית כב

---

גַּאֲוָתוֹ גָּדְלָה עוֹלָם מֵהָכִיל *His greatness has grown beyond what the world can contain.* A hint at the idea, later adumbrated in Lurianic Kabbala, that the light of God was too intense to be contained by a physical universe, which shattered under the impact. Hence we inhabit a broken world which needs repairing.

*Leader:* He taught [Isaac's] offshoots to sound the shofar at the start of this month, / and if the holy Sabbath should happen to fall upon on this day,

*Cong:* Then the remembrance of the sound of the shofar shall serve to sanctify it. *Lev. 23*

*Leader:* Yet should its arrival for a scheduled weekday be announced, then the command should go out that in all your borders the shofar shall sound,

*Cong:* For it shall be a day for you on which the shofar shall resound. *Num. 29*

Refine your deeds so that the covenant may endure.
He who adorns the heavens shall heed your groans, / and your prayers shall be more pleasing to the LORD than an ox or bullock. / O Holy One. *Ps. 69*

*Leader:* May the Rock of my salvation be exalted in the mouth of every nation. / Reveal Your mighty arm to save Your people from those who rise against them.

*Cong:* For Your kingdom is an everlasting kingdom. *Ps. 145*

*Leader:* When You will reveal Yourself to the eyes of all and appear within Your Sanctuary, / congregations and multitudes will come forth to bear testimony:

*Cong:* The LORD shall reign forever and ever. *Ex. 15*

*Leader:* Strength and honor are fitting for You, uttered by / all the world, its inhabitants and all the islands.

*Cong:* Who shall not fear You, O King of all nations? *Jer. 10*

Raise up the tribes that call upon You and let them rule,
as the outstretched branches of their oppressors are cut down and removed,
for the kingdom belongs to the LORD and He rules. / O Holy One. *Ps. 22*

*Leader:* Shatter and destroy the beams placed upon us by our oppressors, gather Your scattered exiles and freely offer them redemption.

*Cong:* Remember the congregation You acquired long ago. *Ps. 74*

*Leader:* The noblest of nations shall be comforted doubly; those who rise against them shall be exposed in humiliation.

*Cong:* May the LORD recall the day of Jerusalem's defeat and visit retribution upon the descendants of Edom. *Ps. 137*

ש״ץ: חֲכָם חֲנִיטָיו לִתְקֹעַ בְּזֶה חֹדֶשׁ
יוֹם זֶה אִם יִקְרֶה בְּשַׁבַּת קוֹדֶשׁ
קהל: זִכְרוֹן תְּרוּעָה מִקְרָא־קֹדֶשׁ: ויקרא כג

ש״ץ: טִבְעוּ אִם בְּחוּל יְבוֹאֲכֶם
צִוּוּ לִתְקֹעַ בְּכָל גְּבוּלְכֶם קהל: יוֹם תְּרוּעָה יִהְיֶה לָכֶם: במדבר כט

שַׁפְּרוּ מַעֲשֵׂיכֶם, וּבְרִית לֹא תוּפַר / נַאֲקַתְכֶם יַאֲזִין, שְׁחָקִים שִׁפַּר
וְתִיטַב לַיהוה מִשּׁוֹר פָּר: / קָדוֹשׁ. תהלים סט

ש״ץ: יָרוּם צוּר יִשְׁעִי בְּפִי כָּל אֻמִּים
חֲשׂף זְרוֹעֲךָ לְהוֹשִׁיעַ מִמִּתְקוֹמְמִים
קהל: מַלְכוּתְךָ מַלְכוּת כָּל־עֹלָמִים: תהלים קמה

ש״ץ: כְּהִגָּלוֹתְךָ לְעֵין כֹּל שִׁכְנְךָ לְהִוָּעֵד
קְהִלּוֹת וּרְבָבוֹת בְּפִימוֹ לְהָעֵד קהל: יהוה יִמְלֹךְ לְעֹלָם וָעֶד: שמות טו

ש״ץ: לְךָ יָאֲתָה כָּבוֹד וָעֹז הֲגוֹיִים
חֶלֶד וְשׁוֹכְנֶיהָ וְכָל הָאִיִּים קהל: מִי לֹא יִרָאֲךָ מֶלֶךְ הַגּוֹיִם: ירמיה י

שִׁבְטֵי מִקְרָאֲךָ עֲלֵה וְהַמְשֵׁל / נְטִישׁוֹת צָרִים בַּהֲתִיזְךָ לְנַשֵּׁל
כִּי לַיהוה הַמְּלוּכָה, וּמֹשֵׁל: / קָדוֹשׁ. תהלים כב

ש״ץ: מוֹטַת צָרִים שַׁבֵּר וְהַכְחִידֵם
זְרוּיֶיךָ קַבֵּץ וְחִנָּם תִּפְדֵּם קהל: זְכֹר עֲדָתְךָ קָנִיתָ קֶּדֶם: תהלים עד

ש״ץ: נְדִיבֵי עַמִּים יְנֻחֲמוּ בְּכִפְלַיִם
קָמֵיהֶם עַל פָּנֵימוֹ גַּלֵּה שׁוּלַיִם
קהל: זְכֹר יהוה לִבְנֵי אֱדוֹם אֵת יוֹם יְרוּשָׁלָיִם: תהלים קלז

---

place where Jacob slept the night he dreamed of a ladder stretching to heaven (*Ḥullin* 91b). It is, spiritually, the center of the universe.

ש״ץ: סְלוּל מְסִלָּתֵנוּ יַשֵּׁר לְצַעַד / וּבֵן יַקִּירְךָ קַרְסֹל לֹא יִמְעַד

קהל: כְּנַמְתָּ, זָכֹר אֶזְכְּרֶנּוּ עוֹד: ירמיה לא

שְׁבוּתֵנוּ מִמֶּרְחָק, עֲלוֹת לְהַר קָדְשׁוֹ / וּנְפָאֲרֵנוּ תָּמִיד בִּדְבִיר מִקְדָּשׁוֹ

כִּי־זָכַר אֶת־דְּבַר קָדְשׁוֹ: / קָדוֹשׁ. תהלים קה

ש״ץ: עֲמוּסֶיךָ תּוֹקְעִים וּמְרִיעִים בַּשּׁוֹפָר

אִמְרָתְךָ לְקַיֵּם כַּחֹק הַמְסֻפָּר קהל: תִּקְעוּ בַחֹדֶשׁ שׁוֹפָר: תהלים פא

ש״ץ: פִּשְׁעָם הַעֲבֵר וַעֲוֹנָם יְכֻפַּר

מַעֲנָם יֶעֱרַב כְּהַקְרָבַת כְּבָשִׂים וָפָר

קהל: בַּחֲצֹצְרוֹת וְקוֹל שׁוֹפָר: תהלים צח

ש״ץ: צֶמְחֵיהֶם יִרְבּוּ כַּחוֹל אֵין מִסְפָּר

צְבָרֵיהֶם יְעוֹרְרוּ וְיַעֲלוּ מֵעָפָר

קהל: כִּנְשֹׂא־נֵס הָרִים תִּרְאוּ, וְכִתְקֹעַ שׁוֹפָר: ישעיה יח

שֶׁבַח מִגְדַּל עֹז, שֵׁם הַגָּדוֹל / נֶצַח בִּתְּתוֹ לְמַלְכּוֹ עֹז וּמִגְדּוֹל

בַּיּוֹם הַהוּא יִתָּקַע בְּשׁוֹפָר גָּדוֹל: קָדוֹשׁ. ישעיה כז

ש״ץ: קִרְיַת מָשׂוֹשׂ, הֵיכָל וְאוּלָם

מִזְבֵּחַ יָשִׁיב, וּכְלֵי שָׁרֵת כֻּלָּם קהל: יהוה יִמְלֹךְ לְעֹלָם: שמות טו

ש״ץ: שָׁמַיִם וָאָרֶץ יְרַנְּנוּ לִשְׁמוֹ

יְעָרוֹת יִמְחֲאוּ כַף לְהַנְעִימוֹ קהל: כִּי־פָקַד יהוה אֶת־עַמּוֹ: רות א

ש״ץ: תֹּקֶף אֶרְאֶלִּים וְכוֹכְבֵי צֶפֶר

תְּהִלּוֹת יִתְּנוּ שֶׁבַח לְהַשְׁפֵּר קהל: הַלְלוּהוּ בְּתֵקַע שׁוֹפָר: תהלים קנ

ישעיה יח כָּל־יֹשְׁבֵי תֵבֵל וְשֹׁכְנֵי אָרֶץ: / יֹאמְרוּ תָמִיד, הִגְדִּיל יהוה לַעֲשׂוֹת בָּאָרֶץ

זכריה יד וְהָיָה יהוה לְמֶלֶךְ עַל־כָּל־הָאָרֶץ: / קָדוֹשׁ.

*The next two verses are said first by the Leader, then the congregation. Originally, these two verses were said by the congregation as alternating refrains after the verses of the following piyut. In recent generations, the custom is to say them only here at the start.*

יִשְׁפֹּט He judges the world with righteousness
and all nations with equity. / O Holy God.

וְהוּא For He alone is LORD – who can refuse Him? Job 23
What His soul desires, He performs. / O Awesome and Holy One.

*All (some congregations omit and continue with "Master, if we are devoid" on page 674):*

אֶתֵּן I shall ascribe righteousness to my Maker / on the day chosen for all deeds to be examined.

His majesty has greatly flourished, / but His humility is equal to His grandeur.

He is Master of the world entire; / who ever hardened his heart against Him and remained whole? Job 9

He recalls those who walk innocently, / He has compassion and takes up the orphan's cause.

He is pure, lofty and sublime, / He made all things becomingly at the proper time.

The Mighty One does not despise / anyone who is lowly in his own eyes.

Glorious, He rides the heavens, / fiery flames and bright light shine before Him.

He cuts down the evil with sharpened swords / on behalf of the orphans and the widows.

He offers man recompense for all his deeds, / He creates mouths to speak and renders speakers dumb.

He created all with compassion, / He is lofty, and lays lofty ones low.

He pardons His creatures with grace, / the works of the true God are perfect.

The earthly judges are vacant in His presence, / astounded and affrighted in their awe of Him. Is. 40

He takes up the cause of His nation, / judging them first to spare them His wrath.

The righteous tremble under His close scrutiny, / though they performed His laws faithfully.

He sees all hidden things, / residing in the lofty heavens.

He foresees events before they occur / and hastens the occurrences of the future.

He proclaims the future of all generations before they come to pass, / searching and examining the inner workings of hearts. Is. 41

▸ He who remembers His covenant with our ancestors, / may He fulfill His oath toward their descendants.

*The next two verses are said first by the* שליח ציבור*, then the* קהל*. Originally, these two verses were said by the* קהל *as alternating refrains after the verses of the following piyut. In recent generations, the custom is to say them only here at the start.*

יִשְׁפֹּט תֵּבֵל בְּצֶדֶק, וּלְאֻמִּים בְּמֵישָׁרִים / הָאֵל קָדוֹשׁ.

איוב כג וְהוּא בְאֶחָד וּמִי יְשִׁיבֶנּוּ, וְנַפְשׁוֹ אִוְּתָה וַיָּעַשׂ: / נוֹרָא וְקָדוֹשׁ.

*All (some congregations omit and continue with* אָדוֹן, אִם מַעֲשִׂים *on page 675):*

אֶתֵּן לְפֹעֲלִי צֶדֶק / בַּיּוֹם הַנִּבְחָר מֵעַשׂ לְהִבָּדֵק.
גַּאֲוָתוֹ מְאֹד גָּדְלָה / דֶּרֶךְ עַנְוָתוֹ לְפִי הַגְּדֻלָּה.
איוב ט הוּא אֲדוֹן הָעוֹלָם / וּמִי־הִקְשָׁה אֵלָיו, וַיִּשְׁלָם:
זוֹכֵר הוֹלֵךְ בַּתֹּם / חוֹנֵן וְעֹשֶׂה דִּין יָתוֹם.
טָהוֹר מָרוֹם וְנִשָּׂא / יָפֶה בְעִתּוֹ הַכֹּל עָשָׂה.
כַּבִּיר לֹא יִמְאַס / לְנִבְזֶה בְעֵינָיו, נִמְאָס.
מְפֹאָר רֹכֵב עֲרָבוֹת / נֹגַהּ נֶגְדּוֹ, וְאֵשׁ לֶהָבוֹת.
סוֹעֵף בַּחֲרָבוֹת שְׁנוּנוֹת / עֲבוּר יְתוֹמִים וְאַלְמָנוֹת.
פֹּעַל אָדָם יְשַׁלֵּם / צָר פֶּה וּמֵשִׂים אִלֵּם.
קֹנֵה הַכֹּל בְּרַחֲמִים / רָם וּמַשְׁפִּיל רָמִים.
שׁוֹפֵט יְצוּרָיו בַּחֲנִינָה / תְּמִים פֹּעַל, אֵל אֱמוּנָה.
ישעיה מ שֹׁפְטֵי אֶרֶץ כַּתֹּהוּ / מִפַּחְדּוֹ יִבָּהֲלוּ וְיִתְמָהוּ.
עוֹשֶׂה מִשְׁפַּט עַמּוֹ / וּתְהִלָּה מְקַדְּמִם מִפְּנֵי זַעְמוֹ.
נְדִיבִים בְּדִקְדּוּקָם יָחִילוּ / בַּאֲשֶׁר מִשְׁפָּטוֹ פָּעֲלוּ.
רוֹאֶה כָּל תַּעֲלוּמוֹת / יוֹשֵׁב בְּגָבְהֵי מְרוֹמוֹת.
צוֹפֶה כָּל נוֹלָדוֹת / חוֹפֵשׂ כָּל הָעֲתִידוֹת.
ישעיה מא קֹרֵא הַדֹּרוֹת מֵרֹאשׁ / חִקְרֵי לֵב לָתוּר וְלִדְרֹשׁ.
◂ זוֹכֵר בְּרִית רִאשׁוֹנִים / קַיֵּם שְׁבוּעָה לָאַחֲרוֹנִים.

---

אֶתֵּן לְפֹעֲלִי צֶדֶק *I shall ascribe righteousness to my Maker.* For commentary see page 391.

*On a Tuesday, Wednesday and Friday the service continues with "Master, if we are devoid" on page 674.*

*The following piyutim, until "The LORD is King" on page 682, share a common triplet structure ending with the word "Holy" – in some this structure is a frame, said before and after the piyut, as "Awaken and sound" below; in others it features as a refrain. Some congregations omit these piyutim, saying responsively only these "Holy" triplets; this is the prevailing custom in Israel.*

*The Leader then the congregation:*

תָּעִיר Awaken and sound the shofar, cut down all evildoers,
and be sanctified by those who know to observe
the sounding of the shofar. O Holy One.

*All (some congregations omit and continue with "O King who offers" on the next page):*

אֲדֶּרֶת The glorious mantle of our royalty – / why was it torn from us? / And we have not returned to rule since / the Babylonian idol Bel was crowned king. / All followed it, so willing, / in contrast to the laws of our religion. / A foreign power has reigned in mastery / over all of our people who will not be free / until the kingdom of the LORD shall appear.

They burned my Temple, / they broke the backs of my innocent ones in slavery / and they have been given allowance to do as they please. / They spread throughout the length and breadth of the land / and drew back their bows, / extending the yoke of their oppression, / frightening the soft nation of Israel, / which now lies there trampled / while still the foreigners rule.

The foundations of the Sanctuary, which sustained the heaps of tithes, / were stripped and confiscated by the enemy horde, / and the Temple was laid bare to its foundation. / They raised their haughty heads in evil / and took crafty counsel against Your people; / they wielded the upper hand. / They burned with evil intentions; / their arrogance extended as far as the heavens / while they girded themselves with Your royal vestments.

They shred my curtains clear away / and plundered my Sanctuary, / turning over the earth till it was plowed clear. / They spread their rule / and adopted royal garb, / angering Your nation. / They plotted and conspired to rebel against God, / and labored to sway Your people to worship strange gods / as they defiled the reign of our LORD.

They oppressed the children of the King, / and before His eyes they uttered the words: / "What king do we have in heaven?" / They spoke arrogantly of the King's throne, / saying, "There is no other king but me; / no other king but I alone." / ▸ O You who are loftier than any earthly king, / remove them and they shall no longer rule, / and reclaim the reign for Yourself alone.

*The Leader then the congregation:*

תָּעִיר Awaken and sound the shofar, cut down all evildoers, and be sanctified by those who know to observe the sounding of the shofar. O Holy One.

*On a Tuesday, Wednesday and Friday the service continues with* אָדוֹן, אִם מַעֲשִׂים *on page 675.*

*The following piyutim, until "*יהוה מֶלֶךְ*" on page 683, share a common triplet structure ending with the word "*קָדוֹשׁ*" – in some this structure is a frame, said before and after the piyut, as* תָּעִיר וְתָרִיעַ *below; in others it features as a refrain. Some congregations omit these piyutim, saying responsively only these "*קָדוֹשׁ*" triplets; this is the prevailing custom in Israel.*

*The* שליח ציבור *then the* קהל*:*

תָּעִיר וְתָרִיעַ, לְהַכְרִית כָּל מֵרִיעַ
וְתִקְדַּשׁ בְּיוֹדְעֵי לְהָרִיעַ. קָדוֹשׁ.

*All (some congregations omit and continue with* מֶלֶךְ מְמַלֵּט *on the next page):*

אַדֶּרֶת מַמְלָכָה / עַל מָה הָשְׁלְכָה / וְעוֹד לֹא מָלְכָה
לְכָל הַמְלִיכָה / וְאַחֲרָיו הָלְכָה / שֶׁלֹּא כַהֲלָכָה
עָלֶיהָ הִמְלִיכָה / גְּבֶרֶת מַמְלָכָה / עַד תּוֹפִיעַ מְלוּכָה.

זְבוּלֵי חֲרֵכָה / מַתְמִימֵי פֶּרֶכָה / וְנִתַּן לָהּ אַרְכָה
רְחָבָה וְאָרְכָה / וְקֶשֶׁת דְּרָכָה / וְעַל הֶאֱרִיכָה
בְּעֵתָהּ בְּרַכָּה / וְהִנֵּה דְרוּכָה / וְעַד עַתָּה מוֹלְכָה.

יְסוֹדוֹת עֲרֵמָה / עֵרָה וְהֶחֱרִימָה / וְעַד יְסוֹד עָרְמָה
רֹאשׁ הֵרִימָה / וְסוֹד הֶעֱרִימָה / וְיָדָהּ רָמָה
בָּעֲרָה מֵעָרְמָה / וְעַד שַׁחַק רוֹמָה / וְתֶאְפַּד מְלוּכָה.

יְרִיעוֹתַי גְּדֻדָה / אָהֳלֵי שֻׁדְּדָה / וְחָרְשָׁה וְשִׁדְּדָה
קְצִינוּת רָפְדָה / וּמַלְכוּת אָפְדָה / וְזֹאת הִקְפִּידָה
יָזְמָה וּמָרְדָה / עֲבוֹד לַזָּר חָרְדָה / וְחִלְּלָה מְלוּכָה.

לְחָצָהּ בְּנֵי מֶלֶךְ / וּפָצָה לְעֵין מֶלֶךְ / מִי לִי בְּדוֹק מֶלֶךְ
יָהֲרָה בְּכֵס מֶלֶךְ / זוּלָתִי אֵין מֶלֶךְ / אֲנִי וְאַפְסִי מֶלֶךְ
◂ רָם עַל כָּל מֶלֶךְ / תַּגְעִילֶנָּה מִמֶּלֶךְ / וּלְךָ תָּשִׁיב מְלוּכָה.

*The* שליח ציבור *then the* קהל*:*

תָּעִיר וְתָרִיעַ, לְהַכְרִית כָּל מֵרִיעַ, וְתִקְדַּשׁ בְּיוֹדְעֵי לְהָרִיעַ. קָדוֹשׁ.

---

אַדֶּרֶת מַמְלָכָה *The glorious mantle of our royalty.* For commentary see page 375.

*The Leader then the congregation:*

מֶלֶךְ O King who offers deliverance from evil,
to those who observe the sounding of the shofar.
O Holy God.

*The Leader then the congregation:*

מֶלֶךְ O King, recall the ram caught by its horns in the thicket,
on behalf of those who sound the ram's horn on this day.
O Awesome and Holy One.

All (*some congregations omit and continue with "His great name is praised" on the next page*):

אַאְפִּיד I shall crown the Awesome One / by proclaiming His holiness threefold in the Kedusha on this day.
Mighty angelic heroes of strength and greatness, / gallop forward to receive Him in the house where His banner is raised!

The angelic camp that raises its voice in rousing sound, / exalts Him with fine words of praise!
For the One who forever recalls the merits of His creatures, / sing a new song of angelic praise!

The Good One bears our burdens for us; / declare His unity as the new moon comes!
He suppresses all sentiments of anger / so as not to implement the issue of His ire.

The angelic servants in His retinue of awe / offer awesome words of praise in the presence of Israel!
Seraphim, who swirl in the stormy ether: / call out to the One who removes His anger!

Wondrous angels, open your mouths to sing / in praise of the One who sees all things!
Congregations of this holy nation: / noisily clamor in your multitudes to elevate Him!

May You listen to the sounding of the call of the shofar, / and cause all guilt to be annulled.
▸ Please, sound the shofar thrice on Your holy mount, / and I shall now proclaim Your threefold holiness in full sanctity.

O King recall the ram caught by its horns in the thicket, on behalf of those who sound the ram's horn on this day. O Awesome and Holy One.

*The* שליח ציבור *then the* קהל:

מֶלֶךְ מְמַלֵּט מֵרָעָה
לְיוֹדְעֵי תְרוּעָה.
הָאֵל קָדוֹשׁ.

*The* שליח ציבור *then the* קהל:

מֶלֶךְ זְכוֹר אֲחוּז קֶרֶן
לְתוֹקְעֵי לְךָ הַיּוֹם בְּקֶרֶן.
נוֹרָא וְקָדוֹשׁ.

*All (some congregations omit and continue with* שֶׁבַח מְגַדֵּל *on the next page):*

אַאְפִּיד נֵזֶר אָיוֹם / בְּשִׁלּוּשׁ קְדֻשָּׁה בַּיּוֹם.
גִּבּוֹרֵי כֹּחַ גְּדֻלָּה / דַּהֲרוּהוּ בְּבֵית דְּגִילָה.

הוֹגֵי הֶגֶה הֲמֻלָּה / וַתְּקוּהוּ בְּהַלֵּל וּמִלָּה.
זוֹכֵר לָעַד זְכֻיּוֹת / חַדְּשׁוּהוּ זֶמֶר חַיּוֹת.

טוֹב עוֹמֵס טֹרַח / יַחֲדוּהוּ בְּחִדּוּשׁ יָרֵחַ.
כּוֹבֵשׁ כָּל כְּעָסִים / לְבַל אַף לְהָשִׂים.

מְשָׁרְתֵי בְּחִיל מוֹרָא / נָכְחַם הַלְלוּ נוֹרָא.
שַׂרְפֵי סְבִיב סְעָרָה / עֱנוּ לְמַעֲבִיר עֶבְרָה.

פְּלִיאִים פִּצְחוּ פֶה / צַלְצְלוּ הַכֹּל צוֹפֶה.
קְהִלּוֹת עַם קְדוֹשִׁים / רוֹמְמוּהוּ רִבְבוֹת רוֹעֲשִׁים.

שְׁמַע קוֹל שׁוֹפָר / תַּאֲזִין, וְאַשְׁמָה תוֹפָר.
◂ תְּשַׁלֵּשׁ שׁוֹפָרוֹת בְּהַר הַקֹּדֶשׁ / וַאֲשַׁלֵּשׁ קְדֻשָּׁה בַּקֹּדֶשׁ.

מֶלֶךְ זְכוֹר אֲחוּז קֶרֶן, לְתוֹקְעֵי לְךָ הַיּוֹם בְּקֶרֶן. נוֹרָא וְקָדוֹשׁ.

*The* שליח ציבור *then the* קהל:

**שֶֽׁבַח מִגְדַּל עֹז, שֵׁם הַגָּדוֹל**
**נֵֽצַח בְּתִתּוֹ לְמַלְכּוֹ עֹז וּמִגְדּוֹל**
**בַּיּוֹם הַהוּא יִתָּקַע בְּשׁוֹפָר גָּדוֹל: קָדוֹשׁ.** ישעיה כז

*Responsively (some congregations omit and continue with* אָדוֹן, אִם מַעֲשִׂים *below):*

ש״ץ: **עֲמוּסֶֽיךָ תּוֹקְעִים וּמְרִיעִים בַּשּׁוֹפָר / אִמְרָתְךָ לְקַיֵּם כַּחֹק הַמְּסֻפָּר**
קהל: **תִּקְעוּ בַחֹֽדֶשׁ שׁוֹפָר:** תהלים פא

ש״ץ: **פִּשְׁעָם הַעֲבֵר וַעֲוֹנָם יְכֻפָּר / מַעֲנָם יֶעֱרַב כְּהַקְרָבַת כְּבָשִׂים וָפָר**
קהל: **בַּחֲצֹצְרוֹת וְקוֹל שׁוֹפָר:** תהלים צח

ש״ץ: **צִמְחֵיהֶם יִרְבּוּ כַּחוֹל אֵין מִסְפָּר / צְבָרֵיהֶם יְעוֹרְרוּ וְיַעֲלוּ מֵעָפָר**
קהל: **כִּנְשֹׂא־נֵס הָרִים תִּרְאוּ, וְכִתְקֹעַ שׁוֹפָר:** ישעיה יח

**שֶֽׁבַח מִגְדַּל עֹז, שֵׁם הַגָּדוֹל / נֵֽצַח בְּתִתּוֹ לְמַלְכּוֹ עֹז וּמִגְדּוֹל**
**בַּיּוֹם הַהוּא יִתָּקַע בְּשׁוֹפָר גָּדוֹל: קָדוֹשׁ.** ישעיה כז

*On all days the service continues:*

*The* שליח ציבור *then the* קהל:

**אָדוֹן, אִם מַעֲשִׂים אֵין בָּֽנוּ**
**שִׁמְךָ הַגָּדוֹל יַעֲמָד לָֽנוּ**
**וְאַל תָּבוֹא בְמִשְׁפָּט עִמָּֽנוּ / קָדוֹשׁ.**

*The* שליח ציבור *then the* קהל:

**הֵן לֹא יַאֲמִין בִּקְדֹשָׁיו**
**וּתְהָלָה יָשִׂים בְּאֵלֵי תַרְשִׁישָׁיו**
**וְאֵיךְ יִצְדְּקוּ קְרוּצֵי גוּשָׁיו / קָדוֹשׁ.**

---

**אָדוֹן, אִם מַעֲשִׂים אֵין בָּֽנוּ** *Master, if we are devoid of good deeds.* On Abraham's words, "Shall the Judge of all the earth not do justice?" (Gen. 18:25), the Midrash comments, "[Abraham said to God:] If You want a world, there cannot be strict justice. If You want strict justice, there cannot be a world. Yet You

*Some congregations recite the piyut "I saw once again" (page 1046) at this point.*

*The Ark is opened.*

*The following piyut is a variation by Rabbi Shimon of Mainz on HaKalir's "The Supreme King" which was recited on the first day. The full version of this piyut is on page 1052.*

וּבְכֵן And so – [The LORD] became King in Yeshurun. *Gen. 33*

The Supreme King –
Powerful and exalted,
exalted above all rulers,
He fulfills His promises,
He is Fortress and Sanctuary,
He is lofty and bears aloft,
He seats kings on their thrones.
He shall reign forever.

The Supreme King –
Mighty in His great works,
He proclaims the future of all generations,
revealing that which is hidden, / His utterances are pure,
He knows the number of stars
and the composition of constellations.
He shall reign forever.

The Supreme King –
Glorified on every tongue,
He is omnipotent,
He takes pity on all,
provides sustenance to all,
concealed from the eyes of all,
yet His eyes roam over all.
He shall reign forever.

---

been removed. Only two remain, just before the end of prayer, said in an undertone and with the Ark closed. It is not clear why the poem was edited in this way. It may have been felt dangerous, even *lèse majesté*, for Jews to

*Some congregations recite the piyut* שַׁבְּתִּי *(page 1047) at this point.*

*The* ארון קודש *is opened.*

*The following piyut is a variation by Rabbi Shimon of Mainz on HaKalir's* מֶלֶךְ עֶלְיוֹן *which was recited on the first day. The full version of this piyut is on page 1053.*

וּבְכֵן, וַיְהִי בִישֻׁרוּן מֶלֶךְ: בראשית לג

מֶלֶךְ עֶלְיוֹן
אַמִּיץ הַמְנֻשָּׂא / לְכֹל לְרֹאשׁ מִתְנַשֵּׂא
אוֹמֵר וְעוֹשֶׂה / מָעוֹז וּמַחְסֶה
נֹשֵׂא וְנוֹשֵׂא / מוֹשִׁיב מְלָכִים לַכִּסֵּא
לַעֲדֵי עַד יִמְלֹךְ.

מֶלֶךְ עֶלְיוֹן
גִּבּוֹר בִּגְבוּרוֹת / קֹרֵא הַדּוֹרוֹת
גּוֹלֶה נִסְתָּרוֹת / אִמְרוֹתָיו טְהוֹרוֹת
יוֹדֵעַ סְפוּרוֹת / לְתוֹצְאוֹת מַזָּרוֹת
לַעֲדֵי עַד יִמְלֹךְ.

מֶלֶךְ עֶלְיוֹן
הַמְפֹאָר בְּפִי כֹל / וְהוּא כֹּל יָכוֹל
הַמְרַחֵם אֶת הַכֹּל / וְנוֹתֵן מִחְיָה לַכֹּל
וְנֶעְלָם מֵעֵין כֹּל / וְעֵינָיו מְשׁוֹטְטוֹת בַּכֹּל
לַעֲדֵי עַד יִמְלֹךְ.

---

מֶלֶךְ עֶלְיוֹן *The Supreme King.* A prayer originally set as a counterpoint between verses describing God, "the Supreme King," and others speaking of a human ruler, "the destitute king." A glance at the initial letters of each verse immediately shows that half the verses, those speaking of the destitute king, have

The Supreme King –
Recalls the forgotten, / examines innards,
His eyes are wide open, / He anticipates all thoughts,
God of spirits, / His words are truthful.
He shall reign forever.

The Supreme King –
Pure in His heavenly abode,
Master of His angelic servants,
none can compare to Him / as He performs His works,
He placed sand as a border
against which the sea waves roar.
He shall reign forever.

The Supreme King –
Gathers the waters of the sea,
stirs up the ocean waves,
causes the tumultuous waves to crash and break
till they are enough to fill the world,
yet He can quiet their power,
causing them to retreat till they cannot be found.
He shall reign forever.

The Supreme King –
Rules with might, / His path is stormy and tempestuous,
clothed in light, / illuminating the night as day,
fog is His concealment, / yet light dwells with Him.
He shall reign forever.

---

denigrate the grandeur of human kings, especially when their very permission to live in a country depended on the will, sometimes the whim, of the king.

Yet the fundamental principle remains true, important and one of Judaism's greatest contributions to human thought: Above all human rulers is the

מֶלֶךְ עֶלְיוֹן
זוֹכֵר נִשְׁכָּחוֹת / חוֹקֵר טְחוֹת
עֵינָיו פְּקֻחוֹת / מַגִּיד שֵׂחוֹת
אֱלֹהֵי הָרוּחוֹת / אִמְרוֹתָיו נְכֹחוֹת
לַעֲדֵי עַד יִמְלֹךְ.

מֶלֶךְ עֶלְיוֹן
טָהוֹר בִּזְבוּלָיו / אוֹת הוּא בְּאֶרְאֶלָּיו
אֵין עֲרֹךְ אֵלָיו / לִפְעֹל כְּמִפְעָלָיו
חוֹל שָׂם גְּבוּלָיו / כַּהֲמוֹת יָם לְגַלָּיו
לַעֲדֵי עַד יִמְלֹךְ.

מֶלֶךְ עֶלְיוֹן
כּוֹנֵס מֵי הַיָּם / רֹגַע גַּלֵּי יָם
סוֹעֵר שְׁאוֹן דָּכְיָם / מְלֹא הָעוֹלָם דַּיָּם
מַשְׁבִּיחָם בַּעְיָם / וְשָׁבִים אָחוֹר וְאַיָּם
לַעֲדֵי עַד יִמְלֹךְ.

מֶלֶךְ עֶלְיוֹן
מוֹשֵׁל בִּגְבוּרָה / דַּרְכּוֹ סוּפָה וּסְעָרָה
עוֹטֶה אוֹרָה / לַיְלָה כַּיּוֹם לְהָאִירָה
עֲרָפֶל לוֹ סִתְרָה / וְעִמֵּהּ שְׁרֵא נְהוֹרָא
לַעֲדֵי עַד יִמְלֹךְ.

The Supreme King –
Hidden in thick clouds, / flames surround Him,
His chariot is Cherubim, / His servants sparks of fire,
constellations and stars / praise Him exceedingly.
He shall reign forever.

The Supreme King –
Opens His hand and provides sustenance,
gathers up waters and causes them to flow,
washing over dry land / in shifts, by thirds and fourths,
each day expressions / of praise are mouthed.
He shall reign forever.

The Supreme King –
Sacred and awesome
with wonders and miraculous works,
He determined the dimensions of the earth
and laid its cornerstone,
and all that was created
was created for His glory.
He shall reign forever.

The Supreme King –
Heeds the destitute / and listens to supplication,
He extends goodwill / and limits wrath,
He is first of the first / and last of the last.
He shall reign forever.

---

Supreme King of kings, Sovereign of the universe. This means that no human rule is absolute, which means in turn that there are moral limits to the use of power. Without this, there may be no check to the abuse of power and the denial of human rights.

מֶלֶךְ עֶלְיוֹן
סִתְרוֹ עָבִים / סְבִיבָיו לְהָבִים
רְכוּבוֹ כְּרוּבִים / מְשָׁרְתָיו שְׁבִיבִים
מַזָּרוֹת וְכוֹכָבִים / הִלּוּלוֹ מַרְבִּים
לַעֲדֵי עַד יִמְלֹךְ.

מֶלֶךְ עֶלְיוֹן
פּוֹתֵחַ יָד וּמַשְׂבִּיעַ / צוֹרֵר מַיִם וּמַנְבִּיעַ
יַבֶּשֶׁת לְהַטְבִּיעַ / לְשְׁלִישׁ וְלִרְבִיעַ
יוֹם לְיוֹם יַבִּיעַ / שִׁבְחוֹ לְהַבִּיעַ
לַעֲדֵי עַד יִמְלֹךְ.

מֶלֶךְ עֶלְיוֹן
קָדוֹשׁ וְנוֹרָא / בְּמוֹפֵת וּבְמוֹרָא
מִמַּדֵּי אֶרֶץ קָרָא / וְאֶבֶן פִּנָּתָהּ יָרָה
וְכָל הַנִּבְרָא / לִכְבוֹדוֹ בָּרָא
לַעֲדֵי עַד יִמְלֹךְ.

מֶלֶךְ עֶלְיוֹן
שׁוֹמֵעַ אֶל אֶבְיוֹנִים / וּמַאֲזִין חִנּוּנִים
מַאֲרִיךְ רְצוֹנִים / וּמְקַצֵּר חֲרוֹנִים
רִאשׁוֹן לָרִאשׁוֹנִים / וְאַחֲרוֹן לָאַחֲרוֹנִים
לַעֲדֵי עַד יִמְלֹךְ.

*The* ארון קודש *is closed and the* קהל *says quietly:*

מֶלֶךְ אֶבְיוֹן
בָּלֶה וְרַד שַׁחַת / בִּשְׁאוֹל וּבְתַחַת / בְּלֵאוּת בְּלִי נַחַת
עַד מָתַי יִמְלֹךְ.

מֶלֶךְ אֶבְיוֹן
תְּנוּמָה תְעוּפֶנּוּ / תַּרְדֵּמָה תְעוֹפְפֶנּוּ / תֹּהוּ יְשׁוּפֶנּוּ
עַד מָתַי יִמְלֹךְ.

*The* ארון קודש *is opened.*

אֲבָל מֶלֶךְ עֶלְיוֹן
שׁוֹפֵט הָאֱמֶת / מַעֲבָדָיו אֱמֶת
עוֹשֶׂה חֶסֶד וֶאֱמֶת / וְרַב חֶסֶד וֶאֱמֶת
נְתִיבָתוֹ אֱמֶת / וְחוֹתָמוֹ אֱמֶת
לַעֲדֵי עַד יִמְלֹךְ.

*Like the previous piyut, this one is also a variation by Rabbi Shimon of Mainz, this time on HaKalir's* יהוה מֶלֶךְ *of the first day. However, instead of the triple alphabetic acrostic, R. Shimon employs a different structure. The first and second lines of each stanza begin with the word* כָּל*, a nod to Hakalir's* קוֹל*, followed by the letters of Rabbi Shimon's name. The second letter of the fourth and fifth words in each line form a double alphabetic acrostic.*

יהוה מֶלֶךְ, יהוה מָלָךְ, יהוה יִמְלֹךְ לְעֹלָם וָעֶד.

כָּל שִׁנְאַנֵּי שַׁחַק בְּאֹמֶר מַאֲמִירִים יהוה מֶלֶךְ.
כָּל שׁוֹכְנֵי שֶׁקֶט בִּבְרָכָה מְבָרְכִים יהוה מָלָךְ.
אֵלּוּ וָאֵלּוּ בְּגֹבַהּ מַגְדִּילִים יהוה יִמְלֹךְ.

יהוה מֶלֶךְ, יהוה מָלָךְ, יהוה יִמְלֹךְ לְעֹלָם וָעֶד.

---

יהוה מֶלֶךְ, יהוה מָלָךְ, יהוה יִמְלֹךְ לְעֹלָם וָעֶד *The* L*ORD is King, the* L*ORD was King, the* L*ORD shall be King forever and ever.* The initial letters of the poem spell out the name of its author, Rabbi Shimon bar Yitzḥak. Its theme is the nature

All the angels above knowingly behold God with The LORD is King.
All the rulers below exult in praise, The LORD was King.
Both assemblies truly admit, The LORD shall be King.
The LORD is King, the LORD was King,
the LORD shall be King forever and ever.

All the mighty in heaven tunefully sing, The LORD is King.
All who come to pass mightily extol, saying, The LORD was King.
Both assemblies tastefully praise, saying, The LORD shall be King.
The LORD is King, the LORD was King,
the LORD shall be King forever and ever.

All those who gather above, rightfully, decorously proclaim,
The LORD is King.
All the pious practitioners crown God dexterously with
The LORD was King.
Both assemblies speak up that The LORD shall be King.
The LORD is King, the LORD was King,
the LORD shall be King forever and ever.

All the beneficent angels murmur the words, The LORD is King.
All those honored by God's pleasant ways musically praise Him,
The LORD was King.
Both assemblies converse aloud, The LORD shall be King.
The LORD is King, the LORD was King,
the LORD shall be King forever and ever.

All those who possess understanding elevate on high, saying,
The LORD is King.
All those creatures of creation burst out with The LORD was King.
Both assemblies chirp softly, The LORD shall be King.
The LORD is King, the LORD was King,
the LORD shall be King forever and ever.

---

how the angels praise God, the second about how we praise Him, and the third about how "both camps," literally "these and those," angels and mortals, join their voices so that from heaven and earth praises stream toward God.

כָּל מַלְאֲכֵי מַעְלָה בְּדֵעָה מַדְגִּילִים יהוה מֶלֶךְ.
כָּל מוֹשְׁלֵי מַטָּה בְּהַלֵּל מְהַלְלִים יהוה מָלָךְ.
אֵלּוּ וָאֵלּוּ בְּוַדַּאי מוֹדִים יהוה יִמְלֹךְ.

יהוה מֶלֶךְ, יהוה מָלָךְ, יהוה יִמְלֹךְ לְעֹלָם וָעֶד.

כָּל עָרִיצֵי עֶלְיוֹנִים בְּזֶמֶר מְזַמְּרִים יהוה מֶלֶךְ.
כָּל עוֹבְרֵי עוֹלָמִים בְּחַיִל מְחַסְּנִים יהוה מָלָךְ.
אֵלּוּ וָאֵלּוּ בְּטַעַם מְטַכְּסִים יהוה יִמְלֹךְ.

יהוה מֶלֶךְ, יהוה מָלָךְ, יהוה יִמְלֹךְ לְעֹלָם וָעֶד.

כָּל וְעוּדֵי וַעַד בְּיֹשֶׁר מְיַפִּים יהוה מֶלֶךְ.
כָּל וָתִיקֵי וֶסֶת בְּכֹשֶׁר מְכַלְּלִים יהוה מָלָךְ.
אֵלּוּ וָאֵלּוּ בְּלַהַג מְלַהֲגִים יהוה יִמְלֹךְ.

יהוה מֶלֶךְ, יהוה מָלָךְ, יהוה יִמְלֹךְ לְעֹלָם וָעֶד.

כָּל נְדִיבֵי נְדָבוֹת בְּמֶלֶל מְמַלְּלִים יהוה מֶלֶךְ.
כָּל נִכְבַּדֵּי נֹעַם בְּנִצּוּחַ מְנַצְּחִים יהוה מָלָךְ.
אֵלּוּ וָאֵלּוּ בְּשִׂיחַ מְשׂוֹחֲחִים יהוה יִמְלֹךְ.

יהוה מֶלֶךְ, יהוה מָלָךְ, יהוה יִמְלֹךְ לְעֹלָם וָעֶד.

כָּל בַּעֲלֵי בִינָה בְּעִלּוּי מְעַלִּים יהוה מֶלֶךְ.
כָּל בְּרוּאֵי בְרִיָּה בְּפֶצַח מְפַצְּחִים יהוה מָלָךְ.
אֵלּוּ וָאֵלּוּ בְּצִפְצוּף מְצַפְצְפִים יהוה יִמְלֹךְ.

יהוה מֶלֶךְ, יהוה מָלָךְ, יהוה יִמְלֹךְ לְעֹלָם וָעֶד.

The flashing angels on high sanctify aloud, The LORD is King.
The first ones to sing below tunefully intone, The LORD was King.
Both assemblies melodically sing, The LORD shall be King.

The LORD is King, the LORD was King,
the LORD shall be King forever and ever.

The precious angels of beauty firmly recount, The LORD is King.
All residents of earth mightily proclaim God's unity as one with
The LORD was King.
Both assemblies mightily proclaim God's splendor with
The LORD shall be King.

The LORD is King, the LORD was King,
the LORD shall be King forever and ever.

All the hosts on high knowingly instruct that The LORD is King.
All those adorned by the crown of Torah rightfully justify saying
The LORD was King.
Both assemblies forcefully respond saying, The LORD shall be King.

The LORD is King, the LORD was King,
the LORD shall be King forever and ever.

The mighty armies of heaven tremblingly await God with
The LORD is King.
All the subjects of God's love strongly reinforce saying
The LORD was King.
Both assemblies melodically sing, The LORD shall be King.

The LORD is King, the LORD was King,
the LORD shall be King forever and ever.

All the sacred servants of the Holy One sanctify in holiness saying,
The LORD is King.
All those gathered in congregations truthfully assert,
The LORD was King.
Both assemblies pleasantly sing, The LORD shall be King.

The LORD is King, the LORD was King,
the LORD shall be King forever and ever.

כָּל רִשְׁפֵי רוּמָה בְּקוֹל מַקְדִּישִׁים יהוה מֶלֶךְ.
כָּל רָאשֵׁי רֹן בְּרֶנֶן מְרַנְּנִים יהוה מָלָךְ.
אֵלּוּ וָאֵלּוּ בְּשִׁירָה מְשׁוֹרְרִים יהוה יִמְלֹךְ.

יהוה מֶלֶךְ, יהוה מָלָךְ, יהוה יִמְלֹךְ לְעֹלָם וָעֶד.

כָּל יַקִּירֵי יֹפִי בְּתֹקֶף מְתַנִּים יהוה מֶלֶךְ.
כָּל יוֹשְׁבֵי יְשׁוּב בְּיִחוּד מְיַחֲדִים יהוה מָלָךְ.
אֵלּוּ וָאֵלּוּ בְּאֶדֶר מְאַדְּרִים יהוה יִמְלֹךְ.

יהוה מֶלֶךְ, יהוה מָלָךְ, יהוה יִמְלֹךְ לְעֹלָם וָעֶד.

כָּל צוֹבְאֵי צָבָא בְּלֶמֶד מְלַמְּדִים יהוה מֶלֶךְ.
כָּל צְנוּפֵי צְפִירָה בְּצֶדֶק מַצְדִּיקִים יהוה מָלָךְ.
אֵלּוּ וָאֵלּוּ בְּחַיִל מְחַזְּרִים יהוה יִמְלֹךְ.

יהוה מֶלֶךְ, יהוה מָלָךְ, יהוה יִמְלֹךְ לְעֹלָם וָעֶד.

כָּל חֲיָלֵי חֹסֶן בַּחֲרָדָה מְחַלִּים יהוה מֶלֶךְ.
כָּל חֲשׁוּקֵי חֶמֶד בְּחָזְקָה מְחַזְּקִים יהוה מָלָךְ.
אֵלּוּ וָאֵלּוּ בְּנִגּוּן מְנַגְּנִים יהוה יִמְלֹךְ.

יהוה מֶלֶךְ, יהוה מָלָךְ, יהוה יִמְלֹךְ לְעֹלָם וָעֶד.

כָּל קְדוֹשֵׁי קָדוֹשׁ בִּקְדֻשָּׁה מַקְדִּישִׁים יהוה מֶלֶךְ.
כָּל קְבוּצֵי קָהָל בְּקֹשֶׁט מְקַשְּׁטִים יהוה מָלָךְ.
אֵלּוּ וָאֵלּוּ בְּנֹעַם מַנְעִימִים יהוה יִמְלֹךְ.

יהוה מֶלֶךְ, יהוה מָלָךְ, יהוה יִמְלֹךְ לְעֹלָם וָעֶד.

All the flashing angels renew their call each day crying, The LORD is King.
All the lofty angels of aquamarine softly whisper, The LORD was King.
Both assemblies announce God's threefold sanctity saying,
The LORD shall be King.

The LORD is King, the LORD was King,
the LORD shall be King forever and ever.

*There follows an ancient piyut, author unknown, which most congregations add before Kedusha. In recent generations the custom to say it responsively has spread; many congregations are accustomed to saying the second stich of each couplet together with the first of the next one. Some sing the entire piyut collectively. However, traditionally this piyut is said only by the Leader, with the congregation joining in at "And so, sanctity will rise up to You."*

*There are differing customs as to whether this piyut is recited now or during Musaf.*

And so, all shall crown You.

The God who renders judgment. / The One who examines hearts on the Day of Judgment.

The One who reveals deep secrets in judgment. / The One who speaks candidly on the Day of Judgment.

The One who voices His wisdom in judgment. / The One who is diligent and performs kindness on the Day of Judgment.

The One who recalls His covenant in judgment. / The One who shows compassion toward His creations on the Day of Judgment.

The One who purifies those who rely on Him in judgment. / The One who knows all inner thoughts on the Day of Judgment.

The One who suppresses His anger in judgment. / The One who clothes Himself with righteousness on the Day of Judgment.

The One who forgives sins in judgment. / The awesome and praiseworthy One on the Day of Judgment.

The One who forgives those He bears in judgment. / The One who answers those who call on Him on the Day of Judgment.

The One who exercises His compassion in judgment. / The One who sees all hidden secrets on the Day of Judgment.

The One who acquires His servants in judgment. / The One who takes pity on His nation on the Day of Judgment.

The One who guards those who love Him in judgment. / The One who supports His innocent ones on the Day of Judgment.

*The Ark is closed.*

כָּל חַשְׁמַלֵּי זִקִּים לַבְּקָרִים מִתְחַדְּשִׁים יהוה מֶלֶךְ.
כָּל תַּרְשִׁישֵׁי גֹּבַהּ בִּדְמָמָה מְלַחֲשִׁים יהוה מָלָךְ.
אֵלּוּ וָאֵלּוּ בְּשִׁלּוּשׁ מְשַׁלְּשִׁים יהוה יִמְלֹךְ.

יהוה מֶלֶךְ, יהוה מָלָךְ, יהוה יִמְלֹךְ לְעֹלָם וָעֶד.

*There follows an ancient piyut, author unknown, which most congregations add before* קדושה*. In recent generations the custom to say it responsively has spread; many congregations are accustomed to saying the second stich of each couplet together with the first of the next one. Some sing the entire piyut collectively. However, traditionally this piyut is said only by the* שליח ציבור*, with the congregation joining in at "*וּבְכֵן לְךָ תַעֲלֶה קְדֻשָּׁה*."*
*There are differing customs as to whether this piyut is recited now or during* מוסף*.*

וּבְכֵן לְךָ הַכֹּל יַכְתִּירוּ.

לְאֵל עוֹרֵךְ דִּין לְבוֹחֵן לְבָבוֹת בְּיוֹם דִּין.
לְגוֹלֶה עֲמֻקּוֹת בַּדִּין לְדוֹבֵר מֵישָׁרִים בְּיוֹם דִּין.
לְהוֹגֶה דֵעוֹת בַּדִּין לְוָתִיק וְעוֹשֶׂה חֶסֶד בְּיוֹם דִּין.
לְזוֹכֵר בְּרִיתוֹ בַּדִּין לְחוֹמֵל מַעֲשָׂיו בְּיוֹם דִּין.
לְטַהֵר חוֹסָיו בַּדִּין לְיוֹדֵעַ מַחֲשָׁבוֹת בְּיוֹם דִּין
לְכוֹבֵשׁ כַּעְסוֹ בַּדִּין לְלוֹבֵשׁ צְדָקוֹת בְּיוֹם דִּין.
לְמוֹחֵל עֲוֹנוֹת בַּדִּין לְנוֹרָא תְהִלּוֹת בְּיוֹם דִּין.
לְסוֹלֵחַ לַעֲמוּסָיו בַּדִּין לְעוֹנֶה לְקוֹרְאָיו בְּיוֹם דִּין.
לְפוֹעֵל רַחֲמָיו בַּדִּין לְצוֹפֶה נִסְתָּרוֹת בְּיוֹם דִּין.
לְקוֹנֶה עֲבָדָיו בַּדִּין לְרַחֵם עַמּוֹ בְּיוֹם דִּין.
לְשׁוֹמֵר אֹהֲבָיו בַּדִּין לְתוֹמֵךְ תְּמִימָיו בְּיוֹם דִּין.

*The* ארון קודש *is closed.*

*All:*

# וּבְכֵן לְךָ תַעֲלֶה קְדֻשָּׁה, כִּי אַתָּה אֱלֹהֵינוּ מֶלֶךְ.

*Some congregations say the piyut* אֲשֶׁר מִי יַעֲשֶׂה *on page 1062 before* קדושה.

## קדושה

*The following is said standing with feet together, rising on the toes at the words indicated by* ˄.

*The* קהל *then the* שליח ציבור*:*

נַקְדִּישְׁךָ וְנַעֲרִיצְךָ כְּנֹעַם שִׂיחַ סוֹד שַׂרְפֵי קֹדֶשׁ
הַמְשַׁלְּשִׁים לְךָ קְדֻשָּׁה
כַּכָּתוּב עַל יַד נְבִיאֶךָ, וְקָרָא זֶה אֶל־זֶה וְאָמַר ישעיה ו

*The* קהל *then the* שליח ציבור*:*

˄קָדוֹשׁ, ˄קָדוֹשׁ, ˄קָדוֹשׁ, יהוה צְבָאוֹת
מְלֹא כָל־הָאָרֶץ כְּבוֹדוֹ:
אָז בְּקוֹל רַעַשׁ גָּדוֹל אַדִּיר וְחָזָק מַשְׁמִיעִים קוֹל
מִתְנַשְּׂאִים לְעֻמַּת שְׂרָפִים, לְעֻמָּתָם מְשַׁבְּחִים וְאוֹמְרִים

*The* קהל *then the* שליח ציבור*:*

˄בָּרוּךְ כְּבוֹד־יהוה מִמְּקוֹמוֹ: יחזקאל ג
מִמְּקוֹמְךָ מַלְכֵּנוּ תוֹפִיעַ וְתִמְלֹךְ עָלֵינוּ
כִּי מְחַכִּים אֲנַחְנוּ לָךְ
מָתַי תִּמְלֹךְ בְּצִיּוֹן, בְּקָרוֹב בְּיָמֵינוּ לְעוֹלָם וָעֶד תִּשְׁכֹּן
תִּתְגַּדַּל וְתִתְקַדַּשׁ בְּתוֹךְ יְרוּשָׁלַיִם עִירְךָ
לְדוֹר וָדוֹר וּלְנֵצַח נְצָחִים.
וְעֵינֵינוּ תִרְאֶינָה מַלְכוּתֶךָ
כַּדָּבָר הָאָמוּר בְּשִׁירֵי עֻזֶּךָ עַל יְדֵי דָוִד מְשִׁיחַ צִדְקֶךָ.

*The* קהל *then the* שליח ציבור*:*

˄יִמְלֹךְ יהוה לְעוֹלָם, אֱלֹהַיִךְ צִיּוֹן לְדֹר וָדֹר, הַלְלוּיָהּ: תהלים קמו

HOLINESS

אַתָּה קָדוֹשׁ You are holy and Your name is holy,
and holy ones praise You daily, Selah!
For You, God, are a great and holy King.

לְדוֹר וָדוֹר From generation to generation declare God King,
for He alone is lofty and holy.

וּבְכֵן יִתְקַדַּשׁ And so may Your name be sanctified, LORD our God,
through Israel Your nation and Jerusalem, Your city,
and Zion, the dwelling place of Your honor
and through the royal house of David Your anointed,
and Your Sanctuary and Your Temple.

וּבְכֵן תֵּן פַּחְדְּךָ And so place the fear of You, LORD our God,
over all that You have made,
and the terror of You over all You have created,
and all who were made will stand in awe of You,
and all of creation will worship You,
and they will be bound all together as one
to carry out Your will with an undivided heart;
for we know, LORD our God,
that all dominion is laid out before You,
strength is in Your palm, and might in Your right hand,
Your name spreading awe over all You have created.

וּבְכֵן תֵּן כָּבוֹד And so place honor, LORD, upon Your people,
praise on those who fear You and hope into those who seek You,
the confidence to speak into all who long for You,
gladness to Your land and joy to Your city,
the flourishing of pride to David Your servant,
and a lamp laid out for his descendant, Your anointed,
soon, in our days.

וּבְכֵן צַדִּיקִים And then righteous people will see and rejoice,
and the upright will exult, and the pious revel in joy,
and injustice will have nothing more to say,
and all wickedness will fade away like smoke
as You sweep the rule of arrogance from the earth.

קדושת השם

אַתָּה קָדוֹשׁ וְשִׁמְךָ קָדוֹשׁ, וּקְדוֹשִׁים בְּכָל יוֹם יְהַלְלוּךָ סֶּלָה
כִּי אֵל מֶלֶךְ גָּדוֹל וְקָדוֹשׁ אָתָּה.

לְדוֹר וָדוֹר הַמְלִיכוּ לָאֵל, כִּי הוּא לְבַדּוֹ מָרוֹם וְקָדוֹשׁ.

וּבְכֵן יִתְקַדַּשׁ שִׁמְךָ יהוה אֱלֹהֵינוּ
עַל יִשְׂרָאֵל עַמֶּךָ וְעַל יְרוּשָׁלַיִם עִירֶךָ
וְעַל צִיּוֹן מִשְׁכַּן כְּבוֹדֶךָ
וְעַל מַלְכוּת בֵּית דָּוִד מְשִׁיחֶךָ
וְעַל מְכוֹנְךָ וְהֵיכָלֶךָ.

וּבְכֵן תֵּן פַּחְדְּךָ יהוה אֱלֹהֵינוּ עַל כָּל מַעֲשֶׂיךָ
וְאֵימָתְךָ עַל כָּל מַה שֶּׁבָּרָאתָ
וְיִירָאוּךָ כָּל הַמַּעֲשִׂים, וְיִשְׁתַּחֲווּ לְפָנֶיךָ כָּל הַבְּרוּאִים
וְיֵעָשׂוּ כֻלָּם אֲגֻדָּה אֶחָת לַעֲשׂוֹת רְצוֹנְךָ בְּלֵבָב שָׁלֵם
כְּמוֹ שֶׁיָּדַעְנוּ יהוה אֱלֹהֵינוּ שֶׁהַשָּׁלְטָן לְפָנֶיךָ
עֹז בְּיָדְךָ וּגְבוּרָה בִּימִינֶךָ, וְשִׁמְךָ נוֹרָא עַל כָּל מַה שֶּׁבָּרָאתָ.

וּבְכֵן תֵּן כָּבוֹד יהוה לְעַמֶּךָ
תְּהִלָּה לִירֵאֶיךָ, וְתִקְוָה טוֹבָה לְדוֹרְשֶׁיךָ
וּפִתְחוֹן פֶּה לַמְיַחֲלִים לָךְ
שִׂמְחָה לְאַרְצֶךָ, וְשָׂשׂוֹן לְעִירֶךָ
וּצְמִיחַת קֶרֶן לְדָוִד עַבְדֶּךָ, וַעֲרִיכַת נֵר לְבֶן יִשַׁי מְשִׁיחֶךָ
בִּמְהֵרָה בְיָמֵינוּ.

וּבְכֵן צַדִּיקִים יִרְאוּ וְיִשְׂמָחוּ, וִישָׁרִים יַעֲלֹזוּ
וַחֲסִידִים בְּרִנָּה יָגִילוּ, וְעוֹלָתָה תִּקְפָּץ פִּיהָ
וְכָל הָרִשְׁעָה כֻּלָּהּ כְּעָשָׁן תִּכְלֶה, כִּי תַעֲבִיר מֶמְשֶׁלֶת זָדוֹן מִן הָאָרֶץ.

וְתִמְלֹךְ And You, who are the LORD our God,
will rule alone over all those You have made,
in Mount Zion, the dwelling of Your glory,
and in Jerusalem, Your holy city,
as it is written in Your holy Writings:
"The LORD shall reign for ever. *Ps. 146*
He is your God, Zion, from generation to generation, Halleluya!"

קָדוֹשׁ אַתָּה You are holy, Your name is awesome,
and there is no god but You, as it is written,
"The LORD of hosts shall be raised up through His judgment, *Is. 5*
the holy God, made holy in righteousness."
Blessed are You, LORD, the holy King.

HOLINESS OF THE DAY

אַתָּה בְחַרְתָּנוּ You have chosen us from among all peoples.
You have loved and favored us.
You have raised us above all tongues.
You have made us holy through Your commandments.
You have brought us near, our King, to Your service,
and have called us by Your great and holy name.

וַתִּתֶּן לָנוּ And You, LORD our God, have given us in love
this Day of Remembrance,
a day of blowing the shofar,
a holy assembly in memory of the exodus from Egypt.

אֱלֹהֵינוּ Our God and God of our ancestors,
may there rise, come, reach, appear, be favored, heard,
regarded and remembered before You,
our recollection and remembrance,
as well as the remembrance of our ancestors,
and of the Messiah, son of David Your servant,
and of Jerusalem Your holy city,
and of all Your people the house of Israel –
for deliverance and well-being,
grace, loving-kindness and compassion,
life and peace, on this Day of Remembrance.

וְתִמְלֹךְ אַתָּה הוּא יהוה אֱלֹהֵינוּ
מְהֵרָה לְבַדֶּךָ עַל כָּל מַעֲשֶׂיךָ
בְּהַר צִיּוֹן מִשְׁכַּן כְּבוֹדֶךָ
וּבִירוּשָׁלַיִם עִיר קָדְשֶׁךָ
כַּכָּתוּב בְּדִבְרֵי קָדְשֶׁךָ
יִמְלֹךְ יהוה לְעוֹלָם, אֱלֹהַיִךְ צִיּוֹן לְדֹר וָדֹר, הַלְלוּיָהּ: תהלים קמו

קָדוֹשׁ אַתָּה וְנוֹרָא שְׁמֶךָ, וְאֵין אֱלוֹהַּ מִבַּלְעָדֶיךָ
כַּכָּתוּב, וַיִּגְבַּהּ יהוה צְבָאוֹת בַּמִּשְׁפָּט ישעיה ה
וְהָאֵל הַקָּדוֹשׁ נִקְדַּשׁ בִּצְדָקָה:
בָּרוּךְ אַתָּה יהוה, הַמֶּלֶךְ הַקָּדוֹשׁ.

קדושת היום

אַתָּה בְחַרְתָּנוּ מִכָּל הָעַמִּים
אָהַבְתָּ אוֹתָנוּ וְרָצִיתָ בָּנוּ, וְרוֹמַמְתָּנוּ מִכָּל הַלְּשׁוֹנוֹת
וְקִדַּשְׁתָּנוּ בְּמִצְוֹתֶיךָ, וְקֵרַבְתָּנוּ מַלְכֵּנוּ לַעֲבוֹדָתֶךָ
וְשִׁמְךָ הַגָּדוֹל וְהַקָּדוֹשׁ עָלֵינוּ קָרָאתָ.

וַתִּתֶּן לָנוּ יהוה אֱלֹהֵינוּ בְּאַהֲבָה אֶת יוֹם הַזִּכָּרוֹן הַזֶּה
יוֹם תְּרוּעָה מִקְרָא קֹדֶשׁ, זֵכֶר לִיצִיאַת מִצְרָיִם.

אֱלֹהֵינוּ וֵאלֹהֵי אֲבוֹתֵינוּ
יַעֲלֶה וְיָבוֹא וְיַגִּיעַ, וְיֵרָאֶה וְיֵרָצֶה וְיִשָּׁמַע
וְיִפָּקֵד וְיִזָּכֵר זִכְרוֹנֵנוּ וּפִקְדוֹנֵנוּ וְזִכְרוֹן אֲבוֹתֵינוּ
וְזִכְרוֹן מָשִׁיחַ בֶּן דָּוִד עַבְדֶּךָ, וְזִכְרוֹן יְרוּשָׁלַיִם עִיר קָדְשֶׁךָ
וְזִכְרוֹן כָּל עַמְּךָ בֵּית יִשְׂרָאֵל, לְפָנֶיךָ
לִפְלֵיטָה לְטוֹבָה, לְחֵן וּלְחֶסֶד וּלְרַחֲמִים, לְחַיִּים וּלְשָׁלוֹם
בְּיוֹם הַזִּכָּרוֹן הַזֶּה.

On it remember us, LORD our God, for good;
recollect us for blessing, and deliver us for a good life.
In accord with Your promise of salvation and compassion,
spare us and be gracious to us;
have compassion on us and deliver us, for our eyes are turned to You
because You, God, are a gracious and compassionate King.

אֱלֹהֵינוּ Our God and God of our ancestors,
rule over all the world in Your honor,
and be raised above all the earth in Your glory,
and appear, in the splendor of Your great might
before all those who live in this world, Your domain.
And all who were made will know that You made them,
and all who were formed will know that You formed them,
and all that have breath in their mouths will declare:
The LORD, God of Israel is King,
and His kingship has dominion over all.
Make us holy through Your commandments
and grant us our share in Your Torah.
Satisfy us with Your goodness,
grant our souls joy in Your salvation,
and purify our hearts to serve You in truth.
For You, LORD, are truth, and Your word is truth
and holds true forever.
Blessed are You, LORD, King over all the earth,
who sanctifies Israel and the Day of Remembrance.

TEMPLE SERVICE

רְצֵה Find favor, LORD our God, in Your people Israel,
and heed their prayer.
Restore the service to Your most holy House,
and accept soon, in love and favor,
the fire-offerings of Israel and their prayer.
May the service of Your people Israel always find favor with You.
And may our eyes witness Your return to Zion in compassion.
Blessed are You, LORD, who restores His Presence to Zion.

זָכְרֵנוּ יהוה אֱלֹהֵינוּ בּוֹ לְטוֹבָה, וּפָקְדֵנוּ בוֹ לִבְרָכָה
וְהוֹשִׁיעֵנוּ בוֹ לְחַיִּים טוֹבִים.
וּבִדְבַר יְשׁוּעָה וְרַחֲמִים חוּס וְחָנֵּנוּ, וְרַחֵם עָלֵינוּ וְהוֹשִׁיעֵנוּ
כִּי אֵלֶיךָ עֵינֵינוּ, כִּי אֵל מֶלֶךְ חַנּוּן וְרַחוּם אָתָּה.

אֱלֹהֵינוּ וֵאלֹהֵי אֲבוֹתֵינוּ
מְלֹךְ עַל כָּל הָעוֹלָם כֻּלּוֹ בִּכְבוֹדֶךָ, וְהִנָּשֵׂא עַל כָּל הָאָרֶץ בִּיקָרֶךָ
וְהוֹפַע בַּהֲדַר גְּאוֹן עֻזֶּךָ עַל כָּל יוֹשְׁבֵי תֵבֵל אַרְצֶךָ.
וְיֵדַע כָּל פָּעוּל כִּי אַתָּה פְעַלְתּוֹ
וְיָבִין כָּל יָצוּר כִּי אַתָּה יְצַרְתּוֹ
וְיֹאמַר כֹּל אֲשֶׁר נְשָׁמָה בְאַפּוֹ
יהוה אֱלֹהֵי יִשְׂרָאֵל מֶלֶךְ וּמַלְכוּתוֹ בַּכֹּל מָשָׁלָה.
קַדְּשֵׁנוּ בְּמִצְוֹתֶיךָ וְתֵן חֶלְקֵנוּ בְּתוֹרָתֶךָ
שַׂבְּעֵנוּ מִטּוּבֶךָ, וְשַׂמַּח נַפְשֵׁנוּ בִּישׁוּעָתֶךָ
וְטַהֵר לִבֵּנוּ לְעָבְדְּךָ בֶּאֱמֶת
כִּי אַתָּה אֱלֹהִים אֱמֶת, וּדְבָרְךָ אֱמֶת וְקַיָּם לָעַד.
בָּרוּךְ אַתָּה יהוה, מֶלֶךְ עַל כָּל הָאָרֶץ
מְקַדֵּשׁ יִשְׂרָאֵל וְיוֹם הַזִּכָּרוֹן.

עבודה

רְצֵה יהוה אֱלֹהֵינוּ בְּעַמְּךָ יִשְׂרָאֵל, וְלִתְפִלָּתָם שְׁעֵה
וְהָשֵׁב אֶת הָעֲבוֹדָה לִדְבִיר בֵּיתֶךָ
וְאִשֵּׁי יִשְׂרָאֵל וּתְפִלָּתָם, מְהֵרָה בְּאַהֲבָה תְקַבֵּל בְּרָצוֹן
וּתְהִי לְרָצוֹן תָּמִיד עֲבוֹדַת יִשְׂרָאֵל עַמֶּךָ.
וְתֶחֱזֶינָה עֵינֵינוּ בְּשׁוּבְךָ לְצִיּוֹן בְּרַחֲמִים.
בָּרוּךְ אַתָּה יהוה, הַמַּחֲזִיר שְׁכִינָתוֹ לְצִיּוֹן.

הודאה

*Bow at the first five words.*

| | *During the* חזרת הש״ץ, *the* קהל *says quietly:* |
|---|---|
| ״מוֹדִים אֲנַחְנוּ לָךְ | ״מוֹדִים אֲנַחְנוּ לָךְ |
| שָׁאַתָּה הוּא יהוה אֱלֹהֵינוּ | שָׁאַתָּה הוּא יהוה אֱלֹהֵינוּ |
| וֵאלֹהֵי אֲבוֹתֵינוּ לְעוֹלָם וָעֶד. | וֵאלֹהֵי אֲבוֹתֵינוּ |
| צוּר חַיֵּינוּ, מָגֵן יִשְׁעֵנוּ | אֱלֹהֵי כָל בָּשָׂר |
| אַתָּה הוּא לְדוֹר וָדוֹר. | יוֹצְרֵנוּ, יוֹצֵר בְּרֵאשִׁית. |
| נוֹדֶה לְּךָ וּנְסַפֵּר תְּהִלָּתֶךָ | בְּרָכוֹת וְהוֹדָאוֹת |
| עַל חַיֵּינוּ הַמְּסוּרִים בְּיָדֶךָ | לְשִׁמְךָ הַגָּדוֹל וְהַקָּדוֹשׁ |
| וְעַל נִשְׁמוֹתֵינוּ הַפְּקוּדוֹת לָךְ | עַל שֶׁהֶחֱיִיתָנוּ וְקִיַּמְתָּנוּ. |
| וְעַל נִסֶּיךָ שֶׁבְּכָל יוֹם עִמָּנוּ | כֵּן תְּחַיֵּנוּ וּתְקַיְּמֵנוּ |
| וְעַל נִפְלְאוֹתֶיךָ וְטוֹבוֹתֶיךָ | וְתֶאֱסֹף גָּלֻיּוֹתֵינוּ |
| שֶׁבְּכָל עֵת, עֶרֶב וָבֹקֶר וְצָהֳרָיִם. | לְחַצְרוֹת קָדְשֶׁךָ |
| הַטּוֹב, כִּי לֹא כָלוּ רַחֲמֶיךָ | לִשְׁמֹר חֻקֶּיךָ וְלַעֲשׂוֹת רְצוֹנֶךָ |
| וְהַמְרַחֵם, כִּי לֹא תַמּוּ חֲסָדֶיךָ | וּלְעָבְדְּךָ בְּלֵבָב שָׁלֵם |
| כִּי מֵעוֹלָם קִוִּינוּ לָךְ. | עַל שֶׁאֲנַחְנוּ מוֹדִים לָךְ. |
| | בָּרוּךְ אֵל הַהוֹדָאוֹת. |

וְעַל כֻּלָּם
יִתְבָּרַךְ וְיִתְרוֹמַם וְיִתְנַשֵּׂא שִׁמְךָ מַלְכֵּנוּ תָּמִיד לְעוֹלָם וָעֶד.

*The* קהל *then the* שליח ציבור*:*

וּכְתֹב לְחַיִּים טוֹבִים כָּל בְּנֵי בְרִיתֶךָ.

וְכֹל הַחַיִּים יוֹדְוּךָ סֶּלָה
וִיהַלְלוּ וִיבָרְכוּ אֶת שִׁמְךָ הַגָּדוֹל בֶּאֱמֶת לְעוֹלָם כִּי טוֹב
הָאֵל יְשׁוּעָתֵנוּ וְעֶזְרָתֵנוּ סֶלָה, הָאֵל הַטּוֹב.
״בָּרוּךְ אַתָּה יהוה, הַטּוֹב שִׁמְךָ וּלְךָ נָאֶה לְהוֹדוֹת.

*In Israel, if Kohanim bless the congregation, turn to page 1002. See laws 91–96.*

אֱלֹהֵינוּ Our God and God of our fathers,
bless us with the threefold blessing in the Torah,
written by the hand of Moses Your servant
and pronounced by Aaron and his sons the priests,
Your holy people, as it is said:

May the LORD bless you and protect you. *Num. 6*
*Cong:* May it be Your will.
May the LORD make His face shine on you and be gracious to you.
*Cong:* May it be Your will.
May the LORD turn His face toward you, and grant you peace.
*Cong:* May it be Your will.

PEACE

שִׂים שָׁלוֹם Grant peace, goodness and blessing,
life, grace, loving-kindness and compassion
to us and all Israel Your people.
Bless us, our Father, all as one, with the light of Your face,
for by the light of Your face You have given us, LORD our God,
the Torah of life and love of kindness,
righteousness, blessing, compassion, life and peace.
May it be good in Your eyes to bless us and all Your people Israel
at every time, in every hour, with Your peace.

*The congregation then the Leader:*

בְּסֵפֶר חַיִּים In the book of life, blessing, peace and prosperity,
and good decrees, salvations and consolations
may we and all Your people the house of Israel
be remembered and written before You
for a good life, and for peace.

Blessed are You, LORD, who blesses His people Israel with peace.

*The following verse concludes the Leader's Repetition of the Amida. See law 64.*

May the words of my mouth and the meditation of my heart *Ps. 19*
find favor before You, LORD, my Rock and Redeemer.

*In* ארץ ישראל*, if* כהנים *say* ברכת כהנים*, turn to page 1003. See laws 91–96.*

אֱלֹהֵינוּ וֵאלֹהֵי אֲבוֹתֵינוּ, בָּרְכֵנוּ בַּבְּרָכָה הַמְשֻׁלֶּשֶׁת בַּתּוֹרָה
הַכְּתוּבָה עַל יְדֵי מֹשֶׁה עַבְדֶּךָ, הָאֲמוּרָה מִפִּי אַהֲרֹן וּבָנָיו
כֹּהֲנִים עַם קְדוֹשֶׁיךָ, כָּאָמוּר

יְבָרֶכְךָ יהוה וְיִשְׁמְרֶךָ: קהל: כֵּן יְהִי רָצוֹן במדבר ו
יָאֵר יהוה פָּנָיו אֵלֶיךָ וִיחֻנֶּךָּ: קהל: כֵּן יְהִי רָצוֹן
יִשָּׂא יהוה פָּנָיו אֵלֶיךָ וְיָשֵׂם לְךָ שָׁלוֹם: קהל: כֵּן יְהִי רָצוֹן

ברכת שלום

שִׂים שָׁלוֹם טוֹבָה וּבְרָכָה, חַיִּים חֵן וָחֶסֶד וְרַחֲמִים
עָלֵינוּ וְעַל כָּל יִשְׂרָאֵל עַמֶּךָ.
בָּרְכֵנוּ אָבִינוּ כֻּלָּנוּ כְּאֶחָד בְּאוֹר פָּנֶיךָ
כִּי בְאוֹר פָּנֶיךָ נָתַתָּ לָּנוּ יהוה אֱלֹהֵינוּ
תּוֹרַת חַיִּים וְאַהֲבַת חֶסֶד
וּצְדָקָה וּבְרָכָה וְרַחֲמִים וְחַיִּים וְשָׁלוֹם.
וְטוֹב יִהְיֶה בְעֵינֶיךָ לְבָרְכֵנוּ וּלְבָרֵךְ אֶת כָּל עַמְּךָ יִשְׂרָאֵל
בְּכָל עֵת וּבְכָל שָׁעָה בִּשְׁלוֹמֶךָ.

*The* קהל *then the* שליח ציבור*:*

בְּסֵפֶר חַיִּים, בְּרָכָה וְשָׁלוֹם, וּפַרְנָסָה טוֹבָה
וּגְזֵרוֹת טוֹבוֹת, יְשׁוּעוֹת וְנֶחָמוֹת, נִזָּכֵר וְנִכָּתֵב לְפָנֶיךָ
אֲנַחְנוּ וְכָל עַמְּךָ בֵּית יִשְׂרָאֵל לְחַיִּים טוֹבִים וּלְשָׁלוֹם.

בָּרוּךְ אַתָּה יהוה, הַמְבָרֵךְ אֶת עַמּוֹ יִשְׂרָאֵל בַּשָּׁלוֹם.

*The following verse concludes the* חזרת הש״ץ*. See law 64.*

יִהְיוּ לְרָצוֹן אִמְרֵי־פִי וְהֶגְיוֹן לִבִּי לְפָנֶיךָ, יהוה צוּרִי וְגֹאֲלִי: תהלים יט

*The Ark is opened.*

*Some omit the first line, "We have sinned before You", in order to avoid calling attention to our sins on Rosh HaShana.*

אָבִינוּ מַלְכֵּנוּ Our Father, our King, we have sinned before You.

Our Father, our King, we have no king but You.

Our Father, our King, deal kindly with us for the sake of Your name.

Our Father our King, renew for us a good year.

Our Father, our King, nullify all harsh decrees against us.

Our Father, our King, nullify the plans of those who hate us.

Our Father, our King, thwart the counsel of our enemies.

Our Father, our King, rid us of every oppressor and adversary.

Our Father, our King, close the mouths of our adversaries and accusers.

Our Father, our King, efface pestilence, sword, famine,
captivity and destruction, iniquity and eradication
from the people of Your covenant.

Our Father, our King, withhold the plague from Your heritage.

Our Father, our King, forgive and pardon all our iniquities.

---

So we experience God in two ways: in awe and in love. In awe, for He is our Sovereign, the supreme power of the universe. But also in love, for He brought us into being. He is to us as a parent.

Between a servant and a king there can be estrangement. A king can send a servant into exile. But between a father and a child there can be no estrangement. However far removed they are from one another, the bond between parent and child still holds.

The beauty of Rabbi Akiva's prayer is the way he orders the words *Avinu Malkenu*. God is our King, and a king rules by justice. But before God is a king He is a parent. A parent loves. A parent lets love override strict justice. A parent forgives.

In the words "Our Father, our King," Rabbi Akiva was saying: Yes, You are our King but remember that You are also our Parent. Therefore, though we have sinned, forgive us. If our words are honest and penetrate to our heart, they penetrate to God's heart also, and God forgives.

There is a beauty and simplicity in this idea. The scientist Stephen Hawking once wrote that if we discovered a unified field theory that would explain the

*The* ארון קודש *is opened.*

*Some omit the first line,* חָטָאנוּ לְפָנֶיךָ, *in order to avoid calling attention to our sins on* ראש השנה.

אָבִינוּ מַלְכֵּנוּ, חָטָאנוּ לְפָנֶיךָ.
אָבִינוּ מַלְכֵּנוּ, אֵין לָנוּ מֶלֶךְ אֶלָּא אָתָּה.
אָבִינוּ מַלְכֵּנוּ, עֲשֵׂה עִמָּנוּ לְמַעַן שְׁמֶךָ.
אָבִינוּ מַלְכֵּנוּ, חַדֵּשׁ עָלֵינוּ שָׁנָה טוֹבָה.
אָבִינוּ מַלְכֵּנוּ, בַּטֵּל מֵעָלֵינוּ כָּל גְּזֵרוֹת קָשׁוֹת.
אָבִינוּ מַלְכֵּנוּ, בַּטֵּל מַחְשְׁבוֹת שׂוֹנְאֵינוּ.
אָבִינוּ מַלְכֵּנוּ, הָפֵר עֲצַת אוֹיְבֵינוּ.
אָבִינוּ מַלְכֵּנוּ, כַּלֵּה כָּל צַר וּמַשְׂטִין מֵעָלֵינוּ.
אָבִינוּ מַלְכֵּנוּ, סְתֹם פִּיּוֹת מַשְׂטִינֵנוּ וּמְקַטְרְגֵנוּ.
אָבִינוּ מַלְכֵּנוּ, כַּלֵּה דֶּבֶר וְחֶרֶב וְרָעָב וּשְׁבִי וּמַשְׁחִית וְעָוֹן וּשְׁמַד
מִבְּנֵי בְרִיתֶךָ.
אָבִינוּ מַלְכֵּנוּ, מְנַע מַגֵּפָה מִנַּחֲלָתֶךָ.
אָבִינוּ מַלְכֵּנוּ, סְלַח וּמְחַל לְכָל עֲוֹנוֹתֵינוּ.

---

AVINU MALKENU – OUR FATHER, OUR KING

Once a great naval ship sailed into the port. On the hillside overlooking the sea a crowd had gathered to watch it enter. Among them was a small child, who waved to the ship. An adult asked the child to whom he was waving. The child replied, "I am waving to the captain of the ship." The man asked, "Do you think the captain of such a great ship would notice a small child like you?" "I am sure of it," said the child. "Why?" said the adult. "You see," answered the child, "the captain of the ship is my father."

On the one hand God is our King and we are His servants. But on the other, He is our Father and we are His children. When God told Moses to lead the Israelites to freedom, He told him to say to Pharaoh: "My child, My firstborn, Israel" (Ex. 4:22). When Moses commanded the Israelites not to lacerate themselves nor divide themselves into factions, he said: "You are the children of the Lord your God" (Deut. 14:1).

Our Father, our King, wipe away and remove our transgressions and sins from Your sight.

Our Father, our King, erase in Your abundant mercy all records of our sins.

*The following nine verses are said responsively, first by the Leader, then by the congregation:*

Our Father, our King, bring us back to You in perfect repentance.

Our Father, our King, send a complete healing to the sick of Your people.

Our Father, our King, tear up the evil decree against us.

Our Father, our King, remember us with a memory of favorable deeds before You.

Our Father, our King, write us in the book of good life.

Our Father, our King, write us in the book of redemption and salvation.

Our Father, our King, write us in the book of livelihood and sustenance.

Our Father, our King, write us in the book of merit.

Our Father, our King, write us in the book of pardon and forgiveness.

*End of responsive reading.*

Our Father, our King, let salvation soon flourish for us.

Our Father, our King, raise the honor of Your people Israel.

Our Father, our King, raise the honor of Your anointed.

Our Father, our King, fill our hands with Your blessings.

Our Father, our King, fill our storehouses with abundance.

Our Father, our King, hear our voice, pity and be compassionate to us.

Our Father, our King, accept, with compassion and favor, our prayer.

Our Father, our King, open the gates of heaven to our prayer.

Our Father, our King, remember that we are dust.

---

understand the Infinite, we do not need cosmology and theoretical physics. We need to understand what it is to be a parent. A parent cannot forsake his or her child, whatever wrong they may have done. God's love for us is like that but deeper: "Were my father and mother to forsake me, the LORD would take me in" (Psalms 27:10).

אָבִינוּ מַלְכֵּנוּ, מְחֵה וְהַעֲבֵר פְּשָׁעֵינוּ וְחַטֹּאתֵינוּ מִנֶּגֶד עֵינֶיךָ.
אָבִינוּ מַלְכֵּנוּ, מְחֹק בְּרַחֲמֶיךָ הָרַבִּים כָּל שִׁטְרֵי חוֹבוֹתֵינוּ.

*The following nine verses are said responsively, first by the* שליח ציבור*, then by the* קהל*:*

אָבִינוּ מַלְכֵּנוּ, הַחֲזִירֵנוּ בִּתְשׁוּבָה שְׁלֵמָה לְפָנֶיךָ.
אָבִינוּ מַלְכֵּנוּ, שְׁלַח רְפוּאָה שְׁלֵמָה לְחוֹלֵי עַמֶּךָ.
אָבִינוּ מַלְכֵּנוּ, קְרַע רֹעַ גְּזַר דִּינֵנוּ.
אָבִינוּ מַלְכֵּנוּ, זָכְרֵנוּ בְּזִכָּרוֹן טוֹב לְפָנֶיךָ.
אָבִינוּ מַלְכֵּנוּ, כָּתְבֵנוּ בְּסֵפֶר חַיִּים טוֹבִים.
אָבִינוּ מַלְכֵּנוּ, כָּתְבֵנוּ בְּסֵפֶר גְּאֻלָּה וִישׁוּעָה.
אָבִינוּ מַלְכֵּנוּ, כָּתְבֵנוּ בְּסֵפֶר פַּרְנָסָה וְכַלְכָּלָה.
אָבִינוּ מַלְכֵּנוּ, כָּתְבֵנוּ בְּסֵפֶר זְכֻיּוֹת.
אָבִינוּ מַלְכֵּנוּ, כָּתְבֵנוּ בְּסֵפֶר סְלִיחָה וּמְחִילָה.

*End of responsive reading.*

אָבִינוּ מַלְכֵּנוּ, הַצְמַח לָנוּ יְשׁוּעָה בְּקָרוֹב.
אָבִינוּ מַלְכֵּנוּ, הָרֵם קֶרֶן יִשְׂרָאֵל עַמֶּךָ.
אָבִינוּ מַלְכֵּנוּ, הָרֵם קֶרֶן מְשִׁיחֶךָ.
אָבִינוּ מַלְכֵּנוּ, מַלֵּא יָדֵינוּ מִבִּרְכוֹתֶיךָ.
אָבִינוּ מַלְכֵּנוּ, מַלֵּא אֲסָמֵינוּ שָׂבָע.
אָבִינוּ מַלְכֵּנוּ, שְׁמַע קוֹלֵנוּ, חוּס וְרַחֵם עָלֵינוּ.
אָבִינוּ מַלְכֵּנוּ, קַבֵּל בְּרַחֲמִים וּבְרָצוֹן אֶת תְּפִלָּתֵנוּ.
אָבִינוּ מַלְכֵּנוּ, פְּתַח שַׁעֲרֵי שָׁמַיִם לִתְפִלָּתֵנוּ.
אָבִינוּ מַלְכֵּנוּ, זְכֹר כִּי עָפָר אֲנָחְנוּ.

---

entire structure of the physical universe, we would "know the mind of God." Judaism holds that to know the mind of God as much as a finite being can ever

אָבִינוּ מַלְכֵּנוּ, נָא אַל תְּשִׁיבֵנוּ רֵיקָם מִלְּפָנֶיךָ.
אָבִינוּ מַלְכֵּנוּ, תְּהֵא הַשָּׁעָה הַזֹּאת שְׁעַת רַחֲמִים וְעֵת רָצוֹן מִלְּפָנֶיךָ.
אָבִינוּ מַלְכֵּנוּ, חֲמֹל עָלֵינוּ וְעַל עוֹלָלֵינוּ וְטַפֵּנוּ.
אָבִינוּ מַלְכֵּנוּ, עֲשֵׂה לְמַעַן הֲרוּגִים עַל שֵׁם קָדְשֶׁךָ.
אָבִינוּ מַלְכֵּנוּ, עֲשֵׂה לְמַעַן טְבוּחִים עַל יִחוּדֶךָ.
אָבִינוּ מַלְכֵּנוּ, עֲשֵׂה לְמַעַן בָּאֵי בָאֵשׁ וּבַמַּיִם עַל קִדּוּשׁ שְׁמֶךָ.
אָבִינוּ מַלְכֵּנוּ, נְקֹם לְעֵינֵינוּ נִקְמַת דַּם עֲבָדֶיךָ הַשָּׁפוּךְ.
אָבִינוּ מַלְכֵּנוּ, עֲשֵׂה לְמַעַנְךָ אִם לֹא לְמַעֲנֵנוּ.
אָבִינוּ מַלְכֵּנוּ, עֲשֵׂה לְמַעַנְךָ וְהוֹשִׁיעֵנוּ.
אָבִינוּ מַלְכֵּנוּ, עֲשֵׂה לְמַעַן רַחֲמֶיךָ הָרַבִּים.
אָבִינוּ מַלְכֵּנוּ, עֲשֵׂה לְמַעַן שִׁמְךָ הַגָּדוֹל הַגִּבּוֹר וְהַנּוֹרָא
שֶׁנִּקְרָא עָלֵינוּ.
◂ אָבִינוּ מַלְכֵּנוּ, חָנֵּנוּ וַעֲנֵנוּ, כִּי אֵין בָּנוּ מַעֲשִׂים
עֲשֵׂה עִמָּנוּ צְדָקָה וָחֶסֶד וְהוֹשִׁיעֵנוּ.

*The* ארון קודש *is closed.*

---

חָנֵּנוּ וַעֲנֵנוּ, כִּי אֵין בָּנוּ מַעֲשִׂים *Be gracious to us and answer us, though we have no worthy deeds.* Rabbi Levi Yitzḥak of Berditchev (c. 1740–1810), one of the third generation of Hasidic leaders, was legendary for his daring prayers on behalf of the Jewish people on the Days of Awe. Elie Wiesel writes of him, "As a child, I visualized him as a powerful, invincible defender of the weak, a dispenser of mercy ready to risk all and lose all in the pursuit of truth and justice. He was my hero then, he still is."* With love, audacity, humor and compassion, he spoke to God in the intimate grammar and conversational closeness that has made Jewish prayer distinctive since the days of Abraham.

One year, he presented this claim to God: "Master of the Universe, there was a time when You offered Your Law to every nation. Each in turn declined

* Elie Wiesel, *Souls on Fire: Portraits and Legends of Hasidic Masters* (New York: Summit Books, 1982), p. 90.

FULL KADDISH

*Leader:* יִתְגַּדַּל Magnified and sanctified may His great name be,
in the world He created by His will.
May He establish His kingdom,
make His salvation flourish,
and hasten His messiah,
in your lifetime and in your days,
and in the lifetime of all the house of Israel,
swiftly and soon –
and say: Amen.

*All:* May His great name be blessed
for ever and all time.

*Leader:* Blessed and praised, glorified and exalted,
raised and honored,
uplifted and lauded be
the name of the Holy One,
blessed be He,
beyond any blessing,
song, praise and consolation
uttered in the world –
and say: Amen.

May the prayers and pleas of all the house of Israel
be accepted by their Father in heaven –
and say: Amen.

May there be great peace from heaven,
and a good life for us and all Israel –
and say: Amen.

*Bow, take three steps back, as if taking leave of the Divine Presence, then bow, first left, then right, then center, while saying:*

May He who makes peace in His high places,
make peace for us and all Israel –
and say: Amen.

## קדיש שלם

ש״ץ: יִתְגַּדַּל וְיִתְקַדַּשׁ שְׁמֵהּ רַבָּא (קהל: אָמֵן)
בְּעָלְמָא דִּי בְרָא כִרְעוּתֵהּ
וְיַמְלִיךְ מַלְכוּתֵהּ וְיַצְמַח פֻּרְקָנֵהּ וִיקָרֵב מְשִׁיחֵהּ (קהל: אָמֵן)
בְּחַיֵּיכוֹן וּבְיוֹמֵיכוֹן וּבְחַיֵּי דְכָל בֵּית יִשְׂרָאֵל
בַּעֲגָלָא וּבִזְמַן קָרִיב
וְאִמְרוּ אָמֵן. (קהל: אָמֵן)

קהל וש״ץ: יְהֵא שְׁמֵהּ רַבָּא מְבָרַךְ לְעָלַם וּלְעָלְמֵי עָלְמַיָּא.

ש״ץ: יִתְבָּרַךְ וְיִשְׁתַּבַּח וְיִתְפָּאַר וְיִתְרוֹמַם וְיִתְנַשֵּׂא
וְיִתְהַדָּר וְיִתְעַלֶּה וְיִתְהַלָּל
שְׁמֵהּ דְּקֻדְשָׁא בְּרִיךְ הוּא (קהל: אָמֵן)
לְעֵלָּא לְעֵלָּא מִכָּל בִּרְכָתָא וְשִׁירָתָא, תֻּשְׁבְּחָתָא וְנֶחֱמָתָא
דַּאֲמִירָן בְּעָלְמָא
וְאִמְרוּ אָמֵן. (קהל: אָמֵן)

תִּתְקַבַּל צְלוֹתְהוֹן וּבָעוּתְהוֹן דְּכָל בֵּית יִשְׂרָאֵל
קֳדָם אֲבוּהוֹן דִּי בִשְׁמַיָּא
וְאִמְרוּ אָמֵן. (קהל: אָמֵן)

יְהֵא שְׁלָמָא רַבָּא מִן שְׁמַיָּא
וְחַיִּים טוֹבִים עָלֵינוּ וְעַל כָּל יִשְׂרָאֵל
וְאִמְרוּ אָמֵן. (קהל: אָמֵן)

*Bow, take three steps back, as if taking leave of the Divine Presence, then bow, first left, then right, then center, while saying:*

עֹשֶׂה הַשָּׁלוֹם בִּמְרוֹמָיו
הוּא יַעֲשֶׂה שָׁלוֹם עָלֵינוּ וְעַל כָּל יִשְׂרָאֵל
וְאִמְרוּ אָמֵן. (קהל: אָמֵן)

THE DAILY PSALM

*One of the following psalms is said on the appropriate day of the week as indicated. After the psalm, the Mourner's Kaddish is said.*

*Sunday:* Today is the first day of the week,
on which the Levites used to say this psalm in the Temple:

לְדָוִד מִזְמוֹר A psalm of David. The earth is the LORD's and all it contains, the world and all who live in it. For He founded it on the seas and established it on the streams. Who may climb the mountain of the LORD? Who may stand in His holy place? He who has clean hands and a pure heart, who has not taken My name in vain or sworn deceitfully. He shall receive a blessing from the LORD, and just reward from the God of his salvation. This is a generation of those who seek Him, the descendants of Jacob who seek Your presence, Selah! Lift up your heads, O gates; be uplifted, eternal doors, so that the King of glory may enter. Who is the King of glory? It is the LORD, strong and mighty, the LORD mighty in battle. Lift up your heads, O gates; lift them up, eternal doors, that the King of glory may enter. ▸ Who is He, the King of glory? The LORD of hosts, He is the King of glory, Selah! *Ps. 24*

*Mourner's Kaddish (page 714)*

*Tuesday:* Today is the third day of the week,
on which the Levites used to say this psalm in the Temple:

מִזְמוֹר לְאָסָף A psalm of Asaph. God stands in the divine assembly. Among the judges He delivers judgment. How long will you judge unjustly, showing favor to the wicked? Selah. Do justice to the weak and the orphaned. Vindicate the poor and destitute. Rescue the weak and needy. Save them from the hand of the wicked. They do not know nor do they understand. They walk about in darkness while all the earth's foundations shake. I once said, "You are like gods, all of you are sons of the Most High." But you shall die like mere men, you will fall like any prince. ▸ Arise, O LORD, judge the earth, for all the nations are Your possession. *Ps. 82*

*Mourner's Kaddish (page 714)*

*Wednesday:* Today is the fourth day of the week,
on which the Levites used to say this psalm in the Temple:

אֵל־נְקָמוֹת God of retribution, LORD, God of retribution, appear! Rise up, Judge of the earth. Repay to the arrogant what they deserve. How long shall the wicked, LORD, how long shall the wicked triumph? They pour out insolent words. All the evildoers are full of boasting. They crush Your people, LORD, and oppress Your inheritance. They kill the widow and the stranger. They murder the orphaned. They say, "The LORD does not see. The God of Jacob pays no heed." Take heed, you most brutish people. You fools, when will you grow wise? Will He who implants the ear not hear? Will He who formed the eye not see? Will He who *Ps. 94*

## שיר של יום

*One of the following psalms is said on the appropriate day of the week as indicated. After the psalm,* קדיש יתום *is said.*

*Sunday* הַיּוֹם יוֹם רִאשׁוֹן בְּשַׁבָּת, שֶׁבּוֹ הָיוּ הַלְוִיִּם אוֹמְרִים בְּבֵית הַמִּקְדָּשׁ:

תהלים כד
לְדָוִד מִזְמוֹר, לַיהוה הָאָרֶץ וּמְלוֹאָהּ, תֵּבֵל וְיֹשְׁבֵי בָהּ: כִּי־הוּא עַל־יַמִּים יְסָדָהּ, וְעַל־נְהָרוֹת יְכוֹנְנֶהָ: מִי־יַעֲלֶה בְהַר־יהוה, וּמִי־יָקוּם בִּמְקוֹם קָדְשׁוֹ: נְקִי כַפַּיִם וּבַר־לֵבָב, אֲשֶׁר לֹא־נָשָׂא לַשָּׁוְא נַפְשִׁי, וְלֹא נִשְׁבַּע לְמִרְמָה: יִשָּׂא בְרָכָה מֵאֵת יהוה, וּצְדָקָה מֵאֱלֹהֵי יִשְׁעוֹ: זֶה דּוֹר דֹּרְשָׁו, מְבַקְשֵׁי פָנֶיךָ יַעֲקֹב סֶלָה: שְׂאוּ שְׁעָרִים רָאשֵׁיכֶם, וְהִנָּשְׂאוּ פִּתְחֵי עוֹלָם, וְיָבוֹא מֶלֶךְ הַכָּבוֹד: מִי זֶה מֶלֶךְ הַכָּבוֹד, יהוה עִזּוּז וְגִבּוֹר, יהוה גִּבּוֹר מִלְחָמָה: שְׂאוּ שְׁעָרִים רָאשֵׁיכֶם, וּשְׂאוּ פִּתְחֵי עוֹלָם, וְיָבֹא מֶלֶךְ הַכָּבוֹד: › מִי הוּא זֶה מֶלֶךְ הַכָּבוֹד, יהוה צְבָאוֹת הוּא מֶלֶךְ הַכָּבוֹד סֶלָה:

קדיש יתום (*page 715*)

*Tuesday* הַיּוֹם יוֹם שְׁלִישִׁי בְּשַׁבָּת, שֶׁבּוֹ הָיוּ הַלְוִיִּם אוֹמְרִים בְּבֵית הַמִּקְדָּשׁ:

תהלים פב
מִזְמוֹר לְאָסָף, אֱלֹהִים נִצָּב בַּעֲדַת־אֵל, בְּקֶרֶב אֱלֹהִים יִשְׁפֹּט: עַד־מָתַי תִּשְׁפְּטוּ־עָוֶל, וּפְנֵי רְשָׁעִים תִּשְׂאוּ־סֶלָה: שִׁפְטוּ־דַל וְיָתוֹם, עָנִי וָרָשׁ הַצְדִּיקוּ: פַּלְּטוּ־דַל וְאֶבְיוֹן, מִיַּד רְשָׁעִים הַצִּילוּ: לֹא יָדְעוּ וְלֹא יָבִינוּ, בַּחֲשֵׁכָה יִתְהַלָּכוּ, יִמּוֹטוּ כָּל־מוֹסְדֵי אָרֶץ: אֲנִי־אָמַרְתִּי אֱלֹהִים אַתֶּם, וּבְנֵי עֶלְיוֹן כֻּלְּכֶם: אָכֵן כְּאָדָם תְּמוּתוּן, וּכְאַחַד הַשָּׂרִים תִּפֹּלוּ: › קוּמָה אֱלֹהִים שָׁפְטָה הָאָרֶץ, כִּי־אַתָּה תִנְחַל בְּכָל־הַגּוֹיִם:

קדיש יתום (*page 715*)

*Wednesday* הַיּוֹם יוֹם רְבִיעִי בְּשַׁבָּת, שֶׁבּוֹ הָיוּ הַלְוִיִּם אוֹמְרִים בְּבֵית הַמִּקְדָּשׁ:

תהלים צד
אֵל־נְקָמוֹת יהוה, אֵל נְקָמוֹת הוֹפִיעַ: הִנָּשֵׂא שֹׁפֵט הָאָרֶץ, הָשֵׁב גְּמוּל עַל־גֵּאִים: עַד־מָתַי רְשָׁעִים, יהוה, עַד־מָתַי רְשָׁעִים יַעֲלֹזוּ: יַבִּיעוּ יְדַבְּרוּ עָתָק, יִתְאַמְּרוּ כָּל־פֹּעֲלֵי אָוֶן: עַמְּךָ יהוה יְדַכְּאוּ, וְנַחֲלָתְךָ יְעַנּוּ: אַלְמָנָה וְגֵר יַהֲרֹגוּ, וִיתוֹמִים יְרַצֵּחוּ: וַיֹּאמְרוּ לֹא יִרְאֶה־יָּהּ, וְלֹא־יָבִין אֱלֹהֵי יַעֲקֹב: בִּינוּ בֹּעֲרִים בָּעָם, וּכְסִילִים מָתַי תַּשְׂכִּילוּ: הֲנֹטַע אֹזֶן הֲלֹא יִשְׁמָע, אִם־

disciplines nations – He who teaches man knowledge – not punish? The LORD knows that the thoughts of man are a mere fleeting breath. Happy is the man whom You discipline, LORD, the one You instruct in Your Torah, giving him tranquility in days of trouble, until a pit is dug for the wicked. For the LORD will not forsake His people, nor abandon His heritage. Judgment shall again accord with justice, and all the upright in heart will follow it. Who will rise up for me against the wicked? Who will stand up for me against wrongdoers? Had the LORD not been my help, I would soon have dwelt in death's silence. When I thought my foot was slipping, Your loving-kindness, LORD, gave me support. When I was filled with anxiety, Your consolations soothed my soul. Can a corrupt throne be allied with You? Can injustice be framed into law? They join forces against the life of the righteous, and condemn the innocent to death. But the LORD is my stronghold, my God is the Rock of my refuge. He will bring back on them their wickedness, and destroy them for their evil deeds. The LORD our God will destroy them.

▸ Come, let us sing for joy to the LORD; let us shout aloud to the Rock of our salvation. Let us greet Him with thanksgiving, shout aloud to Him with songs of praise. For the LORD is the great God, the King great above all powers. *Ps. 95*

*Mourner's Kaddish (on the next page)*

*Friday:* Today is the sixth day of the week,
on which the Levites used to say this psalm in the Temple:

יהוה מָלָךְ The LORD reigns. He is robed in majesty. The LORD is robed, girded with strength. The world is firmly established; it cannot be moved. Your throne stands firm as of old; You are eternal. Rivers lift up, LORD, rivers lift up their voice, rivers lift up their crashing waves. Mightier than the noise of many waters, than the mighty waves of the sea is the LORD on high. ▸ Your testimonies are very sure; holiness adorns Your House, LORD, for evermore. *Ps. 93*

*Mourner's Kaddish (on the next page)*

*The following psalm is said on all days. Some congregations recite it at the end of Musaf.*

לְדָוִד By David. The LORD is my light and my salvation – whom then shall I fear? The LORD is the stronghold of my life – of whom shall I be afraid? When evil men close in on me to devour my flesh, it is they, my enemies and foes, who stumble and fall. Should an army besiege me, my heart would not fear. Should war break out against me, still I would be confident. One thing I ask of the LORD, only this do I seek: to live in the House of the LORD all the days of my life, to gaze on the beauty of the LORD and worship in His Temple. For He will keep me safe in His pavilion on the day of trouble. He will hide me under the cover of His tent. He will set me high upon a rock. Now my head is high above my enemies who surround me. I will sacrifice in His tent with shouts of joy. I *Ps. 27*

יֹצֵר עַיִן הֲלֹא יַבִּיט: הֲיֹסֵר גּוֹיִם הֲלֹא יוֹכִיחַ, הַמְלַמֵּד אָדָם דָּעַת: יהוה
יֹדֵעַ מַחְשְׁבוֹת אָדָם, כִּי־הֵמָּה הָבֶל: אַשְׁרֵי הַגֶּבֶר אֲשֶׁר־תְּיַסְּרֶנּוּ יָּהּ,
וּמִתּוֹרָתְךָ תְלַמְּדֶנּוּ: לְהַשְׁקִיט לוֹ מִימֵי רָע, עַד יִכָּרֶה לָרָשָׁע שָׁחַת:
כִּי לֹא־יִטֹּשׁ יהוה עַמּוֹ, וְנַחֲלָתוֹ לֹא יַעֲזֹב: כִּי־עַד־צֶדֶק יָשׁוּב מִשְׁפָּט,
וְאַחֲרָיו כָּל־יִשְׁרֵי־לֵב: מִי־יָקוּם לִי עִם־מְרֵעִים, מִי־יִתְיַצֵּב לִי עִם־פֹּעֲלֵי
אָוֶן: לוּלֵי יהוה עֶזְרָתָה לִּי, כִּמְעַט שָׁכְנָה דוּמָה נַפְשִׁי: אִם־אָמַרְתִּי מָטָה
רַגְלִי, חַסְדְּךָ יהוה יִסְעָדֵנִי: בְּרֹב שַׂרְעַפַּי בְּקִרְבִּי, תַּנְחוּמֶיךָ יְשַׁעַשְׁעוּ
נַפְשִׁי: הַיְחָבְרְךָ כִּסֵּא הַוּוֹת, יֹצֵר עָמָל עֲלֵי־חֹק: יָגוֹדּוּ עַל־נֶפֶשׁ צַדִּיק,
וְדָם נָקִי יַרְשִׁיעוּ: וַיְהִי יהוה לִי לְמִשְׂגָּב, וֵאלֹהַי לְצוּר מַחְסִי: וַיָּשֶׁב
עֲלֵיהֶם אֶת־אוֹנָם, וּבְרָעָתָם יַצְמִיתֵם, יַצְמִיתֵם יהוה אֱלֹהֵינוּ:

תהלים צה ▸ לְכוּ נְרַנְּנָה לַיהוה, נָרִיעָה לְצוּר יִשְׁעֵנוּ: נְקַדְּמָה פָנָיו בְּתוֹדָה, בִּזְמִרוֹת
נָרִיעַ לוֹ: כִּי אֵל גָּדוֹל יהוה, וּמֶלֶךְ גָּדוֹל עַל־כָּל־אֱלֹהִים:

קדיש יתום (*on the next page*)

*Friday* הַיּוֹם יוֹם שִׁשִּׁי בְּשַׁבָּת, שֶׁבּוֹ הָיוּ הַלְוִיִּם אוֹמְרִים בְּבֵית הַמִּקְדָּשׁ:

תהלים צג יהוה מָלָךְ, גֵּאוּת לָבֵשׁ, לָבֵשׁ יהוה עֹז הִתְאַזָּר, אַף־תִּכּוֹן תֵּבֵל בַּל־
תִּמּוֹט: נָכוֹן כִּסְאֲךָ מֵאָז, מֵעוֹלָם אָתָּה: נָשְׂאוּ נְהָרוֹת יהוה, נָשְׂאוּ נְהָרוֹת
קוֹלָם, יִשְׂאוּ נְהָרוֹת דָּכְיָם: מִקֹּלוֹת מַיִם רַבִּים, אַדִּירִים מִשְׁבְּרֵי־יָם,
אַדִּיר בַּמָּרוֹם יהוה: ▸ עֵדֹתֶיךָ נֶאֶמְנוּ מְאֹד, לְבֵיתְךָ נַאֲוָה־קֹדֶשׁ, יהוה
לְאֹרֶךְ יָמִים:

קדיש יתום (*on the next page*)

*The following psalm is said on all days. Some congregations recite it at the end of* מוסף.

תהלים כז לְדָוִד, יהוה אוֹרִי וְיִשְׁעִי, מִמִּי אִירָא, יהוה מָעוֹז־חַיַּי, מִמִּי אֶפְחָד: בִּקְרֹב
עָלַי מְרֵעִים לֶאֱכֹל אֶת־בְּשָׂרִי, צָרַי וְאֹיְבַי לִי, הֵמָּה כָשְׁלוּ וְנָפָלוּ: אִם־
תַּחֲנֶה עָלַי מַחֲנֶה, לֹא־יִירָא לִבִּי, אִם־תָּקוּם עָלַי מִלְחָמָה, בְּזֹאת אֲנִי
בוֹטֵחַ: אַחַת שָׁאַלְתִּי מֵאֵת־יהוה, אוֹתָהּ אֲבַקֵּשׁ, שִׁבְתִּי בְּבֵית־יהוה
כָּל־יְמֵי חַיַּי, לַחֲזוֹת בְּנֹעַם־יהוה, וּלְבַקֵּר בְּהֵיכָלוֹ: כִּי יִצְפְּנֵנִי בְּסֻכֹּה
בְּיוֹם רָעָה, יַסְתִּרֵנִי בְּסֵתֶר אָהֳלוֹ, בְּצוּר יְרוֹמְמֵנִי: וְעַתָּה יָרוּם רֹאשִׁי
עַל אֹיְבַי סְבִיבוֹתַי, וְאֶזְבְּחָה בְאָהֳלוֹ זִבְחֵי תְרוּעָה, אָשִׁירָה וַאֲזַמְּרָה

לַיהוה: שְׁמַע־יהוה קוֹלִי אֶקְרָא, וְחָנֵּנִי וַעֲנֵנִי: לְךָ אָמַר לִבִּי בַּקְּשׁוּ פָנָי, אֶת־פָּנֶיךָ יהוה אֲבַקֵּשׁ: אַל־תַּסְתֵּר פָּנֶיךָ מִמֶּנִּי, אַל תַּט־בְּאַף עַבְדֶּךָ, עֶזְרָתִי הָיִיתָ, אַל־תִּטְּשֵׁנִי וְאַל־תַּעַזְבֵנִי, אֱלֹהֵי יִשְׁעִי: כִּי־אָבִי וְאִמִּי עֲזָבוּנִי, וַיהוה יַאַסְפֵנִי: הוֹרֵנִי יהוה דַּרְכֶּךָ, וּנְחֵנִי בְּאֹרַח מִישׁוֹר, לְמַעַן שׁוֹרְרָי: אַל־תִּתְּנֵנִי בְּנֶפֶשׁ צָרָי, כִּי קָמוּ־בִי עֵדֵי־שֶׁקֶר, וִיפֵחַ חָמָס: ◦ לוּלֵא הֶאֱמַנְתִּי לִרְאוֹת בְּטוּב־יהוה בְּאֶרֶץ חַיִּים: קַוֵּה אֶל־יהוה, חֲזַק וְיַאֲמֵץ לִבֶּךָ, וְקַוֵּה אֶל־יהוה:

קדיש יתום (*below*)

*In some congregations,* אַנְעִים זְמִירוֹת *(page 887) is recited here.*

## קדיש יתום

*The following prayer, said by mourners, requires the presence of a* מנין.
*A transliteration can be found on page 1095.*

אבל: יִתְגַּדַּל וְיִתְקַדַּשׁ שְׁמֵהּ רַבָּא (קהל: אָמֵן)
בְּעָלְמָא דִּי בְרָא כִרְעוּתֵהּ
וְיַמְלִיךְ מַלְכוּתֵהּ וְיַצְמַח פֻּרְקָנֵהּ וִיקָרֵב מְשִׁיחֵהּ (קהל: אָמֵן)
בְּחַיֵּיכוֹן וּבְיוֹמֵיכוֹן וּבְחַיֵּי דְכָל בֵּית יִשְׂרָאֵל
בַּעֲגָלָא וּבִזְמַן קָרִיב, וְאִמְרוּ אָמֵן. (קהל: אָמֵן)

קהל ואבל: יְהֵא שְׁמֵהּ רַבָּא מְבָרַךְ לְעָלַם וּלְעָלְמֵי עָלְמַיָּא.

אבל: יִתְבָּרַךְ וְיִשְׁתַּבַּח וְיִתְפָּאַר וְיִתְרוֹמַם וְיִתְנַשֵּׂא
וְיִתְהַדָּר וְיִתְעַלֶּה וְיִתְהַלָּל שְׁמֵהּ דְּקֻדְשָׁא בְּרִיךְ הוּא (קהל: אָמֵן)
לְעֵלָּא לְעֵלָּא מִכָּל בִּרְכָתָא וְשִׁירָתָא, תֻּשְׁבְּחָתָא וְנֶחֱמָתָא
דַּאֲמִירָן בְּעָלְמָא, וְאִמְרוּ אָמֵן. (קהל: אָמֵן)

יְהֵא שְׁלָמָא רַבָּא מִן שְׁמַיָּא
וְחַיִּים טוֹבִים עָלֵינוּ וְעַל כָּל יִשְׂרָאֵל, וְאִמְרוּ אָמֵן. (קהל: אָמֵן)

*Bow, take three steps back, as if taking leave of the Divine Presence, then bow, first left, then right, then center, while saying:*

עֹשֶׂה הַשָּׁלוֹם בִּמְרוֹמָיו
הוּא יַעֲשֶׂה שָׁלוֹם עָלֵינוּ וְעַל כָּל יִשְׂרָאֵל, וְאִמְרוּ אָמֵן. (קהל: אָמֵן)

## REMOVING THE TORAH FROM THE ARK

אַתָּה הָרְאֵתָ You have been shown [these things] so that you may know that the LORD is God; besides Him there is no other. *Deut. 4*
There is none like You among the heavenly powers, LORD, and there are no works like Yours. *Ps. 86*
Your kingdom is an eternal kingdom, and Your dominion is for all generations. *Ps. 145*

The LORD is King, the LORD was King,
the LORD shall be King for ever and all time.
The LORD will give strength to His people; *Ps. 29*
the LORD will bless His people with peace.

Father of compassion,
favor Zion with Your goodness; rebuild the walls of Jerusalem. *Ps. 51*
For we trust in You alone, King, God,
high and exalted, Master of worlds.

*The Ark is opened and the congregation stands. All say:*

וַיְהִי בִּנְסֹעַ Whenever the Ark set out, Moses would say, *Num. 10*
"Arise, LORD, and may Your enemies be scattered.
May those who hate You flee before You."
For the Torah shall come forth from Zion, *Is. 2*
and the word of the LORD from Jerusalem.
Blessed is He who, in His holiness, gave the Torah to His people Israel.

*The following (The Thirteen Attributes of Mercy) is said three times:*

יהוה The LORD, the LORD, compassionate and gracious God, *Ex. 34*
slow to anger, abounding in loving-kindness and truth,
extending loving-kindness to a thousand generations, forgiving iniquity,
rebellion and sin, and absolving [the guilty who repent].

רִבּוֹנוֹ Master of the Universe, fulfill my requests for good. Satisfy my desire, grant my request, and pardon me for all my iniquities and all iniquities of the members of my household, with the pardon of loving-kindness and compassion.

---

כִּי מִצִּיּוֹן תֵּצֵא תוֹרָה *For the Torah shall come forth from Zion.* Part of Isaiah's famous vision (2:2–4) of the end of days.

רִבּוֹנוֹ שֶׁל עוֹלָם *Master of the Universe.* The festivals are heightened times of holiness, and the Opening of the Ark a moment when we most intensely

## הוצאת ספר תורה

אַתָּה הָרְאֵתָ לָדַעַת, כִּי יהוה הוּא הָאֱלֹהִים, אֵין עוֹד מִלְּבַדּוֹ: דברים ד

אֵין־כָּמְוֹךָ בָאֱלֹהִים, אֲדֹנָי, וְאֵין כְּמַעֲשֶׂיךָ: תהלים פו

מַלְכוּתְךָ מַלְכוּת כָּל־עֹלָמִים, וּמֶמְשַׁלְתְּךָ בְּכָל־דּוֹר וָדֹר: תהלים קמה

יהוה מֶלֶךְ, יהוה מָלָךְ, יהוה יִמְלֹךְ לְעֹלָם וָעֶד.

יהוה עֹז לְעַמּוֹ יִתֵּן, יהוה יְבָרֵךְ אֶת־עַמּוֹ בַשָּׁלוֹם: תהלים כט

אַב הָרַחֲמִים, הֵיטִיבָה בִרְצוֹנְךָ אֶת־צִיּוֹן תִּבְנֶה חוֹמוֹת יְרוּשָׁלָםִ: תהלים נא

כִּי בְךָ לְבַד בָּטָחְנוּ, מֶלֶךְ אֵל רָם וְנִשָּׂא, אֲדוֹן עוֹלָמִים.

*The* ארון קודש *is opened and the* קהל *stands. All say:*

וַיְהִי בִּנְסֹעַ הָאָרֹן וַיֹּאמֶר מֹשֶׁה במדבר י

קוּמָה יהוה וְיָפֻצוּ אֹיְבֶיךָ וְיָנֻסוּ מְשַׂנְאֶיךָ מִפָּנֶיךָ:

כִּי מִצִּיּוֹן תֵּצֵא תוֹרָה וּדְבַר־יהוה מִירוּשָׁלָםִ: ישעיה ב

בָּרוּךְ שֶׁנָּתַן תּוֹרָה לְעַמּוֹ יִשְׂרָאֵל בִּקְדֻשָּׁתוֹ.

*The following* (י״ג מידות הרחמים) *is said three times:*

יהוה, יהוה, אֵל רַחוּם וְחַנּוּן, אֶרֶךְ אַפַּיִם וְרַב־חֶסֶד וֶאֱמֶת: שמות לד

נֹצֵר חֶסֶד לָאֲלָפִים, נֹשֵׂא עָוֹן וָפֶשַׁע וְחַטָּאָה, וְנַקֵּה:

רִבּוֹנוֹ שֶׁל עוֹלָם, מַלֵּא מִשְׁאֲלוֹתַי לְטוֹבָה, וְהָפֵק רְצוֹנִי וְתֵן שְׁאֵלָתִי, וּמְחֹל לִי עַל כָּל עֲוֹנוֹתַי וְעַל כָּל עֲוֹנוֹת אַנְשֵׁי בֵיתִי, מְחִילָה בְּחֶסֶד מְחִילָה בְּרַחֲמִים, וְטַהֲרֵנוּ מֵחֲטָאֵינוּ וּמֵעֲוֹנוֹתֵינוּ וּמִפְּשָׁעֵינוּ, וְזָכְרֵנוּ בְּזִכְרוֹן טוֹב לְפָנֶיךָ, וּפָקְדֵנוּ

---

אֵין־כָּמְוֹךָ בָאֱלֹהִים *There is none like You among the heavenly powers.* A collection of verses and phrases from the book of Psalms.

וַיְהִי בִּנְסֹעַ *Whenever the Ark set out.* A description of the Ark during the journeys of the Israelites in the wilderness. The parallel verse, "When it came to rest," is recited when the Torah is returned to the Ark. Thus the taking of the *Sefer Torah* from the Ark and its return, recall the Ark of the Covenant which accompanied the Israelites in the days of Moses.

Purify us from our sins, our iniquities and our transgressions; remember us with a memory of favorable deeds before You and be mindful of us in salvation and compassion. Remember us for a good life, for peace, for livelihood and sustenance, for bread to eat and clothes to wear, for wealth, honor and length of days dedicated to Your Torah and its commandments. Grant us discernment and understanding that we may understand and discern its deep secrets. Send healing for all our pain, and bless all the work of our hands. Ordain for us decrees of good, salvation and consolation, and nullify all hard and harsh decrees against us. And may the hearts of the government, its advisers and ministers / *In Israel:* And may the hearts of our ministers and their advisers, / be favorable toward us. Amen. May this be Your will. May the words of my mouth and the meditation *Ps. 19* of my heart find favor before You, Lord, my Rock and Redeemer.

*Say the following verse three times:*

וַאֲנִי As for me, may my prayer come to You, Lord, *Ps. 69*
at a time of favor. O God, in Your great love,
answer me with Your faithful salvation.

בְּרִיךְ Blessed is the name of the Master of the Universe. Blessed is Your crown *Zohar, Vayak-hel* and Your place. May Your favor always be with Your people Israel. Show Your people the salvation of Your right hand in Your Temple. Grant us the gift of Your good light, and accept our prayers in mercy. May it be Your will to prolong our life in goodness. May I be counted among the righteous, so that You will have compassion on me and protect me and all that is mine and all that is Your people Israel's. You feed all; You sustain all; You rule over all; You rule over kings, for sovereignty is Yours. I am a servant of the Holy One, blessed be He, before whom and before whose glorious Torah I bow at all times. Not in man do I trust, nor on any angel do I rely, but on the God of heaven who is the God of truth, whose Torah is truth, whose prophets speak truth, and who abounds in acts of love and truth. ▸ In Him I trust, and to His holy and glorious name I offer praises. May it be Your will to open my heart to the Torah, and to fulfill the wishes of my heart and of the hearts of all Your people Israel for good, for life, and for peace.

---

בְּרִיךְ שְׁמֵהּ *Blessed is the name.* This passage, from the mystical text, the *Zohar,* is prefaced in its original context with the words: "Rabbi Shimon said: When the scroll of the Torah is taken out to be read in public, the Gates of Compassion are opened, and love is aroused on high. Therefore one should say [at this time]…" The words "Blessed is the name" then follow. The custom of reciting it has its origins in the circle of mystics in Safed associated with Rabbi Isaac Luria.

בְּפְקֻדַּת יְשׁוּעָה וְרַחֲמִים. וְזָכְרֵנוּ לְחַיִּים טוֹבִים וּלְשָׁלוֹם, וּפַרְנָסָה וְכַלְכָּלָה, וְלֶחֶם לֶאֱכֹל וּבֶגֶד לִלְבֹּשׁ, וְעֹשֶׁר וְכָבוֹד, וְאֹרֶךְ יָמִים לַהֲגוֹת בְּתוֹרָתֶךָ וּלְקַיֵּם מִצְוֹתֶיהָ, וְשֵׂכֶל וּבִינָה לְהָבִין וּלְהַשְׂכִּיל עִמְקֵי סוֹדוֹתֶיהָ. וְהָפֵק רְפוּאָה לְכָל מַכְאוֹבֵינוּ, וּבָרֵךְ כָּל מַעֲשֵׂה יָדֵינוּ, וּגְזֹר עָלֵינוּ גְּזֵרוֹת טוֹבוֹת יְשׁוּעוֹת וְנֶחָמוֹת, וּבַטֵּל מֵעָלֵינוּ כָּל גְּזֵרוֹת קָשׁוֹת וְרָעוֹת, וְתֵן בְּלֵב הַמַּלְכוּת וְיוֹעֲצֶיהָ וְשָׂרֶיהָ / בארץ ישראל: וְתֵן בְּלֵב שָׂרֵינוּ וְיוֹעֲצֵיהֶם/ עָלֵינוּ לְטוֹבָה. אָמֵן וְכֵן יְהִי רָצוֹן.

תהלים יט יִהְיוּ לְרָצוֹן אִמְרֵי־פִי וְהֶגְיוֹן לִבִּי לְפָנֶיךָ, יהוה צוּרִי וְגֹאֲלִי:

*Say the following verse three times:*

תהלים סט וַאֲנִי תְפִלָּתִי־לְךָ יהוה, עֵת רָצוֹן, אֱלֹהִים בְּרָב־חַסְדֶּךָ עֲנֵנִי בֶּאֱמֶת יִשְׁעֶךָ:

זוהר ויקהל בְּרִיךְ שְׁמֵהּ דְּמָרֵא עָלְמָא, בְּרִיךְ כִּתְרָךְ וְאַתְרָךְ. יְהֵא רְעוּתָךְ עִם עַמָּךְ יִשְׂרָאֵל לְעָלַם, וּפֻרְקַן יְמִינָךְ אַחֲזִי לְעַמָּךְ בְּבֵית מַקְדְּשָׁךְ, וּלְאַמְטוֹיֵי לָנָא מִטּוּב נְהוֹרָךְ, וּלְקַבֵּל צְלוֹתָנָא בְּרַחֲמִין. יְהֵא רַעֲוָא קֳדָמָךְ דְּתוֹרִיךְ לַן חַיִּין בְּטִיבוּ, וְלֶהֱוֵי אֲנָא פְּקִידָא בְּגוֹ צַדִּיקַיָּא, לְמִרְחַם עָלַי וּלְמִנְטַר יָתִי וְיַת כָּל דִּי לִי וְדִי לְעַמָּךְ יִשְׂרָאֵל. אַנְתְּ הוּא זָן לְכֹלָּא וּמְפַרְנֵס לְכֹלָּא, אַנְתְּ הוּא שַׁלִּיט עַל כֹּלָּא, אַנְתְּ הוּא דְשַׁלִּיט עַל מַלְכַיָּא, וּמַלְכוּתָא דִּילָךְ הִיא. אֲנָא עַבְדָּא דְקֻדְשָׁא בְּרִיךְ הוּא, דְּסָגֵדְנָא קַמֵּהּ וּמִקַּמֵּי דִּיקַר אוֹרַיְתֵהּ בְּכָל עִדָּן וְעִדָּן. לָא עַל אֱנָשׁ רְחִיצְנָא וְלָא עַל בַּר אֱלָהִין סָמִיכְנָא, אֶלָּא בֵּאלָהָא דִשְׁמַיָּא, דְּהוּא אֱלָהָא קְשׁוֹט, וְאוֹרַיְתֵהּ קְשׁוֹט, וּנְבִיאוֹהִי קְשׁוֹט, וּמַסְגֵּא לְמֶעְבַּד טַבְוָן וּקְשׁוֹט. ◂ בֵּהּ אֲנָא רָחִיץ, וְלִשְׁמֵהּ קַדִּישָׁא יַקִּירָא אֲנָא אֵמַר תֻּשְׁבְּחָן. יְהֵא רַעֲוָא קֳדָמָךְ דְּתִפְתַּח לִבַּאי בְּאוֹרַיְתָא, וְתַשְׁלִים מִשְׁאֲלִין דְּלִבַּאי וְלִבָּא דְכָל עַמָּךְ יִשְׂרָאֵל לְטָב וּלְחַיִּין וְלִשְׁלָם.

---

feel the transformative energy of the Divine Presence. Thus, when these two sacred moments coincide, we say a personal prayer for God's blessing in our lives and the lives of our family. The version of the prayer on Rosh HaShana emphasizes the idea that at this time the fate of the coming year is under review. The prayer is preceded by the Thirteen Attributes of Mercy, invoked by Moses when praying for mercy and forgiveness, and taught to him, according the Talmud, by God Himself.

*Two Torah scrolls are removed from the Ark. The Leader takes one in his right arm and, followed by the congregation, says:*

Listen, Israel: the LORD is our God, the LORD is One. *Deut. 6*

*Leader then congregation:*

One is our God; great is our Master;
holy and awesome is His name.

*The Leader turns to face the Ark, bows and says:*

Magnify the LORD with me, and let us exalt His name together. *Ps. 34*

*The Ark is closed. The Leader carries the Torah scroll to the bima and the congregation says:*

לְךָ Yours, LORD, are the greatness and the power, the glory and the majesty and splendor, for everything in heaven and earth is Yours. Yours, LORD, is the kingdom; You are exalted as Head over all. *1 Chr. 29*

רוֹמְמוּ Exalt the LORD our God and bow to His footstool; He is holy. Exalt the LORD our God, and bow at His holy mountain, for holy is the LORD our God. *Ps. 99*

Over all may the name of the Supreme King of kings, the Holy One blessed be He, be magnified and sanctified, praised and glorified, exalted and extolled, in the worlds that He has created – this world and the World to Come – in accordance with His will, and the will of those who fear Him, and the will of the whole house of Israel. He is the Rock of worlds, LORD of all creatures, God of all souls, who dwells in the spacious heights and inhabits the high heavens of old. His holiness is over the Ḥayyot and over the throne of glory. Therefore may Your name, LORD our God, be sanctified among us in the sight of all that
lives. Let us sing before Him a new song, as it is written: "Sing to God, make *Ps. 68*
music for His name, extol Him who rides the clouds – the LORD is His name – and exult before Him." And may we see Him eye to eye when He returns to
His abode as it is written: "For they shall see eye to eye when the LORD returns *Is. 52*
to Zion." And it is said: "Then will the glory of the LORD be revealed, and all *Is. 40*
mankind together shall see that the mouth of the LORD has spoken."

Father of mercy, have compassion on the people borne by Him. May He remember the covenant with the mighty (patriarchs), and deliver us from evil times. May He reproach the evil instinct in the people by Him, and graciously grant that we be an eternal remnant. May He fulfill in good measure our requests for salvation and compassion.

*Two* ספרי תורה *are removed from the* ארון קודש*. The* שליח ציבור *takes one in his right arm and, followed by the* קהל*, says:*

דברים ו

**שְׁמַע יִשְׂרָאֵל, יהוה אֱלֹהֵינוּ, יהוה אֶחָד:**

קהל *then* שליח ציבור*:*

**אֶחָד אֱלֹהֵינוּ, גָּדוֹל אֲדוֹנֵינוּ, קָדוֹשׁ וְנוֹרָא שְׁמוֹ.**

*The* שליח ציבור *turns to face the* ארון קודש*, bows and says:*

תהלים לד

**גַּדְּלוּ לַיהוה אִתִּי וּנְרוֹמְמָה שְׁמוֹ יַחְדָּו:**

*The* ארון קודש *is closed. The* שליח ציבור *carries the* ספר תורה *to the* בימה *and the* קהל *says:*

דברי הימים א׳ כט

לְךָ יהוה הַגְּדֻלָּה וְהַגְּבוּרָה וְהַתִּפְאֶרֶת וְהַנֵּצַח וְהַהוֹד, כִּי־כֹל בַּשָּׁמַיִם וּבָאָרֶץ, לְךָ יהוה הַמַּמְלָכָה וְהַמִּתְנַשֵּׂא לְכֹל לְרֹאשׁ:

תהלים צט

רוֹמְמוּ יהוה אֱלֹהֵינוּ וְהִשְׁתַּחֲווּ לַהֲדֹם רַגְלָיו, קָדוֹשׁ הוּא: רוֹמְמוּ יהוה אֱלֹהֵינוּ וְהִשְׁתַּחֲווּ לְהַר קָדְשׁוֹ, כִּי־קָדוֹשׁ יהוה אֱלֹהֵינוּ:

עַל הַכֹּל יִתְגַּדַּל וְיִתְקַדַּשׁ וְיִשְׁתַּבַּח וְיִתְפָּאַר וְיִתְרוֹמַם וְיִתְנַשֵּׂא שְׁמוֹ
שֶׁל מֶלֶךְ מַלְכֵי הַמְּלָכִים הַקָּדוֹשׁ בָּרוּךְ הוּא בָּעוֹלָמוֹת שֶׁבָּרָא, הָעוֹלָם
הַזֶּה וְהָעוֹלָם הַבָּא, כִּרְצוֹנוֹ וְכִרְצוֹן יְרֵאָיו וְכִרְצוֹן כָּל בֵּית יִשְׂרָאֵל. צוּר
הָעוֹלָמִים, אֲדוֹן כָּל הַבְּרִיּוֹת, אֱלוֹהַּ כָּל הַנְּפָשׁוֹת, הַיּוֹשֵׁב בְּמֶרְחֲבֵי
מָרוֹם, הַשּׁוֹכֵן בִּשְׁמֵי שְׁמֵי קֶדֶם, קְדֻשָּׁתוֹ עַל הַחַיּוֹת, וּקְדֻשָּׁתוֹ עַל כִּסֵּא
הַכָּבוֹד. וּבְכֵן יִתְקַדַּשׁ שִׁמְךָ בָּנוּ יהוה אֱלֹהֵינוּ לְעֵינֵי כָּל חָי, וְנֹאמַר לְפָנָיו
תהלים סח שִׁיר חָדָשׁ, כַּכָּתוּב: שִׁירוּ לֵאלֹהִים זַמְּרוּ שְׁמוֹ, סֹלּוּ לָרֹכֵב בָּעֲרָבוֹת, בְּיָהּ
ישעיה נב שְׁמוֹ, וְעִלְזוּ לְפָנָיו: וְנִרְאֵהוּ עַיִן בְּעַיִן בְּשׁוּבוֹ אֶל נָוֵהוּ, כַּכָּתוּב: כִּי עַיִן
ישעיה מ בְּעַיִן יִרְאוּ בְּשׁוּב יהוה צִיּוֹן: וְנֶאֱמַר: וְנִגְלָה כְּבוֹד יהוה, וְרָאוּ כָל־בָּשָׂר
יַחְדָּו כִּי פִּי יהוה דִּבֵּר:

אַב הָרַחֲמִים הוּא יְרַחֵם עַם עֲמוּסִים, וְיִזְכֹּר בְּרִית אֵיתָנִים, וְיַצִּיל נַפְשׁוֹתֵינוּ מִן הַשָּׁעוֹת הָרָעוֹת, וְיִגְעַר בְּיֵצֶר הָרָע מִן הַנְּשׂוּאִים, וְיָחֹן אוֹתָנוּ לִפְלֵיטַת עוֹלָמִים, וִימַלֵּא מִשְׁאֲלוֹתֵינוּ בְּמִדָּה טוֹבָה יְשׁוּעָה וְרַחֲמִים.

*The* ספר תורה *is placed on the* שולחן *and the* גבאי *calls a* כהן *to the* תורה*. See law 69.*

וְיַעֲזֹר וְיָגֵן וְיוֹשִׁיעַ לְכָל הַחוֹסִים בּוֹ, וְנֹאמַר אָמֵן. הַכֹּל הָבוּ גֹדֶל לֵאלֹהֵינוּ וּתְנוּ כָבוֹד לַתּוֹרָה. *כֹּהֵן קְרַב, יַעֲמֹד (פלוני בֶּן פלוני) הַכֹּהֵן.

**If no* כהן *is present, a* לוי *or* ישראל *is called up as follows:*

/אֵין כָּאן כֹּהֵן, יַעֲמֹד (פלוני בֶּן פלוני) בִּמְקוֹם כֹּהֵן./

בָּרוּךְ שֶׁנָּתַן תּוֹרָה לְעַמּוֹ יִשְׂרָאֵל בִּקְדֻשָּׁתוֹ.

*The* קהל *followed by the* גבאי*:*

דברים ד וְאַתֶּם הַדְּבֵקִים בַּיהוה אֱלֹהֵיכֶם חַיִּים כֻּלְּכֶם הַיּוֹם:

*The* קורא *shows the* עולה *the section to be read. The* עולה *touches the scroll at that place with the* ציצית *of his* טלית*, which he then kisses. Holding the handles of the scroll, he says:*

עולה: בָּרְכוּ אֶת יהוה הַמְבֹרָךְ.

קהל: בָּרוּךְ יהוה הַמְבֹרָךְ לְעוֹלָם וָעֶד.

עולה: בָּרוּךְ יהוה הַמְבֹרָךְ לְעוֹלָם וָעֶד.

בָּרוּךְ אַתָּה יהוה, אֱלֹהֵינוּ מֶלֶךְ הָעוֹלָם
אֲשֶׁר בָּחַר בָּנוּ מִכָּל הָעַמִּים
וְנָתַן לָנוּ אֶת תּוֹרָתוֹ.
בָּרוּךְ אַתָּה יהוה, נוֹתֵן הַתּוֹרָה.

*After the* קריאת התורה*, the* עולה *says:*

עולה: בָּרוּךְ אַתָּה יהוה אֱלֹהֵינוּ מֶלֶךְ הָעוֹלָם
אֲשֶׁר נָתַן לָנוּ תּוֹרַת אֱמֶת וְחַיֵּי עוֹלָם נָטַע בְּתוֹכֵנוּ.
בָּרוּךְ אַתָּה יהוה, נוֹתֵן הַתּוֹרָה.

---

**בָּרוּךְ יהוה** *Bless the* Lord. An invitation to the congregation to join in blessing God, similar to the one that precedes communal prayer in the morning and evening services.

*One who has survived a situation of danger (see commentary on page 437) says:*

Blessed are You, Lord our God, King of the Universe, who bestows good on the unworthy, who has bestowed on me much good.

*The congregation responds:*

Amen. May He who bestowed much good on you continue to bestow on you much good, Selah.

FOR AN OLEH

May He who blessed our fathers, Abraham, Isaac and Jacob, bless (*name*, son of *father's name*) who has been called up in honor of the All-Present, in honor of the Torah, and in honor of the Day of Judgment. As a reward for this, may the Holy One, blessed be He, protect and deliver him from all trouble and distress, all infection and illness, and send blessing and success to all the work of his hands, and write him and seal him for a good life on this Day of Judgment, together with all Israel, his brethren, and let us say: Amen.

FOR A SICK MAN

May He who blessed our fathers, Abraham, Isaac and Jacob, Moses and Aaron, David and Solomon, bless and heal one who is ill, (*sick person's name*, son of *mother's name*), on whose behalf (*name of the one making the offering*) is making a contribution to charity. As a reward for this, may the Holy One, blessed be He, be filled with compassion for him, to restore his health, cure him, strengthen and revive him, sending him a swift and full recovery from heaven to all his 248 organs and 365 sinews, amongst the other sick ones in Israel, a healing of the spirit and a healing of the body – may healing be quick to come – now, swiftly and soon, and let us say: Amen.

FOR A SICK WOMAN

May He who blessed our fathers, Abraham, Isaac and Jacob, Moses and Aaron, David and Solomon, bless and heal one who is ill, (*sick person's name*, daughter of *mother's name*), on whose behalf (*name of the one making the offering*) is making a contribution to charity. As a reward for this, may the Holy One, blessed be He, be filled with compassion for her, to restore her health, cure her, strengthen and revive her, sending her a swift and full recovery from heaven to all her organs and sinews, amongst the other sick ones in Israel, a healing of the spirit and a healing of the body – may healing be quick to come – now, swiftly and soon, and let us say: Amen.

*One who has survived a situation of danger (see commentary on page 437) says:*

בָּרוּךְ אַתָּה יהוה אֱלֹהֵינוּ מֶלֶךְ הָעוֹלָם הַגּוֹמֵל לְחַיָּבִים טוֹבוֹת שֶׁגְּמָלַנִי כָּל טוֹב.

*The* קהל *responds:*

אָמֵן. מִי שֶׁגְּמָלְךָ כָּל טוֹב הוּא יִגְמָלְךָ כָּל טוֹב, סֶלָה.

מי שברך לעולה לתורה

מִי שֶׁבֵּרַךְ אֲבוֹתֵינוּ אַבְרָהָם יִצְחָק וְיַעֲקֹב, הוּא יְבָרֵךְ אֶת (פלוני בֶּן פלוני), בַּעֲבוּר שֶׁעָלָה לִכְבוֹד הַמָּקוֹם וְלִכְבוֹד הַתּוֹרָה וְלִכְבוֹד יוֹם הַדִּין. בִּשְׂכַר זֶה הַקָּדוֹשׁ בָּרוּךְ הוּא יִשְׁמְרֵהוּ וְיַצִּילֵהוּ מִכָּל צָרָה וְצוּקָה וּמִכָּל נֶגַע וּמַחֲלָה, וְיִשְׁלַח בְּרָכָה וְהַצְלָחָה בְּכָל מַעֲשֵׂה יָדָיו, וְיִכְתְּבֵהוּ וְיַחְתְּמֵהוּ לְחַיִּים טוֹבִים בְּיוֹם הַדִּין הַזֶּה עִם כָּל יִשְׂרָאֵל אֶחָיו, וְנֹאמַר אָמֵן.

מי שברך לחולה

מִי שֶׁבֵּרַךְ אֲבוֹתֵינוּ אַבְרָהָם יִצְחָק וְיַעֲקֹב, מֹשֶׁה וְאַהֲרֹן דָּוִד וּשְׁלֹמֹה הוּא יְבָרֵךְ וִירַפֵּא אֶת הַחוֹלֶה (פלוני בֶּן פלונית) בַּעֲבוּר שֶׁ(פלוני בֶּן פלוני) נוֹדֵר צְדָקָה בַּעֲבוּרוֹ. בִּשְׂכַר זֶה הַקָּדוֹשׁ בָּרוּךְ הוּא יִמָּלֵא רַחֲמִים עָלָיו לְהַחֲלִימוֹ וּלְרַפְּאתוֹ וּלְהַחֲזִיקוֹ וּלְהַחֲיוֹתוֹ וְיִשְׁלַח לוֹ מְהֵרָה רְפוּאָה שְׁלֵמָה מִן הַשָּׁמַיִם לִרְמַ״ח אֵבָרָיו וּשְׁסָ״ה גִּידָיו בְּתוֹךְ שְׁאָר חוֹלֵי יִשְׂרָאֵל, רְפוּאַת הַנֶּפֶשׁ וּרְפוּאַת הַגּוּף. הַשְׁתָּא בַּעֲגָלָא וּבִזְמַן קָרִיב, וְנֹאמַר אָמֵן.

מי שברך לחולָה

מִי שֶׁבֵּרַךְ אֲבוֹתֵינוּ אַבְרָהָם יִצְחָק וְיַעֲקֹב, מֹשֶׁה וְאַהֲרֹן דָּוִד וּשְׁלֹמֹה הוּא יְבָרֵךְ וִירַפֵּא אֶת הַחוֹלָה (פלונית בַּת פלונית) בַּעֲבוּר שֶׁ(פלוני בֶּן פלוני) נוֹדֵר צְדָקָה בַּעֲבוּרָהּ. בִּשְׂכַר זֶה הַקָּדוֹשׁ בָּרוּךְ הוּא יִמָּלֵא רַחֲמִים עָלֶיהָ לְהַחֲלִימָהּ וּלְרַפְּאתָהּ וּלְהַחֲזִיקָהּ וּלְהַחֲיוֹתָהּ וְיִשְׁלַח לָהּ מְהֵרָה רְפוּאָה שְׁלֵמָה מִן הַשָּׁמַיִם לְכָל אֵבָרֶיהָ וּלְכָל גִּידֶיהָ בְּתוֹךְ שְׁאָר חוֹלֵי יִשְׂרָאֵל, רְפוּאַת הַנֶּפֶשׁ וּרְפוּאַת הַגּוּף. הַשְׁתָּא בַּעֲגָלָא וּבִזְמַן קָרִיב, וְנֹאמַר אָמֵן.

TORAH READING FOR THE SECOND DAY

It happened after these things that God tested Abraham. He said to him, *Gen. 22*
"Abraham!" "Here I am," he replied. He said, "Take your son, your only
son, Isaac, whom you love, and go to the land of Moriah and offer him
there as a burnt-offering on one of the mountains which I shall say to
you." Early the next morning Abraham rose and saddled his donkey
and took his two lads with him, and Isaac his son, and he cut wood for
the burnt-offering, and he set out for the place of which God had told
him. On the third day Abraham looked up and saw the place from afar. LEVI
Abraham said to his lads, "Stay here with the donkey while I and the
boy go on ahead. We will worship and we will return to you." Abraham
took the wood for the burnt-offering and placed it on Isaac his son,
and he took in his hand the fire and the knife, and the two of them
went together. Isaac said to Abraham his father, "Father?" and he said
"Here I am, my son." And he said, "Here are the fire and the wood, but
where is the sheep for the burnt-offering?" Abraham said, "God will
see to the sheep for the burnt-offering, my son." And the two of them
went together. They came to the place God had told him about, and SHELISHI
Abraham built there an altar and arranged the wood and bound Isaac
his son and laid him on the altar on top of the wood. He reached out
his hand and took the knife to slay his son. Then an angel of the Lord
called out to him from heaven, "Abraham! Abraham!" He said, "Here I

---

There is yet another promise: "God took him outside and said, 'Look up at the heavens and count the stars – if indeed you can count them.' Then He said to him, 'So shall your children be'" (Gen. 15:5). Three escalating promises: a great nation, as many children as the dust of the earth, as the stars of the sky.

What though was the reality? Early on in the story, after his brief stay in Egypt, we read that Abraham was "very wealthy in livestock and silver and gold" (Gen. 13:2). He had everything except one thing: a child. His first words to God were, "O Lord God, what will You give me if I remain childless?" (Gen. 15:2). *The first recorded words of man to God in the history of the covenant are a plea for there to be future generations.* The first Jew feared he would be the last.

Then Abraham has a child, Ishmael, born to Sarah's handmaid Hagar. But God tells him: he is not the one. He will be blessed but he will not con-

## קריאת התורה ליום ב׳

וַיְהִי אַחַר הַדְּבָרִים הָאֵלֶּה וְהָאֱלֹהִים נִסָּה אֶת־אַבְרָהָם וַיֹּאמֶר בראשית כב
אֵלָיו אַבְרָהָם וַיֹּאמֶר הִנֵּנִי: וַיֹּאמֶר קַח־נָא אֶת־בִּנְךָ אֶת־יְחִידְךָ
אֲשֶׁר־אָהַבְתָּ אֶת־יִצְחָק וְלֶךְ־לְךָ אֶל־אֶרֶץ הַמֹּרִיָּה וְהַעֲלֵהוּ שָׁם
לְעֹלָה עַל אַחַד הֶהָרִים אֲשֶׁר אֹמַר אֵלֶיךָ: וַיַּשְׁכֵּם אַבְרָהָם בַּבֹּקֶר
וַיַּחֲבֹשׁ אֶת־חֲמֹרוֹ וַיִּקַּח אֶת־שְׁנֵי נְעָרָיו אִתּוֹ וְאֵת יִצְחָק בְּנוֹ וַיְבַקַּע
עֲצֵי עֹלָה וַיָּקָם וַיֵּלֶךְ אֶל־הַמָּקוֹם אֲשֶׁר־אָמַר־לוֹ הָאֱלֹהִים: בַּיּוֹם לוי
הַשְּׁלִישִׁי וַיִּשָּׂא אַבְרָהָם אֶת־עֵינָיו וַיַּרְא אֶת־הַמָּקוֹם מֵרָחֹק: וַיֹּאמֶר
אַבְרָהָם אֶל־נְעָרָיו שְׁבוּ־לָכֶם פֹּה עִם־הַחֲמוֹר וַאֲנִי וְהַנַּעַר נֵלְכָה
עַד־כֹּה וְנִשְׁתַּחֲוֶה וְנָשׁוּבָה אֲלֵיכֶם: וַיִּקַּח אַבְרָהָם אֶת־עֲצֵי הָעֹלָה
וַיָּשֶׂם עַל־יִצְחָק בְּנוֹ וַיִּקַּח בְּיָדוֹ אֶת־הָאֵשׁ וְאֶת־הַמַּאֲכֶלֶת וַיֵּלְכוּ
שְׁנֵיהֶם יַחְדָּו: וַיֹּאמֶר יִצְחָק אֶל־אַבְרָהָם אָבִיו וַיֹּאמֶר אָבִי וַיֹּאמֶר
הִנֶּנִּי בְנִי וַיֹּאמֶר הִנֵּה הָאֵשׁ וְהָעֵצִים וְאַיֵּה הַשֶּׂה לְעֹלָה: וַיֹּאמֶר
אַבְרָהָם אֱלֹהִים יִרְאֶה־לּוֹ הַשֶּׂה לְעֹלָה בְּנִי וַיֵּלְכוּ שְׁנֵיהֶם יַחְדָּו:
וַיָּבֹאוּ אֶל־הַמָּקוֹם אֲשֶׁר אָמַר־לוֹ הָאֱלֹהִים וַיִּבֶן שָׁם אַבְרָהָם שלישי
אֶת־הַמִּזְבֵּחַ וַיַּעֲרֹךְ אֶת־הָעֵצִים וַיַּעֲקֹד אֶת־יִצְחָק בְּנוֹ וַיָּשֶׂם אֹתוֹ
עַל־הַמִּזְבֵּחַ מִמַּעַל לָעֵצִים: וַיִּשְׁלַח אַבְרָהָם אֶת־יָדוֹ וַיִּקַּח אֶת־
הַמַּאֲכֶלֶת לִשְׁחֹט אֶת־בְּנוֹ: וַיִּקְרָא אֵלָיו מַלְאַךְ יהוה מִן־הַשָּׁמַיִם
וַיֹּאמֶר אַבְרָהָם ׀ אַבְרָהָם וַיֹּאמֶר הִנֵּנִי: וַיֹּאמֶר אַל־תִּשְׁלַח יָדְךָ

---

TORAH READING – SECOND DAY: THE BINDING OF ISAAC

There is a mystery at the heart of Jewish existence, and it is written into the first syllables of our recorded time.

The first words of God to Abraham were, "Leave your land, your birthplace and your father's house … And I will make you a great nation" (Gen. 12:1–2). Then Abraham receives another promise, "I will make your children like the dust of the earth, so that if anyone could count the dust of the earth, then could your offspring be counted" (Gen. 13:16).

am." He said, "Do not reach out your hand against the boy; do not do anything to him, for now I know that you fear God, because you have not held back your son, your only son, from Me." Abraham looked up and there he saw a ram caught in a thicket by its horns, and Abraham went and took the ram and offered it as a burnt-offering instead of his son. Abraham called that place "The LORD will see," as is said to this day,
"On the mountain of the LORD He will be seen." The angel of the LORD REVI'I
called to Abraham a second time from heaven, and said, "By Myself I swear, declares the LORD, that because you have done this and have not held back your son, your only son, I will greatly bless you and greatly multiply your descendants, as the stars of heaven and the sand of the seashore, and your descendants shall take possession of the gates of their enemies. Through your descendants, all the nations of the earth will be blessed, because you have heeded My voice." Then Abraham returned to his lads, and they rose and went together to Beersheba, and Abraham stayed in Beersheba.

---

have been no Jewish people. On such slender avoidance of the probable does Jewish continuity rest.

It is as if from the beginning a message was woven into our being. To move from one generation to the next requires a series of miracles. At every stage in the transition from Abraham and Sarah to Isaac, continuity seemed impossible. Nature was against it. Prediction ruled otherwise. At times even Heaven itself seemed to decree against it. We are Jews today by virtue of miracles. How then do we survive?

We cherish what we most risk losing. Might it be that our nation was born in slavery so that we would cherish freedom? That we were condemned to live most of our history in exile so that love of the Promised Land and Jerusalem the holy city would be engraved on our hearts? That we were forced so often to walk through the valley of the shadow of death so that we would never forget the sanctity of life? That, like Jonah and the gourd, we learn to cherish what must be cherished by having it taken away from us?

The story of Abraham and Sarah and their longing for a child, the promises, the delay, the hope, the despair, the torments and trials, could have no other effect than to create, at the very beginning of Jewish time, a focus bordering on an obsession with Jewish children.

No people have cared more for their children, invested more energy in them and shaped the whole of their religious life in order to hand on to them

אֶל־הַנַּעַר וְאַל־תַּעַשׂ לוֹ מְאוּמָה כִּי ׀ עַתָּה יָדַעְתִּי כִּי־יְרֵא אֱלֹהִים
אַתָּה וְלֹא חָשַׂכְתָּ אֶת־בִּנְךָ אֶת־יְחִידְךָ מִמֶּנִּי׃ וַיִּשָּׂא אַבְרָהָם אֶת־
עֵינָיו וַיַּרְא וְהִנֵּה־אַיִל אַחַר נֶאֱחַז בַּסְּבַךְ בְּקַרְנָיו וַיֵּלֶךְ אַבְרָהָם
וַיִּקַּח אֶת־הָאַיִל וַיַּעֲלֵהוּ לְעֹלָה תַּחַת בְּנוֹ׃ וַיִּקְרָא אַבְרָהָם שֵׁם־
הַמָּקוֹם הַהוּא יְהוָה ׀ יִרְאֶה אֲשֶׁר יֵאָמֵר הַיּוֹם בְּהַר יְהוָה יֵרָאֶה׃
רביעי וַיִּקְרָא מַלְאַךְ יְהוָה אֶל־אַבְרָהָם שֵׁנִית מִן־הַשָּׁמָיִם׃ וַיֹּאמֶר בִּי
נִשְׁבַּעְתִּי נְאֻם־יְהוָה כִּי יַעַן אֲשֶׁר עָשִׂיתָ אֶת־הַדָּבָר הַזֶּה וְלֹא
חָשַׂכְתָּ אֶת־בִּנְךָ אֶת־יְחִידֶךָ׃ כִּי־בָרֵךְ אֲבָרֶכְךָ וְהַרְבָּה אַרְבֶּה אֶת־
זַרְעֲךָ כְּכוֹכְבֵי הַשָּׁמַיִם וְכַחוֹל אֲשֶׁר עַל־שְׂפַת הַיָּם וְיִרַשׁ זַרְעֲךָ אֵת
שַׁעַר אֹיְבָיו׃ וְהִתְבָּרְכוּ בְזַרְעֲךָ כֹּל גּוֹיֵי הָאָרֶץ עֵקֶב אֲשֶׁר שָׁמַעְתָּ
בְּקֹלִי׃ וַיָּשָׁב אַבְרָהָם אֶל־נְעָרָיו וַיָּקֻמוּ וַיֵּלְכוּ יַחְדָּו אֶל־בְּאֵר שָׁבַע
וַיֵּשֶׁב אַבְרָהָם בִּבְאֵר שָׁבַע׃

---

tinue the covenant. Abraham has to part company with him. Another son is promised, and Sarah will bear him. This is a biological impossibility. Sarah is already post-menopausal. Yet, against possibility, Isaac is born. We read of Sarah's joy. The story seems to have a happy ending.

Then, in words that over the centuries have not lost their power to shock, we hear God's call to Abraham to offer his son as a sacrifice. Abraham takes the child, travels for three days, climbs the mountain, prepares the wood, ties his son, takes the knife and raises his hand. Then a voice is heard from heaven: "Do not reach out your hand against the boy." The trial is over. Isaac lives.

The enigma is almost overpowering. On the one hand the promises, on the other, the years of childlessness – then the child who was sent away, then the child who could not be born, then the trial countermanded at the last moment. What is the Torah telling us, not for that time but for all time?

The story of Jewish continuity is a mystery. According to the Torah, had nature taken its course, Sarah would not have had a child and there would be no Jewish people. If Abraham had had his way and been content with Ishmael, there would have been no Jewish people. If Isaac had been born but the word from heaven telling Abraham to stay his hand had been delayed, there would

וַיְהִ֗י אַחֲרֵי֙ הַדְּבָרִ֣ים הָאֵ֔לֶּה וַיֻּגַּ֥ד לְאַבְרָהָ֖ם לֵאמֹ֑ר הִ֠נֵּה יָלְדָ֨ה מִלְכָּ֥ה חמישי
גַם־הִ֛וא בָּנִ֖ים לְנָח֥וֹר אָחִֽיךָ׃ אֶת־ע֥וּץ בְּכֹר֖וֹ וְאֶת־בּ֣וּז אָחִ֑יו וְאֶת־
קְמוּאֵ֖ל אֲבִ֥י אֲרָֽם׃ וְאֶת־כֶּ֣שֶׂד וְאֶת־חֲז֔וֹ וְאֶת־פִּלְדָּ֖שׁ וְאֶת־יִדְלָ֑ף
וְאֵ֖ת בְּתוּאֵֽל׃ וּבְתוּאֵ֖ל יָלַ֣ד אֶת־רִבְקָ֑ה שְׁמֹנָ֥ה אֵ֙לֶּה֙ יָלְדָ֣ה מִלְכָּ֔ה
לְנָח֖וֹר אֲחִ֥י אַבְרָהָֽם׃ וּפִֽילַגְשׁ֖וֹ וּשְׁמָ֣הּ רְאוּמָ֑ה וַתֵּ֤לֶד גַּם־הִוא֙ אֶת־
טֶ֣בַח וְאֶת־גַּ֔חַם וְאֶת־תַּ֖חַשׁ וְאֶת־מַעֲכָֽה׃

## חצי קדיש

*Before* מפטיר *is read, the* קורא *says* חצי קדיש:

קורא: **יִתְגַּדַּל וְיִתְקַדַּשׁ שְׁמֵהּ רַבָּא** (קהל: אָמֵן)
**בְּעָלְמָא דִּי בְרָא כִרְעוּתֵהּ**
**וְיַמְלִיךְ מַלְכוּתֵהּ**
**וְיַצְמַח פֻּרְקָנֵהּ וִיקָרֵב מְשִׁיחֵהּ** (קהל: אָמֵן)
**בְּחַיֵּיכוֹן וּבְיוֹמֵיכוֹן וּבְחַיֵּי דְכָל בֵּית יִשְׂרָאֵל**
**בַּעֲגָלָא וּבִזְמַן קָרִיב, וְאִמְרוּ אָמֵן.** (קהל: אָמֵן)

קהל וקורא: **יְהֵא שְׁמֵהּ רַבָּא מְבָרַךְ לְעָלַם וּלְעָלְמֵי עָלְמַיָּא.**

קורא: **יִתְבָּרַךְ וְיִשְׁתַּבַּח וְיִתְפָּאַר וְיִתְרוֹמַם וְיִתְנַשֵּׂא**
**וְיִתְהַדָּר וְיִתְעַלֶּה וְיִתְהַלָּל**
**שְׁמֵהּ דְּקֻדְשָׁא בְּרִיךְ הוּא** (קהל: אָמֵן)
**לְעֵלָּא לְעֵלָּא מִכָּל בִּרְכָתָא וְשִׁירָתָא, תֻּשְׁבְּחָתָא וְנֶחֱמָתָא**
**דַּאֲמִירָן בְּעָלְמָא, וְאִמְרוּ אָמֵן.** (קהל: אָמֵן)

---

what they find precious. *Abraham and Sarah had a child because they so nearly did not have a child.* Other cultures take children for granted. Judaism has never taken its children for granted, because Jews have known what it is like to be an Abraham or Sarah.

So often were we in danger of losing our children, through persecution or assimilation, that they became our driving concern. Do not lose your

## HAGBAHA AND GELILA

*The first Torah scroll is lifted and the congregation says:*

וְזֹאת הַתּוֹרָה This is the Torah Deut. 4
that Moses placed before the children of Israel,
at the LORD's commandment, by the hand of Moses. Num. 9

*Some add:* It is a tree of life to those who grasp it, and those who uphold it are happy. Prov. 3
Its ways are ways of pleasantness, and all its paths are peace.
Long life is in its right hand; in its left, riches and honor.
It pleased the LORD for the sake of [Israel's] righteousness, Is. 42
to make the Torah great and glorious.

*The first Torah scroll is bound and covered and the oleh for Maftir is called to the second Torah scroll.*

## MAFTIR

On the first day of the seventh month you shall hold a sacred assembly. You shall do no laborious work, and it shall be a day of the blowing of the shofar for you. You shall make a burnt-offering of pleasing aroma to the LORD: a young bullock, a ram, and seven yearling male lambs; they shall be without blemish. And their meal-offerings, fine flour mixed with oil, three-tenths of an ephah for the bull, two-tenths of an ephah for the ram, and one-tenth of an ephah for each of the seven lambs, one male goat for atonement. All this aside from the burnt-offering of the New Moon and its meal-offering, and the regular daily burnt-offering with its meal-offering, and their libations according to their ordinance, a burnt-offering of pleasing odor to the LORD. Num. 29:1–6

## HAGBAHA AND GELILA

*The second Torah scroll is lifted and the congregation says:*

וְזֹאת הַתּוֹרָה This is the Torah Deut. 4
that Moses placed before the children of Israel,
at the LORD's commandment, by the hand of Moses. Num. 9

*Some add:* It is a tree of life to those who grasp it, and those who uphold it are happy. Prov. 3
Its ways are ways of pleasantness, and all its paths are peace.
Long life is in its right hand; in its left, riches and honor.
It pleased the LORD for the sake of [Israel's] righteousness, Is. 42
to make the Torah great and glorious.

*The second Torah scroll is bound and covered and the oleh for Maftir reads the Haftara.*

## הגבהה וגלילה

*The first* ספר תורה *is lifted and the* קהל *says:*

וְזֹאת הַתּוֹרָה אֲשֶׁר־שָׂם מֹשֶׁה לִפְנֵי בְּנֵי יִשְׂרָאֵל׃ דברים ד

עַל־פִּי יהוה בְּיַד מֹשֶׁה׃ במדבר ט

*Some add* עֵץ־חַיִּים הִיא לַמַּחֲזִיקִים בָּהּ וְתֹמְכֶיהָ מְאֻשָּׁר׃ משלי ג

דְּרָכֶיהָ דַרְכֵי־נֹעַם וְכָל־נְתִיבֹתֶיהָ שָׁלוֹם׃

אֹרֶךְ יָמִים בִּימִינָהּ, בִּשְׂמֹאולָהּ עֹשֶׁר וְכָבוֹד׃

יהוה חָפֵץ לְמַעַן צִדְקוֹ יַגְדִּיל תּוֹרָה וְיַאְדִּיר׃ ישעיה מב

*The first* ספר תורה *is bound and covered*
*and the* עולה *for* מפטיר *is called to the second* ספר תורה.

## מפטיר

וּבַחֹדֶשׁ הַשְּׁבִיעִי בְּאֶחָד לַחֹדֶשׁ מִקְרָא־קֹדֶשׁ יִהְיֶה לָכֶם כָּל־מְלֶאכֶת במדבר כט: א–ו
עֲבֹדָה לֹא תַעֲשׂוּ יוֹם תְּרוּעָה יִהְיֶה לָכֶם׃ וַעֲשִׂיתֶם עֹלָה לְרֵיחַ נִיחֹחַ
לַיהוה פַּר בֶּן־בָּקָר אֶחָד אַיִל אֶחָד כְּבָשִׂים בְּנֵי־שָׁנָה שִׁבְעָה תְּמִימִם׃
וּמִנְחָתָם סֹלֶת בְּלוּלָה בַשָּׁמֶן שְׁלֹשָׁה עֶשְׂרֹנִים לַפָּר שְׁנֵי עֶשְׂרֹנִים
לָאָיִל׃ וְעִשָּׂרוֹן אֶחָד לַכֶּבֶשׂ הָאֶחָד לְשִׁבְעַת הַכְּבָשִׂים׃ וּשְׂעִיר־עִזִּים
אֶחָד חַטָּאת לְכַפֵּר עֲלֵיכֶם׃ מִלְּבַד עֹלַת הַחֹדֶשׁ וּמִנְחָתָהּ וְעֹלַת
הַתָּמִיד וּמִנְחָתָהּ וְנִסְכֵּיהֶם כְּמִשְׁפָּטָם לְרֵיחַ נִיחֹחַ אִשֶּׁה לַיהוה׃

## הגבהה וגלילה

*The second* ספר תורה *is lifted and the* קהל *says:*

וְזֹאת הַתּוֹרָה אֲשֶׁר־שָׂם מֹשֶׁה לִפְנֵי בְּנֵי יִשְׂרָאֵל׃ דברים ד

עַל־פִּי יהוה בְּיַד מֹשֶׁה׃ במדבר ט

*Some add* עֵץ־חַיִּים הִיא לַמַּחֲזִיקִים בָּהּ וְתֹמְכֶיהָ מְאֻשָּׁר׃ משלי ג

דְּרָכֶיהָ דַרְכֵי־נֹעַם וְכָל־נְתִיבֹתֶיהָ שָׁלוֹם׃

אֹרֶךְ יָמִים בִּימִינָהּ, בִּשְׂמֹאולָהּ עֹשֶׁר וְכָבוֹד׃

יהוה חָפֵץ לְמַעַן צִדְקוֹ יַגְדִּיל תּוֹרָה וְיַאְדִּיר׃ ישעיה מב

*The second* ספר תורה *is bound and covered and the* עולה *for* מפטיר *reads the* הפטרה.

### BLESSING BEFORE READING THE HAFTARA

*Before reading the Haftara, the person called up for Maftir says:*

בָּרוּךְ Blessed are You, Lord our God, King of the Universe, who chose good prophets and was pleased with their words, spoken in truth. Blessed are You, Lord, who chose the Torah, His servant Moses, His people Israel, and the prophets of truth and righteousness.

### HAFTARA FOR THE SECOND DAY

This is what the Lord has said: "The people who outlived the sword found grace in the desert; Israel, as they moved toward their resting place." From far away the Lord appeared to me: "I have loved you with an everlasting love, and so by cords of kindness I draw you. I shall build you up once more, you will be built, young maiden Israel. Once more you will adorn yourself with drums and go out dancing to your own music. You shall once more plant vineyards in the hills of Samaria; the planters will plant and will redeem their fruit to eat. The day is coming, watchmen will cry out from Mount Ephraim, 'Come, let us go up to Zion to the Lord our God.'" *Jer. 31:1–19*

For this is what the Lord has said: "Sing out with the happiness of Jacob, revel on the crests of nations, make it known, sing praises, say: 'Lord, save Your people, the remnant of Israel! 'Watch Me bring them from a northern land; I shall gather them in from the ends of the earth. Blind and limping men, pregnant women, all together, birthing mothers, a great flock of people will come back here; in tears they will come, and in mercy will I lead them, to rivers of water, along an open road, they will not stumble, for I have been Father to Israel, and Ephraim is My firstborn."

---

survived. During the dark centuries, voices of those like Jeremiah sustained the unshakable conviction on the part of successive generations of Jews that they or their children or their children's children would return. The Jewish people kept hope alive. Hope kept the Jewish people alive.

The echoes between the Haftara and Rosh HaShana are many. There is the verse that plays a prominent part in the Musaf Amida, "Is Ephraim not a treasured son to Me?" There is an evocation of the sound of the shofar as weeping, in the idea of Rachel "weeping for her children." Rachel is the

### ברכה קודם ההפטרה

*Before reading the* הפטרה, *the person called up for* מפטיר *says:*

בָּרוּךְ אַתָּה יהוה אֱלֹהֵינוּ מֶלֶךְ הָעוֹלָם אֲשֶׁר בָּחַר בִּנְבִיאִים טוֹבִים,
וְרָצָה בְדִבְרֵיהֶם הַנֶּאֱמָרִים בֶּאֱמֶת. בָּרוּךְ אַתָּה יהוה, הַבּוֹחֵר
בַּתּוֹרָה וּבְמֹשֶׁה עַבְדּוֹ וּבְיִשְׂרָאֵל עַמּוֹ וּבִנְבִיאֵי הָאֱמֶת וָצֶדֶק.

### הפטרה ליום ב׳

ירמיה לא א–יט כֹּה אָמַר יהוה מָצָא חֵן בַּמִּדְבָּר עַם שְׂרִידֵי חָרֶב הָלוֹךְ לְהַרְגִּיעוֹ
יִשְׂרָאֵל: מֵרָחוֹק יהוה נִרְאָה לִי וְאַהֲבַת עוֹלָם אֲהַבְתִּיךְ עַל־כֵּן
מְשַׁכְתִּיךְ חָסֶד: עוֹד אֶבְנֵךְ וְנִבְנֵית בְּתוּלַת יִשְׂרָאֵל עוֹד תַּעְדִּי
תֻפַּיִךְ וְיָצָאת בִּמְחוֹל מְשַׂחֲקִים: עוֹד תִּטְּעִי כְרָמִים בְּהָרֵי שֹׁמְרוֹן
נָטְעוּ נֹטְעִים וְחִלֵּלוּ: כִּי יֶשׁ־יוֹם קָרְאוּ נֹצְרִים בְּהַר אֶפְרָיִם קוּמוּ
וְנַעֲלֶה צִיּוֹן אֶל־יהוה אֱלֹהֵינוּ: כִּי־כֹה ׀ אָמַר יהוה רָנּוּ
לְיַעֲקֹב שִׂמְחָה וְצַהֲלוּ בְּרֹאשׁ הַגּוֹיִם הַשְׁמִיעוּ הַלְלוּ וְאִמְרוּ הוֹשַׁע
יהוה אֶת־עַמְּךָ אֵת שְׁאֵרִית יִשְׂרָאֵל: הִנְנִי מֵבִיא אוֹתָם מֵאֶרֶץ
צָפוֹן וְקִבַּצְתִּים מִיַּרְכְּתֵי־אָרֶץ בָּם עִוֵּר וּפִסֵּחַ הָרָה וְיֹלֶדֶת יַחְדָּו
קָהָל גָּדוֹל יָשׁוּבוּ הֵנָּה: בִּבְכִי יָבֹאוּ וּבְתַחֲנוּנִים אוֹבִילֵם אוֹלִיכֵם
אֶל־נַחֲלֵי מַיִם בְּדֶרֶךְ יָשָׁר לֹא יִכָּשְׁלוּ בָּהּ כִּי־הָיִיתִי לְיִשְׂרָאֵל לְאָב
וְאֶפְרַיִם בְּכֹרִי הוּא: שִׁמְעוּ דְבַר־יהוה גּוֹיִם וְהַגִּידוּ

---

HAFTARA – SECOND DAY: RACHEL'S TEARS, JEREMIAH'S PROMISE

Jeremiah, the prophet who warned of national catastrophe and became known as the voice of warning and grief, was also a supreme prophet of hope. Convinced that the Babylonian conquest and exile were only temporary and that the people would return, he delivered in this passage a majestic vision of the people's return to their land, a vision re-enacted in our time.

Jews did indeed return from Babylon, yet they were later to endure a further exile that lasted longer than any other people has known and yet

Listen, nations, to the word of the LORD; tell them in distant lands, far from here. And say, "The One who scattered Israel to the winds has gathered them, He guards them now as a shepherd does his flock." Yes, the LORD has claimed back Jacob, has redeemed him from enslavement in stronger hands than his, and they will come singing joy from the heights of Zion, streaming down to the goodness of the LORD, [singing] of grain and of new wine and fresh oil, of the young of the flock and the cattle, and they will be like a garden watered lush, and they will not know this aching any more. Then the young girls will go out dancing to their happiness, boys and old men all together. "I shall turn all their mourning into joy, console them, and make happiness of grief. I shall have the priests sated with the offerings' lushness, and My people will eat of My goodness and be full," says the LORD.

This is what the LORD has said: "A voice is heard in Ramah – lamenting, bitter weeping. Rachel is weeping for her children, refusing to be consoled over her children, for they are not."

This is what the LORD has said: "Hold back your voice from weeping, your eyes from tears: there is reward for what you do," says the LORD; "They will return from hostile land. There is hope for your future, and children will return to their own borders. I have heard it; I heard Ephraim rocking back and forth, saying, 'You have punished me, I took punishment, I was like a calf untamed. Return me – let me return, for You are the LORD my

---

Israel. For Israel is the Jewish people's place of destiny: a tiny land for a tiny people, yet one whose role in religious history is vast. It is the land to which Moses and the Israelites traveled across the desert, the land from which they were exiled twice, the land to which our ancestors journeyed whenever they could and which they never voluntarily left, never relinquished. Jewish history is the story of the longing for a land.

The Holy Land remains the place where Jews were summoned to create a society of justice and compassion under the sovereignty of God. And though it was subsequently held holy by Christianity and Islam, it was so only in a derivative sense – because it was the land promised to Abraham, from whom first Christians, then Muslims, claimed to be descended. The centers of these other faiths were elsewhere: for Western Christians, Rome; for Eastern Christians, Constantinople; for Muslims, Mecca and Medina. Israel remains the

בָאִיִּים מִמֶּרְחָק וְאִמְרוּ מְזָרֵה יִשְׂרָאֵל יְקַבְּצֶנּוּ וּשְׁמָרוֹ כְּרֹעֶה
עֶדְרוֹ׃ כִּי־פָדָה יהוה אֶת־יַעֲקֹב וּגְאָלוֹ מִיַּד חָזָק מִמֶּנּוּ׃ וּבָאוּ וְרִנְּנוּ
בִמְרוֹם־צִיּוֹן וְנָהֲרוּ אֶל־טוּב יהוה עַל־דָּגָן וְעַל־תִּירֹשׁ וְעַל־יִצְהָר
וְעַל־בְּנֵי־צֹאן וּבָקָר וְהָיְתָה נַפְשָׁם כְּגַן רָוֶה וְלֹא־יוֹסִיפוּ לְדַאֲבָה
עוֹד׃ אָז תִּשְׂמַח בְּתוּלָה בְּמָחוֹל וּבַחֻרִים וּזְקֵנִים יַחְדָּו וְהָפַכְתִּי
אֶבְלָם לְשָׂשׂוֹן וְנִחַמְתִּים וְשִׂמַּחְתִּים מִיגוֹנָם׃ וְרִוֵּיתִי נֶפֶשׁ הַכֹּהֲנִים
דָּשֶׁן וְעַמִּי אֶת־טוּבִי יִשְׂבָּעוּ נְאֻם־יהוה׃ כֹּה ׀ אָמַר
יהוה קוֹל בְּרָמָה נִשְׁמָע נְהִי בְּכִי תַמְרוּרִים רָחֵל מְבַכָּה עַל־בָּנֶיהָ
מֵאֲנָה לְהִנָּחֵם עַל־בָּנֶיהָ כִּי אֵינֶנּוּ׃ כֹּה ׀ אָמַר יהוה
מִנְעִי קוֹלֵךְ מִבֶּכִי וְעֵינַיִךְ מִדִּמְעָה כִּי יֵשׁ שָׂכָר לִפְעֻלָּתֵךְ נְאֻם־יהוה
וְשָׁבוּ מֵאֶרֶץ אוֹיֵב׃ וְיֵשׁ־תִּקְוָה לְאַחֲרִיתֵךְ נְאֻם־יהוה וְשָׁבוּ בָנִים
לִגְבוּלָם׃ שָׁמוֹעַ שָׁמַעְתִּי אֶפְרַיִם מִתְנוֹדֵד יִסַּרְתַּנִי וָאִוָּסֵר כְּעֵגֶל
לֹא לֻמָּד הֲשִׁבֵנִי וְאָשׁוּבָה כִּי אַתָּה יהוה אֱלֹהָי׃ כִּי־אַחֲרֵי שׁוּבִי
נִחַמְתִּי וְאַחֲרֵי הִוָּדְעִי סָפַקְתִּי עַל־יָרֵךְ בֹּשְׁתִּי וְגַם־נִכְלַמְתִּי כִּי

---

one matriarch who is buried on the people's route to Babylon, and thus has come to symbolize the spirit of the Jewish people lamenting its exile. There is also an echo of another kind of shofar sound, the great shofar that will accompany the ingathering of exiles, as Jeremiah paints a vivid picture of the people coming back to their land – some blind, some limping, some pregnant, some carrying young children – a scene enacted many times in the course of the twentieth century.

No religion in history has been as closely tied to a land as has Judaism. That connection goes back four thousand years, from the first words of God to Abraham: "Leave your country, your birthplace and your father's house and go to the land I will show you." No sooner had he arrived than God said, "To your offspring I will give this land." Seven times God promised the land to Abraham, and promised it again to Isaac and Jacob.

The word *teshuva*, often translated as "repentance," literally means "homecoming" in a double sense: spiritually to God, and physically to the land of

נְשָׂאתִי חֶרְפַּת נְעוּרָי: הֲבֵן יַקִּיר לִי אֶפְרַיִם אִם יֶלֶד שַׁעֲשֻׁעִים כִּי־מִדֵּי דַבְּרִי בּוֹ זָכֹר אֶזְכְּרֶנּוּ עוֹד עַל־כֵּן הָמוּ מֵעַי לוֹ רַחֵם אֲרַחֲמֶנּוּ נְאֻם־יְהוָה:

ברכות לאחר ההפטרה

*After the* הפטרה*, the person called up for* מפטיר *says the following blessings:*

בָּרוּךְ אַתָּה יהוה אֱלֹהֵינוּ מֶלֶךְ הָעוֹלָם, צוּר כָּל הָעוֹלָמִים, צַדִּיק בְּכָל הַדּוֹרוֹת, הָאֵל הַנֶּאֱמָן, הָאוֹמֵר וְעוֹשֶׂה, הַמְדַבֵּר וּמְקַיֵּם, שֶׁכָּל דְּבָרָיו אֱמֶת וָצֶדֶק. נֶאֱמָן אַתָּה הוּא יהוה אֱלֹהֵינוּ וְנֶאֱמָנִים דְּבָרֶיךָ, וְדָבָר אֶחָד מִדְּבָרֶיךָ אָחוֹר לֹא יָשׁוּב רֵיקָם, כִּי אֵל מֶלֶךְ נֶאֱמָן וְרַחֲמָן אָתָּה. בָּרוּךְ אַתָּה יהוה, הָאֵל הַנֶּאֱמָן בְּכָל דְּבָרָיו.

רַחֵם עַל צִיּוֹן כִּי הִיא בֵּית חַיֵּינוּ, וְלַעֲלוּבַת נֶפֶשׁ תּוֹשִׁיעַ בִּמְהֵרָה בְיָמֵינוּ. בָּרוּךְ אַתָּה יהוה, מְשַׂמֵּחַ צִיּוֹן בְּבָנֶיהָ.

שַׂמְּחֵנוּ יהוה אֱלֹהֵינוּ בְּאֵלִיָּהוּ הַנָּבִיא עַבְדֶּךָ, וּבְמַלְכוּת בֵּית דָּוִד מְשִׁיחֶךָ, בִּמְהֵרָה יָבוֹא וְיָגֵל לִבֵּנוּ. עַל כִּסְאוֹ לֹא יֵשֶׁב זָר, וְלֹא יִנְחֲלוּ עוֹד אֲחֵרִים אֶת כְּבוֹדוֹ, כִּי בְשֵׁם קָדְשְׁךָ נִשְׁבַּעְתָּ לּוֹ שֶׁלֹּא יִכְבֶּה נֵרוֹ לְעוֹלָם וָעֶד. בָּרוּךְ אַתָּה יהוה, מָגֵן דָּוִד.

עַל הַתּוֹרָה וְעַל הָעֲבוֹדָה וְעַל הַנְּבִיאִים וְעַל יוֹם הַזִּכָּרוֹן הַזֶּה, שֶׁנָּתַתָּ לָּנוּ יהוה אֱלֹהֵינוּ לְכָבוֹד וּלְתִפְאָרֶת. עַל הַכֹּל יהוה אֱלֹהֵינוּ אֲנַחְנוּ מוֹדִים לָךְ וּמְבָרְכִים אוֹתָךְ, יִתְבָּרַךְ שִׁמְךָ בְּפִי כָּל חַי תָּמִיד לְעוֹלָם וָעֶד, וּדְבָרְךָ אֱמֶת וְקַיָּם לָעַד. בָּרוּךְ אַתָּה יהוה, מֶלֶךְ עַל כָּל הָאָרֶץ, מְקַדֵּשׁ יִשְׂרָאֵל וְיוֹם הַזִּכָּרוֹן.

---

only place on earth where Jews are a majority, where they enjoy self-rule, and where they are able to build a society and shape a culture as Jews.

If anyone doubts the power of faith to shape history, they might ask wheth-

*The Prayer for the Welfare of the Canadian Government is on the next page.*

## PRAYER FOR THE WELFARE OF THE AMERICAN GOVERNMENT

*The Leader says the following:*

הַנּוֹתֵן תְּשׁוּעָה May He who gives salvation to kings and dominion to princes, whose kingdom is an everlasting kingdom, who delivers His servant David from the evil sword, who makes a way in the sea and a path through the mighty waters, bless and protect, guard and help, exalt, magnify and uplift the President, Vice President and all officials of this land. May the Supreme King of kings in His mercy put into their hearts and the hearts of all their counselors and officials, to deal kindly with us and all Israel. In their days and in ours, may Judah be saved and Israel dwell in safety, and may the Redeemer come to Zion. May this be His will, and let us say: Amen.

## PRAYER FOR THE SAFETY OF THE AMERICAN MILITARY FORCES

*The Leader says the following:*

אַדִּיר בַּמָּרוֹם God on high who dwells in might, the King to whom peace belongs, look down from Your holy habitation and bless the soldiers of the American military forces who risk their lives for the sake of peace on earth. Be their shelter and stronghold, and let them not falter. Give them the strength and courage to thwart the plans of the enemy and end the rule of evil. May their enemies be scattered and their foes flee before them, and may they rejoice in Your salvation. Bring them back safely to their homes, as is
written: "The LORD will guard you from all harm, He will guard *Ps. 121*
your life. The LORD will guard your going and coming, now and
for evermore." And may there be fulfilled for us the verse: "Nation *Is. 2*
shall not lift up sword against nation, nor shall they learn war any more." Let all the inhabitants on earth know that sovereignty is Yours and Your name inspires awe over all You have created – and let us say: Amen.

*The Prayer for the Welfare of the Canadian Government is on the next page.*

## תפילה לשלום המלכות

*The* שליח ציבור *says the following:*

הַנּוֹתֵן תְּשׁוּעָה לַמְּלָכִים וּמֶמְשָׁלָה לַנְּסִיכִים, מַלְכוּתוֹ מַלְכוּת כָּל עוֹלָמִים, הַפּוֹצֶה אֶת דָּוִד עַבְדּוֹ מֵחֶרֶב רָעָה, הַנּוֹתֵן בַּיָּם דֶּרֶךְ וּבְמַיִם עַזִּים נְתִיבָה, הוּא יְבָרֵךְ וְיִשְׁמֹר וְיִנְצֹר וְיַעֲזֹר וִירוֹמֵם וִיגַדֵּל וִינַשֵּׂא לְמַעְלָה אֶת הַנָּשִׂיא וְאֵת מִשְׁנֵהוּ וְאֶת כָּל שָׂרֵי הָאָרֶץ הַזֹּאת. מֶלֶךְ מַלְכֵי הַמְּלָכִים, בְּרַחֲמָיו יִתֵּן בְּלִבָּם וּבְלֵב כָּל יוֹעֲצֵיהֶם וְשָׂרֵיהֶם לַעֲשׂוֹת טוֹבָה עִמָּנוּ וְעִם כָּל יִשְׂרָאֵל. בִּימֵיהֶם וּבְיָמֵינוּ תִּוָּשַׁע יְהוּדָה, וְיִשְׂרָאֵל יִשְׁכֹּן לָבֶטַח, וּבָא לְצִיּוֹן גּוֹאֵל. וְכֵן יְהִי רָצוֹן, וְנֹאמַר אָמֵן.

## תפילה לשלום חיילי צבא ארצות הברית

*The* שליח ציבור *says the following:*

אַדִּיר בַּמָּרוֹם שׁוֹכֵן בִּגְבוּרָה, מֶלֶךְ שֶׁהַשָּׁלוֹם שֶׁלּוֹ, הַשְׁקִיפָה מִמְּעוֹן קָדְשְׁךָ, וּבָרֵךְ אֶת חַיָּלֵי צְבָא אַרְצוֹת הַבְּרִית, הַמְחָרְפִים נַפְשָׁם בְּלֶכְתָּם לָשִׂים שָׁלוֹם בָּאָרֶץ. הֱיֵה נָא לָהֶם מַחֲסֶה וּמָעוֹז, וְאַל תִּתֵּן לַמּוֹט רַגְלָם, חַזֵּק יְדֵיהֶם וְאַמֵּץ רוּחָם לְהָפֵר עֲצַת אוֹיֵב וּלְהַעֲבִיר מֶמְשֶׁלֶת זָדוֹן, יָפֽוּצוּ אוֹיְבֵיהֶם וְיָנֽוּסוּ מְשַׂנְאֵיהֶם מִפְּנֵיהֶם, וְיִשְׂמְחוּ בִּישׁוּעָתֶךָ. הֲשִׁיבֵם בְּשָׁלוֹם אֶל בֵּיתָם, כַּכָּתוּב
בְּדִבְרֵי קָדְשֶׁךָ: יהוה יִשְׁמָרְךָ מִכָּל־רָע, יִשְׁמֹר אֶת־נַפְשֶׁךָ: יהוה תהלים קכא
יִשְׁמָר־צֵאתְךָ וּבוֹאֶךָ, מֵעַתָּה וְעַד־עוֹלָם: וְקַיֵּם בָּֽנוּ מִקְרָא
שֶׁכָּתוּב: לֹא־יִשָּׂא גוֹי אֶל־גּוֹי חֶרֶב, וְלֹא־יִלְמְדוּ עוֹד מִלְחָמָה: ישעיה ב
וְיֵדְעוּ כָּל יוֹשְׁבֵי תֵבֵל כִּי לְךָ מְלוּכָה יָאֲתָה, וְשִׁמְךָ נוֹרָא עַל כָּל מַה שֶּׁבָּרָאתָ. וְנֹאמַר אָמֵן.

### PRAYER FOR THE WELFARE OF THE CANADIAN GOVERNMENT

*The Leader says the following:*

הַנּוֹתֵן תְּשׁוּעָה May He who gives salvation to kings and dominion to princes, whose kingdom is an everlasting kingdom, who delivers His servant David from the evil sword, who makes a way in the sea and a path through the mighty waters, bless and protect, guard and help, exalt, magnify and uplift the Prime Minister and all the elected and appointed officials of Canada. May the Supreme King of kings in His mercy put into their hearts and the hearts of all their counselors and officials, to deal kindly with us and all Israel. In their days and in ours, may Judah be saved and Israel dwell in safety, and may the Redeemer come to Zion. May this be His will, and let us say: Amen.

### PRAYER FOR THE SAFETY OF THE CANADIAN MILITARY FORCES

*The Leader says the following:*

אַדִּיר בַּמָּרוֹם God on high who dwells in might, the King to whom peace belongs, look down from Your holy habitation and bless the soldiers of the Canadian Forces who risk their lives for the sake of peace on earth. Be their shelter and stronghold, and let them not falter. Give them the strength and courage to thwart the plans of the enemy and end the rule of evil. May their enemies be scattered and their foes flee before them, and may they rejoice in Your salvation. Bring them back safely to their homes, as is written: "The Lord will guard you from all harm, He will guard your life. *Ps. 121*
The Lord will guard your going and coming, now and for evermore." And may there be fulfilled for us the verse: "Nation shall *Is. 2*
not lift up sword against nation, nor shall they learn war any more." Let all the inhabitants on earth know that sovereignty is Yours and Your name inspires awe over all You have created – and let us say: Amen.

## תפילה לשלום המלכות

*The* שליח ציבור *says the following:*

הַנּוֹתֵן תְּשׁוּעָה לַמְּלָכִים וּמֶמְשָׁלָה לַנְּסִיכִים, מַלְכוּתוֹ מַלְכוּת כָּל עוֹלָמִים, הַפּוֹצֶה אֶת דָּוִד עַבְדּוֹ מֵחֶרֶב רָעָה, הַנּוֹתֵן בַּיָּם דֶּרֶךְ וּבְמַיִם עַזִּים נְתִיבָה, הוּא יְבָרֵךְ וְיִשְׁמֹר וְיִנְצֹר וְיַעֲזֹר וִירוֹמֵם וִיגַדֵּל וִינַשֵּׂא לְמַעְלָה אֶת רֹאשׁ הַמֶּמְשָׁלָה וְאֶת כָּל שָׂרֵי הָאָרֶץ הַזֹּאת. מֶלֶךְ מַלְכֵי הַמְּלָכִים, בְּרַחֲמָיו יִתֵּן בְּלִבָּם וּבְלֵב כָּל יוֹעֲצֵיהֶם וְשָׂרֵיהֶם לַעֲשׂוֹת טוֹבָה עִמָּנוּ וְעִם כָּל יִשְׂרָאֵל. בִּימֵיהֶם וּבְיָמֵינוּ תִּוָּשַׁע יְהוּדָה, וְיִשְׂרָאֵל יִשְׁכֹּן לָבֶטַח, וּבָא לְצִיּוֹן גּוֹאֵל. וְכֵן יְהִי רָצוֹן, וְנֹאמַר אָמֵן.

## תפילה לשלום חיילי צבא קנדה

*The* שליח ציבור *says the following:*

אַדִּיר בַּמָּרוֹם שׁוֹכֵן בִּגְבוּרָה, מֶלֶךְ שֶׁהַשָּׁלוֹם שֶׁלּוֹ, הַשְׁקִיפָה מִמְּעוֹן קָדְשְׁךָ, וּבָרֵךְ אֶת חַיָּלֵי צְבָא קָנָדָה, הַמְחָרְפִים נַפְשָׁם בְּלֶכְתָּם לָשִׂים שָׁלוֹם בָּאָרֶץ. הֱיֵה נָא לָהֶם מַחֲסֶה וּמָעוֹז, וְאַל תִּתֵּן לַמּוֹט רַגְלָם, חַזֵּק יְדֵיהֶם וְאַמֵּץ רוּחָם לְהָפֵר עֲצַת אוֹיֵב וּלְהַעֲבִיר מֶמְשֶׁלֶת זָדוֹן, יָפֽוּצוּ אוֹיְבֵיהֶם וְיָנֽוּסוּ מְשַׂנְאֵיהֶם מִפְּנֵיהֶם, וְיִשְׂמְחוּ בִּישׁוּעָתֶךָ. הֲשִׁיבֵם בְּשָׁלוֹם אֶל בֵּיתָם, כַּכָּתוּב
בְּדִבְרֵי קָדְשֶׁךָ: יהוה יִשְׁמָרְךָ מִכָּל־רָע, יִשְׁמֹר אֶת־נַפְשֶׁךָ: יהוה תהלים קכא
יִשְׁמָר־צֵאתְךָ וּבוֹאֶךָ, מֵעַתָּה וְעַד־עוֹלָם: וְקַיֵּם בָּנוּ מִקְרָא
שֶׁכָּתוּב: לֹא־יִשָּׂא גוֹי אֶל־גּוֹי חֶרֶב, וְלֹא־יִלְמְדוּ עוֹד מִלְחָמָה: ישעיה ב
וְיֵדְעוּ כָּל יוֹשְׁבֵי תֵבֵל כִּי לְךָ מְלוּכָה יָאֲתָה, וְשִׁמְךָ נוֹרָא עַל כָּל מַה שֶּׁבָּרָאתָ. וְנֹאמַר אָמֵן.

## PRAYER FOR THE STATE OF ISRAEL

*The Leader says the following prayer:*

אָבִינוּ שֶׁבַּשָּׁמַיִם Heavenly Father, Israel's Rock and Redeemer, bless the State of Israel, the first flowering of our redemption. Shield it under the wings of Your loving-kindness and spread over it the Tabernacle of Your peace. Send Your light and truth to its leaders, ministers and counselors, and direct them with good counsel before You.

Strengthen the hands of the defenders of our Holy Land; grant them deliverance, our God, and crown them with the crown of victory. Grant peace in the land and everlasting joy to its inhabitants.

As for our brothers, the whole house of Israel, remember them in all the lands of our (*In Israel:* their) dispersion, and swiftly lead us (*In Israel:* them) upright to Zion Your city, and Jerusalem Your dwelling place, as is written in the Torah of Moses Your servant: "Even *Deut. 30* if you are scattered to the furthermost lands under the heavens, from there the LORD your God will gather you and take you back. The LORD your God will bring you to the land your ancestors possessed and you will possess it; and He will make you more prosperous and numerous than your ancestors. Then the LORD your God will open up your heart and the heart of your descendants, to love the LORD your God with all your heart and with all your soul, that you may live."

Unite our hearts to love and revere Your name and observe all the words of Your Torah, and swiftly send us Your righteous anointed one of the house of David, to redeem those who long for Your salvation.

Appear in Your glorious majesty over all the dwellers on earth, and let all who breathe declare: The LORD God of Israel is King and His kingship has dominion over all. Amen, Selah.

## תפילה לשלום מדינת ישראל

*The* שליח ציבור *says the following prayer:*

אָבִינוּ שֶׁבַּשָּׁמַיִם, צוּר יִשְׂרָאֵל וְגוֹאֲלוֹ, בָּרֵךְ אֶת מְדִינַת יִשְׂרָאֵל, רֵאשִׁית צְמִיחַת גְּאֻלָּתֵנוּ. הָגֵן עָלֶיהָ בְּאֶבְרַת חַסְדֶּךָ וּפְרֹשׂ עָלֶיהָ סֻכַּת שְׁלוֹמֶךָ, וּשְׁלַח אוֹרְךָ וַאֲמִתְּךָ לְרָאשֶׁיהָ, שָׂרֶיהָ וְיוֹעֲצֶיהָ, וְתַקְּנֵם בְּעֵצָה טוֹבָה מִלְּפָנֶיךָ.

חַזֵּק אֶת יְדֵי מְגִנֵּי אֶרֶץ קָדְשֵׁנוּ, וְהַנְחִילֵם אֱלֹהֵינוּ יְשׁוּעָה וַעֲטֶרֶת נִצָּחוֹן תְּעַטְּרֵם, וְנָתַתָּ שָׁלוֹם בָּאָרֶץ וְשִׂמְחַת עוֹלָם לְיוֹשְׁבֶיהָ.

וְאֶת אַחֵינוּ כָּל בֵּית יִשְׂרָאֵל, פְּקָד נָא בְּכָל אַרְצוֹת פְּזוּרֵינוּ, וְתוֹלִיכֵנוּ /בארץ ישראל: פְּזוּרֵיהֶם, וְתוֹלִיכֵם/ מְהֵרָה קוֹמְמִיּוּת לְצִיּוֹן עִירֶךָ וְלִירוּשָׁלַיִם מִשְׁכַּן שְׁמֶךָ, כַּכָּתוּב בְּתוֹרַת מֹשֶׁה עַבְדֶּךָ:
אִם־יִהְיֶה נִדַּחֲךָ בִּקְצֵה הַשָּׁמָיִם, מִשָּׁם יְקַבֶּצְךָ יהוה אֱלֹהֶיךָ דברים ל
וּמִשָּׁם יִקָּחֶךָ: וֶהֱבִיאֲךָ יהוה אֱלֹהֶיךָ אֶל־הָאָרֶץ אֲשֶׁר־יָרְשׁוּ
אֲבֹתֶיךָ וִירִשְׁתָּהּ, וְהֵיטִבְךָ וְהִרְבְּךָ מֵאֲבֹתֶיךָ: וּמָל יהוה אֱלֹהֶיךָ
אֶת־לְבָבְךָ וְאֶת־לְבַב זַרְעֶךָ, לְאַהֲבָה אֶת־יהוה אֱלֹהֶיךָ בְּכָל־
לְבָבְךָ וּבְכָל־נַפְשְׁךָ, לְמַעַן חַיֶּיךָ:

וְיַחֵד לְבָבֵנוּ לְאַהֲבָה וּלְיִרְאָה אֶת שְׁמֶךָ, וְלִשְׁמֹר אֶת כָּל דִּבְרֵי תוֹרָתֶךָ, וּשְׁלַח לָנוּ מְהֵרָה בֶּן דָּוִד מְשִׁיחַ צִדְקֶךָ, לִפְדּוֹת מְחַכֵּי קֵץ יְשׁוּעָתֶךָ.

וְהוֹפַע בַּהֲדַר גְּאוֹן עֻזֶּךָ עַל כָּל יוֹשְׁבֵי תֵּבֵל אַרְצֶךָ וְיֹאמַר כֹּל אֲשֶׁר נְשָׁמָה בְאַפּוֹ, יהוה אֱלֹהֵי יִשְׂרָאֵל מֶלֶךְ וּמַלְכוּתוֹ בַּכֹּל מָשָׁלָה, אָמֵן סֶלָה.

## מי שברך לחיילי צה״ל

*The* שליח ציבור *says the following prayer:*

מִי שֶׁבֵּרַךְ אֲבוֹתֵינוּ אַבְרָהָם יִצְחָק וְיַעֲקֹב הוּא יְבָרֵךְ אֶת חַיָּלֵי צְבָא הַהֲגָנָה לְיִשְׂרָאֵל וְאַנְשֵׁי כֹּחוֹת הַבִּטָּחוֹן, הָעוֹמְדִים עַל מִשְׁמַר אַרְצֵנוּ וְעָרֵי אֱלֹהֵינוּ, מִגְּבוּל הַלְּבָנוֹן וְעַד מִדְבַּר מִצְרַיִם וּמִן הַיָּם הַגָּדוֹל עַד לְבוֹא הָעֲרָבָה וּבְכָל מָקוֹם שֶׁהֵם, בַּיַּבָּשָׁה, בָּאֲוִיר וּבַיָּם. יִתֵּן יהוה אֶת אוֹיְבֵינוּ הַקָּמִים עָלֵינוּ נִגָּפִים לִפְנֵיהֶם. הַקָּדוֹשׁ בָּרוּךְ הוּא יִשְׁמֹר וְיַצִּיל אֶת חַיָּלֵינוּ מִכָּל צָרָה וְצוּקָה וּמִכָּל נֶגַע וּמַחֲלָה, וְיִשְׁלַח בְּרָכָה וְהַצְלָחָה בְּכָל מַעֲשֵׂי יְדֵיהֶם. יַדְבֵּר שׂוֹנְאֵינוּ תַּחְתֵּיהֶם וִיעַטְּרֵם בְּכֶתֶר יְשׁוּעָה וּבַעֲטֶרֶת נִצָּחוֹן.
דברים כ וִיקֻיַּם בָּהֶם הַכָּתוּב: כִּי יהוה אֱלֹהֵיכֶם הַהֹלֵךְ עִמָּכֶם לְהִלָּחֵם לָכֶם עִם־אֹיְבֵיכֶם לְהוֹשִׁיעַ אֶתְכֶם: וְנֹאמַר אָמֵן.

## מי שברך לשבויים

*If Israeli soldiers or civilians are being held in captivity, the* שליח ציבור *says the following:*

מִי שֶׁבֵּרַךְ אֲבוֹתֵינוּ אַבְרָהָם יִצְחָק וְיַעֲקֹב, יוֹסֵף מֹשֶׁה וְאַהֲרֹן, דָּוִד וּשְׁלֹמֹה, הוּא יְבָרֵךְ וְיִשְׁמֹר וְיִנְצֹר אֶת נֶעְדְּרֵי צְבָא הַהֲגָנָה לְיִשְׂרָאֵל וּשְׁבוּיָו, וְאֶת כָּל אַחֵינוּ הַנְּתוּנִים בְּצָרָה וּבְשִׁבְיָה, בַּעֲבוּר שֶׁכָּל הַקָּהָל הַקָּדוֹשׁ הַזֶּה מִתְפַּלֵּל בַּעֲבוּרָם. הַקָּדוֹשׁ בָּרוּךְ הוּא יִמָּלֵא רַחֲמִים עֲלֵיהֶם, וְיוֹצִיאֵם מֵחֹשֶׁךְ וְצַלְמָוֶת, וּמוֹסְרוֹתֵיהֶם יְנַתֵּק, וּמִמְּצוּקוֹתֵיהֶם יוֹשִׁיעֵם, וִישִׁיבֵם מְהֵרָה
תהלים קז לְחֵיק מִשְׁפְּחוֹתֵיהֶם. יוֹדוּ לַיהוה חַסְדּוֹ וְנִפְלְאוֹתָיו לִבְנֵי אָדָם:
ישעיה לה וִיקֻיַּם בָּהֶם מִקְרָא שֶׁכָּתוּב: וּפְדוּיֵי יהוה יְשֻׁבוּן, וּבָאוּ צִיּוֹן בְּרִנָּה, וְשִׂמְחַת עוֹלָם עַל־רֹאשָׁם, שָׂשׂוֹן וְשִׂמְחָה יַשִּׂיגוּ, וְנָסוּ יָגוֹן וַאֲנָחָה: וְנֹאמַר אָמֵן.

*If there is a* ברית מילה*, it takes place at this point before* תקיעת שופר *(see page 997)*.

## THE BLOWING OF THE SHOFAR

*In most congregations all say seven times:*

For the conductor of music. A psalm of the sons of Korah. Ps. 47
Sound your hands together, all peoples, make a voice of joy
resound to God,
for the LORD is most high, awesome, great King over all the earth.
It is He who subjugates peoples under us, nations beneath our feet.
He chooses our legacy for us: the pride of this Jacob He loves, Selah!
God is raised up in sound,
raised, the LORD, in the voice of the shofar.
Sing out to God, sing! Sing out to our King, sing!
For God is King over all the earth – Sing out: a psalm.
God reigns over nations,
God takes His place on the throne of His holiness.
The noble men of peoples have gathered; the people of Abraham's God.
For all the earth's defenses are of God, and He is raised high above.

### PRAYER FOR THE TOKE'A (SHOFAR BLOWER)

*In many congregations, the Toke'a recites the following prayer quietly:*

Master of all worlds, Your children, the children of Your beloved ones, have turned their faces toward You, placing their trust in Your vast loving-kindness, and have appointed me their emissary to blow the shofar before You, as You commanded us in Your Torah. Remember for their sake the merit of our forefather Abraham, who walked before You in innocence, and the merit of our forefather Isaac, and his binding upon the altar, and the merit of our forefather Jacob, an innocent man, dwelling in tents, and the merit of Moses and Aaron, David and Solomon, and all the righteous people of the world. Stand up from Your throne of judgment and sit upon Your throne of compassion, as it is said, "God has been raised up in sound, raised, the LORD, in the voice of the shofar." Ps. 47
I know of myself that I am not worthy to ask anything of You, even for myself, to say nothing of other people, and certainly that I do not have the understanding or wisdom to hold the correct intentions, with the right holy names, while blowing the shofar – but I place my trust in Your compassion, and know that You will not turn me away empty-handed from Your presence. In Your goodness, awaken Your compassion, and may the pleasantness of the LORD our God be Ps. 90
upon us. Establish for us the work of our hands, O establish the work of our

# סדר תקיעת שופר

*In most congregations all say seven times:*

תהלים מז
לַמְנַצֵּחַ לִבְנֵי־קֹרַח מִזְמוֹר:
כָּל־הָעַמִּים תִּקְעוּ־כָף, הָרִיעוּ לֵאלֹהִים בְּקוֹל רִנָּה:
כִּי־יהוה עֶלְיוֹן נוֹרָא, מֶלֶךְ גָּדוֹל עַל־כָּל־הָאָרֶץ:
יַדְבֵּר עַמִּים תַּחְתֵּינוּ, וּלְאֻמִּים תַּחַת רַגְלֵינוּ:
יִבְחַר־לָנוּ אֶת־נַחֲלָתֵנוּ, אֶת גְּאוֹן יַעֲקֹב אֲשֶׁר־אָהֵב סֶלָה:
עָלָה אֱלֹהִים בִּתְרוּעָה, יהוה בְּקוֹל שׁוֹפָר:
זַמְּרוּ אֱלֹהִים זַמֵּרוּ, זַמְּרוּ לְמַלְכֵּנוּ זַמֵּרוּ:
כִּי מֶלֶךְ כָּל־הָאָרֶץ אֱלֹהִים, זַמְּרוּ מַשְׂכִּיל:
מָלַךְ אֱלֹהִים עַל־גּוֹיִם, אֱלֹהִים יָשַׁב עַל־כִּסֵּא קָדְשׁוֹ:
נְדִיבֵי עַמִּים נֶאֱסָפוּ, עַם אֱלֹהֵי אַבְרָהָם
כִּי לֵאלֹהִים מָגִנֵּי־אֶרֶץ, מְאֹד נַעֲלָה:

תחינה לתוקע

*In many congregations, the* תוקע *recites the following prayer quietly:*

רִבּוֹן הָעוֹלָמִים, בָּנֶיךָ בְּנֵי רְחוּמֶיךָ שָׂמוּ פְּנֵיהֶם לְנֶגְדְּךָ וּבָטְחוּ עַל רֹב חֲסָדֶיךָ, וְשָׂמוּנִי שָׁלִיחַ לִתְקֹעַ בְּשׁוֹפָר לְפָנֶיךָ כְּמוֹ שֶׁצִּוִּיתָנוּ בְּתוֹרָתֶךָ, וְאַתָּה תִּזְכֹּר לָהֶם זְכוּת אַבְרָהָם אָבִינוּ אֲשֶׁר הִתְהַלֵּךְ לְפָנֶיךָ וְהָיָה תָמִים, וּזְכוּת יִצְחָק אָבִינוּ וַעֲקֵדָתוֹ כְּשֶׁנֶּעֱקַד עַל גַּב הַמִּזְבֵּחַ, וּזְכוּת יַעֲקֹב אָבִינוּ אִישׁ תָּם יֹשֵׁב אֹהָלִים, וּזְכוּת שֶׁל מֹשֶׁה וְאַהֲרֹן דָּוִד וּשְׁלֹמֹה וְכָל צַדִּיקֵי עוֹלָם, וְתַעֲמֹד מִכִּסֵּא הַדִּין וְתֵשֵׁב עַל כִּסֵּא הָרַחֲמִים, כַּדָּבָר שֶׁנֶּאֱמַר:
תהלים מז
עָלָה אֱלֹהִים בִּתְרוּעָה, יהוה בְּקוֹל שׁוֹפָר: וַאֲנִי יוֹדֵעַ בְּעַצְמִי שֶׁאֵינֶנִּי כְּדַאי לְבַקֵּשׁ עַל עַצְמִי, וְכָל שֶׁכֵּן עַל אֲחֵרִים, וְכָל שֶׁכֵּן שֶׁאֵין בִּי לֹא דַעַת וְלֹא חָכְמָה לְכַוֵּן כַּוָּנוֹת הַתְּקִיעוֹת וְצֵרוּפֵי שְׁמוֹתֶיךָ הַקְּדוֹשִׁים,

hands. And connect our good intentions to actual deeds, as if we had blown the shofar with all the correct intentions. May our shofar notes rise up to awaken Your compassion; show compassion for Your children, and turn judgment to kindness and compassion for them through these sounds, and step beyond the rule of law for their sake. Shut and seal the mouth of the Adversary, and do not let him accuse us. And when recriminations against us come before You, do not wipe our names out of Your book, and write for a good life, all the children of Your covenant. May the words of my mouth and the meditation of my heart find favor before You, LORD, my Rock and Redeemer. Amen. *Ps. 19*

*Some add:*

May it be Your will, LORD my God, the God of judgment, that now may be a time of favor before You. Please, in Your great compassion and vast loving-kindness, tear away all the partitions that separate You from Your people Israel on this day, and send away all adversaries and accusers of Your people Israel. Close the mouth of the Adversary, and do not let him accuse us, for our eyes are turned toward You. I will exalt You, my God, King, the God of judgment, who listens to the prayers and shofar notes of Your people Israel today, with compassion. Amen.

*The following is said responsively, Toke'a then congregation.*

מִן־הַמֵּצַר In my distress I called on the LORD. *Ps. 118*
The LORD answered me and set me free.
You have heard my voice, do not close Your ear *Lam. 3*
to my need, from my pleading.
Your first word is truth; *Ps. 119*
and each of Your righteous laws is eternal.
Be Your slave's guarantor for good; *Ibid.*
do not let the arrogant oppress me.
I revel in Your words *Ibid.*
as if discovering great spoils.
Teach me goodness of sense and insight, *Ibid.*
for I have faith in Your commands.
Desire the offerings of my mouth, please, LORD, *Ibid.*
and teach me Your laws.

*The Toke'a adds:*

עָלָה God has been raised up in sound; *Ps. 47*
raised, the LORD, in the voice of the shofar.

אֲבָל בָּטַחְתִּי בְּרַחֲמֶיךָ הָרַבִּים וְיָדַעְתִּי כִּי לֹא תְשִׁיבֵנִי רֵיקָם מִלְּפָנֶיךָ,
וְאַתָּה בְּטוּבְךָ תְּעוֹרֵר רַחֲמֶיךָ, וִיהִי נֹעַם אֲדֹנָי אֱלֹהֵינוּ עָלֵינוּ, וּמַעֲשֵׂה תהלים צ
יָדֵינוּ כּוֹנְנָה עָלֵינוּ, וּמַעֲשֵׂה יָדֵינוּ כּוֹנְנֵהוּ: וּתְצָרֵף מַחֲשַׁבְתֵּנוּ הַטּוֹבָה
לְמַעֲשֶׂה, כְּאִלּוּ נִתְכַּוַּנּוּ בְּכָל כַּוָּנוֹת הַתְּקִיעוֹת, וְיַעֲלוּ תְּקִיעוֹתֵינוּ לְעוֹרֵר
רַחֲמֶיךָ, וּתְרַחֵם עַל בָּנֶיךָ, וְתַהֲפֹךְ לָהֶם עַל יְדֵי תְקִיעוֹת אֵלֶּה מִדַּת
הַדִּין לְמִדַּת הַחֶסֶד וְהָרַחֲמִים, וְתִכָּנֵס לָהֶם לִפְנִים מִשּׁוּרַת הַדִּין. סְתֹם
וַחֲתֹם פֶּה שָׂטָן וְאַל יַשְׂטִין עָלֵינוּ, וּבְבֹא תוֹכֵחָה לְנֶגְדְּךָ שְׁמֵנוּ מִסִּפְרְךָ
אַל תִּמַח, וּכְתֹב לְחַיִּים טוֹבִים כָּל בְּנֵי בְרִיתֶךָ. יִהְיוּ לְרָצוֹן אִמְרֵי־פִי תהלים יט
וְהֶגְיוֹן לִבִּי לְפָנֶיךָ, יהוה צוּרִי וְגֹאֲלִי: אָמֵן.

*Some add:*

יְהִי רָצוֹן מִלְּפָנֶיךָ יהוה אֱלֹהֵי אֱלֹהֵי הַמִּשְׁפָּט, שֶׁתְּהִי עַתָּה עֵת רָצוֹן לְפָנֶיךָ, וְתִקְרַע בְּרַחֲמֶיךָ הָרַבִּים וַחֲסָדֶיךָ הַגְּדוֹלִים אֶת כָּל הַמָּסַכִים אֲשֶׁר הֵם מַבְדִּילִים בֵּינְךָ וּבֵין עַמְּךָ יִשְׂרָאֵל הַיּוֹם הַזֶּה, וְהַעֲבֵר מִלְּפָנֶיךָ כָּל הַמַּשְׂטִינִים וְהַמְקַטְרְגִים עַל עַמְּךָ יִשְׂרָאֵל, סְתֹם פֶּה שָׂטָן וְאַל יַשְׂטִין עָלֵינוּ, כִּי אֵלֶיךָ תְּלוּיוֹת עֵינֵינוּ. אֲרוֹמִמְךָ אֱלוֹהַי הַמֶּלֶךְ אֱלֹהֵי הַמִּשְׁפָּט שׁוֹמֵעַ קוֹל תְּפִלּוֹת וּתְרוּעוֹת עַמְּךָ יִשְׂרָאֵל הַיּוֹם בְּרַחֲמִים, אָמֵן.

*The following is said responsively, תוקע then קהל.*

תהלים קיח מִן־הַמֵּצַר קָרָאתִי יָּהּ, עָנָנִי בַמֶּרְחָב יָהּ:
איכה ג קוֹלִי שָׁמָעְתָּ, אַל־תַּעְלֵם אָזְנְךָ לְרַוְחָתִי לְשַׁוְעָתִי:
תהלים קיט רֹאשׁ־דְּבָרְךָ אֱמֶת, וּלְעוֹלָם כָּל־מִשְׁפַּט צִדְקֶךָ:
שם עֲרֹב עַבְדְּךָ לְטוֹב, אַל־יַעַשְׁקֻנִי זֵדִים:
שם שָׂשׂ אָנֹכִי עַל־אִמְרָתֶךָ, כְּמוֹצֵא שָׁלָל רָב:
שם טוּב טַעַם וָדַעַת לַמְּדֵנִי, כִּי בְמִצְוֹתֶיךָ הֶאֱמָנְתִּי:
שם נִדְבוֹת פִּי רְצֵה־נָא יהוה, וּמִשְׁפָּטֶיךָ לַמְּדֵנִי:

*The תוקע adds:*

תהלים מז עָלָה אֱלֹהִים בִּתְרוּעָה, יהוה בְּקוֹל שׁוֹפָר:

*The Toke'a says:*

I am prepared and ready to fulfill the commandment that our Creator has commanded us, to blow the shofar on this day, as is written in the Torah: "It shall be a day of the sounding of the shofar to you."

*The Toke'a recites the following blessings on behalf of the congregation. The blessings apply to all the shofar blasts sounded throughout Musaf, and for this reason, no unnecessary interruptions may be made until the final blasts are sounded at the end of Musaf.*

בָּרוּךְ Blessed are You, Lord our God, King of the Universe, who has made us holy through His commandments, and has commanded us to listen to the sound of the shofar.

בָּרוּךְ Blessed are You, Lord our God, King of the Universe, who has given us life, sustained us, and brought us to this time.

*The Makri calls out the shofar sounds one by one and the Toke'a blows the shofar.*

TEKIA SHEVARIM TERUA TEKIA
TEKIA SHEVARIM TERUA TEKIA
TEKIA SHEVARIM TERUA TEKIA

*Some congregations say the following prayer (although many authorities rule that this constitutes an interruption and therefore should not be said). The angelic names that appear in parentheses should not be spoken.*

May it be Your will, Lord my God and God of my ancestors, that the sound of TaSHRaT [tekia-shevarim-terua-tekia] that we sound may be made into a crown for You by the angel (שרשי"ה) who is assigned to this role, and may rise up and rest upon Your head, my God; and make us a sign of good favor, and be filled with compassion for us. Blessed are You, Master of compassion.

*The Makri calls out the shofar sounds one by one and the Toke'a blows the shofar.*

TEKIA SHEVARIM TEKIA
TEKIA SHEVARIM TEKIA
TEKIA SHEVARIM TEKIA

*Some congregations say the following prayer (although many authorities rule that this constitutes an interruption and therefore should not be said). The angelic names that appear in parentheses should not be spoken.*

May it be Your will, Lord my God and God of my ancestors, that the sound of TaSHaT [tekia-shevarim-tekia] that we sound today be stitched across the curtain before You by the angel (טרטיא"ל) who is assigned to this role, and be accepted by

*The* תוקע *says:*

הֲרֵי אֲנִי מוּכָן וּמְזֻמָּן לְקַיֵּם הַמִּצְוָה שֶׁצִּוָּנוּ בּוֹרְאֵנוּ לִתְקוֹעַ בְּשׁוֹפָר הַיּוֹם הַזֶּה כְּמוֹ שֶׁכָּתוּב בַּתּוֹרָה יוֹם תְּרוּעָה יִהְיֶה לָכֶם.

*The* תוקע *recites the following* ברכות *on behalf of the* קהל*. The* ברכות *apply to all the* שופר *blasts sounded throughout* מוסף*, and for this reason, no unnecessary interruptions may be made until the final blasts are sounded at the end of* מוסף*.*

בָּרוּךְ אַתָּה יהוה אֱלֹהֵינוּ מֶלֶךְ הָעוֹלָם
אֲשֶׁר קִדְּשָׁנוּ בְּמִצְוֹתָיו, וְצִוָּנוּ לִשְׁמֹעַ קוֹל שׁוֹפָר.

בָּרוּךְ אַתָּה יהוה אֱלֹהֵינוּ מֶלֶךְ הָעוֹלָם
שֶׁהֶחֱיָנוּ וְקִיְּמָנוּ, וְהִגִּיעָנוּ לַזְּמַן הַזֶּה.

*The* מקריא *calls out the* תקיעות *one by one and the* תוקע *blows the* שופר*.*

תקיעה שברים תרועה תקיעה
תקיעה שברים תרועה תקיעה
תקיעה שברים תרועה תקיעה

*Some congregations say the following prayer (although many authorities rule that this constitutes an interruption and therefore should not be said). The angelic names that appear in parentheses should not be spoken.*

יְהִי רָצוֹן מִלְּפָנֶיךָ יהוה אֱלֹהַי וֵאלֹהֵי אֲבוֹתַי שֶׁתְּקִיעַת תשר״ת שֶׁאֲנַחְנוּ תוֹקְעִים הַיּוֹם תֵּעָשֶׂה מִמֶּנָּה עֲטָרָה עַל יַד הַמְמֻנֶּה (שרשי״ה) לִהְיוֹת עוֹלָה וְלֵישֵׁב בְּרֹאשְׁךָ אֱלֹהַי, וַעֲשֵׂה עִמָּנוּ אוֹת לְטוֹבָה וְהִמָּלֵא עָלֵינוּ רַחֲמִים. בָּרוּךְ אַתָּה בַּעַל הָרַחֲמִים.

*The* מקריא *calls out the* תקיעות *one by one and the* תוקע *blows the* שופר*.*

תקיעה שברים תקיעה
תקיעה שברים תקיעה
תקיעה שברים תקיעה

*Some congregations say the following prayer (although many authorities rule that this constitutes an interruption and therefore should not be said). The angelic names that appear in parentheses should not be spoken.*

יְהִי רָצוֹן לְפָנֶיךָ יהוה אֱלֹהַי וֵאלֹהֵי אֲבוֹתַי שֶׁתְּקִיעַת תש״ת שֶׁאֲנַחְנוּ תוֹקְעִים הַיּוֹם תְּהִי מְרֻקֶּמֶת עַל הַיְרִיעָה עַל יַד הַמְמֻנֶּה (טרטיא״ל) וּתְקַבְּלֶנָּה עַל יַד

אֵלִיָּהוּ זָכוּר לַטּוֹב וְ(ישעיה״ה) שַׂר הַפָּנִים שַׂר (מטטרו״ן), וְהִמָּלֵא עָלֵינוּ רַחֲמִים. בָּרוּךְ אַתָּה בַּעַל הָרַחֲמִים.

*The* מקריא *calls out the* תקיעות *one by one and the* תוקע *blows the* שופר.

| | | |
|---|---|---|
| תקיעה | תרועה | תקיעה |
| תקיעה | תרועה | תקיעה |
| תקיעה | תרועה | תקיעה גדולה |

*Some congregations say the following prayer (although many authorities rule that this constitutes an interruption and therefore should not be said).*

וּבְכֵן יְהִי רָצוֹן לְפָנֶיךָ יהוה אֱלֹהֵינוּ וֵאלֹהֵי אֲבוֹתֵינוּ שֶׁיַּעֲלוּ כָּל הַמַּלְאָכִים הַמְמֻנִּים עַל הַשּׁוֹפָר וְעַל הַתְּקִיעָה וְעַל הַשְּׁבָרִים וְעַל הַתְּרוּעָה לִפְנֵי כִּסֵּא כְבוֹדֶךָ וְיַמְלִיצוּ טוֹב בַּעֲדֵנוּ לְכַפֵּר עַל כָּל חַטֹּאתֵינוּ.

*The next three verses are recited responsively,* שליח ציבור *then* קהל:

אַשְׁרֵי הָעָם יוֹדְעֵי תְרוּעָה, יהוה בְּאוֹר־פָּנֶיךָ יְהַלֵּכוּן: תהלים פט

בְּשִׁמְךָ יְגִילוּן כָּל־הַיּוֹם, וּבְצִדְקָתְךָ יָרוּמוּ:

כִּי־תִפְאֶרֶת עֻזָּמוֹ אָתָּה, וּבִרְצוֹנְךָ תָּרוּם קַרְנֵנוּ:

*The* שליח ציבור *says the first verse of* אשרי *aloud and all continue:*

אַשְׁרֵי יוֹשְׁבֵי בֵיתֶךָ, עוֹד יְהַלְלוּךָ סֶּלָה: תהלים פד

אַשְׁרֵי הָעָם שֶׁכָּכָה לּוֹ, אַשְׁרֵי הָעָם שֶׁיהוה אֱלֹהָיו: תהלים קמד

תְּהִלָּה לְדָוִד תהלים קמה

אֲרוֹמִמְךָ אֱלוֹהַי הַמֶּלֶךְ, וַאֲבָרְכָה שִׁמְךָ לְעוֹלָם וָעֶד:

בְּכָל־יוֹם אֲבָרְכֶךָּ, וַאֲהַלְלָה שִׁמְךָ לְעוֹלָם וָעֶד:

גָּדוֹל יהוה וּמְהֻלָּל מְאֹד, וְלִגְדֻלָּתוֹ אֵין חֵקֶר:

דּוֹר לְדוֹר יְשַׁבַּח מַעֲשֶׂיךָ, וּגְבוּרֹתֶיךָ יַגִּידוּ:

הֲדַר כְּבוֹד הוֹדֶךָ, וְדִבְרֵי נִפְלְאֹתֶיךָ אָשִׂיחָה:

וֶעֱזוּז נוֹרְאֹתֶיךָ יֹאמֵרוּ, וּגְדוּלָּתְךָ אֲסַפְּרֶנָּה:

shall recite the record of Your great goodness, and sing with joy of Your righteousness. The LORD is gracious and compassionate, slow to anger and great in loving-kindness. The LORD is good to all, and His compassion extends to all His works. All Your works shall thank You, LORD, and Your devoted ones shall bless You. They shall talk of the glory of Your kingship, and speak of Your might. To make known to mankind His mighty deeds and the glorious majesty of His kingship. Your kingdom is an everlasting kingdom, and Your reign is for all generations. The LORD supports all who fall, and raises all who are bowed down. All raise their eyes to You in hope, and You give them their food in due season. You open Your hand, and satisfy every living thing with favor. The LORD is righteous in all His ways, and kind in all He does. The LORD is close to all who call on Him, to all who call on Him in truth. He fulfills the will of those who revere Him; He hears their cry and saves them. The LORD guards all who love Him, but all the wicked He will destroy. ▸ My mouth shall speak the praise of the LORD, and all creatures shall bless His holy name for ever and all time.

We will bless the LORD now and for ever. Halleluya! *Ps. 115*

## RETURNING THE TORAH TO THE ARK

*The Ark is opened. All stand. The Leader takes one of the Torah scrolls and says:*

יְהַלְלוּ Let them praise the name of the LORD, *Ps. 148*
for His name alone is sublime.

*The congregation responds:*

הוֹדוֹ His majesty is above earth and heaven.
He has raised the horn of His people,
for the glory of all His devoted ones,
the children of Israel, the people close to Him.
Halleluya!

זֵכֶר רַב־טוּבְךָ יַבִּיעוּ, וְצִדְקָתְךָ יְרַנֵּנוּ:
חַנּוּן וְרַחוּם יהוה, אֶרֶךְ אַפַּיִם וּגְדָל־חָסֶד:
טוֹב־יהוה לַכֹּל, וְרַחֲמָיו עַל־כָּל־מַעֲשָׂיו:
יוֹדְוּךָ יהוה כָּל־מַעֲשֶׂיךָ, וַחֲסִידֶיךָ יְבָרְכוּכָה:
כְּבוֹד מַלְכוּתְךָ יֹאמֵרוּ, וּגְבוּרָתְךָ יְדַבֵּרוּ:
לְהוֹדִיעַ לִבְנֵי הָאָדָם גְּבוּרֹתָיו, וּכְבוֹד הֲדַר מַלְכוּתוֹ:
מַלְכוּתְךָ מַלְכוּת כָּל־עֹלָמִים, וּמֶמְשַׁלְתְּךָ בְּכָל־דּוֹר וָדֹר:
סוֹמֵךְ יהוה לְכָל־הַנֹּפְלִים, וְזוֹקֵף לְכָל־הַכְּפוּפִים:
עֵינֵי־כֹל אֵלֶיךָ יְשַׂבֵּרוּ, וְאַתָּה נוֹתֵן־לָהֶם אֶת־אָכְלָם בְּעִתּוֹ:
פּוֹתֵחַ אֶת־יָדֶךָ, וּמַשְׂבִּיעַ לְכָל־חַי רָצוֹן:
צַדִּיק יהוה בְּכָל־דְּרָכָיו, וְחָסִיד בְּכָל־מַעֲשָׂיו:
קָרוֹב יהוה לְכָל־קֹרְאָיו, לְכֹל אֲשֶׁר יִקְרָאֻהוּ בֶאֱמֶת:
רְצוֹן־יְרֵאָיו יַעֲשֶׂה, וְאֶת־שַׁוְעָתָם יִשְׁמַע, וְיוֹשִׁיעֵם:
שׁוֹמֵר יהוה אֶת־כָּל־אֹהֲבָיו, וְאֵת כָּל־הָרְשָׁעִים יַשְׁמִיד:
◂ תְּהִלַּת יהוה יְדַבֶּר פִּי, וִיבָרֵךְ כָּל־בָּשָׂר שֵׁם קָדְשׁוֹ לְעוֹלָם וָעֶד:
תהלים קטו וַאֲנַחְנוּ נְבָרֵךְ יָהּ מֵעַתָּה וְעַד־עוֹלָם, הַלְלוּיָהּ:

## הכנסת ספר תורה

*The* ארון קודש *is opened. All stand. The* שליח ציבור *takes one of the* ספרי תורה *and says:*

תהלים קמח יְהַלְלוּ אֶת־שֵׁם יהוה, כִּי־נִשְׂגָּב שְׁמוֹ, לְבַדּוֹ

*The* קהל *responds:*

הוֹדוֹ עַל־אֶרֶץ וְשָׁמָיִם:
וַיָּרֶם קֶרֶן לְעַמּוֹ
תְּהִלָּה לְכָל־חֲסִידָיו
לִבְנֵי יִשְׂרָאֵל עַם קְרֹבוֹ
הַלְלוּיָהּ:

*While the Torah scrolls are being returned to the Ark the following is said:*

לְדָוִד מִזְמוֹר A psalm of David. The earth is the LORD's and all it contains, the world and all who live in it. For He founded it on the seas and established it on the streams. Who may climb the mountain of the LORD? Who may stand in His holy place? He who has clean hands and a pure heart, who has not taken My name in vain, or sworn deceitfully. He shall receive blessing from the LORD, and just reward from God, his salvation. This is a generation of those who seek Him, the descendants of Jacob who seek Your presence, Selah! Lift up your heads, O gates; be uplifted, eternal doors, so that the King of glory may enter. Who is the King of glory? It is the LORD, strong and mighty, the LORD mighty in battle. Lift up your heads, O gates; lift them up, eternal doors, so that the King of glory may enter. Who is He, the King of glory? The LORD of hosts, He is the King of glory, Selah! *Ps. 24*

*As the Torah scrolls are placed into the Ark, all say:*

וּבְנֻחֹה יֹאמַר When the Ark came to rest, Moses would say:
"Return, O LORD, to the myriad thousands of Israel." *Num. 10*
Advance, LORD, to Your resting place, *Ps. 132*
You and Your mighty Ark.
Your priests are clothed in righteousness,
and Your devoted ones sing in joy.
For the sake of Your servant David,
do not reject Your anointed one.
For I give you good instruction; do not forsake My Torah. *Prov. 4*
▸ It is a tree of life to those who grasp it, *Prov. 3*
and those who uphold it are happy.
Its ways are ways of pleasantness, and all its paths are peace.
Turn us back, O LORD, to You, and we will return. *Lam. 5*
Renew our days as of old.

*The Ark is closed.*

*While the* ספרי תורה *are being returned to the* ארון קודש*, the following is said:*

תהלים כד

לְדָוִד מִזְמוֹר, לַיהוה הָאָרֶץ וּמְלוֹאָהּ, תֵּבֵל וְיֹשְׁבֵי בָהּ: כִּי־הוּא עַל־יַמִּים יְסָדָהּ, וְעַל־נְהָרוֹת יְכוֹנְנֶהָ: מִי־יַעֲלֶה בְהַר־יהוה, וּמִי־יָקוּם בִּמְקוֹם קָדְשׁוֹ: נְקִי כַפַּיִם וּבַר־לֵבָב, אֲשֶׁר לֹא־נָשָׂא לַשָּׁוְא נַפְשִׁי וְלֹא נִשְׁבַּע לְמִרְמָה: יִשָּׂא בְרָכָה מֵאֵת יהוה, וּצְדָקָה מֵאֱלֹהֵי יִשְׁעוֹ: זֶה דּוֹר דֹּרְשָׁו, מְבַקְשֵׁי פָנֶיךָ, יַעֲקֹב, סֶלָה: שְׂאוּ שְׁעָרִים רָאשֵׁיכֶם, וְהִנָּשְׂאוּ פִּתְחֵי עוֹלָם, וְיָבוֹא מֶלֶךְ הַכָּבוֹד: מִי זֶה מֶלֶךְ הַכָּבוֹד, יהוה עִזּוּז וְגִבּוֹר, יהוה גִּבּוֹר מִלְחָמָה: שְׂאוּ שְׁעָרִים רָאשֵׁיכֶם, וּשְׂאוּ פִּתְחֵי עוֹלָם, וְיָבֹא מֶלֶךְ הַכָּבוֹד: מִי הוּא זֶה מֶלֶךְ הַכָּבוֹד, יהוה צְבָאוֹת הוּא מֶלֶךְ הַכָּבוֹד, סֶלָה:

*As the* ספרי תורה *are placed into the* ארון קודש*, all say:*

במדבר י
וּבְנֻחֹה יֹאמַר, שׁוּבָה יהוה רִבְבוֹת אַלְפֵי יִשְׂרָאֵל:

תהלים קלב
קוּמָה יהוה לִמְנוּחָתֶךָ, אַתָּה וַאֲרוֹן עֻזֶּךָ:
כֹּהֲנֶיךָ יִלְבְּשׁוּ־צֶדֶק, וַחֲסִידֶיךָ יְרַנֵּנוּ:
בַּעֲבוּר דָּוִד עַבְדֶּךָ אַל־תָּשֵׁב פְּנֵי מְשִׁיחֶךָ:

משלי ד
כִּי לֶקַח טוֹב נָתַתִּי לָכֶם, תּוֹרָתִי אַל־תַּעֲזֹבוּ:

משלי ג
◂ עֵץ־חַיִּים הִיא לַמַּחֲזִיקִים בָּהּ, וְתֹמְכֶיהָ מְאֻשָּׁר:
דְּרָכֶיהָ דַרְכֵי־נֹעַם וְכָל־נְתִיבוֹתֶיהָ שָׁלוֹם:

איכה ה
הֲשִׁיבֵנוּ יהוה אֵלֶיךָ וְנָשׁוּבָה, חַדֵּשׁ יָמֵינוּ כְּקֶדֶם:

*The* ארון קודש *is closed.*

*The Leader says the following before Musaf:*

הִנְנִי Here I am, empty of deeds, in turmoil, fearing the One who sits enthroned on the praises of Israel. I have come here to stand up and plead with You for Your people Israel who have sent me, even though I am not worthy or fitting to come. And so I ask of You, God of Abraham, God of Isaac and God of Jacob, the LORD, the LORD, compassionate and gracious God, my God, Almighty, fearful and awesome, please, give me success along the road that I tread, to stand and ask for compassion for me and for those who have sent me, and please, do not condemn them for my sins, do not hold them liable for my crimes, for I am a sinner, I do wrong, do not let them be disgraced by my sins, let them not be ashamed of me, nor me of them. Accept my prayer as if it were the prayer of an old man, experienced and fluent, one whose past is becoming and whose beard is long and his voice pleasant, and whose mind is involved with the concerns of others. Banish the Adversary, that he should not draw me aside. Let the banner that we fly for You be love, cover all our crimes over with love, and turn all our fast days and torments to happiness and joy – ours and those of all Israel – to life and to peace; [let us] love truth and peace, and let there be no obstacle to my prayer.

And may it be Your will, LORD God of Abraham, God of Isaac and God of Jacob, the great and mighty and awesome God, God Most High, "I shall be what I shall be," that all the angels who carry our prayers should bring my prayer before the throne of Your glory, and lay it out before You, for the sake of all the righteous and honest, innocent and upright people, and for the sake of Your great and mighty and awesome name's glory, for You listen with compassion to the prayers of Your people Israel. Blessed are You, who listens to prayers.

*Some add:*

I know, Lord, that Your laws are righteous; *Ps. 119*
that in faithfulness You gave me suffering.
Listen to me and answer me; I tremble as I speak, and I cry. *Ps. 55*
But my soul will rejoice in the Lord, will exult in His salvation; *Ps. 35*
He who gives salvation to kings, *Ps. 144*
who saved His servant David from the cruel sword.

*The* שליח ציבור *says the following before* מוסף*:*

הִנְנִי הֶעָנִי מִמַּעַשׂ, נִרְעָשׁ וְנִפְחָד מִפַּחַד יוֹשֵׁב תְּהִלּוֹת יִשְׂרָאֵל, בָּאתִי לַעֲמוֹד וּלְחַנֵּן לְפָנֶיךָ עַל עַמְּךָ יִשְׂרָאֵל אֲשֶׁר שְׁלָחְוּנִי, וְאַף עַל פִּי שֶׁאֵינִי כְדַאי וְהָגוּן לְכָךְ. עַל כֵּן אֲבַקֶּשְׁךָ אֱלֹהֵי אַבְרָהָם אֱלֹהֵי יִצְחָק וֵאלֹהֵי יַעֲקֹב, יהוה יהוה, אֵל רַחוּם וְחַנּוּן, אֱלֹהִים, שַׁדַּי אָיוֹם וְנוֹרָא, הֱיֵה נָא מַצְלִיחַ דַּרְכִּי אֲשֶׁר אָנֹכִי הוֹלֵךְ לַעֲמוֹד לְבַקֵּשׁ רַחֲמִים עָלַי וְעַל שׁוֹלְחָי, וְנָא אַל תַּפְשִׁיעֵם בְּחַטֹּאתַי וְאַל תְּחַיְּבֵם בַּעֲוֹנוֹתַי, כִּי חוֹטֵא וּפוֹשֵׁעַ אָנִי, וְאַל יִכָּלְמוּ בִּפְשָׁעַי, וְאַל יֵבֹשׁוּ בִּי וְאַל אֵבוֹשָׁה בָּהֶם. וְקַבֵּל תְּפִלָּתִי כִּתְפִלַּת זָקֵן וְרָגִיל, וּפִרְקוֹ נָאֶה וּזְקָנוֹ מְגֻדָּל וְקוֹלוֹ נָעִים, וּמְעֹרָב בְּדַעַת עִם הַבְּרִיּוֹת. וְתִגְעַר בְּשָׂטָן לְבַל יַשְׂטִינֵנוּ, וִיהִי נָא דִגְלֵנוּ עָלֶיךָ אַהֲבָה, וְעַל כָּל פְּשָׁעִים תְּכַסֶּה בְּאַהֲבָה, וְכָל צוֹמוֹתֵינוּ וְעִנּוּיֵינוּ הֲפָךְ לָנוּ וּלְכָל יִשְׂרָאֵל לְשָׂשׂוֹן וּלְשִׂמְחָה לְחַיִּים וּלְשָׁלוֹם, הָאֱמֶת וְהַשָּׁלוֹם אֱהָבוּ, וְאַל יְהִי שׁוּם מִכְשׁוֹל בִּתְפִלָּתִי.

וִיהִי רָצוֹן לְפָנֶיךָ יהוה אֱלֹהֵי אַבְרָהָם אֱלֹהֵי יִצְחָק וֵאלֹהֵי יַעֲקֹב, הָאֵל הַגָּדוֹל הַגִּבּוֹר וְהַנּוֹרָא אֵל עֶלְיוֹן אֶהְיֶה אֲשֶׁר אֶהְיֶה, שֶׁכָּל הַמַּלְאָכִים שֶׁהֵם בַּעֲלֵי תְפִלּוֹת יָבִיאוּ תְפִלָּתִי לִפְנֵי כִּסֵּא כְבוֹדֶךָ וְיָפִיצוּ אוֹתָהּ לְפָנֶיךָ, בַּעֲבוּר כָּל הַצַּדִּיקִים וְהַחֲסִידִים הַתְּמִימִים וְהַיְשָׁרִים, וּבַעֲבוּר כְּבוֹד שִׁמְךָ הַגָּדוֹל הַגִּבּוֹר וְהַנּוֹרָא. כִּי אַתָּה שׁוֹמֵעַ תְּפִלַּת עַמְּךָ יִשְׂרָאֵל בְּרַחֲמִים, בָּרוּךְ אַתָּה שׁוֹמֵעַ תְּפִלָּה.

*Some add:*

יָדַעְתִּי יהוה כִּי־צֶדֶק מִשְׁפָּטֶיךָ, וֶאֱמוּנָה עִנִּיתָנִי: תהלים קיט

הַקְשִׁיבָה לִּי וַעֲנֵנִי אָרִיד, בְּשִׂיחִי וְאָהִימָה: תהלים נה

וְנַפְשִׁי תָּגִיל בַּיהוה, תָּשִׂישׂ בִּישׁוּעָתוֹ: תהלים לה

הַנּוֹתֵן תְּשׁוּעָה לַמְּלָכִים, הַפּוֹצֶה אֶת־דָּוִד עַבְדּוֹ מֵחֶרֶב רָעָה: תהלים קמד

## חצי קדיש

ש״ץ: יִתְגַּדַּל וְיִתְקַדַּשׁ שְׁמֵהּ רַבָּא (קהל: אָמֵן)
בְּעָלְמָא דִּי בְרָא כִרְעוּתֵהּ
וְיַמְלִיךְ מַלְכוּתֵהּ
וְיַצְמַח פֻּרְקָנֵהּ וִיקָרֵב מְשִׁיחֵהּ (קהל: אָמֵן)
בְּחַיֵּיכוֹן וּבְיוֹמֵיכוֹן וּבְחַיֵּי דְכָל בֵּית יִשְׂרָאֵל
בַּעֲגָלָא וּבִזְמַן קָרִיב
וְאִמְרוּ אָמֵן. (קהל: אָמֵן)

קהל וש״ץ: יְהֵא שְׁמֵהּ רַבָּא מְבָרַךְ לְעָלַם וּלְעָלְמֵי עָלְמַיָּא.

ש״ץ: יִתְבָּרַךְ וְיִשְׁתַּבַּח וְיִתְפָּאַר וְיִתְרוֹמַם וְיִתְנַשֵּׂא
וְיִתְהַדָּר וְיִתְעַלֶּה וְיִתְהַלָּל
שְׁמֵהּ דְּקֻדְשָׁא בְּרִיךְ הוּא (קהל: אָמֵן)
לְעֵלָּא לְעֵלָּא מִכָּל בִּרְכָתָא וְשִׁירָתָא
תֻּשְׁבְּחָתָא וְנֶחֱמָתָא
דַּאֲמִירָן בְּעָלְמָא
וְאִמְרוּ אָמֵן. (קהל: אָמֵן)

# Musaf for the Second Day

## THE AMIDA

*The following prayer, until "in former years" on page 800, is said silently, standing with feet together. If there is a minyan, the Amida is repeated aloud by the Leader. Take three steps forward and at the points indicated by ▾, bend the knees at the first word, bow at the second, and stand straight before saying God's name.*

When I proclaim the LORD's name, give glory to our God. *Deut. 32*
O LORD, open my lips, so that my mouth may declare Your praise. *Ps. 51*

PATRIARCHS

▾בָּרוּךְ▾ Blessed are You, LORD our God and God of our fathers,
God of Abraham, God of Isaac and God of Jacob;
the great, mighty and awesome God, God Most High,
who bestows acts of loving-kindness, who creates all,
who remembers the loving-kindness of the fathers
and will bring a Redeemer to their children's children
for the sake of His name, in love.

זָכְרֵנוּ לְחַיִּים Remember us for life,
O King who desires life,
and write us in the book of life –
for Your sake, O God of life.

King, Helper, Savior, Shield:
▾Blessed are You, LORD, Shield of Abraham.

---

stone and it seems that your prayer makes no impression on it, still, as the days and years pass, it too will be penetrated. (Rabbi Naḥman of Bratslav)

Once, one of the followers of Rabbi Naḥman of Bratslav asked him the difference between depression and a broken heart. He replied: "When you have a broken heart, you can be standing in the middle of a crowd and still turn around and say, 'Master of the Universe.'"

The Maggid of Mezeritch said: "Every lock has a key which opens it. But there are strong thieves who know how to open it without a key. They break the lock. So, every spiritual mystery can be opened by the appropriate meditation.

# מוסף ליום ב׳

## עמידה

*The following prayer, until* קַדְמֹנִיּוֹת *on page 801, is said silently, standing with feet together. If there is a* מנין*, the* עמידה *is repeated aloud by the* שליח ציבור*. Take three steps forward and at the points indicated by* ˅*, bend the knees at the first word, bow at the second, and stand straight before saying God's name.*

דברים לב כִּי שֵׁם יהוה אֶקְרָא, הָבוּ גֹדֶל לֵאלֹהֵינוּ:

תהלים נא אֲדֹנָי, שְׂפָתַי תִּפְתָּח, וּפִי יַגִּיד תְּהִלָּתֶךָ:

אבות

˅בָּרוּךְ אַתָּה יהוה, אֱלֹהֵינוּ וֵאלֹהֵי אֲבוֹתֵינוּ
אֱלֹהֵי אַבְרָהָם, אֱלֹהֵי יִצְחָק, וֵאלֹהֵי יַעֲקֹב
הָאֵל הַגָּדוֹל הַגִּבּוֹר וְהַנּוֹרָא, אֵל עֶלְיוֹן
גּוֹמֵל חֲסָדִים טוֹבִים, קוֹנֵה הַכֹּל
וְזוֹכֵר חַסְדֵי אָבוֹת
וּמֵבִיא גוֹאֵל לִבְנֵי בְנֵיהֶם לְמַעַן שְׁמוֹ בְּאַהֲבָה.

זָכְרֵנוּ לְחַיִּים, מֶלֶךְ חָפֵץ בַּחַיִּים
וְכָתְבֵנוּ בְּסֵפֶר הַחַיִּים, לְמַעַנְךָ אֱלֹהִים חַיִּים.

מֶלֶךְ עוֹזֵר וּמוֹשִׁיעַ וּמָגֵן.
˅בָּרוּךְ אַתָּה יהוה, מָגֵן אַבְרָהָם.

---

PREPARING TO PRAY

A person should pray with such devotion that his heart is as if it were poured out like water before the Lord.

God listens to every word of prayer. No word goes to waste, and the effect of prayer accumulates until God's mercies are brought down.

It is written, "Water wears away stone" (Job 14:19). It may seem that water dripping on a stone cannot make any impression. Nevertheless, after many years it can actually make a hole in the stone. Even if your heart feels like

DIVINE MIGHT

אַתָּה גִּבּוֹר You are eternally mighty, LORD.
You give life to the dead and have great power to save.

*In Israel:* He causes the dew to fall.

He sustains the living with loving-kindness,
and with great compassion revives the dead.
He supports the fallen,
heals the sick,
sets captives free,
and keeps His faith with those who sleep in the dust.
Who is like You, Master of might,
and to whom can You be compared,
O King who brings death and gives life,
and makes salvation grow?

מִי כָמְוֹךָ Who is like You, compassionate Father,
who remembers His creatures in compassion, for life?

Faithful are You to revive the dead.
Blessed are You, LORD, who revives the dead.

---

The Amida, the "Standing" prayer, is the core of prayer as such, and when saying it we must see ourselves as if we stood directly in God's presence. For this reason we take three steps forward and bow, using body language to convey the motion of the mind.

The first and last three blessings of the Amida are essentially the same throughout the year, though specific additions are made at special times. The first three are collectively about Praise of God, the last three about Thanksgiving.

אַתָּה גִּבּוֹר לְעוֹלָם *You are eternally mighty.* A paragraph that five times refers to the resurrection of the dead, that is, that those who died will one day live again. This was a major controversy in the late Second Temple era, between the Pharisees, who believed in the resurrection, and the Sadducees who did not. Shortly after the destruction of the Temple, the Sadducees ceased to be

גבורות

אַתָּה גִּבּוֹר לְעוֹלָם, אֲדֹנָי
מְחַיֵּה מֵתִים אַתָּה, רַב לְהוֹשִׁיעַ

בארץ ישראל: מוֹרִיד הַטָּל

מְכַלְכֵּל חַיִּים בְּחֶסֶד, מְחַיֵּה מֵתִים בְּרַחֲמִים רַבִּים
סוֹמֵךְ נוֹפְלִים, וְרוֹפֵא חוֹלִים, וּמַתִּיר אֲסוּרִים
וּמְקַיֵּם אֱמוּנָתוֹ לִישֵׁנֵי עָפָר.
מִי כָמְוֹךָ, בַּעַל גְּבוּרוֹת, וּמִי דּוֹמֶה לָּךְ
מֶלֶךְ, מֵמִית וּמְחַיֶּה וּמַצְמִיחַ יְשׁוּעָה.

מִי כָמְוֹךָ אַב הָרַחֲמָן
זוֹכֵר יְצוּרָיו לְחַיִּים בְּרַחֲמִים.

וְנֶאֱמָן אַתָּה לְהַחֲיוֹת מֵתִים.
בָּרוּךְ אַתָּה יהוה, מְחַיֵּה הַמֵּתִים.

---

But God loves the thief who breaks the lock open: I mean the person who prays with a broken heart."

Before beginning to pray, Rabbi Yeḥiel Mikhal of Zlotchov was in the habit of saying, "I join myself to all of Israel, to those who are more than I, that through them my prayer may rise – and to those who are less than I, that they may rise through my prayer."

The Siddur and Maḥzor are the books of Jewish faith, and prayer is its language. In Judaism we do not primarily philosophize about faith; we pray it. We do not talk *about* God; we speak *to* Him. Rabbi Menaḥem Mendel of Kotzk once asked his disciples, "Where does God live?" Confounded, they asked him, "What does the Rabbi mean: Where does God live? Where does God not live?" But the Rabbi replied, "God lives where we let Him in." Prayer is where we open ourselves to God. It is where we let God in.

HOLINESS

אַתָּה קָדוֹשׁ You are holy and Your name is holy,
and holy ones praise You daily, Selah!
For You, God, are a great and holy King.

לְדוֹר וָדוֹר From generation to generation declare God King,
for He alone is lofty and holy.

וּבְכֵן יִתְקַדַּשׁ And so may Your name be sanctified, LORD our God,
through Israel Your nation
and Jerusalem, Your city,
and Zion, the dwelling place of Your honor
and through the royal house of David Your anointed,
and Your Sanctuary and Your Temple.

וּבְכֵן תֵּן פַּחְדְּךָ And so place the fear of You, LORD our God,
over all that You have made,
and the terror of You over all You have created,
and all who were made will stand in awe of You,
and all of creation will worship You,
and they will be bound all together as one
to carry out Your will with an undivided heart;
for we know, LORD our God,
that all dominion is laid out before You,
strength is in Your palm, and might in Your right hand,
Your name spreading awe over all You have created.

---

אַתָּה קָדוֹשׁ *You are holy.* The word "holy" in Judaism means "standing apart, outside, beyond." God is holy because He is transcendent, that is, He exists outside and beyond the universe. We become holy when we become subjects, not objects; when we demonstrate our freedom and distinctiveness, thereby showing that not everything in the human realm is the result of inexorable causation, be it economic (Marx), psychological (Freud), or genetic (neo-Darwinism).

קדושת השם

אַתָּה קָדוֹשׁ וְשִׁמְךָ קָדוֹשׁ
וּקְדוֹשִׁים בְּכָל יוֹם יְהַלְלוּךָ סֶּלָה
כִּי אֵל מֶלֶךְ גָּדוֹל וְקָדוֹשׁ אָתָּה.

לְדוֹר וָדוֹר הַמְלִיכוּ לָאֵל
כִּי הוּא לְבַדּוֹ מָרוֹם וְקָדוֹשׁ.

וּבְכֵן יִתְקַדַּשׁ שִׁמְךָ יהוה אֱלֹהֵינוּ
עַל יִשְׂרָאֵל עַמֶּךָ וְעַל יְרוּשָׁלַיִם עִירֶךָ
וְעַל צִיּוֹן מִשְׁכַּן כְּבוֹדֶךָ וְעַל מַלְכוּת בֵּית דָּוִד מְשִׁיחֶךָ
וְעַל מְכוֹנְךָ וְהֵיכָלֶךָ.

וּבְכֵן תֵּן פַּחְדְּךָ יהוה אֱלֹהֵינוּ עַל כָּל מַעֲשֶׂיךָ
וְאֵימָתְךָ עַל כָּל מַה שֶּׁבָּרָאתָ
וְיִירָאוּךָ כָּל הַמַּעֲשִׂים
וְיִשְׁתַּחֲווּ לְפָנֶיךָ כָּל הַבְּרוּאִים
וְיֵעָשׂוּ כֻלָּם אֲגֻדָּה אַחַת לַעֲשׂוֹת רְצוֹנְךָ בְּלֵבָב שָׁלֵם
כְּמוֹ שֶׁיָּדַעְנוּ יהוה אֱלֹהֵינוּ שֶׁהַשָּׁלְטָן לְפָנֶיךָ
עֹז בְּיָדְךָ וּגְבוּרָה בִּימִינֶךָ
וְשִׁמְךָ נוֹרָא עַל כָּל מַה שֶּׁבָּרָאתָ.

---

a force in Jewish life. The idea of resurrection is essential to the Jewish belief in justice: that those who died before their time, whether through illness, oppression or violence, will, at the end of days, have life restored to them in a way we cannot yet understand.

וּבְכֵן תֵּן כָּבוֹד יהוה לְעַמֶּךָ
תְּהִלָּה לִירֵאֶיךָ,
וְתִקְוָה טוֹבָה לְדוֹרְשֶׁיךָ
וּפִתְחוֹן פֶּה לַמְיַחֲלִים לָךְ.
שִׂמְחָה לְאַרְצֶךָ, וְשָׂשׂוֹן לְעִירֶךָ
וּצְמִיחַת קֶרֶן לְדָוִד עַבְדֶּךָ
וַעֲרִיכַת נֵר לְבֶן יִשַׁי מְשִׁיחֶךָ
בִּמְהֵרָה בְיָמֵינוּ.

וּבְכֵן צַדִּיקִים יִרְאוּ וְיִשְׂמָחוּ, וִישָׁרִים יַעֲלֹזוּ
וַחֲסִידִים בְּרִנָּה יָגִילוּ, וְעוֹלָתָה תִּקְפָּץ פִּיהָ
וְכָל הָרִשְׁעָה כֻּלָּהּ כְּעָשָׁן תִּכְלֶה
כִּי תַעֲבִיר מֶמְשֶׁלֶת זָדוֹן מִן הָאָרֶץ.

וְתִמְלֹךְ אַתָּה הוּא יהוה אֱלֹהֵינוּ
מְהֵרָה לְבַדֶּךָ עַל כָּל מַעֲשֶׂיךָ
בְּהַר צִיּוֹן מִשְׁכַּן כְּבוֹדֶךָ
וּבִירוּשָׁלַיִם עִיר קָדְשֶׁךָ
כַּכָּתוּב בְּדִבְרֵי קָדְשֶׁךָ
יִמְלֹךְ יהוה לְעוֹלָם, אֱלֹהַיִךְ צִיּוֹן לְדֹר וָדֹר, הַלְלוּיָהּ: תהלים קמו

קָדוֹשׁ אַתָּה וְנוֹרָא שְׁמֶךָ, וְאֵין אֱלוֹהַּ מִבַּלְעָדֶיךָ
כַּכָּתוּב, וַיִּגְבַּהּ יהוה צְבָאוֹת בַּמִּשְׁפָּט ישעיה ה
וְהָאֵל הַקָּדוֹשׁ נִקְדַּשׁ בִּצְדָקָה:
בָּרוּךְ אַתָּה יהוה, הַמֶּלֶךְ הַקָּדוֹשׁ.

HOLINESS OF THE DAY AND KINGSHIP

אַתָּה בְחַרְתָּנוּ You have chosen us from among all peoples.
You have loved and favored us.
You have raised us above all tongues.
You have made us holy through Your commandments.
You have brought us near, our King, to Your service,
and have called us by Your great and holy name.

וַתִּתֶּן לָנוּ And You, Lord our God, have given us in love
this Day of Remembrance,
a day of blowing the shofar,
a holy assembly in memory of the exodus from Egypt.

וּמִפְּנֵי חֲטָאֵינוּ But because of our sins
we were exiled from our land and driven far from our country.
We cannot perform our duties in Your chosen House,
the great and holy Temple that was called by Your name,
because of the hand that was stretched out
against Your Sanctuary.
May it be Your will, Lord our God and God of our ancestors,
merciful King,
that You in Your abounding compassion may once more
have mercy on us and on Your Sanctuary,
rebuilding it swiftly and adding to its glory.
Our Father, our King,
reveal the glory of Your kingdom to us swiftly.
Appear and be exalted over us in the sight of all that lives.
Bring back our scattered ones from among the nations,
and gather our dispersed people from the ends of the earth.

וַהֲבִיאֵנוּ לְצִיּוֹן Lead us to Zion, Your city, in jubilation,
and to Jerusalem, home of Your Temple, with everlasting joy.
There we will prepare for You our obligatory offerings:
the regular daily offerings in their order
and the additional offerings according to their law.

קדושת היום ומלכויות

אַתָּה בְחַרְתָּנוּ מִכָּל הָעַמִּים
אָהַבְתָּ אוֹתָנוּ וְרָצִיתָ בָּנוּ
וְרוֹמַמְתָּנוּ מִכָּל הַלְּשׁוֹנוֹת
וְקִדַּשְׁתָּנוּ בְּמִצְוֹתֶיךָ
וְקֵרַבְתָּנוּ מַלְכֵּנוּ לַעֲבוֹדָתֶךָ
וְשִׁמְךָ הַגָּדוֹל וְהַקָּדוֹשׁ עָלֵינוּ קָרָאתָ.

וַתִּתֶּן לָנוּ יהוה אֱלֹהֵינוּ בְּאַהֲבָה אֶת יוֹם הַזִּכָּרוֹן הַזֶּה
יוֹם תְּרוּעָה, מִקְרָא קֹדֶשׁ, זֵכֶר לִיצִיאַת מִצְרָיִם.

וּמִפְּנֵי חֲטָאֵינוּ גָּלִינוּ מֵאַרְצֵנוּ, וְנִתְרַחַקְנוּ מֵעַל אַדְמָתֵנוּ
וְאֵין אֲנוּ יְכוֹלִים לַעֲשׂוֹת חוֹבוֹתֵינוּ בְּבֵית בְּחִירָתֶךָ
בַּבַּיִת הַגָּדוֹל וְהַקָּדוֹשׁ שֶׁנִּקְרָא שִׁמְךָ עָלָיו
מִפְּנֵי הַיָּד שֶׁנִּשְׁתַּלְּחָה בְּמִקְדָּשֶׁךָ.
יְהִי רָצוֹן מִלְּפָנֶיךָ יהוה אֱלֹהֵינוּ וֵאלֹהֵי אֲבוֹתֵינוּ, מֶלֶךְ רַחֲמָן
שֶׁתָּשׁוּב וּתְרַחֵם עָלֵינוּ וְעַל מִקְדָּשְׁךָ בְּרַחֲמֶיךָ הָרַבִּים
וְתִבְנֵהוּ מְהֵרָה וּתְגַדֵּל כְּבוֹדוֹ.
אָבִינוּ מַלְכֵּנוּ, גַּלֵּה כְּבוֹד מַלְכוּתְךָ עָלֵינוּ מְהֵרָה
וְהוֹפַע וְהִנָּשֵׂא עָלֵינוּ לְעֵינֵי כָּל חָי
וְקָרֵב פְּזוּרֵינוּ מִבֵּין הַגּוֹיִם, וּנְפוּצוֹתֵינוּ כַּנֵּס מִיַּרְכְּתֵי אָרֶץ.

וַהֲבִיאֵנוּ לְצִיּוֹן עִירְךָ בְּרִנָּה
וְלִירוּשָׁלַיִם בֵּית מִקְדָּשְׁךָ בְּשִׂמְחַת עוֹלָם
וְשָׁם נַעֲשֶׂה לְפָנֶיךָ אֶת קָרְבְּנוֹת חוֹבוֹתֵינוּ
תְּמִידִים כְּסִדְרָם וּמוּסָפִים כְּהִלְכָתָם

And the additional offerings of this Day of Remembrance
we will prepare and offer before You in love,
in accord with Your will's commandment,
as You wrote for us in Your Torah
through Your servant Moses, by Your own word, as it is said:

וּבַחֹדֶשׁ הַשְּׁבִיעִי On the first day of the seventh month you shall hold a sacred assembly. You shall do no laborious work, and you shall mark a Day of the Blowing of the Shofar. You shall make a burnt-offering of pleasing aroma to the LORD: a young bullock, a ram, and seven yearling male lambs; they shall be without blemish. *Num. 29*

וּמִנְחָתָם וְנִסְכֵּיהֶם And their meal offerings and wine-libations as ordained: three-tenths of an ephah for the bull, two-tenths of an ephah for the ram, one-tenth of an ephah for each of the seven lambs, wine for the libations, two male goats for atonement, and two regular daily offerings according to their law.

מִלְּבַד All this aside from the burnt-offering of the New Moon and its meal-offering, and the regular daily burnt-offering with its meal-offering, and their libations according to their ordinance, a burnt-offering of pleasing odor to the LORD. *Num. 29*

עָלֵינוּ It is our duty to praise the Master of all,
and ascribe greatness to the Author of creation,
who has not made us like the nations of the lands,
nor placed us like the families of the earth;
who has not made our portion like theirs,
nor our destiny like all their multitudes.
(For they worship vanity and emptiness,
and pray to a god who cannot save.)
But we bow in worship
and thank the Supreme King of kings, the Holy One, blessed be He,
who extends the heavens and establishes the earth,
whose throne of glory is in the heavens above,
and whose power's Presence is in the highest of heights.
He is our God; there is no other.

וְאֶת מוּסְפֵי יוֹם הַזִּכָּרוֹן הַזֶּה
נַעֲשֶׂה וְנַקְרִיב לְפָנֶיךָ בְּאַהֲבָה כְּמִצְוַת רְצוֹנֶךָ
כְּמוֹ שֶׁכָּתַבְתָּ עָלֵינוּ בְּתוֹרָתֶךָ
עַל יְדֵי מֹשֶׁה עַבְדֶּךָ מִפִּי כְבוֹדֶךָ, כָּאָמוּר

וּבַחֹדֶשׁ הַשְּׁבִיעִי בְּאֶחָד לַחֹדֶשׁ מִקְרָא־קֹדֶשׁ יִהְיֶה לָכֶם, כָּל־ במדבר כט
מְלֶאכֶת עֲבֹדָה לֹא תַעֲשׂוּ, יוֹם תְּרוּעָה יִהְיֶה לָכֶם: וַעֲשִׂיתֶם
עֹלָה לְרֵיחַ נִיחֹחַ לַיהוה, פַּר בֶּן־בָּקָר אֶחָד, אַיִל אֶחָד, כְּבָשִׂים
בְּנֵי־שָׁנָה שִׁבְעָה תְּמִימִם:

וּמִנְחָתָם וְנִסְכֵּיהֶם כִּמְדֻבָּר, שְׁלֹשָׁה עֶשְׂרֹנִים לַפָּר וּשְׁנֵי עֶשְׂרֹנִים
לָאָיִל, וְעִשָּׂרוֹן לַכֶּבֶשׂ, וְיַיִן כְּנִסְכּוֹ, וּשְׁנֵי שְׂעִירִים לְכַפֵּר, וּשְׁנֵי
תְמִידִים כְּהִלְכָתָם.

מִלְּבַד עֹלַת הַחֹדֶשׁ וּמִנְחָתָהּ, וְעֹלַת הַתָּמִיד וּמִנְחָתָהּ, וְנִסְכֵּיהֶם במדבר כט
כְּמִשְׁפָּטָם, לְרֵיחַ נִיחֹחַ, אִשֶּׁה לַיהוה:

עָלֵינוּ לְשַׁבֵּחַ לַאֲדוֹן הַכֹּל, לָתֵת גְּדֻלָּה לְיוֹצֵר בְּרֵאשִׁית
שֶׁלֹּא עָשָׂנוּ כְּגוֹיֵי הָאֲרָצוֹת, וְלֹא שָׂמָנוּ כְּמִשְׁפְּחוֹת הָאֲדָמָה
שֶׁלֹּא שָׂם חֶלְקֵנוּ כָּהֶם וְגוֹרָלֵנוּ כְּכָל הֲמוֹנָם.
(שֶׁהֵם מִשְׁתַּחֲוִים לְהֶבֶל וָרִיק וּמִתְפַּלְלִים אֶל אֵל לֹא יוֹשִׁיעַ.)
וַאֲנַחְנוּ כּוֹרְעִים וּמִשְׁתַּחֲוִים וּמוֹדִים
לִפְנֵי מֶלֶךְ מַלְכֵי הַמְּלָכִים, הַקָּדוֹשׁ בָּרוּךְ הוּא
שֶׁהוּא נוֹטֶה שָׁמַיִם וְיוֹסֵד אָרֶץ
וּמוֹשַׁב יְקָרוֹ בַּשָּׁמַיִם מִמַּעַל
וּשְׁכִינַת עֻזּוֹ בְּגָבְהֵי מְרוֹמִים.
הוּא אֱלֹהֵינוּ, אֵין עוֹד.

Truly He is our King; there is none else,
as it is written in His Torah:
"You shall know and take to heart this day that the LORD is God, *Deut. 4*
in the heavens above and on the earth below.
There is no other."

Therefore, we place our hope in You, LORD our God,
that we may soon see the glory of Your power,
when You will remove abominations from the earth,
and idols will be utterly destroyed,
when the world will be perfected
under the sovereignty of the Almighty,
when all humanity will call on Your name,
to turn all the earth's wicked toward You.
All the world's inhabitants will realize and know
that to You every knee must bow and every tongue swear loyalty.
Before You, LORD our God, they will kneel and bow down
and give honor to Your glorious name.
They will all accept the yoke of Your kingdom,
and You will reign over them soon and for ever.
For the kingdom is Yours, and to all eternity You will reign in glory,
as it is written in Your Torah:
"The LORD will reign for ever and ever." *Ex. 15*

And it is said:
He saw no injustice in Jacob, *Num. 23*
no deceit did He witness in Israel,
the LORD their God is with them,
and a King's adulation resounds among them.

And it is said:
[The LORD] became King in Yeshurun, *Deut. 33*
when the heads of the people gathered,
all the tribes of Israel together.

And in Your holy Writings it is said,
For kingship is the LORD's and He rules over the nations. *Ps. 22*

אֱמֶת מַלְכֵּנוּ, אֶפֶס זוּלָתוֹ

כַּכָּתוּב בְּתוֹרָתוֹ, וְיָדַעְתָּ הַיּוֹם וַהֲשֵׁבֹתָ אֶל־לְבָבֶךָ דברים ד

כִּי יהוה הוּא הָאֱלֹהִים בַּשָּׁמַיִם מִמַּעַל וְעַל־הָאָרֶץ מִתָּחַת

אֵין עוֹד:

וְעַל כֵּן נְקַוֶּה לְּךָ יהוה אֱלֹהֵינוּ, לִרְאוֹת מְהֵרָה בְּתִפְאֶרֶת עֻזֶּךָ

לְהַעֲבִיר גִּלּוּלִים מִן הָאָרֶץ, וְהָאֱלִילִים כָּרוֹת יִכָּרֵתוּן

לְתַקֵּן עוֹלָם בְּמַלְכוּת שַׁדַּי.

וְכָל בְּנֵי בָשָׂר יִקְרְאוּ בִשְׁמֶךָ לְהַפְנוֹת אֵלֶיךָ כָּל רִשְׁעֵי אָרֶץ.

יַכִּירוּ וְיֵדְעוּ כָּל יוֹשְׁבֵי תֵבֵל

כִּי לְךָ תִּכְרַע כָּל בֶּרֶךְ, תִּשָּׁבַע כָּל לָשׁוֹן.

לְפָנֶיךָ יהוה אֱלֹהֵינוּ יִכְרְעוּ וְיִפֹּלוּ, וְלִכְבוֹד שִׁמְךָ יְקָר יִתֵּנוּ

וִיקַבְּלוּ כֻלָּם אֶת עֹל מַלְכוּתֶךָ

וְתִמְלֹךְ עֲלֵיהֶם מְהֵרָה לְעוֹלָם וָעֶד.

כִּי הַמַּלְכוּת שֶׁלְּךָ הִיא וּלְעוֹלְמֵי עַד תִּמְלֹךְ בְּכָבוֹד

כַּכָּתוּב בְּתוֹרָתֶךָ

יהוה יִמְלֹךְ לְעֹלָם וָעֶד: שמות טו

וְנֶאֱמַר

לֹא־הִבִּיט אָוֶן בְּיַעֲקֹב, וְלֹא־רָאָה עָמָל בְּיִשְׂרָאֵל במדבר כג

יהוה אֱלֹהָיו עִמּוֹ, וּתְרוּעַת מֶלֶךְ בּוֹ:

וְנֶאֱמַר

וַיְהִי בִישֻׁרוּן מֶלֶךְ, בְּהִתְאַסֵּף רָאשֵׁי עָם דברים לג

יַחַד שִׁבְטֵי יִשְׂרָאֵל:

וּבְדִבְרֵי קָדְשְׁךָ כָּתוּב לֵאמֹר

כִּי לַיהוה הַמְּלוּכָה וּמֹשֵׁל בַּגּוֹיִם: תהלים כב

וְנֶאֱמַר
יהוה מָלָךְ, גֵּאוּת לָבֵשׁ תהלים צג
לָבֵשׁ יהוה עֹז הִתְאַזָּר, אַף־תִּכּוֹן תֵּבֵל בַּל־תִּמּוֹט:

וְנֶאֱמַר
שְׂאוּ שְׁעָרִים רָאשֵׁיכֶם, וְהִנָּשְׂאוּ פִּתְחֵי עוֹלָם תהלים כד
וְיָבוֹא מֶלֶךְ הַכָּבוֹד:
מִי זֶה מֶלֶךְ הַכָּבוֹד, יהוה עִזּוּז וְגִבּוֹר
יהוה גִּבּוֹר מִלְחָמָה:
שְׂאוּ שְׁעָרִים רָאשֵׁיכֶם, וּשְׂאוּ פִּתְחֵי עוֹלָם
וְיָבֹא מֶלֶךְ הַכָּבוֹד:
מִי הוּא זֶה מֶלֶךְ הַכָּבוֹד
יהוה צְבָאוֹת הוּא מֶלֶךְ הַכָּבוֹד סֶלָה:

וְעַל יְדֵי עֲבָדֶיךָ הַנְּבִיאִים כָּתוּב לֵאמֹר
כֹּה־אָמַר יהוה מֶלֶךְ־יִשְׂרָאֵל וְגֹאֲלוֹ, יהוה צְבָאוֹת ישעיה מד
אֲנִי רִאשׁוֹן וַאֲנִי אַחֲרוֹן, וּמִבַּלְעָדַי אֵין אֱלֹהִים:

וְנֶאֱמַר
וְעָלוּ מוֹשִׁעִים בְּהַר צִיּוֹן לִשְׁפֹּט אֶת־הַר עֵשָׂו עובדיה א
וְהָיְתָה לַיהוה הַמְּלוּכָה:

וְנֶאֱמַר
וְהָיָה יהוה לְמֶלֶךְ עַל־כָּל־הָאָרֶץ זכריה יד
בַּיּוֹם הַהוּא יִהְיֶה יהוה אֶחָד וּשְׁמוֹ אֶחָד:

וּבְתוֹרָתְךָ כָּתוּב לֵאמֹר
שְׁמַע יִשְׂרָאֵל, יהוה אֱלֹהֵינוּ יהוה אֶחָד: דברים ו

אֱלֹהֵינוּ Our God and God of our ancestors,
rule over all the world in Your honor,
and be raised above all the earth in Your glory,
and appear, in the splendor of Your great might
before all those who live in this world, Your domain.
And all who were made will know that You made them,
and all who were formed will know that You formed them,
and all that have breath in their mouths will declare:
The LORD, God of Israel is King,
and His kingship has dominion over all.
Make us holy through Your commandments
and grant us our share in Your Torah.
Satisfy us with Your goodness,
grant our souls joy in Your salvation,
and purify our hearts to serve You in truth.
For You, LORD, are truth,
and Your word is truth and holds true forever.
Blessed are You, LORD, King over all the earth,
who sanctifies Israel and the Day of Remembrance.

*In many congregations, the shofar is sounded.*

TEKIA SHEVARIM TERUA TEKIA
TEKIA SHEVARIM TEKIA
TEKIA TERUA TEKIA

הַיּוֹם This day is the birth of the world.
This day stands all the world's creations up in judgment,
stands them as sons or as slaves –
If as sons, have compassion for us,
as a father has compassion for his sons.
And if as slaves, our eyes are raised and fixed on You
until You show us favor, and bring out our judgment like sunlight,
Awesome, Holy.

---

of the day ("Who sanctifies Israel and the Day of Remembrance"). It is rare for a single blessing to combine two themes.

אֱלֹהֵינוּ וֵאלֹהֵי אֲבוֹתֵינוּ
מְלֹךְ עַל כָּל הָעוֹלָם כֻּלּוֹ בִּכְבוֹדֶךָ, וְהִנָּשֵׂא עַל כָּל הָאָרֶץ בִּיקָרֶךָ
וְהוֹפַע בַּהֲדַר גְּאוֹן עֻזֶּךָ עַל כָּל יוֹשְׁבֵי תֵבֵל אַרְצֶךָ.
וְיֵדַע כָּל פָּעוּל כִּי אַתָּה פְעַלְתּוֹ
וְיָבִין כָּל יָצוּר כִּי אַתָּה יְצַרְתּוֹ
וְיֹאמַר כֹּל אֲשֶׁר נְשָׁמָה בְאַפּוֹ
יהוה אֱלֹהֵי יִשְׂרָאֵל מֶלֶךְ וּמַלְכוּתוֹ בַּכֹּל מָשָׁלָה.
קַדְּשֵׁנוּ בְּמִצְוֹתֶיךָ וְתֵן חֶלְקֵנוּ בְּתוֹרָתֶךָ
שַׂבְּעֵנוּ מִטּוּבֶךָ וְשַׂמַּח נַפְשֵׁנוּ בִּישׁוּעָתֶךָ
וְטַהֵר לִבֵּנוּ לְעָבְדְּךָ בֶּאֱמֶת
כִּי אַתָּה אֱלֹהִים אֱמֶת, וּדְבָרְךָ אֱמֶת וְקַיָּם לָעַד.
בָּרוּךְ אַתָּה יהוה, מֶלֶךְ עַל כָּל הָאָרֶץ
מְקַדֵּשׁ יִשְׂרָאֵל וְיוֹם הַזִּכָּרוֹן.

*In many congregations, the* שופר *is sounded.*

| | | |
|---|---|---|
| תקיעה | שברים תרועה | תקיעה |
| תקיעה | שברים | תקיעה |
| תקיעה | תרועה | תקיעה |

הַיּוֹם הֲרַת עוֹלָם, הַיּוֹם יַעֲמִיד בַּמִּשְׁפָּט כָּל יְצוּרֵי עוֹלָמִים
אִם כְּבָנִים אִם כַּעֲבָדִים.
אִם כְּבָנִים, רַחֲמֵנוּ כְּרַחֵם אָב עַל בָּנִים
וְאִם כַּעֲבָדִים, עֵינֵינוּ לְךָ תְלוּיוֹת עַד שֶׁתְּחָנֵּנוּ
וְתוֹצִיא כָאוֹר מִשְׁפָּטֵנוּ, אָיֹם קָדוֹשׁ.

---

בָּרוּךְ אַתָּה יהוה, מֶלֶךְ עַל כָּל הָאָרֶץ *Blessed are You, Lord, King over all the earth.* Note that the concluding blessing of the *Malkhiyot* section combines both the concept of Kingship ("King over all the earth") and the special sanctity

REMEMBRANCES

אַתָּה זוֹכֵר You remember the making of the world;
You come to all those formed long ago.
Under Your gaze, all hidden things come to light,
all the many secrets buried since the Beginning.
For nothing is forgotten before the throne of Your glory,
and nothing is hidden from Your eyes.

You remember all of creation,
and all things that were formed – none is shrouded from You.
All is revealed and known before You, Lord our God,
who gazes and looks on to the last of all the ages.
For You bring a day decreed for remembrance
to come to each spirit and soul;
that Your many works be remembered,
Your numerous, endless creations.
From the very beginning You made it known,
long before this time You revealed it,
for this day is the opening of all Your works,
a remembrance of the very first day.
"For it is a decree for Israel, an ordinance of the God of Jacob." *Ps. 81*

And on it, it is said of every province
which will come to the sword and which to peace,
which will succumb to hunger and which find plenty.
And all creations are regarded on this day;
remembered for life, or for death.

מִי לֹא נִפְקַד Who may be overlooked on this day,
when the memory of every being formed comes before You;
each person's works, his purpose, the path that he chooses and follows?
the thoughts and the plans of all mankind,
and the impulses behind each person's acts?
Happy the one who does not forget You,
the child of man who takes courage in You.
For one who seeks You will never stumble,
they need never be ashamed, who seek shelter in You.
For the memory of all that You have made passes before You,
You examine what each one does.

זכרונות

אַתָּה זוֹכֵר מַעֲשֵׂה עוֹלָם, וּפוֹקֵד כָּל יְצוּרֵי קֶדֶם
לְפָנֶיךָ נִגְלוּ כָּל תַּעֲלוּמוֹת וַהֲמוֹן נִסְתָּרוֹת שֶׁמִּבְּרֵאשִׁית
כִּי אֵין שִׁכְחָה לִפְנֵי כִסֵּא כְבוֹדֶךָ, וְאֵין נִסְתָּר מִנֶּגֶד עֵינֶיךָ.

אַתָּה זוֹכֵר אֶת כָּל הַמִּפְעָל, וְגַם כָּל הַיְצוּר לֹא נִכְחַד מִמֶּךָּ.
הַכֹּל גָּלוּי וְיָדוּעַ לְפָנֶיךָ יהוה אֱלֹהֵינוּ
צוֹפֶה וּמַבִּיט עַד סוֹף כָּל הַדּוֹרוֹת
כִּי תָבִיא חֹק זִכָּרוֹן לְהִפָּקֵד כָּל רוּחַ וָנֶפֶשׁ
לְהִזָּכֵר מַעֲשִׂים רַבִּים, וַהֲמוֹן בְּרִיּוֹת לְאֵין תַּכְלִית.
מֵרֵאשִׁית כָּזֹאת הוֹדַעְתָּ, וּמִלְּפָנִים אוֹתָהּ גִּלִּיתָ.
זֶה הַיּוֹם תְּחִלַּת מַעֲשֶׂיךָ, זִכָּרוֹן לְיוֹם רִאשׁוֹן
כִּי חֹק לְיִשְׂרָאֵל הוּא, מִשְׁפָּט לֵאלֹהֵי יַעֲקֹב: תהלים פא

וְעַל הַמְּדִינוֹת בּוֹ יֵאָמֵר
אֵיזוֹ לַחֶרֶב, וְאֵיזוֹ לַשָּׁלוֹם
אֵיזוֹ לָרָעָב, וְאֵיזוֹ לַשֹּׂבַע
וּבְרִיּוֹת בּוֹ יִפָּקֵדוּ, לְהַזְכִּירָם לְחַיִּים וְלַמָּוֶת.

מִי לֹא נִפְקַד כְּהַיּוֹם הַזֶּה
כִּי זֵכֶר כָּל הַיְצוּר לְפָנֶיךָ בָּא
מַעֲשֵׂה אִישׁ וּפְקֻדָּתוֹ, וַעֲלִילוֹת מִצְעֲדֵי גָבֶר
מַחְשְׁבוֹת אָדָם וְתַחְבּוּלוֹתָיו, וְיִצְרֵי מַעַלְלֵי אִישׁ.
אַשְׁרֵי אִישׁ שֶׁלֹּא יִשְׁכָּחֶךָּ, וּבֶן אָדָם יִתְאַמֶּץ בָּךְ
כִּי דוֹרְשֶׁיךָ לְעוֹלָם לֹא יִכָּשֵׁלוּ
וְלֹא יִכָּלְמוּ לָנֶצַח כָּל הַחוֹסִים בָּךְ.
כִּי זֵכֶר כָּל הַמַּעֲשִׂים לְפָנֶיךָ בָּא, וְאַתָּה דוֹרֵשׁ מַעֲשֵׂה כֻלָּם.

And Noah also, You remembered with love,
and You came to him with words of salvation, compassion,
when You brought on the waters of the great flood,
to destroy all creatures of flesh
because the practices they followed were corrupt.
And so let [Noah's] memory come to You, LORD our God,
that You multiply His children like the dust of the earth,
his descendants like sand of the sea.

As it is written in Your Torah:
"God remembered Noah *Gen. 8*
and all the animals and all the cattle
that were with him in the ark,
and God made a wind blow across the earth,
and the waters grew calm."

And it is said:
"God heard their groaning, *Ex. 2*
and God remembered His covenant
with Abraham, with Isaac and with Jacob."

And it is said:
"I will remember My covenant with Jacob, *Lev. 26*
and also My covenant with Isaac,
and also My covenant with Abraham I will remember,
and the land I will remember."

And in Your holy Writings it is written thus:
"He has made remembrance for His wonders; *Ps. 111*
gracious and compassionate is the LORD."

And it is said:
"He has given food to those who revere Him, *Ibid.*
He will remember His covenant forever."

And it is said:
"He remembered His covenant for their sake, *Ps. 106*
and relented in His great love."

וְגַם אֶת נֹחַ בְּאַהֲבָה זָכַרְתָּ, וַתִּפְקְדֵהוּ בִּדְבַר יְשׁוּעָה וְרַחֲמִים
בַּהֲבִיאֲךָ אֶת מֵי הַמַּבּוּל לְשַׁחֵת כָּל בָּשָׂר מִפְּנֵי רֹעַ מַעַלְלֵיהֶם
עַל כֵּן זִכְרוֹנוֹ בָּא לְפָנֶיךָ, יהוה אֱלֹהֵינוּ
לְהַרְבּוֹת זַרְעוֹ כְּעַפְרוֹת תֵּבֵל, וְצֶאֱצָאָיו כְּחוֹל הַיָּם.

כַּכָּתוּב בְּתוֹרָתֶךָ
וַיִּזְכֹּר אֱלֹהִים אֶת־נֹחַ בראשית ח
וְאֵת כָּל־הַחַיָּה וְאֶת־כָּל־הַבְּהֵמָה אֲשֶׁר אִתּוֹ בַּתֵּבָה
וַיַּעֲבֵר אֱלֹהִים רוּחַ עַל־הָאָרֶץ, וַיָּשֹׁכּוּ הַמָּיִם:

וְנֶאֱמַר
וַיִּשְׁמַע אֱלֹהִים אֶת־נַאֲקָתָם שמות ב
וַיִּזְכֹּר אֱלֹהִים אֶת־בְּרִיתוֹ
אֶת־אַבְרָהָם אֶת־יִצְחָק וְאֶת־יַעֲקֹב:

וְנֶאֱמַר
וְזָכַרְתִּי אֶת־בְּרִיתִי יַעֲקוֹב ויקרא כו
וְאַף אֶת־בְּרִיתִי יִצְחָק
וְאַף אֶת־בְּרִיתִי אַבְרָהָם אֶזְכֹּר
וְהָאָרֶץ אֶזְכֹּר:

וּבְדִבְרֵי קָדְשְׁךָ כָּתוּב לֵאמֹר
זֵכֶר עָשָׂה לְנִפְלְאוֹתָיו, חַנּוּן וְרַחוּם יהוה: תהלים קיא

וְנֶאֱמַר
טֶרֶף נָתַן לִירֵאָיו, יִזְכֹּר לְעוֹלָם בְּרִיתוֹ: שם

וְנֶאֱמַר
וַיִּזְכֹּר לָהֶם בְּרִיתוֹ, וַיִּנָּחֵם כְּרֹב חֲסָדָו: תהלים קו

וְעַל יְדֵי עֲבָדֶיךָ הַנְּבִיאִים כָּתוּב לֵאמֹר
ירמיה ב
הָלֹךְ וְקָרָאתָ בְאָזְנֵי יְרוּשָׁלַיִם לֵאמֹר
כֹּה אָמַר יהוה
זָכַרְתִּי לָךְ חֶסֶד נְעוּרַיִךְ, אַהֲבַת כְּלוּלֹתָיִךְ
לֶכְתֵּךְ אַחֲרַי בַּמִּדְבָּר, בְּאֶרֶץ לֹא זְרוּעָה:

וְנֶאֱמַר
יחזקאל טז
וְזָכַרְתִּי אֲנִי אֶת־בְּרִיתִי אוֹתָךְ בִּימֵי נְעוּרָיִךְ
וַהֲקִימוֹתִי לָךְ בְּרִית עוֹלָם:

וְנֶאֱמַר
ירמיה לא
הֲבֵן יַקִּיר לִי אֶפְרַיִם, אִם יֶלֶד שַׁעֲשׁוּעִים
כִּי־מִדֵּי דַבְּרִי בּוֹ, זָכֹר אֶזְכְּרֶנּוּ עוֹד
עַל־כֵּן הָמוּ מֵעַי לוֹ
רַחֵם אֲרַחֲמֶנּוּ נְאֻם־יהוה:

אֱלֹהֵינוּ וֵאלֹהֵי אֲבוֹתֵינוּ
זָכְרֵנוּ בְּזִכְרוֹן טוֹב לְפָנֶיךָ
וּפָקְדֵנוּ בִּפְקֻדַּת יְשׁוּעָה וְרַחֲמִים מִשְּׁמֵי שְׁמֵי קֶדֶם
וּזְכָר לָנוּ יהוה אֱלֹהֵינוּ
אֶת הַבְּרִית וְאֶת הַחֶסֶד וְאֶת הַשְּׁבוּעָה
אֲשֶׁר נִשְׁבַּעְתָּ לְאַבְרָהָם אָבִינוּ בְּהַר הַמּוֹרִיָּה
וְתֵרָאֶה לְפָנֶיךָ עֲקֵדָה
שֶׁעָקַד אַבְרָהָם אָבִינוּ אֶת יִצְחָק בְּנוֹ עַל גַּבֵּי הַמִּזְבֵּחַ
וְכָבַשׁ רַחֲמָיו, לַעֲשׂוֹת רְצוֹנְךָ בְּלֵבָב שָׁלֵם.

So, too, let Your compassion wrest Your anger from us,
and in Your great goodness may Your anger be turned away
from Your people, Your city, Your land and Your inheritance.
Fulfill for us, LORD our God, the promise You made in Your Torah,
at the hand of Moses Your servant and by Your own word,
as it is said:
"And I remembered, for their sake, *Lev. 26*
the covenant of the early ones,
whom I brought out of the land of Egypt
before the eyes of all nations,
to be God to them, I am the LORD."

כִּי זוֹכֵר For it has always been You
who remembered all forgotten things,
and there is no forgetfulness before the throne of Your glory,
and today in Your compassion, You remember
the binding of Isaac, for his descendants' sake.
Blessed are You, LORD, who remembers the covenant.

*In many congregations, the shofar is sounded.*

| TEKIA | SHEVARIM TERUA | TEKIA |
|---|---|---|
| TEKIA | SHEVARIM | TEKIA |
| TEKIA | TERUA | TEKIA |

הַיּוֹם This day is the birth of the world.
This day stands all the world's creations up in judgment,
stands them as sons or as slaves –
If as sons, have compassion for us,
as a father has compassion for his sons.
And if as slaves, our eyes are raised and fixed on You
until You show us favor,
and bring out our judgment like sunlight,
Awesome, Holy.

כֵּן יִכְבְּשׁוּ רַחֲמֶיךָ אֶת כַּעַסְךָ מֵעָלֵינוּ
וּבְטוּבְךָ הַגָּדוֹל יָשׁוּב חֲרוֹן אַפְּךָ מֵעַמְּךָ
וּמֵעִירְךָ וּמֵאַרְצְךָ וּמִנַּחֲלָתֶךָ.
וְקַיֶּם לָנוּ יהוה אֱלֹהֵינוּ אֶת הַדָּבָר שֶׁהִבְטַחְתָּנוּ בְּתוֹרָתֶךָ
עַל יְדֵי מֹשֶׁה עַבְדֶּךָ, מִפִּי כְבוֹדֶךָ
כָּאָמוּר

וְזָכַרְתִּי לָהֶם בְּרִית רִאשֹׁנִים ויקרא כו
אֲשֶׁר הוֹצֵאתִי־אֹתָם מֵאֶרֶץ מִצְרַיִם לְעֵינֵי הַגּוֹיִם
לִהְיוֹת לָהֶם לֵאלֹהִים, אֲנִי יהוה:

כִּי זוֹכֵר כָּל הַנִּשְׁכָּחוֹת אַתָּה הוּא מֵעוֹלָם
וְאֵין שִׁכְחָה לִפְנֵי כִסֵּא כְבוֹדֶךָ
וַעֲקֵדַת יִצְחָק לְזַרְעוֹ הַיּוֹם בְּרַחֲמִים תִּזְכֹּר.
בָּרוּךְ אַתָּה יהוה, זוֹכֵר הַבְּרִית.

*In many congregations, the* שופר *is sounded.*

תקיעה שברים תרועה תקיעה

תקיעה שברים תקיעה

תקיעה תרועה תקיעה

הַיּוֹם הֲרַת עוֹלָם, הַיּוֹם יַעֲמִיד בַּמִּשְׁפָּט כָּל יְצוּרֵי עוֹלָמִים
אִם כְּבָנִים אִם כַּעֲבָדִים.
אִם כְּבָנִים, רַחֲמֵנוּ כְּרַחֵם אָב עַל בָּנִים
וְאִם כַּעֲבָדִים, עֵינֵינוּ לְךָ תְלוּיוֹת עַד שֶׁתְּחָנֵּנוּ
וְתוֹצִיא כָאוֹר מִשְׁפָּטֵנוּ, אָיֹם קָדוֹשׁ.

SHOFAROT

אַתָּה נִגְלֵיתָ You were revealed in a cloud of Your glory,
to Your holy nation, to speak with them.
Out of the heavens Your voice was heard;
You revealed Yourself in mists of purity.
And all the wide world quaked before You,
the works of creation shook in Your presence,
as You revealed Yourself, our King, on Mount Sinai,
to teach Your people Torah and the commandments,
to have them hear the majesty of Your voice –
Your sacred words amid flames of fire.
In thunder and lightning You revealed Yourself to them,
and amid the sound of the shofar You appeared.

As it is written in Your Torah:
"Then on the third day, in the morning – *Ex. 19*
thunder and lightning;
heavy cloud covered the mountain,
there was a very loud sound of the shofar,
and all of the people in the camp quaked."

And it is said:
"And the sound of the shofar grew ever louder – *Ibid.*
Moses spoke, and the LORD answered him with a voice."

And it is said:
"And all the people saw the thunder and the flames, *Ex. 20*
and the sound of the shofar, and the mountain asmoke;
the people saw and they staggered, and stood far back."

And by Your servants the prophets it is written:
"God has been raised up in sound; *Ps. 47*
raised, the LORD, in the voice of the shofar."

---

God's sovereignty was proclaimed, and in the future, with the ingathering of exiles.

שופרות

אַתָּה נִגְלֵיתָ בַּעֲנַן כְּבוֹדֶךָ עַל עַם קָדְשֶׁךָ לְדַבֵּר עִמָּם
מִן הַשָּׁמַיִם הִשְׁמַעְתָּם קוֹלֶךָ, וְנִגְלֵיתָ עֲלֵיהֶם בְּעַרְפְלֵּי טֹהַר.
גַּם כָּל הָעוֹלָם כֻּלּוֹ חָל מִפָּנֶיךָ, וּבְרִיּוֹת בְּרֵאשִׁית חָרְדוּ מִמֶּךָּ
בְּהִגָּלוֹתְךָ מַלְכֵּנוּ עַל הַר סִינַי, לְלַמֵּד לְעַמְּךָ תּוֹרָה וּמִצְוֹת
וַתַּשְׁמִיעֵם אֶת הוֹד קוֹלֶךָ, וְדִבְּרוֹת קָדְשְׁךָ מִלַּהֲבוֹת אֵשׁ.
בְּקוֹלוֹת וּבְרָקִים עֲלֵיהֶם נִגְלֵיתָ, וּבְקוֹל שׁוֹפָר עֲלֵיהֶם הוֹפָעְתָּ.

כַּכָּתוּב בְּתוֹרָתֶךָ

שמות יט וַיְהִי בַיּוֹם הַשְּׁלִישִׁי בִּהְיֹת הַבֹּקֶר
וַיְהִי קֹלֹת וּבְרָקִים וְעָנָן כָּבֵד עַל־הָהָר
וְקֹל שֹׁפָר חָזָק מְאֹד
וַיֶּחֱרַד כָּל־הָעָם אֲשֶׁר בַּמַּחֲנֶה:

וְנֶאֱמַר

שם וַיְהִי קוֹל הַשֹּׁפָר הוֹלֵךְ וְחָזֵק מְאֹד
מֹשֶׁה יְדַבֵּר, וְהָאֱלֹהִים יַעֲנֶנּוּ בְקוֹל:

וְנֶאֱמַר

שמות כ וְכָל־הָעָם רֹאִים אֶת־הַקּוֹלֹת וְאֶת־הַלַּפִּידִם
וְאֵת קוֹל הַשֹּׁפָר, וְאֶת־הָהָר עָשֵׁן
וַיַּרְא הָעָם וַיָּנֻעוּ, וַיַּעַמְדוּ מֵרָחֹק:

וּבְדִבְרֵי קָדְשְׁךָ כָּתוּב לֵאמֹר

תהלים מז עָלָה אֱלֹהִים בִּתְרוּעָה, יהוה בְּקוֹל שׁוֹפָר:

---

**אַתָּה נִגְלֵיתָ** *You were revealed.* A rich tapestry of references to the shofar throughout history: at the revelation at Mount Sinai, in the Temple as

And it is said,
"With trumpets and the sound of the shofar, *Ps. 98*
shout for joy before the LORD, the King."
And it is said:
"Sound the shofar on the new moon, *Ps. 81*
on our feast day when the moon is hidden.
For it is a statute for Israel, an ordinance of the God of Jacob."
And it is said:
"Halleluya! Praise God in His holy place; *Ps. 150*
praise Him in the heavens of His power.
Praise Him for His mighty deeds;
praise Him for His surpassing greatness.
Praise Him with blasts of the shofar;
praise Him with the harp and lyre.
Praise Him with timbrel and dance;
praise Him with strings and flute.
Praise Him with clashing cymbals;
praise Him with resounding cymbals.
Let all that breathes praise the LORD. Halleluya!"

And by Your servants the prophets it is written:
"All the inhabitants of the world, all the dwellers on this earth, *Is. 18*
when He lifts up a banner on the mountains, you will see it,
and when He sounds the shofar you shall hear."
And it is said:
"On that day a great shofar will be sounded, *Is. 27*
and those who are lost will come from the land of Assyria,
and those who were banished, from the land of Egypt,
and they will worship the LORD
at the holy mountain in Jerusalem."
And it is said:
"The LORD will appear to them, *Zech. 9*
His arrow will come out like lightning,
and the LORD God will sound the shofar,
and will move in stormwinds of the south.
The LORD of hosts will protect them –"
So, protect Your people Israel with Your peace.

וְנֶאֱמַר

בַּחֲצֹצְרוֹת וְקוֹל שׁוֹפָר, הָרִיעוּ לִפְנֵי הַמֶּלֶךְ יהוה: תהלים צח

וְנֶאֱמַר

תִּקְעוּ בַחֹדֶשׁ שׁוֹפָר, בַּכֵּסֶה לְיוֹם חַגֵּנוּ: תהלים פא
כִּי חֹק לְיִשְׂרָאֵל הוּא, מִשְׁפָּט לֵאלֹהֵי יַעֲקֹב:

וְנֶאֱמַר

הַלְלוּיָהּ, הַלְלוּ־אֵל בְּקָדְשׁוֹ   הַלְלוּהוּ בִּרְקִיעַ עֻזּוֹ: תהלים קנ
הַלְלוּהוּ בִגְבוּרֹתָיו   הַלְלוּהוּ כְּרֹב גֻּדְלוֹ:
הַלְלוּהוּ בְּתֵקַע שׁוֹפָר   הַלְלוּהוּ בְּנֵבֶל וְכִנּוֹר:
הַלְלוּהוּ בְתֹף וּמָחוֹל   הַלְלוּהוּ בְּמִנִּים וְעֻגָב:
הַלְלוּהוּ בְצִלְצְלֵי־שָׁמַע   הַלְלוּהוּ בְּצִלְצְלֵי תְרוּעָה:
כֹּל הַנְּשָׁמָה תְּהַלֵּל יָהּ
הַלְלוּיָהּ:

וְעַל יְדֵי עֲבָדֶיךָ הַנְּבִיאִים כָּתוּב לֵאמֹר

כָּל־יֹשְׁבֵי תֵבֵל וְשֹׁכְנֵי אָרֶץ ישעיה יח
כִּנְשֹׂא־נֵס הָרִים תִּרְאוּ, וְכִתְקֹעַ שׁוֹפָר תִּשְׁמָעוּ:

וְנֶאֱמַר

וְהָיָה בַּיּוֹם הַהוּא יִתָּקַע בְּשׁוֹפָר גָּדוֹל ישעיה כז
וּבָאוּ הָאֹבְדִים בְּאֶרֶץ אַשּׁוּר, וְהַנִּדָּחִים בְּאֶרֶץ מִצְרָיִם
וְהִשְׁתַּחֲווּ לַיהוה בְּהַר הַקֹּדֶשׁ בִּירוּשָׁלָםִ:

וְנֶאֱמַר

וַיהוה עֲלֵיהֶם יֵרָאֶה, וְיָצָא כַבָּרָק חִצּוֹ זכריה ט
וַאדֹנָי יֱהוִה בַּשּׁוֹפָר יִתְקָע
וְהָלַךְ בְּסַעֲרוֹת תֵּימָן:
יהוה צְבָאוֹת יָגֵן עֲלֵיהֶם:

כֵּן תָּגֵן עַל עַמְּךָ יִשְׂרָאֵל בִּשְׁלוֹמֶךָ.

*All:* May His great name be blessed for ever and all time.

*Mourner:* Blessed and praised,
glorified and exalted,
raised and honored,
uplifted and lauded
be the name of the Holy One,
blessed be He,
beyond any blessing,
song, praise and consolation
uttered in the world –
and say: Amen.

To Israel, to the teachers,
their disciples and their disciples' disciples,
and to all who engage
in the study of Torah,
in this (*in Israel add:* holy) place or elsewhere,
may there come to them and you great peace,
grace, kindness and compassion,
long life, ample sustenance
and deliverance, from their Father
who is in heaven and on earth –
and say: Amen.

May there be great peace from heaven,
and a good life for us and all Israel –
and say: Amen.

*Bow, take three steps back, as if taking leave of the Divine Presence, then bow, first left, then right, then center, while saying:*

May He who makes peace in His high places,
in His compassion make peace
for us and all Israel –
and say: Amen.

*Leader:* Like a youth's, His hair in locks unfurls;
Its black tresses flowing in curls.

*Cong:* Jerusalem, His splendor, is the dwelling place of right;
may He prize it as His highest delight.

*Leader:* Like a crown in His hand may His treasured people be,
a turban of beauty and of majesty.

*Cong:* He bore them, carried them, with a crown He adorned them.
They were precious in His sight, and He honored them.

*Leader:* His glory is on me; my glory is on Him.
He is near to me when I call to Him.

*Cong:* He is bright and rosy; red will be His dress,
when He comes from Edom, treading the winepress.

*Leader:* He showed the tefillin-knot to Moses, humble, wise,
when the LORD's likeness was before his eyes.

*Cong:* He delights in His people; the humble He does raise –
He glories in them; He sits enthroned upon their praise.

*Leader:* Your first word, Your call to every age, is true:
O seek the people who seek You.

*Cong:* My many songs please take and hear
and may my hymn of joy to You come near.

*Leader:* May my praise be a crown for Your head,
and like incense before You, the prayers I have said.

*Cong:* May a poor man's song be precious in Your eyes,
like a song sung over sacrifice.

*Leader:* To the One who sustains all, may my blessing take flight:
Creator, Life-Giver, God of right and might.

*Cong:* And when I offer blessing, to me Your head incline:
accepting it as spice, fragrant and fine.

*Leader:* May my prayer be to You sweet song.
For You my soul will always long.

*The Ark is closed.*

Yours, LORD, are the greatness and the power, the glory, the majesty and *1 Chr. 29*
splendor, for everything in heaven and earth is Yours. Yours, LORD, is the
kingdom; You are exalted as Head over all. ▸ Who can tell of the mighty *Ps. 106*
acts of the LORD and make all His praise be heard?

May You recall the actions of Abraham; / may his righteousness speak on our behalf and seal the mouths of those who accuse us.

He accepted Your fear upon himself and recognized Your Oneness; / he hastened to act properly and glorify You by performing Your commandments.

He was found to be perfect in all that he was commanded, / and God gladdened him on this day by appointing him with offspring. /

▸ He took care to offer praise to the Almighty who had taken pity upon him, / as his beloved wife gave birth at the hour that had been determined.

*All:* We have relied on God always and He has answered us with wonders. / May You willingly accept our supplications as if we had sacrificed animals.

▸ Rescue us with Your shield and deliver us from all deathly afflictions: / "As birds hovering overhead so shall the LORD of hosts protect us." *Is. 31*

*The Leader continues:*

**זָכְרֵנוּ לְחַיִּים** Remember us for life, O King who desires life,
and write us in the book of life – for Your sake, O God of life.
King, Helper, Savior, Shield:
▾Blessed are You, LORD, Shield of Abraham.

DIVINE MIGHT

**אַתָּה גִּבּוֹר** You are eternally mighty, LORD.
You give life to the dead and have great power to save.
*In Israel:* He causes the dew to fall.
He sustains the living with loving-kindness,
and with great compassion revives the dead.
He supports the fallen, heals the sick, sets captives free,
and keeps His faith with those who sleep in the dust.
Who is like You, Master of might, and to whom can You be compared,
O King who brings death and gives life, and makes salvation grow?

---

in Psalms 68:21, "To the LORD God belong the issues [*totza'ot*] of death" as referring to 903 (the numerical value of *totza'ot*) different ways of dying (*Berakhot* 8a).

*The congregation says the next two verses aloud, followed by the Leader:*

The LORD shall reign for ever. Ps. 146
He is your God, Zion,
from generation to generation,
Halleluya!

You are the Holy One, Ps. 22
enthroned on the praises of Israel.

*There follows an ancient piyut, author unknown, which most congregations add after the Meshalesh. In recent generations the custom to say it responsively has spread; many congregations are accustomed to saying the second stich of each couplet together with the first of the next one. However, traditionally this piyut is said only by the Leader, with the congregation joining in at "He is alive and everlasting."*

*The Ark is opened.*

God, please.

You are our God, in heaven and on earth.
Mighty and revered, encircled with myriads.
He spoke and it was, commanded and it came into being.

His memory is forever, His life is everlasting.
Pure of eye, He sits concealed.
His crown is salvation, His garment is righteousness.
His cloak is jealousy, His coat is vengeance.
His counsel is candor, His wisdom is faith.
His deeds are truth, He is righteous and upright.
He is close to those who call upon Him in truth, He is sublime and lofty.
He resides in the heavens, and hangs the earth over emptiness.

*All:*

He is alive and everlasting, awesome, lofty and holy.

*The Ark is closed.*

*Leader:* Pave a straight road for us that we might stride, / and do not allow the ankles of Your precious child to falter.

*Cong:* As You have spoken: "I will remember him always." *Jer. 31*

May He return our captives from afar to His holy mount,
that we might glorify Him always in His holy Sanctuary,
for He has remembered His holy vow. / O Holy One. *Ps. 105*

*Leader:* The nation You have borne shall blast and sound the shofar, adhering to Your command according to the prescribed ritual.

*Cong:* Sound the shofar at the New Moon. *Ps. 81*

*Leader:* Please remove their sins that their iniquity might be forgiven. May their prayer be as delightful to You as an offering of sheep or young bull.

*Cong:* Among trumpets and the sound of the shofar. *Ps. 98*

*Leader:* May their offshoots multiply like the immeasurable sand, and their buried ones awaken and rise from the dust.

*Cong:* You shall witness it like a raised banner on a mountain and like the sound of a shofar. *Is. 18*

His great name is praised as a tower of strength;
He shall eternally give His Messianic king strength and greatness.
On that day, a great shofar shall be sounded. O Holy One. *Is. 27*

*Leader:* May there be joy in the city, in the Sanctuary and hall. May He restore the altar and all the attendant vessels.

*Cong:* The LORD shall reign forever. *Ex. 15*

*Leader:* The heavens and earth shall sing in His honor. The forests shall clap hands to offer pleasant sounds to Him,

*Cong:* For the LORD has finally appointed His people. *Ruth 1*

*Leader:* The splendor of angels and the morning stars / shall offer praise and pleasant song.

*Cong:* Praise Him with the sounding of the shofar. *Ps. 150*

All inhabitants of the world and those who reside on the earth / shall *Is. 18*
forever say that the LORD has done great things in the world, / and the *Zech. 14*
LORD shall reign as King over the entire world. / O Holy One.

*The Leader then the congregation:*

שֶׁבַח His great name is praised as a tower of strength;
He shall eternally give His Messianic king strength and greatness.
On that day, a great shofar shall be sounded. O Holy One. *Is. 27*

*Responsively (some congregations omit and continue with "Master, if we are devoid" below):*

*Leader:* The nation You have borne shall blast and sound the shofar,
adhering to Your command according to the prescribed ritual.
*Cong:* Sound the shofar at the New Moon. *Ps. 81*

*Leader:* Please remove their sins that their iniquity might be forgiven.
May their prayer be as delightful to You as an offering of sheep
or young bull.
*Cong:* Among trumpets and the sound of the shofar. *Ps. 98*

*Leader:* May their offshoots multiply like the immeasurable sand,
and their buried ones awaken and rise from the dust.
*Cong:* You shall witness it like a raised banner on a *Is. 18*
mountain and like the sound of a shofar.

His great name is praised as a tower of strength;
He shall eternally give His Messianic king strength and greatness.
On that day, a great shofar shall be sounded. O Holy One. *Is. 27*

*On all days the service continues:*

*The Leader then the congregation:*

אָדוֹן Master, if we are devoid of good deeds,
let Your great name still remain with us.
Do not approach to judge us. / O Holy One.

*The Leader then the congregation:*

הֵן For He believes not even in His holy beings,
and casts aspersions on His angels of aquamarine.
And how then will those who were but culled
from clods of earth be vindicated? / O Holy One.

---

seek to hold the rope by both ends, desiring both strict justice and a world. Unless You forgo a little, the world cannot endure" (*Bereshit Raba* 49:9).

*The Ark is closed and the congregation says quietly:*

The destitute king
Worn and relegated to decay / in uppermost hell and beneath,
weary without rest –
till when shall he reign?

The destitute king
Sleep hovers over him, / deep sleep enfolds him,
confusion overwhelms him –
till when shall he reign?

*The Ark is opened.*

Yet the Supreme King –
Truthful Judge, / His works are true,
He performs kindness and truth, / He is abundantly kind and true,
His path is truth / and His seal is truth.
He shall reign forever.

*Like the previous piyut, this one is also a variation by Rabbi Shimon of Mainz, this time on HaKalir's "The Lord is King" of the first day. However, instead of the triple alphabetic acrostic, R. Shimon employs a different structure. The first and second lines of each stanza begin with the word "Kol," meaning "all," a nod to Hakalir's "Kol," meaning "voice," followed by the letters of Rabbi Shimon's name. The second letter of the fourth and fifth words in each line form a double alphabetic acrostic.*

The Lord is King, the Lord was King,
the Lord shall be King forever and ever.

All the angels of heaven utter in praise, The Lord is King.
All the residents of the silent earth blessedly exalt, The Lord was King.
Both assemblies extol on high, The Lord shall be King.

The Lord is King, the Lord was King,
the Lord shall be King forever and ever.

---

of the *Kedusha* we are about to say. Recall that the key lines of the *Kedusha*, "Holy, holy, holy" and "Blessed is the Lord's glory from His place," are the words the prophets Isaiah and Ezekiel heard the angels singing in their respective visions of heaven. Yet in the *Kedusha* we say them down here on earth. In this daring act, we live the idea that we and the angels sing in harmony when we sing God's praise. In the poem, the first line of each verse speaks of

*All:*

וּבְכֵן לְךָ And so, sanctity will rise up to You;
for You, our God, are King.

*Some congregations say the piyut "Asher Mi Ya'aseh" on page 1062 before Kedusha.*

## KEDUSHA

*The following is said standing with feet together, rising on the toes at the words indicated by ▴.*

*The congregation then the Leader:*

נְקַדֵּשׁךָ We will sanctify and revere You
with the song sung by the holy Seraphim,
who speak the threefold declaration of Your holiness,
as is written by Your prophet,
"And they [the angels] call to one another saying: *Is. 6*

*The congregation then the Leader:*

▴Holy, ▴holy, ▴holy is the Lord of hosts;
the whole world is filled with His glory."
Then with a sound of mighty noise, majestic and strong,
they make their voice heard, raising themselves
toward the Seraphim, and facing them praise You and say:

*The congregation then the Leader:*

▴"Blessed is the Lord's glory from His place." *Ezek. 3*
Reveal Yourself from Your place, O our King, and reign over us,
for we are waiting for You.
When will You reign in Zion?
May it be soon in our days,
and may You dwell there for ever and all time.
May You be exalted and sanctified in the midst of Jerusalem,
Your city, from generation to generation for evermore.
May our eyes see Your kingdom,
as is said in the songs of Your splendor,
written by David Your righteous anointed one:

*The congregation then the Leader:*

▴"The Lord shall reign for ever. He is your God, Zion, *Ps. 146*
from generation to generation, Halleluya!"

## THANKSGIVING

*Bow at the first nine words.*

▾מוֹדִים We give thanks to You,
for You are the LORD our God
and God of our ancestors
for ever and all time.
You are the Rock of our lives,
Shield of our salvation
from generation to generation.
We will thank You and
declare Your praise for our lives,
which are entrusted into Your hand;
for our souls,
which are placed in Your charge;
for Your miracles
which are with us every day;
and for Your wonders and favors
at all times, evening,
morning and midday.
You are good –
for Your compassion never fails.
You are compassionate –
for Your loving-kindnesses never cease.
We have always placed our hope in You.

*As the Leader recites Modim, the congregation says quietly:*

▾מוֹדִים We give thanks to You,
for You are the LORD our God
and God of our ancestors,
God of all flesh,
who formed us
and formed the universe.
Blessings and thanks
are due to Your great
and holy name for giving us
life and sustaining us.
May You continue
to give us life
and sustain us;
and may You gather our
exiles to Your holy courts,
to keep Your decrees,
do Your will
and serve You
with a perfect heart,
for it is for us
to give You thanks.
Blessed be God to whom
thanksgiving is due.

וְעַל כֻּלָּם For all these things may Your name be blessed and exalted and raised up, our King, continually, for ever and all time.

*The congregation then the Leader:*

וּכְתֹב And write for a good life,
all the children of Your covenant.

Let all that lives thank You, Selah! and praise and bless Your great name in truth, always, because it is good, God, our Savior and Help, Selah! the beneficent God.
▾Blessed are You, LORD, whose name is "the Good" and to whom thanks are due.

Our Father, our King, please do not turn us away from You empty-handed.

Our Father, our King, may this moment be a moment of compassion
and a time of favor before You.

Our Father, our King, have pity on us, our children and our infants.

Our Father, our King, act for the sake of those who were killed
for Your holy name.

Our Father, our King, act for the sake of those who were slaughtered
for proclaiming Your Unity.

Our Father, our King, act for the sake of those
who went through fire and water
to sanctify Your name.

Our Father, our King, avenge before our eyes
the spilt blood of Your servants.

Our Father, our King, act for Your sake, if not for ours.

Our Father, our King, act for Your sake, and save us.

Our Father, our King, act for the sake of Your abundant compassion.

Our Father, our King, act for the sake of Your great, mighty and awesome
name by which we are called.

▸ Our Father, our King, be gracious to us and answer us, though we have
no worthy deeds; act with us in charity and
loving-kindness and save us.

*The Ark is closed.*

---

it. Only we, the children of Israel, accepted it. Therefore I have a proposal to make. We have many sins. You have much forgiveness. Let us exchange our sins for Your forgiveness. And should You say that is not a fair exchange, I ask: Without our sins, of what use would Your forgiveness be?"

Once on his way to the synagogue on Shabbat he met an "enlightened" young man who, in defiance, was smoking in the street. "Surely you have forgotten it is Shabbat," he said. "No," said the young man, "I haven't forgotten." "Then surely you have forgotten that on Shabbat you may not smoke." "No, I know the law." The rabbi paused for a while, then turned to heaven and said, "Master of the Universe, admit this about Your people. They may sin, but they cannot tell a lie."

will sing and chant praises to the LORD. LORD, hear my voice when I call. Be gracious to me and answer me. On Your behalf my heart says, "Seek My face." Your face, LORD, will I seek. Do not hide Your face from me. Do not turn Your servant away in anger. You have been my help. Do not reject or forsake me, God, my Savior. Were my father and my mother to forsake me, the LORD would take me in. Teach me Your way, LORD, and lead me on a level path, because of my oppressors. Do not abandon me to the will of my foes, for false witnesses have risen against me, breathing violence. ▸ Were it not for my faith that I shall see the LORD's goodness in the land of the living. Hope in the LORD. Be strong and of good courage, and hope in the LORD!

*Mourner's Kaddish (below)*

*In some congregations, the Song of Glory (page 886) is recited here.*

## MOURNER'S KADDISH

*The following prayer, said by mourners, requires the presence of a minyan.*
*A transliteration can be found on page 1095.*

*Mourner:* יִתְגַּדַּל Magnified and sanctified may His great name be,
in the world He created by His will.
May He establish His kingdom,
make His salvation flourish,
and hasten His messiah,
in your lifetime and in your days,
and in the lifetime of all the house of Israel,
swiftly and soon – and say: Amen.

*All:* May His great name be blessed for ever and all time.

*Mourner:* Blessed and praised, glorified and exalted,
raised and honored, uplifted and lauded
be the name of the Holy One, blessed be He,
beyond any blessing, song,
praise and consolation
uttered in the world – and say: Amen.

May there be great peace from heaven,
and a good life for us and all Israel – and say: Amen.

*Bow, take three steps back, as if taking leave of the Divine Presence, then bow, first left, then right, then center, while saying:*

May He who makes peace in His high places,
make peace for us and all Israel – and say: Amen.

*The Torah scroll is placed on the bima and the Gabbai calls a Kohen to the Torah. See law 69.*

וְיַעֲזֹר May He help, shield and save all who seek refuge in Him,
and let us say: Amen. Let us all render greatness to our God
and give honor to the Torah. *Let the Kohen come forward.
Arise (*name* son of *father's name*), the Kohen.

**If no Kohen is present, a Levi or Yisrael is called up as follows:*
/As there is no Kohen, arise (*name* son of *father's name*) in place of a Kohen./

Blessed is He who, in His holiness, gave the Torah to His people Israel.

*The congregation followed by the Gabbai:*

You who cling to the LORD your God are all alive today. Deut. 4

*The Reader shows the oleh the section to be read. The oleh touches the scroll at that place with the tzitzit of his tallit, which he then kisses. Holding the handles of the scroll, he says:*

*Oleh:* Bless the LORD, the blessed One.

*Cong:* Bless the LORD, the blessed One, for ever and all time.

*Oleh:* Bless the LORD, the blessed One, for ever and all time.
Blessed are You, LORD our God, King of the Universe,
who has chosen us from all peoples
and has given us His Torah.
Blessed are You, LORD, Giver of the Torah.

*After the reading, the oleh says:*

*Oleh:* Blessed are You, LORD our God, King of the Universe,
who has given us the Torah of truth,
planting everlasting life in our midst.
Blessed are You, LORD, Giver of the Torah.

---

אֲשֶׁר בָּחַר בָּנוּ מִכָּל הָעַמִּים *Who has chosen us from all peoples.* This ancient blessing, to be said before Torah study as well as before the public reading of the Torah, makes it clear that chosenness is not a right but a responsibility.

אֲשֶׁר נָתַן לָנוּ תּוֹרַת אֱמֶת *Who has given us the Torah of truth.* An act of affirmation following the reading. The blessing, simply but beautifully, expresses the thought that in reading, studying and observing the word of the Eternal, we touch eternity.

After these events it was said to Abraham: Milka too has borne sons, to Naḥor your brother: Utz his firstborn, and his brother Buz, and Kemuel the father of Aram. And Kesed and Ḥazo and Pildash and Yidlaf and Betuel, (and to Betuel, Rebecca was born); Milka bore these eight to Abraham's brother, Naḥor. And his concubine, whose name was Re'uma, also bore Tevaḥ, and Gaḥam, and Taḥash and Ma'akha. ḤAMISHI

## HALF KADDISH

*Before Maftir is read, the Reader says Half Kaddish:*

*Reader:* יִתְגַּדַּל Magnified and sanctified may His great name be,
in the world He created by His will.
May He establish His kingdom,
make His salvation flourish,
and hasten His messiah,
in your lifetime and in your days,
and in the lifetime of all the house of Israel,
swiftly and soon – and say: Amen.

*All:* May His great name be blessed for ever and all time.

*Reader:* Blessed and praised, glorified and exalted,
raised and honored, uplifted and lauded
be the name of the Holy One,
blessed be He,
above and beyond any blessing,
song, praise and consolation
uttered in the world – and say: Amen.

---

children through carelessness, neglect, ambivalence, false values, dominance, indifference, too much intrusion or too little, mixed messages or a desire to integrate into values not your own: that was God's message to Abraham and Sarah's descendants. It is His message to us.

We have lost too many Jewish children. What meaning will our lives or the lives of our ancestors have if they are not lent immortality by our continuity? If we would only remember the many miracles it took to bring us to this hour, we would willingly do our duty to ensure that the next generation stays Jewish, and the generation after that. Jewish continuity is the greatest gift we can bring to the future and the past.

God. For when I returned I regretted it all: when I came to know myself, I beat my thighs, I was ashamed, crushed; I bear the endless disgrace of my youth – Is Ephraim not a treasured son to Me, My child of delights? As I speak of him, always, I remember him once more. And so it is that I long for him within, I will tender him compassion," says the LORD.

## BLESSINGS AFTER THE HAFTARA

*After the Haftara, the person called up for Maftir says the following blessings:*

בָּרוּךְ Blessed are You, LORD our God, King of the Universe, Rock of all worlds, righteous for all generations, the faithful God who says and does, speaks and fulfills, all of whose words are truth and righteousness. You are faithful, LORD our God, and faithful are Your words, not one of which returns unfulfilled, for You, God, are a faithful and compassionate King. Blessed are You, LORD, faithful in all His words.

רַחֵם Have compassion on Zion for it is the source of our life, and save the one grieved in spirit swiftly in our days. Blessed are You, LORD, who makes Zion rejoice in her children.

שַׂמְּחֵנוּ Grant us joy, LORD our God, through Elijah the prophet Your servant, and through the kingdom of the house of David Your anointed – may he soon come and make our hearts glad. May no stranger sit on his throne, and may others not continue to inherit his glory, for You promised him by Your holy name that his light would never be extinguished. Blessed are You, LORD, Shield of David.

עַל הַתּוֹרָה For the Torah, for Divine worship, for the prophets, and for this Day of Remembrance, which You, LORD our God, have given us, for honor and glory – for all these we thank and bless You, LORD our God, and may Your name be blessed by the mouth of all that lives, continually, for ever and all time. For You, LORD, are truth, and Your word is true and endures for ever. Blessed are You, LORD, King over all the earth, who sanctifies Israel and the Day of Remembrance.

---

er the return to Zion could ever have happened without the hope incubated in visions like that of Jeremiah seeing God comforting Rachel, telling her to restrain her voice from weeping and assuring her of a future in which her children would return to their own land.

## PRAYER FOR ISRAEL'S DEFENSE FORCES

*The Leader says the following prayer:*

מִי שֶׁבֵּרַךְ May He who blessed our ancestors, Abraham, Isaac and Jacob, bless the members of Israel's Defense Forces and its security services who stand guard over our land and the cities of our God, from the Lebanese border to the Egyptian desert, from the Mediterranean sea to the approach of the Aravah, and wherever else they are, on land, in air and at sea. May the LORD make the enemies who rise against us be struck down before them. May the Holy One, blessed be He, protect and deliver them from all trouble and distress, affliction and illness, and send blessing and success to all the work of their hands. May He subdue our enemies under them and crown them with deliverance and victory. And may there be fulfilled in them the verse, "It is the LORD your God who goes with you to fight for you against your enemies, to deliver you." And let us say: Amen. *Deut. 20*

## PRAYER FOR THOSE BEING HELD IN CAPTIVITY

*If Israeli soldiers or civilians are being held in captivity, the Leader says the following:*

מִי שֶׁבֵּרַךְ May He who blessed our ancestors, Abraham, Isaac and Jacob, Joseph, Moses and Aaron, David and Solomon, bless, protect and guard the members of Israel's Defense Forces missing in action or held captive, and other captives among our brethren, the whole house of Israel, who are in distress or captivity, as we, the members of this holy congregation, pray on their behalf. May the Holy One, blessed be He, have compassion on them and bring them out from darkness and the shadow of death; may He break their bonds, deliver them from their distress, and bring them swiftly back to their families' embrace. Give thanks to the LORD for His loving-kindness and for the wonders He does for the children of men; and may there be fulfilled in them the verse: "Those redeemed by the LORD will return; they will enter Zion with singing, and everlasting joy will crown their heads. Gladness and joy will overtake them, and sorrow and sighing will flee away." And let us say: Amen. *Ps. 107* *Is. 35*

*If there is a Brit Mila, it takes place at this point before the blowing of the shofar* *(see page 996)*.

Elijah of blessed memory and (ישעיה״ה) the minister of the Face, the ministering angel (מטטרו״ן); and be filled with compassion for us. Blessed are You, Master of compassion.

*The Makri calls out the shofar sounds one by one and the Toke'a blows the shofar.*

| | | |
|---|---|---|
| TEKIA | TERUA | TEKIA |
| TEKIA | TERUA | TEKIA |
| TEKIA | TERUA | TEKIA GEDOLA |

*Some congregations say the following prayer (although many authorities rule that this constitutes an interruption and therefore should not be said).*

And so may it be Your will, LORD our God and God of our ancestors, that all the angels responsible for the shofar and for the tekia and for the shevarim and for the terua may rise up before the throne of Your glory, and may advocate for us before You, to atone for all our sins.

*The next three verses are recited responsively, Leader then congregation:*

אַשְׁרֵי Happy is the people who know this sound. Ps. 89
LORD, they shall walk by the light of Your face.
All day long they will rejoice in Your name,
and be raised up in Your righteousness.
For You are the splendor of their strength,
and our power is raised through Your desire.

*The Leader says the first verse of Ashrei aloud and all continue:*

אַשְׁרֵי Happy are those who dwell in Your House; Ps. 84
they shall continue to praise You, Selah!
Happy are the people for whom this is so; Ps. 144
happy are the people whose God is the LORD.
A song of praise by David. Ps. 145

I will exalt You, my God, the King, and bless Your name for ever and all time. Every day I will bless You, and praise Your name for ever and all time. Great is the LORD and greatly to be praised; His greatness is unfathomable. One generation will praise Your works to the next, and tell of Your mighty deeds. On the glorious splendor of Your majesty I will meditate, and on the acts of Your wonders. They shall talk of the power of Your awesome deeds, and I will tell of Your greatness. They

HALF KADDISH

*Leader:* יִתְגַּדַּל Magnified and sanctified
may His great name be,
in the world He created by His will.
May He establish His kingdom,
make His salvation flourish,
and hasten His messiah,
in your lifetime and in your days,
and in the lifetime of all the house of Israel,
swiftly and soon –
and say: Amen.

*All:* May His great name be blessed for ever and all time.

*Leader:* Blessed and praised,
glorified and exalted,
raised and honored,
uplifted and lauded
be the name of the Holy One,
blessed be He,
above and beyond any blessing,
song, praise and consolation
uttered in the world –
and say: Amen.

**וּבְכֵן תֵּן כָּבוֹד** And so place honor, Lord, upon Your people,
praise on those who fear You
and hope into those who seek You,
the confidence to speak
into all who long for You,
gladness to Your land and joy to Your city,
the flourishing of pride to David Your servant,
and a lamp laid out for his descendant, Your anointed,
soon, in our days.

**וּבְכֵן צַדִּיקִים** And then righteous people will see and rejoice,
and the upright will exult,
and the pious revel in joy,
and injustice will have nothing more to say,
and all wickedness will fade away like smoke
as You sweep the rule of arrogance from the earth.

**וְתִמְלֹךְ** And You, who are the Lord our God,
will rule alone over all those You have made,
in Mount Zion, the dwelling of Your glory,
and in Jerusalem, Your holy city,
as it is written in Your holy Writings:
"The Lord shall reign for ever. *Ps. 146*
He is your God, Zion,
from generation to generation, Halleluya!"

**קָדוֹשׁ אַתָּה** You are holy, Your name is awesome,
and there is no god but You,
as it is written,
"The Lord of hosts shall be raised up through His judgment, *Is. 5*
the Holy God, made holy in righteousness."
Blessed are You, Lord,
the holy King.

And it is said:
The LORD reigns. He is robed in majesty. *Ps. 93*
The LORD is robed, girded with strength.
The world is firmly established; it cannot be moved.

And it is said:
Lift up your heads, O gates; be uplifted, eternal doors, *Ps. 24*
so that the King of glory may enter.
Who is the King of glory?
It is the LORD, strong and mighty,
the LORD mighty in battle.
Lift up your heads, O gates;
lift them up, eternal doors,
so that the King of glory may enter.
Who is He, the King of glory?
The LORD of hosts, He is the King of glory, Selah!

And by Your servants the prophets it is written:
This is what the LORD, King of Israel and its Savior, *Is. 44*
the LORD of hosts has said:
"I am the first and I shall be the last,
and there is no other god but Me."

And it is said:
Saviors shall go up to Mount Zion *Ob. 1*
to judge Mount Esau,
and the LORD's shall be the kingdom.

And it is said:
Then shall the LORD be King over all the earth. *Zech. 14*
On that day shall the LORD be One
and His name One.

And in Your Torah it is written:
Listen, Israel: the LORD is our God, the LORD is One. *Deut. 6*

And by Your servants the prophets it is written:
"Go and call out to Jerusalem, *Jer. 2*
This is what the LORD has said.
'I remember of you the kindness of your youth,
your love when you were a bride;
how you walked after Me in the desert,
through a land not sown.'"

And it is said:
"I will remember the covenant I had with you *Ezek. 16*
in the days of your youth,
and I will establish with you an everlasting covenant."

And it is said:
"'Is Ephraim not a treasured son to Me, My child of delights? *Jer. 31*
As I speak of him, always,
I remember him again.
And so it is that I long for him within,
I will tender him compassion,' says the LORD."

**אֱלֹהֵינוּ** Our God and God of our ancestors,
remember us with a favorable memory,
and recall us with a remembrance
of salvation and compassion
from the highest ancient heaven.
Remember for our sake, LORD our God,
the covenant, the loving-kindness,
and the oath that You swore to Abraham our father
on Mount Moriah.
And let the image of that binding,
when our father Abraham bound Isaac his son upon the altar,
be present before You;
when he suppressed his compassion,
to do Your will wholeheartedly.

**אֱלֹהֵינוּ** Our God and God of our ancestors,
sound the great shofar for our freedom,
raise high the banner to gather our exiles,
bring close our scattered ones from among the nations,
and gather our exiles from the very ends of the earth.
Bring us to Zion, Your city, in joy,
and to Jerusalem, Your Temple, in everlasting happiness.
There we will prepare for You our obligatory offerings,
as we were commanded in Your Torah,
at the hand of Your servant Moses and by Your own word, as it is said:
On the days of your celebration, *Num. 10*
and at your times of gathering and at your New Moons,
sound the trumpets over your offerings
and over your peace-offerings,
and those days will be remembrance for you before your God,
I am the Lord your God.

**כִּי אַתָּה שׁוֹמֵעַ** For You hear the call of the shofar,
and listen to its sounding, and there is none to be compared to You.
Blessed are You, Lord, who listens to the sound of Your people,
Israel's trumpet-blasts in compassion.

*In many congregations, the shofar is sounded (except on Shabbat).*

| | | |
|---|---|---|
| TEKIA | SHEVARIM TERUA | TEKIA |
| TEKIA | SHEVARIM | TEKIA |
| TEKIA | TERUA | TEKIA |

**הַיּוֹם** This day is the birth of the world.
This day stands all the world's creations up in judgment,
stands them as sons or as slaves –
If as sons, have compassion for us,
as a father has compassion for his sons.
And if as slaves, our eyes are raised and fixed on You
until You show us favor, and bring out our judgment like sunlight,
Awesome, Holy.

## LEADER'S REPETITION FOR THE SECOND DAY

*The Ark is opened.*

*The Leader takes three steps forward and at the points indicated by ▾, bends the knees at the first word, bows at the second, and stands straight before saying God's name.*

When I proclaim the LORD's name, give glory to our God. *Deut. 32*
O LORD, open my lips, so that my mouth may declare Your praise. *Ps. 51*

PATRIARCHS

▾בָּרוּךְ Blessed are You, LORD our God and God of our fathers,
God of Abraham, God of Isaac and God of Jacob;
the great, mighty and awesome God, God Most High,
who bestows acts of loving-kindness, who creates all,
who remembers the loving-kindness of the fathers
and will bring a Redeemer to their children's children
for the sake of His name, in love.

זָכְרֵנוּ לְחַיִּים Remember us for life, O King who desires life,
and write us in the book of life – for Your sake, O God of life.
King, Helper, Savior, Shield:
▾Blessed are You, LORD, Shield of Abraham.

DIVINE MIGHT

אַתָּה גִּבּוֹר You are eternally mighty, LORD.
You give life to the dead and have great power to save.
*In Israel:* He causes the dew to fall.
He sustains the living with loving-kindness,
and with great compassion revives the dead.
He supports the fallen, heals the sick, sets captives free,
and keeps His faith with those who sleep in the dust.

---

two types of people who believe in God. The first believes because he follows the way of his fathers, strongly maintaining their tradition of faith. The second is the one who gains his faith through reason and philosophical thought.

There is an important difference between these two individuals. The first has the advantage that he cannot be tempted, even if he is confronted with philosophical arguments that challenge his faith. His faith remains strong because of the traditions that he has from his fathers. Besides this, he has never depended on philosophical speculation. On the other hand, this person

*All:*

כִּי כְשִׁמְךָ For as Your name is, so is Your renown:
hard to anger, and readily appeased.
For You do not desire the condemned man's death,
but that he may come back from his ways, and live.
To the very day he dies, You wait for him;
and if he comes back: You welcome him at once.

Truly, it was You who formed them,
You know the forces moving them:/ they are but flesh and blood.

---

Sleep is strong, but death stands over it.
What is stronger than death?
Acts of charity (*tzedaka*), for it is written [Prov. 10:2],
"*Tzedaka* delivers from death." (*Bava Batra* 10a)

There are eight degrees of charity, each one higher than the other.

The highest degree, exceeded by none, is that of one who assists a poor person by providing him with a gift or a loan or by accepting him into a business partnership or by helping him find employment – in a word, by putting him in a situation where he can dispense with other people's aid. With reference to such aid it is said, "You shall strengthen him, be he a stranger or a settler, he shall live with you" (Lev. 25:35), which means: strengthen him in such a manner that his falling into want is prevented.

A step below this is one who gives alms to the needy in such a way that the giver does not know to whom he gives and the recipient does not know from whom he takes. This exemplifies doing a good deed for its own sake. One example was the Hall of Secrecy in the Temple, where the righteous would place their gift clandestinely and where poor people from noble families could come and secretly help themselves to aid. Close to this is putting money in a charity box…

One step lower is where the giver knows to whom he gives, but the poor person does not know from whom he receives. Thus the great sages would go and secretly put money into poor people's doorways…

A step lower is when the poor person knows from whom he is taking, but the giver does not known to whom he is giving. Thus the great sages would tie coins in their scarves, which they would fling over their shoulders, so that the poor could help themselves without suffering shame.

Lower than this, is where someone gives the poor person a gift before he asks.

אֱלֹהֵינוּ וֵאלֹהֵי אֲבוֹתֵינוּ
תְּקַע בְּשׁוֹפָר גָּדוֹל לְחֵרוּתֵנוּ, וְשָׂא נֵס לְקַבֵּץ גָּלֻיּוֹתֵינוּ
וְקָרֵב פְּזוּרֵינוּ מִבֵּין הַגּוֹיִם, וּנְפוּצוֹתֵינוּ כַּנֵּס מִיַּרְכְּתֵי אָרֶץ.
וַהֲבִיאֵנוּ לְצִיּוֹן עִירְךָ בְּרִנָּה
וְלִירוּשָׁלַיִם בֵּית מִקְדָּשְׁךָ בְּשִׂמְחַת עוֹלָם
וְשָׁם נַעֲשֶׂה לְפָנֶיךָ אֶת קָרְבְּנוֹת חוֹבוֹתֵינוּ
כִּמְצֻוֶּה עָלֵינוּ בְּתוֹרָתֶךָ עַל יְדֵי מֹשֶׁה עַבְדֶּךָ, מִפִּי כְבוֹדֶךָ
כָּאָמוּר

וּבְיוֹם שִׂמְחַתְכֶם וּבְמוֹעֲדֵיכֶם וּבְרָאשֵׁי חָדְשֵׁכֶם במדבר י
וּתְקַעְתֶּם בַּחֲצֹצְרֹת עַל עֹלֹתֵיכֶם וְעַל זִבְחֵי שַׁלְמֵיכֶם
וְהָיוּ לָכֶם לְזִכָּרוֹן לִפְנֵי אֱלֹהֵיכֶם
אֲנִי יהוה אֱלֹהֵיכֶם:

כִּי אַתָּה שׁוֹמֵעַ קוֹל שׁוֹפָר וּמַאֲזִין תְּרוּעָה, וְאֵין דּוֹמֶה לָּךְ.
בָּרוּךְ אַתָּה יהוה, שׁוֹמֵעַ קוֹל תְּרוּעַת עַמּוֹ יִשְׂרָאֵל בְּרַחֲמִים.

*In many congregations, the* שופר *is sounded* (*except on* שבת).

| | | |
|---|---|---|
| תקיעה | שברים תרועה | תקיעה |
| תקיעה | שברים | תקיעה |
| תקיעה | תרועה | תקיעה |

הַיּוֹם הֲרַת עוֹלָם, הַיּוֹם יַעֲמִיד בַּמִּשְׁפָּט כָּל יְצוּרֵי עוֹלָמִים
אִם כְּבָנִים אִם כַּעֲבָדִים.
אִם כְּבָנִים, רַחֲמֵנוּ כְּרַחֵם אָב עַל בָּנִים
וְאִם כַּעֲבָדִים, עֵינֵינוּ לְךָ תְלוּיוֹת עַד שֶׁתְּחָנֵּנוּ
וְתוֹצִיא כָאוֹר מִשְׁפָּטֵנוּ, אָיֹם קָדוֹשׁ.

TEMPLE SERVICE

רְצֵה Find favor, LORD our God, in Your people Israel,
and heed their prayer.
Restore the service to Your most holy House,
and accept soon, in love and favor,
the fire-offerings of Israel and their prayer.
May the service of Your people Israel always find favor with You.
And may our eyes witness Your return to Zion in compassion.
Blessed are You, LORD, who restores His Presence to Zion.

THANKSGIVING

*Bow at the first nine words.*

מוֹדִים▾ We give thanks to You,
for You are the LORD our God and God of our ancestors
for ever and all time.
You are the Rock of our lives,
Shield of our salvation from generation to generation.
We will thank You and declare Your praise for our lives,
which are entrusted into Your hand;
for our souls, which are placed in Your charge;
for Your miracles which are with us every day;
and for Your wonders and favors
at all times, evening, morning and midday.
You are good – for Your compassion never fails.
You are compassionate – for Your loving-kindnesses never cease;
for we have always placed our hope in You.
For all these things
may Your name be blessed and exalted and raised up, our King,
continually, for ever and all time.

וּכְתֹב And write, for a good life, all the children of Your covenant.

Let all that lives thank You, Selah! and praise and bless
Your great name in truth, always, because it is good,
God, our Savior and Help, Selah! the beneficent God.
▾Blessed are You, LORD, whose name is "the Good"
and to whom thanks are due.

עבודה

רְצֵה יהוה אֱלֹהֵינוּ בְּעַמְּךָ יִשְׂרָאֵל, וְלִתְפִלָּתָם שְׁעֵה
וְהָשֵׁב אֶת הָעֲבוֹדָה לִדְבִיר בֵּיתֶךָ
וְאִשֵּׁי יִשְׂרָאֵל וּתְפִלָּתָם, מְהֵרָה בְּאַהֲבָה תְקַבֵּל בְּרָצוֹן
וּתְהִי לְרָצוֹן תָּמִיד עֲבוֹדַת יִשְׂרָאֵל עַמֶּךָ.
וְתֶחֱזֶינָה עֵינֵינוּ בְּשׁוּבְךָ לְצִיּוֹן בְּרַחֲמִים.
בָּרוּךְ אַתָּה יהוה, הַמַּחֲזִיר שְׁכִינָתוֹ לְצִיּוֹן.

הודאה

*Bow at the first five words.*

מוֹדִים אֲנַחְנוּ לָךְ
שָׁאַתָּה הוּא יהוה אֱלֹהֵינוּ וֵאלֹהֵי אֲבוֹתֵינוּ לְעוֹלָם וָעֶד.
צוּר חַיֵּינוּ, מָגֵן יִשְׁעֵנוּ, אַתָּה הוּא לְדוֹר וָדוֹר.
נוֹדֶה לְּךָ וּנְסַפֵּר תְּהִלָּתֶךָ
עַל חַיֵּינוּ הַמְּסוּרִים בְּיָדֶךָ, וְעַל נִשְׁמוֹתֵינוּ הַפְּקוּדוֹת לָךְ
וְעַל נִסֶּיךָ שֶׁבְּכָל יוֹם עִמָּנוּ
וְעַל נִפְלְאוֹתֶיךָ וְטוֹבוֹתֶיךָ שֶׁבְּכָל עֵת, עֶרֶב וָבֹקֶר וְצָהֳרָיִם.
הַטּוֹב, כִּי לֹא כָלוּ רַחֲמֶיךָ וְהַמְרַחֵם, כִּי לֹא תַמּוּ חֲסָדֶיךָ
כִּי מֵעוֹלָם קִוִּינוּ לָךְ.
וְעַל כֻּלָּם
יִתְבָּרַךְ וְיִתְרוֹמַם וְיִתְנַשֵּׂא שִׁמְךָ מַלְכֵּנוּ תָּמִיד לְעוֹלָם וָעֶד.
וּכְתֹב לְחַיִּים טוֹבִים כָּל בְּנֵי בְרִיתֶךָ.
וְכֹל הַחַיִּים יוֹדְוּךָ סֶּלָה
וִיהַלְלוּ וִיבָרְכוּ אֶת שִׁמְךָ הַגָּדוֹל בֶּאֱמֶת לְעוֹלָם כִּי טוֹב
הָאֵל יְשׁוּעָתֵנוּ וְעֶזְרָתֵנוּ סֶלָה, הָאֵל הַטּוֹב.
בָּרוּךְ אַתָּה יהוה, הַטּוֹב שִׁמְךָ וּלְךָ נָאֶה לְהוֹדוֹת.

PEACE

שִׂים שָׁלוֹם Grant peace, goodness and blessing,
life, grace, loving-kindness and compassion
to us and all Israel Your people.
Bless us, our Father, all as one,
with the light of Your face,
for by the light of Your face
You have given us, LORD our God,
the Torah of life and love of kindness,
righteousness, blessing, compassion, life and peace.
May it be good in Your eyes
to bless us and all Your people Israel
at every time, in every hour, with Your peace.

בְּסֵפֶר חַיִּים In the book of life, blessing, peace and prosperity,
and good decrees, salvations and consolations
may we and all Your people the house of Israel
be remembered and written before You
for a good life, and for peace.

Blessed are You, LORD,
who blesses His people Israel with peace.

*The following verse concludes the Leader's Repetition of the Amida. Some also say it here as part of the silent Amida. See law 64.*

May the words of my mouth and the meditation of my heart *Ps. 19*
find favor before You, LORD, my Rock and Redeemer.

אֱלֹהַי My God, *Berakhot 17a*
guard my tongue from evil and my lips from deceitful speech.
To those who curse me, let my soul be silent;
may my soul be to all like the dust.
Open my heart to Your Torah
and let my soul pursue Your commandments.
As for all who rise up or plan evil against me,
swiftly thwart their counsel and frustrate their plans.

ברכת שלום

שִׂים שָׁלוֹם טוֹבָה וּבְרָכָה
חַיִּים חֵן וָחֶסֶד וְרַחֲמִים
עָלֵינוּ וְעַל כָּל יִשְׂרָאֵל עַמֶּךָ.
בָּרְכֵנוּ אָבִינוּ כֻּלָּנוּ כְּאֶחָד בְּאוֹר פָּנֶיךָ
כִּי בְאוֹר פָּנֶיךָ נָתַתָּ לָּנוּ יהוה אֱלֹהֵינוּ
תּוֹרַת חַיִּים וְאַהֲבַת חֶסֶד
וּצְדָקָה וּבְרָכָה וְרַחֲמִים וְחַיִּים וְשָׁלוֹם.
וְטוֹב יִהְיֶה בְּעֵינֶיךָ לְבָרְכֵנוּ וּלְבָרֵךְ אֶת כָּל עַמְּךָ יִשְׂרָאֵל
בְּכָל עֵת וּבְכָל שָׁעָה בִּשְׁלוֹמֶךָ.

בְּסֵפֶר חַיִּים, בְּרָכָה וְשָׁלוֹם, וּפַרְנָסָה טוֹבָה
וּגְזֵרוֹת טוֹבוֹת, יְשׁוּעוֹת וְנֶחָמוֹת
נִזָּכֵר וְנִכָּתֵב לְפָנֶיךָ
אֲנַחְנוּ וְכָל עַמְּךָ בֵּית יִשְׂרָאֵל לְחַיִּים טוֹבִים וּלְשָׁלוֹם.

בָּרוּךְ אַתָּה יהוה, הַמְבָרֵךְ אֶת עַמּוֹ יִשְׂרָאֵל בַּשָּׁלוֹם.

*The following verse concludes the* חזרת הש״ץ.
*Some also say it here as part of the silent* עמידה. *See law 64.*

תהלים יט יִהְיוּ לְרָצוֹן אִמְרֵי־פִי וְהֶגְיוֹן לִבִּי לְפָנֶיךָ, יהוה צוּרִי וְגֹאֲלִי:

ברכות יז. אֱלֹהַי
נְצֹר לְשׁוֹנִי מֵרָע וּשְׂפָתַי מִדַּבֵּר מִרְמָה
וְלִמְקַלְלַי נַפְשִׁי תִדֹּם, וְנַפְשִׁי כֶּעָפָר לַכֹּל תִּהְיֶה.
פְּתַח לִבִּי בְּתוֹרָתֶךָ, וְאַחֲרֵי מִצְוֹתֶיךָ תִּרְדֹּף נַפְשִׁי.
וְכָל הַקָּמִים וְהַחוֹשְׁבִים עָלַי רָעָה
מְהֵרָה הָפֵר עֲצָתָם וְקַלְקֵל מַחֲשַׁבְתָּם.

*Some add this prayer:*

יְהִי רָצוֹן May it be Your will, Lord my God, God of my ancestors,
that envy of no man may rise up in me, nor envy of me in any other;
that I will not be angry today, nor make You angry;
and save me from my evil impulse,
placing humility and modesty into my heart.
Our King and God, make Your name One in Your world;
build up Your city, establish Your House and complete Your Sanctuary,
gather in the exiles, redeem Your flock,
and have Your congregation rejoice.

Act for the sake of Your name; act for the sake of Your right hand;
act for the sake of Your Torah; act for the sake of Your holiness.
That Your beloved ones may be delivered, *Ps. 60*
save with Your right hand and answer me.
May the words of my mouth and the meditation of my heart *Ps. 19*
find favor before You, Lord, my Rock and Redeemer.

*Bow, take three steps back, then bow, first left, then right, then center, while saying:*

May He who makes peace in His high places,
make peace for us and all Israel – and say: Amen.

יְהִי רָצוֹן May it be Your will, Lord our God and God of our ancestors,
that the Temple be rebuilt speedily in our days,
and grant us a share in Your Torah.
And there we will serve You with reverence,
as in the days of old and as in former years.
Then the offering of Judah and Jerusalem *Mal. 3*
will be pleasing to the Lord as in the days of old and as in former years.

*Some add this prayer:*

יְהִי רָצוֹן מִלְּפָנֶיךָ יהוה אֱלֹהַי וֵאלֹהֵי אֲבוֹתַי
שֶׁלֹּא תַעֲלֶה קִנְאַת אָדָם עָלַי, וְלֹא קִנְאָתִי עַל אֲחֵרִים
וְשֶׁלֹּא אֶכְעֹס הַיּוֹם, וְשֶׁלֹּא אַכְעִיסֶךָ
וְתַצִּילֵנִי מִיֵּצֶר הָרָע, וְתֵן בְּלִבִּי הַכְנָעָה וַעֲנָוָה.
מַלְכֵּנוּ וֵאלֹהֵינוּ, יַחֵד שִׁמְךָ בְּעוֹלָמֶךָ
בְּנֵה עִירָךְ, יַסֵּד בֵּיתְךָ וְשַׁכְלֵל הֵיכָלֶךָ
וְקַבֵּץ קִבּוּץ גָּלֻיּוֹת, וּפְדֵה צֹאנֶךָ וְשַׂמַּח עֲדָתֶךָ.

עֲשֵׂה לְמַעַן שְׁמֶךָ, עֲשֵׂה לְמַעַן יְמִינֶךָ
עֲשֵׂה לְמַעַן תּוֹרָתֶךָ, עֲשֵׂה לְמַעַן קְדֻשָּׁתֶךָ.
לְמַעַן יֵחָלְצוּן יְדִידֶיךָ, הוֹשִׁיעָה יְמִינְךָ וַעֲנֵנִי: תהלים ס
יִהְיוּ לְרָצוֹן אִמְרֵי־פִי וְהֶגְיוֹן לִבִּי לְפָנֶיךָ, יהוה צוּרִי וְגֹאֲלִי: תהלים יט

*Bow, take three steps back, then bow, first left, then right, then center, while saying:*

עֹשֶׂה הַשָּׁלוֹם בִּמְרוֹמָיו
הוּא יַעֲשֶׂה שָׁלוֹם עָלֵינוּ וְעַל כָּל יִשְׂרָאֵל, וְאִמְרוּ אָמֵן.

יְהִי רָצוֹן מִלְּפָנֶיךָ יהוה אֱלֹהֵינוּ וֵאלֹהֵי אֲבוֹתֵינוּ
שֶׁיִּבָּנֶה בֵּית הַמִּקְדָּשׁ בִּמְהֵרָה בְיָמֵינוּ
וְתֵן חֶלְקֵנוּ בְּתוֹרָתֶךָ
וְשָׁם נַעֲבָדְךָ בְּיִרְאָה כִּימֵי עוֹלָם וּכְשָׁנִים קַדְמֹנִיּוֹת.
וְעָרְבָה לַיהוה מִנְחַת יְהוּדָה וִירוּשָׁלָםִ כִּימֵי עוֹלָם וּכְשָׁנִים קַדְמֹנִיּוֹת: מלאכי ג

# חזרת הש״ץ למוסף ליום השני

*The* ארון קודש *is opened.*

*The* שליח ציבור *takes three steps forward and at the points indicated by* ▾*, bends the knees at the first word, bows at the second, and stands straight before saying God's name.*

כִּי שֵׁם יהוה אֶקְרָא, הָבוּ גֹדֶל לֵאלֹהֵינוּ: דברים לב

אֲדֹנָי, שְׂפָתַי תִּפְתָּח, וּפִי יַגִּיד תְּהִלָּתֶךָ: תהלים נא

אבות

▾בָּרוּךְ אַתָּה יהוה, אֱלֹהֵינוּ וֵאלֹהֵי אֲבוֹתֵינוּ
אֱלֹהֵי אַבְרָהָם, אֱלֹהֵי יִצְחָק, וֵאלֹהֵי יַעֲקֹב
הָאֵל הַגָּדוֹל הַגִּבּוֹר וְהַנּוֹרָא, אֵל עֶלְיוֹן
גּוֹמֵל חֲסָדִים טוֹבִים, קוֹנֵה הַכֹּל
וְזוֹכֵר חַסְדֵי אָבוֹת
וּמֵבִיא גוֹאֵל לִבְנֵי בְנֵיהֶם לְמַעַן שְׁמוֹ בְּאַהֲבָה.

זָכְרֵנוּ לְחַיִּים, מֶלֶךְ חָפֵץ בַּחַיִּים
וְכָתְבֵנוּ בְּסֵפֶר הַחַיִּים, לְמַעַנְךָ אֱלֹהִים חַיִּים.

מֶלֶךְ עוֹזֵר וּמוֹשִׁיעַ וּמָגֵן.
▾בָּרוּךְ אַתָּה יהוה, מָגֵן אַבְרָהָם.

גבורות

אַתָּה גִּבּוֹר לְעוֹלָם, אֲדֹנָי
מְחַיֵּה מֵתִים אַתָּה, רַב לְהוֹשִׁיעַ
בארץ ישראל: מוֹרִיד הַטָּל
מְכַלְכֵּל חַיִּים בְּחֶסֶד, מְחַיֵּה מֵתִים בְּרַחֲמִים רַבִּים
סוֹמֵךְ נוֹפְלִים, וְרוֹפֵא חוֹלִים, וּמַתִּיר אֲסוּרִים
וּמְקַיֵּם אֱמוּנָתוֹ לִישֵׁנֵי עָפָר.

---

אֱלֹהֵינוּ וֵאלֹהֵי אֲבוֹתֵינוּ *Our God and God of our fathers.* The Ba'al Shem Tov taught: The reason we say "Our God and God of our fathers" is that there are

Who is like You, Master of might, and to whom can You be compared,
O King who brings death and gives life, and makes salvation grow?

**מִי כָמוֹךָ** Who is like You, compassionate Father,
who remembers His creatures in compassion, for life?
Faithful are You to revive the dead.
Blessed are You, LORD, who revives the dead.

*In Musaf of the second day of Rosh HaShana no kerovot are said, as was the custom of European Jews since the Middle Ages (with the exception of the now-extinct, old French nusaḥ). However, those congregations that omitted the following piyut in Shaḥarit (page 688), say it here in Musaf. Customs vary in the recitation of this piyut (see page 396).*

And so, all shall crown You.

The God who renders judgment. / The One who examines hearts on the Day of Judgment.
The One who reveals deep secrets in judgment. / The One who speaks candidly on the Day of Judgment.
The One who voices His wisdom in judgment. / The One who is diligent and performs kindness on the Day of Judgment.
The One who recalls His covenant in judgment. / The One who shows compassion toward His creations on the Day of Judgment.
The One who purifies those who rely on Him in judgment. / The One who knows all inner thoughts on the Day of Judgment.
The One who suppresses His anger in judgment. / The One who clothes Himself with righteousness on the Day of Judgment.
The One who forgives sins in judgment. / The awesome and praiseworthy One on the Day of Judgment.
The One who forgives those He bears in judgment. / The One who answers those who call on Him on the Day of Judgment.
The One who exercises His compassion in judgment. / The One who sees all hidden secrets on the Day of Judgment.
The One who acquires His servants in judgment. / The One who takes pity on His nation on the Day of Judgment.
The One who guards those who love Him in judgment. / The One who supports His innocent ones on the Day of Judgment.

---

depends strongly on the traditions of his forefathers, while at the same time taking advantage of his logic in thinking things out. He thus has the best and most perfect faith.

When we say, "Our God and God of our fathers," we thus allude to both paths to faith in God.

*In some congregations the Ark is closed and then reopened by another honoree.*
*The Siluk – the last of the piyutim before Kedusha.*

*All:*

וּבְכֵן לְךָ And so, sanctity will rise up to You; for You, our God, are King.

*All:*

וּנְתַנֶּה תֹּקֶף Let us voice the power of this day's sanctity – it is awesome, terrible; / on this day Your kingship is raised, / Your throne is founded upon love, / and You, with truth, sit upon it. / In truth, it is You: Judge / and Accuser, Knowing One and Witness, / writing and sealing, counting, numbering, / remembering all forgotten things, You open the book of memories – / it is read of itself, / and every man's name is signed there.

וּבְשׁוֹפָר גָּדוֹל A great shofar sounds, / and a still small voice is heard, / angels rush forward / and are held by trembling, shaking; / they say, "Here is the Day of Judgment / visiting all the heavenly host for judgment –" / for they are not cleared in Your eyes in judgment. / And all who have come into this world pass before You like sheep.

כְּבַקָּרַת רוֹעֶה As a shepherd's searching gaze meets his flock, / as he passes every sheep beneath his rod, / so You too pass Yours, count and number, / and regard the soul of every living thing; / and You rule off the limit of each creation's life, / and write down the verdict for each.

*In most congregations the following is said first by the congregation and then the Leader; in some by the Leader alone.*

בְּרֹאשׁ הַשָּׁנָה On Rosh HaShana it is written / and on Yom Kippur it is sealed: / how many will pass away and how many will be born; / who will live and who will die; / who in his due time and who before; / who by water and who by fire; / who by sword and who by beast; / who of hunger and who of thirst; / who by earthquake and who by plague; / who by strangling and who by stoning; / who will rest and who will wander; / who will be calm and who will be harassed; / who will be at ease and who will suffer; / who will become poor and who will grow rich; / who cast down and who raised high.

מִי כָמְוֹךָ, בַּעַל גְּבוּרוֹת, וּמִי דּוֹמֶה לָּךְ
מֶלֶךְ, מֵמִית וּמְחַיֶּה וּמַצְמִיחַ יְשׁוּעָה.

מִי כָמְוֹךָ אַב הָרַחֲמָן, זוֹכֵר יְצוּרָיו לְחַיִּים בְּרַחֲמִים.

וְנֶאֱמָן אַתָּה לְהַחֲיוֹת מֵתִים.
בָּרוּךְ אַתָּה יהוה, מְחַיֵּה הַמֵּתִים.

*In* מוסף *of the second day of* ראש השנה *no kerovot are said, as was the custom of European Jews since the Middle Ages (with the exception of the now-extinct, old French* נוסח*). However, those congregations that omitted the following piyut in* שחרית *(page 689), say it here in* מוסף*.*

*Customs vary in the recitation of this piyut (see page 397).*

וּבְכֵן לְךָ הַכֹּל יַכְתִּירוּ.

לְאֵל עוֹרֵךְ דִּין — לְבוֹחֵן לְבָבוֹת בְּיוֹם דִּין.
לְגוֹלֶה עֲמֻקּוֹת בַּדִּין — לְדוֹבֵר מֵישָׁרִים בְּיוֹם דִּין.
לְהוֹגֶה דֵעוֹת בַּדִּין — לְוָתִיק וְעוֹשֶׂה חֶסֶד בְּיוֹם דִּין.
לְזוֹכֵר בְּרִיתוֹ בַּדִּין — לְחוֹמֵל מַעֲשָׂיו בְּיוֹם דִּין.
לְטַהֵר חוֹסָיו בַּדִּין — לְיוֹדֵעַ מַחֲשָׁבוֹת בְּיוֹם דִּין.
לְכוֹבֵשׁ כַּעְסוֹ בַּדִּין — לְלוֹבֵשׁ צְדָקוֹת בְּיוֹם דִּין.
לְמוֹחֵל עֲוֹנוֹת בַּדִּין — לְנוֹרָא תְהִלּוֹת בְּיוֹם דִּין.
לְסוֹלֵחַ לַעֲמוּסָיו בַּדִּין — לְעוֹנֶה לְקוֹרְאָיו בְּיוֹם דִּין.
לְפוֹעֵל רַחֲמָיו בַּדִּין — לְצוֹפֶה נִסְתָּרוֹת בְּיוֹם דִּין.
לְקוֹנֶה עֲבָדָיו בַּדִּין — לְרַחֵם עַמּוֹ בְּיוֹם דִּין.
לְשׁוֹמֵר אֹהֲבָיו בַּדִּין — לְתוֹמֵךְ תְּמִימָיו בְּיוֹם דִּין.

---

also has a disadvantage. His faith is not well reasoned, nor thought out, and is essentially the result of habit.

The second also has an advantage. He has discovered God with his logic, and is very strong in his faith. However, he also has a disadvantage. He can be persuaded by logic, and if confronted with the arguments that tear down the logical structure of his faith, he can be tempted away.

The person who gains his faith in both these ways has every advantage. He

*In some congregations the ארון קודש is closed and then reopened by another honoree.*

*The סילוק – the last of the piyutim before קדושה.*

*All:*

וּבְכֵן לְךָ תַעֲלֶה קְדֻשָּׁה, כִּי אַתָּה אֱלֹהֵינוּ מֶלֶךְ.

*All:*

וּנְתַנֶּה תֹּקֶף קְדֻשַּׁת הַיּוֹם / כִּי הוּא נוֹרָא וְאָיֹם
וּבוֹ תִנָּשֵׂא מַלְכוּתֶךָ / וְיִכּוֹן בְּחֶסֶד כִּסְאֶךָ / וְתֵשֵׁב עָלָיו בֶּאֱמֶת.
אֱמֶת, כִּי אַתָּה הוּא דַיָּן וּמוֹכִיחַ, וְיוֹדֵעַ וָעֵד
וְכוֹתֵב וְחוֹתֵם וְסוֹפֵר וּמוֹנֶה
וְתִזְכֹּר כָּל הַנִּשְׁכָּחוֹת / וְתִפְתַּח אֶת סֵפֶר הַזִּכְרוֹנוֹת
וּמֵאֵלָיו יִקָּרֵא / וְחוֹתָם יַד כָּל אָדָם בּוֹ.

וּבְשׁוֹפָר גָּדוֹל יִתָּקַע / וְקוֹל דְּמָמָה דַקָּה יִשָּׁמַע
וּמַלְאָכִים יֵחָפֵזוּן / וְחִיל וּרְעָדָה יֹאחֵזוּן
וְיֹאמְרוּ, הִנֵּה יוֹם הַדִּין / לִפְקֹד עַל צְבָא מָרוֹם בַּדִּין
כִּי לֹא יִזְכּוּ בְעֵינֶיךָ בַּדִּין / וְכָל בָּאֵי עוֹלָם יַעַבְרוּן לְפָנֶיךָ כִּבְנֵי מָרוֹן.

כְּבַקָּרַת רוֹעֶה עֶדְרוֹ / מַעֲבִיר צֹאנוֹ תַּחַת שִׁבְטוֹ
כֵּן תַּעֲבִיר וְתִסְפֹּר וְתִמְנֶה / וְתִפְקֹד נֶפֶשׁ כָּל חָי
וְתַחְתֹּךְ קִצְבָה לְכָל בְּרִיָּה / וְתִכְתֹּב אֶת גְּזַר דִּינָם.

*In most congregations the following is said first by the קהל and then the שליח ציבור; in some by the שליח ציבור alone.*

בְּרֹאשׁ הַשָּׁנָה יִכָּתֵבוּן / וּבְיוֹם צוֹם כִּפּוּר יֵחָתֵמוּן.
כַּמָּה יַעַבְרוּן וְכַמָּה יִבָּרֵאוּן
מִי יִחְיֶה וּמִי יָמוּת / מִי בְקִצּוֹ וּמִי לֹא בְקִצּוֹ
מִי בַמַּיִם וּמִי בָאֵשׁ / מִי בַחֶרֶב וּמִי בַחַיָּה / מִי בָרָעָב וּמִי בַצָּמָא
מִי בָרַעַשׁ וּמִי בַמַּגֵּפָה / מִי בַחֲנִיקָה וּמִי בַסְּקִילָה.
מִי יָנוּחַ וּמִי יָנוּעַ / מִי יִשָּׁקֵט וּמִי יִטָּרֵף
מִי יִשָּׁלֵו וּמִי יִתְיַסָּר / מִי יֵעָנִי וּמִי יֵעָשֵׁר / מִי יִשָּׁפֵל וּמִי יָרוּם.

*In many editions of the maḥzor, the words Repentance, Prayer and Charity are accompanied by three corresponding words: fasting, crying, giving. The numerical value (gematria) of each Hebrew word being 136, these words indicate that the three modes of approaching God are equivalent (Minhagim of Rabbi Isaac Tirna, fifteenth century).*

*The congregation says aloud, followed by the Leader:*

*FASTING* *CRYING* *GIVING*

But REPENTANCE, PRAYER and CHARITY
avert the evil of the decree.

---

the darkness disappears completely. The same is true when a person repents. Even though he was previously in a place of darkness, when it is illuminated with the light of Torah, the darkness disappears completely.

Rabbi Bunam of Pzhysha said to his disciples: The sins that a person commits – those are not his great crime. Temptation is powerful and our strength is frail. The great crime is that he can repent at any moment, and yet does not do so.

Said Rabbi Abraham Kook: Sudden penitence comes about as a result of a certain spiritual flash that enters the soul. At once the person senses all the evil and the ugliness of sin and he is converted into a new being; already he experiences inside himself a complete transformation for the better.

There is also a gradual form of penitence. No sudden flash of illumination dawns upon the person to make him change from the depths of evil to the good, but he feels that he must mend his way of life, his will, his pattern of thought. By heeding this impulse he gradually acquires the ways of equity, he corrects his morals, he improves his actions, and he conditions himself increasingly to becoming a good person, until he reaches a high level of purity and perfection.

There is another kind of feeling of penitence, unspecified and general. A person does not conjure up the memory of the past sin or sins, but in a general way he feels terribly depressed. He feels himself pervaded by sin; that the divine light does not shine on him; that there is nothing noble in him; that his heart is unfeeling, his moral behavior does not follow the right course, worthy of sustaining a meaningful life for a wholesome human being. For this state of spiritual malaise, penitence comes as the therapy from a master physician. A sense of assurance in the healing, the general renewal that penitence extends to all who embrace it, distills in him a spirit of grace and acceptance.

Penitence is always present in the heart. At the very time of sin, penitence is hidden in the soul, and it releases its impulses, which become manifest

*In many editions of the* מחזור*, the words* וּתְשׁוּבָה וּתְפִלָּה וּצְדָקָה *are accompanied by three corresponding words:* צום, קול, ממון*. The numerical value (*גימטריה*) of each word being 136, these words indicate that the three modes of approaching God are equivalent (Minhagim of Rabbi Isaac Tirna, fifteenth century).*

*The* קהל *says aloud, followed by the* שליח ציבור*:*

צום קול ממון

**וּתְשׁוּבָה וּתְפִלָּה וּצְדָקָה / מַעֲבִירִין אֶת רֹעַ הַגְּזֵרָה.**

---

REPENTANCE, PRAYER AND CHARITY

Rabbi Menaḥem Mendel Schneerson, the Lubavitcher Rebbe, pointed out that the usual translation of these words is inaccurate. *Teshuva* does not mean penitence. *Tefilla* does not mean prayer. *Tzedaka* does not mean charity.

The word for penitence in Hebrew is *ḥarata*, meaning remorse for the wrong we have done. *Teshuva* means return. It tells us that every sin is a form of being lost; we are not where we are meant to be. *Teshuva* means coming home.

The word for prayer, in the sense of request, is *bakasha*. *Tefilla* comes from the verb meaning "to judge." *Lehitpalel* means "to judge oneself." In *tefilla* we are both subject and object, the doer and the judge of what we do. It is this capacity for self-judgment that makes us capable of moral growth.

The word for charity is *gemilut ḥasadim*. *Tzedaka* means justice, or justice and charity combined. There is no word for this in English. In Judaism we give, not out of charity but out of justice.

מַעֲבִירִין אֶת רֹעַ הַגְּזֵרָה *Avert the evil of the decree.* In these four Hebrew words lies the difference between a hope culture and a tragic culture. In ancient Greece, there was a belief that once a decree had been sealed there was no way of averting it. Every act taken to frustrate it merely brought it closer to fulfillment. That forms the heart of the tragedy of Oedipus and Laius.

In Judaism every decree can be averted by sincere repentance. That is the significance of the story of Jonah and the people of Nineveh. Jonah came and announced the decree: In forty days Nineveh will be destroyed. But the people repented and the decree was annulled. There is no fate that is final, no destiny that cannot be changed. Therefore there is always hope.

Greece gave the world its greatest tragedies, those of Sophocles, Aeschylus and Euripides. Israel was and remains the supreme culture of hope.

REPENTANCE

The Ba'al Shem Tov said: When a person brings a candle into a dark place,

*All:*

כִּי כְּשִׁמְךָ כֵּן תְּהִלָּתֶךָ / קָשֶׁה לִכְעֹס וְנְוֹחַ לִרְצוֹת
כִּי לֹא תַחְפֹּץ בְּמוֹת הַמֵּת / כִּי אִם בְּשׁוּבוֹ מִדַּרְכּוֹ, וְחָיָה
וְעַד יוֹם מוֹתוֹ תְּחַכֶּה לּוֹ / אִם יָשׁוּב, מִיַּד תְּקַבְּלוֹ.

אֱמֶת, כִּי אַתָּה הוּא יוֹצְרָם / וְיוֹדֵעַ יִצְרָם / כִּי הֵם בָּשָׂר וָדָם.

---

when remorse comes summoning to repent. Nothing is more certain than penitence, and in the end everything will be redressed and perfected. (*The Lights of Penitence*)

PRAYER

Once Rabbi Levi Yitzḥak of Berditchev walked over to a group of his disciples after prayers had ended and welcomed them: "*Shalom aleikhem.*" The disciples were surprised and asked the Rebbe what he meant. They hadn't been away. "I was speaking," he said, "not to your bodies but your minds. I saw that while you were praying, you were thinking about other things. Your bodies were here but your minds were far away. Now that they have returned, I wished them *shalom aleikhem.*"

All beings long for the very source of their origin. Every plant, every grain of sand, every clod of earth, small creatures and great, the heavens and the angels, every substance and its particles – all of them are longing, yearning, panting to attain the state of holy perfection. Human beings suffer constantly from this homesickness of the soul, and it is in prayer that we cure it. When praying, we feel at one with the whole creation, and raise it to the very source of blessing and life. (Rabbi Abraham Kook, *Olat Re'iya*)

CHARITY

There are ten strong things in the world:
Rock is strong, but iron breaks it.
Iron is strong, but fire melts it.
Fire is strong, but water extinguishes it.
Water is strong, but the clouds carry it.
The clouds are strong, but the wind drives them.
The wind is strong, but man withstands it.
Man is strong, but fear weakens him.
Fear is strong, but wine removes it.
Wine is strong, but sleep overcomes it.

Man is founded in dust / and ends in dust.
He lays down his soul to bring home bread.
He is like a broken shard,
like grass dried up, like a faded flower,
like a fleeting shadow, like a passing cloud,
like a breath of wind, like whirling dust,
like a dream that slips away.

*The congregation says aloud, followed by the Leader:*

**AND YOU ARE KING –**
**THE LIVING, EVERLASTING GOD.**

*The Ark is closed.*

---

created us in love and forgiveness. We are here because He wanted us to be, because there is a task He wants us to perform.

Each one of us is unique. Even genetically identical twins are different. There are things only we can do, we who are what we are, in this time, this place, these circumstances. For each of us God has a task, work to perform, a kindness to show, a gift to give, love to share, loneliness to ease, pain to heal, broken lives to mend, and discerning that task, hearing God's call, is one of the great spiritual challenges for each of us. Where what we want to do meets what needs to be done, that is where God wants us to be.

And when we are there, our lives take on a meaning that no thought of mortality can defeat. "There are those who acquire their share of eternity in a single hour" (*Avoda Zara* 10b, 17a). The good we do lives after us and beyond us, inspiring others to do good in turn, creating ever widening ripples.

Our lives are short, but just as we do not judge a book by its size or a symphony by its length, so a life is not measured by its years but by its generosity, its moral beauty, the blessings it creates in the lives of others.

Rabbi Moshe of Kobryn taught: It is written, "And he dreamed, and behold a ladder set up on the earth." That is every person. Everyone must know: I am earth, mere dust of the earth. But "the top of it reached to heaven" – my soul can still reach to heaven. "And behold the angels of God ascending and descending on it" – even the ascent and descent of the angels depend on my deeds.

**אָדָם יְסוֹדוֹ מֵעָפָר / וְסוֹפוֹ לֶעָפָר**
**בְּנַפְשׁוֹ יָבִיא לַחְמוֹ / מָשׁוּל כַּחֶרֶס הַנִּשְׁבָּר**
**כְּחָצִיר יָבֵשׁ, וּכְצִיץ נוֹבֵל / כְּצֵל עוֹבֵר, וּכְעָנָן כָּלֶה**
**וּכְרוּחַ נוֹשָׁבֶת, וּכְאָבָק פּוֹרֵחַ, וְכַחֲלוֹם יָעוּף.**

*The* קהל *says aloud, followed by the* שליח ציבור*:*

**וְאַתָּה הוּא מֶלֶךְ, אֵל חַי וְקַיָּם.**

*The* ארון קודש *is closed.*

---

Lower still is one who gives only after the poor person asks.

Lower than this is one who gives less than is fitting, but does so with a friendly countenance.

The lowest level is one who gives ungraciously. (Maimonides, Laws of Gifts to the Poor 10:7–14)

The Kaminker Rebbe once resolved to devote a whole day to reciting Psalms. Toward evening, he was still reciting when a messenger came to tell him that his mentor, the Maggid of Tzidnov, wanted to see him. The rebbe said he would come as soon as he was finished, but the messenger returned, saying that the Maggid insisted that he come immediately. When he arrived, the Maggid asked him why he had delayed. The rebbe explained that he had been reciting Psalms. The Maggid told him that he had summoned the rebbe to collect money for a poor person in need. He continued: "Psalms can be sung by angels, but only human beings can help the poor. Charity is greater than reciting Psalms, because angels cannot perform charity."

**אָדָם יְסוֹדוֹ מֵעָפָר** *Man is founded in dust and ends in dust.* Our time on earth is all too short. Our most precious commodity – given to each of us on roughly equal terms – is time. However rich or powerful we are there are still only twenty-four hours in a day, 365 days in a solar year, and a span of years that is all too short. The most important decision we make in our lives is how to spend our time.

Looked at from the perspective of eternity we are nothing: a wave in the ocean, a grain of sand on the sea shore, dust on the surface of infinity. Yet we are not alone in a universe bereft of meaning. We are here because God

*The congregation then the Leader:*

אֵין קִצְבָה There is no end to Your years,
no limit to the days of Your life.
One cannot grasp the measure of Your glorious chariot;
one may not articulate Your most concealed name.
Your name is befitting to You / and You befit Your name.
By that name You have named us.
Act for Your name's sake. Sanctify Your name
through those who sanctify Your name,
for the sake of the glory of Your name, revered and sanctified,
with the words uttered by the holy Seraphim
who sanctify Your name in the Sanctuary,
those who live in heaven with those who live on earth
cry out and three times repeat
the threefold declaration of holiness to the Holy One,

**KEDUSHA**

*During the Leader's Repetition, the following is said standing with feet together, rising on the toes at the words indicated by ▴.*

*Cong. then Leader:* כֶּתֶר They will crown You, LORD our God, the angels, the multitudes of heaven, together with Your nation Israel, gathering here below –

*Cong. then Leader:* Together all of them will speak the threefold declaration of Your holi ness, as is said by Your prophet:
"They call out to one another, saying: *Is. 6*

*Cong. then Leader:* ▴Holy, ▴holy, ▴holy is the LORD of hosts; the whole world is filled with His glory."

His glory fills the universe. His ministering angels ask each other: Where is the place of His glory, that we may revere Him there? Those facing them praise Him and say:

*Cong. then Leader:* ▴"Blessed is the LORD's glory from His place." *Ezek. 3*

---

by angelic hosts. Their visions, though, were profoundly different. Isaiah said, "The whole world is filled with His glory." Ezekiel saw "the LORD's glory from

*The* קהל *then the* שליח ציבור:

אֵין קִצְבָה לִשְׁנוֹתֶיךָ / וְאֵין קֵץ לְאֹרֶךְ יָמֶיךָ
וְאֵין לְשַׁעֵר מַרְכְּבוֹת כְּבוֹדֶךָ / וְאֵין לְפָרֵשׁ עֵילוּם שְׁמֶךָ.
שִׁמְךָ נָאֶה לְךָ / וְאַתָּה נָאֶה לִשְׁמֶךָ / וּשְׁמֵנוּ קָרָאתָ בִשְׁמֶךָ.
עֲשֵׂה לְמַעַן שְׁמֶךָ, וְקַדֵּשׁ אֶת שִׁמְךָ עַל מַקְדִּישֵׁי שְׁמֶךָ
בַּעֲבוּר כְּבוֹד שִׁמְךָ הַנַּעֲרָץ וְהַנִּקְדָּשׁ
כְּסוֹד שִׂיחַ שַׂרְפֵי קֹדֶשׁ, הַמַּקְדִּישִׁים שִׁמְךָ בַּקֹּדֶשׁ
דָּרֵי מַעְלָה עִם דָּרֵי מַטָּה
קוֹרְאִים וּמְשַׁלְּשִׁים בְּשִׁלּוּשׁ קְדֻשָּׁה בַּקֹּדֶשׁ.

## קדושה

*During the* חזרת הש״ץ*, the following is said standing with feet together, rising on the toes at the words indicated by* ˄.

קהל *then* ש״ץ: כֶּתֶר יִתְּנוּ לְךָ, יהוה אֱלֹהֵינוּ, מַלְאָכִים הֲמוֹנֵי מַעְלָה
עִם עַמְּךָ יִשְׂרָאֵל קְבוּצֵי מַטָּה

קהל *then* ש״ץ: יַחַד כֻּלָּם קְדֻשָּׁה לְךָ יְשַׁלֵּשׁוּ כַּדָּבָר הָאָמוּר עַל יַד נְבִיאֶךָ
ישעיה ו וְקָרָא זֶה אֶל־זֶה וְאָמַר

קהל *then* ש״ץ: ˄קָדוֹשׁ, ˄קָדוֹשׁ, ˄קָדוֹשׁ, יהוה צְבָאוֹת, מְלֹא כָל הָאָרֶץ כְּבוֹדוֹ:
כְּבוֹדוֹ מָלֵא עוֹלָם
מְשָׁרְתָיו שׁוֹאֲלִים זֶה לָזֶה, אַיֵּה מְקוֹם כְּבוֹדוֹ לְהַעֲרִיצוֹ
לְעֻמָּתָם מְשַׁבְּחִים וְאוֹמְרִים

קהל *then* ש״ץ: ˄בָּרוּךְ כְּבוֹד־יהוה מִמְּקוֹמוֹ: יחזקאל ג

---

בָּרוּךְ כְּבוֹד־יהוה מִמְּקוֹמוֹ *Blessed is the* L*ORD's glory from His place.* Two prophets, Isaiah and Ezekiel, saw visions of God enthroned in the heavens surrounded

From His place may He turn,
in His compassion, to His nation,
and be gracious to the people who proclaim the unity
of His name, morning and evening, every day, continually,
twice each day reciting in love the Shema:

*Cong. then Leader:* "Listen, Israel, the LORD is our God, the LORD is One." *Deut. 6*

He is our God, He is our Father, He is our King,
He is our Savior – and He will save us
and redeem us again,
and, in His compassion He will let us hear Him say,
in the presence of all that lives: I have redeemed you again,
as I did at the beginning, "to be your God. *Num. 15*
I am the LORD your God."

*Cong. then Leader:* Glorious is our Glorious One, LORD our Master, *Ps. 8*
and glorious is Your name throughout the earth.
Then the LORD shall be King over all the earth; *Zech. 14*
on that day the LORD shall be One and His name One.

*Leader:* And in Your holy Writings it is written:

*Cong. then Leader:* ▲"The LORD shall reign for ever. *Ps. 146*
He is your God, Zion, from generation to generation,
Halleluya!"

*Leader:* From generation to generation
we will declare Your greatness,
and we will proclaim Your holiness for evermore.
Your praise, our God, shall not leave our mouth forever,
for You, God, are a great and holy King.

---

לְדוֹר וָדוֹר *From generation to generation.* Rabbi Yaakov Yitzḥak of Pzhysha said: If anyone is asked why he toils so hard, he replies: "To bring up my children to be good Jews." And when the children grow up, they forget why their parents toiled, and they toil in their turn, and if you ask them why, they will say, "To bring up my children to be good Jews." And so it goes on from generation to generation. But when will someone say, "Let me be a good Jew"?

מִמְּקוֹמוֹ הוּא יִפֶן בְּרַחֲמָיו לְעַמּוֹ
וְיָחֹן עַם הַמְיַחֲדִים שְׁמוֹ, עֶרֶב וָבְקֶר בְּכָל יוֹם תָּמִיד
פַּעֲמַיִם בְּאַהֲבָה שְׁמַע אוֹמְרִים

*then* קהל ש״ץ: שְׁמַע יִשְׂרָאֵל, יהוה אֱלֹהֵינוּ, יהוה אֶחָד: דברים ו
הוּא אֱלֹהֵינוּ, הוּא אָבִינוּ, הוּא מַלְכֵּנוּ, הוּא מוֹשִׁיעֵנוּ
וְהוּא יוֹשִׁיעֵנוּ וְיִגְאָלֵנוּ שֵׁנִית
וְיַשְׁמִיעֵנוּ בְּרַחֲמָיו לְעֵינֵי כָּל חַי לֵאמֹר
הֵן גָּאַלְתִּי אֶתְכֶם אַחֲרִית כְּרֵאשִׁית
לִהְיוֹת לָכֶם לֵאלֹהִים במדבר טו
אֲנִי יהוה אֱלֹהֵיכֶם:

*then* קהל ש״ץ: אַדִּיר אַדִּירֵנוּ, יהוה אֲדֹנֵינוּ, מָה־אַדִּיר שִׁמְךָ בְּכָל־הָאָרֶץ: תהלים ח
וְהָיָה יהוה לְמֶלֶךְ עַל־כָּל־הָאָרֶץ זכריה יד
בַּיּוֹם הַהוּא יִהְיֶה יהוה אֶחָד וּשְׁמוֹ אֶחָד:

ש״ץ: וּבְדִבְרֵי קָדְשְׁךָ כָּתוּב לֵאמֹר
*then* קהל ש״ץ: יִמְלֹךְ יהוה לְעוֹלָם, אֱלֹהַיִךְ צִיּוֹן לְדֹר וָדֹר, הַלְלוּיָהּ: תהלים קמו

ש״ץ: לְדוֹר וָדוֹר נַגִּיד גָּדְלֶךָ, וּלְנֵצַח נְצָחִים קְדֻשָּׁתְךָ נַקְדִּישׁ
וְשִׁבְחֲךָ אֱלֹהֵינוּ מִפִּינוּ לֹא יָמוּשׁ לְעוֹלָם וָעֶד
כִּי אֵל מֶלֶךְ גָּדוֹל וְקָדוֹשׁ אָתָּה.

---

His place." The difference is that Isaiah prophesied when Israel was in its land, the Temple stood, the priests performed their service and the Levites sang their song. Ezekiel prophesied from Babylon, in exile. He was in mourning, a prisoner of war. He saw God's glory confined, as it were, to heaven. There are times when we see God's glory in the world, but there are other times when there is *hester panim,* when it is as if God were hiding His face. (Rabbi Joseph Soloveitchik)

לְדוֹר וָדוֹר From generation to generation declare God King,
for He alone is lofty and holy.

*The following prayer originally began at "For with Your holiness." Nowadays, it is commonly sung as one stanza together with the later addition of the opening verse "Have mercy on those You have made."*

חֲמֹל Have mercy on those You have made,
take joy in those You made,
and those who shelter in You will say,
as You absolve the ones You bear,
"Be sanctified, Lord, through all that You have made."

כִּי מַקְדִּישֶׁיךָ For with Your holiness You sanctify
all who affirm You holy;
it is fitting that the Holy One be glorified by holy ones.

*Leader:*

וּבְכֵן יִתְקַדַּשׁ And so may Your name be sanctified, Lord our God,
through Israel Your nation
and Jerusalem, Your city,
and Zion, the dwelling place of Your honor,
and through the royal house of David Your anointed,
and Your Sanctuary and Your Temple.

He, our Lord,
will yet remember for us the love of [Abraham] the steadfast one.
And for [Isaac] the son who was bound,
He will still the enmity against us.
And for the merit of [Jacob] the innocent man,
He will bring today our judgment out to the good,
for this day is holy to our Lord. *Neh. 8*

With no one to advocate for us,
against the accuser of sin,
speak words of law and of justice to Jacob,
and absolve us in the judgment, King of judgment.

לְדוֹר וָדוֹר הַמְלִיכוּ לָאֵל
כִּי הוּא לְבַדּוֹ מָרוֹם וְקָדוֹשׁ.

*The following prayer originally began at* כִּי מַקְדִּישֶׁיךָ. *Nowadays, it is commonly sung as one stanza together with the later addition of the opening verse* חֲמֹל עַל מַעֲשֶׂיךָ.

חֲמֹל עַל מַעֲשֶׂיךָ וְתִשְׂמַח בְּמַעֲשֶׂיךָ
וְיֹאמְרוּ לְךָ חוֹסֶיךָ בְּצַדֶּקְךָ עֲמוּסֶיךָ
תֻּקְדַּשׁ אָדוֹן עַל כָּל מַעֲשֶׂיךָ

כִּי מַקְדִּישֶׁיךָ בִּקְדֻשָּׁתְךָ קִדַּשְׁתָּ
נָאֶה לְקָדוֹשׁ פְּאֵר מִקְּדוֹשִׁים.

*The* שליח ציבור*:*

וּבְכֵן יִתְקַדַּשׁ שִׁמְךָ יהוה אֱלֹהֵינוּ
עַל יִשְׂרָאֵל עַמֶּךָ
וְעַל יְרוּשָׁלַיִם עִירֶךָ
וְעַל צִיּוֹן מִשְׁכַּן כְּבוֹדֶךָ
וְעַל מַלְכוּת בֵּית דָּוִד מְשִׁיחֶךָ
וְעַל מְכוֹנְךָ וְהֵיכָלֶךָ.

עוֹד יִזְכֹּר לָנוּ אַהֲבַת אֵיתָן, אֲדוֹנֵינוּ
וּבַבֵּן הַנֶּעֱקָד יַשְׁבִּית מְדַיְּנֵינוּ
וּבִזְכוּת הַתָּם יוֹצִיא הַיּוֹם לְצֶדֶק דִּינֵנוּ
נחמיה ח כִּי־קָדוֹשׁ הַיּוֹם לַאֲדֹנֵינוּ:

בְּאֵין מֵלִיץ יֹשֶׁר מוּל מַגִּיד פֶּשַׁע
תַּגִּיד לְיַעֲקֹב דָּבָר, חֹק וּמִשְׁפָּט
וְצַדְּקֵנוּ בַּמִּשְׁפָּט, הַמֶּלֶךְ הַמִּשְׁפָּט.

*This piyut, with its double alphabetic acrostic, is attributed to Yannai (a poet who lived in Israel in the Byzantine era). In recent generations the custom to say it responsively has spread; many congregations are accustomed to saying the second stich of each couplet together with the first of the next one. Some sing the entire piyut collectively.*

*The Ark is opened.*

הָאוֹחֵז בְּיַד The One who holds in His hand the trait of stern judgment.
And all believe that He is the faithful God.

The One who examines and scrutinizes the hidden stores.
And all believe that He examines the conscience of all.

The One who redeems from death and ransoms from hell.
And all believe that He is a mighty Redeemer.

The sole Judge of all who enter the world.
And all believe that He is a truthful Judge.

The One whose name was pronounced "I will ever be what I am now."
And all believe that He was, is, and shall forever be.

The One whose praise is as affirmed as His name.
And all believe that He is One and there is no other.

The One who recalls kindly those who utter His name.
And all believe that He recalls His covenant.

The One who allots life to all the living.
And all believe that He lives and is everlasting.

The One who acts kindly with both the good and evil.
And all believe that He is kind to all.

The One who knows the devices of all creatures.
And all believe that He is the One who forms them in the womb.

*This piyut, with its double alphabetic acrostic, is attributed to Yannai (a poet who lived in ארץ ישראל in the Byzantine era). In recent generations the custom to say it responsively has spread; many congregations are accustomed to saying the second stich of each couplet together with the first of the next one. Some sing the entire piyut collectively.*

*The ארון קודש is opened.*

הָאוֹחֵז בְּיָד מִדַּת מִשְׁפָּט
וְכֹל מַאֲמִינִים שֶׁהוּא אֵל אֱמוּנָה.

הַבּוֹחֵן וּבוֹדֵק גִּנְזֵי נִסְתָּרוֹת
וְכֹל מַאֲמִינִים שֶׁהוּא בּוֹחֵן כְּלָיוֹת.

הַגּוֹאֵל מִמָּוֶת וּפוֹדֶה מִשַּׁחַת
וְכֹל מַאֲמִינִים שֶׁהוּא גּוֹאֵל חָזָק.

הַדָּן יְחִידִי לְבָאֵי עוֹלָם
וְכֹל מַאֲמִינִים שֶׁהוּא דַּיַּן אֱמֶת.

הֶהָגוּי בְּאֶהְיֶה אֲשֶׁר אֶהְיֶה
וְכֹל מַאֲמִינִים שֶׁהוּא הָיָה וְהֹוֶה וְיִהְיֶה.

הַוַּדַּאי, כִּשְׁמוֹ כֵּן תְּהִלָּתוֹ
וְכֹל מַאֲמִינִים שֶׁהוּא וְאֵין בִּלְתּוֹ.

הַזּוֹכֵר לְמַזְכִּירָיו טוֹבוֹת זִכְרוֹנוֹת
וְכֹל מַאֲמִינִים שֶׁהוּא זוֹכֵר הַבְּרִית.

הַחוֹתֵךְ חַיִּים לְכָל חָי
וְכֹל מַאֲמִינִים שֶׁהוּא חַי וְקַיָּם.

הַטּוֹב וּמֵיטִיב לָרָעִים וְלַטּוֹבִים
וְכֹל מַאֲמִינִים שֶׁהוּא טוֹב לַכֹּל.

הַיּוֹדֵעַ יֵצֶר כָּל יְצוּרִים
וְכֹל מַאֲמִינִים שֶׁהוּא יוֹצְרָם בַּבָּטֶן.

The One who is omnipotent and formed the world at once.
And all believe that He is all-powerful.

The One who dwells concealed in His holy shade.
And all believe that He alone is God.

The One who crowns kings yet the reign is His alone.
And all believe that He is an everlasting King.

The One who acts kindly with each generation.
And all believe that He reserves kindness.

The One who acts patiently with evildoers
and turns a blind eye to the wayward.
And all believe that He is forgiving and exalted.

The lofty One whose eyes are turned to those who fear Him.
And all believe that He answers whispered prayers.

The One who opens the gates
to those who come knocking penitently.
And all believe that His hand is ever open.

The One who espies the evildoer and wishes to justify him.
And all believe that He is righteous and upright.

The One who is slow to anger and defers wrath.
And all believe that His ire is hard to arouse.

The compassionate One who lets pity precede rage.
And all believe that He is easily appeased.

The constant One who considers great and small equally.
And all believe that He is a righteous Judge.

הַכֹּל יָכוֹל, וְכוֹלְלָם יַחַד
וְכֹל מַאֲמִינִים שֶׁהוּא כֹּל יָכוֹל.

הַלָּן בְּסֵתֶר בְּצֵל שַׁדָּי
וְכֹל מַאֲמִינִים שֶׁהוּא לְבַדּוֹ הוּא.

הַמַּמְלִיךְ מְלָכִים, וְלוֹ הַמְּלוּכָה
וְכֹל מַאֲמִינִים שֶׁהוּא מֶלֶךְ עוֹלָם.

הַנּוֹהֵג בְּחַסְדּוֹ עִם כָּל דּוֹר
וְכֹל מַאֲמִינִים שֶׁהוּא נוֹצֵר חֶסֶד.

הַסּוֹבֵל, וּמַעֲלִים עַיִן מִסּוֹרְרִים
וְכֹל מַאֲמִינִים שֶׁהוּא סוֹלֵחַ סֶלָה.

הָעֶלְיוֹן, וְעֵינָיו עַל יְרֵאָיו
וְכֹל מַאֲמִינִים שֶׁהוּא עוֹנֶה לָחַשׁ.

הַפּוֹתֵחַ שַׁעַר לְדוֹפְקֵי בִתְשׁוּבָה
וְכֹל מַאֲמִינִים שֶׁהוּא פְּתוּחָה יָדוֹ.

הַצּוֹפֶה רָשָׁע, וְחָפֵץ לְהַצְדִּיקוֹ
וְכֹל מַאֲמִינִים שֶׁהוּא צַדִּיק וְיָשָׁר.

הַקָּצָר בְּזַעַם, וּמַאֲרִיךְ אַף
וְכֹל מַאֲמִינִים שֶׁהוּא קָשֶׁה לִכְעֹס.

הָרַחוּם, וּמַקְדִּים רַחֲמִים לְרֹגֶז
וְכֹל מַאֲמִינִים שֶׁהוּא רַךְ לִרְצוֹת.

הַשָּׁוֶה, וּמַשְׁוֶה קָטֹן וְגָדוֹל
וְכֹל מַאֲמִינִים שֶׁהוּא שׁוֹפֵט צֶדֶק.

The perfect One who deals in integrity with the innocent.
And all believe that His works are perfect and complete.

*The Ark is closed (in some communities, the Ark remains open until the end of the next paragraph).*

תִּשְׂגַּב לְבַדֶּךָ You will be elevated, peerless,
and will rule over all that is, alone,
as is written by Your prophet,
"Then the LORD shall be King over all the earth; *Zech. 14*
on that day the LORD shall be One and His name One."

וּבְכֵן תֵּן פַּחְדְּךָ And so place the fear of You, LORD our God,
over all that You have made,
and the terror of You over all You have created,
and all who were made will stand in awe of You,
and all of creation will worship You,
and they will be bound all together as one
to carry out Your will with an undivided heart;
for we know, LORD our God,
that all dominion is laid out before You,
strength is in Your palm, and might in Your right hand,
Your name spreading awe over all You have created.

וּבְכֵן תֵּן כָּבוֹד And so place honor, LORD, upon Your people,
praise on those who fear You and hope into those who seek You,
the confidence to speak into all who long for You,
gladness to Your land, and joy to Your city,
the flourishing of pride to David Your servant,
and a lamp laid out for his descendant, Your anointed,
soon, in our days.

---

will always hear this one maxim: fear God. And this one is the whole. There is not a single thing in all the world that does not show you a way to fear God and to serve Him.

הַתָּם, וּמִתַּמֵּם עִם תְּמִימִים
וְכֹל מַאֲמִינִים שֶׁהוּא תָּמִים פָּעֳלוֹ.

*The* ארון קודש *is closed (in some communities, the* ארון קודש *remains open until the end of the next paragraph).*

תִּשְׂגַּב לְבַדֶּךָ, וְתִמְלֹךְ עַל כֹּל בְּיִחוּד
כַּכָּתוּב עַל יַד נְבִיאֶךָ
וְהָיָה יהוה לְמֶלֶךְ עַל־כָּל־הָאָרֶץ זכריה יד
בַּיּוֹם הַהוּא יִהְיֶה יהוה אֶחָד וּשְׁמוֹ אֶחָד:

וּבְכֵן תֵּן פַּחְדְּךָ יהוה אֱלֹהֵינוּ עַל כָּל מַעֲשֶׂיךָ
וְאֵימָתְךָ עַל כָּל מַה שֶּׁבָּרָאתָ
וְיִירָאוּךָ כָּל הַמַּעֲשִׂים, וְיִשְׁתַּחֲווּ לְפָנֶיךָ כָּל הַבְּרוּאִים
וְיֵעָשׂוּ כֻלָּם אֲגֻדָּה אַחַת לַעֲשׂוֹת רְצוֹנְךָ בְּלֵבָב שָׁלֵם
כְּמוֹ שֶׁיָּדַעְנוּ יהוה אֱלֹהֵינוּ שֶׁהַשָּׁלְטָן לְפָנֶיךָ
עֹז בְּיָדְךָ וּגְבוּרָה בִּימִינֶךָ
וְשִׁמְךָ נוֹרָא עַל כָּל מַה שֶּׁבָּרָאתָ.

וּבְכֵן תֵּן כָּבוֹד יהוה לְעַמֶּךָ
תְּהִלָּה לִירֵאֶיךָ וְתִקְוָה טוֹבָה לְדוֹרְשֶׁיךָ
וּפִתְחוֹן פֶּה לַמְיַחֲלִים לָךְ, שִׂמְחָה לְאַרְצֶךָ, וְשָׂשׂוֹן לְעִירֶךָ
וּצְמִיחַת קֶרֶן לְדָוִד עַבְדֶּךָ
וַעֲרִיכַת נֵר לְבֶן יִשַׁי מְשִׁיחֶךָ בִּמְהֵרָה בְיָמֵינוּ.

---

וּבְכֵן תֵּן פַּחְדְּךָ *And so place the fear of You.* Rabbi Moshe of Kobryn taught: At the end of Ecclesiastes we read, "The end of the matter, all having been heard: fear God" (12:13). Now whatever matter you come to the end of, you

וּבְכֵן צַדִּיקִים And then righteous people will see and rejoice,
and the upright will exult, and the pious revel in joy,
and injustice will have nothing more to say,
and all wickedness will fade away like smoke
as You sweep the rule of arrogance from the earth.

*This alphabetic piyut, author unknown, celebrates the future universal recognition of God by all the nations. It is usually sung collectively.*

וְיֶאֱתָיוּ And all shall come forth to worship You
and they shall bless Your honorable name.
And they shall tell of Your righteousness in the islands,
and nations that have not known You shall seek You out.
And all the ends of the earth shall praise You
and shall always say, "May the Lord forever be exalted."
And they shall spurn their idols
and be ashamed of their graven images.
And they shall turn their shoulder as one to worship You,
and those who seek Your presence
shall see You with the rising sun forever.
And they shall recognize Your majestic power,
and the errant ones shall learn to understand.
And they shall speak of Your might
and they shall exalt You who are exalted above all rulers.
And they shall leap back in fear in Your presence,
and they shall crown You with a diadem of glory.
And the mountains themselves shall break out in song,
and the islands shall joyfully shout as You are crowned.
And they shall accept the yoke of Your reign over them,
and You shall be exalted among assembled multitudes.
And they shall hear from far and wide and come
to offer You the royal crown.

וְתִמְלֹךְ And You, who are the Lord our God,
will rule alone over all those You have made,
in Mount Zion, the dwelling of Your glory,
and in Jerusalem, Your holy city,
as it is written in Your holy Writings:
"The Lord shall reign for ever. *Ps. 146*
He is your God, Zion, from generation to generation, Halleluya!"

וּבְכֵן צַדִּיקִים יִרְאוּ וְיִשְׂמָחוּ, וִישָׁרִים יַעֲלֹזוּ
וַחֲסִידִים בְּרִנָּה יָגִילוּ
וְעוֹלָתָה תִּקְפָּץ פִּיהָ
וְכָל הָרִשְׁעָה כֻּלָּהּ כְּעָשָׁן תִּכְלֶה
כִּי תַעֲבִיר מֶמְשֶׁלֶת זָדוֹן מִן הָאָרֶץ.

*This alphabetic piyut, author unknown, celebrates the future universal recognition of God by all the nations. It is usually sung collectively.*

וְיֶאֱתָיוּ כֹּל לְעָבְדֶךָ / וִיבָרְכוּ שֵׁם כְּבוֹדֶךָ
וְיַגִּידוּ בָאִיִּים צִדְקֶךָ / וְיִדְרְשׁוּךָ עַמִּים לֹא יְדָעוּךָ
וִיהַלְלְוּךָ כָּל אַפְסֵי אָרֶץ / וְיֹאמְרוּ תָמִיד יִגְדַּל יהוה
וְיִזְנְחוּ אֶת עֲצַבֵּיהֶם / וְיַחְפְּרוּ עִם פְּסִילֵיהֶם
וְיַטּוּ שְׁכֶם אֶחָד לְעָבְדֶךָ / וְיִירָאְוּךָ עִם שֶׁמֶשׁ מְבַקְשֵׁי פָנֶיךָ
וְיַכִּירוּ כֹּחַ מַלְכוּתֶךָ / וְיִלְמְדוּ תוֹעִים בִּינָה
וִימַלְּלוּ אֶת גְּבוּרָתֶךָ / וִינַשְּׂאוּךָ, מִתְנַשֵּׂא לְכֹל לְרֹאשׁ
וִיסַלְּדוּ בְחִילָה פָּנֶיךָ / וִיעַטְּרוּךָ נֵזֶר תִּפְאָרָה
וְיִפְצְחוּ הָרִים רִנָּה / וְיִצְהֲלוּ אִיִּים בְּמָלְכֶךָ
וִיקַבְּלוּ עֹל מַלְכוּתְךָ עֲלֵיהֶם / וִירוֹמְמוּךָ בִּקְהַל עָם
וְיִשְׁמְעוּ רְחוֹקִים וְיָבוֹאוּ / וְיִתְּנוּ לְךָ כֶּתֶר מְלוּכָה.

וְתִמְלֹךְ אַתָּה הוּא יהוה אֱלֹהֵינוּ
מְהֵרָה לְבַדֶּךָ עַל כָּל מַעֲשֶׂיךָ
בְּהַר צִיּוֹן מִשְׁכַּן כְּבוֹדֶךָ
וּבִירוּשָׁלַיִם עִיר קָדְשֶׁךָ
כַּכָּתוּב בְּדִבְרֵי קָדְשֶׁךָ
תהלים קמו יִמְלֹךְ יהוה לְעוֹלָם, אֱלֹהַיִךְ צִיּוֹן לְדֹר וָדֹר, הַלְלוּיָהּ:

קָדוֹשׁ אַתָּה You are holy, Your name is awesome,
and there is no god but You, as it is written,
"The LORD of hosts shall be raised up through His judgment, Is. 5
the Holy God, made holy in righteousness."
Blessed are You, LORD, the holy King.

HOLINESS OF THE DAY AND MALKHIYOT

אַתָּה בְחַרְתָּנוּ You have chosen us from among all peoples.
You have loved and favored us. You have raised us above all tongues.
You have made us holy through Your commandments.
You have brought us near, our King, to Your service,
and have called us by Your great and holy name.

וַתִּתֶּן לָנוּ And You, LORD our God, have given us in love
this Day of Remembrance, a day of blowing the shofar,
a holy assembly in memory of the exodus from Egypt.

וּמִפְּנֵי חֲטָאֵינוּ But because of our sins we were exiled from our land
and driven far from our country.
We cannot perform our duties in Your chosen House,
the great and holy Temple that was called by Your name,
because of the hand that was stretched out against Your Sanctuary.
May it be Your will, LORD our God and God of our ancestors,
merciful King,
that You in Your abounding compassion may once more
have mercy on us and on Your Sanctuary,
rebuilding it swiftly and adding to its glory.
Our Father, our King,
reveal the glory of Your kingdom to us swiftly.
Appear and be exalted over us in the sight of all that lives.
Bring back our scattered ones from among the nations,
and gather our dispersed people from the ends of the earth.

---

וּמִפְּנֵי חֲטָאֵינוּ *But because of our sins we were exiled from our land.* Rabbi Ḥanokh of Alexander said: "The worst exile is to forget that you are in exile."

קָדוֹשׁ אַתָּה וְנוֹרָא שְׁמֶךָ, וְאֵין אֱלוֹהַּ מִבַּלְעָדֶיךָ
כַּכָּתוּב, וַיִּגְבַּה יהוה צְבָאוֹת בַּמִּשְׁפָּט ישעיה ה
וְהָאֵל הַקָּדוֹשׁ נִקְדַּשׁ בִּצְדָקָה:
בָּרוּךְ אַתָּה יהוה, הַמֶּלֶךְ הַקָּדוֹשׁ.

קדושת היום ומלכיות

אַתָּה בְחַרְתָּנוּ מִכָּל הָעַמִּים
אָהַבְתָּ אוֹתָנוּ וְרָצִיתָ בָּנוּ, וְרוֹמַמְתָּנוּ מִכָּל הַלְּשׁוֹנוֹת
וְקִדַּשְׁתָּנוּ בְּמִצְוֹתֶיךָ וְקֵרַבְתָּנוּ מַלְכֵּנוּ לַעֲבוֹדָתֶךָ
וְשִׁמְךָ הַגָּדוֹל וְהַקָּדוֹשׁ עָלֵינוּ קָרָאתָ.

וַתִּתֶּן לָנוּ יהוה אֱלֹהֵינוּ בְּאַהֲבָה
אֶת יוֹם הַזִּכָּרוֹן הַזֶּה יוֹם תְּרוּעָה
מִקְרָא קֹדֶשׁ, זֵכֶר לִיצִיאַת מִצְרָיִם.

וּמִפְּנֵי חֲטָאֵינוּ גָּלִינוּ מֵאַרְצֵנוּ, וְנִתְרַחַקְנוּ מֵעַל אַדְמָתֵנוּ
וְאֵין אֲנוּ יְכוֹלִים לַעֲשׂוֹת חוֹבוֹתֵינוּ בְּבֵית בְּחִירָתֶךָ
בַּבַּיִת הַגָּדוֹל וְהַקָּדוֹשׁ שֶׁנִּקְרָא שִׁמְךָ עָלָיו
מִפְּנֵי הַיָּד שֶׁנִּשְׁתַּלְּחָה בְּמִקְדָּשֶׁךָ.
יְהִי רָצוֹן מִלְּפָנֶיךָ יהוה אֱלֹהֵינוּ וֵאלֹהֵי אֲבוֹתֵינוּ, מֶלֶךְ רַחֲמָן
שֶׁתָּשׁוּב וּתְרַחֵם עָלֵינוּ וְעַל מִקְדָּשְׁךָ בְּרַחֲמֶיךָ הָרַבִּים
וְתִבְנֵהוּ מְהֵרָה וּתְגַדֵּל כְּבוֹדוֹ.
אָבִינוּ מַלְכֵּנוּ, גַּלֵּה כְּבוֹד מַלְכוּתְךָ עָלֵינוּ מְהֵרָה
וְהוֹפַע וְהִנָּשֵׂא עָלֵינוּ לְעֵינֵי כָּל חָי
וְקָרֵב פְּזוּרֵינוּ מִבֵּין הַגּוֹיִם, וּנְפוּצוֹתֵינוּ כַּנֵּס מִיַּרְכְּתֵי אָרֶץ.

וַהֲבִיאֵנוּ לְצִיּוֹן Lead us to Zion, Your city, in jubilation,
and to Jerusalem, home of Your Temple, with everlasting joy.
There we will prepare for You our obligatory offerings:
the regular daily offerings in their order
and the additional offerings according to their law.
And the additional offerings of this Day of Remembrance we will prepare and offer before You in love,
in accord with Your will's commandment,
as You wrote for us in Your Torah
through Your servant Moses, by Your own word, as it is said:

וּבַחֹדֶשׁ הַשְּׁבִיעִי On the first day of the seventh month *Num. 29*
you shall hold a sacred assembly.
You shall do no laborious work,
and you shall mark a Day of the Blowing of the Shofar.
You shall make a burnt-offering of pleasing aroma to the Lord:
a young bullock, a ram, and seven yearling male lambs;
they shall be without blemish.

וּמִנְחָתָם וְנִסְכֵּיהֶם And their meal offerings
and wine-libations as ordained:
three-tenths of an ephah for the bull,
two-tenths of an ephah for the ram,
one-tenth of an ephah for each of the seven lambs,
wine for the libations,
two male goats for atonement,
and two regular daily offerings
according to their law.

מִלְּבַד All this aside from the burnt-offering *Num. 29*
of the New Moon and its meal-offering,
and the regular daily burnt-offering with its meal-offering,
and their libations according to their ordinance,
a burnt-offering of pleasing odor to the Lord.

וַהֲבִיאֵנוּ לְצִיּוֹן עִירְךָ בְּרִנָּה
וְלִירוּשָׁלַיִם בֵּית מִקְדָּשְׁךָ בְּשִׂמְחַת עוֹלָם
וְשָׁם נַעֲשֶׂה לְפָנֶיךָ אֶת קָרְבְּנוֹת חוֹבוֹתֵינוּ
תְּמִידִים כְּסִדְרָם וּמוּסָפִים כְּהִלְכָתָם
וְאֶת מוּסְפֵי יוֹם הַזִּכָּרוֹן הַזֶּה
נַעֲשֶׂה וְנַקְרִיב לְפָנֶיךָ בְּאַהֲבָה כְּמִצְוַת רְצוֹנֶךָ
כְּמוֹ שֶׁכָּתַבְתָּ עָלֵינוּ בְּתוֹרָתֶךָ
עַל יְדֵי מֹשֶׁה עַבְדֶּךָ מִפִּי כְבוֹדֶךָ, כָּאָמוּר

וּבַחֹדֶשׁ הַשְּׁבִיעִי בְּאֶחָד לַחֹדֶשׁ מִקְרָא־קֹדֶשׁ יִהְיֶה לָכֶם במדבר כט
כָּל־מְלֶאכֶת עֲבֹדָה לֹא תַעֲשׂוּ
יוֹם תְּרוּעָה יִהְיֶה לָכֶם:
וַעֲשִׂיתֶם עֹלָה לְרֵיחַ נִיחֹחַ לַיהוה
פַּר בֶּן־בָּקָר אֶחָד, אַיִל אֶחָד
כְּבָשִׂים בְּנֵי־שָׁנָה שִׁבְעָה תְּמִימִם:

וּמִנְחָתָם וְנִסְכֵּיהֶם כִּמְדֻבָּר
שְׁלֹשָׁה עֶשְׂרֹנִים לַפָּר וּשְׁנֵי עֶשְׂרֹנִים לָאָיִל
וְעִשָּׂרוֹן לַכֶּבֶשׂ, וְיַיִן כְּנִסְכּוֹ
וּשְׁנֵי שְׂעִירִים לְכַפֵּר, וּשְׁנֵי תְמִידִים כְּהִלְכָתָם.

מִלְּבַד עֹלַת הַחֹדֶשׁ וּמִנְחָתָהּ במדבר כט
וְעֹלַת הַתָּמִיד וּמִנְחָתָהּ, וְנִסְכֵּיהֶם כְּמִשְׁפָּטָם
לְרֵיחַ נִיחֹחַ, אִשֶּׁה לַיהוה:

*The Ark is opened.*

עָלֵינוּ It is our duty to praise the Master of all,
and ascribe greatness to the Author of creation,
who has not made us like the nations of the lands,
nor placed us like the families of the earth;

*The Ark is closed.*

who has not made our portion like theirs,
nor our destiny like all their multitudes.
(For they worship vanity and emptiness,
and pray to a god who cannot save.)

*The Ark is opened and the congregation (in some congregations, only the Leader) kneels on the floor at "bow."*

▾But we bow in worship
and thank the Supreme King of kings, the Holy One, blessed be He,
who extends the heavens and establishes the earth,
whose throne of glory is in the heavens above,
and whose power's Presence is in the highest of heights.

*In some congregations, the Leader says "You have been shown" (below) while the congregation continues here with "He is our God."*

He is our God; there is no other.
Truly He is our King; there is none else, as it is written in His Torah:
"You shall know and take to heart this day that the LORD is God, *Deut. 4*
in the heavens above and on the earth below.
There is no other."

---

*The Leader says the following while the congregation says "He is our God" (above).*

אַתָּה הָרְאֵתָ You have been shown, that you may know, that the LORD is our God: there is no other besides him. You shall know and take to heart this day that the LORD is God, in the heavens above and on the earth below. There is no other. Listen, Israel: the LORD is our God, the LORD is One. For heaven, the highest heaven, the earth and all that it contains, belong to the LORD your God. For the LORD your God is the God of gods, the LORD of lords, the great, mighty and awesome God, God, who does not discriminate or accept any bribe. When I proclaim the LORD's name, give glory to our God. Blessed be the name of the LORD, now and for evermore.

*Deut. 4* · *Deut. 6* · *Deut. 10* · *Ibid.* · *Deut. 32* · *Ps. 113*

---

*The Ark is closed.*

*The* ארון קודש *is opened.*

עָלֵינוּ לְשַׁבֵּחַ לַאֲדוֹן הַכֹּל, לָתֵת גְּדֻלָּה לְיוֹצֵר בְּרֵאשִׁית
שֶׁלֹּא עָשָׂנוּ כְּגוֹיֵי הָאֲרָצוֹת, וְלֹא שָׂמָנוּ כְּמִשְׁפְּחוֹת הָאֲדָמָה

*The* ארון קודש *is closed.*

שֶׁלֹּא שָׂם חֶלְקֵנוּ כָּהֶם וְגוֹרָלֵנוּ כְּכָל הֲמוֹנָם.
(שֶׁהֵם מִשְׁתַּחֲוִים לְהֶבֶל וָרִיק וּמִתְפַּלְלִים אֶל אֵל לֹא יוֹשִׁיעַ.)

*The* ארון קודש *is opened and the* קהל *(in some congregations, only the* שליח ציבור*) kneels on the floor at* כּוֹרְעִים.

וַאֲנַחְנוּ כּוֹרְעִים וּמִשְׁתַּחֲוִים וּמוֹדִים
לִפְנֵי מֶלֶךְ מַלְכֵי הַמְּלָכִים, הַקָּדוֹשׁ בָּרוּךְ הוּא
שֶׁהוּא נוֹטֶה שָׁמַיִם וְיוֹסֵד אָרֶץ
וּמוֹשַׁב יְקָרוֹ בַּשָּׁמַיִם מִמַּעַל, וּשְׁכִינַת עֻזּוֹ בְּגָבְהֵי מְרוֹמִים.

*In some congregations, the* שליח ציבור *says* אַתָּה הָרְאֵתָ *(below) while the* קהל *continues here with* הוּא אֱלֹהֵינוּ.

הוּא אֱלֹהֵינוּ, אֵין עוֹד.
אֱמֶת מַלְכֵּנוּ, אֶפֶס זוּלָתוֹ, כַּכָּתוּב בְּתוֹרָתוֹ
דברים ד וְיָדַעְתָּ הַיּוֹם וַהֲשֵׁבֹתָ אֶל־לְבָבֶךָ
כִּי יהוה הוּא הָאֱלֹהִים בַּשָּׁמַיִם מִמַּעַל וְעַל־הָאָרֶץ מִתָּחַת
אֵין עוֹד:

---

*The* שליח ציבור *says the following while the* קהל *says* הוּא אֱלֹהֵינוּ *(above).*

אַתָּה הָרְאֵתָ לָדַעַת, כִּי יהוה הוּא הָאֱלֹהִים, אֵין עוֹד מִלְּבַדּוֹ: וְיָדַעְתָּ דברים ד
הַיּוֹם וַהֲשֵׁבֹתָ אֶל־לְבָבֶךָ, כִּי יהוה הוּא הָאֱלֹהִים בַּשָּׁמַיִם מִמַּעַל וְעַל־
הָאָרֶץ מִתָּחַת, אֵין עוֹד: שְׁמַע יִשְׂרָאֵל, יהוה אֱלֹהֵינוּ, יהוה אֶחָד: הֵן דברים ו דברים י
לַיהוה אֱלֹהֶיךָ הַשָּׁמַיִם וּשְׁמֵי הַשָּׁמָיִם, הָאָרֶץ וְכָל־אֲשֶׁר־בָּהּ: כִּי יהוה שם
אֱלֹהֵיכֶם הוּא אֱלֹהֵי הָאֱלֹהִים וַאֲדֹנֵי הָאֲדֹנִים, הָאֵל הַגָּדֹל הַגִּבֹּר וְהַנּוֹרָא
אֲשֶׁר לֹא־יִשָּׂא פָנִים וְלֹא יִקַּח שֹׁחַד: כִּי שֵׁם יהוה אֶקְרָא, הָבוּ גֹדֶל דברים לב
לֵאלֹהֵינוּ: יְהִי שֵׁם יהוה מְבֹרָךְ, מֵעַתָּה וְעַד־עוֹלָם: תהלים קיג

---

*The* ארון קודש *is closed.*

*A prefatory piyut before the verses of Malkhiyot, Zikhronot and Shofarot, the core of the day's service, in which the congregation asks that the prayers of the Leader be accepted.*

אֱלֹהֵינוּ Our God and the God of our forefathers:
May You stand by the mouths of the emissaries of Your nation,
the house of Israel,
who stand before You to entreat You with prayer and supplication
on behalf of Your nation, the house of Israel.

Instruct them in what to say,
lend them understanding that they may know what to speak.
Let them know what they might ask You,
make known to them how they might glorify You.
May they walk in the light of Your countenance, *Ps. 89*
may they bend their knees before You.
May they bless Your nation with their speech,
and may they all receive blessing through Your uttered blessings.

May they pass Your nation before You,
while they stand in the midst of the congregation.
The eyes of Your nation hang on their word,
and their eyes await You in turn.
They approach the Holy Ark in fear, / trying to abate Your anger and wrath.
Your nation surrounds them as a wall,
and You on high, shall gaze upon them compassionately.

They raise their eyes heavenward to You,
and pour out their hearts like water before You.
And You shall hear them from the heavens. *II Chr. 6*

*In many congregations the following (until "O Lord of Israel") is said quietly by all.*

Please, do not allow their tongues to falter,
may their words not ensnare them.
And may they not be ashamed of their congregation, their support,
and may their congregation not be ashamed of them.
And may their mouths utter no words that negate Your will.
For those You show favor, Lord our God, are graced,
and it is those whom You teach who are learned.

כְּמָה שֶׁיָּדַעְנוּ Just as we have known, O Lord, that You show grace to those You favor, and compassion to those You deem deserving of compassion. As it is written in Your Torah, "And He said, I shall cause all My good to pass *Ex. 33* before you and I shall call out the Tetragrammaton before you, and I will show grace to those I favor and compassion to those I deem deserving of

*A prefatory piyut before the verses of מלכיות זכרונות ושופרות, the core of the day's service, in which the קהל asks that the prayers of the שליח ציבור be accepted.*

אֱלֹהֵינוּ וֵאלֹהֵי אֲבוֹתֵינוּ
הֱיֵה עִם פִּיפִיּוֹת שְׁלוּחֵי עַמְּךָ בֵּית יִשְׂרָאֵל
הָעוֹמְדִים לְבַקֵּשׁ תְּפִלָּה וְתַחֲנוּנִים מִלְּפָנֶיךָ עַל עַמְּךָ בֵּית יִשְׂרָאֵל.

הוֹרֵם מַה שֶּׁיֹּאמְרוּ / הֲבִינֵם מַה שֶּׁיְּדַבֵּרוּ
הֲשִׁיבֵם מַה שֶּׁיִּשְׁאֲלוּ / יַדְּעֵם הֵיךְ יְפָאֵרוּ.

תהלים פט בְּאוֹר פָּנֶיךָ יְהַלֵּכוּן / בֶּרֶךְ לְךָ יִבְרְכוּן
עַמְּךָ בְּפִיהֶם יְבָרְכוּן / וּמִבִּרְכוֹת פִּיךָ כֻּלָּם יִתְבָּרְכוּן.

עַמְּךָ לְפָנֶיךָ יַעֲבִירוּן / וְהֵם בַּתָּוֶךְ יַעֲבֹרוּן
עֵינֵי עַמְּךָ בָּם תְּלוּיוֹת / וְעֵינֵיהֶם לְךָ מְיַחֲלוֹת.

גָּשִׁים מוּל אֲרוֹן הַקֹּדֶשׁ בְּאֵימָה / לְשַׁכֵּךְ כַּעַס וְחֵימָה
וְעַמְּךָ מַסְבִּיבִים אוֹתָם כַּחוֹמָה /
וְאַתָּה מִן הַשָּׁמַיִם תַּשְׁגִּיחַ, אוֹתָם לְרַחֲמָה.

עַיִן נוֹשְׂאִים לְךָ לַשָּׁמַיִם / לֵב שׁוֹפְכִים נִכְחֲךָ כַּמַּיִם
דברי הימים ב, ו וְאַתָּה תִּשְׁמַע מִן הַשָּׁמַיִם.

*In many congregations the following (until אֱלֹהֵי יִשְׂרָאֵל) is said quietly by all.*

שֶׁלֹּא יִכָּשְׁלוּ בִלְשׁוֹנָם / וְלֹא יִנָּקְשׁוּ בְשִׁנּוּנָם
וְלֹא יֵבוֹשׁוּ בְּמַשְׁעֵנָם / וְלֹא יִכָּלְמוּ בָם שְׁאוֹנָם
וְאַל יֹאמַר פִּיהֶם דָּבָר שֶׁלֹּא כִרְצוֹנֶךָ.
כִּי חֲנוּנֶיךָ יהוה אֱלֹהֵינוּ הֵמָּה חֲנוּנִים /
וּמְלֻמָּדֶיךָ הֵמָּה מְלֻמָּדִים.

כְּמָה שֶּׁיָּדַעְנוּ יהוה אֱלֹהֵינוּ, אֵת אֲשֶׁר תָּחֹן יוּחָן, וְאֵת אֲשֶׁר תְּרַחֵם
שמות לג יְרֻחָם. כַּכָּתוּב בְּתוֹרָתֶךָ: וַיֹּאמֶר, אֲנִי אַעֲבִיר כָּל־טוּבִי עַל־פָּנֶיךָ,
וְקָרָאתִי בְשֵׁם יהוה לְפָנֶיךָ, וְחַנֹּתִי אֶת־אֲשֶׁר אָחֹן וְרִחַמְתִּי אֶת־

compassion." And it is written, "May those who await You not be ashamed of Ps. 69
me, O God, LORD of hosts; may those who seek You out not be humiliated
through me, O LORD of Israel."

*The Ark is opened.*

*A second prefatory piyut, said by the Leader.*

אוֹחִילָה I shall await the LORD, I shall entreat His favor,
I shall ask Him to grant my tongue eloquence.

אֲשֶׁר In the midst of the congregated nation I shall sing of His strength;
I shall burst out in joyous melodies for His works.

לְאָדָם The thoughts in man's heart are his to arrange, Prov. 16
but the tongue's eloquence comes from the LORD.

אֲדֹנָי O LORD, open my lips, Ps. 51
so that my mouth may declare Your praise.

*In some congregations, the following verse is said quietly.*

יִהְיוּ May the words of my mouth and the meditation of my heart Ps. 19
find favor before You, LORD, my Rock and Redeemer.

*The Ark is closed.*

*Some congregations say a prefatory piyut before the Malkhiyot verses.*
*On a Sunday, "Ansikha Malki" on page 1032; on other days, "Ahalela" on page 1068.*

וְעַל כֵּן Therefore, we place our hope in You, LORD our God,
that we may soon see the glory of Your power,
when You will remove abominations from the earth,
and idols will be utterly destroyed,
when the world will be perfected
under the sovereignty of the Almighty,
when all humanity will call on Your name,
to turn all the earth's wicked toward You.
All the world's inhabitants will realize and know
that to You every knee must bow and every tongue swear loyalty.
Before You, LORD our God, they will kneel and bow down
and give honor to Your glorious name.
They will all accept the yoke of Your kingdom,
and You will reign over them soon and for ever.

אֲשֶׁר אֲרַחֵם: וְנֶאֱמַר: אַל־יֵבֹשׁוּ בִי קֹוֶיךָ, אֲדֹנָי יֱהֹוִה צְבָאוֹת, תהלים סט
אַל־יִכָּלְמוּ בִי מְבַקְשֶׁיךָ, אֱלֹהֵי יִשְׂרָאֵל:

*The* ארון קודש *is opened.*

*A second prefatory piyut, said by the* שליח ציבור.

אוֹחִילָה לָאֵל, אֲחַלֶּה פָנָיו
אֶשְׁאֲלָה מִמֶּנּוּ מַעֲנֵה לָשׁוֹן.

אֲשֶׁר בִּקְהַל עָם אָשִׁירָה עֻזּוֹ
אַבִּיעָה רְנָנוֹת בְּעַד מִפְעָלָיו.

משלי טז לְאָדָם מַעַרְכֵי־לֵב וּמֵיהוה מַעֲנֵה לָשׁוֹן:

תהלים נא אֲדֹנָי, שְׂפָתַי תִּפְתָּח, וּפִי יַגִּיד תְּהִלָּתֶךָ:

*In some congregations, the following verse is said quietly.*

תהלים יט יִהְיוּ לְרָצוֹן אִמְרֵי־פִי וְהֶגְיוֹן לִבִּי לְפָנֶיךָ, יהוה צוּרִי וְגֹאֲלִי:

*The* ארון קודש *is closed.*

*Some congregations say a prefatory piyut before the* מלכיות *verses.*
*On a Sunday,* אַנְסִיכָה מַלְכִּי *on page 1032; on other days,* אֲהַלְלָה *on page 1068.*

וְעַל כֵּן נְקַוֶּה לְּךָ יהוה אֱלֹהֵינוּ, לִרְאוֹת מְהֵרָה בְּתִפְאֶרֶת עֻזֶּךָ
לְהַעֲבִיר גִּלּוּלִים מִן הָאָרֶץ, וְהָאֱלִילִים כָּרוֹת יִכָּרֵתוּן
לְתַקֵּן עוֹלָם בְּמַלְכוּת שַׁדַּי.
וְכָל בְּנֵי בָשָׂר יִקְרְאוּ בִשְׁמֶךָ לְהַפְנוֹת אֵלֶיךָ כָּל רִשְׁעֵי אָרֶץ.
יַכִּירוּ וְיֵדְעוּ כָּל יוֹשְׁבֵי תֵבֵל
כִּי לְךָ תִּכְרַע כָּל בֶּרֶךְ, תִּשָּׁבַע כָּל לָשׁוֹן.
לְפָנֶיךָ יהוה אֱלֹהֵינוּ יִכְרְעוּ וְיִפֹּלוּ, וְלִכְבוֹד שִׁמְךָ יְקָר יִתֵּנוּ
וִיקַבְּלוּ כֻלָּם אֶת עֹל מַלְכוּתֶךָ
וְתִמְלֹךְ עֲלֵיהֶם מְהֵרָה לְעוֹלָם וָעֶד.

VERSES OF MALKHIYOT

For the kingdom is Yours,
and to all eternity You will reign in glory,
as it is written in Your Torah:
"The LORD will reign for ever and ever." *Ex. 15*

And it is said:
He saw no injustice in Jacob, *Num. 23*
no deceit did He witness in Israel,
the LORD their God is with them,
and a King's adulation resounds among them.

And it is said:
[The LORD] became King in Yeshurun, *Deut. 33*
when the heads of the people gathered,
all the tribes of Israel together.

And in Your holy Writings it is said,
For kingship is the LORD's *Ps. 22*
and He rules over the nations.

And it is said:
The LORD reigns. He is robed in majesty. *Ps. 93*
The LORD is robed, girded with strength.
The world is firmly established;
it cannot be moved.

And it is said:
Lift up your heads, O gates; be uplifted, eternal doors, *Ps. 24*
so that the King of glory may enter.
Who is the King of glory?
It is the LORD, strong and mighty,
the LORD mighty in battle.
Lift up your heads, O gates; lift them up, eternal doors,
so that the King of glory may enter.
Who is He, the King of glory?
The LORD of hosts, He is the King of glory, Selah!

פסוקי מלכיות

## כִּי הַמַּלְכוּת שֶׁלְּךָ הִיא וּלְעוֹלְמֵי עַד תִּמְלֹךְ בְּכָבוֹד
## כַּכָּתוּב בְּתוֹרָתֶךָ

יהוה יִמְלֹךְ לְעֹלָם וָעֶד: שמות טו

**וְנֶאֱמַר**

לֹא־הִבִּיט אָוֶן בְּיַעֲקֹב, וְלֹא־רָאָה עָמָל בְּיִשְׂרָאֵל במדבר כג
יהוה אֱלֹהָיו עִמּוֹ, וּתְרוּעַת מֶלֶךְ בּוֹ:

**וְנֶאֱמַר**

וַיְהִי בִישֻׁרוּן מֶלֶךְ, בְּהִתְאַסֵּף רָאשֵׁי עָם דברים לג
יַחַד שִׁבְטֵי יִשְׂרָאֵל:

**וּבְדִבְרֵי קָדְשְׁךָ כָּתוּב לֵאמֹר**

כִּי לַיהוה הַמְּלוּכָה וּמֹשֵׁל בַּגּוֹיִם: תהלים כב

**וְנֶאֱמַר**

יהוה מָלָךְ, גֵּאוּת לָבֵשׁ תהלים צג
לָבֵשׁ יהוה עֹז הִתְאַזָּר, אַף־תִּכּוֹן תֵּבֵל בַּל־תִּמּוֹט:

**וְנֶאֱמַר**

שְׂאוּ שְׁעָרִים רָאשֵׁיכֶם, וְהִנָּשְׂאוּ פִּתְחֵי עוֹלָם תהלים כד
וְיָבוֹא מֶלֶךְ הַכָּבוֹד:
מִי זֶה מֶלֶךְ הַכָּבוֹד, יהוה עִזּוּז וְגִבּוֹר
יהוה גִּבּוֹר מִלְחָמָה:
שְׂאוּ שְׁעָרִים רָאשֵׁיכֶם, וּשְׂאוּ פִּתְחֵי עוֹלָם
וְיָבֹא מֶלֶךְ הַכָּבוֹד:
מִי הוּא זֶה מֶלֶךְ הַכָּבוֹד
יהוה צְבָאוֹת הוּא מֶלֶךְ הַכָּבוֹד סֶלָה:

And by Your servants the prophets it is written:
This is what the LORD, King of Israel and its Savior, *Is. 44*
the LORD of hosts has said:
"I am the first and I shall be the last,
and there is no other god but Me."

And it is said:
Saviors shall go up to Mount Zion *Ob. 1*
to judge Mount Esau,
and the LORD's shall be the kingdom.

And it is said:
Then shall the LORD be King over all the earth. *Zech. 14*
On that day shall the LORD be One
and His name One.

And in Your Torah it is written:
Listen, Israel: the LORD is our God, *Deut. 6*
the LORD is One.

אֱלֹהֵינוּ Our God and God of our ancestors,
rule over all the world in Your honor,
and be raised above all the earth in Your glory,
and appear, in the splendor of Your great might
before all those who live in this world, Your domain.
And all who were made will know that You made them,
and all who were formed will know that You formed them,
and all that have breath in their mouths will declare:
The LORD, God of Israel is King,
and His kingship has dominion over all.
Make us holy through Your commandments
and grant us our share in Your Torah.
Satisfy us with Your goodness, grant our souls joy in Your salvation,
and purify our hearts to serve You in truth.
For You, LORD, are truth, and Your word is truth
and holds true forever.
Blessed are You, LORD, King over all the earth,
who sanctifies Israel and the Day of Remembrance.

וְעַל יְדֵי עֲבָדֶיךָ הַנְּבִיאִים כָּתוּב לֵאמֹר

כֹּה־אָמַר יהוה מֶלֶךְ־יִשְׂרָאֵל וְגֹאֲלוֹ, יהוה צְבָאוֹת ישעיה מד
אֲנִי רִאשׁוֹן וַאֲנִי אַחֲרוֹן, וּמִבַּלְעָדַי אֵין אֱלֹהִים:

וְנֶאֱמַר

וְעָלוּ מוֹשִׁעִים בְּהַר צִיּוֹן לִשְׁפֹּט אֶת־הַר עֵשָׂו עובדיה א
וְהָיְתָה לַיהוה הַמְּלוּכָה:

וְנֶאֱמַר

וְהָיָה יהוה לְמֶלֶךְ עַל־כָּל־הָאָרֶץ זכריה יד
בַּיּוֹם הַהוּא יִהְיֶה יהוה אֶחָד וּשְׁמוֹ אֶחָד:

וּבְתוֹרָתְךָ כָּתוּב לֵאמֹר

שְׁמַע יִשְׂרָאֵל, יהוה אֱלֹהֵינוּ יהוה אֶחָד: דברים ו

אֱלֹהֵינוּ וֵאלֹהֵי אֲבוֹתֵינוּ
מְלֹךְ עַל כָּל הָעוֹלָם כֻּלּוֹ בִּכְבוֹדֶךָ
וְהִנָּשֵׂא עַל כָּל הָאָרֶץ בִּיקָרֶךָ
וְהוֹפַע בַּהֲדַר גְּאוֹן עֻזֶּךָ עַל כָּל יוֹשְׁבֵי תֵבֵל אַרְצֶךָ.
וְיֵדַע כָּל פָּעוּל כִּי אַתָּה פְעַלְתּוֹ
וְיָבִין כָּל יָצוּר כִּי אַתָּה יְצַרְתּוֹ
וְיֹאמַר כֹּל אֲשֶׁר נְשָׁמָה בְאַפּוֹ
יהוה אֱלֹהֵי יִשְׂרָאֵל מֶלֶךְ וּמַלְכוּתוֹ בַּכֹּל מָשָׁלָה.
קַדְּשֵׁנוּ בְּמִצְוֹתֶיךָ וְתֵן חֶלְקֵנוּ בְּתוֹרָתֶךָ
שַׂבְּעֵנוּ מִטּוּבֶךָ וְשַׂמַּח נַפְשֵׁנוּ בִּישׁוּעָתֶךָ
וְטַהֵר לִבֵּנוּ לְעָבְדְּךָ בֶּאֱמֶת
כִּי אַתָּה אֱלֹהִים אֱמֶת, וּדְבָרְךָ אֱמֶת וְקַיָּם לָעַד.
בָּרוּךְ אַתָּה יהוה, מֶלֶךְ עַל כָּל הָאָרֶץ
מְקַדֵּשׁ יִשְׂרָאֵל וְיוֹם הַזִּכָּרוֹן.

*The congregation stands and the shofar is sounded.*

| | | |
|---|---|---|
| TEKIA | SHEVARIM TERUA | TEKIA |
| TEKIA | SHEVARIM | TEKIA |
| TEKIA | TERUA | TEKIA |

*The congregation, then the Leader:*

היום This day is the birth of the world.
This day stands all the world's creations up in judgment,
stands them as sons or as slaves –
If as sons, have compassion for us,
as a father has compassion for his sons.
And if as slaves, our eyes are raised and fixed on You
until You show us favor, and bring out our judgment like sunlight,
Awesome, Holy.

*The congregation, then the Leader:*

אֲרֶשֶׁת May our mouths' words rise beautiful before You,
most high and elevated God, who understands and heeds,
looks on and listens to the sounds of our shofarot.
Accept, with compassion and favor, our Order of the Kingship.

*Some congregations say a prefatory piyut before the Zikhronot. On a Sunday, "Zekher Teḥilat Kol Ma'as" on page 1034; on other days, "Efḥad Bema'asai" on page 1070.*

REMEMBRANCES

אַתָּה זוֹכֵר You remember the making of the world;
You come to all those formed long ago.
Under Your gaze, all hidden things come to light,
all the many secrets buried since the Beginning.
For nothing is forgotten before the throne of Your glory,
and nothing is hidden from Your eyes.

---

God. What else has he to depend on? And how hard it is for a rich man to depend on God. All his possessions call out to him: Depend on us.

*The* קהל *stands and the* שופר *is sounded.*

| | | |
|---|---|---|
| תקיעה | שברים תרועה | תקיעה |
| תקיעה | שברים | תקיעה |
| תקיעה | תרועה | תקיעה |

*The* קהל*, then the* שליח ציבור*:*

הַיּוֹם הֲרַת עוֹלָם, הַיּוֹם יַעֲמִיד בַּמִּשְׁפָּט כָּל יְצוּרֵי עוֹלָמִים
אִם כְּבָנִים אִם כַּעֲבָדִים.
אִם כְּבָנִים, רַחֲמֵנוּ כְּרַחֵם אָב עַל בָּנִים
וְאִם כַּעֲבָדִים, עֵינֵינוּ לְךָ תְלוּיוֹת עַד שֶׁתְּחָנֵּנוּ
וְתוֹצִיא כָאוֹר מִשְׁפָּטֵנוּ, אָיֹם קָדוֹשׁ.

*The* קהל*, then the* שליח ציבור*:*

אֲרֶשֶׁת שְׂפָתֵינוּ יֶעֱרַב לְפָנֶיךָ
אֵל רָם וְנִשָּׂא, מֵבִין וּמַאֲזִין, מַבִּיט וּמַקְשִׁיב לְקוֹל תְּקִיעָתֵנוּ.
וּתְקַבֵּל בְּרַחֲמִים וּבְרָצוֹן סֵדֶר מַלְכִיּוֹתֵינוּ.

*Some congregations say a prefatory piyut before the* זכרונות*.*
*On a Sunday,* זֵכֶר תְּחִלַּת כָּל מַעַשׂ *on page 1034; on other days,* אֶפְחַד בְּמַעֲשַׂי *on page 1070.*

זכרונות

אַתָּה זוֹכֵר מַעֲשֵׂה עוֹלָם, וּפוֹקֵד כָּל יְצוּרֵי קֶדֶם
לְפָנֶיךָ נִגְלוּ כָּל תַּעֲלוּמוֹת וַהֲמוֹן נִסְתָּרוֹת שֶׁמִּבְּרֵאשִׁית
כִּי אֵין שִׁכְחָה לִפְנֵי כִסֵּא כְבוֹדֶךָ וְאֵין נִסְתָּר מִנֶּגֶד עֵינֶיךָ.

---

וְאִם כַּעֲבָדִים, עֵינֵינוּ לְךָ תְלוּיוֹת *And if as slaves, our eyes are raised and fixed on You.* Rabbi Moshe Leib of Sasov said: How easy it is for a poor man to depend on

You remember all of creation,
and all things that were formed – none is shrouded from You.
All is revealed and known before You, LORD our God,
who gaze and look on to the last of all the ages.
For You bring a day decreed for remembrance
to come to each spirit and soul;
that Your many works shall be remembered,
Your numerous, endless creations.
From the very beginning You made it known,
long before this time You revealed it,
for this day is the opening of all Your works,
a remembrance of the very first day.
"For it is a decree for Israel, an ordinance of the God of Jacob." *Ps. 81*
And on it, it is said of every province
which will come to the sword and which to peace,
which will succumb to hunger and which find plenty.
And all creations are regarded on this day;
remembered for life, or for death.

מִי לֹא נִפְקַד Who may be overlooked on this day,
when the memory of every being formed comes before You;
each person's works, his purpose, the path that he chooses and follows?
the thoughts and the plans of all mankind,
and the impulses behind each person's acts?
Happy the one who does not forget You,
the child of man who takes courage in You.
For one who seeks You will never stumble,
they need never be ashamed, who seek shelter in You.
For the memory of all that You have made passes before You,
You examine what each one does.

וְגַם And Noah also, You remembered with love,
and You came to him with words of salvation, compassion,
when You brought on the waters of the great flood,
to destroy all creatures of flesh
because the practices they followed were corrupt.
And so let [Noah's] memory come to You, LORD our God,
that You multiply His children like the dust of the earth,
his descendants like sand of the sea.

אַתָּה זוֹכֵר אֶת כָּל הַמִּפְעָל, וְגַם כָּל הַיְצוּר לֹא נִכְחַד מִמֶּךָּ.
הַכֹּל גָּלוּי וְיָדוּעַ לְפָנֶיךָ יהוה אֱלֹהֵינוּ
צוֹפֶה וּמַבִּיט עַד סוֹף כָּל הַדּוֹרוֹת
כִּי תָבִיא חֹק זִכָּרוֹן לְהִפָּקֵד כָּל רוּחַ וָנֶפֶשׁ
לְהִזָּכֵר מַעֲשִׂים רַבִּים, וַהֲמוֹן בְּרִיּוֹת לְאֵין תַּכְלִית.
מֵרֵאשִׁית כָּזֹאת הוֹדַעְתָּ וּמִלְּפָנִים אוֹתָהּ גִּלִּיתָ.
זֶה הַיּוֹם תְּחִלַּת מַעֲשֶׂיךָ, זִכָּרוֹן לְיוֹם רִאשׁוֹן
כִּי חֹק לְיִשְׂרָאֵל הוּא, מִשְׁפָּט לֵאלֹהֵי יַעֲקֹב: תהלים פא
וְעַל הַמְּדִינוֹת בּוֹ יֵאָמֵר
אֵיזוֹ לַחֶרֶב, וְאֵיזוֹ לַשָּׁלוֹם
אֵיזוֹ לָרָעָב, וְאֵיזוֹ לַשֹּׂבַע
וּבְרִיּוֹת בּוֹ יִפָּקֵדוּ, לְהַזְכִּירָם לְחַיִּים וְלַמָּוֶת.

מִי לֹא נִפְקַד כְּהַיּוֹם הַזֶּה
כִּי זֵכֶר כָּל הַיְצוּר לְפָנֶיךָ בָּא
מַעֲשֵׂה אִישׁ וּפְקֻדָּתוֹ, וַעֲלִילוֹת מִצְעֲדֵי גָבֶר
מַחְשְׁבוֹת אָדָם וְתַחְבּוּלוֹתָיו, וְיִצְרֵי מַעַלְלֵי אִישׁ.
אַשְׁרֵי אִישׁ שֶׁלֹּא יִשְׁכָּחֶךָּ, וּבֶן אָדָם יִתְאַמֶּץ בָּךְ
כִּי דוֹרְשֶׁיךָ לְעוֹלָם לֹא יִכָּשֵׁלוּ
וְלֹא יִכָּלְמוּ לָנֶצַח כָּל הַחוֹסִים בָּךְ.
כִּי זֵכֶר כָּל הַמַּעֲשִׂים לְפָנֶיךָ בָּא, וְאַתָּה דוֹרֵשׁ מַעֲשֵׂה כֻלָּם.

וְגַם אֶת נֹחַ בְּאַהֲבָה זָכַרְתָּ, וַתִּפְקְדֵהוּ בִּדְבַר יְשׁוּעָה וְרַחֲמִים
בַּהֲבִיאֲךָ אֶת מֵי הַמַּבּוּל לְשַׁחֵת כָּל בָּשָׂר מִפְּנֵי רֹעַ מַעַלְלֵיהֶם
עַל כֵּן זִכְרוֹנוֹ בָּא לְפָנֶיךָ, יהוה אֱלֹהֵינוּ
לְהַרְבּוֹת זַרְעוֹ כְּעַפְרוֹת תֵּבֵל, וְצֶאֱצָאָיו כְּחוֹל הַיָּם.

VERSES OF ZIKHRONOT

As it is written in Your Torah:

“God remembered Noah and all the animals *Gen. 8*
and all the cattle that were with him in the ark,
and God made a wind blow across the earth,
and the waters grew calm.”

And it is said:

“God heard their groaning, *Ex. 2*
and God remembered His covenant
with Abraham, with Isaac and with Jacob.”

And it is said:

“I will remember My covenant with Jacob, *Lev. 26*
and also My covenant with Isaac,
and also My covenant with Abraham I will remember,
and the land I will remember.”

And in Your holy Writings it is written thus:

“He has made remembrance for His wonders; *Ps. 111*
gracious and compassionate is the Lord.”

And it is said:

“He has given food to those who revere Him, *Ibid.*
He will remember His covenant forever.”

And it is said:

“He remembered His covenant for their sake, *Ps. 106*
and relented in His great love.”

And by Your servants the prophets it is written:

“Go and call out to Jerusalem, *Jer. 2*
This is what the Lord has said.
‘I remember of you the kindness of your youth,
your love when you were a bride;
how you walked after Me in the desert,
through a land not sown.’”

And it is said:

“I will remember the covenant I had with you *Ezek. 16*
in the days of your youth,
and I will establish with you an everlasting covenant.”

פסוקי זכרונות

כַּכָּתוּב בְּתוֹרָתֶךָ

וַיִּזְכֹּר אֱלֹהִים אֶת־נֹחַ בראשית ח

וְאֵת כָּל־הַחַיָּה וְאֶת־כָּל־הַבְּהֵמָה אֲשֶׁר אִתּוֹ בַּתֵּבָה

וַיַּעֲבֵר אֱלֹהִים רוּחַ עַל־הָאָרֶץ, וַיָּשֹׁכּוּ הַמָּיִם:

וְנֶאֱמַר

וַיִּשְׁמַע אֱלֹהִים אֶת־נַאֲקָתָם שמות ב

וַיִּזְכֹּר אֱלֹהִים אֶת־בְּרִיתוֹ

אֶת־אַבְרָהָם אֶת־יִצְחָק וְאֶת־יַעֲקֹב:

וְנֶאֱמַר

וְזָכַרְתִּי אֶת־בְּרִיתִי יַעֲקוֹב ויקרא כו

וְאַף אֶת־בְּרִיתִי יִצְחָק, וְאַף אֶת־בְּרִיתִי אַבְרָהָם אֶזְכֹּר

וְהָאָרֶץ אֶזְכֹּר:

וּבְדִבְרֵי קָדְשְׁךָ כָּתוּב לֵאמֹר

זֵכֶר עָשָׂה לְנִפְלְאוֹתָיו, חַנּוּן וְרַחוּם יהוה: תהלים קיא

וְנֶאֱמַר

טֶרֶף נָתַן לִירֵאָיו, יִזְכֹּר לְעוֹלָם בְּרִיתוֹ: שם

וְנֶאֱמַר

וַיִּזְכֹּר לָהֶם בְּרִיתוֹ, וַיִּנָּחֵם כְּרֹב חֲסָדָו: תהלים קו

וְעַל יְדֵי עֲבָדֶיךָ הַנְּבִיאִים כָּתוּב לֵאמֹר

הָלֹךְ וְקָרָאתָ בְאָזְנֵי יְרוּשָׁלַיִם לֵאמֹר ירמיה ב

כֹּה אָמַר יהוה, זָכַרְתִּי לָךְ חֶסֶד נְעוּרַיִךְ, אַהֲבַת כְּלוּלֹתָיִךְ

לֶכְתֵּךְ אַחֲרַי בַּמִּדְבָּר, בְּאֶרֶץ לֹא זְרוּעָה:

וְנֶאֱמַר

וְזָכַרְתִּי אֲנִי אֶת־בְּרִיתִי אוֹתָךְ בִּימֵי נְעוּרָיִךְ יחזקאל טז

וַהֲקִימוֹתִי לָךְ בְּרִית עוֹלָם:

And it is said:

"'Is Ephraim not a treasured son to Me, My child of delights? *Jer. 31*
As I speak of him, always, I remember him again.
And so it is that I long for him within,
I will tender him compassion,' says the LORD."

אֱלֹהֵינוּ Our God and God of our ancestors,
remember us with a favorable memory,
and recall us with a remembrance of salvation and compassion
from the highest ancient heaven.
Remember for our sake, LORD our God,
the covenant, the loving-kindness,
and the oath that You swore to Abraham our father on Mount Moriah,
And let the image of that binding,
when our father Abraham bound Isaac his son upon the altar,
be present before You;
when he suppressed his compassion, to do Your will wholeheartedly.
So, too, let Your compassion wrest Your anger from us,
and in Your great goodness
may Your anger be turned away from Your people,
Your city, Your land and Your inheritance.
Fulfill for us, LORD our God, the promise You made in Your Torah,
at the hand of Moses Your servant
and by Your own word, as it is said:

"And I remembered, for their sake, the covenant of the early ones, *Lev. 26*
whom I brought out of the land of Egypt
before the eyes of all nations,
to be God to them, I am the LORD."

כִּי זוֹכֵר For it has always been You who remembered all forgotten things,
and there is no forgetfulness before the throne of Your glory,
and today in Your compassion, You remember
the binding of Isaac, for his descendants' sake.
Blessed are You, LORD, who remembers the covenant.

---

to do anything for them," he said, "and now they won't have anything to do with me." Silently the rabbi raised his eyes to Heaven. "That's how it is," he said softly. "The father shares in the sorrow of his sons, but the sons do not share in the sorrow of their father."

וְנֶאֱמַר

הֲבֵן יַקִּיר לִי אֶפְרַיִם, אִם יֶלֶד שַׁעֲשֻׁעִים ירמיה לא

כִּי־מִדֵּי דַבְּרִי בּוֹ, זָכֹר אֶזְכְּרֶנּוּ עוֹד

עַל־כֵּן הָמוּ מֵעַי לוֹ, רַחֵם אֲרַחֲמֶנּוּ נְאֻם־יהוה:

אֱלֹהֵינוּ וֵאלֹהֵי אֲבוֹתֵינוּ זָכְרֵנוּ בְּזִכְרוֹן טוֹב לְפָנֶיךָ

וּפָקְדֵנוּ בִּפְקֻדַּת יְשׁוּעָה וְרַחֲמִים מִשְּׁמֵי שְׁמֵי קֶדֶם

וּזְכָר לָנוּ יהוה אֱלֹהֵינוּ אֶת הַבְּרִית וְאֶת הַחֶסֶד וְאֶת הַשְּׁבוּעָה

אֲשֶׁר נִשְׁבַּעְתָּ לְאַבְרָהָם אָבִינוּ בְּהַר הַמּוֹרִיָּה

וְתֵרָאֶה לְפָנֶיךָ עֲקֵדָה

שֶׁעָקַד אַבְרָהָם אָבִינוּ אֶת יִצְחָק בְּנוֹ עַל גַּבֵּי הַמִּזְבֵּחַ

וְכָבַשׁ רַחֲמָיו, לַעֲשׂוֹת רְצוֹנְךָ בְּלֵבָב שָׁלֵם.

כֵּן יִכְבְּשׁוּ רַחֲמֶיךָ אֶת כַּעַסְךָ מֵעָלֵינוּ

וּבְטוּבְךָ הַגָּדוֹל יָשׁוּב חֲרוֹן אַפְּךָ

מֵעַמְּךָ וּמֵעִירְךָ וּמֵאַרְצְךָ וּמִנַּחֲלָתֶךָ.

וְקַיֶּם לָנוּ יהוה אֱלֹהֵינוּ אֶת הַדָּבָר שֶׁהִבְטַחְתָּנוּ בְּתוֹרָתֶךָ

עַל יְדֵי מֹשֶׁה עַבְדֶּךָ מִפִּי כְבוֹדֶךָ, כָּאָמוּר

וְזָכַרְתִּי לָהֶם בְּרִית רִאשֹׁנִים ויקרא כו

אֲשֶׁר הוֹצֵאתִי־אֹתָם מֵאֶרֶץ מִצְרַיִם לְעֵינֵי הַגּוֹיִם

לִהְיוֹת לָהֶם לֵאלֹהִים, אֲנִי יהוה:

כִּי זוֹכֵר כָּל הַנִּשְׁכָּחוֹת אַתָּה הוּא מֵעוֹלָם

וְאֵין שִׁכְחָה לִפְנֵי כִסֵּא כְבוֹדֶךָ

וַעֲקֵדַת יִצְחָק לְזַרְעוֹ הַיּוֹם בְּרַחֲמִים תִּזְכֹּר.

בָּרוּךְ אַתָּה יהוה, זוֹכֵר הַבְּרִית.

---

עַל־כֵּן הָמוּ מֵעַי לוֹ *And so it is that I long for him within.* A man came to the Rabbi of Kotzk and complained of his sons who refused to support him, though he was old and no longer able to earn his own livelihood. “I was always ready

*The congregation stands and the shofar is sounded.*

| | | |
|---|---|---|
| TEKIA | SHEVARIM TERUA | TEKIA |
| TEKIA | SHEVARIM | TEKIA |
| TEKIA | TERUA | TEKIA |

*The congregation, then the Leader:*

הַיּוֹם This day is the birth of the world.
This day stands all the world's creations up in judgment,
stands them as sons or as slaves –
If as sons, have compassion for us,
as a father has compassion for his sons.
And if as slaves, our eyes are raised and fixed on You
until You show us favor, and bring out our judgment like sunlight,
Awesome, Holy.

*The congregation, then the Leader:*

אֲרֶשֶׁת May our mouths' words rise beautiful before You,
most high and elevated God, who understands and heeds,
looks on and listens to the sounds of our shofarot.
Accept, with compassion and favor, our Order of the Remembrances.

*Some congregations say a prefatory piyut before the Shofarot.*
*On a Sunday, "Esa De'i" on page 1037; on other days, "Anusa LeEzra" on page 1072.*

SHOFAROT

אַתָּה נִגְלֵיתָ You were revealed in a cloud of Your glory,
to Your holy nation, to speak with them.
Out of the heavens Your voice was heard;
You revealed Yourself in mists of purity.
And all the wide world quaked before You,
the works of creation shook in Your presence,
as You revealed Yourself, our King, on Mount Sinai,
to teach Your people Torah and the commandments,
to have them hear the majesty of Your voice –
Your sacred words amid flames of fire.
In thunder and lightning You revealed Yourself to them,
and amid the sound of the shofar You appeared.

*The* קהל *stands and the* שופר *is sounded.*

תקיעה שברים תרועה תקיעה

תקיעה שברים תקיעה

תקיעה תרועה תקיעה

*The* קהל*, then the* שליח ציבור*:*

הַיּוֹם הֲרַת עוֹלָם, הַיּוֹם יַעֲמִיד בַּמִּשְׁפָּט כָּל יְצוּרֵי עוֹלָמִים
אִם כְּבָנִים אִם כַּעֲבָדִים.
אִם כְּבָנִים, רַחֲמֵנוּ כְּרַחֵם אָב עַל בָּנִים
וְאִם כַּעֲבָדִים, עֵינֵינוּ לְךָ תְלוּיוֹת עַד שֶׁתְּחָנֵּנוּ
וְתוֹצִיא כָאוֹר מִשְׁפָּטֵנוּ, אָיֹם קָדוֹשׁ.

*The* קהל*, then the* שליח ציבור*:*

אֲרֶשֶׁת שְׂפָתֵינוּ יֶעֱרַב לְפָנֶיךָ
אֵל רָם וְנִשָּׂא, מֵבִין וּמַאֲזִין, מַבִּיט וּמַקְשִׁיב לְקוֹל תְּקִיעָתֵנוּ.
וּתְקַבֵּל בְּרַחֲמִים וּבְרָצוֹן סֵדֶר זִכְרוֹנוֹתֵינוּ.

*Some congregations say a prefatory piyut before the* שופרות*.*
*On a Sunday,* אֶשָּׂא דֵעִי*, on page 1037; on other days,* אֲנוּסָה לְעֶזְרָה *on page 1072.*

שופרות

אַתָּה נִגְלֵיתָ בַּעֲנַן כְּבוֹדֶךָ עַל עַם קָדְשְׁךָ לְדַבֵּר עִמָּם
מִן הַשָּׁמַיִם הִשְׁמַעְתָּם קוֹלֶךָ, וְנִגְלֵיתָ עֲלֵיהֶם בְּעַרְפִלֵּי טֹהַר.
גַּם כָּל הָעוֹלָם כֻּלּוֹ חָל מִפָּנֶיךָ, וּבְרִיּוֹת בְּרֵאשִׁית חָרְדוּ מִמֶּךָּ
בְּהִגָּלוֹתְךָ מַלְכֵּנוּ עַל הַר סִינַי, לְלַמֵּד לְעַמְּךָ תּוֹרָה וּמִצְוֹת
וַתַּשְׁמִיעֵם אֶת הוֹד קוֹלֶךָ, וְדִבְּרוֹת קָדְשְׁךָ מִלַּהֲבוֹת אֵשׁ.
בְּקוֹלוֹת וּבְרָקִים עֲלֵיהֶם נִגְלֵיתָ, וּבְקוֹל שׁוֹפָר עֲלֵיהֶם הוֹפָעְתָּ.

VERSES OF SHOFAROT

As it is written in Your Torah:

"Then on the third day, in the morning – *Ex. 19*
thunder and lightning; heavy cloud covered the mountain,
there was a very loud sound of the shofar,
and all of the people in the camp quaked."

And it is said:

"And the sound of the shofar grew ever louder – *Ibid.*
Moses spoke, and the LORD answered him with a voice."

And it is said:

"And all the people saw the thunder and the flames, *Ex. 20*
and the sound of the shofar, and the mountain asmoke;
the people saw and they staggered, and stood far back."

And by Your servants the prophets it is written:

"God has been raised up in sound; *Ps. 47*
raised, the LORD, in the voice of the shofar."

And it is said,

"With trumpets and the sound of the shofar, *Ps. 98*
shout for joy before the LORD, the King."

And it is said:

"Sound the shofar on the new moon, *Ps. 81*
on our feast day when the moon is hidden.
For it is a statute for Israel, an ordinance of the God of Jacob."

And it is said:

"Halleluya! Praise God in His holy place; *Ps. 150*
praise Him in the heavens of His power.
Praise Him for His mighty deeds;
praise Him for His surpassing greatness.
Praise Him with blasts of the shofar;
praise Him with the harp and lyre.
Praise Him with timbrel and dance;
praise Him with strings and flute.
Praise Him with clashing cymbals;
praise Him with resounding cymbals.
Let all that breathes praise the LORD. Halleluya!"

פסוקי שופרות

כַּכָּתוּב בְּתוֹרָתֶךָ

שמות יט
וַיְהִי בַיּוֹם הַשְּׁלִישִׁי בִּהְיֹת הַבֹּקֶר
וַיְהִי קֹלֹת וּבְרָקִים וְעָנָן כָּבֵד עַל־הָהָר
וְקֹל שֹׁפָר חָזָק מְאֹד, וַיֶּחֱרַד כָּל־הָעָם אֲשֶׁר בַּמַּחֲנֶה:

וְנֶאֱמַר

שם
וַיְהִי קוֹל הַשֹּׁפָר הוֹלֵךְ וְחָזֵק מְאֹד
מֹשֶׁה יְדַבֵּר, וְהָאֱלֹהִים יַעֲנֶנּוּ בְקוֹל:

וְנֶאֱמַר

שמות כ
וְכָל־הָעָם רֹאִים אֶת־הַקּוֹלֹת וְאֶת־הַלַּפִּידִם
וְאֵת קוֹל הַשֹּׁפָר, וְאֶת־הָהָר עָשֵׁן
וַיַּרְא הָעָם וַיָּנֻעוּ, וַיַּעַמְדוּ מֵרָחֹק:

וּבְדִבְרֵי קָדְשְׁךָ כָּתוּב לֵאמֹר

תהלים מז
עָלָה אֱלֹהִים בִּתְרוּעָה, יהוה בְּקוֹל שׁוֹפָר:

וְנֶאֱמַר

תהלים צח
בַּחֲצֹצְרוֹת וְקוֹל שׁוֹפָר, הָרִיעוּ לִפְנֵי הַמֶּלֶךְ יהוה:

וְנֶאֱמַר

תהלים פא
תִּקְעוּ בַחֹדֶשׁ שׁוֹפָר, בַּכֵּסֶה לְיוֹם חַגֵּנוּ:
כִּי חֹק לְיִשְׂרָאֵל הוּא, מִשְׁפָּט לֵאלֹהֵי יַעֲקֹב:

וְנֶאֱמַר

תהלים קנ
הַלְלוּיָהּ, הַלְלוּ־אֵל בְּקָדְשׁוֹ    הַלְלוּהוּ בִּרְקִיעַ עֻזּוֹ:
הַלְלוּהוּ בִגְבוּרֹתָיו    הַלְלוּהוּ כְּרֹב גֻּדְלוֹ:
הַלְלוּהוּ בְּתֵקַע שׁוֹפָר    הַלְלוּהוּ בְּנֵבֶל וְכִנּוֹר:
הַלְלוּהוּ בְתֹף וּמָחוֹל    הַלְלוּהוּ בְּמִנִּים וְעֻגָב:
הַלְלוּהוּ בְצִלְצְלֵי־שָׁמַע    הַלְלוּהוּ בְּצִלְצְלֵי תְרוּעָה:
כֹּל הַנְּשָׁמָה תְּהַלֵּל יָהּ, הַלְלוּיָהּ:

And by Your servants the prophets it is written:
"All the inhabitants of the world, *Is. 18*
all the dwellers on this earth,
when He lifts up a banner on the mountains,
you will see it,
and when He sounds the shofar you shall hear."
And it is said:
"On that day a great shofar will be sounded, *Is. 27*
and those who are lost will come from the land of Assyria,
and those who were banished, from the land of Egypt,
and they will worship the LORD
at the holy mountain in Jerusalem."
And it is said:
"The LORD will appear to them, *Zech. 9*
His arrow will come out like lightning,
and the LORD God will sound the shofar,
and will move in stormwinds of the south.
The LORD of hosts will protect them –"
so, protect Your people Israel with Your peace.

אֱלֹהֵינוּ Our God and God of our ancestors,
sound the great shofar for our freedom,
raise high the banner to gather our exiles,
bring close our scattered ones from among the nations,
and gather our exiles from the very ends of the earth.
Bring us to Zion, Your city, in joy,
and to Jerusalem, Your Temple,
in everlasting happiness.
There we will prepare for You our obligatory offerings,
as we were commanded in Your Torah,
at the hand of Your servant Moses
and by Your own word,
as it is said:

וְעַל יְדֵי עֲבָדֶיךָ הַנְּבִיאִים כָּתוּב לֵאמֹר

כָּל־יֹשְׁבֵי תֵבֵל וְשֹׁכְנֵי אָרֶץ ישעיה יח
כִּנְשֹׂא־נֵס הָרִים תִּרְאוּ, וְכִתְקֹעַ שׁוֹפָר תִּשְׁמָעוּ:

וְנֶאֱמַר

וְהָיָה בַּיּוֹם הַהוּא יִתָּקַע בְּשׁוֹפָר גָּדוֹל ישעיה כז
וּבָאוּ הָאֹבְדִים בְּאֶרֶץ אַשּׁוּר
וְהַנִּדָּחִים בְּאֶרֶץ מִצְרָיִם
וְהִשְׁתַּחֲווּ לַיהוה בְּהַר הַקֹּדֶשׁ בִּירוּשָׁלָם:

וְנֶאֱמַר

וַיהוה עֲלֵיהֶם יֵרָאֶה, וְיָצָא כַבָּרָק חִצּוֹ זכריה ט
וַאדֹנָי יֱהֹוִה בַּשּׁוֹפָר יִתְקָע
וְהָלַךְ בְּסַעֲרוֹת תֵּימָן:
יהוה צְבָאוֹת יָגֵן עֲלֵיהֶם:

כֵּן תָּגֵן עַל עַמְּךָ יִשְׂרָאֵל בִּשְׁלוֹמֶךָ.

אֱלֹהֵינוּ וֵאלֹהֵי אֲבוֹתֵינוּ
תְּקַע בְּשׁוֹפָר גָּדוֹל לְחֵרוּתֵנוּ
וְשָׂא נֵס לְקַבֵּץ גָּלֻיּוֹתֵינוּ
וְקָרֵב פְּזוּרֵינוּ מִבֵּין הַגּוֹיִם
וּנְפוּצוֹתֵינוּ כַּנֵּס מִיַּרְכְּתֵי אָרֶץ.
וַהֲבִיאֵנוּ לְצִיּוֹן עִירְךָ בְּרִנָּה
וְלִירוּשָׁלַיִם בֵּית מִקְדָּשְׁךָ בְּשִׂמְחַת עוֹלָם
וְשָׁם נַעֲשֶׂה לְפָנֶיךָ אֶת קָרְבְּנוֹת חוֹבוֹתֵינוּ
כִּמְצֻוֶּה עָלֵינוּ בְּתוֹרָתֶךָ עַל יְדֵי מֹשֶׁה עַבְדֶּךָ, מִפִּי כְבוֹדֶךָ
כָּאָמוּר

On the days of your celebration, *Num. 10*
and at your times of gathering and at your New Moons,
sound the trumpets over your offerings
and over your peace-offerings,
and those days will be remembrance for you before your God,
I am the LORD your God.

כִּי אַתָּה שׁוֹמֵעַ For You hear the call of the shofar,
and listen to its sounding,
and there is none to be compared to You.
Blessed are You, LORD,
who listens to the sound of Your people,
Israel's trumpet-blasts in compassion.

*The congregation stands and the shofar is sounded.*

| | | |
|---|---|---|
| TEKIA | SHEVARIM TERUA | TEKIA |
| TEKIA | SHEVARIM | TEKIA |
| TEKIA | TERUA | TEKIA |

*The congregation, then the Leader:*

הַיּוֹם This day is the birth of the world.
This day stands all the world's creations up in judgment,
stands them as sons or as slaves –
If as sons, have compassion for us,
as a father has compassion for his sons.
And if as slaves, our eyes are raised and fixed on You
until You show us favor, and bring out our judgment like sunlight,
Awesome, Holy.

*The congregation, then the Leader:*

אֲרֶשֶׁת May our mouths' words rise beautiful before You,
most high and elevated God,
who understands and heeds,
looks on and listens to the sounds of our shofarot.
Accept, with compassion and favor, our Order of the Shofarot.

וּבְיוֹם שִׂמְחַתְכֶם וּבְמוֹעֲדֵיכֶם וּבְרָאשֵׁי חָדְשֵׁכֶם במדבר י
וּתְקַעְתֶּם בַּחֲצֹצְרֹת עַל עֹלֹתֵיכֶם וְעַל זִבְחֵי שַׁלְמֵיכֶם
וְהָיוּ לָכֶם לְזִכָּרוֹן לִפְנֵי אֱלֹהֵיכֶם, אֲנִי יהוה אֱלֹהֵיכֶם:

כִּי אַתָּה שׁוֹמֵעַ קוֹל שׁוֹפָר וּמַאֲזִין תְּרוּעָה, וְאֵין דּוֹמֶה לָּךְ.
בָּרוּךְ אַתָּה יהוה
שׁוֹמֵעַ קוֹל תְּרוּעַת עַמּוֹ יִשְׂרָאֵל בְּרַחֲמִים.

*The* קהל *stands and the* שופר *is sounded.*

| | | |
|---|---|---|
| תקיעה | שברים תרועה | תקיעה |
| תקיעה | שברים | תקיעה |
| תקיעה | תרועה | תקיעה |

*The* קהל*, then the* שליח ציבור*:*

הַיּוֹם הֲרַת עוֹלָם, הַיּוֹם יַעֲמִיד בַּמִּשְׁפָּט כָּל יְצוּרֵי עוֹלָמִים
אִם כְּבָנִים אִם כַּעֲבָדִים.
אִם כְּבָנִים, רַחֲמֵנוּ כְּרַחֵם אָב עַל בָּנִים
וְאִם כַּעֲבָדִים, עֵינֵינוּ לְךָ תְלוּיוֹת עַד שֶׁתְּחָנֵּנוּ
וְתוֹצִיא כָאוֹר מִשְׁפָּטֵנוּ, אָיֹם קָדוֹשׁ.

*The* קהל*, then the* שליח ציבור*:*

אֲרֶשֶׁת שְׂפָתֵינוּ יֶעֱרַב לְפָנֶיךָ
אֵל רָם וְנִשָּׂא, מֵבִין וּמַאֲזִין, מַבִּיט וּמַקְשִׁיב לְקוֹל תְּקִיעָתֵנוּ.
וּתְקַבֵּל בְּרַחֲמִים וּבְרָצוֹן סֵדֶר שׁוֹפְרוֹתֵינוּ.

---

**כִּי אַתָּה שׁוֹמֵעַ קוֹל שׁוֹפָר** *For You hear the call of the shofar.* Rabbi Pinehas of Koretz said: It is written, "Lift up your voice like a shofar" (Isaiah 58:1). Just as a shofar cannot emit any sound except when blown by man, no man can raise his voice in prayer except when the Divine Presence prays through him.

TEMPLE SERVICE

רְצֵה Find favor, LORD our God, in Your people Israel,
and heed their prayer.
Restore the service to Your most holy House,
and accept soon, in love and favor,
the fire-offerings of Israel and their prayer.
May the service of Your people Israel always find favor with You.

*If Kohanim say the Priestly Blessing during the Leader's Repetition, the following is said, otherwise the Leader continues with "And may our eyes" below.*

*In Israel, see below.*

*All:* וְתֶעֱרַב May our entreaty be as pleasing to You as a burnt-offering and sacrifice. Please, Compassionate One, in Your abounding mercy restore Your Presence to Zion, Your city, and the order of the Temple service to Jerusalem. And may our eyes witness Your return to Zion in compassion, that there we may serve You with reverence as in the days of old and as in former years.

*Leader:* Blessed are You, LORD, for You alone do we serve with reverence.

*The service continues with "We give thanks" on the next page.*

---

*In Israel the following formula is used instead:*

*All:* וְתֶעֱרַב May our entreaty be as pleasing to You as a burnt-offering and sacrifice. Please, Compassionate One, in Your abounding mercy restore Your Presence to Zion, Your city, and the order of the Temple service to Jerusalem. That there we may serve You with reverence as in the days of old and as in former years.

---

*When the Priestly Blessing is not said, and also in Israel, the Leader continues:*

And may our eyes witness Your return
to Zion in compassion.
Blessed are You, LORD, who restores His Presence to Zion.

עבודה

רְצֵה יהוה אֱלֹהֵינוּ בְּעַמְּךָ יִשְׂרָאֵל
וְלִתְפִלָּתָם שְׁעֵה
וְהָשֵׁב אֶת הָעֲבוֹדָה לִדְבִיר בֵּיתֶךָ
וְאִשֵּׁי יִשְׂרָאֵל וּתְפִלָּתָם, מְהֵרָה בְּאַהֲבָה תְקַבֵּל בְּרָצוֹן
וּתְהִי לְרָצוֹן תָּמִיד עֲבוֹדַת יִשְׂרָאֵל עַמֶּךָ.

*If* כהנים *say* ברכת כהנים *during* חזרת הש״ץ*, the following is said, otherwise the* שליח ציבור *continues with* וְתֶחֱזֶינָה *below.*

*In Israel, see below.*

קהל וש״ץ: וְתֶעֱרַב עָלֶיךָ עֲתִירָתֵנוּ כְּעוֹלָה וּכְקָרְבָּן. אָנָּא רַחוּם, בְּרַחֲמֶיךָ הָרַבִּים הָשֵׁב שְׁכִינָתְךָ לְצִיּוֹן עִירְךָ, וְסֵדֶר הָעֲבוֹדָה לִירוּשָׁלָיִם. וְתֶחֱזֶינָה עֵינֵינוּ בְּשׁוּבְךָ לְצִיּוֹן בְּרַחֲמִים. וְשָׁם נַעֲבָדְךָ בְּיִרְאָה כִּימֵי עוֹלָם וּכְשָׁנִים קַדְמוֹנִיּוֹת.

ש״ץ: בָּרוּךְ אַתָּה יהוה שֶׁאוֹתְךָ לְבַדְּךָ בְּיִרְאָה נַעֲבֹד.

*The service continues with* מוֹדִים *on the next page.*

---

*In* ארץ ישראל *the following formula is used instead:*

קהל וש״ץ: וְתֶעֱרַב עָלֶיךָ עֲתִירָתֵנוּ כְּעוֹלָה וּכְקָרְבָּן. אָנָּא רַחוּם, בְּרַחֲמֶיךָ הָרַבִּים הָשֵׁב שְׁכִינָתְךָ לְצִיּוֹן עִירְךָ, וְסֵדֶר הָעֲבוֹדָה לִירוּשָׁלָיִם. וְשָׁם נַעֲבָדְךָ בְּיִרְאָה כִּימֵי עוֹלָם וּכְשָׁנִים קַדְמוֹנִיּוֹת.

---

*When* ברכת כהנים *is not said, and also in* ארץ ישראל*, the* שליח ציבור *continues:*

וְתֶחֱזֶינָה עֵינֵינוּ בְּשׁוּבְךָ לְצִיּוֹן בְּרַחֲמִים.
בָּרוּךְ אַתָּה יהוה, הַמַּחֲזִיר שְׁכִינָתוֹ לְצִיּוֹן.

THANKSGIVING

*Bow at the first nine words.*

מוֹדִים We give thanks to You,
for You are the LORD our God
and God of our ancestors
for ever and all time.
You are the Rock of our lives,
Shield of our salvation
from generation to generation.
We will thank You and
declare Your praise for our lives,
which are entrusted into Your hand;
for our souls,
which are placed in Your charge;
for Your miracles
which are with us every day;
and for Your wonders and favors
at all times, evening, morning and
midday.
You are good –
for Your compassion never fails.
You are compassionate –
for Your loving-kindnesses never cease,
for we have always placed
our hope in You.

*As the Leader recites Modim, the congregation says quietly:*

מוֹדִים We give thanks to You,
for You are the LORD our God
and God of our ancestors,
God of all flesh,
who formed us
and formed the universe.
Blessings and thanks
are due to Your great
and holy name for giving us
life and sustaining us.
May You continue
to give us life
and sustain us;
and may You gather our
exiles to Your holy courts,
to keep Your decrees,
do Your will and serve You
with a perfect heart,
for it is for us
to give You thanks.
Blessed be God to whom
thanksgiving is due.

וְעַל כֻּלָּם For all these things
may Your name be blessed and exalted
and raised up, our King, continually, for ever and all time.

*The congregation, then the Leader:*

אָבִינוּ מַלְכֵּנוּ Our Father, our King, remember Your compassion
and overcome Your anger, and efface pestilence, sword, famine,
captivity and destruction, iniquity and plague and bad mishap
and all illness, any harm or feud, and all kinds of afflictions
and all harsh decrees and baseless hatred,
from us and from all the people of Your covenant.

הודאה

*Bow at the first five words.*

ימוֹדִים אֲנַחְנוּ לָךְ
שָׁאַתָּה הוּא יהוה אֱלֹהֵינוּ
וֵאלֹהֵי אֲבוֹתֵינוּ לְעוֹלָם וָעֶד.
צוּר חַיֵּינוּ, מָגֵן יִשְׁעֵנוּ
אַתָּה הוּא לְדוֹר וָדוֹר.
נוֹדֶה לְּךָ וּנְסַפֵּר תְּהִלָּתֶךָ
עַל חַיֵּינוּ הַמְּסוּרִים בְּיָדֶךָ
וְעַל נִשְׁמוֹתֵינוּ הַפְּקוּדוֹת לָךְ
וְעַל נִסֶּיךָ שֶׁבְּכָל יוֹם עִמָּנוּ
וְעַל נִפְלְאוֹתֶיךָ וְטוֹבוֹתֶיךָ
שֶׁבְּכָל עֵת, עֶרֶב וָבֹקֶר וְצָהֳרָיִם.
הַטּוֹב, כִּי לֹא כָלוּ רַחֲמֶיךָ
וְהַמְרַחֵם, כִּי לֹא תַמּוּ חֲסָדֶיךָ
כִּי מֵעוֹלָם קִוִּינוּ לָךְ.

*As the* שליח ציבור *recites* מודים, *the* קהל *says quietly:*

ימוֹדִים אֲנַחְנוּ לָךְ
שָׁאַתָּה הוּא יהוה אֱלֹהֵינוּ
וֵאלֹהֵי אֲבוֹתֵינוּ
אֱלֹהֵי כָל בָּשָׂר
יוֹצְרֵנוּ, יוֹצֵר בְּרֵאשִׁית.
בְּרָכוֹת וְהוֹדָאוֹת
לְשִׁמְךָ הַגָּדוֹל וְהַקָּדוֹשׁ
עַל שֶׁהֶחֱיִיתָנוּ וְקִיַּמְתָּנוּ.
כֵּן תְּחַיֵּנוּ וּתְקַיְּמֵנוּ
וְתֶאֱסֹף גָּלֻיּוֹתֵינוּ
לְחַצְרוֹת קָדְשֶׁךָ
לִשְׁמֹר חֻקֶּיךָ וְלַעֲשׂוֹת רְצוֹנֶךָ
וּלְעָבְדְּךָ בְּלֵבָב שָׁלֵם
עַל שֶׁאֲנוּ מוֹדִים לָךְ.
בָּרוּךְ אֵל הַהוֹדָאוֹת.

וְעַל כֻּלָּם
יִתְבָּרַךְ וְיִתְרוֹמַם וְיִתְנַשֵּׂא שִׁמְךָ מַלְכֵּנוּ תָּמִיד לְעוֹלָם וָעֶד.

*The* קהל*, then the* שליח ציבור*:*

אָבִינוּ מַלְכֵּנוּ, זְכֹר רַחֲמֶיךָ וּכְבֹשׁ כַּעַסְךָ
וְכַלֵּה דֶבֶר, וְחֶרֶב, וְרָעָב
וּשְׁבִי, וּמַשְׁחִית, וְעָוֹן, וּמַגֵּפָה, וּפֶגַע רַע
וְכָל מַחֲלָה, וְכָל תַּקָּלָה, וְכָל קְטָטָה
וְכָל מִינֵי פֻרְעָנִיּוֹת, וְכָל גְּזֵרָה רָעָה, וְשִׂנְאַת חִנָּם
מֵעָלֵינוּ וּמֵעַל כָּל בְּנֵי בְרִיתֶךָ.

*The congregation then the Leader:*

וּכְתֹב And write for a good life,
all the children of Your covenant.

וְכֹל Let all that lives thank You, Selah!
and praise and bless Your great name in truth, always,
because it is good,
God, our Savior and Help, Selah! the beneficent God.
▼Blessed are You, LORD, whose name is "the Good"
and to whom thanks are due.

*The following supplication is recited quietly while the Leader says "Let all that lives" above.*

*The Kohanim say:*

יְהִי רָצוֹן May it be Your will, LORD our God and God of our ancestors, that this blessing with which You have commanded us to bless Your people Israel should be a complete blessing, with neither hindrance nor sin, now and forever.

*In some communities, the congregation says:*

יְהִי רָצוֹן May it be Your will, LORD our God and God of our ancestors, that this blessing with which You have commanded to bless Your people Israel should be a complete blessing, with neither hindrance nor sin, now and forever.

*In Israel the Priestly Blessing on page 1002 is said.*
*When the Priestly Blessing is not said, the Leader says the formula on page 868.*

*The following is recited quietly by the Leader:*

אֱלֹהֵינוּ Our God and God of our fathers,
bless us with the threefold blessing in the Torah,
written by the hand of Moses Your servant
and pronounced by Aaron and his sons:

*The Leader says aloud:*

Kohanim!

*In most places, the congregation responds:*

Your holy people, as it said:

*The Kohanim say the following blessing in unison:*

בָּרוּךְ Blessed are You, LORD our God, King of the Universe, who has made us holy with the holiness of Aaron, and has commanded us to bless His people Israel with love.

*The* קהל *then the* שליח ציבור:

**וּכְתֹב לְחַיִּים טוֹבִים כָּל בְּנֵי בְרִיתֶךָ.**

**וְכֹל הַחַיִּים יוֹדְוּךָ סֶּלָה**
**וִיהַלְלוּ וִיבָרְכוּ אֶת שִׁמְךָ הַגָּדוֹל בֶּאֱמֶת לְעוֹלָם כִּי טוֹב**
**הָאֵל יְשׁוּעָתֵנוּ וְעֶזְרָתֵנוּ סֶלָה, הָאֵל הַטּוֹב.**
**·בָּרוּךְ אַתָּה יהוה, הַטּוֹב שִׁמְךָ וּלְךָ נָאֶה לְהוֹדוֹת.**

*The following supplication is recited quietly while the* שליח ציבור *says* וְכֹל הַחַיִּים *above.*

*The* כהנים *say:*

יְהִי רָצוֹן מִלְּפָנֶיךָ, יהוה אֱלֹהֵינוּ וֵאלֹהֵי אֲבוֹתֵינוּ, שֶׁתְּהֵא הַבְּרָכָה הַזֹּאת שֶׁצִּוִּיתָנוּ לְבָרֵךְ אֶת עַמְּךָ יִשְׂרָאֵל בְּרָכָה שְׁלֵמָה, וְלֹא יִהְיֶה בָּהּ שׁוּם מִכְשׁוֹל וְעָוֹן מֵעַתָּה וְעַד עוֹלָם.

*In some communities, the* קהל *says:*

יְהִי רָצוֹן מִלְּפָנֶיךָ, יהוה אֱלֹהֵינוּ וֵאלֹהֵי אֲבוֹתֵינוּ, שֶׁתְּהֵא הַבְּרָכָה הַזֹּאת שֶׁצִּוִּיתָ לְבָרֵךְ אֶת עַמְּךָ יִשְׂרָאֵל בְּרָכָה שְׁלֵמָה, וְלֹא יִהְיֶה בָּהּ שׁוּם מִכְשׁוֹל וְעָוֹן מֵעַתָּה וְעַד עוֹלָם.

*In* ארץ ישראל *the* ברכת כהנים *on page 1003 is said.*
*When* ברכת כהנים *is not said, the* שליח ציבור *says the formula on page 869.*

*The following is recited quietly by the* שליח ציבור:

**אֱלֹהֵינוּ וֵאלֹהֵי אֲבוֹתֵינוּ, בָּרְכֵנוּ בַּבְּרָכָה הַמְשֻׁלֶּשֶׁת בַּתּוֹרָה הַכְּתוּבָה עַל יְדֵי מֹשֶׁה עַבְדֶּךָ, הָאֲמוּרָה מִפִּי אַהֲרֹן וּבָנָיו**

*The* שליח ציבור *says aloud:*

**כֹּהֲנִים**

*In most places, the* קהל *responds:*

עַם קְדוֹשֶׁךָ, כָּאָמוּר:

*The* כהנים *say the following blessing in unison:*

**בָּרוּךְ אַתָּה יהוה אֱלֹהֵינוּ מֶלֶךְ הָעוֹלָם, אֲשֶׁר קִדְּשָׁנוּ בִּקְדֻשָּׁתוֹ שֶׁל אַהֲרֹן, וְצִוָּנוּ לְבָרֵךְ אֶת עַמּוֹ יִשְׂרָאֵל בְּאַהֲבָה.**

*The first word in each sentence is said by the Leader, followed by the Kohanim. Some read silently the accompanying verses. One should remain silent and not look at the Kohanim while the blessings are being said.*

| | | |
|---|---|---|
| May [He] bless you | May the LORD, Maker of heaven and earth, bless you from Zion. | *Ps. 134* |
| The LORD | LORD, our LORD, how majestic is Your name throughout the earth. | *Ps. 8* |
| And protect you. | Protect me, God, for in You I take refuge. | *Ps. 16* |

*Read the following silently while the Kohanim chant.*

Master of the Universe, I am Yours and my dreams are Yours. I have dreamt a dream and I do not know what it means. May it be Your will, LORD my God and God of my fathers, that all my dreams be, for me and all Israel, for good, whether I have dreamt about myself, or about others, or others have dreamt about me. If they are good, strengthen and reinforce them, and may they be fulfilled in me and them like the dreams of the righteous Joseph. If, though, they need healing, heal them as You healed Hezekiah King of Judah from his illness, like Miriam the prophetess from her leprosy, like Na'aman from his leprosy, like the waters of Mara by Moses our teacher, and like the waters of Jericho by Elisha. And just as You turned the curses of Balaam the wicked from curse to blessing, so turn all my dreams about me and all Israel to good; protect me, be gracious to me and accept me. Amen.

| | | |
|---|---|---|
| May [He] make shine | May God be gracious to us and bless us; may He make His face shine upon us, Selah. | *Ps. 67* |
| The LORD | The LORD, the LORD, compassionate and gracious God, slow to anger, abounding in kindness and truth. | *Ex. 34* |
| His face | Turn to me and be gracious to me, for I am alone and afflicted. | *Ps. 25* |
| On you | To You, LORD, I lift up my soul. | *Ibid.* |
| And be gracious to you. | As the eyes of slaves turn to their master's hand, or the eyes of a slave-girl to the hand of her mistress, so our eyes are turned to the LORD our God, awaiting His favor. | *Ps. 123* |

*Read the following silently while the Kohanim chant.*

Master of the Universe, I am Yours and my dreams are Yours. I have dreamt a dream and I do not know what it means. May it be Your will, LORD my God and God of my fathers, that all my dreams be, for me and all Israel, for good, whether I

*The first word in each sentence is said by the* שליח ציבור*, followed by the* כהנים*. Some read silently the accompanying verses. One should remain silent and not look at the* כהנים *while the blessings are being said.*

תהלים קלד **יְבָרֶכְךָ** יְבָרֶכְךָ יהוה מִצִּיּוֹן, עֹשֵׂה שָׁמַיִם וָאָרֶץ:

תהלים ח **יהוה** יהוה אֲדֹנֵינוּ, מָה־אַדִּיר שִׁמְךָ בְּכָל־הָאָרֶץ:

תהלים טז **וְיִשְׁמְרֶךָ:** שָׁמְרֵנִי אֵל, כִּי־חָסִיתִי בָךְ:

*Read the following silently while the* כהנים *chant.*

רִבּוֹנוֹ שֶׁל עוֹלָם, אֲנִי שֶׁלָּךְ וַחֲלוֹמוֹתַי שֶׁלָּךְ. חֲלוֹם חָלַמְתִּי וְאֵינִי יוֹדֵעַ מַה הוּא. יְהִי רָצוֹן מִלְּפָנֶיךָ, יהוה אֱלֹהַי וֵאלֹהֵי אֲבוֹתַי, שֶׁיִּהְיוּ כָּל חֲלוֹמוֹתַי עָלַי וְעַל כָּל יִשְׂרָאֵל לְטוֹבָה, בֵּין שֶׁחָלַמְתִּי עַל עַצְמִי, וּבֵין שֶׁחָלַמְתִּי עַל אֲחֵרִים, וּבֵין שֶׁחָלְמוּ אֲחֵרִים עָלָי. אִם טוֹבִים הֵם, חַזְּקֵם וְאַמְּצֵם, וְיִתְקַיְּמוּ בִי וּבָהֶם, כַּחֲלוֹמוֹתָיו שֶׁל יוֹסֵף הַצַּדִּיק. וְאִם צְרִיכִים רְפוּאָה, רְפָאֵם כְּחִזְקִיָּהוּ מֶלֶךְ יְהוּדָה מֵחָלְיוֹ, וּכְמִרְיָם הַנְּבִיאָה מִצָּרַעְתָּהּ, וּכְנַעֲמָן מִצָּרַעְתּוֹ, וּכְמֵי מָרָה עַל יְדֵי מֹשֶׁה רַבֵּנוּ, וּכְמֵי יְרִיחוֹ עַל יְדֵי אֱלִישָׁע. וּכְשֵׁם שֶׁהָפַכְתָּ אֶת קִלְלַת בִּלְעָם הָרָשָׁע מִקְּלָלָה לִבְרָכָה, כֵּן תַּהֲפֹךְ כָּל חֲלוֹמוֹתַי עָלַי וְעַל כָּל יִשְׂרָאֵל לְטוֹבָה, וְתִשְׁמְרֵנִי וּתְחָנֵּנִי וְתִרְצֵנִי. אָמֵן.

תהלים סז **יָאֵר** אֱלֹהִים יְחָנֵּנוּ וִיבָרְכֵנוּ, יָאֵר פָּנָיו אִתָּנוּ סֶלָה:

שמות לד **יהוה** יהוה, יהוה, אֵל רַחוּם וְחַנּוּן
אֶרֶךְ אַפַּיִם וְרַב־חֶסֶד וֶאֱמֶת:

תהלים כה **פָּנָיו** פְּנֵה־אֵלַי וְחָנֵּנִי, כִּי־יָחִיד וְעָנִי אָנִי:

שם **אֵלֶיךָ** אֵלֶיךָ יהוה נַפְשִׁי אֶשָּׂא:

תהלים קכג **וִיחֻנֶּךָּ:** הִנֵּה כְעֵינֵי עֲבָדִים אֶל־יַד אֲדוֹנֵיהֶם
כְּעֵינֵי שִׁפְחָה אֶל־יַד גְּבִרְתָּהּ, כֵּן עֵינֵינוּ אֶל־יהוה אֱלֹהֵינוּ
עַד שֶׁיְּחָנֵּנוּ:

*Read the following silently while the* כהנים *chant.*

רִבּוֹנוֹ שֶׁל עוֹלָם, אֲנִי שֶׁלָּךְ וַחֲלוֹמוֹתַי שֶׁלָּךְ. חֲלוֹם חָלַמְתִּי וְאֵינִי יוֹדֵעַ מַה הוּא. יְהִי רָצוֹן מִלְּפָנֶיךָ, יהוה אֱלֹהַי וֵאלֹהֵי אֲבוֹתַי, שֶׁיִּהְיוּ כָּל חֲלוֹמוֹתַי עָלַי וְעַל כָּל

have dreamt about myself, or about others, or others have dreamt about me. If they are good, strengthen and reinforce them, and may they be fulfilled in me and them like the dreams of the righteous Joseph. If, though, they need healing, heal them as You healed Hezekiah King of Judah from his illness, like Miriam the prophetess from her leprosy, like Na'aman from his leprosy, like the waters of Mara by Moses our teacher, and like the waters of Jericho by Elisha. And just as You turned the curses of Balaam the wicked from curse to blessing, so turn all my dreams about me and all Israel to good; protect me, be gracious to me and accept me. Amen.

| | | |
|---|---|---|
| May [He] turn | May he receive a blessing from the LORD and a just reward from the God of his salvation. And he will win grace and good favor in the eyes of God and man. | *Ps. 24*<br>*Prov. 3* |
| The LORD | LORD, be gracious to us; we yearn for You. Be their strength every morning, our salvation in time of distress. | *Is. 33* |
| His face | Do not hide Your face from me in the day of my distress. Turn Your ear to me; on the day I call, swiftly answer me. | *Ps. 102* |
| Toward you | To You, enthroned in heaven, I lift my eyes. | *Ps. 123* |
| And grant | They shall place My name on the children of Israel, and I will bless them. | *Num. 6* |
| You | Yours, LORD, are the greatness and the power, the glory, majesty and splendor, for everything in heaven and earth is Yours. Yours, LORD, is the kingdom; You are exalted as Head over all. | *1 Chr. 29* |
| Peace. | "Peace, peace, to those far and near," says the LORD, "and I will heal him." | *Is. 57* |

---

in God. Then they will be able to find their fulfillment, their equitable and satisfying state. If a person should seek for himself less than this exalted state, he will at once become like a ship tossed about at sea. Stormy waves, raging in opposite directions, will continually rob him of peace. He will be thrown from wave to wave, and he will be unable to find himself. If he should be able to immerse himself in some crude and vulgar preoccupation, he may succeed for a time in reducing the perspective of his life, and it will seem to him that he has finally found peace. But it will not take long for the spirit to break out of its imprisonment and the maddening agitation will begin to act in all its fury. The place where it may find peace is only in God. (*Orot*)

יִשְׂרָאֵל לְטוֹבָה, בֵּין שֶׁחָלַמְתִּי עַל עַצְמִי, וּבֵין שֶׁחָלַמְתִּי עַל אֲחֵרִים, וּבֵין שֶׁחָלְמוּ אֲחֵרִים עָלָי. אִם טוֹבִים הֵם, חַזְּקֵם וְאַמְּצֵם, וְיִתְקַיְּמוּ בִי וּבָהֶם, כַּחֲלוֹמוֹתָיו שֶׁל יוֹסֵף הַצַּדִּיק. וְאִם צְרִיכִים רְפוּאָה, רְפָאֵם כְּחִזְקִיָּהוּ מֶלֶךְ יְהוּדָה מֵחָלְיוֹ, וּכְמִרְיָם הַנְּבִיאָה מִצָּרַעְתָּהּ, וּכְנַעֲמָן מִצָּרַעְתּוֹ, וּכְמֵי מָרָה עַל יְדֵי מֹשֶׁה רַבֵּנוּ, וּכְמֵי יְרִיחוֹ עַל יְדֵי אֱלִישָׁע. וּכְשֵׁם שֶׁהָפַכְתָּ אֶת קִלְלַת בִּלְעָם הָרָשָׁע מִקְּלָלָה לִבְרָכָה, כֵּן תַּהֲפֹךְ כָּל חֲלוֹמוֹתַי עָלַי וְעַל כָּל יִשְׂרָאֵל לְטוֹבָה, וְתִשְׁמְרֵנִי וּתְחָנֵּנִי וְתִרְצֵנִי. אָמֵן.

**יִשָּׂא** יִשָּׂא בְרָכָה מֵאֵת יהוה, וּצְדָקָה מֵאֱלֹהֵי יִשְׁעוֹ: — תהלים כד
וּמְצָא־חֵן וְשֵׂכֶל־טוֹב בְּעֵינֵי אֱלֹהִים וְאָדָם: — משלי ג

**יהוה** יהוה חָנֵּנוּ, לְךָ קִוִּינוּ, הֱיֵה זְרֹעָם לַבְּקָרִים אַף־יְשׁוּעָתֵנוּ בְּעֵת צָרָה: — ישעיה לג

**פָּנָיו** אַל־תַּסְתֵּר פָּנֶיךָ מִמֶּנִּי בְּיוֹם צַר לִי, הַטֵּה־אֵלַי אָזְנֶךָ בְּיוֹם אֶקְרָא מַהֵר עֲנֵנִי: — תהלים קב

**אֵלֶיךָ** אֵלֶיךָ נָשָׂאתִי אֶת־עֵינַי, הַיֹּשְׁבִי בַּשָּׁמָיִם: — תהלים קכג

**וְיָשֵׂם** וְשָׂמוּ אֶת־שְׁמִי עַל־בְּנֵי יִשְׂרָאֵל, וַאֲנִי אֲבָרְכֵם: — במדבר ו

**לְךָ** לְךָ יהוה הַגְּדֻלָּה וְהַגְּבוּרָה וְהַתִּפְאֶרֶת וְהַנֵּצַח וְהַהוֹד כִּי־כֹל בַּשָּׁמַיִם וּבָאָרֶץ, לְךָ יהוה הַמַּמְלָכָה וְהַמִּתְנַשֵּׂא לְכֹל לְרֹאשׁ: — דברי הימים א׳ כט

**שָׁלוֹם:** שָׁלוֹם שָׁלוֹם לָרָחוֹק וְלַקָּרוֹב, אָמַר יהוה, וּרְפָאתִיו: — ישעיה נז

---

**יִשָּׂא יהוה פָּנָיו אֵלֶיךָ וְיָשֵׂם לְךָ שָׁלוֹם** *May the Lord turn His face toward you and grant you peace.* Rabbi Bunam of Pzhysha taught: Our sages say, "Seek peace in your own place." You cannot find peace anywhere other than in your own self. In Psalms we read: "There is no peace in my bones because of my sin" (38:4). When a person has made peace within himself, he will be able to make peace in the whole world.

Said Rabbi Abraham Kook: The spirit cannot find its stability except in a life oriented toward God. Knowledge, feeling, the imagination and the will, in their inner and outer manifestations, all condition people to center their lives

*Read the following silently while the Kohanim chant.*

May it be Your will, Lord my God and God of my fathers, that You act for the sake of Your simple, sacred kindness and great compassion, and for the purity of Your great, mighty and awesome name of twenty-two letters derived from the verses of the priestly blessing spoken by Aaron and his sons, Your holy people. May You be close to me when I call to You. May You hear my prayer, plea and cry as You did the cry of Jacob Your perfect one who was called "a plain man." May You grant me and all the members of my household our food and sustenance, generously not meagerly, honestly not otherwise, with satisfaction not pain, from Your generous hand, just as You gave a portion of bread to eat and clothes to wear to Jacob our father who was called "a plain man." May we find love, grace, kindness and compassion in Your sight and in the eyes of all who see us. May my words in service to You be heard, as You granted Joseph Your righteous one, at the time when he was robed by his father in a cloak of fine wool, that he find grace, kindness and compassion in Your sight and in the eyes of all who saw him. May You do wonders and miracles with me, and a sign for good. Grant me success in my paths, and set in my heart understanding that I may understand, discern and fulfill all the words of Your Torah's teachings and mysteries. Save me from errors and purify my thoughts and my heart to serve You and be in awe of You. Prolong my days (*add, where appropriate:* and those of my father, mother, wife, husband, son/s, and daughter/s) in joy and happiness, with much strength and peace. Amen, Selah.

*The Leader continues with "Grant peace" on the next page.*

*The congregation says:*
אַדִּיר Majestic One on high who dwells in power: You are peace and Your name is peace. May it be Your will to bestow on us and on Your people the house of Israel, life and blessing as a safeguard for peace.

*The Kohanim say:*
רִבּוֹנוֹ Master of the Universe: we have done what You have decreed for us. So too may You deal with us as You have promised us. Look down from Your holy dwelling place, from heaven, and bless Your people Israel and the land You have given us as You promised on oath to our ancestors, a land flowing with milk and honey. *Deut. 26*

---

*If the Priestly Blessing is not said, the following is said by the Leader:*

Our God and God of our fathers, bless us with the threefold blessing in the Torah, written by the hand of Moses Your servant and pronounced by Aaron and his sons the priests, Your holy people, as it is said:

May the Lord bless you and protect you. *Num. 6*
*Cong:* May it be Your will.
May the Lord make His face shine on you and be gracious to you.
*Cong:* May it be Your will.
May the Lord turn His face toward you, and grant you peace.
*Cong:* May it be Your will.

---

*Read the following silently while the* כהנים *chant.*

יְהִי רָצוֹן מִלְּפָנֶיךָ, יהוה אֱלֹהַי וֵאלֹהֵי אֲבוֹתַי, שֶׁתַּעֲשֶׂה לְמַעַן קְדֻשַּׁת חֲסָדֶיךָ וְגֹדֶל רַחֲמֶיךָ הַפְּשׁוּטִים, וּלְמַעַן טָהֳרַת שִׁמְךָ הַגָּדוֹל הַגִּבּוֹר וְהַנּוֹרָא, בֶּן עֶשְׂרִים וּשְׁתַּיִם אוֹתִיּוֹת הַיּוֹצֵא מִפְּסוּקִים שֶׁל בִּרְכַּת כֹּהֲנִים הָאֲמוּרָה מִפִּי אַהֲרֹן וּבָנָיו עַם קְדוֹשֶׁךָ, שֶׁתִּהְיֶה קָרוֹב לִי בְּקָרְאִי לָךְ, וְתִשְׁמַע תְּפִלָּתִי נַאֲקָתִי וְאֶנְקָתִי תָּמִיד, כְּשֵׁם שֶׁשָּׁמַעְתָּ אֶנְקַת יַעֲקֹב תְּמִימֶךָ הַנִּקְרָא אִישׁ תָּם. וְתִתֶּן לִי וּלְכָל נַפְשׁוֹת בֵּיתִי מְזוֹנוֹתֵינוּ וּפַרְנָסָתֵנוּ בְּרֶוַח וְלֹא בְצִמְצוּם, בְּהֶתֵּר וְלֹא בְאִסּוּר, בְּנַחַת וְלֹא בְצַעַר, מִתַּחַת יָדְךָ הָרְחָבָה, כְּשֵׁם שֶׁנָּתַתָּ פִּסַּת לֶחֶם לֶאֱכֹל וּבֶגֶד לִלְבֹּשׁ לְיַעֲקֹב אָבִינוּ הַנִּקְרָא אִישׁ תָּם. וְתִתְּנֵנוּ לְאַהֲבָה, לְחֵן וּלְחֶסֶד וּלְרַחֲמִים בְּעֵינֶיךָ וּבְעֵינֵי כָל רוֹאֵינוּ, וְיִהְיוּ דְבָרַי נִשְׁמָעִים לַעֲבוֹדָתֶךָ, כְּשֵׁם שֶׁנָּתַתָּ אֶת יוֹסֵף צַדִּיקֶךָ בְּשָׁעָה שֶׁהִלְבִּישׁוֹ אָבִיו כְּתֹנֶת פַּסִּים לְחֵן וּלְחֶסֶד וּלְרַחֲמִים בְּעֵינֶיךָ וּבְעֵינֵי כָל רוֹאָיו. וְתַעֲשֶׂה עִמִּי נִפְלָאוֹת וְנִסִּים, וּלְטוֹבָה אוֹת, וְתַצְלִיחֵנִי בִּדְרָכַי, וְתֵן בְּלִבִּי בִּינָה לְהָבִין וּלְהַשְׂכִּיל וּלְקַיֵּם אֶת כָּל דִּבְרֵי תַלְמוּד תּוֹרָתֶךָ וְסוֹדוֹתֶיהָ, וְתַצִּילֵנִי מִשְּׁגִיאוֹת, וּתְטַהֵר רַעְיוֹנַי וְלִבִּי לַעֲבוֹדָתֶךָ, וְתַאֲרִיךְ יָמַי (וִימֵי אָבִי וְאִמִּי / וְאִשְׁתִּי / וּבַעְלִי / וּבָנַי וּבְנוֹתַי) בְּטוֹב וּבִנְעִימוּת, בְּרֹב עֹז וְשָׁלוֹם, אָמֵן סֶלָה.

*The* שליח ציבור *continues with* שִׂים שָׁלוֹם *on the next page.*

*The* קהל *says:*

אַדִּיר בַּמָּרוֹם שׁוֹכֵן בִּגְבוּרָה, אַתָּה שָׁלוֹם וְשִׁמְךָ שָׁלוֹם. יְהִי רָצוֹן שֶׁתָּשִׂים עָלֵינוּ וְעַל כָּל עַמְּךָ בֵּית יִשְׂרָאֵל חַיִּים וּבְרָכָה לְמִשְׁמֶרֶת שָׁלוֹם.

*The* כהנים *say:*

רִבּוֹנוֹ שֶׁל עוֹלָם, עָשִׂינוּ מַה שֶּׁגָּזַרְתָּ עָלֵינוּ, אַף אַתָּה
דברים כו עֲשֵׂה עִמָּנוּ כְּמוֹ שֶׁהִבְטַחְתָּנוּ. הַשְׁקִיפָה מִמְּעוֹן קָדְשְׁךָ מִן־הַשָּׁמַיִם, וּבָרֵךְ אֶת־עַמְּךָ אֶת־יִשְׂרָאֵל, וְאֵת הָאֲדָמָה אֲשֶׁר נָתַתָּה לָנוּ, כַּאֲשֶׁר נִשְׁבַּעְתָּ לַאֲבֹתֵינוּ, אֶרֶץ זָבַת חָלָב וּדְבָשׁ:

---

*If* ברכת כהנים *is not said, the following is said by the* שליח ציבור:

אֱלֹהֵינוּ וֵאלֹהֵי אֲבוֹתֵינוּ, בָּרְכֵנוּ בַּבְּרָכָה הַמְשֻׁלֶּשֶׁת בַּתּוֹרָה, הַכְּתוּבָה עַל יְדֵי מֹשֶׁה עַבְדֶּךָ, הָאֲמוּרָה מִפִּי אַהֲרֹן וּבָנָיו כֹּהֲנִים עַם קְדוֹשֶׁיךָ, כָּאָמוּר

במדבר ו יְבָרֶכְךָ יהוה וְיִשְׁמְרֶךָ: קהל: כֵּן יְהִי רָצוֹן

יָאֵר יהוה פָּנָיו אֵלֶיךָ וִיחֻנֶּךָּ: קהל: כֵּן יְהִי רָצוֹן

יִשָּׂא יהוה פָּנָיו אֵלֶיךָ וְיָשֵׂם לְךָ שָׁלוֹם: קהל: כֵּן יְהִי רָצוֹן

---

PEACE

שִׂים שָׁלוֹם Grant peace, goodness and blessing,
life, grace, loving-kindness and compassion
to us and all Israel Your people.
Bless us, our Father, all as one, with the light of Your face,
for by the light of Your face You have given us, LORD our God,
the Torah of life and love of kindness,
righteousness, blessing, compassion, life and peace.
May it be good in Your eyes to bless us and all Your people Israel
at every time, in every hour, with Your peace.

*The congregation then the Leader:*

בְּסֵפֶר חַיִּים In the book of life, blessing, peace and prosperity,
and good decrees, salvations and consolations
may we and all Your people the house of Israel
be remembered and written before You for a good life, and for peace.

*The congregation then the Leader:*

וְנֶאֱמַר It is said, "Through Me your days will grow many, *Prov. 9*
and years of life will be added to your lot." Write us down for good lives,
O God of life, and write us in the book of life.
As is written, "You who cling to the LORD your God are all alive today." *Deut. 4*

*The Ark is opened by one of the Kohanim.*
*The Leader recites each phrase, and the congregation responds Amen and recites the next phrase. The full version of this piyut can be found on page 1074.*

הַיּוֹם This day, may You strengthen us. AMEN
This day, may You bless us. AMEN
This day, may You give us greatness. AMEN
This day, may You deal with us kindly. AMEN
This day, may You hear our cry. AMEN
This day, may You accept our prayers
compassionately and willingly. AMEN
This day, may You support us
with Your hand of righteousness. AMEN

*The Ark is closed.*

---

בָּרְכֵנוּ אָבִינוּ כֻּלָּנוּ כְּאֶחָד *Bless us, our Father, all as one.* Rabbi Yaakov Yosef of Polnoye said: Jews are likened in the Torah to sand (Gen. 32:12). Each

ברכת שלום

שִׂים שָׁלוֹם טוֹבָה וּבְרָכָה
חַיִּים חֵן וָחֶסֶד וְרַחֲמִים עָלֵינוּ וְעַל כָּל יִשְׂרָאֵל עַמֶּךָ.
בָּרְכֵנוּ אָבִינוּ כֻּלָּנוּ כְּאֶחָד בְּאוֹר פָּנֶיךָ
כִּי בְאוֹר פָּנֶיךָ נָתַתָּ לָנוּ יהוה אֱלֹהֵינוּ
תּוֹרַת חַיִּים וְאַהֲבַת חֶסֶד, וּצְדָקָה וּבְרָכָה וְרַחֲמִים וְחַיִּים וְשָׁלוֹם.
וְטוֹב יִהְיֶה בְּעֵינֶיךָ לְבָרְכֵנוּ וּלְבָרֵךְ אֶת כָּל עַמְּךָ יִשְׂרָאֵל
בְּכָל עֵת וּבְכָל שָׁעָה בִּשְׁלוֹמֶךָ.

*The* קהל *then the* שליח ציבור*:*

בְּסֵפֶר חַיִּים, בְּרָכָה וְשָׁלוֹם, וּפַרְנָסָה טוֹבָה
וּגְזֵרוֹת טוֹבוֹת, יְשׁוּעוֹת וְנֶחָמוֹת, נִזָּכֵר וְנִכָּתֵב לְפָנֶיךָ
אֲנַחְנוּ וְכָל עַמְּךָ בֵּית יִשְׂרָאֵל לְחַיִּים טוֹבִים וּלְשָׁלוֹם.

*The* קהל *then the* שליח ציבור*:*

וְנֶאֱמַר: כִּי־בִי יִרְבּוּ יָמֶיךָ, וְיוֹסִיפוּ לְךָ שְׁנוֹת חַיִּים: משלי ט
לְחַיִּים טוֹבִים תִּכְתְּבֵנוּ, אֱלֹהִים חַיִּים, כָּתְבֵנוּ בְּסֵפֶר הַחַיִּים.
כַּכָּתוּב: וְאַתֶּם הַדְּבֵקִים בַּיהוה אֱלֹהֵיכֶם, חַיִּים כֻּלְּכֶם הַיּוֹם: דברים ד

*The* ארון קודש *is opened by one of the* כהנים*.*
*The* שליח ציבור *recites each phrase, and the* קהל *responds* אמן *and recites the next phrase. The full version of this piyut can be found on page 1075.*

הַיּוֹם תְּאַמְּצֵנוּ. אָמֵן
הַיּוֹם תְּבָרְכֵנוּ. אָמֵן
הַיּוֹם תְּגַדְּלֵנוּ. אָמֵן
הַיּוֹם תִּדְרְשֵׁנוּ לְטוֹבָה. אָמֵן
הַיּוֹם תִּשְׁמַע שַׁוְעָתֵנוּ. אָמֵן
הַיּוֹם תְּקַבֵּל בְּרַחֲמִים וּבְרָצוֹן אֶת תְּפִלָּתֵנוּ. אָמֵן
הַיּוֹם תִּתְמְכֵנוּ בִּימִין צִדְקֶךָ. אָמֵן

*The* ארון קודש *is closed.*

*The congregation then the Leader:*

כְּהַיּוֹם Bring us this day, happy, rejoicing, to a House restored,
as is written:

"I shall bring them to My holy mountain, *Is. 56*
and I shall have them rejoice in My house of prayer;
their offerings and their sacrifices
shall be accepted, desired on My altar,
for My House will be called a house of prayer for all peoples."

And it is said,

"And the Lord commanded You to perform all these statutes, *Deut. 6*
to fear the Lord our God, that it may be good for us all our
days; to give us life as on this day."

And it is said,

"Righteousness will be in our hands, *Ibid.*
when we take care to fulfill all these commands
before the Lord our God, as He has commanded."

Righteousness and blessing, compassion and life and peace –
may these be with us and with all Israel, forever.

*The Leader concludes:*

Blessed are You, Lord, who blesses His people Israel with peace.

*The following verse concludes the Leader's Repetition of the Amida. See law 64.*

May the words of my mouth and the meditation of my heart *Ps. 19*
find favor before You, Lord, my Rock and Redeemer.

---

Help all of us that we may always hold fast to the attribute of peace,
So that true and abundant peace prevail between man and man,
between husband and wife,
And no strife separate humankind even in thought.
You make peace in Your heaven, You bring contrary elements together:
Extend abundant peace to us and to the whole world,
So that all discords be resolved in great love and peace,
And with one mind, one heart, all come near to You and Your law in truth,
And all form one union to do Your will with a whole heart.
Lord of peace, bless us with peace. (*Likkutei Tefillot*, 1:95)

*The* קהל *then the* שליח ציבור*:*

כְּהַיּוֹם הַזֶּה תְּבִיאֵנוּ, שָׂשִׂים וּשְׂמֵחִים בְּבִנְיַן שָׁלֵם.
כַּכָּתוּב
וַהֲבִיאוֹתִים אֶל־הַר קָדְשִׁי וְשִׂמַּחְתִּים בְּבֵית תְּפִלָּתִי ישעיה נו
עוֹלֹתֵיהֶם וְזִבְחֵיהֶם לְרָצוֹן עַל־מִזְבְּחִי
כִּי בֵיתִי בֵּית־תְּפִלָּה יִקָּרֵא לְכָל־הָעַמִּים:
וְנֶאֱמַר
וַיְצַוֵּנוּ יהוה לַעֲשׂוֹת אֶת־כָּל־הַחֻקִּים הָאֵלֶּה דברים ו
לְיִרְאָה אֶת־יהוה אֱלֹהֵינוּ
לְטוֹב לָנוּ כָּל־הַיָּמִים לְחַיֹּתֵנוּ כְּהַיּוֹם הַזֶּה:
וְנֶאֱמַר
וּצְדָקָה תִּהְיֶה־לָּנוּ שם
כִּי־נִשְׁמֹר לַעֲשׂוֹת אֶת־כָּל־הַמִּצְוָה הַזֹּאת
לִפְנֵי יהוה אֱלֹהֵינוּ, כַּאֲשֶׁר צִוָּנוּ:

וּצְדָקָה וּבְרָכָה וְרַחֲמִים וְחַיִּים וְשָׁלוֹם
יִהְיֶה לָנוּ וּלְכָל יִשְׂרָאֵל עַד הָעוֹלָם.

*The* שליח ציבור *concludes:*

בָּרוּךְ אַתָּה יהוה, הַמְבָרֵךְ אֶת עַמּוֹ יִשְׂרָאֵל בַּשָּׁלוֹם.

*The following verse concludes the* חזרת הש״ץ*. See law 64.*

יִהְיוּ לְרָצוֹן אִמְרֵי־פִי וְהֶגְיוֹן לִבִּי לְפָנֶיךָ, יהוה צוּרִי וְגֹאֲלִי: תהלים יט

---

particle of sand is distinct, and only through fire do they become fused into glass. Likewise the Israelites are usually divided among themselves, and only calamities unite them.

**הַמְבָרֵךְ אֶת עַמּוֹ יִשְׂרָאֵל בַּשָּׁלוֹם** *Who blesses His people Israel with peace.* Rabbi Naḥman of Bratslav used to pray:

LORD and King of Peace,
Who makes peace and creates all things:

*The most common custom is to sound ten notes in the middle of Full Kaddish, before "May the prayers...", in order to complete one hundred notes (see law 81). Congregations who did not blew the shofar during the silent Amida ,blow forty additional notes; some sound all forty before "May the prayers...", and others sound thirty notes after ,Full Kaddish and ten more before the concluding Aleinu .*

FULL KADDISH

*Leader:* יִתְגַּדַּל Magnified and sanctified may His great name be,
in the world He created by His will.
May He establish His kingdom,
make His salvation flourish,
and hasten His messiah,
in your lifetime and in your days,
and in the lifetime of all the house of Israel,
swiftly and soon – and say: Amen.

*All:* May His great name be blessed for ever and all time.

*Leader:* Blessed and praised, glorified and exalted,
raised and honored, uplifted and lauded be
the name of the Holy One,
blessed be He,
beyond any blessing, song, praise and consolation
uttered in the world – and say: Amen.

TEKIA SHEVARIM TERUA TEKIA
TEKIA SHEVARIM TEKIA
TEKIA TERUA TEKIA GEDOLA

May the prayers and pleas of all the house of Israel
be accepted by their Father in heaven – and say: Amen.

May there be great peace from heaven,
and a good life for us and all Israel – and say: Amen.

*Bow, take three steps back, as if taking leave of the Divine Presence, then bow, first left, then right, then center, while saying:*

May He who makes peace in His high places,
make peace for us and all Israel – and say: Amen.

*The most common custom is to sound ten notes in the middle of* קדיש שלם, *before* תתקבל, *in order to complete one hundred notes (see law 81).*

*Congregations who did not blew the* שופר *during the silent* עמידה, *blow forty additional notes; some sound all forty before* תתקבל, *and others sound thirty notes after* קדיש שלם, *and ten more before the concluding* עָלֵינוּ.

## קדיש שלם

ש״ץ: יִתְגַּדַּל וְיִתְקַדַּשׁ שְׁמֵהּ רַבָּא (קהל: אָמֵן)
בְּעָלְמָא דִּי בְרָא כִרְעוּתֵהּ
וְיַמְלִיךְ מַלְכוּתֵהּ וְיַצְמַח פֻּרְקָנֵהּ וִיקָרֵב מְשִׁיחֵהּ (קהל: אָמֵן)
בְּחַיֵּיכוֹן וּבְיוֹמֵיכוֹן וּבְחַיֵּי דְכָל בֵּית יִשְׂרָאֵל
בַּעֲגָלָא וּבִזְמַן קָרִיב, וְאִמְרוּ אָמֵן. (קהל: אָמֵן)

קהל וש״ץ: יְהֵא שְׁמֵהּ רַבָּא מְבָרַךְ לְעָלַם וּלְעָלְמֵי עָלְמַיָּא.

ש״ץ: יִתְבָּרַךְ וְיִשְׁתַּבַּח וְיִתְפָּאַר וְיִתְרוֹמַם וְיִתְנַשֵּׂא
וְיִתְהַדָּר וְיִתְעַלֶּה וְיִתְהַלָּל
שְׁמֵהּ דְּקֻדְשָׁא בְּרִיךְ הוּא (קהל: אָמֵן)
לְעֵלָּא לְעֵלָּא מִכָּל בִּרְכָתָא וְשִׁירָתָא, תֻּשְׁבְּחָתָא וְנֶחֱמָתָא
דַּאֲמִירָן בְּעָלְמָא, וְאִמְרוּ אָמֵן. (קהל: אָמֵן)

תקיעה שברים תרועה תקיעה
תקיעה שברים תקיעה
תקיעה תרועה תקיעה גדולה

תִּתְקַבַּל צְלוֹתְהוֹן וּבָעוּתְהוֹן דְּכָל בֵּית יִשְׂרָאֵל
קֳדָם אֲבוּהוֹן דִּי בִשְׁמַיָּא, וְאִמְרוּ אָמֵן. (קהל: אָמֵן)

יְהֵא שְׁלָמָא רַבָּא מִן שְׁמַיָּא
וְחַיִּים טוֹבִים עָלֵינוּ וְעַל כָּל יִשְׂרָאֵל, וְאִמְרוּ אָמֵן. (קהל: אָמֵן)

*Bow, take three steps back, as if taking leave of the Divine Presence, then bow, first left, then right, then center, while saying:*

עֹשֶׂה הַשָּׁלוֹם בִּמְרוֹמָיו, הוּא יַעֲשֶׂה שָׁלוֹם עָלֵינוּ
וְעַל כָּל יִשְׂרָאֵל, וְאִמְרוּ אָמֵן. (קהל: אָמֵן)

קַוֵּה Hope in the LORD. Be strong and of good courage, and hope in the LORD! *Ps. 27*

There is no other one holy like the LORD, for there is none besides You, there is no Rock like our God. *I Sam. 2*

For who but the LORD is God; who is a Rock apart from our God? *Ps. 18*

אֵין כֵּאלֹהֵינוּ There is none like our God, none like our LORD,
none like our King, none like our Savior.
Who is like our God? Who is like our LORD?
Who is like our King? Who is like our Savior?
We will thank our God, we will thank our LORD,
we will thank our King, we will thank our Savior.
Blessed is our God, blessed is our LORD,
blessed is our King, blessed is our Savior.
You are our God, You are our LORD,
You are our King, You are our Savior.
You are He to whom our ancestors offered the fragrant incense.

פִּטּוּם הַקְּטֹרֶת The incense mixture consisted of balsam, onycha, galbanum and frankincense, each weighing seventy manehs; myrrh, cassia, spikenard and saffron, each weighing sixteen manehs; twelve manehs of costus, three of aromatic bark; nine of cinnamon; nine kabs of Carsina lye; three seahs and three kabs of Cyprus wine. If Cyprus wine was not available, old white wine might be used. A quarter of a kab of Sodom salt, and a minute amount of a smoke-raising herb. Rabbi Nathan says: Also a minute amount of Jordan amber. If one added honey to the mixture, he rendered it unfit for sacred use. If he omitted any one of its ingredients, he is guilty of a capital offense. *Keritot 6a*

Rabban Shimon ben Gamliel says: "Balsam" refers to the sap that drips from the balsam tree. The Carsina lye was used for bleaching the onycha to improve it. The Cyprus wine was used to soak the onycha in it to make it pungent. Though urine is suitable for this purpose, it is not brought into the Temple out of respect.

These were the psalms which the Levites used to recite in the Temple: *Mishna, Tamid 7*

On the first day of the week they used to say: "The earth is the LORD's and all it contains, the world and all who live in it." *Ps. 24*

On the second day they used to say: "Great is the LORD and greatly to be praised in the city of God, on His holy mountain." *Ps. 48*

קַוֵּה אֶל־יהוה, חֲזַק וְיַאֲמֵץ לִבֶּךָ, וְקַוֵּה אֶל־יהוה: תהלים כז
אֵין־קָדוֹשׁ כַּיהוה, כִּי־אֵין בִּלְתֶּךָ, וְאֵין צוּר כֵּאלֹהֵינוּ: שמואל א׳ ב
כִּי מִי אֱלוֹהַּ מִבַּלְעֲדֵי יהוה, וּמִי צוּר זוּלָתִי אֱלֹהֵינוּ: תהלים יח

אֵין כֵּאלֹהֵינוּ, אֵין כַּאדוֹנֵינוּ, אֵין כְּמַלְכֵּנוּ, אֵין כְּמוֹשִׁיעֵנוּ.
מִי כֵאלֹהֵינוּ, מִי כַאדוֹנֵינוּ, מִי כְמַלְכֵּנוּ, מִי כְמוֹשִׁיעֵנוּ.
נוֹדֶה לֵאלֹהֵינוּ, נוֹדֶה לַאדוֹנֵינוּ, נוֹדֶה לְמַלְכֵּנוּ, נוֹדֶה לְמוֹשִׁיעֵנוּ.
בָּרוּךְ אֱלֹהֵינוּ, בָּרוּךְ אֲדוֹנֵינוּ, בָּרוּךְ מַלְכֵּנוּ, בָּרוּךְ מוֹשִׁיעֵנוּ.
אַתָּה הוּא אֱלֹהֵינוּ, אַתָּה הוּא אֲדוֹנֵינוּ
אַתָּה הוּא מַלְכֵּנוּ, אַתָּה הוּא מוֹשִׁיעֵנוּ.
אַתָּה הוּא שֶׁהִקְטִירוּ אֲבוֹתֵינוּ לְפָנֶיךָ אֶת קְטֹרֶת הַסַּמִּים.

כריתות ו. פִּטּוּם הַקְּטֹרֶת. הַצֳּרִי, וְהַצִּפֹּרֶן, וְהַחֶלְבְּנָה, וְהַלְּבוֹנָה מִשְׁקַל שִׁבְעִים שִׁבְעִים מָנֶה, מֹר, וּקְצִיעָה, שִׁבֹּלֶת נֵרְדְּ, וְכַרְכֹּם מִשְׁקַל שִׁשָּׁה עָשָׂר שִׁשָּׁה עָשָׂר מָנֶה, הַקֹּשְׁטְ שְׁנֵים עָשָׂר, קִלּוּפָה שְׁלֹשָׁה, וְקִנָּמוֹן תִּשְׁעָה, בֹּרִית כַּרְשִׁינָה תִּשְׁעָה קַבִּין, יֵין קַפְרִיסִין סְאִין תְּלָת וְקַבִּין תְּלָתָא וְאִם אֵין לוֹ יֵין קַפְרִיסִין, מֵבִיא חֲמַר חִוַּרְיָן עַתִּיק. מֶלַח סְדוֹמִית רֹבַע, מַעֲלֶה עָשָׁן כָּל שֶׁהוּא. רַבִּי נָתָן הַבַּבְלִי אוֹמֵר: אַף כִּפַּת הַיַּרְדֵּן כָּל שֶׁהוּא, וְאִם נָתַן בָּהּ דְּבַשׁ פְּסָלָהּ, וְאִם חִסַּר אֶחָד מִכָּל סַמָּנֶיהָ, חַיָּב מִיתָה.

רַבָּן שִׁמְעוֹן בֶּן גַּמְלִיאֵל אוֹמֵר: הַצֳּרִי אֵינוֹ אֶלָּא שְׂרָף הַנּוֹטֵף מֵעֲצֵי הַקְּטָף. בֹּרִית כַּרְשִׁינָה שֶׁשָּׁפִין בָּהּ אֶת הַצִּפֹּרֶן כְּדֵי שֶׁתְּהֵא נָאָה, יֵין קַפְרִיסִין שֶׁשּׁוֹרִין בּוֹ אֶת הַצִּפֹּרֶן כְּדֵי שֶׁתְּהֵא עַזָּה, וַהֲלֹא מֵי רַגְלַיִם יָפִין לָהּ, אֶלָּא שֶׁאֵין מַכְנִיסִין מֵי רַגְלַיִם בַּמִּקְדָּשׁ מִפְּנֵי הַכָּבוֹד.

משנה תמיד ז הַשִּׁיר שֶׁהַלְוִיִּם הָיוּ אוֹמְרִים בְּבֵית הַמִּקְדָּשׁ:
בַּיּוֹם הָרִאשׁוֹן הָיוּ אוֹמְרִים, לַיהוה הָאָרֶץ וּמְלוֹאָהּ, תֵּבֵל וְיֽשְׁבֵי בָהּ: תהלים כד
בַּשֵּׁנִי הָיוּ אוֹמְרִים, גָּדוֹל יהוה וּמְהֻלָּל מְאֹד, בְּעִיר אֱלֹהֵינוּ הַר־קָדְשׁוֹ: תהלים מח

On the third day they used to say: "God stands in the divine assembly. *Ps. 82*
Among the judges He delivers judgment."
On the fourth day they used to say: "God of retribution, LORD, *Ps. 94*
God of retribution, appear."
On the fifth day they used to say: "Sing for joy to God, our strength. *Ps. 81*
Shout aloud to the God of Jacob."
On the sixth day they used to say: "The LORD reigns: He is robed in majesty; *Ps. 93*
the LORD is robed, girded with strength;
the world is firmly established; it cannot be moved."
On the Sabbath they used to say: "A psalm, a song for the Sabbath day" – *Ps. 92*
[meaning] a psalm and song for the time to come,
for the day which will be entirely Sabbath and rest for life everlasting.

It was taught in the Academy of Elijah: Whoever studies [Torah] laws every day *Megilla 28b* is assured that he will be destined for the World to Come, as it is said, "The ways of the world are His" – read not, "ways" [*halikhot*] but "laws" [*halakhot*]. *Hab. 3*

Rabbi Elazar said in the name of Rabbi Ḥanina: The disciples of the sages increase *Berakhot 64a* peace in the world, as it is said, "And all your children shall be taught of the LORD, *Is. 54* and great shall be the peace of your children [*banayikh*]." Read not *banayikh*, "your children," but *bonayikh*, "your builders." Those who love Your Torah have *Ps. 119* great peace; there is no stumbling block for them. May there be peace within your *Ps. 122* ramparts, prosperity in your palaces. For the sake of my brothers and friends, I shall say, "Peace be within you." For the sake of the House of the LORD our God, I will seek your good. ▸ May the LORD grant strength to His people; may the *Ps. 29* LORD bless His people with peace.

## THE RABBIS' KADDISH

*The following prayer requires the presence of a minyan.*
*A transliteration can be found on page 1094.*

*Mourner:* יִתְגַּדַּל Magnified and sanctified may His great name be,
in the world He created by His will.
May He establish His kingdom,
make His salvation flourish,
and hasten His messiah,
in your lifetime and in your days,
and in the lifetime of all the house of Israel,
swiftly and soon – and say: Amen.

בַּשְּׁלִישִׁי הָיוּ אוֹמְרִים, אֱלֹהִים נִצָּב בַּעֲדַת־אֵל, בְּקֶרֶב אֱלֹהִים יִשְׁפֹּט: תהלים פב
בָּרְבִיעִי הָיוּ אוֹמְרִים, אֵל־נְקָמוֹת יהוה, אֵל נְקָמוֹת הוֹפִיעַ: תהלים צד
בַּחֲמִישִׁי הָיוּ אוֹמְרִים, הַרְנִינוּ לֵאלֹהִים עוּזֵּנוּ, הָרִיעוּ לֵאלֹהֵי יַעֲקֹב: תהלים פא
בַּשִּׁשִּׁי הָיוּ אוֹמְרִים, יהוה מָלָךְ גֵּאוּת לָבֵשׁ, לָבֵשׁ יהוה עֹז הִתְאַזָּר תהלים צג
אַף־תִּכּוֹן תֵּבֵל בַּל־תִּמּוֹט:
בַּשַּׁבָּת הָיוּ אוֹמְרִים, מִזְמוֹר שִׁיר לְיוֹם הַשַּׁבָּת: תהלים צב
מִזְמוֹר שִׁיר לֶעָתִיד לָבוֹא, לְיוֹם שֶׁכֻּלּוֹ שַׁבָּת וּמְנוּחָה
לְחַיֵּי הָעוֹלָמִים.

תָּנָא דְבֵי אֵלִיָּהוּ: כָּל הַשּׁוֹנֶה הֲלָכוֹת בְּכָל יוֹם, מֻבְטָח לוֹ שֶׁהוּא בֶּן עוֹלָם מגילה כח:
הַבָּא, שֶׁנֶּאֱמַר, הֲלִיכוֹת עוֹלָם לוֹ: אַל תִּקְרֵי הֲלִיכוֹת אֶלָּא הֲלָכוֹת. חבקוק ג

אָמַר רַבִּי אֶלְעָזָר, אָמַר רַבִּי חֲנִינָא: תַּלְמִידֵי חֲכָמִים מַרְבִּים שָׁלוֹם בָּעוֹלָם, ברכות סד.
שֶׁנֶּאֱמַר, וְכָל־בָּנַיִךְ לִמּוּדֵי יהוה, וְרַב שְׁלוֹם בָּנָיִךְ: אַל תִּקְרֵי בָּנָיִךְ, אֶלָּא ישעיה נד
בּוֹנָיִךְ. שָׁלוֹם רָב לְאֹהֲבֵי תוֹרָתֶךָ, וְאֵין־לָמוֹ מִכְשׁוֹל: יְהִי־שָׁלוֹם בְּחֵילֵךְ, תהלים קיט תהלים קכב
שַׁלְוָה בְּאַרְמְנוֹתָיִךְ: לְמַעַן אַחַי וְרֵעָי אֲדַבְּרָה־נָּא שָׁלוֹם בָּךְ: לְמַעַן
בֵּית־יהוה אֱלֹהֵינוּ אֲבַקְשָׁה טוֹב לָךְ: ◂ יהוה עֹז לְעַמּוֹ יִתֵּן, יהוה יְבָרֵךְ תהלים כט
אֶת־עַמּוֹ בַשָּׁלוֹם:

## קדיש דרבנן

*The following prayer, said by mourners, requires the presence of a* מנין*.*
*A transliteration can be found on page 1094.*

יִתְגַּדַּל וְיִתְקַדַּשׁ שְׁמֵהּ רַבָּא (קהל: אָמֵן)
בְּעָלְמָא דִּי בְרָא כִרְעוּתֵהּ
וְיַמְלִיךְ מַלְכוּתֵהּ וְיַצְמַח פֻּרְקָנֵהּ וִיקָרֵב מְשִׁיחֵהּ (קהל: אָמֵן)
בְּחַיֵּיכוֹן וּבְיוֹמֵיכוֹן וּבְחַיֵּי דְכָל בֵּית יִשְׂרָאֵל
בַּעֲגָלָא וּבִזְמַן קָרִיב
וְאִמְרוּ אָמֵן. (קהל: אָמֵן)

*All:* May His great name be blessed for ever and all time.

*Mourner:* Blessed and praised,
glorified and exalted,
raised and honored,
uplifted and lauded
be the name of the Holy One,
blessed be He,
beyond any blessing,
song, praise and consolation
uttered in the world –
and say: Amen.

To Israel, to the teachers,
their disciples and their disciples' disciples,
and to all who engage
in the study of Torah,
in this (*in Israel add:* holy) place or elsewhere,
may there come to them and you great peace,
grace, kindness and compassion,
long life, ample sustenance
and deliverance, from their Father
who is in heaven and on earth –
and say: Amen.

May there be great peace from heaven,
and a good life for us and all Israel –
and say: Amen.

*Bow, take three steps back, as if taking leave of the Divine Presence, then bow, first left, then right, then center, while saying:*

May He who makes peace in His high places,
in His compassion make peace
for us and all Israel –
and say: Amen.

קהל ואבל: יְהֵא שְׁמֵהּ רַבָּא מְבָרַךְ לְעָלַם וּלְעָלְמֵי עָלְמַיָּא.

אבל: יִתְבָּרַךְ וְיִשְׁתַּבַּח וְיִתְפָּאַר וְיִתְרוֹמַם וְיִתְנַשֵּׂא
וְיִתְהַדָּר וְיִתְעַלֶּה וְיִתְהַלָּל
שְׁמֵהּ דְּקֻדְשָׁא בְּרִיךְ הוּא (קהל: אָמֵן)
לְעֵלָּא לְעֵלָּא מִכָּל בִּרְכָתָא וְשִׁירָתָא, תֻּשְׁבְּחָתָא וְנֶחֱמָתָא
דַּאֲמִירָן בְּעָלְמָא
וְאִמְרוּ אָמֵן. (קהל: אָמֵן)

עַל יִשְׂרָאֵל וְעַל רַבָּנָן
וְעַל תַּלְמִידֵיהוֹן וְעַל כָּל תַּלְמִידֵי תַלְמִידֵיהוֹן
וְעַל כָּל מָאן דְּעָסְקִין בְּאוֹרַיְתָא
דִּי בְּאַתְרָא (בארץ ישראל: קַדִּישָׁא) הָדֵין, וְדִי בְּכָל אֲתַר וַאֲתַר
יְהֵא לְהוֹן וּלְכוֹן שְׁלָמָא רַבָּא
חִנָּא וְחִסְדָּא, וְרַחֲמֵי, וְחַיֵּי אֲרִיכֵי, וּמְזוֹנֵי רְוִיחֵי
וּפֻרְקָנָא מִן קֳדָם אֲבוּהוֹן
דִּי בִשְׁמַיָּא וְאַרְעָא
וְאִמְרוּ אָמֵן. (קהל: אָמֵן)

יְהֵא שְׁלָמָא רַבָּא מִן שְׁמַיָּא
וְחַיִּים טוֹבִים עָלֵינוּ וְעַל כָּל יִשְׂרָאֵל
וְאִמְרוּ אָמֵן. (קהל: אָמֵן)

*Bow, take three steps back, as if taking leave of the Divine Presence, then bow, first left, then right, then center, while saying:*

עֹשֶׂה הַשָּׁלוֹם בִּמְרוֹמָיו
הוּא בְּרַחֲמָיו יַעֲשֶׂה שָׁלוֹם עָלֵינוּ וְעַל כָּל יִשְׂרָאֵל
וְאִמְרוּ אָמֵן. (קהל: אָמֵן)

*Stand while saying Aleinu. Bow at* ▾.

עָלֵינוּ It is our duty to praise the Master of all,
and ascribe greatness to the Author of creation,
who has not made us like the nations of the lands
nor placed us like the families of the earth;
who has not made our portion like theirs,
nor our destiny like all their multitudes.
(For they worship vanity and emptiness,
and pray to a god who cannot save.)
▾But we bow in worship
and thank the Supreme King of kings, the Holy One, blessed be He,
who extends the heavens and establishes the earth,
whose throne of glory is in the heavens above,
and whose power's Presence is in the highest of heights.
He is our God; there is no other.
Truly He is our King, there is none else, as it is written in His Torah:
"You shall know and take to heart this day *Deut. 4*
that the LORD is God, in the heavens above and on the earth below.
There is no other."

Therefore, we place our hope in You, LORD our God,
that we may soon see the glory of Your power,
when You will remove abominations from the earth,
and idols will be utterly destroyed,
when the world will be perfected under the sovereignty of the Almighty,
when all humanity will call on Your name,
to turn all the earth's wicked toward You.
All the world's inhabitants will realize and know
that to You every knee must bow and every tongue swear loyalty.
Before You, LORD our God, they will kneel and bow down
and give honor to Your glorious name.
They will all accept the yoke of Your kingdom,
and You will reign over them soon and for ever.
For the kingdom is Yours, and to all eternity You will reign in glory,
as it is written in Your Torah: "The LORD will reign for ever and ever." *Ex. 15*
▸ And it is said: "Then the LORD shall be King over all the earth; *Zech. 14*
on that day the LORD shall be One and His name One."

*Stand while saying* עָלֵינוּ. *Bow at* ▾.

עָלֵינוּ לְשַׁבֵּחַ לַאֲדוֹן הַכֹּל, לָתֵת גְּדֻלָּה לְיוֹצֵר בְּרֵאשִׁית
שֶׁלֹּא עָשָׂנוּ כְּגוֹיֵי הָאֲרָצוֹת, וְלֹא שָׂמָנוּ כְּמִשְׁפְּחוֹת הָאֲדָמָה
שֶׁלֹּא שָׂם חֶלְקֵנוּ כָּהֶם וְגוֹרָלֵנוּ כְּכָל הֲמוֹנָם.
(שֶׁהֵם מִשְׁתַּחֲוִים לְהֶבֶל וָרִיק וּמִתְפַּלְלִים אֶל אֵל לֹא יוֹשִׁיעַ.)
▾וַאֲנַחְנוּ כּוֹרְעִים וּמִשְׁתַּחֲוִים וּמוֹדִים
לִפְנֵי מֶלֶךְ מַלְכֵי הַמְּלָכִים, הַקָּדוֹשׁ בָּרוּךְ הוּא
שֶׁהוּא נוֹטֶה שָׁמַיִם וְיוֹסֵד אָרֶץ, וּמוֹשַׁב יְקָרוֹ בַּשָּׁמַיִם מִמַּעַל
וּשְׁכִינַת עֻזּוֹ בְּגָבְהֵי מְרוֹמִים.
הוּא אֱלֹהֵינוּ, אֵין עוֹד.
אֱמֶת מַלְכֵּנוּ, אֶפֶס זוּלָתוֹ כַּכָּתוּב בְּתוֹרָתוֹ
דברים ד וְיָדַעְתָּ הַיּוֹם וַהֲשֵׁבֹתָ אֶל־לְבָבֶךָ
כִּי יהוה הוּא הָאֱלֹהִים בַּשָּׁמַיִם מִמַּעַל וְעַל־הָאָרֶץ מִתָּחַת, אֵין עוֹד:

וְעַל כֵּן נְקַוֶּה לְּךָ יהוה אֱלֹהֵינוּ, לִרְאוֹת מְהֵרָה בְּתִפְאֶרֶת עֻזֶּךָ
לְהַעֲבִיר גִּלּוּלִים מִן הָאָרֶץ, וְהָאֱלִילִים כָּרוֹת יִכָּרֵתוּן
לְתַקֵּן עוֹלָם בְּמַלְכוּת שַׁדַּי.
וְכָל בְּנֵי בָשָׂר יִקְרְאוּ בִשְׁמֶךָ לְהַפְנוֹת אֵלֶיךָ כָּל רִשְׁעֵי אָרֶץ.
יַכִּירוּ וְיֵדְעוּ כָּל יוֹשְׁבֵי תֵבֵל
כִּי לְךָ תִּכְרַע כָּל בֶּרֶךְ, תִּשָּׁבַע כָּל לָשׁוֹן.
לְפָנֶיךָ יהוה אֱלֹהֵינוּ יִכְרְעוּ וְיִפֹּלוּ, וְלִכְבוֹד שִׁמְךָ יְקָר יִתֵּנוּ
וִיקַבְּלוּ כֻלָּם אֶת עֹל מַלְכוּתֶךָ
וְתִמְלֹךְ עֲלֵיהֶם מְהֵרָה לְעוֹלָם וָעֶד.
כִּי הַמַּלְכוּת שֶׁלְּךָ הִיא וּלְעוֹלְמֵי עַד תִּמְלֹךְ בְּכָבוֹד
שמות טו כַּכָּתוּב בְּתוֹרָתֶךָ, יהוה יִמְלֹךְ לְעֹלָם וָעֶד:
זכריה יד ◂ וְנֶאֱמַר, וְהָיָה יהוה לְמֶלֶךְ עַל־כָּל־הָאָרֶץ
בַּיּוֹם הַהוּא יִהְיֶה יהוה אֶחָד וּשְׁמוֹ אֶחָד:

*Some add:*

Have no fear of sudden terror or of the ruin when it overtakes the wicked. *Prov. 3*
Devise your strategy, but it will be thwarted; propose your plan, *Is. 8*
but it will not stand, for God is with us.
When you grow old, I will still be the same. *Is. 46*
When your hair turns gray, I will still carry you.
I made you, I will bear you, I will carry you, and I will rescue you.

## MOURNER'S KADDISH

*The following prayer, said by mourners, requires the presence of a minyan. A transliteration can be found on page 1095.*

*Mourner:* יִתְגַּדַּל Magnified and sanctified may His great name be,
in the world He created by His will.
May He establish His kingdom,
make His salvation flourish, and hasten His messiah,
in your lifetime and in your days,
and in the lifetime of all the house of Israel,
swiftly and soon –
and say: Amen.

*All:* May His great name be blessed for ever and all time.

*Mourner:* Blessed and praised, glorified and exalted,
raised and honored, uplifted and lauded
be the name of the Holy One,
blessed be He,
beyond any blessing, song, praise and consolation
uttered in the world –
and say: Amen.

May there be great peace from heaven,
and a good life for us and all Israel –
and say: Amen.

*Bow, take three steps back, as if taking leave of the Divine Presence, then bow, first left, then right, then center, while saying:*

May He who makes peace in His high places,
make peace for us and all Israel –
and say: Amen.

*Some add:*

אַל־תִּירָא מִפַּחַד פִּתְאֹם וּמִשֹּׁאַת רְשָׁעִים כִּי תָבֹא: משלי ג

עֻצוּ עֵצָה וְתֻפָר, דַּבְּרוּ דָבָר וְלֹא יָקוּם, כִּי עִמָּנוּ אֵל: ישעיה ח

וְעַד־זִקְנָה אֲנִי הוּא, וְעַד־שֵׂיבָה אֲנִי אֶסְבֹּל ישעיה מו

אֲנִי עָשִׂיתִי וַאֲנִי אֶשָּׂא וַאֲנִי אֶסְבֹּל וַאֲמַלֵּט:

## קדיש יתום

*The following prayer, said by mourners, requires the presence of a* מנין*.*
*A transliteration can be found on page 1095.*

אבל: יִתְגַּדַּל וְיִתְקַדַּשׁ שְׁמֵהּ רַבָּא (קהל: אָמֵן)

בְּעָלְמָא דִּי בְרָא כִרְעוּתֵהּ

וְיַמְלִיךְ מַלְכוּתֵהּ

וְיַצְמַח פֻּרְקָנֵהּ וִיקָרֵב מְשִׁיחֵהּ (קהל: אָמֵן)

בְּחַיֵּיכוֹן וּבְיוֹמֵיכוֹן וּבְחַיֵּי דְכָל בֵּית יִשְׂרָאֵל

בַּעֲגָלָא וּבִזְמַן קָרִיב, וְאִמְרוּ אָמֵן. (קהל: אָמֵן)

קהל ואבל: יְהֵא שְׁמֵהּ רַבָּא מְבָרַךְ לְעָלַם וּלְעָלְמֵי עָלְמַיָּא.

אבל: יִתְבָּרַךְ וְיִשְׁתַּבַּח וְיִתְפָּאַר

וְיִתְרוֹמַם וְיִתְנַשֵּׂא וְיִתְהַדָּר וְיִתְעַלֶּה וְיִתְהַלָּל

שְׁמֵהּ דְּקֻדְשָׁא בְּרִיךְ הוּא (קהל: אָמֵן)

לְעֵלָּא לְעֵלָּא מִכָּל בִּרְכָתָא

וְשִׁירָתָא, תֻּשְׁבְּחָתָא וְנֶחֱמָתָא

דַּאֲמִירָן בְּעָלְמָא, וְאִמְרוּ אָמֵן. (קהל: אָמֵן)

יְהֵא שְׁלָמָא רַבָּא מִן שְׁמַיָּא

וְחַיִּים טוֹבִים עָלֵינוּ וְעַל כָּל יִשְׂרָאֵל, וְאִמְרוּ אָמֵן. (קהל: אָמֵן)

*Bow, take three steps back, as if taking leave of the Divine Presence,*
*then bow, first left, then right, then center, while saying:*

עֹשֶׂה הַשָּׁלוֹם בִּמְרוֹמָיו, הוּא יַעֲשֶׂה שָׁלוֹם עָלֵינוּ

וְעַל כָּל יִשְׂרָאֵל, וְאִמְרוּ אָמֵן. (קהל: אָמֵן)

## SONG OF GLORY

*The Ark is opened and all stand.*

*Leader:* I will sing sweet psalms and I will weave songs,
to You for whom my soul longs.

*Cong:* My soul yearns for the shelter of Your hand,
that all Your mystic secrets I might understand.

*Leader:* Whenever I speak of Your glory above,
my heart is yearning for Your love.

*Cong:* So Your glories I will proclaim,
and in songs of love give honor to Your name.

*Leader:* I will tell of Your glory though I have not seen You;
imagine and describe You, though I have not known You.

*Cong:* By the hand of Your prophets, through Your servants' mystery,
You gave a glimpse of Your wondrous majesty.

*Leader:* Recounting Your grandeur and Your glory,
of Your great deeds they told the story.

*Cong:* They depicted You, though not as You are,
but as You do: Your acts, Your power.

*Leader:* They represented You in many visions;
through them all You are One without divisions.

*Cong:* They saw You, now old, then young,
Your head with gray, with black hair hung.

*Leader:* Aged on the day of judgment, yet on the day of war,
a young warrior with mighty hands they saw.

*Cong:* Triumph like a helmet He wore on His head;
His right hand and holy arm to victory have led.

*Leader:* His curls are filled with dew drops of light,
His locks with fragments of the night.

*Cong:* He will glory in me, for He delights in me;
My diadem of beauty He shall be.

*Leader:* His head is like pure beaten gold;
Engraved on His brow, His sacred name behold.

*Cong:* For grace and glory, beauty and renown,
His people have adorned Him with a crown.

# שיר הכבוד

*The* ארון קודש *is opened and all stand.*

ש״ץ: אַנְעִים זְמִירוֹת וְשִׁירִים אֶאֱרֹג, כִּי אֵלֶיךָ נַפְשִׁי תַעֲרֹג.

קהל: נַפְשִׁי חִמְּדָה בְּצֵל יָדֶךָ, לָדַעַת כָּל רָז סוֹדֶךָ.

ש״ץ: מִדֵּי דַבְּרִי בִּכְבוֹדֶךָ, הוֹמֶה לִבִּי אֶל דּוֹדֶיךָ.

קהל: עַל כֵּן אֲדַבֵּר בְּךָ נִכְבָּדוֹת, וְשִׁמְךָ אֲכַבֵּד בְּשִׁירֵי יְדִידוֹת.

ש״ץ: אֲסַפְּרָה כְבוֹדְךָ וְלֹא רְאִיתִיךָ, אֲדַמְּךָ אֲכַנְּךָ וְלֹא יְדַעְתִּיךָ.

קהל: בְּיַד נְבִיאֶיךָ בְּסוֹד עֲבָדֶיךָ, דִּמִּיתָ הֲדַר כְּבוֹד הוֹדֶךָ.

ש״ץ: גְּדֻלָּתְךָ וּגְבוּרָתֶךָ, כִּנּוּ לְתֹקֶף פְּעֻלָּתֶךָ.

קהל: דִּמּוּ אוֹתְךָ וְלֹא כְפִי יֶשְׁךָ, וַיְשַׁוּוּךָ לְפִי מַעֲשֶׂיךָ.

ש״ץ: הִמְשִׁילְוּךָ בְּרֹב חֶזְיוֹנוֹת, הִנְּךָ אֶחָד בְּכָל דִּמְיוֹנוֹת.

קהל: וַיֶּחֱזוּ בְךָ זִקְנָה וּבַחֲרוּת, וּשְׂעַר רֹאשְׁךָ בְּשֵׂיבָה וְשַׁחֲרוּת.

ש״ץ: זִקְנָה בְּיוֹם דִּין וּבַחֲרוּת בְּיוֹם קְרָב, כְּאִישׁ מִלְחָמוֹת יָדָיו לוֹ רָב.

קהל: חָבַשׁ כּוֹבַע יְשׁוּעָה בְּרֹאשׁוֹ, הוֹשִׁיעָה לּוֹ יְמִינוֹ וּזְרוֹעַ קָדְשׁוֹ.

ש״ץ: טַלְלֵי אוֹרוֹת רֹאשׁוֹ נִמְלָא, קְוֻצּוֹתָיו רְסִיסֵי לָיְלָה.

קהל: יִתְפָּאֵר בִּי כִּי חָפֵץ בִּי, וְהוּא יִהְיֶה לִּי לַעֲטֶרֶת צְבִי.

ש״ץ: כֶּתֶם טָהוֹר פָּז דְּמוּת רֹאשׁוֹ, וְחַק עַל מֵצַח כְּבוֹד שֵׁם קָדְשׁוֹ.

קהל: לְחֵן וּלְכָבוֹד צְבִי תִפְאָרָה, אֻמָּתוֹ לוֹ עִטְּרָה עֲטָרָה.

*Leader:* Like a youth's, His hair in locks unfurls;
Its black tresses flowing in curls.

*Cong:* Jerusalem, His splendor, is the dwelling place of right;
may He prize it as His highest delight.

*Leader:* Like a crown in His hand may His treasured people be,
a turban of beauty and of majesty.

*Cong:* He bore them, carried them, with a crown He adorned them.
They were precious in His sight, and He honored them.

*Leader:* His glory is on me; my glory is on Him.
He is near to me when I call to Him.

*Cong:* He is bright and rosy; red will be His dress,
when He comes from Edom, treading the winepress.

*Leader:* He showed the tefillin-knot to Moses, humble, wise,
when the LORD's likeness was before his eyes.

*Cong:* He delights in His people; the humble He does raise –
He glories in them; He sits enthroned upon their praise.

*Leader:* Your first word, Your call to every age, is true:
O seek the people who seek You.

*Cong:* My many songs please take and hear
and may my hymn of joy to You come near.

*Leader:* May my praise be a crown for Your head,
and like incense before You, the prayers I have said.

*Cong:* May a poor man's song be precious in Your eyes,
like a song sung over sacrifice.

*Leader:* To the One who sustains all, may my blessing take flight:
Creator, Life-Giver, God of right and might.

*Cong:* And when I offer blessing, to me Your head incline:
accepting it as spice, fragrant and fine.

*Leader:* May my prayer be to You sweet song.
For You my soul will always long.

*The Ark is closed.*

Yours, LORD, are the greatness and the power, the glory, the majesty and *I Chr. 29*
splendor, for everything in heaven and earth is Yours. Yours, LORD, is the
kingdom; You are exalted as Head over all. ▸ Who can tell of the mighty *Ps. 106*
acts of the LORD and make all His praise be heard?

ש״ץ: מַחְלְפוֹת רֹאשׁוֹ כְּבִימֵי בְחוּרוֹת, קְוֻצּוֹתָיו תַּלְתַּלִּים שְׁחוֹרוֹת.
קהל: נְוֵה הַצֶּדֶק צְבִי תִפְאַרְתּוֹ, יַעֲלֶה נָּא עַל רֹאשׁ שִׂמְחָתוֹ.

ש״ץ: סְגֻלָּתוֹ תְּהִי בְיָדוֹ עֲטֶרֶת, וּצְנִיף מְלוּכָה צְבִי תִפְאֶרֶת.
קהל: עֲמוּסִים נְשָׂאָם, עֲטֶרֶת עִנְּדָם, מֵאֲשֶׁר יָקְרוּ בְעֵינָיו כִּבְּדָם.

ש״ץ: פְּאֵרוֹ עָלַי וּפְאֵרִי עָלָיו, וְקָרוֹב אֵלַי בְּקָרְאִי אֵלָיו.
קהל: צַח וְאָדֹם לִלְבוּשׁוֹ אָדֹם, פּוּרָה בְדָרְכוֹ בְּבוֹאוֹ מֵאֱדוֹם.

ש״ץ: קֶשֶׁר תְּפִלִּין הֶרְאָה לֶעָנָו, תְּמוּנַת יהוה לְנֶגֶד עֵינָיו.
קהל: רוֹצֶה בְעַמּוֹ עֲנָוִים יְפָאֵר, יוֹשֵׁב תְּהִלּוֹת בָּם לְהִתְפָּאֵר.

ש״ץ: רֹאשׁ דְּבָרְךָ אֱמֶת קוֹרֵא מֵרֹאשׁ דּוֹר וָדוֹר, עַם דּוֹרֶשְׁךָ דְּרֹשׁ.
קהל: שִׁית הֲמוֹן שִׁירַי נָא עָלֶיךָ, וְרִנָּתִי תִּקְרַב אֵלֶיךָ.

ש״ץ: תְּהִלָּתִי תְּהִי לְרֹאשְׁךָ עֲטֶרֶת, וּתְפִלָּתִי תִּכּוֹן קְטֹרֶת.
קהל: תִּיקַר שִׁירַת רָשׁ בְּעֵינֶיךָ, כַּשִּׁיר יוּשַׁר עַל קָרְבָּנֶיךָ.

ש״ץ: בִּרְכָתִי תַעֲלֶה לְרֹאשׁ מַשְׁבִּיר, מְחוֹלֵל וּמוֹלִיד, צַדִּיק כַּבִּיר.
קהל: וּבְבִרְכָתִי תְנַעֲנַע לִי רֹאשׁ, וְאוֹתָהּ קַח לְךָ כִּבְשָׂמִים רֹאשׁ.

ש״ץ: יֶעֱרַב נָא שִׂיחִי עָלֶיךָ, כִּי נַפְשִׁי תַעֲרֹג אֵלֶיךָ.

*The* ארון קודש *is closed.*

לְךָ יהוה הַגְּדֻלָּה וְהַגְּבוּרָה וְהַתִּפְאֶרֶת וְהַנֵּצַח וְהַהוֹד דברי הימים א׳ כט
כִּי־כֹל בַּשָּׁמַיִם וּבָאָרֶץ
לְךָ יהוה הַמַּמְלָכָה וְהַמִּתְנַשֵּׂא לְכֹל לְרֹאשׁ:
◂ מִי יְמַלֵּל גְּבוּרוֹת יהוה, יַשְׁמִיעַ כָּל־תְּהִלָּתוֹ: תהלים קו

## MOURNER'S KADDISH

*The following prayer, said by mourners, requires the presence of a minyan. A transliteration can be found on page 1095.*

*Mourner:* יִתְגַּדַּל Magnified and sanctified
may His great name be,
in the world He created by His will.
May He establish His kingdom,
make His salvation flourish,
and hasten His messiah,
in your lifetime and in your days,
and in the lifetime of all the house of Israel,
swiftly and soon –
and say: Amen.

*All:* May His great name be blessed for ever and all time.

*Mourner:* Blessed and praised, glorified and exalted,
raised and honored, uplifted and lauded
be the name of the Holy One,
blessed be He,
beyond any blessing,
song, praise and consolation
uttered in the world –
and say: Amen.

May there be great peace from heaven,
and a good life for us and all Israel –
and say: Amen.

*Bow, take three steps back, as if taking leave of the Divine Presence, then bow, first left, then right, then center, while saying:*

May He who makes peace in His high places,
make peace for us and all Israel –
and say: Amen.

*Many congregations conclude the service with Adon Olam (page 220) and/or Yigdal (page 222).*

## קדיש יתום

*The following prayer, said by mourners, requires the presence of a* מנין*.*
*A transliteration can be found on page 1095.*

אבל: יִתְגַּדַּל וְיִתְקַדַּשׁ שְׁמֵהּ רַבָּא (קהל: אָמֵן)
בְּעָלְמָא דִּי בְרָא כִרְעוּתֵהּ
וְיַמְלִיךְ מַלְכוּתֵהּ
וְיַצְמַח פֻּרְקָנֵהּ וִיקָרֵב מְשִׁיחֵהּ (קהל: אָמֵן)
בְּחַיֵּיכוֹן וּבְיוֹמֵיכוֹן וּבְחַיֵּי דְכָל בֵּית יִשְׂרָאֵל
בַּעֲגָלָא וּבִזְמַן קָרִיב, וְאִמְרוּ אָמֵן. (קהל: אָמֵן)

קהל ואבל: יְהֵא שְׁמֵהּ רַבָּא מְבָרַךְ לְעָלַם וּלְעָלְמֵי עָלְמַיָּא.

אבל: יִתְבָּרַךְ וְיִשְׁתַּבַּח וְיִתְפָּאַר
וְיִתְרוֹמַם וְיִתְנַשֵּׂא וְיִתְהַדָּר וְיִתְעַלֶּה וְיִתְהַלָּל
שְׁמֵהּ דְּקֻדְשָׁא בְּרִיךְ הוּא (קהל: אָמֵן)
לְעֵלָּא לְעֵלָּא מִכָּל בִּרְכָתָא
וְשִׁירָתָא, תֻּשְׁבְּחָתָא וְנֶחֱמָתָא
דַּאֲמִירָן בְּעָלְמָא, וְאִמְרוּ אָמֵן. (קהל: אָמֵן)

יְהֵא שְׁלָמָא רַבָּא מִן שְׁמַיָּא
וְחַיִּים טוֹבִים עָלֵינוּ וְעַל כָּל יִשְׂרָאֵל, וְאִמְרוּ אָמֵן. (קהל: אָמֵן)

*Bow, take three steps back, as if taking leave of the Divine Presence, then bow, first left, then right, then center, while saying:*

עֹשֶׂה הַשָּׁלוֹם בִּמְרוֹמָיו
הוּא יַעֲשֶׂה שָׁלוֹם עָלֵינוּ
וְעַל כָּל יִשְׂרָאֵל, וְאִמְרוּ אָמֵן. (קהל: אָמֵן)

*Many congregations conclude the service with* אֲדוֹן עוֹלָם *(page 221) and/or* יִגְדַּל *(page 223).*

## KIDDUSH FOR ROSH HASHANA DAY

*On Yom Tov that falls on a weekday, some start here:*

אֵלֶּה These are the appointed times of the Lord, sacred assemblies, which you shall announce in their due season. Thus Moses announced the Lord's appointed seasons to the children of Israel. *Lev. 23*

*On Yom Tov that falls on a weekday, start here:*

תִּקְעוּ Sound the shofar on the new moon, *Ps. 81*
on our feast day when the moon is hidden.
For it is a statute for Israel, an ordinance of the God of Jacob.

*When saying Kiddush for others:* Please pay attention, my masters.

בָּרוּךְ Blessed are You, Lord our God, King of the Universe, who creates the fruit of the vine.

*Birkat HaMazon can be found on page 124.*

## BLESSING AFTER FOOD – AL HAMIḤYA

*Grace after eating from the "seven species" of produce with which Israel is blessed: food made from the five grains (but not bread); wine or grape juice; grapes, figs, pomegranates, olives, or dates.*

בָּרוּךְ Blessed are You, Lord our God, King of the Universe,

| *After grain products (but not bread or matza):* | *After wine or grape juice:* | *After grapes, figs, olives, pomegranates or dates:* |
|---|---|---|
| for the nourishment and sustenance, | for the vine and the fruit of the vine, | for the tree and the fruit of the tree, |

*After grain products (but not bread or matza), and wine or grape juice:*
for the nourishment and sustenance and for the vine and the fruit of the vine,

and for the produce of the field; for the desirable, good and spacious land that You willingly gave as heritage to our ancestors, that they might eat of its fruit and be satisfied with its goodness. Have compassion, please, Lord our God, on Israel Your people, on Jerusalem, Your city, on Zion the home of Your glory, on Your altar and Your Temple. May You rebuild Jerusalem, the holy city swiftly in our time, and may You bring us back there, rejoicing in its rebuilding, eating from its fruit, satisfied by its goodness, and blessing You for it in holiness and purity. Remember us for good on this Day of Remembrance. For You, God, are good and do good to all and we thank You for the land

# קידושא רבה לראש השנה

*On* יום טוב *that falls on a weekday, some start here:*

ויקרא כג
אֵלֶּה מוֹעֲדֵי יהוה מִקְרָאֵי קֹדֶשׁ אֲשֶׁר־תִּקְרְאוּ אֹתָם בְּמוֹעֲדָם:
וַיְדַבֵּר מֹשֶׁה אֶת־מֹעֲדֵי יהוה אֶל־בְּנֵי יִשְׂרָאֵל:

*On* יום טוב *that falls on a weekday, start here:*

תהלים פא
תִּקְעוּ בַחֹדֶשׁ שׁוֹפָר, בַּכֶּסֶה לְיוֹם חַגֵּנוּ:
כִּי חֹק לְיִשְׂרָאֵל הוּא, מִשְׁפָּט לֵאלֹהֵי יַעֲקֹב:

*When saying* קידוש *for others* סַבְרִי מָרָנָן

בָּרוּךְ אַתָּה יהוה אֱלֹהֵינוּ מֶלֶךְ הָעוֹלָם, בּוֹרֵא פְּרִי הַגָּפֶן.

ברכת המזון *can be found on page 125.*

# ברכה מעין שלוש

*Grace after eating from the "seven species" of produce with which* ארץ ישראל *is blessed: food made from the five grains (but not bread); wine or grape juice; grapes, figs, pomegranates, olives, or dates.*

בָּרוּךְ אַתָּה יהוה אֱלֹהֵינוּ מֶלֶךְ הָעוֹלָם, עַל

*After grain products (but not bread or* מצה*):*
הַמִּחְיָה וְעַל הַכַּלְכָּלָה

*After wine or grape juice:*
הַגֶּפֶן וְעַל פְּרִי הַגֶּפֶן

*After grapes, figs, olives, pomegranates or dates:*
הָעֵץ וְעַל פְּרִי הָעֵץ

*After grain products (but not bread or* מצה*), and wine or grape juice:*
הַמִּחְיָה וְעַל הַכַּלְכָּלָה וְעַל הַגֶּפֶן וְעַל פְּרִי הַגֶּפֶן

וְעַל תְּנוּבַת הַשָּׂדֶה וְעַל אֶרֶץ חֶמְדָּה טוֹבָה וּרְחָבָה, שֶׁרָצִיתָ וְהִנְחַלְתָּ לַאֲבוֹתֵינוּ לֶאֱכֹל מִפִּרְיָהּ וְלִשְׂבֹּעַ מִטּוּבָהּ. רַחֵם נָא יהוה אֱלֹהֵינוּ עַל יִשְׂרָאֵל עַמֶּךָ וְעַל יְרוּשָׁלַיִם עִירֶךָ וְעַל צִיּוֹן מִשְׁכַּן כְּבוֹדֶךָ וְעַל מִזְבְּחֲךָ וְעַל הֵיכָלֶךָ. וּבְנֵה יְרוּשָׁלַיִם עִיר הַקֹּדֶשׁ בִּמְהֵרָה בְיָמֵינוּ, וְהַעֲלֵנוּ לְתוֹכָהּ וְשַׂמְּחֵנוּ בְּבִנְיָנָהּ וְנֹאכַל מִפִּרְיָהּ וְנִשְׂבַּע מִטּוּבָהּ, וּנְבָרֶכְךָ עָלֶיהָ בִּקְדֻשָּׁה וּבְטָהֳרָה. וְזָכְרֵנוּ לְטוֹבָה בְּיוֹם הַזִּכָּרוֹן הַזֶּה, כִּי אַתָּה יהוה טוֹב וּמֵטִיב לַכֹּל, וְנוֹדֶה לְּךָ עַל הָאָרֶץ

| *After grain products (but not bread or matza):* | *After wine or grape juice:* | *After grapes, figs, olives, pomegranates or dates:* |
|---|---|---|
| and for the nourishment. Blessed are You, LORD, for the land and for the nourishment. | and for the fruit of the vine. Blessed are You, LORD, for the land and for the fruit of the vine. | and for the fruit. Blessed are You, LORD, for the land and for the fruit. |

*After grain products (but not bread or matza), and wine or grape juice:*

and for the nourishment and for the fruit of the vine.
Blessed are You, LORD,
for the land and for the nourishment
and the fruit of the vine.

## BLESSING AFTER FOOD – BOREH NEFASHOT

*After food or drink that does not require Birkat HaMazon or Al HaMiḥya – such as meat, fish, dairy products, vegetables, beverages, or fruit other than grapes, figs, pomegranates, olives or dates – say:*

בָּרוּךְ Blessed are You, LORD our God, King of the Universe,
who creates the many forms of life and their needs.
For all You have created to sustain the life of all that lives,
blessed be He, Giver of life to the worlds.

*After grain products (but not bread or מצה):*

וְעַל הַמִּחְיָה.
בָּרוּךְ אַתָּה יהוה עַל
הָאָרֶץ וְעַל הַמִּחְיָה.

*After wine or grape juice:*

וְעַל פְּרִי הַגָּפֶן.*
בָּרוּךְ אַתָּה יהוה עַל
הָאָרֶץ וְעַל פְּרִי הַגָּפֶן.*

*After grapes, figs, olives, pomegranates or dates:*

וְעַל הַפֵּרוֹת.**
בָּרוּךְ אַתָּה יהוה עַל
הָאָרֶץ וְעַל הַפֵּרוֹת.**

*After grain products (but not bread or מצה), and wine or grape juice:*

וְעַל הַמִּחְיָה וְעַל פְּרִי הַגָּפֶן.*
בָּרוּךְ אַתָּה יהוה, עַל הָאָרֶץ וְעַל הַמִּחְיָה וְעַל פְּרִי הַגָּפֶן.*

**If the wine is from ארץ ישראל, then substitute גַּפְנָהּ for הַגָּפֶן.*
***If the fruit is from ארץ ישראל, then substitute פֵּרוֹתֶיהָ for הַפֵּרוֹת.*

## בורא נפשות

*After food or drink that does not require ברכת המזון or מעין שלוש – such as meat, fish, dairy products, vegetables, beverages, or fruit other than grapes, figs, pomegranates, olives or dates – say:*

בָּרוּךְ אַתָּה יהוה אֱלֹהֵינוּ מֶלֶךְ הָעוֹלָם
בּוֹרֵא נְפָשׁוֹת רַבּוֹת וְחֶסְרוֹנָן
עַל כָּל מַה שֶּׁבָּרָאתָ לְהַחֲיוֹת בָּהֶם נֶפֶשׁ כָּל חָי.
בָּרוּךְ חֵי הָעוֹלָמִים.

# Minḥa for Both Days

*Some have the custom to recite before Minḥa the Daily Sacrifice (page 240) or the Korbanot/Offerings (pages 238–244), omitting the Taking of the Ashes and the Order of the Priestly Functions.*

אַשְׁרֵי Happy are those who dwell in Your House; Ps. 84
they shall continue to praise You, Selah!
Happy are the people for whom this is so; Ps. 144
happy are the people whose God is the LORD.
A song of praise by David. Ps. 145

I will exalt You, my God, the King, and bless Your name for ever and all time. Every day I will bless You, and praise Your name for ever and all time. Great is the LORD and greatly to be praised; His greatness is unfathomable. One generation will praise Your works to the next, and tell of Your mighty deeds. On the glorious splendor of Your majesty I will meditate, and on the acts of Your wonders. They shall talk of the power of Your awesome deeds, and I will tell of Your greatness. They shall recite the record of Your great goodness, and sing with joy of Your righteousness. The LORD is gracious and compassionate, slow to anger and great in loving-kindness. The LORD is good to all, and His compassion extends to all His works. All Your works shall thank You, LORD, and Your devoted ones shall bless You. They shall talk of the glory of Your kingship, and speak of Your might. To make known to mankind His mighty deeds and the glorious majesty of His kingship. Your kingdom is an everlasting kingdom, and Your reign is for all generations. The LORD supports all who fall, and raises all who are bowed down. All raise their eyes to You in hope, and

---

ture (praising God with every letter of the alphabet except for the missing *nun*, omitted because of its association with *nefila*, "falling") and because it is the only one of the 150 explicitly to be called a "psalm" – *tehilla*. Added to it are two verses beginning with *Ashrei*, the first word of the book of Psalms, and one ending with *Halleluya*, the last word of the book. It thus becomes a miniature version of Psalms as a whole.

# מנחה לשני ימים

*Some have the custom to recite before* מנחה*,* פרשת קרבן התמיד
*(page 241) or* סדר הקרבנות *(pages 239–245),*
*omitting* פרשת תרומת הדשן *and* סדר המערכה.

אַשְׁרֵי יוֹשְׁבֵי בֵיתֶךָ, עוֹד יְהַלְלוּךָ סֶּלָה: תהלים פד
אַשְׁרֵי הָעָם שֶׁכָּכָה לּוֹ, אַשְׁרֵי הָעָם שֶׁיהוה אֱלֹהָיו: תהלים קמד
תְּהִלָּה לְדָוִד תהלים קמה
אֲרוֹמִמְךָ אֱלוֹהַי הַמֶּלֶךְ, וַאֲבָרְכָה שִׁמְךָ לְעוֹלָם וָעֶד:
בְּכָל־יוֹם אֲבָרְכֶךָּ, וַאֲהַלְלָה שִׁמְךָ לְעוֹלָם וָעֶד:
גָּדוֹל יהוה וּמְהֻלָּל מְאֹד, וְלִגְדֻלָּתוֹ אֵין חֵקֶר:
דּוֹר לְדוֹר יְשַׁבַּח מַעֲשֶׂיךָ, וּגְבוּרֹתֶיךָ יַגִּידוּ:
הֲדַר כְּבוֹד הוֹדֶךָ, וְדִבְרֵי נִפְלְאֹתֶיךָ אָשִׂיחָה:
וֶעֱזוּז נוֹרְאֹתֶיךָ יֹאמֵרוּ, וּגְדוּלָּתְךָ אֲסַפְּרֶנָּה:
זֵכֶר רַב־טוּבְךָ יַבִּיעוּ, וְצִדְקָתְךָ יְרַנֵּנוּ:
חַנּוּן וְרַחוּם יהוה, אֶרֶךְ אַפַּיִם וּגְדָל־חָסֶד:
טוֹב־יהוה לַכֹּל, וְרַחֲמָיו עַל־כָּל־מַעֲשָׂיו:
יוֹדְוּךָ יהוה כָּל־מַעֲשֶׂיךָ, וַחֲסִידֶיךָ יְבָרְכוּכָה:
כְּבוֹד מַלְכוּתְךָ יֹאמֵרוּ, וּגְבוּרָתְךָ יְדַבֵּרוּ:
לְהוֹדִיעַ לִבְנֵי הָאָדָם גְּבוּרֹתָיו, וּכְבוֹד הֲדַר מַלְכוּתוֹ:
מַלְכוּתְךָ מַלְכוּת כָּל־עֹלָמִים, וּמֶמְשַׁלְתְּךָ בְּכָל־דּוֹר וָדֹר:
סוֹמֵךְ יהוה לְכָל־הַנֹּפְלִים, וְזוֹקֵף לְכָל־הַכְּפוּפִים:

---

MINḤA – ASHREI

*Ashrei* is to the Afternoon Service as all of the Verses of Praise are to the Morning Service. It represents a highly abridged form of preparation for, and meditative prelude to, the Amida that follows. It is constructed out of Psalm 145, a key text in the book of Psalms because of its alphabetical struc-

You give them their food in due season. You open Your hand, and satisfy every living thing with favor. The LORD is righteous in all His ways, and kind in all He does. The LORD is close to all who call on Him, to all who call on Him in truth. He fulfills the will of those who revere Him; He hears their cry and saves them. The LORD guards all who love Him, but all the wicked He will destroy. ▸ My mouth shall speak the praise of the LORD, and all creatures shall bless His holy name for ever and all time.

We will bless the LORD now and for ever. Halleluya! *Ps. 115*

וּבָא לְצִיּוֹן גּוֹאֵל "A redeemer will come to Zion, *Is. 59*
to those of Jacob who repent of their sins," declares the LORD.
"As for Me, this is My covenant with them," says the LORD.
"My spirit, that is on you, and My words I have placed in your mouth will not depart from your mouth, or from the mouth of your children, or from the mouth of their descendants from this time on and for ever," says the LORD.

▸ You are the Holy One, enthroned on the praises of Israel. *Ps. 22*
And [the angels] call to one another, saying, ◂ "Holy, holy, holy *Is. 6*
is the LORD of hosts; the whole world is filled with His glory."

And they receive permission from one another, saying: *Targum Yonatan Is. 6*
"Holy in the highest heavens, home of His Presence; holy on earth, the work of His strength; holy for ever and all time is the LORD of hosts; the whole earth is full of His radiant glory."

---

with God's help, for redemption. Just as Moses led the people out of slavery, David established them as a united kingdom with Jerusalem as its capital, and Solomon built the Temple, so a redeemer will one day come to Zion to restore Israel to freedom, unity and peace – an independent nation under the sovereignty of God and a role model to humankind in its commitment to the good, the right, the just and the holy.

קָדוֹשׁ, קָדוֹשׁ, קָדוֹשׁ *Holy, holy, holy.* This entire sequence – similar to the *Kedusha* said in the Repetition of the Amida, but set out as verses from Isaiah, Ezekiel and Exodus together with their Aramaic translations – is known as the *Kedusha deSidra*. Its origin is in the ancient custom of studying the prophetic

עֵינֵי־כֹל אֵלֶיךָ יְשַׂבֵּרוּ, וְאַתָּה נוֹתֵן־לָהֶם אֶת־אָכְלָם בְּעִתּוֹ:
פּוֹתֵחַ אֶת־יָדֶךָ, וּמַשְׂבִּיעַ לְכָל־חַי רָצוֹן:
צַדִּיק יהוה בְּכָל־דְּרָכָיו, וְחָסִיד בְּכָל־מַעֲשָׂיו:
קָרוֹב יהוה לְכָל־קֹרְאָיו, לְכֹל אֲשֶׁר יִקְרָאֻהוּ בֶאֱמֶת:
רְצוֹן־יְרֵאָיו יַעֲשֶׂה, וְאֶת־שַׁוְעָתָם יִשְׁמַע, וְיוֹשִׁיעֵם:
שׁוֹמֵר יהוה אֶת־כָּל־אֹהֲבָיו, וְאֵת כָּל־הָרְשָׁעִים יַשְׁמִיד:
◄ תְּהִלַּת יהוה יְדַבֶּר פִּי, וִיבָרֵךְ כָּל־בָּשָׂר שֵׁם קָדְשׁוֹ לְעוֹלָם וָעֶד:
וַאֲנַחְנוּ נְבָרֵךְ יָהּ מֵעַתָּה וְעַד־עוֹלָם, הַלְלוּיָהּ: תהלים קטו

וּבָא לְצִיּוֹן גּוֹאֵל, וּלְשָׁבֵי פֶשַׁע בְּיַעֲקֹב, נְאֻם יהוה: ישעיה נט
וַאֲנִי זֹאת בְּרִיתִי אוֹתָם, אָמַר יהוה
רוּחִי אֲשֶׁר עָלֶיךָ וּדְבָרַי אֲשֶׁר־שַׂמְתִּי בְּפִיךָ
לֹא־יָמוּשׁוּ מִפִּיךָ וּמִפִּי זַרְעֲךָ וּמִפִּי זֶרַע זַרְעֲךָ
אָמַר יהוה, מֵעַתָּה וְעַד־עוֹלָם:

◄ וְאַתָּה קָדוֹשׁ יוֹשֵׁב תְּהִלּוֹת יִשְׂרָאֵל: וְקָרָא זֶה אֶל־זֶה וְאָמַר ◄ תהלים כב / ישעיה ו
קָדוֹשׁ, קָדוֹשׁ, קָדוֹשׁ, יהוה צְבָאוֹת, מְלֹא כָל־הָאָרֶץ כְּבוֹדוֹ:
וּמְקַבְּלִין דֵּין מִן דֵּין וְאָמְרִין, קַדִּישׁ בִּשְׁמֵי מְרוֹמָא עִלָּאָה בֵּית שְׁכִינְתֵהּ תרגום יונתן / ישעיה ו
קַדִּישׁ עַל אַרְעָא עוֹבַד גְּבוּרְתֵהּ, קַדִּישׁ לְעָלַם וּלְעָלְמֵי עָלְמַיָּא
יהוה צְבָאוֹת, מַלְיָא כָל אַרְעָא זִיו יְקָרֵהּ.

---

**וּבָא לְצִיּוֹן גּוֹאֵל** *A redeemer will come to Zion.* A key verse from the prophet Isaiah, the poet laureate of hope and the great visionary of Israel's redemption from exile and persecution. The concept of redemption, *ge'ula,* is one of Judaism's most striking beliefs. Other religions have found solace in other worlds – paradise, the afterlife, the realm of the soul after death – believing that justice, truth and the encounter with God are impossible in a finite universe with all its failings. Judaism, to the contrary, believes that it is precisely here, in this physical world and its history of humanity, that we are to strive,

▸ Then a wind lifted me up and I heard behind me the sound of a great noise, saying, ◂ "Blessed is the LORD's glory from His place." *Ezek. 3*

Then a wind lifted me up and I heard behind me
the sound of a great tempest of those who uttered praise, saying,
"Blessed is the LORD's glory from the place of the home of His Presence." *Targum Yonatan Ezek. 3*

The LORD shall reign for ever and all time. *Ex. 15*

The LORD's kingdom is established for ever and all time. *Targum Onkelos Ex. 15*

יהוה LORD, God of Abraham, Isaac and Yisrael, our ancestors, may *1 Chr. 29*
You keep this for ever so that it forms the thoughts in Your people's
heart, and directs their heart toward You. He is compassionate. He *Ps. 78*
forgives iniquity and does not destroy. Repeatedly He suppresses
His anger, not rousing His full wrath. For You, my LORD, are good *Ps. 86*
and forgiving, abundantly kind to all who call on You. Your righ- *Ps. 119*
teousness is eternally righteous, and Your Torah is truth. Grant *Mic. 7*
truth to Jacob, loving-kindness to Abraham, as You promised our
ancestors in ancient times. Blessed is my LORD for day after day *Ps. 68*
He burdens us [with His blessings]; God is our salvation, Selah!
The LORD of hosts is with us; the God of Jacob is our refuge, Selah! *Ps. 46*
LORD of hosts, happy is the one who trusts in You. LORD, save. May *Ps. 84* *Ps. 20*
the King answer us on the day we call.

בָּרוּךְ Blessed is He, our God, who created us for His glory, separating us from those who go astray; who gave us the Torah of truth, planting within us eternal life. May He open our heart to His Torah, imbuing our heart with the love and awe of Him, that we may do His will and serve Him with a perfect heart, so that we neither toil in vain nor give birth to confusion.

---

Kedusha sequence beginning "Holy, holy, holy" tells us how the angels praise God in heaven, according to the visions of Isaiah and Ezekiel. It appears in three forms during the prayers: (1) In the first blessing before the Shema in the morning service, we *recite* it; (2) During the Repetition of the Amida, we *enact* it; (3) During the *Kedusha deSidra,* as here, we *study* it.

◂ וַתִּשָּׂאֵנִי רוּחַ, וָאֶשְׁמַע אַחֲרַי קוֹל רַעַשׁ גָּדוֹל ◂ יחזקאל ג
בָּרוּךְ כְּבוֹד־יהוה מִמְּקוֹמוֹ:
וּנְטָלַתְנִי רוּחָא, וּשְׁמָעִית בַּתְרַי קָל זִיעַ סַגִּיא, דִּמְשַׁבְּחִין וְאָמְרִין תרגום יונתן יחזקאל ג
בְּרִיךְ יְקָרָא דַיהוה מֵאֲתַר בֵּית שְׁכִינְתֵּהּ.

יהוה יִמְלֹךְ לְעֹלָם וָעֶד: שמות טו
יהוה מַלְכוּתֵהּ קָאֵם לְעָלַם וּלְעָלְמֵי עָלְמַיָּא. תרגום אונקלוס שמות טו

יהוה אֱלֹהֵי אַבְרָהָם יִצְחָק וְיִשְׂרָאֵל אֲבֹתֵינוּ, שָׁמְרָה־זֹּאת לְעוֹלָם דברי הימים א, כט
לְיֵצֶר מַחְשְׁבוֹת לְבַב עַמֶּךָ, וְהָכֵן לְבָבָם אֵלֶיךָ: וְהוּא רַחוּם יְכַפֵּר תהלים עח
עָוֹן וְלֹא־יַשְׁחִית, וְהִרְבָּה לְהָשִׁיב אַפּוֹ, וְלֹא־יָעִיר כָּל־חֲמָתוֹ:
כִּי־אַתָּה אֲדֹנָי טוֹב וְסַלָּח, וְרַב־חֶסֶד לְכָל־קֹרְאֶיךָ: צִדְקָתְךָ תהלים פו תהלים קיט
צֶדֶק לְעוֹלָם וְתוֹרָתְךָ אֱמֶת: תִּתֵּן אֱמֶת לְיַעֲקֹב, חֶסֶד לְאַבְרָהָם, מיכה ז
אֲשֶׁר־נִשְׁבַּעְתָּ לַאֲבֹתֵינוּ מִימֵי קֶדֶם: בָּרוּךְ אֲדֹנָי יוֹם יוֹם יַעֲמָס־ תהלים סח
לָנוּ, הָאֵל יְשׁוּעָתֵנוּ סֶלָה: יהוה צְבָאוֹת עִמָּנוּ, מִשְׂגָּב לָנוּ אֱלֹהֵי תהלים מו
יַעֲקֹב סֶלָה: יהוה צְבָאוֹת, אַשְׁרֵי אָדָם בֹּטֵחַ בָּךְ: יהוה הוֹשִׁיעָה, תהלים פד תהלים כ
הַמֶּלֶךְ יַעֲנֵנוּ בְיוֹם־קָרְאֵנוּ:

בָּרוּךְ הוּא אֱלֹהֵינוּ שֶׁבְּרָאָנוּ לִכְבוֹדוֹ, וְהִבְדִּילָנוּ מִן הַתּוֹעִים, וְנָתַן לָנוּ תּוֹרַת אֱמֶת, וְחַיֵּי עוֹלָם נָטַע בְּתוֹכֵנוּ. הוּא יִפְתַּח לִבֵּנוּ בְּתוֹרָתוֹ, וְיָשֵׂם בְּלִבֵּנוּ אַהֲבָתוֹ וְיִרְאָתוֹ וְלַעֲשׂוֹת רְצוֹנוֹ וּלְעָבְדוֹ בְּלֵבָב שָׁלֵם, לְמַעַן לֹא נִיגַע לָרִיק וְלֹא נֵלֵד לַבֶּהָלָה.

---

books immediately after prayer. Study usually involved translation since not everyone understood the original Hebrew. The language they spoke from the late Second Temple era to that of the Babylonian Talmud, was Aramaic, and it was thus into Aramaic that the biblical verses were translated. The

יְהִי רָצוֹן May it be Your will, O LORD our God and God of our ancestors, that we keep Your laws in this world, and thus be worthy to live, see and inherit goodness and blessing in the Messianic Age and in
the life of the World to Come. So that my soul may sing to You and Ps. 30
not be silent. LORD, my God, for ever I will thank You. Blessed is Jer. 17
the man who trusts in the LORD, whose trust is in the LORD alone.
Trust in the LORD for evermore, for God, the LORD, is an everlast- Is. 26
ing Rock. ▸ Those who know Your name trust in You, for You, LORD, Ps. 9
do not forsake those who seek You. The LORD desired, for the sake Is. 42
of Israel's merit, to make the Torah great and glorious.

### HALF KADDISH

*Before Maftir is read, the Reader says Half Kaddish:*

*Reader:* יִתְגַּדַּל Magnified and sanctified
may His great name be,
in the world He created by His will.
May He establish His kingdom,
make His salvation flourish,
and hasten His messiah,
in your lifetime and in your days,
and in the lifetime of all the house of Israel,
swiftly and soon – and say: Amen.

*All:* May His great name be blessed for ever and all time.

*Leader:* Blessed and praised, glorified and exalted,
raised and honored,
uplifted and lauded
be the name of the Holy One, blessed be He,
above and beyond any blessing,
song, praise and consolation
uttered in the world –
and say: Amen.

*On Shabbat continue on the next page.*
*On a weekday, the service continues with the Amida on page 916.*

יְהִי רָצוֹן מִלְּפָנֶיךָ יהוה אֱלֹהֵינוּ וֵאלֹהֵי אֲבוֹתֵינוּ, שֶׁנִּשְׁמֹר חֻקֶּיךָ
בָּעוֹלָם הַזֶּה, וְנִזְכֶּה וְנִחְיֶה וְנִרְאֶה וְנִירַשׁ טוֹבָה וּבְרָכָה, לִשְׁנֵי
תהלים ל יְמוֹת הַמָּשִׁיחַ וּלְחַיֵּי הָעוֹלָם הַבָּא. לְמַעַן יְזַמֶּרְךָ כָבוֹד וְלֹא יִדֹּם,
ירמיה יז יהוה אֱלֹהַי, לְעוֹלָם אוֹדֶךָּ: בָּרוּךְ הַגֶּבֶר אֲשֶׁר יִבְטַח בַּיהוה,
ישעיה כו וְהָיָה יהוה מִבְטַחוֹ: בִּטְחוּ בַיהוה עֲדֵי־עַד, כִּי בְּיָהּ יהוה צוּר
תהלים ט עוֹלָמִים: › וְיִבְטְחוּ בְךָ יוֹדְעֵי שְׁמֶךָ, כִּי לֹא־עָזַבְתָּ דֹרְשֶׁיךָ, יהוה:
ישעיה מב יהוה חָפֵץ לְמַעַן צִדְקוֹ, יַגְדִּיל תּוֹרָה וְיַאְדִּיר:

## חצי קדיש

ש״ץ: יִתְגַּדַּל וְיִתְקַדַּשׁ שְׁמֵהּ רַבָּא (קהל: אָמֵן)
בְּעָלְמָא דִּי בְרָא כִרְעוּתֵהּ
וְיַמְלִיךְ מַלְכוּתֵהּ
וְיַצְמַח פֻּרְקָנֵהּ וִיקָרֵב מְשִׁיחֵהּ (קהל: אָמֵן)
בְּחַיֵּיכוֹן וּבְיוֹמֵיכוֹן וּבְחַיֵּי דְכָל בֵּית יִשְׂרָאֵל
בַּעֲגָלָא וּבִזְמַן קָרִיב
וְאִמְרוּ אָמֵן. (קהל: אָמֵן)

קהל וש״ץ: יְהֵא שְׁמֵהּ רַבָּא מְבָרַךְ לְעָלַם וּלְעָלְמֵי עָלְמַיָּא.

ש״ץ: יִתְבָּרַךְ וְיִשְׁתַּבַּח וְיִתְפָּאַר וְיִתְרוֹמַם וְיִתְנַשֵּׂא
וְיִתְהַדָּר וְיִתְעַלֶּה וְיִתְהַלָּל
שְׁמֵהּ דְּקֻדְשָׁא בְּרִיךְ הוּא (קהל: אָמֵן)
לְעֵלָּא לְעֵלָּא מִכָּל בִּרְכָתָא וְשִׁירָתָא, תֻּשְׁבְּחָתָא וְנֶחֱמָתָא
דַּאֲמִירָן בְּעָלְמָא
וְאִמְרוּ אָמֵן. (קהל: אָמֵן)

*On* שבת *continue on the next page.*
*On a weekday, the service continues with the* עמידה *on page 917.*

וַאֲנִי As for me, may my prayer come to You, LORD, Ps. 69
at a time of favor. O God, in Your great love,
answer me with Your faithful salvation.

*The Ark is opened and the congregation stands. All say:*

וַיְהִי בִּנְסֹעַ Whenever the Ark set out, Moses would say, Num. 10
"Arise, LORD, and may Your enemies be scattered.
May those who hate You flee before You."
For the Torah shall come forth from Zion, Is. 2
and the word of the LORD from Jerusalem.
Blessed is He who, in His holiness,
gave the Torah to His people Israel.

Blessed is the name of the Master of the Universe. Blessed is Your crown and Your place. May Your favor always be with Your people Israel. Show Your people the salvation of Your right hand in Your Temple. Grant us the gift of Your good light, and accept our prayers in mercy. May it be Your will to prolong our life in goodness. May I be counted among the righteous, so that You will have compassion on me and protect me and all that is mine and all that is Your people Israel's. You feed all; You sustain all; You rule over all; You rule over kings, for sovereignty is Yours. I am a servant of the Holy One, blessed be He, before whom and before whose glorious Torah I bow at all times. Not in man do I trust, nor on any angel do I rely, but on the God of heaven who is the God of truth, whose Torah is truth, whose prophets speak truth, and who abounds in acts of love and truth. ▸ In Him I trust, and to His holy and glorious name I offer praises. May it be Your will to open my heart to the Torah, and to fulfill the wishes of my heart and of the hearts of all Your people Israel for good, for life, and for peace. *Zohar, Vayak-hel*

*The Leader takes the Torah scroll in his right arm, bows toward the Ark and says:*

Magnify the LORD with me, and let us exalt His name together. Ps. 34

---

people would not have to go more than three days without hearing the words of Torah. Behind this institution is the remarkable assumption that just as the body needs water so the soul needs the word of God. It is dangerous for the body to go three days without water, equally so for the soul to be deprived for three days of spiritual sustenance.

וַאֲנִי תְפִלָּתִי־לְךָ יהוה, עֵת רָצוֹן, אֱלֹהִים בְּרָב־חַסְדֶּךָ תהלים סט
עֲנֵנִי בֶּאֱמֶת יִשְׁעֶךָ:

*The* ארון קודש *is opened and the* קהל *stands. All say:*

וַיְהִי בִּנְסֹעַ הָאָרֹן וַיֹּאמֶר מֹשֶׁה במדבר י
קוּמָה יהוה וְיָפֻצוּ אֹיְבֶיךָ וְיָנֻסוּ מְשַׂנְאֶיךָ מִפָּנֶיךָ:
כִּי מִצִּיּוֹן תֵּצֵא תוֹרָה וּדְבַר־יהוה מִירוּשָׁלָםִ: ישעיה ב
בָּרוּךְ שֶׁנָּתַן תּוֹרָה לְעַמּוֹ יִשְׂרָאֵל בִּקְדֻשָּׁתוֹ.

בְּרִיךְ שְׁמֵהּ דְּמָרֵא עָלְמָא, בְּרִיךְ כִּתְרָךְ וְאַתְרָךְ. יְהֵא רְעוּתָךְ עִם עַמָּךְ יִשְׂרָאֵל זוהר ויקהל
לְעָלַם, וּפֻרְקַן יְמִינָךְ אַחֲזִי לְעַמָּךְ בְּבֵית מַקְדְּשָׁךְ, וּלְאַמְטוֹיֵי לַנָא מִטּוּב
נְהוֹרָךְ, וּלְקַבֵּל צְלוֹתַנָא בְּרַחֲמִין. יְהֵא רַעֲוָא קֳדָמָךְ דְּתוֹרִיךְ לַן חַיִּין בְּטִיבוּ,
וְלֶהֱוֵי אֲנָא פְקִידָא בְּגוֹ צַדִּיקַיָּא, לְמִרְחַם עֲלַי וּלְמִנְטַר יָתִי וְיַת כָּל דִּי לִי וְדִי
לְעַמָּךְ יִשְׂרָאֵל. אַנְתְּ הוּא זָן לְכֹלָּא וּמְפַרְנֵס לְכֹלָּא, אַנְתְּ הוּא שַׁלִּיט עַל כֹּלָּא,
אַנְתְּ הוּא דְּשַׁלִּיט עַל מַלְכַיָּא, וּמַלְכוּתָא דִּילָךְ הִיא. אֲנָא עַבְדָּא דְקֻדְשָׁא
בְּרִיךְ הוּא, דְּסָגֵדְנָא קַמֵּהּ וּמִקַּמֵּי דִּיקַר אוֹרַיְתֵהּ בְּכָל עִדָּן וְעִדָּן. לָא עַל אֱנָשׁ
רָחִיצְנָא וְלָא עַל בַּר אֱלָהִין סָמִיכְנָא, אֶלָּא בֶּאֱלָהָא דִשְׁמַיָּא, דְּהוּא אֱלָהָא
קְשׁוֹט, וְאוֹרַיְתֵהּ קְשׁוֹט, וּנְבִיאוֹהִי קְשׁוֹט, וּמַסְגֵּא לְמֶעְבַּד טַבְוָן וּקְשׁוֹט. ◂ בֵּהּ
אֲנָא רָחִיץ, וְלִשְׁמֵהּ קַדִּישָׁא יַקִּירָא אֲנָא אֵמַר תֻּשְׁבְּחָן. יְהֵא רַעֲוָא קֳדָמָךְ
דְּתִפְתַּח לִבַּאי בְּאוֹרַיְתָא, וְתַשְׁלִים מִשְׁאֲלִין דְּלִבַּאי וְלִבָּא דְכָל עַמָּךְ יִשְׂרָאֵל
לְטָב וּלְחַיִּין וְלִשְׁלָם.

*The* שליח ציבור *takes the* ספר תורה *in his right arm, bows toward the* ארון קודש *and says:*

גַּדְּלוּ לַיהוה אִתִּי וּנְרוֹמְמָה שְׁמוֹ יַחְדָּו: תהלים לד

---

READING OF THE TORAH

Reading the Torah on Shabbat and festival afternoons was ordained by Ezra for the sake of those unable to come to the synagogue on Mondays and Thursdays to hear the beginning of the Torah portion of the coming Shabbat (*Bava Kamma* 82a). According to the Talmud, though the midweek readings may have existed earlier, it was Ezra who gave them their present form so that

*The Ark is closed. The Leader carries the Torah scroll to the bima and the congregation says:*

לְךָ Yours, LORD, are the greatness and the power, the glory and the majesty and splendor, for everything in heaven and earth is Yours. Yours, LORD, is the kingdom; You are exalted as Head over all. *I Chr. 29*

רוֹמְמוּ Exalt the LORD our God and bow to His footstool; He is holy. Exalt the LORD our God, and bow at His holy mountain, for holy is the LORD our God. *Ps. 99*

אַב הָרַחֲמִים May the Father of compassion have compassion on the people borne by Him. May He remember the covenant with the mighty [patriarchs], and deliver us from evil times. May He reproach the evil instinct in the people carried by Him, and graciously grant that we be an everlasting remnant. May He fulfill in good measure our requests for salvation and compassion.

*The Torah scroll is placed on the bima and the Gabbai calls a Kohen to the Torah. See law 68.*

וְתִגָּלֶה May His kingship over us be soon revealed and made manifest. May He be gracious to our surviving remnant, the remnant of His people the house of Israel in grace, loving-kindness, compassion and favor, and let us say: Amen. Let us all render greatness to our God and give honor to the Torah. *Let the Kohen come forward. Arise (*name* son of *father's name*), the Kohen.

**If no Kohen is present, a Levi or Yisrael is called up as follows:*

/As there is no Kohen, arise (*name* son of *father's name*) in place of a Kohen./

Blessed is He who, in His holiness, gave the Torah to His people Israel.

*The congregation followed by the Gabbai:*

You who cling to the LORD your God are all alive today. *Deut. 4*

*The Reader shows the oleh the section to be read. The oleh touches the scroll at that place with the tzitzit of his tallit or the fabric belt of the Torah scroll, which he then kisses. Holding the handles of the scroll, he says:*

*Oleh:* Bless the LORD, the blessed One.

*Cong:* Bless the LORD, the blessed One, for ever and all time.

*Oleh:* Bless the LORD, the blessed One, for ever and all time.

Blessed are You, LORD our God, King of the Universe, who has chosen us from all peoples and has given us His Torah. Blessed are You, LORD, Giver of the Torah.

*After the reading, the oleh says:*

*Oleh:* Blessed are You, LORD our God, King of the Universe, who has given us the Torah of truth, planting everlasting life in our midst. Blessed are You, LORD, Giver of the Torah.

*The* ארון קודש *is closed. The* שליח ציבור *carries the* ספר תורה *to the* בימה *and the* קהל *says:*

דברי הימים א׳ כט לְךָ יהוה הַגְּדֻלָּה וְהַגְּבוּרָה וְהַתִּפְאֶרֶת וְהַנֵּצַח וְהַהוֹד, כִּי־כֹל בַּשָּׁמַיִם וּבָאָרֶץ: לְךָ יהוה הַמַּמְלָכָה וְהַמִּתְנַשֵּׂא לְכֹל לְרֹאשׁ:

תהלים צט רוֹמְמוּ יהוה אֱלֹהֵינוּ וְהִשְׁתַּחֲווּ לַהֲדֹם רַגְלָיו, קָדוֹשׁ הוּא: רוֹמְמוּ יהוה אֱלֹהֵינוּ וְהִשְׁתַּחֲווּ לְהַר קָדְשׁוֹ, כִּי־קָדוֹשׁ יהוה אֱלֹהֵינוּ:

אַב הָרַחֲמִים הוּא יְרַחֵם עַם עֲמוּסִים, וְיִזְכֹּר בְּרִית אֵיתָנִים, וְיַצִּיל נַפְשׁוֹתֵינוּ מִן הַשָּׁעוֹת הָרָעוֹת, וְיִגְעַר בְּיֵצֶר הָרָע מִן הַנְּשׂוּאִים, וְיָחֹן אוֹתָנוּ לִפְלֵיטַת עוֹלָמִים, וִימַלֵּא מִשְׁאֲלוֹתֵינוּ בְּמִדָּה טוֹבָה יְשׁוּעָה וְרַחֲמִים.

*The* ספר תורה *is placed on the* שולחן *and the* גבאי *calls a* כהן *to the* תורה. *See law 68.*

וְתִגָּלֶה וְתֵרָאֶה מַלְכוּתוֹ עָלֵינוּ בִּזְמַן קָרוֹב, וְיָחֹן פְּלֵיטָתֵנוּ וּפְלֵיטַת עַמּוֹ בֵּית יִשְׂרָאֵל לְחֵן וּלְחֶסֶד וּלְרַחֲמִים וּלְרָצוֹן וְנֹאמַר אָמֵן. הַכֹּל הָבוּ גֹדֶל לֵאלֹהֵינוּ וּתְנוּ כָבוֹד לַתּוֹרָה. *כֹּהֵן קְרַב, יַעֲמֹד (פלוני בֶּן פלוני) הַכֹּהֵן.

**If no* כהן *is present, a* לוי *or* ישראל *is called up as follows:*

/אֵין כָּאן כֹּהֵן, יַעֲמֹד (פלוני בֶּן פלוני) בִּמְקוֹם כֹּהֵן./

בָּרוּךְ שֶׁנָּתַן תּוֹרָה לְעַמּוֹ יִשְׂרָאֵל בִּקְדֻשָּׁתוֹ.

*The* קהל *followed by the* גבאי*:*

דברים ד וְאַתֶּם הַדְּבֵקִים בַּיהוה אֱלֹהֵיכֶם חַיִּים כֻּלְּכֶם הַיּוֹם:

*The* קורא *shows the* עולה *the section to be read. The* עולה *touches the scroll at that place with the* ציצית *of his* טלית *or the gartel of the* ספר תורה*, which he then kisses. Holding the handles of the scroll, he says:*

עולה: בָּרְכוּ אֶת יהוה הַמְבֹרָךְ.

קהל: בָּרוּךְ יהוה הַמְבֹרָךְ לְעוֹלָם וָעֶד.

עולה: בָּרוּךְ יהוה הַמְבֹרָךְ לְעוֹלָם וָעֶד.

בָּרוּךְ אַתָּה יהוה, אֱלֹהֵינוּ מֶלֶךְ הָעוֹלָם אֲשֶׁר בָּחַר בָּנוּ מִכָּל הָעַמִּים וְנָתַן לָנוּ אֶת תּוֹרָתוֹ. בָּרוּךְ אַתָּה יהוה, נוֹתֵן הַתּוֹרָה.

*After the* קריאת התורה*, the* עולה *says:*

עולה: בָּרוּךְ אַתָּה יהוה אֱלֹהֵינוּ מֶלֶךְ הָעוֹלָם אֲשֶׁר נָתַן לָנוּ תּוֹרַת אֱמֶת וְחַיֵּי עוֹלָם נָטַע בְּתוֹכֵנוּ. בָּרוּךְ אַתָּה יהוה, נוֹתֵן הַתּוֹרָה.

## TORAH READING

Heavens, take heed and I shall speak; and earth, you must hear my words. *Deut. 32:1–18*
My lesson will pour down like rain, my words will fall like the dew,
like a wind blowing rain over grasslands, like drops on the stems.
As I call out the name of the LORD – come, attribute greatness to our God.
*The Rock, His work is whole, and all of His ways are just, LEVI *(in most congregations)*
a God of truth, He knows no injustice, He is righteous and upstanding.
Is this devastation His? No, His sons – it is their flaw, it is this base and twisted generation.
Can it be the LORD you repay thus, you boorish people, and not wise?
Is He not your Father, your Maker? He formed you – He set you on your feet.

*Some start the Levi portion here:*

Remember the earliest of days; YISRAEL
grasp the years of generations that have been.
Ask your father – he will tell you all; ask the elders of your kin and they will say:
When the Most High bequeathed the lands of nations,
when He sent mankind their different ways,
He laid out the boundaries of peoples
by the number of the Israelites;
the LORD's own estate is His people; the plot of His legacy is Jacob.
In a desert land He found him, in the wailing emptiness of wastelands.
He encircled him, watched over him;
He guarded him close as the reflection in His eye.
As an eagle awakens its nest, as it hovers above its young,
spreads out its plumes and takes them, and carries them on its wings,
so the LORD led them, alone, and no strange god was with Him.

---

הַצּוּר תָּמִים פָּעֳלוֹ *The Rock, His work is whole.* A classic expression of *tzidduk hadin*, acceptance of God's judgment. Even when faced with suffering, persecution or loss, Jews continue to have faith in God.

זְכֹר יְמוֹת עוֹלָם *Remember the earliest of days.* The command to remember, *Zakhor*, is fundamental to Judaism. The verb appears 169 times in Tanakh. Jews were the first to see God in history, the first to see history as a single extended narrative with a beginning, middle and anticipated end, the first to see time as the arena within which the Divine-human encounter is played out, and the first to see memory as a religious obligation.

## קריאת התורה

הַאֲזִינוּ הַשָּׁמַיִם וַאֲדַבֵּרָה     וְתִשְׁמַע הָאָרֶץ אִמְרֵי־פִי׃ דברים לב: א–יח
יַעֲרֹף כַּמָּטָר לִקְחִי     תִּזַּל כַּטַּל אִמְרָתִי
כִּשְׂעִירִם עֲלֵי־דֶשֶׁא     וְכִרְבִיבִים עֲלֵי־עֵשֶׂב׃
כִּי שֵׁם יְהֹוָה אֶקְרָא     הָבוּ גֹדֶל לֵאלֹהֵינוּ׃
*הַצּוּר תָּמִים פָּעֳלוֹ     כִּי כָל־דְּרָכָיו מִשְׁפָּט לוי (ברוב הקהילות)
אֵל אֱמוּנָה וְאֵין עָוֶל     צַדִּיק וְיָשָׁר הוּא׃
שִׁחֵת לוֹ לֹא בָּנָיו מוּמָם     דּוֹר עִקֵּשׁ וּפְתַלְתֹּל׃
הַ לְיהֹוָה תִּגְמְלוּ־זֹאת     עַם נָבָל וְלֹא חָכָם
הֲלוֹא־הוּא אָבִיךָ קָּנֶךָ     הוּא עָשְׂךָ וַיְכֹנְנֶךָ׃

*Some start the* לוי *portion here:*

*זְכֹר יְמוֹת עוֹלָם     בִּינוּ שְׁנוֹת דֹּר־וָדֹר ישראל
שְׁאַל אָבִיךָ וְיַגֵּדְךָ     זְקֵנֶיךָ וְיֹאמְרוּ לָךְ׃
בְּהַנְחֵל עֶלְיוֹן גּוֹיִם     בְּהַפְרִידוֹ בְּנֵי אָדָם
יַצֵּב גְּבֻלֹת עַמִּים     לְמִסְפַּר בְּנֵי יִשְׂרָאֵל׃
כִּי חֵלֶק יְהֹוָה עַמּוֹ     יַעֲקֹב חֶבֶל נַחֲלָתוֹ׃
יִמְצָאֵהוּ בְּאֶרֶץ מִדְבָּר     וּבְתֹהוּ יְלֵל יְשִׁמֹן
יְסֹבְבֶנְהוּ יְבוֹנְנֵהוּ     יִצְּרֶנְהוּ כְּאִישׁוֹן עֵינוֹ׃
כְּנֶשֶׁר יָעִיר קִנּוֹ     עַל־גּוֹזָלָיו יְרַחֵף
יִפְרֹשׂ כְּנָפָיו יִקָּחֵהוּ     יִשָּׂאֵהוּ עַל־אֶבְרָתוֹ׃
יְהֹוָה בָּדָד יַנְחֶנּוּ     וְאֵין עִמּוֹ אֵל נֵכָר׃

---

הַאֲזִינוּ הַשָּׁמַיִם *Heavens, take heed.* Moses, nearing the end of his life, calls heaven and earth as witnesses to the terms of Israel's history as the people of the covenant. In majestic poetry he contrasts the faithfulness of God with the faithlessness of the people. God has continually shown the people His loving care, rescuing them from danger the way an eagle does with its young, sheltering them under its wings, but the people have acted like wayward children. Do not blame God when bad things happen, Moses warns. God is just. The explanation lies elsewhere.

*Most congregations end the Torah reading here. Some start the Yisrael portion here:*

*He set them upon the high places of the world,
had them eat of the bounty of meadows;
He let them suckle honey from the rock, and oil from flint.
They fed on the cream of cattle, fat of the flock, the fat of the lambs,
and the good Bashan sheep and the goats, with the lushest kernels of wheat,
and the rich blood of grapes they drank –
and Yeshurun grew fat and kicked –
you grew fat, you thickened, you bloated –
he rejected the God who made him,
and cursed the Rock of his salvation.
They incensed Him with strange gods,
and angered Him with abominable things. They gave offerings to demons
not God,
to gods they had not known; new things rising up but lately,
that your ancestors never did fear. You abandoned the Rock that bore you,
and forgot the God of whom You were conceived.

*The Torah scroll is lifted and the congregation says:*

וְזֹאת הַתּוֹרָה This is the Torah that *Deut. 4*
Moses placed before the children of Israel,
at the LORD's commandment, by the hand of Moses. *Num. 9*

*Some add:* It is a tree of life to those who grasp it, and those who uphold it are happy. *Prov. 3*
Its ways are ways of pleasantness, and all its paths are peace. Long life is
in its right hand; in its left, riches and honor. It pleased the LORD for the *Is. 42*
sake of [Israel's] righteousness, to make the Torah great and glorious.

*The congregation says the following two psalms while the Torah scroll is being bound:*

הַלְלוּיָהּ I shall give thanks to the LORD with all my heart, in a group of noble *Ps. 111* people, this congregation. The LORD's works are great; all who long for them may find them. Majestic and splendid are His acts, and His righteousness stands forever. He made remembrance for His wonders, He is gracious and loving. He gives meat to those who hold Him in awe, He will remember His covenant always. He made known to His people the power of His acts, as He bequeathed them the inheritance of nations. The works of His hands are truth and justice, and all His commands unswerving; all of them are steadfast forever and all time, and made in truth and in uprightness. He sends His people redemption; His covenant once made is eternal. His name is holy and awesome. The awe of the LORD is where wisdom begins, and success comes to all who follow His laws. His praise stands true forever.

*Most congregations end the* תורה *reading here. Some start the* ישראל *portion here:*

*יַרְכִּבֵ֙הוּ֙ עַל־בָּ֣מותי אָ֔רֶץ וַיֹּאכַ֖ל תְּנוּבֹ֣ת שָׂדָ֑י בָּ֣מֳתֵי
וַיֵּנִקֵ֤הוּ דְבַשׁ֙ מִסֶּ֔לַע וְשֶׁ֖מֶן מֵחַלְמִ֥ישׁ צֽוּר׃
חֶמְאַ֨ת בָּקָ֜ר וַחֲלֵ֣ב צֹ֗אן עִם־חֵ֨לֶב כָּרִ֜ים
וְאֵילִ֤ים בְּנֵֽי־בָשָׁן֙ וְעַתּוּדִ֔ים עִם־חֵ֖לֶב כִּלְי֣וֹת חִטָּ֑ה
וְדַם־עֵנָ֖ב תִּשְׁתֶּה־חָֽמֶר׃ וַיִּשְׁמַ֤ן יְשֻׁרוּן֙ וַיִּבְעָ֔ט
שָׁמַ֖נְתָּ עָבִ֣יתָ כָּשִׂ֑יתָ וַיִּטֹּשׁ֙ אֱל֣וֹהַ עָשָׂ֔הוּ
וַיְנַבֵּ֖ל צ֥וּר יְשֻׁעָתֽוֹ׃ יַקְנִאֻ֖הוּ בְּזָרִ֑ים
בְּתוֹעֵבֹ֖ת יַכְעִיסֻֽהוּ׃ יִזְבְּח֗וּ לַשֵּׁדִים֙ לֹ֣א אֱלֹ֔הַ
אֱלֹהִ֖ים לֹ֣א יְדָע֑וּם חֲדָשִׁים֙ מִקָּרֹ֣ב בָּ֔אוּ
לֹ֥א שְׂעָר֖וּם אֲבֹתֵיכֶֽם׃ צ֥וּר יְלָדְךָ֖ תֶּ֑שִׁי
וַתִּשְׁכַּ֖ח אֵ֥ל מְחֹלְלֶֽךָ׃

*The* ספר תורה *is lifted and the* קהל *says:*

דברים ד וְזֹאת הַתּוֹרָה אֲשֶׁר־שָׂם מֹשֶׁה לִפְנֵי בְּנֵי יִשְׂרָאֵל:
במדבר ט עַל־פִּי יהוה בְּיַד מֹשֶׁה:

משלי ג *Some add* עֵץ־חַיִּים הִיא לַמַּחֲזִיקִים בָּהּ וְתֹמְכֶיהָ מְאֻשָּׁר: דְּרָכֶיהָ דַרְכֵי־נֹעַם
וְכָל־נְתִיבוֹתֶיהָ שָׁלוֹם: אֹרֶךְ יָמִים בִּימִינָהּ, בִּשְׂמֹאולָהּ עֹשֶׁר וְכָבוֹד:
ישעיה מב יהוה חָפֵץ לְמַעַן צִדְקוֹ יַגְדִּיל תּוֹרָה וְיַאְדִּיר:

*The* קהל *says the following two psalms while the* ספר תורה *is being bound:*

תהלים קיא הַלְלוּיָהּ, אוֹדֶה יהוה בְּכָל־לֵבָב, בְּסוֹד יְשָׁרִים וְעֵדָה: גְּדֹלִים מַעֲשֵׂי יהוה, דְּרוּשִׁים לְכָל־חֶפְצֵיהֶם: הוֹד־וְהָדָר פָּעֳלוֹ, וְצִדְקָתוֹ עֹמֶדֶת לָעַד: זֵכֶר עָשָׂה לְנִפְלְאֹתָיו, חַנּוּן וְרַחוּם יהוה: טֶרֶף נָתַן לִירֵאָיו, יִזְכֹּר לְעוֹלָם בְּרִיתוֹ: כֹּחַ מַעֲשָׂיו הִגִּיד לְעַמּוֹ, לָתֵת לָהֶם נַחֲלַת גּוֹיִם: מַעֲשֵׂי יָדָיו אֱמֶת וּמִשְׁפָּט, נֶאֱמָנִים כָּל־פִּקּוּדָיו: סְמוּכִים לָעַד לְעוֹלָם, עֲשׂוּיִם בֶּאֱמֶת וְיָשָׁר: פְּדוּת שָׁלַח לְעַמּוֹ, צִוָּה־לְעוֹלָם בְּרִיתוֹ, קָדוֹשׁ וְנוֹרָא שְׁמוֹ: רֵאשִׁית חָכְמָה יִרְאַת יהוה, שֵׂכֶל טוֹב לְכָל־עֹשֵׂיהֶם, תְּהִלָּתוֹ עֹמֶדֶת לָעַד:

הַלְלוּיָהּ Halleluya! Happy is the one who holds the LORD in awe; who desires His commandments with all his might. His offspring will be heroes in the land, a blessed generation of noble people. Wealth and richness will be in his house, and his righteousness will stand firm forever. A light shines in darkness for the noble-hearted; for one who is compassionate, loving and righteous. It is good to be such a one as shows compassion and lends to those in need; one who arranges justly all that he does. For such a man will never be shaken – a righteous person is remembered forever. He need never be afraid when bad news comes; one who trusts in the LORD may have a steady heart. His heart will be steadfast and will not fear, till that time when he shall see his tormentors overcome. He is generous, he gives to the destitute – and his righteousness will stand firm forever; his horn will be raised in honor. The wicked man who sees it will grind his teeth in anger and be gone. Any urge of such a person comes to nothing. *Ps. 112*

*The Torah scroll is bound and covered. The Ark is opened.*
*The Leader takes the Torah scroll and says:*

יְהַלְלוּ Let them praise the name of the LORD, *Ps. 148*
for His name alone is sublime.

*The congregation responds:*

הוֹדוֹ His majesty is above earth and heaven.
He has raised the horn of His people,
for the glory of all His devoted ones,
the children of Israel, the people close to Him. Halleluya!

*As the Torah scroll is returned to the Ark say:*

לְדָוִד מִזְמוֹר A psalm of David. The earth is the LORD's and all it contains, the world and all who live in it. For He founded it on the seas and established it on the streams. Who may climb the mountain of the LORD? Who may stand in His holy place? He who has clean hands and a pure heart, who has not taken My name in vain, or sworn deceitfully. He shall receive blessing from the LORD, and just reward from God, his salvation. This is a generation of those who seek Him, the descendants of Jacob who seek Your presence, Selah! Lift up your heads, O gates; be uplifted, eternal doors, so that the King of glory may enter. Who is the King of glory? It is the LORD, strong and mighty, the LORD mighty in battle. Lift up your heads, O gates; lift them up, eternal doors, so that the King of glory may enter. Who is He, the King of glory? The LORD of hosts, He is the King of glory, Selah! *Ps. 24*

הַלְלוּיָהּ, אַשְׁרֵי־אִישׁ יָרֵא אֶת־יהוה, בְּמִצְוֹתָיו חָפֵץ מְאֹד: גִּבּוֹר בָּאָרֶץ יִהְיֶה זַרְעוֹ, דּוֹר יְשָׁרִים יְבֹרָךְ: הוֹן־וָעֹשֶׁר בְּבֵיתוֹ, וְצִדְקָתוֹ עֹמֶדֶת לָעַד: זָרַח בַּחֹשֶׁךְ אוֹר לַיְשָׁרִים, חַנּוּן וְרַחוּם וְצַדִּיק: טוֹב־אִישׁ חוֹנֵן וּמַלְוֶה, יְכַלְכֵּל דְּבָרָיו בְּמִשְׁפָּט: כִּי־לְעוֹלָם לֹא יִמּוֹט, לְזֵכֶר עוֹלָם יִהְיֶה צַדִּיק: מִשְּׁמוּעָה רָעָה לֹא יִירָא, נָכוֹן לִבּוֹ בָּטֻחַ בַּיהוה: סָמוּךְ לִבּוֹ לֹא יִירָא, עַד אֲשֶׁר־יִרְאֶה בְצָרָיו: פִּזַּר, נָתַן לָאֶבְיוֹנִים, צִדְקָתוֹ עֹמֶדֶת לָעַד, קַרְנוֹ תָּרוּם בְּכָבוֹד: רָשָׁע יִרְאֶה וְכָעָס, שִׁנָּיו יַחֲרֹק וְנָמָס, תַּאֲוַת רְשָׁעִים תֹּאבֵד: תהלים קיב

*The* ספר תורה *is bound and covered. The* ארון קודש *is opened.*
*The* שליח ציבור *takes the* ספר תורה *and says:*

יְהַלְלוּ אֶת־שֵׁם יהוה, כִּי־נִשְׂגָּב שְׁמוֹ, לְבַדּוֹ תהלים קמח

*The* קהל *responds:*

הוֹדוֹ עַל־אֶרֶץ וְשָׁמָיִם:
וַיָּרֶם קֶרֶן לְעַמּוֹ, תְּהִלָּה לְכָל־חֲסִידָיו
לִבְנֵי יִשְׂרָאֵל עַם קְרֹבוֹ, הַלְלוּיָהּ:

*As the* ספר תורה *is returned to the* ארון קודש*, say:*

לְדָוִד מִזְמוֹר, לַיהוה הָאָרֶץ וּמְלוֹאָהּ, תֵּבֵל וְיֹשְׁבֵי בָהּ: כִּי־הוּא עַל־יַמִּים יְסָדָהּ, וְעַל־נְהָרוֹת יְכוֹנְנֶהָ: מִי־יַעֲלֶה בְהַר־יהוה, וּמִי־יָקוּם בִּמְקוֹם קָדְשׁוֹ: נְקִי כַפַּיִם וּבַר־לֵבָב, אֲשֶׁר לֹא־נָשָׂא לַשָּׁוְא נַפְשִׁי וְלֹא נִשְׁבַּע לְמִרְמָה: יִשָּׂא בְרָכָה מֵאֵת יהוה, וּצְדָקָה מֵאֱלֹהֵי יִשְׁעוֹ: זֶה דּוֹר דֹּרְשָׁו, מְבַקְשֵׁי פָנֶיךָ, יַעֲקֹב, סֶלָה: שְׂאוּ שְׁעָרִים רָאשֵׁיכֶם, וְהִנָּשְׂאוּ פִּתְחֵי עוֹלָם, וְיָבוֹא מֶלֶךְ הַכָּבוֹד: מִי זֶה מֶלֶךְ הַכָּבוֹד, יהוה עִזּוּז וְגִבּוֹר, יהוה גִּבּוֹר מִלְחָמָה: שְׂאוּ שְׁעָרִים רָאשֵׁיכֶם, וּשְׂאוּ פִּתְחֵי עוֹלָם, וְיָבֹא מֶלֶךְ הַכָּבוֹד: מִי הוּא זֶה מֶלֶךְ הַכָּבוֹד, יהוה צְבָאוֹת הוּא מֶלֶךְ הַכָּבוֹד, סֶלָה: תהלים כד

*As the Torah scroll is placed into the Ark, say:*

וּבְנֻחֹה יֹאמַר When the Ark came to rest, Moses would say: "Return, *Num. 10*
O Lord, to the myriad thousands of Israel." Advance, Lord, to Your *Ps. 132*
resting place, You and Your mighty Ark. Your priests are clothed in
righteousness, and Your devoted ones sing in joy. For the sake of Your
servant David, do not reject Your anointed one. For I give you good *Prov. 4*
instruction; do not forsake My Torah. ▸ It is a tree of life to those *Prov. 3*
who grasp it, and those who uphold it are happy. Its ways are ways of
pleasantness, and all its paths are peace. Turn us back, O Lord, to You, *Lam. 5*
and we will return. Renew our days as of old.

*The Ark is closed.*

## HALF KADDISH

*Reader:* יִתְגַּדַּל Magnified and sanctified
may His great name be,
in the world He created by His will.
May He establish His kingdom,
make His salvation flourish,
and hasten His messiah,
in your lifetime and in your days,
and in the lifetime of all the house of Israel,
swiftly and soon –
and say: Amen.

*All:* May His great name be blessed for ever and all time.

*Leader:* Blessed and praised, glorified and exalted,
raised and honored,
uplifted and lauded
be the name of the Holy One,
blessed be He,
above and beyond any blessing,
song, praise and consolation
uttered in the world –
and say: Amen.

*As the* ספר תורה *is placed into the* ארון קודש*, say:*

וּבְנֻחֹה יֹאמַר, שׁוּבָה יהוה רִבְבוֹת אַלְפֵי יִשְׂרָאֵל: קוּמָה יהוה במדבר י / תהלים קלב
לִמְנוּחָתֶךָ, אַתָּה וַאֲרוֹן עֻזֶּךָ: כֹּהֲנֶיךָ יִלְבְּשׁוּ־צֶדֶק, וַחֲסִידֶיךָ יְרַנֵּנוּ:
בַּעֲבוּר דָּוִד עַבְדֶּךָ אַל־תָּשֵׁב פְּנֵי מְשִׁיחֶךָ: כִּי לֶקַח טוֹב נָתַתִּי משלי ד
לָכֶם, תּוֹרָתִי אַל־תַּעֲזֹבוּ: › עֵץ־חַיִּים הִיא לַמַּחֲזִיקִים בָּהּ, וְתֹמְכֶיהָ משלי ג
מְאֻשָּׁר: דְּרָכֶיהָ דַרְכֵי־נֹעַם וְכָל־נְתִיבֹתֶיהָ שָׁלוֹם: הֲשִׁיבֵנוּ יהוה איכה ה
אֵלֶיךָ וְנָשׁוּבָה, חַדֵּשׁ יָמֵינוּ כְּקֶדֶם:

*The* ארון קודש *is closed.*

חצי קדיש

ש״ץ: יִתְגַּדַּל וְיִתְקַדַּשׁ שְׁמֵהּ רַבָּא (קהל: אָמֵן)
בְּעָלְמָא דִּי בְרָא כִרְעוּתֵהּ
וְיַמְלִיךְ מַלְכוּתֵהּ
וְיַצְמַח פֻּרְקָנֵהּ וִיקָרֵב מְשִׁיחֵהּ (קהל: אָמֵן)
בְּחַיֵּיכוֹן וּבְיוֹמֵיכוֹן, וּבְחַיֵּי דְכָל בֵּית יִשְׂרָאֵל
בַּעֲגָלָא וּבִזְמַן קָרִיב
וְאִמְרוּ אָמֵן. (קהל: אָמֵן)

קהל וש״ץ: יְהֵא שְׁמֵהּ רַבָּא מְבָרַךְ לְעָלַם וּלְעָלְמֵי עָלְמַיָּא.

ש״ץ: יִתְבָּרַךְ וְיִשְׁתַּבַּח וְיִתְפָּאַר וְיִתְרוֹמַם וְיִתְנַשֵּׂא
וְיִתְהַדָּר וְיִתְעַלֶּה וְיִתְהַלָּל
שְׁמֵהּ דְּקֻדְשָׁא בְּרִיךְ הוּא (קהל: אָמֵן)
לְעֵלָּא לְעֵלָּא מִכָּל בִּרְכָתָא וְשִׁירָתָא
תֻּשְׁבְּחָתָא וְנֶחֱמָתָא
דַּאֲמִירָן בְּעָלְמָא
וְאִמְרוּ אָמֵן. (קהל: אָמֵן)

## THE AMIDA

*The following prayer, until "in former years" on page 930, is said silently, standing with feet together. If there is a minyan, the Amida is repeated aloud by the Leader. Take three steps forward and at the points indicated by ▾, bend the knees at the first word, bow at the second, and stand straight before saying God's name.*

When I proclaim the LORD's name, give glory to our God. *Deut. 32*
O LORD, open my lips, so that my mouth may declare Your praise. *Ps. 51*

PATRIARCHS

▾בָּרוּךְ▾ Blessed are You, LORD our God and God of our fathers,
God of Abraham, God of Isaac and God of Jacob;
the great, mighty and awesome God, God Most High,
who bestows acts of loving-kindness, who creates all,
who remembers the loving-kindness of the fathers
and will bring a Redeemer to their children's children
for the sake of His name, in love.

זָכְרֵנוּ לְחַיִּים Remember us for life, O King who desires life,
and write us in the book of life –
for Your sake, O God of life.
King, Helper, Savior, Shield:
▾Blessed are You, LORD,
Shield of Abraham.

DIVINE MIGHT

אַתָּה גִּבּוֹר You are eternally mighty, LORD.
You give life to the dead and have great power to save.

*In Israel:* He causes the dew to fall.

He sustains the living with loving-kindness,
and with great compassion revives the dead.
He supports the fallen, heals the sick, sets captives free,
and keeps His faith with those who sleep in the dust.
Who is like You, Master of might,
and to whom can You be compared,
O King who brings death and gives life,
and makes salvation grow?

# עמידה

*The following prayer, until* קַדְמֹנִיּוֹת *on page 931, is said silently, standing with feet together. If there is a* מנין*, the* עמידה *is repeated aloud by the* שליח ציבור*. Take three steps forward and at the points indicated by* ᵛ*, bend the knees at the first word, bow at the second, and stand straight before saying God's name.*

דברים לב כִּי שֵׁם יהוה אֶקְרָא, הָבוּ גֹדֶל לֵאלֹהֵינוּ:

תהלים נא אֲדֹנָי, שְׂפָתַי תִּפְתָּח, וּפִי יַגִּיד תְּהִלָּתֶךָ:

אבות

ᵛבָּרוּךְ אַתָּה יהוה, אֱלֹהֵינוּ וֵאלֹהֵי אֲבוֹתֵינוּ
אֱלֹהֵי אַבְרָהָם, אֱלֹהֵי יִצְחָק, וֵאלֹהֵי יַעֲקֹב
הָאֵל הַגָּדוֹל הַגִּבּוֹר וְהַנּוֹרָא, אֵל עֶלְיוֹן
גּוֹמֵל חֲסָדִים טוֹבִים, קוֹנֵה הַכֹּל
וְזוֹכֵר חַסְדֵי אָבוֹת
וּמֵבִיא גוֹאֵל לִבְנֵי בְנֵיהֶם לְמַעַן שְׁמוֹ בְּאַהֲבָה.

זָכְרֵנוּ לְחַיִּים, מֶלֶךְ חָפֵץ בַּחַיִּים
וְכָתְבֵנוּ בְּסֵפֶר הַחַיִּים, לְמַעַנְךָ אֱלֹהִים חַיִּים.
מֶלֶךְ עוֹזֵר וּמוֹשִׁיעַ וּמָגֵן.
ᵛבָּרוּךְ אַתָּה יהוה, מָגֵן אַבְרָהָם.

גבורות

אַתָּה גִּבּוֹר לְעוֹלָם, אֲדֹנָי
מְחַיֵּה מֵתִים אַתָּה, רַב לְהוֹשִׁיעַ
בארץ ישראל: מוֹרִיד הַטָּל
מְכַלְכֵּל חַיִּים בְּחֶסֶד, מְחַיֵּה מֵתִים בְּרַחֲמִים רַבִּים
סוֹמֵךְ נוֹפְלִים, וְרוֹפֵא חוֹלִים, וּמַתִּיר אֲסוּרִים
וּמְקַיֵּם אֱמוּנָתוֹ לִישֵׁנֵי עָפָר.
מִי כָמוֹךָ, בַּעַל גְּבוּרוֹת, וּמִי דּוֹמֶה לָּךְ
מֶלֶךְ, מֵמִית וּמְחַיֶּה וּמַצְמִיחַ יְשׁוּעָה.

מִי כָמְוֹךָ Who is like You, compassionate Father,
who remembers His creatures in compassion, for life?
Faithful are You to revive the dead.
Blessed are You, LORD,
who revives the dead.

---

KEDUSHA

*During the Leader's Repetition, the following is said standing with feet together, rising on the toes at the words indicated by ▲.*

*Cong. then Leader:* נְקַדֵּשָׁךְ We will sanctify and revere You with the song
sung by the holy Seraphim,
who speak the threefold declaration of Your holiness,
as is written by Your prophet,
"And they [the angels] call to one another saying: *Is. 6*

*Cong. then Leader:* ▲Holy, ▲holy, ▲holy is the LORD of hosts;
the whole world is filled with His glory."
Those facing them praise You and say:

*Cong. then Leader:* ▲"Blessed is the LORD's glory from His place." *Ezek. 3*
And in Your holy Writings it is written thus:

*Cong. then Leader:* ▲"The LORD shall reign for ever. He is your God, Zion, *Ps. 146*
from generation to generation, Halleluya!"

---

HOLINESS

אַתָּה קָדוֹשׁ You are holy and Your name is holy,
and holy ones praise You daily, Selah!
For You, God, are a great and holy King.

לְדוֹר וָדוֹר From generation to generation declare God King,
for He alone is lofty and holy.

וּבְכֵן יִתְקַדַּשׁ And so may Your name be sanctified, LORD our God,
through Israel Your nation and Jerusalem, Your city,
and Zion, the dwelling place of Your honor
and through the royal house of David Your anointed,
and Your Sanctuary and Your Temple.

מִי כָמְוֹךָ אַב הָרַחֲמָן, זוֹכֵר יְצוּרָיו לְחַיִּים בְּרַחֲמִים.
וְנֶאֱמָן אַתָּה לְהַחֲיוֹת מֵתִים.
בָּרוּךְ אַתָּה יהוה, מְחַיֵּה הַמֵּתִים.

---

קדושה

*During the* חזרת הש״ץ, *the following is said standing with feet together, rising on the toes at the words indicated by* ˄.

קהל then ש״ץ: נְקַדֵּשׁךָ וְנַעֲרִיצְךָ כְּנֹעַם שִׂיחַ סוֹד שַׂרְפֵי קֹדֶשׁ
הַמְשַׁלְּשִׁים לְךָ קְדֻשָּׁה
ישעיה ו כַּכָּתוּב עַל יַד נְבִיאֶךָ, וְקָרָא זֶה אֶל־זֶה וְאָמַר

קהל then ש״ץ: ˄קָדוֹשׁ, ˄קָדוֹשׁ, ˄קָדוֹשׁ, יהוה צְבָאוֹת, מְלֹא כָל־הָאָרֶץ כְּבוֹדוֹ:
לְעֻמָּתָם מְשַׁבְּחִים וְאוֹמְרִים

יחזקאל ג קהל then ש״ץ: ˄בָּרוּךְ כְּבוֹד־יהוה מִמְּקוֹמוֹ:
וּבְדִבְרֵי קָדְשְׁךָ כָּתוּב לֵאמֹר

תהלים קמו קהל then ש״ץ: ˄יִמְלֹךְ יהוה לְעוֹלָם, אֱלֹהַיִךְ צִיּוֹן לְדֹר וָדֹר, הַלְלוּיָהּ:

---

קדושת השם

אַתָּה קָדוֹשׁ וְשִׁמְךָ קָדוֹשׁ
וּקְדוֹשִׁים בְּכָל יוֹם יְהַלְלְוּךָ סֶּלָה
כִּי אֵל מֶלֶךְ גָּדוֹל וְקָדוֹשׁ אָתָּה.

לְדוֹר וָדוֹר הַמְלִיכוּ לָאֵל
כִּי הוּא לְבַדּוֹ מָרוֹם וְקָדוֹשׁ.

וּבְכֵן יִתְקַדַּשׁ שִׁמְךָ יהוה אֱלֹהֵינוּ
עַל יִשְׂרָאֵל עַמֶּךָ וְעַל יְרוּשָׁלַיִם עִירֶךָ
וְעַל צִיּוֹן מִשְׁכַּן כְּבוֹדֶךָ
וְעַל מַלְכוּת בֵּית דָּוִד מְשִׁיחֶךָ
וְעַל מְכוֹנְךָ וְהֵיכָלֶךָ.

וּבְכֵן תֵּן פַּחְדְּךָ And so place the fear of You, Lord our God,
over all that You have made,
and the terror of You over all You have created,
and all who were made will stand in awe of You,
and all of creation will worship You,
and they will be bound all together as one
to carry out Your will with an undivided heart;
for we know, Lord our God,
that all dominion is laid out before You,
strength is in Your palm,
and might in Your right hand,
Your name spreading awe over all You have created.

וּבְכֵן תֵּן כָּבוֹד And so place honor, Lord, upon Your people,
praise on those who fear You and hope into those who seek You,
the confidence to speak into all who long for You,
gladness to Your land and joy to Your city,
the flourishing of pride to David Your servant,
and a lamp laid out for his descendant, Your anointed,
soon, in our days.

וּבְכֵן צַדִּיקִים And then righteous people will see and rejoice,
and the upright will exult,
and the pious revel in joy,
and injustice will have nothing more to say,
and all wickedness will fade away like smoke
as You sweep the rule of arrogance from the earth.

וְתִמְלֹךְ And You, who are the Lord our God,
will rule alone over all those You have made,
in Mount Zion, the dwelling of Your glory,
and in Jerusalem, Your holy city,
as it is written in Your holy Writings:
"The Lord shall reign for ever. *Ps. 146*
He is your God, Zion, from generation to generation, Halleluya!"

וּבְכֵן תֵּן פַּחְדְּךָ יהוה אֱלֹהֵינוּ עַל כָּל מַעֲשֶׂיךָ
וְאֵימָתְךָ עַל כָּל מַה שֶּׁבָּרָאתָ
וְיִירָאוּךָ כָּל הַמַּעֲשִׂים, וְיִשְׁתַּחֲווּ לְפָנֶיךָ כָּל הַבְּרוּאִים
וְיֵעָשׂוּ כֻלָּם אֲגֻדָּה אֶחָת לַעֲשׂוֹת רְצוֹנְךָ בְּלֵבָב שָׁלֵם
כְּמוֹ שֶׁיָּדַעְנוּ יהוה אֱלֹהֵינוּ שֶׁהַשָּׁלְטָן לְפָנֶיךָ
עֹז בְּיָדְךָ וּגְבוּרָה בִּימִינֶךָ
וְשִׁמְךָ נוֹרָא עַל כָּל מַה שֶּׁבָּרָאתָ.

וּבְכֵן תֵּן כָּבוֹד יהוה לְעַמֶּךָ
תְּהִלָּה לִירֵאֶיךָ וְתִקְוָה טוֹבָה לְדוֹרְשֶׁיךָ
וּפִתְחוֹן פֶּה לַמְיַחֲלִים לָךְ
שִׂמְחָה לְאַרְצֶךָ, וְשָׂשׂוֹן לְעִירֶךָ
וּצְמִיחַת קֶרֶן לְדָוִד עַבְדֶּךָ
וַעֲרִיכַת נֵר לְבֶן יִשַׁי מְשִׁיחֶךָ
בִּמְהֵרָה בְיָמֵינוּ.

וּבְכֵן צַדִּיקִים יִרְאוּ וְיִשְׂמָחוּ, וִישָׁרִים יַעֲלֹזוּ
וַחֲסִידִים בְּרִנָּה יָגִילוּ, וְעוֹלָתָה תִּקְפָּץ פִּיהָ
וְכָל הָרִשְׁעָה כֻּלָּהּ כְּעָשָׁן תִּכְלֶה
כִּי תַעֲבִיר מֶמְשֶׁלֶת זָדוֹן מִן הָאָרֶץ.

וְתִמְלֹךְ אַתָּה הוּא יהוה אֱלֹהֵינוּ
מְהֵרָה לְבַדֶּךָ עַל כָּל מַעֲשֶׂיךָ
בְּהַר צִיּוֹן מִשְׁכַּן כְּבוֹדֶךָ
וּבִירוּשָׁלַיִם עִיר קָדְשֶׁךָ
כַּכָּתוּב בְּדִבְרֵי קָדְשֶׁךָ
יִמְלֹךְ יהוה לְעוֹלָם, אֱלֹהַיִךְ צִיּוֹן לְדֹר וָדֹר, הַלְלוּיָהּ: תהלים קמו

קָדוֹשׁ אַתָּה You are holy, Your name is awesome,
and there is no god but You, as it is written,
"The LORD of hosts shall be raised up through His judgment, *Is. 5*
the Holy God, made holy in righteousness."
Blessed are You, LORD, the holy King.

### HOLINESS OF THE DAY

אַתָּה בְחַרְתָּנוּ You have chosen us from among all peoples.
You have loved and favored us.
You have raised us above all tongues.
You have made us holy through Your commandments.
You have brought us near, our King, to Your service,
and have called us by Your great and holy name.

*On Shabbat, add the words in parentheses:*

וַתִּתֶּן לָנוּ And You, LORD our God, have given us in love
(this Sabbath day and) this Day of Remembrance,
a day of (recalling) blowing the shofar.
(with love,) a holy assembly in memory of the exodus from Egypt.

אֱלֹהֵינוּ Our God and God of our ancestors,
may there rise, come, reach, appear, be favored, heard,
regarded and remembered before You,
our recollection and remembrance,
as well as the remembrance of our ancestors,
and of the Messiah, son of David Your servant,
and of Jerusalem Your holy city,
and of all Your people the house of Israel –
for deliverance and well-being,
grace, loving-kindness and compassion,
life and peace, on this Day of Remembrance.
On it remember us, LORD our God, for good;
recollect us for blessing, and deliver us for a good life.
In accord with Your promise of salvation and compassion,
spare us and be gracious to us;
have compassion on us and deliver us, for our eyes are turned to You
because You, God, are a gracious and compassionate King.

קָדוֹשׁ אַתָּה וְנוֹרָא שְׁמֶךָ, וְאֵין אֱלוֹהַּ מִבַּלְעָדֶיךָ
כַּכָּתוּב, וַיִּגְבַּהּ יהוה צְבָאוֹת בַּמִּשְׁפָּט ישעיה ה
וְהָאֵל הַקָּדוֹשׁ נִקְדַּשׁ בִּצְדָקָה:
בָּרוּךְ אַתָּה יהוה, הַמֶּלֶךְ הַקָּדוֹשׁ.

קדושת היום

אַתָּה בְחַרְתָּנוּ מִכָּל הָעַמִּים
אָהַבְתָּ אוֹתָנוּ וְרָצִיתָ בָּנוּ
וְרוֹמַמְתָּנוּ מִכָּל הַלְּשׁוֹנוֹת
וְקִדַּשְׁתָּנוּ בְּמִצְוֹתֶיךָ וְקֵרַבְתָּנוּ מַלְכֵּנוּ לַעֲבוֹדָתֶךָ
וְשִׁמְךָ הַגָּדוֹל וְהַקָּדוֹשׁ עָלֵינוּ קָרָאתָ.

*On שבת, add the words in parentheses:*

וַתִּתֶּן לָנוּ יהוה אֱלֹהֵינוּ בְּאַהֲבָה
אֶת יוֹם (הַשַּׁבָּת הַזֶּה וְאֶת יוֹם) הַזִּכָּרוֹן הַזֶּה
יוֹם (זִכְרוֹן) תְּרוּעָה (בְּאַהֲבָה) מִקְרָא קֹדֶשׁ, זֵכֶר לִיצִיאַת מִצְרָיִם.

אֱלֹהֵינוּ וֵאלֹהֵי אֲבוֹתֵינוּ
יַעֲלֶה וְיָבוֹא וְיַגִּיעַ, וְיֵרָאֶה וְיֵרָצֶה וְיִשָּׁמַע
וְיִפָּקֵד וְיִזָּכֵר זִכְרוֹנֵנוּ וּפִקְדוֹנֵנוּ וְזִכְרוֹן אֲבוֹתֵינוּ
וְזִכְרוֹן מָשִׁיחַ בֶּן דָּוִד עַבְדֶּךָ, וְזִכְרוֹן יְרוּשָׁלַיִם עִיר קָדְשֶׁךָ
וְזִכְרוֹן כָּל עַמְּךָ בֵּית יִשְׂרָאֵל, לְפָנֶיךָ
לִפְלֵיטָה לְטוֹבָה, לְחֵן וּלְחֶסֶד וּלְרַחֲמִים, לְחַיִּים וּלְשָׁלוֹם
בְּיוֹם הַזִּכָּרוֹן הַזֶּה.
זָכְרֵנוּ יהוה אֱלֹהֵינוּ בּוֹ לְטוֹבָה, וּפָקְדֵנוּ בוֹ לִבְרָכָה
וְהוֹשִׁיעֵנוּ בוֹ לְחַיִּים טוֹבִים.
וּבִדְבַר יְשׁוּעָה וְרַחֲמִים חוּס וְחָנֵּנוּ, וְרַחֵם עָלֵינוּ וְהוֹשִׁיעֵנוּ
כִּי אֵלֶיךָ עֵינֵינוּ, כִּי אֵל מֶלֶךְ חַנּוּן וְרַחוּם אָתָּה.

אֱלֹהֵינוּ Our God and God of our ancestors,
rule over all the world in Your honor,
and be raised above all the earth in Your glory,
and appear, in the splendor of Your great might
before all those who live in this world, Your domain.
And all who were made will know that You made them,
and all who were formed will know that You formed them,
and all that have breath in their mouths will declare:
The LORD, God of Israel is King,
and His kingship has dominion over all.

*On Shabbat, add the words in parentheses:*

(Our God and God of our ancestors,
find favor, please, in our rest.)

Make us holy through Your commandments
and grant us our share in Your Torah.
Satisfy us with Your goodness,
grant our souls joy in Your salvation
(in love and favor, LORD our God,
grant us as our heritage Your holy Sabbaths,
so that all Israel, who sanctify Your name may find rest on them),
and purify our hearts to serve You in truth.
For You, LORD, are truth, and Your word is truth
and holds true forever.
Blessed are You, LORD, King over all the earth,
who sanctifies (the Sabbath,)
Israel and the Day of Remembrance.

TEMPLE SERVICE

רְצֵה Find favor, LORD our God, in Your people Israel,
and heed their prayer.
Restore the service to Your most holy House,
and accept soon, in love and favor,
the fire-offerings of Israel and their prayer.
May the service of Your people Israel always find favor with You.

אֱלֹהֵינוּ וֵאלֹהֵי אֲבוֹתֵינוּ
מְלֹךְ עַל כָּל הָעוֹלָם כֻּלּוֹ בִּכְבוֹדֶךָ
וְהִנָּשֵׂא עַל כָּל הָאָרֶץ בִּיקָרֶךָ
וְהוֹפַע בַּהֲדַר גְּאוֹן עֻזֶּךָ
עַל כָּל יוֹשְׁבֵי תֵבֵל אַרְצֶךָ.
וְיֵדַע כָּל פָּעוּל כִּי אַתָּה פְעַלְתּוֹ
וְיָבִין כָּל יָצוּר כִּי אַתָּה יְצַרְתּוֹ
וְיֹאמַר כֹּל אֲשֶׁר נְשָׁמָה בְאַפּוֹ
יהוה אֱלֹהֵי יִשְׂרָאֵל מֶלֶךְ וּמַלְכוּתוֹ בַּכֹּל מָשָׁלָה.

*On שבת, add the words in parentheses:*

(אֱלֹהֵינוּ וֵאלֹהֵי אֲבוֹתֵינוּ, רְצֵה נָא בִמְנוּחָתֵנוּ)
קַדְּשֵׁנוּ בְּמִצְוֹתֶיךָ וְתֵן חֶלְקֵנוּ בְּתוֹרָתֶךָ
שַׂבְּעֵנוּ מִטּוּבֶךָ וְשַׂמַּח נַפְשֵׁנוּ בִּישׁוּעָתֶךָ
(וְהַנְחִילֵנוּ יהוה אֱלֹהֵינוּ בְּאַהֲבָה וּבְרָצוֹן שַׁבְּתוֹת קָדְשֶׁךָ
וְיָנוּחוּ בָם כָּל יִשְׂרָאֵל מְקַדְּשֵׁי שְׁמֶךָ)
וְטַהֵר לִבֵּנוּ לְעָבְדְּךָ בֶּאֱמֶת
כִּי אַתָּה אֱלֹהִים אֱמֶת, וּדְבָרְךָ אֱמֶת וְקַיָּם לָעַד.
בָּרוּךְ אַתָּה יהוה, מֶלֶךְ עַל כָּל הָאָרֶץ
מְקַדֵּשׁ (הַשַּׁבָּת וְ) יִשְׂרָאֵל וְיוֹם הַזִּכָּרוֹן.

עבודה

רְצֵה יהוה אֱלֹהֵינוּ בְּעַמְּךָ יִשְׂרָאֵל, וְלִתְפִלָּתָם שְׁעֵה
וְהָשֵׁב אֶת הָעֲבוֹדָה לִדְבִיר בֵּיתֶךָ
וְאִשֵּׁי יִשְׂרָאֵל וּתְפִלָּתָם, מְהֵרָה בְּאַהֲבָה תְקַבֵּל בְּרָצוֹן
וּתְהִי לְרָצוֹן תָּמִיד עֲבוֹדַת יִשְׂרָאֵל עַמֶּךָ.

And may our eyes witness Your return to Zion in compassion.
Blessed are You, Lord, who restores His Presence to Zion.

THANKSGIVING

*Bow at the first nine words.*

ᵛמוֹדִים We give thanks to You,
for You are the Lord our God
and God of our ancestors
for ever and all time.
You are the Rock of our lives,
Shield of our salvation
from generation to generation.
We will thank You and
declare Your praise for our lives,
which are entrusted into Your hand;
for our souls,
which are placed in Your charge;
for Your miracles
which are with us every day;
and for Your wonders and favors
at all times, evening,
morning and midday.
You are good –
for Your compassion never fails.
You are compassionate –
for Your loving-kindnesses never cease.
For we have always placed
our hope in You.

*During the Leader's Repetition, the congregation says quietly:*

ᵛמוֹדִים We give thanks to You,
for You are the Lord our God
and God of our ancestors,
God of all flesh,
who formed us
and formed the universe.
Blessings and thanks
are due to Your great
and holy name for giving us
life and sustaining us.
May You continue
to give us life
and sustain us;
and may You gather our
exiles to Your holy courts,
to keep Your decrees,
do Your will
and serve You
with a perfect heart,
for it is for us
to give You thanks.
Blessed be God to whom
thanksgiving is due.

וְעַל כֻּלָּם For all these things may Your name be blessed and exalted and raised up, our King, continually, for ever and all time.

וּכְתֹב And write for a good life, all the children of Your covenant.

Let all that lives thank You, Selah! and praise and bless
Your great name in truth, always, because it is good,
God, our Savior and Help, Selah! the beneficent God.
ᵛBlessed are You, Lord, whose name is "the Good"
and to whom thanks are due.

וְתֶחֱזֶינָה עֵינֵינוּ בְּשׁוּבְךָ לְצִיּוֹן בְּרַחֲמִים.
בָּרוּךְ אַתָּה יהוה, הַמַּחֲזִיר שְׁכִינָתוֹ לְצִיּוֹן.

הודאה

*Bow at the first five words.*

ׄמוֹדִים אֲנַחְנוּ לָךְ
שָׁאַתָּה הוּא יהוה אֱלֹהֵינוּ
וֵאלֹהֵי אֲבוֹתֵינוּ לְעוֹלָם וָעֶד.
צוּר חַיֵּינוּ, מָגֵן יִשְׁעֵנוּ
אַתָּה הוּא לְדוֹר וָדוֹר.
נוֹדֶה לְּךָ וּנְסַפֵּר תְּהִלָּתֶךָ
עַל חַיֵּינוּ הַמְּסוּרִים בְּיָדֶךָ
וְעַל נִשְׁמוֹתֵינוּ הַפְּקוּדוֹת לָךְ
וְעַל נִסֶּיךָ שֶׁבְּכָל יוֹם עִמָּנוּ
וְעַל נִפְלְאוֹתֶיךָ וְטוֹבוֹתֶיךָ
שֶׁבְּכָל עֵת, עֶרֶב וָבֹקֶר וְצָהֳרָיִם.
הַטּוֹב, כִּי לֹא כָלוּ רַחֲמֶיךָ
וְהַמְרַחֵם, כִּי לֹא תַמּוּ חֲסָדֶיךָ
כִּי מֵעוֹלָם קִוִּינוּ לָךְ.

*During the* חזרת הש״ץ, *the* קהל *says quietly:*

ׄמוֹדִים אֲנַחְנוּ לָךְ
שָׁאַתָּה הוּא יהוה אֱלֹהֵינוּ
וֵאלֹהֵי אֲבוֹתֵינוּ
אֱלֹהֵי כָל בָּשָׂר
יוֹצְרֵנוּ, יוֹצֵר בְּרֵאשִׁית.
בְּרָכוֹת וְהוֹדָאוֹת
לְשִׁמְךָ הַגָּדוֹל וְהַקָּדוֹשׁ
עַל שֶׁהֶחֱיִיתָנוּ וְקִיַּמְתָּנוּ.
כֵּן תְּחַיֵּנוּ וּתְקַיְּמֵנוּ
וְתֶאֱסֹף גָּלֻיּוֹתֵינוּ
לְחַצְרוֹת קָדְשֶׁךָ
לִשְׁמֹר חֻקֶּיךָ וְלַעֲשׂוֹת רְצוֹנֶךָ
וּלְעָבְדְּךָ בְּלֵבָב שָׁלֵם
עַל שֶׁאֲנַחְנוּ מוֹדִים לָךְ.
בָּרוּךְ אֵל הַהוֹדָאוֹת.

וְעַל כֻּלָּם
יִתְבָּרַךְ וְיִתְרוֹמַם וְיִתְנַשֵּׂא שִׁמְךָ מַלְכֵּנוּ תָּמִיד לְעוֹלָם וָעֶד.

וּכְתֹב לְחַיִּים טוֹבִים כָּל בְּנֵי בְרִיתֶךָ.

וְכֹל הַחַיִּים יוֹדְוּךָ סֶּלָה
וִיהַלְלוּ וִיבָרְכוּ אֶת שִׁמְךָ הַגָּדוֹל בֶּאֱמֶת לְעוֹלָם כִּי טוֹב
הָאֵל יְשׁוּעָתֵנוּ וְעֶזְרָתֵנוּ סֶלָה, הָאֵל הַטּוֹב.
ׄבָּרוּךְ אַתָּה יהוה, הַטּוֹב שִׁמְךָ וּלְךָ נָאֶה לְהוֹדוֹת.

PEACE

שִׂים שָׁלוֹם Grant peace, goodness and blessing,
life, grace, loving-kindness and compassion
to us and all Israel Your people.
Bless us, our Father, all as one, with the light of Your face,
for by the light of Your face You have given us, Lord our God,
the Torah of life and love of kindness,
righteousness, blessing,
compassion, life and peace.
May it be good in Your eyes
to bless us and all Your people Israel
at every time, in every hour, with Your peace.

בְּסֵפֶר חַיִּים In the book of life, blessing, peace and prosperity,
and good decrees, salvations and consolations
may we and all Your people the house of Israel
be remembered and written before You
for a good life, and for peace.

Blessed are You, Lord,
who blesses His people Israel with peace.

*The following verse concludes the Leader's Repetition of the Amida.*
*Some also say it here as part of the silent Amida. See law 64.*

May the words of my mouth and the meditation of my heart *Ps. 19*
find favor before You, Lord, my Rock and Redeemer.

אֱלֹהַי My God, *Berakhot 17a*
guard my tongue from evil
and my lips from deceitful speech.
To those who curse me, let my soul be silent;
may my soul be to all like the dust.
Open my heart to Your Torah
and let my soul pursue Your commandments.
As for all who rise up or plan evil against me,
swiftly thwart their counsel and frustrate their plans.

ברכת שלום

שִׂים שָׁלוֹם טוֹבָה וּבְרָכָה
חַיִּים חֵן וָחֶסֶד וְרַחֲמִים
עָלֵינוּ וְעַל כָּל יִשְׂרָאֵל עַמֶּךָ.
בָּרְכֵנוּ אָבִינוּ כֻּלָּנוּ כְּאֶחָד בְּאוֹר פָּנֶיךָ
כִּי בְאוֹר פָּנֶיךָ נָתַתָּ לָּנוּ יהוה אֱלֹהֵינוּ
תּוֹרַת חַיִּים וְאַהֲבַת חֶסֶד
וּצְדָקָה וּבְרָכָה וְרַחֲמִים וְחַיִּים וְשָׁלוֹם.
וְטוֹב יִהְיֶה בְּעֵינֶיךָ לְבָרְכֵנוּ וּלְבָרֵךְ אֶת כָּל עַמְּךָ יִשְׂרָאֵל
בְּכָל עֵת וּבְכָל שָׁעָה בִּשְׁלוֹמֶךָ.

בְּסֵפֶר חַיִּים, בְּרָכָה וְשָׁלוֹם, וּפַרְנָסָה טוֹבָה
וּגְזֵרוֹת טוֹבוֹת, יְשׁוּעוֹת וְנֶחָמוֹת, נִזָּכֵר וְנִכָּתֵב לְפָנֶיךָ
אֲנַחְנוּ וְכָל עַמְּךָ בֵּית יִשְׂרָאֵל לְחַיִּים טוֹבִים וּלְשָׁלוֹם.

בָּרוּךְ אַתָּה יהוה, הַמְבָרֵךְ אֶת עַמּוֹ יִשְׂרָאֵל בַּשָּׁלוֹם.

*The following verse concludes the* חזרת הש״ץ.
*Some also say it here as part of the silent* עמידה. *See law 64.*

תהלים יט
יִהְיוּ לְרָצוֹן אִמְרֵי־פִי וְהֶגְיוֹן לִבִּי לְפָנֶיךָ, יהוה צוּרִי וְגֹאֲלִי:

ברכות יז.
אֱלֹהַי
נְצֹר לְשׁוֹנִי מֵרָע וּשְׂפָתַי מִדַּבֵּר מִרְמָה
וְלִמְקַלְלַי נַפְשִׁי תִדֹּם, וְנַפְשִׁי כֶּעָפָר לַכֹּל תִּהְיֶה.
פְּתַח לִבִּי בְּתוֹרָתֶךָ, וְאַחֲרֵי מִצְוֹתֶיךָ תִּרְדֹּף נַפְשִׁי.
וְכָל הַקָּמִים וְהַחוֹשְׁבִים עָלַי רָעָה
מְהֵרָה הָפֵר עֲצָתָם וְקַלְקֵל מַחֲשַׁבְתָּם.

*Some add this prayer:*
יְהִי רָצוֹן May it be Your will, Lord my God, God of my ancestors,
that envy of no man may rise up in me, nor envy of me in any other;
that I will not be angry today, nor make You angry;
and save me from my evil impulse, placing humility and modesty into my heart.
Our King and God, make Your name One in Your world;
build up Your city, establish Your House and complete Your Sanctuary,
gather in the exiles, redeem Your flock, and have Your congregation rejoice.

Act for the sake of Your name;
act for the sake of Your right hand;
act for the sake of Your Torah;
act for the sake of Your holiness.
That Your beloved ones may be delivered, *Ps. 60*
save with Your right hand and answer me.
May the words of my mouth and the meditation of my heart *Ps. 19*
find favor before You, Lord, my Rock and Redeemer.

*Bow, take three steps back, then bow, first left, then right, then center, while saying:*
May He who makes peace in His high places,
make peace for us and all Israel –
and say: Amen.

יְהִי רָצוֹן May it be Your will, Lord our God and God of our ancestors,
that the Temple be rebuilt speedily in our days,
and grant us a share in Your Torah.
And there we will serve You with reverence,
as in the days of old and as in former years.
Then the offering of Judah and Jerusalem *Mal. 3*
will be pleasing to the Lord as in the days of old and as in former years.

*On Friday or Shabbat, Avinu Malkenu is not said*
*and the service continues with Full Kaddish on page 936.*

*The Ark is opened.*

אָבִינוּ מַלְכֵּנוּ Our Father, our King, we have sinned before You.

Our Father, our King, we have no king but You.

Our Father, our King, deal kindly with us for the sake of Your name.

Our Father our King, renew for us a good year.

Our Father, our King, nullify all harsh decrees against us.

*Some add this prayer:*

יְהִי רָצוֹן מִלְּפָנֶיךָ, יהוה אֱלֹהַי וֵאלֹהֵי אֲבוֹתַי
שֶׁלֹּא תַעֲלֶה קִנְאַת אָדָם עָלַי, וְלֹא קִנְאָתִי עַל אֲחֵרִים
וְשֶׁלֹּא אֶכְעֹס הַיּוֹם, וְשֶׁלֹּא אַכְעִיסֶךָ
וְתַצִּילֵנִי מִיֵּצֶר הָרָע, וְתֵן בְּלִבִּי הַכְנָעָה וַעֲנָוָה.
מַלְכֵּנוּ וֵאלֹהֵינוּ, יַחֵד שִׁמְךָ בְּעוֹלָמֶךָ
בְּנֵה עִירְךָ, יַסֵּד בֵּיתְךָ וְשַׁכְלֵל הֵיכָלֶךָ
וְקַבֵּץ קִבּוּץ גָּלֻיּוֹת, וּפְדֵה צֹאנֶךָ וְשַׂמַּח עֲדָתֶךָ.

עֲשֵׂה לְמַעַן שְׁמֶךָ, עֲשֵׂה לְמַעַן יְמִינֶךָ
עֲשֵׂה לְמַעַן תּוֹרָתֶךָ, עֲשֵׂה לְמַעַן קְדֻשָּׁתֶךָ.
תהלים ס לְמַעַן יֵחָלְצוּן יְדִידֶיךָ, הוֹשִׁיעָה יְמִינְךָ וַעֲנֵנִי:
תהלים יט יִהְיוּ לְרָצוֹן אִמְרֵי־פִי וְהֶגְיוֹן לִבִּי לְפָנֶיךָ, יהוה צוּרִי וְגֹאֲלִי:

*Bow, take three steps back, then bow, first left, then right, then center, while saying:*

עֹשֶׂה הַשָּׁלוֹם בִּמְרוֹמָיו
הוּא יַעֲשֶׂה שָׁלוֹם עָלֵינוּ וְעַל כָּל יִשְׂרָאֵל, וְאִמְרוּ אָמֵן.

יְהִי רָצוֹן מִלְּפָנֶיךָ יהוה אֱלֹהֵינוּ וֵאלֹהֵי אֲבוֹתֵינוּ
שֶׁיִּבָּנֶה בֵּית הַמִּקְדָּשׁ בִּמְהֵרָה בְיָמֵינוּ, וְתֵן חֶלְקֵנוּ בְּתוֹרָתֶךָ
וְשָׁם נַעֲבָדְךָ בְּיִרְאָה כִּימֵי עוֹלָם וּכְשָׁנִים קַדְמֹנִיּוֹת.
מלאכי ג וְעָרְבָה לַיהוה מִנְחַת יְהוּדָה וִירוּשָׁלָםִ כִּימֵי עוֹלָם וּכְשָׁנִים קַדְמֹנִיּוֹת:

*On Friday or* שבת*,* אָבִינוּ מַלְכֵּנוּ *is not said*
*and the service continues with* קדיש שלם *on page 937.*

*The* ארון קודש *is opened.*

אָבִינוּ מַלְכֵּנוּ, חָטָאנוּ לְפָנֶיךָ.
אָבִינוּ מַלְכֵּנוּ, אֵין לָנוּ מֶלֶךְ אֶלָּא אָתָּה.
אָבִינוּ מַלְכֵּנוּ, עֲשֵׂה עִמָּנוּ לְמַעַן שְׁמֶךָ.
אָבִינוּ מַלְכֵּנוּ, חַדֵּשׁ עָלֵינוּ שָׁנָה טוֹבָה.
אָבִינוּ מַלְכֵּנוּ, בַּטֵּל מֵעָלֵינוּ כָּל גְּזֵרוֹת קָשׁוֹת.

Our Father, our King, nullify the plans of those who hate us.

Our Father, our King, thwart the counsel of our enemies.

Our Father, our King, rid us of every oppressor and adversary.

Our Father, our King, close the mouths of our adversaries
and accusers.

Our Father, our King, efface pestilence, sword, famine,
captivity and destruction, iniquity and eradication
from the people of Your covenant.

Our Father, our King, withhold the plague from Your heritage.

Our Father, our King, forgive and pardon all our iniquities.

Our Father, our King, wipe away and remove our transgressions and
sins from Your sight.

Our Father, our King, erase in Your abundant mercy all records
of our sins.

*The following nine verses are said responsively, first by the Leader, then by the congregation:*

Our Father, our King, bring us back to You in perfect repentance.

Our Father, our King, send a complete healing to the sick of Your people.

Our Father, our King, tear up the evil decree against us.

Our Father, our King, remember us with a memory of favorable deeds
before You.

Our Father, our King, write us in the book of good life.

Our Father, our King, write us in the book of redemption and salvation.

Our Father, our King, write us in the book of livelihood and sustenance.

Our Father, our King, write us in the book of merit.

Our Father, our King, write us in the book of pardon and forgiveness.

*End of responsive reading.*

Our Father, our King, let salvation soon flourish for us.

Our Father, our King, raise the honor of Your people Israel.

אָבִינוּ מַלְכֵּנוּ, בַּטֵּל מַחְשְׁבוֹת שׂוֹנְאֵינוּ.
אָבִינוּ מַלְכֵּנוּ, הָפֵר עֲצַת אוֹיְבֵינוּ.
אָבִינוּ מַלְכֵּנוּ, כַּלֵּה כָּל צַר וּמַשְׂטִין מֵעָלֵינוּ.
אָבִינוּ מַלְכֵּנוּ, סְתֹם פִּיּוֹת מַשְׂטִינֵנוּ וּמְקַטְרְגֵינוּ.
אָבִינוּ מַלְכֵּנוּ, כַּלֵּה דֶּבֶר וְחֶרֶב וְרָעָב וּשְׁבִי וּמַשְׁחִית וְעָוֹן וּשְׁמַד מִבְּנֵי בְרִיתֶךָ.
אָבִינוּ מַלְכֵּנוּ, מְנַע מַגֵּפָה מִנַּחֲלָתֶךָ.
אָבִינוּ מַלְכֵּנוּ, סְלַח וּמְחַל לְכָל עֲוֹנוֹתֵינוּ.
אָבִינוּ מַלְכֵּנוּ, מְחֵה וְהַעֲבֵר פְּשָׁעֵינוּ וְחַטֹּאתֵינוּ מִנֶּגֶד עֵינֶיךָ.
אָבִינוּ מַלְכֵּנוּ, מְחֹק בְּרַחֲמֶיךָ הָרַבִּים כָּל שִׁטְרֵי חוֹבוֹתֵינוּ.

*The following nine verses are said responsively, first by the* שליח ציבור*, then by the* קהל*:*

אָבִינוּ מַלְכֵּנוּ, הַחֲזִירֵנוּ בִּתְשׁוּבָה שְׁלֵמָה לְפָנֶיךָ.
אָבִינוּ מַלְכֵּנוּ, שְׁלַח רְפוּאָה שְׁלֵמָה לְחוֹלֵי עַמֶּךָ.
אָבִינוּ מַלְכֵּנוּ, קְרַע רֹעַ גְּזַר דִּינֵנוּ.
אָבִינוּ מַלְכֵּנוּ, זָכְרֵנוּ בְּזִכְרוֹן טוֹב לְפָנֶיךָ.
אָבִינוּ מַלְכֵּנוּ, כָּתְבֵנוּ בְּסֵפֶר חַיִּים טוֹבִים.
אָבִינוּ מַלְכֵּנוּ, כָּתְבֵנוּ בְּסֵפֶר גְּאֻלָּה וִישׁוּעָה.
אָבִינוּ מַלְכֵּנוּ, כָּתְבֵנוּ בְּסֵפֶר פַּרְנָסָה וְכַלְכָּלָה.
אָבִינוּ מַלְכֵּנוּ, כָּתְבֵנוּ בְּסֵפֶר זְכֻיּוֹת.
אָבִינוּ מַלְכֵּנוּ, כָּתְבֵנוּ בְּסֵפֶר סְלִיחָה וּמְחִילָה.

*End of responsive reading.*

אָבִינוּ מַלְכֵּנוּ, הַצְמַח לָנוּ יְשׁוּעָה בְּקָרוֹב.
אָבִינוּ מַלְכֵּנוּ, הָרֵם קֶרֶן יִשְׂרָאֵל עַמֶּךָ.

Our Father, our King, raise the honor of Your anointed.

Our Father, our King, fill our hands with Your blessings.

Our Father, our King, fill our storehouses with abundance.

Our Father, our King, hear our voice, pity and be compassionate to us.

Our Father, our King, accept, with compassion and favor, our prayer.

Our Father, our King, open the gates of heaven to our prayer.

Our Father, our King, remember that we are dust.

Our Father, our King, please do not turn us away from You empty-handed.

Our Father, our King, may this moment be a moment of compassion
and a time of favor before You.

Our Father, our King, have pity on us, our children and our infants.

Our Father, our King, act for the sake of those who were killed
for Your holy name.

Our Father, our King, act for the sake of those who were slaughtered
for proclaiming Your Unity.

Our Father, our King, act for the sake of those
who went through fire and water
to sanctify Your name.

Our Father, our King, avenge before our eyes
the spilt blood of Your servants.

Our Father, our King, act for Your sake, if not for ours.

Our Father, our King, act for Your sake, and save us.

Our Father, our King, act for the sake of Your abundant compassion.

Our Father, our King, act for the sake of Your great, mighty and
awesome name by which we are called.

▸ Our Father, our King, be gracious to us and answer us, though we have
no worthy deeds; act with us in charity and
loving-kindness and save us.

*The Ark is closed.*

אָבִינוּ מַלְכֵּנוּ, הָרֵם קֶרֶן מְשִׁיחֶךָ.

אָבִינוּ מַלְכֵּנוּ, מַלֵּא יָדֵינוּ מִבִּרְכוֹתֶיךָ.

אָבִינוּ מַלְכֵּנוּ, מַלֵּא אֲסָמֵינוּ שָׂבָע.

אָבִינוּ מַלְכֵּנוּ, שְׁמַע קוֹלֵנוּ, חוּס וְרַחֵם עָלֵינוּ.

אָבִינוּ מַלְכֵּנוּ, קַבֵּל בְּרַחֲמִים וּבְרָצוֹן אֶת תְּפִלָּתֵנוּ.

אָבִינוּ מַלְכֵּנוּ, פְּתַח שַׁעֲרֵי שָׁמַיִם לִתְפִלָּתֵנוּ.

אָבִינוּ מַלְכֵּנוּ, זְכֹר כִּי עָפָר אֲנָחְנוּ.

אָבִינוּ מַלְכֵּנוּ, נָא אַל תְּשִׁיבֵנוּ רֵיקָם מִלְּפָנֶיךָ.

אָבִינוּ מַלְכֵּנוּ, תְּהֵא הַשָּׁעָה הַזֹּאת שְׁעַת רַחֲמִים וְעֵת רָצוֹן מִלְּפָנֶיךָ.

אָבִינוּ מַלְכֵּנוּ, חֲמֹל עָלֵינוּ וְעַל עוֹלָלֵינוּ וְטַפֵּנוּ.

אָבִינוּ מַלְכֵּנוּ, עֲשֵׂה לְמַעַן הֲרוּגִים עַל שֵׁם קָדְשֶׁךָ.

אָבִינוּ מַלְכֵּנוּ, עֲשֵׂה לְמַעַן טְבוּחִים עַל יִחוּדֶךָ.

אָבִינוּ מַלְכֵּנוּ, עֲשֵׂה לְמַעַן בָּאֵי בָאֵשׁ וּבַמַּיִם עַל קִדּוּשׁ שְׁמֶךָ.

אָבִינוּ מַלְכֵּנוּ, נְקֹם לְעֵינֵינוּ נִקְמַת דַּם עֲבָדֶיךָ הַשָּׁפוּךְ.

אָבִינוּ מַלְכֵּנוּ, עֲשֵׂה לְמַעַנְךָ אִם לֹא לְמַעֲנֵנוּ.

אָבִינוּ מַלְכֵּנוּ, עֲשֵׂה לְמַעַנְךָ וְהוֹשִׁיעֵנוּ.

אָבִינוּ מַלְכֵּנוּ, עֲשֵׂה לְמַעַן רַחֲמֶיךָ הָרַבִּים.

אָבִינוּ מַלְכֵּנוּ, עֲשֵׂה לְמַעַן שִׁמְךָ הַגָּדוֹל הַגִּבּוֹר וְהַנּוֹרָא
שֶׁנִּקְרָא עָלֵינוּ.

◂ אָבִינוּ מַלְכֵּנוּ, חָנֵּנוּ וַעֲנֵנוּ, כִּי אֵין בָּנוּ מַעֲשִׂים
עֲשֵׂה עִמָּנוּ צְדָקָה וָחֶסֶד וְהוֹשִׁיעֵנוּ.

*The* ארון קודש *is closed.*

## FULL KADDISH

*Leader:* יִתְגַּדַּל Magnified and sanctified may His great name be,
in the world He created by His will.
May He establish His kingdom,
make His salvation flourish,
and hasten His messiah,
in your lifetime and in your days,
and in the lifetime of all the house of Israel,
swiftly and soon –
and say: Amen.

*All:* May His great name be blessed for ever and all time.

*Leader:* Blessed and praised, glorified and exalted,
raised and honored,
uplifted and lauded be
the name of the Holy One,
blessed be He, beyond any blessing,
song, praise and consolation
uttered in the world –
and say: Amen.

May the prayers and pleas of all the house of Israel
be accepted by their Father in heaven –
and say: Amen.

May there be great peace from heaven,
and a good life for us and all Israel –
and say: Amen.

*Bow, take three steps back, as if taking leave of the Divine Presence, then bow, first left, then right, then center, while saying:*

May He who makes peace in His high places,
make peace for us and all Israel –
and say: Amen.

## קדיש שלם

ש״ץ: יִתְגַּדַּל וְיִתְקַדַּשׁ שְׁמֵהּ רַבָּא (קהל: אָמֵן)
בְּעָלְמָא דִּי בְרָא כִרְעוּתֵהּ
וְיַמְלִיךְ מַלְכוּתֵהּ
וְיַצְמַח פֻּרְקָנֵהּ וִיקָרֵב מְשִׁיחֵהּ (קהל: אָמֵן)
בְּחַיֵּיכוֹן וּבְיוֹמֵיכוֹן וּבְחַיֵּי דְכָל בֵּית יִשְׂרָאֵל
בַּעֲגָלָא וּבִזְמַן קָרִיב, וְאִמְרוּ אָמֵן. (קהל: אָמֵן)

קהל וש״ץ: יְהֵא שְׁמֵהּ רַבָּא מְבָרַךְ לְעָלַם וּלְעָלְמֵי עָלְמַיָּא.

ש״ץ: יִתְבָּרַךְ וְיִשְׁתַּבַּח וְיִתְפָּאַר וְיִתְרוֹמַם וְיִתְנַשֵּׂא
וְיִתְהַדָּר וְיִתְעַלֶּה וְיִתְהַלָּל
שְׁמֵהּ דְּקֻדְשָׁא בְּרִיךְ הוּא (קהל: אָמֵן)
לְעֵלָּא לְעֵלָּא מִכָּל בִּרְכָתָא
וְשִׁירָתָא, תֻּשְׁבְּחָתָא וְנֶחֱמָתָא
דַּאֲמִירָן בְּעָלְמָא, וְאִמְרוּ אָמֵן. (קהל: אָמֵן)

תִּתְקַבַּל צְלוֹתְהוֹן וּבָעוּתְהוֹן דְּכָל בֵּית יִשְׂרָאֵל
קֳדָם אֲבוּהוֹן דִּי בִשְׁמַיָּא, וְאִמְרוּ אָמֵן. (קהל: אָמֵן)

יְהֵא שְׁלָמָא רַבָּא מִן שְׁמַיָּא
וְחַיִּים טוֹבִים עָלֵינוּ וְעַל כָּל יִשְׂרָאֵל, וְאִמְרוּ אָמֵן. (קהל: אָמֵן)

*Bow, take three steps back, as if taking leave of the Divine Presence, then bow, first left, then right, then center, while saying:*

עֹשֶׂה הַשָּׁלוֹם בִּמְרוֹמָיו
הוּא יַעֲשֶׂה שָׁלוֹם עָלֵינוּ
וְעַל כָּל יִשְׂרָאֵל, וְאִמְרוּ אָמֵן. (קהל: אָמֵן)

*Stand while saying Aleinu. Bow at* ▾.

עָלֵינוּ It is our duty to praise the Master of all,
and ascribe greatness to the Author of creation,
who has not made us like the nations of the lands,
nor placed us like the families of the earth;
who has not made our portion like theirs,
nor our destiny like all their multitudes.
(For they worship vanity and emptiness,
and pray to a god who cannot save.)
▾But we bow in worship
and thank the Supreme King of kings,
the Holy One, blessed be He,
who extends the heavens and establishes the earth,
whose throne of glory is in the heavens above,
and whose power's Presence is in the highest of heights.
He is our God; there is no other.
Truly He is our King; there is none else,
as it is written in His Torah:
"You shall know and take to heart this day *Deut. 4*
that the LORD is God,
in the heavens above and on the earth below.
There is no other."

Therefore, we place our hope in You, LORD our God,
that we may soon see the glory of Your power,
when You will remove abominations from the earth,
and idols will be utterly destroyed,
when the world will be perfected
under the sovereignty of the Almighty,
when all humanity will call on Your name,
to turn all the earth's wicked toward You.
All the world's inhabitants will realize and know that to You
every knee must bow
and every tongue swear loyalty.

*Stand while saying* עָלֵינוּ. *Bow at* ▼.

עָלֵינוּ לְשַׁבֵּחַ לַאֲדוֹן הַכֹּל, לָתֵת גְּדֻלָּה לְיוֹצֵר בְּרֵאשִׁית
שֶׁלֹּא עָשָׂנוּ כְּגוֹיֵי הָאֲרָצוֹת, וְלֹא שָׂמָנוּ כְּמִשְׁפְּחוֹת הָאֲדָמָה
שֶׁלֹּא שָׂם חֶלְקֵנוּ כָּהֶם וְגוֹרָלֵנוּ כְּכָל הֲמוֹנָם.
(שֶׁהֵם מִשְׁתַּחֲוִים לְהֶבֶל וָרִיק וּמִתְפַּלְלִים אֶל אֵל לֹא יוֹשִׁיעַ.)
▼וַאֲנַחְנוּ כּוֹרְעִים וּמִשְׁתַּחֲוִים וּמוֹדִים
לִפְנֵי מֶלֶךְ מַלְכֵי הַמְּלָכִים, הַקָּדוֹשׁ בָּרוּךְ הוּא
שֶׁהוּא נוֹטֶה שָׁמַיִם וְיוֹסֵד אָרֶץ
וּמוֹשַׁב יְקָרוֹ בַּשָּׁמַיִם מִמַּעַל
וּשְׁכִינַת עֻזּוֹ בְּגָבְהֵי מְרוֹמִים.
הוּא אֱלֹהֵינוּ, אֵין עוֹד.
אֱמֶת מַלְכֵּנוּ, אֶפֶס זוּלָתוֹ
כַּכָּתוּב בְּתוֹרָתוֹ
וְיָדַעְתָּ הַיּוֹם וַהֲשֵׁבֹתָ אֶל־לְבָבֶךָ דברים ד
כִּי יהוה הוּא הָאֱלֹהִים בַּשָּׁמַיִם מִמַּעַל וְעַל־הָאָרֶץ מִתָּחַת
אֵין עוֹד:

וְעַל כֵּן נְקַוֶּה לְךָ יהוה אֱלֹהֵינוּ, לִרְאוֹת מְהֵרָה בְּתִפְאֶרֶת עֻזֶּךָ
לְהַעֲבִיר גִּלּוּלִים מִן הָאָרֶץ, וְהָאֱלִילִים כָּרוֹת יִכָּרֵתוּן
לְתַקֵּן עוֹלָם בְּמַלְכוּת שַׁדַּי.
וְכָל בְּנֵי בָשָׂר יִקְרְאוּ בִשְׁמֶךָ
לְהַפְנוֹת אֵלֶיךָ כָּל רִשְׁעֵי אָרֶץ.
יַכִּירוּ וְיֵדְעוּ כָּל יוֹשְׁבֵי תֵבֵל
כִּי לְךָ תִּכְרַע כָּל בֶּרֶךְ, תִּשָּׁבַע כָּל לָשׁוֹן.

Before You, LORD our God, they will kneel and bow down
and give honor to Your glorious name.
They will all accept the yoke of Your kingdom,
and You will reign over them soon and for ever.
For the kingdom is Yours, and to all eternity You will reign in glory,
as it is written in Your Torah:
"The LORD will reign for ever and ever." *Ex. 15*
▸ And it is said:
"Then the LORD shall be King over all the earth; *Zech. 14*
on that day the LORD shall be One and His name One."

*Some add:*

Have no fear of sudden terror or of the ruin when it overtakes the wicked. *Prov. 3*
Devise your strategy, but it will be thwarted; propose your plan, *Is. 8*
but it will not stand, for God is with us.
When you grow old, I will still be the same. *Is. 46*
When your hair turns gray, I will still carry you.
I made you, I will bear you, I will carry you, and I will rescue you.

## MOURNER'S KADDISH

*The following prayer, said by mourners, requires the presence of a minyan.*
*A transliteration can be found on page 1095.*

*Mourner:* יִתְגַּדַּל Magnified and sanctified may His great name be,
in the world He created by His will.
May He establish His kingdom,
make His salvation flourish,
and hasten His messiah,
in your lifetime and in your days,
and in the lifetime of all the house of Israel,
swiftly and soon –
and say: Amen.

*All:* May His great name be blessed for ever and all time.

*Mourner:* Blessed and praised, glorified and exalted,
raised and honored, uplifted and lauded
be the name of the Holy One,
blessed be He,

לְפָנֶיךָ יהוה אֱלֹהֵינוּ יִכְרְעוּ וְיִפֹּלוּ
וְלִכְבוֹד שִׁמְךָ יְקָר יִתֵּנוּ
וִיקַבְּלוּ כֻלָּם אֶת עֹל מַלְכוּתֶךָ
וְתִמְלֹךְ עֲלֵיהֶם מְהֵרָה לְעוֹלָם וָעֶד.
כִּי הַמַּלְכוּת שֶׁלְּךָ הִיא וּלְעוֹלְמֵי עַד תִּמְלֹךְ בְּכָבוֹד
כַּכָּתוּב בְּתוֹרָתֶךָ, יהוה יִמְלֹךְ לְעֹלָם וָעֶד: שמות טו
▸ וְנֶאֱמַר, וְהָיָה יהוה לְמֶלֶךְ עַל־כָּל־הָאָרֶץ זכריה יד
בַּיּוֹם הַהוּא יִהְיֶה יהוה אֶחָד וּשְׁמוֹ אֶחָד:

*Some add:*

אַל־תִּירָא מִפַּחַד פִּתְאֹם וּמִשֹּׁאַת רְשָׁעִים כִּי תָבֹא: משלי ג
עֻצוּ עֵצָה וְתֻפָר, דַּבְּרוּ דָבָר וְלֹא יָקוּם, כִּי עִמָּנוּ אֵל: ישעיה ח
וְעַד־זִקְנָה אֲנִי הוּא, וְעַד־שֵׂיבָה אֲנִי אֶסְבֹּל ישעיה מו
אֲנִי עָשִׂיתִי וַאֲנִי אֶשָּׂא וַאֲנִי אֶסְבֹּל וַאֲמַלֵּט:

## קדיש יתום

*The following prayer, said by mourners, requires the presence of a* מנין.
*A transliteration can be found on page 1095.*

אבל: יִתְגַּדַּל וְיִתְקַדַּשׁ שְׁמֵהּ רַבָּא (קהל: אָמֵן)
בְּעָלְמָא דִּי בְרָא כִרְעוּתֵהּ
וְיַמְלִיךְ מַלְכוּתֵהּ
וְיַצְמַח פֻּרְקָנֵהּ וִיקָרֵב מְשִׁיחֵהּ (קהל: אָמֵן)
בְּחַיֵּיכוֹן וּבְיוֹמֵיכוֹן וּבְחַיֵּי דְכָל בֵּית יִשְׂרָאֵל
בַּעֲגָלָא וּבִזְמַן קָרִיב, וְאִמְרוּ אָמֵן. (קהל: אָמֵן)

קהל ואבל: יְהֵא שְׁמֵהּ רַבָּא מְבָרַךְ לְעָלַם וּלְעָלְמֵי עָלְמַיָּא.

אבל: יִתְבָּרַךְ וְיִשְׁתַּבַּח וְיִתְפָּאַר
וְיִתְרוֹמַם וְיִתְנַשֵּׂא וְיִתְהַדָּר וְיִתְעַלֶּה וְיִתְהַלָּל
שְׁמֵהּ דְּקֻדְשָׁא בְּרִיךְ הוּא (קהל: אָמֵן)

beyond any blessing, song, praise and consolation
uttered in the world –
and say: Amen.

May there be great peace from heaven,
and a good life for us and all Israel –
and say: Amen.

*Bow, take three steps back, as if taking leave of the Divine Presence, then bow, first left, then right, then center, while saying:*

May He who makes peace in His high places,
make peace for us and all Israel –
and say: Amen.

*The following psalm is said on all days.*

לְדָוִד By David. The LORD is my light and my salvation – whom then shall I fear? The LORD is the stronghold of my life – of whom shall I be afraid? When evil men close in on me to devour my flesh, it is they, my enemies and foes, who stumble and fall. Should an army besiege me, my heart would not fear. Should war break out against me, still I would be confident. One thing I ask of the LORD, only this do I seek: to live in the House of the LORD all the days of my life, to gaze on the beauty of the LORD and worship in His Temple. For He will keep me safe in His pavilion on the day of trouble. He will hide me under the cover of His tent. He will set me high upon a rock. Now my head is high above my enemies who surround me. I will sacrifice in His tent with shouts of joy. I will sing and chant praises to the LORD. LORD, hear my voice when I call. Be gracious to me and answer me. On Your behalf my heart says, "Seek My face." Your face, LORD, will I seek. Do not hide Your face from me. Do not turn Your servant away in anger. You have been my help. Do not reject or forsake me, God, my Savior. Were my father and my mother to forsake me, the LORD would take me in. Teach me Your way, LORD, and lead me on a level path, because of my oppressors. Do not abandon me to the will of my foes, for false witnesses have risen against me, breathing violence. ▸ Were it not for my faith that I shall see the LORD's goodness in the land of the living. Hope in the LORD. Be strong and of good courage, and hope in the LORD! *Ps. 27*

*Mourner's Kaddish (previous page)*

לְעֵלָּא לְעֵלָּא מִכָּל בִּרְכָתָא
וְשִׁירָתָא, תֻּשְׁבְּחָתָא וְנֶחֱמָתָא
דַּאֲמִירָן בְּעָלְמָא, וְאִמְרוּ אָמֵן. (קהל: אָמֵן)

יְהֵא שְׁלָמָא רַבָּא מִן שְׁמַיָּא
וְחַיִּים טוֹבִים עָלֵינוּ וְעַל כָּל יִשְׂרָאֵל, וְאִמְרוּ אָמֵן. (קהל: אָמֵן)

*Bow, take three steps back, as if taking leave of the Divine Presence, then bow, first left, then right, then center, while saying:*

עֹשֶׂה הַשָּׁלוֹם בִּמְרוֹמָיו
הוּא יַעֲשֶׂה שָׁלוֹם
עָלֵינוּ וְעַל כָּל יִשְׂרָאֵל, וְאִמְרוּ אָמֵן. (קהל: אָמֵן)

*The following psalm is said on all days.*

תהלים כז
לְדָוִד, יהוה אוֹרִי וְיִשְׁעִי, מִמִּי אִירָא, יהוה מָעוֹז־חַיַּי, מִמִּי אֶפְחָד: בִּקְרֹב עָלַי מְרֵעִים לֶאֱכֹל אֶת־בְּשָׂרִי, צָרַי וְאֹיְבַי לִי, הֵמָּה כָשְׁלוּ וְנָפָלוּ: אִם־תַּחֲנֶה עָלַי מַחֲנֶה, לֹא־יִירָא לִבִּי, אִם־תָּקוּם עָלַי מִלְחָמָה, בְּזֹאת אֲנִי בוֹטֵחַ: אַחַת שָׁאַלְתִּי מֵאֵת־יהוה, אוֹתָהּ אֲבַקֵּשׁ, שִׁבְתִּי בְּבֵית־יהוה כָּל־יְמֵי חַיַּי, לַחֲזוֹת בְּנֹעַם־יהוה, וּלְבַקֵּר בְּהֵיכָלוֹ: כִּי יִצְפְּנֵנִי בְּסֻכֹּה בְּיוֹם רָעָה, יַסְתִּרֵנִי בְּסֵתֶר אָהֳלוֹ, בְּצוּר יְרוֹמְמֵנִי: וְעַתָּה יָרוּם רֹאשִׁי עַל אֹיְבַי סְבִיבוֹתַי, וְאֶזְבְּחָה בְאָהֳלוֹ זִבְחֵי תְרוּעָה, אָשִׁירָה וַאֲזַמְּרָה לַיהוה: שְׁמַע־יהוה קוֹלִי אֶקְרָא, וְחָנֵּנִי וַעֲנֵנִי: לְךָ אָמַר לִבִּי בַּקְּשׁוּ פָנָי, אֶת־פָּנֶיךָ יהוה אֲבַקֵּשׁ: אַל־תַּסְתֵּר פָּנֶיךָ מִמֶּנִּי, אַל תַּט־בְּאַף עַבְדֶּךָ, עֶזְרָתִי הָיִיתָ, אַל־תִּטְּשֵׁנִי וְאַל־תַּעַזְבֵנִי, אֱלֹהֵי יִשְׁעִי: כִּי־אָבִי וְאִמִּי עֲזָבוּנִי, וַיהוה יַאַסְפֵנִי: הוֹרֵנִי יהוה דַּרְכֶּךָ, וּנְחֵנִי בְּאֹרַח מִישׁוֹר, לְמַעַן שׁוֹרְרָי: אַל־תִּתְּנֵנִי בְּנֶפֶשׁ צָרָי, כִּי קָמוּ־בִי עֵדֵי־שֶׁקֶר, וִיפֵחַ חָמָס: ◂ לוּלֵא הֶאֱמַנְתִּי לִרְאוֹת בְּטוּב־יהוה בְּאֶרֶץ חַיִּים: קַוֵּה אֶל־יהוה, חֲזַק וְיַאֲמֵץ לִבֶּךָ, וְקַוֵּה אֶל־יהוה:

קדיש יתום (*previous page*)

# Tashlikh

*On the first day of Rosh HaShana (or, if that day is Shabbat, on the second day), it is customary, in the afternoon after Minḥa, to go to the banks of a river, or any stretch of flowing water, and say the following (see law 101):*

מִי־אֵל כָּמְוֹךָ Who, God, is like You, *Mic. 7*
who pardons iniquity and forgives the transgression
of the remnant of His heritage?
He does not stay angry for ever,
but delights in loving-kindness.
He will again have compassion on us, suppress our iniquities,
and cast into the depths of the sea all their sins.
Grant truth to Jacob, kindness to Abraham,
as You promised our ancestors in ancient times.

מִן־הַמֵּצַר In my distress I called on the LORD. *Ps. 118*
The LORD answered me and set me free.
The LORD is with me; I will not be afraid.
What can man do to me? The LORD is with me.
He is my Helper. I will see the downfall of my enemies.
It is better to take refuge in the LORD than to trust in man.
It is better to take refuge in the LORD than to trust in princes.

*Many add:*

רַנְּנוּ Sing joyfully to the LORD, you righteous, for praise from the upright is seemly. *Ps. 33* Give thanks to the LORD with the harp; make music to Him on the ten-stringed lute. Sing Him a new song, play skillfully with shouts of joy. For the LORD's word is right, and all His deeds are done in faith. He loves righteousness and justice; the earth is full of the LORD's loving-kindness. By the LORD's word the heavens were made, and all their starry host by the breath of His mouth. He gathers the sea waters as a heap, and places the deep in storehouses. Let all the earth fear the LORD, and all the world's

---

(Micah 7:19). In Jerusalem the custom is to perform the ceremony by a well or water cistern. In towns in the north of Israel where rivers are not accessible, many go to high points from which Lake Kinneret is visible.

The first mention of the custom is in *Sefer Maharil* of Rabbi Jacob Moellin (d. 1425). Various explanations have been given. Rabbi Moellin himself relates it

# תשליך

*On the first day of* ראש השנה *(or, if that day is* שבת*, on the second day), it is customary, in the afternoon after* מנחה*, to go to the banks of a river, or any stretch of flowing water, and say the following (see law 101):*

מיכה ז
מִי־אֵל כָּמְוֹךָ
נֹשֵׂא עָוֹן וְעֹבֵר עַל־פֶּשַׁע לִשְׁאֵרִית נַחֲלָתוֹ
לֹא־הֶחֱזִיק לָעַד אַפּוֹ
כִּי־חָפֵץ חֶסֶד הוּא:
יָשׁוּב יְרַחֲמֵנוּ, יִכְבֹּשׁ עֲוֺנֹתֵינוּ
וְתַשְׁלִיךְ בִּמְצֻלוֹת יָם כָּל־חַטֹּאתָם:
תִּתֵּן אֱמֶת לְיַעֲקֹב, חֶסֶד לְאַבְרָהָם
אֲשֶׁר־נִשְׁבַּעְתָּ לַאֲבֹתֵינוּ מִימֵי קֶדֶם:

תהלים קיח
מִן־הַמֵּצַר קָרָאתִי יָּהּ, עָנָנִי בַמֶּרְחָב יָהּ:
יהוה לִי לֹא אִירָא, מַה־יַּעֲשֶׂה לִי אָדָם:
יהוה לִי בְּעֹזְרָי, וַאֲנִי אֶרְאֶה בְשֹׂנְאָי:
טוֹב לַחֲסוֹת בַּיהוה, מִבְּטֹחַ בָּאָדָם:
טוֹב לַחֲסוֹת בַּיהוה, מִבְּטֹחַ בִּנְדִיבִים:

*Many add:*

תהלים לג
רַנְּנוּ צַדִּיקִים בַּיהוה, לַיְשָׁרִים נָאוָה תְהִלָּה: הוֹדוּ לַיהוה בְּכִנּוֹר, בְּנֵבֶל עָשׂוֹר
זַמְּרוּ־לוֹ: שִׁירוּ־לוֹ שִׁיר חָדָשׁ, הֵיטִיבוּ נַגֵּן בִּתְרוּעָה: כִּי־יָשָׁר דְּבַר־יהוה, וְכָל־
מַעֲשֵׂהוּ בֶּאֱמוּנָה: אֹהֵב צְדָקָה וּמִשְׁפָּט, חֶסֶד יהוה מָלְאָה הָאָרֶץ: בִּדְבַר יהוה

---

TASHLIKH: THE CASTING

It is a custom, on the afternoon of the first day of Rosh HaShana (or second, if the first is Shabbat) to go to the shore of the sea, the bank of a river, or other running stream of water, as a symbolic enactment of the words of the prophet Micah: "He [God] will cast (*tashlikh*) into the depths of the sea all their sins"

inhabitants stand in awe of Him. For He spoke, and it was; He commanded, and it stood firm. The LORD foils the plans of nations; He thwarts the intentions of peoples. The LORD's plans stand for ever, His heart's intents for all generations. Happy is the nation whose God is the LORD, the people He has chosen as His own. From heaven the LORD looks down and sees all mankind; from His dwelling place He oversees all who live on earth. He forms the hearts of all, and discerns all their deeds. No king is saved by the size of his army; no warrior is delivered by great strength. A horse is a vain hope for deliverance; despite its great strength, it cannot save. The eye of the LORD is on those who fear Him, on those who place their hope in His unfailing love, to rescue their soul from death, and keep them alive in famine. Our soul waits for the LORD; He is our Help and Shield. In Him our hearts rejoice, for we trust in His holy name. Let Your unfailing love be upon us, LORD, as we have put our hope in You.

*Some omit the following and conclude with "For no one will do evil" on page 954.*

A psalm of David. The earth is the LORD's and all it contains, the world and all who live in it. For He founded it on the seas and established it on the streams. Who may climb the mountain of the LORD? Who may stand in His holy place? He who has clean hands and a pure heart, who has not taken My name in vain, or sworn deceitfully. He shall receive blessing from the LORD, and just reward from God, his salvation. This is a generation of those who seek Him, the descendants of Jacob who seek Your presence, Selah! Lift up your heads, O gates; be uplifted, eternal doors, so that the King of glory may enter. Who is the King of glory? It is the LORD, strong and mighty, the LORD mighty in battle. Lift up your heads, O gates; lift them up, eternal doors, so that the King of glory may enter. Who is He, the King of glory? The LORD of hosts, He is the King of glory, Selah! *Ps. 24*

Master of the Universe, as we now take to our hearts our many shortcomings in Your service, and in our involvement in Your holy Torah and in fulfilling Your commands, all our bones are seized with trembling, and our hearts melt away to water. What will we answer now, what can we say, for the Adversary who works with grimy clay against us, has blackened our lives; and with them the imprisonment, as we are beaten in harsh exiles, exiles of the body and soul. Even so, it is known and revealed before You that our will is to perform Your will, and to watch outside Your doors, for "a day in Your courtyard is better than a thousand": this is what we have chosen; and we are afraid and trembling before Your holy judgment. And so we have come to You with bowed heads, low stature, feeble of strength, to recall and awaken to Your mercy.

---

to a midrashic tradition about the binding of Isaac (on Rosh HaShana we blow the ram's horn in memory of the ram Abraham offered as a sacrifice in place of his son). On the journey, the Accuser placed a river in his way. Abraham was undeterred and walked straight through (*Tanḥuma, VaYera 22*). Thus, as with the blowing of the shofar, we ask God to forgive us in the merit of Abraham.

שָׁמַֽיִם נַעֲשׂוּ, וּבְרֽוּחַ פִּיו כָּל־צְבָאָם: כֹּנֵס כַּנֵּד מֵי הַיָּם, נֹתֵן בְּאוֹצָרוֹת תְּהוֹמוֹת:
יִירְאוּ מֵיהוה כָּל־הָאָֽרֶץ, מִמֶּנּוּ יָגֽוּרוּ כָּל־יֹשְׁבֵי תֵבֵל: כִּי הוּא אָמַר וַיֶּֽהִי, הוּא־
צִוָּה וַיַּעֲמֹד: יהוה הֵפִיר עֲצַת־גּוֹיִם, הֵנִיא מַחְשְׁבוֹת עַמִּים: עֲצַת יהוה לְעוֹלָם
תַּעֲמֹד, מַחְשְׁבוֹת לִבּוֹ לְדֹר וָדֹר: אַשְׁרֵי הַגּוֹי אֲשֶׁר־יהוה אֱלֹהָיו, הָעָם בָּחַר
לְנַחֲלָה לוֹ: מִשָּׁמַֽיִם הִבִּיט יהוה, רָאָה אֶת־כָּל־בְּנֵי הָאָדָם: מִמְּכוֹן־שִׁבְתּוֹ
הִשְׁגִּֽיחַ, אֶל כָּל־יֹשְׁבֵי הָאָֽרֶץ: הַיֹּצֵר יַחַד לִבָּם, הַמֵּבִין אֶל־כָּל־מַעֲשֵׂיהֶם:
אֵין־הַמֶּֽלֶךְ נוֹשָׁע בְּרָב־חָֽיִל, גִּבּוֹר לֹא־יִנָּצֵל בְּרָב־כֹּֽחַ: שֶֽׁקֶר הַסּוּס לִתְשׁוּעָה,
וּבְרֹב חֵילוֹ לֹא יְמַלֵּט: הִנֵּה עֵין יהוה אֶל־יְרֵאָיו, לַמְיַחֲלִים לְחַסְדּוֹ: לְהַצִּיל
מִמָּֽוֶת נַפְשָׁם, וּלְחַיּוֹתָם בָּרָעָב: נַפְשֵֽׁנוּ חִכְּתָה לַיהוה, עֶזְרֵֽנוּ וּמָגִנֵּֽנוּ הוּא:
כִּי־בוֹ יִשְׂמַח לִבֵּֽנוּ, כִּי בְשֵׁם קָדְשׁוֹ בָטָֽחְנוּ: יְהִי־חַסְדְּךָ יהוה עָלֵֽינוּ, כַּאֲשֶׁר
יִחַֽלְנוּ לָךְ:

*Some omit the following and conclude with לֹא־יָרֵֽעוּ, on page 955.*

לְדָוִד מִזְמוֹר, לַיהוה הָאָֽרֶץ וּמְלוֹאָהּ, תֵּבֵל וְיֹֽשְׁבֵי בָהּ: כִּי־הוּא עַל־יַמִּים תהלים כד
יְסָדָהּ, וְעַל־נְהָרוֹת יְכוֹנְנֶֽהָ: מִי־יַעֲלֶה בְהַר־יהוה, וּמִי־יָקוּם בִּמְקוֹם קָדְשׁוֹ:
נְקִי כַפַּֽיִם וּבַר־לֵבָב, אֲשֶׁר לֹא־נָשָׂא לַשָּׁוְא נַפְשִׁי, וְלֹא נִשְׁבַּע לְמִרְמָה: יִשָּׂא
בְרָכָה מֵאֵת יהוה, וּצְדָקָה מֵאֱלֹהֵי יִשְׁעוֹ: זֶה דּוֹר דֹּרְשָׁו, מְבַקְשֵׁי פָנֶֽיךָ יַעֲקֹב
סֶֽלָה: שְׂאוּ שְׁעָרִים רָאשֵׁיכֶם, וְהִנָּשְׂאוּ פִּתְחֵי עוֹלָם, וְיָבוֹא מֶֽלֶךְ הַכָּבוֹד: מִי
זֶה מֶֽלֶךְ הַכָּבוֹד, יהוה עִזּוּז וְגִבּוֹר, יהוה גִּבּוֹר מִלְחָמָה: שְׂאוּ שְׁעָרִים רָאשֵׁיכֶם,
וּשְׂאוּ פִּתְחֵי עוֹלָם, וְיָבֹא מֶֽלֶךְ הַכָּבוֹד: מִי הוּא זֶה מֶֽלֶךְ הַכָּבוֹד, יהוה צְבָאוֹת
הוּא מֶֽלֶךְ הַכָּבוֹד סֶֽלָה:

רִבּוֹנוֹ שֶׁל עוֹלָם, בְּהַעֲלוֹתֵֽנוּ עַל לְבָבֵֽנוּ רֹב קִצּוּרֵֽנוּ בַּעֲבוֹדָתֶֽךָ וּבְעֵֽסֶק תּוֹרָתְךָ הַקְּדוֹשָׁה וְקִיּוּם מִצְוֹתֶֽיךָ, כָּל עַצְמוֹתֵֽינוּ יֹאחֲזֵֽמוֹ רָֽעַד, וְנָמֵס לִבֵּֽנוּ וְהָיָה לְמָֽיִם. מַה נַּעֲנֶה וּמַה נֹּאמַר, כִּי הַצַּר הַצּוֹרֵר בְּחֶבְרַת הַחֹֽמֶר הֶעָכוּר הָיָה בְּעוֹכְרֵֽנוּ, גַּם אָסוּר נִלְוָה עִמָּם, אֲסוּרִים וּלְטוּשִׁים בְּגַלְיוֹת קָשִׁים, גָּלוּת הַנֶּֽפֶשׁ וְהַגּוּף. הָאָמְנָם גָּלוּי וְיָדֽוּעַ לְפָנֶֽיךָ שֶׁרְצוֹנֵֽנוּ לַעֲשׂוֹת רְצוֹנֶֽךָ וְלִשְׁקֹד עַל דַּלְתוֹתֶֽיךָ, כִּי טוֹב יוֹם בַּחֲצֵרֶֽיךָ מֵאֶֽלֶף בָּחַֽרְנוּ, וִירֵאִים וַחֲרֵדִים אֲנַֽחְנוּ מֵאֵימַת דִּינְךָ הַקָּדוֹשׁ. עַל כֵּן בָּֽאנוּ אֵלֶֽיךָ בִּכְפִיפַת רֹאשׁ וּנְמִיכַת קוֹמָה וַחֲלִישַׁת חָֽיִל לְהַזְכִּיר וּלְעוֹרֵר רַחֲמֶֽיךָ.

May it be Your will, LORD my God and God of my ancestors, God Most High, crowned with thirteen paths of mercy, that this hour will be a time of favor before You, and that the reading of the thirteen attributes of mercy that are found in the verses "Who is God like You" [etc.] may rise up in correspondence with the Thirteen Attributes, "Compassionate and gracious God" etc., that we have read before You, as if we had somehow grasped all the secrets and combinations of names that arise from them, and the partnerships of attributes that will step forward one with another to sweeten harsh judgments. Please, cast all our sins to the depths of the sea. And You, in Your goodness, awaken Your compassion and let us be clean of all impurity and filth and pollution, and let all the sparks of holiness that have been scattered rise up again, and let them be sifted and bleached white in Your attribute of goodness, God of our salvation, extending loving-kindness to a thousand generations. And in Your great compassion, grant us each a long life, a life of peace, a life of goodness, a life of blessing, a life of sustenance, a life of physical health, a life marked by reverence for Heaven and dread of sin, a life without shame or disgrace, a life of wealth and honor with which to serve You, a life in which we have love for the Torah and reverence for Heaven, a life in which our hearts' desires are fulfilled for good. And remember us for life, O King who desires life, and write us in the book of life – for Your sake, O God of life. Tear up the evil decree against us, and let our merit be read out before You.

God full of compassion, may Your compassion whisper to You, willingly to accept our submission and the repentant thoughts that form sparks within us, even while, with our sealed and blocked and locked-up hearts, there is none among us who even knows by which way we may come to You, by which to return; who we are, and what we have come to repair. You who have great power to save, light up our eyes as You promised in Your vast compassion, "Open a pinprick's opening for Me, and I shall open the doors of a great hall for you." See that our power is gone; that no one is left, either bonded or free, and there is none to be gracious and none to show compassion but You, for those You show grace shall have grace, and those You show compassion
enjoy compassion, as it is written, "I will be gracious to whom I will be gracious, and *Ex. 33*
show compassion to whom I will have compassion." And so, create a pure heart for us, God, and renew a strong spirit within us, and let the flames of our hearts' awakening
in love for You, and in Your Torah, ever burn and grow stronger without pause. Help *Ps. 79*

---

first life forms (Gen. 1:20) and thus the first witnesses to creation (Matteh Moshe).

There are other symbolic associations. Water is a symbol of Torah, of the knowledge that leads to virtue and peace: "They will neither harm nor destroy on all My holy Mountain, for the earth will be full of the knowledge of the LORD as the waters cover the sea" (Isaiah 11:9).

Rivers are a symbol of tears (*Avot deRabbi Natan*, ch. 31) and thus a sign

וִיהִי רָצוֹן מִלְּפָנֶיךָ יהוה אֱלֹהַי וֵאלֹהֵי אֲבוֹתַי, אֵל עֶלְיוֹן מְכֻתָּר בִּתְלֵיסַר מְכִילִין דְּרַחֲמֵי, שֶׁתְּהֵא שָׁעָה זוֹ עֵת רָצוֹן לְפָנֶיךָ, וְתִהְיֶה עוֹלָה לְפָנֶיךָ קְרִיאַת שְׁלֹשׁ עֶשְׂרֵה מִדּוֹת שֶׁל רַחֲמִים שֶׁבַּפְּסוּקִים מִי אֵל כָּמוֹךָ, הַמְכֻוָּנִים אֶל שְׁלֹשׁ עֶשְׂרֵה מִדּוֹת אֵל רַחוּם וְחַנּוּן וגו׳, אֲשֶׁר קָרִינוּ לְפָנֶיךָ, כְּאִלּוּ הִשַּׂגְנוּ כָּל הַסּוֹדוֹת וְצֵרוּפֵי שֵׁמוֹת הַיּוֹצְאִים מֵהֶם וְזִוּוּגֵי מִדּוֹתֵיהֶם, אֲשֶׁר אֶחָד בְּאֶחָד יִגָּשׁוּ לְהַמְתִּיק הַדִּינִים תַּקִּיפִים, וְתַשְׁלִיךְ בִּמְצוּלוֹת יָם כָּל חַטֹּאתֵינוּ. וְאַתָּה בְּטוּבְךָ תְּעוֹרֵר רַחֲמֶיךָ, וְנִהְיֶה נְקִיִּים מִכָּל טֻמְאָה וְחֶלְאָה וְזֻהֲמָא, וְיַעֲלוּ כָּל נִיצוֹצֵי הַקְּדֻשָּׁה אֲשֶׁר נִתְפַּזְּרוּ, וְיִתְבָּרְרוּ וְיִתְלַבְּנוּ בְּמִדַּת טוּבְךָ, אַתָּה אֵל יְשׁוּעָתֵנוּ נֹצֵר חֶסֶד לָאֲלָפִים, וּבְרֹב רַחֲמֶיךָ תִּתֵּן לָנוּ חַיִּים אֲרוּכִים, חַיִּים שֶׁל שָׁלוֹם, חַיִּים שֶׁל טוֹבָה, חַיִּים שֶׁל בְּרָכָה, חַיִּים שֶׁל פַּרְנָסָה טוֹבָה, חַיִּים שֶׁל חִלּוּץ עֲצָמוֹת, חַיִּים שֶׁיֵּשׁ בָּהֶם יִרְאַת שָׁמַיִם וְיִרְאַת חֵטְא, חַיִּים שֶׁאֵין בָּהֶם בּוּשָׁה וּכְלִמָּה, חַיִּים שֶׁל עֹשֶׁר וְכָבוֹד לַעֲבוֹדָתֶךָ, חַיִּים שֶׁתְּהֵא בָנוּ אַהֲבַת תּוֹרָה וְיִרְאַת שָׁמַיִם, חַיִּים שֶׁתְּמַלֵּא כָּל מִשְׁאֲלוֹת לִבֵּנוּ לְטוֹבָה, וְזָכְרֵנוּ לְחַיִּים מֶלֶךְ חָפֵץ בַּחַיִּים, וְכָתְבֵנוּ בְּסֵפֶר הַחַיִּים לְמַעַנְךָ אֱלֹהִים חַיִּים, וּקְרַע רֹעַ גְּזַר דִּינֵנוּ, וְיִקָּרְאוּ לְפָנֶיךָ זָכִיּוֹתֵינוּ.

אֵל מָלֵא רַחֲמִים, יֶהֱמוּ נָא רַחֲמֶיךָ לְקַבֵּל בְּרָצוֹן הַכְנָעָתֵנוּ וְהַרְהוּרֵי תְשׁוּבָה הַמִּתְנוֹצְצִים בָּנוּ, בְּשַׁגָּם לִבֵּנוּ אָטוּם סָתוּם וְחָתוּם, לֹא אִתָּנוּ יוֹדֵעַ זוֹ הִיא בִּיאָה זוֹ הִיא שִׁיבָה, מָה אָנוּ וּמַה בָּאנוּ לְתַקֵּן. רַב לְהוֹשִׁיעַ, הָאֵר עֵינֵינוּ כַּאֲשֶׁר בְּגֹדֶל רַחֲמֶיךָ הִבְטַחְתָּנוּ: פִּתְחוּ לִי פֶּתַח כְּחֻדּוֹ שֶׁל מַחַט, וַאֲנִי אֶפְתַּח לָכֶם פֶּתַח כְּפִתְחוֹ שֶׁל אוּלָם, וּרְאֵה כִּי אָזְלַת יָד, וְאֶפֶס עָצוּר וְעָזוּב, וְאֵין חוֹנֵן וְאֵין מְרַחֵם זוּלָתֶךָ, כִּי חֲנוּנֶיךָ הֵם חֲנוּנִים וּמְרֻחָמֶיךָ הֵם מְרֻחָמִים, כְּדִכְתִיב:
וְחַנֹּתִי אֶת־אֲשֶׁר אָחֹן, וְרִחַמְתִּי אֶת־אֲשֶׁר אֲרַחֵם: וּבְכֵן, לֵב טָהוֹר בְּרָא לָנוּ שמות לג
אֱלֹהִים, וְרוּחַ נָכוֹן חַדֵּשׁ בְּקִרְבֵּנוּ, וְרִשְׁפֵּי הִתְעוֹרְרוּת לִבֵּנוּ בְּאַהֲבָתֶךָ וּבְתוֹרָתֶךָ
יַתְמִידוּ וְיִתְרַבּוּ בְּלִי הֶפְסֵק. עָזְרֵנוּ אֱלֹהֵי יִשְׁעֵנוּ עַל־דְּבַר כְּבוֹד־שְׁמֶךָ: תָּחֵל תהלים עט

Rabbi Isaiah Horowitz says that the water reminds us of fish: just as they never close their eyes, so God's eyes are ever-open, watching over the deeds of humankind (Shenei Luḥot HaBerit).

Rabbi Moses of Przemysl relates the ceremony to the creation of the universe of which Rosh HaShana is the anniversary. Marine creatures were the

us, God of our salvation, for the sake of the glory of Your name, and bring on the New Year and the blessings that it harbors. And let us merit that our hearts be strong and committed into our own hands, and let us not anger others or You. Give our hands the strength to distance ourselves from all the bad and forbidden attributes, and in particular, let us be distant from pride and anger and severity and from all kinds of arrogance. Let us be settled in our minds, and aware of our low worth and let our souls be like dust to everyone; and let us not anger ourselves or show severity. Let us love peace and increase peace, and shelter in the shadow of Your wings. Let us merit to remain at a distance from cynical laughter and lies and from hypocrisy and slander and from worldly conversation on Shabbat, and all forbidden speech. And may the greater part of our speech concern the Torah, and the order and methods of Your service, the holy service. And let us gird strength to guard our mouths against bringing our own tongues to sin.

Compassionate Father, give us strength and health and allow us the merit of distancing ourselves from any appetite for the indulgences and empty things of this world, and let us eat to satisfy our souls – and so with all our various needs; may all our actions be done for the sake of Heaven. And grant us the merit that it be in happiness that we engage with Your Torah and with Your commands, and that our trust may be habitually in You, and may we have a joyful heart with which to serve You.

Please, compassionate and gracious King, the spirit is Yours, and the body Your creation. Spare those You have formed. And so, may Your compassion whisper of us and find us worthy to complete the Tikkun of the soul, spirit and higher soul in this incarnation, and let us not die [first], Heaven forbid; and emanate an outpouring of holiness on our soul, spirit and higher soul, that we may be tenacious in our service of You, and may make Your will as ours all the days of our lives, we and all our children and their descendants, and allow us the merit to engage with Your holy Torah for its own sake, and to direct ourselves to the truth of that Torah, and spare our minds from mistakes in the law and in teaching others, and do not screen any word of truth from our mouths ever. And may we and our descendants and their descendants all know Your name and study Your Torah for its own sake, and fulfill Your commandments. Let no fault or flaw be found in us or in our descendants or theirs. And let Your name never be desecrated through us, Heaven forbid.

And see that Your nation is this great nation, the children of Your beloved ones, Abraham, Isaac and Jacob Your servants, the children of those You have tested, and

---

full" (Eccl. 1:4, 7), and consciousness of mortality is a fundamental theme of Rosh HaShana.

Rivers, for Jews in the Diaspora, were places where they felt a special connection with the Divine Presence. Ezekiel, in exile in Babylon, prophesied by the banks of the river Chebar (Ezek. 1:3). Daniel, also in Babylon, had a vision "by the stream Ulai" (Dan. 8:2). Thus, when the prophets outside

שָׁנָה וּבִרְכוֹתֶיהָ, וּתְזַכֵּנוּ שֶׁיְּהֵא לִבֵּנוּ נָכוֹן וּמָסוּר בְּיָדֵינוּ, וְלֹא נִכְעַס וְלֹא נַכְעִיסֶךָ, וְתַסְפִּיק בְּיָדֵינוּ לְהִתְרַחֵק מִכָּל הַמִּדּוֹת הָרָעוֹת וְהָאֲסוּרוֹת, וּבִפְרָט זַכֵּנוּ לְהִתְרַחֵק מֵהַגַּאֲוָה וְהַכַּעַס וְהַהַקְפָּדָה וְכָל גֹּבַהּ לֵב, וְנִהְיֶה מְיֻשָּׁבִים בְּדַעְתֵּנוּ וְנַכִּיר מִעוּט עֶרְכֵּנוּ, וְנַפְשֵׁנוּ כֶּעָפָר לַכֹּל תִּהְיֶה, וְלֹא נִתְכַּעֵס וְלֹא נַקְפִּיד, וְנִהְיֶה אוֹהֲבֵי שָׁלוֹם וּמַרְבִּים שָׁלוֹם, וּבְצֵל כְּנָפֶיךָ נֶחֱסֶה. וּתְזַכֵּנוּ לְהִתְרַחֵק מִלֵּיצָנוּת וְשֶׁקֶר וַחֲנֻפָּה וְלָשׁוֹן הָרָע וְדִבּוּר חֹל בְּשַׁבָּת וְכָל דִּבּוּר אָסוּר, וִיהִי רֹב דִּבּוּרֵנוּ בַּתּוֹרָה וּבְסֵדֶר וְאֹפֶן עֲבוֹדָתֶךָ עֲבוֹדַת הַקֹּדֶשׁ. וּתְאַזְּרֵנוּ חַיִל לִשְׁמֹר לְפִינוּ מֵחֲטוֹא בִּלְשׁוֹנֵנוּ.

אָב הָרַחֲמָן, תֵּן בָּנוּ כֹּחַ וּבְרִיאוּת, וְזַכֵּנוּ לְהִתְרַחֵק מִתַּאֲוַת תַּעֲנוּגֵי וְהַבְלֵי הָעוֹלָם הַזֶּה, וְנֹאכַל לָשֹׂבַע נַפְשֵׁנוּ, וְכֵן בְּכָל צְרָכֵינוּ יִהְיוּ כָּל מַעֲשֵׂינוּ לְשֵׁם שָׁמַיִם. וּתְזַכֵּנוּ לִהְיוֹת שְׂמֵחִים בְּעֵסֶק תּוֹרָתֶךָ וּבְמִצְוֹתֶיךָ, וְלִהְיוֹת בִּטְחוֹנֵנוּ בְּךָ תָּדִיר, וְיִהְיֶה לָנוּ לֵב שָׂמֵחַ לַעֲבוֹדָתֶךָ.

אָנָּא מֶלֶךְ רַחוּם וְחַנּוּן, הַנְּשָׁמָה לָךְ וְהַגּוּף פָּעֳלָךְ, חוּסָה עַל עֲמָלָךְ. וּבְכֵן יֶהֱמוּ נָא רַחֲמֶיךָ עָלֵינוּ, וּתְזַכֵּנוּ לְהַשְׁלִים תִּקּוּן נר״ן בְּגִלְגּוּל זֶה וְלֹא נֹאבַד חַס וְשָׁלוֹם, וְתַשְׁפִּיעַ שֶׁפַע קֹדֶשׁ עַל נר״ן לְהַתְמִיד בַּעֲבוֹדָתֶךָ וְלַעֲשׂוֹת רְצוֹנֵנוּ כִּרְצוֹנְךָ כָּל יְמֵי חַיֵּינוּ, אֲנַחְנוּ וְזַרְעֵנוּ וְזֶרַע זַרְעֵנוּ, וּתְזַכֵּנוּ לַעֲסֹק בְּתוֹרָתְךָ הַקְּדוֹשָׁה לִשְׁמָהּ וּלְכַוֵּן לַאֲמִתָּהּ שֶׁל תּוֹרָה, וְתַצִּיל מִלִּבֵּנוּ טָעוּת בַּהֲלָכָה וּבְהוֹרָאָה, וְאַל תַּצֵּל מִפִּינוּ דְּבַר אֱמֶת לְעוֹלָם. וְנִהְיֶה אֲנַחְנוּ וְצֶאֱצָאֵינוּ וְצֶאֱצָאֵי צֶאֱצָאֵינוּ כֻּלָּנוּ יוֹדְעֵי שְׁמֶךָ, וְלוֹמְדֵי תוֹרָתֶךָ לִשְׁמָהּ וּמְקַיְּמֵי מִצְוֹתֶיךָ. וְלֹא יִמָּצֵא בָּנוּ וְלֹא בְּזַרְעֵנוּ וְלֹא בְּזֶרַע זַרְעֵנוּ שׁוּם פְּגַם וְשׁוּם פְּסוּל. וְלֹא יִתְחַלֵּל שִׁמְךָ עַל יָדֵינוּ חַס וְשָׁלוֹם.

וּרְאֵה כִּי עַמְּךָ הַגּוֹי הַגָּדוֹל הַזֶּה, זֶרַע אוֹהֲבֶיךָ אַבְרָהָם יִצְחָק וְיִשְׂרָאֵל, עֲבָדֶיךָ בְּנֵי בְחוּנֶיךָ, וּבְגָלוּתָם וְדַלּוּתָם וְשִׁפְלוּתָם וְלַחֲצָם וְדָחְקָם זֶה כַּמָּה מֵאוֹת שָׁנִים

---

of repentance and remorse. "By the rivers of Babylon, there we sat and wept as we remembered Zion" (Psalms 137:1). Flowing water is also a symbol of time (as in Isaac Watts' paraphrase of Psalm 90: "Time, like an ever-flowing stream, bears all its sons away"). It represents mortality: "One generation goes, another comes… All streams flow into the sea, yet the sea is never

that throughout their exile and want and shame and oppression and hardship these several hundred years, they have continued calling Your name and believing in You and in Your Torah, and thousands and myriads have offered themselves up to be killed and burned for the sanctification of Your name. Please, Mighty One, guard like the pupil of the eye those who seek Your unity. And be filled with compassion for all our brothers, the house of Israel, scattered in the four corners of the earth, and in particular for those who live in the land of Israel and for the inhabitants of this town, and for all this holy congregation. Have compassion for us and for them, and save us from evil and famine and captivity and from all sin, and bring a complete recovery to all the sick among Your nation Israel; God, please, heal them please, and fulfill in each one of them the verse, "The LORD will support him on his sickbed; every time he is laid low, You turn his fate about in his illness." And as for the healthy members of Your people Israel – maintain their health that they may never become ill, Heaven forbid. And save us, save all Israel, from every kind of damage, from every enemy and adversary and accuser and from depression and the nagging worries of poverty and from all the afflictions that trouble the world. And recall us, bringing healthy children, holy children, to all those who are deprived of descendants. And bring women in labor out from darkness to light, and let their babies emerge at the right time, with no trouble or harm coming either to the mothers or to their babies, and let the plague and demons and spirits and liliths never exert power on any of the children of Your people, the house of Israel, and let them grow up to Torah and to Your commandments, while their fathers and mothers yet live.

*Ps. 41*

And those of Israel Your nation who go to sea – redeem them and save them from great waters and from strangers, save them from mud and do not let them drown, let them survive the surge of the waves and the depths of the sea. And those of Your children Israel who travel on land – lead them along a straight path to reach a settled town, and rescue them from any enemy or ambush on the way. And as for any of Your people Israel who are imprisoned – release their chains and bring them out to broad spaces, and bring back to the awe of You all those who have been forced by the arrogant to convert away from the faith. Grace them with the merit of ancestors and bring our judgment out to daylight, and write us in the book of life for Your sake, O God of life, and let Your face shine upon Your desolate Sanctuary, for Your sake, O LORD.

*Dan. 9*

Our God and God of our ancestors, merciful God, have compassion for us. You who are good and do good, respond to our call. Return to us in Your abounding mercy, for

---

a symbolic gesture to accompany the process of repentance, begun on Rosh HaShana, as if we were "casting away" our sins.

This practice was dismissed by some halakhic authorities and ridiculed by gentiles. However it is less ridiculous than it seems. Maimonides writes about the scapegoat on Yom Kippur, over which the High Priest confessed the sins of the people, and which was then sent out into the wilderness:

קוֹרְאִים בְּשִׁמְךָ וּמַאֲמִינִים בְּךָ וּבְתוֹרָתֶךָ, וְכַמָּה אֲלָפִים וּרְבָבוֹת מָסְרוּ עַצְמָן לַהֲרִיגָה וְלִשְׂרֵפָה עַל קְדֻשַּׁת שְׁמֶךָ. נָא גִּבּוֹר דּוֹרְשֵׁי יִחוּדְךָ כְּבָבַת שָׁמְרֵם. וְתִתְמַלֵּא רַחֲמִים עַל כָּל אַחֵינוּ בֵּית יִשְׂרָאֵל הַנְּפוּצִים בְּאַרְבַּע כַּנְפוֹת הָאָרֶץ, וּבִפְרָט עַל יוֹשְׁבֵי אֶרֶץ יִשְׂרָאֵל, וְעַל יוֹשְׁבֵי הָעִיר הַזֹּאת וְעַל כָּל הַקָּהָל הַקָּדוֹשׁ הַזֶּה, וּתְרַחֵם עָלֵינוּ וַעֲלֵיהֶם, וְתַצִּילֵנוּ מֵרָעָה וּמֵרָעָב וּמִשְּׁבִי וּבִזָּה וּמִכָּל חֵטְא, וְתִשְׁלַח רְפוּאָה שְׁלֵמָה לְכָל חוֹלֵי עַמְּךָ יִשְׂרָאֵל, אֵל נָא רְפָא נָא לָהֶם וּתְקַיֵּם
תהלים מא בְּכָל אֶחָד מֵהֶם מִקְרָא שֶׁכָּתוּב: יהוה יִסְעָדֶנּוּ עַל־עֶרֶשׂ דְּוָי, כָּל־מִשְׁכָּבוֹ הָפַכְתָּ בְחָלְיוֹ: וְהַבְּרִיאִים מֵעַמְּךָ יִשְׂרָאֵל תַּתְמִיד בְּרִיאוּתָם, שֶׁלֹּא יֶחֱלוּ חַס וְשָׁלוֹם. וְתַצִּילֵנוּ וְתַצִּיל לְכָל יִשְׂרָאֵל מִכָּל נֶזֶק וּמִכָּל צַר וּמַשְׂטִין וּמְקַטְרֵג וּמֵרוּחַ רָעָה וּמִדִּקְדּוּקֵי עֲנִיּוּת, וּמִכָּל מִינֵי פֻּרְעָנִיּוֹת הַמִּתְרַגְּשׁוֹת בָּעוֹלָם. וְתִפְקֹד בְּזֶרַע שֶׁל קַיָּמָא זֶרַע קֹדֶשׁ לְכָל חֲשׂוּכֵי בָנִים, וְהַיּוֹשְׁבוֹת עַל הַמַּשְׁבֵּר תּוֹצִיא אוֹתָן מֵאֲפֵלָה לְאוֹרָה, וְיֵצֵא הַוָּלָד בְּשָׁעָה טוֹבָה וְלֹא יֶאֱרַע שׁוּם צַעַר וְשׁוּם נֶזֶק לֹא לַיּוֹלְדוֹת וְלֹא לְיַלְדֵיהֶן, וְאַל יִמְשׁוֹל אַסְכְּרָה וְשֵׁדִין וְרוּחִין וְלִילִין לְכָל יַלְדֵי עַמְּךָ בֵּית יִשְׂרָאֵל, וּתְגַדְּלֵם לְתוֹרָתֶךָ וּלְמִצְוֹתֶיךָ בְּחַיֵּי אֲבִיהֶם וְאִמָּם.

וּבְנֵי יִשְׂרָאֵל עַמְּךָ יוֹרְדֵי הַיָּם, פְּצֵם וְהַצִּילֵם מִמַּיִם רַבִּים, מִיַּד בְּנֵי נֵכָר, הַצִּילֵם מִטִּיט וְאַל יִטְבָּעוּ, יִנָּצְלוּ מִשּׂוֹנְאֵיהֶם וּמִמַּעֲמַקֵּי מָיִם. וּבְנֵי יִשְׂרָאֵל הַהוֹלְכִים בַּיַּבָּשָׁה, הַדְרִיכֵם בְּדֶרֶךְ יְשָׁרָה לָלֶכֶת אֶל עִיר מוֹשָׁב, וְתַצִּילֵם מִכַּף כָּל אוֹיֵב וְאוֹרֵב בַּדֶּרֶךְ. וְכָל הָאֲסוּרִים בְּבֵית הַכֶּלֶא מֵעַמְּךָ יִשְׂרָאֵל, הַתֵּר מַאֲסְרֵיהֶם וְתוֹצִיאֵם לִרְוָחָה, וְהָשֵׁב לְיִרְאָתְךָ כָּל הָאֲנוּסִים בְּיַד גֵּאִים, וְתָחֹן זְכוּת אָבוֹת לְהוֹצִיא
דניאל ט לָאוֹר מִשְׁפָּטֵנוּ, כָּתְבֵנוּ בְּסֵפֶר חַיִּים לְמַעַנְךָ אֱלֹהִים חַיִּים, וְהָאֵר פָּנֶיךָ עַל־מִקְדָּשְׁךָ הַשָּׁמֵם לְמַעַן אֲדֹנָי:

אֱלֹהֵינוּ וֵאלֹהֵי אֲבוֹתֵינוּ מֶלֶךְ רַחֲמָן רַחֵם עָלֵינוּ, טוֹב וּמֵטִיב הִדָּרֶשׁ לָנוּ, שׁוּבָה אֵלֵינוּ בַּהֲמוֹן רַחֲמֶיךָ, בִּגְלַל אָבוֹת שֶׁעָשׂוּ רְצוֹנֶךָ. בְּנֵה בֵיתְךָ כְּבַתְּחִלָּה, וְכוֹנֵן

Israel sought inspiration they found it by going to a river (*Mekhilta deRabbi Shimon bar Yoḥai, Bo* 12:1).

Some have the custom to shake the hems of their clothing, in accordance with Nehemiah 5:13, "Also I shook out my lap, and said: so may God shake out…" (*Maḥzor Oholei Yaakov*). Many folk customs have become associated with *Tashlikh,* among them the custom of throwing crumbs into the water as

the sake of our fathers who did Your will. Rebuild Your Temple as at the beginning, and establish Your Temple on its site. Let us witness its rebuilding and gladden us with its restoration. Bring the priests back to their service, the Levites to their platform and their song and music, and the Israelites to their homes.

And the earth shall be filled with the knowledge of God, of awe and of love for Your great and awesome name; Amen – may this be Your will.

No weapon that is made will succeed against you, and whatever tongue may rise up against you, you will prove in the judgment to be wicked. This is the legacy of the servants of the LORD, and it is from Me that their righteousness comes, says the LORD. *Is. 54*

For no one will do evil, they will make no devastation, *Is. 11*
anywhere on My holy mountain.
For the earth will be filled with the knowledge of the LORD,
as water covers over the sea.

May it be Your will that through the light that the "Holy Ancient One" will shed along its paths to the "Small Face" of the "Large Face" [mystical terms for aspects of the Divine], Your compassion will wrest away Your anger, and will overcome Your other attributes; and You will deal with us through Your attribute of compassion, and grant us long, good lives, engaging with Your Torah and observing Your commands and performing Your will; Amen – may this be Your will.

שִׁיר הַמַּעֲלוֹת A song of ascents. From the depths I have called to You, LORD. LORD, hear my voice; let Your ears be attentive to my plea. If You, LORD, should keep account of sins, O LORD, who could stand? But with You there is forgiveness, that You may be held in awe. I wait for the LORD, my soul waits, and in His word I put my hope. My soul waits for the LORD more than watchmen wait for the morning, more than watchmen wait for the morning. Israel, put your hope in the LORD, for with the LORD there is loving-kindness, and great is His power to redeem. It is He who will redeem Israel from all their sins. *Ps. 130*

*Seven times:*

Forever, LORD, Your word stands firm in the heavens. *Ps. 119*

---

and that the past is in some sense erased (the root meaning of *kippur* in Yom Kippur). Feelings of stigma, shame, self-reproach, dishonor, disgrace, even defilement, may remain, trapping us in the past and barring our way to a new beginning. If a symbolic act was needed in biblical times, might it not be needed even now, for though the world has changed, human psychology remains? There is, therefore, in the custom of throwing away crumbs – as often with Jewish folkways – a psychological depth not to be lightly dismissed. It is a gesture of breaking with the past and letting it be carried away on the river of time while we set out on a new journey in a different direction.

מִקְדָּשְׁךָ עַל מְכוֹנוֹ, וְהַרְאֵנוּ בְּבִנְיָנוֹ וְשַׂמְּחֵנוּ בְּתִקּוּנוֹ, וְהָשֵׁב כֹּהֲנִים לַעֲבוֹדָתָם,
וּלְוִיִּם לְשִׁירָם וּלְזִמְרָם, וְהָשֵׁב יִשְׂרָאֵל לִנְוֵיהֶם.

וּמָלְאָה הָאָרֶץ דֵּעָה אֶת יהוה, לְיִרְאָה וּלְאַהֲבָה אֶת שִׁמְךָ הַגָּדוֹל וְהַנּוֹרָא,
אָמֵן כֵּן יְהִי רָצוֹן.

כָּל־כְּלִי יוּצַר עָלַיִךְ לֹא יִצְלָח, וְכָל־לָשׁוֹן תָּקוּם־אִתָּךְ לַמִּשְׁפָּט תַּרְשִׁיעִי ישעיה נד
זֹאת נַחֲלַת עַבְדֵי יהוה וְצִדְקָתָם מֵאִתִּי נְאֻם־יהוה:

לֹא־יָרֵעוּ וְלֹא־יַשְׁחִיתוּ בְּכָל־הַר קָדְשִׁי ישעיה יא
כִּי־מָלְאָה הָאָרֶץ דֵּעָה אֶת־יהוה, כַּמַּיִם לַיָּם מְכַסִּים:

יְהִי רָצוֹן מִלְּפָנֶיךָ, עַל יְדֵי הֶאָרַת תִּקּוּנִים, עַתִּיקָא קַדִּישָׁא דְעַתִּיקִין בִּזְעֵר
שֶׁבְּאָרִיךְ, יִכְבְּשׁוּ רַחֲמֶיךָ אֶת כַּעַסְךָ, וְיִגֹּלּוּ רַחֲמֶיךָ עַל מִדּוֹתֶיךָ, וְתִתְנַהֵג עִמָּנוּ
בְּמִדַּת הָרַחֲמִים, וְתִתֶּן לָנוּ חַיִּים אֲרוּכִים וְטוֹבִים בְּעִסְקֵי תוֹרָתֶךָ, וּלְקַיֵּם
מִצְוֹתֶיךָ וְלַעֲשׂוֹת רְצוֹנֶךָ, אָמֵן כֵּן יְהִי רָצוֹן.

שִׁיר הַמַּעֲלוֹת, מִמַּעֲמַקִּים קְרָאתִיךָ יהוה: אֲדֹנָי שִׁמְעָה בְקוֹלִי, תִּהְיֶינָה תהלים קל
אָזְנֶיךָ קַשֻּׁבוֹת לְקוֹל תַּחֲנוּנָי: אִם־עֲוֹנוֹת תִּשְׁמָר־יָהּ, אֲדֹנָי מִי יַעֲמֹד: כִּי־עִמְּךָ
הַסְּלִיחָה, לְמַעַן תִּוָּרֵא: קִוִּיתִי יהוה קִוְּתָה נַפְשִׁי, וְלִדְבָרוֹ הוֹחָלְתִּי: נַפְשִׁי
לַאדֹנָי, מִשֹּׁמְרִים לַבֹּקֶר, שֹׁמְרִים לַבֹּקֶר: יַחֵל יִשְׂרָאֵל אֶל־יהוה, כִּי־עִם־יהוה
הַחֶסֶד, וְהַרְבֵּה עִמּוֹ פְדוּת: וְהוּא יִפְדֶּה אֶת־יִשְׂרָאֵל, מִכֹּל עֲוֹנוֹתָיו:

*Seven times:*

לְעוֹלָם יהוה דְּבָרְךָ נִצָּב בַּשָּׁמָיִם: תהלים קיט

---

> There is no doubt that sins cannot be carried like a burden, and taken off the shoulder of one being and laid on that of another. But these ceremonies are of a symbolic character, and serve to impress people with a certain idea, and to induce them to repent, as if to say: we have freed ourselves of our previous deeds, have cast them behind our backs, and removed them from us as far as possible. (*Guide for the Perplexed*, III:46)

That, undoubtedly, is the underlying psychology of the folk custom of casting away crumbs as sins: a symbolic gesture, no more, no less. The Judaic concept of *teshuva*, repentance, is not psychologically straightforward. For those who feel a strong sense of guilt it is not easy to believe that God forgives

# Ma'ariv for Motza'ei Rosh HaShana

וְהוּא רַחוּם He is compassionate. *Ps. 78*
He forgives iniquity and does not destroy.
Repeatedly He suppresses His anger, not rousing His full wrath.
LORD, save! May the King answer us on the day we call. *Ps. 20*

## BLESSINGS OF THE SHEMA

*The Leader says the following, bowing at "Bless," standing straight at "the LORD"; the congregation, followed by the Leader, responds, bowing at "Bless," standing straight at "the LORD":*

*Leader:* **BLESS**
the LORD, the blessed One.

*Congregation:* Bless the LORD, the blessed One,
for ever and all time.

*Leader:* Bless the LORD, the blessed One,
for ever and all time.

בָּרוּךְ Blessed are You, LORD our God, King of the Universe,
who by His word brings on evenings,
by His wisdom opens the gates of heaven,
with understanding makes time change
and the seasons rotate,
and by His will
orders the stars in their constellations in the sky.
He creates day and night,
rolling away the light before the darkness,
and darkness before the light.
▸ He makes the day pass and brings on night,
distinguishing day from night:
the LORD of hosts is His name.

# מעריב למוצאי ראש השנה

וְהוּא רַחוּם, יְכַפֵּר עָוֹן וְלֹא־יַשְׁחִית תהלים עח
וְהִרְבָּה לְהָשִׁיב אַפּוֹ, וְלֹא־יָעִיר כָּל־חֲמָתוֹ:
יהוה הוֹשִׁיעָה, הַמֶּלֶךְ יַעֲנֵנוּ בְיוֹם־קָרְאֵנוּ: תהלים כ

## קריאת שמע וברכותיה

*The* שליח ציבור *says the following, bowing at* בָּרְכוּ*, standing straight at* ה׳*; the* קהל*, followed by the* שליח ציבור*, responds, bowing at* בָּרוּךְ*, standing straight at* ה׳*:*

ש״ץ: בָּרְכוּ
אֶת יהוה הַמְבֹרָךְ.

קהל: בָּרוּךְ יהוה הַמְבֹרָךְ לְעוֹלָם וָעֶד.

ש״ץ: בָּרוּךְ יהוה הַמְבֹרָךְ לְעוֹלָם וָעֶד.

בָּרוּךְ אַתָּה יהוה אֱלֹהֵינוּ מֶלֶךְ הָעוֹלָם
אֲשֶׁר בִּדְבָרוֹ מַעֲרִיב עֲרָבִים
בְּחָכְמָה פּוֹתֵחַ שְׁעָרִים
וּבִתְבוּנָה מְשַׁנֶּה עִתִּים וּמַחֲלִיף אֶת הַזְּמַנִּים
וּמְסַדֵּר אֶת הַכּוֹכָבִים בְּמִשְׁמְרוֹתֵיהֶם בָּרָקִיעַ כִּרְצוֹנוֹ.
בּוֹרֵא יוֹם וָלָיְלָה, גּוֹלֵל אוֹר מִפְּנֵי חֹשֶׁךְ וְחֹשֶׁךְ מִפְּנֵי אוֹר
◂ וּמַעֲבִיר יוֹם וּמֵבִיא לָיְלָה
וּמַבְדִּיל בֵּין יוֹם וּבֵין לָיְלָה
יהוה צְבָאוֹת שְׁמוֹ.

May the living and forever enduring God rule over us for all time.
Blessed are You, LORD, who brings on evenings.

אַהֲבַת עוֹלָם With everlasting love
have You loved Your people, the house of Israel.
You have taught us Torah and commandments,
decrees and laws of justice.
Therefore, LORD our God, when we lie down and when we rise up
we will speak of Your decrees,
rejoicing in studying the words of Your Torah
and Your commandments for ever.
▸ For they are our life and the length of our days;
on them will we meditate day and night.
May You never take away Your love from us.
Blessed are You, LORD, who loves His people Israel.

*The Shema must be said with intense concentration. See laws 10–14.*

*When not with a minyan, say:*

God, faithful King!

*The following verse should be said aloud, while covering the eyes with the right hand.*

## Listen, Israel: the LORD is our God, the LORD is One. *Deut. 6*

*Quietly:* Blessed be the name of His glorious kingdom for ever and all time.

וְאָהַבְתָּ Love the LORD your God with all your heart, with all your soul, and with all your might. These words which I command you today shall be on your heart. Teach them repeatedly to your children, speaking of them when you sit at home and when you travel on the way, when you lie down and when you rise. Bind them as a sign on your hand, and they shall be an emblem between your eyes. Write them on the doorposts of your house and gates. *Deut. 6*

וְהָיָה If you indeed heed My commandments with which I charge you today, to love the LORD your God and worship Him with all your heart and with all your soul, I will give rain in your land in its season, the early and late rain; and you shall gather in your grain, *Deut. 11*

אֵל חַי וְקַיָּם תָּמִיד, יִמְלֹךְ עָלֵינוּ לְעוֹלָם וָעֶד.
בָּרוּךְ אַתָּה יהוה, הַמַּעֲרִיב עֲרָבִים.

אַהֲבַת עוֹלָם בֵּית יִשְׂרָאֵל עַמְּךָ אָהָבְתָּ
תּוֹרָה וּמִצְוֹת, חֻקִּים וּמִשְׁפָּטִים, אוֹתָנוּ לִמַּדְתָּ
עַל כֵּן יהוה אֱלֹהֵינוּ בְּשָׁכְבֵנוּ וּבְקוּמֵנוּ נָשִׂיחַ בְּחֻקֶּיךָ
וְנִשְׂמַח בְּדִבְרֵי תַלְמוּד תּוֹרָתֶךָ וּבְמִצְוֹתֶיךָ לְעוֹלָם וָעֶד
◄ כִּי הֵם חַיֵּינוּ וְאֹרֶךְ יָמֵינוּ, וּבָהֶם נֶהְגֶּה יוֹמָם וָלָיְלָה.
וְאַהֲבָתְךָ אַל תָּסִיר מִמֶּנּוּ לְעוֹלָמִים.
בָּרוּךְ אַתָּה יהוה, אוֹהֵב עַמּוֹ יִשְׂרָאֵל.

*The שמע must be said with intense concentration. See laws 10–14.*

*When not with a מנין, say:*

אֵל מֶלֶךְ נֶאֱמָן

*The following verse should be said aloud, while covering the eyes with the right hand.*

דברים ו **שְׁמַע יִשְׂרָאֵל, יהוה אֱלֹהֵינוּ, יהוה ׀ אֶחָד׃**

*Quietly* בָּרוּךְ שֵׁם כְּבוֹד מַלְכוּתוֹ לְעוֹלָם וָעֶד.

דברים ו וְאָהַבְתָּ אֵת יהוה אֱלֹהֶיךָ, בְּכָל־לְבָבְךָ וּבְכָל־נַפְשְׁךָ וּבְכָל־מְאֹדֶךָ׃
וְהָיוּ הַדְּבָרִים הָאֵלֶּה, אֲשֶׁר אָנֹכִי מְצַוְּךָ הַיּוֹם, עַל־לְבָבֶךָ׃ וְשִׁנַּנְתָּם
לְבָנֶיךָ וְדִבַּרְתָּ בָּם, בְּשִׁבְתְּךָ בְּבֵיתֶךָ וּבְלֶכְתְּךָ בַדֶּרֶךְ, וּבְשָׁכְבְּךָ
וּבְקוּמֶךָ׃ וּקְשַׁרְתָּם לְאוֹת עַל־יָדֶךָ וְהָיוּ לְטֹטָפֹת בֵּין עֵינֶיךָ׃
וּכְתַבְתָּם עַל־מְזֻזוֹת בֵּיתֶךָ וּבִשְׁעָרֶיךָ׃

דברים יא וְהָיָה אִם־שָׁמֹעַ תִּשְׁמְעוּ אֶל־מִצְוֺתַי אֲשֶׁר אָנֹכִי מְצַוֶּה אֶתְכֶם
הַיּוֹם, לְאַהֲבָה אֶת־יהוה אֱלֹהֵיכֶם וּלְעָבְדוֹ, בְּכָל־לְבַבְכֶם וּבְכָל־
נַפְשְׁכֶם׃ וְנָתַתִּי מְטַר־אַרְצְכֶם בְּעִתּוֹ, יוֹרֶה וּמַלְקוֹשׁ, וְאָסַפְתָּ דְגָנֶךָ
וְתִירֹשְׁךָ וְיִצְהָרֶךָ׃ וְנָתַתִּי עֵשֶׂב בְּשָׂדְךָ לִבְהֶמְתֶּךָ, וְאָכַלְתָּ וְשָׂבָעְתָּ׃

wine and oil. I will give grass in your field for your cattle, and you shall eat and be satisfied. Be careful lest your heart be tempted and you go astray and worship other gods, bowing down to them. Then the LORD's anger will flare against you and He will close the heavens so that there will be no rain. The land will not yield its crops, and you will perish swiftly from the good land that the LORD is giving you. Therefore, set these, My words, on your heart and soul. Bind them as a sign on your hand, and they shall be an emblem between your eyes. Teach them to your children, speaking of them when you sit at home and when you travel on the way, when you lie down and when you rise. Write them on the doorposts of your house and gates, so that you and your children may live long in the land that the LORD swore to your ancestors to give them, for as long as the heavens are above the earth.

וַיֹּאמֶר The LORD spoke to Moses, saying: Speak to the Israelites *Num. 15*
and tell them to make tassels on the corners of their garments for all generations. They shall attach to the tassel at each corner a thread of blue. This shall be your tassel, and you shall see it and remember all of the LORD's commandments and keep them, not straying after your heart and after your eyes, following your own sinful desires. Thus you will be reminded to keep all My commandments, and be holy to your God. I am the LORD your God, who brought you out of the land of Egypt to be your God. I am the LORD your God.

## True –

*The Leader repeats:*

▸ The LORD your God is true –

**וֶאֱמוּנָה** – and faithful is all this, and firmly established for us
that He is the LORD our God,
and there is none besides Him,
and that we, Israel, are His people.
He is our King, who redeems us from the hand of kings
and delivers us from the grasp of all tyrants.

הִשָּׁמְרוּ לָכֶם פֶּן־יִפְתֶּה לְבַבְכֶם, וְסַרְתֶּם וַעֲבַדְתֶּם אֱלֹהִים אֲחֵרִים וְהִשְׁתַּחֲוִיתֶם לָהֶם: וְחָרָה אַף־יהוה בָּכֶם, וְעָצַר אֶת־הַשָּׁמַיִם וְלֹא־יִהְיֶה מָטָר, וְהָאֲדָמָה לֹא תִתֵּן אֶת־יְבוּלָהּ, וַאֲבַדְתֶּם מְהֵרָה מֵעַל הָאָרֶץ הַטֹּבָה אֲשֶׁר יהוה נֹתֵן לָכֶם: וְשַׂמְתֶּם אֶת־דְּבָרַי אֵלֶּה עַל־לְבַבְכֶם וְעַל־נַפְשְׁכֶם, וּקְשַׁרְתֶּם אֹתָם לְאוֹת עַל־יֶדְכֶם, וְהָיוּ לְטוֹטָפֹת בֵּין עֵינֵיכֶם: וְלִמַּדְתֶּם אֹתָם אֶת־בְּנֵיכֶם לְדַבֵּר בָּם, בְּשִׁבְתְּךָ בְּבֵיתֶךָ וּבְלֶכְתְּךָ בַדֶּרֶךְ, וּבְשָׁכְבְּךָ וּבְקוּמֶךָ: וּכְתַבְתָּם עַל־מְזוּזוֹת בֵּיתֶךָ וּבִשְׁעָרֶיךָ: לְמַעַן יִרְבּוּ יְמֵיכֶם וִימֵי בְנֵיכֶם עַל הָאֲדָמָה אֲשֶׁר נִשְׁבַּע יהוה לַאֲבֹתֵיכֶם לָתֵת לָהֶם, כִּימֵי הַשָּׁמַיִם עַל־הָאָרֶץ:

במדבר טו וַיֹּאמֶר יהוה אֶל־מֹשֶׁה לֵּאמֹר: דַּבֵּר אֶל־בְּנֵי יִשְׂרָאֵל וְאָמַרְתָּ אֲלֵהֶם, וְעָשׂוּ לָהֶם צִיצִת עַל־כַּנְפֵי בִגְדֵיהֶם לְדֹרֹתָם, וְנָתְנוּ עַל־צִיצִת הַכָּנָף פְּתִיל תְּכֵלֶת: וְהָיָה לָכֶם לְצִיצִת, וּרְאִיתֶם אֹתוֹ וּזְכַרְתֶּם אֶת־כָּל־מִצְוֹת יהוה וַעֲשִׂיתֶם אֹתָם, וְלֹא תָתוּרוּ אַחֲרֵי לְבַבְכֶם וְאַחֲרֵי עֵינֵיכֶם, אֲשֶׁר־אַתֶּם זֹנִים אַחֲרֵיהֶם: לְמַעַן תִּזְכְּרוּ וַעֲשִׂיתֶם אֶת־כָּל־מִצְוֹתָי, וִהְיִיתֶם קְדֹשִׁים לֵאלֹהֵיכֶם: אֲנִי יהוה אֱלֹהֵיכֶם, אֲשֶׁר הוֹצֵאתִי אֶתְכֶם מֵאֶרֶץ מִצְרַיִם, לִהְיוֹת לָכֶם לֵאלֹהִים, אֲנִי יהוה אֱלֹהֵיכֶם:

# אֱמֶת

*The* שליח ציבור *repeats:*

◂ יהוה אֱלֹהֵיכֶם אֱמֶת

וֶאֱמוּנָה כָּל זֹאת וְקַיָּם עָלֵינוּ
כִּי הוּא יהוה אֱלֹהֵינוּ וְאֵין זוּלָתוֹ
וַאֲנַחְנוּ יִשְׂרָאֵל עַמּוֹ.
הַפּוֹדֵנוּ מִיַּד מְלָכִים
מַלְכֵּנוּ הַגּוֹאֲלֵנוּ מִכַּף כָּל הֶעָרִיצִים.

He is our God,
who on our behalf repays our foes
and brings just retribution on our mortal enemies;
who performs great deeds beyond understanding;
miracles and wonders beyond number;
who kept us alive, not letting our foot slip;
who led us on the high places of our enemies,
raising our pride above all our foes;
who did miracles for us
and brought vengeance against Pharaoh;
who performed signs and wonders
in the land of Ham's children;
who smote in His wrath all the firstborn of Egypt,
and brought out His people Israel from their midst
into everlasting freedom;
who led His children through the divided Reed Sea,
plunging their pursuers and enemies into the depths.
When His children saw His might,
they gave praise and thanks to His name,
▸ and willingly accepted His Sovereignty.
Moses and the children of Israel
then sang a song to You with great joy,
and they all exclaimed:

מִי־כָמֹכָה "Who is like You, LORD, among the mighty? *Ex. 15*
Who is like You, majestic in holiness,
awesome in praises, doing wonders?"

▸ Your children beheld Your majesty
as You parted the sea before Moses.
"This is my God!" they responded, and then said:

"The LORD shall reign for ever and ever." *Ibid.*

▸ And it is said, "For the LORD has redeemed Jacob *Jer. 31*
and rescued him from a power stronger than his own."
Blessed are You, LORD, who redeemed Israel.

הָאֵל הַנִּפְרָע לָנוּ מִצָּרֵינוּ
וְהַמְשַׁלֵּם גְּמוּל לְכָל אוֹיְבֵי נַפְשֵׁנוּ.
הָעוֹשֶׂה גְדוֹלוֹת עַד אֵין חֵקֶר
נִסִּים וְנִפְלָאוֹת עַד אֵין מִסְפָּר
הַשָּׂם נַפְשֵׁנוּ בַּחַיִּים, וְלֹא נָתַן לַמּוֹט רַגְלֵנוּ
הַמַּדְרִיכֵנוּ עַל בָּמוֹת אוֹיְבֵינוּ
וַיָּרֶם קַרְנֵנוּ עַל כָּל שׂוֹנְאֵינוּ.
הָעוֹשֶׂה לָּנוּ נִסִּים וּנְקָמָה בְּפַרְעֹה
אוֹתוֹת וּמוֹפְתִים בְּאַדְמַת בְּנֵי חָם.
הַמַּכֶּה בְעֶבְרָתוֹ כָּל בְּכוֹרֵי מִצְרָיִם
וַיּוֹצֵא אֶת עַמּוֹ יִשְׂרָאֵל מִתּוֹכָם לְחֵרוּת עוֹלָם.
הַמַּעֲבִיר בָּנָיו בֵּין גִּזְרֵי יַם סוּף
אֶת רוֹדְפֵיהֶם וְאֶת שׂוֹנְאֵיהֶם בִּתְהוֹמוֹת טִבַּע
וְרָאוּ בָנָיו גְּבוּרָתוֹ, שִׁבְּחוּ וְהוֹדוּ לִשְׁמוֹ
◂ וּמַלְכוּתוֹ בְּרָצוֹן קִבְּלוּ עֲלֵיהֶם.
מֹשֶׁה וּבְנֵי יִשְׂרָאֵל, לְךָ עָנוּ שִׁירָה בְּשִׂמְחָה רַבָּה
וְאָמְרוּ כֻלָּם

מִי־כָמֹכָה בָּאֵלִם יהוה שמות טו
מִי כָּמֹכָה נֶאְדָּר בַּקֹּדֶשׁ
נוֹרָא תְהִלֹּת עֹשֵׂה פֶלֶא:

◂ מַלְכוּתְךָ רָאוּ בָנֶיךָ, בּוֹקֵעַ יָם לִפְנֵי מֹשֶׁה
זֶה אֵלִי עָנוּ, וְאָמְרוּ

יהוה יִמְלֹךְ לְעֹלָם וָעֶד: שם

◂ וְנֶאֱמַר

כִּי־פָדָה יהוה אֶת־יַעֲקֹב, וּגְאָלוֹ מִיַּד חָזָק מִמֶּנּוּ: ירמיה לא

בָּרוּךְ אַתָּה יהוה, גָּאַל יִשְׂרָאֵל.

הַשְׁכִּיבֵנוּ Help us lie down, O Lord our God, in peace,
and rise up, O our King, to good lives and to peace.
Spread over us Your canopy of peace.
Direct us with Your good counsel,
and save us quickly for the sake of Your name.
Shield us and remove from us every enemy,
plague, sword, famine and sorrow.
Remove the adversary from before and behind us.
Shelter us in the shadow of Your wings,
for You, God, are our Guardian and Deliverer;
You, God, are a gracious and compassionate King.
▸ Guard our going out and our coming in,
for life and peace, from now and for ever.
Blessed are You, Lord, who guards His people Israel for ever.

*In Israel the service continues with Half Kaddish on page 968.*

בָּרוּךְ Blessed be the Lord for ever. Amen and Amen. *Ps. 89*
Blessed from Zion be the Lord *Ps. 135*
who dwells in Jerusalem. Halleluya!
Blessed be the Lord, God of Israel, *Ps. 72*
who alone does wonders.
Blessed be His glorious name for ever,
and may all the earth be filled with His glory. Amen and Amen.
May the glory of the Lord endure for ever; *Ps. 104*
may the Lord rejoice in His works.
May the name of the Lord be blessed now and for all time. *Ps. 113*
For the sake of His great name *I Sam. 12*
the Lord will not abandon His people,
for the Lord vowed to make you a people of His own.
When all the people saw [God's wonders] they fell on their faces *I Kings 18*
and said: "The Lord, He is God; the Lord, He is God."
Then the Lord shall be King over all the earth; *Zech. 14*
on that day the Lord shall be One and His name One.
May Your love, Lord, be upon us, as we have put our hope in You. *Ps. 33*

הַשְׁכִּיבֵנוּ יהוה אֱלֹהֵינוּ לְשָׁלוֹם
וְהַעֲמִידֵנוּ מַלְכֵּנוּ לְחַיִּים טוֹבִים וּלְשָׁלוֹם
וּפְרֹשׂ עָלֵינוּ סֻכַּת שְׁלוֹמֶךָ, וְתַקְּנֵנוּ בְּעֵצָה טוֹבָה מִלְּפָנֶיךָ
וְהוֹשִׁיעֵנוּ מְהֵרָה לְמַעַן שְׁמֶךָ.
וְהָגֵן בַּעֲדֵנוּ, וְהָסֵר מֵעָלֵינוּ אוֹיֵב, דֶּבֶר וְחֶרֶב וְרָעָב וְיָגוֹן
וְהָסֵר שָׂטָן מִלְּפָנֵינוּ וּמֵאַחֲרֵינוּ, וּבְצֵל כְּנָפֶיךָ תַּסְתִּירֵנוּ
כִּי אֵל שׁוֹמְרֵנוּ וּמַצִּילֵנוּ אָתָּה
כִּי אֵל מֶלֶךְ חַנּוּן וְרַחוּם אָתָּה.
◂ וּשְׁמֹר צֵאתֵנוּ וּבוֹאֵנוּ לְחַיִּים וּלְשָׁלוֹם מֵעַתָּה וְעַד עוֹלָם.
בָּרוּךְ אַתָּה יהוה, שׁוֹמֵר עַמּוֹ יִשְׂרָאֵל לָעַד.

*In* ארץ ישראל *the service continues with* חצי קדיש *on page 969.*

בָּרוּךְ יהוה לְעוֹלָם, אָמֵן וְאָמֵן: תהלים פט
בָּרוּךְ יהוה מִצִּיּוֹן, שֹׁכֵן יְרוּשָׁלָםִ, הַלְלוּיָהּ: תהלים קלה
בָּרוּךְ יהוה אֱלֹהִים אֱלֹהֵי יִשְׂרָאֵל, עֹשֵׂה נִפְלָאוֹת לְבַדּוֹ: תהלים עב
וּבָרוּךְ שֵׁם כְּבוֹדוֹ לְעוֹלָם
וְיִמָּלֵא כְבוֹדוֹ אֶת־כָּל־הָאָרֶץ, אָמֵן וְאָמֵן:
יְהִי כְבוֹד יהוה לְעוֹלָם, יִשְׂמַח יהוה בְּמַעֲשָׂיו: תהלים קד
יְהִי שֵׁם יהוה מְבֹרָךְ מֵעַתָּה וְעַד־עוֹלָם: תהלים קיג
כִּי לֹא־יִטֹּשׁ יהוה אֶת־עַמּוֹ בַּעֲבוּר שְׁמוֹ הַגָּדוֹל שמואל א, יב
כִּי הוֹאִיל יהוה לַעֲשׂוֹת אֶתְכֶם לוֹ לְעָם:
וַיַּרְא כָּל־הָעָם וַיִּפְּלוּ עַל־פְּנֵיהֶם מלכים א, יח
וַיֹּאמְרוּ, יהוה הוּא הָאֱלֹהִים, יהוה הוּא הָאֱלֹהִים:
וְהָיָה יהוה לְמֶלֶךְ עַל־כָּל־הָאָרֶץ זכריה יד
בַּיּוֹם הַהוּא יִהְיֶה יהוה אֶחָד וּשְׁמוֹ אֶחָד:
יְהִי־חַסְדְּךָ יהוה עָלֵינוּ, כַּאֲשֶׁר יִחַלְנוּ לָךְ: תהלים לג

הוֹשִׁיעֵנוּ Save us, LORD our God, gather us Ps. 106
and deliver us from the nations,
to thank Your holy name, and glory in Your praise.
All the nations You made shall come and bow before You, LORD, Ps. 86
and pay honor to Your name,
for You are great and You perform wonders:
You alone are God.
We, Your people, the flock of Your pasture, Ps. 79
will praise You for ever.
For all generations we will relate Your praise.

בָּרוּךְ Blessed is the LORD by day,
blessed is the LORD by night.
Blessed is the LORD when we lie down;
blessed is the LORD when we rise.
For in Your hand are the souls of the living and the dead,
[as it is written:] "In His hand is every living soul, Job 12
and the breath of all mankind."
Into Your hand I entrust my spirit: Ps. 31
You redeemed me, LORD, God of truth.
Our God in heaven, bring unity to Your name,
establish Your kingdom constantly
and reign over us for ever and all time.

יִרְאוּ May our eyes see, our hearts rejoice,
and our souls be glad in Your true salvation,
when Zion is told, "Your God reigns." Is. 52
The LORD is King, the LORD was King,
the LORD will be King for ever and all time.
▸ For sovereignty is Yours,
and to all eternity You will reign in glory,
for we have no king but You.
Blessed are You, LORD,
the King who in His constant glory will reign over us
and all His creation for ever and all time.

הוֹשִׁיעֵנוּ יהוה אֱלֹהֵינוּ, וְקַבְּצֵנוּ מִן־הַגּוֹיִם תהלים קו
לְהוֹדוֹת לְשֵׁם קָדְשֶׁךָ, לְהִשְׁתַּבֵּחַ בִּתְהִלָּתֶךָ:
כָּל־גּוֹיִם אֲשֶׁר עָשִׂיתָ, יָבוֹאוּ וְיִשְׁתַּחֲווּ לְפָנֶיךָ, אֲדֹנָי תהלים פו
וִיכַבְּדוּ לִשְׁמֶךָ:
כִּי־גָדוֹל אַתָּה וְעֹשֵׂה נִפְלָאוֹת, אַתָּה אֱלֹהִים לְבַדֶּךָ:
וַאֲנַחְנוּ עַמְּךָ וְצֹאן מַרְעִיתֶךָ, נוֹדֶה לְּךָ לְעוֹלָם תהלים עט
לְדוֹר וָדֹר נְסַפֵּר תְּהִלָּתֶךָ:

בָּרוּךְ יהוה בַּיּוֹם, בָּרוּךְ יהוה בַּלָּיְלָה
בָּרוּךְ יהוה בְּשָׁכְבֵנוּ, בָּרוּךְ יהוה בְּקוּמֵנוּ.
כִּי בְיָדְךָ נַפְשׁוֹת הַחַיִּים וְהַמֵּתִים.
אֲשֶׁר בְּיָדוֹ נֶפֶשׁ כָּל־חָי, וְרוּחַ כָּל־בְּשַׂר־אִישׁ: איוב יב
בְּיָדְךָ אַפְקִיד רוּחִי, פָּדִיתָה אוֹתִי יהוה אֵל אֱמֶת: תהלים לא
אֱלֹהֵינוּ שֶׁבַּשָּׁמַיִם, יַחֵד שִׁמְךָ וְקַיֵּם מַלְכוּתְךָ תָּמִיד
וּמְלֹךְ עָלֵינוּ לְעוֹלָם וָעֶד.

יִרְאוּ עֵינֵינוּ וְיִשְׂמַח לִבֵּנוּ
וְתָגֵל נַפְשֵׁנוּ בִּישׁוּעָתְךָ בֶּאֱמֶת
בֶּאֱמֹר לְצִיּוֹן מָלַךְ אֱלֹהָיִךְ. ישעיה נב
יהוה מֶלֶךְ, יהוה מָלָךְ, יהוה יִמְלֹךְ לְעֹלָם וָעֶד.
◂ כִּי הַמַּלְכוּת שֶׁלְּךָ הִיא, וּלְעוֹלְמֵי עַד תִּמְלֹךְ בְּכָבוֹד
כִּי אֵין לָנוּ מֶלֶךְ אֶלָּא אָתָּה.
בָּרוּךְ אַתָּה יהוה
הַמֶּלֶךְ בִּכְבוֹדוֹ תָּמִיד, יִמְלֹךְ עָלֵינוּ לְעוֹלָם וָעֶד
וְעַל כָּל מַעֲשָׂיו.

HALF KADDISH

*Reader:* יִתְגַּדַּל Magnified and sanctified may His great name be,
in the world He created by His will.
May He establish His kingdom,
make His salvation flourish,
and hasten His messiah,
in your lifetime and in your days,
and in the lifetime of all the house of Israel,
swiftly and soon – and say: Amen.

*All:* May His great name be blessed for ever and all time.

*Leader:* Blessed and praised, glorified and exalted,
raised and honored, uplifted and lauded
be the name of the Holy One,
blessed be He,
above and beyond any blessing,
song, praise and consolation
uttered in the world – and say: Amen.

## THE AMIDA

*The following prayer, until "in former years" on page 984, is said silently, standing with feet together. Take three steps forward and at the points indicated by ▾, bend the knees at the first word, bow at the second, and stand straight before saying God's name.*

O Lord, open my lips, *Ps. 51*
so that my mouth may declare Your praise.

PATRIARCHS

▾ בָּרוּךְ Blessed are You, Lord our God and God of our fathers,
God of Abraham, God of Isaac and God of Jacob;
the great, mighty and awesome God, God Most High,
who bestows acts of loving-kindness, who creates all,
who remembers the loving-kindness of the fathers
and will bring a Redeemer to their children's children
for the sake of His name, in love.

חצי קדיש

ש״ץ: יִתְגַּדַּל וְיִתְקַדַּשׁ שְׁמֵהּ רַבָּא (קהל: אָמֵן)
בְּעָלְמָא דִּי בְרָא כִרְעוּתֵהּ
וְיַמְלִיךְ מַלְכוּתֵהּ
וְיַצְמַח פֻּרְקָנֵהּ וִיקָרֵב מְשִׁיחֵהּ (קהל: אָמֵן)
בְּחַיֵּיכוֹן וּבְיוֹמֵיכוֹן, וּבְחַיֵּי דְכָל בֵּית יִשְׂרָאֵל
בַּעֲגָלָא וּבִזְמַן קָרִיב, וְאִמְרוּ אָמֵן. (קהל: אָמֵן)

קהל וש״ץ: יְהֵא שְׁמֵהּ רַבָּא מְבָרַךְ לְעָלַם וּלְעָלְמֵי עָלְמַיָּא.

ש״ץ: יִתְבָּרַךְ וְיִשְׁתַּבַּח וְיִתְפָּאַר וְיִתְרוֹמַם וְיִתְנַשֵּׂא
וְיִתְהַדָּר וְיִתְעַלֶּה וְיִתְהַלָּל
שְׁמֵהּ דְּקֻדְשָׁא בְּרִיךְ הוּא (קהל: אָמֵן)
לְעֵלָּא לְעֵלָּא מִכָּל בִּרְכָתָא וְשִׁירָתָא, תֻּשְׁבְּחָתָא וְנֶחֱמָתָא
דַּאֲמִירָן בְּעָלְמָא, וְאִמְרוּ אָמֵן. (קהל: אָמֵן)

## עמידה

*The following prayer, until* קַדְמֹנִיּוֹת *on page 985, is said silently, standing with feet together. Take three steps forward and at the points indicated by* ▾*, bend the knees at the first word, bow at the second, and stand straight before saying God's name.*

תהלים נא אֲדֹנָי, שְׂפָתַי תִּפְתָּח, וּפִי יַגִּיד תְּהִלָּתֶךָ:

אבות

▾בָּרוּךְ אַתָּה יהוה, אֱלֹהֵינוּ וֵאלֹהֵי אֲבוֹתֵינוּ
אֱלֹהֵי אַבְרָהָם, אֱלֹהֵי יִצְחָק, וֵאלֹהֵי יַעֲקֹב
הָאֵל הַגָּדוֹל הַגִּבּוֹר וְהַנּוֹרָא, אֵל עֶלְיוֹן
גּוֹמֵל חֲסָדִים טוֹבִים, קוֹנֵה הַכֹּל
וְזוֹכֵר חַסְדֵי אָבוֹת
וּמֵבִיא גוֹאֵל לִבְנֵי בְנֵיהֶם לְמַעַן שְׁמוֹ בְּאַהֲבָה.

זָכְרֵנוּ לְחַיִּים Remember us for life, O King who desires life,
and write us in the book of life – for Your sake, O God of life.

*If forgotten, the Amida is not repeated.*

King, Helper, Savior, Shield:
▾Blessed are You, LORD,
Shield of Abraham.

DIVINE MIGHT

אַתָּה גִּבּוֹר You are eternally mighty, LORD.
You give life to the dead
and have great power to save.

*In Israel:* He causes the dew to fall.

He sustains the living with loving-kindness,
and with great compassion revives the dead.
He supports the fallen, heals the sick, sets captives free,
and keeps His faith with those who sleep in the dust.
Who is like You, Master of might,
and to whom can You be compared,
O King who brings death and gives life,
and makes salvation grow?

מִי כָמְוֹךָ Who is like You, compassionate Father,
who remembers His creatures in compassion, for life?

*If forgotten, the Amida is not repeated.*

Faithful are You to revive the dead.
Blessed are You, LORD,
who revives the dead.

HOLINESS

אַתָּה קָדוֹשׁ You are holy and Your name is holy,
and holy ones praise You daily, Selah!
For You, God, are a great and holy King.
Blessed are You, LORD,
the holy King.

*If "holy God" is said, then the Amida is repeated.*

זָכְרֵנוּ לְחַיִּים, מֶלֶךְ חָפֵץ בַּחַיִּים
וְכָתְבֵנוּ בְּסֵפֶר הַחַיִּים, לְמַעַנְךָ אֱלֹהִים חַיִּים.

*If forgotten, the* עמידה *is not repeated.*

מֶלֶךְ עוֹזֵר וּמוֹשִׁיעַ וּמָגֵן.
בָּרוּךְ אַתָּה יהוה, מָגֵן אַבְרָהָם.

גבורות

אַתָּה גִּבּוֹר לְעוֹלָם, אֲדֹנָי
מְחַיֵּה מֵתִים אַתָּה, רַב לְהוֹשִׁיעַ
בארץ ישראל: מוֹרִיד הַטָּל
מְכַלְכֵּל חַיִּים בְּחֶסֶד, מְחַיֵּה מֵתִים בְּרַחֲמִים רַבִּים
סוֹמֵךְ נוֹפְלִים, וְרוֹפֵא חוֹלִים, וּמַתִּיר אֲסוּרִים
וּמְקַיֵּם אֱמוּנָתוֹ לִישֵׁנֵי עָפָר.
מִי כָמוֹךָ, בַּעַל גְּבוּרוֹת, וּמִי דּוֹמֶה לָּךְ
מֶלֶךְ, מֵמִית וּמְחַיֶּה וּמַצְמִיחַ יְשׁוּעָה.
מִי כָמוֹךָ אַב הָרַחֲמָן, זוֹכֵר יְצוּרָיו לְחַיִּים בְּרַחֲמִים.

*If forgotten, the* עמידה *is not repeated.*

וְנֶאֱמָן אַתָּה לְהַחֲיוֹת מֵתִים.
בָּרוּךְ אַתָּה יהוה, מְחַיֵּה הַמֵּתִים.

קדושת השם

אַתָּה קָדוֹשׁ וְשִׁמְךָ קָדוֹשׁ
וּקְדוֹשִׁים בְּכָל יוֹם יְהַלְלוּךָ סֶּלָה
כִּי אֵל מֶלֶךְ גָּדוֹל וְקָדוֹשׁ אָתָּה.
בָּרוּךְ אַתָּה יהוה, הַמֶּלֶךְ הַקָּדוֹשׁ.

*If* הָאֵל הַקָּדוֹשׁ *is said, then the* עמידה *is repeated.*

KNOWLEDGE

אַתָּה חוֹנֵן You grace humanity with knowledge
and teach mortals understanding.
You have graced us with the knowledge of Your Torah,
and taught us to perform the statutes of Your will.
You have distinguished, LORD our God,
between sacred and profane,
light and darkness, Israel and the nations,
and between the seventh day and the six days of work.
Our Father, our King,
may the days approaching us bring peace;
may we be free from all sin, cleansed from all iniquity,
holding fast to our reverence of You.
And grace us with the wisdom, understanding
and knowledge that come from You.
Blessed are You, LORD,
who graciously grants knowledge.

REPENTANCE

הֲשִׁיבֵנוּ Bring us back, our Father, to Your Torah.
Draw us near, our King, to Your service.
Lead us back to You in perfect repentance.
Blessed are You, LORD,
who desires repentance.

FORGIVENESS

*Strike the left side of the chest at °.*

סְלַח לָנוּ Forgive us, our Father,
for we have °sinned.
Pardon us, our King,
for we have °transgressed;
for You are the good and forgiving God.
Blessed are You, LORD,
the gracious One who repeatedly forgives.

דעת

אַתָּה חוֹנֵן לְאָדָם דַּעַת, וּמְלַמֵּד לֶאֱנוֹשׁ בִּינָה.
אַתָּה חוֹנַנְתָּנוּ לְמַדַּע תּוֹרָתֶךָ
וַתְּלַמְּדֵנוּ לַעֲשׂוֹת חֻקֵּי רְצוֹנֶךָ
וַתַּבְדֵּל יהוה אֱלֹהֵינוּ בֵּין קֹדֶשׁ לְחֹל
בֵּין אוֹר לְחֹשֶׁךְ, בֵּין יִשְׂרָאֵל לָעַמִּים
בֵּין יוֹם הַשְּׁבִיעִי לְשֵׁשֶׁת יְמֵי הַמַּעֲשֶׂה.
אָבִינוּ מַלְכֵּנוּ
הָחֵל עָלֵינוּ הַיָּמִים הַבָּאִים לִקְרָאתֵנוּ לְשָׁלוֹם
חֲשׂוּכִים מִכָּל חֵטְא וּמְנֻקִּים מִכָּל עָוֹן וּמְדֻבָּקִים בְּיִרְאָתֶךָ.
וְחָנֵּנוּ מֵאִתְּךָ חָכְמָה בִּינָה וָדָעַת.
בָּרוּךְ אַתָּה יהוה, חוֹנֵן הַדָּעַת.

תשובה

הֲשִׁיבֵנוּ אָבִינוּ לְתוֹרָתֶךָ
וְקָרְבֵנוּ מַלְכֵּנוּ לַעֲבוֹדָתֶךָ
וְהַחֲזִירֵנוּ בִּתְשׁוּבָה שְׁלֵמָה לְפָנֶיךָ.
בָּרוּךְ אַתָּה יהוה, הָרוֹצֶה בִּתְשׁוּבָה.

סליחה

*Strike the left side of the chest at °.*

סְלַח לָנוּ אָבִינוּ כִּי °חָטָאנוּ
מְחַל לָנוּ מַלְכֵּנוּ כִּי °פָשָׁעְנוּ
כִּי אֵל טוֹב וְסַלָּח אָתָּה.
בָּרוּךְ אַתָּה יהוה, חַנּוּן הַמַּרְבֶּה לִסְלֹחַ.

REDEMPTION

רְאֵה Look, please, on our affliction,
plead our cause,
and redeem us with a complete redemption,
soon, for Your name's sake,
for You are a powerful God and Redeemer.
Blessed are You, Lord,
the Redeemer of Israel.

HEALING

רְפָאֵנוּ Heal us, Lord, and we shall be healed.
Save us and we shall be saved, for You are our praise.
Bring remedy and healing to all our illnesses and pains,
complete recovery for all our ailments,

---

*The following prayer for a sick person may be said here:*
May it be Your will, O Lord my God and God of my ancestors, that You speedily send a complete recovery from heaven, a healing of both soul and body, to the patient (*name*), son/daughter of (*mother's name*) among the other afflicted of Israel.

---

for You, God, King, are a faithful and compassionate Healer.
Blessed are You, Lord,
Healer of the sick of His people Israel.

PROSPERITY

בָּרֵךְ Bless this year for us, Lord our God,
and all its types of produce for good.
Grant blessing on the face of the earth,
and from its goodness satisfy us,
and grace our year as the best of years, as a blessing,
for You are the good and beneficent God,
who gives the years their blessing.
Blessed are You, Lord,
who blesses the years.

גאולה

רְאֵה נָא בְעָנְיֵנוּ, וְרִיבָה רִיבֵנוּ
וּגְאָלֵנוּ גְאֻלָּה שְׁלֵמָה מְהֵרָה לְמַעַן שְׁמֶךָ
כִּי אֵל גּוֹאֵל חָזָק אָתָּה.
בָּרוּךְ אַתָּה יהוה, גּוֹאֵל יִשְׂרָאֵל.

רפואה

רְפָאֵנוּ יהוה וְנֵרָפֵא
הוֹשִׁיעֵנוּ וְנִוָּשֵׁעָה, כִּי תְהִלָּתֵנוּ אָתָּה
וְהַעֲלֵה אֲרוּכָה וּמַרְפֵּא לְכָל תַּחֲלוּאֵינוּ וּלְכָל מַכְאוֹבֵינוּ
וּרְפוּאָה שְׁלֵמָה לְכָל מַכּוֹתֵינוּ

---

*The following prayer for a sick person may be said here:*

יְהִי רָצוֹן מִלְּפָנֶיךָ יהוה אֱלֹהַי וֵאלֹהֵי אֲבוֹתַי, שֶׁתִּשְׁלַח מְהֵרָה רְפוּאָה שְׁלֵמָה מִן הַשָּׁמַיִם רְפוּאַת הַנֶּפֶשׁ וּרְפוּאַת הַגּוּף לַחוֹלֶה/לַחוֹלָה *name of patient* בֶּן/בַּת *mother's name* בְּתוֹךְ שְׁאָר חוֹלֵי יִשְׂרָאֵל.

---

כִּי אֵל מֶלֶךְ רוֹפֵא נֶאֱמָן וְרַחֲמָן אָתָּה.
בָּרוּךְ אַתָּה יהוה, רוֹפֵא חוֹלֵי עַמּוֹ יִשְׂרָאֵל.

ברכת השנים

בָּרֵךְ עָלֵינוּ יהוה אֱלֹהֵינוּ אֶת הַשָּׁנָה הַזֹּאת
וְאֶת כָּל מִינֵי תְבוּאָתָהּ, לְטוֹבָה
וְתֵן בְּרָכָה עַל פְּנֵי הָאֲדָמָה, וְשַׂבְּעֵנוּ מִטּוּבָהּ
וּבָרֵךְ שְׁנָתֵנוּ כַּשָּׁנִים הַטּוֹבוֹת לִבְרָכָה
כִּי אֵל טוֹב וּמֵטִיב אַתָּה, וּמְבָרֵךְ הַשָּׁנִים.
בָּרוּךְ אַתָּה יהוה, מְבָרֵךְ הַשָּׁנִים.

INGATHERING OF EXILES

תְּקַע Sound the great shofar for our freedom,
raise high the banner to gather our exiles,
and gather us together speedily
from the four quarters of the earth back to our land.
Blessed are You, Lord,
who gathers the dispersed
of His people Israel.

JUSTICE

הָשִׁיבָה Restore our judges as at first,
and our counselors as at the beginning,
and remove from us sorrow and sighing.
May You alone, Lord,
reign over us soon
with loving-kindness and compassion,
with righteousness and justice.
Blessed are You, Lord,
the King of justice.

*If "the King who loves righteousness and justice" is said,*
*then the Amida is not repeated.*

AGAINST INFORMERS

וְלַמַּלְשִׁינִים For the slanderers
let there be no hope,
and may all heretics perish in an instant.
May all Your people's enemies swiftly be cut down.
May You swiftly uproot,
crush, cast down the arrogant,
and obliterate and bring them low and humble them
swiftly in our days.
Blessed are You, Lord,
who destroys enemies and humbles the arrogant.

קיבוץ גלויות

תְּקַע בְּשׁוֹפָר גָּדוֹל לְחֵרוּתֵנוּ
וְשָׂא נֵס לְקַבֵּץ גָּלֻיּוֹתֵינוּ
וְקַבְּצֵנוּ יַחַד מְהֵרָה מֵאַרְבַּע כַּנְפוֹת הָאָרֶץ לְאַרְצֵנוּ.
בָּרוּךְ אַתָּה יהוה
מְקַבֵּץ נִדְחֵי עַמּוֹ יִשְׂרָאֵל.

השבת המשפט

הָשִׁיבָה שׁוֹפְטֵינוּ כְּבָרִאשׁוֹנָה
וְיוֹעֲצֵינוּ כְּבַתְּחִלָּה
וְהָסֵר מִמֶּנּוּ יָגוֹן וַאֲנָחָה
וּמְלֹךְ עָלֵינוּ מְהֵרָה אַתָּה יהוה לְבַדְּךָ
בְּחֶסֶד וּבְרַחֲמִים, בְּצֶדֶק וּבְמִשְׁפָּט.
בָּרוּךְ אַתָּה יהוה
הַמֶּלֶךְ הַמִּשְׁפָּט.

*If* מֶלֶךְ אוֹהֵב צְדָקָה וּמִשְׁפָּט *is said, then the* עמידה *is not repeated.*

ברכת המינים

וְלַמַּלְשִׁינִים אַל תְּהִי תִקְוָה
וְכָל הַמִּינִים כְּרֶגַע יֹאבֵדוּ
וְכָל אוֹיְבֵי עַמְּךָ מְהֵרָה יִכָּרֵתוּ
וְהַזֵּדִים מְהֵרָה
תְעַקֵּר וּתְשַׁבֵּר וּתְמַגֵּר וּתְכַלֵּם וְתַשְׁפִּילֵם וְתַכְנִיעֵם
בִּמְהֵרָה בְיָמֵינוּ.
בָּרוּךְ אַתָּה יהוה
שׁוֹבֵר אוֹיְבִים וּמַכְנִיעַ זֵדִים.

THE RIGHTEOUS

עַל הַצַּדִּיקִים To the righteous, the pious,
the elders of the remnant of Your people the house of Israel,
the survivors among their scholars,
the righteous converts, and to us,
may Your compassion be aroused, please, LORD our God.
Grant a good reward to all
who sincerely trust in Your name.
Set our lot with them,
so that we may never be ashamed,
for in You we trust,
and upon Your great loving-kindness we truly depend.
Blessed are You, LORD,
who is the support and trust of the righteous.

REBUILDING JERUSALEM

וְלִירוּשָׁלַיִם To Jerusalem, Your city,
may You return in compassion,
and may You dwell in it as You promised.
May You rebuild it rapidly in our days
as an everlasting structure,
and install within it soon the throne of David, Your servant.
Blessed are You, LORD,
who builds Jerusalem.

KINGDOM OF DAVID

אֶת צֶמַח May the offshoot of Your servant David soon flower,
and may his pride be raised high
by Your salvation,
for we wait for Your salvation all day.
Blessed are You, LORD,
who makes the glory of salvation flourish.

על הצדיקים

עַל הַצַּדִּיקִים וְעַל הַחֲסִידִים
וְעַל זִקְנֵי שְׁאֵרִית עַמְּךָ בֵּית יִשְׂרָאֵל
וְעַל פְּלֵיטַת בֵּית סוֹפְרֵיהֶם
וְעַל גֵּרֵי הַצֶּדֶק, וְעָלֵינוּ
יֶהֱמוּ נָא רַחֲמֶיךָ, יהוה אֱלֹהֵינוּ
וְתֵן שָׂכָר טוֹב לְכָל הַבּוֹטְחִים בְּשִׁמְךָ בֶּאֱמֶת
וְשִׂים חֶלְקֵנוּ עִמָּהֶם
וּלְעוֹלָם לֹא נֵבוֹשׁ, כִּי בְךָ בָּטָחְנוּ
וְעַל חַסְדְּךָ הַגָּדוֹל בֶּאֱמֶת נִשְׁעָנְנוּ.
בָּרוּךְ אַתָּה יהוה, מִשְׁעָן וּמִבְטָח לַצַּדִּיקִים.

בנין ירושלים

וְלִירוּשָׁלַיִם עִירְךָ בְּרַחֲמִים תָּשׁוּב
וְתִשְׁכֹּן בְּתוֹכָהּ כַּאֲשֶׁר דִּבַּרְתָּ
וּבְנֵה אוֹתָהּ בְּקָרוֹב בְּיָמֵינוּ בִּנְיַן עוֹלָם
וְכִסֵּא דָוִד עַבְדְּךָ מְהֵרָה לְתוֹכָהּ תָּכִין.
בָּרוּךְ אַתָּה יהוה, בּוֹנֵה יְרוּשָׁלָיִם.

משיח בן דוד

אֶת צֶמַח דָּוִד עַבְדְּךָ מְהֵרָה תַצְמִיחַ
וְקַרְנוֹ תָּרוּם בִּישׁוּעָתֶךָ
כִּי לִישׁוּעָתְךָ קִוִּינוּ כָּל הַיּוֹם.
בָּרוּךְ אַתָּה יהוה
מַצְמִיחַ קֶרֶן יְשׁוּעָה.

RESPONSE TO PRAYER

אָב הָרַחֲמָן Compassionate Father,
listen to our voice, LORD our God.
Spare us and have compassion on us,
and in compassion and favor accept our prayer,
for You, God, listen to prayers and pleas.
Do not turn us away, O our King,
empty-handed from Your presence,
Be gracious to us, answer us and listen to our prayer.
For You listen
to the prayer of every mouth.
Blessed are You, LORD,
who listens to prayer.

TEMPLE SERVICE

רְצֵה Find favor, LORD our God, in Your people Israel,
and heed their prayer.
Restore the service to Your most holy House,
and accept soon, in love and favor,
the fire-offerings of Israel and their prayer.
May the service of Your people Israel always find favor with You.
And may our eyes witness Your return to Zion in compassion.
Blessed are You, LORD,
who restores His Presence to Zion.

THANKSGIVING

*Bow at the first nine words.*

מוֹדִים ▾ We give thanks to You,
for You are the LORD our God and God of our ancestors
for ever and all time.
You are the Rock of our lives,
Shield of our salvation from generation to generation.
We will thank You and declare Your praise for our lives,
which are entrusted into Your hand;

שומע תפלה

אָב הָרַחֲמָן, שְׁמַע קוֹלֵנוּ יהוה אֱלֹהֵינוּ
חוּס וְרַחֵם עָלֵינוּ
וְקַבֵּל בְּרַחֲמִים וּבְרָצוֹן אֶת תְּפִלָּתֵנוּ
כִּי אֵל שׁוֹמֵעַ תְּפִלּוֹת וְתַחֲנוּנִים אָתָּה
וּמִלְּפָנֶיךָ מַלְכֵּנוּ רֵיקָם אַל תְּשִׁיבֵנוּ
חָנֵּנוּ וַעֲנֵנוּ וּשְׁמַע תְּפִלָּתֵנוּ
כִּי אַתָּה שׁוֹמֵעַ תְּפִלַּת כָּל פֶּה.
בָּרוּךְ אַתָּה יהוה, שׁוֹמֵעַ תְּפִלָּה.

עבודה

רְצֵה יהוה אֱלֹהֵינוּ בְּעַמְּךָ יִשְׂרָאֵל, וְלִתְפִלָּתָם שְׁעֵה
וְהָשֵׁב אֶת הָעֲבוֹדָה לִדְבִיר בֵּיתֶךָ
וְאִשֵּׁי יִשְׂרָאֵל וּתְפִלָּתָם, מְהֵרָה בְּאַהֲבָה תְקַבֵּל בְּרָצוֹן
וּתְהִי לְרָצוֹן תָּמִיד עֲבוֹדַת יִשְׂרָאֵל עַמֶּךָ.
וְתֶחֱזֶינָה עֵינֵינוּ בְּשׁוּבְךָ לְצִיּוֹן בְּרַחֲמִים.
בָּרוּךְ אַתָּה יהוה, הַמַּחֲזִיר שְׁכִינָתוֹ לְצִיּוֹן.

הודאה

*Bow at the first five words.*

ימוֹדִים אֲנַחְנוּ לָךְ
שָׁאַתָּה הוּא יהוה אֱלֹהֵינוּ וֵאלֹהֵי אֲבוֹתֵינוּ לְעוֹלָם וָעֶד.
צוּר חַיֵּינוּ, מָגֵן יִשְׁעֵנוּ
אַתָּה הוּא לְדוֹר וָדוֹר.
נוֹדֶה לְּךָ וּנְסַפֵּר תְּהִלָּתֶךָ
עַל חַיֵּינוּ הַמְּסוּרִים בְּיָדֶךָ

for our souls, which are placed in Your charge;
for Your miracles which are with us every day;
and for Your wonders and favors at all times,
evening, morning and midday.
You are good – for Your compassion never fails.
You are compassionate – for Your loving-kindnesses never cease.
For we have always placed our hope in You.
For all these things may Your name be blessed
and exalted and raised up,
our King, continually, for ever and all time.

וּכְתֹב And write for a good life,
all the children of Your covenant.

*If forgotten, the Amida is not repeated.*

Let all that lives thank You, Selah! and praise and bless
Your great name in truth, always, because it is good,
God, our Savior and Help, Selah! the beneficent God.
▾Blessed are You, LORD, whose name is "the Good"
and to whom thanks are due.

PEACE

שָׁלוֹם רָב Grant great peace to Your people Israel for ever,
for You are the sovereign LORD of all peace;
And may it be good in Your eyes to bless us
and all Your people Israel
at every time, in every hour, with Your peace.

בְּסֵפֶר חַיִּים In the book of life, blessing, peace and prosperity,
and good decrees, salvations and consolations
may we and all Your people the house of Israel
be remembered and written before You
for a good life, and for peace.

*If forgotten, the Amida is not repeated.*

Blessed are You, LORD, who blesses His people Israel with peace.

וְעַל נִשְׁמוֹתֵינוּ הַפְּקוּדוֹת לָךְ, וְעַל נִסֶּיךָ שֶׁבְּכָל יוֹם עִמָּנוּ
וְעַל נִפְלְאוֹתֶיךָ וְטוֹבוֹתֶיךָ שֶׁבְּכָל עֵת, עֶרֶב וָבֹקֶר וְצָהֳרָיִם.
הַטּוֹב, כִּי לֹא כָלוּ רַחֲמֶיךָ
וְהַמְרַחֵם, כִּי לֹא תַמּוּ חֲסָדֶיךָ
כִּי מֵעוֹלָם קִוִּינוּ לָךְ.
וְעַל כֻּלָּם
יִתְבָּרַךְ וְיִתְרוֹמַם וְיִתְנַשֵּׂא שִׁמְךָ מַלְכֵּנוּ תָּמִיד לְעוֹלָם וָעֶד.

וּכְתֹב לְחַיִּים טוֹבִים כָּל בְּנֵי בְרִיתֶךָ.

*If forgotten, the* עמידה *is not repeated.*

וְכֹל הַחַיִּים יוֹדוּךָ סֶּלָה
וִיהַלְלוּ וִיבָרְכוּ אֶת שִׁמְךָ הַגָּדוֹל בֶּאֱמֶת לְעוֹלָם כִּי טוֹב
הָאֵל יְשׁוּעָתֵנוּ וְעֶזְרָתֵנוּ סֶלָה, הָאֵל הַטּוֹב.
בָּרוּךְ אַתָּה יהוה, הַטּוֹב שִׁמְךָ וּלְךָ נָאֶה לְהוֹדוֹת.

ברכת שלום

שָׁלוֹם רָב עַל יִשְׂרָאֵל עַמְּךָ תָּשִׂים לְעוֹלָם
כִּי אַתָּה הוּא מֶלֶךְ אָדוֹן לְכָל הַשָּׁלוֹם.
וְטוֹב יִהְיֶה בְּעֵינֶיךָ לְבָרְכֵנוּ, וּלְבָרֵךְ אֶת כָּל עַמְּךָ יִשְׂרָאֵל
בְּכָל עֵת וּבְכָל שָׁעָה בִּשְׁלוֹמֶךָ.

בְּסֵפֶר חַיִּים, בְּרָכָה וְשָׁלוֹם, וּפַרְנָסָה טוֹבָה
וּגְזֵרוֹת טוֹבוֹת, יְשׁוּעוֹת וְנֶחָמוֹת, נִזָּכֵר וְנִכָּתֵב לְפָנֶיךָ
אֲנַחְנוּ וְכָל עַמְּךָ בֵּית יִשְׂרָאֵל לְחַיִּים טוֹבִים וּלְשָׁלוֹם.

*If forgotten, the* עמידה *is not repeated.*

בָּרוּךְ אַתָּה יהוה, הַמְבָרֵךְ אֶת עַמּוֹ יִשְׂרָאֵל בַּשָּׁלוֹם.

*Some say the following verse. See law 64.*

May the words of my mouth and the meditation of my heart *Ps. 19*
find favor before You, LORD, my Rock and Redeemer.

אֱלֹהַי My God, *Berakhot 17a*
guard my tongue from evil and my lips from deceitful speech.
To those who curse me, let my soul be silent;
may my soul be to all like the dust.
Open my heart to Your Torah
and let my soul pursue Your commandments.
As for all who rise up or plan evil against me,
swiftly thwart their counsel and frustrate their plans.

*Some add this prayer:*

יְהִי רָצוֹן May it be Your will, LORD my God, God of my ancestors,
that envy of no man may rise up in me, nor envy of me in any other;
that I will not be angry today, nor make You angry;
and save me from my evil impulse, placing humility and modesty into my heart.
Our King and God, make Your name One in Your world;
build up Your city, establish Your House and complete Your Sanctuary,
gather in the exiles, redeem Your flock, and have Your congregation rejoice.

Act for the sake of Your name;
act for the sake of Your right hand;
act for the sake of Your Torah;
act for the sake of Your holiness.
That Your beloved ones may be delivered, *Ps. 60*
save with Your right hand and answer me.
May the words of my mouth and the meditation of my heart *Ps. 19*
find favor before You, LORD, my Rock and Redeemer.

*Bow, take three steps back, then bow, first left, then right, then center, while saying:*

May He who makes peace in His high places,
make peace for us and all Israel – and say: Amen.

יְהִי רָצוֹן May it be Your will, LORD our God and God of our ancestors,
that the Temple be rebuilt speedily in our days, and grant us a share in Your Torah.
And there we will serve You with reverence,
as in the days of old and as in former years.
Then the offering of Judah and Jerusalem *Mal. 3*
will be pleasing to the LORD as in the days of old and as in former years.

*Some say the following verse. See law 64.*

יִהְיוּ לְרָצוֹן אִמְרֵי־פִי וְהֶגְיוֹן לִבִּי לְפָנֶיךָ, יהוה צוּרִי וְגֹאֲלִי: תהלים יט

ברכות יז.

אֱלֹהַי
נְצֹר לְשׁוֹנִי מֵרָע וּשְׂפָתַי מִדַּבֵּר מִרְמָה
וְלִמְקַלְלַי נַפְשִׁי תִדֹּם, וְנַפְשִׁי כֶּעָפָר לַכֹּל תִּהְיֶה.
פְּתַח לִבִּי בְּתוֹרָתֶךָ, וְאַחֲרֵי מִצְוֹתֶיךָ תִּרְדֹּף נַפְשִׁי.
וְכָל הַקָּמִים וְהַחוֹשְׁבִים עָלַי רָעָה
מְהֵרָה הָפֵר עֲצָתָם וְקַלְקֵל מַחֲשַׁבְתָּם.

*Some add this prayer:*

יְהִי רָצוֹן מִלְּפָנֶיךָ, יהוה אֱלֹהַי וֵאלֹהֵי אֲבוֹתַי
שֶׁלֹּא תַעֲלֶה קִנְאַת אָדָם עָלַי, וְלֹא קִנְאָתִי עַל אֲחֵרִים
וְשֶׁלֹּא אֶכְעֹס הַיּוֹם, וְשֶׁלֹּא אַכְעִיסֶךָ
וְתַצִּילֵנִי מִיֵּצֶר הָרָע, וְתֵן בְּלִבִּי הַכְנָעָה וַעֲנָוָה.
מַלְכֵּנוּ וֵאלֹהֵינוּ, יַחֵד שִׁמְךָ בְּעוֹלָמֶךָ
בְּנֵה עִירָךְ, יַסֵּד בֵּיתְךָ וְשַׁכְלֵל הֵיכָלֶךָ
וְקַבֵּץ קִבּוּץ גָּלֻיּוֹת, וּפְדֵה צֹאנֶךָ וְשַׂמַּח עֲדָתֶךָ.

עֲשֵׂה לְמַעַן שְׁמֶךָ, עֲשֵׂה לְמַעַן יְמִינֶךָ
עֲשֵׂה לְמַעַן תּוֹרָתֶךָ, עֲשֵׂה לְמַעַן קְדֻשָּׁתֶךָ.
לְמַעַן יֵחָלְצוּן יְדִידֶיךָ, הוֹשִׁיעָה יְמִינְךָ וַעֲנֵנִי: תהלים ס
יִהְיוּ לְרָצוֹן אִמְרֵי־פִי וְהֶגְיוֹן לִבִּי לְפָנֶיךָ, יהוה צוּרִי וְגֹאֲלִי: תהלים יט

*Bow, take three steps back, then bow, first left, then right, then center, while saying:*

עֹשֶׂה הַשָּׁלוֹם בִּמְרוֹמָיו
הוּא יַעֲשֶׂה שָׁלוֹם עָלֵינוּ וְעַל כָּל יִשְׂרָאֵל, וְאִמְרוּ אָמֵן.

יְהִי רָצוֹן מִלְּפָנֶיךָ יהוה אֱלֹהֵינוּ וֵאלֹהֵי אֲבוֹתֵינוּ
שֶׁיִּבָּנֶה בֵּית הַמִּקְדָּשׁ בִּמְהֵרָה בְיָמֵינוּ, וְתֵן חֶלְקֵנוּ בְּתוֹרָתֶךָ
וְשָׁם נַעֲבָדְךָ בְּיִרְאָה כִּימֵי עוֹלָם וּכְשָׁנִים קַדְמֹנִיּוֹת.
וְעָרְבָה לַיהוה מִנְחַת יְהוּדָה וִירוּשָׁלָםִ כִּימֵי עוֹלָם וּכְשָׁנִים קַדְמֹנִיּוֹת: מלאכי ג

FULL KADDISH

*Leader:* יִתְגַּדַּל Magnified and sanctified may His great name be,
in the world He created by His will.
May He establish His kingdom,
make His salvation flourish,
and hasten His messiah,
in your lifetime and in your days,
and in the lifetime of all the house of Israel,
swiftly and soon –
and say: Amen.

*All:* May His great name be blessed for ever and all time.

*Leader:* Blessed and praised, glorified and exalted,
raised and honored,
uplifted and lauded be
the name of the Holy One,
blessed be He, beyond any blessing,
song, praise and consolation
uttered in the world –
and say: Amen.

May the prayers and pleas of all the house of Israel
be accepted by their Father in heaven –
and say: Amen.

May there be great peace from heaven,
and a good life for us and all Israel –
and say: Amen.

*Bow, take three steps back, as if taking leave of the Divine Presence, then bow, first left, then right, then center, while saying:*

May He who makes peace in His high places,
make peace for us and all Israel –
and say: Amen.

## קדיש שלם

ש״ץ: יִתְגַּדַּל וְיִתְקַדַּשׁ שְׁמֵהּ רַבָּא (קהל: אָמֵן)
בְּעָלְמָא דִּי בְרָא כִרְעוּתֵהּ
וְיַמְלִיךְ מַלְכוּתֵהּ
וְיַצְמַח פֻּרְקָנֵהּ וִיקָרֵב מְשִׁיחֵהּ (קהל: אָמֵן)
בְּחַיֵּיכוֹן וּבְיוֹמֵיכוֹן וּבְחַיֵּי דְכָל בֵּית יִשְׂרָאֵל
בַּעֲגָלָא וּבִזְמַן קָרִיב, וְאִמְרוּ אָמֵן. (קהל: אָמֵן)

קהל וש״ץ: יְהֵא שְׁמֵהּ רַבָּא מְבָרַךְ לְעָלַם וּלְעָלְמֵי עָלְמַיָּא.

ש״ץ: יִתְבָּרַךְ וְיִשְׁתַּבַּח וְיִתְפָּאַר וְיִתְרוֹמַם וְיִתְנַשֵּׂא
וְיִתְהַדָּר וְיִתְעַלֶּה וְיִתְהַלָּל
שְׁמֵהּ דְּקֻדְשָׁא בְּרִיךְ הוּא (קהל: אָמֵן)
לְעֵלָּא לְעֵלָּא מִכָּל בִּרְכָתָא
וְשִׁירָתָא, תֻּשְׁבְּחָתָא וְנֶחֱמָתָא
דַּאֲמִירָן בְּעָלְמָא, וְאִמְרוּ אָמֵן. (קהל: אָמֵן)

תִּתְקַבַּל צְלוֹתְהוֹן וּבָעוּתְהוֹן דְּכָל בֵּית יִשְׂרָאֵל
קֳדָם אֲבוּהוֹן דִּי בִשְׁמַיָּא, וְאִמְרוּ אָמֵן. (קהל: אָמֵן)

יְהֵא שְׁלָמָא רַבָּא מִן שְׁמַיָּא
וְחַיִּים טוֹבִים עָלֵינוּ וְעַל כָּל יִשְׂרָאֵל, וְאִמְרוּ אָמֵן. (קהל: אָמֵן)

*Bow, take three steps back, as if taking leave of the Divine Presence, then bow, first left, then right, then center, while saying:*

עֹשֶׂה הַשָּׁלוֹם בִּמְרוֹמָיו
הוּא יַעֲשֶׂה שָׁלוֹם עָלֵינוּ
וְעַל כָּל יִשְׂרָאֵל, וְאִמְרוּ אָמֵן. (קהל: אָמֵן)

## HAVDALA

*Holding the cup of wine in the right hand, say:*

Please pay attention, my masters.

Blessed are You, LORD our God, King of the Universe,
who creates the fruit of the vine.

Blessed are You, LORD our God, King of the Universe,
who distinguishes between sacred and secular,
between light and darkness, between Israel and the nations,
between the seventh day and the six days of work.
Blessed are You, LORD, who distinguishes between sacred and secular.

*Some communities say Psalm 121, followed by Mourner's Kaddish and Barekhu, "Bless the LORD":*

שִׁיר לַמַּעֲלוֹת A song of ascents. I lift my eyes up to the hills; from where will my help come? My help comes from the LORD, Maker of heaven and earth. He will not let your foot stumble; He who guards you does not slumber. See: the Guardian of Israel neither slumbers nor sleeps. The LORD is your Guardian; the LORD is your Shade at your right hand. The sun will not strike you by day, nor the moon by night. The LORD will guard you from all harm; He will guard your life. The LORD will guard your going and coming, now and for evermore. *Ps. 121*

### MOURNER'S KADDISH

*The following prayer, said by mourners, requires the presence of a minyan.*
*A transliteration can be found on page 1095.*

*Mourner:* יִתְגַּדַּל Magnified and sanctified may His great name be,
in the world He created by His will.
May He establish His kingdom,
make His salvation flourish,
and hasten His messiah,
in your lifetime and in your days,
and in the lifetime of all the house of Israel,
swiftly and soon –
and say: Amen.

# הבדלה

*Holding the cup of wine in the right hand, say:*

סַבְרִי מָרָנָן

בָּרוּךְ אַתָּה יהוה אֱלֹהֵינוּ מֶלֶךְ הָעוֹלָם, בּוֹרֵא פְּרִי הַגָּפֶן.

בָּרוּךְ אַתָּה יהוה אֱלֹהֵינוּ מֶלֶךְ הָעוֹלָם
הַמַּבְדִּיל בֵּין קֹדֶשׁ לְחֹל, בֵּין אוֹר לְחֹשֶׁךְ
בֵּין יִשְׂרָאֵל לָעַמִּים, בֵּין יוֹם הַשְּׁבִיעִי לְשֵׁשֶׁת יְמֵי הַמַּעֲשֶׂה.
בָּרוּךְ אַתָּה יהוה, הַמַּבְדִּיל בֵּין קֹדֶשׁ לְחֹל.

*Some communities say* שִׁיר לַמַּעֲלוֹת *followed by* קדיש יתום *and* בָּרְכוּ:

שִׁיר לַמַּעֲלוֹת, אֶשָּׂא עֵינַי אֶל־הֶהָרִים, מֵאַיִן יָבֹא עֶזְרִי: עֶזְרִי מֵעִם תהלים קכא
יהוה, עֹשֵׂה שָׁמַיִם וָאָרֶץ: אַל־יִתֵּן לַמּוֹט רַגְלֶךָ, אַל־יָנוּם שֹׁמְרֶךָ:
הִנֵּה לֹא־יָנוּם וְלֹא יִישָׁן שׁוֹמֵר יִשְׂרָאֵל: יהוה שֹׁמְרֶךָ, יהוה צִלְּךָ
עַל־יַד יְמִינֶךָ: יוֹמָם הַשֶּׁמֶשׁ לֹא־יַכֶּכָּה, וְיָרֵחַ בַּלָּיְלָה: יהוה יִשְׁמָרְךָ
מִכָּל־רָע, יִשְׁמֹר אֶת־נַפְשֶׁךָ: יהוה יִשְׁמָר־צֵאתְךָ וּבוֹאֶךָ, מֵעַתָּה
וְעַד־עוֹלָם:

### קדיש יתום

*The following prayer, said by mourners, requires the presence of a* מנין.
*A transliteration can be found on page 1095.*

אבל: יִתְגַּדַּל וְיִתְקַדַּשׁ שְׁמֵהּ רַבָּא (קהל: אָמֵן)
בְּעָלְמָא דִּי בְרָא כִרְעוּתֵהּ
וְיַמְלִיךְ מַלְכוּתֵהּ
וְיַצְמַח פֻּרְקָנֵהּ וִיקָרֵב מְשִׁיחֵהּ (קהל: אָמֵן)
בְּחַיֵּיכוֹן וּבְיוֹמֵיכוֹן וּבְחַיֵּי דְכָל בֵּית יִשְׂרָאֵל
בַּעֲגָלָא וּבִזְמַן קָרִיב, וְאִמְרוּ אָמֵן. (קהל: אָמֵן)

*All:* May His great name be blessed for ever and all time.

*Mourner:* Blessed and praised, glorified and exalted,
raised and honored, uplifted and lauded
be the name of the Holy One,
blessed be He,
beyond any blessing, song, praise and consolation
uttered in the world –
and say: Amen.

May there be great peace from heaven,
and a good life for us and all Israel –
and say: Amen.

*Bow, take three steps back, as if taking leave of the Divine Presence, then bow, first left, then right, then center, while saying:*

May He who makes peace in His high places,
make peace for us and all Israel –
and say: Amen.

*The person saying Kaddish adds:*
Bless the LORD, the blessed One.

*Cong:* Bless the LORD, the blessed One,
for ever and all time.

*Mourner:* Bless the LORD, the blessed One,
for ever and all time.

*Stand while saying Aleinu. Bow at ▾.*

עָלֵינוּ It is our duty to praise the Master of all,
and ascribe greatness to the Author of creation,
who has not made us like the nations of the lands,
nor placed us like the families of the earth;
who has not made our portion like theirs,
nor our destiny like all their multitudes.
(For they worship vanity and emptiness,
and pray to a god who cannot save.)

קהל ואבל: יְהֵא שְׁמֵהּ רַבָּא מְבָרַךְ לְעָלַם וּלְעָלְמֵי עָלְמַיָּא.

אבל: יִתְבָּרַךְ וְיִשְׁתַּבַּח וְיִתְפָּאַר
וְיִתְרוֹמַם וְיִתְנַשֵּׂא וְיִתְהַדָּר וְיִתְעַלֶּה וְיִתְהַלָּל
שְׁמֵהּ דְּקֻדְשָׁא בְּרִיךְ הוּא (קהל: אָמֵן)
לְעֵלָּא לְעֵלָּא מִכָּל בִּרְכָתָא
וְשִׁירָתָא, תֻּשְׁבְּחָתָא וְנֶחֱמָתָא
דַּאֲמִירָן בְּעָלְמָא, וְאִמְרוּ אָמֵן. (קהל: אָמֵן)

יְהֵא שְׁלָמָא רַבָּא מִן שְׁמַיָּא
וְחַיִּים טוֹבִים עָלֵינוּ וְעַל כָּל יִשְׂרָאֵל, וְאִמְרוּ אָמֵן. (קהל: אָמֵן)

*Bow, take three steps back, as if taking leave of the Divine Presence, then bow, first left, then right, then center, while saying:*

עֹשֶׂה הַשָּׁלוֹם בִּמְרוֹמָיו
הוּא יַעֲשֶׂה שָׁלוֹם
עָלֵינוּ וְעַל כָּל יִשְׂרָאֵל, וְאִמְרוּ אָמֵן. (קהל: אָמֵן)

*The person saying* קדיש *adds:*

בָּרְכוּ אֶת יהוה הַמְבֹרָךְ.
קהל: בָּרוּךְ יהוה הַמְבֹרָךְ לְעוֹלָם וָעֶד.
אבל: בָּרוּךְ יהוה הַמְבֹרָךְ לְעוֹלָם וָעֶד.

*Stand while saying* עָלֵינוּ*. Bow at* ▾.

עָלֵינוּ לְשַׁבֵּחַ לַאֲדוֹן הַכֹּל, לָתֵת גְּדֻלָּה לְיוֹצֵר בְּרֵאשִׁית
שֶׁלֹּא עָשָׂנוּ כְּגוֹיֵי הָאֲרָצוֹת, וְלֹא שָׂמָנוּ כְּמִשְׁפְּחוֹת הָאֲדָמָה
שֶׁלֹּא שָׂם חֶלְקֵנוּ כָּהֶם וְגוֹרָלֵנוּ כְּכָל הֲמוֹנָם.
(שֶׁהֵם מִשְׁתַּחֲוִים לְהֶבֶל וָרִיק וּמִתְפַּלְלִים אֶל אֵל לֹא יוֹשִׁיעַ.)

▾But we bow in worship and thank the Supreme King of kings,
the Holy One, blessed be He,
who extends the heavens and establishes the earth,
whose throne of glory is in the heavens above,
and whose power's Presence is in the highest of heights.
He is our God; there is no other.
Truly He is our King, there is none else, as it is written in His Torah:
"You shall know and take to heart this day *Deut. 4*
that the LORD is God,
in the heavens above and on the earth below.
There is no other."

Therefore, we place our hope in You, LORD our God,
that we may soon see the glory of Your power,
when You will remove abominations from the earth,
and idols will be utterly destroyed,
when the world will be perfected
under the sovereignty of the Almighty,
when all humanity will call on Your name,
to turn all the earth's wicked toward You.
All the world's inhabitants will realize and know
that to You every knee must bow and every tongue swear loyalty.
Before You, LORD our God, they will kneel and bow down
and give honor to Your glorious name.
They will all accept the yoke of Your kingdom,
and You will reign over them soon and for ever.
For the kingdom is Yours, and to all eternity You will reign in glory,
as it is written in Your Torah: "The LORD will reign for ever and ever." *Ex. 15*
▸ And it is said: "Then the LORD shall be King over all the earth; *Zech. 14*
on that day the LORD shall be One and His name One."

*Some add:*

Have no fear of sudden terror or of the ruin when it overtakes the wicked. *Prov. 3*
Devise your strategy, but it will be thwarted; propose your plan, *Is. 8*
but it will not stand, for God is with us. When you grow old, I will still be the same. *Is. 46*
When your hair turns gray, I will still carry you. I made you, I will bear you,
I will carry you, and I will rescue you.

וַאֲנַחְנוּ כּוֹרְעִים וּמִשְׁתַּחֲוִים וּמוֹדִים
לִפְנֵי מֶלֶךְ מַלְכֵי הַמְּלָכִים, הַקָּדוֹשׁ בָּרוּךְ הוּא
שֶׁהוּא נוֹטֶה שָׁמַיִם וְיוֹסֵד אָרֶץ
וּמוֹשַׁב יְקָרוֹ בַּשָּׁמַיִם מִמַּעַל, וּשְׁכִינַת עֻזּוֹ בְּגָבְהֵי מְרוֹמִים.
הוּא אֱלֹהֵינוּ, אֵין עוֹד.
אֱמֶת מַלְכֵּנוּ, אֶפֶס זוּלָתוֹ, כַּכָּתוּב בְּתוֹרָתוֹ
וְיָדַעְתָּ הַיּוֹם וַהֲשֵׁבֹתָ אֶל־לְבָבֶךָ דברים ד
כִּי יהוה הוּא הָאֱלֹהִים בַּשָּׁמַיִם מִמַּעַל וְעַל־הָאָרֶץ מִתָּחַת
אֵין עוֹד:

וְעַל כֵּן נְקַוֶּה לְּךָ יהוה אֱלֹהֵינוּ, לִרְאוֹת מְהֵרָה בְּתִפְאֶרֶת עֻזֶּךָ
לְהַעֲבִיר גִּלּוּלִים מִן הָאָרֶץ, וְהָאֱלִילִים כָּרוֹת יִכָּרֵתוּן
לְתַקֵּן עוֹלָם בְּמַלְכוּת שַׁדַּי.
וְכָל בְּנֵי בָשָׂר יִקְרְאוּ בִשְׁמֶךָ לְהַפְנוֹת אֵלֶיךָ כָּל רִשְׁעֵי אָרֶץ.
יַכִּירוּ וְיֵדְעוּ כָּל יוֹשְׁבֵי תֵבֵל
כִּי לְךָ תִּכְרַע כָּל בֶּרֶךְ, תִּשָּׁבַע כָּל לָשׁוֹן.
לְפָנֶיךָ יהוה אֱלֹהֵינוּ יִכְרְעוּ וְיִפֹּלוּ, וְלִכְבוֹד שִׁמְךָ יְקָר יִתֵּנוּ
וִיקַבְּלוּ כֻלָּם אֶת עֹל מַלְכוּתֶךָ
וְתִמְלֹךְ עֲלֵיהֶם מְהֵרָה לְעוֹלָם וָעֶד.
כִּי הַמַּלְכוּת שֶׁלְּךָ הִיא וּלְעוֹלְמֵי עַד תִּמְלֹךְ בְּכָבוֹד
כַּכָּתוּב בְּתוֹרָתֶךָ, יהוה יִמְלֹךְ לְעֹלָם וָעֶד: שמות טו
◂ וְנֶאֱמַר, וְהָיָה יהוה לְמֶלֶךְ עַל־כָּל־הָאָרֶץ זכריה יד
בַּיּוֹם הַהוּא יִהְיֶה יהוה אֶחָד וּשְׁמוֹ אֶחָד:

*Some add:*

אַל־תִּירָא מִפַּחַד פִּתְאֹם וּמִשֹּׁאַת רְשָׁעִים כִּי תָבֹא: משלי ג
עֻצוּ עֵצָה וְתֻפָר, דַּבְּרוּ דָבָר וְלֹא יָקוּם, כִּי עִמָּנוּ אֵל: ישעיה ח
וְעַד־זִקְנָה אֲנִי הוּא, וְעַד־שֵׂיבָה אֲנִי אֶסְבֹּל, אֲנִי עָשִׂיתִי וַאֲנִי אֶשָּׂא וַאֲנִי אֶסְבֹּל וַאֲמַלֵּט: ישעיה מו

## MOURNER'S KADDISH

*The following prayer, said by mourners, requires the presence of a minyan. A transliteration can be found on page 1095.*

*Mourner:* יִתְגַּדַּל Magnified and sanctified
may His great name be,
in the world He created by His will.
May He establish His kingdom,
make His salvation flourish,
and hasten His messiah,
in your lifetime and in your days,
and in the lifetime of all the house of Israel,
swiftly and soon –
and say: Amen.

*All:* May His great name be blessed
for ever and all time.

*Mourner:* Blessed and praised, glorified and exalted,
raised and honored, uplifted and lauded
be the name of the Holy One,
blessed be He,
beyond any blessing,
song, praise and consolation
uttered in the world –
and say: Amen.

May there be great peace from heaven,
and a good life for us and all Israel –
and say: Amen.

*Bow, take three steps back, as if taking leave of the Divine Presence, then bow, first left, then right, then center, while saying:*

May He who makes peace in His high places,
make peace for us and all Israel –
and say: Amen.

## קדיש יתום

*The following prayer, said by mourners, requires the presence of a* מנין.
*A transliteration can be found on page 1095.*

*A transliteration can be found on page 1095.*

אבל: יִתְגַּדַּל וְיִתְקַדַּשׁ שְׁמֵהּ רַבָּא (קהל: אָמֵן)
בְּעָלְמָא דִּי בְרָא כִרְעוּתֵהּ
וְיַמְלִיךְ מַלְכוּתֵהּ
וְיַצְמַח פֻּרְקָנֵהּ וִיקָרֵב מְשִׁיחֵהּ (קהל: אָמֵן)
בְּחַיֵּיכוֹן וּבְיוֹמֵיכוֹן וּבְחַיֵּי דְכָל בֵּית יִשְׂרָאֵל
בַּעֲגָלָא וּבִזְמַן קָרִיב
וְאִמְרוּ אָמֵן. (קהל: אָמֵן)

קהל ואבל: יְהֵא שְׁמֵהּ רַבָּא מְבָרַךְ לְעָלַם וּלְעָלְמֵי עָלְמַיָּא.

אבל: יִתְבָּרַךְ וְיִשְׁתַּבַּח וְיִתְפָּאַר
וְיִתְרוֹמַם וְיִתְנַשֵּׂא וְיִתְהַדָּר וְיִתְעַלֶּה וְיִתְהַלָּל
שְׁמֵהּ דְּקֻדְשָׁא בְּרִיךְ הוּא (קהל: אָמֵן)
לְעֵלָּא לְעֵלָּא מִכָּל בִּרְכָתָא
וְשִׁירָתָא, תֻּשְׁבְּחָתָא וְנֶחֱמָתָא, דַּאֲמִירָן בְּעָלְמָא,
וְאִמְרוּ אָמֵן. (קהל: אָמֵן)

יְהֵא שְׁלָמָא רַבָּא מִן שְׁמַיָּא
וְחַיִּים טוֹבִים עָלֵינוּ וְעַל כָּל יִשְׂרָאֵל
וְאִמְרוּ אָמֵן. (קהל: אָמֵן)

*Bow, take three steps back, as if taking leave of the Divine Presence, then bow, first left, then right, then center, while saying:*

עֹשֶׂה הַשָּׁלוֹם בִּמְרוֹמָיו
הוּא יַעֲשֶׂה שָׁלוֹם עָלֵינוּ וְעַל כָּל יִשְׂרָאֵל
וְאִמְרוּ אָמֵן. (קהל: אָמֵן)

## BRIT MILA

*When the baby is brought in, all stand and say:*

Blessed is he who comes.

*The mohel (in some congregations, all) say (in Israel omit):*

וַיְדַבֵּר The LORD spoke to Moses, saying: Pinehas the son of Elazar, the son of Aaron the priest, turned back My rage from the children of Israel, when he was zealous for Me among them, and I did not annihilate the children of Israel in My own zeal. And so tell him, that I now give him My covenant for peace. *Num. 25*

*The following verses, through "LORD, please, grant us success," are only said in Israel.*

*Mohel:* Happy are those You choose and bring near to dwell in Your courts. *Ps. 65*

*All:* May we be sated with the goodness of Your House,
Your holy Temple.

*The father takes the baby in his hands and says quietly:*

אִם אֶשְׁכָּחֵךְ If I forget you, O Jerusalem, may my right hand forget its skill. May my tongue cling to the roof of my mouth, if I do not remember you, if I do not set Jerusalem above my highest joy. *Ps. 137*

*The father says aloud, followed by the congregation:*

Listen, Israel: the LORD is our God, the LORD is One. *Deut. 6*

*The Mohel, followed by the congregation,*
*recites each of the following three phrases twice:*

The LORD is King, the LORD was King,
the LORD shall be King for ever and all time.
LORD, please, save us. *Ps. 118*
LORD, please, grant us success.

*The baby is placed on Eliyahu's seat, and the Mohel says:*

This is the throne of Elijah the prophet, may he be remembered for good.

*The Mohel continues:*

לִישׁוּעָתְךָ For Your salvation I wait, O LORD. I await Your deliverance, LORD, and I observe Your commandments. Elijah, angel of the covenant, behold: yours is before you. Stand at my right hand and be close to me. *Gen. 49 Ps. 119*
I await Your deliverance, LORD. I rejoice in Your word like one who finds *Ibid.*

# סדר ברית מילה

*When the baby is brought in, all stand and say:*

## בָּרוּךְ הַבָּא.

*The* מוהל *(in some congregations, all) say (in* ארץ ישראל *omit):*

במדבר כה וַיְדַבֵּר יהוה אֶל־מֹשֶׁה לֵּאמֹר: פִּינְחָס בֶּן־אֶלְעָזָר בֶּן־אַהֲרֹן הַכֹּהֵן הֵשִׁיב אֶת־חֲמָתִי מֵעַל בְּנֵי־יִשְׂרָאֵל, בְּקַנְאוֹ אֶת־קִנְאָתִי בְּתוֹכָם, וְלֹא־כִלִּיתִי אֶת־בְּנֵי־יִשְׂרָאֵל בְּקִנְאָתִי: לָכֵן אֱמֹר, הִנְנִי נֹתֵן לוֹ אֶת־בְּרִיתִי שָׁלוֹם:

*The following verses, through* אָנָּא יהוה הַצְלִיחָה נָּא *are only said in Israel.*

תהלים סה המוהל: אַשְׁרֵי תִּבְחַר וּתְקָרֵב, יִשְׁכֹּן חֲצֵרֶיךָ

הקהל: נִשְׂבְּעָה בְּטוּב בֵּיתֶךָ, קְדֹשׁ הֵיכָלֶךָ:

*The father takes the baby in his hands and says quietly:*

תהלים קלז אִם־אֶשְׁכָּחֵךְ יְרוּשָׁלָםִ, תִּשְׁכַּח יְמִינִי: תִּדְבַּק לְשׁוֹנִי לְחִכִּי אִם־לֹא אֶזְכְּרֵכִי, אִם־לֹא אַעֲלֶה אֶת־יְרוּשָׁלַםִ עַל רֹאשׁ שִׂמְחָתִי:

*The father says aloud, followed by the* קהל*:*

דברים ו שְׁמַע יִשְׂרָאֵל, יהוה אֱלֹהֵינוּ, יהוה אֶחָד:

*The* מוהל*, followed by the* קהל*, recites each of the following three phrases twice:*

יהוה מֶלֶךְ, יהוה מָלָךְ, יהוה יִמְלֹךְ לְעוֹלָם וָעֶד.

תהלים קיח אָנָּא יהוה הוֹשִׁיעָה נָּא

אָנָּא יהוה הַצְלִיחָה נָא:

*The baby is placed on the* כסא של אליהו*, and the* מוהל *says:*

## זֶה הַכִּסֵּא שֶׁל אֵלִיָּהוּ הַנָּבִיא זָכוּר לַטּוֹב.

*The* מוהל *continues:*

בראשית מט תהלים קיט לִישׁוּעָתְךָ קִוִּיתִי יהוה: שִׂבַּרְתִּי לִישׁוּעָתְךָ יהוה, וּמִצְוֹתֶיךָ עָשִׂיתִי: אֵלִיָּהוּ מַלְאַךְ הַבְּרִית, הִנֵּה שֶׁלְּךָ לְפָנֶיךָ, עֲמֹד עַל יְמִינִי וְסָמְכֵנִי.

תהלים קיט שִׂבַּרְתִּי לִישׁוּעָתְךָ יהוה: שָׂשׂ אָנֹכִי עַל־אִמְרָתֶךָ, כְּמוֹצֵא שָׁלָל רָב:

much spoil. Those who love Your Torah have great peace, and there is no stumbling block before them. Happy are those You choose and bring near to dwell in Your courts. *Ps. 65*

*All respond:*

May we be sated with the goodness of Your House, Your holy Temple.

*The baby is placed on the knees of the Sandak, and the Mohel says:*

בָּרוּךְ Blessed are You, LORD our God, King of the Universe,
who has made us holy through His commandments,
and has commanded us concerning circumcision.

*Immediately after the circumcision, the father says:*

בָּרוּךְ Blessed are You, LORD our God, King of the Universe,
who has made us holy through His commandments,
and has commanded us to bring him [our son]
into the covenant of Abraham, our father.

*In Israel the father adds (some outside Israel add it as well):*

בָּרוּךְ Blessed are You, LORD our God, King of the Universe,
who has given us life, sustained us, and brought us to this time.

*All respond:*

אָמֵן Amen. Just as he has entered into the covenant,
so may he enter into Torah, marriage and good deeds.

---

*the covenant of Abraham, our father* – a separate blessing, referring not to the circumcision itself, but what it is a sign of – namely entry into the life of the covenant, under the sheltering wings of the Divine Presence (*Arukh HaShulḥan, Yoreh De'ah* 365:5); (3) *Who made the beloved one* [*Isaac*] *holy from the womb* – a blessing of acknowledgment. Isaac was the first child to have a circumcision at the age of eight days. He was consecrated before birth, Abraham having been told that it would be Isaac who would continue the covenant (Gen. 17:19, 21).

כְּשֵׁם שֶׁנִּכְנַס לַבְּרִית *Just as he has entered into the covenant:* Mentioned already in early rabbinic sources as the response of those present. The three phrases refer to the duties of a parent to a child: (1) to teach him Torah; (2) to ensure that he marries; and (3) to train him to do good deeds, as the Torah says in the case of Abraham: "For I have singled him out so that he may instruct his children and his posterity to keep the way of the LORD by doing what is just and right" (Gen. 18:19).

שָׁלוֹם רָב לְאֹהֲבֵי תוֹרָתֶךָ, וְאֵין־לָמוֹ מִכְשׁוֹל: אַשְׁרֵי תִּבְחַר וּתְקָרֵב, יִשְׁכֹּן חֲצֵרֶיךָ תהלים סה

*All respond:*

נִשְׂבְּעָה בְּטוּב בֵּיתֶךָ, קְדֹשׁ הֵיכָלֶךָ:

*The baby is placed on the knees of the* סנדק*, and the* מוהל *says:*

בָּרוּךְ אַתָּה יהוה אֱלֹהֵינוּ מֶלֶךְ הָעוֹלָם
אֲשֶׁר קִדְּשָׁנוּ בְּמִצְוֹתָיו, וְצִוָּנוּ עַל הַמִּילָה.

*Immediately after the circumcision, the father says:*

בָּרוּךְ אַתָּה יהוה אֱלֹהֵינוּ מֶלֶךְ הָעוֹלָם, אֲשֶׁר קִדְּשָׁנוּ
בְּמִצְוֹתָיו, וְצִוָּנוּ לְהַכְנִיסוֹ בִּבְרִיתוֹ שֶׁל אַבְרָהָם אָבִינוּ.

*In* ארץ ישראל *the father adds (some in* חוץ לארץ *add it as well):*

בָּרוּךְ אַתָּה יהוה אֱלֹהֵינוּ מֶלֶךְ הָעוֹלָם
שֶׁהֶחֱיָנוּ וְקִיְּמָנוּ וְהִגִּיעָנוּ לַזְּמַן הַזֶּה.

*All respond:*

אָמֵן. כְּשֵׁם שֶׁנִּכְנַס לַבְּרִית
כֵּן יִכָּנֵס לְתוֹרָה וּלְחֻפָּה וּלְמַעֲשִׂים טוֹבִים.

---

SERVICE AT A CIRCUMCISION

Since the days of Abraham (Gen. 17:4–14), circumcision has been the sign, for Jewish males, of the covenant between God and His people. Despite the fact that the law was restated by Moses (Lev. 12:3), it remains known as the "Covenant of Abraham." The ceremony – always performed on the eighth day, even on Shabbat, unless there are medical reasons for delay – marks the entry of the child into the covenant of Jewish fate and destiny. The duty of circumcision devolves, in principle, on the father of the child; in practice it is performed only by a qualified *mohel.*

בָּרוּךְ *Blessed are You:* There are three blessings to be said at a circumcision: (1) *And has commanded us concerning circumcision* – a blessing over the commandment itself, the "about" formula signaling that the *mohel* is performing the commandment on behalf of the father; (2) *To bring him [our son] into*

*After the circumcision has been completed, the Mohel (or another honoree) takes a cup of wine and says:*

בָּרוּךְ Blessed are You, LORD our God, King of the Universe, who creates the fruit of the vine.

בָּרוּךְ Blessed are You, LORD our God, King of the Universe, who made the beloved one [Isaac] holy from the womb, marked the decree of circumcision in his flesh, and gave his descendants the seal and sign of the holy covenant. As a reward for this, the Living God, our Portion, our Rock, did order deliverance from destruction for the beloved of our flesh, for the sake of His covenant that He set in our flesh. Blessed are You, LORD, who establishes the covenant.

אֱלֹהֵינוּ Our God and God of our fathers, preserve this child to his father and mother, and let his name be called in Israel (*baby's name* son of *father's name*). May the father rejoice in the issue of his body, and
the mother be glad with the fruit of her womb, as is written, "May your father and mother rejoice, and she who bore you be glad." And it is said, *Prov. 23*
"Then I passed by you and saw you downtrodden in your blood, and I said to you: In your blood, live; and I said to you: In your blood, live." *Ezek. 16*

וְנֶאֱמַר And it is said, "He remembered His covenant for ever; the word He ordained for a thousand generations; the covenant He made with Abraham and gave on oath to Isaac, confirming it as a statute for Jacob, an everlasting covenant for Israel." And it is said, *Ps. 105*
"And Abraham circumcised his son Isaac at the age of eight days, as God had commanded him." *Gen. 21*
Thank the LORD for He is good; His loving-kindness is for ever. *Ps. 118*

*All respond:*

Thank the LORD for He is good; His loving-kindness is for ever.

*The Mohel (or honoree) continues:*

May this child (*baby's name* son of *father's name*) become great. Just as he has entered into the covenant, so may he enter into Torah, marriage and good deeds.

*The Sandak also drinks some of the wine; some drops are given to the baby. The cup is then sent to the mother, who also drinks from it.*

*All say Aleinu on page 990, and Mourner's Kaddish on page 994 is said.*

*After the circumcision has been completed, the* מוהל *(or another honoree), takes a cup of wine and says:*

בָּרוּךְ אַתָּה יהוה אֱלֹהֵינוּ מֶלֶךְ הָעוֹלָם, בּוֹרֵא פְּרִי הַגָּפֶן.

בָּרוּךְ אַתָּה יהוה אֱלֹהֵינוּ מֶלֶךְ הָעוֹלָם, אֲשֶׁר קִדַּשׁ יְדִיד מִבֶּטֶן, וְחֹק בִּשְׁאֵרוֹ שָׂם, וְצֶאֱצָאָיו חָתַם בְּאוֹת בְּרִית קֹדֶשׁ. עַל כֵּן בִּשְׂכַר זֹאת, אֵל חַי חֶלְקֵנוּ צוּרֵנוּ צַוֵּה לְהַצִּיל יְדִידוּת שְׁאֵרֵנוּ מִשַּׁחַת, לְמַעַן בְּרִיתוֹ אֲשֶׁר שָׂם בִּבְשָׂרֵנוּ. בָּרוּךְ אַתָּה יהוה, כּוֹרֵת הַבְּרִית.

אֱלֹהֵינוּ וֵאלֹהֵי אֲבוֹתֵינוּ, קַיֵּם אֶת הַיֶּלֶד הַזֶּה לְאָבִיו וּלְאִמּוֹ, וְיִקָּרֵא שְׁמוֹ בְּיִשְׂרָאֵל (פלוני בֶּן פלוני). יִשְׂמַח הָאָב בְּיוֹצֵא חֲלָצָיו וְתָגֵל
אִמּוֹ בִּפְרִי בִטְנָהּ, כַּכָּתוּב: יִשְׂמַח־אָבִיךָ וְאִמֶּךָ, וְתָגֵל יוֹלַדְתֶּךָ: משלי כג
וְנֶאֱמַר: וָאֶעֱבֹר עָלַיִךְ וָאֶרְאֵךְ מִתְבּוֹסֶסֶת בְּדָמָיִךְ, וָאֹמַר לָךְ יחזקאל טז
בְּדָמַיִךְ חֲיִי, וָאֹמַר לָךְ בְּדָמַיִךְ חֲיִי:

וְנֶאֱמַר: זָכַר לְעוֹלָם בְּרִיתוֹ, דָּבָר צִוָּה לְאֶלֶף דּוֹר: אֲשֶׁר כָּרַת אֶת־ תהלים קה
אַבְרָהָם, וּשְׁבוּעָתוֹ לְיִשְׂחָק: וַיַּעֲמִידֶהָ לְיַעֲקֹב לְחֹק, לְיִשְׂרָאֵל
בְּרִית עוֹלָם: וְנֶאֱמַר: וַיָּמָל אַבְרָהָם אֶת־יִצְחָק בְּנוֹ בֶּן־שְׁמֹנַת בראשית כא
יָמִים, כַּאֲשֶׁר צִוָּה אֹתוֹ אֱלֹהִים: הוֹדוּ לַיהוה כִּי־טוֹב, כִּי לְעוֹלָם תהלים קיח
חַסְדּוֹ:

*All respond:*

הוֹדוּ לַיהוה כִּי־טוֹב, כִּי לְעוֹלָם חַסְדּוֹ:

*The* מוהל *(or honoree) continues:*

(פלוני בֶּן פלוני) זֶה הַקָּטָן גָּדוֹל יִהְיֶה, כְּשֵׁם שֶׁנִּכְנַס לַבְּרִית, כֵּן יִכָּנֵס לְתוֹרָה וּלְחֻפָּה וּלְמַעֲשִׂים טוֹבִים.

*The* סנדק *also drinks some of the wine; some drops are given to the baby. The cup is then sent to the mother, who also drinks from it.*

*All say* עָלֵינוּ*,* *on page 991,* *and* קדיש יתום *on page 995* *is said.*

## BIRKAT KOHANIM IN ISRAEL

*In Israel, the following is said by the Leader during the Repetition of the Amida when Kohanim bless the congregation.*

*If there is more than one Kohen, a member of the congregation calls:* (*See laws 91–96.*)

Kohanim!

*The Kohanim respond:*

Blessed are You, LORD our God, King of the Universe,
who has made us holy with the holiness of Aaron,
and has commanded us to bless His people Israel with love.

*The Leader calls word by word, followed by the Kohanim:*

יְבָרֶכְךָ May the LORD bless you and protect you. (*Cong:* Amen.) *Num. 6*
May the LORD make His face shine on you
and be gracious to you. (*Cong:* Amen.)
May the LORD turn His face toward you,
and grant you peace. (*Cong:* Amen.)

*The congregation says:*

אַדִּיר Majestic One on high who dwells in power: You are peace and Your name is peace. May it be Your will to bestow on us and on Your people the house of Israel, life and blessing as a safeguard for peace.

*The Kohanim say:*

רִבּוֹנוֹ Master of the Universe: we have done what You have decreed for us. So too may You deal with us as You have promised us. Look down from Your holy dwelling place, from heaven, and bless Your people Israel and the land You have given us as You promised on oath to our ancestors, a land flowing with milk and honey. *Deut. 26*

*In Shaḥarit continue with "Grant peace" on page 410 on the first day, and on page 700 on the second day.*

*Musaf continues with "Grant peace" on page 614 on the first day, and on page 870 on the second day.*

# ברכת כהנים בארץ ישראל

*In* ארץ ישראל, *the following is said by the* שליח ציבור *during the* חזרת הש״ץ *when* כהנים *say* ברכת כהנים.
*If there is more than one* כהן, *a member of the* קהל *calls:* (*See laws 91–96.*)

## כֹּהֲנִים

*The* כהנים *respond:*

בָּרוּךְ אַתָּה יהוה אֱלֹהֵינוּ מֶלֶךְ הָעוֹלָם
אֲשֶׁר קִדְּשָׁנוּ בִּקְדֻשָּׁתוֹ שֶׁל אַהֲרֹן
וְצִוָּנוּ לְבָרֵךְ אֶת עַמּוֹ יִשְׂרָאֵל בְּאַהֲבָה.

*The* שליח ציבור *calls word by word, followed by the* כהנים:

יְבָרֶכְךָ יהוה וְיִשְׁמְרֶךָ: קהל: אָמֵן במדבר ו
יָאֵר יהוה פָּנָיו אֵלֶיךָ וִיחֻנֶּךָּ: קהל: אָמֵן
יִשָּׂא יהוה פָּנָיו אֵלֶיךָ וְיָשֵׂם לְךָ שָׁלוֹם: קהל: אָמֵן

*The* קהל *says:*

אַדִּיר בַּמָּרוֹם שׁוֹכֵן בִּגְבוּרָה, אַתָּה שָׁלוֹם וְשִׁמְךָ שָׁלוֹם. יְהִי רָצוֹן שֶׁתָּשִׂים עָלֵינוּ וְעַל כָּל עַמְּךָ בֵּית יִשְׂרָאֵל חַיִּים וּבְרָכָה לְמִשְׁמֶרֶת שָׁלוֹם.

*The* כהנים *say:*

רִבּוֹנוֹ שֶׁל עוֹלָם, עָשִׂינוּ מַה שֶּׁגָּזַרְתָּ עָלֵינוּ, אַף אַתָּה
עֲשֵׂה עִמָּנוּ כְּמוֹ שֶׁהִבְטַחְתָּנוּ. הַשְׁקִיפָה מִמְּעוֹן דברים כו
קָדְשְׁךָ מִן־הַשָּׁמַיִם, וּבָרֵךְ אֶת־עַמְּךָ אֶת־יִשְׂרָאֵל,
וְאֵת הָאֲדָמָה אֲשֶׁר נָתַתָּה לָנוּ, כַּאֲשֶׁר נִשְׁבַּעְתָּ
לַאֲבֹתֵינוּ, אֶרֶץ זָבַת חָלָב וּדְבָשׁ:

*In* שחרית *continue with* שִׂים שָׁלוֹם *on page 411 on the first day, and on page 701 on the second day.*

מוסף *continues with* שִׂים שָׁלוֹם *on page 615 on the first day, and on page 871 on the second day.*

# פיוטים נוספים ליום א׳

# ADDITIONAL PIYUTIM FOR THE FIRST DAY

## ADDITIONAL PIYUTIM FOR FIRST DAY SHAḤARIT

*The piyutim said by the Leader in Shaḥarit are commonly called Yotzerot; however, the Yotzer refers only to the first piyut, said at the beginning of the first blessing of the Shema. The theme of the Yotzerot for both days of Rosh HaShana is God's kingship.*

*All:*

O King girded with strength, / the greatness of Your name is in Your mighty deeds; / Yours is an arm of strength. *Ps. 89*

O King with garments made of vengeance, / donned on the day of vengeance, / He shall bring back His enemies' crimes to punish them.

O King clothed in majesty, / whose ire can cause the very seas to run dry / and subdue the rivers when they rise haughtily.

▸ O King clothed in ten mythical garments, girded with Your holy nation,
O God, feared in the council of the holy angels. / O Holy One. *Ibid.*

*All continue:*

O King who lives in light / and clothes Himself with light, / He shall bring forth our judgment into the light.

O King girded with might, / whose right hand resonates with might, / to challenge You no man shall dare.

O King who dons righteousness / and is sanctified in righteousness, / with You, O Lord, is the right. *Dan. 9*

O King majestically robed, / with a helmet of salvation upon His head, / God seated upon the throne of His holiness. *Is. 63* *Is. 59* *Ps. 47*

O King with clothes of crimson hue, / when He tramples the traitors underfoot / He shall bring low the spirits of princes. *Ps. 76*

O King with a cloak as pure as snow, / pristine, in His purity He shall cleanse / those who polish their actions to triumph in judgment.

O King clad with a cloak of zeal, / zealous indeed, He has revealed His strength, / like a man of war He shall stir up ardor. *Is. 42*

O King over all the ends of the earth, / may all bow before the King of the earth, / for He comes to judge the earth. *I Chr. 16*

O King, on the day He rises for all eternity, / every creature shall tremble before Him, / O high and lofty One who exists until eternity. *Is. 57*

---

of poetry-as-prayer, and his work combines multiple references to rabbinic tradition, stated in such brief and labyrinthine Hebrew that it can be difficult

# פיוטים נוספים לשחרית של יום א׳

*The piyutim said by the* שליח ציבור *in* שחרית *are commonly called* יוצרות*; however, the* יוצר *refers only to the first piyut, said at the beginning of the first blessing of the* שמע*. The theme of the* יוצרות *for both days of* ראש השנה *is God's kingship.*

*All:*

מֶלֶךְ אָזוּר גְּבוּרָה / גָּדוֹל שִׁמְךָ בִּגְבוּרָה / לְךָ זְרוֹעַ עִם־גְּבוּרָה: תהלים פט

מֶלֶךְ בִּגְדֵי נָקָם / לָבַשׁ בְּיוֹם נָקָם / לְצָרָיו יָשִׁיב אֵל חֵיקָם.

מֶלֶךְ גֵּאוּת לָבֵשׁ / יַמִּים מְיַבֵּשׁ / וְגַאֲוַת אֲפִיקִים מְכַבֵּשׁ.

› מֶלֶךְ בַּעֲשָׂרָה לְבוּשִׁים
הִתְאַזָּר בִּקְדוֹשִׁים
אֵל נַעֲרָץ בְּסוֹד־קְדֹשִׁים: / קָדוֹשׁ. שם

*All continue:*

מֶלֶךְ דָּר בִּנְהוֹרָא / עוֹטֶה אוֹרָה / מִשְׁפָּטֵנוּ יוֹצִיא לָאוֹרָה.

מֶלֶךְ הִתְאַזָּר עוֹז / יְמִינוֹ תָּעֹז / וֶאֱנוֹשׁ אַל יָעֹז.

מֶלֶךְ וַיִּלְבַּשׁ צְדָקָה / וְנִקְדַּשׁ בִּצְדָקָה / לְךָ יהוה הַצְּדָקָה: דניאל ט

מֶלֶךְ זֶה הָדוּר בִּלְבוּשׁוֹ: / וְכוֹבַע יְשׁוּעָה בְּרֹאשׁוֹ: / ישעיה סג ישעיה נט
אֱלֹהִים יָשַׁב עַל־כִּסֵּא קָדְשׁוֹ: תהלים מז

מֶלֶךְ חָמוּץ בְּגָדִים / בְּדָרְכוֹ בוֹגְדִים / יִבְצֹר רוּחַ נְגִידִים: תהלים עו

מֶלֶךְ טַלִּיתוֹ כַּשֶּׁלֶג מְצֻחְצָח / צַח וּבְצַחְצָחוֹת יְצַחְצַח /
מְצַחְצְחִים פָּעֳלָם לָנֶצַח.

מֶלֶךְ יָעַט קִנְאָה / קַנֹּא קִנֵּא, גָּאֹה גָּאָה / כְּאִישׁ מִלְחָמוֹת יָעִיר קִנְאָה: ישעיה מב

מֶלֶךְ כָּל אַפְסֵי אָרֶץ / יִשְׁתַּחֲווּ לַמֶּלֶךְ עַל כָּל הָאָרֶץ /
כִּי־בָא לִשְׁפּוֹט אֶת־הָאָרֶץ: דברי הימים א׳ טז

מֶלֶךְ לְיוֹם קוּמוֹ לָעַד / כָּל יְצוּר לְפָנָיו יִרְעַד / רָם וְנִשָּׂא, שֹׁכֵן עַד: ישעיה נז

---

מֶלֶךְ אָזוּר גְּבוּרָה *O King girded with strength.* This poem was written by the great master of Hebrew liturgical poetry, Rabbi Elazar HaKalir. He lived in Israel but we do not know exactly when: conjectures vary from the tenth century to the fourth or perhaps even earlier. He was the greatest virtuoso

O King who in His strength rules the world, / the mountains quake before His majesty,/ leaping like rams at His reproach. *Ps. 46*

O King, fearsome to all kings of the earth, / the land shall writhe in fear; / before the One enthroned among the Cherubim, let the earth tremble!

O King whose power none can gather strength to withstand, / who in His might bears all, / who gives strength to the weary. *Is. 40*

O King who rises to preside in judgment / on the Day of Judgment, / who examines the haughty ones in judgment.

O King who reveals the secrets of those who seek / to hide their counsel in deep places; / the LORD shall expose and reveal all deep secrets.

O King who commands all four directions, / and envelops the haughty tyrants / with a great current of wind.

O King who shall gather the earthly kings, / who will deliver the vision of Duma in a stormy wind, / visiting punishment upon the haughty legions.

O King so high and lofty in justice, / whose royal might is His love of justice, / the foundation of His throne is righteousness and justice.

O King, O righteous Judge, / righteousness shall always go before Him, / pleading for those who pursue righteousness.

O King who governs with might, / whose throne is suspended in heaven above / and His kingdom has dominion over all. *Ps. 103*

O King who lowered the universe with a glance, / whose gaze caused the very foundation of the universe to quake, / His eyes wander throughout the land.

O King who seeks out every creature / to determine how to act, / on the earth below and in heaven above.

▸ O King, O Eternal God,
crown Him, O eternal nation!
May the LORD God rule for all eternity. / O Holy One.

*On a weekday, continue with "In compassion" (page 316);*
*on Shabbat, with "All will thank You" (page 318).*

---

The concept of a "garment" is that God cannot be seen or known directly. We see the effects of His actions and no more. These signals of transcendence are referred to poetically and mystically as "garments."

מֶלֶךְ מֹשֵׁל עוֹלָם בִּגְבוּרָתוֹ / יִרְעֲשׁוּ־הָרִים בְּגַאֲוָתוֹ: / תהלים מו
וּכְאֵילִים יִרְקְדוּ מִגַּעֲרָתוֹ.
מֶלֶךְ נוֹרָא לְמַלְכֵי אֶרֶץ / חוּל תָּחוּל הָאָרֶץ /
מִיּשֵׁב הַכְּרוּבִים תָּנוּט הָאָרֶץ.
מֶלֶךְ שְׂאֵתוֹ מִי יַעֲצָר כֹּחַ / וְהוּא נוֹשֵׂא כֹל בַּכֹּחַ / נֹתֵן לַיָּעֵף כֹּחַ: ישעיה מ
מֶלֶךְ עָמְדוּ לָדִין / בְּיוֹם הַדִּין / שׁוֹפֵט גֵּאִים בַּדִּין.
מֶלֶךְ פִּלֵּשׁ סוֹד הַמַּעֲמִיקִים / לַסְתִּיר עֵצָה בְּמַעֲמַקִּים /
יַחְשֹׂף וִיגַלֶּה עֲמֻקִּים.
מֶלֶךְ צִוָּה מִכָּל רוּחַ / עָרִיצֵי גַּסֵּי הָרוּחַ / לְאַפְּפָם בְּשֶׁטֶף רוּחַ.
מֶלֶךְ קָהֵל מַלְכֵי אֲדָמָה / בְּסַעֲרוֹ מַשָּׂא דוּמָה / יִפְקֹד עַל צְבָא רוּמָה.
מֶלֶךְ רָם וְגָבֹהַּ בַּמִּשְׁפָּט / וְעֹז מֶלֶךְ אָהֵב מִשְׁפָּט /
מְכוֹן כִּסְאוֹ צֶדֶק וּמִשְׁפָּט.
מֶלֶךְ שׁוֹפֵט צֶדֶק / לְפָנָיו יְהַלֵּךְ צֶדֶק / לְהָלִיץ בְּעַד רוֹדְפֵי צֶדֶק.
מֶלֶךְ תַּקִּיף בְּמֶמְשָׁלָה / כִּסְאוֹ תָּלָה לְמַעְלָה / וּמַלְכוּתוֹ בַּכֹּל מָשָׁלָה: תהלים קג
מֶלֶךְ תַּחַת חֶלֶד מֵהַבִּיטוֹ / מַרְעִיד יְסוֹד בְּהַבִּיטוֹ / בַּכֹּל מְשׁוֹטֵט מַבָּטוֹ.
מֶלֶךְ תָּר בְּכָל פֹּעַל / בַּכֹּל מַה יִּפְעַל / בְּמַטָּה וּבְמָעַל.
› מֶלֶךְ אֱלֹהֵי עוֹלָם
הַמְלִיכוּהוּ עַם עוֹלָם
יהוה יִמְלֹךְ לְעֹלָם / קָדוֹשׁ.

*On a weekday continue with* הַמֵּאִיר *(page 317); on* שבת*, with* הַכֹּל יוֹדוּךָ *(page 319).*

---

to decode. The theme of this poem, however, is clear. It is the central theme of Rosh HaShana: God as King.

The prophets and poets of Tanakh occasionally described God as "robed" in a variety of ways, each representing a different revelation of God in history or creation. There are ten such descriptions in the books of Isaiah, Psalms and Daniel: God is spoken of as being robed in *might, vengeance, majesty, radiance, strength, triumph, grandeur, crimson, white,* and *zeal*. Hence, the "ten garments" of the poem.

*This piyut comprises the second part of the Yotzer.*
*It is known as the Ofan, and is said on both days.*
*All say:*

כְּבוֹדוֹ His glory He canopied over the earth
in His compassion on this day – the King
He who examines the thoughts of the young and old – the King
He girds Himself with glory and might – the King
Heaven and earth tremble in awe of the King
He who fashions all their hearts, show them favor, O King
He who fathoms all their actions, vindicate them, O King
It is a call to remembrance, this day the shofar is sounded for the King
▸ It is the law and custom in Israel,
that they might be found innocent, O King
He has provided sustenance for those who fear Him,
He who crowns every earthly king
He shall forever recall His covenant favorably – the King

*All continue:*

Do not wipe out the last remnant of the children of the King
It is for this reason that we have come before You our King, O King
We began to prepare ourselves to entreat You already yesterday, O King
▸ Please reserve Your kindness for the descendants of the one
who was visited by the three angels of the King
Listen to those who come before You in prayer, for the sake of the
one on whose behalf bitter tears were shed by the angels of the King
Do not scorn their utterances for the sake of the one who slept
where there ascended and descended angels of the King

---

In the middle of the poem there is a very poignant line: "Do not wipe out the last remnant of the children of the King." There were times when the very future of the Jewish people seemed in doubt. Yet Jews remained "children of the King" – recall God's command to Moses to tell Pharaoh: "My child, My firstborn, Israel" (Ex. 4:22). Redeem us, forgive us, for we are Your children, and the children of Abraham, Isaac and Jacob whom You loved.

מֵאֶתְמוֹל קִדַּמְנוּךָ *We began to prepare ourselves… already yesterday.* A reference to the extended *Seliḥot* prayers said on the day before Rosh HaShana, and to the ancient custom of fasting on that day.

*This piyut comprises the second part of the* יוצר*.*
*It is known as the* אופן*, and is said on both days.*

*All say:*

כְּבוֹדוֹ אִהֵל כְּהַיּוֹם בְּרַחֲמִים מֶלֶךְ.
בּוֹחֵן כָּל עֶשְׁתּוֹנוֹת צָעִיר וָרַב מֶלֶךְ.
גֵּאוּת וָעֹז הִתְאַזָּר מֶלֶךְ.
דּוֹק וָחֶלֶד יֶחֶרְדוּן מֵאֵימַת מֶלֶךְ.
הַיּוֹצֵר יַחַד לִבָּם יָחוֹן מֶלֶךְ.
וּמֵבִין אֶל כָּל מַעֲשֵׂיהֶם יַצְדִּיק מֶלֶךְ.
זִכָּרוֹן הוּא יוֹם תְּרוּעַת מֶלֶךְ.
‹ חֹק לְיִשְׂרָאֵל הוּא לְזַכּוֹתָם מֶלֶךְ.
טֶרֶף נָתַן לִירֵאָיו מַמְלִיךְ כָּל מֶלֶךְ.
יִזְכֹּר לְעוֹלָם בְּרִיתוֹ בְּזִכְרוֹן טוֹב מֶלֶךְ.

*All continue:*

כָּלָה אַל תַּעַשׂ לִשְׁאֵרִית בְּנֵי מֶלֶךְ.
לָכֵן אָתָנוּ לְךָ מַלְכֵּנוּ מֶלֶךְ.
מֵאֶתְמוֹל קִדַּמְנוּךָ לְחַלּוֹתְךָ מֶלֶךְ.
‹ נָא נְצֹר חֶסֶד לְנִינֵי שֶׁלְּחוּ לוֹ שְׁלֹשֶׁת אֵילֵי מֶלֶךְ.
סְכוּת בָּאֵי בְתַחַן לְמַר בָּכוּ אֶרְאֶלֵּי מֶלֶךְ.
עֲנוּתָם בַּל תֶּבֶז לָלָן בְּמָקוֹם עָלוּ וְיָרְדוּ בוֹ מַלְאֲכֵי מֶלֶךְ.

---

כְּבוֹדוֹ אִהֵל *His glory He canopied.* A poem composed by Elazar HaKalir, each line ending with the keyword of the day, *Melekh,* “King.” It begins with an account of God as creator and judge of the universe, and then passes to the three patriarchs. “The one who was visited by the three angels” is Abraham. The one “on whose behalf bitter tears were shed by the angels” is Isaac – a reference to the midrashic tradition that when God commanded Abraham to sacrifice his son, the angels wept. “The one who slept where there ascended and descended angels,” is Jacob.

*All continue:*

Redeem them today from any decided verdict,
so they shall not be condemned, O King
▸ Vindicate them in Your compassion and recall them favorably, O King
*on a weekday:* Hearken to the sound
of the shofar blown for You this day, O King
*on Shabbat:* Hearken to the remembrance
of the sound of the shofar
sounded by those who recall You this day, O King
Awaken Your compassion on behalf of those who long for You, O King

*All continue:*

Heed the cries of the nation that seeks You earnestly, O King
Turn to the supporters of the Blessed One,
that we might bless You, O Living God and King.

*Congregations that say the above piyut conclude with the following formula:*

The Ḥayyot sing out, / and the Cherubim glorify,
and the Seraphim pray, / and the Erelim bless,
with the face of each Ḥayya and Ophan and Cherub
turned toward the Seraphim.
Facing these, they give praise, saying:

*Continue with "Blessed is the LORD's glory" on page 326.*

*All continue:*

פְּדֵם הַיּוֹם מִדִּין גָּמוּר מִלְּחַיְּבָם מֶלֶךְ.
‹ צַדְּקֵם בְּרַחֲמִים לְפָקְדָם לְטוֹבָה מֶלֶךְ.
*on a weekday* קְשֹׁב קוֹל תְּקִיעָה מְתוֹקְעֵי לְךָ הַיּוֹם מֶלֶךְ.
בשבת: קְשֹׁב זִכְרוֹן תְּקִיעָה מִזּוֹכְרֵי לְךָ הַיּוֹם מֶלֶךְ.
רַחֲמִים תְּעוֹרֵר לִמְחַכֶּיךָ מֶלֶךְ.

*All continue:*

שְׁעֵה שַׁוְעַת עַם מְשַׁחֲרֶיךָ מֶלֶךְ.
תֵּיֶפֶן בְּתוֹמְכֵי בָרוּךְ, וּנְבָרֶכְךָ אֱלֹהִים חַיִּים וָמֶלֶךְ.

*Congregations that say the above piyut conclude with the following* נוסח*:*

וְהַחַיּוֹת יְשׁוֹרֵרוּ / וּכְרוּבִים יְפָאֵרוּ
וּשְׂרָפִים יָרֹנּוּ / וְאֶרְאֶלִּים יְבָרֵכוּ
פְּנֵי כָל חַיָּה וְאוֹפָן וּכְרוּב לְעֻמַּת שְׂרָפִים
לְעֻמָּתָם מְשַׁבְּחִים וְאוֹמְרִים.

*Continue with* בָּרוּךְ כְּבוֹד־יהוה מִמְּקוֹמוֹ *on page 327.*

*Originally the last piyut before קדושה, the סילוק is composed of twelve internally rhyming stanzas. Three of these stanzas feature the same word at the end of each stich – "אֶרֶץ – world," "דִּין – judgment," or "צְדָקָה – righteousness," indicating the overall theme of God's judgment of the universe.*

מֶלֶךְ בְּמִשְׁפָּט יַעֲמִיד אָרֶץ: / עֶלְיוֹן עַל־כָּל־הָאָרֶץ: משלי כט / תהלים צז
יַכִּירוּ וְיֵדְעוּ כָּל הָאָרֶץ / כָּל־יֹשְׁבֵי תֵבֵל וְשֹׁכְנֵי אָרֶץ: ישעיה יח
מִקְצֵה הָאָרֶץ וְעַד־קְצֵה הָאָרֶץ: / כִּי הוּא בּוֹרֵא קְצוֹת כָּל הָאָרֶץ דברים יג
עֹשֶׂה מִשְׁפָּט וּצְדָקָה בָּאָרֶץ: / בְּקוּמוֹ לַמִּשְׁפָּט יַשְׁקִיט הָאָרֶץ ירמיה ט
לְהוֹשִׁיעַ כָּל עַנְוֵי הָאָרֶץ / לַעֲשׂוֹת כְּתֹהוּ שׁוֹפְטֵי הָאָרֶץ
לֶאֱחֹז בְּאַרְבַּע כַּנְפוֹת הָאָרֶץ / לְנַעֵר כָּל רִשְׁעֵי אָרֶץ
וְקוֹל יַשְׁמִיעוּ בַּשָּׁמַיִם וּבָאָרֶץ / מָה־אַדִּיר שִׁמְךָ בְּכָל־הָאָרֶץ: תהלים ח
וּבְמָלְכוֹ עַל כָּל הָאָרֶץ / אָז יָרִיעוּ תַּחְתִּיּוֹת אָרֶץ
יִשְׂמְחוּ הַשָּׁמַיִם וְתָגֵל הָאָרֶץ: / וַאֲשֶׁר בַּשָּׁמַיִם מִמַּעַל לָאָרֶץ תהלים צו
וַאֲשֶׁר בַּמַּיִם מִתַּחַת לָאָרֶץ: / וְאָז יִפְצְחוּ רֶנֶן בְּאֶרֶץ שמות כ
כְּבוֹדוֹ מְלֹא כָּל הָאָרֶץ / יהוה מָלָךְ תָּגֵל הָאָרֶץ: תהלים צז
וּבְכֵן יְשַׁלֵּשׁ שׁוֹפָרוֹת עָרֶץ / וַיַּפְחִיד חוֹרֵי יוֹשְׁבֵי הָאָרֶץ
וַיַּהֲפֹךְ כִּסֵּא מַמְלְכוֹת הָאָרֶץ / וַיֹּאמַר כָּל אֲשֶׁר נְשָׁמָה בְּאַפּוֹ בָּאָרֶץ
מָה־אַדִּיר שִׁמְךָ בְּכָל־הָאָרֶץ: / וְיִכּוֹנֵן מָשׂוֹשׂ כָּל הָאָרֶץ תהלים ח
וַיְעוֹרֵר כָּל יְשֵׁנֵי אָרֶץ / וַיַּעֲלוּ זְמִירוֹת מִכְּנַף הָאָרֶץ
שִׁירוּ לַיהוה כָּל־הָאָרֶץ: תהלים צו

אֶרֶץ וְדָרֶיהָ יִצָּפוּ לַדִּין / וְיֵחַתּוּ וְיֶחֶרְדוּ מֵאֵימַת הַדִּין
כִּי גָדוֹל יוֹם הַדִּין / וּמִי יְכִילֶנּוּ, לְהִצְטַדֵּק בַּדִּין
וְכָל יוֹשְׁבֵי עַל מִדִּין / וְכָל יוֹדְעֵי דָּת וָדִין
וְכָל שֶׁנַּעֲשָׂה בוֹ דִין / אוּלַי יֵחָנֵן בִּשְׁעַת הַדִּין
כִּי אֵין רַחֲמִים בַּדִּין / וְלֹא יִשָּׂא פָנִים בַּדִּין
וְהוּא עֵד וּבַעַל דִּין / לָדַעַת בָּאֶרֶץ מַעֲשֵׂהוּ בַּדִּין

וּבְיַד כָּל אָדָם יְחַתֵּם דִּין / וּלְפִי מִשְׁטָרוֹ יַעֲשֶׂה לוֹ דִין
וּכְפָעֳלוֹ יִפְעַל לוֹ דִין / וּמַעֲשָׂיו יוֹכִיחוּ אוֹתוֹ בַּדִּין
וְאֶבֶן מִקִּיר תִּזְעַק בַּדִּין / וְכָפִיס מֵעֵץ יַעֲנֶנָּה בַדִּין
הַכֹּל בֶּאֱמֶת וְהַכֹּל בַּדִּין / בְּמִדַּת רַחֲמִים וּבְמִדַּת הַדִּין
וְהַיּוֹם הוּכַן עַמִּים בּוֹ לָדִין / לַעֲשׂוֹת אוֹת לְיוֹם הַדִּין
וְכָל נְפָשׁוֹת בּוֹ יָדִין.

וְהוּא עָשׂוּי חֹק זִכָּרוֹן / לְיוֹם רִאשׁוֹן וּלְיוֹם אַחֲרוֹן
לְהִזָּכֵר בּוֹ יְשֵׁנֵי חֶבְרוֹן / בְּצִלָּם לְהֵחָבְאוֹת חֲבַצֶּלֶת הַשָּׁרוֹן
בָּם לְהַצְדִּיק שָׁבִים לְבִצָּרוֹן / תּוֹקְעֵי בַּשּׁוֹפָר וְקוֹרְאֵי בְגָרוֹן
לִמְצֹא בְצִדְקָם מַעֲשֵׂה כִשְׁרוֹן / בָּם לְהִנָּצֵל מֵאַף וְחָרוֹן.

וּכְשָׁמַר אָב דֶּרֶךְ מִשְׁפָּט וּצְדָקָה / יַעֲשֶׂה לְנִינָיו מִשְׁפָּט וּצְדָקָה
וּכְיוֹנַת אֵלֶם זָרַע לִצְדָקָה / יִקְצְרוּ נִינָיו אֱמֶת וּצְדָקָה
וּכְנִתַּן לְתָם בֶּאֱמֶת צְדָקָה / יִנָּתֵן לְנִינָיו אֱמֶת וּצְדָקָה
וְכִסֵּא כָבוֹד מְתֻקָּן בִּצְדָקָה / לְפָנָיו יַעֲמֹד מֵלִיץ וִילַמֵּד צְדָקָה
וְכַעֲלוֹת שׁוֹפָר מִדַּלֵּי צְדָקָה / יְחַנְּנוּ וְיַפְגִּיעוּ אֲבוֹת הַצְּדָקָה
וְיֹאמְרוּ לִפְנֵי אוֹהֵב צְדָקָה / חָלִילָה לְּךָ מְדַבֵּר בִּצְדָקָה
מֵעֲשׂוֹת מִשְׁפָּט בְּלֹא צְדָקָה / וּבִמְקוֹם מִשְׁפָּט אֵין צְדָקָה
וּבְאֵין מִשְׁפָּט יֵשׁ צְדָקָה / וְאַתָּה בְּמִשְׁפָּט תַּעֲשֶׂה צְדָקָה
לִשְׁפֹּט תֵּבֵל בְּמַעֲשֵׂה הַצְּדָקָה / וּמְכוֹן כִּסְאֲךָ מִשְׁפָּט וּצְדָקָה
וּבְחֶפְשְׁךָ מַעֲשִׂים מִבְּלִי צְדָקָה / הִזָּכֵר לְטוֹב מְעַט בִּצְדָקָה
וּבְמַתְּנַת חִנָּם תַּעֲשֶׂה צְדָקָה / לִפְתּוֹחַ לָמוֹ אוֹצְרוֹת הַצְּדָקָה.

וְאִם יָצְאָה גְּזֵרָה דְחוּקָה / לְחַבֵּל יוֹשְׁבֵי אַרְקָא
בְּבוּקָה וּמְבוּקָה וּמְבֻלָּקָה / הִסְתַּכֵּל בַּתַּבְנִית אֲשֶׁר בַּכִּסֵּא חֲקוּקָה
וּבַתֵּבָה אֲשֶׁר תַּחְתָּיו פְּקוּקָה / וְנַפְשׁוֹת צוּרִים בְּתוֹכָהּ נְקוּקָה

וּבַעֲטָרָה אֲשֶׁר בְּרֹאשְׁךָ זְקוּקָה / וּבְשֵׁם יִשְׂרָאֵל בְּכִנּוּי מְחֻזָּקָה
וּבִדְמוּת שְׁבָטִים מְעֻזָּקָה / וּבֵין כְּתֵפָיו שָׁכֵן בְּחָזְקָה
בָּם אֶשָּׁעֲנָה, וּבָם אֶתְחַזְּקָה.

כִּי בְשִׁבְתּוֹ בַּכִּסֵּא לִשְׁפֹּטִי / יַעַמְדוּ כֻּלָּם לִפְנֵי שׁוֹפְטִי
לְהַדְמִים בַּשּׁוֹפָר בַּעַל מִשְׁפָּטִי / לְהָלִיץ בַּעֲדִי וּלְזַכּוֹת יִשְׁפְּטִי
וּבְמִשְׁפְּטֵי הַגּוֹיִם בְּלִי לִשְׁפְּטִי / כִּי לָאוֹר יוֹצִיא מִשְׁפָּטִי
וְנֹגַהּ כָּאוֹר תִּהְיֶה בְּהִשָּׁפְטִי.

רֹאשׁוֹ כֶּתֶם פָּז לְצַדְּקִי / לְבוּשֵׁהּ כִּתְלַג חִוָּר לְנַקִּי
וּשְׂעַר רֵאשֵׁהּ כַּעֲמַר נָקִי / בְּנַקֵּה לֹא יְנַקֶּה לְנַקִּי
בְּאֹמֶר יְמַלֵּט אִי נָקִי / וְהוּא רוֹכֵב בָּעֲרָבוֹת מַבְהִיקִי
וְיוֹשֵׁב בְּחַדְרֵי תֵימָן כְּבָקִי / בִּגְבוּל בִּנְיָמִין בְּצֶלְצַח לְנַקִּי.

וְרַגְלֵי הַחַיּוֹת אֲשֶׁר בְּמִישׁוֹר עֲרָבוֹת / וְעַד לְמַעְלָה לְמַעְלָה רָבוֹת
וְסִלְסוּל לְבָרוּךְ מִמְּקוֹמוֹ מַרְבּוֹת / וּפוֹרְדוֹת וּמַשִּׁיקוֹת סְלִיחָה לְהַרְבּוֹת
לְהַצְדִּיק בְּמִשְׁפָּט אַלְפֵי רְבָבוֹת / כְּמַרְאֵה בָזָק רָצוֹת וְשָׁבוֹת
וּמַרְאוֹת תְּמוּנַת דִּמְיוֹן מִתְחַבְּאוֹת / וּמַטִּיפוֹת כְּנֹפֶת רִשְׁפֵּי שַׁלְהָבוֹת
לְהֵעָשׂוֹת נְהַר דִּינוּר אֵשׁ וְלֶהָבוֹת.

וְעַל רָאשֵׁיהֶם נָטוּי בְּמוֹרָא / דְּמוּת רָקִיעַ כְּקֶרַח הַנּוֹרָא
וּשְׁמֵי מְעוֹנָה מְקוֹם מַה נּוֹרָא / וְשָׁם אִתּוֹ שְׁרֵא נְהוֹרָא
וּמִמַּעַל לָרָקִיעַ כְּאֶבֶן יְקָרָה / כְּמַרְאֵה סַפִּיר כֵּס תִּפְאָרָה
וּבוֹ יוֹשֵׁב עוֹטֶה אוֹרָה / חוֹצֵב מִפִּיו תַּלְמוּד תּוֹרָה
וּמִשָּׁם שׁוֹמֵעַ שַׁוְעַת עֲתִירָה / וּמִימִינוֹ אֵשׁ דָּת כַּתּוֹרָה.

וְשָׁם בְּיָמִין יֵשׁ חַלּוֹנוֹת / בְּצַד רָאשֵׁי הַכְּרוּבִים בִּמְעוֹנוֹת
כִּי דֶרֶךְ אוֹתָן הַחַלּוֹנוֹת / יַאֲזִין תְּפִלּוֹת וְיַקְשִׁיב תְּחִנּוֹת
פְּעָמִים פְּתוּחוֹת וּפְעָמִים צְפוּנוֹת / בְּכֵן עִתִּים הֵם לְהִתְעַנּוֹת
בְּעֵת רָצוֹן לְהִפָּתֵחַ וּלְהֵעָנוֹת / וּכְשֶׁיַּחְפֹּץ רַחוּם לִשְׁעוֹת וְלַעֲנוֹת
יִגְזֹר וְיִפָּתְחוּ אוֹתָן הַחַלּוֹנוֹת.

וְיֵצְאוּ בָם אֶלֶף וּשְׁמוֹנֶה מֵאוֹת / הַמְּלִיצִים יֹשֶׁר מִשְׁפָּט לְנָאוֹת
וִיקַבְּלוּ תְּפִלּוֹת מִלְּבּוֹת בָּאוֹת / וְיִתְּנוּם בְּרֹאשׁ אֱלֹהֵי צְבָאוֹת
בְּכֶתֶר וָנֵזֶר בְּרֹאשׁוֹ לְהֵרָאוֹת / עֲשׂוֹת בָּמוֹ לְטוֹבָה אוֹת
בְּיוֹם תְּרוּעָה מוֹפֵת לְהַרְאוֹת.

וְאָז אֵלִים יְשַׁלְּשׁוּ קְדֻשּׁוֹת / שְׁתַּיִם לְעַם קָדוֹשׁ מִתְפָּרְשׁוֹת
וְאַחַת בְּרֹאשׁ קָדוֹשׁ מַקְדִּישׁוֹת / קָדוֹשׁ בְּכָל מִינֵי קְדֻשּׁוֹת
וּמִיָּדוֹ נָתַן שְׁתֵּי קְדֻשּׁוֹת / וְיִקַדֵּשׁ בְּאַחַת בְּשָׁלוֹשׁ קְדֻשּׁוֹת
וְיֶעֱרַב לוֹ מִלְּמַטָּה שָׁלוֹשׁ תְּקִיעוֹת / כְּמוֹ מִלְּמַעְלָה שָׁלוֹשׁ קְדֻשּׁוֹת.

*The service continues with* קדושה *on page 399.*

# PIYUTIM FOR FIRST DAY MUSAF

*This piyut, which enlarges upon the two refrains "O God of faith" and "If He shall not do it on His own behalf," is nowadays omitted by many congregations. It emphasizes how, throughout history, even the most righteous of men were at fault before God, and ends with a plea for His mercy. The author signed his name, "Elazar BiRabi Kalir," in the first letters of each stanza.*

אָמֶץ אַדִּירֵי The mighty representatives desired by God,
were sentenced to destruction when inspected in judgment,
like a vessel that had no use anymore.

Man is a creature formed from the dust of the earth,
compared to the angels of heaven,
but he failed to understand and became like a vain breath.

He was set aside to work and tend the garden,
but he violated His commandments and was banished.
Yet this day is the one when he was cared for and reprieved.

O faithful God, as You prepare to pass judgment,
were You to press the letter of the law in judgment,
who would ever be found righteous before You and acquitted by such judgment? / O Holy One.

When Abraham woke the world from obscurity,
the world was one of confusion and darkness.
Twenty despicable and lowly generations had inhabited it.

He made the straight path known to those who were perverse,
yet, because he questioned God's gift of land, saying: "How shall I know?" *Gen. 15*
his descendants were sentenced to the hard line of slavery:
"You shall know [they will be strangers]." *Ibid.*

Were those who walk in the tearful valley of sin to be examined closely,
were He to regard their actions precisely in judgment,
who then might be exonerated before the Judge?

If He shall not do it on His own behalf, / and remove all ire and wrath,
then no inquiry of man's actions will yield any merits. / O Holy One.

The innocent Isaac, who willingly offered up his soul to sacrifice,
found no respite in old age
as his eyes grew dim from the smoke of idolatrous offerings,
burned by his foolish son's wives.

His other offspring, Jacob, frequented the tents of Torah learning,
but because he claimed his path was concealed from God,
the fruitful bough, Joseph, was hidden away from him.

# פיוטים למוסף של יום א׳

*This piyut, which enlarges upon the two refrains "אֵל אֱמוּנָה" and "אִם לֹא לְמַעֲנוֹ יַעַשׂ," is nowadays omitted by many congregations. It emphasizes how, throughout history, even the most righteous of men were at fault before God, and ends with a plea for His mercy. The author signed his name, "אלעזר בירבי קליר," in the first letters of each stanza.*

אֹמֶץ אַדִּירֵי כָּל חֵפֶץ / בְּהִתְבַּקְּרָם בַּדִּין חֻיְּבוּ לְנַפֵּץ
כְּלֹא נִמְצָא בָהֶם חֵפֶץ.

אָדָם יְצִיר עָפָר מֵאֲדָמָה / לְאֵילֵי מָרוֹם אוֹתוֹ דִּמָּה
לֹא בָן וְלַהֶבֶל דָּמָה.

לַעֲבֹד וְלִשְׁמֹר גַּן, הִפְרִישׁוֹ / וְעָבַר עַל צִוּוּיו וַיְגָרְשׁוֹ
וְיוֹם זֶה לְיֹשֶׁר דְּרָשׁוֹ.

אֵל אֱמוּנָה, בְּעָרְכְּךָ דִין / אִם תְּמַצֶּה עֹמֶק הַדִּין / מִי יִצְדַּק לְפָנֶיךָ בַּדִּין / קָדוֹשׁ.

לְעֵת הֵעִיר אֶזְרָח מִמַּאֲפָל / עוֹלָם הָיָה תֹהוּ וּמְאֻפָּל
עֶשְׂרִים דּוֹר בָּזוּי וְשָׁפָל.

עִקְּשִׁים לְמִישׁוֹר מַסְלוּל יִדַּע / וְעַל נְאָמוֹ, בַּמָּה אֵדַע בראשית טו
נִדּוֹן בְּקַו, יָדֹעַ תֵּדַע. שם

עוֹבְרֵי בְּעֵמֶק הַבָּכָא לְהִבָּדֵק / אִם כְּפָעֳלָם בְּרִיב יְדֻקְדַּק
לִפְנֵי שׁוֹפֵט מִי יִצְטַדֵּק.

אִם לֹא לְמַעֲנוֹ יַעַשׂ / וְיָסִיר חֲרוֹן אַף וָכַעַס / אֵין לְבַקֵּר וְלִמְצֹא מַעַשׂ / קָדוֹשׁ.

זָךְ הַמַּשְׁלִים בְּעֵקֶד נֶפֶשׁ / בְּזָקְנוֹ לֹא מָצָא נֹפֶשׁ
וַתִּכְהֶיןָ עֵינָיו בַּעֲשַׁן טִפֵּשׁ.

זַרְעוֹ רִגֵּל בְּאָהֳלֵי תוֹרָה / וְעַל אָמְרוֹ דַּרְכִּי נִסְתְּרָה
נִכְסָה מֶנּוּ פּוֹרַת בְּסִתִירָה.

So, too, the evil ones who dig a hiding place for themselves,
shall find righteousness walking before them, leaping toward them.
And perhaps they shall be hidden away on the day of the LORD's anger.

O faithful God, as You prepare to pass judgment,
were You to press the letter of the law in judgment,
who would ever be found righteous before You and acquitted by such judgment? / O Holy One.

When the twelve brothers were examined,
He did not exonerate them in judgment,
for they had sold their righteous brother into bondage for money. *Amos 2*

The evil men of no name, who sold God's chosen ones
into whoring, drunkenness, thievery and violence,
shall have punishment heaped upon them when they stand for judgment.

When God rises to the case and stands in judgment,
He will punish these men for all they have done,
that they shall know there is a God who renders judgment.

If He shall not do it on His own behalf, / and remove all ire and wrath,
then no inquiry of man's actions will yield any merits. / O Holy One.

The descendant who brought down the holy commandments,
and freed the firstborn bullock, Israel, from servitude to the asses of Egypt,
yet suffered punishment because of his harsh words:
"Listen, you rebellious people." *Num. 20*

As a result of his ensnarement in the ten tests the people set for God,
his death merited ten different biblical mentions.
And when he reached the border of the holy land,
he was chained and bound and was not allowed to enter.

The leaders who issue judgment while taking bribes –
how can they hope to be judged with a measuring-line of exoneration?
Rather, just as they judged so shall they be judged.

O faithful God, as You prepare to pass judgment,
were You to press the letter of the law in judgment,
who would ever be found righteous before You and acquitted by such judgment? / O Holy One.

The youths – Aaron's sons – who offered their foreign flame,
were killed by God's decree when the holy fire entered their nostrils,
as a lesson to the sinners of God's scattered nation.

Achan, the lowly man who desired consecrated booty from Jericho,
was seized and destroyed together with all that was his,
from stacks and standing grain to vineyards.

רָשָׁע אֲשֶׁר בְּמַחֲבֵא יְחַתֵּר / צֶדֶק לְפָנָיו יְהַלֵּךְ וִינַתֵּר
אוּלַי בְּיוֹם אַף יִסָּתֵר.

אֵל אֱמוּנָה, בְּעָרְכְּךָ דִין / אִם תְּמַצֶּה עֹמֶק הַדִּין / מִי יִצְדַּק לְפָנֶיךָ בַּדִּין / קָדוֹשׁ.

רֵעִים שְׁנֵים עָשָׂר כְּהִבְדִּיק / בְּרִיב אוֹתָם לֹא הִצְדִּיק
עַל־מִכְרָם בַּכֶּסֶף צַדִּיק: עמוס ב

בְּנֵי בְלִי שֵׁם, בְּמָכְרָם עֲמוּסִים / בְּזוֹנָה וּבְיַיִן וּבְשֹׁד חֲמָסִים
אֵיךְ בַּדִּין יִהְיוּ נֶעֱמָסִים.

בְּהִתְיַצְּבוֹ לָרִיב, בְּעָמְדוֹ לָדִין / עַל זֹאת אוֹתָם יָדִין
לְמַעַן יֵדְעוּן שַׁדּוּן בַּדִּין.

אִם לֹא לְמַעֲנוֹ יַעַשׂ / וְיָסִיר חֲרוֹן אַף וָכַעַס / אֵין לְבַקֵּר וְלִמְצֹא מַעַשׂ / קָדוֹשׁ.

יֶרֶד אֲשֶׁר הוֹרִיד אֲמָרִים / וְהִדְרִיד בְּכוֹר שׁוֹר מֵחֲמוֹרִים
וְנֶעֱנַשׁ בְּשָׁמְעוּ נָא הַמּוֹרִים. במדבר כ

יַעַן אֲשֶׁר נוֹקַשׁ בְּעֶשֶׂר / נֶחֱרְתוּ בוֹ מִיתוֹת עֶשֶׂר
וּכְגָע גְּבוּל, כְּבַל בְּאֹסֶר.

רָאשֶׁיהָ אֲשֶׁר בְּשֹׁחַד יִשְׁפֹּטוּ / אֵיךְ בְּקַו צֶדֶק יִשָּׁפֵטוּ
כִּי אִם כְּמוֹ שָׁפָטוּ.

אֵל אֱמוּנָה, בְּעָרְכְּךָ דִין / אִם תְּמַצֶּה עֹמֶק הַדִּין / מִי יִצְדַּק לְפָנֶיךָ בַּדִּין / קָדוֹשׁ.

רוֹבִים עֲלֵי אֵשׁ זָרָה / פָּגְעָה בָם בְּאַף גְּזֵרָה
לְלַמֵּד בָּם פּוֹשְׁעֵי פְזוּרָה.

בְּעַר חָמַד מִן הַחֵרֶם / וְנִלְכַּד הוּא וְכָל אֲשֶׁר לוֹ בַּחֵרֶם
מִגָּדִישׁ וְעַד קָמָה וָכָרֶם.

What good comes from being a traitor and thief,
for riches profit not on the day of the Lord's wrath.
They will not help to beseech the One who teaches all for their own benefit.

If He shall not do it on His own behalf, / and remove all ire and wrath,
then no inquiry of man's actions will yield any merits. / O Holy One.

Uzzah sent forth his hand to take hold of the holy Ark,
so he was judged severely as God's anger was aroused.
What then can those who pass before God like sheep hope for?

When the minstrel – David – burst forth with "God, examine me,"
he was indeed scrutinized and pleaded with God – "Be gracious to me
and do not approach to judge me harshly."

Those who call loudly with their voices and shofar,
though their sins shall be recounted in their judgment,
may they find atonement in a gift of grace.

O faithful God, as You prepare to pass judgment,
were You to press the letter of the law in judgment,
who would ever be found righteous before You and acquitted by such judgment? / O Holy One.

When the King – Uzziah – haughtily offered incense to God,
leprosy appeared on his forehead as a sign.
He was judged for not knowing what was forbidden in God's law,
and was found culpable.

When the feet of the evildoers shall weaken,
those who entered the holy Sanctuary to intentionally sin
shall be judged when the Lord subdues rebellious nations.

When those who amass wealth through lies shall be judged,
in meticulous, wrathful proceedings before the Lord,
then the mouths of those slanderers shall be stopped up. *Ps. 63*

If He shall not do it on His own behalf, / and remove all ire and wrath,
then no inquiry of man's actions will yield any merits. / O Holy One.

The upright Hezekiah who walked before the Lord faithfully –
how is it that despite the righteous things he had done and his faithful deeds,
the God of truth judged him for bragging of the Temple treasures?

Josiah, God's confidant, before whom and after
no other comparable leader ever rose from His chosen nation,
nevertheless fell in battle when God judged him meticulously.

בּוֹגֵד וְשׁוֹדֵד מַה מּוֹעִיל / וְהוֹן בְּעֶבְרָה לֹא יוֹעִיל
לְחַלּוֹת פְּנֵי מְלַמֵּד לְהוֹעִיל.

אִם לֹא לְמַעֲנוֹ יַעַשׂ / וְיָסִיר חֲרוֹן אַף וָכַעַס / אֵין לְבַקֵּר וְלִמְצֹא מַעַשׂ / קָדוֹשׁ.

יָד שָׁלַח אֶחָז בָּאָרוֹן / וְנַעֲשָׂה בּוֹ מִשְׁפָּט וְחָרוֹן
מַה יַּעֲשׂוּ עוֹבְרֵי כִּבְנֵי מָרוֹן.

יוֹדֵעַ נַגֵּן כְּפָץ בְּחָנְנִי / נִבְחַן וְנָם חִנָּם חָנֵּנִי
וְאַל תָּבֹא בְמִשְׁפָּט לְדַיְּנֵנִי.

קוֹרְאֵי בְגָרוֹן וְקוֹל שׁוֹפָר / אִם פִּשְׁעָם בַּדִּין יְסֻפָּר
בְּמַתְּנַת חִנָּם הַיּוֹם יְכֻפָּר.

אֵל אֱמוּנָה, בְּעָרְכְּךָ דִּין / אִם תְּמַצֶּה עֹמֶק הַדִּין / מִי יִצְדַּק לְפָנֶיךָ בַּדִּין / קָדוֹשׁ.

קָצִין כְּגָאָה לְקַטֵּר לַשֵּׁם / נֶגַע בְּמִצְחוֹ זָרַח לְהֵרָשֵׁם
וְנִשְׁפַּט בְּלֹא יָדַע וְאָשֵׁם.

לְעֵת תָּמוּט רֶגֶל זֵדִים / אֲשֶׁר בָּאוּ לְהֵיכָל מְזִידִים
יִשָּׁפְטוּ בְּמַכְנִיעַ עַם זֵדִים.

לְעֵת יְבֻקְּרוּ פּוֹעֲלֵי שֶׁקֶר / לְהִשָּׁפֵט בְּבוֹחֵן אַף וָחֵקֶר
יִסָּכֵר פִּי דוֹבְרֵי שָׁקֶר. תהלים סג

אִם לֹא לְמַעֲנוֹ יַעַשׂ / וְיָסִיר חֲרוֹן אַף וָכַעַס / אֵין לְבַקֵּר וְלִמְצֹא מַעַשׂ / קָדוֹשׁ.

יָשָׁר מִתְהַלֵּךְ לְפָנָיו בֶּאֱמֶת / אֵיךְ אַחֲרֵי הַדְּבָרִים וְהָאֱמֶת
חִשֵּׁב פָּעֳלוֹ אֱלֹהִים אֱמֶת.

יְדִיד אֲשֶׁר לְפָנָיו וְאַחֲרָיו / לֹא קָם כָּמוֹהוּ בִּבְחִירָיו
וְאַחֲרֵי כָּל זֹאת דִּקְדֵּק אַחֲרָיו.

Thus shall all the creatures of the world understand,
that if this is the case for the very pillars of the Lord's earth,
what can the earth's wicked hope for?

O faithful God, as You prepare to pass judgment,
were You to press the letter of the law in judgment,
who would ever be found righteous before You and acquitted by such judgment? / O Holy One.

Thus men, like trees of the field, shall indeed see,
for if fire took hold of the righteous who are saturated with merits like dew,
then no doubt the evil, who are like dry, cut-down thorns, shall quiver.

Behold there is no one left at all / to entreat on behalf of man,
for You are God and not a mortal.

I shall speak of that which is recorded in Your truthful record,
of the deeds that were done throughout this year,
as we seek to appease You with the sound (*On Shabbat:* remembrance)
of the shofar, on this Rosh HaShana Day.

If He shall not do it on His own behalf, / and remove all ire and wrath,
then no inquiry of man's actions will yield any merits. / O Holy One.

*Most communities continue with "And so – [The Lord] became King in Yeshurun" on* *page 538.* *However, nowadays only half the original piyut is recited; the full text is given below.*

וּבְכֵן And so – [The Lord] became King in Yeshurun.

The Supreme King
God who resides on high, / mighty on high,
May He lift the strength of His hand high –
He shall reign forever.

The destitute king
Worn and relegated to decay / in uppermost hell and beneath,
weary without rest –
till when shall he reign?

The Supreme King
Mighty in His assemblies, / He decrees and fulfills
and reveals hidden truths –
He shall reign forever.

The destitute king
Faint as a plague, / He speaks and fades, / and is as a blind man –
till when shall he reign?

יָבִינוּ כָּל יְצוּרֵי אֶרֶץ / אִם כֵּן בִּמְצוּקֵי אֶרֶץ
מַה יַּעֲשׂוּ רִשְׁעֵי אָרֶץ.

אֵל אֱמוּנָה, בְּעָרְכְּךָ דִין / אִם תְּמַצֶּה עְמֶק הַדִּין / מִי יִצְדַּק לְפָנֶיךָ בַּדִּין / קָדוֹשׁ.

רָאֹה יִרְאוּ יַעֲרֵי שִׂיחִים / אִם אֵשׁ אָחֲזָה בַּלַּחִים
אָז יָנְוּעוּ יְבֵשִׁים כְּסוּחִים.

רְאֵה כִּי אֵין אִישׁ / לְהַפְגִּיעַ בְּעַד בְּנֵי אִישׁ
וְאַתָּה אֵל וְלֹא אִישׁ.

רָשׁוּם בִּכְתָב אֱמֶת אֲשַׁנְּנָה / מַעֲשֵׂה כָּל יְמוֹת הַשָּׁנָה
לְרַצּוֹתְךָ בְּשׁוֹפָר (*On* שבת *substitute* בְּזִכְרוֹן שׁוֹפָר) בְּזֶה רֹאשׁ הַשָּׁנָה.

אִם לֹא לְמַעֲנוֹ יַעַשׂ / וְיָסִיר חֲרוֹן אַף וָכַעַס / אֵין לְבַקֵּר וְלִמְצֹא מַעַשׂ / קָדוֹשׁ.

*Most communities continue with* וּבְכֵן, וַיְהִי בִישֻׁרוּן מֶלֶךְ *on page 539.*
*However, nowadays only half the original piyut is recited; the full text is given below.*

וּבְכֵן, וַיְהִי בִישֻׁרוּן מֶלֶךְ

מֶלֶךְ עֶלְיוֹן
אֵל דָּר בַּמָּרוֹם / אַדִּיר בַּמָּרוֹם / אֹמֶץ יָדוֹ תָּרֹם
לַעֲדֵי עַד יִמְלֹךְ.

מֶלֶךְ אֶבְיוֹן
בָּלֶה וְיֹרֵד שַׁחַת / בִּשְׁאוֹל וּבְתַחַת / בְּלֵאוּת בְּלִי נַחַת
עַד מָתַי יִמְלֹךְ.

מֶלֶךְ עֶלְיוֹן
גִּבּוֹר לְהָקִים / גּוֹזֵר וּמֵקִים / גּוֹלֶה עֲמֻקִּים
לַעֲדֵי עַד יִמְלֹךְ.

מֶלֶךְ אֶבְיוֹן
דָּוֶה כַדֶּבֶר / דּוֹבֵר וְעוֹבֵר / דּוֹמֶה לְעִוֵּר
עַד מָתַי יִמְלֹךְ.

The Supreme King
He speaks righteously, / garbed in righteousness, /
He hearkens to our cries –
He shall reign forever.

The destitute king
Desirous of evil, / working evil, / ready for sin and evil –
till when shall he reign?

The Supreme King
He recalls our ancestors / to vindicate His creatures,
wrathful to our oppressors –
He shall reign forever.

The destitute king
He plans and forgets, / hastens to forget, / sins and argues yet –
till when shall he reign?

The Supreme King
Good is He who lives forever, / His kindness lasts forever, /
He laid out the eternal heavens –
He shall reign forever.

The destitute king
His days are short, / filled with disappointment, /
conceived for a brief duration –
till when shall he reign?

The Supreme King
Clothed in light like a garment, / all the luminaries of light,
He is mighty and luminous –
He shall reign forever.

The destitute king
Shall be lowered into darkness, / dimmed like a clod of earth,
folded into obscurity –
till when shall he reign?

מֶלֶךְ עֶלְיוֹן
**הַמְדַבֵּר בִּצְדָקָה / הַלּוֹבֵשׁ צְדָקָה / הַמַּאֲזִין צְעָקָה**
לַעֲדֵי עַד יִמְלֹךְ.

מֶלֶךְ אֶבְיוֹן
וְחָפֵץ בְּרֶשַׁע / וְעוֹשֶׂה רֶשַׁע / וּמוּכָן לְפֶשַׁע
עַד מָתַי יִמְלֹךְ.

מֶלֶךְ עֶלְיוֹן
**זוֹכֵר צוּרִים / זַכּוּת יְצוּרִים / זוֹעֵם צָרִים**
לַעֲדֵי עַד יִמְלֹךְ.

מֶלֶךְ אֶבְיוֹן
חוֹשֵׁב וְשׁוֹכֵחַ / חָשׁ וּמִשְׁתַּכֵּחַ / חָב וּמִתְוַכֵּחַ
עַד מָתַי יִמְלֹךְ.

מֶלֶךְ עֶלְיוֹן
**טוֹב שׁוֹכֵן עַד / טוּבוֹ לָעַד / טִפַּח שְׁמֵי עַד**
לַעֲדֵי עַד יִמְלֹךְ.

מֶלֶךְ אֶבְיוֹן
יָמָיו טְפָחוֹת / יוֹמוֹ לְמַפָּחוֹת / יָחוּם טִפּוּחוֹת
עַד מָתַי יִמְלֹךְ.

מֶלֶךְ עֶלְיוֹן
**כַּשַּׂלְמָה עוֹטֶה אוֹר / כָּל מְאוֹרֵי אוֹר / כַּבִּיר וְנָאוֹר**
לַעֲדֵי עַד יִמְלֹךְ.

מֶלֶךְ אֶבְיוֹן
לְצַלְמָוֶת יְשֻׁפַּל / לְרֶגֶב יְאֻפַּל / לְאַשְׁמַן יְקֻפַּל
עַד מָתַי יִמְלֹךְ.

The Supreme King
King who reigns forever, / He deciphers hidden mysteries
and puts speech in the mouth of the mute –
He shall reign forever.

The destitute king
Frequently shaken, / troubled by chance, / terrified with madness –
till when shall he reign?

The Supreme King
Bears all His creatures, / encompasses and consumes all,
looks upon all –
He shall reign forever.

The destitute king
He shall pass and traverse, / his eyelids shall grow dim,
his dust shall be heaped up –
till when shall he reign?

The Supreme King
His glory is might, / the works of His right hand are mighty,
the Redeemer and Fortress –
He shall reign forever.

The destitute king
His stench shall reek, / clothed in excrement, / desolation shall be his lot –
till when shall he reign?

The Supreme King
His holy angels are like flames,
calling forth the waters of angelic name,
close to those who call upon Him in love –
He shall reign forever.

The destitute king
Clothed in worms, / whether wet or dry, / engulfed in water and flames –
till when shall he reign?

מֶֽלֶךְ עֶלְיוֹן
מֶֽלֶךְ עוֹלָמִים / מְפַעְנֵֽחַ נֶעֱלָמִים / מֵשִֽׂיחַ אִלְּמִים
לַעֲדֵי עַד יִמְלֹךְ.

מֶֽלֶךְ אֶבְיוֹן
נָע לִרְגָעִים / נֶחְפָּז מִפְּגָעִים / נִבְהָל בְּשִׁגּוּעִים
עַד מָתַי יִמְלֹךְ.

מֶֽלֶךְ עֶלְיוֹן
סוֹבֵל כֹּל / סָב וּמְבַלֶּה כֹל / סוֹקֵר בַּכֹּל
לַעֲדֵי עַד יִמְלֹךְ.

מֶֽלֶךְ אֶבְיוֹן
עוֹבֵר וּמִתְעַבֵּר / עַפְעַפָּיו מְעַוֵּר / עֲפָרוֹ צוֹבֵר
עַד מָתַי יִמְלֹךְ.

מֶֽלֶךְ עֶלְיוֹן
פְּאֵרוֹ עֹז / פָּעַל יְמִינוֹ תָּעֹז / פּוֹדֶה וּמָעוֹז
לַעֲדֵי עַד יִמְלֹךְ.

מֶֽלֶךְ אֶבְיוֹן
צַחֲנָה תְבִאִישֶֽׁנּוּ / צוֹאָה תַלְבִּישֶֽׁנּוּ / צִיָּה תִירָשֶֽׁנּוּ
עַד מָתַי יִמְלֹךְ.

מֶֽלֶךְ עֶלְיוֹן
קְדוֹשָׁיו לַהַב / קוֹרֵא מֵי רַהַב / קָרוֹב לְקוֹרְאָיו בְּאַהַב
לַעֲדֵי עַד יִמְלֹךְ.

מֶֽלֶךְ אֶבְיוֹן
רִמָּה לוֹבֵשׁ / רָטֹב וְיָבֵשׁ / רָשׁוּף בְּמַֽיִם וּבְאֵשׁ
עַד מָתַי יִמְלֹךְ.

The Supreme King
He does not know sleep, / His nearest angelic servants are at peace,
fine praise for the righteous fills His treasury –
He shall reign forever.

The destitute king
Sleep hovers over him, / deep sleep enfolds him,
confusion overwhelms him –
till when shall he reign?

Yet the Supreme King
His vigor is eternal, / His glory forever and ever,
His praise stands eternally –
He shall reign forever.

*The service continues with "And so, sanctity" on page 542.*

מֶלֶךְ עֶלְיוֹן
שֵׁנָה אֵין לְפָנָיו / שֶׁקֶט בִּפְנִינָיו / שֶֽׁבַח טוֹב בְּמַצְפּוּנָיו
לַעֲדֵי עַד יִמְלֹךְ.

מֶלֶךְ אֶבְיוֹן
תְּנוּמָה תְעוּפֶֽנּוּ / תַּרְדֵּמָה תְעוֹפְפֶֽנּוּ / תֹּֽהוּ יְשׁוּפֶֽנּוּ
עַד מָתַי יִמְלֹךְ.

אֲבָל מֶלֶךְ עֶלְיוֹן
תָּקְפּוֹ לָעַד / תִּפְאַרְתּוֹ עֲדֵי עַד / תְּהִלָּתוֹ עוֹמֶֽדֶת לָעַד
לַעֲדֵי עַד יִמְלֹךְ.

*The service continues with* וּבְכֵן לְךָ תַעֲלֶה *on page 543.*

*Traditionally, special piyutim (תקיעתות) were said before the* מלכיות *verses, and before the* זכרונות *and* שופרות *blessings, originally incorporating the verses of* מלכיות *into the piyutim themselves. The* תקיעתא *for the first-day* מלכיות *was composed by Rabbi Elazar HaKalir. It has a quadruple acrostic form, and its theme is the future kingdom of God. Because it mentions the* שופר *several times, it is not said on* שבת *– in which case the second-day piyut, "אֲהַלְלָה," (page 1068) is substituted, and "אַנְסִיכָה" is said on the second day.*

אַנְסִיכָה מַלְכִּי / לְפָנָיו בְּהִתְהַלְּכִי / אָמְצוֹ בְּהַמְלִיכִי / יֶאְזֹר עֹז וְיִמְלֹךְ.
אֱלִיל בְּהַשְׁלִיכִי / לִפְנֵי בּוֹא יוֹם מַלְכִּי / אִישׁ מַלְאָכִי / יִשְׁלַח, וְאָז יִמְלֹךְ.

בְּבוֹאוֹ לַהֲלֹךְ / נִתַּשׁ חָנֵף מִמֶּלֶךְ / בֵּית גֵּאִים בְּלִי מְלֹךְ / יִסַּח, לְבַל יִמְלֹךְ.
בְּתוֹכִי יַהֲלֹךְ / בְּהוֹפִיעוֹ לִמְלֹךְ / בְּמַלְכוּתוֹ אֶמְלֹךְ / וְאָז יִמְלֹךְ.

גְּבֶרֶת מַמְלָכוֹת / בְּמַגְּרוֹ מַמְלָכוֹת / גּוֹיִם וּמַמְלָכוֹת / יָהֹם, וְהוּא יִמְלֹךְ.
גִּלְיוֹן הֲלִיכוֹת / וְסֵפֶר תַּהֲלוּכוֹת / גַּל הַיּוֹם לְזַכּוֹת / חוֹכָיו לִמְלֹךְ.

דּוֹרֶכֶת נְסִיכוֹת / בְּחִנּוּן קוֹל בָּכוֹת / דִּבְּרָה, אֲנִי בְּמַלְכוּת /
וּמִי יוּכַל לִמְלֹךְ.
דַּכְּאֵי רְוַח נְמִיכוֹת / מְחַפְּשֵׂי בְּיוֹם דִּין זְכוּת / דֶּשָׁה בְּעֹל מַלְכוּת /
עַד צוּר יִמְלֹךְ.

הִלּוּךְ מַהֲלַךְ / חֲמֵשׁ מֵאוֹת הִלַּךְ / הָדוּר עַד הַמְלַךְ / בְּעֻזּוֹ לִמְלֹךְ.
הֲבֵל הַמְּמְלָךְ / עַל מֶה מָלַךְ / הֲלֹא בְּמִי נִמְלַךְ / כִּי אָץ לִמְלֹךְ.

וּמִלִּפְנֵי מְלָךְ מֶלֶךְ / חַי מִלְּפָנִים מֶלֶךְ / וְעַד תֶּהֱלֶה כָּל מֶלֶךְ /
הוּא לְבַד יִמְלֹךְ.
וּמַה יָּעֹז מוֹלֵךְ / בְּעֹז מִשְׁפַּט מֶלֶךְ / וְכַעֲבוֹר סוּפָה בְּהֵלֶךְ / יַחֲלֹף מִמְּלֹךְ.

זָךְ, דִּין בְּעָרְכוֹ / יֹאחֵז דַּרְכּוֹ / זֵדִים בְּדָרְכוֹ / נָקָם יָעַט, וְיִמְלֹךְ.
זֵר זֵד בְּשַׁלְּכוֹ / יִתֵּן עֹז לְמַלְכּוֹ / זַכִּים בְּהַמְלִיכוֹ / עַל כֹּל יִמְלֹךְ.

חַדְּשׁוּ מְלוּכָה / כַּדָּת וְכַהֲלָכָה / חֹטֶר מַמְלָכָה / בְּמִישׁוֹר יִמְלֹךְ.
חֹבֶשׁ אֲרוּכָה / לְאֶרֶךְ יוֹם מְבוּכָה / חֲתֻלָּה לְמַכָּה / יַעַל בְּעֵת יִמְלֹךְ.

טֹרַח מַלְכֻיוֹת / עוֹבְדֵי מַשְׂכִּיּוֹת / טִמְּאוּ חֱמֶד שְׂכִיּוֹת / בְּגַאֲוָה לִמְלֹךְ.
טֹהַר זָכִיּוֹת / וְשַׁאַג קוֹל בְּכִיּוֹת / טֶבַע צוּל דָּכִיּוֹת / יִפֶן, וּבָם יִמְלֹךְ.

יָהָב מַשְׁלִיכִים / עָלָיו בְּנֵי מְלָכִים / יוֹם זֶה לוֹ מְחַכִּים / בֹּא יָבֹא לִמְלֹךְ.
יַעַבְרוּ, מִתְהַלְּכִים / לְפָנָיו כְּמַלְאָכִים / יַחַד מַמְלִיכִים / יהוה יִמְלֹךְ.

כִּתִּים בְּכִתָּתוֹ / אִיֵּים בְּהַכּוֹתוֹ / כֵּס מִמַּלְכוּתוֹ / יִכּוֹן וְיִמְלֹךְ.
כְּבוֹד מַלְכוּתוֹ / וְקִדּוּשׁ הֲלִיכָתוֹ / כְּגָמְרוֹ מְלַאכְתּוֹ / לְעֵין כֹּל יִמְלֹךְ.

לְכָל גֹּבַהּ יַפִּיל / וְהַר וְגֶבַע יַשְׁפִּיל / לְכָל אֹם יַאְפִּיל / וּכְאוֹר זָרוּעַ יִמְלֹךְ.
לְרֹאִי יַקְפִּיל / וַחֲדָשִׁים יַכְפִּיל / לְיוֹם זֶה פּוּר הִפִּיל / מִצִּיּוֹן לִמְלֹךְ.

מֻטּוּ גוֹיִם / הָמוּ גֵאִים / מָעֲדוּ מִתְגָּאִים / גֵּאֶה בְּבֹאוֹ לִמְלֹךְ.
מָלְכוּ דְגוּיִם / נֻטְּלוּ סְגוּיִם / מֶלֶךְ הַגּוֹיִם / עֵת אָתָא לִמְלֹךְ.

נְדִיבֵי עַמִּים / יֵאָסְפוּ מֵעַמִּים / נְשֹׂא מְעוּטֵי עַמִּים / אֶל מְקוֹמָם לִמְלֹךְ.
נִגּוּן נְעִימִים / לְמוּלָם מַנְעִימִים / נְשָׂאָם מֵעֲמָמִים / עֲלֵיהֶם לִמְלֹךְ.

סִכּוּת אֱלִילִים / כִּיּוּן גִּלּוּלִים / סָחֹב כְּמוֹ חֲלָלִים / יַשְׁלְכוּ בְּלִי לִמְלֹךְ.
סוֹד אֵל אֵלִים / הָבוּ בְּנֵי אֵלִים / שְׂאוּ זִמְרָה וְהִלּוּלִים / לְאָדוֹן, כִּי יִמְלֹךְ.

עִזּוּז יָד בְּהַשִּׂיאוֹ / לְהָרִים נְשִׂיאוֹ / עֲמוּסָיו בְּנַשְּׂאוֹ / יָעֹז וְיִמְלֹךְ.
עַל רוּם מַשָּׂאוֹ / יְדֵיהוּ בְּנַשְּׂאוֹ / עַל הוֹד כִּסְאוֹ / יֵשֵׁב וְיִמְלֹךְ.

פּוּר תְּפוֹרַר אֶרֶץ / בְּכִלָּיוֹן וְחָרֶץ / פַּח בְּיוֹשְׁבֵי הָאָרֶץ / יַרְגִּיז וְיִמְלֹךְ.
פַּחַד שׁוֹפָרוֹת עֶרֶץ / יְשַׁלֵּשׁ, וּבָם יֶרֶץ / פְּאֵר מִכְּנַף הָאָרֶץ /
יַעֲלוּ, כִּי יִמְלֹךְ.

צְבִי מֵהֲדֹם יַעַל / וְאֶדֶר מִשַּׁעַל / צַהַל מִשְּׁמֵי מַעַל / יְרַנְּנוּ, כִּי יִמְלֹךְ.
צְבָאוֹת כָּל פֹּעַל / לְצַלְעָם יִרְטִי תַּעַל / צְפִירַת פְּאֵר לְהַעַל /
הֵן לְצֶדֶק יִמְלֹךְ.

קְצִינִים אֲשֶׁר מָלְכוּ / אַדֶּרֶת יַשְׁלִיכוּ / קוֹל יִתְּנוּ, וְיַמְלִיכוּ /
לַמֶּלֶךְ, כִּי יִמְלֹךְ.

קְרוּאִים יִמְלֹכוּ / וְאַחֲרָיו יַהֲלֹכוּ / קוֹמְמִיּוּת יֵלֵכוּ / וּבְרֹאשָׁם יִמְלֹךְ.
רָז הַמֻּכְמָן / לְיוֹם זֶה מְזֻמָּן / רָשׁוּם לְמוֹעֵד וּזְמָן / וּבוֹ נוֹקֵם יִמְלֹךְ.
רוֹעֶה נֶאֱמָן / בְּבֹאוֹ מִתֵּימָן / רְוּחַ יַסְעִיר בְּתֵימָן / בְּגִלְעָד יִמְלֹךְ.

שִׁנְאַן עֲלִיּוֹת / וְסוֹד פְּלִיאִיּוֹת / שִׁיר מִתְּלוּלִיּוֹת / יִפְצְחוּ, כִּי יִמְלֹךְ.
שְׂאִיּוֹת תַּחְתִּיּוֹת / וְהוֹד אוֹתִיּוֹת / שְׁאוֹן הֲמוֹן בְּרִיּוֹת / יָרִיעוּ, כִּי יִמְלֹךְ.

תְּכַן כֵּס כַּשֶּׁמֶשׁ / שְׁמוֹ לִפְנֵי שֶׁמֶשׁ / תָּאֳרוֹ כְּצֵאת הַשֶּׁמֶשׁ /
בְּמָלְכוֹ יִמְלֹךְ.
תּוֹמֵךְ מִמִּזְרַח שֶׁמֶשׁ / וְעַד מְבוֹאַת שֶׁמֶשׁ / תַּמָּה, בָּרָה כַּשֶּׁמֶשׁ /
יְרוֹמֵם וְיִמְלֹךְ.

*The* תקיעתא *for the first-day* זכרונות *was composed by Rabbi Elazar HaKalir. It also has a quadruple acrostic form (following the reverse order* תשר״ת*), every stanza opens with the word* זְכֹר *("In memory of"), and each line ends with the word* יִזְכֹּר *("He will remember"). Like the* תקיעתא *for* מלכיות*, it is not said on* שבת *– in which case the piyut for the second day, "*אֶפְחַד בְּמַעֲשַׂי*," (page 1070) is said, and "*זְכֹר תְּחִלַּת*" is said on the second day.*

זְכֹר תְּחִלַּת כָּל מַעַשׂ / אֲשֶׁר בְּכָל שָׁנָה נַעַשׂ / תּוֹחַלְתָּם לִמְאַס /
יוֹצֵר בַּל יִזְכֹּר.
תּוֹכַחַת מַעַשׂ / אִם יָצְאָה בְּכַעַס / תּוֹמֵךְ לְמַעֲנוֹ יַעַשׂ /
וִיצוּרִים יִזְכֹּר.

זְכֹר שֶׁמִּבְּרֵאשִׁית / תְּבוּאַת רֵאשִׁית / שֹׁרֶשׁ בִּכּוּר רֵאשִׁית / יְרֵא וְיִזְכֹּר.
שֶׁצֶף חֲרִישִׁית / אִם חָר לְהָשִׁית / שׁוּבָה אֲשֶׁר הֵשִׁית /
לַשּׁוֹבָבִים יִזְכֹּר.

זְכֹר רֹאשׁ עֲפָרוֹת / וְתוֹלָדוֹת סְפוּרוֹת / רִשּׁוּם סְפוּרוֹת /
לְמִסְפַּר חוֹל יִזְכֹּר.
רֹבַע מִסְפָּרוֹת / מַחֲנֵי לְכַפָּרוֹת / רֶגֶשׁ שׁוֹפָרוֹת / לְשַׁפְּרָם יִזְכֹּר.

זְכֹר קְרִיאַת סֵפֶר / אֲשֶׁר גָּלְמִי שִׁפֵּר / קָצַב לוֹ בַּסֵּפֶר /
בְּכָל דּוֹר וָדוֹר לִזְכֹּר.
קֶצֶף אִם הֶחֱרַט בַּסֵּפֶר / לְבִלְתִּי מְצֹא כֹפֶר /
קִיּוּם זִכְרוֹן זֶה סֵפֶר לְפָנָיו יִזְכֹּר.

זְכֹר צְפוּן מוֹרְדֵי אוֹר / תְּמִים דּוֹר כָּאוֹר / צִיָּה כְּחַר לָאוֹר / קֹנָיו יִזְכֹּר.
צִפּוּפִים פְּנֵי נָאוֹר / מִשְׁפָּטָם תֵּת לָאוֹר / צַחַן רֹעַ שְׂאוֹר /
בְּרִיב בַּל יִזְכֹּר.

זְכֹר פְּעֻלַּת אֶזְרָח / הֶעֱרָתָהּ מִמִּזְרָח / פָּעֳלוֹ יִזְרַח / בְּקֶרֶב שָׁנִים יִזְכֹּר.
פַּח אִם הֻטְרַח / פְּרָחָיו לְמֵרַח / פִּלּוּלוֹ יִצְרַח / בַּעֲדָם יִזְכֹּר.

זְכֹר עֲקֵדַת מוֹרִיָּה / כְּהִיּת רְאִיָּה / עֲדֵי עֵרֹם וְעֶרְיָה / סִבּוּכוֹ יִזְכֹּר.
עֶצֶב טְרִיָּה / אִם כּוֹאֲבָה פּוּרִיָּה / עֲתָרוֹ לְרָאִיָּה / וְלִזְכוּת יִזְכֹּר.

זְכֹר סֻלָּם חֲלָם / וְעָלָיו מְחוּלָּלָם / שָׂרֵי אַרְבַּע וְעֵלָם / בּוֹ כְּמֵאָז יִזְכֹּר.
שָׂרִיגָיו בִּמְעָלָם / וַיֹּאמֶר לְגַעְלָם / שִׂיחוֹ יוֹעִילָם / בְּרִית לִזְכֹּר.

זְכֹר נְקוּבֵי מַטּוֹת / שְׁבוּעוֹת מַטּוֹת / נְדִידוֹת הַמִּטּוֹת / לְאַמְּצָם יִזְכֹּר.
נוֹשְׂאֵי עַל מוֹטוֹת / אִם פֶּץ לְהַמְטוֹת / נֶפֶץ חֲדַר הַמִּטּוֹת /
לְכִפּוּר יִזְכֹּר.

זְכֹר מְצוּקִים / יְסוֹד מוּצָקִים / מִפְּעָלָם לְצוֹעֲקִים / בְּפוּט חָשׁ לִזְכּוֹר.
מִפִּי יוֹנְקִים / אֲשֶׁר בַּסּוּף נוֹאֲקִים / מַאֲמַר בְּרִית וְחֻקִּים /
דְּבַר קָדְשׁוֹ יִזְכֹּר.

זְכֹר לִין כְּפָרִים / וְאִמְרֵי שְׁפָרִים / לִמְשַׁלְּמֵי פָרִים / בְּשָׂפָה יִזְכֹּר.
לְעֵת בִּקּוּר סְפָרִים / סְתָרִים מְסַפְּרִים / לִשְׁנֵי עֳפָרִים / לְצֶדֶק יִזְכֹּר.

זְכֹר כְּבוֹד מִשְׁכָּן / מְקוֹם דּוֹד שָׁכַן / כְּרוּבִים בּוֹ שִׁכַּן /
חֶסֶד נְעוּרִים יִזְכֹּר.
כִּיּוֹר עִם כַּן / וְנֹעַם קוֹל דּוּכָן / כַּבִּיר בְּיוֹם מוּכָן / לַנְּבוֹנִים יִזְכֹּר.

זְכֹר יְלִיד נוּן / וּמִשְׁפְּטֵי אוּרֵי אֶפְנוּן / יֶזְכְּרוּ בְּרִנּוּן / פִּלְאָם לִזְכּוֹר.
יָקֶשׁ בְּרַק הַשָּׁנוּן / אִם הֻשְׁלַף לְתַאֲנוּן / יַקְשִׁיב תַּחֲנוּן /
חֲנוּנָיו לִזְכּוֹר.

זְכֹר טַעַם שׁוֹפְטִים / וְאוֹת קְצִיר חִטִּים / טֶפֶשׁ שׁוֹטִים / יְחַתֵּל מִלִּזְכּוֹר.
טֹרַח אַרְבַּעַת שְׁבָטִים / אִם נֶעֶנְשׁוּ נִשְׁפָּטִים / טֶבַע מִשְׁפָּטִים /
אֲשֶׁר שָׁם יִזְכֹּר.

זְכֹר חֲצוֹת לַיְלָה / וְתוֹדוֹת מִשְׁפְּטֵי לַיְלָה / חֹשֶׁךְ בְּאִישׁוֹן לַיְלָה /
נִגּוּנוֹ יִזְכֹּר.
חֵקֶר מִפְקַד לַיְלָה / יַגִּיהַּ בְּלַהַב לַיְלָה / חֹק הֶגֶה יוֹמָם וָלַיְלָה /
לַגִּיהָם יִזְכֹּר.

זְכֹר זֶה זְבוּל / אֲשֶׁר בְּבִצְעֵי חָבוּל / זְדוֹנוֹת סָבוּל / עוֹד בַּל יִזְכֹּר.
זַעַם כַּמַּבּוּל / אִם יָצָא לַחְבּוּל / זִכְרוֹן יֶרַח בּוּל / לְחֶמְלָה יִזְכֹּר.

זְכֹר וְכַח כָּל פֹּעַל / בְּקַו וָפֶלֶס יַעַל / וְאִם בְּמֶרֶד וְאִם בְּמַעַל /
רַב חֶסֶד יִזְכֹּר.
וְאִם טוֹב וְאִם רַע / אֲשֶׁר בּוֹ יֶאֱרַע / וְסִתּוֹ יִפָּרַע /
בְּסַאסְּאָה מִלִּזְכּוֹר.

זָכַר הַחַיִּים / עַד כַּמֶּה הֵם חַיִּים / הֵן אִם לַמָּוֶת אִם לַחַיִּים /
חַי חַי יִזְכֹּר.
הֲמוֹן שְׁאוֹן בְּרוּאִים / יַעַבְרוּ לְפָנָיו כִּמְרִיאִים / הֲלֹא כְּמוֹ רְאוּיִים/
לְכָל אֶחָד יִזְכֹּר.

זָכַר דַּלּוּת וָעֹשֶׁר / בַּצָּרַת וָחֹשֶׁר / דְּפִי וְגַם יֹשֶׁר / בַּדִּין הוּא יִזְכֹּר.
דְּבַר גָּלוּי וָסֵתֶר / בֵּינוֹנוּת וְסוֹתֵר / דֵּי חָסֵר וְיָתֵר / לְקֶצֶב יִזְכֹּר.

זָכַר גְּנוּנִים לְיַשֵּׁב / בַּמִּדְבָּר וְיוֹשֵׁב / גֶּשֶׁם וָרוּחַ לְנַשֵּׁב / מֵהַיּוֹם יִזְכֹּר.
גָּרוֹן לְהַקְשֵׁב / מֵעַם שְׁמוֹ חוֹשֵׁב / גָּלֻיּוֹת לְהָשֵׁב / בְּיוֹם תֵּקַע יִזְכֹּר.

זָכַר בֶּהָל וְחֵמָה / קְרָב וּמִלְחָמָה / בְּקוֹעַ חוֹמָה / לְחוֹמַת יָם יִזְכֹּר.
בְּאָדָם וּבִבְהֵמָה / אִם הֻקְנַס מְהוּמָה / בְּצוּר קוֹל הוֹמָה /
לַאֲדָמָה יִזְכֹּר.

זָכַר אֱמוּנָה וָשֶׁקֶר / אִזּוּן שִׂיחַ וָסֶקֶר / אוֹת פְּקֻדַּת בֹּקֶר / לִרְגָעִים יִזְכֹּר.
אִם לְזוֹל אִם לְיֹקֶר / אִם לָטַעַת אִם לַעֲקֹר /
אֱנוֹשׁ בְּדִקְדּוּק וָחֵקֶר/ לַמִּשְׁפָּט יִזְכֹּר.

*In the Middle Ages, the following lines were added to the* תקיעתא*,*
*in memory of those massacred during the Crusades.*

זָכַר בְּחוּנֵי שְׁמַד / טֶבַח זֵד מְשַׁמֵּד / בְּיוֹם תַּעַן וּמַעֲמָד / זִכְרוֹנָם לְפָנֶיךָ
יַעֲמֹד לִזְכֹּר.
כִּמְלֹא גְוִיּוֹת בְּנֵי נֵכָר / דְּמָם הֱיוֹת מֻנְכָּר / בְּהַבְדִּילוֹ בְּנֵי נֵכָר / דּוֹרֵשׁ
דָּמִים אוֹתָם זָכַר וְיִזְכֹּר.

זָכַר בָּאֵי בָאֵשׁ וּבַמַּיִם / נוֹשְׂאֵי לְךָ עַיִן לַשָּׁמַיִם / בְּיוֹם מְיֻמִּים / זִכְרוֹן
פְּגִיעַת פַּעֲמַיִם יִזְכֹּר.
בְּרַחֲמֵי מִדָּתְךָ / תִּשְׁפֹּט יְחִידָתְךָ / בִּרְצוֹן עֲבוֹדָתְךָ /
קִנְיַן עֲדָתְךָ זָכוֹר תִּזְכֹּר.

*The service continues with* אַתָּה זוֹכֵר *on page 587.*

*The author of the* תקיעתא *for first-day* מוסף *is unknown. It has a quadruple acrostic form, and its theme is the sound of the* שופר, *for which reason it is not said on* שבת. *Instead the piyut for the second day, "*אֲנוּסָה לְעֶזְרָה*," (page 1072) is said, and "*אֶשָּׂא דֵעִי*" on the second day.*

אֶשָּׂא דֵעִי בְּצֶדֶק / תֵּת לְפוֹעֲלִי צֶדֶק / אֶשְׁאֲלָה מִשְׁפְּטֵי צֶדֶק / קוֹל לְהָרִים כַּשּׁוֹפָר.
אֵין קוֹרֵא בְצֶדֶק / רוֹדֵף צֶדֶק צֶדֶק / אֶקְרָא שִׁמְעָה צֶדֶק / בְּקוֹל בָּלוּל בַּשּׁוֹפָר

בַּנְתִּי בְּמַדָּעִי / לְמֵרָחוֹק שְׂאֵת דֵעִי / בִּטּוּי תְּרוּעָה בְּיִדְּעִי / בְּקוֹל מַתַּן שׁוֹפָר.
בּוֹ בַּהֲרִיעִי / אֲרַצֶּה לִי רוֹעִי / בְּאַמְּצוֹ זְרוֹעִי / בְּקוֹל כֹּחַ שׁוֹפָר.

גַּשְׁתִּי בְּיוֹם דִּין / לְהִתְוַכֵּחַ בַּדִּין / גּוֹלֶה עֹמֶק הַדִּין / בְּקוֹל קִפְאוֹן שׁוֹפָר.
גְּזֵרַת דָּת וָדִין / אִם חֻיַּבְתִּי בַּדִּין / גְּרוֹנִי יְעַכֵּב מוֹרַע דִּין / בְּקוֹל עִם שׁוֹפָר.

דְּרֹשׁ וְהַעַל רְטִיָּה / לִפְנֵי טְרִיָּה / דַּעַת לִטְרוּיָה / בְּקוֹל חֹבֶשׁ שׁוֹפָר.
דָּחוּי לִכְרוּיָה / בְּעַד נָכְרִיָּה / דְּרוֹר לְכָל בְּרִיָּה / בְּקוֹל עֲבָרַת שׁוֹפָר.

הֻכְשַׁל בְּנַאֲפוּף / בְּזָרַת גִּפּוּף / הֻצַּג בְּרִיב צָפוּף / בְּקוֹל חֶרְדַּת שׁוֹפָר.
הָעֳנַשׁ בְּאִפּוּף / וְשָׁב הֱיוֹת חָפוּף / הוֹעִילוֹ לֵב כָּפוּף / בְּקוֹל כְּפִיפַת שׁוֹפָר.

וְאִם שׁוֹד יַעֲלְזוּ / וּבַדִּין יְלִיזוּ / וְצֶדֶק יָרוּץ לֶאֱחֹזוּ / בְּקוֹל חִיל שׁוֹפָר.
וּכְמוֹ מַכְנִיס בְּזוֹ / וּמוֹצִיא בְּזוֹ / וְכֵן מֶנּוּ יְגִיזוּ / בְּקוֹל רְוַח שׁוֹפָר.

זֶה מִכָּל קוֹלוֹת / אֲשֶׁר בְּמַקְהֵלוֹת / זִקֵּק לִקְהִלּוֹת / קוֹל תֵּקַע שׁוֹפָר.
זוֹמְמֵי עֲקַלְקַלּוֹת / מְחַיְּבֵי סְקִילוֹת / זָעוּ בְּגִדּוּעַ מַקְלוֹת / בְּקוֹל שֵׁמַע שׁוֹפָר.

חַי מִכָּל שָׁנָה / יוֹם זֶה שִׁנָּה / חָקוּק לְשׁוֹשַׁנָּה / בְּקוֹל חֵרוּת שׁוֹפָר.
חִבָּתוֹ מִשְׁנָה / שְׁנִיָּה מֵרִאשׁוֹנָה / חֵטְא כָּל הַשָּׁנָה / דְּחוֹת בְּקוֹל שׁוֹפָר.

טֶבַע בְּרָכוֹת תֵּשַׁע / מוּל שׁוֹפָרוֹת תֵּשַׁע / טָהוֹר מֵהֶם יִשַׁע / בְּקוֹל דָּת שׁוֹפָר.
טֶנֶף צְחוּנֵי רֶשַׁע / בְּשׁוּבָם מִפֶּשַׁע / טְרִיָּתָם תְּשַׁעֲשַׁע / בְּקוֹל שֵׁוַע שׁוֹפָר.

יוֹטַב מִשּׁוֹר פָּר / וּמֵאֵיל הַמְּשֻׁפָּר / יוֹם הַמְּסֻפָּר / לְקוֹל חִדּוּשׁ שׁוֹפָר.
יְקֹשׁ יוּפַר / וְסוֹטֵן יְחֻפַּר / יֹשֶׁר לֵב יְשֻׁפַּר / בְּקוֹל שִׁפּוּר שׁוֹפָר.

כְּעֵת הֵם תּוֹקְעִים / גַּיְא מַבְקִיעִים / כְּרַכִּים מַשְׁקִיעִים / בְּקוֹל שְׁאוֹן שׁוֹפָר.
כָּל הֲמוֹן מְרֵעִים / בְּחִילוֹ מִתְרוֹעֲעִים / כַּאֲשֶׁר הֵם מַתְרִיעִים / קוֹל יָרִיַע כַּשּׁוֹפָר.

לְקוֹלוֹ כִּיקָשַׁב / יְבַעֵת כָּל מוֹשָׁב / לְאֻמִּים בְּסַעַר יְנַשֵּׁב / בְּקוֹל סַעֲרַת שׁוֹפָר.
לְיוֹדְעָיו יוֹשֵׁב / לְאוֹת טוֹב יִתְחַשֵּׁב / לְעֵת יִתְיַשֵּׁב / בְּקוֹל טַעַם שׁוֹפָר.

מוֹאֲסָיו לְהַבְקִיעַ / בּוֹגְדָיו לְקַעְקֵעַ / מוֹרְדָיו לְהַשְׁקִיעַ / בְּקוֹל חִזּוּק שׁוֹפָר.
מַאֲרִיךְ בְּהִתָּקְעַ / מְקַצֵּר בְּהִבָּקֵעַ / מֵרִיעַ וְתוֹקֵעַ / בְּקוֹל שִׁלּוּשׁ שׁוֹפָר.

נוֹתֵן אֵימוֹת / מַחְפִּיז אֻמּוֹת / נוֹסוּ נוֹאֲמוֹת / מִקּוֹל בּוּךְ שׁוֹפָר.
נוֹתֵן חוֹמוֹת / מַשְׁבִּית מִלְחָמוֹת / נוֹהֵם כַּהֲמוֹת / בְּקוֹל שַׁאַג שׁוֹפָר.

סוֹדוֹ כְּגִלָּה / בְּסִין לִסְגֻלָּה / סִיּוּם מְגִלָּה / בְּקוֹל הִלּוּךְ שׁוֹפָר.
סוֹד יוֹם גְּאֻלָּה / בְּחָסְפּוֹ לַדְּגוּלָה / שָׂשׂוֹן וְגִילָה / בְּקוֹל יַשְׁמִיעַ שׁוֹפָר.

עָשׂוֹר דּוֹחֶה / עֹנֶג מַדְחֶה / עֲבֵרוֹת מַמְחֶה / בְּקוֹל צֶוַח שׁוֹפָר.
עֲוֹנוֹת מוֹחֶה / עַבְדוּת מַנְחֶה / עֲבוֹדוֹת מְאַחֶה / קוֹל חִצּוּר שׁוֹפָר.

פַּגֵּר וְהַסְעִיר / מַמְלְכוּת שָׂעִיר / פִּשְׁעָה תָּעִיר / בְּקוֹל קוֹלוֹת שׁוֹפָר.
פִּתְחֵי הָעִיר / תַּשְׁקִיעַ וְתַבְעִיר / פַּחַד רַב וְצָעִיר / מִקּוֹל הֶמְיַת שׁוֹפָר.

צִיּוּן רֶמֶז אוֹת / שׁוֹפָרוֹת שְׁלֹשׁ מֵאוֹת / צָוְחָה בְּמִדְיָן דְּאוֹת / בְּקוֹל שִׁתּוּף שׁוֹפָר.

צִפְצְפוּ צְבָאוֹת / כְּשָׁרוּ פְּלָאוֹת / צוּר כְּעָשׂ נִפְלָאוֹת / בְּקוֹל עֵרֶב שׁוֹפָר.

קוֹל חֲלוּשָׁה / בְּאַרְקָא חֲלָשָׁה / קוֹלוֹת מַתַּן שְׁלֹשָׁה / קוֹלוֹת כְּנִתְּנוּ בַשּׁוֹפָר.
קֶרֶן מְשֻׁלָּשָׁה / הַיּוֹם לְזֶכֶר אֲשַׁלְּשָׁה / קְרוֹא עוֹד שְׁלֹשָׁה / בְּקוֹל עִתּוּד שׁוֹפָר.

רָחַשְׁתִּי לַעֲלִיּוֹת / וְעֵינַי תְּלוּיוֹת / רְאוֹת כִּנּוּס גָּלֻיּוֹת / בְּקוֹל גֹּדֶל שׁוֹפָר.
רְבִיעִית חַיּוֹת / לִיקוּד לִהְיוֹת / רֶשֶׁף שַׁלְהֲבִיּוֹת / בְּקוֹל לַהַב שׁוֹפָר.

שֵׁנָה תְּעוֹרֵר / לְשַׁלֵּם גְּמוּל לְצוֹרֵר / שְׁאוֹנוֹ תְּפוֹרֵר / בְּקוֹל גְּבוּרוֹת שׁוֹפָר.
שׁוֹשָׁן תַּדְרֵר / גְּאֻלָּה תְּבָרֵר / שׁוֹכְנִים תְּזוֹרֵר / בְּקוֹל הֲעָרַת שׁוֹפָר.

תְּיַשֵּׁר מֵחֶרְמוֹן / לְרוֹעֵה אַדְמוֹן / תַּשְׁלֵג בְּצַלְמוֹן / בְּקוֹל הֲמוֹן שׁוֹפָר.
תִּצְעַד כְּבִישִׁימוֹן / בְּמַתַּן אָמוֹן / תַּשְׁמִיעַ בְּאַרְמוֹן / קוֹל קוֹרֵא כַּשּׁוֹפָר.

*The service continues with* אַתָּה נִגְלֵיתָ *on page 597.*

# פיוטים נוספים ליום ב׳

# ADDITIONAL PIYUTIM FOR THE SECOND DAY

## PIYUTIM FOR SECOND DAY SHAḤARIT

*The Yotzer for the second day.*

O King, Your words are true, firmly set since times of old. / May Your name be glorified when You rise within Your congregation.
O Lord, Your word shall stand for eternity. *Ps. 119*

O King, on this day when You finished the work of Your art, / and You saved from condemnation the one wrought in Your image,
Your faith shall endure for all generations. *Ibid.*

O King, You likewise ordered salvation for his progeny, / that they might be delivered from Your fearful verdict. / On this day, *Ibid.*
they all stand before Your judgment.

▸ Those who observe Your commandments,
Your witnesses and worshipers,
lift them up and carry them to proliferate Your honor.
For all are Your servants. / O Holy One. *Ibid.*

*All continue:*

Remember those who seek You for life and grant them strength.
Restore their vigor with compassionate anticipation.
Remember the congregation you acquired long ago. *Ps. 74*

Remember those who are drawn to You and beseech You with love,
who are sustained by the delight of Your laws that burn like embers, / the tribe of Your inheritance that You redeemed. *Ibid.*

Remember and hasten Your day of salvation to bring it near, / that they might bow in Your Temple and enter the place of Your Presence, /on this Mount Zion where You once dwelled. *Ibid.*

▸ Hold dear the tender flock in Your compassion.
Provide them with internal and external sustenance.
As for me, may my prayer come to You, Lord, *Ps. 69*
at a time of favor. / O Holy One.

---

words. The sequence is then repeated, and the seventh paragraph returns to the theme of kingship.

The poet spells out his name, Shimon bar Yitzḥak, in the form of an acrostic made up of the first letters of the second phrase of each three-phrase stanza. He does so a second time in a code embedded in the fourth and eighth lines. In the twelfth, sixteenth, twentieth and twenty-fourth lines he has encoded

# פיוטים לשחרית של יום ב׳

*The* יוצר *for the second day.*

מֶלֶךְ אָמוֹן מַאֲמָרְךָ מֵרָחוֹק מֻצָּב / שִׁמְךָ יִתְפָּאֵר בַּעֲדָתְךָ תִּתְיַצָּב
לְעוֹלָם יהוה דְּבָרְךָ נִצָּב: תהלים קיט

מֶלֶךְ בִּכְלוֹתְךָ הַיּוֹם מַעַשׂ אֳמָנוּתֶךָ / מִדִּין הַצֶּלֶת מְרֻקָּם בִּתְמוּנָתֶךָ
לְדֹר וָדֹר אֱמוּנָתֶךָ: שם

מֶלֶךְ גְּזֵרַתְךָ כְּמוֹ כֵן לְצֶאֱצָאָיו פִּדְיוֹם / עֲבוּר לְהִמָּלֵט מִשְּׁאֵתְךָ אָיוֹם
לְמִשְׁפָּטֶיךָ עָמְדוּ הַיּוֹם: שם

› שׁוֹמְרֵי מִצְוֹת, עֵדֶיךָ וַעֲבָדֶיךָ
נַטְּלֵם וְנַשְּׂאֵם לְהַרְבּוֹת כְּבוֹדֶךָ
כִּי הַכֹּל עֲבָדֶיךָ: / קָדוֹשׁ. שם

*All continue:*

זְכֹר דּוֹרְשֶׁיךָ, לְתֶחִי לְעוֹדְדֵם / וְהָרֵם קַרְנָם בְּרַחֲמֶיךָ לְהַקְדֵּם
זְכֹר עֲדָתְךָ קָנִיתָ קֶּדֶם: תהלים עד

זְכֹר הַמְשׁוּכָה אַחֲרֶיךָ בְּאַהַב לְחַלּוֹתֶךָ / נִסְמֶכֶת בְּשַׁעֲשׁוּעַ דַּת נַחֲלָתֶךָ
גָּאַלְתָּ שֵׁבֶט נַחֲלָתֶךָ: שם

זְכֹר וּמַהֵר יוֹם יִשְׁעֲךָ לְקָרְבוֹ / בִּדְבִירְךָ לְהִשְׁתַּחֲוֹת וּבְמִשְׁכְּנוֹתֶיךָ לָבֹא
הַר־צִיּוֹן זֶה שָׁכַנְתָּ בּוֹ: שם

› בְּרַחֲמִים יַקֵּר צְעִירֵי הַצֹּאן
חָקָם הַטְרִיפֵם, פְּנִימִי וְחִיצוֹן
וַאֲנִי תְפִלָּתִי־לְךָ יהוה, עֵת רָצוֹן: / קָדוֹשׁ. תהלים סט

---

מֶלֶךְ אָמוֹן מַאֲמָרְךָ *O King, Your words are True.* This poem, like many for the second day, was composed by Rabbi Shimon bar Yitzḥak of Mainz (950–c. 1020), one of the earliest German-Jewish liturgical poets, also known as Rabbi Shimon HaGadol, "the Great." Its theme is the threefold motif of Rosh HaShana on which the Musaf Amida is based: *malkhiyot,* references to God as King; *zikhronot,* remembrances; and *shofarot,* mentions of the shofar. Each paragraph consists of three lines beginning with one of these

*All continue:*

O Shofar whose time has come and is sounded as is fitting, / using a ram's horn to remind You of those who withstood / Your tests when a ram was found. / It was caught by its horns in the thicket. *Gen. 22*

O Shofar that caused the camp to tremble and stand from afar.
O Compassionate One, recall it and desire vindication for us.
And the sound of the shofar resounded and grew strong. *Ex. 19*

O Shofar that You ordained for this feast day for those innumerable as dust, / that they might turn away from iniquity on Yom Kippur and be forgiven. / Sound the shofar at the new moon. *Ps. 81*

▸ O Lord who favors His inheritance
and adorns them with pleasantness,
who taught them to read the account of His sacrifices
so that their prayers might be more pleasing *Ps. 69*
to the Lord than an ox or bullock. / O Holy One.

*All continue:*

O King who judges peoples with uprightness that they might exalt Him, / who keeps careful watch upon them in judgment as He is exalted. / You whose throne is prepared for judgment. *Ps. 9*

O King, almighty, sanctified alone in righteousness, / the Living One who shall be exalted and glorified in judgment, / may He render the judgment of His servant. *1 Kings 8*

O King, You shall recall Your compassion despite Your anger, in accordance with Your word, / and draw near to vindicate the nation that acclaims Your Oneness – / Your nation, Israel, that worships You each and every day. *Ibid.*

▸ May Your actions and glory appear to Your innocent ones,
those who shall live in the safety of Your shade forever.
For Your kingdom is an everlasting kingdom. / O Holy One. *Ps. 145*

---

chess, father and son recognized one another. The pope then annulled the decree and returned to his family and faith (or, according to another version, committed suicide). Hence, Rabbi Shimon's prayer that his son be granted eternal life.

*All continue:*

שׁוֹפָר זְמַנּוֹ בָּא תְּקוֹעַ בְּעִנְיָנָיו / בְּקֶרֶן אַיִל לְהִזָּכֵר בְּחוּנָיו
אַחַר נֶאֱחַז בַּסְּבַךְ בְּקַרְנָיו: בראשית כב

שׁוֹפָר חָרַד הַמַּחֲנֶה מֵרָחוֹק לַעֲמֹד / רַחוּם זָכְרֵהוּ וּלְצַדְּקֵהוּ תַּחְמֹד
הַשֹּׁפָר הוֹלֵךְ וְחָזֵק מְאֹד: שמות יט

שׁוֹפָר טִכַּסְתָּ בַּכֶּסֶה לְמִי מָנָה עָפָר / יְשׁוּבוּן מֵאָוֶן, בְּכִפּוּר לְהִתְכַּפָּר
תִּקְעוּ בַחֹדֶשׁ שׁוֹפָר: תהלים פא

› אֵל חָנַן נַחֲלָתוֹ בְּנֹעַם לְהַשְׁפַּר
יְדָעָם קְרֹא קָרְבְּנוֹתָיו בְּמִסְפָּר
וְתִיטַב לַיהוה מִשּׁוֹר פָּר: / קָדוֹשׁ. תהלים סט

*All continue:*

מֶלֶךְ יִשְׁפֹּט עַמִּים בְּמֵישָׁרִים לְנַשְּׂאוֹ / צוֹפֶה לְדַקְדֵּק בְּדִינָם בְּהִתְנַשְּׂאוֹ
כּוֹנֵן לַמִּשְׁפָּט כִּסְאוֹ: תהלים ט

מֶלֶךְ כַּבִּיר, נִקְדָּשׁ בִּצְדָקָה לְבַדּוֹ / חַי יִגְבַּהּ בַּמִּשְׁפָּט בְּהִתְכַּבְּדוֹ
לַעֲשׂוֹת מִשְׁפַּט עַבְדּוֹ: מלכים א׳ ח

מֶלֶךְ לְרֹגֶז רַחֵם יִזְכֹּר כְּנָאֳמוֹ / קָרוֹב לְהַצְדִּיק עַם הַמְיַחֲדִים שְׁמוֹ
עַמּוֹ יִשְׂרָאֵל דְּבַר־יוֹם בְּיוֹמוֹ: שם

› יֵרָאֶה פָעָלְךָ וַהֲדָרְךָ לִתְמִימִים
חֲיוֹת בְּצִלְּךָ לְאֹרֶךְ יָמִים
מַלְכוּתְךָ מַלְכוּת כָּל־עֹלָמִים: / קָדוֹשׁ. תהלים קמה

---

the message *Elḥanan beni yeḥi leḥayyei olam, Amen*, "May my son Elḥanan be granted eternal life, Amen." Behind this lies a story.

It is said that Elḥanan, the son of Rabbi Shimon, was kidnapped as a child, raised as a Christian, and eventually became pope. As pope, he issued an edict ordering the Jews of Mainz to become Christians. The Jews sent Rabbi Shimon to plead with the pope. During the visit, in the course of a game of

*All continue:*

Remember those who wait for You that You might set Your table with satisfying plenty, / that Your glory might be praised in their mouths, as it is said, / the memory of the Righteous One is blessed. *Prov. 10*

Remember the benevolent ones among the nations, those ancestors of the world, / and spare Your servant from sins both unintentional and presumptuous. / For the kindness of the LORD lasts forever and ever. *Ps. 103*

Remember the sanctuary of Shalem that now sits so alone; / hasten to reestablish it and sustain it. / Let there be joy on Mount Zion and may the daughters of Judah rejoice. *Ps. 48*

▸ May Your faithful be written for a lengthy life,
and merit to behold the glory of the LORD *Ps. 27*
as a remembrance before Him of those who fear the LORD. / O Holy One. *Mal. 3*

*All continue:*

O Shofar the proclamation of its sound is heard with glee. / They shall be adorned with ornaments of everlasting joy, / as the lost ones in the land of Assyria return. *Is. 27*

O Shofar whose sound shall blast beyond all rivers of exile, / sounding freedom to Judah and Ephraim / and for the banished ones in the land of Egypt. *Ibid.*

O Shofar that shall cry throughout the Diaspora in Tzarfat and Sepharad to sanctify Him. / Those scattered to the four winds shall be renewed for all eternity, / and they shall bow before the LORD on the holy mountain. *Ibid.*

▸ Your words of comfort shall cause us twofold delight,
and they shall worship You, Selah, forever in all their regions,
on the holy mountain in Jerusalem. / O Holy One. *Ibid.*

*All continue:*

O King, O Holy One, residing in the awesome heavens, / hasten the arrival of the herald who shall announce the Redeemer's ascent. The LORD reigns; let the earth rejoice. *Ps. 97*

O King, O high and lofty One, Knowing One and Witness, / rebuild Your city for the time has come. / The LORD shall reign forever and ever. *Ex. 15*

O King whose rule is forever and reigns over all, / prepare a path of uprightness for those who fear You, that they might benefit. The LORD shall reign forever. *Ps. 146*

▸ May You guide us through the land of the living.
Come, let us walk in the light of the LORD.
And the kingdom shall be the LORD's alone. / O Holy One. *Ob. 1*

*Continue with "In compassion" (page 316).*

*All continue:*

זְכֹר מְקַוֶּיךָ, נַחַת שֻׁלְחָנְךָ לְעָרְכָה / אֱדֶר תְּהִלָּתְךָ בְּפִימוֹ לְהִתְבָּרְכָה
זֵכֶר צַדִּיק לִבְרָכָה: משלי י

זְכֹר נְדִיבֵי עַמִּים אֲבוֹת הָעוֹלָם / חֲשֹׂךְ עֲבָדֶיךָ מִזָּדוֹן וְנֶעְלָם
וְחֶסֶד יהוה מֵעוֹלָם וְעַד־עוֹלָם: תהלים קג

זְכֹר סֻכַּת שָׁלֵם הַיּוֹשֶׁבֶת בְּדוּדָה / חוּשָׁה לְהָכִין אֹתָהּ וּלְסַעֲדָהּ
יִשְׂמַח הַר־צִיּוֹן תָּגֵלְנָה בְּנוֹת יְהוּדָה: תהלים מח

‹ לְחַיֵּי עוֹלָם יִכָּתְבוּ אֱמוּנַי / יִזְכּוּ לַחֲזוֹת בְּנֹעַם יהוה תהלים כז
זִכָּרוֹן לְפָנָיו לְיִרְאֵי יהוה: / קָדוֹשׁ. מלאכי ג

*All continue:*

שׁוֹפָר עֲבָרַת קוֹלוֹ נִשְׁמַע בְּאַשּׁוּר / לְהֵעָטוֹת שִׂמְחַת עוֹלָם בְּקִשּׁוּר
וּבָאוּ הָאֹבְדִים בְּאֶרֶץ אַשּׁוּר: ישעיה כז

שׁוֹפָר פּוֹצֵץ קוֹלוֹ בְּעֶבְרֵי נַהֲרַיִם / חֵרוּת לְהַשְׁמִיעַ יְהוּדָה וְאֶפְרַיִם
וְהַנִּדָּחִים בְּאֶרֶץ מִצְרָיִם: שם

שׁוֹפָר צָרְפַת וּסְפָרַד יִצְרַח לְהִתְקַדֵּשׁ / נְפוּצִים בְּאַרְבַּע נֵצַח יְחַדֵּשׁ
וְהִשְׁתַּחֲווּ לַיהוה בְּהַר הַקֹּדֶשׁ: שם

‹ אִמְרֵי נְחוּמֶיךָ יְשַׁעַשְׁעוּנוּ בְּכִפְלַיִם / סֶלָה לְעָבְדְּךָ בְּכָל גְּבוּלַיִם
בְּהַר הַקֹּדֶשׁ בִּירוּשָׁלָיִם: / קָדוֹשׁ. שם

*All continue:*

מֶלֶךְ קָדוֹשׁ שׁוֹכֵן שְׁמֵי עֶרֶץ / נַחֵץ מְבַשֵּׂר עֲלוֹת הַפֹּרֵץ
יהוה מָלָךְ תָּגֵל הָאָרֶץ: תהלים צז

מֶלֶךְ רָם וְנִשָּׂא הַיּוֹדֵעַ וָעֵד / בְּנֵה קִרְיָתְךָ כִּי בָא מוֹעֵד
יהוה יִמְלֹךְ לְעֹלָם וָעֶד: שמות טו

מֶלֶךְ שִׁלְטוֹנְךָ לָעַד בְּכֹל מָשְׁלָם / יַשֵּׁר לִירֵאֶיךָ דֶּרֶךְ לְהוֹעִילָם
יִמְלֹךְ יהוה לְעוֹלָם: תהלים קמו

‹ תְּנַהֲגֵנוּ בְּאַרְצוֹת הַחַיִּים לְהִתְהַלְּכָה / בְּאוֹר יהוה לְכוּ וְנֵלְכָה
וְהָיְתָה לַיהוה הַמְּלוּכָה: / קָדוֹשׁ. עובדיה א

*Continue with* הַמֵּאִיר *(page 317).*

*This piyut, which enlarges upon the two refrains "Master, if we are devoid of good deeds" and "For He believes not," is omitted today by many congregations. As in many piyutim by Rabbi Shimon bar Yitzhak, his name appears in the acrostic.*

שַׁבְתִּי I saw once again under the sun / that nothing is better than arming oneself, / strengthening oneself in the fear of God's greatness, never to yield. *Eccl. 9*

The application of the full extent of the law my eyes have seen, / as we learn from Adam, the first man, / who was created in the image of God in the Garden of Eden.

From the time he violated the royal word of God, / he was not allowed to abide in honor and was banished as the leaves fell. / And there, God *Gen. 3*
placed the bright blade of the ever-turning sword.

Master, if we are devoid of good deeds, / let Your great name still remain with us / and do not approach to judge us, / O Holy One.

Abraham was guided along the goodly path for his own benefit, / as God shone from the East to dissipate the darkness, / He heralded *Is. 41*
righteousness wherever he set his feet.

The One who tested him and gave him His promise, he tested. / As he opened his mouth to ask how he might know that he was to inherit it, so his offspring was dragged away to exile for four hundred years.

Awaken, O noble ones, and overcome desire; / aspire to righteousness *Zeph. 2*
and humility. / Perhaps there is hope still. *Lam. 3*

For He believes not even in His holy beings, / and casts aspersions on His angels of aquamarine, / and how then will those who were but culled from clods of earth be vindicated, / O Holy One?

The bound one who was offered upon one of the mountains, / was circumcised on the eighth day, fulfilling the covenant of flesh. / And Isaac planted seeds and reaped a hundredfold.

He was given offspring – one troublesome son and one delightful son – at the age of sixty, / and as he grew old his eyes grew dim till he could no longer see, / for he had tolerated Esau's evil.

Place upon your hearts the fear of heaven, / remove your hands from injustice that you might avoid hardship. / Perhaps the Lord God of *Amos 5*
hosts will be gracious and pardon.

Master, if we are devoid of good deeds, / let Your great name still remain with us / and do not approach to judge us, / O Holy One.

*This piyut, which enlarges upon the two refrains "אָדוֹן, אִם מַעֲשִׂים אֵין בָּנוּ" and "הֵן לֹא יַאֲמִין," is omitted today by many congregations. As in many piyutim by Rabbi Shimon bar Yitzḥak, his name appears in the acrostic.*

שַׁבְתִּי וְרָאֹה תַּחַת־הַשָּׁמֶשׁ: / אֵין טוֹב לֶאֱנוֹשׁ מֵהִתְחַמֵּשׁ קהלת ט
בְּיִרְאַת מָעֻזּוֹ לְהִתְחַזֵּק, וְלֹא לְהָמֵשׁ.

שׁוּרַת הַדִּין רָאֲתָה עֵינִי / נָבִין תְּחִלָּה מֵאָדָם הַקַּדְמוֹנִי
בְּצֶלֶם אֱלֹהִים נִבְרָא, בְּעֵדֶן גַּנִּי.

מֵעֵת הֵפֵר פִּי מַמְלֶכֶת / בִּיקָר לֹא לָן, וְנִגְרַשׁ בְּשַׁלֶּכֶת
וְאֵת לַהַט הַחֶרֶב הַמִּתְהַפֶּכֶת: בראשית ג

אָדוֹן, אִם מַעֲשִׂים אֵין בָּנוּ / שִׁמְךָ הַגָּדוֹל יַעֲמָד לָנוּ
וְאַל תָּבוֹא בְמִשְׁפָּט עִמָּנוּ / קָדוֹשׁ.

מְדָרֵךְ בְּדֶרֶךְ טוֹבִים לְהוֹעִילוֹ / מִמִּזְרַח הֵאִיר עֶלֶט מַאֲפֵלוֹ
צֶדֶק יִקְרָאֵהוּ לְרַגְלוֹ: ישעיה מא

עַל נַסּוֹתוֹ מַבְטִיחוֹ בִּבְחִינָה / וּפָץ לְהוֹדִיעוֹ אִם יִירָשֶׁנָּה
נִגְרְרוּ גְזָעָיו גֵּרוּת אַרְבַּע מֵאוֹת שָׁנָה:

עוּרוּ נְדִיבִים וְהִתְאוֹשְׁשׁוּ לְתַאֲוָה / בַּקְּשׁוּ צֶדֶק, בַּקְּשׁוּ עֲנָוָה צפניה ב
אוּלַי יֵשׁ תִּקְוָה. איכה ג

הֵן לֹא יַאֲמִין בִּקְדֹשָׁיו / וְתָהֳלָה יָשִׂים בְּאֵלֵי תַרְשִׁישָׁיו
וְאֵיךְ יִצְדְּקוּ קְרוּצֵי גוּשָׁיו / קָדוֹשׁ.

וָתִיק הַנַּעֲלֶה בְּאַחַד הֶהָרִים / לִשְׁמוֹנָה קִיֵּם בְּרִית בְּשָׂרִים
וְזָרַע וּמָצָא מֵאָה שְׁעָרִים.

וּלְשִׁשִּׁים נֶחֱנַט בְּמֵצִיק וּמְשַׁעֲשֵׁעַ / וּלְשֵׂיבָה כָּהֲה מְאוֹרוֹ לְהָשַׁע
עֲבוּר שְׂאֵתוֹ פְּנֵי הָרָשָׁע.

נָא שִׂימוּ עַל לֵב מוֹרָאוֹת / וְהָשִׁיבוּ יָד מֵעָוֶל לְהִמָּלֵט מִתְּלָאוֹת
אוּלַי יֶחֱנַן יהוה אֱלֹהֵי־צְבָאוֹת: עמוס ה

אָדוֹן, אִם מַעֲשִׂים אֵין בָּנוּ / שִׁמְךָ הַגָּדוֹל יַעֲמָד לָנוּ
וְאַל תָּבוֹא בְמִשְׁפָּט עִמָּנוּ / קָדוֹשׁ.

Jacob, the pleasing one, with his goodly tents / and his image engraved in God's throne in heaven: / And behold, God stood above him. *Gen. 28*

As he returned from Padan and was rescued from hardship, / his vow to the God who had appeared to him he delayed to fulfill. / His downfall came through the incident of Dina, daughter of Leah.

Take care, creatures, to merit God's compassion; / be fearful of the stormy anger of God. / Perhaps you will be safely hidden on the day of God's wrath. *Zeph. 2*

For He believes not even in His holy beings, / and casts aspersions on His angels of aquamarine, / and how then will those who were but culled from clods of earth be vindicated, / O Holy One?

Aaron and Moses, anointed brothers and friends, / who made haste like the gazelle to perform God's mission / and set limits for God's chosen people at the foot of the mountain.

They wrote down the greatness of the Torah for the nation, / and showed them the just path and the pleasing laws. / But they were visited by God's indignation at the waters of Meriva.

Let this be known by all inhabitants of the earth, / for if this is what occurs to the innocent and wise, / what can those who are full of deceit hope to accomplish?

Master, if we are devoid of good deeds, / let Your great name still remain with us / and do not approach to judge us, / O Holy One.

Saul, the descendant of Benjamin – the LORD's dear son – who first became king, / free from sin as a year-old babe, / he did not shy away from war to save his nation.

He was commanded to erase the Amalekites who attacked Israel from the rear, / but he deviated from God's command and was shamed like a discovered thief, / as he took pity on their spoiled king who used black magic to disappear.

God, our rock, regretted making him king, / and had him fall into the hands of his enemies to be extinguished. / What then can those who violate the laws hope for when God holds judgment?

For He believes not even in His holy beings, / and casts aspersions on His angels of aquamarine, / and how then will those who were but culled from clods of earth be vindicated, / O Holy One?

נָעִים אֲשֶׁר טֹבוּ אֹהָלָיו / וְתָאֳרוּ חָקוּק בְּכֵס זְבוּלָיו
וְהִנֵּה יהוה נִצָּב עָלָיו: בראשית כח

בְּשׁוּבוֹ מִפַּדָּן וְנֶחֱלַץ מִתְּלָאָה / וְנִדְּרוֹ אֵחַר לְאֵל לוֹ נִרְאָה
נִכְשַׁל בְּדִינָה בַּת לֵאָה.

בִּינוּ יְצוּרִים לְרַחֲמָיו לִשְׁאַף / גּוּרוּ לָכֶם מִפְּנֵי סַעֲרַת חֲרוֹן אַף
אוּלַי תִּסָּתְרוּ בְּיוֹם אַף: צפניה ב

הֵן לֹא יַאֲמִין בִּקְדֹשָׁיו / וְתָהֳלָה יָשִׂים בְּאֵלֵי תַרְשִׁישָׁיו
וְאֵיךְ יִצְדְּקוּ קְרוּצֵי גוּשָׁיו / קָדוֹשׁ.

רֵעִים וְאַחִים, בְּנֵי הַיִּצְהָר / אֲשֶׁר אָצוּ בְּמִשְׁלַחְתָּם כִּצְבִי לְמַהֵר
וְהִגְבִּילוּ סְגֻלָּה בְּתַחְתִּית הָהָר.

רְבֵּי תוֹרָה כָּתְבוּ לָעָם / וְהוֹרוּם דַּרְכֵי יֹשֶׁר וּמִשְׁפְּטֵי נֹעַם
וּבְמֵי מְרִיבָה הָפְקְדוּ בְּזָעַם.

יֵדְעוּ זֹאת כָּל יוֹשְׁבֵי אֲדָמָה / אִם כֵּן בִּתְמִימֵי חָכְמָה
מַה יַּעֲשׂוּ מְלֵאֵי מִרְמָה.

אָדוֹן, אִם מַעֲשִׂים אֵין בָּנוּ / שִׁמְךָ הַגָּדוֹל יַעֲמָד לָנוּ
וְאַל תָּבוֹא בְמִשְׁפָּט עִמָּנוּ / קָדוֹשׁ.

יְדִיד יהוה אֲשֶׁר מָלַךְ תְּחִלָּה / כְּבֶן שָׁנָה נָקִי מִכָּל עַוְלָה
וְלֹא נֶעֱצַל מִמִּלְחֶמֶת עֲבוּר הַצָּלָה.

צִוָּה עַל מְחִיַּת הַמְזַנֵּב / שָׁנָה מִפְקָד וְהוֹבִישׁ כְּגוֹנֵב
בְּחָמְלוֹ מַעֲדַנּוֹת בִּכְשָׁפָיו מִתְגַּנֵּב.

צוּר נִחַם כִּי הִמְלִיכוֹ / וּבְיַד אֹיְבָיו הִפִּילוֹ לְדַכְּאוֹ
וּמַה יַּעֲשׂוּ מְפִירֵי דִין כְּעֶרְכּוֹ.

הֵן לֹא יַאֲמִין בִּקְדֹשָׁיו / וְתָהֳלָה יָשִׂים בְּאֵלֵי תַרְשִׁישָׁיו
וְאֵיךְ יִצְדְּקוּ קְרוּצֵי גוּשָׁיו / קָדוֹשׁ.

The pious king, David, who composed pleasing songs for his Creator, whose majestic throne was established through the kindness of his Maker, / and who acted justly and righteously with all the multitudes of his people.

He was forced to flee before his own offspring, / and was met along the way by a slanderer who told lies about his master. / David later divided the field between this slanderer and his master with a smooth tongue.

When God heard these words from His dwelling on high, / He divided his kingdom between David's descendant and his servant. / What then can the common slanderer hope for in the face of God's ire?

Master, if we are devoid of good deeds, / let Your great name still remain with us / and do not approach to judge us, / O Holy One.

Congregations, thousands and multitudes / that did precede us have passed like a wind, / and they were not able to justify their innocence.

The very heavens themselves are not pristine in His eyes, / and all the legions of heaven expire like a flaxen wick. / So how shall the repugnant corrupt ones be exonerated?

They heap deceit upon deceit and secretly perform their deeds. / But though they say in their hearts: "Who will testify against me before Him?" – / yet the very walls and furniture and beams and stones of their houses shall bear witness.

For He believes not even in His holy beings, / and casts aspersions on His angels of aquamarine, / and how then will those who were but culled from clods of earth be vindicated, / O Holy One?

O You who are too pure to behold evil, / cast our sins into the hidden depths of the sea, / and show us a sign that all will be well.

If we have done evil and turned away from You, / recall the ancestors of the world, Your chosen ones, / and do not ignore the pleas of those who seek You eagerly.

Let our prayers come in place of the proper young bulls and meal-offerings, / recall our utterances and show us favor, / preserve us for a good life on this day of Rosh HaShana.

Master, if we are devoid of good deeds, / let Your great name still remain with us / and do not approach to judge us, / O Holy One.

*The service continues with "And so" on page 676.*

חָסִיד הַמְּנְעִים זְמִירוֹת לְקוֹנוֹ / וְהוּכַן בַּחֶסֶד כִּסֵּא גְאוֹנוֹ
וְעָשָׂה מִשְׁפָּט וּצְדָקָה לַהֲמוֹנוֹ.

חָתַף לִבְרֹחַ מִפְּנֵי פְּרִי בִטְנוֹ / וְהִקְדִּימוּ רָכִיל, מְשַׁקֵּר עַל אֲדוֹנוֹ
וְחִלֵּק לוֹ שָׂדֶה בְּחֵלֶק לְשׁוֹנוֹ.

קוֹל הַחִלּוּק כְּהִסְכִּית מִמְּעוֹנוֹ / חִלֵּק מַלְכוּתוֹ בֵּין עַבְדּוֹ וּבֵין בְּנוֹ
וּמַה יַּעֲשֶׂה מְלָשְׁנִי כִּפְקֹד עָלָיו חֲרוֹנוֹ.

אָדוֹן, אִם מַעֲשִׂים אֵין בָּנוּ / שִׁמְךָ הַגָּדוֹל יַעֲמָד לָנוּ
וְאַל תָּבוֹא בְּמִשְׁפָּט עִמָּנוּ / קָדוֹשׁ.

קְהִלּוֹת וּרְבָבוֹת וַאֲלָפִים / אֲשֶׁר לְפָנֵינוּ עָבְרוּ חֲלוּפִים
וְלֹא יָכְלוּ לְהִצְטַדֵּק הֱיוֹת חַפִּים.

הֵן שָׁמַיִם בְּעֵינָיו לֹא זַכּוּ / וְכָל לִגְיוֹנֵי שַׁחַק כַּפִּשְׁתָּה דָּעֵכוּ
וְנִתְעָב וְנֶאֱלָח מַה יִּזְכּוּ.

קוֹבֵץ מִרְמָה וּמִסְתַּתֵּר בְּעִנְיָנָיו / אִם יֹאמַר בְּלִבּוֹ מִי יְעִידֵנִי לְפָנָיו
קוֹרוֹתָיו וְרָהִיטָיו עֵצָיו וַאֲבָנָיו.

הֵן לֹא יַאֲמִין בִּקְדֹשָׁיו / וְתָהֳלָה יָשִׂים בְּאֶלֵי תַרְשִׁישָׁיו
וְאֵיךְ יִצְדְּקוּ קְרוּצֵי גוּשָׁיו / קָדוֹשׁ.

טְהוֹר עֵינַיִם בְּרֶגַע מֵרְאוֹת / הַצְלֵל חֲטָאֵינוּ בְּעִמְקֵי מַחֲבוֹאוֹת
וַעֲשֵׂה עִמָּנוּ לְטוֹבָה אוֹת.

נַחְנוּ אִם פָּשַׁעְנוּ מֵאַחֲרֶיךָ / הִזָּכֵר לַאֲבוֹת הָעוֹלָם בְּחִירֶיךָ
וְאַל תִּתְעַלַּם מִתַּחַן מְשַׁחֲרֶיךָ.

חֵלֶף פָּרִים וּמִנְחָה הֲגוּנָה / זְכֹר הֶגְיוֹנֵנוּ וְתֵן לָנוּ חֲנִינָה
קַיְּמֵנוּ לְחַיִּים טוֹבִים בְּזֶה רֹאשׁ הַשָּׁנָה.

אָדוֹן, אִם מַעֲשִׂים אֵין בָּנוּ / שִׁמְךָ הַגָּדוֹל יַעֲמָד לָנוּ
וְאַל תָּבוֹא בְּמִשְׁפָּט עִמָּנוּ / קָדוֹשׁ.

*The service continues with* וּבְכֵן, וַיְהִי בִישֻׁרוּן מֶלֶךְ *on page 677.*

*The following is the full text of Rabbi Shimon bar Yitzḥak's variation of "The Supreme King," which is said on the second day.*

The Supreme King –
Powerful and exalted, / exalted above all rulers,
He fulfills His promises,
He is Fortress and Sanctuary,
He is lofty and bears aloft,
He seats kings on their thrones.
He shall reign forever.

The destitute king –
Despised and plundered, / he conceals his sins;
frightened and weakened, / his iniquity spreads;
every deed is inspected, / his treasury has been pillaged.
How then will he rule?

The Supreme King –
Mighty in His great works,
He proclaims the future of all generations;
revealing that which is hidden,
His utterances are pure;
He knows the number of stars
and the composition of constellations.
He shall reign forever.

The destitute king –
Hatched from dust, / his failure is sin;
he shall be brought to burial, / locked up in prison,
he falls into deep pits, / destined for desolation.
How then will he rule?

The Supreme King –
Glorified on every tongue, / He is omnipotent;
He takes pity on all, / provides sustenance to all,
concealed from the eyes of all,
yet His eyes roam over all.
He shall reign forever.

*The following is the full text of Rabbi Shimon bar Yitzhak's variation of "מֶלֶךְ עֶלְיוֹן," which is said on the second day.*

מֶלֶךְ עֶלְיוֹן
אַמִּיץ הַמְנֻשָּׂא / לְכֹל לְרֹאשׁ מִתְנַשֵּׂא
אוֹמֵר וְעוֹשֶׂה / מָעוֹז וּמַחְסֶה
נִשָּׂא וְנוֹשֵׂא / מוֹשִׁיב מְלָכִים לַכִּסֵּא
לַעֲדֵי עַד יִמְלֹךְ.

מֶלֶךְ אֶבְיוֹן
בָּזוּי וּמְשֻׁסֶּה / פְּשָׁעָיו מְכַסֶּה
בָּהוּל וּמִתְקַשֶּׁה / עָוֹן פּוֹשֶׂה
נִבְחָן בְּכָל מַעֲשֶׂה / וְאוֹצָרוֹ יִשָּׁסֶה
וְאֵיךְ יִמְלֹךְ.

מֶלֶךְ עֶלְיוֹן
גִּבּוֹר בִּגְבוּרוֹת / קֹרֵא הַדּוֹרוֹת
גּוֹלֶה נִסְתָּרוֹת / אִמְרוֹתָיו טְהוֹרוֹת
יוֹדֵעַ סְפוֹרוֹת / לְתוֹצְאוֹת מַזָּרוֹת
לַעֲדֵי עַד יִמְלֹךְ.

מֶלֶךְ אֶבְיוֹן
דָּגוּר מֵעֲפָרוֹת / נִכְשָׁל בַּעֲבֵרוֹת
יוּבַל לִקְבָרוֹת / נִסְגָּר בְּמַסְגֵּרוֹת
נוֹפֵל בְּמַהֲמוֹרוֹת / וְגָזוּר בִּגְזֵרוֹת
וְאֵיךְ יִמְלֹךְ.

מֶלֶךְ עֶלְיוֹן
הַמְפֹאָר בְּפִי כֹל / וְהוּא כֹּל יָכוֹל
הַמְרַחֵם אֶת הַכֹּל / וְנוֹתֵן מִחְיָה לַכֹּל
וְנֶעְלָם מֵעֵין כֹּל / וְעֵינָיו מְשׁוֹטְטוֹת בַּכֹּל
לַעֲדֵי עַד יִמְלֹךְ.

The destitute king –
Pained by his sickness, / his quiver is depleted;
his tears increase, / he perishes and is no more;
yet as if that were not enough,
he shall be brought to justice.
How then will he rule?

The Supreme King –
Recalls the forgotten, / examines innards,
His eyes are wide open, / He anticipates all thoughts,
God of spirits, / His words are truthful.
He shall reign forever.

The destitute king –
Profane and errant, / shepherds foolishly,
he storms and rushes / growling over his prey,
but when trapped,
he cries out like a woman in childbirth.
How then will he rule?

The Supreme King –
Pure in His heavenly abode,
Master of His angelic servants,
none can compare to Him
as He performs His works;
He placed sand as a border
against which the sea waves roar.
He shall reign forever.

The destitute king –
Arrogantly evil, / stirring up strife,
he is condemned in his lifetime / to oblivion in death;
his spirit shall know strife
and he shall know that there is justice.
How then will he rule?

מֶלֶךְ אֶבְיוֹן
וְנִכְאָב בְּחָלְיוֹ / וְנִגְרָע תְּלְיוֹ
וְנוֹסָף בִּכְיוֹ / וְיִגְוַע וְאַיּוֹ
וְלֹא דַיּוֹ / לַמִּשְׁפָּט יְבִיאוֹ
וְאֵיךְ יִמְלֹךְ.

מֶלֶךְ עֶלְיוֹן
זוֹכֵר נִשְׁכָּחוֹת / חוֹקֵר טְחוֹת
עֵינָיו פְּקְחוֹת / מַגִּיד שֵׂחוֹת
אֱלֹהֵי הָרוּחוֹת / אִמְרוֹתָיו נְכֹחוֹת
לַעֲדֵי עַד יִמְלֹךְ.

מֶלֶךְ אֶבְיוֹן
חוֹנֵף וְתוֹעֶה / אֱוִילֵי רוֹעֶה
סוֹעֵר וְסוֹעֶה / לְטַרְפּוֹ גוֹעֶה
בִּסְגוֹר צוֹעֶה / כַּיּוֹלֵדָה יִפְעֶה
וְאֵיךְ יִמְלֹךְ.

מֶלֶךְ עֶלְיוֹן
טָהוֹר בִּזְבוּלָיו / אוֹת הוּא בְּאֶרְאֶלָּיו
אֵין עֲרֹךְ אֵלָיו / לִפְעֹל כְּמִפְעָלָיו
חוֹל שָׂם גְּבוּלָיו / כַּהֲמוֹת יָם לְגַלָּיו
לַעֲדֵי עַד יִמְלֹךְ.

מֶלֶךְ אֶבְיוֹן
יָהִיר בְּזָדוֹן / מְגָרֶה מָדוֹן
בְּחַיָּיו נִדּוֹן / בְּמוֹתוֹ לַאֲבַדּוֹן
רוּחוֹ יָדוֹן / וְיֵדַע שַׁדּוּן
וְאֵיךְ יִמְלֹךְ.

The Supreme King –
Gathers the waters of the sea, / stirs up the ocean waves,
causes the tumultuous waves to crash and break
till they are enough to fill the world.
Yet He can quiet their power,
causing them to retreat till they cannot be found.
He shall reign forever.

The destitute king –
Cowardly of heart, / crying out as if wronged;
as if afflicted, he begs for kindness;
he bears a heavy yoke,
he is trod like clay / and melts like wax.
How then will he rule?

The Supreme King –
Rules with might,
His path is stormy and tempestuous,
clothed in light, / illuminating the night as day,
fog is His concealment,
yet light dwells with Him.
He shall reign forever.

The destitute king –
Forgotten by good, / saddened by pain,
strife and animosity / are his kin,
excess sin / shall be his ruin.
How then will he rule?

The Supreme King –
Hidden in thick clouds, / flames surround Him,
His chariot is Cherubim,
His servants sparks of fire,
constellations and stars / praise Him exceedingly.
He shall reign forever.

מֶלֶךְ עֶלְיוֹן
כּוֹנֵס מֵי הַיָּם / רֹגַע גַּלֵּי יָם
סוֹעֵר שְׁאוֹן דָּכְיָם / מְלֹא הָעוֹלָם דַּיָּם
מַשְׁבִּיחָם בַּעְיָם / וְשָׁבִים אָחוֹר וְאַיָּם
לַעֲדֵי עַד יִמְלֹךְ.

מֶלֶךְ אֶבְיוֹן
לִבּוֹ יִמַּס / זוֹעֵק חָמָס
חֶסֶד לַמָּס / עֹל נֶעֱמָס
כְּטִיט נִרְמָס / וְכַדּוֹנַג נָמָס
וְאֵיךְ יִמְלֹךְ.

מֶלֶךְ עֶלְיוֹן
מוֹשֵׁל בִּגְבוּרָה / דַּרְכּוֹ סוּפָה וּסְעָרָה
עוֹטֶה אוֹרָה / לַיְלָה כַּיּוֹם לְהָאִירָה
עֲרָפֶל לוֹ סִתְרָה / וְעִמֵּהּ שְׁרֵא נְהוֹרָא
לַעֲדֵי עַד יִמְלֹךְ.

מֶלֶךְ אֶבְיוֹן
נְשׁוּי טוֹבָה / בְּעֶצֶב לְהַעֲצִיבָה
תַּחֲרוּת וְאֵיבָה / אֵלָיו קְרוֹבָה
בְּרֹב חוֹבָה / יִהְיֶה לְחָרְבָּה
וְאֵיךְ יִמְלֹךְ.

מֶלֶךְ עֶלְיוֹן
סִתְרוֹ עָבִים / סְבִיבָיו לְהָבִים
רְכוּבוֹ כְּרוּבִים / מְשָׁרְתָיו שְׁבִיבִים
מַזָּרוֹת וְכוֹכָבִים / הִלּוּלוֹ מַרְבִּים
לַעֲדֵי עַד יִמְלֹךְ.

The destitute king –
Pitiful and humiliated, / shadowed in darkness,
his iniquity has doubled, / his sin clings to him,
because of it he was laid low / and fell from heights.
How then will he rule?

The Supreme King –
Opens His hand and provides sustenance,
gathers up waters and causes them to flow,
washing over dry land / in shifts, by thirds and fourths;
each day expressions / of praise are mouthed.
He shall reign forever.

The destitute king –
The sword awaits him / night and day,
the cold and heat / shall freeze and scorch him,
he is excised from the midst of his people
as death waits to ambush him.
How then will he rule?

The Supreme King –
Sacred and awesome / with wonders and miraculous works,
He determined the dimensions of the earth
and laid its cornerstone,
and all that was created / was created for His glory.
He shall reign forever.

The destitute king –
His compassion is corrupted, /
his good character traits are few,
his path is filled with terror, / his sins are engraved,
his lifeblood is given over to death-dealers /
like cattle in a shed.
How then will he rule?

מֶלֶךְ אֶבְיוֹן
עָלוּב וְשָׁפָל / בְּחֹשֶׁךְ מְאֻפָּל
עֲוֹנוֹ מְכֻפָּל / חֶטְאוֹ מְטֻפָּל
בִּגְלָלוֹ יְשֻׁפָּל / מִגָּבְהוֹ נָפָל
וְאֵיךְ יִמְלֹךְ.

מֶלֶךְ עֶלְיוֹן
פּוֹתֵחַ יָד וּמַשְׂבִּיעַ / צוֹרֵר מַיִם וּמַנְבִּיעַ
יַבֶּשֶׁת לְהַטְבִּיעַ / לְשַׁלִּישׁ וְלְרַבִּיעַ
יוֹם לְיוֹם יַבִּיעַ / שִׁבְחוֹ לְהַבִּיעַ
לַעֲדֵי עַד יִמְלֹךְ.

מֶלֶךְ אֶבְיוֹן
צָפוּי אֱלֵי חֶרֶב / בַּבֹּקֶר וּבָעֶרֶב
מִקֹּר וּמֵחֹרֶב / יְזֹרַב וְיִשְׁתָּרֵב
נִכְרַת מִקֶּרֶב / מָוֶת לוֹ מְאָרֵב
וְאֵיךְ יִמְלֹךְ.

מֶלֶךְ עֶלְיוֹן
קָדוֹשׁ וְנוֹרָא / בְּמוֹפֵת וּבְמוֹרָא
מְמַדֵּי אֶרֶץ קָרָא / וְאֶבֶן פִּנָּתָהּ יָרָה
וְכָל הַנִּבְרָא / לִכְבוֹדוֹ בָּרָא
לַעֲדֵי עַד יִמְלֹךְ.

מֶלֶךְ אֶבְיוֹן
רַחֲמָיו שְׁחוּתִים / מִדּוֹתָיו פְּחוּתִים
דְּרָכָיו חַתְחַתִּים / פְּשָׁעָיו חֲרוּתִים
וְחַיָּתוֹ לַמְמִיתִים / כְּבִקְרֵי רְפָתִים
וְאֵיךְ יִמְלֹךְ.

The Supreme King –
Heeds the destitute / and listens to supplication,
He extends goodwill / and limits wrath,
He is first of the first / and last of the last.
He shall reign forever.

The destitute king –
His hopes have deceived, /
his expectations shamefully turned away,
his carcass rots, / his soul is in pain,
he is broken and held captive /
by the fervor of the approaching day.
How then will he rule?

Yet the Supreme King –
Truthful Judge, / His works are true,
He performs kindness and truth,
He is abundantly kind and true,
His path is truth / and His seal is truth.
He shall reign forever.

מֶלֶךְ עֶלְיוֹן
שׁוֹמֵעַ אֶל אֶבְיוֹנִים / וּמַאֲזִין חִנּוּנִים
מַאֲרִיךְ רְצוֹנִים / וּמְקַצֵּר חֲרוֹנִים
רִאשׁוֹן לָרִאשׁוֹנִים / וְאַחֲרוֹן לָאַחֲרוֹנִים
לַעֲדֵי עַד יִמְלֹךְ.

מֶלֶךְ אֶבְיוֹן
תּוֹחַלְתּוֹ נִכְזָבָה / תִּקְוָתוֹ נֶעֱלָבָה
גְּוִיָּתוֹ נִרְקָבָה / נִשְׁמָתוֹ נִכְאָבָה
נִשְׁבָּר וְנִשְׁבָּה / מִלַּהַט הַיּוֹם הַבָּא
וְאֵיךְ יִמְלֹךְ.

אֲבָל מֶלֶךְ עֶלְיוֹן
שׁוֹפֵט הָאֱמֶת / מַעֲבָדָיו אֱמֶת
עוֹשֶׂה חֶסֶד וֶאֱמֶת / וְרַב חֶסֶד וֶאֱמֶת
נְתִיבָתוֹ אֱמֶת / וְחוֹתָמוֹ אֱמֶת
לַעֲדֵי עַד יִמְלֹךְ.

*The* סילוק*, the culmination of the* קרובה *by Rabbi Shimon bar Yitzhak, said in* שחרית *of the second day. Today, it is omitted by most congregations.*

אֲשֶׁר מִי יַעֲשֶׂה כְּמַעֲשֶׂיךָ וְכִגְבוּרֹתֶיךָ / וּמִי יְהַרְהֵר אַחַר מִדּוֹתֶיךָ
וּמִי יְמַלֵּל קְצָת תִּפְאַרְתֶּךָ / וּמִי יַשְׁמִיעַ כָּל תְּהִלָּתֶךָ
וּמִי יַעֲרִיץ הוֹד קְדֻשָּׁתֶךָ / שָׁמַיִם וּשְׁמֵי הַשָּׁמַיִם לֹא יְכַלְכְּלוּ אֵימָתֶךָ
הָאָרֶץ וְעַמּוּדֶיהָ יִתְפַּלָּצוּן מִגַּעֲרָתֶךָ / אֵין כָּמְוֹךָ וְאֵין כְּעֶרְכְּךָ וְאֵין בִּלְתֶּךָ
אַתָּה רִאשׁוֹן וְאַתָּה אַחֲרוֹן וְאֶפֶס זוּלָתֶךָ / אֵין קֵץ וְחֵקֶר וְסוֹף לִתְבוּנָתֶךָ
צָפוּן וְנֶעְלָם וְנִסְתָּר, גְּלוּיִים לְעָמְתֶךָ / לְךָ הַהוֹד וְהַתִּפְאֶרֶת וְהַנֵּצַח הֲדָרָתֶךָ
לְךָ הַגְּדֻלָּה וְהַגְּבוּרָה, וּכְיִרְאָתְךָ עֶבְרָתֶךָ

מֵאֵין כָּמְוֹךָ יהוה גָּדוֹל אַתָּה וְגָדוֹל שִׁמְךָ בִּגְדֻלָּתֶךָ

לְךָ הַשָּׁמַיִם, וְכָל צְבָאָם נִבְרְאוּ לְשָׁרְתֶךָ

לְךָ הָאָרֶץ וּמְלוֹאָהּ, הֲדֹם מַרְגְּלוֹתֶיךָ

לְךָ הַיָּם וְהַיַּבָּשָׁה, וְהַכֹּל כּוֹנְנוּ אֶצְבְּעוֹתֶיךָ

לְךָ הַכֶּסֶף וְהַזָּהָב, וְכָל שְׂכִיּוֹת חֶמְדָּתֶךָ

לְךָ כָּל הַנְּפָשׁוֹת יַחַד מְפֻקָּדוֹת בְּאוֹצְרוֹתֶיךָ

לְךָ הַחָכְמָה וְהַתְּבוּנָה וְהַשֵּׂכֶל מִבִּינָתֶךָ

חֲכַם לֵבָב וְאַמִּיץ כֹּחַ, וְתִתְנַהֵג בַּחֲסִידוּתֶךָ

כִּי מִי בַשַּׁחַק יַעֲרָךְ לְךָ לְדַמּוֹתֶךָ

מִי כָמְוֹךָ חֲסִין יָהּ, אוֹת בִּצְבָאוֹתֶיךָ

אֵל נַעֲרָץ בְּסוֹד קְדֹשִׁים רַבָּה, וְנוֹרָא עַל כָּל סְבִיבוֹתֶיךָ

חֹשֶׁךְ סִתְרְךָ, וַעֲרָפֶל סֻכָּתֶךָ / מִנֹּגַהּ נֶגְדְּךָ, בָּרָד וְאֵשׁ גַּחֲלָתֶךָ
הָאֵל הַנֶּאֱמָן, שֹׁמֵר הַבְּרִית וְהַחֶסֶד בְּמִשְׁמַרְתֶּךָ

לָתֵת לְאִישׁ כִּדְרָכָיו, בְּשַׁלֶּמְךָ מַשְׂכֻּרְתֶּךָ

הַצּוּר תָּמִים פָּעֳלוֹ, וְאֵין עָוֶל, אֱמֶת פְּעֻלָּתֶךָ

מִשְׁפָּטֶיךָ תְּהוֹם רַבָּה, וּכְהַרְרֵי אֵל צִדְקָתֶךָ

עוֹזֵר וְסוֹמֵךְ לְכָל מְהִירֵי מְלַאכְתֶּךָ / אֶת הַכֹּל עָשִׂיתָ יָפֶה בְעִתּוֹ בְּחָכְמָתֶךָ
בְּטֶרֶם הָרִים יֻלָּדוּ, וַתְּחוֹלֵל אַדְמָתֶךָ / בָּרָאתָ תְּשׁוּבָה לְמַרְפֵּא אֲרוּכָתֶךָ
וְעַד לֹא מַכָּה, הִקְדַּמְתָּ תְּעָלָתֶךָ / וְעַד לֹא מָזוֹר, הִגְהִיתָ רְפוּאָתֶךָ
כִּי גָלוּי וְצָפוּי לִפְנֵי כֵס שְׁכִינָתֶךָ

כִּי אָדָם אֵין צַדִּיק בָּאָרֶץ, לְהִזָּהֵר מִגַּחֲלָתֶךָ

אֲשֶׁר יַעֲשֶׂה טוֹב, וְלֹא יַעֲבֹר מִתּוֹרָתֶךָ
כִּי לֹא תַאֲמִין בַּעֲבָדֶיךָ וּבִמְשָׁרְתֶיךָ
וְתָהֳלָה תָשִׂים בִּגְדוּדֵי מַחֲנוֹתֶיךָ / אַף שֹׁכְנֵי בָתֵּי חֹמֶר עַפְרוֹתֶיךָ
הַגְּדֵלִים בְּעָוֹן, וְעוֹבְרִים עַל מִצְוֹתֶיךָ
וְתָשֵׂם בַּסַּד רַגְלָם, כִּי יָסוּרוּ מֵאָרְחוֹתֶיךָ
וּבְיַד כָּל אָדָם יַחְתֹּם בִּגְזֵרוֹתֶיךָ / וְתַגֵּד לָהֶם פִּשְׁעָם בְּתוֹכְחוֹתֶיךָ
וְהִתְוַדּוּ אֶת עֲוֹנָם, וְיַצְדִּיקוּ דִין אֲמִתֶּךָ / וְלָכֵן הִקְדַּמְתָּ צֳרִי לִטְרִיָּתֶךָ
כִּי יְשׁוּבוּן מֵאָוֶן, וִיבַקְשׁוּ מְחִילָתֶךָ
וְאַתָּה קָרוֹב לְקוֹרְאֶיךָ, לְהָשִׁיב מֵהֶם חֲמָתֶךָ
וְיוֹם זֶה בָּחַרְתָּ, לֵישֵׁב בְּמִשְׁפָּט עַל בְּרִיּוֹתֶיךָ
וְכִבְנֵי מָרוֹן יַעַבְרוּן לְפָנֶיךָ בִּסְפִירָתֶךָ
וְכֻלָּם נִסְקָרִין בִּסְקִירַת צְפִיָּתֶךָ / וְתִרְאֶה יַחַד לִבָּם בִּרְאִיָּתֶךָ
וְתִגְזֹר עֲלֵיהֶם כָּל גְּזֵרוֹתֶיךָ / וְתִקְצֹב מְזוֹנוֹתֵיהֶם וּפַרְנָסָתָם בְּאִמְרָתֶךָ
וְעַמְּךָ בְּחִנּוּנָם מִתְוַעֲדִים לְחַלּוֹתֶךָ / וְתוֹקְעִים וּמְרִיעִים, כְּאָמוּר בְּתוֹרָתֶךָ
וּמְעַרְבְּבִים קַטֵּגוֹר, בְּלִי לְהַשְׂטִינָם לִקְרָאתֶךָ
וְתִזְכֹּר לָמוֹ עֲקֵדַת יִצְחָק כִּשְׁבוּעָתֶךָ
וְתַהֲפֹךְ מִדַּת הַדִּין לְרַחֲמִים, כִּי כֵן מִדָּתֶךָ / וּתְרַחֵם עֲלֵיהֶם בְּרֹב חֶמְלָתֶךָ
כִּי הֵם בָּנֶיךָ וְצֹאן מַרְעִיתֶךָ.

וְהַיּוֹם יִפָּתְחוּ שְׁלֹשָׁה סְפָרִים מְנֻקָּדִים / שֶׁל צַדִּיקִים שׁוֹמְרֵי פִקּוּדִים
שֶׁל בֵּינוֹנִים, וְשֶׁל זֵדִים / צַדִּיקִים נִכְתָּבִים לְחַיֵּי עַד שְׁקוּדִים
וּרְשָׁעִים נִכְתָּבִים לְתַבְעֵרַת יְקוּדִים
וּבֵינוֹנִים עַד יוֹם כִּפּוּר תְּלוּיִים וְעוֹמְדִים
אִם יָשׁוּבוּ מִמַּעֲשֵׂיהֶם הָרָעִים, וְיִהְיוּ חֲרֵדִים
וִיתַקְּנוּ מַעַלְלֵיהֶם וְיֵיטִיבוּ צְעָדִים
חֶלְקָם בַּחַיִּים יִזְכּוּ נֶחֱמָדִים / וְאִם לֹא זָכוּ, לְמִיתָה יִהְיוּ נֶאֱחָדִים
וּכְמוֹ כֵן יֵעָשֶׂה לְיוֹם הַדִּין / וְיָבֹאוּ מַעֲשֵׂיהֶם לְהָעִיד כְּעֵדִים
וּבְמֹאזְנַיִם יַעֲלוּ מִשְּׁנֵי צְדָדִים
אִם יַכְרִיעוּ טוֹבִים עַל הָרָעִים, לִהְיוֹת כְּבֵדִים
בְּעָלִים יִהְיוּ בְטוּחִים, וְלֹא פְחוּדִים / וְאִם מֶחֱצָה עַל מֶחֱצָה יִהְיוּ אֲגוּדִים

וְרַב חֶסֶד מַטֶּה כְלַפֵּי חֲסָדִים / יָשׁוּב יְרַחֵם, יִכְבֹּשׁ עָוֹן מוֹרְדִים
וְיִשָּׂא עָוֹן, וְיַגְבִּיהַּ מְרָדִים / וְיַכְרִיעוּ נְעִימִים וַעֲנוּדִים
וְיַעֲבִיר רִאשׁוֹן רִאשׁוֹן אֲחָדִים / כִּי צַדִּיק יהוה בְּכָל דְּרָכָיו, וּמַעֲשָׂיו חֲסָדִים
רוֹצֶה בִתְשׁוּבָה מִכָּל עוֹלוֹת וּתְמִידִים
הַתְּשׁוּבָה וּמַעֲשֵׂה הַטּוֹב כִּתְרִיס בִּפְנֵי שׁוֹדְדִים.

אָנָּא אָדוֹן מָלֵא רַחֲמִים / בְּקוּמְךָ לַמִּשְׁפָּט עַל יְצוּרֵי עוֹלָמִים
רְגֶז בַּל תָּעִיר עַל מְעוּטֵי עַמִּים / הַמְיַחֲדִים שִׁמְךָ לֵילוֹת וְיָמִים
וּלְנַצְּחָךְ תָּמִיד מַעֲרִיבִים וּמַשְׁכִּימִים / וּכְאָב עַל בֵּן, יִכָּמְרוּ רַחֲמֶיךָ בְּנִחוּמִים
לְנַקּוֹתָם מִכֹּבֶד עָוֹן וַאֲשָׁמִים / וְהִזָּכֵר לִבְרִית שְׁלֹשֶׁת תְּמִימִים
וּלְאַב הָמוֹן, אֲשֶׁר הָיָה תָמִים / וְנִתְנַסָּה בַּעֲשָׂרָה נִסְיוֹנוֹת עֲצוּמִים
וְנִמְצָא שָׁלֵם בְּכָל פְּעָמִים.

הַנֵּס הָרִאשׁוֹן, בְּהִוָּלְדוֹ נִתְיָעֲצוּ הַחַרְטֻמִּים
וּבִקְשׁוּ לְהָרְגוֹ גְּדוֹלֵי הַמַּלְכוּת וְהַקּוֹסְמִים
וְנֶחְבָּא בָּאָרֶץ שְׁלֹשׁ עֶשְׂרֵה שָׁנָה שְׁלֵמִים
וְלֹא רָאָה שֶׁמֶשׁ וְיָרֵחַ וְכוֹכְבֵי מְרוֹמִים
וּלְאַחַר שְׁלֹשׁ עֶשְׂרֵה שָׁנָה יָצָא מְחֻכָּם בְּחִכּוּמִים
וּמָאַס אֱלִילִים וְשִׁקֵּץ צְלָמִים / וּבָטַח בְּיוֹצְרוֹ, וְנָפַל חֶבְלוֹ בַּנְּעִימִים.
הַשֵּׁנִי, הִשְׁלִיכוּהוּ לְכִבְשַׁן אֵשׁ פֶּחָמִים
וּמֶלֶךְ הַכָּבוֹד פָּשַׁט יְמִינוֹ וְהִצִּילוֹ בְּרַחֲמִים
וְנָם, אֲנִי יהוה אֲשֶׁר הוֹצֵאתִיךָ מֵאוּר כַּשְׂדִּים, בִּנְאוּמִים.
הַשְּׁלִישִׁי, הֶגְלָהוּ מִמּוֹלַדְתּוֹ הָגְלַת שְׁלוּמִים.
הָרְבִיעִי, הֵבִיא רָעָב בְּאוֹתָן הַיָּמִים
הוּא הָרָעָב הָרִאשׁוֹן אֲשֶׁר בָּא לְעוֹלָמִים
וְלֹא בְּכָל הָאֲרָצוֹת וּבְכָל הַתְּחוּמִים
כִּי אִם בְּאֶרֶץ כְּנַעַן, לְנַסּוֹתוֹ וּלְהוֹרִידוֹ לְאַדְמַת עֲנָמִים.
הַחֲמִישִׁי, נִלְקְחָה שָׂרָה לְמוֹשֵׁל עַמִּים / בְּלֵיל שִׁמֻּרִים, הַנִּשְׁמָר לִבְכוֹרֵי חָמִים
וַיְנַגַּע יהוה אֶת פַּרְעֹה נְגָעִים גְּדֹלִים וְאֵימִים
וַיָּגָר בְּאֶרֶץ פְּלִשְׁתִּים רַבִּים יָמִים / וְשָׁלַח מֶלֶךְ גְּרָר, וְלָקַח יְפַת פְּעָמִים

וְנַעֲשָׂה הוּא וְכָל בְּנֵי בֵיתוֹ טְמְטוּמִים / וַיֵּרֶד מִיכָאֵל הַמַּלְאָךְ לְהָרְגוֹ בִּזְעָמִים
וְזָעַק, הֲגוֹי גַּם צַדִּיק תַּהֲרֹג, וְתִשְׁפֹּךְ דָּמִים
וְאָמַר לוֹ, הָשֵׁב אֵשֶׁת הָאִישׁ, כִּי נָבִיא הוּא וְאָב לַחֲכָמִים
וְלָקַח צֹאן וּבָקָר וַעֲבָדִים וּשְׁפָחוֹת, וְהֵשִׁיב לוֹ תַּשְׁלוּמִים
וַיִּתְפַּלֵּל אַבְרָהָם אֶל הָאֱלֹהִים, וַיֵּעָתֵר לוֹ מִמְּרוֹמִים
וַיִּרְפָּא אֹתָם מֵעֲצִירַת רְחָמִים.
הַשִּׁשִּׁי, בְּבוֹא עָלָיו הַמְּלָכִים הַקְּדוּמִים / עִם כְּדָרְלָעֹמֶר מֶלֶךְ עֵילָמִים
וּבְבֶן אָחִיו הִתְחִילוּ תְחִלָּה שׁוֹטְמִים / וּבִשְׁבִילוֹ לָקְחוּ אֶת כָּל רְכוּשׁ סְדוֹמִים
וַיָּבֹא הַפָּלִיט, וְהִגִּיד מֶה עָשׂוּ קָמִים
וַיָּרֶק אֶת חֲנִיכָיו יְלִידֵי בֵיתוֹ רְשׁוּמִים
הֵם עָנֵר, אֶשְׁכֹּל וּמַמְרֵא, וֶאֱלִיעֶזֶר מְסֻיָּמִים
וַיֵּחָלֵק עֲלֵיהֶם לַיְלָה, וַיַּכֵּם בְּמַהֲלֻמִּים / הוּא הַלַּיְלָה אֲשֶׁר הָיָה מִקְּדוּמִים
וַיָּשֶׁב אֵת כָּל הָרְכֻשׁ, בְּעֶזְרַת מַשְׁפִּיל רָמִים.
הַשְּׁבִיעִי, כְּשֶׁנִּדְבַּר עִמּוֹ בֵּין הַבְּתָרִים / וְהֶרְאָהוּ אַרְבַּע מַלְכֻיּוֹת כַּבִּירִים
שֶׁמּוֹשְׁלִים בִּזְמַנָּם, וְיֹאבְדוּ לְדוֹר דּוֹרִים
עֶגְלָה מְשֻׁלֶּשֶׁת, זוֹ מַלְכוּת אֲדוֹמִים אֲרוּרִים
אֲשֶׁר הִיא כְּעֶגְלָה דָשָׁה, וְכַחֲזִירֵי יְעָרִים
וְעֵז מְשֻׁלֶּשֶׁת אֵלּוּ יְוָנִים, שֶׁנִּמְשְׁלוּ לִצְפִירִים
וְאַיִל מְשֻׁלָּשׁ, זוֹ מַלְכוּת מָדַי וּפָרַס חֲבֵרִים
כְּעִנְיָן שֶׁנֶּאֱמַר, הָאַיִל אֲשֶׁר רָאִיתָ בְּבֵרוּרִים
וְתוֹר אֵלּוּ בְּנֵי יִשְׁמָעֵאל, שֶׁנִּמְשְׁלוּ לְשְׁוָרִים
וְגוֹזָל אֵלּוּ יִשְׂרָאֵל, שֶׁנִּמְשְׁלוּ לְיוֹנִים וְתֹרִים
כְּעִנְיָן שֶׁנֶּאֱמַר, יוֹנָתִי בְּחַגְוֵי הַסֶּלַע וּבִסְתָרִים
וְלָקַח וּבִתְּרָם לִשְׁנֵי בְתָרִים / כְּדֵי לְהַתִּישׁ כֹּחָם, וְזִכְרָם לְהַחֲרִים
וַיֵּרֶד הָעַיִט לְאַבְּדָם, זֶה דָוִד רֹאשׁ הַגִּבּוֹרִים
כְּצֵאת הַשֶּׁמֶשׁ הָיָה מֵנִיף עֲלֵיהֶם בְּסוּדָרִים
שֶׁלֹּא יִמְשֹׁל בָּהֶם הָעַיִט עַד הָעֶרֶב, כְּסוֹד מוֹרִים
לְהוֹדִיעַ שֶׁאֵין מוֹשְׁלִים, אֶלָּא יוֹם אֶחָד מִיּוֹמוֹ שֶׁל יוֹצֵר הָרִים
חוּץ מִשְּׁתֵּי יָדוֹת שָׁעָה בְּשִׁעוּרִים

כְּשֶׁהַחַמָּה נוֹטָה לְמַעֲרָב, שְׁתֵּי יָדוֹת שָׁעָה מַכְהָה אוֹרִים
כֵּן עַד שֶׁלֹּא יָבֹא הָעֶרֶב יִצְמַח אוֹר לַיְשָׁרִים
וְהָיָה לְעֵת עֶרֶב יִהְיֶה אוֹר לַהֲדוּרִים.
הַשְּׁמִינִי, בְּהִמּוֹלוֹ עָרְלַת בְּשָׂרִים / בֶּעָשׂוֹר לַחֹדֶשׁ, בְּיוֹם הַכִּפּוּרִים
וּבְכָל שָׁנָה נִרְאֵית דַּם מִילָתוֹ, כְּדַם פָּרִים וְאֵמוּרִים
וּמְכַפֵּר עֲוֹנוֹת עַמּוֹ, לְהַצְדִּיקָם כִּישָׁרִים.
הַתְּשִׁיעִי, בְּשַׁלְּחוֹ יִשְׁמָעֵאל וְאִמּוֹ לַמִּדְבָּרִים
מֵעַל יָחִיד, הַנַּעֲלָה בְּאַחַד הֶהָרִים / מִזֶּה וְלַבָּא לְדוֹר דּוֹרִים.
הָעֲשִׂירִי הָיָה אַחַר הַדְּבָרִים הָאֵלֶּה בְּמִלָּה
וְנִסָּהוּ, קַח נָא אֶת בִּנְךָ, וְהַעֲלֵהוּ לִי לְעֹלָה
וֶהֱשִׁיבוֹ, לְאֵיזֶה בֵן, לְבֶן הָעָרְלָה אוֹ לְבֶן הַמִּילָה
אֶת יְחִידְךָ, אֲשֶׁר אָהַבְתָּ בְּחֶמְלָה / עַל הָהָר אֲשֶׁר עָלָיו שְׁכִינָה מְכֻלָּלָה
וְהִשְׁכִּים בַּבֹּקֶר וְלֹא נִתְעַצֵּל בְּעַצְלָה
וְחָבַשׁ הַחֲמוֹר בְּעַצְמוֹ, בְּגִילָה
הוּא הַחֲמוֹר אֲשֶׁר רָכַב עָלָיו דָּלָה דָלָה
וְהוּא שֶׁעָתִיד עָנִי לִרְכֹּב עָלָיו בְּעֵת הַגְּאֻלָּה
וְהָלְכוּ לְדַרְכָּם בְּיֹשֶׁר מְסִלָּה
כְּשֶׁהִגִּיעוּ לַצּוֹפִים, רָאוּ שַׁלְהֶבֶת תְּלוּלָה / וְהֵבִין, כִּי הוּא הָהָר לִתְהִלָּה
וּבְאֶצְבַּע הֶרְאָהוּ הַמִּזְבֵּחַ שֶׁל שׁוֹכֵן מַעְלָה / הוּא הַמִּזְבֵּחַ אֲשֶׁר הָיָה מִתְּחִלָּה
וְצִוָּה יָחִיד לִקְשֹׁר יָדָיו וְרַגְלָיו לְרַגְלָה / שֶׁלֹּא יִבְעַט, מִצְוַת כַּבֵּד לְחַלְּלָה
וַעֲקָדוֹ עַל הַמִּזְבֵּחַ כְּטָלֵה עֹלָה / וְעָרַךְ הָאֵשׁ, וְהָעֵצִים הֶעֱלָה
וְלָקַח הַמַּאֲכֶלֶת לְשָׁחֲטוֹ בְּחַלְחָלָה / וּכְכֹהֵן גָּדוֹל הִגִּישׁ מִנְחָה בְלוּלָה
וְיוֹשֵׁב וְרוֹאֶה נוֹרָא עֲלִילָה / הָאָב מַעֲקִיד וְהַבֵּן נֶעֱקָד בְּחִילָה
הֵן אֶרְאֶלָּם צָעֲקוּ חֻצָה בִּילָלָה
וְהִשְׁמִיעַ, אַל תִּשְׁלַח יָדְךָ אֶל הַנַּעַר לַעֲשׂוֹתוֹ כָלָה
וְהָאַיִל אֲשֶׁר הָצְפַּן מִשֵּׁשֶׁת יְמֵי בְרֵאשִׁית לְעוֹלָה
נִתַּן כָּפְרוֹ, וְהֻחְשַׁב לוֹ לְשֵׁם וְלִתְהִלָּה
וְנִשְׁבַּע לְבָרְכוֹ בִּבְרָכָה מְעֻלָּה / וְלִזְכֹּר עֲקֵדָתוֹ לְאֹם נִדְגָּלָה

לְמַלְּטָם מִכָּל עָוֹן וְעַוְלָה / וְלִקְנוֹתָם, לִהְיוֹת לוֹ לְעַם סְגֻלָּה
לִהְיוֹת יְשׁוּעָתֵנוּ וְעֶזְרָתֵנוּ, סֶלָה.
וְהַיּוֹם הַזֶּה, לְפָנֶיךָ יִפָּקֵד / כְּשֵׁר מִפְעֲלוֹת עוֹקֵד וְנֶעֱקָד
וְיוֹשִׁיבַת הַתָּם, אָהֳלֶיךָ שָׁקַד / זְכֹר אָדוֹן בְּרַחֲמִים לִפְקֹד
וְתַרְשִׁישֵׁי חַשְׁמַל, חֲשָׁשֵׁי יְקָד / יִכְרְעוּ וְיִשְׁתַּחֲווּ לְפָנֶיךָ לִקֹּד.
וְזֶה אֶל זֶה יַעֲרִיצוּ / וְזֶה אֶל זֶה יַקְדִּישׁוּ
וְשִׁלּוּשׁ קְדֻשָּׁה לַקָּדוֹשׁ מַקְדִּישִׁים.

*The service continues with* קדושה *on page 691.*

# פיוטים למוסף של יום ב׳

*This תקיעתא, composed by Rabbi Yose ben Yose (see commentary on page 317), is less complex than its parallel "אֲנַסִּיכָה" – it employs only a double acrostic, and no internal rhyme. The poet calls on the audience to praise God, and accept His kingship, culminating with a vision of the future redemption. If the first day of ראש השנה is שבת, "אֲהַלְלָה" is recited; otherwise it is said on the second day.*

אֲהַלְלָה אֱלֹהַי / אָשִׁירָה עֻזּוֹ / אֲסַפְּרָה כְבוֹדוֹ / אֲאַפְּדֶנּוּ מְלוּכָה.
אֲשַׂגֵּב לַפּוֹעֵל / אֲשֶׁר שָׂח וּפָעַל / אַנְוֵהוּ כִּי לוֹ / יָאֲתָה מְלוּכָה.

בְּעֻזּוֹ נֶצַח אֲשַׁנֵּן / כִּי צְבָאוֹ אֲנִי / וְלוֹ נָאֶה שִׂיחַ / גֹּדֶל הַמְּלוּכָה.
בַּקָּהָל אֲבַשֵּׂר / בְּרָב עָם אֲדַבֵּר / לְמִי שְׂאֵת וְיֶתֶר עֹז / וּלְמִי הַמְּלוּכָה.

גְּשׁוּ גוֹיִם / וּבוֹאוּ מַמְלָכוֹת / רְאוּ מַה נֶּהְדָּר / בְּמֵזַח הַמְּלוּכָה.
גַּדְּלוּהוּ אִתִּי / וּנְרוֹמְמֶנְהוּ יַחַד / וְאַל תִּתְגָּאוּ / בְּנֵזֶר הַמְּלוּכָה.

דְּרָכִים בְּעֵת / נֶעֶשְׂתָה מְצוּלָה / הִתְבּוֹנְנוּ יַחַד / לְמִי נֶזְרְקָה הַמְּלוּכָה.
דָּרַךְ סוּס בַּיָּם / כְּנֶגֶד שֵׁשׁ מֵאוֹת רֶכֶב / וּמַה יּוֹעִיל גֶּבֶר / עֹז בִּמְלוּכָה.

הֶאֱזִינוּ רוֹזְנִים / אָז, וַיִּרְגָּזוּ / הִבִּיטוּ חֲתַת / וּמָאֲסוּ מְלוּכָה.
הִגִּידוּ כֹּחוֹ / לְאֻמִּים, וְדִבְּרוּ / לָזֶה יִכָּתֵב / שֵׁם הַמְּלוּכָה.

וְנִלְחַם רֵאשִׁית / גּוֹיִם, וְאָבָד / כִּי נִשְׁבַּע חַי / בְּכִסֵּא מְלוּכָה.
וַיִּלְעַג בְּכָל דּוֹר / כִּי לֹא לָמַד / מִי נִלְחַם בַּיָּם / וְעָטָה מְלוּכָה.

זָד עַל אֲדוֹנָיו / עֶבֶד יוֹשֵׁב נֶגֶב / בְּזֹאת תִּרְגַּז אֶרֶץ / בִּשְׂאֵת עֶבֶד מְלוּכָה.
זֶרַע בְּרוּכִים / הֶחֱרִימוּ אֲרוּרִים / כִּי נָתְנוּ קוֹל / לְאַדִּיר הַמְּלוּכָה.

חֶשְׁבּוֹן וּבָשָׁן / עוֹרְרוּ מִלְחָמֶת / בְּלִי לָתֵת דֶּרֶךְ / לִצְבְאוֹת מְלוּכָה.
חֵילָם נִשְׁמַד / וְאַרְצָם חֻלָּקָה / וּמֵעַל זְרוֹעָם / נָפְלָה מְלוּכָה.

טָפְשׁוּ בְּנֵי כְנַעַן / כִּי נָכְרִים הֵם / בְּאַדְמַת בְּנֵי שֵׁם / זֶרַע הַמְּלוּכָה.
טְבָחָם בִּן נוּן / עַד פִּנָּה אֶרֶץ / לִפְנֵי אֲרוֹן הַבְּרִית / אֲדוֹן הַמְּלוּכָה.

יוֹשְׁבֵי חֲרֹשֶׁת / אָז הִקְשָׁה לַחַץ / עֲזָרוּהוּ בְּלִי בֶצַע / אַפְסֵי מְלוּכָה.
יָהּ הִלְחִים בָּם / צָבָא בְּלִי בֶצַע / כֵּן יֹאבְדוּ שְׁאָר / וְלַיהוה הַמְּלוּכָה.

כְּאֶרֶז בַּלְּבָנוֹן / אַשּׁוּר גָּדַל / וְחֵרֵף, אוֹרִיד / כַּבִּיר מְלוּכָה.
כְּלִיל אֵשׁ הֲמָמָם / בְּלֵיל שִׁמּוּרִים / וְאָז יֵדְעוּ כֹל / כִּי לָאֵל הַמְּלוּכָה.

לַשַּׁחַת כָּרַע בֵּל / כְּחָשְׁבוּ עֲלוֹת לַשַּׁחַק / וְסָר מֶנּוּ לְבַב אֱנוֹשׁ / וְיָרַד מִמְּלוּכָה.
לְכַנּוּ הוּשַׁב / וְכֹחַ אֵל הִכִּיר / לְמֵרִים וּמַשְׁפִּיל / הַשְׁלִים מְלוּכָה.

מְגֻרָה צֹאן לַטֶּבַח / וְנִתְכְּנוּ עֲלִילוֹת / בִּלְבוּשׁ צָעִיר / רוֹדֵם הַמְּלוּכָה.
מְכוּרֵי בְּלֹא הוֹן / פְּדוּיֵי בְּלֹא כֶסֶף / סֹלּוּ לְמַטֵּה כְּמַיִם / לֵב הַמְּלוּכָה.

נִמְכְּרוּ יוֹנִים / לִבְנֵי יְוָנִים / וְרִחֲקוּם מֵעַל / גְּבוּל הַמְּלוּכָה.
נֵאֲרוּ בְּרִית וָדָת / וְהִמְרִידוּ עַם בְּאֵל / וּמִגְּרוּם בְּלֹא כֹחַ / מְכַהֲנֵי מְלוּכָה.

שָׂעִיר הֶחֱנִיף / לְהוֹרֵהוּ בְּצֵידוֹ / וַיִּירַשׁ בְּקוֹל בֶּכִי / חֶרֶב וּמְלוּכָה.
שְׂגַב חֵלֶק / הֱיוֹת גְּבִיר לְאֶחָיו / וְעוֹד תִּסֹּב / לִישֻׁרוּן הַמְּלוּכָה.

עֲשֵׂה לְךָ בְּצִיּוֹן / שֵׁם נוֹרָאוֹת / כְּאָז תַּצְלִיחֶנָּה / בְּכִסֵּא מְלוּכָה.
עוֹרֵר וְהָקֵץ / מְשׂוֹשׂ כָּל הָאָרֶץ / וְכוֹנֵן כִּסְאֲךָ / בְּקִרְיַת מְלוּכָה.

פְּנֵי מְאוֹר לְבָנָה / וְחַמָּה תַּחְפִּיר / וְיֵבוֹשׁוּ עוֹבְדֵימוֹ / בְּשְׂאֵתְךָ מְלוּכָה.
פָּאֵר עִיר יֹפִי / לְבָרָה כַּחַמָּה / וְגַלֵּה לְנֶגְדֵּנוּ / כְּבוֹד מְלוּכָה.

צִבְאוֹת גְּאוּלֵי צֹעַן / שׁוֹרְרוּ בְּלֵיל חָג / וְהוּא לַיְלָה נִשְׁמָר / לְסַחֵף מְלוּכָה.
צָעֲדוּ בְּמֵי שֹׁעַל / צָפוּ בְּרוּחַ שֶׂכֶל / אָנָה יִנְטָעוּ / וִיקַבְּלוּ מְלוּכָה.

קָמְטוּ שַׁעֲרֵי זְבוּל / בֵּית עוֹלָמִים / כִּי מִבֵּינֵימוֹ / שָׁבְתָה מְלוּכָה.
קָדוֹשׁ יָבוֹא בָם / לְעוֹלָמִים / וְאָז יִשְׂאוּ רֹאשׁ / בְּחַדְּשׁוֹ מְלוּכָה.

רָבְצָה עֲדִינָה / שָׁקְטָה מֵאַלְמוֹן / כִּי אָרַךְ לָהּ / קֵץ הַמְּלוּכָה.
רִיבוּ מוֹשִׁיעִים / שְׂאוּ אֶדֶר מֵאֱדוֹם / וְשִׁיתוּ עַל אָדוֹן / הוֹד הַמְּלוּכָה.

שָׁוְא שָׂנֵא אֵל / וְהוּא עַל לְשׁוֹנֵנוּ / בִּקֵּשׁ אֱמֶת וָאַיִן / וְרָחֲקָה מְלוּכָה.
שַׁדַּי הָסֵר / אָוֶן מִצְּבָאֶיךָ / וְיָרִיעוּ לָךְ / תְּרוּעַת מְלוּכָה.

תַּחְגֹּר גֵּאוּת / תִּתְאַזַּר עֹז / לְבַל יִשְׂתָּרֵר / זָר בִּמְלוּכָה.
תִּכּוֹן תֵּבֵל / כִּי יִנָּעֵר רָשָׁע / וְשָׂם צֶדֶק לְרַגְלָיו / וְיִצְנֹף מְלוּכָה.
תְּקַס גּוֹיִם / תּוֹכִיחַ לְאֻמִּים / תִּשְׁבֹּר מַטֵּה רֶשַׁע / מוֹשֵׁל הַמְּלוּכָה.
תַּחֲלִיף אֱלִילִים / תִּשְׂגַּב לְבַדֶּךָ / תִּקָּרֵא נֶצַח / יָחִיד בִּמְלוּכָה.

*The service continues with* וְעַל כֵּן *on a weekday on page 837; and on a* שבת *on page 581.*

*This* תקיעתא*, author unknown, features a double acrostic and no internal rhyme. Each line ends with the word "*לְזִכָּרוֹן*" – "for remembrance." The intention was probably to incorporate the verses of* זכרונות*. If the first day of* ראש השנה *is a* שבת*, "*בְּמַעֲשַׂי אֶפְחַד*" is recited; otherwise it is said on the second day.*

אֶפְחַד בְּמַעֲשַׂי / אֶדְאַג בְּכָל עֵת / אִירָא מִיּוֹם דִּין / בְּבוֹאִי לְזִכָּרוֹן.

אֶדְרֹשׁ לְחַנּוּן / אֲחַלֶּה לְרַחוּם / אֲחַנֵּן לְחֹק לִי / יוֹם זִכָּרוֹן.

בְּבוֹאִי לַמִּשְׁפָּט / בְּמִי אֶשָּׁעֵן / וּמִי יְחַפֶּשׂ לִי / צֶדֶק לְזִכָּרוֹן.

בָּאָבוֹת בָּטַחְתִּי / וּפָעֳלָם אִכַּלְתִּי / וְהֵם הָיוּ לִי / קֶדֶם לְזִכָּרוֹן.

גְּבוּרָה זְרוֹעִי / כְּשָׁת מִחְנֵי נָא / לְבַל יִמַּח מֶנִּי / שֵׁם וְזִכָּרוֹן.

גֶּבֶר אִם יַעֲמֹד / לְפָנָיו, הֲיוֹעִיל / בְּעֵת יְבַקֵּשׁ מֶנִּי / זְכוּת לְזִכָּרוֹן.

דַּצְתִּי בְּלוֹבֵשׁ אֵפוֹד / וְחֹשֶׁן הַמִּשְׁפָּט / אֲשֶׁר בָּם הוּחַק / שְׁמִי לְזִכָּרוֹן.

דִּלֵּג בְּמַחְתָּה / עַד יֵעָצַר נֶגֶף / בְּגֶשֶׁת זָר מְכַהֵן / יָקוּד לְזִכָּרוֹן.

הַבִּיטָה אֵל / בְּעָמְדִי לְפָנֶיךָ / אֵין בְּקִרְבִּי אֱנוֹשׁ / תָּוִי לְזִכָּרוֹן.

הֲיֵשׁ מִי יְפַלֵּל / וְיָשִׁיב חֵמָה / וְיוּחַק לְדוֹרוֹת / שְׁמוֹ לְזִכָּרוֹן.

וּמִי שׂוֹנֵא בֶצַע / יְדַבֵּר עֱנוּ בִי / וַיַּעַן וַיֹּאמַר עֵד / אָדוֹן לְזִכָּרוֹן.

וּבְטָלֶה חָלָב / יְכַפֵּר בַּעֲדֵנוּ / וּכְנֶגֶד שְׁנֵי עֳפָרִים / יַעַל לְזִכָּרוֹן.

זַעַף יָרֵא, וַיֹּאמַר / תְּהִי יָדְךָ בִּי / אֲשֶׁר כְּלֵב אֱלֹהָיו / הוּא לְזִכָּרוֹן.

זָעַק, וְהֵשִׁיב / חֶרֶב אֶל נְדָנָהּ / וְהוּשַׁת לוֹ כַּשֶּׁמֶשׁ / כֵּס לְזִכָּרוֹן.

חִכִּיתִי בְּעֵת עֹצֶר / לְפוֹתֵחַ וּמַמְטִיר / כִּמְשִׁיב רְוּחַ לַיֶּלֶד / אָבוּד מִזִּכָּרוֹן.

חַי לִרְאוֹת בְּרִית / בְּדַבְּרוֹ קִנֵּאתִי / כִּי עָזְבוּ עָם / בְּרִית וְזִכָּרוֹן.

טֶרֶם הָיָה לִי / מְכַפֵּר פָּנִים / מִנְחָה הוֹלֶכֶת / כְּשֹׁחַד לְזִכָּרוֹן.

טֶרֶף נֵרְדְּ וְסַמִּים / לְמֵסַב חֲדָרָיו / דָּם וְחֵלֶב לְנִיחוֹחַ / וְלֶחֶם לְזִכָּרוֹן.

יֻצַּגְתִּי וְהוּשַׁמְתִּי / עַל גֶּחָלֵי רֵקָה / כִּי לֹא אַלְמָן / שַׁתִּי לְזִכָּרוֹן.

יָהּ אֶבְטַח בָּךְ / וְלֹא בִנְדִיבִים / כִּי הֵם בַּקֶּבֶר / וְלָנֶצַח שִׁמְךָ לְזִכָּרוֹן.

כָּל אֵלֶּה סְמָכוּנִי / וְרַחֲמֶיךָ בִּקַּשְׁתִּי / לוּלֵי הֵם תַּמְתִּי / וְאֵינִי לְזִכָּרוֹן.

כִּי הֵם בִּזְרוֹעַ / עָדֶיךָ לֹא בָאוּ / רוֹמְמוֹתֶיךָ בְּפִיהֶם / שָׂמוּ לְזִכָּרוֹן.

לְיוֹם זֶה נִכְמַס / סֶכֶם חֶשְׁבּוֹנוֹת / תְּחִלָּה לְיָמִים / וְרֹאשׁ לְזִכָּרוֹן.

לְהִקָּרֵא בוֹ / כְּתָב עֵט וְשָׁמִיר / גָּלוּי וּבָאֵר / וְיָדוּעַ לְזִכָּרוֹן.

מָוֶת וְחַיִּים / שָׁלוֹם וּמִלְחֶמֶת / צַחְצָחוֹת וָשֹׂבַע / בָּאוּ לְזִכָּרוֹן.

מַעַלְלֵי גֶבֶר / וּמִסְפַּר צְעָדָיו / נִשְׁכְּחוּ מֵאֱנוֹשׁ / וְלָאֵל לְזִכָּרוֹן.
נִסְתְּרָה דַרְכִּי / מִי יוּכַל שִׂיחַ / לַשָּׁוְא נִכְתַּב לִי / חֵטְא לְזִכָּרוֹן.
נֶגֶד פְּנֵי גֶבֶר / מַעֲשָׂיו יוֹכִיחוּ / וְיַעֲנֶה בּוֹ כַּחְשׁוֹ / עֵד לְזִכָּרוֹן.
שִׂיחוּ מְזִמּוֹת אֵל / יַחַד כָּל בְּנֵי אִישׁ / עוֹבְרֵי תַּחַת שֵׁבֶט / כַּצֹּאן לְזִכָּרוֹן.
סוֹגֵר דֶּלֶת / בְּעַד תְּמִימִים בְּזַעַם / עַד בּוֹא קִצָּם / צֵאת לְזִכָּרוֹן.
עֲשֵׂה פֶלֶא לַחַיִּים / לְבַל יִהְיוּ כַּמֵּתִים / הֲיֵשׁ אֲמִתֶּךָ / בַּקֶּבֶר לְזִכָּרוֹן.
עוֹרַרְתָּ אָז בְּפֹעַל / עוֹרְרֵנוּ בְּלֹא פֹעַל / הֲלֹא לְנִפְלְאוֹתֶיךָ / תַּעַשׂ זִכָּרוֹן.
פְּנֵה אֱלֹהִים / בְּיוֹשְׁבֵי גַנִּים / מַקְשִׁיב לְנִדְבָּרֵימוֹ / בְּדָת לְזִכָּרוֹן.
פְּעָלָם לְפָנֶיךָ / וּשְׂכָרָם אִתָּךְ / אוֹכְלֵי לֶחֶם הָעֲצָבִים / בְּסֵפֶר לְזִכָּרוֹן.
צָצוּ שׁוּעָלִים / מְחַבְּלִים כְּרָמִים / לְהַכְרִית מִגֶּפֶן / שֹׁרֶשׁ וְזִכָּרוֹן.
צְרוּרִים בְּפֶרֶךְ / נָאֲקוּ וְנוֹשָׁעוּ / בְּכֹשֶׁר הֲרָרֵי קֶדֶם / הוּחַק לְזִכָּרוֹן.
קֶדֶם בְּנִתָּהּ לַדּוֹרוֹת / נַמְתָּה אֵין בָּהֶם חֵפֶץ / חִלַּפְתָּם וְאִבַּדְתָּם / מִהְיוֹת לְזִכָּרוֹן.
קָחְתָּה דוֹר מֵאֶלֶף / הֶאֱרַכְתָּ הַנְחָלָתָם / לְמַעַנָם בְּכָל דּוֹר / חַקֹּתָ לְזִכָּרוֹן.
רָם חָשַׁק מְאֹד / בְּכַלַּת נְעוּרִים / הֲרוּגֶיהָ וַעֲנִיֶּיהָ / תִּתָּה לְזִכָּרוֹן.
רָצָה אַחֲרֶיךָ / בְּגֵיא צִיָּה וְצַלְמָוֶת / אַהֲבַת כְּלוּלוֹתֶיהָ / תַּעַשׂ לְזִכָּרוֹן.
שִׁחֲתוּ עָם / שְׂאֵת שִׁמְצָה בְּקָמֵיהֶם / שָׂם פֶּסֶל וְלֹא אֵל / שָׁתוּ לְזִכָּרוֹן.
שְׁכָלוּ כִּמְעַט רֶגַע / לוּלֵא קָם בַּפֶּרֶץ / מְעוֹרֵר שְׁבוּעָה / וּבְרִית לְזִכָּרוֹן.
תִּעַבְתָּ מֵאָז / עֲדַת כָּל לְאֻמִּים / חֲשַׁקְתָּנוּ מֵהֶם / עֵדוּת לְזִכָּרוֹן.
תְּמוּר כֶּסֶף נִמְאַס / דּוֹר נִשְׁכַּח קָחְתָּ / קְנֵנוּ שֵׁנִית / כִּי שְׁכַחְנוּ מִזִּכָּרוֹן.
תָּר אִישׁ תָּם / בְּמִי זַרְעוֹ יְכֻנֶּה / שִׂכֵּל יָדָיו / לְאוֹת וְזִכָּרוֹן.
תְּרַפֵּק מְשׁוּל אֶפְרַיִם / בְּשַׁעֲשׁוּעַ יֶלֶד / כְּיֶלֶד וּבֵן יַקִּיר / חַקֹּתָ לְזִכָּרוֹן.

*The service continues with* אַתָּה זוֹכֵר *on a weekday on page 843; and on a* שבת *on page 587.*

*The initial letters of each line in this anonymous* תקיעתא*, follow a double alphabetic acrostic. Each line ends with the word* קול*, meaning "voice," but also has the connotation of prayer, and plea. If the first day of* ראש השנה *is* שבת*, "*אֲנוּסָה לְעֶזְרָה*" is recited; otherwise it is said on the second day.*

אֲנוּסָה לְעֶזְרָה / אֶמְצָא נֶגְדִּי / אֵל קָרוֹב לִי / בְּעֵת קָרְאִי בְּקוֹל.
אֲשֶׁר בַּעֲדַת אֵל / בְּקִרְבִּי נִצָּב / פֹּה בְּמִקְדָּשׁ מְעַט / אֲצַפְצֵף לוֹ בְּקוֹל.

בַּקְּרָנִי, דְּרָשַׁנִי / שֶׂה פְזוּרָה אֲנִי / נִגְזַזְתִּי וְנֶאֱלַמְתִּי / בְּלִי לְהָרִים קוֹל.
בֶּאֱמֹר גּוֹזְזַי / נִדָּחָה הִיא / שׁוֹמְרָה וְצַלָּה / לֹא יִשְׁאַג בְּקוֹל.

גָּלְתִי שִׂיחַ בְּחֻקָּיו / וְחִכִּי עָרֵב / כְּהִטָּה אֹזֶן, וְשָׁח / הַשְׁמִיעֵנִי קוֹל.
גָּז וּבָרַח מֶנִּי / כְּעֹפֶר עַל הָרֵי בָתֶר / בְּבַקְשׁוֹ דָּת וָאוֹת / בְּמִשְׁכְּנוֹתַי, וְאֵין קוֹל.

דִּלֵּג מִבֶּתֶר לְבֶתֶר / הֲשִׁיבֵהוּ אֵלַי / אוּלַי יִשָּׂא פָנֶיךָ / עֵקֶב שָׁמְעֲךָ בְּקוֹל.
דְּרוֹשׁ טוֹבָה לַמּוֹרָאָה / וּרְאֵה שֵׂה מוֹרִיָּה / אֱלֶם פִּיהוּ יְהִי צֶדֶק / לְלֹא שָׁמְעָה בְּקוֹל.

הָסֵר מֵחָלָק / יָדַיִם שְׂעִירוֹת / הוֹגֶה בְתַחֲנוּנִים / כִּי לְךָ הַקּוֹל.
הוֹשַׁע אֲשֶׁר / לֹא תִשָּׁכַח עֵדוּת / וּמִפִּי זַרְעוֹ / לֹא יָסוּף קוֹל.

וְחוֹזַי וּמְלִיצַי / הֵם בְּנֵי אִמִּי / אָז נִחֲרוּ בִי / לְמַעַן אֶשְׁמַע קוֹל.
וְעַל מִשְׁמַרְתָּם / יַעַמְדוּ וְיִזְעָקוּ / וְגַל לָהֶם סוֹד / וְהוּא יַעֲנֵם בְּקוֹל.

זֶה חָמַק מֶנִּי / אֲסוֹבֵב וַאֲבַקְשֶׁנּוּ / בְּכָל מָקוֹם הוּא / אָנָה אֶשָּׂא קוֹל.
זֶכֶר דּוֹדִי לְמַטָּה / אַדִּיר בַּמָּרוֹם / מְלֹא כָל הָאָרֶץ כְּבוֹדוֹ / לְמַעְלָה קוֹרְאִים בְּקוֹל.

חֵילֵי מַיִם / אֲשֶׁר בָּם תִּכֵּן שְׁבִילוֹ / דִּבְּרוּ, תְּמוּנָה לֹא שָׁרְנוּ / זוּלָתִי קוֹל.
חִפַּשְׂתִּי יְשִׁימוֹן הֲיֵשׁ / וְאָמַר אָיִן / קֶדֶם תִּתּוֹ עֹז / בִּעֲתַנִי קוֹל.

טָהוֹר דִּלֵּג / הָרִים, וְעָבַר / וּמִמְּעוֹן הַר מוֹר / אָז נָתַן קוֹל.
טִמֵּאתִי יְדִידוּת / שִׁכְנוֹ, וְעָלָה / לְיוֹם כֶּסֶא יָבוֹא / בְּאָזְנַי קוֹל.

יָקַרְתִּי בְּעֵינָיו / וְנִלְוָה לִי בַּשֶּׁבִי / עִמּוֹ אָנֹכִי / הִבְטִיחַנִי בְּקוֹל.
יָרַד לְשִׁנְעָר / וְשָׂם כֵּס בְּעֵילָם / הִשְׁמִיעַ כַּאֲרִי / וּכְנָחָשׁ קוֹל.

כִּלָּה מֶנִּי דֹּב / כְּהִתְרַפָּה מִמְּלֶאכֶת / אֲשֶׁר חָק בַּמִּכְתָּב / וַיַּעֲבֶר קוֹל.
כָּבַשׁ לִי אַרְבָּעָה / רָאשֵׁי נָמֵר / וְגַם אֲנִי בְּהוֹדָיוֹת סֶלָה / אַשְׁמִיעַ לוֹ קוֹל.

לְחַיַּת קָנֶה / אָז מָכַר אֶרֶץ / מִי לִי בַשָּׁמַיִם / אָז הֵרִימָה קוֹל.
לֵאלֹהֵי יִשְׁעִי / מִשִּׁנֵּי בַרְזֶל שַׁוְעָתִי / וּמֵרֶגֶל עַבְטִיט / הִצְרַחְתִּי בְקוֹל.

מִדַּת קִצִּי / לֹא הוֹדִיעַנִי / מָתַי בְּאַרְצִי / תּוֹר יַשְׁמִיעַ קוֹל.
מִיּוֹדְעֵי סֵפֶר / חָתַם קִצִּי / לְבַל דַּעַת צוֹפַי / עֵת יִשְׂאוּ קוֹל.

נָא הַבֵּט וּרְאֵה / עָנְיִי וּמְרוּדִי / אֵין לִי מַכִּיר / לְמִי אֶשָּׂא קוֹל.
נֶצַח אֲקַוֶּה / כִּי לֹא יִפֹּל דָּבָר / מִמַּקְשִׁיבַי / דְּמָמָה וָקוֹל.

שׂוֹשׂ יָשִׂישׂ לִבִּי / בְּקִרְבִּי בְּשָׁמְעִי / דּוֹדִי דּוֹפֵק / עַל פְּתָחַי בְּקוֹל.
סֶלָה יְשִׂימֵנִי / כַּחוֹתָם עַל לֵב / כְּאָז תַּחַת הַתַּפּוּחַ / עוֹרַרְנִי בְקוֹל.

עִלִּיתַנִי אֵל / עַל כָּל בָּנוֹת / כִּי בַעֲבוּרִי / בְּחוֹרֵב תַּתָּה קוֹל.
עַל כָּל אֱלֹהִים / מְאֹד נִתְעַלֵּיתָה / וְנֶצַח תִּתְעַלֶּה / בִּתְרוּעַת קוֹל.

פָּדָה מִמִּדְבָּר / צִפּוֹר מִמִּצְרַיִם / וְיוֹנָה הִשְׁמִיעָה / מֵאַשּׁוּר קוֹל.
פְּקֹד צִפּוֹר בַּיִת / דְּרֹשׁ יוֹנַת אֵלֶם / תְּקַע לָמוֹ בַּשּׁוֹפָר / וּשְׁרֹק לָמוֹ בְקוֹל.

צוּר חֻקִּים מֶנִּי / בַּל יָעוּפוּ כַּנֶּשֶׁר / וּבַל יִכָּנְפוּ / מַשְׁמִיעֵי קוֹל.
צְרוּפָה אֶלְמַד / וְעֵינַי לְמוֹרַי / כְּאָז צִיר מְדַבֵּר / וְאֵל מְשִׁיבוֹ בְקוֹל.

קָרַב קֵץ / בָּא עֵת מִשְׁפָּט / קָם מֵלִיץ יֹשֶׁר / לְהִתְחַנֵּן בְּקוֹל.
קַדֵּשׁ חֹדֶשׁ / וְהוּכַן מוֹעֵד / אֶתְקַע בַּשּׁוֹפָר / וְיַעֲנֶה לִי בְקוֹל.

רֶגֶשׁ מִקֶּבֶר / צְוָחָה מִסֶּלַע / בְּתֵת יְבֵשֵׁי עֶצֶם / מֵעָפָר קוֹל.
רְאוּ נֵס בֶּהָרִים / וְקוֹל שׁוֹפָר בָּאָרֶץ / לְהַשְׁמִיעַ רֶנֶן / מִדְּמוּמֵי קוֹל.

שֶׁגֶג לֵב הוּתַל / עוֹד בַּל יַטֶּנּוּ / בְּלִי לְהַכְבִּיד אֹזֶן / מִשְּׁמוֹעַ קוֹל.
שׁוֹבֵב לִי כְקֶדֶם / דָּת מוֹרָשָׁה / אֲשֶׁר בָּהּ עִלַּפְתַּנִי / בְּלַפִּידִים וְקוֹל.

תְּבוּנָה הֵפִיק / אִישׁ נְבוֹן דָּבָר / וְחַךְ נֹעַם זְמִירוֹת / בִּנְעִימוֹת קוֹל.
תְּהִלָּה יְתַנּוּ / אָז לַכֹּל הִשְׁמִיעַ / לָאֵל מוֹשֵׁל בַּכֹּל / יַמְתִּיקוּ קוֹל.

תַּחַת בְּנֵי צִיּוֹן / בְּנֵי יָוָן שָׁחוּ / הִבְרַקְתָּ חִצִּים / וַתְּהֻמֵּם בְּקוֹל.
תַּרְעֵם לְבוֹזְזַי / תִּתְקַע בַּשּׁוֹפָר / בְּסַעֲרוֹת תֵּימָן / אָז יֵלֵךְ קוֹל.

*The service continues with* אַתָּה נִגְלֵיתָ *on a weekday on page 851; and on a* שבת *on page 597.*

*Nowadays, the piyut "This day, may You strengthen us" which is said at the end of Musaf (see page 616 for the first day and page 870 for the second), is recited in its abridged form. Most communities say seven stichs from the following complete version.*

הַיּוֹם This day, may You strengthen us.
This day, may You bless us.

This day, may You give us greatness.
This day, may You deal with us kindly.

This day, may You glorify us.
This day, may You be with us.

This day, may You recall us
with compassion.
This day, may You protect us.

This day, may You purify us of all sins.
This day, may You straighten us
out before You.

This day, may You grant us respect.
This day, May You give us wisdom.

This day, may You save us from all evil.
This day, may You cleanse us of all iniquity.

This day, may You support us.
This day, may You answer us.

This day, may You appoint us
for life and blessings.
This day, may You vindicate us.

This day, may You raise us up.
This day, may You have pity on us.

This day, may You hear our cry.
This day, may You give us succor.

*Nowadays, the piyut "הַיּוֹם תְּאַמְּצֵנוּ" which is said at the end of מוסף (see page 617 for the first day and page 871 for the second), is recited in its abridged form. Most communities say seven stichs from the following complete version.*

הַיּוֹם תְּאַמְּצֵנוּ.

הַיּוֹם תְּבָרְכֵנוּ.

הַיּוֹם תְּגַדְּלֵנוּ.

הַיּוֹם תִּדְרְשֵׁנוּ לְטוֹבָה.

הַיּוֹם תְּהַדְּרֵנוּ.

הַיּוֹם תְּוַעֲדֵנוּ.

הַיּוֹם תִּזְכְּרֵנוּ בְּרַחֲמֶיךָ.

הַיּוֹם תְּחַסְּנֵנוּ.

הַיּוֹם תְּטַהֲרֵנוּ מִכָּל חֵטְא.

הַיּוֹם תְּיַשְּׁרֵנוּ לְפָנֶיךָ.

הַיּוֹם תְּכַבְּדֵנוּ.

הַיּוֹם תְּלַבְּבֵנוּ.

הַיּוֹם תְּמַלְּטֵנוּ מִכָּל רָע.

הַיּוֹם תְּנַקֵּנוּ מֵעָוֹן.

הַיּוֹם תִּסְמְכֵנוּ.

הַיּוֹם תַּעֲנֵנוּ.

הַיּוֹם תִּפְקְדֵנוּ לְחַיִּים וְלִבְרָכָה.

הַיּוֹם תְּצַדְּקֵנוּ.

הַיּוֹם תְּקוֹמְמֵנוּ.

הַיּוֹם תְּרַחֲמֵנוּ.

הַיּוֹם תִּשְׁמַע שַׁוְעָתֵנוּ.

הַיּוֹם תִּתְמְכֵנוּ.

# הלכות תפילה

## HALAKHA GUIDE

# GUIDE TO ROSH HASHANA

## EREV ROSH HASHANA

1 The recitation of *Seliḥot* precedes regular Shaḥarit for weekdays. The congregation omits *Taḥanun* and shofar blowing [שו״ע ורמ״א או״ח, תקפא: ג].

2 It is customary to say the formula of **התרת נדרים**, the Annulment of Vows (page 3) in front of three adult males after Shaḥarit [חיי אדם, קלח: ח]. The formula may be said at any time of the day [שו״ע יו״ד רלד: נו] and any day prior to Yom Kippur.

3 Some have the custom to immerse in the *mikveh*. Other customs include fasting and visiting the graves of departed relatives [שו״ע או״ח, תקפא: ב; רמ״א, שם: ד].

4 If one has uncollected loans outstanding at the end of a *shemitta* year (the seventh year in the *shemitta* cycle), the loans will be canceled unless prior to Rosh HaShana one signs a *prozbul* (page 7); the *prozbul* permits one to collect the loans after the end of the *shemitta* year.

5 When Rosh HaShana falls on Thursday and Friday, each household must prepare an *Eiruv Tavshilin* (page 9); this makes it permissible to prepare food on Friday for the Shabbat meals [שו״ע או״ח, תקכז].

▸ LAWS OF ROSH HASHANA EVE

6 Candle lighting: Two blessings are said: (1) **לְהַדְלִיק נֵר שֶׁל יוֹם טוֹב** ("to light the festival light") and (2) **שֶׁהֶחֱיָנוּ** ("Who has given us life…"). When Rosh HaShana eve falls on Friday night, the conclusion of the first blessing is modified as follows: **לְהַדְלִיק נֵר שֶׁל שַׁבָּת וְיוֹם טוֹב** ("to light the Shabbat and Festival light") (page 11).

7 Candles should be lit before sunset in order to "add from the weekday to the holiday," i.e., beginning the holiday before the objective starting time of the holiday [שו״ע או״ח, רסא: ב ומשנ״ב שם: י].

## ▸ LAWS OF THE THE EVENING SHEMA

8 Saying the three paragraphs of the Shema each morning and each night fulfills an affirmative mitzva from the Torah. As saying the Shema is a time-bound mitzva, women are exempt [שו״ע או״ח, ע: א]. Nevertheless, women are required to say the first verse to express their acceptance of עול מלכות שמים (the yoke of the kingdom of Heaven) [ב״ח שם]. Women are permitted to say the Shema and the blessings preceding and following [משנ״ב שם: ב].

9 There is a set time period every night during which the Shema may be said: At the earliest, the Shema may be said from nightfall [שו״ע או״ח, רלה: א]. The Shema should be said before midnight (measured from nightfall to daybreak), but one is permitted to say the Shema until daybreak [שם: ג].

10 The Shema must be said with concentration and awe [שו״ע או״ח, סא: א]. Each word and syllable should be pronounced correctly and carefully, without slurring consonants [שו״ע או״ח, סא: טו–כא].

11 Some authorities ruled that one should say the Shema with *Ta'amei HaMikra*. Today, however, most people do not do so [שו״ע ורמ״א, שם: כד].

12 The custom is to cover the eyes with the right hand while saying the first verse, so as not to look at anything that might disturb one's concentration [שו״ע או״ח, סא: ה].

13 The custom is to draw out one's pronunciation of the letters ח and ד in the word אחד to emphasize God's sovereignty over creation [שו״ע או״ח, סא: ו].

14 The sentence בָּרוּךְ שֵׁם כְּבוֹד מַלְכוּתוֹ לְעוֹלָם וָעֶד is said quietly, because it does not appear in the biblical text of the Shema [שו״ע שם: יג; משנ״ב, שם: ל].

15 If one enters the synagogue and hears the congregation about to begin saying the Shema, one is required to say the first verse of the Shema together with the congregation [שו״ע או״ח, סה: ב].

16 If one enters the synagogue and hears the congregation about to begin saying the Amida, for Ma'ariv, one should say the Amida together with the congregation, then afterward say the Shema with the blessings before and after [שו״ע או״ח, רלו: ג].

17 Most congregations begin Ma'ariv services for Rosh HaShana after nightfall. If the Ma'ariv services are held early, the communal recitation of the Shema in Ma'ariv may take place too early to fulfill the halakhic obligation. Under such circumstances, it is recommended to repeat all three paragraphs of Shema after nightfall [שו״ע או״ח, רלה: א].

▸ MA'ARIV FOR ROSH HASHANA

18 Ma'ariv for Rosh HaShana generally follows the format of Ma'ariv for Shabbat and Yom Tov, with the following variations:

a Before saying the Amida, a special verse for the day: תִּקְעוּ בַחֹדֶשׁ שׁוֹפָר (Ps. 81:4–5), is said (page 77).

b The Amida for Rosh HaShana includes special additions as discussed in further detail in law 20 below.

c After the Amida, the Ark is opened and the *Shaliaḥ Tzibbur* and congregation say responsively Psalm 24, לְדָוִד מִזְמוֹר, לַה׳ הָאָרֶץ וּמְלוֹאָהּ (page 99).

19 Changes to the Kaddish: It is customary to replace the phrase לְעֵלָּא מִן כָּל ("beyond any") with לְעֵלָּא לְעֵלָּא מִכָּל ("above and beyond any") [משנ״ב, נו: ב] and to change the phrase עֹשֶׂה שָׁלוֹם ("He who makes peace") to עֹשֶׂה הַשָּׁלוֹם ("He who makes the peace") [ערוה״ש או״ח, תקפב: ח]. One who forgets either of these changes is not required to repeat the Kaddish.

20 Special additions to the Amida: On Rosh HaShana (and Yom Kippur), additional phrases are added to the Amida: זָכְרֵנוּ לְחַיִּים... is added in the first blessing; מִי כָמְוֹךָ... in the second blessing; four paragraphs are added to the third blessing, and its ending is changed to הַמֶּלֶךְ הַקָּדוֹשׁ; וּכְתֹב is added to the penultimate blessing, and בְּסֵפֶר חַיִּים... is added to the final blessing. One who forgets to say any of these passages is not required to repeat the Amida with the forgotten additions [שו״ע ורמ״א או״ח, תקפב: ה]. However, one who forgets to change the ending of the third blessing to הַמֶּלֶךְ הַקָּדוֹשׁ must repeat the Amida from the beginning, unless one corrects the error תּוֹךְ כְּדֵי דִבּוּר, (see source in the *Shulḥan Arukh* for a discussion of this rule.) [שו״ע או״ח, תקפא: ג].

▸ LAWS OF MOURNER'S KADDISH

21 The Mourner's Kaddish is generally said after specific chapters of Psalms at the beginning and end of the prayer service. It is said by one who is either (a) in mourning for a relative, or (b) commemorating the *yahrzeit* of a relative. When no such person is present, the Mourner's Kaddish is generally omitted, except after *Aleinu* at the end of the morning service [רמ״א או״ח, קלב: ב], when it is said by one whose parents have died or whose parents do not object to their child saying the Mourner's Kaddish [שם].

22 Historically, the Mourner's Kaddish was recited by one individual; a set of rules developed for allocating among different mourners the various opportunities for saying the Mourner's Kaddish. [ביאור הלכה שם, קונטרוס מאמר קדישין, י] Today, most

congregations allow group recitation of the Mourner's Kaddish. In such case, they should say the words in unison [סידור יעב״ץ].

▸ ROSH HASHANA ON SHABBAT EVE

23 When Rosh HaShana eve falls on Friday night, Ma'ariv is preceded by an abbreviated version of Kabbalat Shabbat: Psalm 29, the first two and last two stanzas of לְכָה דוֹדִי, מִזְמוֹר שִׁיר לְיוֹם הַשַּׁבָּת and יהוה מָלָךְ, גֵּאוּת לָבֵשׁ (pages 57–61). כְּגַוְנָא is omitted. The Amida is said with additions for Shabbat. After the Amida, before saying Psalm 24 the congregation says וַיְכֻלּוּ הַשָּׁמַיִם, and the *Shaliaḥ Tzibbur* says the abbreviated Repetition of the Amida as is customary on Shabbat eve [שו״ע או״ח, תריט: ג]. This is followed by Full Kaddish, Psalm 23, Half Kaddish and *Barekhu*.

▸ ROSH HASHANA EVE – AFTER CONCLUSION OF MA'ARIV

24 On the eve of Rosh HaShana, it is customary to greet one another with wishes for inscription for a good new year: "לְשָׁנָה טוֹבָה תִּכָּתֵב וְתֵחָתֵם" [רמ״א או״ח, תקפב: ט].

25 Upon returning home, one says the Kiddush for Rosh HaShana. When Rosh HaShana eve falls on Friday night, the additions for Shabbat are said (page 115).

26 On the first night of Rosh HaShana, after eating the *ḥalla*, it is customary to say the blessing on fruit, eat a slice of apple dipped in honey, then say a prayer for a sweet new year [רמ״א או״ח, תקפג: א]. Some have the custom to eat additional symbolic foods, each preceded by an appropriate prayer (*Simanim*, page 121). יַעֲלֶה וְיָבוֹא is added to *Birkat HaMazon* (page 131).

# ROSH HASHANA DAY

▸ ON WAKING

27 The custom is to say מוֹדֶה אֲנִי (page 209) immediately on waking, even before washing hands [משנ״ב, א: ח].

▸ LAWS OF WASHING HANDS; ברכת אשר יצר; אלהי נשמה

28 Upon waking, one is obligated to wash hands [שבת, קח:]. Some hold that one should not walk even four *amot* (around six feet) prior to washing hands [משנ״ב, א:ב (בשם הזוהר)].

29 According to some authorities, there is a separate obligation to wash hands prior to prayer [ערוה״ש או״ח, ד:ה]. One who washes and says the blessing of עַל נְטִילַת יָדַיִם after waking does not repeat the blessing when washing prior to prayer [רמ״א או״ח, ו:ב].

30 Hands should preferably be washed using a cup, but a cup is not required [שו״ע ורמ״א או״ח, ד:ז]. The custom is to pour water from the cup onto the right hand, then the left, and repeat a total of three times [משנ״ב שם:י]. Where water is unavailable, one may clean one's hands using any appropriate material; in that case, the blessing is changed to עַל נְקִיּוּת יָדַיִם [שו״ע או״ח, ד:כב].

31 The blessing of עַל נְטִילַת יָדַיִם may be said before drying one's hands or afterward [משנ״ב, ד:ב].

32 A number of reasons have been offered for washing hands upon waking. The Gemara states that, during the night, hands are enveloped by an "evil vapor," רוּחַ רָעָה, which is removed by washing one's hands [שבת, קח:]. In addition, there is a concern that, while sleeping, one's hands may have touched an unclean part of the body [רא״ש ברכות, פ״ט:כג]. Finally, it is noted that a person who wakes is like a newborn; therefore one needs to sanctify oneself by washing [שו״ת רשב״א ח״א, קצא].

33 The blessing of אֲשֶׁר יָצַר should be said each time after relieving oneself. It is recommended that one should go to the bathroom immediately after washing hands, then say the blessings of עַל נְטִילַת יָדַיִם followed by אֲשֶׁר יָצַר. However, even if one does not relieve oneself, one is permitted to say the blessing of אֲשֶׁר יָצַר after washing hands [רמ״א או״ח, ד:א]. One should not postpone going to the bathroom [שו״ע או״ח, ג:יז].

34 According to the Gemara, the blessing of אֱלֹהַי נְשָׁמָה (page 211) should be said upon waking [ברכות, ס:]. The contemporary custom is to say אֱלֹהַי נְשָׁמָה immediately after אֲשֶׁר יָצַר [משנ״ב, שם:יב]. However, some rule that one who stays up all night should not say אֱלֹהַי נְשָׁמָה and the blessing הַמַּעֲבִיר שֵׁנָה מֵעֵינַי, and should instead hear them from others [משנ״ב, מו:כד].

35 The custom is to say the *Birkhot HaTorah* (page 213) after אֲשֶׁר יָצַר, because one should not read or recite Torah verses before making the requisite blessings on Torah study [שו״ע ורמ״א, או״ח: מו, ט].

### ▸ LAWS OF TZITZIT

36 Putting on a four-cornered garment with tzitzit attached fulfills an affirmative mitzva from the Torah. The obligation applies only during daytime [מנחות,

מג]. Since wearing tzitzit is a time-bound mitzva, women are exempt [שו״ע או״ח, יז: ב].

37 The accepted practice is to wear a *tallit katan* all day long and to wear a *tallit gadol* during Shaḥarit and Musaf [שו״ע או״ח, כד: א]. The dominant Ashkenazi custom is to begin wearing a *tallit gadol* when one marries [משנ״ב, יז: י], but Jews of German and Sephardi descent begin wearing the *tallit gadol* at an earlier age. Nevertheless, the custom is to wear a *tallit gadol* – even if unmarried – when acting as *Shaliaḥ Tzibbur*, reading from or being called up to the Torah, opening the Ark or performing *hagbaha* or *gelila*.

38 One should put on the *tallit katan* immediately upon dressing. One should first examine the strings of the tzitzit to ensure that they are not torn [שו״ע או״ח, ח: ט]. Then, while standing [שו״ע או״ח, ח: א], one should say the blessing of עַל מִצְוַת צִיצִית (page 211) and immediately put on the garment [רמ״א או״ח, ח: ו]. One does not say the blessing if (a) one is about to put on a *tallit gadol*, and (b) one will have in mind the *tallit katan* when saying the blessing on the *tallit gadol*. On the other hand, if there is a substantial interruption between the time one puts on the *tallit katan* and one puts on the *tallit gadol*, one should say the separate blessing on the *tallit katan* [שו״ע או״ח, ח: יג].

39 The blessing on *tzitzit* may be said at daybreak, but not before [רמ״א או״ח, יח: ג].

40 Similarly with the *tallit gadol*, one should first examine the strings, then while standing, say the blessing לְהִתְעַטֵּף בַּצִּיצִית (page 217) and put on the *tallit gadol*. The word לְהִתְעַטֵּף means to wrap oneself; one should initially wrap the *tallit gadol* around to cover one's head and face for a few moments, after which it is sufficient that it cover the torso [מג״א, ח: ב].

41 If one removes the *tallit gadol* for any reason, one should repeat the blessing when putting the tallit back on [שו״ע או״ח, ח: יד]. The blessing is not repeated if the *tallit gadol* is put back on soon after taking it off, and either (a) one was wearing a *tallit katan* all along, or (b) one's original intention was to put the tallit back on shortly [משנ״ב, שם: לז].

42 If one's head is otherwise covered, there is no requirement to cover one's head with the *tallit gadol* [ט״ז או״ח, ח: ג]. Some authorities nevertheless require married men to cover their heads with the *tallit gadol* throughout Shaḥarit and Musaf, because it promotes reverence in prayer [ב״ח או״ח, ח: ג (בשם הרדב״ז)]. Others have the custom to cover their heads during the Amida only, or from *Barekhu* through the end of the Amida. Unmarried persons should not wear the *tallit gadol* over their heads [קידושין, כט:].

▸ LAWS OF BIRKOT HASHAḤAR AND PESUKEI DEZIMRA

43 According to the Gemara [ברכות, ס:], *Birkhot HaShaḥar* (Morning Blessings, page 225) were originally said individually, in conjunction with the performance of the associated activity. Thus, upon dressing one would say the blessing of מַלְבִּישׁ עֲרֻמִּים, and upon standing up one would say the blessing of זוֹקֵף כְּפוּפִים. However, the custom now is to say all of the blessings together in the synagogue [שו״ע או״ח, מו: ב].

44 The insertion of the verses of Shema after *Birkhot HaShaḥar* (page 235) was not meant to satisfy the individual's obligation to say the Shema every morning [רמ״א שם: ט]. However, as discussed in further detail in law 51 below, the three paragraphs of Shema must be said within the first half of the morning (measured as ¼ of the time from daybreak to nightfall). Since some congregations hold Shaḥarit services late, and as such the communal recitation of the Shema in Shaḥarit may take place too late to fulfill the halakhic obligation, under such circumstances, it is recommended to say all three paragraphs of Shema after *Birkhot HaShaḥar* [משנ״ב, שם: לא].

45 One should say the biblical verses describing the קרבן תמיד (page 241), preferably with the congregation [רמ״א או״ח, מח]. Some authorities require one to stand [משנ״ב, שם: ב].

46 The fifth chapter of מסכת זבחים (page 247) and the ברייתא דרבי ישמעאל (page 251) were added after the biblical passages regarding sacrifices to institutionalize the daily study of Scripture, Mishna and Gemara [שו״ע או״ח, נ: א].

47 Saying Kaddish, *Barekhu* or *Kedusha* requires the presence of a *minyan* (ten adult males) [שו״ע או״ח, נה: א].

48 One should not utter idle speech from the beginning of the words בָּרוּךְ אַתָּה ה׳ in *Barukh SheAmar* until one completes the Amida [שו״ע או״ח, נא: ד].

49 If one comes late to the synagogue, one may skip all, or portions, of *Pesukei DeZimra* as follows:

a If there is sufficient time, say *Pesukei DeZimra,* omitting the additional psalms for Shabbat and Yom Tov (pages 263–281; 285–287).

b If there is less time, say *Barukh SheAmar,* Psalms 145–150, then continue with נִשְׁמַת כָּל חַי.

c If there is less time, say *Barukh SheAmar,* Psalms 145, 148, 150, then continue with נִשְׁמַת כָּל חַי.

d If there is less time, say *Barukh SheAmar,* Psalm 145, then continue with נִשְׁמַת כָּל חַי.

**e** If there is less time, omit *Pesukei DeZimra* altogether. Complete the rest of the service with the congregation, then say *Pesukei DeZimra* privately, omitting *Barukh SheAmar* and from נִשְׁמַת כָּל חַי to the end [רמ״א ושו״ע או״ח, נב].

### ▸ SHAḤARIT FOR ROSH HASHANA

50 Shaḥarit for Rosh HaShana generally follows the format of Shaḥarit for Shabbat and Yom Tov, with the following variations:

**a** The *Shaliaḥ Tzibbur* for Shaḥarit begins from the words הַמֶּלֶךְ יוֹשֵׁב.

**b** After *Yishtabaḥ*, the Ark is opened and the congregation says Psalm 130 responsively. (Some say Psalm 130 before נִשְׁמַת כָּל חַי.)

**c** Some congregations add *piyutim* in the first blessing preceding the Shema.

**d** During the Repetition of the Amida, the *Shaliaḥ Tzibbur* adds *piyutim* before the *Kedusha*.

**e** After the Repetition of the Amida, the congregation says *Avinu Malkenu* (pages 413 and 703), but not on Shabbat [רמ״א או״ח, תקפד:א].

### ▸ LAWS OF THE MORNING SHEMA – קריאת שמע של שחרית

51 There is a set time period every morning during which the Shema may be said. The optimal time is immediately before sunrise, when there is assumed to be sufficient light to recognize an acquaintance from a distance of four *amot* (around 6 feet). If necessary, the Shema may be said from daybreak [שו״ע או״ח, נח:ג]. After sunrise, the earlier the Shema is said, the better [שם:ב]. At the latest, the Shema must be said during the first quarter of the day (in halakhic terminology, three halakhic "hours," where each hour represents 1⁄12 of the day); there is a dispute between halakhic authorities whether the day is measured from daybreak to nightfall (*Magen Avraham*) or from sunrise to sunset (Vilna Gaon) [שם:א]. After that time, one is permitted to say Shema with the blessings during the fourth halakhic "hour," that is, until the end of the first third of the day. After that, the Shema may be said without the blessings, but this does not fulfill the mitzva [שם:ו].

52 If one says the Shema without its preceding and following blessings, one has still fulfilled the mitzva. However, one should say the blessings afterward, preferably repeating the Shema as well [שו״ע או״ח, ס:ב].

For additional laws relating the Shema, see laws 8–17 above.

### ▸ LAWS OF THE SHAḤARIT AMIDA

53 There is a set time period every morning during which the Amida may be said. In general, the Amida should be said at or after sunrise. At the latest, the Amida should be said during the first third of the day (four halakhic "hours"; regarding the measure of a "day," see law 51). If the Amida was said between daybreak and sunrise, the mitzva has been fulfilled. If necessary, it is permissible to say the Amida after the first third of the day, but before midday [שו״ע או״ח, פט:א].

54 If one did not say the Amida for Shaḥarit prior to midday, one should say the Amida for Minḥa twice [משנ״ב שם:ו].

55 One should not eat or drink before saying the Amida, although drinking water is permitted. Moreover, anyone who needs to eat or drink in order to concentrate on his prayers is permitted to do so [שו״ע או״ח, פט:ג-ד].

56 The Amida is said facing the site of the Temple in Jerusalem. Thus, outside Israel, one faces the land of Israel; inside Israel, one faces Jerusalem; and inside Jerusalem, one faces the Temple Mount [שו״ע או״ח, צד:א]. If one is praying in a synagogue that does not face Jerusalem, one should pray facing the Ark [משנ״ב שם:י].

57 The Amida is said standing with feet together in imitation of the angels who, according to tradition, present the appearance of having only one leg [ברכות, י:, רש״י ד״ה ״ורגליהם״]. One should bow one's head and imagine one is standing in the Temple, like a servant before his master [שו״ע או״ח, צה:א-ב].

58 When saying the Shaḥarit Amida, one may not allow any interruption or disruption between the conclusion of the blessing גָּאַל יִשְׂרָאֵל and the introductory words to the Amida [ושם, קיא:א שו״ע או״ח, סו:ח]. This includes not responding to Kaddish, *Barekhu*, *Kedusha* or *Modim* [רמ״א, שם]. One may also answer "Amen" if one hears someone else concluding the blessing גָּאַל יִשְׂרָאֵל [רמ״א או״ח, סו:ז].

### ▸ LAWS OF THE REPETITION OF THE AMIDA – חזרת הש״ץ

59 During the Repetition of the Amida, the congregation is required to listen attentively to the blessings and respond "Amen" [שו״ע או״ח, קכד:ד].

60 In order to begin the Repetition of the Amida, a minimum of nine men are required to be listening attentively [שם].

61 Some require the congregation to stand during the Repetition of the Amida [רמ״א שם], but the custom is to be lenient on this matter, especially on days, like Rosh HaShana, when the Repetition is particularly lengthy.

62 There are different customs regarding what the congregation says during *Kedusha*: (1) The congregation says only the biblical verses (קָדוֹשׁ קָדוֹשׁ קָדוֹשׁ,

(בָּרוּךְ כְּבוֹד, יִמְלֹךְ) [שו״ע או״ח, קכה: א]. (2) The congregation says every word of the Kedusha, with the *Shaliaḥ Tzibbur* repeating each sentence [בה״ט שם בשם האר״י]. (3) The congregation says נַקְדִּישָׁךְ and all the biblical verses [ערוה״ש שם: ב].

63 In most congregations in Israel, *Birkat Kohanim* is said in Shaharit as well as in Musaf [שו״ע או״ח, קכט: א]. Outside Israel, or in Israel when no Kohen is present, the *Shaliaḥ Tzibbur* says **אֱלֹהֵינוּ וֵאלֹהֵי אֲבוֹתֵינוּ**.

64 At the conclusion of the Repetition of the Shaharit Amida, it is recommended that the *Shaliaḥ Tzibbur* say quietly the verse יִהְיוּ לְרָצוֹן אִמְרֵי־פִי, except on Shabbat when Full Kaddish immediately follows the Repetition of the Amida [משנ״ב, קכג: כא]. Some also say this verse at the conclusion of the silent Amida.

## ▸ TORAH READING AND HAFTARA

65 Prior to taking the Torah from the Ark, the Daily Psalm and Psalm 27 are said, each followed by the Mourner's Kaddish. When the Torah is taken from the Ark, most congregations say the "Thirteen Attributes of Mercy" and a special supplication (pages 431 and 717), except on Shabbat.

66 Torah Reading: first day – Gen. 21:1–34; second day – Gen. 22:1–24. Maftir (both days): Num. 29:1–6. Haftara: first day – I Sam. 1:1–2:10; second day – Jer. 31:1–19 [שו״ע או״ח, תקפד: ב; שם, תרא: א].

## ▸ LAWS OF TORAH READING

67 Five men are called up, seven on Shabbat [שו״ע או״ח, רפב: א].

68 If a Kohen is present, he is called up first. If a Levi is also present, he is called up second; for subsequent *aliyot*, one calls up a Yisrael [שו״ע או״ח, קלה: ג]. If a Kohen is present, but a Levi is not, the same Kohen is called up for the first two *aliyot* [שם: ח]. If a Levi is present and a Kohen is not, the Levi need not be called up, but if the Levi is called up, he should be first [שו״ע ורמ״א או״ח, קלה: ו].

69 The custom is to avoid calling up a Kohen after a Yisrael, except for Maftir and, in some communities, for אחרון, provided it is a *hosafa* [רמ״א, שם: י].

70 It is considered bad luck to call up two brothers or a father and son one after the other [שו״ע או״ח, קמא: ו]. While the custom is to avoid this practice, if one is called up after one's brother or father, one should accept the *aliya*.

71 One who is called up to the Torah should take the shortest route to the *bima* [שו״ע, שם: ו]. He should open the scroll to locate where the *aliya* begins. Still holding the handle, he should say the blessing, taking care to look away from the Torah (or close the scroll or his eyes), so as not to appear to be reading the blessing from the scroll itself [שו״ע ורמ״א או״ח, קלט: ד].

72 If, after the blessing is said, the *ba'al koreh* discovers that the blessing was said over the wrong passage of the Torah, the scroll is rolled to the correct location and the *oleh* repeats the blessing. The blessing does not need to be repeated if the correct passage was visible when the blessing was said [שו״ע או״ח, קמ: ג ומשנ״ב שם: ט].

73 The Torah is read standing [שו״ע או״ח, קמא: א]. The *oleh* is also required to stand. The rest of the congregation is not required to stand, but it is proper to do so [ערוה״ש, שם: ב].

74 The *oleh* should read the words quietly along with the *ba'al koreh* [שו״ע או״ח, קמא: ב].

75 If the *ba'al koreh* makes an error that affects the meaning of the words, he needs to re-read the Torah portion from the location of the error [שו״ע ורמ״א או״ח, קמב: א].

76 If an error is found in the Torah scroll, the reading is stopped, a new scroll is brought out, and the reading is continued from the location of the error [שו״ע או״ח, קמג: ד]. It is not required to call up all of the *aliyot* a second time to read from the new scroll, but if the remainder of the reading can be divided into the appropriate number of *aliyot* for that day, it is preferable to do so [משנ״ב, שם: טו].

77 It is customary to say a prayer (מי שברך, pages 437 and 725) for the ill at the conclusion of the Torah reading or between *aliyot*.

78 After completing the reading from a Torah scroll, the open scroll is raised and displayed to the entire congregation. The congregation says וְזֹאת הַתּוֹרָה [שו״ע ורמ״א או״ח, קלד: ב].

79 The Haftara is followed by (*Yekum Purkan* on Shabbat [page 455], then the prayers for the government and the State of Israel (pages 459 and 741). It is customary for the rabbi to deliver a sermon prior to the sounding of the shofar. If there is a Brit Mila, it takes place before the shofar blowing (page 997).

### ▸ LAWS OF SHOFAR BLOWING

80 Hearing the sound of the shofar is an affirmative mitzva from the Torah. A deaf person is exempt from this mitzva, but a blind person is not; consequently, a blind person may blow the shofar for others, but a deaf person may not. Women are exempt from this mitzva, but a woman is permitted to blow shofar for herself and other women. If a man is blowing shofar for one or more women, the women should say the blessings for themselves [שו״ע ורמ״א או״ח, תקפט: ג].

81 The first thirty shofar blasts sounded prior to Musaf represent the minimum number of shofar sounds that one is required to hear [שו״ע או״ח, תקצ: א]. However, it is customary to blow a hundred blasts. The Sephardi custom, which is followed by most congregations, is to blow the shofar during the silent Amida, rather

than after the Repetition (see law 97). Some congregations follow the Ashkenazi custom, which is to blow thirty before Musaf, thirty during the Repetition of the Amida and forty more in sets of thirty and ten during the Full Kaddish after Musaf [משנ״ב, תקצב: ד].

82 The person blowing the shofar is required to stand; the congregation is permitted to sit during the first set of shofar sounds, although the custom is to stand [שו״ע או״ח, תקפה: א; משנ״ב, שם: ב].

83 Two blessings are said by the person blowing the shofar: (1) לִשְׁמֹעַ קוֹל שׁוֹפָר and (2) שֶׁהֶחֱיָנוּ [שו״ע או״ח, תקפה: ב] (pages 471 and 753).

84 To prevent distractions while performing the mitzva of hearing the shofar, the congregation is, until completion of the first thirty shofar blasts, forbidden to speak about matters unrelated to shofar and, until completion of the hundredth blast, forbidden to speak about matters unrelated to prayer [שו״ע או״ח, תקצב: ג].

85 The rabbis ruled that we do not blow the shofar when Rosh HaShana falls on Shabbat [ראש השנה, כט: ושו״ע או״ח, תקפח: ה].

86 After the shofar is blown, *Ashrei* is said and the Torah scrolls are returned to the Ark. The *Shaliaḥ Tzibbur* for Musaf says a special prefatory prayer, הִנְנִי הֶעָנִי מִמַּעַשׂ ("Here I am, empty of deeds") and Half Kaddish (pages 485 and 761).

▸ MUSAF FOR ROSH HASHANA

87 Unique among the Amidot said on Shabbat and Yom Tov, the Musaf for Rosh HaShana comprises nine blessings, rather than seven. Instead of one blessing devoted to the Festival, there are three extended blessings dedicated to three separate Rosh HaShana themes: Kingship, Remembrance and the Shofar [שו״ע או״ח, תקצא: א; שם: ד]. Upon completion by the congregation of each of the three middle blessings of the Amida, ten shofar blasts are sounded. If Rosh HaShana falls on Shabbat, the shofar is not sounded.

88 Before *Kedusha*, וּנְתַנֶּה תֹּקֶף is said, preceded on the first day with *piyutim*.

89 The fourth blessing contains *Aleinu*. During the Repetition of the Amida, the Ark is opened before *Aleinu* and the *Shaliaḥ Tzibbur* (and, in most communities, the entire congregation) kneels in prostration at the words וַאֲנַחְנוּ כּוֹרְעִים. Because one is forbidden to touch one's head against the bare stone floor when kneeling, one should place a piece of cloth or paper between one's head and the floor [רמ״א או״ח, קלא: ח].

90 Upon completion by the *Shaliaḥ Tzibbur* of each of the three middle blessings of the Amida, ten shofar blasts are sounded, and the congregation sings הַיּוֹם הֲרַת עוֹלָם

and אֲרֶשֶׁת שְׂפָתֵינוּ. If Rosh HaShana falls on Shabbat, the shofar is not sounded and אֲרֶשֶׁת שְׂפָתֵינוּ is omitted. The Kohanim say *Birkat Kohanim* (pages 609 and 863).

▸ LAWS OF BIRKAT KOHANIM

91 The Kohen has an affirmative obligation from the Torah to bless the congregation, provided there are at least ten males aged thirteen or over (including the Kohen himself) [שו״ע או״ח, קכח: א-ב].

92 The Kohen is required to wash his hands (without a blessing) before saying *Birkat Kohanim*. The custom is for a Levi to pour the water [שם: ו]. If there is no water, or if the Kohen did not have enough time to wash, he may say *Birkat Kohanim*, provided that: (a) he washed his hands before Shaḥarit, and (b) since washing for Shaḥarit he has not touched anything unclean, even his own shoes [משנ״ב, שם: כ].

93 Each Kohen removes his shoes before ascending to say *Birkat Kohanim* [שם: ה]. When the *Shaliaḥ Tzibbur* begins רְצֵה, the Kohanim ascend to the Ark and stand with their backs to the congregation [שם: ח, י]. After the congregation answers "Amen" to the blessing הַטּוֹב שִׁמְךָ וּלְךָ נָאֶה לְהוֹדוֹת, if there is more than one Kohen, the *Shaliaḥ Tzibbur* calls out "Kohanim," and they turn around and say the blessing. If only one Kohen has ascended, he starts the blessing without being prompted [שם: י–יא]. The *Shaliaḥ Tzibbur* does not answer "Amen" at the end of the blessing [משנ״ב, שם: עא].

94 The *Shaliaḥ Tzibbur* reads each word of *Birkat Kohanim* and the Kohanim repeat it in unison. At the end of each verse, the congregation answers "Amen" [שו״ע ורמ״א שם: יג]. The *Shaliaḥ Tzibbur* does not answer "Amen" at the end of each verse [שו״ע שם: יט].

95 If the *Shaliaḥ Tzibbur* is himself a Kohen, some rule that he should not say the blessing, unless no other Kohanim are in the synagogue [שו״ע שם: יט]. However, the custom today is for the *Shaliaḥ Tzibbur* to participate in the blessing [משנ״ב, שם: עה].

96 During *Birkat Kohanim*, the congregation should stand silently with eyes lowered and concentrate on the words of the Kohanim. One should not look at the faces or fingers of the Kohanim [שו״ע, שם: כג].

▸ CONCLUSION OF THE SERVICE

97 After Musaf, the Shaliaḥ Tzibbur says Full Kaddish. Ten more shofar blasts are sounded. Some congregations pause during the Full Kaddish to blow the ten blasts; others sound the ten after the completion of the Full Kaddish. The

service continues with *Ein Kelokeinu*; the Rabbis' Kaddish; *Aleinu*; Mourner's Kaddish; *Anim Zemirot*; Mourner's Kaddish and *Adon Olam*.

▸ MINḤA FOR ROSH HASHANA

98 Minḥa for Rosh HaShana generally follows the format of Minḥa for Shabbat and Yom Tov. When Rosh HaShana falls on Shabbat, the beginning of *Ha'azinu* is read. The Amida is identical to that said during Shaḥarit, except that it is preceded by the verse beginning כִּי שֵׁם ה׳ אֶקְרָא (Deut. 32:3). After the *Shaliaḥ Tzibbur* repeats the Amida, the congregation says *Avinu Malkenu* (page 931), except when Rosh HaShana falls on Shabbat.

99 There is a set time period every afternoon during which the Minḥa Amida may be said: At the earliest, one may say the Amida one half of a halakhic "hour" from midday (a halakhic hour is 1/12 of the day). At the latest, the Amida must be said before nightfall. It is preferable to say the Amida at least three and a half halakhic "hours" after midday [שו״ע או״ח, רלג: א].

100 One should wash hands before saying Minḥa, even if they are not dirty, but if no water is available, one need not wash [שם: ב]. No blessing is said on the hand-washing.

101 After Minḥa, it is customary to say *Tashlikh* beside a source of running water (page 945). If the first day of Rosh HaShana falls on Shabbat, *Tashlikh* is said on the second day [רמ״א או״ח, תקפג: ב].

▸ ROSH HASHANA – SECOND DAY

102 Candle lighting for the second day and preparations for the meal must be performed after nightfall.

103 If the first day of Rosh HaShana fell on Shabbat, the congregation adds the paragraph וַתּוֹדִיעֵנוּ in the middle section of the Amida (page 87). Similarly, in Kiddush, the two blessings for Havdala are inserted prior to the blessing שֶׁהֶחֱיָנוּ; thus the order of blessings is: wine, Kiddush, flame, Havdala, שֶׁהֶחֱיָנוּ (pages 103 and 118).

104 On the second night of Rosh HaShana, it is customary to eat a new fruit or wear a new garment. However, one says שֶׁהֶחֱיָנוּ during Kiddush even if there is no new fruit or garment [שו״ע או״ח, תר: ב]. Similarly, שֶׁהֶחֱיָנוּ is said before blowing shofar on the second day, even if the shofar was blown on the first day [שם: ג].

105 Ma'ariv, Shaḥarit and Minḥa: Except as noted above, the prayers for the second day of Rosh HaShana parallel the prayers for the first.

▸ MOTZA'EI ROSH HASHANA

106 Ma'ariv for weekdays is said. In the fourth blessing of the Amida, the paragraph of אַתָּה חוֹנַנְתָּנוּ is added (page 973). Havdala (page 989) is said over a cup of wine or grape juice; no blessing is made over spices or a flame [שו"ע או"ח, תרא: א].

RABBIS' KADDISH

*Mourner:* Yitgadal ve-yitkadash shemeh raba. (*Cong:* Amen)
Be-alema di vera khir'uteh, ve-yamlikh malkhuteh,
ve-yatzmaḥ purkaneh vi-karev meshiḥeh (*Cong:* Amen)
be-ḥayyeikhon, uv-yomeikhon, uv-ḥayyei de-khol beit
Yisrael, ba-agala uvi-zman kariv,
ve-imru Amen. (*Cong:* Amen)

*All:* Yeheh shemeh raba mevarakh le'alam ul-alemei alemaya.

*Mourner:* Yitbarakh ve-yishtabaḥ ve-yitpa'ar ve-yitromam ve-yitnaseh
ve-yit-hadar ve-yit'aleh ve-yit-hallal
shemeh dekudsha, berikh hu. (*Cong:* Amen)
Le-ela le-ela mi-kol birkhata ve-shirata,
tushbeḥata ve-neḥemata, da-amiran be-alema,
ve-imru, Amen. (*Cong:* Amen)

Al Yisrael, ve-al rabanan,
ve-al talmideihon, ve-al kol talmidei talmideihon,
ve-al kol man de-asekin be-oraita
di be-atra (*In Israel:* kadisha) ha-dein ve-di be-khol atar va-atar,
yeheh lehon ul-khon shelama raba,
ḥina ve-ḥisda, ve-raḥamei,
ve-ḥayyei arikhei, um-zonei re-viḥei,
u-furkana min kodam avuhon di vish-maya,
ve-imru Amen. (*Cong:* Amen)

Yeheh shelama raba min shemaya
ve-ḥayyim tovim aleinu ve-al kol Yisrael,
ve-imru Amen. (*Cong:* Amen)

*Bow, take three steps back, as if taking leave of the Divine Presence, then bow, first left, then right, then center, while saying:*

Oseh ha-shalom bim-romav,
hu ve-raḥamav ya'aseh shalom aleinu, ve-al kol Yisrael,
ve-imru Amen. (*Cong:* Amen)

## MOURNER'S KADDISH

*Mourner:* Yitgadal ve-yitkadash shemeh raba. (*Cong:* Amen)
Be-alema di vera khir'uteh, ve-yamlikh malkhuteh,
ve-yatzmaḥ purkaneh vi-karev meshiḥeh (*Cong:* Amen)
be-ḥayyeikhon, uv-yomeikhon, uv-ḥayyei de-khol beit Yisrael,
ba-agala uvi-zman kariv,
ve-imru Amen. (*Cong:* Amen)

*All:* Yeheh shemeh raba mevarakh le'alam ul-alemei alemaya.

*Mourner:* Yitbarakh ve-yishtabaḥ ve-yitpa'ar ve-yitromam ve-yitnaseh
ve-yit-hadar ve-yit'aleh ve-yit-hallal
shemeh dekudsha, berikh hu. (*Cong:* Amen)
Le-ela le-ela mi-kol birkhata ve-shirata,
/ *In Minḥa of Erev Rosh HaShana:* Le-ela min kol birkhata ve-shirata,/
tushbeḥata ve-neḥemata, da-amiran be-alema,
ve-imru, Amen. (*Cong:* Amen)

Yeheh shelama raba min shemaya
ve-ḥayyim tovim aleinu ve-al kol Yisrael,
ve-imru Amen. (*Cong:* Amen)

*Bow, take three steps back, as if taking leave of the Divine Presence, then bow, first left, then right, then center, while saying:*
Oseh ha-shalom bim-romav,
hu ya'aseh shalom aleinu, ve-al kol Yisrael,
ve-imru Amen. (*Cong:* Amen)

קורן ירושלים